D1560897

THE HOLLYWOOD WALK OF FAME

UPCOMING BOOKS ALSO
BY SAMANTHA HART

Fiction

First Family in Space

A hilarious family comedy,
suitable for all ages.

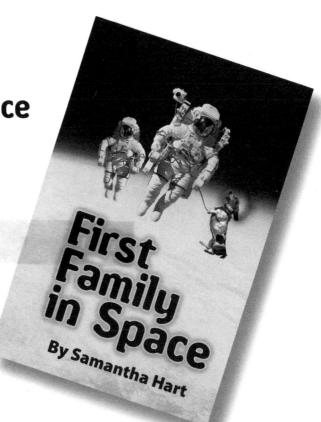

Hollywood

MAX FACTOR: HOLLYWOOD'S 100 GREATEST BEAUTY SECRETS AND CELEBRITY STORIES

Regarding the world as a stage, this indispensable book documents how the heroes and villains, and the winners and losers were created by the legendary Max Factor, Makeup King to the Stars. From Hollywood's earliest accounts of the stars through the Golden Era, from its black and white silent days to its stunning Technicolor glory, each chapter reflects not only a great deal about the growing entertainment industry, but how entertainment has evolved. The world's biggest stars—from Valentino to Jean Harlow, Clark Gable to Marlene Dietrich—the moguls and their studios, all turned to Max Factor to set the standard of appearance, as did the world at large. One of the most powerful men in Hollywood, this book reveals original makeup recipes, Max Factor's theories on color, beauty, behind-the-scenes revelations, and more.

For frequent updates and more information, visit: www.hollywoodfame.com.
Or, E-mail: shart@hollywoodfame.com
You may also write to: Crybaby Books and Entertainment
P.O. Box 1416,
LCF, CA 91012-5416

THE HOLLYWOOD WALK OF FAME

The World's #1 Book on the Stars

SPECIAL MILLENNIUM EDITION

By Samantha Hart

Introduction by Johnny Grant

Edited by Sir Michael Teilmann

An Officially Licensed Product of the Hollywood Chamber of Commerce
Official Licensed Trademarks of the Hollywood Chamber of Commerce
Licensed by CMG Worldwide

2000

Crybaby Books and Entertainment

Samantha Hart
Visit: www.hollywoodfame.com
E-mail: shart@hollywoodfame.com

Hollywood photographer Bob Freeman, E-mail: bfphoto@earthlink.net

®/TM 2000 Hollywood Chamber of Commerce
Licensed by CMG Worldwide Indianapolis, Indiana 46202 U.S.A.
All Rights Reserved Internet Page: http://www.cmgww.com

CP Graphics, Glendale, California
Telephone: 818.241.0861; E-mail: cpg@cp-graphics.com

Publisher's Cataloging-in-Publication Data
    (Provided by Quality Books, Inc.)
Hart, Samantha
        The Hollywood Walk of Fame : 2000 stars,
    star-makers & legends! / by Samantha Hart ;
    introduction by Johnny Grant ; edited by Michael
    Teilmann. — 2nd ed., special millennium ed.
        p. cm.
        Includes index.
        "The world's #1 book on the stars."
        ISBN 0-9665787-0-8

        1. Hollywood Boulevard (Los Angeles, Calif.)
    2. Motion picture actors and actresses—Biography.
    3. Hollywood (Los Angeles, Calif.)—Biography
    I. Title

    PN1993.5.U65H37 2000   791.43/092/2
        [B]   QBI99-1401

    10 9 8 7 6 5 4 3 2 1

Manufactured in the United States of America

To Johnny Grant
He taught me the whole world lives next door to Hollywood.

TABLE OF CONTENTS

ACKNOWLEDGMENTS

I would like to thank the celebrities, entertainers, their families and friends for so kindly supplying photographs and granting interviews. Many of you were in various corners of the globe, but did not hesitate to participate; I value your efforts. Some were working on a film, a television show, on Broadway, or in a recording studio, but still made time to talk with me and review written material. I offer my thanks to Paramount Pictures, the Walt Disney Company, Warner Bros., Universal Studios, Sony/Columbia, MGM/UA, 20th Century-Fox, and the various guilds and unions—Screen Actors Guild, AFTRA, Society of Singers, the Director's Guild of America, the Producer's Guild and the Writer's Guild of America—for their superb help. Mike Hawks and Peter Bateman at Larry Edmunds Bookshop, the Academy of Motion Picture Arts and Sciences, and the Academy of Television Arts and Sciences also offered outstanding assistance in this monumental project. The networks, CBS, NBC and ABC, and cable stations AMC, Turner Classics, and HBO participated as well. Many record companies proved to be a fountain of information and photographs, including Arista, MCA Music, Virgin, Warner Music, Concord Jazz, Columbia, Honest, Rhino, and Food Chain.

The Hollywood Chamber of Commerce—especially Ana Martinez-Holler, Leron Gubler, and the late Bill Welsh—endorsed me from day one and continued throughout the years of research and writing. I am grateful to their former Walk of Fame photographer, Buzz Lawrence (who has continued in other high profile Hollywood jobs), and to their current official photographer for many years, the esteemed Bob Freeman.

World-class support was given by Aloke Bosu, CPA, and the entertainment law firm of Myman, Abell, Fineman, Greenspan, & Light, LLP, with special thanks to Leslie Abell and Robert Myman.

To those who sustained me, Margaret Wright Ellis, Dr. Irving Posalski M.D., architect Stephen L. Ball AIA, Dr. Darcy Spicer, Dr. Arthur L. Wisot, Dr. Margaret E. Bates, Dr. Mark Alan Dwight, Arlene Curry, Andre Blocker, and Johnny, Michelle, Luis and Angela Mion (at Tito's famous Argentinean Market and Delicatessen, in El Monte, CA), as well as Scherr Lillico, Women in Show Business...*for children* (for information on WSB, refer to the back of this book). I am grateful to you all.

Kent and Susan Chesney, owners of CP Graphics, and their capable staff—especially Glendon Schnepf, Berj Boghosian, Patrick Holland, Tony Camarena, Ariel Lust, Tracy Dragoo, Suzi Braun, William Paul, Diane Toomey, Marianne Pearson, Johnny Garcia, Paul Escoto and Luis Martinez—provided a highly professional printing and graphics environment.

Photo editor Joseph C. Hooper, A.S.I.D., worked tirelessly and handled the multitude of difficult artistic tasks in the layout of this book.

My heartfelt gratitude to Arthur M. Kassel, my international security expert, great friend and husband of my publishing role model, Tichi Wilkerson Kassel, herself a Walk of Fame star honoree (see her bio in this book). Tichi is the former owner, publisher and editor-in-chief of *The Hollywood Reporter*, and is the founder and president emerita of the prestigious organization, Women in Film. Over the years they have graciously contributed their time, energy and advice, which has been invaluable to me.

My editor, Sir Michael Teilmann, has a soul of patience. He greatly lightened my burden with his intelligence working on this encyclopedic volume.

The author wishes to express her deep appreciation to Dr. Tarek M.A. Shawaf, for his unfailing and generous help.

And last but not least, my mentor and friend Johnny Grant who consistently cheered me on, shared great Hollywood stories and anecdotes, supplied countless photographs, and stood by me star by star. Johnny Grant *never* let me down. *I am indebted to him, for without his support this book would not have been possible.*

I thank them all.

The beautiful terrazzo star-studded sidewalks have attracted millions of sight-seers since the first dedication ceremony in 1958.

CREDITS

BOOK WRITTEN BY
SAMANTHA HART

INTRODUCTION BY
JOHNNY GRANT

EDITED BY
SIR MICHAEL TEILMANN

PHOTO EDITING BY
JOSEPH C. HOOPER

LETTER BY
LERON GUBLER

LETTER BY
TICHI WILKERSON KASSEL

PUBLISHED BY
Crybaby Books and
Entertainment, Inc.
All Rights Reserved

PROUDLY PRINTED IN THE U.S.A.
cp graphics

HOW to USE THIS BOOK

I have designed this book so that the stars on the Walk of Fame are laid out geographically, starting at one of the most well-known spots on the globe.

The book begins in front of the world-famous Grauman's Chinese Theatre. Starting at Harry Langdon's star next to the box office, the Hollywood Walk of Fame continues eastward to Vine Street, heads north, then south, and wraps around the entire 2.3 miles of the star-studded boulevard. You will end your tour at Barbra Streisand's star, back in front of the movie palace.

If you are reading this book from outside Hollywood, you can still enjoy the excitement of actually walking the Walk, and identifying these many talented celebrities.

Of course, if you are interested in a specific star or stars, simply refer to the index for easy access.

I wish to thank my readers from around the world for making this the #1 book on the stars. I appreciate your correspondence, communications, and reader loyalty.

In expression of gratitude to Hollywood fans everywhere, I have researched and interviewed extensively to obtain some of the most fascinating quotes, entertaining anecdotes and studio stories. More than 750 *extra* photographs were added for your enjoyment.

I sincerely hope that you and your family will treasure this special volume and will find it a lively and informative edition to your library.

Samantha Hart

Samantha Hart

*"The key to immortality is first living
a life worth remembering."*
St. Augustine

REFERENCE MAP

Map of Hollywood Boulevard and Vine, Block by block

NORTH

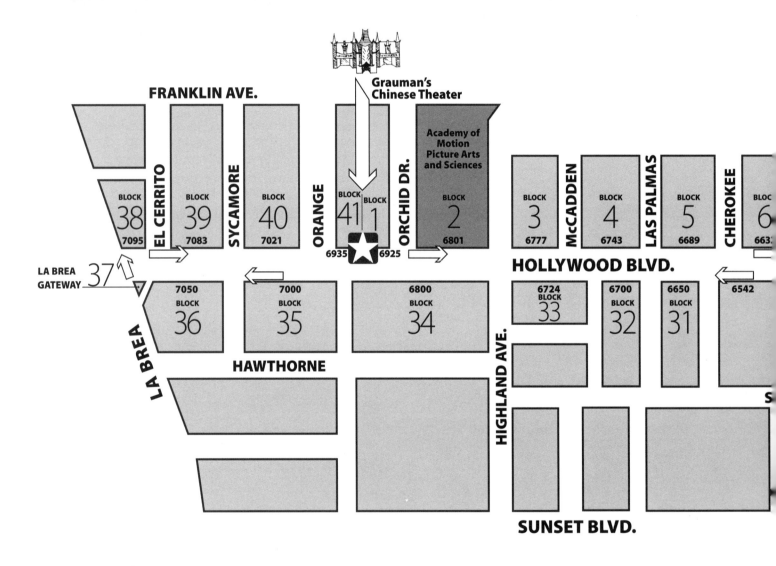

Grauman's Chinese Theater

FRANKLIN AVE.

Academy of Motion Picture Arts and Sciences

BLOCK 38	EL CERRITO	BLOCK 39	SYCAMORE	BLOCK 40	ORANGE	BLOCK 41	BLOCK 1	ORCHID DR.	BLOCK 2
7095		7083		7021			6935 6925		6801

BLOCK 3 — 6777

McCADDEN

BLOCK 4 — 6743

LAS PALMAS

BLOCK 5 — 6689

CHEROKEE

BLOC 6 — 663

HOLLYWOOD BLVD.

LA BREA GATEWAY 37

7050 BLOCK 36	7000 BLOCK 35	6800 BLOCK 34	6724 BLOCK 33	6700 BLOCK 32	6650 BLOCK 31

6542

LA BREA

HAWTHORNE

HIGHLAND AVE.

SUNSET BLVD.

References:

BLOCK
1 : Indicates block, as well as chapter in book

1234 : Indicates street address

⇒ : Recommended self-tour

★ : Recommended start point

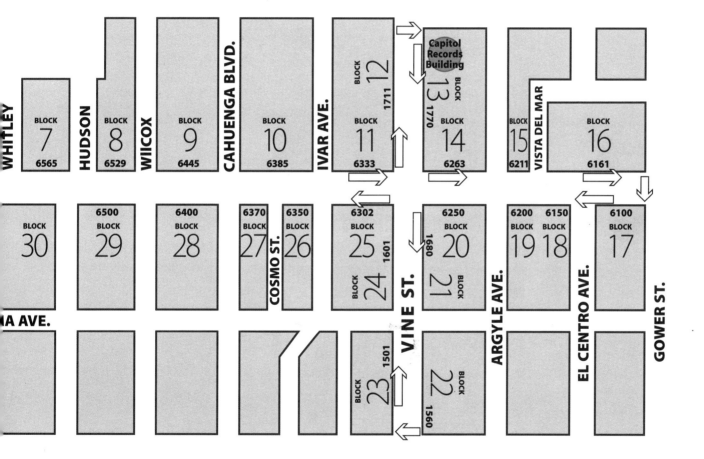

HOLLYWOOD

WHITLEY

BLOCK
7
6565

HUDSON

BLOCK
8
6529

WILCOX

BLOCK
9
6445

CAHUENGA BLVD.

BLOCK
10
6385

IVAR AVE.

BLOCK **12**
1711
BLOCK **11**
6333

BLOCK **13** 1770
Capitol Records Building

BLOCK **14**
6263

VISTA DEL MAR
BLOCK **15**
6211

BLOCK **16**
6161

BLOCK
30

6500 BLOCK
29

6400 BLOCK
28

6370 BLOCK
27
COSMO ST.
6350 BLOCK
26

6302 BLOCK
25
1601
BLOCK **24**

VINE ST.

1680
6250 BLOCK
20
BLOCK **21**

6200 BLOCK
19
6150 BLOCK
18

ARGYLE AVE.

6100 BLOCK
17

EL CENTRO AVE.

GOWER ST.

BLOCK **23** 1501
BLOCK **22** 1560

*Hollywood's Honorary Mayor Johnny Grant and fellow Walk of Fame honoree President Ronald Reagan
share a moment at a White House reception (official White House photo).*

JOHNNY GRANT

The Hollywood Walk of Fame, along with the Hollywood sign, are the most famous and popular public symbols of a community that has brought unprecedented entertainment and happiness to the world.

No doubt about it, the Walk of Fame's street-level monument to our industry's most famous and illustrious has been instrumental in making Hollywood Boulevard the most famous thoroughfare in the world!

When the stars of film, television, radio, the recording industry and live theatre receive their prestigious Oscars, Emmys, Grammys, Golden Microphones and Tonys, the public who helped them win these awards are only able to catch a quick glimpse during the inevitable award shows. However, when a star on the Hollywood Walk of Fame is awarded and dedicated, the exciting and colorful ceremonies are open to the public free of charge! Not only can the fans see history being made as we ceremonially uncover the star for the first time, but they can actually touch the star, pose with it, participate with friends in its mystique and enjoy it forever. It is the most unique honor an entertainer can be accorded, an honor that can be shared with the people who helped make it happen!

People often ask how a star on the Walk of Fame comes to fruition. In concise terms, an entertainer or person from the five categories—Film, TV, Recording, Radio or Live Theatre—must have achieved a level of recognized professional achievement. He or she has to have a minimum of five years of public longevity in that category, and have demonstrated their commitment to contribute something back to the community. These are the basic requirements for consideration. The selection committee keeps in mind the fact that visitors to the Walk of Fame often search for the stars of contemporary artists as well as the legendary entertainers. To keep the walk current, we try to honor many of the newer generation of stars who meet the criteria.

It startles many people to learn that anyone can nominate a celebrity for a star on the Walk of Fame. Before doing so, however, they must be able to guarantee two primary things. First, that the individual they are nominating will agree to participate in the ceremony, and second, that the costs of the star, ie: permits, manufacture, installation, etc. will be provided for. Applications for nomination, as well as full details of the requirements can be obtained from the Hollywood Chamber of Commerce.

As chairman of the Hollywood Walk of Fame Selection Committee and host of the dedication ceremonies, I have witnessed, firsthand, the reactions of those honored with a star. Whoever says that stars are intolerant and unappreciative of their fans would learn differently if they could see these famous folks as their names are immortalized on "The Boulevard of Dreams" for all-time. It is more than just a delightful experience to see their reaction. They are, after all, just people, like you and me. Some of the most famous and popular stars worry if anybody will show up! Imagine that!! Some of the most accomplished actors in the world simply forget their well-rehearsed "thank you" lines, and still others are brought to tears when their stars are uncovered and the crowds of fans and officials enthusiastically cheer their approval! Of all the roles I have played in Hollywood for more than fifty years, actor, producer, TV host, newsman, special event producer and mayor, this particular assignment is one of the most enjoyable a person could hope for!

Some of the highlights of recent Walk of Fame ceremonies included: Awarding the world's most famous and popular cowboy, Gene Autry, his fifth star. He is the only entertainer to have earned and received a star in each of the Walk's five categories. With the current trend of specialization in one, or maybe two areas, I doubt if anyone else will ever equal that unique accomplishment. I also recall when the famed Native American Indian actor Iron Eyes Cody did a rain dance as a publicity stunt and the clouds opened-up with such a downpour we almost had to cancel the ceremony.

Other memorable Walk of Fame moments included having the 100-year-old Oscar-winning producer Hal Roach, one of the industry's most legendary figures, join his friend Maureen O'Sullivan, the Irish beauty, as she received her much-deserved star. Then there was our friend Bob Hope, ready with a host of legendary show business pals, a couple dozen sharp quips and even the U.S. Marine Corps band on hand as he received his fourth star on the Walk of Fame.

And how appropriate that we honored the memory of the late screen star Natalie Wood with a star on Hollywood's 100th birthday, February 1st, 1987. Natalie's husband, Robert Wagner, along with their children and her mother participated in this most poignant moment.

I pride myself as an emcee on absolute correctness, but it all came apart when at her star ceremony I introduced Joan Rivers as Joan Collins! Before I could publicly recover, Ms. Rivers grabbed the microphone and advised the World that "I've been called a witch (with a "B") before!" It was hilarious and all in good fun.

When I had a bit of trouble getting up from my knees during the unveiling of the Rev. Billy Graham's star, the world-famed preacher alerted the crowd and media to another of my foibles by announcing in his sonorous tones that "...I don't think that Johnny's had a lot of practice being on his knees!" My pals haven't let me forget that one!

Needless-to-say, there have been other magic moments helping to honor colleagues and some of my long-time friends like Autry, Hope, Angie Dickinson, Sammy Davis, Jr., Jane Russell, Pat Buttram. and even re-dedicating the star of our friend, the legendary Marilyn Monroe.

For many of us "old-timers," the Hollywood walk of Fame is like a walk down "Memory Lane." It is so appropriate that we honor these talented and wonderful stars in this very special manner.

As one of Hollywood's most popular tourist attractions, the Walk of Fame is a proven winner. It was a visionary project created by the Hollywood Chamber of Commerce more than four decades ago. The first stars were dedicated in 1958. The idea was to honor the celebrities, bring back some of the glamour and excitement of Hollywood's "Golden Years," showcase the names of more contemporary entertainers, sharing all of them with the fans, and to increase tourism and business along Hollywood's main street. It has done all of that and a great deal more!

The Hollywood Walk of Fame has inspired similar attractions in communities around the world. A few years back, then Los Angeles Mayor Tom Bradley and I participated in the dedication of a Walk of Fame in Nagoya, Japan with 25 exact-replica stars from the Hollywood attraction honoring some of the entertainment world's greatest names. I was also honored to officiate at the inaugural events of the Walk of Fame—Europe in Rotterdam, Holland, The Walk of Stars in Palm Springs, California and numerous others. These public attractions should not be thought of as "copycat" versions of our original Hollywood Walk of Fame, but rather as positive efforts of communities throughout the world to honor their citizens who have achieved distinction in everything from entertainment and the arts to science, politics, charitable activities, sports and business. More power to them. Hollywood has, once again, provided them an image that they can mold into their own for the enjoyment and inspiration of all.

The book you are about to read has been a mainstay in my library. It is packed with information on well-known stars and other entertainment personalities, and with a lot of lesser-known facts and information on Hollywood and this most famous attraction. I am confident that this book will be read, re-read, shared and enjoyed for years to come.

I hope that each of you will have an opportunity to personally stroll along the Hollywood Walk of Fame and experience for yourself one of the greatest attractions in the world.

And, to author Samantha Hart, thank you.

JOHNNY GRANT

On behalf of the Hollywood Chamber of Commerce, I would like to express our congratulations to Samantha Hart on the production of this Special Millennium Edition Walk of Fame Book.

The history of Hollywood lives on through these five acres of terrazzo stars. The great men, women, animals and animated characters honored herein have entertained millions of people over the years. Their names are memorialized here to be remembered and recalled forever.

Conceived originally as a tribute to the stars, the Hollywood Walk of Fame has grown into an international icon. Today, it is the number one tourist attraction in Hollywood. The Hollywood Chamber of Commerce is proud of the role it has played in conceiving, developing and maintaining this Walk. It is indeed a cherished treasure, not only for our community, but for the world.

We look forward to continuing our role in fostering, preserving, and enhancing the Hollywood Walk of Fame into the third Millennium.

Sincerely

Leron Gubler
President & CEO

The only independent producer to win five Oscars is Hollywood Walk of Fame honoree Arthur Cohn.

Academy Award-winning writers-movie stars Ben Affleck (left) and Matt Damon (right) with Hollywood Walk of Fame photographer Bob Freeman

Oscar-winning motion picture director James Cameron (of Titanic fame) with president and CEO of the Hollywood Chamber of Commerce Leron Gubler (right), at the Guinness Museum.

Producer-publisher Dr. Tarek Shawaf (seated, right), actress-writer Lydia Cornell, advisor and former Congressman Barry Goldwater, Jr. (left), and Walk of Fame photo editor Joseph C. Hooper, A.S.I.D.

Child model and actress Natasha Holler dreams of following in the footsteps of the world's most famous child star ever.

Some people break into the movies from behind-the scenes, as did technical advisor Capt. Joseph R. John (left) in Under Seige (1992), starring Steven Seagal (right) and Tommy Lee Jones.

WOMEN IN FILM

Dear Samantha:

Your continuing interest in the Hollywood Walk of Fame has culminated into one of the most comprehensive and detailed publications ever to be printed about Hollywood. This 600-page coffee table volume, which took you more than seven years to research and complete is a tribute to your ability to finish what you start. You were also a wonderful resource to me in my role as Publisher and Editor-in-Chief of *The Hollywood Reporter.*

Johnny Grant, one of Hollywood's treasures, presided over my own star-presentation ceremony ten years ago. With his love for Hollywood, the Walk of Fame, the Hollywood Sign, the Hollywood Christmas Parade, and your unique Walk of Fame trip through Hollywood's intriguing history, you will both continue to bring Hollywood to millions of people throughout the world and encourage countless visitors to our wonderful city.

I am proud to sponsor you as a lifetime member of Women in Film. I know you will bring the same commitment to Women in Film that you have to this impressive book about the 'stars' of Hollywood.

Warm regards,

Tichi

Tichi Wilkerson Kassel
Founder-President Emerita

Hollywood's powerful, world famous sign had its humble beginnings as an advertisement for a real estate development. Each letter, at 30 feet wide and 50 feet high, was pulled up the hillside by a team of mules. It was completed for a total cost of $21,000 in 1923.

WHAT IS HOLLYWOOD?

At the turn of the last century, Hollywood resembled a vast ranch, with evergreen eucalyptus, tropical palms and California oak trees dotting the landscape. The air was fragrant with heady orange blossoms, and the small community of 4,999 residents took great pride in their main street, Hollywood Boulevard. That pride motivated them to enact a city ordinance prohibiting the driving of more than 5,000 sheep in one band at any single time down the boulevard.

Hollywood was barely noticeable on the map when Eastern filmmakers discovered Southern California's mild climate ideal for "silent moving pictures." Most pictures were made outdoors, even interior shots were frequently shot on revolving exterior stages with sliding curtains, using the sun for illumination. The state offered 300 days of sunshine, glistening beaches, tree-topped mountains, citrus orchards, and arid deserts. The most popular movie of the day was the trusty Western; the area's wide open valleys, replete with dusty floors and tumbleweeds proved perfect shooting grounds. Land was cheap at $150 to $400 per lot, on easy terms, or for the less monied, rooms rented for $5 a month, breakfast and dinner included. Word spread like wildfire; to the quiet citizens of Hollywood it seemed like the entire entertainment industry had overrun their peaceful town. To counter this onslaught, they imposed laws forbidding the selling of liquor—even California's splendid zinfandel at 50 cents a gallon, and thirst-quenching beer from the microbrewery for five cents a large glass were restricted. Pharmacists were allowed to dispense liquor, but only with a physician's prescription. The district's self-imposed prohibition forced the Cahuenga House Saloon's owner into near bankruptcy; he regrouped by leasing his property to the Nestor Film Company. This presented another problem as even more "players" and hopefuls poured into their little suburb. Next, the city council placed signs on various businesses which read: "No Dogs or Actors Allowed." (Notice "actors" got second billing.) Still, the city thrived as money from the "theater people" spoke louder than words and became a driving force for commerce. The residents slowly began to view the picture-making studios cropping up in their neighborhood with curiosity. In 1923, the area's population numbered 100,000, and soon tripled that. Rudolph Valentino built his palatial home just east of Highland Boulevard (in an affluent area where no home could cost less than $3,000), and Charlie Chaplin lived a few blocks away in a Spanish-Californian house on Argyle. Hollywood Boulevard became the familiar stomping grounds of Mary Pickford, Douglas Fairbanks, Norma Shearer, the Barrymores, the Gish sisters, Pola Negri, Anita Loos, Pearl White, Theda Bara, among dozens of world-class entertainers. Hollywood citizens were beginning to accept the notion that movie stars were America's own "royalty." Nearby, no self-respecting, blue-blooded Pasadena resident—many with ties to the United States oldest financial institutions—would dare be seen in "the new glamour center of the world."

The motion picture business converted the haughty and the contemptuous, as it quickly became one of the world's greatest and richest industries, with Hollywood at its center.

"Hollywood: No Dogs or Actors Allowed."

MGM's famous Leo the Lion makes his roaring debut.

The most famous gate in Hollywood: The Bronson Gate at Paramount Pictures.

THE FIRST STAR

By the 1920s, the world knew Hollywood. The mere mention of the word conjured up images of movie studios, stars and glamour. Year after year, thousands poured into an area that had become as famous as her people. The path to fame and fortune was lined with palm trees, while the night's darkness was pierced by klieg lights.

Although films were produced elsewhere around the globe, Hollywood was the supreme place to make movies. A factory town, Hollywood had become the ideal center of the universe.

In 1927, the Hollywood Roosevelt Hotel (named after President Theodore "Teddy" Roosevelt) opened its doors on Hollywood Boulevard. Several of its backers, film greats Mary Pickford, Douglas Fairbanks, Joseph Schenck, Louis B. Mayer, and Marcus Loew, toasted this palatial "home of the stars" with champagne and caviar. Lured by its beauty, charm, and elegance, the Academy of Motion Picture Arts and Sciences headquartered there that same year.

The following year, in 1928, the organization held the first Academy Awards ceremony in the hotel's Blossom Room.

In 1934, a starry-eyed hopeful entered Hollywood to become a movie star. He wandered into the Blossom Room dreaming about winning his own Oscar one day. David Niven later recalled, "When I first arrived in California, broke and twenty-two years old, I had no training as an actor. I met Al Weingard, the reception clerk at the Hollywood Roosevelt Hotel, and he gave me a room in the servants' quarters. I am eternally grateful to him and the hotel...All that thinking about the Oscar paid off, too. Dammit, I must say I wanted to win and I'm happy I did." (Niven won a 1958 Best Actor Oscar for *Separate Tables*.)

Another transplanted Britisher, Sir Cedric Hardwicke, made this comment about his new home: "I believe that God felt sorry for actors, so He created Hollywood to give them a place in the sun and a swimming pool."

A little more than half a century had passed since the community's founding when the Hollywood Chamber of Commerce voted to give the stars a permanent home on Hollywood Boulevard.

In 1958, the Academy Award-winning actress, Joanne Woodward, received the first star on the Hollywood Walk of Fame. Five other celebrities who received stars on that same northwest corner of Hollywood Boulevard and Highland Avenue were silent screen comedienne Louise Fazenda, the versatile actor Preston Foster, leading man Burt Lancaster, the great beauty Olive Borden and director Edward Sedgwick. This elite group had been selected from a list of more than 1,000 motion picture personalities to best represent the old and new.

Marilyn Monroe, who had been ignored by the Academy of Motion Picture Arts and Sciences, was thrilled to learn that she would be honored with her own beautiful terrazzo Walk of Fame star. Within sixteen months, 1,558 luminaries had been forever immortalized in one sweeping, continuing installation—much to the dismay of local shopkeepers who were none too pleased with the sidewalk disruption. Yet, the community swelled with justifiable pride at the official dedication ceremony on February 8, 1960. The Chamber had actually scheduled the completion one week earlier on February 1 to coincide with Hollywood's birthday, but the construction could not be completed on time.

Eight years would pass before a new star was born. On December 11, 1968, actor/comedian Danny Thomas hosted the momentous star unveiling for producer/studio executive Richard D. Zanuck. The ceremony, held in front of the world famous Grauman's Chinese Theater, attracted worldwide attention and exacted this quip from Thomas, "My star is at 6901 Hollywood Boulevard. Let's move this show down there."

The show has been going on ever since. As we enter the new millennium, there are more than 2,150 stars on the world-famous Hollywood Walk of Fame.

Joanne Woodward is honored with the first star on the Hollywood Walk of Fame in 1958.

THE NOMINATION PROCEEDINGS

"Popularity is the easiest thing in the world to gain and the hardest thing to hold."

—Will Rogers

The Hollywood Walk of Fame is, in part, a key to immortality. The gleaming bronze landmarks testify that silent screen star Clara Bow was the "It" girl, that a German shepherd dog named Rin-Tin-tin ruled the box office, and that Charlie Chaplin's little tramp inspired the world to laughter and tears with his art of pantomime.

The star-studded boulevard speaks volumes about its recipients, including the enterprising businessmen who founded this town, such as William Fox, who arrived in the States poor, but with a burning ambition and founded the Fox Corporation (later known as 20th Century-Fox), immigrant Carl Laemmle who founded Universal Studios, and the four siblings who became known around the world as Warner Bros. These are a handful of moguls whose names sparkle in the sidewalks. From these outstanding men's lengthened shadows global communications grew. The Hollywood Walk of Fame shares a thousand stories like those and more from the beginnings of Hollywood through today.

HOW A STAR GETS ON THE WALK OF FAME

To be honored with a star in Hollywood's Walk of Fame is a tribute as coveted and sought after as any of the entertainment industry's equally prestigious awards, including the Oscar, Emmy, Grammy, Tony and Golden Mike. A unique honor, it recognizes a lifelong contribution to the arts, and embraces both public and peer appreciation. In a class by itself, the Hollywood Walk of Fame is a permanent monument of the past, as well as the present.

The Hollywood Chamber of Commerce and the Hollywood Historic Trust are the guardians of these landmarks. Neither organization nominates stars. And unlike the privileged members of the Academy who alone decide the winners of the Oscars, anyone (yes, really, anyone) can nominate a star for the Walk of Fame. After all, the fans truly decide who is a star and who is not.

Any individual, or family or friend, fan club, studio, manager, and/or agent can nominate their favorite entertainer. However, it would be inappropriate for the artist to nominate himself or herself. A few nervy celebrities have personally asked for the tribute and were rejected by the selection committee for that year's consideration because of it.

WHO CAN BE CHOSEN FOR A STAR?

There are five categories on the Walk of Fame:

Motion Pictures	Television

Recording	Radio	Live Theater

Each category encompasses a wide range of individuals. The lists below include many "job profiles" of recipients, but by no means includes every "job description." There are those involved in show business whose work defies labeling.

Motion picture and television categories honor on-camera and behind-the-scenes talent, including actors, hosts, comedians, writers, producers, directors, animators, inventors, special effects technicians, composers, dancers, stuntmen/women, costume designers, cinematographers, choreographers, and makeup artists.

Recording celebrates the world's finest talent in music, including opera, classical, jazz, gospel, blues, rock 'n' roll, pop, country and western, and even novelty.

Radio applauds newscasters, talk show hosts, advice columnists, disc jockeys, sportscasters, shock jocks, singers, musicians, comedians, educators, preachers and announcers. Live Theater salutes stage, concert, rodeo, and other arenas of live performance.

THE APPLICATION PROCESS

To receive a star nomination application, send a $10. nonrefundable check or money order (please do *not* send cash) to:

> The Hollywood Chamber of Commerce
> Attn: Star Nomination Applications
> 7018 Hollywood Boulevard
> Hollywood, CA 90028

Or, visit their website at: chamber.hollywood.com

Complete the questions on the official Hollywood Walk of Fame nomination application. Besides the nominee's name, you must *select only one* of the five categories in which the nominee is to be evaluated.

Next, confirm your nominee does not already have a star. In past decades, some celebrities received two, three, four and even five stars in the different categories. For example, Lucille Ball has two stars: one in television, and the other in motion pictures. Frank Sinatra has three stars: one in recording, a second in motion pictures and the third in television. In the new millennium, it is rare for an individual to be honored more than once.

On the other hand, there are important names missing from the Walk of Fame. For example, director/producer Steven Spielberg does not have a star on the Walk of Fame. Why? Because everyone assumes he has one, so no one has nominated him *yet*. Let's fill out an imaginary form nominating the very worthy Spielberg in the motion picture category. First, describe the qualifications of the nominee.

I would write four words: *"Steven Spielberg. Enough said."*

You, however, should describe the director's outstanding films and colossal box office appeal of his movies, including

Jaws (1975), *Close Encounters of the Third Kind* (1977), *Raiders of the Lost Ark* (1981), *E.T. the Extra-Terrestrial* (1982), *The Color Purple* (1985), *Jurassic Park* (1993), *Schindler's List* (1993), and *Saving Private Ryan* (1998), for which he was named best director and won an Oscar. He has earned many awards, including the honorary Irving G. Thalberg Memorial Award in 1987.

The Walk of Fame selection committee weighs contributions to society, too. You may want to mention one of Spielberg's many charitable works. He cares about education and has donated considerable sums to various institutions of higher learning. For instance, he gave to the University of Southern California film school. Ironically, USC had rejected the young Spielberg when he applied as a student many years earlier. Later, at the donation ceremony, an embarrassed school administrator spoke half-jokingly about the great Spielberg, stating, "He didn't tell us who he was."

Oprah Winfrey's name is noticeably missing from the television category as of 2000. Again, most people assume she already has a star, and so she has never been nominated. Winfrey is a cherished TV icon, a talk show host, a producer, and a gifted motion picture actress. She is a leading, multi-faceted talent of both the 20th and 21st centuries.

On her application form, I would write: *"Oprah Winfrey. Our Beloved."*

You, however, will want to detail her numerous Emmy Awards, her highly acclaimed, popular and long-running "Oprah" television show, and her roles as actress and producer. Her inspirational capacity as a tremendous humanitarian counts, too.

What does the Walk of Fame selection committee consider when reviewing a potential nominee's application? First, professional accomplishments and achievements. For example, a recording star should be represented by a string of hit records, complemented by Grammy or other music awards. Non-entertainment awards are taken into consideration, too, so list any. Second, longevity in the business is a must. In Hollywood that is five years. (That illustrates how tough it is to break into show business, as well as stay on top; audiences can be very fickle.) Third, contributions to society are counted. Walk of Fame honorees, for the most part, are good Samaritans. They must donate their time, talent, and/or money to help those less fortunate then themselves. Finally, if selected, the honoree must agree to be present at the dedication ceremony.

Follow the other instructions on the application, and submit a photograph in your package.

Next, return the application during the official nomination period, April 7 to May 31. The May 31 deadline must be met for consideration in the upcoming year's ceremonies.

The award process is now ready to begin. Johnny Grant, honorary mayor of Hollywood and chairman of the Selection Committee, calls the secret panel of experts to begin reviewing applications in June.

These entertainment specialists, one representing each of the five categories, judge and vote on hundreds of applications. The ones with the highest scores get set aside. The Selection Committee carefully scrutinizes the merits of each nominee. Discussions are held, shows may be watched, records listened to, etc. Finally, after a very difficult period with so many worthy talents to review, all votes are cast. Anywhere

Two Hollywood Walk of Fame honorees
are participating in the U.S. Marshal Association America's Star Award gala. Award recipient Julio Iglesias, presenter Charlton Heston, recipient Los Angeles Mayor Richard Riordan, and executive vice president, producer Arthur M. Kassel.

Superstar Mel Gibson and Director of Publicity, Ana Martinez-Holler

from 24 to 36 lucky artists will have their stars implanted in the following 12-month period. Dedication ceremonies will occur at the rate of one or two and occasionally three a month. Anyone may attend these events free of charge.*

Next, the fee must be paid. When the Walk of Fame started, store owners were assessed taxes according to their square front footage for the sidewalk improvements. Calculated at 1.25 million dollars, no one was happy with the taxation. A non-taxation system eventually replaced it. An award is currently funded by the nominee's sponsor. Very often, an individual sponsor can persuade a studio, network, record or radio corporation, or an independent organization to foot the bill.

This, however, does *not* mean a star can be bought, it *cannot*. It is a tribute bestowed upon a worthy artist. The Hollywood Historic trust is a non-profit organization, and is not able to fund the award and the ceremony, but they do care for the upkeep of the stars.

Sometimes a sponsor is simply an adoring fan, or fan club, who helped their idol land a tribute on the world's most famous sidewalk.

Singer Billie Holiday would have been very proud of the musicians, fans and restaurateurs who rallied on her behalf to obtain a recording star in her memory. This dedication ceremony occurred posthumously, and in her particular case, there was no corporate interest to pick up the tab. Instead, the sponsors held a successful fund raiser in the Lady's memory. Many stars have been honored posthumously, including Vivian Vance (from TV's "I Love Lucy" fame; the star was dedicated on Valentine's Day), Jim Henson (puppeteer creator of "The Muppet Show"—the star was unveiled on what would have been his 55th birthday), and recording legends Jimi Hendrix, and Patsy Cline.

At Tom Selleck's 1986 dedication ceremony, John Hillerman, that very fine and capable Texas-born actor who played Jonathan Quale Higgens III on "Magnum P.I.," asked me how much a star costs. After I told him $3,500, he looked at me with a twinkle in his eyes and a mischievous grin and said: "Hmmm, (3-second pause), not a bad price to pay for a bit of immortality."

In 2000, the $15,000 payment covers the actual cost of time, labor and materials to jackhammer out the blank star and replace it with a newly made one, complete with category emblem and name of recipient. Other labor, freight, city permits, traffic control, and security are also paid from the fee. Depending on the size of the ceremony, streets are blocked off. The director of publicity for the Walk of Fame, Ana Martinez-Holler, handles all private celebrity details, coordination of the international media, VIP passes to the ceremonies, and other special event aspects.

The one-time fee does not cover cleaning, maintenance, repair and replacement of damaged stars. The Hollywood Walk of Fame and Historic Trust rely in part on licensing fees to help cover these expenses. The stars are actually cleaned by hand, one at a time by paid workers. In some cases, a fan club "adopts" their favorite stars on the Walk to clean bi-monthly, at no charge. With upwards of 15 million visitors annually, the Walk gets a lot of wear and tear. It is one of the world's most popular tourist attractions, and all the better that it is free for visitors to enjoy.

If there is a significant personality missing from the Hollywood Walk of Fame, you can bet it is because he or she (1) has never been nominated; (2) was nominated, but could not beat the stiff competition that year and was asked to resubmit the following term (it may take several consecutive nominations before a nominee is finally selected); or (3) was unable to schedule attendance at the dedication ceremony, which is a stipulation for acceptance.

Who picks the location of the star? The recipient is asked for his or her placement preference. For many motion picture stars, one highly desirable location—which is now limited to a few blank spaces—is in front of the world-famous Grauman's Chinese Theater. Singer Tina Turner chose to have hers placed in front of Capitol Records on Vine Street. Hers lies in front of the circular building, which resembles a stack of records, appropriately enough. Others have their Walk of Fame star embedded near their mentors' or friends' stars. Talk show host Larry King wished to be near Arthur Godfrey, while game show host Pat Sajak asked to be next to

Recording giant David Bowie and famed publicity director Ana Martinez-Holler

Jack Paar. Dick Van Dyke's star was dedicated adjacent to his friend and mentor, Stan Laurel's. For years, W.C. Fields radio star was in front of a liquor store—a choice deliberately made to honor his memory. Although this may not be politically correct in today's climate, W.C. Fields was a man who *loved* his martinis, and he *certainly* would have appreciated the gesture. Fields' motion picture star lies in front of the Hollywood Roosevelt Hotel, next to Hugh M. Hefner's and Eddie Murphy's stars.

From those gifted pioneers of yesteryear whose hard work laid the foundation, to the global superstar generation, the Hollywood Walk of Fame serves to both rejoice in the talents and preserve the memories of America's unique cultural gift to the world—*entertainment.*

6925 HOLLYWOOD

Harry Langdon 🎬
Comedian

Harry Langdon

John Green 🎬
Composer, arranger, conductor

BORN Oct. 10, 1908, in New York, NY. **SPOTLIGHTS** Known by everyone as Johnny, he entered Harvard University at age 16. During his sophomore year, this genius had his first hit song "Coquette." Yet Johnny had no interest in pursuing a musical career. After graduating with a degree in economics in 1928, he headed to Wall Street. The disastrous stock market collapse on Black Friday, Oct. 29, 1929 decimated his chosen profession. He switched full-time to music and had a number of hit Broadway tunes, including "Body and Soul." This creative force collaborated with such greats as Ira Gershwin, Yip Harburg, and Johnny Mercer, to score some of Hollywood's finest: *Easter Parade* (1948), *An American in Paris* (1951), *West Side Story* (1961), *Bye Bye Birdie* (1963), and *Oliver* (1968). **ACHIEVEMENTS** 1948, 1951, 1961, and 1968 Academy Awards. Died: 1989.

Basil Rathbone 📺
See page 86

Billy Crystal 🎬
Actor, comedian, director, writer, producer, host

BORN Mar. 14, 1947, in Long Island, NY. **SPOTLIGHTS** Crystal is one of Hollywood's most beloved personalities. Raised in a show business environment, he hit the stand-up comedy circuit at an early age. Smart as a whip and fast with

6925 Hollywood

BORN June 15, 1884, in Council Bluffs, IA. **SPOTLIGHTS** A master of comic timing, Langdon's cute baby face enhanced his movie persona. He portrayed a man of complete innocence, so trusting and naive he did not realize when someone had wronged him, thus altering the final outcome in his favor. This very funny, bewildered-looking clown in two-and three-reelers caused hysterics with his lovable, confused personality in *There He Goes* (1925), and *Fiddlesticks* (1926). In the same comedy league as the big boys—Charlie Chaplin, Buster Keaton, and Harold Lloyd—Langdon's favorite feature comedies were *Tramp, Tramp, Tramp* (1926; probably his best work; written by Frank Capra) and *The Strong Man* (1926). Died: 1944.

6925 Hollywood

6925 Hollywood

6925 Hollywood

a quip, he swept TV talk shows. He missed out as a regular cast member in the brand new, hip and original "Saturday Night Live," but made headway in the progressive prime time series "Soap" (1977-'81). Crystal got another shot at "SNL" in 1984, and this time made it stick. He gained wide fame with his engaging characterizations. One of the public's favorites was the smooth talking Fernando, whose catchphrase *"You look mahvelous"* became American slang. His two comedy videos

Billy Crystal

are: *Billy Crystal—Don't Get Me Started* (1986), and *Billy Crystal—Midnight Train to Moscow* (1989). He made his silver screen debut in *Rabbit Test* (1978). He followed with *This Is Spinal Tap* (1984), *Running Scared* (1986), and *The Princess Bride* (1987). This critically acclaimed talent did not want to *Throw Mama from the Train* (1987), but took audiences for a joyride anyway in this superb black comedy with Danny De Vito. He pondered the question can women and men "just be friends" in the smash hit *When Harry Met Sally...*(1989), in which he distinguishes himself in the genre of romantic comedy. His portrayal of a New Yorker experiencing a mid-life crisis, who yearns to be a cowboy in *City Slickers* (1991), taught us all a funny thing or two about cattle drives. Motion pictures include *Mr. Saturday Night* (1992—his directorial debut; also co-screenplay, and producer), and *Forget Paris* (1995). He bravely tested Elizabethan waters in *Hamlet* (1996). In 1999, Crystal appears in America's #1 smash comedy hit, *Analyze This*, co-starring Robert De Niro and Lisa Kudrow. He received rave reviews for his hilarious portrayal of a nervous psychiatrist who treats a dangerous mobster (De Niro). He was also executive producer. **ACHIEVEMENTS** Known as the "Master of the Ad-lib," this intelligent, funny gentleman has hosted several Academy Awards ceremonies. Crystal has surpassed Johnny Carson's record of five hosting stints, but has not surpassed Bob Hope's 17 times. (In 2000, he hosted the 72nd Academy Awards; it was Crystal's seventh stint.) He is co-host of HBO's "Comic Relief," along with Whoopi Goldberg and Robin Williams, benefitting the nation's homeless. A six-time Emmy Award-winner, his Walk of Fame star was dedicated on June 4, 1991. About the joyous event, he commented, "I feel blessed."

Chill Wills 🎬
Actor, singer

6925 Hollywood

BORN July 18, 1903, in Seagoville, TX. **SPOTLIGHTS** Born on a sizzling hot day in Texas, his good-humored parents

Chill Wills

christened him Chill. As a tot, he performed in tent shows across Texas, Oklahoma and Nevada. Warned that his scratchy, funny sounding voice would kill any hopes of a movie career, Wills used it to his advantage, turning it into his personal gold mine. He even sings in *Bar 20 Rides Again* (1935). He made 50 pictures—frequently cast as a cowboy in supporting roles. He was wonderful in *Boom Town* (1940), and gave a great performance in *Giant* (1956), starring James Dean and Elizabeth Taylor. He was Oscar-nominated for best supporting actor in *The Alamo* (1960). He provided the offscreen voice of *Francis the Talking Mule* in a film series first starring Donald O'Connor, then later, Mickey Rooney. Died: 1978.

Jack Nicholson 🎥   6925 Hollywood
Actor, director, screenwriter

Jack Nicholson (right) with Johnny Grant

BORN John J. Nicholson; April 22, 1937, most likely in New Jersey, or New York. (No official birth certificate exists.) **SPOTLIGHTS** It might surprise many of you that as a child Nicholson himself sought out religion, was baptized in the Catholic Church at age six, enjoyed singing in the church choir, received Holy Communion, and was confirmed at the proper age. (He, in fact, would later reflect, "Catholicism was the only official dogma training I've had. I liked it. It's a smart religion.") Nicholson, too, is smart. He skipped seventh grade, but pretended not to be brainy, already putting to use his natural acting abilities. After graduating from Manasquan High School in the seaside town of Spring Lake, the gregarious 17-year-old traveled to Los Angeles for a visit. Instead of return-

ing home to follow his loose plans to attend an Eastern college, he surrendered to the hypnotic lure of the movie studios. Nicholson landed a job as an office boy in MGM's cartoon department, working under William Hanna (of Hanna-Barbera fame). The teenager glibly talked to everyone on the lot, famous, or not. Producer Joe Pasternak, whose keen eye for talent was legendary, offered him a screen test. Originally Nicholson said "no," then when he accepted, failed it. Pasternak, though, was encouraging—in a bizarre way. The producer told him, "Well, Jack, you're such an *unusual* person that I don't know exactly how we would use you, but when we need you, we'll need you very badly." The 20-year-old Nicholson was puzzled. (He commented, "I did not, quite frankly, think of myself as that strange, just as I don't today.") He made his interesting screen debut in Roger Corman's low-budget flick, *The Cry Baby Killer* (1958). He worked in several Corman pictures, including *The Little Shop of Horrors* (1960). That campy work—a black comedy horror film—was made in a record two days for principal photography and, for decades, has been a cult classic. Nicholson also wrote obscure "B" pictures for the director/producer. As the years passed, a frustrated Nicholson got very close to giving up acting all

Jack Nicholson

together in favor of his writing career. Then, he got his big break in the landmark road picture, *Easy Rider* (1969). His role as the drunken, disillusioned Southern lawyer who hits the highway with Peter Fonda and Dennis Hopper earned him his first Oscar nomination and catapulted him to stardom. Nicholson—a mysterious bundle of instinctive talent—has acted out both demons and angels. He is both lusty and lovable. His red-hot temper can send blue chills down any spine. He is as quickly humorous and unbelievably delightful. He is a movie star in the grandest scheme; an actor that even the best of the Golden Era talents would have been proud to call their colleague. Motion pictures include *Five Easy Pieces* (1970--in an Oscar-nominated performance), *Carnal Knowledge* (1971), *The Last Detail* (1973--in an Oscar-nominated performance), *Chinatown* (1974--in an Oscar-nominated performance), *The Passenger* (1975), *The Shining* (1980), *Reds* (1981--in an Oscar-nominated performance),*Prizzi's Honor* (1985--in an Oscar-nominated performance), *The Witches of Eastwick* (1987), *Ironweed* (1987--in an Oscar-nominated performance), *Batman* (1989), *A Few Good Men* (1992--in an Oscar-nominated performance), *Hoffa* (1992), and *The Evening Star* (1996). Worldwide audiences have come to know his trademark soulful musical drawl, arched eyebrows and unique charisma. **ACHIEVEMENTS** Winner of three Academy Awards: 1975 Best Actor in *One Flew Over the Cuckoo's Nest*, 1983 Best Supporting Actor in *Terms of Endearment*, and 1998 Best Actor in *As Good as It Gets*. Backstage at the 1998 Academy Awards Nicholson stated, "Well, welcome to the '90s. I like a career that covers three decades. I won one in the 1970s, one in the '80s and now this is the '90s. One of the things I meant to say in my speech is, if you have young children, you always wish they'd get to see you do something big, so I knew they were sitting home having a ball. They don't know the difference between this and bowling, but they know dad won." **QUOTE** Cheering family, friends and fans watched his Hollywood Walk of Fame star dedication ceremony on Dec. 4, 1996. Nicholson mused, "The first time I ever came to Hollywood, I came right over here, directly from the shores of New Jersey. I'm sure somewhere on this street is somebody exactly like me, who's gonna wind up standing exactly where I am, and that's the tradition I am very proud to be part of."

Marion Martin 🎥   6925 Hollywood
Actress
BORN June 7, 1916, in Philadelphia, PA. **SPOTLIGHTS** A tall, platinum blonde, she fluttered her long, dark eyelashes and utilized her sexy voice to seduce both stage and screen. On Broadway, she worked for Ziegfeld in the "Pretty Follies of 1933." She made her screen debut in Josef von Sternberg's *Sergeant Madden* (1939), a drama about a police officer whose son breaks his heart by becoming a gangster. She was a reliable supporting talent in *The Man in the Iron Mask* (1939). In *Boom Town* (1940) and *The Lady From Cheyenne* (1941), she appears as a feisty Western dance-hall hostess. For MGM, she had a terrific time playing with the Marx Brothers in *The Big*

Marion Martin

Store (1941), and another famous comedy team in *Abbott and Costello in Hollywood* (1945). Martin was solid in *George White's Scandals* (1945),*Cinderella Jones* (1946), and *Angel on My Shoulder* (1946). Although often typecast as a "loud" dame, this beauty descended from one of Philadelphia's finest families and was educated in exclusive European schools. Died: 1985.

Elton John 🎵   6925 Hollywood
Singer, composer, pianist

Elton John

BORN Reginald Kenneth Dwight; March 25, 1947, in Pinner, England. **SPOTLIGHTS** A legendary performer and recording artist, John was introduced to the piano at age three by his grandmother. He was semi-professional by age 14, then teamed with lyricist Bernie Taupin in 1967 to launch the most successful rock-'n'-roll song writing team since the Beatles' Paul McCartney and John Lennon. (Taupin writes the words, John the music.) His breakthrough *Elton John* was released in April 1970, with hits "Border Song," "Take Me To The Pilot," and "Your Song." In 1973 he had his first chart-topping album, *Don't Shoot Me I'm Only the Piano Player*. Throughout the decade, the master showman won incredible worldwide popularity with the now-classic pop hits: "Rocket Man," "Crocodile Rock," "Bennie and the Jets," "Philadelphia Freedom," "Candle In the Wind" (a tribute to movie star Marilyn Monroe), "Goodbye Yellow Brick Road," and "Someone Saved My Life Tonight." Possessing an incomparable, playful, and remarkable stage presence, he also became known for his outlandish and extravagant costumes, colorful eyeglasses and accessories. In the 1980s, gold/platinum hits include "I Guess That's Why They Call It the Blues," "Sad Songs (Say So Much)" and "That's What Friends Are For." In August of 1997 Taupin reworked the lyrics to "Candle In the Wind" for the funeral of John's friend, the beloved Diana, Princess of Wales. John performed live in Westminster Abbey. TV cameras were pointed away from her children, Prince William and Prince Harry, as mourners swallowed their hearts while John's rich tenor voice sang the opening lyrics "Goodbye England's Rose," moving the two young princes to tears. The funeral was watched by an estimated billion people worldwide and the song became one of the best-selling singles (song proceeds were donated to Diana's favorite causes and charities). **ACHIEVEMENTS** He and new lyric partner Tim Rice won Academy Awards for Disney's *The Lion King* (1994), and two Grammys. The movie's popular songs include "Can You See the Love Tonight," "Circle of Life," "I Just Can't Wait to Be King," and "Hakuna Matata." In 1998 he was honored to receive a British knighthood. **QUOTE** He spoke publicly about his battle with demons— drugs, alcohol and depression—stating, "I had to change because I was frightened. I didn't want to die angry and bitter and sad."

Joel Silver 🎥 6915 Hollywood
Producer

Joel Silver (holding star plaque on right side) with Johnny Grant and celebrity friends: Geena Davis (far left), Wesley Snipes (middle), Sly Stallone, and Joe Pesci (far right)

BORN July 14, 1952, in South Orange, NJ. **SPOTLIGHTS** A powerhouse producer, his movies serve up great excitement and big effects. He began as assistant/co-producer on such films as *Hooper* and *The End* (both 1978), both starring Burt Reynolds. But Silver was his own man, and soon enough was running his own company, Silver Pictures. His first production was *Commando* (1985), starring Arnold Schwarzenegger, followed by *Predator* (1987). The action just got bigger with *Lethal Weapon* (1987) and *Lethal Weapon 2* (1989), starring Mel Gibson and Danny Glover. Their characters maintain a genuine relationship even amid all the chaos. The mayhem of *Die Hard* (1988) and *Die Hard 2* (1990), starring Bruce Willis was explosive. Other Silver credits, in various capacities,

include *48 Hours* (1982), *Weird Science* (1985), *Lethal Weapon 3* (1992), *Demolition Man* (1993), *Executive Decision* (1996), and *Conspiracy Theory* (1997). He produced *House on Haunted Hill* (1999), and the Oscar-winning sci-fi movie, *The Matrix* (1999), starring Keanu Reeves. In 2000, he produced the action picture *Romeo Must Die,* starring Jet Li, Aaliyah, and Delrow Lindo, and *Dungeons and Dragons,* starring Jeromy Irons. **ACHIEVEMENTS** Recipient of an Image Award from the NAACP in recognition of his utilization of minority actors in a wide variety of roles.

Dick Powell 🎥 6915 Hollywood
Actor, singer, dancer, director, producer

Dick Powell

BORN Nov. 14, 1904, in Mountain View, AR. **SPOTLIGHTS** A memorable wavy-haired, clean-cut, boyish tenor of Busby Berkeley classic musicals, he stars opposite sweet-faced Ruby Keeler in *42nd Street* (1933) and *Gold Diggers of 1933.* He co-stars in the musical *Thanks a Million* (1935), with Ann Dvorak. About his days as a song-and-dance man in musicals, the former crooner said, "That was a wonderful period in my life, a beautiful experience and thoroughly enjoyable, but it's over. You look ahead, or at least you try to in this business." He became a surprise sensation as gumshoe Philip Marlowe, in *Murder, My Sweet* (1944), opposite Claire Trevor. The movie had been carefully adapted from one of Raymond Chandler's best novels, *Farewell, My Lovely.* In addition to the terrific story, this film had it all: perfect casting, style and great dialogue. Audiences loved Powell as a two-fisted tough guy. He followed up as an ex-serviceman—set on revenge—who travels the globe in pursuit of the Nazi who killed his wife in the taut thriller *Cornered* (1945). With a new second acting career in motion, he played steely heroes in thrillers and dramas: *Johnny O'Clock* (1947), and *The Bad and the Beautiful* (1952). He appears in *Station West* (1948), opposite Jane Greer. He produced *The Hunters* (1958). **TV** Hosted "Dick Powell's Zane Gray Theater" (1955-'61)...Married to Joan Blondell (1935-'45), and June Allyson (from 1945 on). **QUOTE** "This is a wonderful business, you know. One hit, and you're in. There's no business quite like it." Died: 1963.

Richard D. Zanuck 🎥 6915 Hollywood
Producer

BORN Dec. 13, 1934, in Los Angeles, CA. **SPOTLIGHTS** Born into a family with a passion for motion picture making, Richard is the son of mogul Darryl F. Zanuck (co-founder of 20th Century-Fox, production head and president). The son, though, brought his many talents to the table after graduating

Richard D. Zanuck

from Stanford University. Creative in his own right, he started in 20th Century-Fox's story department, then worked his way up to president in 1969. While Head of Production, 20th Century-Fox won three Best Picture Academy Awards for *The Sound of Music* (1965), *Patton* (1970), and *The French Connection* (1971). Credits as producer with David Brown include *Jaws* (1975), *The Verdict* (1982), *The Sting* (1973), and *Deep Impact* (1998). With his wife Lili, the Zanucks produced *Cocoon* (1985), *Cocoon: The Return* (1988), *Wild Bill* (1995), *Mulholland Falls* (1996), *Rush* (1991) and *Driving Miss Daisy* (1989). With his wife Lili Fini Zanuck, they became first-time Oscar show producers with the 72nd Annual Academy Award ceremonies in 2000. It was also the first time that either had produced a live show. **ACHIEVEMENTS** 1973 Oscar for *The Sting*. 1989 Best Picture for *Driving Miss Daisy* (co-produced with wife Lili). In 1990 Zanuck won the Academy's prestigious Irving Thalberg Humanitarian Award. **QUOTE** Regarding *Driving Miss Daisy*: "I'd talk to head of production at a studio and say, 'I've got a little picture about a black chauffeur and a white lady in the South, and it will only cost about seven million dollars.' Before I even finish the sentence I know I'm in trouble. We went down on our knees and everybody turned us down. We went to a group of dentists—they were going to use it as a tax shelter, and they turned us down! But we hung on, got the picture made and it went on to be hugely successful. You'd think after that experience people might pay more attention, but we still have to beg."

Zsa Zsa Gabor 📺   6915 Hollywood
Actress

Zsa Zsa Gabor

BORN Sari Gabor; Feb. 6, 1920, in Budapest, Hungary. **SPOTLIGHTS** A stunning teenager, she came in second in a 1936 Miss Hungary beauty contest. About her placing she remarked, "I should of been vurst. It vass a feex." A slinky-looking blonde, Gabor was wonderful in her screen debut —a musical comedy— *Lovely to Look At* (1952). That same year she appears in the dramatic story of French artist Toulouse-Lautrec in *Moulin Rouge*. The lavish picture captures Parisian nightlife during that era and won an Oscar for art direction. In 1953 she worked in the family musical *Lili,* and in the romantic ocean tale *The Story of Three Loves*. In 1959 she appeared in the musical *For the First Time* with the great tenor, Mario Lanza. She was delightful in the sexy comedy *Boys' Night Out* (1962), starring Kim Novak. This glamour puss became famous for her society headlines, fabulous collection of jewels and her good-humored, witty TV guest spots. In addition she has appeared on Broadway. She is known for her "Dollink" Hungarian speech pattern and her terrific sense of humor. Her sister is actress Eva Gabor of TV's "Green Acres" fame. **QUOTE** "I believe in beeg families. Every woman should have three husbands...I'm a vunderful housekeeper. Every time I get a divorce, I keep ze house."

Johnny Grant and Babe Ruth (right) in 1946

Johnny Grant 📺   6915 Hollywood
Entertainer, host, producer

BORN May 9, 1923, in Goldsboro, NC. **SPOTLIGHTS** The names Johnny Grant and Hollywood are synonymous. He is the Honorary Mayor of Hollywood (for life), dedicating himself to the betterment of the community. Perhaps President Ronald Reagan stated it best: "I can't even begin to recount your vast record of service to the Hollywood community, as well as your unswerving commitment to making our society a better place. From the first days of the Hollywood Christmas Parade, through a long and storied movie and television career, to your countless appearances at charity functions, you have always been the number one booster of America's most famous community—Hollywood. In fact, when one thinks of 'Tinseltown,' it's hard not to think of Johnny Grant." Considered movieland's International Ambassador of Goodwill, Grant's efforts on behalf of Hollywood are not simply *legendary*, they are continuous! Hardly a day goes by where the "Mayor of Hollywood" is not seen on television somewhere around the world. He served for decades as Executive Producer of the "Hollywood Christmas Parade" and telecast, having taken the reins of the then-local event back in 1978. Through his leadership, this annual spectacular grew to become the world's largest celebrity parade. Presented live to a million spectators on the streets of Hollywood, it is televised throughout the U.S. and to 88 foreign countries. In 1997 Bob Hope declared, "When you want to get something done in Hollywood, Johnny Grant is the man!" Grant has been an active and effective force in the splendid renovation of Hollywood, bringing the town back to its former glory—or better! An enthusiastic supporter of America's men and women in uniform, Grant holds the world record for overseas USO tours and visits. After serving in the Army Air Corps in World War II, he traveled to Korea 14 times to bring cheer to our troops; also to Vietnam, 14 times; to Beirut, Saudi Arabia and Bosnia. In late 1999, Grant flew to Macedonia and Kosovo to visit American peacekeepers in preparation for the Millennium USO Tour. In all, he has made 53 USO and personal "handshake" tours entertaining GIs around the globe. General William C. Westmoreland, America's long-time commander in Vietnam wrote to Grant: "Your patriotic contribution to the morale and welfare of the United States and Free World Military Assistance Forces has earned you the lasting respect and admiration of this command and reflects the highest credit upon yourself and your profession." Among his credits is the *first national telethon* ever produced. It raised funds to send our Olympic athletes to Helsinki in 1952. Grant's 60-year career in the entertainment industry encompasses motion pictures (we see him every year in *White Christmas*), television and radio. In 1997 Johnny Grant received one of filmdom's greatest honors, he was the 190th celebrity to have his hand and footprints enshrined in cement in "the forecourt of honor" at the world-famous Grauman's Chinese Theatre. While joining the elite ranks of the world's greatest entertainers at that landmark location, Johnny made one of his few ever permanent mistakes...in the excitement of the moment he left out one of the n's in Johnny! That ceremony created a new Hollywood trivia question: Who are the only three people to have their hands and footprints AND their Walk of Fame stars in front of the Chinese Theatre? Johnny is in good company with Jack Nicholson and Robin Williams. **ACHIEVEMENTS** Two Emmy Awards, including the "Governor's Award," and 14 Emmy nominations; 1982 "Wrangler Award" in the Cowboy Hall of Fame for "outstanding contributions to Western heritage through TV programming." He holds the rank of Major General in the California State Military Reserve; honored by the California Army National Guard with two awards of the Order of California—the State's highest decoration for service; USO's Distinguished American Award. The Department of Defense, the U.S. Army, and the U.S. Navy (on behalf of the Marine Corps) have decorated General Grant with an unprecedented three Distinguished Service Medals for Public Service. Recipient of the first-ever "Spirit of Hollywood" award, and hundreds of other honors.

Glenn Miller 🔴 **6915 Hollywood**

Major Glenn Miller (r) confers with military colleague Johnny Grant

Band leader, arranger, trombonist
BORN Alton Glenn Miller; March 1, 1904, in Clarinda, IA. **SPOTLIGHTS** Glenn Miller was one of the most romantic, outstanding popular dance band leaders of the swing era. The band's music exuded many moods, much contrast and always generated colossal excitement. Miller's artistic sensitivity, imagination and confidence helped create the jazzy, hot environment of the late 1930s and '40s. His music was easily identifiable as having that "Glenn Miller sound." Noted for the band's precise playing of arrangements, his special device was doubling a melody on saxophone with a clarinet an octave higher. He became a celebrity with his gigantic hits: "Little Brown Jug," "Humoresque," "A String of Pearls," "Pennsylvania Six Five Thousand" (the Hotel Pennsylvania's telephone number), "That Old Black Magic," "Tuxedo Junction," "At Last," "Serenade in Blue," "Chattanooga Choo-Choo" and "Moonlight Serenade," his theme song. Miller's biggest hit of all time was "In the Mood." His best-loved, most enchanting and romantic waltz was "Alice Blue Gown." He had his own radio show starting in 1941, where his well-known medley was "something old, something new, something borrowed, something blue." Amazingly, the Glenn Miller band only played for eight years; most critics dismiss the first two as "terrible," but praise the last six as "outstanding." It was America's best-loved dance band. Miller and his band performed in two movies: *Sun Valley Serenade* (1941) and *Orchestra Wives* (1942). A film based on his life, *The Glenn Miller Story* (1953), stars James Stewart in the title role, and June Allyson as his devoted wife Helen. **QUOTE** Although too old to be drafted, the patriotic Miller felt compelled to serve in WWII. He stated, "I, like every American, have an obligation to fulfill. That obligation is to lend as much support as I can to winning the war. It is not enough for me to sit back and buy bonds...The mere fact that I have had the privilege of exercising the rights to live and work as a free man puts me in the same position as every man in uniform, for it was the freedom and the democratic way of life we have that enabled me to make strides in the right direction." Ironically, Miller, who had a fear of flying, accepted a commission in the U.S. Army Air Corps (Air Force) in September 1942. His Army serial number was 0505273. His expanded all-soldier orchestra was heard via radio broadcasts in the U.S., and entertained GIs fighting in Western Europe. Band members came from some of the country's best big swing bands: Artie Shaw's, Harry James', Tommy Dorsey's, and Vaughn Monroe's. Some musicians were culled from leading symphony orchestras. Miller created the most spectacular and exciting

sound since John Philip Sousa. Marching music included "St. Louis Blues," and "Blues On the Night." Died: Dec. 15, 1944, in a plane crash between London and Paris, over the English Channel. At first, it was speculated that the plane was downed in the heavy fog. Other sources asserted Miller had been flying in a small aircraft associated with the statesman, Sir Winston Churchill. The Nazis suspected the war leader was on board and shot it out of the air. The truth will never be known.

Leon Shamroy 🎥   6915 Hollywood
Cinematographer

BORN July 16, 1901, in New York, NY. **SPOTLIGHTS** Known to his friends as "Shamy," those who did not like him called him "Grumble Guts." As temperamental as any prima donna, "Grumble Guts" never shied from telling anyone off, including the movie stars with whom he worked. He could be both rude and arrogant. But the technicians who worked alongside him recognized "Shamy" as a tough guy on the outside with a heart of...gold? If it were gold, he spent it at the track; he loved thoroughbred racing. At work, Shamroy did get the job done in outstanding fashion, as confirmed by his many Academy Awards. Shamroy was a brilliant cinematographer, whose use of light was wholly unique. **ACHIEVEMENTS** Oscars: *The Black Swan* (1942), *Wilson* (1944), *Leave Her to Heaven* (1945), and *Cleopatra* (1963). Died: 1974.

Creighton Hale 🎥   6901 Hollywood
Actor

Creighton Hale

BORN Patrick Fitzgerald; May 13, 1883, in Cork, Ireland. **SPOTLIGHTS** His theatrical father, who was with a touring company, introduced Hale to the stage when he was an infant. By age 30, and following in his father's footsteps, Creighton traveled to America with an Irish troupe. Within a year, he had made his screen debut in *The Million Dollar Mystery* (1914--serial). It only took a few years for the rambunctious lad to become a star. By 1917, Hale was one of the top-salaried film personalities, a real who's who in silents. His winning ways seduced audiences in *Forbidden Love* (1921). His best known starring role was *The Cat and the Canary* (1927). Those who graced the silver screen discovered, for the first time in their theatrical lives, that being a movie star meant swimming in Tinseltown's goldfish bowl. The debonair Hale did not seem to mind the strain, nor the admiration. His movies as a supporting actor include *Hollywood Boulevard* (1936), *The Return of Doctor X* (1939), *Larceny, Inc.* (1942), and *The Perils of Pauline* (1947). Died: 1965.

Tom Selleck 🎥   6901 Hollywood
Actor, producer

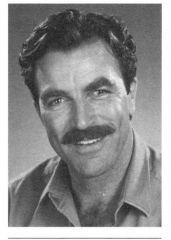
Tom Selleck

BORN Jan. 29, 1945, in Detroit, MI. **SPOTLIGHTS** Tom Selleck is the definitive "Jeopardy" answer to "Who's tall, dark and handsome?" Like many of Hollywood's Golden Era leading men, Selleck shares movieland traits and history that will serve him in future works. For instance, Cary Grant—arguably one of the finest, most charming and important actors in cinema—got his break from Mae West in *She Done Him Wrong*. Selleck, too, was chosen by West—albeit in a dreadful film, but nonetheless she could spot desirable characteristics that would translate well on film—in *Myra Breckinridge* (1970). And like Clark Gable, star of *Gone With the Wind* (1939), both he and Selleck share the same knowing smile and a twinkle in the eyes that ladies find irresistible. Selleck's own path would have mirrored Gable's more closely had he been able to play the film role for which he had been originally cast—that of Indiana Jones of *Raiders of the Lost Ark* (1981). Selleck, unfortunately, could not get released from his TV series "Magnum P.I."(1980-'88) in what must have been one of the biggest blows to his career. He did earn an Emmy and Golden Globe for his role as the Honolulu-based private eye for that show, and enjoyed tremendous worldwide popularity. Still it was not the action-packed motion picture career he could have easily won in the Indiana Jones role. Selleck made eight movies before his first hit, the smash comedy *Three Men and a Baby* (1987). Then, he turned in a must-see performance in *Quigley Down Under* (1990), as an American cowboy who travels to Australia for work. Underrated during its first release, this film has a huge, growing audience of fans proving that critics don't always know best out of the box. Selleck was truly superb in the black comedy *Folks* (1992), opposite Don Ameche who plays his infirm father. This clever picture about aging in America is wickedly humorous and Selleck carries it off as Cary Grant would have. It is an impressive performance that unfortunately had to compete with the L.A. riots when released. He received high marks for his role in the film *In & Out* (1997). He co-stars opposite the talented Kate Capshaw in the romantic comedy *The Love Letter* (1999). Other TV work includes "Broken Trust" (1995), the Western "Last Stand at Saber River" (1997)—for which he received the Cowboy Hall of Fame Heritage Award as star and executive producer—and in 1996 he joined the popular cast of "Friends" for a recurring comic role. **QUOTE** On June 4, 1986, a bevy of family, celebrity friends, fans and international media attended his star dedication ceremony. He said, "You have to believe in yourself and you have to follow your dreams because your talent, whether it's acting or anything, generally lies where your dreams are."

William Dieterle 🎥
Director

6901 Hollywood

William Dieterle (right) with Buddy Adler

BORN July 15, 1893, in Germany. **SPOTLIGHTS** He presented a strong anti-war statement when he showed battered human nature in *The Last Flight* (1931). This WWI postwar study stars Richard Barthelmess and Helen Chandler. In 1935 he worked with fellow countryman, producer Max Reinhardt, in Warner Bros.' *A Midsummer's Night Dream*. The cameraman, Hal Mohr, won an Academy Award for his work on the fantasy piece, but the film suffers from major flaws. Dieterle fared better the next decade. He didn't sell his soul for *All That Money Can Buy* (1941), but the "farmer" in this wonderful picture did. One of his most memorable motion pictures, *I'll Be Seeing You* (1944), stars Ginger Rogers, Joseph Cotten and Shirley Temple in a touching love story about a convict and a shell-shocked veteran...The director always wore white gloves, but he was not a gentleman on the set. Backstage, he unleashed his inner tyrant, terrifying actors into submission. Died: 1972.

William Shatner 📺
Actor, director

6901 Hollywood

William Shatner

BORN March 22, 1931, in Montreal, Canada. **SPOTLIGHTS** An actor idolized by millions, Shatner earned immortalization playing the intelligent, passionate Captain James T. Kirk in TV's "Star Trek" (1966-'69). In fact, it was this good-looking, energetic actor who launched the original sci-fi series. The first pilot--with a different lead actor in the role--was rejected. A rare second pilot was requested by the network, and with Shatner at the helm, the cast came together. His mission to "boldly go where no man has gone before" on the Starship U.S.S. Enterprise won an immediate loyal following. And its many spin-off series are as popular—if not more popular—today. Shatner co-stars in a number of related movies, starting with *Star Trek—The Motion Picture* (1979). Others include *Star Trek II: The Wrath of Khan* (1982), *Star Trek III: The Search for Spock* (1984), *Star Trek IV: The Voyage Home* (1986), *Star Trek V: The Final Frontier* (1989; also dir., co-story), *Star Trek VI: The Undiscovered Country* (1991), and *Star Trek: Generations* (1994). Before working in

"Star Trek," this solid actor was an accomplished Broadway stage performer and a pioneer actor in live TV. Shatner made his powerful silver screen debut in *The Brothers Karamazov* (1958). He delivers a compelling performance as Alexei Karamazov in Fyodor Dostoyevsky's family saga. The MGM motion picture was the #1 film of the year. He is wonderful in the engrossing drama *Judgment at Nuremberg* (1961), appears in several other films, then co-stars opposite Angie Dickinson in Roger Corman's *Big Bad Mama* (1974). His uniquely paced voice and sense of timing proved zany in comedy, too: *Airplane II, The Sequel* (1982), and *National Lampoon's Loaded Weapon I* (1993). In 1999, he appears in the parody *Free Enterprise*. The funny, campy comedy is about two zealous "Star Trek" fans (Trekkies), who worship Shatner until they meet him. Other TV: He came down to earth in 1982 to star in the police drama as Sergeant "T. J. Hooker." He also directed a number of episodes. Since 1991, he has hosted "Rescue 911."...His autobiography is entitled *Star Trek Memories* (1993), and he has penned sci-fi novels. (See the bios of Gene Roddenberry, Leonard Nimoy, DeForest Kelley, George Takei and Nichelle Nichols in this book.) **QUOTE** At his May 19, 1983 star dedication ceremony, Shatner remarked, "Life is full of surprises, both uplifting and degrading. The Walk of Fame, with its bubble gum and doggy doo, and its steps of admiration, is also the way of life. I'm humbled and grateful to be included here."

Danny Thomas 📺
Actor, singer, comedian

6901 Hollywood

Danny Thomas

BORN Amos Muzyad Jacobs; Jan. 6, 1912, in Deerfield, MI. **SPOTLIGHTS** The fifth born of nine children from struggling Lebanese immigrants, young Amos was raised by his doting, childless aunt because of his mother's ill health. When he got a job selling candy in a burlesque theatre, he discovered a sweet tooth for show business. Although the Great Depression was not the best time to be trying this, Thomas dropped out of high school to be a comic. He worked in dingy, shabby rooms in Chicago, where he was ashamed to use his real name, so he took his stage name from two of his brothers. He earned $2 a night. On this salary he had to get his wife and newborn daughter, Margaret (later, Marlo) out of the hospital. He prayed to St. Jude, patron saint of hopeless causes: *"Help me find a way in life and I will build you a shrine."* (He later stated, "I never said make me rich and famous. I said 'help me find a way...'") His prayers were answered immediately. The very next day he landed a job entertaining and received just enough money to pay the hospital bills. He began playing upscale clubs, hooked up with a veteran publicist, and was invited to Hollywood for "The Baby Snooks Show." Known as *comedy's* *greatest storyteller*, he never rushed his jokes. The experience of hearing Thomas tell the winding stories to get to the end was as enjoyable as the punch line itself. All the while, he never forgot his promise to St. Jude. He generated massive amounts of dollars for the building of his shrine, the St. Jude Children's Research Hospital, in Memphis, Tennessee. In 1953 he starred in the Emmy-award winning "Make Room for Daddy." It became one of the longest-running family comedies, lasting 18 years (also under the names "The Danny Thomas Show," and "Make Room for Granddaddy"). The show remains a rarity, where the father exudes warmth, humor, and human frailty, but is not depicted as a fool. His promise to St. Jude was realized in the early 1960s. In 1962, when the survival rate of children with acute lymphocytic leukemia was less than 5%, the first sick child was admitted to the hospital. His words were as good as gold when he stated, "We are the pediatric research center of the world." *In his lifetime he raised $1 billion dollars to help sick children, and lived to see their survival rate improve to 50%.* **ACHIEVEMENTS** Thomas said, "St. Jude's Hospital is the greatest accomplishment of my life, something that will live long after the celluloid turns yellow." For his Good Works, Pope Pius XII made the Roman Catholic Maronite a Knight of Malta. Pope Paul VI decorated him as a Knight Commander of the Holy Sepulcher of Jerusalem. In 1985 President Reagan honored him with a Congressional Gold Medal, declaring Thomas "a pioneer in wholesome entertainment." His daughter Marlo has a star (see her bio in this book), and his son Tony is a successful producer. At Thomas' funeral, Catholic Archbishop Roger Mahony spoke of Thomas as "a special meteor, a person of unusual brilliance and light." Bob Hope commented that his friend "didn't wish for things to be better and brighter—he went out and made them that way." Tearfully Hope added, "I have it on good authority that God said, 'Move over—make room for Danny.'" **QUOTE** Thomas was a religious man, but never evangelized his beliefs. He said, "My purpose in life is to propagate the philosophy of man's faith in man, based upon my own belief that unless man re-establishes his faith in his fellow beings, he can never establish a faith in God." This great man died in 1991.

Charles Bronson 🎥   6901 Hollywood

Actor

BORN Charles Bunchinsky; Nov. 3, 1922, in Ehronfeld, PA. **SPOTLIGHTS** A man of few words, Bronson's tough-looking, droopy-eyed, rock-hard face and macho physique originally got him cast as a villain. He played such characters as the notorious *Machine Gun Kelly* (1958), in Roger Corman's classic B picture. Over the decades his face softened into craggy lines, and his ruggedness proved safe, honorable and believable as the hero. He became best known in roles that used justified homicide against evil creeps. Among his many credits are *House of Wax* (1953), *The Magnificent Seven* (1960), *The Dirty Dozen* (1967), *The Valachi Papers* (1972), *The Stone Killer* (1973), *Death Wish* (1974, plus successful sequels through 1994), *The*

Charles Bronson

White Buffalo (1977—as Wild Bill Hickok), and *The Evil That Men Do* (1984). Many critics consider the brutal Depression-era boxing/action picture *Hard Times* (1975) his best work. His co-stars: James Coburn and Jill Ireland. **ACHIEVEMENTS** 1968 top box office star in Europe; 1971 world's most popular actor (Golden Globe); 1973-'81 one of the world's top box office stars. Married to actress Jill Ireland, she also has a star on the Walk of Fame (see her bio).

Dinah Shore 🔴   6901 Hollywood

See page 490

Robin Williams 🎥   6925 Hollywood

Actor, comedian, producer

Robin Williams (holding star plaque)

BORN July 21, 1952, in Chicago, IL. **SPOTLIGHTS** A versatile leading actor, he first came to America's attention as the manic, misfit extraterrestrial in TV's smash hit "Mork and Mindy." A comic virtuoso, he possesses a superb verbal dexterity with lightning speed. His improvisational talents are unmatched. From the small screen, he leaped into feature films, astounding critics and surprising everyone alike with his ability to perform in serious dramatic roles. Films include *The World According to Garp* (1982), *Good Morning, Vietnam* (1988) and *Dead Poets Society* (1989)—the last two earned him Academy Award nominations. He delivers a gripping performance in the must-see drama, *The Fisher King* (1991). His fun, flexible and expressive voice can be heard in Disney's animated feature film *Aladdin* (1992). Then, Williams is delightful in *Mrs. Doubtfire* (1993), as a devoted father who dresses in drag to be his children's nanny. He is hilarious in *The Birdcage* (1996). That same year, he co-stars in *Hamlet*, proving Shakespeare was not out of his thespian reach. He received rave reviews for his sensitive performance in *What Dreams May Come* (1998), as a loving husband who mourns for his wife after *his* death. Then, he stars in *Patch Adams*, based on a physician's true story. In 1999, he stars in *Jakob the Liar*, and in *Bicentennial Man.* **ACHIEVEMENTS** 1997 Best Supporting Actor Academy Award for *Good Will Hunting.* Thrilled beyond belief, Williams quickly named the Oscar statuette his "golden dude." In 1986, he was the first solo comedian to perform at the NY Metropolitan Opera. He is a primary force, along with Billy Crystal and Whoopi Goldberg, for more than a decade in HBO's annual "Comic Relief," a telethon to benefit the homeless. Williams is a clown in the best sense of the word, he can make us laugh and cry. A true sweetheart, this beloved talent received his Hollywood Walk of Fame star on Dec. 12, 1990 with much adoration.

Broderick Crawford 🎥   6901 Hollywood
See page 451

John Travolta 🎥   6901 Hollywood
Actor, singer, dancer

John Travolta

BORN Feb. 18, 1954, in Englewood, NJ. **SPOTLIGHTS**: Known as a triple threat for his ability to sing, dance and act, this handsome, dark-haired, cleft-chinned talent was destined for the world's stage. His energetic Broadway performances led to TV's "Welcome Back Kotter," as the not-too-bright Vinnie Barbarino, and introduced him to America-at-large. Travolta leaped into international superstardom with his breakthrough movie *Saturday Night Fever* (1977), as an egotistic Brooklynite. The show stopper was his famous dance number in the now-historic white suit; it mesmerized the world. Travolta launched a global disco dance craze with the Bee Gees hits "Stayin' Alive," "Night Fever," and "How Deep Is Your Love." *Time* magazine wrote: "When Travolta first appears in *Saturday Night Fever* there's an instant charge...No one can fully define star quality, but...in 1978, that walk is the best one around." He stars in the nostalgic 1950s musical *Grease* (1978), opposite Olivia Newton-John, and creates another vivid character. The movie's soundtrack remains one of the most popular, highest-selling in history. As a macho oil field worker who plays hard in *Urban Cowboy* (1980), he started another international fad. City folks everywhere donned Western duds and packed into noisy honky-tonks to ride mechanical bulls. After he misfired on a couple of flops, he

took a respite from acting to do what he likes best—flying. He also settled down with his beautiful actress-wife Kelly Preston, and started a family. Re-energized, he appears in a film comedy series called *Look Who's Talking* (1989; 1991; 1993). It did not get critics, nor Travolta devotees talking, but children loved it. Next, this actor pulled off the most amazing feat of all—when nobody in Hollywood was expecting it. He delivered a gritty performance in *Pulp Fiction* (1994). He enjoyed immediate critical and commercial success, while still hypnotizing audiences with his dancing. "The Comeback Kid" grabbed the crown of superstardom *again*. (It couldn't happen to a nicer guy; he is so gracious.) He followed with a divine performance in *Get Shorty* (1995). In 1996, he was a grubby angel, not a saint, in *Michael*. Films include *Broken Arrow* (1996), *Face/Off* (1997), *Primary Colors* (1997), *The Thin Red Line* (1998), *A Civil Action* (1998), and *The General's Daughter* (1999). **QUOTE** "We're all flawed, but despite that we can all do great things." When he received his star on June 5, 1985, he said, "Now this *is* perfect. Thank you!"

Buster Crabbe 📺   6901 Hollywood
Actor

Buster Crabbe

BORN: Clarence Lindon Crabbe; Feb. 17, 1907, in Oakland, CA. **SPOTLIGHTS**: Fished out of an Olympic-sized chlorinated pool by Paramount Pictures and placed on jungle vines, he wrestled with beasts in *King of the Jungle*, and *Tarzan the Fearless* (both 1933). After appearing in a number of the feature films and serial version, he moved into other hero roles in both science fiction movies and Westerns. In the late 1930s and early 1940s, he appears in the title roles in both *Flash Gordon* and *Buck Rogers*. He won a new generation of young fans when his edited *Rogers* movies were shown as a TV serial. Crabbe was also starred in TV's "Captain Gallant." He made 50 movies. **ACHIEVEMENTS** Winner of the 1928 Olympic bronze medal in swimming. 1932 gold medal in swimming. In 1971 he broke the world's record in 400-meter free style for people older than sixty. Died: 1983.

Wayne Newton 🎵   6901 Hollywood
Singer, musician, actor

BORN April 3, 1942, in Roanoke, VA. **SPOTLIGHTS** This handsome, dark-haired, all-around entertainer is descended from Native American Powhatan/Cherokee blood; a heritage

Wayne Newton

Newton is extremely proud of. At age four, his parents took him to see Hank Williams and Kitty Wells perform in a Grand Ole Opry road show. After the show he told his mother, "This is what I want to do." "What?" she asked. "That," he answered, pointing toward the stage. A natural, he learned the piano, guitar and steel guitar by ear with the help of a few lessons. Two years later this precocious, big-voiced kid was doing his own daily radio show before school. He was in first grade when selected to perform in a show for President Truman! As an adult he became Las Vegas' favorite entertainer, performing live to more than 20,000,000 people. He is known for giving each show his all, working hard to deliver the goods. In *Spin* magazine Jim Greer wrote "...his show is the standard by which I will henceforth judge each future concert of any genre. I'm not talking about camp, or kitsch...I'm talking about full-blooded American entertainment." Devoted fans come from all corners of the earth to hear him. His nickname is "Mr. Las Vegas." Among his hit recordings are: "Heart," "Danke Schoen," "Red Roses for a Blue Lady," "Summer Wind," "Dreams of a Everyday Housewife," "Daddy, Don't You Walk So Fast," "Years," "She Believes in Me," and "While the Feeling's Good." Newton's feature films include *License to Kill* (1989), *The Adventures of Ford Fairlane* (1990), and *Vegas Vacation* (1997). Also as an actor, he has worked in countless TV shows like "Ally McBeal," "Roseanne," and "LA Law," as well as mini-series and cable shows. **ACHIEVEMENTS** The U.S. Department of Defense awarded Wayne its highest civilian award for performing in several dangerous locales, including Vietnam, Beirut (after the 1983 bombing of the Marine barracks in Lebanon), and the Persian Gulf. He is also the recipient of numerous prestigious medals and honors, such as the Founder's Award of the St. Jude Children's Hospital, and the American Legion's Exceptional Citizen Award.

Beniamino Gigli ●   6901 Hollywood

Opera singer

BORN March 20, 1890, in Recanati, Italy. **SPOTLIGHTS**: A great, bel canto lyric tenor in a class with Enrico Caruso, he possessed a powerful, superb, sweet tonal quality. Recordings include *La Boheme* on EMI; *Puccini's Tosca* on Victor label; and Leoncavallo's *Pagliacci*. At the Metropolitan Opera, Gigli was frequently cast in romantic roles opposite the soprano, Maria Jeritz. Offstage, they loathed each other. In one scene of *Fedora,* Gigli had to reject her. Keeping in character, he violently pushed Jeritz. She stumbled backwards onstage—just missing a dive into the orchestra pit—and ended up lying smack on the floor. To everyone's surprise, the diva sang the rest of the scene on her back. When the two went backstage, Gigli explained it had been an accident, but Jeritz claimed he tried to kill her. Her husband, Baron von Popper, challenged Gigli to a duel. The press had a field day, reporting that they were at each other's throat in front of their fans. The prima donna swore to the press she would never sing with him again. For the record: in two weeks they performed beautifully together in *Tosca*...That's show business, no matter how high the art form. Died: 1957.

Billy Graham ▮   6901 Hollywood

Evangelist

The Rev. and Mrs. Billy Graham

BORN William F. Graham; Nov. 7, 1918, in Charlotte, NC. **SPOTLIGHTS** This beloved evangelist has covered the globe preaching the Gospel to princes and paupers alike. Reared on a dairy farm, at age 16 the tall teen accepted Christ at a revival meeting. Ordained in 1940 by the Southern Baptist Convention, he received a solid foundation in the Scriptures at Florida Bible Institute (now Trinity College). The 1949 Los Angeles Crusade vaulted the Reverend Graham onto the public stage, and to this day he continues his Good Works. In 1950, he founded the Billy Graham Evangelistic Association. In his rich Southern drawl and baritone voice, he has carried his live sermons to more than 160 million people at revival meetings (often in stadiums), where he has preached the Gospel. These crusades have reached hundreds of millions more —with the message of faith and love—through radio, television, film, and newspaper columns around the globe. In response to objections raised about using media to reach souls, the Reverend said, "I am selling the greatest product in the world. Why shouldn't it be promoted as well as soap?" He also observed, "St. Paul didn't have television. We can reach more people by TV probably than the population of the world was then." His extremely popular weekly radio program is broadcast worldwide and his television specials air during prime time. He encourages the young and old alike to avoid temptation. He declared, "When Satan knocks, I just send Christ to the door." He received the Congressional Gold Medal with his wife Ruth in 1996. He marked the occasion with a fine sermon. He preached, "We must commit our lives to God and to the moral and spiritual truths that have made this nation great." The Rev. is regularly listed by the Gallup polls as one of the "Ten Most Admired Men in the World." His autobiography *Just As I Am*, was published by Harper Collins. **QUOTE** Based on Biblical Revelation 21, Verse 16, he calculates the dimensions of Heaven at: "1,600 miles long, 1,600 miles wide and 1,600 miles high."

Judy Holliday 🎥   6901 Hollywood
Actress

Judy Holliday

BORN Judith Tuvim; June 21, 1922, in New York, NY. (Her translated last name "Tuvim" means holiday in Hebrew.) **SPOTLIGHTS** A perky Broadway stage star with a uniquely pitched voice, she was a master of comedy. Holliday made a mint playing the ever-popular shrewd dumb blonde. But she was hardly stupid in real life, her genius IQ was 172. Movies include *Adam's Rib* (1949) opposite Katherine Hepburn and Spencer Tracy, *The Marrying Kind* (1952) with Aldo Ray, *Phffft!* (1954) with Jack Lemmon and Kim Novak, *It Should Happen to You* (1954) co-starring Peter Lawford and Lemmon, *The Solid Gold Cadillac* (1956) with Paul Douglas, and *Full of Life* (1957). **ACHIEVEMENTS** 1950 Best Actress Oscar for *Born Yesterday*, in her first movie role. **QUOTE** "It takes smarts to play dumb." Died: 1965.

Julie Andrews 🎥   6901 Hollywood
Actress, singer

Julie Andrews

BORN Julia Elizabeth Wells; Oct. 1, 1935, at Walton-on-Thames, England. **SPOTLIGHTS** As a child her name was changed to that of her stepfather, Ted Andrews, who was a music hall tenor. Her own voice was discovered to have magical qualities when, as an eight-year-old, her stepfather gave her singing lessons. Her mother first took her to a throat specialist to check out this remarkable instrument, then to a singing coach, one Lillian Stiles-Allen. At age 12, she made her professional debut singing the "Polonaise" from *Mignon* at London's Hippodrome Theater. Thereafter, she toured all over England, appearing in music halls, doing concerts, performing a Christmas spectacular every year and doing a radio series. At age 18, she was cast as Polly Brown in the Broadway production of "The Boyfriend," for which she received rave reviews and her name was placed above the title on the marquee. Before she turned 21 years old, she had been cast as Eliza, the female lead in the Lerner-Loewe production of "My Fair Lady," opposite Rex Harrison, who played Professor Higgins. She was a smash on Broadway and triumphant in the same role when it went to London. This was followed by Lerner and Loewe's "Camelot," where she played the role of Guinevere opposite Richard Burton's King Arthur. It was hoped that she would win the film role of Eliza in "My Fair Lady." That went to Audrey Hepburn instead, the studios thinking that the latter was well known to cinema audiences whereas Julie Andrews had never made a film. Thankfully, Walt Disney welcomed the actress at his studio and cast her as the English nursemaid in the musical *Mary Poppins* (1964). Andrews sparkled as the crisp nanny. Her performance was luminous, and earned her an Academy Award. The very next year she was immortalized in yet *another* role, that of a postulant turned governess in *The Sound of Music*. This superb classic became one of the best-loved films of all time, for which she received her second Academy Award nomination. Director Robert Wise said, "There is a genuineness about her, an unphoniness. She goes right through the camera onto film and out to the audience. Julie seems to have born with that magic gene that comes through on the screen." The adapted true life story of the Von Trapp family became the highest grossing box office movie at the time, toppling the blockbuster #1 longtime winner, *Gone with the Wind*, off its record-holding throne, and taking all of Hollywood by storm. Among her other credits are *The Americanization of Emily* (1964), *Hawaii* (1966), *Thoroughly Modern Millie* (1967), *10* (1980), *S.O.B.* (1981), and *That's Life!* (1986). In 1983, she starred as a woman impersonating a man impersonating a woman in *Victor/Victoria*, which earned her a third Academy Award nomination. More than a decade later she reprised the role on the Broadway stage. **ACHIEVEMENTS** 1964 Best Actress Oscar for *Mary Poppins*. (Only a handful of actresses have won this prestigious trophy their first time out.) Three Golden Globes, one for *Mary Poppins*, one for *Sound of Music*, and one for *Victor/Victoria*. Emmy-nominated six times for her excellent television specials and series, in 1973 she won an Emmy Award for "The Julie Andrews Hour" (outstanding variety musical series). She is the recipient of countless honors. In 2000, she was designated Dame Julie (the female version of the British Knight) by Queen Elizabeth...She is married to director Blake Edwards (see his bio in this book), and they have five children. She and her husband contribute to various charities, and are on the board of Operation USA, an international relief agency which rushes help to disaster areas worldwide. They are also on the board of the Foundation for Hereditary Disease, and Ms. Andrews is a Goodwill Ambassador for UNIFEM, the United Nations international fund for women. Two of her children's books have been published and another two are expected. **QUOTE** "I never dreamed, when I lived in the small village of Walton-on-Thames in Surrey, England, that one day I would have my name on the Hollywood Walk of Fame. I consider it a tremendous honor."

Edgar Kennedy 🎥   6901 Hollywood
Actor, comedian

BORN April 26, 1890, in Monterey, CA. **SPOTLIGHTS** He clowned with the best, including Charlie Chaplin and Laurel and Hardy. He co-stars with the Marx Brothers in *Duck Soup* (1933). Died: 1948.

Olivia Newton-John    6901 Hollywood
Singer, actress

Olivia Newton-John

BORN Sept. 26, 1948, in Cambridge, England. **SPOTLIGHTS** The granddaughter of the 1954 Nobel Prize laureate physicist Max Born (who was also a Cambridge University professor), and the daughter of a university professor, Newton-John was raised in Australia since age five. As a teenager, she formed her first band, the Sol Four. After she won a talent contest at age 16, Newton-John quit school and headed to England to seek her fame and fortune. There, she hooked up with music producer/ promoter Don Kirshner. In 1971 she had her first hit single, Bob Dylan's "If Not for You." She followed up with George Harrison's "What Is Life," and John Denver's "Take Me Home Country Roads." By 1973 she had her first two American gold albums, *Let Me Be There* and *If You Love Me, Let Me Know*. The latter included the hit song "I Honestly Love You." Her music ranges from pop-country to pop-rock 'n' roll. She enjoyed a number of hits that crossed over from the pop to country charts, including "Have You Never Been Mellow," and "Please Mr. Please." She made her American film debut in *Grease* (1978), opposite John Travolta. A sweet, spunky, fresh face blonde, the 30-year-old played a teenager convincingly. Blessed with the clean girl-next-door sex appeal, she is transformed from a shy student to a popular leather girl. Her delightful characterization of a teen in the nostalgic 1950s helped *Grease* to become one of the highest grossing musical films of all time. Its soundtrack remains a best-seller more than 22 years later. Hits from the movie are "You're the One I Want," "Summer Lovin'," "Hopelessly Devoted to You," and the title song. Later albums include *Xanadu* with the hits "Physical" and "Magic," *Totally Hot and Physical, Gaia, Warm and Tender* (a collection of children's songs), and *Back With a Heart*. **ACHIEVEMENTS** Winner of four Grammy Awards, she is the recipient of numerous awards given by by the Country Music Association, and People's Choice Awards, and has numerous gold and platinum recordings. She has charted seven movie songs. She was honored with an Order of the British Empire (OBE). Newton-John received her Hollywood Walk of Fame star on Aug. 5, 1981. She is a breast cancer survivor, a tireless crusader against the insidious disease (early detection counts), and an inspiration to millions.

Greta Garbo    6901 Hollywood
Actress

Greta Garbo

BORN Greta Gustafsson, Sept. 18, 1905, in Stockholm, Sweden. **SPOTLIGHTS** Known as "the Face," she was mysterious, divine, chic, and haunting. Widely acclaimed for her great beauty, Garbo made dozens of films—both silents and talkies. This glamorous blonde became a legendary talent in the eyes of her adoring international public. She was *the* love goddess. A few of her classics are: *Flesh and the Devil* (1927), *Love* (1927), *Anna Christie* (1930—the publicity campaign ran posters that read, "GARBO TALKS!"), *Mata Hari* (1932), *Grand Hotel* (1932), *Queen Christina* (1933), *Anna Karenina* (1935), *Camille* (1937), and *Ninotchka* (1939). Offscreen, she was a serious, intensely private person. Due to her stoic reserve, she was nicknamed the "Swedish Sphinx." She retired from acting in 1942, never revealing why she had quit. Gossip mongers reported Garbo had declared, "Ay vant to be *let* alonnn." About two decades after she had retired, actor David Niven caught up with her at an outdoor restaurant. Niven recalled, "I often wondered if something of (vertigo) had overtaken Garbo at the pinnacle of her career, so seeing her before me, carefree and happy, munching away contentedly with the rain cascading off the table, I decided it might be a propitious moment to try and find out. 'Why *did* you give up the movies?' I asked. She considered her answer so carefully that I wondered if she had decided to ignore my personal question. At last, almost to herself, she said, 'I had made enough faces.'" She remained a recluse—primarily in the city of Manhattan—until her death. **ACHIEVEMENTS** Garbo never won an Academy Award for a specific performance, but was honored in 1954 with a Special Oscar for her "unforgettable screen performances." **HIGHLIGHTS** During the silent era Garbo learned that screen actress Lillian Gish was making $400,000-a-year, while she pulled in $18,000. Garbo decided to demand more money from MGM. Although she spoke little English and had no business background, she knew her films were box office hits. She approached mogul Louis B. Mayer and asked him for a raise from her $350 to $5,000-a-week. The studio boss threatened to fire her and have her deported. His publicity men began spreading ugly rumors about her. Garbo apparently remained unfazed. She simply told Mayer, "I tank I go home." She went to her hotel and stayed there for months until Mayer agreed to her terms. **QUOTE** "In America you are all so happy. Why are you happy all the time?" Died: 1990.

Earl Holliman   6901 Hollywood

Actor

Earl Holliman

BORN Sept. 11, 1931, in Tennessa Swamp, LA. **SPOTLIGHTS** Born the seventh child of a Louisiana farmer who died shortly before his birth, Holliman was adopted when he was one week old. He spent his boyhood in Texas, never missing a new movie at the local theatre. The restless youth celebrated his 15th birthday by hitchhiking to Hollywood. He ran out of money in one week and thumbed his way back home. Three months later he falsified his age and joined the Navy. The Navy sent him to radio school in Los Angeles; the young seaman spent all his free time at the Hollywood Canteen with the entertainers, until the Navy discovered his true age. Back home he enrolled in high school, maintained an "A" average, worked in the oil fields after school and discovered first hand the joy of performing on stage. After finishing both high school and his Navy duty, Holliman studied drama at USC and the Pasadena Playhouse. He found a clever way to get past the guard at Paramount Pictures by telling him he was going in to see Victor, the barber. He visited every casting director and eventually grabbed a one-liner in the Dean Martin-Jerry Lewis vehicle *Scared Stiff* (1953). With his rugged appeal, he got roles in a huge slate of feature films and theatrical credits: *The Rainmaker* (1956), *Giant* (1956), *Gunfight at the O.K. Corral* (1957), and *The Sons of Katie Elder* (1965). TV: His countless performances include the acclaimed mini-series "The Thorn Birds," but he is best known as "Sgt. Bill Crowley" on the long-running dramatic series "Police Woman" with Angie Dickinson. **HIGHLIGHTS** President of Actors and Others for Animals; he is dedicated to animal welfare.

Joel McCrea    6901 Hollywood
Actor

Joel McCrea

BORN Nov. 5, 1905, in South Pasadena, CA. **SPOTLIGHTS** He was one of the very first stars to rise from the ranks of the extras. By 1920 he stunt doubled for both actors and actresses, falling off horses, stagecoaches, cliffs, and buildings. The tall, handsome gent's first notable picture was the *Jazz Age* (1929). Within a few years, the likable, capable performer became a leading man. He co-stars opposite Sylvia Sidney, Humphrey Bogart, Wendy Barrie and Claire Trevor in the socially conscious movie, *Dead End* (1937). Director Alfred Hitchcock saw him as "every man, the man next door" and cast him in the thriller *Foreign Correspondent* (1940). He is must-see in this masterpiece; watch for the windmill scene. McCrea was outstanding in Preston Sturges' savvy classic, *Sullivan's Travels* (1941), and Sturges' screwball farce *The Palm Beach Story* (1942). Even with several tremendous successes in thrillers and comedies, McCrea is best remembered for his 85 Westerns, including *Union Pacific* (1939), *The Virginian* (1946), *Colorado Territory* (1949), *Stars in My Crown* (1950), and *Ride the High Country* (1962). He retired wealthy to live the remainder of his life on his ranch with his family. **QUOTE** He and Will Rogers became friends while working in the movie *Lightin'* (1930). He credited Rogers for his own financial success. In 1970 he recalled, "Will taught me real estate values. I bought a piece of land (1,200 acres) in 1931 for $19,500. Then, a few years later, I leased a small parcel of it to Union Oil for a million. When they were no longer interested in the lease, I sold it to another party for $1.3 million. You can't beat sound advice like that." Died: 1990.

Joan Collins    6901 Hollywood
Actress, producer, author

Joan Collins

BORN May 23, 1933, in London, England. **SPOTLIGHTS** Blondes don't always have more fun. This sultry, dark-haired, determined beauty took Hollywood by storm, and swept up a legion of men with her. After studying at the prestigious Royal Academy of Dramatic Arts for 18 months, she was signed to an exclusive contract by the Rank Organization. Then, Collins made her screen debut in the British farce, *Lady Godiva Rides Again* (1951). The temptress worked in nine more English films, including the action picture, *The Good Die Young* (1954), before crossing the Atlantic. She made her Hollywood film debut in Howard Hawks' cult classic, *Land of the Pharaohs* (1955). The interesting screenplay about the building of the pyramids in Ancient Egypt was co-written by the Nobel Prize and multiple Pulitzer Prize-winner William Faulkner, and is celebrated for its ending. Among top directors such as Martin Scorsese and Francis Ford Coppola, as well as movie buffs, this one scores with certain entertainment values. However, its director was less than pleased with its results—no fault of Collins—revealing to director Peter Bogdanovich that is was his least favorite motion picture. Hawks stated, "I don't know how a pharaoh talks. And Faulkner didn't know. None of us knew." Collins' first important dramatic role in America was in *The Virgin Queen* (1955), opposite Bette Davis and Richard Todd. Collins plays one of the queen's ladies-in-waiting, who is caught in a love triangle with Sir Walter Raleigh and Queen Elizabeth I. Next, she portrays Evelyn Nesbit Thaw in *The Girl in the Red Velvet Swing* (1955). Based on a true turn-of-the-century love scandal involving the famed New York architect Stanford White, Collins co-stars opposite Ray Milland and Farley Granger. When you see her in this film, it is easy to see how her stunning face and provocative figure could drive men wild. She appears in the all-star cast of MGM's *The Opposite Sex* (1956), with June Allyson, Dolores Gray, Ann Sheridan, Agnes Moorehead, and Joan Blondell. Next, Collins co-stars opposite Richard Burton in a story about shipwreck survivors in *The Sea Wife*. The only problem is that as the relationship progresses, Burton does not realize she is a nun! Among her motion picture credits are *Island in the Sun* (1957) with James Mason, Joan Fontaine and Dorothy Dandridge, *Rally 'Round the Flag, Boys!* (1958) opposite Paul Newman and Joanne Woodward, *Seven Thieves* (1960) co-starring Edward G. Robinson and Rod Steiger, *If It's Tuesday, It Must Be Belgium* (1969) with Suzanne Pleshette, *Tales from the Crypt* (1972), *The Bawdy Adventures of Tom Jones* (1976), *The Nutcracker* (1982), *Decadence* (1994), Kenneth Branaugh's *In the Bleak Mid-Winter* (1996), *The Clandestine Marriage* (1999) co-starring Sir Nigel Hawthorne, and Universal's prequel *The Flintstones: Viva Rock Vegas* (2000—as Wilma Flintstone's mother, Pearl). **TV** During the 1980s, Collins won over another generation of fans on television's prime time glossy soap opera, "Dynasty." This glamour queen played the sexy, rich, powerful, manipulative Alexis Carrington Colby. The talent was so good at being bad that she acquired tens of millions of new devotees worldwide. When she appears in television movies, mini-series like "Sins" (also producer), or guest stars in a series, ratings go through the roof. She is one of the most popular television stars of all time. Collins is also an accomplished stage actress. Her autobiography is entitled *Past Imperfect*. Her younger sister, Jackie Collins, is a best-selling author. **ACHIEVEMENTS** In March of 1997, Her Majesty, Queen Elizabeth II, presented Collins with one of Great Britain's most distinguished awards—the Officer of the British Empire (O.B.E.) for her lifetime contributions to the arts and her continuing charity work. A devoted humanitarian, she is an honorary founding member of the National Society for the Prevention of Cruelty to Children, and is a patron of the International Foundation for Children with Learning Disabilities. In May 1988, the Joan Collins Wing of the Children's Hospital of Michigan opened. Collins is also a Golden Globe and People's Choice Award winner. She received her Hollywood Walk of Fame star on Dec. 14, 1983. **QUOTE** In 1957, she observed the staggering differences between the two acting communities of Great Britain and America. She said, "In London they kept saying learn to be an actress. In Hollywood they say you're great when they mean you're good, and they say you're good when they mean you're awful."

Ellen Drew 🎥   6901 Hollywood
Actress

BORN Terry Ray; Nov. 23, 1915, in Kansas City, MO. **SPOTLIGHTS** A former Kansas City beauty queen, with large hazel eyes, full lips, and thick hair, she made a total of 40 films. She made her screen debut in *College Holiday* (1936), in a bit part, then became a desirable leading lady. As star or in supporting roles, movies include *Hollywood Boulevard* (1936), *The Gracie Allen Murder Case* (1939), *Christmas in July* (1940), *My Favorite Spy* (1942),

Ellen Drew

The Imposter (1944), *China Sky* (1945), *Johnny O'Clock* (1948), *Davy Crockett Indian Scout* (1950), and *Man in the Saddle* (1951).

Leonard Goldberg 📺   6901 Hollywood
Producer, executive

BORN Jan. 24, 1937, in New York, NY. **SPOTLIGHTS** A graduate of the Wharton School of Finance and Commerce, Goldberg began his career with ABC's research department. He quickly rose to V.P. of Daytime Programming where he originated the phenomenally successful game shows "The Dating Game," and "The Newlywed Game." But it was a year later, when he was named Head of All Programming that he developed a breakthrough concept that changed the face of prime time. Goldberg introduced

Leonard and Wendy Goldberg

"Made-for-TV-Movies." (Previously, only former motion pictures had been shown on TV.) His new concept instantly became a favorite with viewers, expanding the medium with fresh possibilities. He moved into production at Screen Gems, setting into motion the landmark television film "Brian's Song," which brought him the prestigious Peabody Award, then entertained the country (as it turned out for several generations) with the hit TV series "Bewitched," and "The Partridge Family." When he formed a partnership with Aaron Spelling, the duo launched a generous portion of the most popular series in TV history: "Charlie's Angels," "T.J. Hooker," "Starsky and Hutch," "Fantasy Island," "Hart to Hart," and the beloved, award-winning "Family." Under the aegis of his

Leonard Goldberg Company and Mandy films, the producer presented "Something About Amelia," in 1984 starring Glenn Close and Ted Danson. Internationally acclaimed for the frank and sensitive handling of the all-important subject matter, Goldberg won an Emmy Award for "Outstanding Drama Special," and an award from the National Committee for Prevention of Child Abuse. Later works include the outstanding television adaptation of the award-winning play "Love Letters" (1999). Hit movies produced by Goldberg—some prior to (and some after) his tenure at Twentieth Century-Fox as President—include *All Night Long* (1981), *War Games* (1983), *Sleeping with the Enemy* (1991), and *Double Jeopardy* (1999). One of his many admirable qualities is his dedication to giving newcomers a chance and place to shine. He helped launch Richard Gere, John Travolta, Matthew Broderick, Jaclyn Smith, Farrah Fawcett, Kristy McNichol, and Darryl Hannah. And, on the executive side, both Barry Diller and Michael Eisner were given their starts by Leonard Goldberg at ABC. This gentleman is extremely well-liked throughout the industry. **HIGHLIGHTS** He and his wife Wendy live on both coasts with their three children. Wendy is actively involved in community affairs and fund-raisers for the arts. She co-wrote the book *Marry Me*, which had two TV specials. **QUOTE** "Unlike the engineer who builds a bridge to span a specific space, or the lawyer who deals with the finite laws of our society, we, in the entertainment industry provide only flickering images on a television or movie screen. All we are bound by is our imagination, our creativity and our passion."

William Friedkin 🎥   6925 Hollywood

Director

Born: Aug. 29, 1939, in Chicago, Illinois. **SPOTLIGHTS** During high school, Friedkin focused more on basketball than classroom studies. After graduation, it came as no surprise that he found himself flipping through the "Help Wanted" classifieds, instead of college textbooks. He spotted an ad for a job at WBBM-TV, but mistakenly applied at nearby station WGN-TV. "They needed a mail room boy, too, so they hired me," he said. Within two years, he was directing live television. He had found his passion in life. He also discovered that "work is my education." By age 20, he had more than 2,000 live broadcasts under his belt! "Those were the golden days of Chicago television, a time it was possible to do such things," Friedkin later remarked. From the small screen, he moved to the medium of 16mm film documentary. He chronicled the story of a man who spent years on death row in *The People vs. Paul Crump*. The controversial piece was banned by the station for which it was made, but Friedkin won critical acclaim and the Golden Gate Award at the 1962 San Francisco Film Festival. This caught the attention of a competitor at the event. Producer David Wolper (who lost to Friedkin) hired him to make several television documentary specials: "The Thin Blue Line," "Mayhem on a Sunday Afternoon," and "The Bold Men." From this non-fiction genre he leaped to a musical, *Good Times* (1968), starring

Sonny and Cher in their movie debut. Friedkin directed the picture, "because I felt it was a chance to present a parable in popular, comedy form. The plot is funny, but it is really about a guy who nearly sells himself to the devil." He directed three more movies—the 1920s comedy, *The Night They Raided Minsky's* (1968), the dramatic adaptation of Harold Pinter's play, *The Birthday Party* (1969), and the adaptation of

William Friedkin and Sherry Lansing

Mort Crowley's Broadway production, *The Boys in the Band* (1970)—ground breaking in its honest handling of homosexuality. His next motion picture had as much to do with the historic period in American history as with the subject matter itself. Drug smuggling had become exceedingly profitable during the late 1960s when Free Love, Woodstock, the Hippie Revolution and rebellion against the senseless and bloody Vietnam War made using drugs an integral part of the counterculture. *The French Connection* (1971)—bold, gritty, and fast-paced—won both Best Picture and Best Director Academy Awards. He followed with *The Exorcist* (1973), terrifying audiences with diabolic possession. It scared the hell out of men and women, and drew the longest lines around the theater. A blockbuster, it received 10 Oscar nominations. Motion pictures include *The Brink's Job* (1979), *Deal of the Century* (1983), *To Live and Die in L.A.* (1985), *Rampage* (1992), and *Blue Chips* (1994). Returning to his roots he directed the classic jury drama, "12 Angry Men" in 1997 for Showtime/MGM TV with an all-star cast. Next, he journeyed to Florence, Italy, to direct Alban Berg's opera "Wozzeck." Zubin Mehta conducted, and with Friedkin's brave staging of the work, it premiered in May of 1997 to outstanding reviews. In 2000, he directed Tommy Lee Jones, Samuel L. Jackson, and Anne Archer in the drama, *Rules of Engagement*. He is married to Sherry Lansing, the beautiful and savvy chairman of Paramount Pictures. (See Lansing's bio in this book.) His exciting Hollywood Walk of Fame star dedication ceremony took place on August 14, 1997.

The genius Charles ("Charlie") Chaplin as the Little Tramp. (See his bio in Block Three.)

Hollywood in Red Square

The Red Army Drum and Bugle Corps welcomed Hollywood showmen Honorary Mayor Johnny Grant (center) and writer-producer
Sir Michael Teilmann (left) to Moscow's Red Square. The Kremlin sought their advice for producing Russia's 50th anniversary
of WWII commemoration events. That morning, Russian helicopters and troops cleared the snow from in front of Saint Basil's Church
for this historic photograph. Russian host Alexi Novareski helps balance the replica of the world-famous Hollywood sign.

6801 HOLLYWOOD

Penny Singleton 🎙   **6801 Hollywood**
See page 86

Bee Gees 💿   **6801 Hollywood**
Musicians, singers
BORN Barry, Sept. 1, 1946, in Manchester, England; Maurice and Robin (twins); Dec. 22, 1949; on the Isle of Man, England. **SPOTLIGHTS** The Bee Gees' famous singing trademark—close high harmonies—became instantly recognizable with their first performance in 1955. Although they hosted an Australian TV show, and later enjoyed hit singles "How Can You Mend a Broken Heart," it was the soundtrack album for *Saturday Night Fever* (1977) that brought them international fame. *Fever* kept at the top of the charts for two years. This best-of-disco classic includes "Stayin' Alive," "Night Fever," and "How Deep Is Your Love."

Sammy Kaye 🎙   **6801 Hollywood**
See page 108

James Mason 🎥   **6801 Hollywood**
Actor

James Mason

BORN May 15, 1909, in England. **SPOTLIGHTS** Mason earned an architecture degree from Cambridge University before deciding on a theatrical career. An extraordinary performer who glowered on-screen, he brought intelligence, class and cruelty to his roles, making more than 100 films. About his work in *I Met a Murderer* (1939—also wrote and produced), the dark-haired Brit stated: "My acting creaked abominably." *The Man in Grey* (1943) was a gigantic box-office success, but Mason declared it: "The worst hit ever made." Critics called him brilliant in *Odd Man Out* (1947) and Mason responded: "It was my one completely satisfactory role." Later, he commented that *Lolita* (1962) was his best film, with *Odd Man Out* a close second. A bona fide movie star, other pictures include *The Seventh Veil* (1946), *Pandora and the Flying Dutchman* (1951), *The Desert Fox* (1951), *5 Fingers* (1952), *The Prisoner of Zenda* (1952), and Shakespeare's *Julius Caesar* (1953--as "the noblest Roman of them all"). About Mason's performance in *A Star Is Born* (1954), director George Cukor said, "He is a complete actor. He is a man who has the greatest discretion...rather reserved by nature, a mysterious creature. To see that man break down was very moving. But all the credit for that goes to James." Movies include *20,000 Leagues*

Under the Sea (1954), *Bigger Than Life* (1956—also prod.), *Cry Terror* (1958), *North by Northwest* (1959), *Journey to the Center of the Earth* (1959), *The Man with the Green Carnation* (1960), *Fall of the Roman Empire* (1964), *The Blue Max* (1966), *Georgy Girl* (1966), *The Deadly Affair* (1966), *The Seagull* (1968--the first successful filming of a Chekhov play), *Age of Consent* (1969), *Heaven Can Wait* (1978), and *Murder by Decree* (1979). Died: 1984.

Robert Rossen 🎥   **6801 Hollywood**
Director, screenwriter
BORN Robert Rosen; March 16, 1908, in New York, NY. **SPOTLIGHTS** His directorial debut was based on a story he wrote, *Johnny O'Clock* (1947), a *noir* crime drama starring Dick Powell. His next movie, *Body and Soul* (1947), became a boxing classic. It stars John Garfield in his finest performance; the only one in which he was Oscar-nominated. Rossen received critical and commercial acclaim for producing, scripting and directing *All the King's Men* (1949) about a backwoods politician who ascends to power, while his corruption level rises with it: "absolute power corrupts absolutely." It won Oscars for Best Picture, Best Actor (Broderick Crawford), and Best Supporting Actress (Mercedes McCambridge). He directed Shelley Winters in *Mambo* (1954), shot on location in Venice, Italy, and Paul Newman as a pool shark in *The Hustler* (1961). *Lilith* (1964--his last film) was shot in England, and stars Warren Beatty as a therapist-in-training who falls for an asylum patient (Jean Seberg). Died: 1966.

Gig Young 📺   **6801 Hollywood**
Actor

Gig Young (left) and David Niven

BORN Byron Barr; Nov. 4, 1913, in St. Cloud, MN. **SPOTLIGHTS** An Oscar nominee for *Come Fill the Cup* (1951) and *Teacher's Pet* (1958), Young is best remembered for his light-hearted fare in a series of Doris Day comedies, including *The Tunnel of Love* (1958), and *That Touch of Mink* (1962). Powerful in dramas., he worked with Humphrey Bogart in *The Desperate Hours* (1955), then won an Academy Award for his brilliant performance in *They Shoot Horses, Don't They?* (1969). In the action picture *The Killer Elite* (1975), Young played James

Caan's cynical boss. He appeared in TV plays, specials, and starred opposite David Niven and Charles Boyer in TV's 1960s series *The Rogues*. He played scoundrel Tony Fleming, who believed in "honor before honesty." **SIDELIGHTS** Actress Elizabeth Montgomery was one of his five wives, as was Beverly Hills real estate broker, Elaine Young, who sells/leases multi-million dollar properties in the exclusive 5.5 square miles. Their union produced Jennifer Young, a pop singer-songwriter. Gig Young died in 1978.

Ida Lupino 🎥   6801 Hollywood
Actress, director, screenwriter

Ida Lupino

BORN Feb. 4, 1918, in London, England. **SPOTLIGHTS** Trained at the Royal Academy of Dramatic Arts, Lupino followed in her parents' theatrical footsteps. Her urge to act was stronger than that; she was one in a long line of an old British stage family dating back to the 17th Century. Hollywood saw Lupino as a beautiful, perky brunette and cast her in lightweight ingenue roles. She quickly grew tiresome of these standard female characters, and urged she be given more riveting scripts. When given the chance, she proved to be more than a pretty face. She played randy, bossy, street-wise *femmes fatales* convincingly. Lupino once referred to herself as "The poor man's Bette Davis." Films include *The Adventures of Sherlock Holmes* (1939), *The Light That Failed* (1939), *They Drive By Night* (1940), *High Sierra* (1941), *The Sea Wolf* (1941), *Out of the Fog* (1941), *The Hard Way* (1942), *Devotion* (1946), *Road House* (1948), and *While the City Sleeps* (1956). Postwar, she became the sole female in Hollywood who sat on a director's chair. Lupino's *The Hitch-Hiker* (1953), a classic thriller, established her as a talent on equal footing with the men. She was tough and quick with *The Bigamist* (1953), a splendid *film noir* crime drama, in which she also appears. Later, Lupino directed the family comedy *The Trouble with Angels* (1966), and directed TV. **QUOTE** "If you give me a funeral, I won't go." Died: 1995.

Bob Thomas 🎥   6801 Hollywood
Reporter, author, narrator, producer

BORN Robert Joseph Thomas; Jan. 26, 1922, in San Diego, CA. **SPOTLIGHTS** One of Hollywood's most respected journalists, his accurate, incisive reporting chronicles the past, present, and future possibilities of the entertainment industry. At age 22, he became a Hollywood columnist and has been going strong ever since, with magazine articles, television programs and 30 books. His well-known and widely admired works include biographies of Marlon Brando, Irving Thalberg, Walt Disney, Joan Crawford, Fred Astaire, and Roy O. Disney. Thomas has written, produced and appeared in five TV specials on the Oscars, and has covered 56 consecutive Academy Awards ceremonies. Since 1986, he has co-produced and narrated "Hollywood Stars," a weekly TV show devoted to interviews and film clips. It is syndicated in the United States and appears in Japan, Australia, and other countries. Although most of his career has been reporting the entertainment world, he has also

Bob Thomas and Samantha Hart

covered political campaigns. His most historic story came when he broke the news of the assassination of presidential candidate Robert F. Kennedy on California Primary night in 1968. His byline has appeared in the Associated Press report more times than any other writer in the news agency's 150-year history. In May 1999, Thomas marked 56 years as an AP reporter. **QUOTE** At his Walk of Fame ceremony on Dec. 1, 1988, he quipped, "This is 100% better than attending your own funeral."

Al Lichtman 🎥   6801 Hollywood
Executive

BORN April 9, 1888, in Hungary. **SPOTLIGHTS** He began his career as a theater usher, moved into vaudeville, worked as an exhibitor, then gained valuable knowledge in distribution. He landed a key position with Famous Players (Paramount), and later rose to the top as president of United Artists. He changed desks (and parking spaces) at MGM in 1935. Lichtman finally joined 20th Century-Fox as vice president, and was a founding member of the Motion Picture Pioneers. Died: 1962.

Robert W. Morgan 🎙   6801 Hollywood
Radio personality

SPOTLIGHTS L.A.'s longest-running morning personality arrived on the scene in 1965 for "Boss Radio" KHJ. He replaced the brilliant Dick Whittinghill and the ratings still soared. He joined K-Earth in 1992. As host of "The Robert W. Morgan Special of the Week," he was heard on more than 2000 radio stations across the country, and won Billboard's "Air Personality of the Year." A funny, knowledgeable wit, his show ensured people arrived at work in fine spirits: "Good Morgan, Los Angeles!" Died: 1998.

Celeste Holm 📺   6801 Hollywood
See page 305

Dick Haymes 🎙   6801 Hollywood
See page 233

Paul Lukas 🎥   6801 Hollywood
Actor
BORN May 26, 1894, in Hungary. **SPOTLIGHTS** A handsome leading and supporting actor, he appears in hundreds of films. Movies include *City Streets* (1931—with an original screenplay by Dashiell Hammett), *To Each His Own* (1946) and *Miss Tatlock's Millions* (1948). Died: 1971.

Stuart Hamblen ⚫   6801 Hollywood
Singer, band leader, songwriter
BORN Carl S. Hamblen; Oct. 20, 1908, in Kellyville, TX. **SPOTLIGHTS** He rode the range to Hollywood in 1929, and landed a job at local radio station KFI where he became known as "Cowboy Joe." In 1930 using the name Dave Donner, he became a member of the singing group called the Beverly Hillbillies. Radio's first singing cowboy star, his recordings include "My Mary-My Brown Eyed Texas Rose," "Old Pappy's New Banjo," and "Remember Me, I'm the One Who Loves You." Hamblen was a prolific songwriter who could turn out songs in minutes, like "Open Up Your Heart (And Let The Sun Shine In). He composed Rosemary Clooney's hit "This Ole House" in 1954. **QUOTE** "I'd always been a rough man, but my big problem was not being able to leave the booze alone. My daddy was a Methodist minister and I guess I was the original juvenile delinquent. I just loved to fight, too, and I suppose I did get thrown into jail a few times." This changed when he attended a revival in a tent-show by the Reverend Billy Graham in 1949. Hamblen's conversion occurred that day. He never touched booze or gambled on the ponies again. He said he lived happily as a sober man in God's grace and comfort. Inspired to compose gospel songs, he became equally famous for his spiritual tunes "It Is No Secret (What God Can Do)," and "Known Only to Him" (Elvis Presley recorded both). As a speaker, he was considered the West's best teller of tales since Will Rogers. He started the "Cowboy Church of the Air," where he said, "The one thing I want to make clear is that I'm no preacher. We tell stories instead of sermons. And we don't accept donations." Died: 1989.

Paul Douglas 📺   6801 Hollywood
See page 272

Sons of the Pioneers ⚫   6801 Hollywood
Vocal and instrumental group, songwriters
BORN Members of the group during 40-plus years include: Roy Rogers, Bob Nolan, Tim Spencer, Hugh and Karl Farr, Lloyd Perryman, Pat Brady, Doye O'Dell, Ken Carson, Deuce Spriggins, Tommy Doss, Ken Curtis, Rusty Richards, Dale Warren, and Roy Landham. **SPOTLIGHTS** Roy Rogers formed the Sons of the Pioneers trio in 1930. The band fluctuated in numbers/members over the years, and through many musical Westerns. Hit recordings: "Cool Water," "There's a New Moon Over My Shoulder," "Lie Low, Little Doggies," "Room Full of Roses," and "Cowboy Hymns and Spirituals."

Sons of the Pioneers • Roy Rogers leading

Taylor Holmes 🎥   6801 Hollywood

Actor

BORN May 18, 1872, in Newark, NJ. **SPOTLIGHTS** His family sent the youngster to a diction teacher because of his high-pitched voice; it led to acting. This five-foot, eight-inch, 154-pound actor's career spanned six decades. He started in vaudeville in 1899, turned to legitimate theater in 1901, playing Hamlet at New York's Garden Theater. He became a matinee idol of the early 1900s. Talkies include *Dinner at Eight* (1933), and *Gentlemen Prefer Blondes* (1953). Died: 1959.

Rex Allen 🎥   6801 Hollywood

Singer, actor, muscian, songwriter, narrator

Rex Allen

BORN Dec. 31, 1924, in Willcox, AZ. **SPOTLIGHTS** A rodeo star, he joined America's #1 radio program, WLS' "The National Barn Dance," then landed a recording contract with Mercury in the late 1940s. The epitomy of the singing Western hero, he was nicknamed "Mr. Cowboy," and "The Arizona Cowboy." A prolific songwriter of 300 tunes, he sang new and old songs--like the faithful "On Top of Old Smoky," "Don't Go Near the Indians," "Streets of Laredo," "I Won't Need My Six-Gun in Heaven," and "Crying in the Chapel." With his trusty stallion Koko, he appears in 19 Republic Pictures, including *Old Overland Trail* (1953). With his warm voice, he narrated the majority of Walt Disney's nature films, and narrated Hanna-Barbera's animated classic *Charlotte's Web* (1973). **ACHIEVEMENTS** One of the top Western box office stars of 1951, '52, '53 and '54. He started—and was elected to—the Cowboy Hall of Fame. He fathered three sons; Rex Allen, Jr. became a country singer ("Don't Say Goodbye"). Died: 1999.

Anthony Perkins 🎥   6801 Hollywood

Actor

BORN April 4, 1932, in NY, NY. **SPOTLIGHTS** An intense, tall, dark-haired talent whose portrayal of Norman Bates, the creepy motel keeper in Hitchcock's *Psycho* (1960) made him an international celebrity: "Mother, uh, what is that phrase? She isn't quite herself today." Interestingly, the director feared the film might be a box office dud. It was Hitchcock's most shocking work as it slowly dawns on audiences that the movie focuses on the killer (Perkins), instead of sympathetic and/or potential victims. Perkins delivers a performance of convincing lunacy, and *Psycho* was the second highest grossing film of the year. Motion pictures include *The Tin Star* (1957), *The Lonely Man* (1957), *Desire Under the Elms* (1958), *The Matchmaker* (1958), the end-of-the-world drama *On the Beach* (1959),

Welles' *The Trial* (1963), *The Champagne Murders* (1966), *The Life and Times of Judge Roy Bean* (1972), *Murder on the Orient Express* (1974), *Mahoney* (1975), *Psycho II* (1983), and *Psycho III* (1986—also directed). His acting style—sincere, anxious, and gawky—was bathed in a thin veneer of edgy loneliness. Perkins confessed, "I never studied acting. I never had one lesson." **SIDELIGHTS** The *Psycho* property can be seen at Universal Studios Hollywood where it is revealed that the blood in the

Anthony Perkins

shower scene was really America's favorite chocolate sauce. (Yum.) **QUOTE** "I'm not really suited to be a movie star. I have no confidence in myself. I'm not interested in money. I'm not good-looking. I have a hunch in my spine. I can't see worth a damn. I have a very small head. I haven't many opinions. I have no string of French girls. I'm not tough. I haven't a single quality a movie star should have. Not a single one." Died: 1992.

Frank Parker 🎤   6801 Hollywood

Tenor, actor

BORN Nov. 8, 1900, in Fillmore, MO. **SPOTLIGHTS** One of the earliest singers on radio, he started with A&P (Atlantic and Pacific) on "Gypsies" in 1923, and never stopped. This sweet-voiced, reliable, strong tenor could be heard on shows such as Jack Benny's, Bob Hope's and Arthur Godfrey's. A regular on "The American Album of Familiar Music," he kept busy in many other popular shows. Parker remained one of radio's favorite singers to the end. Died: 1962.

Bill Stern 🎤   6801 Hollywood

Sportscaster, host, storyteller

BORN July 1, 1907, in Rochester, NY. **SPOTLIGHTS** While attending Pennsylvania Military College, Stern won three varsity letters and participated in football (as starring quarterback), tennis, boxing, basketball and crew. He graduated in 1930 and by 1934 had broken into sports broadcasting with the great Graham MacNamee. Stern stayed in radio thereafter and was praised for never missing a broadcast. Known for his emotional delivery and intimate knowledge of sports, Stern's lively, vividly detailed descriptions of Rose Bowl and Army-Navy games, and the Olympics, made both his voice and name familiar to sports-loving Americans. He then added special events and human interest stories. Stern became news himself when, in a race to get to the station, he got in a car accident that resulted in his leg being amputated. **QUOTE** About his stories, he commented: "Some are true, some hearsay, but all so interesting we'd like to pass them along to you." Died: 1971.

Mario Lanza 🎥   6801 Hollywood
Singer, actor

Mario Lanza

BORN Alfredo Cocozza; Jan. 31, 1921, in Philadelphia, PA. **SPOTLIGHTS** As a youth, Lanza was a piano mover; that should give you an idea about his strength and build. His 1947 Hollywood Bowl opera debut in *Madame Butterfly* won him praise as the best male classical vocalist. His outstanding portrayal of *The Great Caruso* (1951) proved a tremendous success at the box office. This handsome, dark-haired, passionate tenor captures the heart of anyone who hears "Vesti La Giubba." His 1951 operatic recording of "Che Gelida Manina" is a direct gift from Heaven. Lanza's incredible voice (not Edmund Purdom's)—packed with heart and profound feeling—was used for *The Student Prince* (1954) music soundtrack, and his singing of "Golden Days" brings watery eyes to most listeners. Films include *That Midnight Kiss* (1949—his movie debut), *The Toast of New Orleans* (1950-with the platinum song "Be My Love"), *Because You're Mine* (1952), *The Seven Hills of Rome* (1958), and *For the First Time* (1959). **ACHIEVEMENTS** Conductor Arturo Toscanini pronounced Lanza as having "the greatest voice of the 20th century." And, the "Three Tenors" (Jose Carreras, Placido Domingo and Luciano Pavarotti) admitted they were swayed to become singers after seeing—and hearing—Mario Lanza in the movies. **HIGHLIGHTS** His voice was so naturally gifted that Lanza himself believed that the ghost of Caruso possessed him. In an interesting "reincarnation" twist of fate, Caruso *died* the year Lanza was *born*. Rent the *The Great Caruso* (1951)--Lanza's best film and enjoy his magnificent arias and Italian folk songs. He seemed born to play the title role. **QUOTE** When asked about his palatial villa in Rome, Lanza remarked, "I'm a movie star. And I think I should live like one." Died: 1959.

Henri Mancini 🌀   6801 Hollywood
Composer, arranger, conductor

BORN April 16, 1924, in Cleveland, OH. **SPOTLIGHTS** His love of music came from his father, a Pennsyvania steel worker, who played the flute in his spare time with the local Sons of Italy band. Mancini was an instant success at Universal Studios in 1952. He was adept at creating sweeping moods ranging from the fun "Pink Panther" to the sadly moving "Days of Wine and Roses." He altered the movie experience by embracing contemporary music in his themes (rather than using classical only as was standard at the time). In doing so, Mancini's name became synonymous with elegant 20th Century film music. He scored more than 100 films. Songs include "Baby Elephant Walk," "Sweetheart Tree," "Arabesque," "Love Story," among countless other treasures. TV theme songs include "Peter Gun," "Mr. Lucky," and "The Thorn Birds," to name a few. Recorded more than 90 albums, including *The Hollywood Musicals; Henri Mancini: As Time Goes By; Mancini: Top Hat.* **ACHIEVEMENTS** Four Oscars: "Moon River," "Days of Wine and Roses," and the scores of "Breakfast at Tiffany's," and "Victor/Victoria." 20 Grammys...His daughter, Monica Mancini, is a singer who has recorded a CD of her father's songs. Her twin sister, Felice, runs The Mr. Holland's Opus Foundation, which provides musical instruments to students. His son, Chris, is involved in music publishing. His wife, Ginny, founded the Society of Singers (a non-profit agency that helps vocalists in need). **QUOTE** When UCLA presented him with a medal of recognition, he quipped: "I was kind of hoping for a diploma." Died: 1994.

Jules C. Stein 🎥   6801 Hollywood
Executive

BORN Julian Caesar Stein; April 26, 1896, in South Bend, IN. **SPOTLIGHTS** This M.D. became one of the most powerful men in show business, not by practicing medicine, but as founder/President of Music Corporation of America, (MCA). MCA became the largest booking agency in the world. For a 10% commission, MCA provided Talent (with a capital T) for any entertainment occasion. Their clients were the top musicians, orchestras, writers, directors, even animals. Ironically he came by show business while helping to pay his way through medical school. As a student he booked the band he played in, and booked other bands—taking a cut of the evening's proceeds. But he still loved medicine. His post-graduate work at the University of Vienna's eye clinic inspired his 1924 treatise entitled *Telescopic Spectacles and Magnifiers as Aids to Poor Vision.* While practicing as an ophthalmologist in Chicago, he partnered with a pianist friend, Billy Goodheart, Jr. They rented a couple of small rooms for their start-up company, and Stein made a personal investment of $1,000. The two envisioned organizing new bands and booking them. But instead of having the same band play at the same club/hotel for months or years as was standard practice at the time, they would constantly rotate them. They charged the club/hotel owners, then hired and booked the musicians and pocketed the difference—at a substantial profit. The doctor thought the agency would be a nice sideline business. It took off like wild fire and before long he had to give up his medical practice. Stein created the concept of the exclusive contract for which MCA would become known as "the star spangled octopus" for its stranglehold on talent and operators. He promised businessmen that if they booked only through MCA "there will be a continuous flow of the right kind of talent at the right prices." In 1938, he conquered Hollywood. Eventually MCA acquired Universal Studios. **ACHIEVEMENTS** 1976 Jean Hersholt Humanitarian Award. He donated millions to hospitals who specialize in eye disorders. **QUOTE** *Time* magazine once reported Jules Stein was one of America's richest men. A friend asked him, "Aren't you surprised to learn that you are one of the richest men in the country?" "No," remarked Stein, "I was only surprised how poor the others were." Died: 1981.

Y Frank Freeman 🎥   6801 Hollywood
Executive

BORN Dec. 14, 1890, In Greenville, GA. **SPOTLIGHTS** The "Y" in his name stands for Young. A true Southerner, he was a top executive during the Golden Era. While chief of production at Paramount, his duties included sending a letter (dated Dec. 21, 1957) to the Army requesting Elvis Presley be given a 60-day deferment to finish shooting *King Creole* (1958). The military stated the request had to come from Presley himself. It did and Memphis Draft Board #86 agreed to the delay..**SIDELIGHTS**.One day Freeman brought his boxer puppies to the studio. A producer stopped by, bent down to pet them, then suddenly straightened up. He glared at Freeman and said, "What am I petting them for? You already took up my option!"...Freeman became chairman of the board of the Assoc. of Motion Picture Producers (1959-'64). Died: 1969.

Anita Louise 🎥   6801 Hollywood
Actress

BORN Anita Louis Fremault; Jan. 9, 1915, in New York, NY. **SPOTLIGHTS** A child stage actress, she blossomed into a blonde beauty queen. Although considered a Hollywood stunner, Louise did more than decorate pictures. Films include *Judge Priest, Madame DuBarry* (both 1934), *A Midsummer Night's Dream* (1935), *The Story of Louis Pasteur* (1935), *Marie Antoinette* (1938), *The Little Princess* (1939), *Wagons Westward* (1940), and *Love Letters* (1945). Died: 1970.

Peter Frampton 🎵   6801 Hollywood
Singer, guitarist, songwriter

BORN April 22, 1950, in Beckingham, England. **SPOTLIGHTS** Artistry runs in his family (his father was an art teacher, who taught David Bowie). Since his earliest memories, he saw himself immersed in music. By age 10, Frampton had made his professional debut. By age 16, he joined the Herd; a band which produced several teenybopper hits. Yearning to be known as a serious musician he formed the British group Humble Pie. By age 21 he left the group to perform sessions with the likes of George Harrison, Harry Nilsson, Ringo Starr and Billy Preston. He toured and hit the big time with his double-album *Frampton Comes Alive!* (1976)--one of the best-selling "Live" albums. Songs include: "Show Me the Way," "Baby I Love Your Way," and "Do You Feel Like We Do." The next year, he had the #2 album with *I'm With You*. His 1990 plans to revamp Humble Pie were destroyed by a fire that took the life of his pal and band cohort Steve Marriot in 1991. You can see his movie debut in *Sgt. Pepper's Lonely Hearts Club Band* (1978). It's no fault of Frampton's, but it's a garish film with hideous sets. Don't expect the flawless 1967 Beatles album of the same name. It's no "Lucy in the Sky with Diamonds."

Jerry Lewis 🎥
6801 Hollywood
Actor, director

Jerry Lewis

BORN Joseph Levitch; March 16, 1926, in Newark, NJ. **SPOTLIGHTS** He was born into a family of performers and blessed with the gift of genius. His father, Danny Lewis, was one of the last vaudevillians. As a child, he was onstage with his parents. At age 16, the intense, creative teen hit the road on his own. His star rose like a rocket in 1946 when he teamed with Dean Martin in clubs. He was 18, Martin age 28. Before he reached 21, Lewis--with partner Martin--were the hottest ticket in show business. In his splendid autobiography, *Jerry Lewis in Person* (with Herb Gluck, published by Atheneum), he wrote, "Sometimes, alone in my hotel room...thinking about what Dean and I had accomplished, of what we were capable of becoming, the adrenaline would pump so hard I'd jump around shouting, 'There's no way to fail--no way!'" Playing comedy as a goofy, rubbery-faced, limber-bodied, occasionally cross-eyed talent, complemented with his signature Kid voice, he became a screen giant. He made 16 motion pictures with co-star Dean Martin. It all started with *My Friend Irma* (1949) and ended with *Hollywood or Bust* (1956). A global, top box-office attraction, he was loved as a bumbling, stumbling, mugging, pantomiming clown, who managed to be both funny and sad. Lewis said his character at the time was, "a nine-year-old boy trapped in a man's body." Along with the pratfalls, the physical aspects and genuine spontaneity, Lewis reflected that "comedy is really simple. It's based on mischief and silliness." His childlike and childish characters were diametrically opposed to his co-star, the handsome, suave, romantic Martin. When their

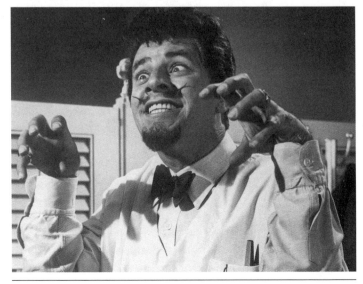

One of a zillion funny faces created by Jerry Lewis.

partnership dissolved in 1956, Lewis wrote, directed, produced and/or stars in *The Bellboy* (1960), *The Errand Boy* (1961), *The Patsy* (1964), *The Nutty Professor* (1963), and *The Family Jewels* (1965), among others. The actor made his Broadway debut in 1995 (at age 69) in "Damn Yankees," playing Mr. Applegate the devil. He quipped, "It's a role made in heaven." **ACHIEVEMENTS** Lewis performed for two and a-half hours for the Queen of England, and for the FIRST time in history, *the Queen stood up to applaud an entertainer!* In France, he is worshipped. *Monsieur* Lewis has received the French government's highest honor: *Chevalier de l'Ordre des Arts et Lettres*...For more than three dedicated decades, he has raised hundreds of millions of dollars during his annual Muscular Dystrophy Labor Day telethons...Lewis is also the author of *The Total Film-Maker*, published in 1971. **HIGHLIGHTS** "Thirteen is my lucky number, (it) has been ever since Grandma Sarah gave me her bar mitzvah present--the gold Star of David." **QUOTE** "I want to do everything I can, to use myself to the fullest. To direct, to write, anything, but use myself as an entertainer. I have to be allowed to work to the utmost...When the light goes on in the refrigerator, I automatically do a 20-minute performance."

Billy Daniels 🎵 6801 Hollywood
Singer, dancer, actor

BORN William Boone Daniels; Sept. 12, 1915, in Jacksonville, FL. **SPOTLIGHTS** A tempestuous entertainer, his early career as a solo artist preceded that of Frank Sinatra's. He sang regularly in the famed 52nd Street swing club before joining Bill "Bojangles" Robinson on Broadway in the musical *Memphis Bound.* He halted his career for military service, enlisted in the Marines and served bravely in WWII. He returned strong criss-crossing the country's leading nightclubs and hotel spots, including Las Vegas. His trademark song "That Old Black Magic" remains a classic. He had soul. His best-selling songs include "On the Sunny Side of the Street," "When You're Smiling," and "Cruising Down the River." He gave eight command performances before the British Royals. Died: 1988.

Mabel Normand 🎥 6801 Hollywood
Comedienne, actress

Mabel Normand

BORN Mabel Fortescue; Nov. 16, 1894, in Boston, MA. **SPOTLIGHTS** One of the leading silent screen comediennes, she would do anything for a laugh. But director Mack Sennett described her "as beautiful as a spring morning." This vivacious brunette had an engaging smile and loads of comic talent. Surprisingly, she was excellent in dramas,

too. Normand was naturally athletic, enjoyed doing her own dangerous stunts, and worked like the devil to make a joke funny. Credits include *Mabel's Adventures* (1912, first in series), *Tillie's Punctured Romance* (1914) with Charlie Chaplin, *Mabel's and Fatty's Wash Day* (1915) with frequent co-star Roscoe "Fatty" Arbuckle, *Mickey* (1917), *Peck's Bad Girl* (1918), *Molly O* (1921), *Susanna* (1923), and *The Extra Girl* (1923—where she leads a lion around by a leash thinking it's the studio dog in makeup), among countless others. This great silent screen star died in 1930 of tuberculous, at the dawn of talkies.

Judy Canova 🎥 6801 Hollywood
See page 34

Frances Drake 🎥 6801 Hollywood
Actress, dancer

BORN Frances Dean; Oct. 22, 1908, in NY, NY. **SPOTLIGHTS** A beautiful brunette talent in *Bolero* (1934), opposite George Raft, *Ladies Should Listen* (1934) co-starring Cary Grant, the classic *Les Miserables* (1935) with Fredric March and Charles Laughton, *Mad Love* (1935) opposite Peter Lorre, *The Invisible Ray* (1936) with Boris Karloff and Bela Lugosi, and *It's a Wonderful World* (1939) co-starring James Stewart. She often specialized in roles as the terrified heroine. Drake retired to marry a son of the 19th Earl of Suffolk in 1939. Died: 2000.

Harriet Nelson 📺 6801 Hollywood
See page 252

Amelita Galli-Curci 🎵 6801 Hollywood
Opera singer

BORN Nov. 18, 1882, in Milan, Italy. **SPOTLIGHTS** Originally trained as a pianist, she was virtually self-taught as a singer. She possessed a sweet girlish timbre. The soprano opened in Chicago at a matinee of *Rigoletto,* then worked with the Met. She performed with tenor Tito Schipa in Bellini's *La Sonnambula.* **SIDELIGHTS** One afternoon, when laborers were working nearby her cabin retreat in the Catskills, she repetitively sang some music. After several hours, the foreman knocked loudly at her door, not knowing who she was. He asked, "You the lady who's been singing all morning?" She nodded yes confidently, then inquired, "Have you enjoyed it? He responded, "Look lady, it's not that, exactly. I just wanted to ask if you'd mind not hanging onto that top note so long next time. My men have knocked off for lunch three times already." Died: 1963.

Groucho Marx 🎤 6801 Hollywood
See page 152

Ted Husing 🎤 6801 Hollywood
Announcer ,sportswriter, screenwriter

BORN Nov. 27, 1902, in Bronx, NY. **SPOTLIGHTS** Born over the saloon owned by his German immigrant parents, after high school he worked as a payroll clerk. On a hunch he applied for a job he saw an advertisement in the newspaper for a radio announcer. The year was 1924 and radio commercial broadcasting had just begun. He won the job due to his distinctively appealing voice. Husing worked 14-hour days announcing news and plugging songs. He branched out, becoming known as one of the best sports broadcasters in America, who always managed to get the inside "scoop." His sensational delivery often made sports events more exciting to listen to than to watch. After a lengthy illness with symptoms that included dizzy spells, it was discovered he had a brain tumor. A few days after his 1956 operation, he asked the nurse to remove the bandages from his eyes. The nurse told him there were no bandages on his eyes. He suddenly realized that he was blind. *My Eyes Are in My Heart* is his autobiography. Died: 1962.

Henry O' Neill 🎥   6801 Hollywood
Actor
BORN Aug. 10, 1891, in Orange, NJ. **SPOTLIGHTS** Film buffs recognize this veteran character talent as the kind soul in more than 150 films from 1930-'57. Movies include Warner's *The Story of Louis Pasteur* (1935), *Wells Fargo* (1937), and MGM's *The Human Comedy* (1943). Died: 1961.

Leon Errol 🎥   6801 Hollywood
Actor, dancer
BORN July 3, 1881, in Sydney, Australia. **SPOTLIGHTS** After attending Sydney University, he joined a repertory company, then experimented as a circus clown. He headed to San Francisco as a comedian and dancer. From there, he went to New York and worked in burlesque. He landed an important pantomime job in Ziegfeld's "Follies of 1911." A regular cast member for five years, he entered vaudeville in 1916, became a headliner at the Palace three years later, then made his screen debut in 1924. *The Lunatic at Large* (1928) and *Pop Always Pays* (1940), glorify his best-loved characterization of a hen-pecked husband who is a rubbery-legged drunk. Errol was excellent teamed with W.C. Fields in *Never Give a Sucker an Even Break* (1941). He was also in the *Mexican Spitfire* and *Joe Palooka* series. He made 65 movies. Died: 1951.

Alice Calhoun 🎥   6801 Hollywood
Actress
BORN Nov. 21, 1900, in Cleveland, OH. **SPOTLIGHTS** Silent screen brunette beauty in 75 Vitagraph and Warner Bros. films from 1916-'32, including *Blue Blood* and *Little Wildcat* (both 1922). Died: 1966.

Edgar Bergen 🎙   6801 Hollywood
Ventriloquist, actor
BORN Feb. 16, 1903, in Chicago, IL. **SPOTLIGHTS** This budding ventriloquist spent the princely sum of $35 back in his high school days to build his wooden creation, Charlie McCarthy. The "little boy" dummy was the master of the piercing joke. He was a wise guy, who chided his boss Bergen

Edgar Bergen and Charlie McCarthy

for moving his lips perceptively. Charlie seemed to take on a mischievous personality of his own, and listeners forgot he was not real. Prepared for fisticuffs, he threatened: "I'll clip 'em! So help me, I'll mowwww 'em down!" Two other alter egos—country bumpkin, Mortimer Snerd, whose catch-phrase was "Duhhh," and the perennial spinster Effie Klinker—joined radio's "The Edgar Bergen and Charlie McCarthy Show." On air from 1937-'55, it was one of NBC's long-running, comedy-variety programs before the advent of TV. Films include *Charlie McCarthy Detective* (1939) and *I Remember Mama* (1948). Bergen was a tremendous wit. **ACHIEVEMENTS** 1937 Special Oscar (Charlie received a wooden Oscar)! Father of actress Candice Bergen...One of the four original Charlie McCarthys is at the Smithsonian. Magician David Copperfield purchased another for $112,500 in 1995. Died: 1978.

J. Peverell Marley 🎥   6801 Hollywood
Cinematographer
BORN Aug. 14, 1901, in San Jose, CA. **SPOTLIGHTS** Marley's keen eye for aesthetics brought symmetry to pictures, and it is evident in his first work, *The Ten Commandments* (1923), where he was the chief cameraman. His work also included *Charlie's Aunt* (1941), and *The Greatest Show on Earth* (1952), with associate cinematographer, George Barnes. Died: 1964.

William Primrose ●   6801 Hollywood
Musician
BORN Aug. 23 1904, in Scotland. **SPOTLIGHTS** A distinguished violinist, he performed in concert halls worldwide. In 1956 he co-founded the Festival Quartet. Died: 1982.

Bobbie Vernon 🎥   6801 Hollywood
Comedian
BORN Silvion Jardins; March 9, 1897, in Chicago, IL. **SPOTLIGHTS** 19-year-old Vernon paired with 19-year-old Mack Sennett for comedy shorts, including *Hearts and Sparks* (1916). Later, he went behind-the-scenes. Died: 1939.

Milburn Stone 📺   6801 Hollywood
Actor
BORN July 5, 1904, in Burton, KS. **SPOTLIGHTS** A supporting and leading actor in 73 movies, including *Young Mr. Lincoln* (1939), *Nick Carter--Master Detective* (1939), *The Great Train Robbery* (1941), *Reap the Wild Wind* (1942), *Sherlock Holmes Faces Death* (1943), *The Mad Ghoul* (1943), *The Spider*

Milburn Stone

Woman Strikes Back (1946), *The Sun Shines Bright* (1953--a remake of *Judge Priest*), *Black Tuesday*, *The Long Gray Line* (both 1955), and *Drango* (1957). Stone won a 1967 Emmy as Dr. Galen (Doc) Adams in TV's Western series, "Gunsmoke" (1955-'75). Died: 1980.

Tony Curtis 🎥
Actor

6801 Hollywood

Tony Curtis

BORN Bernard Schwartz; June 3, 1925, in Bronx, NY. **SPOTLIGHTS** A handsome, beef-cake talent, he turned to acting after being discharged from the Navy. He studied on the GI bill, toured with a stock company in the Borscht Circuit, and was discovered while performing in the stage production of "Golden Boy" in New York. At age 22, he was under contract to Universal Studios making a succession of costume pictures, and receiving premium acting lessons. Curtis stars in *Houdini* (1953) with his then-wife, actress Janet Leigh. He appears with Burt Lancaster and Gina Lollobrigida in his first important film, the classic *Trapeze* (1956), where he gave a solid performance. It was his terrific performance playing the complete heel in *The Sweet Smell of Success* (1957), opposite Burt Lancaster, that made him a superstar. In *The Defiant Ones* (1958), he co-stars with Sidney Poitier as a handcuffed convict on the run from the law. The dramatic, insightful plot explores racial themes in the deep South. The following year, he switched to a military comedy for director Blake Edwards in *Petticoat Junction* (1959). It was a huge commercial success. Curtis struck gold with his subtle, yet hilarious must-see performance in *Some Like It Hot* (1959), with Marilyn Monroe and Jack Lemmon. He is at his comic best, as is the rest of the cast. He was earning a bundle—more than a million a year—to which he remarked, "Man, ain't it crazy!" He appears in the all-star cast of the biblical epic *Spartacus* (1960). Motion pictures include *Great Imposter* (1960), *Captain Newman, M.D.* (1963), *Goodbye, Charlie* (1964), *Paris—When It Sizzles* (1964), *Sex and the Single Girl* (1965), *The Great Race* (1965), *Suppose They Gave a War and Nobody Came* (1970), *Capone* (1975), *The Mirror Crack'd* (1980), *Naked in New York* (1994), and *The Celluloid Closet* (1995). He became an accomplished painter. Father of Jamie Lee Curtis (see her bio in this book).

Louise Fazenda 🎥
Actress, comedienne

6801 Hollywood

BORN June 17, 1889, in Lafayette, IN. **SPOTLIGHTS** Louise Fazenda was one of the greatest slapstick comediennes of the silent movies. A hilarious and outrageous talent, she set the standard for all female comics who have followed in her footsteps. Movies include *Love and Graft* (1914), *The Great Vacuum Robbery* (1915), *A Hash House Fraud* and *Fatty's Tin Type Tangle* (both 1915). This 5'5", 130-pound, brown-haired, hazel-eyed plain-looking woman

Louise Fazenda

pulled stunts like removing villain Mack Swain's hat to smooth down his hairs before hitting him over the head with a baseball bat, or had the flowers on her hat stand straight up when she got frightened. She worked with all the great silent comedians. She appears opposite Ford Sterling in *Her Torpedoed Love* (1917), and W.C. Fields in *Tillie's Punctured Romance* (1928—she played Tillie). Her last film before retirement was *The Old Maid* (1939), based on an Edith Wharton novel. **QUOTE** "It's customary to write nonsense about a comedienne. But the work to get the laugh is harder than the effort to get the tear. I got what success I have by sheer concentration. For five years I toiled in obscurity, as patiently as any clerk over a ledger; was just a bathing girl at Mack Sennett's. Then, I planned in my own mind the gingham dress, the pig-tails and the square-toed shoes, and the comedy that went with it. In a way, it's just as a man builds a house. Of course you modify as you go along, but what I want to stress is that comedy is made from the gray matter of the brain, and it's much harder than it looks...My entrance into the picture world was quite prosaic. I was studying to be a teacher, when a girl living in the apartment next to ours, suggested that I go out and see a casting director with her. It was Christmas time. I thought then of only the extra Christmas presents the work as an extra would buy. But after the holidays I still continued to need money and so went on working in insignificant parts. Then I grew to love the work itself. Probably at that moment my ambition was born. Now I have found my little niche, and I am quite content to go on giving pleasure." Died: 1962.

Telly Savalas 🎥
Actor

6801 Hollywood

BORN Aristotle Savalas; Jan. 21, 1924, in Garden City, NY. **SPOTLIGHTS** A bald, tough-looking talent, he came to acting as a second career. A graduate of Columbia University, Savalas enlisted in the military during World War II. Injured in action, he was decorated with a Purple Heart. After his honorable discharge he went to work at the State Department, then found his way to ABC News. As a senior director he won the prestigious Peabody Award for "Your Voice of America" series. Approaching his 30s he decided to change careers and become

Telly Savalas

an actor. Due to his strong-faced looks with his crooked grin, he was cast in villainous—often psychopathic—parts. He was Oscar-nominated for his role in the *Birdman of Alcatraz* (1962). He portrayed Pontius Pilate in *The Greatest Story Ever Told* (1964). Other films include *Cape Fear* (1961), *Battle of the Bulge* (1965), *The Dirty Dozen* (1967), *Kelly's Heroes* (1970), and *Capricorn One* (1978). He gained a new generation of fans on TV's "Kojak" police drama series. This time, though, he played the hero, who didn't mind stretching the interpretation of the law to crack a case. The Emmy-winning actor played a streetwise New York detective with a cynical sense of humor. No toxic smokes for this macho man, he had a penchant for lollipops. Died: 1994.

Burt Lancaster 🎥 6801 Hollywood
Actor

Burt Lancaster

BORN Burton Stephen Lancaster; Nov. 2, 1913, in New York, NY. **SPOTLIGHTS** A handsome, fair-haired actor, Lancaster possessed a flashy, piercing smile and abundant charm. He was vital, muscular, and athletic. Yet, he could be gentle; moving his body with grace and beauty. Lancaster was soft-spoken, but his gaze could chill. Prior to coming to pictures, he had been an acrobat in the circus for six years, then joined the military for WWII duty. He served in special wartime forces in Italy and North Africa. Lancaster made his New York stage debut in "A Sound of the Hunting" and was discovered by Hollywood. His acting embodied the highest qualities of honesty and hard work. He excelled in thrillers, action films, and dramas, including *The Killers* (1946), *Sorry, Wrong Number* (1948), *Criss Cross* (1949), *Come Back, Little Sheba* (1952), *From Here to Eternity* (1953), *The Rose Tattoo* (1955), *Trapeze* (1956), *The Rainmaker* (1956),

The Sweet Smell of Success (1957—as J.J. Hunsecker), *Gunfight at the OK Corral* (1957), *Separate Tables* (1958), *Judgment at Nuremberg* (1961), *The Leopard* (1963), *The Swimmer* (1966—this film has an unusual, interesting premise), *Airport* (1970), a first-class drama with Dean Martin and George Kennedy, *Ulzana's Raid* (1972), *Cassandra Crossing* (1976), with Sophia Loren and John Phillip Law, and *Atlantic City* (1980), co-starring Susan Saradon. **ACHIEVEMENTS** 1960 Best Actor Oscar for *Elmer Gantry*...His superb performance in the true story, *Birdman of Alcatraz* (1962), is a breathtaking human study. Lancaster became so absorbed in the Robert Stroud persona that every time the character suffered a setback, he broke down. Director John Frankenheimer thought it was great acting, but Lancaster choked back tears and pleaded the age-old actor's saying: "Oh, no, let the audience cry—not me." Died: 1994.

Beverly Garland 📺 6801 Hollywood
Actress

Beverly Garland

BORN Beverly Fessenden; Oct. 17, 1926, in Santa Cruz, CA. **SPOTLIGHTS** This blonde-haired, brown-eyed, pouty-lipped talent played the sultry, assertive dame at the beginning of her career. She made her screen debut in the stylish, tense film noir *D.O.A.* (1949), starring Edmond O'Brien. Then, she appears in a number of low-budget films in the late 1950s, many for director/producer Roger Corman, including the sci-fi horror flick *It Conquered the World*, *Hellfire*, a period piece filmed in Russian, and the Western *Gunslinger*. Other movies include *The Desperate Hours* (1955), opposite Humphrey Bogart, *The Joker is Wild* (1957), co-starring Frank Sinatra, *Chicago Confidential* (1957), *The Alligator People* (1959), and *Where the Red Fern Grows* (1974). Garland became active in TV dramas in the late 1950s, and earned an Emmy nomination in "Medic." Her co-starring role as Bing's wife on "The Bing Crosby Show" led to a new generation of young fans in TV's "My Three Sons" (1969-'72), as Fred MacMurray's irresistibly charming wife. In the 1980s, she played Kate Jackson's mother Dottie West on "Scarecrow and Mrs. King." She has appeared in a number of TV movies, including "The World's Oldest Living Bridesmaid," opposite Donna Mills, and "Mittleman's Hardware," co-starring George C. Scott. Garland became a successful hotelier, with her Beverly Garland's Holiday Inn Universal Studios Hollywood.

Preston Foster 📺 6801 Hollywood
Actor, singer
BORN Oct. 24, 1902, in Ocean City, NJ. **SPOTLIGHTS** A stur-

Preston Foster

dy fellow, he was a former professional wrestler. Then, he leaped into opera singing and acting. At a well-built 6'2", 200 pounds, Foster could easily slip into villainous roles, but with his dashing smile he also played the rugged hero. He made his silver screen debut in *Nothing But the Truth* (1930). He made an impressive 125 films, including *Doctor X* (1932), *I Am a Fugitive from a Chain Gang* (1932), *Hoopla* (1933), *Wharf Angel* (1935), *Annie Oakley* (1935), *The Outcasts of Poker Flat* (1937), *Up the River* (1938), *The Lady in the Morgue* (1938), *Geronimo* (1940), *My Friend Flicka* (1943), *The Harvey Girls* (1946), *Tangier* (1946), *Inside Job* (1946), *I Shot Jesse James* (1949), *Tomahawk* (1951), *The Big Night* (1951), *Kansas City Confidential* (1952), *I the Jury* (1953), and *The Time Travelers* (1964). **TV** He starred as Captain Herrick of the *Cheryl Ann* in the adventure series "Waterfront" (1953-'56). In the 1960s, he played Captain Wingate in the Western "Gunslinger" series. Foster's offscreen recreation included his membership in the California Yacht Club. He frequently raced his sailboat Zoa II in the Pacific Ocean. Died: 1970.

John Beradino 🖾   6801 Hollywood
Actor

BORN May 1, 1917, in Los Angeles, CA. **SPOTLIGHTS** He was lovingly pushed into show business by an adoring stage mother who thought her little *Giovanni* was the cutest thing since spaghetti and meatballs. As a child, he used his real-life experiences of growing up in an Italian-American family for his on-screen antics in the "Our Gang" comedies. The rascal ragamuffin earned "six bucks and a box lunch everyday." His father, though, had other ideas for his son. He recalled, "Everyday Papa put me outside with a glove and a ball." He grew into a super athlete who played second base for the Cleveland Indians (winning a 1948 World Series ring), the St. Louis Browns and the Pittsburgh Pirates during his 16-year pro ball career, with a lifetime batting average of .249. Injured during WWII at Pearl Harbor, he switched hit careers. On April Fool's Day in 1963, he became Dr. Steve Hardy in the soap opera "General Hospital." He celebrated his 30th anniversary as the show's patriarch by receiving his Hollywood Walk of Fame tribute. Died: 1996.

Edward Sedgwick 🎥   6801 Hollywood
Director

BORN Nov. 7, 1892, in Galveston, TX. **SPOTLIGHTS** Sedgwick is credited with some of Hollywood's earliest baseball movies: *Stepping Fast* (1923--a Western with ball scenes), *Hit and Run* (1924), and MGM's *Slide, Kelly, Slide* (1927), where a cocky

player has to win the game for a dying boy in the hospital. (That evergreen scene became standard sports rehash.) In 1934 Sedgwick directed *Death on the Diamond*, a unique mystery melodrama for MGM. He made 100 films in various capacities—acting, writing, or directing, from 1915-'51, including *A Southern Yankee* (1948), and *Ma and Pa Kettle Back on the Farm* (1951). He directed such greats as Charlie Chaplin, Tom Mix, Robert Young and Red Skelton. Died: 1953.

Cliff Robertson 🎥   6801 Hollywood
Actor

Cliff Robertson

BORN Sept. 9, 1925, in La Jolla, CA. **SPOTLIGHTS** A very masculine, handsome, dark-haired leading man, he made his auspicious screen debut in the marvelous slice-of-Americana drama, *Picnic* (1956). That same year, he gave a stirring, psychologically tinged performance in *Autumn Leaves*. He was honored to portray President John F. Kennedy in *PT-109* (1963); he was personally selected for the role by the President. He co-stars with Henry Fonda in the presidential political drama, *The Best Man* (1964). He made his directorial debut with *J.W. Coop* (1972), a Western story about an aging rodeo star. Motion pictures include *Underworld U.S.A.* (1961), *The Honey Pot* (1967), *The Man Without a Country* (1973), *Three Days of the Condor* (1975), *Midway, Obsession* (both 1976), *The Pilot* (1979—also directed, co-screenplay credit), *Brainstorm* (1983), *Malone* (1987), *Wild Hearts Can't Be Broken* (1991), *Wind* (1992), *Renaissance Man* (1994) and *Escape from L.A.* (1996). **ACHIEVEMENTS** 1968 Best Actor Oscar for *Charly*. 1966 Emmy for "The Game."...Before becoming a movie star, he was a busboy, waiter, and taxi driver.

Ronald Colman 🎥   6801 Hollywood
Actor

BORN Feb. 9, 1891, in England. **SPOTLIGHTS** His first film job paid a pound a day, a lowly scale by American standards. In the U.S., both Selznick and Goldwyn recognized that his bracing good looks, calm nature, and ease of movement would translate on the silent screen. He possessed a dreamy, aristocratic presence that was approachable. Heart-throb Colman exuded a wide range of emotions while winning the title of the top male

Ronald Colman

star in 1927 and 1928, in films like *Two Lovers*, opposite Vilma Banky. This charismatic talent readily made the transition to talkies with his mellifluous voice and superb phrasing. He innately underplayed; his acting was ideal for sound. Films include *Arrowsmith* (1931),*Cynara* (1932), *The Masquerader* (1933), *A Tale of Two Cities* (1935), *The Prisoner of Zenda, Lost Horizon* (both 1937), *The Talk of the Town* (1942), *Kismet* (1944), *Champagne for Caesar* (1950). **ACHIEVEMENTS** 1947 Oscar for *A Double Life*. Died: 1958, from pneumonia resulting from an by an old WWI wound.

Jeanne Cooper 📺   6801 Hollywood
Actress

BORN Jan. 21, 1928, in Taft, CA. **SPOTLIGHTS** An accomplished actress of both stage and screen, Cooper became one of television's most popular celebrities. She has starred on the daytime soap opera, "The Young and the Restless," since it premiered on Mar. 23, 1973. This blonde, blue-eyed talent has won numerous Emmy nominations in her role as the proud, wealthy and sometimes ruthless Kay (aka Katherine Chancellor-Sterling—at last count), and formerly portraying Kay's double, Marge, the gum-chewing waitress. In real life, Cooper's parents are from a Native American Cherokee Indian reservation in Oklahoma. They ventured West in the oil business, and she was accepted into the prestigious Pasadena Playhouse School. She subsequently began performing in the Civic Light Opera Company and Revue Theater in Stockton. The pretty youth landed a studio contract with Universal, making her screen debut opposite Maureen O'Hara in *The Redhead from Wyoming* (1953). That same year, she co-stars with Glenn Ford in *The Man from the Alamo*. She appeared in several more pictures, and performed in stage productions like "The Miracle Worker," and "On the Town." As part of television's Golden Age, she became a regular in the series "Maverick." Cooper also contributed as guest star to more than 400 episodic TV shows including "Perry Mason," "Twilight Zone," "The Untouchables," and "Playhouse 90." She was also Emmy-nominated for "Ben Casey," and "L.A. Law." She is mother of actor Corben Bernsen, another son Colin, and a daughter Caren. She is the doting and devoted grandmother of Oliver, Westin and Harrison. Recipient of numerous honors: 1989 "Outstanding Lead Actress," Soap Opera Digest Awards; and "Woman of the Year," Pasadena Playhouse Alumni & Associates. **QUOTE** Part Native American Cherokee Indian, she was honored in 1999 by the First Americans in the Arts. Upon receiving the organization's prestigious award, she declared, "Believe it or not, under this blonde hair is the blackest hair you've ever seen."

Jeanne Cooper

Olive Borden 🎥   6801 Hollywood
Actress

BORN Sybil Tinkle; July 14, 1907, in Richmond, VA. **SPOTLIGHTS** A breathtakingly beautiful silent screen star, she was idealized in a timeless painting by Vargas. Movies include *The Bad Men* (1926), *The Joy Girl* (1927) and *Sinners in Love* (1928), to name three in her more than 50 films. Her career abruptly ended when talkies were introduced. Died: 1941.

Joanne Woodward 🎥   6801 Hollywood
Actress

Joanne Woodward

BORN Feb. 27, 1930, in Thomasville, GA. **SPOTLIGHTS** A lovely, green-eyed, husky-voiced Southerner, she first tried dramatics in high school, then at Louisiana State University. After her studies, she moved to Greenville, SC, where she gained more experience in community theatre. With dreams of establishing a Broadway career, she headed to New York for additional study. While attending New York's Neighborhood Playhouse, she became an understudy in "Picnic" and met future husband, Paul Newman. Woodward moved to Hollywood, and began appearing in TV playhouse dramas. She made her screen debut in *Count Three and Pray* (1955). Motion pictures include *A Kiss Before Dying* (1956), *Rally Round the Flag, Boys!* (1958), *The Fugitive Kind* (1959), *The Stripper* (1962—in a role originally written for Marilyn Monroe), *A Fine Madness* (1966), *Rachel, Rachel* (1968—in an Oscar-nominated performance), *The Effects of Gamma Rays on Man-in-the-Moon Marigolds* (1972), *Summer Wishes, Winter Dreams* (1973—in an Oscar-nominated performance), *Glass Menagerie* (1987), *Mr. and Mrs. Bridge* (1990—in an Oscar-nominated performance), and *Philadelphia* (1993). **ACHIEVEMENTS** 1958 Best Actress Oscar for *The Three Faces of Eve*. It was her third motion picture, and one she initially did not want to do. When she first learned of her Oscar nomination she declared, "It's not my best performance," and stated that it did not matter to her. However, when her name was called as the winner on Oscar night, she burst into tears. She explained, "I guess I cared more than I thought I did." 1958 proved to be a stellar year for the dazzling and youthful Woodward: she won the Oscar; married actor Paul Newman (to date, she has worked with him on 11 films); and became the first to be honored with a star on the Walk of Fame. **QUOTE** "I still can't believe I'm a movie star. The only thing that's really happened to make me believe it is they're now making the Joanne Woodward paper doll box...I guess maybe that proves I've arrived."

Ernest Torrence 🎥 6801 Hollywood
Actor
BORN June 26, 1878, in Scotland. **SPOTLIGHTS** An actor in *Mantrap* (1920), he played opposite the flirty, bouncy "IT" girl Clara Bow. In *Queen Christina* (1933), his co-star was the hauntingly beautiful Greta Garbo. Died: 1933.

Monty Hall 📺 6801 Hollywood
Host, TV personality, actor, singer

Monty Hall

BORN Monte Halperin; August 25, 1926, in Winnipeg, Manitoba, Canada. **SPOTLIGHTS** While attending the University of Manitoba, Monty Hall performed in musical and dramatic college productions, and served as emcee of Canadian Army Shows during WWII. Soldiers appreciated his smooth vocals and quick wit to help steady/entertain them. He graduated with a Bachelor of Science degree in 1945, then moved to Toronto where he resumed his career as actor, singer, emcee and sportscaster. In 1955, Hall landed NBC's "Monitor" in New York. Five years later, CBS pursued him for "Video Village," which brought him to Hollywood. There, he was inspired to package projects and he sold "Your First Impression" to NBC. His next creation won him lasting fame and fortune. "Let's Make a Deal" (1964-'86; also produced and hosted) was Hall's long-running, wacky game show. As the pleasant and cheerful host, he encouraged the costumed audience to participate in the show's zany antics. Sometimes the contestants' greed left them with turkey prizes—much to the delight or disappointment of viewers. But the attractive Hall always remained friendly, fun to watch, and enjoyed one of the largest, most devoted fans of any television host/personality. He produced other shows, starred in his own variety specials for ABC, guest starred on "The Odd Couple," "Love American Style," "The Flip Wilson Show," "The Dean Martin Show," "The Love Boat," and "The Nanny." He headlined at the Sahara Hotel in Las Vegas, and toured the country in the stage show of "High Button Shoes," a musical comedy. ...Known for being extremely reliable—he *never* called in sick. **ACHIEVEMENTS** A tremendous humanitarian, his life away from TV has been as important as that on the stage. He has traveled the United States, Canada, and Europe extensively, speaking and performing for countless charities. He makes more than 100 appearances every year, without compensation, for charitable organizations representing hospitals, diseases, the disabled and underprivileged. He has raised 850 million dollars for these worthy causes. He proudly wears the lifetime label of International Chairman of Variety Clubs International, the world's largest children's charity. He has children's wings named for him at Hahnemann Hospital, UCLA Medical Center, Mount Sinai in Toronto, and Johns Hopkins in Baltimore. In May 1988, the Canadian government bestowed on him their highest award, the prestigious Order of Canada...Amazingly, he was only Emmy-nominated once for "outstanding host in a game show or audience participation show" during the 1974-'75 season. He did not win. "Let's Make a Deal" was Emmy-nominated seven times, but the show never took an Emmy either! No matter, both Hall and his show were winners with fans...He is married to Marilyn, a writer-producer and winner of an Emmy Award as Co-Executive Producer of "Do You Remember Love," a drama concerning Alzheimer's disease. They have three children. Joanna Gleason is a Tony Award-winning Broadway actress. Richard is an Emmy Award-winning television producer. And, Sharon is a television director/writer. **QUOTE** About August 24, 1973, Hall commented, "I'll never forget that day. They blocked off the corner of Highland and Hollywood Boulevards. I told Mayor Bradley, who officiated, not to widen either of those streets because my star was right on the corner and would be the first to disappear! We then went to celebrate at the Palladium with 900 guests. Sammy Davis was M.C. and I felt that at that moment my career was validated."

Monty Hall (right) and family with former City of Los Angeles Mayor Tom Bradley

Mabel Normand

In 1930 Louise Fazenda relaxes in the fresh ocean air with her Scottish terriers.
She leased a Malibu Colony house with 30 feet of Pacific Ocean beach frontage,
at $30-a-month for 10 years.

6777 HOLLYWOOD

Lanny Ross 🎤   6777 Hollywood

Singer

BORN 1906, in Seattle, WA. **SPOTLIGHTS** He made his theatrical stage debut in a Shakespearean production, in London, with his actor father. Later, he attended Yale University where he had to choose between a career in athletics, law, or singing. He turned down an Olympic track opportunity to pursue his law degree. After passing the New York bar, he followed his passion and became a professional singer in radio (he never practiced law). Ross starred on a number of shows including "Maxwell House Showboat." Originally the tenor with the lovely singing voice was forbidden to speak. The network hired a "double" to talk for him because the corporate heads didn't like his speaking voice! In time, he won them over and became known as "the idol of the airwaves." The very patriotic Ross took up arms, enlisting in the army during World War II. He was stationed in the South Pacific, receiving the Medal of Merit in Manila while on General MacArthur's staff. Post war, Procter and Gamble snapped him up for their popular "Ivory Soap" series. Housewives adored his romantic, soft ballads, especially "Moonlight and Roses."

Brian Beirne 🎤   6777 Hollywood

Disc Jockey

Brian Beirne (left) and Jack Lemmon

BORN Nov. 7, 1949, in San Mateo, CA. **SPOTLIGHTS** Known as "Mr. Rock 'n' Roll," this witty K-Earth radio personality is considered *the* authority on rock 'n' roll. One of the top modern music historians in the world, he owns one of the globe's largest private record libraries, numbering more than 40,000, plus a huge collection of rock 'n' roll memorabilia. His intimate story-telling about the lives and legends of the music industry has captivated audiences for years. Beirne's classic oldies show is one of the best in America, popular with an audience ranging in age from teeny boppers to those old enough to have seen the Beatles perform live. **ACHIEVEMENTS** A recipient of *Billboard* magazine's acclaimed honor, he is also an award-winning music producer, and the successful host/producer of the annual "Legends of Rock 'n' Roll" concert held at the Los Angeles Greek Theatre in October each year. **QUOTE** "As a child it was Elvis who really got me hooked on music for life. The minute I heard his first record I knew I had to be on the air playing this music." His admiration of the king has never abated. Beirne makes an annual pilgrimage to Graceland with contest winners.

Richard Mulligan 📺   6777 Hollywood

Actor

Richard Mulligan

BORN Nov. 13, 1932, in Bronx, New York, NY. **SPOTLIGHTS** The son of a New York city policeman, and one of five boys, as a youngster he proved smart as a whip. Mulligan was a serious student and academically inclined. While attending Cardinal Hayes High School he thought about devoting his life to the Catholic Church. Next, he enrolled in Maryknoll Junior Seminary where he gave serious thought to a spiritual life as a priest. He also studied play writing at Columbia University. The course ignited his artistic spark. By now, it was time for his Navy duty. He did his stint as a crash rescue man, in Pensacola, Florida. Off-hour, he wrote. One day while driving to Miami he had a simple accident; his tire went flat. Whether it was divine intervention or simply serendipity, when Mulligan looked up he saw he was stranded in front of a local theater. The aspiring dramatist decided to try to sell his recently written play. Inside, auditions for Eugene O'Neill's play, "Beyond the Horizon" were on. He tried out, won a part and received exceptional reviews. Mulligan headed to the Great White Way. He wowed audiences with his Broadway performance in the Pulitzer Prize-winning "All the Way Home." Other stage productions include "Never Too Late," "Nobody Loves an Albatross," and "The Mating Game." In 1963 this solid character actor made his silver screen debut in *Love with the Proper Stranger*. Motion pictures include *One Potato, Two Potato* (1964), *The Group* (1966), *Little Big Man* (1970—as General Custer), *Visit to a Chief's Son* (1974), *S.O.B.* (1981),

Trail of the Pink Panther (1982), *Micki and Maude* (1984), *The Heavenly Kid* (1985), *A Fine Mess* (1986), *Babes in Toyland* (1986), and *Oliver and Company* (1988—voiceover). Yet even with all his work on stage and screen, Mulligan has found his greatest fame on television. He appeared in dozens of shows: "Route 66" "The Defenders," and "The Dupont Show of the Month," but made his breakthrough in the prime time series, "Soap." He later starred in another hit series, "Empty Nest." (See below.) Among his colleagues, Mulligan is known for his precision delivery and for being exceedingly well-prepared when he arrives on the set. **ACHIEVEMENTS** 1980 Emmy Award for his role as Burt Campbell in TV's off-beat comedy series "Soap." Recipient of the 1989 Emmy Award for Best Actor and Golden Globe Award for his portrayal of the widowed pediatrician Harry Weston in "Empty Nest."

Judy Canova 6777 Hollywood
Singer, comedienne, dancer

Judy Canova

BORN Nov. 20, 1916, in Jacksonville, FL. **SPOTLIGHTS** She was the first hillbilly-comedy act to strike gold on radio. Ear-bursting yodeling was Canova's lovable trademark. One of the biggest stars during the World War II (and post WWII) era, her ultra hick style on "The Judy Canova Show" (NBC) split ribs for a decade. She achieved her fame playing the friendly pig-tailed hayseed, who was always man-hungry, and trying to crash into upper society. *Variety* reported "Miss Canova, when given to songs, spreads her style from scat to rhythm to plain hog calling, but it was all entertaining." Her jokes were simple, fun, and corny. For example: Judy (to a stranger): "Your kisses sure send me." Stranger (to Judy): "Shucks, some people don't care how they travel." Another example: Judy: "I'm gonna sing the Miseries from *Il Travatore*. Mr. Opera Man (to Judy): "Miss Canova, that's the *Miserere*—not the Miseries. Judy: "You ain't heard me sing it yet." An example of a social climbing joke: Mrs Proothwistle: "Most of the families in the Saddle and Hunt Club have been riding to the hounds for 30 years." Judy: "Shucks. My family went to the dogs long before that." Here is her sound country advice to city bigwigs: "Remember more people have been flattened by a right to the back than a left to the jaw." This rural miss, the pride of the Ozarks, also conquered Broadway. The lively, backwoods, rather plain-looking country brunette with a gigantic mouth entertained motion picture audiences from 1935-'76 with hilarious movies. She was famous for her cavorting and grimaces and mugging. But the pig-tailed mimic knew about timing and delivery. A partial listing of her films includes *Scatterbrain* (1940), *Puddin' Head* (1941), *Chatterbox* (1943),

Hit the Hay (1945), and *Honeychile* (1951), among others. **QUOTE** During WWII, she closed her radio show with the theme "Good night, Soldier, wherever you may be...my heart's lonely...without you." After the war, she closed with a sweet nursery song: "Go to sleep-y, little ba-by, Go to sleep-y, little ba-by, When you wake, You'll patty-patty cake, And ride a shiny little po-ny." Died: 1983.

Jascha Heifetz 6777 Hollywood
Violinist

BORN Feb. 2, 1901, in Vilna, Russia. **SPOTLIGHTS** One of the world's greatest violinists, Heifetz recalled, "I picked up my first violin at age three, staged my first recital at age seven, and have been playing ever since." (His father gave a quarter-size violin to him at age three.) At age five, he had already enrolled in the prestigious Royal School of Music in Vilna, Russia. At age nine, his family relocated to St. Petersburg so little Jascha could study with the world renowned instructor, Leopold Auer. This great teacher rarely gave praise to any of his students, in fact, he disliked most of them. Yet, with little Jascha, he declared, "A Heifetz appears in the musical world approximately once in two centuries." Auer dedicated himself to training the youngster. The following year, this child prodigy gave his first official concert. He was already a world famous violinist when he forced to leave Russia due to the turmoil of the Czar Nicholas II's ruined government and the upcoming Bolshevik Revolution. The confident 16-year-old made his Carnegie Hall debut to an astounded audience. He became a U.S. citizen in 1925, enjoying much-deserved popularity and success. He considered his work as serious music for the elite to be performed in presitigious venues. When radio networks wooed him to perform on the air, he flatly rejected their offers. He declared he did not want to stoop to the masses. Without missing a beat, he did a complete turnabout when he realized he could reach millions in one evening's broadcast, instead of thousands in a concert hall. In 1936 he returned to his homeland, where adoring fans rushed him with near-hysteria. Of his overwhelming reception, he said, "The greatest emotional experience of my life." He was also a brave man with a light sense of humor. During World War II he played for American and Allied Forces at the front, telling them, "Whether you like it or not, you're going to get some Bach." The GIs surprised Heifetz by demanding an encore. Widely admired for his virtuosity and technique, he was often compared to the great Paganini. He received numerous Grammys for his recordings. **HIGHLIGHTS** When Heifetz first played in a trio with pianist Artur Rubinstein and cellist Gregor Piatigorsky, the violinist got second billing. When another concert was arranged—and Rubinstein again got top billing—he complained, "If the Almighty himself played the violin, the credits would still read 'Rubinstein, God, and Piatigorsky' in that order!" **QUOTE** "Sometimes we have to do nothing, just sit and think, and to have dreams—to keep on dreaming. Everything in this modern world tends to kill it." Died: 1987.

Bessie Love 🎥   6777 Hollywood

Actress

BORN Juanita Horton; Sept. 10, 1898, in Midland, TX. **SPOTLIGHTS** Discovered by Makeup King Max Factor, Love's career spanned the silents from the classic *Intolerance* (1916), to the first MGM sound musical—*The Broadway Melody* (1929). She kept busy on stage, TV, and wrote plays in America and England. Died: 1986.

Andrew L. Stone 🎥   6777 Hollywood

Director, screenwriter, producer

BORN July 16, 1902, in Oakland, CA. **SPOTLIGHTS** He worked as screenwriter, director, and producer of *The Bachelor's Daughters* (1946), the story of a group of struggling girls who pass themselves off as an upper-crust family to attract rich bachelors. **HIGHLIGHTS** His "thriller" films owe their tension-packed sequences to his editor wife, Virginia Stone: including *Cry Terror!* (1958).

Anna Lee 🎥   6777 Hollywood

Actress

Anna Lee with Johnny Grant

BORN Joan Boniface Winnifrith; Jan. 2, 1913, in Ightham, Kent, England. **SPOTLIGHTS** She studied at the Central School of Speech Training and Dramatic Art at the Royal Albert Hall, in London. Fellow alumni included Laurence Olivier and John Gielgud. She appeared in dozens of films, notably *How Green Was My Valley* (1939), beginning a long-lasting association with director John Ford. Since 1978 she has become best known as matriarch Lila Quartermaine in the daytime soap opera "General Hospital." **ACHIEVEMENTS** Awarded a Member of the Most Excellent Order of the British Empire in 1982. She was received at Buckingham Palace by Her Majesty, Queen Elizabeth II.

Kirsten Flagstad 🎤   6777 Hollywood

Opera singer

BORN July 12, 1895, in Hamar, Norway. **SPOTLIGHTS** Known as the no-nonsense diva, she was professional, determined, pleasant, but cold. While on the verge of retirement she made her Met debut on February 2, 1935, as Sieglinde. The powerful soprano was immortalized in Wagnerian repertory. Her vocal mastery was so colorful, beautiful and legendary, that many wonder if any singer can ever compete with her supremacy in Wagner's roles. Together with Lauritz Melchior, they were able to keep the Met afloat during the dark days of the Depression. She sang two sold-out performances a week, while keeping her salary demands low. This also allowed the rest of America to hear her via the Met Saturday broadcasts. Unlike others in her profession, she offered a direct, concise answer to any question. When asked her secret to singing Wagnerian heroines, she replied, "Always wear comfortable shoes." **SIDELIGHTS** During an especially long recording session of *Die Walkure,* the producer asked the conductor what to do if the singer got tired. The conductor laughed, "Tired? She'll never get tired. She's built like a battleship!" Died: 1962.

Bill Burrud 📺   6777 Hollywood

Host, producer

Bill Burrud

BORN Jan. 12, 1925, in Hollywood, CA. **SPOTLIGHTS** Specializing in wildlife documentaries, the ruggedly handsome host introduced audiences to the earth's wondrous animals and its ecological chain in "Animal World" (1968-'71) and "Safari to Adventure" (1969-'75). Ahead of the times, his programs demonstrated the need for environmental action and protection of endangered species. For proactive, hands-on involvement contact "Earthwatch." Call 800.776.0188; 617.926.8200. Website: www.earthwatch.org Or, to help call 202.293.4800, World Wildlife Fund, 1250 Twenty-Fourth Street, NW, Washington, DC 20037.

Elvis Presley 🎤   6777 Hollywood

Singer, actor, guitarist

Elvis Presley

BORN Jan. 8, 1935, and weighing in at five pounds, in East Tupelo, Mississippi. **SPOTLIGHTS** Known as "the King," he was the first rock 'n' roll star. Inspired by rhythm and blues, local jazz and gospel, Presley combined their elements to create his hip slinging rockabilly style. In 1957 upset critics described him as "the bumping baritone," and "proof of decadence in civilization." Responding to them, Elvis said, "Ah don't do no dirty body movements. When Ah sing, Ah just start jumpin'." His business manager, Colonel Tom Parker, verified, "If I thought he was doing it on purpose, I'd be against it, but he honestly just gets overexcited when he sings." Word spread like wildfire about his hip thrusts and fancy footwork throughout the industry. While auditioning for "The Jackie Gleason Show" (one of the earliest shows Elvis appeared on), Gleason made the young Elvis repeat a song several times. Wanting to avoid the wrath of censors, he ordered the cameraman to shoot only from the waist up. After a few times, Elvis pouted and refused to do it again. Perfectionist Gleason instructed Elvis to do the song one more time. Elvis dropped his head down like a stubborn child. His ever-present manager, Colonel Parker, sensed Gleason's growing frustration with Elvis' moodiness, and approached the singer. He patted on his pocket, saying, "If you do it one more time, I'll give you this." The crew wondered what could be in that pocket, and if it would work. Elvis performed the song again. Afterwards, with all eyes discreetly on Colonel Parker's pocket, the Colonel stunned everyone when he pulled out a chocolate bar and gave it to Elvis! Actress Audrey Meadows commented, "Yes sir, that boy must have quite a sweet tooth." In the fall of 1956, he appeared on "The Ed Sullivan Show," capturing the biggest TV audience of all time. Teens idolized him, copying his sullen expression, long sideburns, blue jeans and unbuttoned plaid shirt. In 1958, when a reporter asked young Elvis why he thought teens took to him, he replied, "Ah don't know what Ah represent to them. But Ah get lonesome without their hollerin'." He served his stint in the U.S. military from 1958-'60. His Army serial number was 53310761, and his paycheck was $78 a month, down from his civilian earnings by approximately $399,922 monthly. That's not the only thing that dropped: he went from his induction weight of 185 pounds, to 170 pounds upon his release. As popular as ever with the public, his songs always turned to gold. Hits include "Jailhouse Rock," "Blue Suede Shoes," "Heartbreak Hotel," "I Was the One," "I Want You, I Need You, I Love You," "Hound Dog," "My Baby Left Me," "Don't Be Cruel," "All Shook Up," "(Let Me Be Your) Teddy Bear," "Stuck on You," "It's Now or Never," "Are You Lonesome Tonight?" "A Big Hunk o' Love," "Good Luck Charm," "Surrender," "Suspicious Minds," and "Love Me Tender." Gospel tunes include "How Great Thou Art" (he sang it as a prayer), "He Touched Me," and "Amazing Grace." He made 33 movies, including *Love Me Tender* (1956--his screen debut), *Loving You* (1957--his first color film), *Jailhouse Rock* (1957--critics consider this his best film, with terrific Leiber/Stoller songs, and Elvis' own choreography of the title song), *G.I. Blues* (1960--it caused a riot in Mexico City; the Mexican government banned all

The beautiful actress Priscilla Presley with club impresario Mark Fleischman

future Elvis films!), *Blue Hawaii* (1961), *Fun in Acapulco* (1963), *Viva Las Vegas* (1964), *Roustabout* (1964), *Girl Happy* (1965), *Tickle Me* (1965), *Frankie and Johnny* (1965), *Paradise, Hawaiian Style* (1966), *Spinout* (1966), and *The Trouble With Girls* (1969). More than one billion compact discs, albums and singles of Elvis' have been sold—more than anyone else ever. The King earned countless awards and generated enough interest to merit an astounding 350 books about him. More than 5,000 performers have earned a living impersonating Elvis, including Danny U (Danny Uwnawich), lead singer of Don Grenough's famed band, Gypsy Magic...Elvis was inspired by Rudolph Valentino and Gilda Gray. (See their respective bios in this book.)...The survivor of identical twins, his still-born brother was named Jesse Garon. Elvis mourned for his brother his entire life. He considered his mother Gladys' death his greatest tragedy...He married the former Priscilla Ann Beaulieu on May 1, 1967, in a private ceremony at the Aladdin Hotel, in Las Vegas. Nine months after their wedding, Lisa Marie Presley was born. The world wept when the King died in 1977.

Ray Charles ●   6775 Hollywood
Singer, pianist, composer

Ray Charles

BORN Ray Charles Robinson; Sept. 23, 1930, in Albany, GA. **SPOTLIGHTS** A legend and one of the most versatile artists of 20th-century music, Charles is the gigantic talent behind Soul music. Although he grew up poverty-stricken, the piano had captured his imagination by age three. At age six, he contracted glaucoma which went untreated, and he went blind. The next year he attended St. Augustine School for the Deaf and Blind, as a charity student, where he learned to play alto saxophone, trumpet, clarinet and piano. He learned to read Braille and studied composition. Before he hit his teens, he was writing music for the school's 15-piece orchestra. He stated, "It wasn't hard for me to do. I could write a whole arrangement without ever touching the paper. If you know what it's going to sound like in your brain, and you've studied harmony and orchestration, you can do it. It's like Beethoven. He went deaf, but he still composed, didn't he?" Other hardships struck during his childhood; he was 10 when his father died, 15 when his mom died. In 1945 he left St. Augustine's to perform in dance bands in Florida and dropped his last name so not to be confused with boxer Sugar Ray Robinson. Two years later, he moved with $500 in savings to Seattle, where he hooked up with Quincy Jones (a lifetime friend and colleague). For a while he crooned in the style of his idol Nat King Cole. When he decided to be himself, Charles quickly rose to the top. Using jazz as his foundation, he easily proved his first-rate improvisational skills and jazz sensibilities on "The Great Ray Charles." But

Charles also possesses a broad repertoire in rhythm & blues, gospel, pop, country, Latin mix, and big band. This 69-year show business veteran recordings include "Georgia on My Mind" (his version is the official state song), "I Got a Woman," "Ruby," "Hit the Road, Jack," "What'd I Say," "Let the Good Times Roll," "Al Di La," "Hallelujah, I Love Her So," "I Can't Stop Loving You," "You Don't Know Me," "Your Cheatin' Heart," "Blue Moon of Kentucky," "I'm Movin' On," "Yesterday," "Without You," and "A Song for You" (President Clinton's favorite song). **ACHIEVEMENTS** Among his hundreds of honors, and national medals are 10 Grammys, a prestigious Kennedy Center Honor, and an inductee of the Rock and Roll Hall of Fame. Charles is a tremendous humanitarian.

Vivien Leigh 🎥   6775 Hollywood
Actress

Vivien Leigh and Laurence Olivier (Lord Olivier)

BORN Vivian Hartley; Nov. 5, 1913, in Darjeeling, India. **SPOTLIGHTS** It was a British director named Victor Saville who first suggested to Leigh that she should read *Gone with the Wind*. He told her, "Vivien, I've just read a great story for the movies about the bitchiest of all bitches, and you're just the person to play the part." Leigh was immortalized as the Southern belle Scarlett O'Hara in *Gone with the Wind* (1939). And well she should be. For she worked harder in that picture—with sheer determination to get every detail right—than anyone in the film. She created one of cinema's most memorable characters. When asked why she thought the character appealed to so many people worldwide, Miss Leigh answered, "It's the rebel in her that draws us to a girl like Scarlett. Most of us have compromised with life. Those who fight for what they want will always thrill us." The film's director Victor Fleming gave her the nickname of "Fiddle-Dee-Dee," and called her that on the set. A ravishing brunette with translucent blue-green eyes, she also graced both the London and Broadway stages with remarkable performances, including Shakespearean roles. Motion pictures include *Waterloo Bridge* (1940), and *Caesar and Cleopatra* (1945). She remains a time-

less screen beauty. **ACHIEVEMENTS** Best Actress Academy Awards for *Gone with the Wind* (1939—in a role considered *la creme de la creme* of all female leading roles), and *A Streetcar Named Desire* (1951—the second Southern belle she played, although Blanche du Bois was more decadent). **HIGHLIGHTS** The Lady was married to Sir Laurence Olivier (1940-'60). They were the most glamorous couple in the world in the 1940s. **SIDELIGHTS** She contracted tuberculosis in England in the 1940s, and was plagued by ill health and physical exhaustion until her death. Died: 1967, in her sleep.

B. B. King 🔴   6771 Hollywood
Singer, musician, songwriter

B. B. King

BORN Riley B. King; Sept. 16, 1925, in Indianola, MS. **SPOTLIGHTS** The world's number one blues singer and leading musician is called the "King of the Modern Blues." Born on a plantation, he picked cotton for 35 cents per 100 pounds. As a teenager, he played on street corners for dimes. When he accidentally wrecked some farm equipment (a tractor), he figured it was a sign for him to move on and pursue his dreams. With his guitar and $2.50, he hitchhiked north to Memphis to pursue his career. He first became a disc jockey known as the "Beale Street Blues Boy." "Blues Boy" stuck as his nickname, but he shortened it to "B.B." He is universally and lovingly referred to as "B." His first break came on Sonny Boy Williamson's radio program. His first recording went nowhere—in fact, the company went belly up—and he felt discouraged. Despite that, he kept on working in the music business, performing in small clubs, jamming, and listening for good songs to record. If money got low, he momentarily returned to agriculture—picking a few hundred pounds of cotton. While performing at a dance hall in the 1950s, a fight broke out between two men. A fire ensued. Everyone escaped, but B.B. ran back in to save his $30 guitar. After learning the brawl was over a woman name Lucille, he named his guitar "Lucille." He also affectionately refers to the instrument as "my best gal, Lucille." He hit big in 1952 with "Three O'Clock Blues." Recorded in a remarkable two takes, it topped *Billboard*'s Rhythm and Blues chart at #1 for three months. As B.B. King put it, "I'm out of the cotton field and in the music field!" He became a household name in the music world and his career soared. During the 1950s, recordings include *Singin' the Blues, The Blues, Do the Boogie! B.B. King's Early 50s, Heart and Soul*, and *My Sweet Little Angel*, among others. In 1965, he recorded *Live at the Regal*, which is considered the definitive blues album. Others that decade: *Blues Is King* and *Lucille*. Crossing over to pop—although there's a lot of bluesy soul to it—"The Thrill is Gone"—rocketed up the charts in 1970. The 1980s saw the releases of two of his Grammy, winners: *There Must Be a Better World Somewhere*, and *Six Silver Strings* ("My Guitar Sings the Blues"). The 1990s Grammy Award-winning hits include *Live at San Quentin*, *Live at the Apollo* and *Blues Summit*. In the 1990s, he opened B.B. King's Blues Club, a restaurant/club at Universal City Walk (next to Universal Studios Hollywood), and another in Memphis. **ACHIEVEMENTS** The world's "Ambassador of the Blues," has toured Russia, South America among other continents. He won his first Grammy Award in 1970 for the Best Rhythm and Blues Vocal Performance, Male: "The Thrill Is Gone." One of his least traditional works, *Blues 'n' Jazz*, won a Grammy for Best Traditional Blues Album. Nominated 17 times, he has won seven Grammys, plus his album *Indianola Mississippi* won one for Best Album cover. In 1987, he received a Grammy Awards Lifetime Achievement Award. In 1990, he received a Songwriters Hall of Fame Lifetime Achievement Award. He has been inducted into four Halls of Fame. King has been recognized and awarded every important musical prize and honor for his singing, guitar playing and song writing. In addition to his countless tributes, he has received an honorary doctorate from Yale University, and a Presidential Medal of the Arts...King refers to Job in the Bible, "The moral is patience. Patience has worked for me, always. Patience is the one thing that's seen me through." **LISTENING** *B.B. King, How Blue Can You Get? Classic Live Performances 1964 to 1994*. And, the four-CD/cassette box, *King of the Blues*, is a superb collection from his stellar career, available on MCA. **RECOMMENDED** His riveting autobiography, *Blues All Around Me*, written with David Ritz and published by Avon Books. **QUOTE** With his world-famous soulful sound, on Sept. 5, 1990, B.B. said, "I'm happy to be stuck in the Hollywood Walk of Fame."

Milton Berle 🎙   6771 Hollywood

See page 194

Al Christie 🎬   6769 Hollywood

Director, screenwriter, producer
BORN Nov. 24, 1886, in Canada. **SPOTLIGHTS** See the bio of his brother, Charles Christie, in this book. Al died in 1951.

Lindsay Wagner 🎬   6767 Hollywood

Actress, singer
BORN June 22, 1949, in Los Angeles, CA. **SPOTLIGHTS** At age 13, Wagner began dance studies. When her inner ballerina failed to emerge, her mentor suggested she study acting. Wagner proved to be a natural born talent, moving to the head of her class with a major part in a showcase production of Tennessee Williams' "This Property is Condemned." Impressed with her abilities, an MGM talent scout immediately offered the teenager the lead in a television series. Her acting instructor, James Best, advised her to resist the opportunity and continue training and personal maturity—promising

Lindsay Wagner

her "other chances will come your way." The beautiful youth soon became a sought-after fashion model for the prestigious Nina Blanchard agency while still attending North Hollywood High School. After graduation, she spent a few months in France, attended the University of Oregon, and sang in a rock 'n' roll band. Ready to pursue her life's passion, she won numerous roles in popular television series: "The F.B.I.," "The Bold Ones," and "The Rockford Files." Then, she hit big as star of the TV action series "The Bionic Woman" (1975-'78), for which she won an Emmy. Wagner played the confident, athletic "superhero," Jaime Sommers (a character introduced on "The Six Million Dollar Man"). With her superhuman powers, she chased and fought criminals. Although it was a comic-book-type character, millions of young females admired her. They learned to believe in themselves, and their own personal power. As a female role model, she inspired girls to be athletic, assertive and to be taken seriously. In historic terms, those early feminist contributions cannot be overestimated. After the series, this intelligent, sensitive performer chose a different route. Wagner makes little distinction between her life as an actress, advocate, mother, humanitarian or author. What unites these various parts is a commitment through her work and her personal life to advance human potential. It is clearly the reason why her career took a direction towards the genre of TV movies with issue-oriented stories. It is a field in which she is the undisputed record holder with more than 30 starring credits. The opportunity to use media as a way to communicate ideas to help people in their personal process is a major criteria in almost all of her choices. "Shattered Dreams" (1991), a film on domestic violence that Wagner produced and starred in, exemplifies this quality best. Wagner championed this film to shatter the socio-economic stereotypes about spousal abuse by portraying the true story of a Washington socialite battered by her husband, a prominent, high-profile government official. Most importantly, she insisted that the film address her character's healing and recovery process, giving an underlying substance and understanding to the story's sensational or violent elements. Other notable credits for this Golden Globe winner are "The Taking of Flight 847: The Uli Derickson Story," "Scruples," "Passions," "I Want to Live," "Callie and Son," "The Incredible Journey of Meg Laurel" (her favorite); "A Mother's Instinct," and "Fighting for My Daughter." Wagner continues to exercise her belief in the need for quality TV—especially in regard to providing meaningful subject matter for viewing by children. Features include her starring role in the Oscar-winning picture, *The Paper Chase* (1973), and the suspenseful crime drama *Nighthawks* (1981). **ACHIEVEMENTS** Both on-screen and off, Wagner has championed these issues: child abuse and domestic violence prevention, environment, animal rights, and learning differences. She is known as the most knowledgeable entertainer on holistic health. Like many other Hollywood celebrities, she practices vegetarianism. She co-penned with Ariane Spade a best-selling vegetarian lifestyle cookbook entitled, *The High Road to Health* (published by Simon & Schuster). Another work is entitled, *Lindsay Wagner's New Beauty: The Acupressure Facelift* (Simon & Schuster; and on Lorimar home video). **FANS** Contact Lindsay Wagner's Official Fan Club, P.O. Box 5087, Sherman Oaks, CA 91403 (website: www.fansource.com). **QUOTE** Her star dedication ceremony took place on Dec. 12, 1984. Wagner said, "I was especially moved to receive my star on the Hollywood Walk of Fame because my fans did it all. Then, they presented it as a surprise to me."

Bing Crosby 🎞   6767 Hollywood
See page 344

Rafael Mendez 💿   6767 Hollywood
Trumpet player

Rafael Mendez

BORN March 26, 1906, in Mexico. **SPOTLIGHTS** He was the third son of 19 children. His father, a composer-arranger , encouraged young Rafael to pursue his favorite instrument. By the early 1930s, Mendez was playing with Rudy Vallee's orchestra. During the 1940s he was a member of MGM's orchestra. A trumpet virtuoso, he recorded "Scherzo in D Minor," "Mendez Jota," and "The Virgin of the Macarena." This world renowned concert trumpet player and recording artist performed with his identical twin sons—both gifted trumpet players—on the Ed Sullivan Show in 1954. Although he quietly *hoped* his sons would pursue a *musical* career, they became doctors. Both Ralph G. Mendez, M.D. and Robert Mendez, M.D. are two of America's leading transplant surgeons—which is music to the ears to their countless patients whose lives they have saved. Rafael Mendez died in 1981.

Edgar Bergen 🎞 6767 Hollywood
See page 26

Roseanne 📺   6767 Hollywood
Actress, producer, comedian, writer
BORN Nov. 3, 1955, in Salt Lake City, UT. **SPOTLIGHTS** Roseanne is America's leading TV female comedian and one of its most innovative entertainment thinkers. A former cocktail waitress, her bar customers urged her to do stand-up downtown because she was so funny. She began making the rounds in local clubs, and by 1983 fans called her the "Queen of Denver Comedy." Her irreverent, fresh, true routines sparkled with jokes about being a "domestic goddess." Since almost every woman can relate to her tales of the drudgery of housework along with hopeless husbands, her monologues were like a hilarious strike of lightning that tickled

Roseanne and Johnny Grant

women right down to their tootsies. Urged by friends to audition at the Comedy Store in Los Angeles, she did, and the quick-witted comic was instantly hired. Discovered there by a talent scout from "The Tonight Show starring Johnny Carson," she was a national smash hit one week later. She came on like gangbusters as a working-class heroine in her landmark "Roseanne" series. This ground breaking situation comedy made its hilarious debut in October, 1988, as one of the top-rated series and quickly rose to the #1 position. Her special brand of comedy made her America's favorite new TV Mom. But the program also handled difficult social, moral, economical and cultural issues with cutting insight. For example, when America was going through one of its worse recessions in history, and unemployment reached one of its all-time highs, Roseanne mirrored our country's problems in her show. Her TV family struggled to pay bills, worried about keeping their house, their jobs, and hiding from bill collectors. She helped millions of viewers emotionally through these ordeals. At the very least, we could all laugh in our misery together. "Roseanne" enjoyed a nine-year run, four Emmy Awards, and countless other honors. In 1998 she switched tracks to become a daytime talk show host on "The Roseanne Show." This nationally syndicated program is seen across the nation and in 32 other countries. She works proudly with three of her daughters, who are on staff. About her talk show, Roseanne commented, "Just having the free exchange of ideas is exciting...with contributing members of society...with mothers to explore children's issues. Information can change lives." With her warmth, kindness and insight, the show has proven to be another glorious creation. Roseanne is also an accomplished stage performer, and film actress. **ACHIEVEMENTS** Two People's Choice Awards for Favorite All-Around Female Television Performer and Favorite All-Around Female Entertainer (1990). Two American Comedy Awards (1988) for Funniest Female Performer in a Television Series and Funniest Female Stand-up Comic. She is the recipient of numerous prestigious awards. Her book, *Roseanne: My Life as a Woman*, became a best-seller (1989). **QUOTE** On Sept. 25, 1992, Roseanne's Walk of Fame star was unveiled. She graciously said, "Ever since I was a child of three, I dreamed of coming to

Hollywood and having my own show with my own name on it. Now I have it and my dreams have come true. Thank you."

Sammy Kaye ● 6765 Hollywood
See page 108

Chick Hearn 🎤 6765 Hollywood
Broadcaster

Chick Hearn

BORN Francis Dayle Hearn; in Aurora, IL. **SPOTLIGHTS** A broadcasting legend, Hearn is nationally famous for his dramatic, accurate play-by-play action. Devoted to the Lakers for more than 38 years (since 1961) he's also the fastest voice in the NBA. Humorous, original and fresh, the "Golden Throat" comes up with something new each broadcast, but more than one of his familiar phrases "is in the refrigerator." His entertaining "words-eye-view" boasts such beauties as "The mustard came off the hot dog," "Faked him into the popcorn machine," "The jell-o is jiggling" and "Give and go." This sports icon got his star on an unusual day for Southern California, a rainy day back in 1986. **ACHIEVEMENTS** "The Iron Man" has not missed a day's—or night's—work since 1965, and that was due to bad weather grounding his plane. Called his 3,000th consecutive Laker game on Martin Luther King day, in Jan. 1998...Two Emmys...1991 Inductee the Basketball Hall of Fame. **QUOTE** After Lakers' player Rick Fox scored on a wild shot, he said, "That was a prayer. The only way that goes in, is if you throw a little extra in the collection plate."

Marie Wilson 📺 6765 Hollywood
See page 81

Eddie Cantor 🎤 6763 Hollywood
See page 429

Robert Merrill ●
6763 Hollywood
Opera singer

Robert Merrill

BORN Robert Miller; June 4, 1917, in Brooklyn, NY. **SPOTLIGHTS** An eminent American baritone, he succeeded first as a singer of popular music in clubs. Then, he made his sensational New York debut at the Metropolitan Opera House in 1945 in *La Traviata*. Adored by the public, he broke the Met's attendance records with his beautiful voice by performing hundreds of times and by becoming its leading baritone. **SIDELIGHTS** The handsome, fair-haired star was assigned the science lab as his dressing room during a university concert. At his break, a beautiful, shapely, brunette co-ed appeared at his door. Merrill declared, "I never sign autographs during the intermission." "I don't want your autograph," she replied. "I want to feed my snake."

Red Skelton 🎤 6763 Hollywood
See page 431

Katherine MacDonald 🎥 6761 Hollywood
Actress, producer

BORN Dec. 14, 1891, in Pennsylvania. **SPOTLIGHTS** A gorgeous silent screen actress who appeared in dozens of silent films, including *Headin' South* (1918) and *The Untamed Women* (1925). Died: 1956.

Ingrid Bergman 🎥   6761 Hollywood
Actress

Ingrid Bergman

BORN Aug. 29, 1915, in Stockholm, Sweden. **SPOTLIGHTS** After both of her parents were killed when she was a child, she was raised by relatives. After high school graduation in 1933, Bergman studied at Stockholm's Royal Dramatic Theater School, where she found she could immerse herself in parts. A natural born talent, she won her first film role in *The Surf* (1934). Although she was a newcomer, her immense gifts were immediately recognized. She appears in Gustaf Molander's *Intermezzo* (1936) in Sweden, then was invited to Hollywood by actor Leslie Howard to co-star in *Intermezzo: A Love Story* (1939). It won her international acclaim. Bergman, though, was immortalized with Humphrey Bogart in the evergreen wartime drama, *Casablanca* (1942). Among her credits are three Alfred Hitchcock vehicles: the outstanding thrillers *Spellbound* (1945) and *Notorious* (1946), as well as *Under Capricorn* (1949), a movie which neither Hitchcock nor Bergman liked. Ditto for the public. (Also see Alfred Hitchcock's bio in this book to learn the acting secret Hitchcock taught her.) About her performance in *The Bells of St. Mary's* (1945), director Leo McCarey said, "She's so great that when she walks on-screen and says 'Hello,' people ask, 'Who wrote that wonderful line of dialogue?'" The sentimental and charming drama co-stars Bing Crosby. Other films include *Dr. Jekyll and Mr. Hyde* (1941), *For Whom the Bell Tolls* (1943), opposite Gary Cooper, *Joan of Arc* (1948), in a role she had successfully performed on

Broadway, *Indiscreet* (1958), with one of her favorite co-stars Cary Grant, and *The Inn of the Sixth Happiness* (1958), opposite Curt Jurgens and Robert Donat. A tall, natural beauty who shied from makeup, she had an open, compassionate face and an air of nobility about her. She played romantic figures as easily as the more challenging role of a haunted or tragic heroine. She was a true woman, not a silly girl-lady. **ACHIEVEMENTS** Best Actress Oscars for *Gaslight* (1944), *Anastasia* (1956), and *Murder on the Orient Express* (1974). 1947 Tony Award for "Joan of Lorraine." One of her daughters is the beautiful, intelligent and talented actress, Isabella Rossellini. **QUOTE** "I am not frightened by age. Just think of the wonderful parts I can play when I am 70. I hope they will put on my gravestone: 'She acted on the very last day of her life. Here lies a good actress.'" Died: 1982.

Lee Strasberg 🎥 6757 Hollywood
Acting teacher, actor
BORN Israel Strasberg; Nov. 17, 1901, in Austria. **SPOTLIGHTS** Immortalized as a legendary acting instructor, Strasberg embraced Method acting. Star pupils number too many to list here, but Marilyn Monroe and Al Pacino were two of his students. **ACHIEVEMENTS** 1930-'37 co-founder and director of the Group Theater; 1948 Artistic director of Actor's Studio in New York. 1969 Founder of the Lee Strasberg Institute in New York and Los Angeles. He was 73 when he made his first screen appearance in *The Godfather, Part II* (1974), as the quiet monster Hyman Roth. Died: 1982.

Fran Allison 📺 6757 Hollywood
Hostess, creator
BORN 1925, in La Porte City, IA. **SPOTLIGHTS** A former radio singer, she won the nation's heart in the well-loved children's puppet show, "Kukla, Fran, and Ollie" (1947-'57). Known as the "lovable chatterbox," she was the only live member of the "cast." Allison played the friendly foil to Kukla, the egg-shaped, bald, bulbous-nosed puppet and the snaggle-toothed Ollie J. Dragon. It opened with "Yes, by Gum, by Golly, It's Kukla, Fran and Ollie." The show's charm was its humanity and innocence. Telecast live, five nights a week, the entire show was improvised. **SIDELIGHTS** Bars around the country made special considerations for people who did not own TV sets. The bar owners turned off their sporting events and stopped serving liquor to allow families to come in and watch the peaceful, popular program. Died: 1989.

Joseph Schenck 🎥 6755 Hollywood
Film pioneer, producer, executive
BORN Dec. 25, 1878, in Rybinsk, Russia. **SPOTLIGHTS** A penniless immigrant who lived the rags-to-riches American dream. An independent producer in 1917, he became the head of United Artists in 1924 before co-founding 20th Century in 1933; two years later boss of 20th Century-Fox. **ACHIEVEMENTS** He was one of the 36 original founders of the Academy. Schenck was awarded a Special Oscar in 1952.

QUOTE "The wisdom of Hollywood is this: when studios get desperate, they drop a few hundred-dollar-a-week employees and then hire a four-thousand-a-week executive." Died: 1961.

Richard Barthelmess 🎥 6755 Hollywood
Actor

Richard Barthelmess

BORN May 9, 1895, in New York, NY. **SPOTLIGHTS** A superior dramatic talent in D.W. Griffith's *Broken Blossoms* (1919), co-starring Lillian Gish, his work inspired headlines and helped to elevate film as an art form. Reviewed by *The New York Times* as a "masterpiece," D.W.'s movie and excellent actors won over hardened critics who wondered if cinema could be "a new art...as important as music and poetry." He and Gish were also splendid in *Way Down East* (1920). He often played the romantic hero, who was sweet, kind and boyish; it compensated for the hardening of women during the Roaring '20s. The screen's dream boy worked with Lillian's sister, Dorothy Gish, in *Fury* (1923). So successful in 1924, he paid $29,995 in income tax, while studio head Louis B. Mayer (MGM) paid $14,000! He earned Oscar nominations for *The Patent Leather Kid* (1927) and *The Noose* (1928). Died: 1963.

Dennis James 📺 6753 Hollywood
Actor, performer

Dennis James

BORN Aug. 24, 1917, in Jersey City, N.J. **SPOTLIGHTS** In front of the TV camera more than any performer for the first few decades of television. James was *the first to*: host a variety show, emcee a game show, provide sports commentary and star in a dramatic show. He held the dubious honor of being the first to announce a TV commercial. (What a trend he started.) Best known as host of the "Nighttime Price is Right" and "Name That Tune." His rallying cry of "Come on down!" fired up contestants and audiences. **ACHIEVEMENTS** Recipient of the "Humanitarian Award" from President Eisenhower (1965.) Official host of the Cerebral Palsy telethons for more than 40 years. He campaigned for ChildHelp USA, more. Raised $1 billion for charities. Died: 1997.

Richard Arlen 🎥 6755 Hollywood
Actor
BORN Cornelius Mattimore; Sept. 1, 1899, in Charlottesville,

VA. **SPOTLIGHTS** Arlen made his screen debut as an extra in a 1920 silent film. The handsome, rugged talent with ruddy cheeks, quickly moved into a bit part in *Ladies Must Lie* (1921), his second film. He moved into the supporting actor category in *Vengeance of the Deep* (1923). After appearing in William Wellman's *Wings* (1927)—which won the very *first* Best Picture Academy Award—his career soared. He co-stars with Gary Cooper in *The Virginian* (1929), before doing a light musical with Bing Crosby, Jack Oakie and George Burns in *College Humor* (1933). He plays the lively Cheshire Cat in *Alice in Wonderland* (1933). He worked in both A and B movies, including horror. Motion pictures include *Artists and Models* (1937), *Raiders of the Desert* (1941), *Hurricane Smith* (1952), and *The Bounty Killer* (1965). Died: 1976.

Joel Grey 🎭   6755 Hollywood
Actor, singer, dancer

Joel Grey

BORN Joel Katz; April 11, 1932, in Cleveland, OH. **SPOTLIGHTS** An American stage star, who sings, dances and wows audiences with phenomenal skill. He is also a fine actor: lithe, precise, and energetic, Grey began performing on stage when he was nine; he starred as Pud in "On Borrowed Time" at the Cleveland Playhouse. By 19, he had entertained at New York's Copacabana and the London Palladium. Broadway plays include "George M!" and "The Grand Tour," among many other successes. He made his silver screen debut in the musical *About Face* (1952). Motion pictures include *Calypso Heat Wave* (1957), *Come September* (1961), *Man on a Swing* (1974), *The Seven Percent Solution* (1976), *Remo Williams: The Adventure Begins* (1985), and *The Music of Chance* (1993). Grey was immortalized in his scintillating role as the Master of Ceremonies in Bob Fosse's *Cabaret* (1972). In television, he has starred in numerous specials and movies, including the 1999 production of "A Christmas Carol." He appears as the ghost to Patrick Stewart's Scrooge. **ACHIEVEMENTS** 1967 Tony Award, Best Supporting Actor for *Cabaret*. He reprised his stage role on film and won a 1972 Oscar Best Supporting Actor. His daughter is actress-dancer Jennifer Grey of *Dirty Dancing* fame.

Ilka Chase 📷   6755 Hollywood
See page 120

Jill Ireland 🎥   6751 Hollywood
Actress

BORN April 24, 1936, in London, England. **SPOTLIGHTS** A saucy blonde beauty whose career spanned three decades in

Charles Bronson and Jill Ireland

Europe and America. She made her professional debut in the London theatre, and appeared in such British films as *Oh Rosalinda* with Sir Michael Redgrave (1955) and *Three Men In A Boat* with Lawrence Harvey (1956). She immigrated to the U.S. in 1962, appearing in the TV series "Ben Casey." Ireland also co-starred with David Carradine in the western TV series "Shane." She co-starred opposite her real-life husband Charles Bronson in 19 feature films, including *The Valachi Papers* (1972), *Hard Times* (1975), and *Breakheart Pass* (1976). **ACHIEVEMENTS** Her book *Life Wish* dealt with cancer. She was recipient of The Courage Award, presented by President and Mrs. Reagan. Died: 1990.

Eddie Bracken 📺   6751 Hollywood
Actor, comedian, singer

Eddie Bracken

BORN Feb. 7, 1920, in Astoria, Long Island, NY. **SPOTLIGHTS** Educated at New York's Professional Children's School, Bracken won a "cute babies" contest at age four and "wowed 'em" ever since. As a child he appeared in "Our Gang" family comedy series (aka "The Little Rascals"), in vaudeville, and on Broadway. He grew into a 5-foot, 10-inch, 165-pound talent who specialized in playing the shy, bumbling type. This blue-eyed, wavy brown-haired actor landed a Paramount Pictures contract and made his screen debut in *Too Many Girls* (1940). One of his best films is the brilliant satirical comedy, *Hail the Conquering Hero* (1944), where he plays a Marine reject whose small hometown thinks he is a war hero. Motion pictures include *Sweater Girl* (1942), *Out of This World* (1945), *Bring on the Girls* (1945), *Duffy's Tavern* (1945), *National Lampoon's Vacation* (1983), *Home Alone 2: Lost in New York* (1992), and *Baby's Day Out* (1994). **SIDELIGHTS** The Walk of Fame "TV" category is a mistake; it should be "Motion Pictures."

Hanna-Barbera: William Hanna and

Joseph Barbera 📺   6751 Hollywood
Animators

William Hanna

Joseph Barbera

BORN William Hanna, July 14, 1910, in Melrose, NM; Joseph Barbera, Mar. 24, 1911, on the Lower East Side (Little Italy), NY. **SPOTLIGHTS** Legendary innovators in early animation, Hanna and Barbera have treasured their more than 60-year prolific partnership. Hanna's enthusiasm for animation started from day one on the job working for Harman-Ising, free-lance producers of cartoons. In his splendid 1996 autobiography entitled, *A Cast of Friends* (co-written with Tom Ito; Taylor Publishing Company, Texas), Hanna stated, "Everyone seemed to enjoy their work and each other, and the family-like atmosphere set a personal precedent for me early on of discovering my closest friendships with the people with whom I worked." On his own, he expanded his work hours without asking for extra pay. He started to "suggest gags and comic situations for the cartoons." He wrote, "A lot of these things just came to me while I was working away painting a cel or maybe chewing on a ham sandwich at noon...zany little stunts...I also began writing little songs that (were incorporated) into Warner Bros.' early Looney Tunes and Merrie Melodies cartoons." Hanna found himself so enthralled with the process that he worked his normal shift, went home for dinner, then returned to the studio and worked until midnight. His normal workday was 14 to 15 hours long. By his third year, Hanna earned $37.50-a-week, then after a meeting with competitor Walt Disney, Harman-Ising raised his salary to $60.00 weekly. In June 1937, MGM Studios hired Hanna as a director and story editor in their new cartoon department. On his second day of work, Hanna met another new MGM animation employee, Joe Barbera. Barbera grew up spending a lot of time daydreaming and drawing. No one else in his large Italian family had the gift of illustration, and he can remember his mother only saving one of his works, but he *knew* he had special talents. In his excellent 1994 autobiography entitled *My Life in 'Toons* (Turner Publishing, Atlanta, Georgia), Barbera wrote, "It seemed to me that God had looked around, saw me, and just said: *You can draw.* And that's all there was to it." He was his high school's champion athlete, drew sketches of pretty girls he wanted to (and did) date, edited and drew cartoons for the school newspaper, and graduated early. He skipped college as times were tough; the Great Depression loomed. Barbera, who was lousy at arithmetic, got a job—through one of his father's contacts—as an assistant tax man at Irving Trust Bank. The year was 1928 and he was paid $16-a-week. He "hated each and every minute of it," but with most of his friends out of work, he was too scared to leave. He likened his six years there to "a tortuous jail sentence." For mental survival, he spent his lunch hour drawing. At noon each Thursday, he submitted his cartoons to the two top magazines of the day, *Redbook* and *Collier's*. He dashed to the local subway and took the ride to Grand Central Station. From there, he made his way to Park Avenue, where both magazines were headquartered. Each week he would pick up his rejects and bring new creations. For *two straight years* his material was rejected. Finally, he sold a single cartoon to *Collier's* magazine for $25, then sold another three. Barbera was awakened to the possibility of *moving* cartoons when he saw Walt Disney's cartoon short, the "Skelton Dance" at the Roxy Theatre. Barbera even wrote his first and only fan letter to Walt Disney and included a sketch he had done of Mickey Mouse. To his surprise, Disney wrote back, thanking him for the drawing and signed the letter with his unique trademark script. Inspired, Barbera took art lessons at 50 cents a piece. Then, like most of the country, he found himself laid off. Instead of sadness, he felt freedom. With moxie, he took his four published cartoons to Van Beuren Studio, and was hired as an "in-betweener" sketch artist at $25-a-week. Like his soon-to-be partner, Hanna, Barbera did not restrict himself to normal work hours. He commented that he worked: "feverishly in my attic (apartment) every night, practicing, practicing, and practicing—for all practical purposes, *inventing* (for myself)—the art and science of animation. After some months I became good enough to ascend to the next rung on the animation ladder, an assistant." He traveled to the West Coast in his '36 Ford roadster, and he landed a job at MGM Studio, where he met Hanna. Their first collaboration, "Puss Gets the Boot" introduced audiences to "Tom and Jerry," the world's most famous cat and mouse team. They received acclaim after merging their "Jerry" animation with live actor Gene Kelly in *Anchors Aweigh* (1945), and providing the "Tom and Jerry" sequence for swim queen Esther Williams in *Dangerous When Wet* (1953), the movie's highlight. When the two collaborated, the result was nothing short of magical. With the onset of TV, the two men formed their own company in 1957. A coin toss determined whose name would be first. In 1958 they released the happy, good-natured blue canine on "The Huckleberry Hound Show." Every kid in America loved this dog. The show became an instant hit and won Hanna-Barbera its first Emmy Award. It was also the first time an animated TV series won an Emmy. Next, the team created the character Quick Draw McGraw in 1959. It featured a cuddly looking horse who walked around on two legs and wore a fine Stetson hat. America also fell in love with Jellystone Park's two most fascinating creatures, Yogi Bear and Boo Boo Bear. Breaking new ground, in 1960 Hanna-Barbera created TV's first animated family sitcom, "The Flintstones," a landmark series for a number of reasons. "The Flintstones" was the first animated series to air in prime time, the first animated series to go beyond the six or seven-minute cartoon format, and the first animated series to feature human characteristics. After its initial six-year run on ABC, it has remained one of the top-ranking animated programs in syndication history, with all original 166 episodes still being viewed worldwide. In a spin-off, there have been two major motion pictures with superstar actors playing the roles. Other Hanna-Barbera prime time cartoons include "The Jetsons," and "Top Cat." Hanna-Barbera also created the precious cowardly Great Dane, Scooby-Doo, who possesses a scratchy voice and foolhardy laugh, "Scooby-Doo, Where Are You?" made its TV debut in 1969 and continues to be one of TV's longest-running animated series. In 1981 Hanna-Barbera did it again with "The Smurfs," which won Daytime Emmy Awards in 1982 and 1983 for Outstanding Children's Entertainment Series and a Humanitas Prize in 1987. Animated features include the tender family tale, *Charlotte's Web* (1973), and *Heidi's Song* (1982) a sweet movie for the very young...Fred Flintstone's "Yabba Dabba Doo" is "an expression of jubilance; a spontaneous, loud exclamation of joy; an exchange of greetings between good friends denoting respect and admiration." Hanna-Barbera became part of the Warner Bros. family in 1996. Warner Bros. houses one of the most impressive animation libraries in the world. **ACHIEVEMENTS** Collected seven Academy Awards for *Tom and Jerry*, eight Emmy Awards, one Academy of Television Arts, and Sciences Governors Award. One Golden Globe. Inducted into the Television Academy Hall of Fame in 1991. Their star dedication ceremony took place on July 21, 1976. **QUOTE** Hanna summed up his feelings in a sweet poem:

> *"For the first few days, Hanna was my name*
> *as it appeared on the Walk of Fame*
> *I thought I heard people say*
> *'is it Hanna or banana?'*
>
> *I told them either name is fine*
> *I'm happy that my star will shine*
> *and it will shine and shine and shine*
> *As long as that big star is mine!"*

Barbera said, "*Only in America*, this phrase certainly applies to a kid born in Brooklyn who started working in a deli at the age of eight. For this kid to be standing on Hollywood Boulevard, staring at a star with his name on it, certainly seems like he's accomplished an impossible dream, but it's happened to me. Many times I have stood on the corner close to my star and have marveled at the reaction of hundreds of tourists from all over the world as they read the names of the stars and pose for pictures with the stars on the great Hollywood Walk of Fame. Some have cameras, others are just laughing and mugging. And, as I watch these fans of Tinseltown, I realize that I've received more than 200 awards in my career, but none has meant as much to me as that fabulous Star on Hollywood Boulevard."

Ken Maynard 🎥   6751 Hollywood

Actor, singer

BORN July 21, 1895, in Vevay, IN. **SPOTLIGHTS** He rode for years in a circus, then became a starring trick rider with the Buffalo Bill and Ringling Brothers Wild West shows. Next, Maynard took on the challenge of the great American rodeo, became a champ, and was invited to come to Hollywood as a stuntman. This tough cowboy quickly jumped into the role of leading man, dazzling millions of children with his nifty riding stunts. His trusty steed was his own palomino horse named Tarzan. As a Saturday matinee idol, he made hundreds of Westerns during the 1920s and 1930s, including *Senor Daredevil* (1926), *The Code of the Scarlet* (1928), *The Wagon Master* (1929), and *Song of the Caballero* (1931). He started the singing cowboy movie trend in the early 1930s sound pictures, although his songs were introduced subtly and played down. When he encouraged vocalist Gene Autry to make a singing appearance *In Old Santa Fe* (1934—a Ken Maynard vehicle), it was the movie's high point. Autry received an astounding reaction from the public and was signed to a 12-part serial. Called *The Phantom Empire,* it was an odd science-fiction Western, but the beginning of Autry's career. Sadly, this grand Western hero (Maynard) died in 1973, of malnutrition.

Charles Chaplin 🎥   6751 Hollywood

Pantomimist, actor, director, producer, screenwriter, composer

BORN Charles Spencer Chaplin; April 16, 1889, in East Lane, Walworth, England. **SPOTLIGHTS** A genius. The silent screen's greatest comedian. Known as Charlie Chaplin, he became most famous for his endearing "Little Tramp" character. This mischievous misfit—with mustache, cocked bowler hat, oversized baggy trousers, tight coat, floppy shoes, and cane—symbolized the simple fellow everywhere. Chaplin personally referred to his character as "The Little Fellow," and described him as: "You know this fellow is many-sided. A tramp, a gentleman, a poet, a dreamer, a lonely fellow, always hopeful of romance and adventure." The "Little Tramp" became the world's most beloved character, while Chaplin himself became the world's biggest star. It was no exaggeration when Chaplin accurately stated of his far-reaching fame, "I am quite well known in Tibetan lamaseries, where the name of Jesus Christ has never been heard." (This was not an indictment of religion, but a statement about the popularity of his films.) A pantomime artist extraordinaire with an unlimited imagination, Chaplin made more people laugh in history than any man had ever before. The clown was brilliant with a story and brought both laughter and tears to his ingeniously made films. He turned comedy into an art form. He was sweet, malicious, melancholy, wise, compassionate, annoying, and innocent. "The Little Fellow" was a creature of sweeping moods and utterly luminous. Early comedy silents include *The Tramp, The Count, The Fireman, Shoulder Arms, The Vagabond, One A.M., The Rink*, and *Easy Street*, among his long list of credits. He brilliantly directed the weepie *A Woman of Paris* (1923),

Charles "Charlie" Chaplin

starring Edna Purviance and Adolphe Menjou. Features include *The Kid* (1921), *The Pilgrim* (1923), *The Gold Rush* (1925) and *City Lights* (1931). About *City Lights*, Chaplin commented, "Action is more generally understood than words." When asked if he would bring his famous Tramp hero into the new age of sound, Chaplin responded, "He would have to talk, and to talk he would have to step off his pedestal, the pedestal of the silent film. The Orientals have gods, but they never take them out of their shrines." Later pictures with sound include *Modern Times* (1936), *The Great Dictator* (1940—his first complete talkie), *Monsieur Verdoux* (1947), and *Limelight* (1952). In 1992 Robert Downey Jr. gave a brilliant performance in the title role of *Chaplin*. This fascinating study of Chaplin's life was directed by Sir Richard Attenborough. Buster Keaton said of him, "At his best, and Chaplin remained at his best for a long time, he was the greatest comedian who ever lived." Stan Laurel stated, "I don't think there's any greater in the business or ever will be. He's the greatest artist that was ever on the screen." Somerset Maugham wrote: "Chaplin will keep you laughing for hours on end without effort; he has a genius for the comic. His fun is simple and spontaneous. And yet all the time you have a feeling that at the back of it all is a profound melancholy." Agnes de Mille recalled, "When Chaplin talked about pictures, we all sat still and listened hard. We knew very well what we had among us. The greatest actor of our time, unique, irreplaceable. He was beyond jealousy. He was an absolute." Charles Laughton declared, "Chaplin is not only the greatest theatrical genius of our time, but one of the greatest in history...If I were to recall the three greatest performances I've ever seen on the screen, all of them would be performances by Charlie Chaplin." W.C. Fields noted, "The son of a bitch is a ballet dancer...He's the best ballet dancer that ever lived, and if I get a good chance, I'll kill him with my bare hands." **ACHIEVEMENTS** 1927-'28 Special Academy Award. 1973 Special Academy Award. Knighted by the Queen of England in 1975 (Sir Charles Spencer Chaplin). Chaplin's *The Immigrant* (1917) rose to icon status based on "historical, cultural or aesthetic significance." and made its prestigious entry into the National Film Registry in 1998. **QUOTE** "I have been asked many times, 'How can I get into the movies?' Even as yet, I do not know and cannot understand why so many are anxious, even crazed, to enter this business." Died: 1977.

Bing Crosby ●   6751 Hollywood

See page 344

Mark & Brian 🎙   6767 Hollywood

Disc jockeys, Broadcasters

Mark & Brian with celebrity friends at their star ceremony.

BORN Mark Thompson, Dec. 1, 1955, in Florence, Alabama; Brian Phelps, May 5, 1959, in Kewanee, Illinois. **SPOTLIGHTS** Unemployed, and with nothing to lose, the two manic humorists were introduced at a radio station in Birmingham, Alabama at the suggestion of a mutual friend. Mark & Brian clicked, becoming the #1 radio team in the area. In 1987 Bill Sommers, president of KLOS/KABC/ KDIS, brought them to Los Angeles. Although some questioned moving one Southern boy and one prairie boy into a huge, urban-based market, Sommers dismissed their doubts by stating, "People are either funny or they're not." In 1987 they joined the Capital Cities/ABC Station, 95.5 KLOS. Since then, they have won *Billboard*'s "Air Personalities of the Year" award twice, the industry's prestigious National Association of Broadcasters' Marconi Awards, and an Emmy. Mark & Brian entertain audiences with celebrity interviews, surprise stunts, listener interaction, comic bits, and their quick wit. Exploits include transforming a Bob's Big Boy statue into "Elvis Bob" and perching it high atop the famous Capitol Records building; dipping themselves in chocolate to become "human candy bars" on Valentine's Day; airing an "Above & Below" show featuring Brian broadcasting live while skydiving and Mark broadcasting live while scuba diving. Their popular morning show is syndicated across the country, and young men particularly enjoy it. Their Hollywood Walk of Fame star was dedicated on Sept. 25, 1997. **QUOTE** "We still make each other laugh. That's core. This show is all about the relationship of two buddies, havin' a great time together."

Elvis Presley (r) is presented an award by Johnny Grant. (Turn this book sideways and notice Presley's Adonis-like reflection in the plaque.)

6743 HOLLYWOOD

Tyrone Power 🎥
Actor

6743 Hollywood

Tyrone Power

BORN May 5, 1913, in Cincinnati, OH. **SPOTLIGHTS** One of Hollywood's most divine Golden Era stars. With his Adonis-like face, sculptured physique, wavy hair and flashing smile, he was a major Top Ten box office attraction. Often cast as the romantic lead in costume pictures, his films include *Cafe Metropole* (1937), *Second Honeymoon* (1937), *Thin Ice* (1937), *Alexander's Ragtime Band* (1938), *Suez* (1938), *Marie Antoinette* (1938), *Jesse James* (1939), *The Rains Came* (1939), *Johnny Apollo* (1940), *The Mark of Zorro* (1940—as title character), *Blood and Sand* (1941—as Juan), and *This Above All* (1942). His military service in WWII interrupted his acting career. When he returned to the screen, it was in a more serious vein. Power expanded into widely different genres, and searched for profound insight into his characters. For his role in *The Razor's Edge* (1946), which had been adapted from W. Somerset Maugham's classic novel, Power tried again and again to grasp the symbolism and the work's essential truth. Frustrated by the slowdown in shooting, producer Darryl Zanuck thought the actor was wasting time splitting hairs. He asked the star, "Do I have to bring my barber here as technical director?" Other postwar films include *Nightmare Alley* (1947), where his acting capacity outshone his beauty, and *The Long Gray Line* (1955) co-starring Maureen O'Hara. He was riveting in *The Sun Also Rises* (1957), based on Hemingway's classic tale, with the beauteous Ava Gardner and Errol Flynn. One of his best films, *Witness for the Prosecution* (1957), was also his last. In all, he made 48 mostly splendid motion pictures. He was the son of matinee idol, Tyrone Power (Sr.). Jr. died in 1958.

Allen Ludden 📺
Television host

6743 Hollywood

BORN Oct. 5, 1917, in Mineral Point, Wisconsin. **SPOTLIGHTS** A Phi Beta Kappa graduate from the University of Texas, Ludden tried his hand at various communications-related occupations: personal manager, press agent, and continuity editor, before creating, writing, producing and hosting the teen radio show "Mind Your Manners." In 1961 he became the famous TV personality of the popular game show "Password." A word-association game, it won more awards and had larger audiences than any game show in television history. It appeared—over a 20-year period—on CBS, ABC and NBC. In addition he hosted "Ludden's Gallery," "Win With

Allen Ludden and Betty White

the Stars," "Liar's Club," and many parades. He also wrote five books "for young people." **ACHIEVEMENTS** 1976 Emmy for Best Game Show Host for "Password." During WWII, Ludden was awarded the Bronze Star while in the Army. He had headed the entertainment section of the Pacific Theater of Operations. Ludden produced more than 50 shows for the GIs while working with numerous well-known entertainers who were then in uniform...Married to actress Betty White, whose Walk of Fame star lies next to his...Along with his real-life leading lady, Ludden was dedicated to many organizations and charities, including assisting the Los Angeles Zoo for improvements, more natural environments for the animals, "Big Brothers," and "Actors & Others for Animals." His star was dedicated posthumously on March 31, 1988. Died: 1981.

Betty White 📺
Actress, comedienne

6743 Hollywood

Betty White

BORN Jan. 17, 1924, in Oak Park, IL. **SPOTLIGHTS** When White was two years old, her family relocated to Los Angeles. While attending Beverly Hills High School, she began setting her sights on a career in show business. After graduation, she utilized her flexible, perky voice to land small roles in radio. When an opportunity presented itself to work in the brand new medium of west coast television—in its early experimental stages—White leaped at the chance. Before long she had her first big break, joining Al Jarvis on a local TV show. It was broadcast five and a half hours a day, six days a week—*live*. After two years she inherited the show. Without question, White had become one of the first and best trained TV talents. With keen acumen White formed her own production company with producer Don Fedderson and writer George Tibbles. In 1952 the trio produced White's first comedy series, "Life with Elizabeth," where she played a newlywed wife trying to make a go of it. White received her first Emmy that same year; the show was a success. White's videogenic personality captured the public's imagination and has not diminished one iota in nearly five decades. In 1957 they produced a network situation comedy, "A Date with the Angels." White played another newlywed wife, this time to an insurance salesman, Gus, whose many schemes brought friends and neighbors to their house. Her own "Betty White Show" has been both a comedy-variety and a situation comedy. She narrated the New Year's Day Tournament of Roses Parade on network television for 20 years, and the Macy's Thanksgiving Day Parade for 10 years. A frequent guest star on major variety and game shows, this sparkling talent was a recurring regular with Jack Paar (more than 70 appearances), Merv Griffin and Johnny Carson. She also subbed as host on all three shows. White was absolutely delicious as the man-hungry Sue Ann Nivens on "The Mary Tyler Moore Show" (1973-77). Her portrayal of the Happy Homemaker brought two Emmys for best supporting actress in 1974-'75 and 1975-'76. She was excellent as the simple, chatty, naive Rose in the long-running "Golden Girls." Nominated seven times for Best Actress in a Comedy Series, she won the Emmy the first season in 1985. Two years later, the American Comedy Awards presented her with the Funniest Female Award. **ACHIEVEMENTS** Six-time Emmy winner. Recipient of the Lifetime Achievement Award in 1990. In 1995 she was inducted into the Television Academy Hall of Fame. President Emeritus of Morris Animal Foundation, on the Board of the Greater Los Angeles Zoo Association since 1974, and was appointed by Mayor Riordan to the new Los Angeles Zoo Commissioner. Recipient of the American Veterinary Medical Association's Humane Award. Author of four best-selling books including *Betty White's Pet Love* and *Here We Go Again: My Life In Television*...Married to TV personality, Allen Ludden, from 1963 until his death in 1981. **QUOTE** "As excited as I was to receive my star in 1960, it couldn't compare to the thrill in 1988 when Ralph Edwards' 'This Is Your Life' presented one next to mine in honor of my beloved Allen Ludden. We are in great company."

Gary Owens 🎙 6743 Hollywood
Disc jockey, broadcaster, actor

BORN May 10, 1939, in Mitchell, SD. **SPOTLIGHTS** Although he started his career as a newspaper cartoonist, his is the voice that launched a thousand quips. From his college broadcasting days, through his years of national recognition on TV's smash hit "Laugh-In" (1968-'73), through his induction into four distinguished Halls of Fame, Gary Owens has become one of America's most recognized and celebrated performers. Combining his renowned baritone with an inspired brand of zaniness, he has won over radio, television and film audiences. His workload is impressive—to say the least. He has performed on more than 1000 network and syndicated TV programs and has (his voice) starred in 3000 animated cartoons, and is one of the busiest commercial "voice-over" and TV promo announcers in the industry (more than 20,000). He made his feature film debut in Disney's *The Love Bug* then went on to appear in a variety of movies. Warmth and heartiness distinguish Owens' rich radio voice from others in his

Gary Owens (left) and Ringo Starr

field, earning him the title of America's top radio personality ten times, and being the number one disc jockey for 40 straight years (1957-97) in L.A. His current daily national radio program, "The Gary Owens Show" is heard by an estimated 15,000,000 listeners. And he's managed to stay one of the sweetest guys around—despite it all. **ACHIEVEMENTS** A golden-voiced superpower, Owens is one of the top ten announcers in the history of television. Named "Outstanding radio personality in the world" at Billboard Magazine's International Radio Forum in Toronto...He has been the master of ceremonies or star humorist at charity events which have raised more than $100,000,000! ...NBC copied his ear and had it encased in cement at their studios. Memorialized in wax at the Hollywood Wax Museum. **QUOTE** "At 16 I kind of knew what I would be doing. Of course, there are different ways to do the same thing: TV, radio, film. Some pay more than others, but versatility is the key. If a person can be versatile...My folks were hurt by the Depression and told me to have a lot of other jobs. That way if things run out on one job you have ten or eleven others."

Walt Disney 📺 6743 Hollywood
See page 567

Rod McKuen ⬤ 6743 Hollywood
Songwriter, singer, author

BORN April 29, 1933, in Oakland, CA. **SPOTLIGHTS** The feel-good 1960s poet/songwriter with tunes "Jean," "Listen to the Warm," "Coming Close to the Earth," and "Stanyan Street." McKuen's "groovy" words and emotions spoke to one restless and totally unique generation. His movie scores include *The Pride of Miss Jane Brody* (1969), and *A Boy Named Charlie Brown* (1970). 1968 Grammy for "Spoken Work."

Dick Powell 📺 6743 Hollywood
See page 4

Shari Lewis 📺   6743 Hollywood
Ventriloquist, puppeteer, musician

Shari Lewis and Lamb Chop

BORN Shari Hurwitz; Jan. 17, 1934, in Bronx, NY. **SPOTLIGHTS** Like a multifaceted diamond, Lewis was world-famous for her sparkling brilliance in the arts. She was especially geared to educate and entertain children. Baby boomers recall growing up with her right hand lamb, Lamb Chop, Charlie Horse, and Hush Puppy. In the late 1990s, children watched her daytime series "The Charlie Horse Music Pizza." Lewis created the show because sadly "school systems have virtually eliminated music education from their curriculum. And I was brought up to be a musician by a mother who was not only a music teacher, but one of the six music coordinators for the New York City board of education. Mother taught teachers *how to teach music*. Also, Mother felt music was important for the heart and the spirit, and that you grow smarter by playing a musical instrument." Children were inspired watching the show while learning the basic principles of music. They could sing along with the TV characters, learn about harmony, and understand that it is okay to hit the wrong notes during practice, because eventually you hit the right notes and make music. An accomplished violinist, she conducted 300 symphony orchestras. Winner of 12 Emmys. Penned dozens of books. Died: 1998.

King Vidor 🎥   6743 Hollywood
Director

BORN Feb. 8, 1894, in Galveston, TX. **SPOTLIGHTS** In 1907 he got a job as a ticket-taker/projectionist in a nickelodeon. He earned $3.50 weekly, for 12-hour workdays, but benefitted artistically by seeing pictures over and over again. He watched *Ben Hur* 147 times. While on vacation from the Peacock Military Academy, in San Antonio, he photographed a 60-mph windstorm and sold it to a Texas newsreel company. He tried his hand at writing, too, creating more than 52 scenarios before he sold his first one. In other words, he was determined, but broke. His luck turned when he and his bride moved to Santa Monica, California. He landed a $12.00-a-week clerk job at Universal Studios. He made his directorial debut with *The Turn in the Road* (1918), followed quickly by the successful romantic comedy, *Better Times* (1919). Vidor's long and distinguished career began in silents, and some of his early movies attempted to make social statements. His later work was motivated by commercial demands. His 1930 sound version of *Billy the Kid* remains a classic today. Made in a 70-mm process called Grandeur Screen, it continues to be of interest to film societies worldwide. One of his best films, *Northwest Passage* (1940), demonstrates full maturity of craftsmanship. Movies include *The Champ* (1931), *The Citadel* (1938), *The Fountainhead* (1949), and *Man Without a Star* (1955). **QUOTE** "Don't think you will become a motion picture star because you are a 'type.' That is

King Vidor

my advice to the screen-struck people who are planning to invade Hollywood to work. I never pick types, but instead select actors for the parts, and *they* create the types. My advice to potential screen favorites is to judge themselves from the ability to ACT, not from their physical appearance." **ACHIEVEMENTS** 1979 Honorary Oscar. Died: 1982.

Harold Robbins 🎥   6743 Hollywood
Author

BORN Francis Kane; May 21, 1916, in Hell's Kitchen, NY. **SPOTLIGHTS** Born poverty-stricken, Robbins was orphaned when he was a baby. As an adult, he worked as a bookkeeper, then began to write when he was 30 years old. He used his real birth name as the hero in his first novel, *Never Love a Stranger*, published in 1948. He described his works as "picturesque novels about doomed people," involving fortunes, love and sex. *The Carpetbaggers* (1967) and *The Betsy* (1967) were two of his novels adapted for the movies. An enormous best-seller, more than 25,000 people a day bought his books, which were translated and sold in 57 foreign countries. Died: 1997.

Anne Baxter 🎥   6743 Hollywood
Actress

Anne Baxter

BORN May 7, 1923, in Michigan City, IN. **SPOTLIGHTS** A sweet, brown-haired talent, she did not follow in her family's footsteps. Her grandfather was the distinguished American architect, Frank Lloyd Wright. Her 1936 Broadway debut in "Seen but Not Heard" launched her screen career. Two of her fine films include *I Confess* (1953), and her *tour-de-force* performance in *The Ten*

Commandments (1956), as the beautiful and tragic Queen. She plays a scheming young actress in *All About Eve* (1950--in an Oscar-nomated performance). She is outstanding in the crime thriller *Chase a Crooked Shadow* (1958). Other movies include *Charley's Aunt* (1941), *The Magnificent Ambersons* (1942), *Sunday Dinner for a Soldier* (1944), *Angel on My Shoulder* (1946), and *Three Violent People* (1956). She often repeated her grandfather's credo: "See into life and don't just look at it." **ACHIEVEMENTS** 1946 Best Supporting Actress Oscar for *The Razor's Edge*. She penned a clever autobiography entitled *Intermission* (1976). She also performed on Broadway, and in TV. **QUOTE** "My recipe for success is this—work with people who care as deeply about what they're doing as you do." Died: 1985.

Sidney Sheldon 6739 Hollywood
Screenwriter, best-selling author

Sidney Sheldon

BORN Feb. 11, 1917, in Chicago, IL. **SPOTLIGHTS** A master storyteller whose novels have sold more than 100 million copies in 30 countries, he considers becoming a writer a miracle. "Both my parents were third-grade dropouts. My father had never read a book in his life. I was the only one in the family to complete high school," Sheldon revealed. He left home at age 17, during the Great Depression. After working for brief periods of time at various jobs, he found work as script reader at Universal Studios. His career took off from there. He became a top Broadway playwright by 25, and later won a Tony Award for "Redhead," starring Gwen Verdon. He won an Oscar for *The Bachelor and the Bobbysoxer* (1947), starring Cary Grant. Movies include *Anything Goes* (1936), *Easter Parade* (1948), and *Annie Get Your Gun* (1950). He created TV's smash hits "The Patty Duke Show," "I Dream of Jeannie" and "Hart to Hart." He turned to writing novels at age 53. His first was entitled *The Naked Face* (1970), a psychological thriller. His best-selling blockbusters adapted to TV include "Rage of Angels," "Master of the Game," and "Windmills of the Gods."...Steve Allen once quipped, "Sidney Sheldon isn't himself today. It's almost noon and he hasn't written a novel yet!"

Liberace 6739 Hollywood
See page 95

Jane Darwell 6737 Hollywood
Actress

BORN Patti Woodward; Oct. 15, 1880, in Palmyra, MO. **SPOTLIGHTS** A stout, solid character actress of stage, screen, radio and television, she possessed "no nonsense" American pilgrim looks. Darwell made her motion picture debut in

Jane Darwell

1912, and never stopped working, making silent after silent. When sound arrived, she barely had time to take a breath; she made more than 200 pictures from 1930-'55 alone! Films include *Rose of the Rancho* (1914), *Huckleberry Finn* (1931), *Back Street* (1932), *Life Begins at Forty* (1935), *Three Godfathers* (1936), *Gone with the Wind* (1939), *The Ox-Bow Incident* (1943), *Sunday Dinner for a Soldier* (1944), *Wagon Master* (1950), *The Lemon Drop Kid* (1951), and *Mary Poppins* (1964), as the bird lady. **ACHIEVEMENTS** 1940 Best Supporting Actress Oscar for *The Grapes of Wrath*, as Ma Joad. In her acceptance speech, she said, "Needless to say this is my favorite role." Died: 1967.

Doris Day 6735 Hollywood
See page 258

Carleton Young 6733 Hollywood
Actor

BORN May 26, 1907, in NY. **SPOTLIGHTS** His countless credits include the title roles in "The Adventures of Ellery Queen," and "The Count of Monte Cristo." Died: 1971.

Ann Blyth 6733 Hollywood
Actress, singer

Ann Blyth

BORN Aug. 16, 1928, in Mt. Kisco, NY. **SPOTLIGHTS** A child radio, opera and Broadway performer, she made her screen debut in *Chip Off the Old Block* (1944) while still in her teens. Her vengeful portrayal of Joan Crawford's daughter in *Mildred Pierce* (1945--in an Oscar-nominated performance) was truly good and despicable. Never typecast, she co-stars with Howard Keel in *Kismet* (1955). A lovely soprano, her well-trained singing voice enhanced MGM musicals. Films include *Brute Force* (1947), *Killer McCoy* (1947), *A Woman's Vengeance* (1947--with an outstanding script by Aldous Huxley), *Another Part of the Forest* (1948), *Mr. Peabody and the Mermaid* (1948), *Our Very Own* (1950), *The Great Caruso* (1951), and *The Student Prince* (1954). She retired too soon.

Ritchie Valens 6733 Hollywood
Singer, songwriter, musician

BORN Richard Valenzuela; May 13, 1941, in Pacoima, CA. **SPOTLIGHTS** Born poverty-stricken, his father died when he

Ritchie Valens

was ten, leaving the family destitute. He lived in a tiny wooden shack and dreamed of buying his mother a new house. Somehow, deep inside, he knew he was going to become a big star. He began playing guitar as a child; by high school he had formed his own band. His first single, "Come on, Let's Go" and his love song "Donna" were two hits. His rock 'n' roll version of the traditional Mexican wedding song "La Bamba" became an international classic. He earned three Gold albums. Film appearances include *Go Johnny Go* (1959). Valens became the first Latino rocker to cross over into popular American music. *La Bamba* (1987) was based on his life; it is an energetic story packed with musical vitality. Amazingly, his career was only eight months long. "The Day The Music Died" refers to the day the plane crashed that took the lives of Valens, Buddy Holly and the Big Bopper (J.P. Richardson) in 1959.

Thomas Ince 🎥　　6727 Hollywood
Producer, director

Thomas Ince

BORN Nov. 6, 1882, in Newport, RI. **SPOTLIGHTS** Known as "The Pioneer Producer-Director of Films," he began acting on the stage as soon as he could walk. Film paid more so he worked in front of the camera until 1911, when he directed his first picture, *Across the Plains.* High quality, strong story, and realism were his trademarks. Innovative—at the time—in his detailed script writing, he brought honesty to American Westerns (starring William S. Hart). *Civilization* (1916) is one of his masterpieces. **QUOTE** "In spite of the fact that the motion picture industry ranks among the biggest in the United States, the public at large cherishes more misconceptions about it than about any other 'big business.' The man who aspires to be the head of a great factory, unless he happens to have some unusual 'pull,' either starts at the bottom, or having received his first training in some similar branch of work wins the coveted place by merit of the work he has done elsewhere. That rule holds good for screen aspirants. Occasionally 'pull' will find an opening that boosts the newcomer over the rank and file, and if the ability to act is there, too, plus the appeal known as 'screen personality,' a new star will arise. This is the rare case. Of the hundreds of men and women who have passed through my studios, 75% of the stars broke into the picture game as 'extras.' They learned the ropes. They knew the disappointments and the difficulties of the long hours, small returns and hard work before their chance came to prove their mettle. One day they were picked for some 'bit.' If they proved themselves real screen material in the hands of the director, they soon found themselves in line for bigger roles and then the public had the chance of stamping them with approval or disapproval. A director or producer may pick stars and give them opportunities, but in the end it is the public which approves or disapproves them by box-office response." Died: 1924.

Owen Moore 🎥　　6725 Hollywood
Actor

BORN Dec. 12, 1886, in Ireland. **SPOTLIGHTS** A romantic leading man during the silent era, he was frequently cast opposite Mary Pickford—America's Sweetheart—to whom he was married. Talkies include *A Star is Born* (1937). Died: 1939.

Philip Dunne 🎥　　6725 Hollywood
Writer, director

BORN Feb. 11, 1908, in New York, NY. **SPOTLIGHTS** He came to Hollywood after the 1929 stock market crash, where his writing career soared. He received two Oscar nominations for Best Screenplay: *How Green Was My Valley* (1941) and *David and Bathsheba* (1951). Credits include *The Count of Monte Cristo* (1934), *The Last of the Mohicans* (1936), *The Ghost and Mrs. Muir* (1947), and *Forever Amber* (1947). **ACHIEVEMENTS** Founding member of the Writers Guild of America. Speech writer for Presidents FDR and JFK. Died: 1992.

Arturo Toscanini 🎙　　6723 Hollywood
See page 376

The Spinners 🎙　　6723 Hollywood
Detroit-based soul harmony group

Original 1957 members: Bobby Smith (born: Apr. 10), tenor voc.; Billy Henderson (born: Aug. 9), tenor-baritone voc.; Henry Fambrough (born: May 10) baritone voc.; Pervis Jackson (born: May 16) bass voc; George W. Dixon, tenor voc. After Dixon left, Edgar "Chico" Edwards (tenor voc.) joined. After Edwards left, G.C. Cameron (tenor voc.) became a member. When Cameron exited, Phillipe Wynne (born: Apr.3, 1941/died: 1984), a tenor voc. signed up. John Edwards replaced Wynne (1977) when Wynne went solo. **SPOTLIGHTS** Known for their close-harmony ballads, the rhythm-and-blues singing sensation were inspired by the doo-wop style of groups such as the Clovers and Flamingos. Classic hits include "I'll always Love You," and "Could It Be I'm Falling in Love." They struck gold again with the medley style remake of The Four Seasons' "Working My Way Back To You." Throughout the 1990s, the Spinners toured regularly...The band's name is Motown's slang for hubcaps.

Aileen Pringle 🎥 6723 Hollywood
Actress

Aileen Pringle

BORN Aileen Bisbee; July 23, 1895, in San Francisco, CA. **SPOTLIGHTS** A dark-haired, 5-foot, 4-inch tall, 119-pound star of the silent screen, her movies include *Redhead* (1919) and *A Kiss in the Dark* (1925). **QUOTE** "Unlike a great many girls, I did not seek a career on the screen from any motive of wanting to earn a living. I gave up a rather useless life of ease because I felt that I had an ability to express myself on the screen. Clinging to that belief, I went to the studios looking, not for a meal ticket, but for a chance to show what I knew I could do. The chance came. I did not fall right into fame. Neither did I languish and grow pale waiting. I think that my advice to girls would be to wait until one had sufficient money to enable one to seek—not a job, but a chance to show what one felt one could do best...for self-expression." Died: 1989.

Ernest Truex 📺 6723 Hollywood
Actor, comedian

Ernest Truex

BORN Sept. 19, 1890, in Kansas City, MO. **SPOTLIGHTS** As a child, he spent his early years in the limelight. Those were the days when kerosene lamps lit the stage. As a young adult, he opened on Broadway dozens of times, and appeared on the London stage in Shakespearean roles. He easily moved into silent films, and was successful in talkies: *Christmas in July* (1940). He often played the hen-pecked husband or a nervous Norman. He was well into his 60s when cast in the comedy "Mr. Peepers" (1952-'55). Died: 1973.

Oscar Micheaux 🎥 6721 Hollywood
Writer, director, producer, cameraman, pioneer filmmaker

BORN 1889, in Metropolis, IL (most likely). **SPOTLIGHTS** Known as the "Father of African American Cinema," he was the son of freed slaves. Raised in poverty, he left home in his late teens. He worked several jobs before homesteading land. At age 24 he anonymously wrote *The Conquest: The Story of a Negro Pioneer*. This autobiographical tale was quickly followed by a second book. He traveled from town to town, selling the books and shares in his own tiny publishing house. An enterprising and intelligent gentleman, his third book generated

Oscar Micheaux

interested in film rights from an African American film company. When acceptable terms could not be reached, Micheaux's *The Homesteader* (1919) was the result. He was the first African American independent filmmaker to actively sustain a film company. In doing so he became the cinema's pioneer black filmmaker. Motion pictures include *Within Our Gates* (1920), *Symbol of the Unconquered* (1921), *Body and Soul* (1924--starring Paul Robeson in his screen debut), *Scar of Shame* (1927), *Underworld* (1936), *Swing* (1936), *God's Stepchildren* (1938), and *Birthright* (1939, a remake of his 1924 version). In a fascinating career that spanned 30 years, he made 44 films, both silents and talkies. He also penned ten novels. This brave innovator's historic contributions to the motion picture industry are invaluable...He encountered countless problems from every imaginable direction, but persevered anyway. The Producers Guild of America annually honors those who achieve film and TV success, despite tough odds, with the prestigious Oscar Micheaux Award. Died: 1951.

Harry Belafonte 💿 6721 Hollywood
Singer, actor, producer

Harry Belafonte

BORN Harold George Belafonte; March 1, 1927, in Harlem, NY. **SPOTLIGHTS** International celebrity of live concerts, motion pictures, recording and television, Belafonte initially gained recognition for his calypso (West Indian) music. His flair for that tempo and beat were influenced by time he spent in Jamaica during his childhood. His velvety, husky voice made classics of "Day-O," "Matilda, Matilda," "When the Saints Go Marching In," & "Mama Look a Boo Boo." He made his screen debut in *Bright Road* (1953), opposite Dorothy Dandridge. He took on the starring role of Joe in *Carmen Jones* (1954). *Island in the Sun* (1957) explores romantic interracial tensions, with Joan Fontaine. About the controversy this film stirred up, he commented, "I haven't wanted to become a symbol, but I have. And, since I want to work, I at least want to do pictures I consider worthwhile and the film industry is not really geared toward pictures of this sort. That's the reason for forming my own company." He gave an intriguing performance in the thriller *Odds Against Tomorrow* (1959). In 1988 his special concert was shot in Zimbabwe: *Harry Belafonte—Global Carnival.* **ACHIEVEMENTS** Recipient of numerous awards including Grammys, a 1953 Tony for his Broadway performance in "John Murray Anderson's Almanac," and a 1960 Emmy...At age 17 he joined the Navy to serve in World War II...His daughter is actress Shari Belafonte. **QUOTE** Reflecting on his difficult childhood in a crowded tenement in a Harlem slum and his alternating years to the island of Jamaica, Belafonte said, "I guess I was a bad kid, but my mother saved me. She tried to teach me love instead of hate. If it weren't for her, I do not think I would have come to anything."

Dorothy Dandridge 🎥 6719 Hollywood
Actress, singer, dancer

Dorothy Dandridge

BORN Nov. 9, 1923, in Cleveland, OH. **SPOTLIGHTS** At age four she began performing in a song-and-acrobatics act known as "The Wonder Children" with her sister Vivian. She grew into a gorgeous creature—compared by some as "a black Marilyn Monroe"— who exuded charisma and personality. This beauty's motion picture debut was a bit part in the Marx Bros.' *A Day at the Races* (1937). With an exquisite cafe au lait complexion and seductress figure, she was a tremendous success as a sultry night club entertainer in the 1940s. She was the first African-American actress to achieve stardom onscreen as the lead, and the first African American to receive an Academy Award nomination in the category of Best Actress for her sizzling performance in *Carmen Jones* (1954), her breakthrough role. She was excellent in *Island in the Sun* (1957), and *Porgy and Bess* (1959). She fought racism, and paved the way for future African American actresses. Halle Berry starred in the award-winning TV movie based on her life. **HIGHLIGHTS** Immortalized twice in Hollywood landmarks, her beautiful likeness is represented in a stainless steel statue at the southeast corner of Hollywood and La Brea. (See "La Brea Gateway" in this book.) Died: 1965.

Barton MacLane 📺 6719 Hollywood
Actor

BORN Dec. 25, 1902, in Columbia, SC. **SPOTLIGHTS** Star of "The Outlaws" (1960-'61), as U. S. Marshal Frank Caine. Played commanding officer, General Martin Peterson (1965-'69), on "I Dream of Jeannie." Made more than 200 pictures, including *The Maltese Falcon* (1941). Died: 1969.

Dr. Frank C. Baxter 📺 6717 Hollywood
Lecturer, host

BORN 1897. **SPOTLIGHTS** This Ph.D. hosted "Telephone Time" where he selected plays from original short stories and used relatively unknown talent in each show. Died: 1982.

Yvonne De Carlo 📺 6715 Hollywood
See page 236

Ken Niles 🎙 6715 Hollywood
Announcer, actor

BORN Dec. 9, 1906, in Livingston, MT. **SPOTLIGHTS** He often acted in dual roles as both an announcer and comedian, and worked in a variety of radio programs. Credits include "The Abbott and Costello Show," "The Beulah Show," "Burns and Allen," "The Danny Kaye Show," "Gateway to Hollywood" (a talent show), "Hollywood Hotel," "The Judy Canova Show," "Kay Kyser's Kollege of Musical Knowledge," "The Life of Riley," and "Take It Or Leave It." Died: 1988.

Fred Allen 🎙 6711 Hollywood
Comedian, writer

BORN John Florence Sullivan; May 31, 1894, in Cambridge, MA. **SPOTLIGHTS** His mother died before he was three. When he was a child, is father got him a job at the public library where he worked as a bookbinder. When Allen was eleven, his father died. He and his brother went to live with his aunt, where his salary of 20 cents an hour helped make end meets. An avid reader, he discovered a library book on juggling that fascinated him. At age 16 he criss-crossed the country, juggling in every small-town theater. Billed as "Freddy James, the World's Worst Juggler," he polished a new act with comedy and traveled the country and abroad. Then, he made the leap to radio. Allen became America's king of satire. He wrote much of his own acerbic material for "The Fred Allen Show" (1932-'49). Skits included "The Average Man's Round Table," and "People You Don't Expect to Meet." No subject was safe from his parodies, dry wit, or nasal voice. Tallulah Bankhead, Hitchcock, and others guested his shows. His "newsreel" was the earliest satire news commentary. Jack Benny declared Allen

Fred Allen (left), Mary Martin, and Jack Benny

"the best wit, the best extemporaneous comedian I know." Ventriloquist Edgar Bergen praised Allen as the "greatest living comedian, a wise materialist who exposes and ridicules the pretensions of his times." The end of his show marked the end of radio's golden years. He was widely admired by the intelligentsia, Pulitzer and Nobel prize-winning author John Steinbeck wrote that Allen was "unquestionably the best humorist of our time." **QUOTE** "You can take all the sincerity in Hollywood, put it in a flea's navel, and have room left over for three caraway seeds and an agent's heart." He was a panelist on the quiz show, "What's My Line?" (1954-'56). It is ironic that he appeared on it and that he was honored with a second Walk of Fame star in the TV category. He despised that form of entertainment, stating, "When vaudeville died, TV was the box that they buried it in." Died: 1956.

George Reeves
Actor   **6709 Hollywood**

George Reeves and Noel Neill

BORN George Besselo; April 6, 1914, in Woodstock, IA. **SPOTLIGHTS** He made his silver screen debut as Brent Tarleton in *Gone With the Wind* (1939). Then, he was "faster than a speeding bullet" starring in TV's "The Adventures of Superman" (1951-'57). Reeves and was a hero to kids everywhere. Died: 1959.

Madeleine Carroll
Actress   **6705 Hollywood**

BORN Marie O'Carroll; Feb. 26, 1906, in West Bromwich, England. **SPOTLIGHTS** An elegant blonde beauty with an exquisitely sculptured face, she graced Hitchcock's *The Thirty-Nine Steps* (1935) and *The Secret Agent* (1936). She was brilliant in *The Prisoner of Zenda* (1937), opposite the dashing Douglas Fairbanks, Jr., and delightful in the comedy *My Favorite Blonde* (1942), co-starring Bob Hope. After her sister was killed in WWII's London blitz, she dedicated her efforts to peace movements and aiding war victims. Active in the Allied Relief Fund and the Red Cross. Died: 1987.

Nils Asther
Actor   **6705 Hollywood**

BORN Jan. 17, 1897 in Sweden. **SPOTLIGHTS** Active in silent films, his career slowed down with the arrival of sound. However, he was extremely popular as the Chinese warlord in Capra's *The Bitter Tea of General Yen* (1933), opposite Barbara Stanwyck. It is a must-see film. Died: 1981.

Mary Livingston
Actress   **6701 Hollywood**

BORN Sadye Marks; June 22, 1909, in Seattle, WA. **SPOTLIGHTS** A "nervous Nellie" vaudeville performer, she got a bad case of "mike fright" when her real-life husband, Jack Benny, insisted she play Mary Livingston on his radio show. She never fully recovered from her on-air jitters, and her nervous laugh was incorporated into the character on "The Jack Benny Show" (1932-'54). A lot of the show's humor derived

from her poking fun at him. After a 47-year marriage, Mary suffered quite a setback when he died. On the morning after his death, she received a single long-stemmed rose without a card. The next day, she received another one. Wondering who was the sending flowers, she called the florist. She was informed that her late husband had said, "If anything should happen to me, I want you to send Mary one perfect, red rose daily for the rest of Mary's life." And he had stipulated it as a clause in his will. Died: 1983.

Roscoe Arbuckle
Comedian, writer, director   **6701 Hollywood**

BORN March 24, 1887, in Smith Center, KS. **SPOTLIGHTS** As a youngster growing up in Santa Ana, California, "Fatty" sold tickets at carnivals and performed in blackface on vaudeville. He landed a $3-a-day job with Mack Sennett's Keystone Kops, where audiences roared at his fat cop routine. Working with such all-time comedy greats as Charlie Chaplin in *The Rounders* (1914), he rose to stardom. He also wrote and directed comedy shorts. In 1917 joined forces with Joseph M. Schenck and recruited stone-faced Buster Keaton—an old vaudeville pal—for *The Butcher Boy* (1917). By 1920 he was on top, earning $7,000 per week. Died: 1933.

Mary Astor
Actress   **6701 Hollywood**

Mary Astor

BORN Lucille Langhanke; May 3, 1906, in Quincy, IL. **SPOTLIGHTS** A leading lady in silents (she co-stars with John Barrymore in *Beau Brummel* in 1924), she easily moved into talkies. Specializing in crime, film noir and drama, her movies include *The Man With Two Faces* (1934), co-starring Edward G. Robinson and Ricardo Cortez, and *Dodsworth* (1936), opposite Walter Huston. A brilliant actress, Astor was immortalized in the classic *The Maltese Falcon* (1941), opposite Humphrey Bogart. Later, she appears in *Hush...Hush, Sweet Charlotte* (1965), with an all-star cast. **ACHIEVEMENTS** 1941 Best Supporting Actress Oscar for *The Great Life*. **QUOTE** "It is a well-known axiom that beauty is as beauty does—but I could also say that beauty does as beauty is. It is by selecting the kind of people who have beautiful ideas, who live beautiful lives and thus are in themselves beautiful personalities, that the screen actress will assimilate a beauty of personality and thought which will make her charming in every way. And charm is the first step to success upon the screen. It is what the public demands—charm plus ability to act." Died: 1987.

Jean Hersholt
     6701 Hollywood
See page 102

6689 HOLLYWOOD

Faye Emerson 📺   6689 Hollywood
See page 95

Ruth Warrick 🎥   6689 Hollywood
Actress

Ruth Warrick

BORN June 29, 1915, in St. Joseph, MO. **SPOTLIGHTS** A former Mercury Theater actress, Warrick next achieved success in radio. She made her impressive screen debut in one of the greatest motion pictures of all time, *Citizen Kane* (1941), as Orson Welles' wife. She appears in 21 movies, including *The Corsican Brothers* (1941), *Journey into Fear* (1942), *China Sky* (1945), *Song of the South* (1946), *Three Husbands* (1950), and *The Great Train Robbery* (1969). She also performed on Broadway, but is best-loved by devoted fans for her many years on ABC's long-running soap opera "All My Children." She *is* Phoebe Tyler. Previously, she enjoyed fame as Hannah Cord in TV's racy melodrama "Peyton Place," and in the daytime soap opera, "As the World Turns." Her autobiography, *The Confessions of Phoebe Tyler*, co-written with Don Preston (Prentice-Hall). **QUOTE** "I can't stop being an actress."

John Payne 📺   6687 Hollywood
See page 222

Myrna Loy 🎥   6685 Hollywood
Actress

Myrna Loy and William Powell

BORN Myrna Williams; Aug. 2, 1905, in Helena, Montana. **SPOTLIGHTS** When Loy recalled her childhood, she described herself as "a little girl who was an ugly duckling. I've never quite gotten over it. My freckled face, slant eyes and red hair—being red-headed isolates you." After her cattleman father died in the flu pandemic of 1918, her family moved to California. She attended Venice High School, but was unable to go to college because her family was too poor. Loy got a job as a Middle Eastern dancer in *The Thief of Bagdad* (1924). The picture, starring Douglas Fairbanks, was the cinematic event of the year. While doing extra and bit parts she earned supplemental income posing as an Asian model. Through photographer Henry Waxman she made the acquaintance of Rudolph Valentino and his wife. She remembered Valentino being quite different from his romantic lover screen image. "He was a dear, sweet, simple, very kind man," Loy said. The Valentinos changed her name and guided her into ethnic parts. "I played Arabic, Japanese, Polynesian, Malayan, Hindu, and Egyptian roles. I became known as an American girl gone native in the Easterly direction," the actress laughed. The "Oriental Vamp" appeared in 59 movies including *The Animal Kingdom* and *The Mask of Fu Manchu* (both 1932). MGM paired her with Clark Gable in *Night Flight* (1933), but co-star William Powell rescued her career in the sophisticated comedy series, *The Thin Man* (1934). She played the "perfect wife," trading wise-cracking barbs, love and martinis with her detective husband. "I adore him," she remarked about Powell. This gorgeous, petite redhead was voted "Queen of Hollywood" by the filmgoing public in 1936. She appeared opposite Clark Gable and Walter Pidgeon in the screwball comedy *Too Hot to Handle* (1938). Loy considered the post-WWII drama *The Best Years of Our Lives* (1946) her most important work. Loy loved working with Cary Grant in the comedy, *Mr. Blandings Builds His Dream House* (1948), and was charming in the turn-of-the-century piece, *Cheaper by the Dozen* (1950). Died: 1993.

Harry James 🎵   6683 Hollywood
Trumpeter

Harry James (right) and Betty Grable present Johnny Grant with a copy of their hit song "I Can't Begin To Tell You."

BORN May 15, 1916, in Albany, GA. **SPOTLIGHTS** Raised in a circus, James started blowing his horn at age 13. By age 20, he signed on as a leading member of Benny Goodman's band.

During this time he recorded "Ridin' High" on Goodman's *Jazz Concert, Number 2* album. He formed his own big band in 1938 with spectacular results. Headlines read "James Jumps!" When reporters interviewed him, James had this to say, "No, I don't think I made any mistake when I left Benny. When I was with Benny, I often had to play sensational horn. I was one of a few featured men in a killer-diller band. Each of us had to impress all the time. Consequently, when I got up to take, say, sixteen bars, I'd have to try to cram everything into that short space." With his newfound freedom, James played more ballads: "Just a Gigolo," "I Surrender, Dear," and "Black and Blue." He was a happier man, stating, "Playing what you want to play is good for a guy's soul, you know." In 1939 he signed "the skinny, boy vocalist named Frank Sinatra" to croon tunes "Melancholy Mood," and "From the Bottom of My Heart" at each show. Sinatra lacked self-confidence in those days, so James positioned himself to encourage him constantly. In 1941 he recorded these swing tunes, adding his trumpet virtuoso "The Flight of the Bumble Bee," and "You Made Me Love You." He continued to turn out great 1940s music with hits "Sleepy Time Gal," and "Sleepy Lagoon." This swing era legend played solidly for four more decades. Listeners may

enjoy the CD *The Best of Harry James: The Capitol Years,* with arrangements by Ray Conniff, Ernie Wilkins and Neal Hefti, and trademark music "Trumpet Blues and Cantabile." It is a surefire winner. Died: 1983.

Gene Roddenberry 📺　6683 Hollywood
Writer, producer

BORN Earth Date: Aug. 19, 1921, in El Paso, TX.
SPOTLIGHTS Raised in Los Angeles, Roddenberry joined the U.S. Army Air Corps six months before Pearl Harbor. During World War II, he was a B-17 bomber pilot who saw combat in the Pacific. After his honorable discharge, he became a commercial pilot for a few years. In 1949 Roddenberry joined the Los Angeles Police Department, and honed his writing skills by creating speeches for the Chief of Police. Moonlighting as a writer, he sold his first television script four years later, then wrote a few spec scripts for "Mr. District Attorney," and "Highway Patrol." In 1954 he passed the police sergeant's exam on first try. Two years later, his creative output surpassed his sergeant's duties, and he resigned from the LAPD. He created and produced of "The Lieutenant" for MGM-TV. In 1964, at age 43, he developed the "Star Trek" concept with a

Gene Roddenberry (center), wife Majel and son Rod, "Star Trek" cast members, Johnny Grant and Bill Welsh

16-page series description and signed with Desilu Productions (Lucille Ball's company). The series sold to NBC, who rejected the first pilot. An unprecedented second pilot was ordered; it was a success with sponsors. "Star Trek" aired from 1966 - '69, but was killed by the network when the air time changed to Fridays at 10 PM—the time its core viewers were out of their houses. In syndication—and broadcast earlier—it was an immediate and stunning hit, captivating college students with Roddenberry's disguised social commentary and positive humanism. Fans recognized, understood and embraced the series, quickly becoming Star Trek devotees. Motion pictures include *Star Trek: The Motion Picture* (1979), *Star Trek II: The Wrath of Khan* (1982), *Star Trek IV: The Voyage Home* (1986), *Star Trek VI: The Undiscovered Country* (1991), *Star Trek VII: Generations* (1994), *Star Trek VIII: First Contact* (1996), and *Star Trek IX: Insurrection* (1998). He created "Star Trek: The Next Generation" in 1986 which went 150 TV episodes, nearly double the original series. After his death, more series were spun off: "Star Trek: Deep Space Nine," and "Star Trek: Voyager." Thousands of products from uniforms and jewelry to model star ships and toy phasers have been made and sold over its 33-year history...The first "Star Trek" convention was held in New York City in 1972 with Roddenberry in attendance. Every week of the year sees a "Star Trek" convention somewhere on the planet...The "Star Trek" franchise has generated $3.5 billion in revenue. Highly illogical? No. As Mr. Spock stated, "Live Long and Prosper." **RECOMMENDED** *Star Trek Creator: The Authorized Biography of Gene Roddenberry*, by David Alexander is the definitive read. This excellent book covers Roddenberry's life and creations in depth and meticulous detail. Available to purchase in paperback online at barnes&noble.com, and amazon.com. If you like "Star Trek" you must own this book. Writer David Alexander is the expert on the subject. **ACHIEVEMENTS** Roddenberry won an Air Medal and Distinguished Flying Cross during the war. Recipient of countless honors, including the prestigious Peabody Award. **QUOTE** His life rule: "Never Complain, Never Explain." **DEATH** A pioneer in death, this legendary talent died in 1991, but the voyage continued. In 1992 he was posthumously honored by NASA for his contributions toward making humanity a space faring race. Astronaut James Weatherbee took a small canister of his ashes into orbit on board the Shuttle Columbia. They were returned to his widow, Majel. Five years later, a small, aluminum cylinder containing some of Roddenberry's ashes went into deep space, this time not to return, on board the "Founders Flight" sponsored by Celestis. It is the first *space memorial* in the history of mankind. Orbiting space at a speed of 14,864 feet per second—for a period of two to six years—it will drop out of orbit. Its high speed reentry into Earth's atmosphere will incinerate it.

Gene Lockhart 　　　 6681 Hollywood
See page 133

George Takei 　　　 6681 Hollywood

George Takei

Actor, author
BORN April 20, 1940, in Los Angeles, CA. **SPOTLIGHTS** He is one of the most famous Asian-American actors with a galaxy full of "Trekkies" (a.k.a."Trekkers") devoted to him. They worship his portrayal of Mr. Sulu, the helmsman of the starship U.S.S. Enterprise, in the acclaimed science fiction series "Star Trek." And out of the 27 feature films he has appeared in, six are *Star Trek* sequels. Yet life has not always been so sweet. With the outbreak of World War II, the young boy and his family were locked behind barbed-wired internment camps—along with 120,000 other Japanese-Americans—in one of the most embarrassing moments in U.S. history. He spent the greater portion of his childhood at Camp Rohwer in the swamps of Arkansas and at the wind-swept CampTule Lake in Northern California. When the government released its citizens, Takei returned to his native Los Angeles wanting nothing more than to work inside the motion picture studios being part of the magic making machinery. He involved himself in every school play and drama club to hone his craft. At UCLA he received a bachelor of arts and master of arts in theater, then attended the Shakespeare Institute at Stratford-Upon-Avon and Sophia University in Tokyo, Japan. He's enjoyed success on stage, TV, feature films, even doing voice-overs for animated cartoon characters with his marvelous baritone voice. "I've always been a ham," he commented. "My mother says that my theatrical debut was in the maternity ward." To keep in shape Takei is a dedicated long-distance runner, having completed many 26.2-mile marathons. He's active in community affairs and serves as co-chairperson for East West Players, America's foremost Asian Pacific American theater company. **QUOTE** "Hollywood is fantastic! My career with 'Star Trek' shot me up to the starry galaxies. And even when I'm back down to earth here in my hometown on the Hollywood Walk of Fame, I'm still part of a galaxy of stars. Except, this time, rather than looking skyward, the fans look down on us."

SIGHT SEEING TIP Trek to the nearby *Hollywood Entertainment Museum* for an out-of-this-world experience. You'll find the Captain's bridge from the Starship Enterprise, and the transporter room where you can beam yourself up. Located at 7021 Hollywood Blvd. Tel. 323.465.7900.

Arthur Kennedy 🎬 　　　 6681 Hollywood
Actor
BORN John A Kennedy; Feb. 17, 1914, in Worcester, MA. **ACHIEVEMENTS** James Cagney caught his wonderful Broadway performance in "International Incident," opposite

Arthur Kennedy

Ethel Barrymore. Able to keep pace with the tremendous actress, he was brought to Hollywood by "Jimmy the Gent" (Cagney). Kennedy made his screen debut in *City for Conquest* (1940). He spent his life splitting his time between Hollywood and Broadway. He appears in Kazan's terrific crime picture, *Boomerang!* (1947), and received an Oscar nomination for Best Supporting Actor for *Champion* (1949). He was an Academy Award nominee for Best Actor for *Bright Victory* (1951). He garnered three more Oscar nominations in the Best Supporting category for *Trial* (1955), *Peyton Place* (1957), and *Some Came Running* (1958). Five times Oscar-nominated, he never won. Movies include *High Sierra* (1941), *The Window* (1949), *Elmer Gantry* (1960), *Lawrence of Arabia* (1962), *Fantastic Voyage* (1966), and *Grandpa* (1990). He made 125 motion pictures, working straight up until his death. **QUOTE** "The only security a man has is not what he's got in the bank, but his own talent." Died: 1990.

Mary Carlisle 🎥   6679 Hollywood

Actress

Mary Carlisle

BORN Feb. 3, 1912, in Boston, MA. **SPOTLIGHTS** Paramount's blonde, blue-eyed darling plays a sweet, well-brought-up co-ed opposite Bing Crosby in *College Humor* (1933), *Double or Nothing* (1937), and *Dr. Rhythm* (1938). She is best remembered for those three musicals. She worked in 18 movies before hitting it big with Crosby. Carlisle, though, tired of playing the good girl. She refused many roles, and retired from show business in 1943 after marrying James Blakely. She raised their son, then after having modeled for Max Factor, she went over to the Elizabeth Arden camp on Wilshire Boulevard, in Beverly Hills, to become the salon's cosmetics and beauty manager.

The Monkees 🔘   6675 Hollywood

Actors, personalities, recording artists

BORN David (Davy) Jones, Dec. 30, 1945, in Manchester, England; Michael Nesmith, Dec. 30, 1942, in Houston, Texas; Peter Tork, Feb. 13, 1944, Washington, D.C.; Micky Dolenz, Mar. 8, 1945, in Tarzana, California. **SPOTLIGHTS** "Hey, hey, we're the Monkees!" Savvy TV executives formed the band in

Johnny Grant and The Monkees: (from left) Mickey Dolenz, Michael Nesmith, Davy Jones, and Peter Tork.

1965 to capitalize on the Beatles success, particularly wishing to duplicate the feel of the Beatles' film *A Hard Day's Night* (1964). Although the Monkees pretended to play their own instruments on the show, professional studio players did most of the work. Gold singles include: "I'm a Believer," "Last Train to Clarksville," and "(I'm Not Your) Steppin' Stone." Pushed by Nesmith, who is also a songwriter, the band did learn to play, and staged sold-out worldwide tours. Their film *Head* (1968)—a long-form music video—is considered by some the forerunner of all music videos. Enjoyed a strong comeback concert tour in 1996. **ACHIEVEMENTS** Spotting the genius talent of rock electric guitarist/vocalist Jimi Hendrix and having him open for them at one of *their* concerts!..Nesmith's mother invented Liquid Paper; a product that first hit big in the old typewriter days to white out a mistake. Nesmith became a novelist, and successful, tough businessman.

Guy Lombardo 🎙   6677 Hollywood

Band Leader

BORN Gideon Lambert; June 19, 1902, in Canada. **SPOTLIGHTS** He started to hit his stride in the late 1920s and was so successful he entertained two generations of dancers. His big band orchestra carried the slogan, "The Royal Canadians, the sweetest music this side of heaven." Initially it was considered more sweet than hot because his musicians could not fit in all the notes with the fast fox trot dances. Lombardo specialized in slow, intimate, dreamy music; as he put it, "I play for people in love, not acrobats." For people who were intimidated by a dance floor and an orchestra they could feel secure dancing to Lombardo's music. Booked for six months out of the year in the New York Roosevelt Hotel, he literally supported many of his siblings. A member of his band remarked: "It's not true that you have to be a relative to work here—but it helps." Of the 15 Royal Canadians, one-third were his brothers and one was his brother-in-law. Among his peers it was commonly said, "Guy Lombardo is the nicest man that's ever been in the music business." Fans thought he was swell, too. He sold more records than any other dance band, created more hit records, and played at more Presidential Inaugural Balls than any other orchestra. Well-respected, he was also loved by almost everyone who came to know him. One of his biggest fans was jazz great Louis Armstrong, who called Lombardo's Royal Canadians "my inspirators!" The band broke countless previous attendance records, including the Savoy Ballroom in Harlem—which is nothing short of astounding. It seemed just about everyone liked his cheerful, upbeat music. Not one to change style or songs, Lombardo's standards include "The Band Played On," "Little White Lies," "Boo Hoo," "Sweethearts on Parade," "Stardust," "Coquette," "Fascination," "Where or When," "We'll Meet Again," "Give Me A Little Kiss," "Seems Like Old Times," "Smoke Gets In Your Eyes," and "Begin the Beguine." He and his band performed "Auld Lang Syne" on annual New Year's Eve radio broadcasts for so many years that listeners thought he had created it. **QUOTE** "Enjoy yourself, enjoy yourself, before it's too late!" (He made a song out of his motto.) Died: 1977.

Robert Guillaume 6675 Hollywood
Actor, singer

Robert Guillaume

BORN Robert Williams; Nov. 30, 1937, in St. Louis, MO. **SPOTLIGHTS** Raised by his grandmother, he interrupted his education with a stint in the United States Army. After his honorable discharge, he attended St. Louis' Washington University as a business administration major, while temporarily burying his true ambition to sing tenor at the Metropolitan Opera. Offered a scholarship at the Aspen (Colorado) Music Festival, his appearance in the Rocky Mountains brought acclaim. This afforded Guillaume an apprenticeship at Cleveland's Karamu Theatre where he made his professional debut in both opera and musical comedy. From there he moved to New York City, becoming one of the stage's best-reviewed actors. **TV** Guillaume, became a household name as "Benson." He won his first Emmy in 1979 for Best Supporting Actor in "Soap" where the character was initially introduced, and a second Emmy in 1985 for Best Actor after "Benson" moved to the series bearing the character's name. In the late 1990s, he starred in "Sports Night." Features include Disney's *The Lion King* (1994—voiceover). His Walk of Fame star was dedicated on Nov. 22, 1984. **QUOTE** "If I had to identify what made me successful, I'd say it was a firmly grounded early education which made me unafraid of the English language. Today, a lot of young people can't speak the language. They think there's nobility in not being able to do so. These youngsters must have totally missed the point."

Betty Furness 6675 Hollywood
Actress

Betty Furness

BORN Jan. 3, 1916, in New York, NY. **SPOTLIGHTS** At 16 years old, this blonde, blue-eyed, 5-foot, 4 inches, 100-pound sophisticate became a leading lady. She became more famous to a nation of TV viewers as a spokeswoman: You can "be sure if it's a Westinghouse" (1949-60). She was also the consumer reporter on NBC's "Today" Show. Her sincerity opened official doors as President Johnson's top adviser on Consumer Affairs. Tough as nails, she tracked down safety malfunctions, and watched for typical consumer rip-offs, such as the amount of water in canned ham. **QUOTE** "Behave well, apply yourself, and do your very best because nothing else is acceptable." Died: 1994.

George Peppard 6675 Hollywood
Actor, producer, director

George Peppard

BORN Oct. 1, 1928, in Detroit, MI. **SPOTLIGHTS** Educated at Purdue University and Carnegie Tech, Peppard brought an intelligence to his variety of roles. The fair-haired, blue-eyed leading man was equally talented in tough or sensitive roles. Movies include *Breakfast at Tiffany's* (1961), co-starring Audrey Hepburn, *How the West Was Won* (1962) with Carroll Baker and Henry Fonda, James Stewart, John Wayne and the voice of Spencer Tracy, *The Carpetbaggers* (1964), opposite Carroll Baker and Alan Ladd, *Operation Crossbow* (1965) opposite Sophia Loren, *The Blue Max* (1966) with James Mason and Ursula Andress, and *House of Cards* (1969) with Orson Welles. He made more than 30 movies, and appeared onstage. **TV** Peppard starred in three series: as the smooth private eye "Banacek" (1972-'74), as Dr. Jake Goodwin on "Doctor's Hospital" (1975-'76), and as Colonel John "Hannibal" Smith of "The A-Team" (1983-'87). Died: 1994.

Ferlin Husky 6675 Hollywood
Guitarist, singer, songwriter, comedian
BORN Dec. 3, 1925, in Flat River, MO. **SPOTLIGHTS** While growing up, the youngster learned to pluck the guitar and dreamed of becoming a famous recording and movie star. As a

singer-musician he recorded his first hit, "A Dear John Letter" in 1953. It was a duet with Jean Shepherd, which was followed with the duet hit "Forgive Me John." Signed with Capitol Records, and actively being part of the Bakersfield Sound movement—where country enjoyed new life with its upbeat, danceable, honky-tonk music—Husky's career soared. Other Husky and His Hush Puppies hits include: "I Feel Better All Over," "Little Tom," "Gone," "Fallen Star," and "On the Wings of a Dove" (gospel). Husky also realized his goal of appearing in TV and movies, including *Mr. Rock and Roll* (1957) and *Country Music Holiday* (1958). He also recorded under the name of Simon Crum (his comic alter ego): "Cuzz You're So Sweet" and "Country Music is Here to Stay." ...Served five years in the Merchant Marines during WWII.

Vin Scully

6675 Hollywood

Broadcaster

Vin Scully

BORN Nov. 29, 1927, in New York. **SPOTLIGHTS** An eternal blue boy of summer, Scully hooked up with the Brooklyn Dodgers in 1949 and has been one of the exceptions to its changing list of players. From Koufax and Drysdale, to Garvey to Gibson, Scully has seen it all and called it all. Among the thrilling games he testified to are: three perfect games (Don Larsen—1956, Sandy Koufax—1965, and Dennis Martinez—1991); 18 no-hitters; Johnny Podres' shutout of the Yankees in Game Seven of the 1955 World Series giving the Dodgers their first World Championship; 18-strikeout games by Sandy Koufax in 1959 and 1962, and Ramon Martinez in 1990; the Dodgers sweeping the New York Yankees in the 1963 World Series; Don Drysdale's scoreless innings streak in 1968; Hank Aaron's 715th career home run in 1974; Orel Hershiser's 59 consecutive scoreless innings in 1988; Kirk Gibson's dramatic game-winning home run in Game One of the 1988 World Series; and the rookie seasons of Fernando Valenzuela and Hideo Nomo. It's easy to see why Scully is one of the most recognizable personalities in sport broadcasting. Known as the "voice of Dodger baseball," Scully's play-by-play descriptions have earned him fans across the United States. In addition to the Dodgers, Scully announces the World Series for the CBS Radio Network. **ACHIEVEMENTS** The recipient of countless honors, this broadcasting icon considers his 1982 induction into the Baseball Hall of Fame his most coveted award. There, he was immortalized alongside his mentor, Red Barber, in its broadcast wing. He holds the longest service and the longest consecutive service of a current major league broadcaster for one team. **HIGHLIGHTS** Sports expert, Justin Dedeaux—of the famed USC baseball coaching clan—recalled how, "Vinny sold

the Dodgers to Los Angeles fans forever when, after a losing 1958 season, the Dodgers of 1959 won a playoff with the Braves to play Chicago in the World Series. As the winning run crossed home plate, Vinny uttered those famous words, 'and we go to Chicago!'"

Tommy Dorsey

6675 Hollywood

Trombonist and band leader

Tommy Dorsey

BORN Thomas Dorsey; Nov. 19, 1905, in Shenandoah, PA. **SPOTLIGHTS** Known as "The Sentimental Gentleman of Swing," he had one of the greatest dance bands of all time. When Frank Sinatra was a vocalist in Dorsey's band he learned a lot about singing by watching Dorsey. Sinatra said, "I studied Tommy's breath control on the trombone. Tommy could make it all sound so musical that you never lost the thread of the message...I learned about dynamics and phrasing and style from the way he played his horn." Songs Sinatra performed with Dorsey include "I'll Walk Alone," "I Think of You," and "If You Are But A Dream." The Tommy Dorsey Orchestra made its radio network debut on "The Kate Smith Evening Hour" and became known for rendering ballads at dance tempos. During the big band, swing-era he gained international "boogie woogie" fame via radio, recording such hit tunes as "Marie," and giving live performances. In 1940 at the Apollo Theater in New York City, Dorsey joined Count Basie, Harry James, Coleman Hawkins, Gene Krupa, Benny Goodman, and other jazz greats in one of the hottest sessions of all time. He made several movie appearances including *The Fabulous Dorseys* (1947), a fictionalized musical account of the two brothers. In 1954 Tommy and brother Jimmy had their own TV musical variety program, "Stage Show," which was produced and closely supervised by Jackie Gleason. The show's theme song: "I'm Getting Sentimental over You." Elvis Presley made a spectacular appearance on "Stage Show" singing "Heartbreak Hotel." A phenomenal success, Presley appeared on the Dorsey show for the next six weeks. **QUOTE** "Organizing the musicians is like putting together the boys for a football team. The soloists are the backfield, in the line are the lead men on first trombone, first sax and first trumpet. Then, you have your boys in the rhythm section, the pianist, guitarist, bassist and drummer." Died: 1956.

Glen A. Larson

6673 Hollywood

Writer, producer, singer, songwriter

BORN Jan. 3, 1942, in Long Beach, CA. **SPOTLIGHTS** One of television's most successful writer/producers, Larson sums up his feelings this way, "I don't think anything in the world can

Glen A. Larson (left) and Fred Astaire

compete with the excitement and immediacy of working in television. I still consider it an honor to drive through the front gate of the studio." A native Californian, Larson spent his first eight years of his life going to the Hitching Post on Hollywood Boulevard to watch *Roy Rogers* movies, the second eight standing in "no ticket" lines to broadcasts in order to watch the most famous of radio's Golden Era talents: Jack Benny, Edgar Bergen with Charlie McCarthy and the Lux Radio Theater. (Larson started life with absolutely no industry connections which might get a ticket to anything.) It was his fascination with broadcasting and its ability to reach millions of people in a single night that impassioned Larson and set into motion his prolific and diverse career. He went from producing radio shows for neighborhood kids in his garage at age 12—using cast out scripts like "The Cisco Kid," "Sam Spade," and "A Man Called X" that he had found behind the NBC and CBS studios—to producing his first national TV show with only one step in between, a love of music which sidetracked him into the record business while still in high school. He attended Hollywood High with such celebrated personalities as David and Rick Nelson, Sally Kellerman, and John Phillip Law. Musically inclined, he participated in the glee club, and as a lark formed the Four Preps. While still in high school, Larson and the Preps began to work as backup singers for buddy Rick Nelson, appearing in a number of television episodes of the legendary all-American family situation comedy, "The Adventures of Ozzie and Harriet." Larson remarked, "I taught Rick his first three chords on a guitar." He added, "Ozzie Nelson took me apart one day in front of the entire 'Ozzie and Harriet' crew for apparently attempting to exert too much influence on how Ozzie did his show. I guess you could say I suffered from over-confidence." The Preps then split from Rick Nelson to record their own hits: "26 Miles," "Big Man," and "Down By the Station," all written by Larson. Through the Preps' relationship with Henry Mancini, Larson was given the chance to submit two different series ideas to Sid Sheinberg, the then-television head of Universal Studios who is credited with giving Steven Spielberg his start. Sheinberg bought both ideas, though both were assigned to other writers and both went nowhere. As a sort of consolation prize for not allowing Larson to be involved with the writing of his own ideas, he was offered a chance to meet with producers on the busy lot to demonstrate, if he could, the writing talents he insisted he had. Every producer turned him down save one, Gene Coon, for a new series called "It Takes A Thief," starring Robert Wagner. "I wrote one script over the weekend and was immediately hired as the show's story editor." Larson wrote

two more scripts. They made him the producer of the show. It was not a fast ride, it was *meteoric*. A workaholic with an endless stream of exciting ideas, he became one of Hollywood's premiere writer/creator/producers specializing in one-hour action dramas in unparalleled numbers, including "Magnum, P.I.," "The Fall Guy," "Knight Rider," "The Six Million Dollar Man," "Quincy," "Buck Rogers in the 25th Century," "Battlestar Galactica," "B.J. and the Bear," "Alias Smith and Jones" "McCloud," and "The Hardy Boys—Nancy Drew Mysteries." He dominated the television marketplace from the late 1960s through the '80s. He attributes this infinitely versatile slate of successes to: "I write what I like to see, aim for the middle of the country and never write down to an audience," Larson stated. **QUOTE** The three most thrilling moments of his professional life: "Watching John Williams conduct the Boston Pops Orchestra playing his great movie compositions including *Star Wars*, *E.T.*, *Close Encounter of the Third Kind*, and *Raiders of the Lost Ark* to which he added the theme from 'Battlestar Galactica.' Second, was doing an episode of 'The Fall Guy' starring Roy Rogers playing himself, as if in one of his own Republic movies in which he rode Trigger, shot bad guys (along with every movie/TV cowboy we could hire), and sang all of his great songs backed by the Sons of the Pioneers. It was a childhood dream come true. And third, was getting my star on the Walk of Fame on Oct. 23, 1985."

Flora Finch 🎥   6673 Hollywood
Comedienne
BORN Feb. 11, 1869, in England. **SPOTLIGHTS** One of the screen's earliest comedy queens, she worked opposite movieland's first fat funnyman, comedian John Bunny. As his sidekick, she co-stars in *A Cure for Pokeritis* (1912), *Bunny's Mistake* (1913), and *Bunny Buys a Harem* (1914), among others. Finch, the skinny, plain-looking half of the comedy team, and Bunny the ugly, sturdy one, had legions of devoted fans worldwide. She played pious, he lacked virtue (as long as his wife didn't catch him). This hilarious team made more than 150 short comedies together until Bunny's sudden death in 1915. Later she played supporting roles in features, right up until her death. Her last two movies were *Show Boat* (1936) and *The Women* (1939). Died: 1940.

Ted Knight 📺 6673 Hollywood
Actor

Ted Knight (right) and Gary Collins

BORN Tadeus Konopka; Dec. 7, 1925, in Terryville, CT. **SPOTLIGHTS** Known for his superb comic timing and delivery, he played Ted Baxter, a bumbling, goofy, egotistic—but lovable—

anchorman at WJM-TV news in TV's long-running "The Mary Tyler Moore Show" (1970-'77). With his rich baritone voice and affable personality, he brought many laughs to the popular series. In another funny series, he starred as Henry Rush in "Too Close for Comfort" (1980-'83). **ACHIEVEMENTS** Knight won two Emmys: 1972 and 1976. Died: 1986.

Licia Albanese    6671 Hollywood
Opera singer
BORN July 22, 1913, in Bari, Italy. **SPOTLIGHTS** From her unglamorous beginnings in an impoverished Italian village, Albanese's voice took her everywhere her heart desired. Known by the singing crowd, but not the public, Albanese had great fortune in Milan. She was called in from the audience to substitute for the ill lead in *Madame Butterfly* and became a star from that unlikely, impromptu debut. Her debut at the Metropolitan Opera was in the same role in 1940. This renowned soprano, remembered for her Puccini heroines, performed a variety of lead roles in Italian and French during her long association with the Met. Recordings: Puccini's *La Boheme*, Verdi's *La Traviata*. She was the only soprano selected to sing more than once for Toscanini radio opera broadcasts. **QUOTE** "It's easier to sing well than to have to explain why you did not sing well."

Jerry Dunphy   6669 Hollywood
Broadcast journalist

Jerry Dunphy

BORN June 9, in Milwaukee, WI. **SPOTLIGHTS** "From the desert to the sea, to all of Southern California, good evening" was "the Dunph's" catchphrase every weekday evening for more than 20 years as the award-winning "Eyewitness News" anchor of Los Angeles' Channel 7, who double dutied as a week-end network anchor for ABC-TV. He switched to KCAL-TV to head up the anchor team, helping to launch the channel into a position of prominence. His career began a half a century ago as a journalism student at Northwestern University. After graduation he worked in radio doing news and sports, then entered the relatively new field of television journalism. He built a reputation of doing the best local news in the nation, reporting from Europe on U.S. NATO bases, from Israel and Kuwait after the six-day war, and going after important global stories. Consistently rated a leader in his field, his long and distinguished anchor position led him to interview five U.S. Presidents. One of his most memorable in-depth accounts was his "Nixon/Dunphy: 90 Minutes Live" (1979)—the first one-on-one with Richard Nixon after Watergate. Respected for his news integrity, his balanced, fair, no-nonsense reporting, his wide collection of awards are a testament to his journalistic accomplishments. **ACHIEVEMENTS** 11 Golden Mikes, Emmys, Academy statuettes (for "Vietnam, the Village War," and "Jerry Visits," intimate interviews with movie stars). As a Captain in the Army Air Corps, he flew 29 combat missions, shot down two enemy planes and became squadron bombardier in his B-29 group.

Patsy Kelly   6669 Hollywood
Actress, dancer
BORN Jan. 10, 1910, in Brooklyn, NY. **SPOTLIGHTS** A strong comedienne who was pretty good at putting her hooves down: *Pigskin Parade* (1936), *Merrily We Live* (1938), and *Topper Returns* (1941). Died: 1981.

Andy Williams    6669 Hollywood
Singer, actor
BORN Howard A. Williams; Dec. 3, 1930, in Wall Lake, IA. **SPOTLIGHTS** The man who made "Moon River" a cherished American standard began singing as a child in the local Presbyterian church choir along with his three older brothers. He made his professional singing debut at age eight on radio station WIIO's "Iowa Barn Dance Show" in Des Moines, then continued through his youth to perform on radio as part of the Williams Brothers Quartet, traveling to Chicago, Cincinnati and Los Angeles. The quartet turned into a nightclub act, performing for audiences in Europe and the U.S. for five years. Williams went solo in 1951. He was offered a sweet deal by Steve Allen—to appear on his "Tonight Show" for two and one-half years. His recording, concert and TV career soared. Hits include: "Hawaiian Wedding Song," "You Do Something to Me," "Alexander's Ragtime Band," "Danny Boy," "Twelfth of Never," "Call Me Irresponsible," "Born Free," "Honey," and "The Impossible Dream." His trademark vocal delivery on "The Days of Wine and Roses," "The Shadow of Your Smile," "Can't Get Used to Losing You," and the love themes for "The

Andy Williams and Debbie Reynolds

Godfather" and "Love Story" has earned Williams both Gold and Platinum albums. His easy listening, smooth, warm vocals were complemented by his showmanship and selection of guest performers, earning him three Emmys for "The Andy Williams Show." This elegant entertainer's TV popularity proved itself as NBC's highest rated series during its nine-year run. President Ronald Reagan praised, "His voice is a national treasure." **HIGHLIGHTS** "The Andy Williams Moon River Theatre" is his own concert theatre located in Branson, Missouri; telephone 417. 334.4500. **QUOTE** "In Vegas the best you can get is a royal flush. But here in Branson the best you can get is a full house."

Frank Lloyd 🎥　　　6667 Hollywood
Director, producer
BORN Feb. 2, 1888, in Scotland. **SPOTLIGHTS** A master of costume pictures and historical pieces, his original Golden Era movie, *Mutiny on the Bounty* (1935), hit big for MGM. It stars Charles Laughton and Clark Gable. His first Western, *Wells Fargo* (1937), stars Frances Dee and Joel McCrea. It told the story of the legendary line, with plenty of action. Ronald Colman stars as swashbuckling poet Villon opposite Basil Rathbone's Louis XI in *If I Were King* (1938). If you like period pieces, it is worth seeing. **ACHIEVEMENTS** 1929 Best Director Oscar for *The Divine Lady*; and a 1933 Best Director Oscar for *Cavalcade*. Died: 1960.

Aaron Spelling 🎥　　　6667 Hollywood
Producer, executive, writer

Aaron Spelling

BORN April 22, 1928, in Dallas, TX. **SPOTLIGHTS** He is the most prolific producer in television history, as recorded in *The Guinness Book of World Records*. Earlier, Spelling had been a successful student playwright at Southern Methodist University. He came to Hollywood with visions of being an important actor. He appeared in a number of projects, but found neither critical acclaim, satisfaction, nor financial security. His first writing job was for "Dick Powell's Zane Grey Theater." From that moment forward his writing, creating and producing skills have never been in question. Spelling produced these hit series with Leonard Goldberg: "Charlie's Angels," "Starsky and Hutch," "Fantasy Island," "Hart to Hart," and "Family." But his credits don't stop there. A continuing list of his hit series—some of them are considered classics—are: "The Love Boat," "Hotel," "Dynasty," "The Rookies," "T.J. Hooker," "Matt Houston," "Vega$," and "The Mod Squad." In the 1990s, Spelling created: "Beverly Hills 90210," "Melrose Place," "7th Heaven," and "Charmed." His first daytime soap opera "Sunset Beach," has a huge following. In addition, he's done numerous network and cable movies, as well as feature films. Aaron Spelling knows his audience—it's the whole world who watches and is entertained by his shows. Seeing his entire television library would require almost five months of 24-hour-a-day watching. **ACHIEVEMENTS** Recipient of countless awards, he received critical acclaim and an Emmy for "Day One," about the conception and building of the atom bomb and the decision to drop it on Japan. He won another Emmy for "And the Band Played On," an HBO program about AIDS that attracted one of the highest viewing audiences in history for a single cable special...His daughter, Tori, is an actress (of "Beverly Hills, 90210" TV fame), and his son, Randy, is an actor ("Sunset Beach"). Before Spelling conquered Hollywood, he had a tough go at it. His star is located in front of the Musso & Frank Grill for sentimental reasons—the restaurant kindly gave him a tab and fed him when he was flat broke.

John Barrymore 🎥　　　6667 Hollywood
Actor

John Barrymore

BORN John Sidney Blythe; Feb. 15, 1882, in Philadelphia, PA. **SPOTLIGHTS** One of the "Fabulous Barrymores," he was known as "The Great Profile," and billed as "The Great Lover." His discerning performances in the silent *Dr. Jekyll and Mr. Hyde* (1920), in which he transformed himself with little makeup, and his spellbinding Hamlet on the London stage in 1922, affirmed his reputation as one of the best. This matinee idol appeared in more than 50 motion pictures and an equal number of stage plays, including numerous Shakespearean roles. Films include *A Bill of Divorcement* and *Grand Hotel* (both 1932), *Rasputin and The Empress* (1933—in the only film he made with brother Lionel and sister Ethel), *Counsellor-at-Law* (1933—in one of his finest performances), and *Dinner at Eight* (1933). Family and friends called this beloved rogue, Jack. He indulged in a hard-drinking, high-spending lifestyle that he thought befitting a great star. Very literate, he loved the *bon mot*. Barrymore once commented, "My head is buried in the sands of tomorrow, while my tail feathers are singed by the hot sun of today." **HIGHLIGHTS** Christopher Plummer starred as "Barrymore" in the Broadway production, for which he won a 1997 Tony Award. **QUOTE** Barrymore descended from American theatrical royalty, but resisted their demands to join them. He wanted to be a cartoonist. When he finally joined the family business by making his stage debut in *Magda* in 1903 he said, "This acting is a new game. But that's superfluous, isn't it? I don't have to tell a critic that I'm new on the stage." After receiving rave reviews he attributed it to, "I fancied it was rather because the audience—that big, funny thing, you know—believed that acting was rather natural to a Barrymore." Slightly superstitious and long on family tradition, he insisted on having a fresh red apple on his dressing table. In 2000, the world knows his granddaughter, actress Drew Barrymore. This legendary talent died in 1942.

Buck Owens ●   6667 Hollywood
Singer, guitarist

Buck Owens

BORN Alvis Edgar Owens, Jr.; Aug. 12, 1929, outside Sherman, TX. **SPOTLIGHTS** A honky-tonk giant, he rose to unimaginable heights from the lowly position born of the Great Depression. His sharecropper parents were devastated by horrendous Dust Bowl conditions; finally they moved westward, picking fruit on farms from Arizona to California. He quickly learned firsthand a phrase he has not let go of, "Poverty sucks." If suffering helps make a

great artist, Buck was truly inspired. For relief as a teenager, he listened to cowboy music in small, rowdy honky tonks. Using the "freight train" sound with its churning speed, Buck hit #1 with "Act Naturally" in 1963. With his unique twanging and plucking, he hit #1 after #1—for a total of 21 #1 country songs: "Love's Gonna Live Here," "Together Again," "My Heart Skips a Beat," "Only You," "Buckaroo," "Waitin' in Your Welfare Line," "Think of Me," "Your Tender Loving Care"; more. He had a #1 hit in 1988 with Dwight Yoakam, "The Streets of Bakersfield." His trademark guitar is a bold red, white and blue. TV: "The Buck Owens Ranch Show" (1966 syndicated), and co-hosted "Hee Haw" (1969-'71 CBS; syndicated since 1971) with Roy Clark. Although "Hee Haw" was corny, Buck ain't nobody's fool, thank you very much. He's an astute businessman who's running the empire he created. He still practices what his daddy taught him: to always be honest—no matter how poor, no matter what the circumstances, no excuses ever. His nickname "Buck" came from a mule the family once owned. The Beatles appreciated him, too. The Fab Four recorded "Act Naturally." When Buck praised the Beatles' work, others in the industry raised eyebrows at the breaking away of the country to rock 'n' roll...Owens owns the first-rate Crystal Palace—a restaurant, museum and nightclub, in Bakersfield, CA. You can dance the night away to Owens' famed Buckaroos band. www.buckowens.com or telephone 805.327.7500. **QUOTE** "I live up to my word. It's the Okie code. I've never been in jail, been arrested, stole anybody's

songs or taken dope. I'm respectful of the flag, and my mommy and daddy were my role models."

Gene Autry 📺   6667 Hollywood
See page 428

Quinn Martin 📺   6667 Hollywood
Executive, producer

Quinn Martin (left) relaxes at home reading Hollywood trade papers with his son, Michael Q. Martin. The tot's mother was busy writing the classic TV show "I Love Lucy."

BORN Irwin Cohn; May 22, 1922, in Brooklyn, NY. **SPOTLIGHTS** With his keen eye for assembling talent and packages for top shows, he produced a slew of television's most memorable dramatic series. Martin's TV contributions include "The Untouchables" (1959-63), starring Robert Stack, "The Fugitive" (1963-67), starring David Janssen, "12 O'Clock High" (1964-67), "The F.B.I." (1965-'74), starring Efrem Zimbalist,Jr., "Cannon" (1971-'76), starring Robert Conrad, "The Streets of San Francisco" (1972-'77), starring Karl Malden and Michael Douglas, and "Barnaby Jones" (1973-'80), with Buddy Ebsen in the title role. Martin was one of the first producers to shoot television at real locations, instead of shooting on the studio's backlot. This gave his shows a sense of immediacy. At one point, he had eight series running simultaneously on the air. Martin's TV legacy paved the way for other realistic, intense character-driven dramas, and shows packed with tension, suspense and action like "NYPD Blue," and "ER." **QUOTE** "If the fans wrote in and said, 'They liked the show,' I knew I was in trouble. But, if they said, 'I like the star,' I knew I had a hit." He reasoned that they might lose interest in the show, but that their fondness for the star would keep them tuning in. Died: 1987.

Harrison Ford 🎬   6667 Hollywood
Actor

BORN March 16, 1892, in Kansas City, MO. **SPOTLIGHTS** This is not the Harrison Ford you think it is. This honoree was a charming, good-looking, box office attraction of the silent screen. Movies include *Passion Flower* (1921) with Norma Talmadge, *Vanity Fair* (1923), and *Little Old New York* (1923), co-starring Marion Davies. Died: 1957.

William Demarest 🎥 6667 Hollywood

Actor

William Demarest

BORN Feb. 27, 1892, in St. Paul, MN. **SPOTLIGHTS** A character actor from vaudeville days, his show business career spanned 60 years and included stage, radio, TV and films. Movies include *The Jazz Singer* (1927), *Mr. Smith Goes to Washington* (1939), *The Jolson Story* (1946—an Oscar-nominated performance), and *Viva Las Vegas* (1964). TV: He played Uncle Charley O'Casey, the crusty old sailor (with a soft heart), opposite Fred MacMurray in "My Three Sons" (1965-'72), a family sitcom. Died: 1983.

Freddie Bartholomew 🎥 6667 Hollywood

Actor

Freddie Bartholomew (right), Spencer Tracy (l), & Lionel Barrymore

BORN Frederick Llewellyn; March 28, 1924, in England. **SPOTLIGHTS** Although little Freddie came from a family of modest means, he had a gentleness about him that indicated he was of aristocratic lineage. His Aunt Cissie spotted the boy's talent while he was reciting. It was under her guidance that he was cast in the title role of *David Copperfield* (1935), and landed a seven-year contract with MGM. Greta Garbo adored him in *Anna Karenina* (1935). He made *Captains Courageous* (1937), opposite Spencer Tracy and Lionel Barrymore. The child's salary? One grand per week. Died: 1992.

Mark Serrurier Moviola 🎥 6667 Hollywood

Inventor

BORN Mark Serrurier. **SPOTLIGHTS** Creator of the Moviola, an editing device, it is an indispensable piece of equipment. It has a small screen, and is controlled by a foot pedal for viewing a film at any speed. It can also freeze a frame for close examination, and handles sound synchronization. His father, Iwan Serrurier, was an inventor and pioneer designer of the Midget, a 1924 film editing bench. The Moviola evolved from this. **ACHIEVEMENTS** 1979 Oscar "for having kept pace effectively to meet the demands of the motion picture technology."

Peter Donald 📺 6665 Hollywood

Comedian

SPOTLIGHTS One of four comedians who told jokes on "Can You Top This?" (1950-'51). Panelist (1952-'53) on "Masquerade Party," an entertaining show on which the clues for the disguised celebrities were their costumes. A regular on "Pantomime Quiz" (1953-'55, 1957).

Harry Ackerman 📺 6665 Hollywood

Executive, producer

BORN Nov. 17, 1912, in New York, NY. **SPOTLIGHTS** A writer and creative force associated with Screen Gems. Many success stories include "Dennis the Menace" (1959-'63), "Hazel" (1961-'65), and "Bewitched" (1964-'72). Died: 1991.

Douglas Fairbanks, Jr. 📺 6665 Hollywood

See page 367

Robert Cummings 🎥 6663 Hollywood

Actor

Robert Cummings

BORN Clarence Cummings; June 10, 1908, in Joplin, MO. **SPOTLIGHTS** Too poor to stay in high school during the Great Depression, Cummings left during his senior year to attend the American Academy of Dramatic Arts, *because they paid male students a salary!* He discovered he liked acting. Fun and cheerful in *College Swing* (1938), the affable actor played to his ever youthful appearance (like Dick Clark). Known for his comic abilities, he was effective in dramas and Westerns, and made 75 films, including *Kings Row* (1942), *Heaven Only Knows* (1947), *The Lost Moment* (1947), and *Dial M for Murder* (1954). He was immortalized in TV's "The Bob Cummings Show" (1955-'59), as playboy bachelor photographer, Bob Collins. His infatuated secretary? Charmain (Shultzy) Schultz...His godfather was the legendary aviation pioneer, Orville Wright. An accomplished pilot himself,

Cummings held the distinction of being issued America's Instructor Pilot License #1. Died: 1990.

Nat "King" Cole  6655 Hollywood
Singer, pianist

Nat "King" Cole

BORN Nathanial Adam Coles; March 17, 1919, in Montgomery, AL. **SPOTLIGHTS** The "King of the Romantic Ballad," Cole was first known as a pianist in the "Chicago Blues" style. But, it was Nat "King" Cole's golden voice that brought him international fame. He sang with a throaty, masculine gentleness which smoothly glided over melodies. Gigantic selling hits include "Mona Lisa," "Looking Back," "Ramblin' Rose," "Send for Me," "Autumn Leaves," "That Sunday That Summer," "The Christmas Song," and "Unforgettable." While none of the above are jazz recordings, this outstanding pianist never completely left jazz behind him. Jazz CDs include *Sweet Lorraine*, and *The Best of the Nat King Cole Trio*. His motion pictures range from crime dramas—*Blue Gardenia* (1953), to action—*China Gate* (1957), to musicals—*St. Louis Blues* (1958—put on your "must-see" list). The legendary all-star musical cast includes Cole, Eartha Kitt, Pearl Bailey, Ruby Dee, Cab Calloway, Ella Fitzgerald, and Mahalia Jackson. **ACHIEVEMENTS** His albums flew off store shelves enabling Capitol Records to build their circular landmark headquarters, resembling a stack of records with a needle on top. It is *the house that Nat built*...He sold more than 50 million records. When a few reviewers criticized his choice of soft music, he quipped, "Critics don't buy records. They get them free."...He made history by becoming the first black entertainer to have his own network television show in the 1950s, "The Nat 'King' Cole Show." Both he and NBC had to tough it out against prejudice from small-minded corporate heads who refused to sponsor the show by buying commercial time. These dunderheads thought no one would want to buy any products associated with "his kind." Cole quit due to the lack of a sponsor. He stated, "This is nonsense. I know I sell to all kinds of people, not just one race." Mr.Cole remained a gentleman throughout the ordeal—as did NBC executives—paving the way for future African-American performers to make a significant contribution to the cultural arts...He is the father of singer Natalie Cole. **SIDELIGHTS** When the U.S. Postal Service released a 29-cent stamp honoring Cole, they listed him born in "1917." When the musician's widow pointed out their mistake at the unveiling ceremony, the error could not be corrected; the U.S. Postal Service had already printed 36 million stamps...The world mourned the loss of this incredible talent when he died in 1965 from cancer caused by smoking.

Reginald Denny 🎥 6655 Hollywood

Actor

Reginald Denny

BORN Reginald Daymore; Nov. 2, 1891, in Richmond, Surrey, England. **SPOTLIGHTS** After coming to America, Denny made his debut in *The Melting Pot* (1912). This versatile talent could play in any type of movie. In comedies he scored big as the slightly foolish Englishman. In romances he was the noble gent who should get the girl but doesn't. In action pics he was the virile man of strength. He made a series of 24 "Leather Pusher" shorts (1922-'24) boxing his way to the top of the ticket office. A wildly popular performer, fans anxiously awaited each new film Denny made. Among his credits are *Oh Doctor!* (1925), *California Straight Ahead* (1925) and *Skinner's Dress Suit* (1926). By 1926 this athletic fellow was Universal Studios biggest asset, and was paid a whopping $8,000 a week for the honor. However, Warner's biggest attraction, Rin-Tin-Tin, was voted the public's favorite performer of the year! This dapper gent survived the transition to talkies. Wonderful films include *The Secret Life of Walter Mitty* (1947), *Mr. Blandings Builds His Dream House* (1948) and *Around the World in 80 Days* (1956). The well-loved Englishman died in 1967.

Fritz Kreisler 💿 6655 Hollywood
Musician, composer

BORN Feb. 2, 1875, in Vienna, Austria. **SPOTLIGHTS** A world-famous violinist, he played so elegantly he could make people cry. Famous in Europe, he first visited America from 1901 - 1903 where he won acclaim as the supreme violinist of the day. He traveled on concert tours around the globe, but became an American citizen in 1941. Kreisler played with warmth, vitality, technical mastery, and a magnificent grasp of form. After hearing him perform at one of his concerts, a fan gushed: "I would give my whole life to play as beautifully as you do." Kreisler responded, "I did." He composed violin pieces: *Liebesfreud* and *Caprice Viennoise*. He made numerous recordings for motion pictures, and wrote several light operas. He played various melodic compositions from the 17th and 18th centuries which turned out to be musical forgeries; it was later discovered they were his *own* compositions. **QUOTE** After he retired at age 75, he stated, "I never play now except for my own pleasure, and there's not much pleasure in playing for yourself." Died: 1962.

Iron Eyes Cody 📺 6655 Hollywood
Actor, consultant

BORN Little Eagle Oskie Cody; April 3, 1916, in Bacone, OK. **SPOTLIGHTS** A Native American actor, he was extremely

Iron Eyes Cody and Samantha Hart

proud of his noble heritage: part-Cree and part Cherokee Indian. Cody became an actor and technical adviser on Native American matters in countless TV and film productions. For example, Cody explained the cultural tradition of painted faces: "The young Indian man has a vision and paints his face accordingly. The different colors symbolize different things. Green is good, red is war, yellow is sun, and blue is for the clouds and the Great Spirit. After a young man has had his vision, he fasts and meditates. Then he takes a sweat bath to purify himself, and dances. Then he is a man." Cody was also one of the few living experts in Sioux sign language. As an actor, he appeared in a number of Westerns in supporting and lead roles. In all, he worked on more than 200 pictures, starting in the silent era. Films include *The Covered Wagon* (1923), *The Iron Horse* (1924), *Cimarron* (1931—the first Western to win a Best Picture Academy Award), *The Plainsman* (1937), *Union Pacific* (1939), *My Little Chickadee* (1940), *Kit Carson* (1940), *They Died With Their Boots On* (1941), *The Outlaw* (1943), *The Paleface* (1948), *Blood on the Moon* (1948), *Broken Arrow* (1950), *Son of Paleface* (1952), *Sitting Bull* (1954—as Chief Crazy Horse), Disney's *Westward Ho the Wagons* (1956), *A Man Called Horse* (1970), *El Condor* (1970) opposite Lee Van Cleef, *Grayeagle* (1977), and *Ernest Goes to Camp* (1987). He played a cowboy once in Tony Bill's *Hearts of the West* (1975). He gained immense popularity and national recognition in the "Pollution: It's a Crying Shame" TV commercials. The "Keep America Beautiful" campaign was launched in 1971. His impact on viewers' minds is staggering. Most baby boomers can easily recall his saddened expression as he looks over the littered, destroyed environment with a tear rolling down his face. It could move a viewer to tears in 60 seconds and is considered the most effective public ad campaign *of all time*. Cody appeared in the TV series "The First Americans," "Davy Crockett," "Daniel Boone," "Wagon Train," and "The Virginian." He was the annual representative in both the Hollywood Christmas Parade and the Tournament of Roses Parade for decades. He penned *Iron Eyes: My Life as a*

Hollywood Indian in 1982, and received his Walk of Fame star on April 20, 1983. **QUOTE** "Nearly all my life, it has been my policy to help those less fortunate. My greatest endeavors have been to dignify my people's image through uplifting portrayals, humility and love of my country." Died: 1999, at age 94.

Dorothy Sebastian 🎥   6655 Hollywood
Actress
BORN April 26, 1903, in Birmingham, AL. **SPOTLIGHTS** Beginning during the silent era, she made 25 pictures: *The Arizona Wildcat* (1927), *Our Dancing Daughters* (1928), *The Arizona Kid* (1939), and *Among the Living* (1941). Died: 1957.

Alan Hale, Jr. 📺   6655 Hollywood
Actor

Alan Hale, Jr. (left) with Tina Louise and Bob Denver

BORN Alan MacKahn; March 8, 1918, in Los Angeles, CA. **SPOTLIGHTS** A robust and merry character, he was immortalized as skipper of the charter boat Minnow, stranded on "Gilligan's Island" (1964-'67). It remains one of the most popular TV series of all time, and is still seen daily in worldwide syndication. He had earlier appeared in TV's "Casey Jones." Films include *The Music Man* (1948), and *Hang 'em High* (1967). The smell of greasepaint runs in the family; his father was actor/director Alan Hale. Died: 1990.

Antonio Moreno 🎥 🎥   6655 Hollywood
Actor
BORN Antonio Garride Monteagudo; Sept. 26, 1886, in Madrid, Spain. **SPOTLIGHTS** He made his silent screen debut in *Voice of Millions* (1912), then delivered an excellence performance in D. W. Griffith's *The Musketeers of Pig Alley* (1912), a realistic gangster drama. He rose to leading man as an aristocratic Latin lover. He romanced the most glamorous leading ladies of the era. He stars opposite Great Garbo in *The Temptress* (1926--her second American film), as her lover. He made more than 100 movies. He aged gracefully, but never fully lost his Spanish accent. When talkies arrived, he kept busy in character roles in talkies. He appears in comedies, dramas and monster movies from the 1930s: *The Bohemian Girl* (1936), *Notorious* (1946), and *Creature from the Black Lagoon* (1954). **QUOTE** "No two screen players have the same abilities. Some are hard working, some are lazy. This one works intelli-

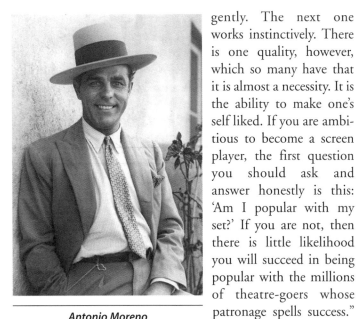

Antonio Moreno

gently. The next one works instinctively. There is one quality, however, which so many have that it is almost a necessity. It is the ability to make one's self liked. If you are ambitious to become a screen player, the first question you should ask and answer honestly is this: 'Am I popular with my set?' If you are not, then there is little likelihood you will succeed in being popular with the millions of theatre-goers whose patronage spells success." Died: 1967.

Dean Martin 📺   6655 Hollywood
See page 96

Phil Harris 🎙   6655 Hollywood
Actor, musician, orchestra leader

Phil Harris

BORN June 24, 1906, in Linton, IN. **SPOTLIGHTS** A big, jovial gentleman, he became equally known as a comedian and a band leader. Harris formed his own band in 1931, and was discovered while playing at L.A.'s Coconut Grove nightclub. He gained national fame in 1932 on radio's "The Jack Benny Show." He played the brash stooge, providing side-splitting antics with his illiterate wolf routines. That gig lasted a decade. A regular on radio's "Kay Kyser's Kollege of Musical Knowledge," Harris had a firm reputation as a happy-go-lucky star. He teamed with wife (since 1941) on radio's "The Phil Harris-Alice Faye Show," comedy-variety starting in 1946. Known as the "Reigning Master of the Patter Song." His trademark song was "That's What I Like About the South." Other hits: "Lazy River," "Ding Dong Daddy from Dumas" and "Old Time Religion." Died: 1995.

Leonard Nimoy 🎥   6655 Hollywood
Actor, director, producer, writer
BORN March 26, 1931, in Boston, MA. **SPOTLIGHTS** Educated at Boston College and Antioch College, he joined an elite group of artists who trained at the Pasadena Playhouse, in California. He made his screen debut in *Queen for a Day* (1951). *Rhubarb* (1951) provided him with his first good sup-

porting role on the silver screen. The farce is about an eccentric man who dies and leaves his fortune—including his baseball team—to his lucky pet cat. Nimoy plays opposite Ray Milland, Jan Sterling, Gene Lockhart, and William Frawley in the comedy. He made a number of other motion pictures, including *Francis Goes to West Point* (1952), *The Balcony* (1963), and the excellent remake of *Invasion of the Body Snatchers* (1978). **TV** Nimoy gained his

Leonard Nimoy

greatest fame in television. He first appeared in the series that opened with the voiceover of Robert Cleveland Johnson: "Good morning, Mr. Phelps. Your mission, should you decide to accept it...Should you or any member of the IM force be caught or killed, the secretary will disavow any knowledge of your actions. This tape will self-destruct in five seconds. Good luck, Jim." He played Paris on the classic adventure series "Mission Impossible" (1967-'71). He was, however, immortalized in the classic sci-fi TV series, "Star Trek" (1966-'69). He portrayed the acutely intelligent, logical, and humorless (although he was occasionally funny) science officer Mr. Spock on the starship U.S.S. Enterprise. His pointy-ear character was half-Vulcan, half-human. After the series initial run ended, his popularity did not. It grew in syndication. He continues to explore new box office potential with a related film series at Paramount. He co-stars in *Star Trek—The Motion Picture* (1979), *Star Trek: The Wrath of Khan* (1982), *Star Trek III: The Search for Spock* (1984—also directed), *Star Trek IV: The Voyage Home* (1986—also directed and co-story--it's one of the best), *Star Trek V: The Final Frontier* (1989), and *Star Trek VI: The Undiscovered Country* (1991—also exec. produced and co-screenplay). Nimoy did not appear in, but directed the smash hit comedy, *Three Men and a Baby* (1987), starring Tom Selleck. In TV, he hosted the series "In Search Of" (1976-'82). Nimoy is also an accomplished Broadway performer. He received rave reviews in "Equus" (1977), and thrilled audiences with his one-man show "Vincent," in which he portrayed the great Dutch postimpressionist painter, Vincent Van Gogh. An intelligent artist in mind, spirit and body, he has written several books of poetry: *You and I* (1973), *I Think of You* (1974), and *We Are All Children Searching for Love* (1977). His autobiography is entitled *I Am Not Spock* (1975)...Also see the bios of Gene Roddenberry, William Shatner, DeForest Kelley, George Takei and Nichelle Nichols in this book. **QUOTE** His star dedication ceremony took place on Jan. 16, 1985. Hundreds of fans, friends, family and global media attended the exciting event. Nimoy commented, "The unveiling of my star on the Walk of Fame was a deeply moving event for me and my entire family. My parents were still with us and it was a great joy to have them be there."

6633 HOLLYWOOD

Robert Vaughn    6633 Hollywood

Robert Vaughn

Actor

BORN Nov. 30, 1932, in New York City. **SPOTLIGHTS** Playing an upper-crust, wealthy scion-gone-bad in *The Young Philadelphians* (1959), Vaughn earned an Oscar nomination. This must-see work was his third motion picture, and the beginning of a stellar screen career. His well-bred good looks, dark hair, and cold eyes were a screenwriter's dream; Vaughn could slip into a superiority complex, as easily as he could flash his dazzling grin in roguish charm. Female fans found him "dashing" and "romantic," but directors often sought him out for an entirely different role, that of a menacing villain. Yet, due to his handsome visage these villains always had a lot more going for them. A versatile talent, his 100 motion pictures run the gamut from Western to comedy: *The Magnificent Seven* (1960), *Bullitt* (1968), *The Bridge at Remagen* (1969), *Julius Caesar* (1970), *The Towering Inferno* (1974), *Superman III* (1983), *Black Moon Rising* (1986), and *BASEketball* (1998). Vaughn became the most popular actor in America with his hit TV show, "The Man From U.N.C.L.E." (1964-'68). He starred as the suave, cosmopolitan super agent, Napoleon Solo. The spy spoof was NBC's response to James Bond. Vaughn requested that his Walk of Fame star be placed at this location (on July 27, 1998) because it was the exact corner where he waited for the bus to take him to Los Angeles City College. He arrived in Hollywood with his mother in 1951, and lived in an apartment building at 1830 N. Cherokee Avenue, a few blocks away. After earning his B.A. degree in drama, he earned his master's and Ph.D. in Political Science.

Mark Stevens    6633 Hollywood

Mark Stevens

Actor, director, producer

BORN Richard Stevens; Dec. 13, 1915, in Cleveland, OH. **SPOTLIGHTS** He excelled as the fatalistic hero in film noir thrillers, including *The Snake Pit* (1948), *Street with No Name* (1948—a gem of a picture) and *Between Midnight and Dawn* (1950). He was strong as the ex-Navy flyboy in the drama, *Torpedo Alley* (1953). He direct-ed, produced, and stars in *Cry Vengeance* (1954). He starred in TV's "Martin Kane, Private Eye" (1953-'54), and as newspaper editor, Steve Wilson, in "Big Town" (1954-'56).

Nichelle Nichols    6633 Hollywood

Nichelle Nichols

Actress, singer, dancer

BORN Grace Nichols; Dec. 28, 1936, in Robbins, IL. **SPOTLIGHTS** A leggy dancer, choreographer and singer with Duke Ellington, this graceful beauty's singing career soared in the late 1950s through the '60s. Summoned to Hollywood she worked in motion pictures, and was featured in *Porgy and Bess* (1959) with Sidney Poitier, Dorothy Dandridge, Pearl Bailey and Sammy Davis, Jr., and *Mister Buddwing* (1966) with James Garner. But it was through her first TV role, guest-starring on Gene Roddenberry's "The Lieutenant" show, that Nichols made her most important Hollywood contact. Roddenberry decided to cast her in his next venture—a science fiction series called "Star Trek." Nichols was immortalized when she beamed up to the Starship Enterprise as the extremely competent communications officer Lieutenant Uhura. A cast member of "Star Trek" for all three seasons, she also worked in the six "Star Trek" motion pictures. Her dignified presence helped break down racial barriers in TV. One of the show's ardent fans was Martin Luther King, Jr. Dr. King observed how the program was about men and women "of all races going forth in peaceful exploration, living as equals." Clearly, the series was making history, and as Dr. King declared, "Miss Nichols is changing the face of television forever." A futurist, she played a real-life role in America's space program. Under contract to NASA, she recruited the first women and minority astronauts for the space shuttle program. **ACHIEVEMENTS** On Jan. 9, 1992, the entire cast beamed down from the bridge to join their shipmate for her dedication ceremony. Nichols declared, "getting a star on the Hollywood Walk of Fame is one of the happiest experiences in my life." She became the first African American to place her hands in the hallowed cement at Grauman's Chinese Theatre, along with her "Star Trek" co-stars.

Anatole Litvak    6633 Hollywood

Director

BORN Mikhal Anatol Litvak; May 10, 1902, in Kiev, Russia. **SPOTLIGHTS** Litvak helped make an international star out of

Charles Boyer in *Mayerling* (1936). This outstanding picture is an imperial romantic tragedy with breathtaking performances. He directed Edward G. Robinson and Paul Lukas in Warner's *Confessions of a Nazi Spy* (1939)—a heartfelt subject for the Jewish artist forced to flee Nazi Germany. He fought in the U.S. military during WWII and was awarded many medals for his service. Litvak directed the original suspense thriller, *Sorry Wrong Number* (Paramount, 1948), starring Barbara Stanwyck and Burt Lancaster. He exposed the harrowing side of a nervous breakdown with the original, classic writhing inmate scene in *The Snake Pit* (1948)—starring Olivia de Havilland and Mark Stevens. Ingrid Bergman returns to American screens in Litvak's *Anastasia* (1956) about a refugee who impersonates Czar Nicholas II's daughter. Died: 1974.

Dustin Farnum 🎥   6633 Hollywood

Dustin Farnum

Actor

BORN May 27, 1874, in Hampton Beach, NH. **SPOTLIGHTS** A stage actor, he earned his rightful place in film history by starring in Hollywood's FIRST feature-length film—*The Squaw Man* (1914)—directed by the great Cecil B. DeMille. *The Squaw Man* had been a successful Broadway play about an Englishman who married a Native American Indian woman in the Wild West. It cost $15,450.25 and took eighteen days to make. It was a phenomenal success, grossing more than $250,000. and began Hollywood's journey into what we watch today—feature length films. Dustin Farnum also starred in Cecil B. DeMille's *The Virginian* (1914). What amazes me— and I'm sure it haunted him throughout his life—was the fact that *he made the BIGGEST financial blunder in all of Hollywood history*. Mr. DeMille offered Dustin a partnership in his studio if the actor would pass on his up front salary on the risky project. After all, money was tight, and DeMille's office was literally in a barn that he shared with animals. But Dustin foolishly insisted an advanced salary for his work in *The Squaw Man*, instead of a piece of what soon became Paramount Pictures! Died: 1929.

Pat Morita 🎥   6633 Hollywood

Actor

BORN Noriyuki Morita; June 28, 1933, in Berkeley, CA. **SPOTLIGHTS** Morita gained worldwide fame, and an Academy nomination, in *The Karate Kid* movie. He portrays, with much honesty, the mysterious karate mentor, Miyagi. His character serves double duty by fatherly role modeling—which won

Pat Morita

Morita millions of devoted fans. In the film he teaches a boy values and morals seen through the wise eyes of Eastern philosophy, as well as physical strength and restraint via the martial arts. Morita has continued his popular, starring role throughout the *Karate* series—which started in 1987 and has continued past 1994. Other motion pictures include *Thoroughly Modern Millie* (1967), *The Shakiest Gun in the West* (1968), *Midway* (1976), *Full Moon High* (1981), *Savannah Smiles* (1982), *Lena's Holiday* (1990), *Honeymoon in Vegas* (1992), and *Even Cowgirls Get the Blues* (1994). The former nightclub comic appeared in TV "Sanford and Son," and "M*A*S*H," before landing a high profile, long-running role in one of the all-time favorite sitcoms, "Happy Days." Had his own detective series, "Ohara," making him the first Japanese-American to star in a series. **ACHIEVEMENTS** Triumphed over tragedy. Hospitalized as a child for nine years with spinal tuberculosis, Morita had to re-learn how to walk. Although born in America, he was detained with his parents for two years during WWII at the infamous Tulelake internment camp in Northern California—a sad chapter in American history...Recipient of numerous awards, he received his Walk of Fame star on August 4, 1994. **QUOTE** "There once was born to immigrant Japanese parents one male child who contracted spinal tuberculosis at age two. The parents were told their son would soon die. Or, at best, never be able to walk. Then, from age nine, medicines and miracles would begin to happen. The kid began to walk—through hospitals, internment camps, high school, young adulthood, the Happy Days of the '50s, the turbulent '60s, three decades of his life's work as an actor/comedian, Academy Award and Emmy nominations, and finally a cherished star of his own on Hollywood's famous Walk of Fame. Not too shabby for a kid whose parents were told he would never walk in his lifetime. Only in America."

H.C. Potter 🎥   6633 Hollywood

Director

BORN Henry "Hank" Codman Potter; Nov. 13, 1904, in New York, NY. **SPOTLIGHTS** Yale-educated, this gentle showman directed stage and screen with equal aplomb. He directed the zany *Hellzapoppin* (1942), with Martha Raye, *The Farmer's Daughter* (1947), starring Loretta Young in an Academy-winning performance, and the original story of the money pit, *Mr. Blandings Builds His Dream House* (1948). Died: 1977.

Jim Henson 📺   6631 Hollywood

Puppeteer, director, producer, creator

Jim Henson

BORN Sept. 24, 1936, in Greenville, MA. **SPOTLIGHTS** Legendary puppeteer. As a child fascinated by visuals on the small screen, Henson knew he wanted to have a career in television. When a local Washington, D.C. station announced an audition for young puppeteers, Henson made a puppet from his mother's old, green spring coat—and won. The teen went on air with "The Junior Morning Show." From there he worked on other local shows, then entered the University of Maryland. During his freshman year he was offered a late evening time slot at WRC-TV, in Washington, D.C. Given freedom to experiment, "Sam and Friends," showcased Henson's technical wizardry complemented by his whimsical story formats. The show introduced the famous frog, Kermit, and the characters were called "The Muppets." The hour-long show won Henson a local Emmy in 1959 for Outstanding Television Entertainment. Still uncertain whether to pursue a lifelong career in puppetry, a vacation in Europe helped him to form a decision. There, Puppet Theater is considered a serious art form. It is enhanced by scenic design and a sophisticated story line, as well as by dishing out social satire. About this realization he observed, "Puppetry is putting a mirror up to ourselves. Just like theater, that's what it's all about. Puppetry gives us the ability to look at ourselves through different perspectives, especially the perspective of humor." During the 1960s the Muppets were appearing on a variety of TV shows, but it was not until 1969 with the advent of "Sesame Street" that the Muppets became a household word. Henson produced the puppet segments for Children's Television Workshop. Aware of the phenomenal influence of television, Henson felt a great need to use it responsibly—to entertain and educate. He stated, "I've seen enough research about violence on TV to believe it doesn't belong there at all. Keep violence off TV as much as possible. It does affect kids. Kids will model their behavior after the violence." With tremendous integrity, Henson modeled the show as if his own children were watching. "Sesame Street" won widespread audiences; its popularity soared to 80 countries. In 1976—with great difficulty—he introduced "The Muppet Show," an entertainment variety program. American network executives thought the premise "too child-oriented for prime time television," and rejected it. But British Lord Lew Grade, a major entertainment figure in Great Britain, backed it and syndicated the show around the world. Within three years more than 235 million viewers watched it in more than 100 countries each week during its five-year run. Henson created other successful family-oriented shows, like "Fraggle Rock" for Home Box Office (HBO). Distributed to more than 90 countries, this entertaining program fostered international understanding and tolerance toward others. Another huge hit is his animated Saturday morning childrens' program, "Muppet Babies." The Oscar-nominated Henson brought the Muppets to the big screen in *The Muppet Movie* (1979), *The Great Muppet Caper* (1981), and *The Muppets Take Manhattan* (1984). His fantasy films, *The Dark Crystal* and *Labyrinth*—with George Lucas—combine unbelievable creations with technological wizardry. **ACHIEVEMENTS** Three Emmys, the prestigious Peabody Award, and a vast collection of international awards and honors for his talent, originality and creativity. Even Miss Piggy would be impressed! **HIGHLIGHTS** The star dedication ceremony took place posthumously on Sept. 24, 1991, on what would have been Henson's 55th birthday. **QUOTE** "Follow your enthusiasm. It's something I've always believed in. Find those parts of your life you enjoy the most. Do what you enjoy doing." Died: 1990.

Perry Como 🔊   6631 Hollywood

Perry Como (seated) and Victor Borge

Singer, actor
BORN Pierino Como; May 18, 1912, in Canonsburg, PA. **SPOTLIGHTS** A hair cutter, the ambitious Como had his own three-chair barber shop by age 15. A friend urged him to take a day off and audition for Frank Carlone's band. He won the job, dropped his scissors and toured for three years. He joined Ted Weems' orchestra as a vocalist in 1937, but when Weems' enlisted in the military for WWII, the group disbanded. Como picked up his scissors and began cutting hair again. CBS called. He moved to New York. Como did a few bits in radio, worked the nightclub circuit, and recorded a few songs. Hollywood put him in a handful of movies, including *Something for the Boys* (1944), *Doll Face* (1946), and *If I'm Lucky* (1946). He was the first recording artist to have two songs reach two million in sales simultaneously: "Till the End of Time," and a tune from Rodgers and Hammerstein's musical, *Carousel*, called "If I Loved You." The year was 1945. He had numerous multi-million selling records, including "Hubba Hubba Hubba," "Lili Marlene," and "Temptation." Yet, his greatest claim to fame came via television. Kraft Foods signed him to a whopping $25,000,000 deal for 66 shows over the course of two years. When Como inked the deal in 1959, it was the biggest contract in television history to date, and far surpassed what Frank Sinatra or Eddie Fisher had been offered. He hosted "The Kraft Music Hall," the most popular musical variety show of the late 1950s and early '60s. Television's "Mr. Nice Guy" enjoyed widespread appeal to pony-tailed bobby-soxers and adults alike. About the show's success "Mr. C"

chuckled, "It's like shooting craps with the dice loaded. I guess we've proven that we've got the right formula." Como possessed a warm, sweet, round, velvety baritone voice, and performed in a low-keyed, relaxed style. Audience favorites include "Catch a Falling Star," "Wanted," "And I Love You So," "Dream On," "Little Dreamer," and "Moon River." His holiday specials were set in interesting spots around the world. "It's Impossible" to say enough about one of the world's most successful crooners. **ACHIEVEMENTS** Emmys: 1954, 1955, 1957, 1959. Grammy: 1958. **QUOTE** "I'm convinced it doesn't matter what you do or even how you sing. People have to like you as a person first. If they like you, you're in. When they stop liking you as a person, you're gone."

Jerry Lee Lewis ●   6631 Hollywood

Singer, songwriter
BORN Sept. 29, 1935, in Ferriday, LA. **SPOTLIGHTS** A pioneer of rock 'n' roll, his beginnings were humble. As an eight-year-old child, his natural musical abilities became apparent when he tinkered on a friend's piano, then played a recognizable version of "Silent Night." His parents realized he "had a God-given gift" and mortgaged their house to buy a piano for him at age nine. He rose to international fame during the 1950s with his rendition of "Whole Lotta Shakin' Going On" (1957).

It became a #1 hit on the pop, country, and rhythm-and-blues charts. It is one of the biggest-selling records in the history of the recording industry. Next came "Great Balls of Fire," selling more than 25 million records and becoming the first disc to go "Gold" in 1958. He appears in the all-star musical motion picture *Jamboree* (1957), where the highlight is his singing "Great Balls of Fire." Other rock 'n' roll hits: "Breathless," "It'll Be Me," "Rockin' My Life Away," "Me and Bobby McGee," "Drinking Wine Spo-Dee O'Dee," and "High School Confidential." With worldwide record sales in excess of 250 million copies, he has appeared on numerous television shows and specials. In the late 1960s he switched to country, and enjoyed a number of hits, including "Middle-Age Crazy," "To Make Love Sweeter For You," "There Must Be More To Love Than This," "Would You Take Another Chance On Me," "Chantilly Lace," and "Thirty-Nine and Holding." Classic country and rock hits total more than 60, and 100 albums. **ACHIEVEMENTS** His songs literally went to the moon in 1969, placed in a time capsule by NASA's Apollo astronauts, Neil Armstrong, Buzz Aldrin and Michael Collins. Lewis is one of the original inductees in the Rock and Roll Hall of Fame in 1986. He received his star on the Hollywood Walk of Fame on June 13, 1989, in conjunction with the motion picture based on his life. The movie, *Great Balls of Fire!* (1989), stars Dennis Quaid (playing Lewis), Winona Ryder and Alec Baldwin, with

Dennis Quaid (left), Johnny Grant, Jerry Lee Lewis (center, holding star plaque), Steve Allen and Bill Welsh

Lewis himself on the soundtrack. **HIGHLIGHTS** Lewis used to call everybody "the Killer." The nickname stuck to him for his wild antics onstage. He also bears the title of "The Greatest Live Show on Earth" (featured on two of his albums).

Tex Ritter    6631 Hollywood

Singer, actor
BORN Woodward Maurice Ritter; Jan. 12, 1905 in rural Murvaul, TX. **SPOTLIGHTS** The Ritters were homesteaders of public land before the Battle of the Alamo. This pioneer family was active in local politics and law enforcement. Influenced more by Southern music than Western, he loved to perform cowboy songs, but decided to pursue a legal career. He kept active in the Glee Club and drama while attend-

Tex Ritter

ing the University of Texas, and met two professors doing a serious research project into cowboy songs. Inspired by their theories, he studied American folk music, Western folklore and the history of Texas and the Southwest. He began presenting a true cowboy song and lecture program. He also sang on a weekly program over Houston's KPRC Radio, then just before graduation won a minor role in a Broadway show. He left college one course shy of finishing his law degree. His move to New York also provided him with a new name—Tex. He worked onstage and in radio, playing a key role as writer and performer in the original "Lone Ranger" series. Tex made his screen debut in 1936 in *Song of the Gringo*, as a singing cowboy. He stars in 78 movies astride his fiery steed White Flash, and was named among the top 10 best money-making Western actors from 1937-'41. He was so popular that *Capitol Records altered corporate policty in 1942 by signing him as their first country artist*. Hits include: "I'm Wasting My Tears on You," "Jingle, Jangle, Jingle," "Rye Whiskey," "Have I Stayed Away Too Long," "Deck of Cards," and "I Dreamed I Was in Hillbilly Heaven." His rendition of "Do Not Forsake Me," the theme song from the classic Western masterpiece, *High Noon,* became a crossover pop hit. **ACHIEVEMENTS** He is the only person to be elected to both the Cowboy Hall of Fame and Country Music Hall of Fame. Inducted into the Country Music Hall of Fame in 1964, his plaque reads: "One of America's most illustrious and versatile stars of radio, television, records, motion pictures and the Broadway stage. Untiring pioneer and champion of the Country and Western music industry, his devotion to his God, his family and his

country is a continuing inspiration to his countless friends throughout the world." His son is actor John Ritter. This legendary cowboy died in 1974.

John Ritter   6631 Hollywood

John Ritter

Actor, host
BORN Sept. 17, 1948, in Burbank, CA. **SPOTLIGHTS** A natural born talent, he is the son of the fabled Western film star and country music legend, Tex Ritter (see bio above). He attended Hollywood High School, then graduated from the University of Southern California with a major in Drama and a minor in Psychology. Active on the stage in "Love Letters," "The Glass Menagerie," "Forty Carats," and "The Tempest," among others,

he received critical praise for his work. Still, the actor came to national prominence starring as Jack Tripper in TV's "Three's Company" (1977-'84). He hit a home run with his impeccable comic delivery, winning an Emmy Award and millions of fans worldwide. Audiences remain affectionate toward Ritter's likable personality. An all-around actor, he has starred capably in more than 20 TV movies, in a variety of genres, including "Unnatural Causes," "The Dreamer of Oz," "Montana," and "A Child's Wish," featuring a special appearance by President Clinton. He has hosted a series of prime time specials like NBC's highly rated "The World's Greatest Magic." He also appeared in Henry Winkler's outstanding Showtime cable series, "Dead Man's Gun." Motion pictures include *Skin Deep* (1989), *Problem Child* (1990), *Noises Off* (1992), *North* (1994)*, Sling Blade* (1997), and *Bride of Chucky* (1998). In 1999-2000, he teamed with Henry Winkler again; this time they co-starred in Neil Simon's record-breaking comedy "The Dinner Party," directed by John Rando...His Hollywood Walk of Fame ceremony took place on Sept. 28, 1983. Ritter is one of America's most appealing personalities and one of the country's favorite actors.

Fred Zinnemann   6627 Hollywood

Director
BORN April 29, 1907, in Vienna, Austria. **SPOTLIGHTS** He stunned the world by making *The Search* (1948), the first movie shot in Germany after WWII. Starring Montgomery Clift, it is an interesting study in its semi-documentary style. His breakthrough Western, *High Noon* (1952), employed the real time of 85 minutes to match the 85 minutes retiring marshall Will Kane (Gary Cooper) sweats it out while waiting to confront an outlaw gang bent on killing him. He bril-

liantly adapted the classic Rodgers and Hammerstein musical *Oklahoma!* (1955) starring Shirley Jones, Gordon MacRae and Rod Steiger. It has a fabulous score and stylized dance numbers by the innovative choreographer Agnes de Mille. For the first time ever in a musical, Miss de Mille integrated dance with story. He followed up with Audrey Hepburn in *The Nun's Story* (1959). He directed so many good pictures, among them the true story, *Julia* (1977) starring Jane Fonda and Vanessa Redgrave. **ACHIEVEMENTS** Out of 21 pictures, he had seven nominations for Best Director. He won a 1938 Oscar for *That Mothers Might Live*; a 1953 Oscar for *From Here to Eternity*; and a 1966 Oscar for *A Man For All Seasons*. **QUOTE** "I've been called a 'sensitive' director, and I think that's a dirty word. I don't like being labeled. I did *The Search* (a picture about a G.I. caring for a concentration camp child), and *The Men* (a picture about paraplegics). Because of these pictures I was called a sensitive director. I discovered it's like having leprosy. Then I did *High Noon* and *From Here to Eternity*, both were very dramatic. No director is taken seriously in the industry until he makes pictures that make money. *High Noon* and *Eternity* did. After that I was a Director." Died: 1997.

Jimi Hendrix 💿   6627 Hollywood

Jimi Hendrix

Musician, songwriter, singer
BORN James Marshall Hendrix; Nov. 27, 1942, in Seattle, WA. **SPOTLIGHTS** One of rock's few true originals and one of the most influential rock artists of all time. Born of African, Native American Cherokee, and Irish ancestry, as a child Jimi taught himself how to play the guitar by listening to the great blues guitarists such as Muddy Waters and B.B. King. By age 12, he was playing for local bands in exchange for hamburgers and Coca-Cola. By 1963 he was on the "chitlin circuit" as backup guitarist, picking up work where he could find it—with Little Richard, the Isley Brothers, Wilson Pickett, King Curtis, Jackie Wilson, and many others. Hendrix formed his own group (Jimi James and the Blue Flames) in 1965 playing in coffee houses in Greenwich Village, New York. The following year in London, England, the retooled band became the Jimi Hendrix Experience. Their first song "Hey Joe" was a #6 hit in the United Kingdom. When Paul McCartney of the Beatles fame heard Hendrix play, he insisted he perform at the rock 'n' roll Monterey Pop Festival, in California. As McCartney knew he would, Jimi exploded onto the international music scene in 1967 at the festival, burning his name as well as his guitar into the pantheon of rock guitarists. (This concert,

filmed as *Monterey Pop*, features outstanding performances by Hendrix, Otis Redding, Janis Joplin, and The Who.) Hendrix expanded the limits of the electric guitar with his phenomenal innovation by combining driving rhythm with electronic feedback. His controlled, fluid technique and phenomenal talent have—to date—not been duplicated. Revered by his peers, his reputation remains as one of the greatest of all time. His rendition of "The Star Spangled Banner" at Woodstock (1969) set the tone for an entire generation. Classic hard rock songs include "Purple Haze," and "Foxy Lady." His tender ballads include "The Wind Cries Mary" and "Little Wing." Yet Hendrix did not forget his deeply blues-rooted soul. His songs "Red House" and "Voodoo Chile" are his eerie blues recordings. Albums include *Are You Experienced?*, *Axis: Bold As Love*, *Electric Ladyland*, *Smash Hits*, *The Cry of Love*, and *Hendrix Band of Gypsys*. **ACHIEVEMENTS** A genius, he changed the face of popular music forever. His name is synonymous with rock guitar playing, and his influence is acknowledged far and wide. Although "the establishment" perceived of Hendrix as an unpatriotic hippie, he enlisted in the U.S. Army in 1959 and received an honorable discharge in 1961 after sustaining parachuting injuries. **HIGHLIGHTS** His theatrical performing style included the left-handed Hendrix playing a right-handed Fender Stratocaster upside down, and picking with his teeth. As Hendrix himself put it, "'Scuse Me While I Kiss the Sky." This legendary talent died in London in 1970.

Art Carney 📺   6627 Hollywood

Art Carney (left) and Jackie Gleason

Actor
BORN Arthur William Matthew Carney; Nov. 4, 1918, in Mount Vernon, NY. **SPOTLIGHTS** He spent a lifetime as best friend and second banana to "The Great One," Jackie Gleason, during the Golden Age of television. Gleason personally selected Carney for the actor's unique approach in underplaying a scene, and his naturalism in comedy. The soft-spoken Carney appeared on "The Jackie Gleason Show" (1952-'57, 1966-'70), and "The Honeymooners" (1955-'56). He was immortalized in the latter, as Ed Norton, a cheerful, naive "underground sanitation worker." About the classic show, Gleason said, "I couldn't do it without Art Carney." Earlier, he had quit his busy career in radio and nightclubs--doing impressions and stand-up comedy--to enlist in the Army. Sent overseas, he was hit by shrapnel in combat at Normandy's Omaha Beach landing. His slight limp was caused by that WWII

injury. Postwar, he became an accomplished Broadway performer, in both comedy and drama. Movies include *The Yellow Rolls-Royce* (1964), *A Guide for the Married Man* (1967), *Firestarter* (1984), *The Muppets Take Manhattan* (1984), and *Last Action Hero* (1993). **ACHIEVEMENTS** 1974 Best Actor Academy Award for *Harry and Tonto*. Emmys: 1953, 1954, and 1955. Special Emmys, 1967 and 1968. **QUOTE** "He (Gleason) turned out to be a delightful companion. We didn't discuss anything serious—no politics, no religion, no philosophy, nothing about our families. When Gleason was partying, it was all frivolous and fun talk, trying to top each other. He was very good at that."

Enrico Caruso 6625 Hollywood

Enrico Caruso

Opera singer
BORN Feb. 25, 1873, in Naples, Italy. **SPOTLIGHTS** Born to poverty-stricken parents, he was the first to survive out of 18 children. Although the horrid conditions of his birthplace would seem like he was destined for anything but an exalted position in life, Caruso became one of the world's greatest tenors and one of the most famous opera singers in history. What made Caruso one of the greatest tenors of all time? As Rossini stated, "Opera is voice, voice and more voice." His outstanding musical instrument set standards that even today's supreme tenors—such as Luciano Pavarotti—cede to. Back at the turn of the century Caruso became the first opera star to record, and the single biggest selling recording artist. This had come about when Fred Gaisberg, a talent scout for the Gramophone Company, heard Caruso perform at La Scala in 1902 and negotiated a deal: the tenor would record ten arias to piano accompaniment for 100 Italian lira (about 500 U.S. dollars). It would take place in one afternoon only, as that is all the time the singer could spare. Gramophone's London head office sent a telegram to their scout reading: "FEE EXORBITANT. FORBID YOU TO RECORD." Gaisberg decided to record that incredible voice anyway—no matter if it cost him his job. And although Caruso was not yet famous, the disc made a bundle. After Caruso made his 1903 debut at the Metropolitan Opera in *Rigoletto,* his voice could be heard on the popular Victrola. The construction of those wind-up, 12-inch players perfectly mated Caruso's voice with its machinery, making it sound as vibrant as if he were performing in your own parlor. In America alone, no self-respecting family would go without a Victrola and a set of Carusos. He was the first artist to sell a million records. In 1916 he recorded the classic "O Sole Mio." In his mastery of music he was tender, yet aggressive, an outstanding artist singing in almost 50 lyric and spinto tenor

roles. In private life, he was loving, thoughtful and polite. **HIGHLIGHTS** The movie based on his life, *The Great Caruso* (1951), stars Mario Lanza. (See Lanza's bio in this book.) Another great singer, Elvis Presley, watched this movie half a dozen times and collected Caruso's recordings. **QUOTE** When asked by a reporter what he thought of Babe Ruth, Caruso replied, "I do not know, as unfortunately I have never heard her sing." The legendary tenor died in his prime in 1921.

Angela Lansbury 🎥 6623 Hollywood

Angela Lansbury

Actress, singer
BORN Oct. 16, 1925, in England. **SPOTLIGHTS** This lovely, porcelain-skinned actress turned in a perfect performance in her movie debut, *Gaslight* (1944)--in an Oscar-nominated performance. The following year, Lansbury could be described as divine in the intriguing, elegant drama, *The Picture of Dorian Gray.* She received her second Oscar nomination. Then, the talent had fun in the Wild West musical, *Harvey Girls* (1946), where she leads her free spirited saloon girls against Judy Garland's ladylike gathering. In *The Long Hot Summer* (1958) she appears in an all-star cast with Paul Newman, Joanne Woodward, and Orson Welles. *The Manchurian Candidate* (1962) was her third Oscar-nominated performance. She was one of the charming voices in Disney's animated *Beauty and the Beast* (1991). **TV** She played mystery writer/sleuth Jessica Fletcher in the long-running, popular series "Murder, She Wrote." Lansbury was nominated multiple times for an Emmy for her starring role, and the program enjoyed a 12-year-run on CBS starting in 1984. She has made several excellent movies-for-television—always with interesting themes and strong characters—including "Mrs. Santa Claus" (1996). **ACHIEVEMENTS** Her multifaceted career spans more than 50 years and includes countless honors. Lansbury is the recipient of four Tony Awards and the Screen Actors Guild Life Achievement Award. She has generously given to the American Red Cross and the Salvation Army.

Margaret Whiting 6623 Hollywood

Singer, actress
BORN July 22, 1926, in Detroit, MI. **SPOTLIGHTS** "Born with a silver tuning fork in her hand," she is the daughter of acclaimed songwriter Richard Whiting (of "Hooray for Hollywood" fame.) She once wrote, "Our house was filled with musicians and movie stars." When Johnny Mercer, a Capitol Records co-founder, came to their house, he asked the 18-year-old teen to sing one of her father's songs on their label.

"My Ideal" sold one million copies and turned Margaret Whiting into a household name. Other hit songs include "Swinging on a Star," "Moonlight in Vermont," "Come Rain or Come Shine," and "It Might as Well Be Spring." Popular radio vocalist: "Club Fifteen" with Bob Crosby and "The Eddie Cantor Show." TV: Co-starred in the sitcom, "Those Whiting Girls" (1955-'57--the summer replacement for "I Love Lucy"), opposite her real-life sister Barbara Whiting.

Drew Pearson 📷   6623 Hollywood

Newscaster, columnist, actor

BORN Andrew Pearson; Dec. 13, 1897, in Evanston, IL. **SPOTLIGHTS** A columnist/investigative reporter, Pearson worked for the *Baltimore Sun* in the early 1930s, while his partner, Robert Allen worked with the *Christian Science Monitor*. With great instinct, they dug up the incredible stories of the day. Often their papers refused to print the articles, so the pair assembled their hottest stories into a book, *Washington Merry-Go-Round*. Although they had taken every precaution, including having it published anonymously, they were found out and fired. United Features picked them up and syndicated their new column, "Merry-Go-Round." Radio quickly followed in 1935. Allen went off to the war, while Pearson stayed on radio through 1953. His individualized reporting style was prophetic. "I predict ..." Died: 1969.

J. M. Kerrigan 🎥   6621 Hollywood

Actor

BORN Dec. 16, 1887, in Dublin, Ireland. **SPOTLIGHTS** A stage and screen star, his career spanned the silent era through the talkies. Films: *Merely Mary Ann* (1931), *Gone With the Wind* (1939), *Mr. Lucky* (1943), *Black Beauty* (1946), *The Luck of the Irish* (1948), *My Cousin Rachel* (1952), and *20,000 Leagues Under the Sea* (1954). Died: 1964.

Buster Keaton 🎥   6621 Hollywood

Comedian, screenwriter, director

BORN Joseph Keaton; Oct. 4, 1895, in Piqua, KS. **SPOTLIGHTS** One of the giants of the silent screen, he was known as the Great Stone Face. His specialty was being able to survive adversity with amazing patience—no matter how crazy the circumstance. A master of comic timing, this brilliant, agile talent came from a vaudeville family who traveled the circuit with Harry Houdini. In fact, it was Houdini who nicknamed the six-year-old after the boy fell down a flight of stairs. The great illusionist turned to Keaton's father and remarked: "That was some buster your baby took!" From then on, little Joseph was known as "Buster." Visited pal "Fatty" Arbuckle shooting *The Butcher Boy* (1917) and wound up in the film. Extremely gifted, this soulful-eyed artist started in shorts and progressed to feature length films. His comedies far surpassed slapstick, they were witty, creative, and even beautiful. A few of his well-

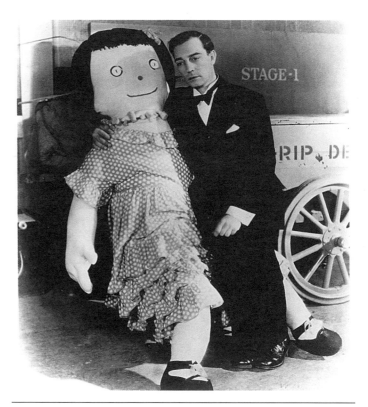

Buster Keaton

loved classics—in which he either starred, wrote, or directed, or worked in all three capacities—include *The Three Ages* (1923), *Our Hospitality* (1923), *Sherlock Jr.* (1924), *The Navigator* (1924), *Seven Chances* (1925), *Go West* (1925), and *The General* (1927—considered his best film). In the latter, he is a confederate engineer who rescues his beloved train from the Yankees during the Civil War. In all, he made hundreds of pictures. *The Great Chase* (1963) compiles fun and exciting chase scenes from his many of his silents. **ACHIEVEMENTS** 1959 Special Oscar. **HIGHLIGHTS** Keaton refused to use stunt men, but still performed what is considered the best stunt of the silent era. In *Steamboat Bill, Jr.* (1928), a front of a house—weighing an astounding 4,000 pounds—falls on top of him; he is spared only by an open window. **QUOTE** "Pie-throwing is not only a matter of the quantity thrown, but a matter of the quality. I not only was the champion pie-thrower, I am the champ." About the art of getting a laugh, Keaton observed, "The audience wants his comic to be human, not clever." Died: February 1, 1966, on Hollywood's 79th Birthday.

Peter Lorre 🎥   6619 Hollywood

Actor

BORN Laszlo Lowenstein; June 26, 1904, in Hungary. **SPOTLIGHTS** Lorre portrayed the maniac—sleepy-eyed psychopaths—like no one ever had ever dreamed (or nightmared). Motion pictures include *M* (1931—in Germany), *The Man Who Knew Too Much* (1934), *Mad Love* (1935), *Crime and Punishment* (as Raskolnikov), *The Maltese Falcon* (1941—in a quasi-comedy role, and cast opposite Sidney Greenstreet; they appear in a number of films together), *Casablanca* (1942), *The*

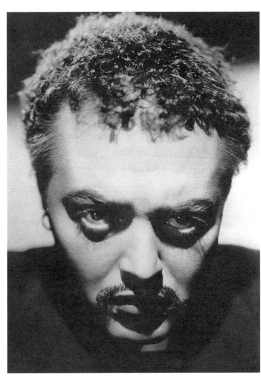

Mask of Dimitrios (1944), *Arsenic and Old Lace* (1944), *Confidential Agent* (1945), *The Verdict* (1946), and *The Big Circus* (1959), to list a few of his 125 film credits, spanning 40 years. He did play against type in a series of *Mr. Moto* detective films (in the same vein as the *Charlie Chan* series, and just as much fun,

Peter Lorre: "He was the vilest of villains on the screen; he was the little man of gigantic crimes."

with Lorre's unique twist). This small, bug-eyed, sinister-looking performer remained one of Hollywood's busiest actors, often working in two to three different pictures at the same time. Lorre's criminal characterizations have left an indelible record. **QUOTE** "I suppose when you win a reputation for doing a certain thing well, no one thinks of asking you to do anything else. At any rate, I don't mind being bad in films, so long as I'm thought good at it." Died: 1964.

Wallace Reid 🎥   6617 Hollywood

Actor, director, screenwriter

Wallace Reid

BORN William W. Reid; April 15, 1891, in St. Louis, MO. **SPOTLIGHTS** This lovable, charming and self-effacing leading man was a #1 box office star. Women threw themselves at his feet. He acted in and/or directed 100 shorts, and had historic participation in D.W. Griffith's *The Birth of a Nation* (1915) and De Mille's *Joan the Woman* (1917). *Valley of the Giants*, *The Lottery Man* (both 1919), *Nice People*, and *Clarence* (both 1922) were a few of his many hits. **TREND**

SETTER Wally was the first actor to wear a soft white shirt—instead of the stiff, three-inch high Errol collar that men of the Victorian era wore. It caused such a stir that the manufacturers of the Errol collar ran to the Motion Picture Producers' Association: "Can't you get Wally Reid to wear a starched collar? All the collar plants are being put out of business." Hollywood answered: "Well, why don't you manufacturer soft white shirts?" They did, and the stiff, high Errol collar was fashion history. Died: 1923.

Billie Burke 🎥   6617 Hollywood

Actress

Billie Burke

BORN Mary Burke; Aug. 7, 1885, in Washington, DC. **SPOTLIGHTS** This pretty stage actress moved to the West Coast to play "bird-witted ladies" in films for $10,000 a week. And, as she often said, "That ain't chicken feed." She was immortalized playing a role that was her personal favorite—that of Glinda the Good Witch in *The Wizard of Oz* (1939). She was the classic screwball in *Topper* (1937), and its sequel, *Topper Returns* (1940), opposite Roland Young. She was terrific in *The Young in Heart* (1938)—voted one of the ten best pictures of the year. Burke was superb in the comedy *The Cheaters* (1945). She was charming in *Father of the Bride* (1950), and its sequel *Father's Little Dividend* (1951). In *Three Husbands* (1950), her suspicious husband tries to determine if she has strayed, after receiving a mysterious letter from a deceased seducer. She appears in more than 100 motion pictures. **HIGHLIGHTS** Married former employer, showman Florenz Ziegfeld, in 1914. **QUOTE** "I have always been called Billie Burke except for those eighteen improbable glittering years when I was also Mrs. Florenz Ziegfeld, Jr. I find Billie a perfectly adequate name for the skitter-witted ladies I play on the screen today, and it suits me, too, because I might as well confess here and now that I am not always saner than I seem." Died: 1970.

Norman Lear 📺   6615 Hollywood

Writer, director, producer

BORN Norman Milton Lear; July 27, 1922, in New Haven, CT. **SPOTLIGHTS** Over 120,000,000 Americans—more than half the nation's population—have watched the television shows of Norman Lear. Generations of fans can instantly match character Archie Bunker with his favorite catchphrase—"stifle yourself." "All in the Family" was brought to America with compliments from producer Lear in 1971; it

Norman Lear

broke all entertainment's rules and stunned the country with its realistic look at life. But Lear had a gigantic success. Within a few months of airing, this controversial sitcom became a #1 hit, and held onto its top position for a solid five years. Thereafter, it remained a popular staple until its conclusion in 1983. (It runs in syndication today.) Paddy Chayefsky—stage, TV, and Academy Award-winning film dramatist—summed up Lear's remarkable conquest, "Norman Lear took television away from dopey wives and dumb fathers, from the pimps, hookers, hustlers, private eyes, junkies, cowboys and rustlers that constituted television chaos and in their place he put the American people. He took the audience and put them on the set." A partial listing of Lear's other television credits are: "Sanford & Son," "Maude," "Good Times," "The Jeffersons," "Mary Hartman, Mary Hartman," and the dramatic series, "Palmerstown, U.S.A." Lear is very proud of the latter. It was a special collaboration with Pulitzer Prize-winning author Alex Haley. Lear is also a motion picture producer. His first film coincided with playwright's Neil Simon's debut move to the silver screen with *Come Blow Your Horn* (1963), starring Frank Sinatra. In 1967 his original screenplay for *Divorce American Style* earned him an Academy Award nomination. Other films include *Stand By Me* (1986), *The Princess Bride* (1987), and *Fried Green Tomatoes* (1991). **ACHIEVEMENTS** Recipient of countless awards, he was one of the first to be inducted into the Television Hall of Fame. In 1977 he received the prestigious Mark Twain Award for being "Mark Twain's successor as America's most delightful humorist, gentle depicter of the virtues and weaknesses of humanity with humor's paintbrush." That same year he received the Peabody Award, for "establishing (with 'All in the Family') the right to express social comment in a social comedy, for devising the technique of humor as a bridge to better understanding of national issues, for providing an excellent production in every way and for providing the public with the greatest of all healers—humor. He received a second Peabody in 1985 for his compelling dramatic special, "Heartsounds." Winner of four Emmys. He is also noted for his activism on behalf of worldwide human rights. In 1980 he formed People for the American Way, a national, nonpartisan constitutional liberties organization. **QUOTE** "I consider myself a writer who loves to show real people in real conflict with all their fears, doubts, hopes and ambitions rubbing against their love for one another."

César Romero 🎥 6615 Hollywood

Actor

César Romero

BORN Feb. 15, 1907, in New York, NY. **SPOTLIGHTS** Known as "the dashing Latin from Manhattan," he came from an affluent family of Cuban émigrés. Romero possessed a natural elegance, as well as eloquence. This handsome, mustached, actor appears in 100 motion pictures—often as the leading man—including *The Thin Man* (1934), *The Good Fairy, Cardinal Richelieu, Diamond Jim* (all 1935), *Dangerously Yours* (1937), *Wee Willie Winkie* (1937), *The Little Princess* (1939), *Return of the Cisco Kid* (1939), *Charlie Chan at Treasure Island* (1939), *Captain from Castille* (1947), and *Crooks and Coronets* (1969). Immortalized as the villainous, maniacal Joker, in the campy 1960s TV series "Batman" (1966-'68). Died: 1994.

Lawrence Welk 💿 6613 Hollywood

Band leader, accordionist
BORN March 11, 1903, in Strasburg, ND. **SPOTLIGHTS**: His parents immigrated to America, and were homesteaders of public land. They turned the real estate into the family's farmland in North Dakota, in 1893. Lawrence was the sixth born of eight children, who were loved dearly, but not educated, and spoke only German. Since his family feared he would learn "worldly ways" if he pursued his musical ambitions, he stayed on the farm until he reached age 21. Without speaking any English, and with only a third grade education, Welk left with his accordion in tow, to seek his fame and fortune. He started off touring with the Lawrence Welk Novelty Orchestra, then formed The Hotsy Totsy Orchestra. He broadcast from his home state with the latter. He became a popular recording artist with such high sellers as "Bubble in

Phil Harris (left), Andy Williams and Lawrence Welk (right)

Wine," and "Sparkling Strings." About his albums, Welk stated, "Basically I'm a musician." He instructed his producer and arranger to: "Watch the lyrics. When children are listening, I don't want to give them a smutty thought." He made the move to television with his orchestra in "Lawrence Welk's Top Tunes and New Talent" and "The Lawrence Welk Show." Tall and upright, with a grand smile and possessing a spirit of gaiety, Welk introduced viewers to his show with: "Ah-one an' ah-two." And when he addressed them, he called them "Folks." His odd, charming pronunciation of the English language endeared him to American audiences. Welk's signature catchphrase "Wunnerful, wunnerful," delighted TV fans for 27 years (1955-'82). (The show still runs in syndication.) The maestro's "champagne music" bubbled with enthusiasm, with emphasis on muted horns and strings, simple arrangements and melody. His music ran the gamut from hymn singing, tap and ballroom dancing, from Porter to polka to pop, in "a good, wholesome, all-American style." His most enchanting and romantic classic was "Anniversary Waltz." He achieved all his heart desired: a musical career his parents could be proud of, a devoted wife and children, and a multimillion-dollar entertainment conglomerate. He was known within the industry for paying his musicians some of the highest salaries on record. An eternal optimist, he even gave them pep talks when they were blue. For himself, he insisted on being happy and working at it daily. And, although famous for his "champagne music," Welk never touched the stuff. He was a teetotaler...His car's California license plate read: NA1NA2. **QUOTE** *Variety* dubbed him "a genius in schmaltz." He responded, "My music is not sophisticated, or new, or clever, or smart, but everyone can understand it. You have to show a little friendliness, let's say it that way, and you do the things you know you can do...As long as I stay with my audience, I'm a winner." Died: 1992.

Hugh O'Brian 6613 Hollywood

Hugh O'Brian

Actor
BORN Hugh Krampke; April 19, 1925, in Rochester, NY. **SPOTLIGHTS** A natural born leader, he enlisted in the Marines at 17, then became the youngest drill instructor in the history of the Corps. Inspired by his acting idol, Spencer Tracy, O'Brian went to Hollywood after WWII and appeared—with little satisfaction—in a number of minor roles. It was not until he was cast as the legendary Marshal of Tombstone (Arizona), that he felt any personal reward in acting. For male viewers, this meant he was sharpshooter Wyatt Earp with a pair of matching .45 pistols.

For the opposite sex, he was tall, dark and handsome, as the dashing, romantic Marshal in "The Life and Legend of Wyatt Earp" (1955-'61). He enjoyed the largest female audience for any TV Western series. About those statistics, O'Brian wryly stated, "Well, I don't know of any other Western that advertises a shampoo." He made 58 motion pictures including *Little Big Horn* (1951) with Lloyd Bridges, *The Man from the Alamo* (1953) opposite Glenn Ford, *There's No Business Like Show Business* (1954) with Marilyn Monroe, Donald O'Connor, Ethel Merman and Dan Dailey, *Broken Lance* (1954) co-starring Spencer Tracy, *Ten Little Indians* (1965), and *The Shootist* (1976) with John Wayne, Lauren Bacall, and Ron Howard. **HIGHLIGHTS** His longtime friend, John Wayne, refereed O'Brian's first boxing match for the U.S. Marine Corps. **ACHIEVEMENTS** Inspired by Albert Schweitzer (winner of 1952 Nobel Peace Prize on behalf of the "Brotherhood of Nations"), he founded "HOBY," the Hugh O'Brian youth leadership in 1958. This international organization (headquartered in Westwood, California) is devoted to developing the leadership qualities in teenagers. Due to the generosity of corporate sponsors and public donations, there is no cost to the student, the parent, or the school. At present, 14,500 high schools participate in the HOBY seminar programs. Visit their website (www.hoby.org). **QUOTE** "I believe every person is created as the steward of his or her own destiny with great power for a specific purpose: to share with others, through service, a reverence for life in a spirit of love."

Mildred Dunnock 6613 Hollywood

Character actress
BORN Jan. 25, 1906, in Baltimore, MD. **SPOTLIGHTS** In high school she discovered her love of drama and planned a career in the theater. Her parents thought otherwise; she graduated from Johns Hopkins and had a teaching career before she dared the stage. Admirers of American literature are thankful she did. Such great writers as Arthur Miller, Tennessee Williams and Lillian Hellman were thrilled with her personas—including that of the long-suffering, loyal wife of Willy Loman in the classic tragedy *Death of a Salesman*, Big Mama in *Cat on a Hot Tin Roof*, and Lavinia in *Another Part of the Forest*. She gave as much to her audiences in regional theater, as she did on Broadway, and in film. She later taught at the Yale Drama School, Harvard University and Barnard College. **ACHIEVEMENTS** Oscar-nominated for two films: *Death of a Salesman* (1951), and *Baby Doll* (1956). During her lifetime, she was recognized and honored as an American theatrical institution. Died: 1991.

James Whitmore 6611 Hollywood

Actor
BORN Oct. 1, 1921, in White Plains, NY. **SPOTLIGHTS** Educated at an Ivy League school, he joined the Yale Drama School Players, and helped establish that university's radio station. He enlisted in the Marines, and bravely served during

James Whitmore

WWII. After his honorable discharge, this stocky, curly-haired, solid actor made his 1947 Broadway debut in "Command Decision." Whitmore made his screen debut in *The Undercover Man* (1949). He was Oscar-nominated in *Battleground* (1949), his second film. Other motion pictures include *The Asphalt Jungle* (1950), *The Next Voice You Hear* (1950--as a man who hears God on the radio), *It's a Big Country* (1951), *Them!* (1954; a classic sci-fi monster movie about giant ants), *The Command* (1954--the first Western shot in CinemaScope), *Battle Cry* (1955), *Black Like Me* (1964), *Planet of the Apes* (1968), *Guns of the Magnificent Seven* (1969), *Tora! Tora! Tora!* (1970), *Where the Red Fern Grows* (1974), his *tour de force* portrayal of President Truman in *Give 'Em Hell Harry!* (1975--in an Oscar-nominated performance), *Bully* (1978--as President Theodore Roosevelt), *Nuts* (1987), *The Shawshank Redemption* (1994), and *The Relic* (1996). He guest-starred on countless TV shows, then became Abraham Lincoln Jones in "The Law and Mr. Jones" (1960-'62), and Dr. Vincent Campanelli in "Temperatures Rising" (1972-'74). His son, James Whitmore, Jr. is also a noted actor.

Kitty Carlisle 🎥 6611 Hollywood

Singer, actress
BORN Catherine Conn; Sept. 3, 1915, in New Orleans, LA. **SPOTLIGHTS** Reared in Europe, she attended a fine French school studying music, dance and theatre before training at the Royal Academy of Dramatic Arts in London. She won a Hollywood contract in her early 20s and made her screen debut in *Murder at the Vanities* (1934). Her clever performance in the zany *A Night at the Opera* (1935), with Groucho, Chico, and Harpo Marx, was also one of her favorite roles. But she had this to say about television's "To Tell the Truth" quiz show: "It was the most delightful job I ever had." She added, "It was a special talent to be a good panelist. You had to have an enormous range of talent, and the ability to make a joke about virtually anything." **QUOTE** Chairwoman of the New York State Council on the Arts, she declared, "What is it that makes us feel we don't need the arts? Children learn better if they experience the arts."

Mary Martin 🎙 6609 Hollywood

See page 300

Vincent Lopez 🎙 6609 Hollywood

Band leader, composer, lyricist
BORN Dec. 30, 1898. **SPOTLIGHTS** "Hello, everybody. Lopez speaking from the beautiful Hotel Taft in that grand city New York" is how the pioneer radio man greeted listeners. The year was 1921, just one year after the birth of radio and introduction of American commercial broadcasting. About his simple, but danceable music Lopez said, "I don't believe in chasing 'em off the floor, especially when it's time to moon around." Many talented personalities worked with him early on in their careers—Xaviar Cugar, Artie Shaw, and the Dorsey Brothers. His most famous recordings include "Three Sisters," "Does a Duck Like Water," and "Knock, Knock, Who's There?" **QUOTE** Early in his career he rejected such entertainers as Rudy Vallee and Ted Lewis. Then, he became a numerologist. Lopez declared, "In reviewing mistakes like these, I've often felt they might have been avoided if I'd known then what I know now about numerology." He made headlines when—using this mystical approach to luck—he correctly predicted that Arthur Godfrey was destined for a major life change in 1959. Died: 1979.

Jane Wyman 🎥 6607 Hollywood

See page 281

Bonita Granville 🎥 6607 Hollywood

Actress, producer
BORN Feb. 2, 1923, in Chicago, IL. **SPOTLIGHTS** Her grandmother, Maria Brambilla, danced as a prima ballerina in the Ballet Russe de Monte Carlo. Her grandfather, Francis Timponi, conducted at La Scala Opera, in Milan. Her father, Bernard Granville, starred in the Ziegfeld Follies and in Broadway musicals. It seems natural then that this little bundle of genetic abilities would be paired with Laurence Olivier and Ann Harding for her film debut at age seven, in *Westward Passage* (1932). Her innocent looks belied her power as a spiteful schoolgirl in Samuel Goldwyn's *These Three* (1936), in which she was nominated for an Academy Award. Two years later Warners gave her the lead in the *Nancy Drew* series (1938-'39). She took *Strike It Rich* (1948) seriously and married an oil-rich Texan. Later, she

Bonita Granville

produced TV's "Lassie." When not in production, Granville went on nationwide lecture tours espousing the preservation of the environment and of traditional family values—these two themes were consistent topics on "Lassie." Her business acumen cannot be understated. Recipient of awards from the White House, to the Boy Scouts of America. Died: 1988.

Victor Jory 🎥　　6605 Hollywood

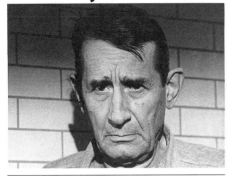
Victor Jory

Actor

BORN Nov. 23, 1902, in Dawson City, AK. **SPOTLIGHTS** In the Coast Guard, Jory was the boxing and wrestling champion. In films, he was the big, menacing villain that audiences loved to "boo." He wore more "black hats" than almost any other character actor. His "bad" face seemed a natural for wicked brutes, which he played in most--but not all--of his more than 100 movies. Films include *State Fair* (1933), *Madame Du Barry* (1934), *A Midsummer Night's Dream* (1935--as King Oberon), *Too Tough to Kill* (1935), *The Adventures of Tom Sawyer* (1937--as Injun Joe), *Dodge City* (1939), *Gone with the Wind* (1939), *Bad Man of Missouri* (1941), *Cave of Outlaws* (1951), *The Man from Alamo* (1953), *The Miracle Worker* (1962), and *Cheyenne Autumn* (1964). His career spanned four decades; his last movie was *Papillon* (1973). Died: 1982.

Marie Wilson 🎥　　6603 Hollywood

Actress

Marie Wilson and Bob Cosby

BORN Katherine Elizabeth Wilson; Dec. 30, 1916, in Anaheim, CA. **SPOTLIGHTS** A buoyant, beautiful, statuesque, wide-eyed talent an expressionless stare. She first gained fame in night clubs with Ken Murray's "Blackouts." Murray described her as "the only girl I know who can stand up in front of an audience and tell jokes." Graduating to radio, screen and television, Wilson baffled everyone as to if she were a wise blonde who plays dumb, or a dumb blonde who succeeded in spite of herself. The consensus bore out that she was smart, but excelled play-

ing dizzy, dumb-dumb dames. She stars with James Cagney in a spoof about the movie business, *Boy Meets Girl* (1938), which also features the future President of the United States, Ronald Reagan. In *The Fabulous Joe* (1947), she competes with a talking dog and a henpecked husband, but still gets her laughs. With her well-practiced verbal ingenuousness, Wilson was the featherbrained lead in *My Friend Irma*, a radio show in 1947, before becoming a 1949 film, and later a TV series (1952-'54). The movie is best known for cinematically introducing the comic duo of Dean Martin and Jerry Lewis. Died: 1972.

Edmund Lowe 📺　　6601 Hollywood

See page 118

George Fitzmaurice 🎥　　6601 Hollywood

Director

BORN Feb. 13, 1885, in Paris. **SPOTLIGHTS** He made idealistic, pictorials during the silent era, with a trend toward realism in the early sound days. *The Son of Sheik* (1926) starring Rudolph Valentino, *The Devil to Pay* (1931) with Ronald Colman, and *As You Desire Me* (1932), with Greta Garbo, are among his movies. **QUOTE** "Hollywood as far as I can see, will always be the home of the motion picture producing industry. It has been my pleasure to experiment and definitely decide whether pictures can be made in other parts of the United States and abroad as effectively from a financial standpoint, as well as from an artistic standpoint. My answer is 'no.' Speaking from a business standpoint, Hollywood is more efficient for us. New York—*and when I say New York I mean every other city*—is entirely unadaptable to our purpose. In Hollywood, the community understands this. It does not expect anyone in the industry that has made it famous to do things as any other businessman would...If you want a thousand people in Hollywood, you can depend on getting them and also know that they will report punctually on location. In New York, the weather is always an uncertainty and often it is necessary to wait until the very morning of the day's work before ordering the crowd to report. If they are instructed to appear the day before, it generally happens that the weather changes and the conditions are such that they have to be sent away, the producer paying salary and expenses...It took years to establish the subsidiary industries and facilities important to motion picture production in Hollywood. There is no reason why the business should go through all this pioneering again elsewhere nor is there any time for it. Hence, Hollywood will always remain the film producing center of the country." Died: 1941.

Melvyn Douglas 📺　　6601 Hollywood

See page 107

*Placido Domingo delivers a powerful,
dramatic performance as Otello.*

*Carmen Miranda (left) and Mickey Rooney
share dancing secrets.*

6565 HOLLYWOOD

Peggy King 🎙   6565 Hollywood

Comedienne, singer
BORN 1931, in Greensburg, PA. **SPOTLIGHTS** A secretary before joining a band, she performed as a regular in radio, then landed a recording contract. She was featured on "The George Gobel Show" (1954-'56).

Clem McCarthy 🎙   6565 Hollywood

Pioneer announcer
BORN Sept. 9, 1882, in Rochester, NY. **SPOTLIGHTS** McCarthy had a hoarse, excitable voice well-suited for early radio in the 1920s. He opened each show with his trademark, "They're off!" This sportscaster knew thoroughbred horse racing inside and out. His aggressive delivery was often imitated by comedians in early broadcast years. Died: 1962.

Danny Kaye 🎥   6563 Hollywood

Danny Kaye

Actor, singer, dancer, mimic
BORN David D. Kaminski; Jan. 18, 1913, in Brooklyn, NY. **SPOTLIGHTS** Kaye was like a wound-up cuckoo clock whose time was immediately following World War II. The tall, thin artist with red-gold hair and a comic-wistful face made his motion picture debut in Goldwyn's *Up in Arms* (1944), then followed with *Wonder Man* (1945). Audiences quickly learned that restraint was not a word in this actor's vocabulary. His biggest movie was *The Secret Life of Walter Mitty* (1947); a film that made the world take notice. Children loved him in the storybook musical *Hans Christian Andersen* (1952), with pretty little songs "The Ugly Duckling," "Thumbelina," and "The Emperor's New Clothes." He did slow down for these tunes. Most often Kaye sang scat, gushing the sounds forth. Every holiday season, *White Christmas* (1952), with Kaye and Bing Crosby, brings the yuletide spirit to melancholy viewers. **ACHIEVEMENTS** 1954 Special Oscar. 1981 Jean Hersholt Humanitarian Award. 1964 Emmy for "The Danny Kaye Show." He was recognized for his unstinting efforts to help needy children worldwide. Kaye traveled 500,000 miles for the U.N. Children's Fund, and more for special UNICEF programs. Died: 1987.

Ruth Etting 🎥   6563 Hollywood

Actress, singer
BORN Nov. 23, 1896, in David City, Nebraska. **SPOTLIGHTS** A popular 1920s torch singer, Etting's career was masterminded by her husband, a scummy small-time mobster named Moe "the Gimp" Schneider. She appeared as the girl vocalist for Paul Whiteman's Orchestra in New York, and enjoyed fame with her recordings on the Columbia label. She became a huge star with the Ziegfeld "Follies" singing a tune Irving Berlin had written "Shaking the Blues Away." Motion pictures include *Ruth Etting Paramount Movietone* (short, 1928), and Ruth Etting, *The Book of Lovers* (short, 1929). She made 30 shorts, and three features through 1936. In the 1930s her radio show had its aural mark of identification—her trademark hit song—"Shine On, Harvest Moon." The musical biography, *Love Me or Leave Me* (1955), was based on her tumultuous life. It stars Doris Day as the manhandled talent, and James Cagney as her vicious lover. The movie's good songs are "Ten Cents a Dance," "I'll Never Stop Loving You," and "Mean to Me." In real life, though, Miss Etting was soft and sensual, not like the cold character portrayed on film. Died: 1978.

Toby Wing 📺   6561 Hollywood

Actress
BORN Martha Wing; July 14, 1913, in Richmond, VA. **SPOTLIGHTS** A gorgeous, vivacious blonde who enjoyed success in *Gold-Diggers of 1933* and *42nd Street* (1933). Retired in 1937 to marry aviator Dick Merrill.

David Butler 🎥   6559 Hollywood

Director, screenwriter
BORN Dec. 17, 1894, in San Francisco, CA. **SPOTLIGHTS** His specialties—musicals and light comedies—were box office hits. Those starring Shirley Temple are classics: *Bright Eyes* (1934)—with the irresistible Temple singing "On the Good Ship Lollipop"; *The Little Colonel* (1935) with Bill "Bojangles" Robinson and Temple in one of cinema's most famous dance sequences—done on the stairs; *The Littlest Rebel* (1935) and *Captain January* (1936). He also did *Kentucky* (1938)—a 1930s take on Romeo and Juliet, which stars Loretta Young (with Walter Brennan winning an Oscar for playing her aristocratic father). *Road to Morocco* (1942) is one of the best "Road" pictures with the Hope-Crosby-Lamour team. *Where's Charley?* (1952) with Ray Bolger is delightful. And, it ain't just "Secret Love" that audiences fell for Butler's *Calamity Jane* starring Doris Day and Howard Keel (1953). Died: 1979.

Ozzie Nelson 📺   6555 Hollywood

See page 252

Gene Barry 🎥   6555 Hollywood

Gene Barry

Actor, singer

BORN Eugene Klass; June 14, 1921, in New York, NY. **SPOTLIGHTS** Born and raised in New York, Gene Barry obtained his start with a singing scholarship at the age of 17. His first theatrical role was in "Pins and Needles," a role which led him on a cross-country tour of America and to join the bright lights of the Great White Way. After its successful run, Barry appeared in operettas, including "New Moon," and "Naughty Marietta," where he sang at Carnegie Hall. His first big break on Broadway came from famed producer Max Reinhardt in the production of "Rosalinda." It opened on 44th Street and ran for several years. He became a famed trouper on the Broadway stage, starring in more than 100 plays and musicals, including "Catherine the Great" starring Mae West, "Glad to See You" by Jules Styne and Sammy Cahn, and "The Would Be Gentleman" produced by Mike Todd. Hollywood beckoned for Barry during a performance of "Idiot's Delight." An agent persuaded him to move West. Barry signed with Paramount Pictures after his first movie, *The Turning Point* (1952) starring William Holden. While at Paramount he played in many films, including his starring role in *War of the Worlds* (1953). Other movies include *Naked Alibi* (1954) with Sterling Hayden, *Soldiers of Fortune* (1955) with Clark Gable, and *Thunder Road* (1958) with Robert Mitchum, to list just a few. A run of television series then took over his career, beginning with the popular Western, "Bat Masterson" (1959-'61). Looking quite the debonair dandy, with a derby hat and gold-topped cane, he battled the bad guys with his wits, not guns. The show was based on the real life of William Bartley "Bat" Masterson, a legendary Old West hero. He played the role with such elegance, sophistication and humor that "the Gene Barry style" became his hallmark. In another series, "Burke's Law" (1963-'66), he played a millionaire homicide detective, who lived in a luxurious mansion and often drove to the crime scene in a glistening Rolls Royce automobile. It became an instant hit. Later his one-man musical "Gene Barry in One," received rave reviews around the world. **ACHIEVEMENTS** Tony Award for the Broadway musical "La Cage Aux Folles." Former first vice-president of the Screen Actors Guild. Served as National Chairman of Multiple Sclerosis and Hope for Hearing Foundation. He received his "Live Theater" star on the Walk of Fame on May, 5, 1988, and is one of only a handful of artists to have achieved a star in that prestigious category. It is a symbol of both public and peer appreciation and remains a permanent monument to the past, as well as to the future...Married for more than 50 years to actress Betty Claire Barry; their union produced two sons and a daughter.

John Cromwell   6555 Hollywood

Director, actor

BORN Elwood Dager; Dec. 23, 1888, in Toledo, OH. **SPOTLIGHTS** He came to Los Angeles at age 40; late by Tinseltown's standards. Cromwell, though, wasted no time in becoming active. He made the family picture *Tom Sawyer* (1930), starring Jackie Coogan and Mitzi Green, then switched to the cruel, gritty revelation *Of Human Bondage* (1934), starring Leslie Howard and Bette Davis. *Little Lord Fauntleroy* (1936) was a charmer starring child actor Freddie Bartholomew. The *Prisoner of Zenda* (1937)—a magical story of a medieval commoner who thwarts a rebel's plot by impersonating his cousin, a kidnapped king—stars dashing Ronald Colman, equally dashing Douglas Fairbanks, Jr., and a terrific Madeleine Carroll. It is one of the best swashbuckler's ever made. Cromwell's *Abe Lincoln in Illinois* (1940), about the 16th President's young life, earned star Raymond Massey an Oscar nomination. *The Enchanted Cottage* (1945) is a touching love story about inner beauty after war disfigures a man. He made the original, non-musical version of *Anna and the King of Siam* (1946), starring Irene Dunne and Rex Harrison. His *Caged* (1950) is generally recognized as the most chilling women's prison picture. He directed *The Goddess* (1957), a drama based on close examination of the Marilyn Monroe phenomenon, scripted by Paddy Chayefsky. Died: 1979.

Jack Klugman   6555 Hollywood

Jack Klugman

Actor

BORN April 27, 1922, Philadelphia, PA. **SPOTLIGHTS** At the conclusion of World War II, the young, energetic soldier decided to follow his lifelong dream of becoming an actor. He used his GI bill to attend Carnegie Tech, in Pittsburgh. With his rough-around-the-edges appearance, gruff voice, and dramatic range from comic to fiendish, Klugman hustled small roles and summer stock parts. In 1949 he landed his first important stage role "Stevedore," with Rod Steiger—who had also trained on the GI bill. In 1952 he got his lucky break on the bright lights of Broadway with his stage debut in "Golden Boy." He followed up with Broadway productions of "Mr. Roberts," "The Odd Couple," and "Gypsy" with Ethel Merman. The performer made the leap to the silver screen in *Timetable* (1956). He proved himself a brilliant actor in *12 Angry Men* (1957), *Cry Terror* (1958), *Days of Wine and Roses* (1962), *Act One* (1962), *Goodbye, Columbus* (1969), and *Dear God* (1996). He became a household name in TV, where he triumphed in the hit comedy series "The Odd Couple" (1970-'75). His hilarious portrayal of the sloppy sportswriter Oscar Madison won him two Emmys and worldwide fame. He scored another home run in the police drama "Quincy M.E." (1976-'83), as a forensic medical examiner. Previously, he won a 1963 Emmy for portraying a blacklisted actor in the "Defenders." In 1998 he celebrated his 50th anniversary in the dramatic arts. **QUOTE** "The only thing that never let me down was acting. That's because I've never let it down."

James Dunn ⚊ 6555 Hollywood

See page 510

The Smothers Brothers ⚊ 6555 Hollywood

Comics, comedy team

Tom (left) and Dick Smothers

BORN Tom Smothers, Feb. 2, 1937; Dick Smothers, Nov. 20,1937, both born in Governor's Island, NY. **SPOTLIGHTS** Starting in the 1950s as wacky folk musicians, their immense popularity fueled concerts, film, television, and their roles as masters of ceremonies. "Off-the-wall" rebel Tom played against Dick the straight man, who "mom always liked best." Their combination proved magical. With their smooth banter and irreverence, their comedy defined the turbulent 1960s. Their classic TV show, "The Smothers Brothers Comedy Hour" (1967-'69) brought their hip, topical satire to national prominence. Unfortunately for fans, their piercing insights into the social condition proved too hot to handle. Especially upsetting to right-wingers were their "left-wing" politics; they protested the Vietnam war, did a skit on interracial marriage, etc. They rocked the establishment. CBS pulled the plug, then was inundated with angry mail for months! The brothers enjoyed a peaceful move to the Sonoma/Napa Valley region of Northern California, where they produce fine wine. The year 2000 marked their 30th anniversary of being fired from the network.

Reed Hadley ⚊ 6553 Hollywood

Actor

Reed Hadley

BORN Reed Herring; Jan. 8, 1911, in Petrolia, TX. **SPOTLIGHTS** With years of stock and small theater behind him, he was a reliable, versatile actor. Able to play the decent man as well as the villain, he made his screen debut in *Female Fugitive* (1938). One of Hollywood's most cooperative actors, he played leading, supporting and character roles without ever rejecting a part. Movies include *Zorro's Fighting Legion* (serial, as Zorro), *Calling Dr. Kildare* (both 1939), *The Bank Dick* (1940), *Adventures of Captain Marvel* (serial, starting in 1941), *Leave Her to Heaven* (1945), and *A Southern Yankee* (1948). As Captain John Braddock in TV's "Racket Squad" (1951-'53), he protected citizens from confidence men. As Bart Matthews in The "Public Defender," he exonerated innocents "wrongly accused of crimes." Died: 1974.

John Forsythe ⚊ 6551 Hollywood

Actor

Sir Michael Teilmann and John Forsythe (right) visiting the French Riviera.

BORN John Freund; Jan. 29, 1918, in Penns Grove, NJ. **SPOTLIGHTS** Although extremely fond of thoroughbred race horses, this very handsome, wavy-haired actor never gambled with his busy career. A huge sports fan and former college baseball player, Forsythe—who possesses a rich voice—began his show business career in a radio booth announcing games for the Brooklyn Dodgers. Urged to try the stage, he found himself first in minor roles on Broadway, then made his silver screen debut in *Destination Tokyo* (1944). In 1947, he took on the challenge of the new medium of television. It was here he found his niche with his extremely videogenic face and personality. After appearing in numerouss dramatic teleplays, this intelligent, elegant actor starred in numerous series. He played Beverly Hills resident, Bentley Gregg, in "Bachelor Father" (1957-'62), among other 1960s starring roles, then became the voice only on "Charlie's Angels" (1976-'81). In 1981 he starred as oil tycoon Blake Carrington in the long-running hit "Dynasty." This popular show held viewers captive through most of the excessive '80s. Forsythe has made some wonderful films, too. He is adept in both comedy and drama. Motion picture credits include *The Glass Web* (1953), *It Happens Every Thursday* (1953), Hitchcock's *The Trouble With Harry* (1955—Shirley MacLaine's screen debut), *In Cold Blood* (1967), Hitchcock's *Topaz* (1969), and *Scrooged* (1988). **HIGHLIGHTS** If he could have had any career of his making, he would have chosen to be a baseball pitcher for the Dodgers. **QUOTE** About his attendance at New York's Actors Studio, Forsythe commented, "It is known as the 'Dirty Sweatshirt School,' but I never wore one. I was known as the Brooks Brothers Bohemian."

Helen Hayes 🎭   6551 Hollywood

See page 251

Basil Rathbone 🎥   6551 Hollywood

Basil Rathbone

Actor
BORN Philip B. Rathbone; June 13, 1892, in South Africa. **SPOTLIGHTS** Sharp. Dangerous. Cruel. Articulate. The screen's most distinguished villain. Rathbone was *the* choice to play against good, yet was immortalized as Sherlock Holmes. From silents to talkies, his 100+ motion pictures include *The Masked Bride* (1925), *Sin Takes a Holiday* (1930), *David Copperfield* (1935), *Anna Karenina, Captain Blood, A Tale of Two Cities* (all 1935), *Romeo and Juliet* (as Tybalt—1936), *The Adventures of Robin Hood* (1938), *The Hound of the Baskervilles* (1939, as Sherlock Holmes, plus 13 more SH features through 1946), *Son of Frankenstein* (1939), *Tower of London* (1939), *The Mark of Zorro* (1940), and *The Last Hurrah* (1958)...About his agent, Rathbone said, "He is the Hollywood version of Robin Hood. He steals from the rich and he steals from the poor." **QUOTE**

Hollywood "is a cruel place—relentless, stern and unforgiving—as I suppose all great industrial centres must be." Died: 1967.

Penny Singleton 🎥   6547 Hollywood

Actress
BORN Dorothy McNulty; Sept. 15, 1908, in Philadelphia, PA. **SPOTLIGHTS** She played the pretty, feather-brained Mrs. Dagwood Bumstead through most of her movie career by audience demand. The original, *Blondie*

Penny Singleton

(1938), based on the comic strip by Chic Young, was a "B" movie. That did not matter to audiences, who found the Bumstead family hilarious, and bought more tickets to it than competing "A" pictures. Singleton captured immediate fame as "Blondie" and found herself in the public spotlight. A natural redhead, she had to keep a tight schedule at the beauty salon to make sure her locks always appeared blonde. A number of comedies followed in this popular film series, including *Blondie Brings Up Baby* (1939). The serial ran from 1938-'50. Singleton reprised her starring role in radio's "Blondie" (1939-'49). The zany CBS show opened with her husband Dagwood Bumstead announcing his arrival at home by calling: "BLONNNNNNNNNNNNNDIE!" Both the film and radio series ran concurrently, with the same lead actors. She was honored with two stars on the Hollywood Walk of Fame (the other is for "radio"). In her lifetime she saw four different regimes run Hollywood, from the pioneers to high tech. **QUOTE** Still vital at age 90, she said, "The key to longevity is being happy and appreciating what you've got. You also have to watch your diet, and drink a lot of water."

Martha Raye 📺   6547 Hollywood

See page 198

Jack Warner 🎥   6547 Hollywood

Film pioneer, producer
BORN Aug. 2, 1892, in Canada. **SPOTLIGHTS**: He was co-

The Warner Bros. (from left to right) Harry, Jack, Sam and Abe

founder of one of the world's largest studios, Warner Brothers, along with his three brothers, Harry, Samuel, and Albert. The youngest of 12 children, he had the artistic, creative sense. The magic of the Warner family was that each member had a unique quality to bring to "the team." Together they were an unbeatable force. Significant early productions include *The Gold Diggers* (1923) and *Beau Brummel* (1924), and the *Rin-Tin-Tin* film series. They bravely went against the silent movement, and introduced the first sound motion picture, *The Jazz Singer* (1927). With a few spoken words and some songs, thye stunned the world and changed film forever. Classics include *Little Caesar* (1931), *Five Star Final* (1931), *I Am a Fugitive from a Chain Gang* (1932), *Of Human Bondage* (1934), *Black Fury* (1935), *The Story of Louis Pasteur* (1935), *The Life of Emile Zola* (1937), *Angels with Dirty Faces* (1938), *Casablanca* (1942), and *A Streetcar Named Desire* (1951). See the bios of Harry Warner and Rin-Tin-Tin in this book. **HIGHLIGHTS** Jack Warner took a nap every afternoon with strict rules not to be disturbed. One day, Bette Davis stormed into his office, ranting over a terrible script she had been given. Keeping his eyes closed, Warner groggily grabbed his phone and told his secretary, "Come in and wake me up. I'm having a terrible nightmare!" Davis burst into laughter, and the script crisis was quickly settled. **QUOTE** In 1924, he said, "Hollywood is and always will be the producing center for the world. The motion picture industry is as important a part of Hollywood as are the steel mills to Pennsylvania. We must remember motion picture people have established their homes here, are rearing families, and expect to live to a ripe old age in Hollywood. These are not to be lightly moved away. Los Angeles should be loathe to see us go, even if such were our mind. For of the 200,000 people who have come to reside here permanently during the last year, it would be fair to hazard that a large percentage were first attracted to this semi-tropical paradise by seeing its charms in a motion picture. My own desire to come here was born, when

as a small boy, I sat in the old nickelodeon, and saw the magnificent palm trees of Southern California. There, I said to myself, *I would go when I grew up.* Hollywood has now become a unique city, attracting artists, poets, writers, from all over the world, and they are here to stay. The movies, of course, are the magnet for them. But they have created a place that has an atmosphere all its own. Here a man without a collar can walk with his head up, the same as anyone else. Caste is gone. This freedom and individuality makes an ideal spot for creative art." Died: 1978, at the "ripe old age" of 86.

Mickey Rooney   6541 Hollywood

See page 183

Nancy Wilson   6541 Hollywood
Singer

Nancy Wilson

BORN Feb. 20, 1937, in Chillicothe, OH. **SPOTLIGHTS** She is a supreme "song stylist," who embraces jazz, pop, blues and soul to create a magic mix of contemporary and classic sounds. At 15, she had her own local television show, "Skyline Melody." Her first big hit, "Tell Me The Truth" (1963), was followed by classics "(You Don't Know) How Glad I Am," "I Wanna Be With You," "Can't Take My Eyes Off You," among others. Wilson has recorded more than 40 albums, and has made numerous TV appearances over the decades, including "The Carol Burnett Show" and "The Sammy Davis, Jr. Show." **ACHIEVEMENTS** Recipient of the Emmy Award for "The Nancy Wilson Show" (1975), and many other honors. She has made diligent efforts for the Martin Luther King Center for Social Change and The National Urban Coalition.

Bob Hope   6541 Hollywood

Bob Hope and Samantha Hart

Comedian, actor, writer, producer, patriot
BORN Leslie Townes Hope; May 29, 1903, in England. **SPOTLIGHTS** In America since age four, Hope trained in vaudeville, taking to the stage like a duck to water. When he

Bob Hope and Ann-Margret entertaining troops.

went to work in the Ziegfeld Follies—a revue famous for its spectacular staging and parading of young, beautiful show girls—he perfected his "greatest lover" routine. He typified the average guy who *is* resistible, but cannot figure out why. He poked fun at the serious pursuit of romance and rose to fame. He would later remark, "I was born with timing and coordination." The funny man was a major ticket attraction on Broadway, in musical comedies in the 1930s, and enjoyed huge success with NBC radio during this period. When he was not performing in those venues, he enjoyed doing stand-up. At one show he quipped, "The hotel room where I'm staying is so small that the rats are round-shouldered." The hotel's owner threatened to sue for damages unless Hope apologized. When his next show opened Hope announced, "I'm sorry I said that the rats in the hotel were round-shouldered. They're not." Hollywood became interested in him. Studios especially liked his popular joke-filled radio shows. He made his motion picture debut in *The Big Broadcast of 1938* (where he first sang "Thanks for the Memory" making it his signature song). But it was with co-star Bing Crosby in the 1940s "Road" film series (seven in all) that the two men proved they were masters of the gag. Four favorites of these funny "anything goes" movies are: *Road to Morocco* (1942--with Bing singing "Moonlight Becomes You"), *Road to Utopia* (1945--playing gold miners), *Road to Rio* (1947--with the Andrew Sisters singing "You Don't

Have to Know the Language"), and *Road to Bali* (1952--in Technicolor, with a cameo appearance by Humphrey Bogart). He was a funny patsy in the spy comedy *My Favorite Blonde* (1942), clever in the detective spoof *My Favorite Brunette* (1947), excellent playing the coward in *Paleface* (1948), and hilarious in *My Favorite Spy* (1951). Other movies include *Monsieur Beaucaire* (1946) with Joan Caulfield, *The Great Lover* (1949) opposite Rhonda Fleming, *Fancy Pants* (1950) co-starring Lucille Ball, *The Lemon Drop Kid* (1951) with Marilyn Maxwell, and *The Seven Little Foys* (1955). TV: He starred in his first annual TV special for NBC in 1950. He also became a longtime host of the Academy Awards. With such a busy schedule over the years, how did he get time to rest? Hope commented, "Laughter is an instant vacation." **ACHIEVEMENTS** Putting his own life on the line, Hope bravely made every wartime tour starting in World War II and ending with Desert Storm. Dedicated to entertaining homesick, anxiety-ridden soldiers during the holidays, Hope also recruited gorgeous dames (top starlets), comedians, singers, dancers, and musicians to help cheer up our troops and those of our allies...He has received two citations from the *Guinness Book of World Records*. One is for the longest continuous contract in the history of radio and television—60 years with NBC. The second is as "The Most Honored Individual in the Entertainment Industry." He has received more than 100 national and international honors; five special Academy Awards, an Emmy, a Peabody, an Order of the British Empire, a British knighthood by Queen Elizabeth II, a papal knighthood by Pope John Paul II, Distinguished Service medals from all branches of the armed forces, and four stars on the Walk of Fame. **QUOTE** "Laughter is therapy."

Bill Conti 🎥   6541 Hollywood

Composer, conductor

BORN April 13, 1942, in Providence, RI. **SPOTLIGHTS** This award-winning composer of motion picture hits, he studied piano as a child under the tutelage of his father—an accomplished pianist, sculptor and painter. By age 15, Conti had organized a band and played for high school dances. As a member of his high school symphony orchestra he won the "Silver Knight Award" from the *Miami Herald* for high achievement in the field of music. After graduation, Conti took bassoon instruction and practiced long hours over the summer. In the fall, he auditioned and received bassoon scholarships from three universities. He attended Louisiana State University with a major in composition. For extra money Conti played jazz piano at local night spots. After receiving his bachelor degree, he auditioned and was accepted at the famed Juilliard School of Music in New York. He graduated with a master's degree. In 1965 he won Juilliard's Marion Freschl Prize for having composed the best song of the year. Two years later, Conti and his wife, Shelby (a ballet student he met at LSU), moved to Italy. They stayed for seven years; Conti played the piano for a sometimes meager living. He made friends with the best-selling author Morris West, who one day altered Conti's life direction. During a conversation West asked Conti what his dreams and aspirations were. Conti admitted he wanted to be a film composer. West challenged him by saying that if he were really a composer, he'd be making a living composing, not playing. Like a divine missive West declared, "You *are* what you *do*." That moment Conti decided to pursue his life's passion. He slowly made headway in he industry; his first score was for an Italian film entitled *Candidate for Killing*. Arriving in California in 1974 with his then-useless European credits, he began to seek work as a film composer. Without a car, and sometimes not even having bus money, he walked or rode a bicycle to visit the heads of music at the various film studios. Lionel Newman admired his ambition and fortitude and gave generously of his time, advice, and introductions—especially to D'Angelo Productions—a powerhouse television production company. Producer/executive Bill D'Angelo hired him to compose the score for "Papa and Me," for which Conti earned an Emmy nomination. Almost one year to the day after his arrival in L.A., director Paul Mazursky asked him to score *Harry & Tonto*. He has scored many motion pictures since, including the famed theme song for *Rocky* (1976, + sequels). Credits include *For Your Eyes Only* (1981—Oscar nominated song), *The Karate Kid* (1984), *Broadcast News* (1987), *Baby Boom* (1987), *Lean on Me* (1989), *Bushwacked* (1995), and *Entertaining Angels* (1997). TV credits include "Dynasty," "Falcon Crest," "Cagney and Lacey," "Lifestyles of the Rich and Famous," "Ohara," and "Business Week." **ACHIEVEMENTS** Oscar for Best Original Score for *The Right Stuff* (1983). He holds an all-time industry record for having composed the themes to nine weekly television series...Conducted the orchestra at the Academy Awards a number of times. **HIGHLIGHTS** The UCLA marching band was on hand to salute Bill Conti at his star dedication ceremony on Nov. 10, 1989. They played their new fight song, "Mighty Bruins," which he composed for them.

Bob Burns 🎙   6541 Hollywood

See page 339

Leslie Nielsen 🎥   6541 Hollywood

Actor
BORN Feb. 11, 1926, in Regina, Saskatchewan, Canada. **SPOTLIGHTS** The son of a Canadian Mounted Policeman, he served bravely during World War II in the Canadian Air Force. With his well-trained baritone voice, Nielsen began his career in radio as an on-air personality. He received a scholarship to the Neighborhood Playhouse in New York, then started in television with a 1949 "Studio One" appearance with Charlton Heston. The tall, strapping, ruggedly handsome talent was offered a contract with MGM. His early films include *The Vagabond King* (1956), and *Tammy and the Bachelor* (1957) with Debbie Reynolds. Throughout the 1960s and '70s he

Leslie Nielsen (holding star plaque)

devoted his attention to TV, guest-starring regularly in adventure series and starring in many series of his own. TV programs include: "Peyton Place," "Hawaii Five-O," and "Bracken's World," to name a few. He was nominated for an Emmy for "Police Squad," where America discovered his comedic side. His riotous deadpan humor soared in *Airplane!* (1980), and turned him into *The Naked Gun* (1988+sequels). Nielsen, who somehow manages to appear cool and hip, enjoys a large following of millions of young fans. He has made more than 55 motion pictures, including *The Poseidon Adventure* (1972), *Creepshow* (1982), *Soul Man* (1986), *Nuts* (1987), *Dracula: Dead and Loving It* (1995), and *Spy Hard* (1996).

José Ferrer 🎥   6541 Hollywood

José Ferrer

Actor, director
BORN Jan. 8, 1909, in Santurce, Puerto Rico. **SPOTLIGHTS** Educated at Princeton, Ferrer surprised his family by deciding against becoming an architect in favor of a show business career. This dark-haired talent proved to be a versatile actor and director, first on the Broadway stage. In 1942-'43 he excelled in the revival of "Othello" as Iago opposite Paul Robeson; some critics wrote that his performance overshadowed Robeson's. He made his cinema debut opposite Ingrid Bergman in *Joan of Arc* (1948). In 1952 he starred in *Moulin Rouge*, the fictional biopic of French artist Toulouse Lautrec, for which he received an Academy nomination. Ferrer turned in a powerful performance in *The Caine Mutiny* (1954) with Humphrey Bogart. The following year he was fascinating to watch in *The Shrike* (1955), opposite June Allyson (playing against type); he also directed. Ferrer directed the 1961 sequel, *Return to Peyton Place*,

and the 1962 remake of *State Fair* starring Pat Boone, Bobbie Darin and Alice Faye. Ferrer, along with the rest of the cast, was brilliant in David Lean's *Lawrence of Arabia* (1962—as the Turkish officer). He played Herod Antipas in George Stevens' *The Greatest Story Ever Told* (1965). He was active both as an actor and director in many other films. **ACHIEVEMENTS** 1950 Best Actor Oscar, *Cyrano de Bergerac*. He went over and beyond the call of duty to aid the World War II effort, and donated heavily to GI welfare. **HIGHLIGHTS** His third wife was singer Rosemary Clooney (1953-'67; see her bio in this book). Their eldest son, out of five, is the talented actor Miguel Ferrer. **QUOTE** "People don't understand that I was never the bundle of energy I seemed to be. I only did one thing at a time, but it happened that at one time everything I had been working on appeared at once." Died: 1992.

José Feliciano ● 6541 Hollywood

Musician, singer, composer

José Feliciano

BORN Sept. 10, 1945, in Lares, Puerto Rico. **SPOTLIGHTS** Born sightless, the second of 12 children to poor parents, he was raised in poverty. In hopes of a better future, the family relocated to New York's Spanish Harlem when he was age five. Feliciano quit school in his teens to help support his large family. A master of many musical instruments—guitar, bass, banjo, keyboards, timbales, mandolin and harmonica—he played at local coffee houses in Greenwich Village. There, he earned more than tips, he was discovered by a recording powerhouse. The brilliant talent rose to spectacular fame. By age 23, he had won two Grammy Awards and was performing internationally to sold-out crowds in four languages. Acclaimed by critics as the world's greatest living guitarist, the incredibly gifted Feliciano specializes in flamenco-flavored versions of pop. He was awarded Best Pop Guitarist for five years running. A few of his many hit recordings include "Light My Fire," "Feliciano!" "California Dreamin'," and "Feliz Navidad." Dozens of gold and platinum albums, and 10 Grammy nominations.

Viola Dana 🎥 6541 Hollywood

Actress
BORN Violet Flugrath; June 28, 1897, in Brooklyn, NY. **SPOTLIGHTS** *Cinderella's Twin* (1920) was how she felt as a screen siren, but the coming of sound was like the clock striking 12—she dropped out of sight! Died: 1987.

William Fox 🎥 6541 Hollywood

Movie pioneer, mogul

William Fox

BORN Wilhelm Fried; Jan. 1, 1879, in Hungary. **SPOTLIGHTS** Hoping for a better life, his impoverished parents immigrated to America when he was nine months old. Fox was the eldest of 13 children, yet only one of six who survived through infancy. As a child he peddled polish, newspaper and candy to help pay for food. Needing more money to support the family, the 11-year-old took a garment sweatshop job working 12 hours a day for low pay. As a young adult he opened his own business sponging fabric (for pre-shrinkage). Although without a formal education, Fox instinctively understood the potential of new entertainment. He purchased a penny arcade, then in 1904, opened his first nickelodeon in New York. He expanded into a theater chain and distributing motion pictures, then in 1914 produced films from his Box Office Attraction Company. Two years later, he changed the growing company's name to Fox Film Corporation. He was known for being a very kind and sweet man, loved by his employees. Blessed with the gift of picking stories, cast, and the correct director to make a film that the public eagerly anticipates, Fox built an empire that had made his personal net worth $200 million by 1919. Died: 1952.

Maureen O'Sullivan 🎥 6541 Hollywood

Actress
BORN May 17, 1911, in Boyle, County Roscommon, Ireland. **SPOTLIGHTS** Educated in convents, she original planned to become a Catholic nun. Spotted at the Dublin International Horse Show by Hollywood director Frank Borzage (who had been scouting locations), the 19-year-old ingenue made

Maureen O'Sullivan

her film debut in his musical *Song O' My Heart* (1930). She became a favorite at MGM. She appears in more than 60 films: *Tugboat Annie* (1933), *The Thin Man* (1934), *David Copperfield* (1934), *Cardinal Richelieu, Anna Karenena* (both 1935), *A Day at the Races* (1937), *Pride and Prejudice* (1940), and *The Big Clock* (1948). But she is best remembered in the role that offered Tarzan this line: "Me, Jane." O'Sullivan was the delicate, curvaceous beauty who, as a scantily clan Jane, drove Johnny Weissmuller ape in the *Tarzan* films. She made a critically acclaimed cameo performance playing a flirtatious mother in *Hannah and Her Sisters* (1986), appearing with real-life daughter Mia Farrow. **QUOTE** "I was not a big movie fan as a child, although I did trade a $6 fountain pen for a picture of Rudolph Valentino," O'Sullivan fondly remembered. Died: 1998.

Johnny Weissmuller 📺 6541 Hollywood

Actor

Johnny Weissmuller

BORN Peter John Weissmuller; June 2, 1904, in Windber, PA. **SPOTLIGHTS** An Olympic swimming champion, Johnny Weissmuller collected five gold medals in 1924 and 1928. He set more than 60 world records, and then was asked to screen test for the lead in Tarzan. Weissmuller looked in shock at the producer and asked, "Me? Tarzan?" (True story.) Strong, graceful, and handsome, he acted in the first talkie version *Tarzan the Ape Man* (1932). A dozen *Tarzan* pictures followed paired with the beautiful Maureen O'Sullivan. Over 17 years MGM studio staffers lovingly called him "the censored Adam." Out of all the subsequent Tarzan movies, no one could hold a candle to Weissmuller. He *was* Tarzan. And, in fact, it was Weissmuller's recognizable Tarzan yell used for the TV series (the other actor opened his mouth in lip-sinc). The athletic hunk also appears in Columbia's "Jungle Jim" series (1944-'55), which were edited for TV. To date, there have been 82 worldwide theatrical releases featuring Tarzan. Died: 1984.

David W. Griffith 🎥 6537 Hollywood

D.W. Griffith (right) and Abel Gance

Director, film pioneer
BORN David Wark Griffith; Jan. 22, 1874, in La Grange, KY. **SPOTLIGHTS** Known as D. W. Griffith, he is the acknowledged "Father of Modern Cinema." Throughout his career, he invented breakthrough filmmaking techniques: the flashback, intense closeups, overhead shots, artistic back-lighting, panoramic shooting, cross-cutting, and epic scope. Prior to Griffith, films were shot like stage plays (the point of view was a fixed spot in one location). He was the first to direct a movie like a movie, showing audiences what was around the corner, what was deep in the background, etc. He also introduced epic films with *The Birth of a Nation* (1915), a three-hour cinematic triumph about the Civil War (when most films were only 15 minutes long). Tickets were costly at $2 each, but people lined up to see it. It was Hollywood's first blockbuster. So precise in his shooting techniques, he studied the camera angle for one scene in *The Birth of a Nation* and said, "Move those ten thousand horses a little to the right." Movies include *Intolerance* (1916), and *Orphan's of the Storm* (1922). He co-formed United Artists in 1919 with Charlie Chaplin, Douglas Fairbanks, and Mary Pickford. **HISTORICAL** *The Birth of a Nation* is considered one of the most important films in the development of cinema art. However, it is the most racist film ever made in America. Based in part on *The Clansman*, a book, it actually revived the Ku Klux Klan. When the film was released, there were relatively few members of the KKK. The movie's bigotry toward African Americans in incendiary scenes roused the KKK back to life and acted like a giant recruitment machine. It did not help that America's President at the time was a prejudiced Southerner. President Woodrow Wilson wholeheartedly approved of the assaults of racism, rampant discrimination, and crushing acts to squash those people whose skin color was darker than his own. He saw the film at the White House before its release and praised *The Birth of a Nation* as "history written in lighting." For the first time ever, credence to hate someone simply because of his or her skin color was given the mass, official, governmental stamp of approval. And, the movie made racism seem right. By 1930, nearly 200 million Americans had seen the picture, and unfortunately many formulated ignorant, negative stereotypes against people of color. Not everyone embraced the hatred. Actor James Stewart called the KKK, "America's homegrown

terrorists." It is an ugly time capsule of racism. Died: 1948.

Duke Ellington 🔘   6535 Hollywood

Jazz composer, pianist, and band leader

Duke Ellington

BORN Edward Kennedy Ellington; April 29, 1899, in Washington, D.C. **SPOTLIGHTS** "At 13, I was a soda jerk and that was the summer I got my nickname Duke. They called me that because I was prideful of the stiff starched uniform I used to wear on my job," he recalled. Inspired in his teens, his first composition was "The Soda Fountain Rag." Duke could also draw, and at one time thought of becoming an illustrator. He was so good at it he won a scholarship to the Pratt Institute of Design. Fortunately, this gigantic talent decided on a musical career. Ellington was one of the most prominent figures in big band jazz and one of jazz kingdom's highest members of royalty. He formed his own band in 1918, and played the Cotton Club for five years starting in 1927. He comprised pure instrumental jazz compositions, production numbers, blues, jungle style, popular songs, dance music, and mood music. His concert debut, "Black, Brown and Beige," musically illustrated the history of African Americans. From 1943-'52, he performed annual concerts at Carnegie Hall. Leading his orchestra from his piano, and never using a baton, his perfectly disciplined orchestra caused envy in the jazz world. His musical magic was known as the "Ellington Effect." Hit recordings include "Choo Choo," "Old Man Blues," "Mood Indigo," "In a Sentimental Mood," "Take the 'A' Train," "Ducky Wucky," "The Mooche," "Satin Doll," "Sophisticated Lady," "Prelude to a Kiss," "Black and Tan Fantasy," "Creole Love Call," "East St. Louis Toodle-oo," and "Do Nothing 'Til You Hear From Me." Movies include *Check and Double Check* (1930), and *Cabin in the Sky* (1943). Extremely productive, his compositions numbered 2,000, and included three-minute instrumental pieces, suites, film scores, etc. RCA released the single CD *Best of the Duke Ellington Centennial Edition* (with 18 excellent selections), and the ultimate collection, *The Duke Ellington Centennial Edition* (with five decades of excellent selections). **ACHIEVEMENTS** A great master of 20th century American jazz, he was the recipient of countless honors and awards, including the prestigious Presidential Medal of Freedom Award in 1969. **QUOTE** "Some want Dixieland. Others want their music to be cool, still others want me to sit around playing 'Mood Indigo.' We give them everything. I don't care what I play. All I'm interested in is communication. We want everyone to come to the party. When they grunt, you know they're communicating." Died: 1974.

Sol Lesser 🎥   6535 Hollywood

Producer

BORN Feb. 17, 1890, in Spokane, WA. **SPOTLIGHTS** Most of the Tarzan pictures were produced under the aegis of Mr. Lesser, starting with *Tarzan the Fearless* (1933) with Buster Crabbe in the lead. Then, a casting problem caused difficulties for Lesser, which turned out to be a good thing for moviegoers. Crabbe opted for a costume with a cowboy hat and two six-guns rather than be typecast as the vine-swinging character. The producer cast Lou Gehrig, the Yankee baseball legend, clean-up man and home-run king, in the Tarzan lead. But, the screen test revealed that Lou Gehrig's massive legs were too beefy in the skimpy costume; completely non-suitable for the ape man. Johnny Weissmuller, the long-legged, perfectly fit Olympic gold medalist in swimming, who had starred in the very first Talkie version, won back the title of Tarzan. And he was the best. As a consolation prize, Lesser would later cast Lou Gehrig in *Rawhide* (1938), a Western with some baseball scenes stuck in. Sol Lesser also produced the serial *Dick Tracy* (1937). Died: 1980.

Morton Gould 🔘   6533 Hollywood

Composer, conductor

BORN Dec. 10, 1913, in Richmond Hill, NY. **SPOTLIGHTS** A piano prodigy, his first composition was published at age six. Conducting and arranging weekly radio programs by age 21, including works "Pavane" and "American Salute." Compositions for symphonies and symphonic band include: "Spirituals for Orchestra"; "Dance Variations for Two Pianos and Orchestra"; "Jekyll and Hyde Variations." Composed more than 1,000 musical scores for Broadway, film, the ballet, TV and radio. Works include three major U.S. Bicentennial commissions. Also composed "American Sing" for the Los Angeles Philharmonic Summer Olympics Concert an the Hollywood Bowl, in July, 1984. **ACHIEVEMENTS** 1966 Grammy for conducting the Chicago Symphony playing Charles Ives symphony No. 1 in D minor. 1983 Gold Baton Award. 1994 Kennedy Center Honor. 1995 Pulitzer Prize for "Stringmusic." **QUOTE** In regard to his somber face, Gould stated, "I'm not a glamour boy. When I'm out on the stage, I'm there to do my work. It's usually pretty grim." Died 1996, peacefully in his sleep.

Clyde Cook 🎥   6531 Hollywood

Actor

Clyde Cook

BORN Dec. 16, 1891, in Australia. **SPOTLIGHTS** Cook's family immigrated to America when he was a small lad. Energetic and acrobatic, he started out as a circus performer before he reached his teens. He excelled in pantomime, and easily made the transition to silent films in Mack Sennett's Keystone comedies. He rose to starring roles opposite Louise Fazenda in the late 1920s. With his expressive, often menacing face, he found plenty of character roles in talkies, including *Oliver Twist* (1933), *Barbary Coast* (1935), *Wee Willie Winkle* (1937), *The Little Princess* (1939), *The Sea Hawk* (1940), and *The Verdict* (1946) and *To Each His Own* (1946). Died: 1984.

John Derek ![tv icon]   6531 Hollywood

Actor, director, producer

John Derek

BORN Derek Harris; Aug. 12, 1926, in Hollywood, C A . **SPOTLIGHTS** The son of an actress mother, and a writer-director father, Derek followed in the family business. This ruggedly handsome actor made his screen debut as an extra in *Since You Went Away* (1944), then landed a bit role in *I'll Be Seeing You* (1945). Movies include *A Double Life* (1947), *Knock on Any Door* (1949), *All the King's Men* (1949), *The Outcast* (1953), *Omar Khayyam* (1957), *The Flesh is Weak* (1957), *The Ten Commandments* (1956), and *Exodus* (1960). Later, he directed his wife, Bo Derek, in *Tarzan the Apeman* (1981), co-starring Richard Harris and John Phillip Law. His directorial efforts on *Tarzan* were not appreciated; he received scathing reviews. Other directing and producing efforts fared better. **TV** Actor Ronald Reagan narrated the show "A Place in the Sun" (1954), which starred Derek. He played Ben Travis in the 1960s Western series "Frontier Circus." **HIGHLIGHTS** Derek married and divorced three beautiful actresses: French starlet Pati Behrs; the Swiss-born Ursula Andress; and American Linda Evans. Nicknamed "the Svengali," he groomed fourth wife Bo Derek's acting career; she is famous for the film *10*. He married her when she was 18, and remained married to her until his death. **QUOTE** "Your looks influence your life. It doesn't matter if you're a man or a woman. Your looks matter *more* than any other thing on earth." Died: 1998.

Phyllis Thaxter ![camera icon]   6531 Hollywood

Actress

Phyllis Thaxter

BORN Phyllis St. Felix Thaxter; Nov. 20, 1921, in Portland, ME. **SPOTLIGHTS** An American blue blood, her father was a Maine Supreme Court justice, and her mother a former celebrated Shakespearean actress. She honed her craft at the Montreal Repertory Theatre and made her Broadway stage debut at age 17. She made her screen debut in the gritty WWII drama, *Thirty Seconds over Tokyo* (1944), starring Spencer Tracy. She appears in Robert Wise's classic dark Western *Blood on the Moon* (1948), opposite Robert Mitchum. Other movies include *Act of Violence* (1949), a post WWII drama, *Jim Thorpe--All American*, *Come Fill the Cup* (both 1951), *Women's Prison* (1955--a cult classic), *Man Afraid* (1957), and *The World of Henry Orient* (1964--a delightful comedy). Talented in heavy drama and light comedy, the versatile Thaxter was also good in Nervous Nellie roles, breathing fresh life into those characters...She contracted polio in 1952, but courageously continued working. Her last film was *Superman* (1978).

Bela Lugosi and Carol Borland in Tod Browning's **Mark of the Vampire** *(1935)*

6529 HOLLYWOOD

Alfred Green 🎥   6529 Hollywood

Director

BORN: July 7, 1889, in Perris, CA. **SPOTLIGHTS** He was the creative force behind America's Sweetheart Mary Pickford in *Little Lord Fauntleroy* (1921). For Warner Bros. he turned out such films as *Disraeli* (1929), *The Green Goddess* (1930), *Smart Money* (1931), *Silver Dollar* (1932), *Baby Face, The Narrow Corner*, and *I Loved a Woman* (all 1933). Bette Davis won her Oscar under Green's direction in *Dangerous* (1935), but it might be considered "soapy" by today's standards. Green diversified with the goofy mystery, *The Gracie Allen Murder Case* (1939), and a fun fantasy in *A Thousand and One Nights* (1945). He captured the essence of a show business legend in the box office smash hit *The Jolson Story* (1946). Died: 1960.

Faye Emerson 🎥   6529 Hollywood

Actress

BORN July 8, 1917, in Elizabeth, LA. **SPOTLIGHTS** A vivacious beauty, she possessed a wry wit and tremendous style. Her film career includes *Wild Bill Hickock Rides* (1941), *Murder in the Big House* (1942), *Hollywood Canteen* (1944), and *A Face in the Crowd* (1957), to name just a few. But this glamorous, brown-eyed, articulate blonde enjoyed greater fame on the small box. She consistently had the highest ratings with her 1950s shows: "The Faye Emerson Show," and "Faye Emerson's Wonderful Town." A chic dresser, who most often wore gowns with a plunging neckline, she married Elliott Roosevelt—the son of then-president Franklin D. Roosevelt. Emerson pulled rank and caused a national scandal by shipping her beloved pooch via a priority Army Air Transport Plane. It led in part to a divorce; thereafter she married and divorced several powerful and influential men. Died: 1983.

Liberace 🎬   6529 Hollywood

Pianist, showman

Liberace

BORN Wladziu Valentino Liberace; May 16, 1919, in West Allis, WI. **SPOTLIGHTS** A child prodigy, he attended Wisconsin College of Music at age seven and was introduced as a soloist with the Chicago Symphony at age 14. During the Depression, he switched from classical music to play jazz tunes in nightclubs—to earn a living. He took the stage name "Walter Buster Keys," adding his tongue-in-cheek trademark humor to his show. He stated, "Wisecracks lifted my income from $150-a-week to more than $1,000,000-a-year." In 1953 he played Carnegie Hall. The next year, he tickled the ivories at the Madison Square Garden in New York where the fans loved him, but the critics loathed him. He stated to the press, "What you said hurt me very much. I cried all the way to the bank." He headed to Las Vegas, Nevada, where his contracts would be valued in the multi-millions at the casinos. The ever-smiling, flamboyant Liberace was known as "Mr. Showmanship" for his bouncy renditions of Chopin and Gershwin, outrageously extravagant sequined costumes, bejeweled pianos, and twinkly-eyed rapport with his audience. His stage sets included his ever-present candelabra, chauffeured Rolls-Royces being driven onstage, colorful, dancing water, and plenty of gilded glamour. **ACHIEVEMENTS** Emmys (two) 1952; and 1953 for his successful ABC daytime series. **QUOTE** "My great virtue is that I have no vanity. People criticize me, but when they meet me nobody can help liking me." Died: 1987.

Betty Grable 🎥   6527 Hollywood

Actress, singer, dancer

Betty Grable in favorite WWII pinup photo.

BORN Elizabeth Grable; Dec. 18, 1916, in St Louis, MO. **SPOTLIGHTS** Famous as the No. 1 Pin-Up girl during World War II (see photo)—due to her shapely legs, peachy complexion and sweet smile, she was one of the best-liked and highest paid female movie stars. Her films include *Million Dollar Legs* (1940) which played off her real-life nickname, *Tin Pan Alley* (1940), *Moon Over Miami* (1941), *Footlight Serenade* (1942), *Springtime in the Rockies* (1942), *Sweet Rosie O'Grady* (1943), *Pin-Up Girl* (1944), *Four Jills in a Jeep* (1944), *Diamond Horseshoe* (1945), *The Dolly Sisters* (1945), and *How to Marry a Millionaire* (1953). **SIDELIGHTS** While Miss Grable's five-year-old niece was staying with her, she asked her Aunt Betty if she could join her in the bubble bath. Betty replied, "Sure, climb on in." Once in the tub, Betty noticed her niece staring at her intently. After a couple of moments, Betty asked her, "What's the matter?" The child responded, "I'm just wondering, why is it that I'm so plain and you're so fancy." Died: 1973.

Merian C. Cooper 6525 Hollywood

Producer, director, screenwriter
BORN Oct. 24, 1893, in Jacksonville, FL. **SPOTLIGHTS** He served in both World War I and II, and retired as a U.S. Air Force Brigadier General. He produced and co-directed the original—and best—*King Kong* (1933). He was the man responsible for creating one of the screen's most memorable moments: Kong perched on top of the Empire State Building fighting off airplanes. He co-produced the classic post Civil War Western, *Fort Apache* (1948), starring John Wayne, Henry Fonda, Shirley Temple, John Agar, Ward Bond, George O'Brien, and Victor McLaglen. **ACHIEVEMENTS** 1952 Special Academy Award for "his many innovations and contributions to the art of motion pictures." Died: 1973.

Edmond O'Brien 6523 Hollywood

See page 146

Roland Young 6523 Hollywood

Actor

Roland Young

BORN Nov. 11, 1887, in England. **SPOTLIGHTS** A superb, sweet, charming character actor, he made whimsy his trademark. Young played the some-what bewildered and droll fellow peeking out from the drawing room. With utmost perfection and hilarious results, he used fluttering mannerisms in 120 pictures. Although trained at the prestigious Royal Academy of Dramatic Arts in London, Shakespeare was not his forte. He did play—quite distinctively—the Earl of Burnstead in *Ruggles of Red Gap* (1935); the title role of Cosmo Topper in *Topper* (1937—a role in which he was nominated for an Oscar and is best remembered and its sequels, including *Topper Returns* (1940). Roland was terrific in *The Young in Heart* (1938)—voted one of the ten best pictures of the year. It is a funny and entertaining comedy. A true darling of the cinema, he appears in *The Philadelphia Story* (1940), in the must-see, all-star cast of *Forever and a Day* (1943), and the marvelous comedy *The Great Lover*. He appears in the very first Agatha Christie novel adapted to the screen *And Then There Were None* (1945). It's a five-star picture. Died: 1953.

Harry Von Zell 6521 Hollywood

Announcer, actor
BORN July 11, 1906, in Indianapolis, IN. **SPOTLIGHTS** A robust, happy announcer-stooge with a lively personality on radio's top Golden Era shows from the 1930s-'40s, including "The George Burns and Gracie Allen Show," "The Eddie Cantor Show," "The Fred Allen Show," "The Dinah Shore Show," and "The Aldrich Family" He was also the announcer for countless situation comedies and dramas. Died: 1981.

Dean Martin 6519 Hollywood

Actor, comedian, singer

Dean Martin

BORN Dino Paul Crocetti; June 7, 1917, in Steubenville, OH. **SPOTLIGHTS** Born to an Italian immigrant father who cut hair for a living, Martin inherited dashing Italian good looks. As a teenager, he cut classes for fun, and boxed instead of studying. He dropped out of high school in the 10th grade. (He lived to regret that decision, as he spent his adulthood embarrassed by his poor English grammar and lack of education.) He boxed under the name of "Kid Crocetti" in the welterweight class. Meeting all sorts of underworld thugs at the rings, "Kid" made extra loot bootlegging booze and stealing hub caps. Then, in Ohio's "Little Chicago" he worked as a blackjack croupier. After hours he sang with a local band at a cafe. He won a gig paying $50 a week as a singer, and billed himself as Dino Martini. "The best thing that ever happened to me was when I found out that you could put on a suit and make a buck singing, which is something I'd done all my life," he revealed. When he got his next singing contract, he changed his name to Dean Martin, but remained "Dino" to his friends. In 1946 he greeted Jerry Lewis at the Glass Hat in New York, where both men were appearing. The twosome created a comedy routine where the handsome, charming playboy Martin crooned, while Lewis interrupted as a goofy, bumbling busboy. 16 popular movies followed, including *My Friend Irma* (1949), *Scared Stiff* (1953), *The Stooge* (1953), and *Hollywood or Bust* (1956). One of his later solo efforts is *Kiss Me, Stupid* (1964), opposite Kim Novak and Ray Walston. **TV** Regarding his comedy-variety program, "The Dean Martin Show" (1965-'74), he stated, "Wanna know why this show's a hit? The reason is that it's me. It ain't nothin' phony; that's really me. You take everybody else on TV they're puttin' on an act, playin' something they aren't." Dressed in a tux, the charmer appeared laid-back, drunk or nonchalant. His most popular recording hits include

"Everybody Loves Somebody," "Memories Are Made of This," "I Will," "That's Amore," "Return to Me," and "Volare." Known for crooning in a melodic baritone voice, the romantic, all-around superb entertainer stated, "I have an easy style."...His best friend was Frank Sinatra, and in Las Vegas Martin became the chief deputy of Sinatra's Rat Pack. When Martin passed away in 1995, Sinatra released this written statement: "Dean was my brother—not through blood but through choice. Our friendship has traveled down many roads over the years and there will always be a special place in my heart and soul for Dean. He has been like the air I breathe—always there, always close by." **QUOTE** "If I am relaxed myself, I can relax an audience. That's one of the secrets of being an entertainer."

Leatrice Joy 🎥   6519 Hollywood

Actress

BORN Leatrice J. Zeidler; Nov. 7, 1896, in New Orleans, LA. **SPOTLIGHTS** Her expressive face and control of body movement helped her get noticed in *The Slave* (1918), opposite the sweet, rotund comedian Oliver Hardy. Others pictures include *The Poverty of Riches* (1921), *Manslaughter* (1922) and *The Ten Commandments* (1923). By the mid-1920s Joy had jumped on the Roaring '20s bandwagon. She wore tailored men's suits and a boyish bob to emulate a top notch business woman in pictures like *For Alimony Only* (1926). As you might imagine the suits did *not* make her look mannish. She was elegance personified, either in pants or the fabulous Adrian gowns she showcased so well. In the late 1920s Joy became Cecil B. DeMille's favorite female star, where she was particularly effective as the sophisticated society girl. Died: 1985.

Madge Bellamy 🎥   6517 Hollywood

Actress

BORN Margaret Philpott; June 30, 1903, in Hillsboro, TX. **SPOTLIGHTS** A leading lady of the silent screen, she made her movie debut in *The Riddle Woman* (1920). Bellamy was the kind beauty in *Blind Hearts* (1921). She plays an outlaw's daughter who is really a kidnapped heiress in *Lorna Doone* (1922). When talkies arrived, she became a character actress. She worked in the *Charlie Chan* detective series (1934 on). Her last film was *Northwest Trail* (1945). Died: 1990.

John Howard 📺   6515 Hollywood

Host, actor

BORN John Cox, Jr.; April 14, 1913, in Cleveland, OH. **SPOTLIGHTS** A businesslike, mustachioed player, he did a fine job in the Bulldog Drummond film series of the late 1930s. He was excellent in the must-see *Lost Horizon* (1937) and in *The Philadelphia Story* (1940). **TV** As Dr. Wayne Hudson in "Dr. Hudson's Secret Journal" his healing touch saved broken hearts and repaired battered bodies. Howard played Dave Welch in "My Three Sons" (1965-'67). **ACHIEVEMENTS**

Howard accepted dangerous military assignments during WWII and became a real-life war hero. Awarded the Navy Cross and France's *Croix de Guerre* for valor, he graduated Phi Beta Kappa at Ohio's Western Reserve University.

Rochester 🎙   6513 Hollywood

Comedian, actor

Rochester

BORN Eddie Anderson; Sept. 18, 1905, in Oakland, CA. **SPOTLIGHTS** One of America's favorite stars, the gravel-voiced Anderson became a household name and gained his greatest fame in network radio and television playing Rochester, the comedic manservant on "The Jack Benny Program." He was first cast in a temporary role as a Pullman train porter on March 28, 1937. Jack Benny found Anderson's impeccable comic timing and characteristic raspy voice hilarious, and signed him to a permanent contract by June of that same year. He became a regular member of the cast in the role of Benny's African-American valet, Rochester Van Jones. In doing so, he was immortalized in the timeless classic. When the show moved to TV in 1950, audiences were thrilled to watch Anderson's mugging and other funny facial expressions and delightful body movements. He enjoyed enormous popularity, and often garnered the biggest laughs on the show for the next 15 years. He also appeared in a variety of films from drama to musicals, including *What Price Hollywood?* (1932), *Show Boat* (1936), *Jezebel* (1938), *Thanks for the Memory* (1938), *Kentucky* (1938), *Gone With the Wind* (1939), *Topper Returns* (1940), *Star Spangled Rhythm* (1942), *Cabin in the Sky* (1943), *Stormy Weather* (1943), and *Brewster's Millions* (1945). He made 28 motion pictures. **HIGHLIGHTS** Anderson wanted his Walk of Fame star to bear his beloved character name of "Rochester." In real life, radio alone had made him a rich man. In 1947 it was reported in the *Saturday Evening Post* that Anderson owned "a block-large estate and has three servants of his own, drives an expensive car, and when not working—which he does two days a week for some $700 per air-time minute—spends his leisure hours either yachting or supervising his well-stocked racing stable." Devastated by Jack Benny's death in 1974, he stated that Benny had been "one of the warmest, kindest men, and I feel blessed by God, and my life enriched, by working with him." Died: 1977.

Clara Kimball Young 🎥 6513 Hollywood

Actress

BORN Clara Kimball; Sept. 6, 1890, in Chicago, IL. **SPOTLIGHTS** Both of her parents were vaudeville performers and they introduced their daughter on stage at age three. A seasoned performer by age 19, she entered films, under the wing of her husband, director-actor James Young. When she was 24 years old, she was voted "the most popular cinema star." Mogul Selznick placed this raven-haired beauty in dramas *Camille* and *Trilby* (both 1915), where she shot to superstardom on the silent screen. Although excellent in heavy emotional roles, she had a true sense of satire, bringing greatness to any of the comedy roles she took. Unfortunately she made the mistake of divorcing her first husband, whose business acumen and devotion had aided her greatly. Although she prospered into the early 1920s, her career—and finances—took a nose dive when she entrusted both to her incompetent, second husband (her former agent who became her producer/director). Died: 1960.

John Sturges 🎥 6511 Hollywood

Director

BORN Jan. 3, 1911, in Oak Park, IL. **SPOTLIGHTS** Tense dramas and action-packed Westerns with climactic gun battles were his impressive trademarks. Motion pictures include *Bad Day at Black Rock* (1954) starring Spencer Tracy, Robert Ryan, and Anne Francis, *Gunfight at the O.K. Corral* (1957) starring Burt Lancaster, Kirk Douglas, Rhonda Fleming, Jo Van Fleet, John Ireland, and Lee Van Cleef, *The Magnificent Seven* (1960) starring Yul Brynner, Steve McQueen, Eli Wallach, Horst Buchholz, James Coburn, Charles Bronson, Robert Vaughn, and Brad Dexter, and *Joe Kidd* (1972) starring Clint Eastwood, Robert Duvall and John Saxon. The classic P.O.W. movie is Sturges' *The Great Escape* (1963), starring Steve McQueen (watch for the Harley Davidson motorcycle escape scene), James Gardner, Richard Attenborough, Charles Bronson, James Coburn, David McCallum and Donald Pleasence. He finished with *The Eagle Has Landed* (1977). Died: 1992.

Art Baker 📺 6509 Hollywood

Actor, announcer

BORN Arthur Shank; Jan. 7, 1898, in New York, NY. **SPOTLIGHTS** An articulate announcer on radio's "The Bob Hope Show" (first broadcast NBC, 1934). TV: Host on "You Asked For It" (1950-'59). Died: 1966.

Spring Byington 🎥 6507 Hollywood

Actress

BORN Oct. 17, 1893, in Colorado Springs, CO. **SPOTLIGHTS** She specialized in female confusion and was one of America's best-loved character actresses. She started her own theatrical company in high school with $500.00 she had inherited. After

Spring Byington

graduation, she walked into a casting office in Kansas City to try out for a stock company. Later she recalled, "Even though it was a professional company, I knew I would get the part. That's the wonderful thing about innocence, or ignorance; you aren't a bit frightened because you just don't know enough to be." She toured Canada with the company, then in 1924 made her Broadway debut in "A Beggar on Horseback." Although she was neither desired by the casting agent, or producer—due to her lack of motion picture experience—RKO Studios cast her as Marmee in David O. Selznick's *Little Women* (1933). The camera picked up her light within; she exuded warmth, a naturalness, and an appealing sweetness. She enjoyed tremendous success. Films include *Mutiny on the Bounty* (1935), *Dodsworth* (1936), *Theodora Goes Wild* (1936), *The Story of Alexander Graham Bell* (1939), *Meet John Doe* (1941), and *I'll I'll Be Seeing You* (1944). She starred in TV's sitcom "December Bride" (1954-'60), as Lily Ruskin, the lovable mother-in-law. In "Laramie" (1961-'63), she played Daisy Cooper, surrogate mother. **QUOTE** "Show business isn't what it used to be. It's all business and no romance." Died: 1971.

Les Brown 6505 Hollywood

Composer, conductor, songwriter

Les Brown

BORN March 14, 1912, in Reinerton, PA. **SPOTLIGHTS** Brown graduated valedictorian from the New York Military Academy. He attended the Ithaca Conservatory of Music, and Duke University, where he became the leader of the "Duke Blue Devils" dance band. After the group toured for a year, Brown free-lanced in New York, arranging for Isham Jones, Jimmy Dorsey and others. In 1938 he started the orchestra that later became Les Brown and His Band of Renown. In 1947 he became the musical director for Bob Hope, performing 18 Christmas USO shows overseas. During one show Hope turned to Brown and stated, "If they drop a bomb, cut my second number." **TV** Among Brown's long list of credits as musical director are "The Steve Allen Show," "The Dean Martin Show," and PBS's "Mel Torme —The Christmas Songs." Enjoyed huge success with recordings of "Sentimental Journey" (which he also wrote; his band girl vocalist was Doris Day in 1945), "I've Got My Love To Keep Me Warm," and "We Wish You The Merriest." Also a guest conductor for the U.S.Air Force—once for the return of the American hostages from Iran. **ACHIEVEMENTS** Received an Honorary Doctor of Music from Ithaca Conservatory of Music. Brown has played for Presidents Nixon's and Reagan's inauguration balls, presidential birthdays, and for Queen Elizabeth.

Jimmy Dorsey   6505 Hollywood

Musician, band leader

BORN James Dorsey; Feb. 29, 1904, in Shenandoah, PA. **SPOTLIGHTS** In the early 1930s, Jimmy and his brother Tommy formed the Dorsey Brothers Orchestra with a big band swing sound. They employed the unique brass set-up of one trumpet and three trombones, among their dozen or so orchestra players. Some of their recording hits include "Stop, Look and Listen," "St. Louis Blues," "I'll Never Say 'Never Again' Again," "Dinah," and "Honeysuckle Rose." Jimmy was known for playing the alto saxophone. He also played the clarinet, and every so often the trumpet. Younger brother Tommy was outstanding on the trombone, and was the determined band leader. As a bonus, they also had the brilliant Glenn Miller working with them for awhile. The two brothers, though, struggled with serious issues of sibling rivalry. Jimmy, who tended to be a relaxed type who enjoyed leisurely rounds of golf and cocktails, ironically possessed a fiery temper and picked on his younger brother. Tommy, a better musician, was contentious and the more driven of the two. Tommy resented all the extra work he was forced to due on his less ambitious brother's behalf. Jimmy and Tommy actually came to blows to settle arguments. Although this was never done in front of the public, their constant fighting is certainly one reason that during a performance in June 1935 Tommy walked away from the band and went his separate way. Jimmy Dorsey took over leadership of the band; it was a responsibility he would have preferred not to have had. As the new Jimmy emerged, he concentrated on working in radio. They broadcast via live radio band remotes that kept the country swinging from the Mocambo in Hollywood, the Trianon and Aragon in Chicago, to hundreds of other ballrooms across the land. Jimmy Dorsey and his orchestra enjoyed such boogie-woogie, up-tempo hits as "Green Eyes," "Amapola," "Tangerine," and "Yours." Other popular tunes include "I Understand," "Embraceable You" (with Helen O'Connell), "Marie Elena," "I'm Glad There Is You," "I Get Along Without You Very Well," and "So Rare." Throughout the years he featured a number of singers, and varied their music with everything from ragtime, to jitter-bugs to Dixieland. **SIDELIGHTS** Jimmy and Tommy Dorsey reunited in 1953 and "worked together but as separately as possible" with their band until 1955. (Also see the bio of Tommy Dorsey

in this book.) **QUOTE** "If you don't feel well, stop thinking about yourself and rise above it." Died: 1957.

Vincent Price   6501 Hollywood

See page 212

Ann-Margret   6501 Hollywood

Actress, singer, dancer

Ann-Margret

BORN Ann-Margret Olsson; April 28, 1941, in Sweden. **SPOTLIGHTS** One of the world's most glamorous and versatile superstars, this ravishing redhead with a perfect figure is the consummate entertainer. As a young girl, Ann-Margret was discovered by the legendary George Burns and given her first big break performing at the Sahara Hotel, in Las Vegas in 1960. At age 20, she made her silver screen debut playing Bette Davis' daughter in Capra's *Pocketful of Miracles* (1961). She was sheer delight to watch. Her real breakthrough, though, was in the energetic musical *Bye Bye Birdie* (1963), where she had her first starring role. Six months after the movie had wrapped, director George Sidney was inspired to add a scene. At his own expense of $60,000, he brought the crew and talent back to the Columbia sound stage to film a new song just for Ann-Margret. This scene would become *Bye Bye Birdie*'s now-classic signature opening and closing number. Dressed in her peach chiffon dress, with the wind blowing through her hair, and sweet as candy with a sugar jolt bang, she exploded on screen singing the title song "Bye Bye Birdie." It catapulted Ann-Margret into superstardom, and captured the imagination of movie audiences. Life magazine wrote that her: "torrid dancing almost replaces central heating in the movie theater." The picture became an immediate box office hit; the studios reimbursed Sidney. Next, Sidney cast her in the fun musical, *Viva Las Vegas* (1964), opposite Elvis Presley. Both leads could sing and dance in perfect sync with each other, and both had ample sex appeal. Offscreen, they shared a lifelong friendship. She made dozens of other films, earning two Oscar nominations for her poignant performances. First for her dramatic portrayal of the bimbo, Bobby Templeton, in Mike Nichols' *Carnal Knowledge* (1971), and then for her role as Nora Walker in Ken Russell's wild rock musical, *Tommy* (1975). Other films include *The Cincinnati Kid* (1965) opposite Steve McQueen, *The Swinger* (1966) with Tony Franciosa, *C.C. & Company* (1970) with Joe Namath, *The Train Robbers*

(1973) co-starring John Wayne, *Magic* (1978) opposite Anthony Hopkins, *I Ought to Be in Pictures* (1982) with Walter Matthau, and *Twice in a Lifetime* (1985) co-starring Gene Hackman. Ann-Margret stole another generation of movie hearts with her comic performances in *Grumpy Old Men* (1993) and its sequel *Grumpier Old Men* (1995). For director Oliver Stone in *Any Given Sunday* (1999), she joins Al Pacino, Dennis Quaid, Cameron Diaz, and Jamie Foxx...In TV, in a role she initially did not want, she horrified TV audiences with an evil, vengeful wife in "Seduced by Madness" (1996). She starred in the title lead in the highly rated "Pamela Harriman: Life of the Party" (1998) for Lifetime Cable TV, earning Lifetime's first Best Actress Golden Globe nomination, as well as the Screen Actors Guild's Best Actress nomination. Ann-Margret has received four Emmy nominations for her acclaimed television work: "A Streetcar Named Desire," "The Two Mrs. Grenvilles," "Who Will Love My Children?" and "Queen." She has also starred in a number of television specials, and guest-starred with Bob Hope, among others. Hanna-Barbera immortalized her in animation in "The Flintstones" television cartoon series. She had a recurring role as Ann-Margrock, in which she did all the voiceovers, including special musical numbers written for her. The glamorous entertainer draws sell out crowds in Las Vegas, Atlantic City and Radio City Music Hall and always dazzles audiences with her performances. It has been said that: "Ann-Margret electrifies the room, not only with her talent and beauty, but with her joy." **ACHIEVEMENTS** The two-time Oscar nominee has won five Golden Globe Awards. A recipient of hundreds of honors, she is a three-time winner of the "Female Star of the Year" award given by the United Motion Pictures Association; has been twice honored as "Outstanding Box Office Star of the Year" by the Theatre Owners of America, and was voted "Song and Dance Star of the Year" by the American Guild of Variety Artists. In 1966 she went to war-torn Vietnam with the Johnny Rivers trio to entertain American troops. In her autobiography, she wrote: "As soon as I heard they wanted me, I was ready. I regarded the trip as a moral responsibility, something I owed to the soldiers and to America. Nothing could deter me." She bravely remained on the front line—in constant danger—for two weeks to boost morale...Her Hollywood Walk of Fame ceremony took place on July 11, 1973...Her best-selling autobiography, *Ann-Margret, My Story*, was published in 1994, by G.P. Putnam's Sons. **FANS** Contact Ann-Margret's Official Fan Club, 5664 Cahuenga Blvd., Ste. 336, North Hollywood, CA 91601. Website: www.fansource.com.

Walter Brennan   6501 Hollywood

Actor, stuntman
BORN July 25, 1894, in Swampscott, MA. **SPOTLIGHTS** A graduate of Massachusetts' Rindge Tech School, Brennan put aside his engineering career to enlist in the U.S. Army in 1917. He served as a private during World War I. After his honorable discharge, he decided to visit Hollywood. Around 1923

Walter Brennan

Brennan broke into silent films as an extra, then advanced to doing stunts in Westerns. It was wild and dangerous work, with few, if any, regulations or controls. He recalled, "I started playing old men when I was 32, because I got my teeth knocked out in a mob scene. I've just now reached the age I've been playing all the years I was in motion pictures." He got his *real* break in 1935 from Samuel Goldwyn, who cast him as "Old Atrocity" in *Barbary Coast*. With his distinctive, craggy voice, loose-limbed body, and unshaven, punchy face, he became one of Hollywood's busiest—and most highly acclaimed—character actors. This superior motion picture talent appears in more than 100 films, including *Man on the Flying Trapeze* (1935), *Fury* (1936), *The Adventures of Tom Sawyer* (1938), *Northwest Passage* (1940), *Meet John Doe* (1941), *My Darling Clementine* (1946), *Red River* (1948), *Bad Day at Black Rock* (1954), *The Far Country* (1955), *The Proud Ones* (1956), *Rio Bravo* (1959), and *Support Your Local Sheriff!* (1969). **TV** He played the folksy, bumbling, busy-body Gran'pa Amos McCoy on the rural comedy "The Real McCoys" (1957-'63). About the show, he said, "Kids won't learn English from this series, but this is one show that won't teach them better ways to ruin the furniture, throw food, or talk back to their elders." **ACHIEVEMENTS** Brennan was the first actor ever to win three Academy Awards. Best Supporting Actor Academy Awards for *Come and Get It* (1936); *Kentucky* (1938); and *The Westerner* (1940). **QUOTE** "My favorite movie line? Why it's from a film I did called *To Have and Have Not* (1945) with Mr. Bogart and Miss Bacall. It goes like this, 'Didja ever get stung by a dead bee?'" Died: 1974.

Alex Trebek   6501 Hollywood

Host, producer
BORN George Alexander Trebek; on July 22, 1940, in Sudbury, Ontario, Canada. **SPOTLIGHTS** The King of Quiz. Before becoming America's favorite television quiz show host, Trebek graduated from the University of Ottawa in 1961 with two degrees in philosophy. He decided against pursuing his graduate degree in favor of a career in broadcasting. He joined the Canadian Broadcasting Company, Canada's premier television network. For the next dozen years he honed his craft as an announcer and reporter, covering a wide range of events, for both radio and TV. He earned a reputation as a newsman who maintained his poise and composure—two of his finest qualities—even in the most nerve-racking situations. Trebek first moved to the quiz show format with a Canadian teen show called "Reach for the Top." Arriving in America in 1973, he

Alex Trebek

landed the host position on the game show "Wizard of Odds." Handsome enough to be a movie star, with brown hair and dark brown eyes, complemented by a fit physique at a sound 6 feet tall, Trebek had ample sex appeal to attract a large female audience. Added to his congenial, debonair personality and quick wit, he became a favorite with viewers, and soon other game shows were vying for his services. The charmer has hosted "High Rollers," "The New Battlestars," "The $128,000 Question," "Classic Concentration," and "To Tell the Truth." Proving a TV personality can be both good-looking and smart as a whip, he gained phenomenal fame and became a household name as host of "Jeopardy!" Trebek was immediately attracted to the fast-paced nature of the show, combined with the sophisticated level of the contestants' knowledge. He stated, "When I began producing and hosting 'Jeopardy!' in 1984, I had no idea that it would become the long-running hit it is. But I did feel the show was the right show for me, because it rewards people for their knowledge, a value I heartily endorse." He added, "It's unlike any show on television. The format is an exciting concept that challenges people to think quickly and make split second decisions under pressure." Under Trebek's deft stewardship, "Jeopardy!" has reigned as TV's #1 quiz show for the past 15 years. It has ranked first among all quiz shows in the Nielsen ratings throughout its run. As its cerebral host, he has posed more than 200,000 answers from thousands of categories, in more than 3,500 shows. One reason for the show's popularity lies with Trebek himself. He is trustworthy, intelligent and of unimpeachable integrity, and the camera beams that with shining clarity. He is also a *bon vivant*, a man of *esprit* and refined sophistication, who brings a subtle joy to the program. Extremely perceptive, Trebek skillfully guides contestants through the ins and outs of TV's most dynamic, stimulating and intellectual game show. His hosting duties on "Jeopardy!" have become legendary. Another key ingredient for its success is Trebek's sincere admiration for the contestants and viewers. He said, "The show challenges viewers to examine their knowledge from the general to the arcane. In terms of our contestants, I am constantly amazed with their breadth of knowledge." Trebek's devoted audience looms in the tens of millions, and are sticklers for not missing a show. They appreciate his genuine nature and have a sense of his honor in both show business and his private life. Offscreen, Trebek is a devoted husband to his wife, Jean, and father to Matthew and Emily. **ACHIEVEMENTS** "Jeopardy!" has won 19 Emmy Awards; Trebek has personally taken two Emmys home. He is the recipient of countless other honors and awards, including an honorary doctorate of philosophy from his alma mater. A tremendous humanitarian, Trebek travels frequently on behalf of World Vision, an international organization that provides for the needy, with emphasis on children. On behalf of World Vision, he has traveled to India, Ethiopia, Ghana, Bosnia, Columbia, as well as other impoverished and/or disaster areas, to lend a helping hand. Trebek also serves on the World Board of Governors for the United Services Organization (USO). He has been on more than ten goodwill tours for the military, improving the troops' morale, including during the holidays. In addition, Trebek is a board member of the National Geographic Society Educational Foundation, for which he hosts the annual National Geographic Bee, and is on the board of the National Advisory Council for the Literacy Volunteers of America...An accomplished chef, Trebek holds a partial interest in a California winery called Creston Vineyards, which produces 50,000 cases annually, and owns Creston Farms, a working Thoroughbred horse ranch. Websites: www.wines.com/creston and www.crestonfarms.com **HIGHLIGHTS** The category is "Tributes" and the answer is: "It's a tribute as coveted and sought after as any of the entertainment industry's equally prestigious awards—including the Oscar, Emmy, Grammy, Golden Mike or Tony. This gleaming landmark recognizes a lifelong contribution to the arts, and is of both public and peer appreciation. It is a permanent monument of the past, as well as the present, and will be admired by countless generations to come. The question? What is Alex Trebek's star on the Hollywood Walk of Fame? **QUOTE** His Walk of Fame star dedication ceremony took place on May 17, 1999. Trebek commented, "There was no television when I was a young boy growing up in Northern Ontario. I had only radio and movies to fire my imagination. To think that nearly a half century later I am in the same block as Betty Grable, Liberace, Dean Martin, Ann-Margret, and Walter Brennan, and across the street from Nelson Eddy, Frank Sinatra, Alfred Hitchcock, Isaac Stern, and many big band leaders boggles my mind. I'm not sure I deserve to be here, but I'm so happy and grateful that I am. I hope that in 50 years, I'll be remembered as warmly as they are."

Julia Faye 🎥   6501 Hollywood

Actress

BORN Sept. 24, 1896, in Richmond, VA. **SPOTLIGHTS** A light-haired lovely with an oval-shaped face and large, dark eyes, Faye was one of Mack Sennett's original bathing beauties. By cinema's standard in the late 1990s, she would be considered chubby, but during the silent area she was voluptuous and desirable. One day she was introduced to the great director, Cecil B. DeMille, who in essence made her a contract player. Faye appears in dozens of his movies as a supporting actress. She worked for half a century in DeMille's films—wearing a variety of historical costumes, in both silents and talkies—including the tremendous success, *The Squaw Man* (1918), *Fool's Paradise* (1921), his religious epic *The Ten Commandments* (1923), *Turkish Delight* (1927), the remake of *The Squaw Man* (1931), *Samson and Delilah* (1949), *The Greatest Show on Earth* (1952), to the remake of *The Ten Commandments* (1956). She made 125 pictures. Died: 1966.

Jean Hersholt 🎥   6501 Hollywood

Actor

BORN July 12, 1886, in Copenhagen, Denmark. **SPOTLIGHTS** The son of theatrical parents, Hersholt was a former Scandinavian stage actor before arriving in America in 1914. He began working in silents in 1915, becoming a busy actor in countless films. With the introduction of sound in the late 1920s, Hersholt decided to specialize in leading character roles. His decision was based on his advancing age and slight accent. He gained tremendous fame in the role of Dr. Allan Roy Dafoe—the real-life backwoods doctor who delivered the Dionne quintuplets in Canada and became an immediate celebrity—in Fox's *The Country Doctor* (1936). Audiences

loved Hersholt in the warm, nurturing and fatherly type role. When he tried to obtain rights to the name for a radio program, his offer was rejected. Hersholt then created the fictional character of "Dr. Christian," which he introduced to radio listeners in 1937. He played the kindly physician-philosopher-Cupid-philanthropist, who lived fundamentally by the Golden Rule. Hersholt certainly became a beloved radio star in this light drama, especially in America's Bible Belt. He played the role so convincingly that listeners wrote to him asking for medical advice. Hersholt had an excellent work ethic; he never missed a single broadcast. This long-running radio series ended in 1954. The heroic character and his traditional values were just as popular in movies: *Meet Dr. Christian* (1939), *The Courageous Dr. Christian* (1940), *Dr. Christian Meets the Women* (1940), *Remedy for Riches* (1940), *Melody for Three* (1941), and *They Meet Again* (1941). In was in this role, as Dr. Paul Christian, that Hersholt was immortalized. **ACHIEVEMENTS** Known for his tremendous humanitarian efforts, in 1939 he received a Special Oscar for his volunteer service and founding of the Motion Picture Relief Fund (which helped ill and/or impoverished, unemployed movie people), and in 1949 he was awarded a Special Oscar "for distinguished service to the motion picture industry." He was also a former president of the Academy of Motion Picture Arts and Sciences. In 1956 the Academy named a special award in his honor. It is presented annually—during the official Academy Awards ceremony—to a deserving individual for humanitarian achievements. Died: 1956.

Samuel Goldwyn (seated left, wearing hat), Flo Ziegfeld (seated with hat on lap), and Roy Rennahan at the camera. They are on the set of Whoopee! *(1930)*

6445 HOLLYWOOD

Yma Sumac 🎵   6445 Hollywood

Singer, actress

BORN Emperatriz Chavarri; Sept. 10, 1927, in Ichocan, Peru. **SPOTLIGHTS** A supreme soprano whose incredible vocal range is from a deep contralto to a high coloratura. She won acclaim in the U.S. from her 1949 appearance at the Hollywood Bowl. The exotic beauty immediately became known as the "Aztec Princess Reincarnated." Recordings include "Legend of the Sun Virgin," "Mambo," and "Voice of Xtabay." Films include *Secret of the Incas* (1954), and *The Loves of Omar-Khayyam* (1957). Critic Virgil Thomson wrote "her vocal technique is impeccable. She sings very low and warm, very high and bird-like . . . the scale is very close to four octaves."

Carlton E. Morse 🎙   6445 Hollywood

Writer, producer, director

BORN June 4, 1901, in Jennings, LA. **SPOTLIGHTS** He was creator, writer and producer of radio's *most* powerful serial, "One Man's Family," which was on the air for 27 years (1932-'59). Much of America listened to this show and kept the program close to their hearts. Children and parents gathered around the radio in the living room to listen to the weekly continuation of "One Man's Family." Listeners aged at the same rate the characters did, and the fans embraced the depicted Barbours family of Sea Cliff, San Francisco as if they were members of their own family. Morse conceived the idea of "One Man's Family" to unite the family unit. He felt that the rise of juvenile delinquency was directly related to the deterioration of the family in post-war America. Through his characters Morse dispensed family philosophy. Morse was also creator, writer, producer and director of "I Love a Mystery" (1939-'52)—one of the greatest radio programs of all time. Completely opposite in content to his other show, it showcased international travel, mystery and murder. It aired late at night when the kiddies were in bed. **QUOTE** His advice to writers? "Be lucky." Died: 1993.

Louis Jordan 🎵   6445 Hollywood

See page 217

Barbara Whiting 📺   6443 Hollywood

Actress, singer

BORN May 19, 1931, in Los Angeles, CA. **SPOTLIGHTS** The daughter of acclaimed songwriter, Richard Whiting, she was a born performer. The funny, plucky 13-year-old lucked into her first film when her next door neighbor had director George Seaton over and he asked to see her. She hopped over the fence into the feature *Junior Miss* (1945). She played Fuffy, the foil, to Peggy Ann Garner's lead. Later, she became "Junior Miss" on the CBS radio series. Her next movie was the musical *Centennial Summer* (1946) packed with wonderful Jerome Kern songs. TV: Played a UCLA co-ed, and her real-life, older sister Margaret played a singer in "Those Whiting Girls" (1955-'57), a sitcom. Although offered her own series, she chose love over TV, marrying and moving to Chicago—the very city her mother had worked so hard to leave.

Eddie Albert 📺   6439 Hollywood

Actor

Eddie Albert and Eva Gabor

BORN Edward Heimberger; April 22, 1908, in Rock Island, IL. **SPOTLIGHTS** An agile and charming youth, he started in show business traveling with a circus. Albert was a star trapeze artist. He made his screen debut in *Brother Rat* (1938), a comedy about three cadets at the Virginia Military Academy. His co-stars were Wayne Morris and Ronald Reagan (the future President of the United States). Albert's impressive filmography includes *Roman Holiday* (1953--in an Oscar-nominated role), *Oklahoma!* (1955), *The Teahouse of the August Moon* (1956), Hemingway's classic tale *The Sun Also Rises* (1957), *The Joker is Wild* (1957), *Captain Newman, M.D.* (1963), *The Heartbreak Kid* (1972--in an Oscar-nominated role), *The Longest Yard* (1974), and *Escape to Witch Mountain* (1975). **TV** Starred as Oliver Douglas in "Green Acres" (1965-'71). He played a successful Manhattan attorney who throws it all away to get closer to nature, in Hooterville, on a 160-acre rundown farm. Still seen in syndication today, a new generation of fans have fallen for this delightful talent. Father of the handsome actor-photographer Edward Albert.

Harry Warner 🎥   6439 Hollywood

Film pioneer, producer

BORN Dec. 12, 1881, in Poland. **SPOTLIGHTS** Out of 12 children, Warner Bros. was started by four brothers: Harry, Albert, Sam and Jack. In 1903, the family risked their savings and hocked everything they owned for $1000 to acquire a Model B Kinetoscope machine, a light-making unit, and one film. They set up a nickelodeon, an early picture palace that charged five cents for admission. It was the stuff dreams were made of, and proved to be the beginning of the legendary Warner Bros. empire. The film was the exciting, 12-minute, one-reeler, *The Great Train Robbery* (1903). This ground breaking "moving" action picture was the first to have a story line. Crowds were ecstatic while watching it, although many did not fully understand the concept of cinema and feared the gunshot from the robbery sequence might hit them! The Warner Bros. made $300 in one week. As brother Sam declared, "$300! My God, that's more money than Pop makes in a month!" By 1907, they decided that nickels were not the most profitable end of show business. They went into film distribution, where they were already considering the possibility that Warner Bros. could be all over the world. As their loving mother and father put it: "When four marvelous boys like you stick together through thick and thin, there is no question but that you will attain all the success you hope for." Filmmaking followed; *My Four Years* (1918) was their first commercial hit. Then, a few years later, when they were $990,000 on bank overdraft and on the verge of bankruptcy, they hit the jackpot with a dog named Rin-Tin-Tin. The German shepherd's movies were so popular around the globe that both Warner Bros. and the exhibitors praised him as "The Mortgage Lifter." (See the bio of Rin-Tin-Tin in this book.) Warner Bros. made motion picture history when it made the very first movie with sound, *The Jazz Singer* (1927). Died: 1958.

Jim Nabors   6435 Hollywood

Actor, singer

Jim Nabors

BORN June 12, 1933, in Sylacauga, AL. **SPOTLIGHTS** The son of a local police officer, Nabors was raised in Alabama. Gifted with a rich classical baritone, he began singing in his high school glee club. His first professional performance was at The Horn in Santa Monica, California, a cabaret theater whose intimate atmosphere was bent toward the showcasing of new talent. His act included hillbilly monologues as well as operatic arias. To his good fortune, he was discovered by Andy Griffith at the small club. Griffith asked him to audition for the role of bumbling gas station attendant Gomer Pyle in TV's "The Andy Griffith Show" (1960-'68). The rest is television history. Nabors became America's "Favorite Southern Country Cousin," and his catchphrase—"Sha-zaam!!!"—was imitated by millions of fans. He became star of the military situation comedy, "Gomer Pyle USMC" (1964-'70). His concerts include his performing with the Dallas and St. Louis symphonies and in numerous theater productions, including "The Music Man." He has recorded 28 albums— including five gold and one platinum. Motion pictures include *The Best Little Whorehouse in Texas* (1982) opposite Burt Reynolds and Dolly Parton, *Stroker Ace* (1983) with Burt Reynolds and Loni Anderson and a cameo role in the star-studded *Cannonball Run II* (1983). **HIGHLIGHTS** One of Carol Burnett's best friends, Nabors was also her good luck charm. She made sure he appeared as the guest star on the first telecast of each new season...Nabors received his Hollywood Walk of Fame star on Jan. 31, 1991.

Jack Haley   6435 Hollywood

Actor, comedian, singer

Jack Haley

BORN Aug. 10, 1899, in Boston, MA. **SPOTLIGHTS** Born at the turn of the century, Haley trained in vaudeville and legit theatre before coming to the big screen. He was a popular light comedian and radio star. On air he hosted his own variety program, "The Jack Haley Show" (CBS, starting in 1938), featuring a 27-year-old comedienne named Lucille Ball. Haley, however, is best remembered for his supporting work in motion pictures: *Alexander's Ragtime Band* (1938) with Tyrone Power, and *Rebecca of Sunnybrook Farm* (1938) with Shirley Temple. But, it was playing the Tin Man in *The Wizard of Oz* (1939) that Haley earned immortality. Father of producer-director-writer Jack Haley, Jr. **QUOTE** His agent asked for an autographed photo. Haley cleverly inscribed, "To Paul Small. In appreciation of what you have done for Paul Small." Died: 1979.

Cloris Leachman   6435 Hollywood

Actress

BORN April 30, 1930, in Des Moines, IA. **SPOTLIGHTS** After winning the Miss Chicago beauty contest, Leachman became runner-up in the 1946 Miss America pageant. This five-foot, four-inch, 108-pound blonde possesses shimmering grey-green eyes and a positive outlook on life. Vivacious and intelligent, she is a star of Broadway, motion pictures and television. Leachman is renowned for her exquisite and solid sense of delivery and timing. She made her silver screen debut in the thriller *Kiss Me Deadly* (1955), opposite Ralph Meeker and Albert Dekker. Based on a Micky Spillane novel, this P.I. Mike Hammer story moves at an interesting, fast base, and Leachman is excellent in it. The following year, she appeared in *The Rack* (1956) starring Paul Newman. This courtroom drama about war, brainwashing and treason was adapted from Rod Serling's TV play, and again, Leachman delivers a powerful performance. Other motion pictures include *Butch Cassidy and the Sundance Kid* (1969), *Lovers and Other Strangers* (1970), *The Muppet Movie* (1979), *Texasville* (1990) and *The Beverly Hillbillies* (1993—as Granny). Her work with Mel Brooks includes *Young Frankenstein* (1974), *High Anxiety*

Cloris Leachman

(1977), and *History of the World, Part I* (1981). She is adept at comedy and drama. **TV** She appeared as the mother in the beloved show "Lassie" (1957-'58). Leachman played the hilariously flaky busybody, Phyllis Lindstrom, on "The Mary Tyler Moore Show" (1970-'75), and in her own popular show "Phyllis" (1975-'77). **ACHIEVEMENTS** 1971 Best Supporting Actress Oscar for *The Last Picture Show*. (In 1990, she appears in the sequel *Texasville*.) The recipient of Six Emmy Awards, mother of five children, she is health-minded. This compassionate one is a vegetarian.

Paul Muni 📽   6433 Hollywood

Actor

Paul Muni

BORN Muni Weisenfreund; Oct. 14, 1895, in Lemberg, (then) Austria. **SPOTLIGHTS** Born into a theatrical family, Muni became appearing on stage with his parents when he was still in diapers. Around the turn of the century, his family emigrated to America. There, they worked in Yiddish Theater in New York's Lower East Side. His first notable performance was playing an old, bearded man. Audiences were convinced they were watching an elderly gentleman, when in fact they were watching the brilliant, intense acting of a 13-year-old boy named Muni. By 1913, the family was touring in stock companies. In 1926, he made his English-speaking Broadway stage debut in "We, Americans." Muni made his silver screen debut in *The Valiant* (1929), playing a killer who hides his true personality from his mother, for which he was nominated for an Academy Award. This dark-haired artist was cast in the title role in *Scarface: The Shame of a Nation* (1932). Loosely based on Al Capone's life, this is one of the original gangster movies. This near-perfect picture also features Ann Dvorak, George Raft, and Boris Karloff. That same year he enjoyed another movie triumph in Mervyn Le Roy's *I Am a Fugitive from a Chain Gang*. He gave a compelling performance as an innocent man who is wrongfully convicted of a crime. It is a brutal story about man's inhumanity to man, and brought real-life reform to the Georgia Penal Code. Other movies include *Bordertown* (1935) opposite Bette Davis, *Doctor Socrates* (1935) co-starring Dvorak again,

in the title role of *The Story of Louis Pasteur* (1935), as Wang Lung in the adaptation of Pearl S. Buck's novel *The Good Earth* (1937), and *We Are Not Alone* (1939) from James Hilton's novel. In the offbeat fantasy, *Angel on My Shoulder* (1946), he plays a murderous gangster who dies, goes straight to hell and makes a deal with the devil (Claude Rains). In his final role, he portrays a cantankerous, but kindly slum doctor who becomes the subject of a television documentary in *The Last Angry Man* (1959), which was based on Gerald Green's novel. The latter was a Royal Performance selection in the United Kingdom. **ACHIEVEMENTS** 1936 Best Actor Oscar for *The Story of Louis Pasteur*. 1956 Tony Award for "Inherit the Wind." **QUOTE** "I wouldn't give a tinker's damn for anyone in the business of facing the public who wasn't bothered by icy butterflies. Every time you step on a stage, a TV or movie set, or a rostrum, it's opening night. A little tingle down your spine is a message that you're not only healthy, but normal." Died: 1967.

Carol Burnett 📺   6433 Hollywood

Comedienne, actress, singer

Carol Burnett and Monty Hall

BORN April 26, 1936, in San Antonio, TX. **SPOTLIGHTS** One of television's greatest female entertainers was born a child of the Great Depression into a troubled family. She was raised in an old, cluttered, single-room apartment with her grandmother, whom she called Nanny, in Hollywood, California. Her divorced mother, a Hollywood wanna-be, lived down the hall. The family survived on welfare checks from the government. But, Burnett herself was determined to make it good in the world. Blessed with the gift of comic genius she did just that. She appeared on stage, then worked in television with puppeteer Paul Winchell, made guest appearances on "The Dinah Shore Show," among others. The comedienne had already received widespread fame on "The Garry Moore Show" before winning the hearts of America with "The Carol Burnett Show" (1967-'79). Her variety program utilized all her talents—singing, dancing, clowning, acting and miming. She also assembled an outstanding cast and crew. In 2000, Burnette returned to Broadway in "Putting It Together," a revue featuring Stephen Sondheim songs. **ACHIEVEMENTS** 1962 Emmy "The Garry Moore Show"; 1963 Emmy "Julie and Carol at Carnegie Hall"; 1972, 1974 and 1975 Emmys for "The Carol Burnett Show"; 1969 Special Tony Award...Her daughter, Erin Hamilton, is an accomplished singer. **STAR PLACEMENT** As a youngster, Carol worked as an usherette at the Hollywood Warner Brothers Theater for 65 cents an hour. Her Walk of Fame star was dedicated on May 21, 1975, at the exact site where she was fired and thrown out onto the street. (The theater no longer exists.) **QUOTE** Getting out of a New York taxi cab, she accidentally shut the door on her coat. The driver quickly pulled away, forcing Burnett to run along side the moving auto to avoid being thrown to the ground (and possibly run over). An alert passer-by saw this and flagged the cab down. The driver stopped, and Burnett released her coat. The panicked cabbie asked, "Are you all right?" "Yes," the comedienne replied breathlessly. "But how much more do I owe you?"

Jesse Lasky 🎥   6433 Hollywood

Pioneer film producer, executive

BORN Sept. 13, 1880, in San Francisco, CA. **SPOTLIGHTS** Lasky and partners Samuel Goldwyn (his brother-in-law) and Cecil B. DeMille made Hollywood's first important film, *The Squaw Man* (1914). This feature-length Western starred Dustin Farnum, and was made in 18 days. Originally budgeted at $15,000, it ended up costing three times that amount (twice what their company was worth). However, the gamble paid off. It was a huge success that legitimized the motion picture business in Hollywood. The film grossed around $250,000 in a few months and enabled the company to make 21 more films. The Jesse L. Lasky Feature Play Company merged with Adolph Zukor's Famous Players Corporation in 1916. They purchased Paramount (then a distributing company), and moved to the site where Paramount Pictures is still located today. Lasky was involved with the production of 500 films. **QUOTE** In 1923 Lasky stated, "Prophets have one great advantage over other people. Provided they deal with a future which is sufficiently remote, no one can dispute their prophecies. The technique of motion picture production changes so rapidly it is difficult to keep abreast and it is infinitely more difficult to foresee accurately the changes of next month or next year. A little over a decade ago, there were many leaders in the world of entertainment who declared the motion picture had no future. And there are some who think it is a passing phase of modern life. They hold these views in the face of facts which are staggering. I believe the motion picture is destined to grow to proportions of which we do not dream at present. Every great invention, once it has proven its practical nature, continues to grow in usefulness. I believe the motion picture will find new ways to serve humanity every year--the schoolroom, the medical clinic, government and private research departments, factories, salesmen and many other industries. The forms of entertainment which the motion picture assumes will be governed in the future, as now, by the popular taste. In this respect, the film will travel through cycles in each of which different types of story will be in vogue." Died: 1958.

Lowell Thomas 🎥   6433 Hollywood

See page 168

Ben Alexander 📺   6433 Hollywood

See page 398

Hal Mohr 🎥   6433 Hollywood

Cameraman, Cinematographer

BORN Aug. 2, 1894, in San Francisco, CA. **SPOTLIGHTS** Born the sixth and last child, Mohr attended parochial school (his mother was Catholic), but was excused from both the religious services and from school during the Jewish holidays (his father was Jewish). After the big 1906 San Francisco earthquake destroyed much of the city, new buildings—variety and vaudeville houses—went up. "At one of the little vaudeville houses, I saw my first motion picture, just a train going by the camera. I got so fascinated, I wanted to find out what it was. I couldn't understand how they did it—which must sound stupid now, but the process was brand new. I was always experimenting, investigating. I had an inquisitive nature." From that moment forward, he devoted himself to the camera, even building his own as a teenager. Much to his parents' dismay, who wanted him to become a doctor, he began his film career in 1910, and became director of photography on 108 motion pictures. Many of his early works were with the screen's #1 star, Mary Pickford in films like *Little Annie Rooney* (1925). He also did *The Jazz Singer* (1927--the first talkie), *Noah's Ark* (1929), *Destry Rides Again* (1939), and *The Wild One* (1954). **ACHIEVEMENTS** 1935 Oscar for *A Midsummer's Night's Dream*; 1943 Oscar for the remake of *The Phantom of the Opera*. **QUOTE** "The intelligent director works creatively with his cameraman, never treating him as a mere photographer. I'm still eager to associate with that kind of man." Died: 1974.

Bob Hawk 🎤   6433 Hollywood

Emcee, quiz show specialist

BORN 1908, in Creaton, IA. **SPOTLIGHTS** One of radio's hardest working quiz masters, this top-rated announcer hosted such shows as "Foolish Questions and Fun Quiz," "Bob Hawk's Quixie Doodle Quiz," "Name Three," "Take It or Leave It," and "How'm I Doin'?" during the 1930s through 1950s. He was known for his provocative one-line tests of knowledge. A good researcher, too, Hawk knew the scientific data to back the correct answer. He was also one of the earliest to do the man-on-the-street interview show. While contestants on his show could win anywhere from $10 up to $3,000, this master of ceremonies was clearing in $300,000 a year in 1952.

Melissa Gilbert 📺   6429 Hollywood

Actress, director

BORN May 8, 1964, in Los Angeles, CA. **SPOTLIGHTS** An endearing child actor, she was immortalized as Laura Ingalls Wilder on "Little House on the Prairie" (1974-'83). Playing the tomboyish farmer's daughter of the struggling Ingalls family in Walnut Grove, Plum Creek, Minnesota, Gilbert won rave reviews. Her winning and charming characterization made her a natural scene-stealer. She has distinguished herself since in a variety of quality TV movies: the remake of "The Diary of Anne Frank," and "The Miracle Worker" (the Helen Keller and Annie Sullivan story), opposite Patty Duke. Other work includes "Blood Vows: Mafia Wives." In 1998 she guest-starred on the highly rated CBS family show, "Touched by An Angel," and although grown-up, looked youthful. In 1999, she tackled "Murder at 75 Birch." In 2000, she starred in the CBS-TV movie "Vision of Murder: The Story of Danielle." Gilbert also directs. Her sister is actress Sara Gilbert of TV's "Roseanne" fame, and her husband is actor Bruce Boxleitner.

Jennifer Jones 🎥   6429 Hollywood

Actress

Jennifer Jones

BORN Phyllis Isley; Mar. 2, 1919, in Tulsa, OK. **SPOTLIGHTS** With her high cheek bones, open-face, and dark-hair beauty, Jones was extremely selective in what she acted in. (She could afford to be picky about her roles due to her various powerhouse husbands.) In the romantic comedy *Cluny Brown* (1946) she deliciously partakes in jabbing some of the absurdity of British upper-class society. That same year she gave an entirely difference performance in *Duel in the Sun* (1946). Her hot-blooded portrayal caused a furor. Other classics include *Since You Went Away* (1944), *Portrait of Jennie* (1948), *Love is a Many-Splendored Thing* (1955), and *The Man in the Gray Flannel Suit* (1956). **ACHIEVEMENTS** 1943 Best Actress Oscar for *The Song of Bernadette*...Her second husband was movie producer David O. Selznick, of *Gone with the Wind* fame. Their marriage began in 1949 and ended with his death in 1965. Married third husband, billionaire industrialist Norton Simon, in 1971.

Gabby Hayes 🎙   6427 Hollywood

Actor

BORN George Hayes; May 7, 1885, in Wellsville, NY. **SPOTLIGHTS** The perennial sidekick and stooge of Western heroes, this well-loved, white-whiskered, toothless comedy rascal with a flapped-back Stetson appeared in some 200 oaters (Westerns). Although he appeared in other genres as well. Movies include *Mr. Deeds Goes to Town* (1936) with Gary Cooper and Jean Arthur, and *Dark Command* (1940) with John Wayne and Claire Trevor. TV: He played Red Connors in

Gabby Hayes

"Hopalong Cassidy" (1945-'48). He also hosted matinee Westerns, usually watched by children. Radio: A regular on "The Roy Rogers Show" (1944-'46) and "The Andrews Sister Eight-to-the-Bar Ranch" (1944-'45). **SIDELIGHTS** When Fred (Mister) Rogers was starting out, he worked behind-the-scenes on Hayes' Saturday morning TV show. Hayes would casually sit on a porch and talk with great ease to the camera. Rogers asked Hayes how he could be so natural in front of the camera. Hayes responded, "Well, I think of just one little buckaroo, and talk directly to him." That advice proved to be a tremendous asset to Rogers, who became famous for his relaxed style. **QUOTE** "You're durn tootin'." Died: 1969.

Edward Everett Horton 🎥 6427 Hollywood

Actor

Edward Everett Horton

BORN March 18, 1886, in Brooklyn, NY. **SPOTLIGHTS** A nervous, befuddled fussbudget, he enjoyed great success as a character actor. Horton made his screen debut in the silent *Too Much Business* (1921), but easily made the transition to sound. Films include *The Merry Widow* (1934) starring Maurice Chevalier and Jeanette MacDonald, *The Gay Divorcee* (1934) and *Top Hat* (1935) with the Astaire-Rogers team, *Lost Horizon* (1937) starring Ronald Colman, *Here Comes Mr. Jordan* (1941) starring Robert Montgomery, and *Arsenic and Old Lace* (1944) with Cary Grant. He made dozens of other pictures. His doomsday catchphrase was: "Oh, dear!" While his goofy screen appearances led some to think he was uneducated, in real life, Horton excelled at Oberlin Academy, Polytechnic Institute, and Columbia University. Died: 1970.

Edgar Bergen 📺   6425 Hollywood

See page 26

Melvyn Douglas 🎥   6425 Hollywood

Actor

BORN Melvyn Hesselberg; April 5, 1901, in Macon, GA. **SPOTLIGHTS** A former Broadway actor, Douglas was brilliant

Melvyn Douglas

in sophisticated, romantic comedies. A dapper gent with a penciled moustache, he carried the air of self-confidence. His trademark was his wry double-take. Films include *As You Desire Me* (1932), *Counsellor-at-Law* (1933), *Theodora Goes Wild* (1936), *Ninotchka* (1939, opposite Greta Garbo; he was billed as "the man who made Garbo laugh"), *The Gorgeous Hussy* (1938), *A Woman's Face* (1940), and *I Never Sang for My Father* (1969). Played Benjamin Franklin on TV's "The Statesman." **ACHIEVEMENTS** Best Supporting Oscars: 1963, *Hud*; 1980, *Being There*. 1967-'68 Emmy Award for "Do Not Go Gently into that Good Night." Died: 1981.

Fred MacMurray 🎥   6421 Hollywood

Fred MacMurray

Actor
BORN Aug. 30, 1908, in Kankakee, IL. **SPOTLIGHTS** The son of a concert violinist, MacMurray started out professionally as a saxophone player and singer. He made his movie debut in *Girls Go Wild* (1934) with a bit role. *The Gilded Lily* (1935), with Claudette Colbert, was a sensational lift for his movie career. With a halting, light comic flair, he appears opposite Carole Lombard in *Hands Across the Table* (1935). MacMurray's acting style was accented by his genial ways, stiff humor and surface romance. He broke away from "Mr. Nice Guy" roles to be a heel in Billy Wilder's *Double Indemnity* (1944), with murder partner Barbara Stanwyck. He received excellent reviews. He also played against type include *The Caine Mutiny* (1954), *Pushover* (1954), and *The Apartment* (1960). He was very good in these pictures, yet audiences preferred him as the affable, neighborly type. Pal Walt Disney cast him in *Shaggy Dog* (1959)—the first of five pictures with that studio. In all, MacMurray made 85 films. **TV** He starred in the sitcom "My Three Sons" (1960-'72), in a fatherly role well-suited for the him. **QUOTE** No *Absent-Minded Professor* (1961) when he re-invested his salary in Disney stock. This keenly minded businessman also owned real estate holdings. MacMurray stated, "There was an article in *Cosmopolitan* some time ago listing the richest people—they called them 'the very, very rich'—of the world. My gardener showed it to me, as he

asked for a raise. I was appalled. There was a picture of Aga Khan. A picture of Barbara Hutton. A picture of Doris Duke. And there was me. How much that article cost me, you'll never imagine." Died: 1991.

Carl Reiner 📺   6421 Hollywood

Carl Reiner

Comic, writer, producer, director
BORN March 29, 1922, in Bronx, NY. **SPOTLIGHTS** Born in the Bronx, Reiner is the son of a watchmaker who taught him the value of time. He was actively involved in baseball, drama, academics and, at age 16, held a job as a machinist helper in the millinery trade. He enlisted in the Army Air Corp (Air Force) during World War II, where he trained as a radio operator. Reiner's comedic talents were discovered and he was reassigned to the Special Services Entertainment Unit, touring for 18 months in the Pacific in G.I. revues. Upon his honorable discharge after the War, he won parts in various musicals on Broadway, then joined Sid Caesar and Imogene Coca on "Your Show of Shows." Reiner conceived "The Dick Van Dyke Show" (1961-'66), which became one of the best-loved sitcoms in TV history. Audiences remember his co-starring role as the toupee-wearing producer, Alan Brady. A truly versatile talent in front of the cameras, as well as behind the scenes, he's written and/or directed these movies: *The Thrill of It All* (1963) with Doris Day and James Garner, *Oh, God!* (1977) starring George Burns, *The Jerk* (1979) starring Steve Martin, and *Fatal Instinct* (1995) with Armand Assante. His acting credits include *It's A Mad, Mad, Mad, Mad World* (1963), *The Russians Are Coming, The Russians Are Coming* (1966) with John Phillip Law, and *Dead Men Don't Wear Plaid* (1982). **ACHIEVEMENTS** He's made us laugh a million times and has 12 Emmys to prove it! 1999 Grammy with Mel Brooks for Best Spoken Comedy Album: *The 2000 Year Old Man in the Year 2000*...Reiner and his wife of 55 years, Estelle, are parents of three children. TV fans of "All in the Family" know his son Rob Reiner, but the Reiners have two daughters, too. **QUOTE** A proud papa, he calls his children, "Terribly civilized, wonderful human beings."

Sammy Kaye 📺   6419 Hollywood

Orchestra leader, composer

BORN March 13, 1910, in Rocky River, OH. **SPOTLIGHTS** The folksy radio host of the "The Sammy Kaye Show," his variety program featured his orchestra playing their popular "swing and sway" rhythms. This long-running program first aired in 1944, and was retitled "Sammy Kaye's Sunday Serenade Room" in 1954. Instead of breaking new ground, Kaye utilized time-tested tunes in simple arrangements. His soothing, but danceable music was reassuring to Americans coming out of World War II. **TV** "The Sammy Kaye Show" entertained audiences for years with the comic routine, "So You Want to Lead a Band?" Kaye would select members of the audience to be guest conductors. The orchestra would musically follow their new leader's baton "instructions" with entertaining results. Kaye and his band had another long run, from 1950-'59. His recordings topped the charts: "Moondust" and "My Buddy." **QUOTE** A homespun fella, Kaye talked to audiences as if they were his good friends: "Mom's out in the kitchen, fishing around in the ice-box for the root beer and the cheese spread. Well, there they are and there we are and pretty soon we're all singing and dancing and having a heck of a time." Died: 1987.

Bert Lytell 🎥   6417 Hollywood

Actor

Bert Lytell

BORN Feb. 24, 1885, in New York, NY. **SPOTLIGHTS** The divinely handsome Lytell was an extremely popular leading man during the silent era. With his dapper presence, dreamy eyes and sly smile, Lytell made female fans swoon in the aisles. He excelled in romantic stories and light comedies. Films include *Alias Jimmy Valentine* (1920), *The Idle Rich* (1921), and *Rupert of Hentzau* (1923). In all, he made 60 pictures. When sound arrived, Lytell returned to the stage; he had started in theatre at age three. Broadway welcomed him with opened arms. He enjoyed a tremendous reception with each new role, and produced one Broadway extravaganza. Died: 1954.

Snub Pollard 🎥   6415 Hollywood

Comedian

BORN Harold Fraser; April 2, 1886, in Australia. **SPOTLIGHTS** A small, expressive, slapstick actor during the silent era, he made 100 shorts and features from 1914-'61. He was a great supporting asset to lead comedians. He occasionally was the star. Pictures include *Luke Laughs Last* (1916), *From Hand to Mouth* (1919), *The Dippy Dentist* (1920), *Are Husbands Human?* (1925), *Man of a Thousand Faces* (1957), and *Pocketful of Miracles* (1961—his last). The exuberant Pollard had an identifiable black, waxed handlebar mustache. Died: 1962.

Fanny Brice 🎥   6415 Hollywood

Fanny Brice

Singer, comedienne

BORN Fannie Borach; Oct. 29, 1891, New York's Lower East Side, NY. (In the 1920s she changed the spelling of her first name from "Fannie" to "Fanny.") **SPOTLIGHTS** A born entertainer, she skipped school to observe the busy streets in Harlem. Brice had a keen ear for dialect, and spent a lot of time listening to and learning how to imitate the Italian, German, Polish, and other immigrants who lived in the area. The jargon would later fit into her comedy skits. As a child, she also frequented Coney Island, where she begged for pennies and nickels, and tearfully sang melancholy songs to the coin-throwing tourists. She readily learned that the more real tears she cried, the more jangling she heard. At age 14, she made her stage debut singing "When You Know You're Not Forgotten by the Girl You Can't Forget" during amateur night at Keeney's Theater, in Brooklyn. She won $10 in prize money and gathered $23 in coins tossed onto the stage. While in her teens, this brash girl worked in burlesque clubs and briefly with George M. Cohan (see his bio in this book). Cohan, though, fired her when he discovered she could not dance. She returned to clubs. To her good fortune, a young songwriter named Irving Berlin handed the music "Sadie Salome" to Brice and advised her to sing it with a Yiddish dialect. That same night, impresario Florenz Ziegfeld was in the Columbia Burlesque House audience scouting talent. Although Brice was not considered attractive (compared to the phenomenal beauties in Ziegfeld's shows), he could spot her rare gifts. While other top-rated shows had rejected her, he had complete confidence in Brice. Ziegfeld put her in his spectacular Broadway extravaganza. In return, she remained extremely loyal to him. In 1910, he signed her to an eight-year contract at $75-a-week for the first year, and $100-a-week the following year. When she first landed the deal, Brice was so overjoyed that she showed her contract to *everyone* and wore the paper out. She returned to Ziegfeld on eight separate occasions for the same contract; finally, on number nine, he refused to give her another. He told her that enough people had seen the written agreement. Brice instantly became the sensational star of the "Ziegfeld Follies" (1910-'23), in a handful of "Midnight Frolic" editions (1915-'23), and after Ziegfeld's death, in Shubert's production of the "Ziegfeld Follies" (1934-'36). A wonderful singer and hilarious comedienne, she mugged a wide variety of funny facial expressions. Her onstage antics have still never been rivaled. Without peer, she was a real show-stopper. Tunes closely associated with her are: her haunting rendition of "My Man," "Secondhand Rose," and "I'd Rather Be Blue over You (Than Be Happy with Somebody Else)." She appears in *The Great Ziegfeld* (1936) and *Ziegfeld Follies* (1946). In 1936, NBC radio first aired "The Baby Snooks Show" starring Brice as the impish little girl. Brice had originated this childlike character for the 1934 "Follies." But radio offered something for the 40-something-year-ish Brice that stage could not—"blind broadcasting." This enabled her to play a young brat with believability. Her show smashed through the ratings, earning her $3,000-a-week (upped to $6,000 weekly). Baby Snooka was so instinctive, that she confessed playing the role was: "like stealing money." **HIGHLIGHTS** The *Funny Girl* play (1964) and film (1968), and *Funny Lady* (1975), were based on her life; all star Barbra Streisand. **QUOTES** Married three times, Brice told Billy Rose, her third husband: "I married Frank White, the barber, because he smelled so good; Nicky Arnstien because he looked so good, and you because you thought so good." Died: 1951.

June Havoc    6415 Hollywood

See page 422

Meredith Willson   6413 Hollywood

Author, lyricist, conductor

BORN Robert M. Reiniger; May 18, 1902, in Mason City, IA. **SPOTLIGHTS** The Music Man. Willson first made news the moment of his birth, weighing in at 14 pounds, seven ounces, he was the biggest baby ever born in Iowa. As a child he played piano, piccolo and the flute. At age 17, he studied at the

Meredith Willson

Juilliard School of Music. Two years later, he began his professional career with John Philip Sousa's big brass band. He played first flute for the New York Philharmonic and other prestigious organizations, and "then one day—without even wanting to—I got into conducting for radio, and that was my career." In radio, he also programmed, and wrote 10 major symphonic and concert pieces. He wrote these popular songs: "Two in Love," "Bless This House," and "You and I." Studios called upon his musical services: Chaplin's *The Great Dictator* (1940), and Wyler's *The Little Foxes* (1941). During WWII, he served as Head of the Armed Forces Radio Service. In 1950, he wrote the now-standard "May the Good Lord Bless and Keep You" as the title song for Tallulah Bankhead's "The Big Show"; it was from recalling his mother's traditional Sunday blessing. His own musical variety show was known for its luxuriant sounds and "chiffon swing." Willson's delightful childhood—playing piccolo and flute in a marching band—inspired his writing the story of a small hometown in America's heartland: *The Music Man*. A hit Broadway musical in 1957, it translated into a 1962 Academy Award-winner. **QUOTE** "I didn't have to make anything up for *The Music Man*, I just remembered." Died: 1984.

Jack Bailey   6411 Hollywood

Actor

BORN Sept. 15, 1907, in Hampton, IA. **SPOTLIGHTS** A former barker at two World's Fairs, and a vaudeville music man, Bailey enjoyed a long and extensive radio career. With his upbeat effervescent personality, Bailey was especially adept at working a crowd and getting their enthusiasm up. With his trademark opening pitch, "Would YOU like to be Queen for a Day?" Bailey's most successful radio program was the lively audience show "Queen for a Day" (1945-'57). The show offered down-on-their-luck women a chance to have their wish come true. But other women won, too, like those who asked for favors for ladies they knew who were in need. One particularly moving show had a survivor of a Nazi concentration camp ask to have her tattoo on her wrist removed. There were many tears shed when these women told their stories. After 12 years of doing the show in radio, he moved to TV, and stayed for eight years. He briefly emceed "Truth or Consequences" during the mid-1950s. He did voiceovers for Disney's animated works. Died: 1980.

Slim Summerville   6409 Hollywood

Actor, comedian

BORN George Summerville; July 10, 1892, in Albuquerque,

Slim Summerville

NM. **SPOTLIGHTS** A lanky, brown-haired talent with big, droopy brown eyes, a large nose and receding chin, his homely looks made him the perfect "hick" character. He made more than 600 pictures, starting as one of Mack Sennett's original Keystone Kops in 1913. When talkies arrived, it was discovered his unique voice had a musical drawl to it. This reliable character actor was solid gold in supporting roles. Specializing in humorous works, his blank stare added comic relief in such films as *Life Begins at Forty* (1935)—a witty Will Rogers vehicle. Summerville is credited with perfecting the technique of understatement in comedy. Yet, the tall, thin talent occasionally took dramatic parts, as in *All Quiet On the Western Front* (1930—a must-see classic war picture), and *Tobacco Road* (1941). He made a number of Westerns, including *Jesse James* (1939), and co-stars with Shirley Temple in *Captain January* (1936), as a lonely lighthouse inspector. In *Rebecca of Sunnybrook Farm* (1938), starring Temple, he lends terrific support. He was also paired opposite Zasu Pitts in a wonderful series of comedies. Died: 1946.

Bennett Cerf 🖵   6407 Hollywood

Panelist, editor, writer, publisher

BORN May 25, 1898, in New York. **SPOTLIGHTS** As keen on humor as he was good in business, Cerf once said, "For me, a hearty belly-laugh is one of the beautiful sounds in the world." Quick-witted, intelligent and a ham at heart, he was one of the longest-running panelists (1951-'67) on TV's "What's My Line?" He participated in the radio version of the guessing game, too. **HIGHLIGHTS** He founded Random House publishing in 1927, and remained at its helm as president as his imprint grew to prominence. He published such noted authors as Joyce, Proust, O'Neill and Faulkner. He declared, "In my years of publishing, I am proud to say that my House has never lost an author it really wanted to keep." He stepped down as its chairman in 1970. Cerf was also a humorist, columnist, journalist and sought-after lecturer. **QUOTE** "An awful lot comes from doing co-related things. The man who really gets into trouble is the one who does too many unrelated jobs. It throws life out of kilter. I have a dream life where everything fits into everything else." Died: 1971. His memorial service was held at his alma mater, Columbia University. The music played— Broadway show tunes—had all been written by his school chum and dear friend, Richard Rodgers.

Graham McNamee 🖳   6405 Hollywood

Reporter, commentator

BORN July 10, 1888, in Washington, DC. **SPOTLIGHTS** Called

"radio's first reporter," sports fans can thank the efforts of "the father of sportscasting" for today's personalities who deliver the play-by-play action with expertise, knowledge, and a true love of the game. McNamee permanently took the ball in 1923 from bored staff announcers, who often had no understanding of the event they were covering. Although he had planned on spending less than six months in the new medium of radio, within one year this hard-working, intelligent broadcaster had become the most famous person on air. He was so popular with listeners that his employers scheduled him to announce everything from opera to political conventions, and every sporting event from prize fights to baseball. McNamee defined sports broadcasting with sports terminology, and gave sports color. **QUOTE** About covering his first outdoor boxing match—a 1923 championship fight between Harry Greb and Johnny Wilson—he said: "I found myself thinking of the 60,000 fans that would line those stands while I was up there by the ring talking to a million more for miles around. And every once in a while I would look up at the sky, praying for rain." The sky stayed clear, he did a great job and stuck around for 19 more years until a brain embolism cut his life short in 1942.

Teresa Wright 📺   6405 Hollywood

See page 268

Del Moore 📺   6403 Hollywood

Actor

BORN 1917. **SPOTLIGHTS** A regular in "Bachelor Father" (1960-62), he also worked in "The Betty White Show" (1958) and "The Jerry Lewis Show" (1963). He appears in humorous movie shorts: *So You Want to Enjoy Life?* (1954); *So You Want to Go to a Nightclub?* (1954); *So You Want to be a Gladiator?* (1955); *So You Want to Be a Vice President?*; and *So You Think the Grass is Greener?* (1956). Died: 1970.

Johnny Maddox 🎙   6401 Hollywood

Pianist

BORN 1929, in Gallatin, TN. **SPOTLIGHTS** A musical prodigy, he first performed in concert at age five. 1950s recordings: "The Crazy Otto," "Heart and Soul," and "Yellow Dog Blues."

Will Rogers 🎥   6401 Hollywood

Actor, humorist, writer

BORN William Rogers; Nov. 4, 1879, in Oologah, Indian Territory, OK. **SPOTLIGHTS** A genius. America's folk hero. Part Native American Cherokee and part Irish, Rogers remarked about his birthplace, "I usually say I was born in Claremore, for convenience, because nobody but an Indian can pronounce Oolo-gah." His homespun humor made him widely admired by Americans. He reached the pinnacle of his popularity during the Great Depression when he used the gentle barb of his wit to make everyone laugh. There were no sacred cows. He touched the untouchables: bankers, lawyers, diplomats, etc. This insightful star was extremely popular in vaudeville, films, on stage, and on radio, but always remained *the* common man—no matter how famous he became. Everyone, both high and low in society, related to him. Rogers was brilliant, swift as lightning with a quip and an all-around lively entertainer. The following is a sample of his remarks. About high finance/white collar crime: "You see there is a lot of things these old boys have done that are within the law, but it's so near the edge that you couldn't slip a safety razor blade between their acts and a prosecution." About diplomats: "Diplomats are nothing but high-class lawyers—some ain't even high class." About the U.S. government: "The government has never been accused of being a businessman." On foreign government: "For a Latin-American dictator he died a natural death—shot in the back." On education: "Everybody is ignorant, only on different subjects." On women: "If we can

Will Rogers on politics: "So much money is being spent on the campaigns that I doubt if either man, as good as they are, are worth what it will cost to elect them."

just improve their marksmanship, we can improve civilization. About every fourth fellow you meet nowadays ought to be shot." Extremely well loved, his most endearing statement is also his best-remembered: "I never met a man I didn't like." When Rogers went to work in Ziegfeld's Midnight Frolic show in 1916, it was a unique experience for impresario Florenz Ziegfeld. Before the show toured, Ziegfeld met with Rogers to negotiate a contract at $600-a-week for the first year and $750-a-week the second; an amount that far exceeded Rogers' expectations. The comedian agreed to the deal, and Ziegfeld told him to drop by his office to sign a contract. Rogers responded, "I don't like contracts. You can trust me and I know I can trust you." After his successful 10-year run, Rogers received a beautiful watch from the flamboyant Broadway producer. It had been engraved with this inscription: "To Will Rogers, in appreciation of a real fellow, whose word is his bond." Motion pictures include *Connecticut Yankee* (1931), *State Fair*, and *Mr. Skitch* (both 1933), *David Harum*, *Handy Andy*, and *Judge Priest* (all 1934), *Life Begins at Forty* (1935), and *Steamboat 'Round the Bend* (1935). This comedian, country philosopher and story teller started in radio in 1922, but did not really enjoy the experience. It frustrated him that he only told jokes "into a cold microphone" and nobody laughed back. This was particularly an issue for him as it was common knowledge that Rogers paid closer attention to his audience cues than any other entertainer. To get him to agree to do a weekly show, executives got the idea of installing a Sunday night audience. In the 1930s Rogers became known as "the biggest one-man show in radio." **ACHIEVEMENTS** A tremendous humanitarian, he often donated **100%** of his salary directly to the needy. Died: 1935.

Josef von Sternberg 🎥 6401 Hollywood

Director
BORN Jonas Jo Sternberg; May 29, 1894, in Austria. **SPOTLIGHTS** As his trademark, he always wore black riding boots around the studio; his attire hinted at his reputation of being a stern taskmaster. He was also an exceptional stylist. Extravagant, proud and moody, this director's glorious accomplishments include *Underworld* (1927), and making a star out of formerly plump Marlene Dietrich as Lola Lola in *The Blue Angel* (1930). He worked with her in a handful of other fine motion pictures, including *Morocco* (1930), *Shanghai Express* (1932), and *The Devil Is a Woman* (1935). Other movies include *Crime and Punishment* (1935), *Sergeant Madden* (1939), and *The Shanghai Gesture* (1941). **ACHIEVEMENTS** In Japan, in 1953, he made *Ana-Ta-Han* (*The Saga of Anatahan*). Based on a true, bizarre story about Japanese soldiers who refused to believe that WWII had ended with Japan's defeat, they continued to man their posts for seven more years. Von Sternberg wrote the screenplay, directed, photographed, and narrated the English-language version. It is considered by many critics to be a masterpiece. Died: 1969.

6385 HOLLYWOOD

Lew Ayres 🎥
6385 Hollywood

Actor, musician

Lew Ayres

BORN Lewis Ayer; Dec. 28, 1908, in Minneapolis, MN. **SPOTLIGHTS** A talented musician on the banjo, guitar, and piano, he was discovered while playing with Ray West's orchestra at the hot Los Angeles night spot, The Cocoanut Grove. The next year, he appears Universal's classic *All Quiet on the Western Front* (1930), as a young German schoolboy drawn into the hellish experience of soldiering in WWI. Later, drawing upon his real-life study of medicine, he played *Young Doctor Kildare* (1939) in the original 'B' movie and played the same role in radio's popular "The Story of Dr. Kildare." He earned an Oscar nomination in *Johnny Belinda* (1948). He traveled the Far East and Near East for two years with a cameraman at his side filming images of Hinduism, Buddhism, Sikhism and the Islamic regions. His finished project—*Altars of the World*—received a Golden Globe award. He did it, he said, "To acquaint the people of the western world to what the rest of the world believes."...A conscientious objector in WWII, he entered the Medical Corps. He was under fire much of the time and in mosquito-infected mud, he served with distinction as an Army medic and chaplain's assistant in war torn New Guinea and the Philippines. He told columnist Hedda Hopper that war "was even more horrible than I had ever imagined it." Died: 1996.

Dorothy Gish 🎥
6385 Hollywood

Actress

Dorothy Gish

BORN Dorothy de Guiche; March 11, 1898, in Dayton, OH. **SPOTLIGHTS** A silent screen star, she was especially good in light comedies. She entered films as a teen with help from friend Mary Pickford in 1912, and older sister Lillian Gish. How *Molly Made Good* (1915) was one of her 90 films. Famed director D. W. Griffith produced a string of comedies for her. She retired at the onset of talkies, with rare film appearances: *The Cardinal* (1963). Died: 1968.

Frankie Laine 🎵
6385 Hollywood

Singer, actor

Frankie Laine

BORN Frank Paul Lo Vecchio; March 30, 1913, in Chicago, IL. **SPOTLIGHTS** Known as "Mr. Rhythm," this smooth and sweet balladeer was a former altar-choir boy and 1932 Depression champion marathon dancer. He remained relatively obscure until his songs "That's My Desire," and "Cry of the Wild Goose" hit big on radio. Laine offered something new to live performances, too, with his flaying and stamping. He said, "I happen to be the first guy who began to move around and project." Known as the "Master of the Ballad" he rode the pop hit parade with 16 gold tunes, including "Mule Train," "That Lucky Old Sun," "The Wild Goose," "Music Maestro," "Please," "Sunny Side of the Street" and "Moonlight Gambler." Movie theme songs: *Blowing Wild* (1953) and *Gunfight at the O.K Corral* (1957). TV theme songs: "Rango," and "Rawhide." His "Frankie Laine Time" (1955-'56) was the summer replacement for "Arthur Godfrey and Friends."

Wally Cox 📺
6385 Hollywood

Actor, comedian

Wally Cox

BORN Dec. 6, 1924, in Detroit, MI. **SPOTLIGHTS** Cox discovered he could even make soldiers laugh during horrible WWII conditions. After his honorable discharge, and an education at NYU, he ran a jewelry store for awhile. Then, he began doing stand-up comedy. Audiences loved him as the bespectacled, "nervous Norman" type. Cox possessed a high-pitched voice, and starred as the shy science teacher on TV's "Mr. Peepers" (1952-'55) with hilarious results. In the 1960s, he was a witty regular on "Hollywood Squares," and a frequent guest in "Love, American Style" (1969-'73). A capable actor in movies, he appears in *State Fair* (1962), *Spencer's Mountain* (1963), *The Yellow Rolls Royce* (1964), *The Bedford Incident* (1965), Gene Kelly's *A Guide for the Married Man* (1967), *The One and Only, Genuine, Original Family Band* (1968), and *The Barefoot Executive* (1971). **QUOTE** "I don't believe that anyone ever started out to be a comedian. Everybody wants to be the ideal one--six feet tall, that's the good height, and with a deep booming voice, and the one who gets chosen to pitch the game--to be Sir Galahad. But when you discover you're the smallest boy in class and they pick you for the team because you're the one that's left, then, when you're young, you try to find ways to make yourself acceptable." Died: 1973.

Forrest Tucker 🎥 6385 Hollywood
Actor

Forrest Tucker

BORN Feb. 12, 1919, in Plainsfield, IN. **SPOTLIGHTS** A six-foot, five-inch tall, robust actor, he appears in 50 films. The rugged blonde made his silver screen debut in *The Westerner* (1940), starring Gary Cooper. Tucker was a very reliable supporting actor. Terrific in action pictures, he works with John Wayne in the *Sands of Iwo Jima* (1949). He appears in the Westerns *Pony Express* (1952), opposite Charlton Heston, Rhonda Fleming, and Jan Sterling, and *Three Violent People* (1956) starring Charlton Heston and Anne Baxter. **TV** Tucker gained national popularity and became a household name as Sgt. Morgan O'Rourke in the military comedy "F Troop" (1965-'67). Died: 1986.

Don Murray 🎥 6385 Hollywood
Actor, director, writer

BORN July 31, 1929, in Hollywood, CA. **SPOTLIGHTS** The son of show business parents, Murray trained at the American Academy of Dramatic Arts. He made his Broadway debut in 1951 in "The Rose Tattoo." Murray had the good fortune to play opposite Marilyn Monroe in *Bus Stop* (1956), his very first picture! He's very good in the slice-of-life drama, *The Bachelor Party* (1957). He co-wrote, produced and starred in *The Hoodlum Priest* (1961), based on a true story of a clergyman who devotes himself to troubled

Don Murray

youths. Directed and co-wrote the screenplay for *The Cross and the Switchblade* (1970). Other films include *A Hatful of Rain* (1957), *Shake Hands with the Devil* (1959), *One Man's Way* (1964—as preacher and positive thinker Norman Vincent Peale), *Baby the Rain Must Fall* (1964) with Steve McQueen and Lee Remick, and *Peggy Sue Got Married* (1986). He follows a strong ethical code in selecting and making movies.

Vikki Carr 🔘 6385 Hollywood
Singer, actress

Vikki Carr

BORN Florencia Bisenta de Casillas Martinez Cardona, July 19, 1942, in El Paso, TX. **SPOTLIGHTS** With her warm, rich voice and charming stage presence, this Latina-American beauty has achieved success in theater, television, night clubs, international concert stages and personal appearances. As an actress, she has appeared in such musicals as "South Pacific," and "The Unsinkable Molly Brown." Her perennial hit "It Must be Him" remains a favorite to fans everywhere and was featured in the film *Moonstruck*. She is a popular singing sensation in English and Spanish. **ACHIEVEMENTS** Three-time Grammy winner for *Simplemente Mujer* (1985), *Cosas del Amor* (1992), and *Recuerdo a Javier Solis* (1995). Released 55 records in two languages, including 17 gold albums. Performed for five U.S. Presidents, the Queen of England at a Royal Command Performance in London, and war-time soldiers in Vietnam. Recipient of countless honors including the top award from the Association of Hispanic Critics, Chicago's Ovation Award, the Founder of Hope Award by the City of Hope, and Hispanic Woman of the Year.

Gail Davis 📺 6385 Hollywood
Actress

Gail Davis

BORN Betty Jeanne Grayson, Oct. 5, 1925, in Little Rock, AR. **SPOTLIGHTS** Gene Autry gave this petite (five-foot, two-inch tall, 95-pound), wiry actress her big break. As a brunette, she co-stars in 15 films, including *The Far Frontier* (1948), *Death Valley Gunfighter*, *Frontier Investigator* and *Law of the Golden West* (all 1949). She gained her greatest fame in the title lead of TV's Western serial "Annie Oakley" (1953-'56).

Tony Orlando 🔘 6389 Hollywood
Singer, writer, producer

BORN Michael Anthony Orlando Cassavitis, Apr. 3, 1944, in New York, NY. **SPOTLIGHTS** At age 12, he formed a corner doo-wop group. By 16, he had auditioned for producer Don Kirshner, and hit the charts with "Halfway to Paradise," and "Bless You." He was the first vocal artist to sign with Epic Records. Then, Orlando hit #1 with "Candida." He also worked behind-the-scenes at CBS Records in the executive suite, as one of their youngest vice presidents. After releasing the #1 song of 1971, "Knock Three Times," the handsome talent felt it was safe to give up his day job. Along with the lovely duo—Telma Louise Hopkins and Joyce Vincent-Wilson—*Tony Orlando and Dawn* became an international sensation. Together they recorded: "Say, Has Anybody Seen My Sweet Gypsy Rose?" and "He Don't Love You (Like I Love You),"

Tony Orlando

among other top songs. Their 1973 #1 hit "Tie A Yellow Ribbon 'Round the Ole Oak Tree" became not only the best-selling single of the year, but the most recorded song of the '70s. During the 1981 Iran Hostage Crisis, yellow ribbons were tied around trees to signify the country's unity in demanding the return of the Americans. Since then, the yellow ribbon has become a national American symbol for hope and homecoming, reunion and renewal. Orlando entertains with warmth and an exhilarating energy. The "Tony Orlando Yellow Ribbon Music Theater" has become a popular club in Branson, Missouri. **HIGHLIGHTS** Veterans are honored each Veterans Day, November 11th, with the *Tony Orlando Yellow Ribbon Salute to Veterans*. This is a specially produced extravaganza, in Branson, which is free to veterans and their families. As part of his salute to Vets, he presents the Yellow Ribbon Medal of Freedom. Past recipients have included Bob Hope, former POW Major Stephen Long, Boxcar Willie and Connie Stevens. **ACHIEVEMENTS** His ground breaking TV show was the first multi-ethnic variety show. Orlando, of Hispanic and Greek orgins, and Hopkins and Wilson, African-Americans, were an instant hit...He is the recipient of three American Music Awards and a People's Choice Award. He received his Hollywood Walk of Fame star on March 21, 1990.

Mel Blanc 🎙   6385 Hollywood

Voice specialist, actor, musician

BORN Melvin Jerome Blanc; May 30, 1908, in San Francisco, CA. **SPOTLIGHTS** Hollywood's greatest voice specialist was known as the "Man of 1,000 voices." This genius' voice was immortalized in Warner Bros. cartoons, and has delighted hundreds of millions over the years. He breathed life, humor and personality into Bugs Bunny ("Eh, what's up, Doc?"), Daffy Duck, Sylvester ("Sufferin' succotash!"), Tweety ("I tawt I taw a puddy tat"), Porky Pig, Road Runner, Yosemite Sam, the Tasmanian Devil, Pepe Le Pew, as well as Hanna-Barbera's Barney Rubble and Dino the Dinosaur (of "The Flintstones"), and Mr. Spacely (of "The Jetsons"), among countless others. It is no exaggeration to state that Blanc provided the voices for essentially every classic Warner Bros. cartoon character. Gifted

Mel Blanc and friends at Warner Bros.

with a keen ear and a remarkable vocal dexterity, he began imitating dialects in his youth. The local grocers were an elderly Jewish couple on the corner, and this was Blanc's first mastery of jargon. Next, he became deft with the sounds of Chinatown, and from there he acquired noises, sounds and idioms at rocket speed. He was a crack-up at high school in Portland, Oregon. After graduation he found sporadic work as an actor in local radio, then in 1927 started his professional career on a show called "The Hoot Owls." Blanc was also a musician for NBC radio; he played the violin, tuba, and bass. In 1933 he became the voice of Joe Penner's famed Goo-Goo duck on "The Baker's Broadcast," becoming more popular on radio than most human counterparts. After landing a job with Warner Bros. in 1934 to provide the offscreen voices for their animated characters in film shorts, Blanc continued to work in radio. In 1939 he joined "The Jack Benny Program" as Carmichael the polar bear. Blanc later reflected in his memoirs that when he auditioned for the role he let out "a roar so savage, I nearly frightened myself." The boss, Jack Benny, signed him to the show as soon as he could stop laughing. Blanc also did the vocal sound effects of the antique Maxwell automobile which sputtered and fell apart at the seams. Blanc's unforgettable roles included a disembodied train station announcer whose catchphrase, "Train leaving on track five for Anaheim, Asuza and Cuc...amonga!" was particularly hilarious because each time Blanc said it, he left a longer silent space between "Cuc" and "amonga!" Eventually, he started the line at the opening of the show, and finally say "amonga!" at the end. Blanc was a genius with comic timing and skits. On "The Burns and Allen Show" he played the Happy Postman. He'd talk in an extremely depressed voice about the most joyous things; his voice would crack as if he were about to cry. This hardworking talent was a sweet, gentle soul, beloved by all within the industry and by anyone who had the pleasure of knowing him. **ACHIEVEMENTS** It is estimated more than 20 million people hear his voice everyday. His career spanned 55 years with Warner Bros. studios, where Blanc worked on more than 850 cartoons, television specials and movies. His son, Noel Blanc, is also a voice specialist. In his autobiography, *That's Not All Folks* (1988), Blanc wrote about San Francisco's melting pot: "For a voice man intent on assimilating new dialects, simply walking down the street provided daily education." "Th-th-th-th-that's all f-f-f-folks!" Died: 1989.

Abbe Lane 📺   6381 Hollywood

Singer, dancer, actress

BORN Dec. 14, 1932, in New York. **SPOTLIGHTS** This popular nightclub entertainer easily made the transisiton to Hollywood. A spectacular knockout beauty with a stunning figure and warm delivery, Lane initially won over audiences in "The Jackie Gleason Show." As colleague Audrey Meadows said, "Abbe could really work a room." This hot number was also a co-star on her husband's program, "The Xavier Cugat Show." Cugie led the band and played his violin, while she sang Latin tunes and danced superbly to the energetic music. Her sensuous wiggle caused quite a sensation. **QUOTE** "Sex appeal is something from within, not from without. You don't turn it on and off like a faucet." About show business: "I'm a

Abbe Lane

ham. I love the theater because I love its glamour, the money, and, most of all, the applause."

Alan Freed 🎙️   6381 Hollywood

Radio personality, producer

BORN Dec. 15, 1922, in Johnstown, PA. **SPOTLIGHTS** Called the "King of the Deejays," and the "Rock 'n' Roll King," he is credited with coining the phrase "rock 'n' roll." With his deep resonant voice that he "word punched with a beat," he became one of the hippest on the airwaves. From his controversial early 1950s "Moon Dog Show" in Cleveland, to his riotous rock 'n' roll stage shows at Brooklyn's Paramount Theatre, he toppled the wall that divided white and black music, and achieved national fame. He was instrumental in launching the careers of Muddy Waters, Bo Diddley and Chuck Berry. Freed brought the music to the big screen with the '50s classics *Rock Around The Clock*; *Rock, Rock, Rock*; *Don't Knock the Rock*; *Mr. Rock 'n' Roll*; and *Go Johnny Go*. **QUOTE** "Just like swing belonged to us, rock 'n' roll belongs to them. Kids are great joiners and this is their club." Died: 1965.

Anna Magnani 🎥   6381 Hollywood

Actress

Anna Magnani

BORN March 7, 1908, in Egypt. **SPOTLIGHTS** Of Italian ancestry, but born in the Middle East, Magnani would have been well-suited to play Cleopatra. Like a swift jungle cat, she could be lusty one moment, ferocious the next. She had no shortage of self-esteem or confidence and was shamelessly emotional. On the first evening of her stay at "the Pink Palace" (the luxurious Beverly Hills Hotel), her private maid knocked on the next-door suite. When its respectable occupant—an important politician—opened the door, the maid asked in her broken English, "Pleasa no flusha the toilet in ta morning. Ta world's greatest actress is trying to sleepa!" One of her greatest admirers and friends was playwright Tennessee Williams. He, like so many others, found her to possess a strange magnetism. It was not that she was a great beauty, yet something profoundly strong about her made her beautiful in an unorthodox way. She inspired his work *The Rose Tattoo* (1955). When adapted for a motion picture, it became Magnani's first Hollywood role. During the shooting of a fight scene between two women Magnani fractured two of Virginia Grey's ribs. Without offering an apology, Magnani declared, "Script says be rough—when I play rough, I play rough." She took home an Academy Award for Best Actress. This incredible muse for Tennesse Williams also inspired his *Orpheus Descending*. When Marlon Brando was offered the role opposite her in the Broadway production, he turned it down stating, "I have no intention of walking out on any stage with Magnani. They'd have to mop me up." He did, however, acquiesce to the dramatic film version which was entitled *The Fugitive Kind* (1959). This picture is considered a hollow version of the original work. Other films include *Wild is the Wind* (1957). **QUOTE** "Myself, I have so much boiling inside, I had to become an actress. If I had not, I think I could have become a great criminal." Died: 1973.

Sid Grauman 🎥   6379 Hollywood
Theater owner, impresario

BORN Sidney Patrick Grauman; March 17, 1897, in Indianapolis, IN. **SPOTLIGHTS** A legendary impresario. With true panache, this flamboyant showman brought Chinese artisans to Hollywood to build the world-famous Grauman's Chinese Theatre. He received official permission from the Chinese government to import temple bells, Fu dogs, pagodas, as well as some scarce artifacts to enhance the authenticity of his opulent theatre. The extraordinarily beautiful Chinese-American actress, Anna May Wong, was selected to drive the first rivet into the steel structure on Nov. 11, 1925, Armistice Day (now known as Veteran's Day). With a number of kleig lights beaming into the night sky, Grauman held its grand opening on May 18, 1927, premiering Cecil B. DeMille's religious epic, *King of Kings*. The magnificent red movie palace is admired for its ornate architecture and its large collection of movie star hand prints, footprints and signatures in cement. This rare and fun array is free and open for everyone to view and feel in the theatre's front courtyard. Each year, millions visit the landmark. The theatre is also renowned for its glamorous star-studded movie premieres. It holds the world record for the most gala premieres at a theatre, and, of course, for holding the most spectacular celebrity events. **NOTE** Although known around the world as "Grauman's Chinese Theatre," its name was changed by its second owner who removed "Grauman" and put his own name "Mann" in its place. Since then, the theatre has been sold and resold. The current owners should give Hollywood a great gift by restoring its rightful name back to *Grauman's Chinese Theatre*. This theatre is a treasured, precious jewel box, and the credit belongs to Grauman. **HIGHLIGHTS** Grauman also had the distinction of building Hollywood's *first* movie palace, the lavish Egyptian Theatre, which is located four blocks east of the Chinese Theatre. With its long open-air courtyard—originally designed to resemble the grounds leading to an Egyptian Temple—Grauman added pillars, elaborate murals and a unique sunburst ceiling pattern interior. Everyone who was anyone showed up for the opening night gala premiere of *Robin Hood* starring Douglas Fairbanks, on Oct. 18, 1922. That night, George Eastman (president of the Hollywood Chamber of Commerce) declared, "This night is a most auspicious one for Los Angeles, but it is still more auspicious for Hollywood. It marks Hollywood's advent from the status of a small town to a city of metropolitan importance where world premieres are shown." Although Hollywood legend had it that Grauman was inspired to build it after the dis-

covery of King Tutankhamen's tomb, the theatre had actually celebrated its opening five weeks before the famed English Egyptologists, Howard Carter and Lord Carnarvon's stupendous findings in the Valley of the Kings on Nov. 26, 1922. Coincidentally, Rudolph Valentino had become Hollywood's hottest property with his exciting movie, *The Sheik* (1921). With the Arabian desert motif, and Valentino's smoldering sex appeal, all things Arabesque were in vogue. The Egyptian Theatre and interest in King Tut's tomb flamed imaginations even more. Societies of Egyptologists popped up around the globe, but especially with the chic in Hollywood, Paris, London and Rome. **SIDELIGHTS** The Egyptian Theatre is located at 6712 Hollywood Boulevard. It now houses the wonderful organization, the American Cinematheque: "a non-profit, viewer-supported film exhibition and cultural organization dedicated to the celebration of the Moving Picture in all of its art forms...Programs range from in-person tributes to filmmakers and actors; screenings of classics, independents, new and retrospective foreign films, boasting state-of-the-art technology at work within an historic shell." For 24-hour information, call 323.466.3456; website: www.egyptiantheatre.com The master showman died in 1950.

Nathan Milstein 💿   6377 Hollywood
Musician extraordinaire

BORN Dec. 31, 1904, in Odessa, Russia. **SPOTLIGHTS** Violin virtuoso who mastered nearly all the world's violin repertoire. He was praised for his integrity. This serene, elegant, scholarly gentleman performed 50 international concerts and recitals annually during the peak decades of his career. He taught master classes at his home in Lausanne, Switzerland, but only for 12 days each year! He instructed his students: "You should be more than an instrument operator...Be a whole person...You cannot play the violin without feeling other things. I don't say *knowing*, I say *feeling*. There is no time to know so much." **ACHIEVEMENTS** 1975 Grammy for his recording of Bach's sonatas and parititas for unaccompanied violin. Died: 1992.

Art Linkletter 📺   6377 Hollywood
See page 291

Harry Carey, Jr. 📺   6363 Hollywood
Actor

BORN May 16, 1921, in Saugus, CA. **SPOTLIGHTS** Greasepaint runs in the family's veins; he made his screen debut with his father in *Red River* (1948). He specialized in Westerns and was a regular for director John Ford: *She Wore a Yellow Ribbon* (1949) starring John Wayne, and *Rio Grande* (1950). Carey was great in *Mister Rogers* (1955). He appeared in many movies, including *Wagonmaster, The Searchers, The Long Riders, Back to the Future, Part III*. Also appeared in TV.

Erroll Garner 💿   6363 Hollywood
Musician

BORN July 15, 1921, in Pittsburgh, PA. **SPOTLIGHTS** A self-taught pianist who started playing at age three, he never learned to read music, but could play in any key. At age seven, he was earning "lunch" money playing at local parties. Playing entirely by ear, he emerged one of the most popular jazz artists. Trying to explain his genius, the self-effacing Garner stated, "I just got the gift. The good Lord give it to me. It comes out what I feel and hear. That's what it completely is." Garner typically worked in trios, and his music ranged from bebop to romantic swing. He was the first jazz man to be booked by the classical impresario Sol Hurok. He recorded with Charlie Parker, and other jazz greats. Wonderful albums include *Concert by the Sea* (on Columbia), *The Original Misty* (on Mercury), *Solitaire* (on Mercury), *The Erroll Garner Collections Volumes 4 & 5: Solo Time!* (on Emarcy), and *Paris Impressions* (on Columbia). This internationally renowned pianist and composer, possessed a style completely his own. He did film scores, too. His record "Laura" sold more than one million copies. He wrote "Misty" in 1954, one of the industry's most covered tunes. He recorded it for Clint Eastwood's *Play Misty For Me* in 1971. **ACHIEVEMENTS** Recipient of every major music award in Europe and America, including the Grand Prix de Disque. In 1958 he performed at Carnegie Hall. **QUOTE** "I don't know what I do, or how I do it. With me, it's the relaxation and the feeling. I re-live my life at the piano, plus all the real that's coming out of me. I just like to look at people and play and smile, and get 'em on my side." Died: 1977.

Victor Young 🔴   6363 Hollywood
Songwriter, arranger, conductor

Victor Young

BORN Aug. 8, 1900, in Chicago, IL. **SPOTLIGHTS** Raised dirt poor in the tenements of the "Windy City," his gifts changed his life. Due to his tough prizefighter looks, movie studio producers found it difficult to believe he had been a solo violinist with the Philharmonic Orchestra, let alone that he was a musical genius. Young was involved with more than 350 film scores (mostly for Paramount). Selections include: "Love Letters," and "Stella By Starlight." He led the orchestra on Judy Garland's classic hit "Over the Rainbow" (1939). He also worked on many Bing Crosby hits. For Goldwyn, Young's song "My Foolish Heart,' was Oscar-Nominated. He co-wrote "Do Not Forsake Me, Oh My Darling," the theme song for *High Noon*, for which he won an Oscar. He also wrote the TV title song "Rawhide." Posthumous Oscar for "Around the World in Eighty Days." Died: 1956.

Jimmy Jam & Terry Lewis 🔴   6363 Hollywood
Producers, writers

BORN Jimmy Jam on June 6, 1959, in Minneapolis, MN; Terry Lewis on Nov. 24, 1956, in Omaha, NE. **SPOTLIGHTS** While in their teens, Jam and Lewis both attended an Upward Bound program—designed to help urban youths compete—at the University of Minnesota. There, they met at a piano and instantly clicked. Jam and Lewis have become two of the most influential musicians/songwriters/producers. Both natural born talents, and both hard workers, their midas touch of writing and producing has spun gold and platinum for a who's who list of recording artists from Janet Jackson (including her No. 1 single "Together Again"), Mariah Carey, and Johnny Gill to George Michael and Karyn White. Together they have written and produced over 40 singles and albums that went Gold or Platinum. Continuing to expand their musical horizons, they have produced movie soundtracks, including *How Stella Got Her Groove Back* (1998). In 1999 they produced Mariah Carey featuring Joe and 98 Degrees' "Thank God I Found You." They launched their own Universal Records joint-venture label Flyte Time Records. **ACHIEVEMENTS** Winner of ASCAP's Writer of the Year Award for four consecutive years. 1986 Grammy, Producer of the Year. Honored by the NAACP with its Heritage Award for their charity efforts. Their exciting Walk of Fame dedication ceremony took place on March 10, 1993.

Edmund Lowe 🎥   6363 Hollywood
Actor

BORN March 3, 1890, in San Jose, CA. **SPOTLIGHTS** Formerly a teacher, this black-haired, mustached, refined, well-dressed leading man appeared in more than 100 pictures. He was surprisingly brilliant in a role that was the antithesis of his personality, as Sergeant Quirt ("a lousy bum") in *What Price Glory?* (1926), and in the comedy *Hagg and Quirt* series that followed. TV: "Front Page Detective" (1951-'53). Died: 1971.

The Pointer Sisters 🔴   6363 Hollywood
Singing group

BORN Ruth, Mar. 19, 1946; Anita, Jan. 23, 1948; Bonnie, July 11, 1950; June, Nov. 30, 1954; all in Oakland, CA. (In 1978 Bonnie signed a solo contract with Motown.) **SPOTLIGHTS** Their mother and father were ministers at the West Oakland Church of God, and that is where they had their musical training. These fabulous siblings sang gospel in church until 1969. Their long string of hits began in 1973 with "Yes We Can Can." The following year, "Fairytale," written by Anita and Bonnie won a Grammy for best Country Single of the Year (and was the first tune recorded by women of color to reach the country charts). The Pointers Sisters' vocal repertoire spans rhythm & blues, country, jazz and pop. They're terrific entertainers, too. Smash hits: "Fire," "He's So Shy," "Slow Hand," "Automatic," "I'm So Excited," "Jump (For My Love)," and "Neutron Dance." They were the first African American female group to perform at the Grand Ole Opry.

Guy Lombardo 🎙   6363 Hollywood
See page 58

The Pointer Sisters

Edward Asner 📺   **6363 Hollywood**

Actor

Edward Asner

BORN November 15, 1935, in Kansas City, MO. **SPOTLIGHTS** Versatile and eloquent, this talented actor excels in both comedy and drama. He is best known for his portrayal of news producer Lou Grant, an ornery and cantankerous all-newsroom professional. (This terrific character was loosely based on the real-life Pete Noyes. Noyes, a Peabody Award winner, was a dominant force in Los Angeles news for most of his career, which spanned decades.) Asner developed the blunt, boisterous, grumpy boss with the heart of gold so brilliantly in the smash comedy "The Mary Tyler Moore Show," and then the spin off series, "Lou Grant," that he won a total of five Emmys for his characterization (1971, 1972, 1975, 1978, and 1980). Other fine actors who worked in these extremely popular series include Mary Tyler Moore, Ted Knight, Gavin MacLeod, and Robert Walden. Asner added two more Emmys for his work in "Rich Man, Poor Man" and "Roots." In addition he is the recipient of five Golden Globe Awards. He also does voice-overs for children's animated series. Adored by millions of television fans, Asner has also delighted audiences with his electrifying stage performances in Broadway productions, and the American and New York Shakespeare Festivals. Must-see feature films include *El Dorado* (1967--a top notch cowboy picture with John Wayne), *Skin Game* (1971-a comedy with James Garner and Louis Gossett, Jr.), and *Fort Apache, The Bronx* (1981-a crime pic with Paul Newman). Offscreen, this lovable guy exudes warmth and strength. He received a special tap dance on his Hollywood Walk of Fame star by friend, actor Martin Sheen, at his dedication ceremony on September 17, 1992. He served as National President of the Screen Actors Guild for two terms from 1981-'85. (Incidentally, that is a post that actor Ronald Reagan served for his *first* political position, when he was a Democrat.) **POLITICAL/CHARITABLE** Asner actively gives time to worthy causes. He is a committed citizen devoted to improving humanities' lot in life. He is a staunch supporter of both national and international programs: "Constitutional Rights Foundation," "ACLU," "Defenders of Wildlife," "Peace Now (Middle East)," "The Heifer Project (assists globally in farming and agriculture for the world's poor)," and local soup kitchens and missions.

William S. Hart 🎥   **6363 Hollywood**

Actor, screenwriter, director

BORN Dec. 6, 1870, in Newburgh, NY. **SPOTLIGHTS** One of the greatest and earliest silent screen Western stars, he began life criss-crossing the Wild West territory with his father, a wandering miller. They stayed with Native Indians and trail herders, and the young Hart developed a profound love of the American West. In his early teens he helped the family by working on cattle drives, becoming an expert horseman. On screen, he insisted on realism, bringing the true flavor of the rugged land and its people to his works. It helped that he wrote and directed many of his films. Pictures include: *The Apostle of*

William S. Hart

Vengeance (1916), *Branding Broadway* (1919—a funny fish-out-of-water story), *The Money Corral* (1919). *Tumbleweeds* (1925) survived the talkie era (it was reissued in 1939 with Hart himself appearing in the eight-minute prologue. It gave audiences an opportunity to hear his finely tuned baritone voice—with the perfect amount of emotion—which he had crafted during 20 years of performing Shakespeare on Broadway before he did movies). The film includes the sensational re-enactment of the Native Cherokee-Indian Strip land rush. **QUOTE** "Exactly as there are always new gold mines for the discoverer, so do I firmly believe there are still new trails to be blazed in that ever-popular form of photoplay since the beginning of motion pictures—the Western drama. The popular conception of a Western picture is one in which the chief element of thrill is hard riding, expert roping and flashing gunplay. These things all have their place, but there is a deep wealth of drama that is less generally known. The cowboy of the ranges will always be popular, and rightly, for he was a romantic figure." Died: 1946.

Ilka Chase 🎥   6361 Hollywood
Actress, author, radio & TV personality
BORN April 8, 1903, in New York, NY. **SPOTLIGHTS** In radio, she was known for her facile wit with gems like this: "America's best buy for a nickel is a telephone call to the right man." As an actress of stage and screen, she played a refined, upper-class lady: *Miss Tatlock's Millions* (1948). TV: Chase was a permanent and delightful panelist of "Masquerade Party," and host of "Glamour-Go-Round." In 1926 she married actor Louis Calhern, but they divorced that same year. A few weeks later, he married somebody else. Without missing a beat, Chase sent her still-intact box of *Mrs. Louis Calhern* calling cards to the new wife, with a note reading, "I hope these reach you in time." Died: 1978.

Jack Carson 🎙   6361 Hollywood
See page 298

Charles Ruggles 🎙   6359 Hollywood
See page 255

Jack Lemmon 🎥   6357 Hollywood
Actor
BORN John Lemmon III; on Feb. 8, 1925, in Boston, MA. **SPOTLIGHTS** At age four, he made his stage debut with his father, John Uhler Lemmon II, in *Gold in Them Thar Hills.* Later, he shined during his college years at Harvard, already becoming known—and loved—for his rather bewildered-looking, fresh approach to acting. He soon discovered that the *gold in them thar hills* referred to the hills surrounding Hollywood. With his humorous flair for sneering and carping, he emerged as one of the greatest light comedians. He captivated audiences in 1954 with *It Should Happen to You,* and *Phfft!* 1955 brought *Three for the Show* and *My Sister Eileen,* then he won an Oscar (see below). He gave an offbeat performance in *Bell, Book and*

Candle (1958), as a whimsical warlock. Lemmon gained immortality in the comic masterpiece, *Some Like It Hot* (1959), opposite Marilyn Monroe and Tony Curtis. He gave a brillant performance. Director Billy Wilder offered Lemmon praise, declaring, "He has the greatest rapport with an audience of anyone since Charlie Chaplin. Just by looking at him people can tell what goes on in his heart." He gave an outstanding dramatic performance in *Days of Wine and Roses* (1962).

Jack Lemmon

Then, a new generation of adoring fans came to know him as the compulsive neat nik in *The Odd Couple* (1968), co-starring Walter Matthau, and in the drama, *The China Syndrome* (1979). Paired with Matthau, he plays a cranky senior citizen in *Grumpy Old Men* (1993) and its 1995 sequel. He appears in *That's Life!* (1986), *JFK* (1991) and *Out to Sea* (1997). **ACHIEVEMENTS** 1955 Best Supporting Actor Oscar for *Mister Roberts.* 1973 Best Actor for *Save the Tiger.* 1996 Kennedy Center Honor. **QUOTE** "I've never cared whether or not I've gotten the lead. But I've gotten some pretty good seconds and I've managed to sneak into some big ones."

Walter Matthau 🎥   6357 Hollywood
Actor
BORN Walter Matuschanskavasky; Oct. 1, 1920, in New York, NY. **SPOTLIGHTS** This national acting treasure had a tough beginning in life. His father, a Russian Orthodox priest who immigrated to America, deserted his family. His mother was forced to work long hours for meager wages, leaving the youngster to be raised by the Daughters of Israel Day Nursery. He grew up impoverished on the Lower East Side in the cold-

Walter Matthau and Lauren Bacall

water tenements. Instead of changing to suit the polished screen needs of the West Coast, he used his Lower East Side growl, tinge of sadness, and slouchy posture as an asset. Matthau plays the lovable crank in *The Odd Couple* (1968), teamed with pal Jack Lemmon, and excels in the comedy. Motion pictures include *Goodbye Charlie* (1964), *Cactus Flower* (1969), *Plaza Suite* (1971), *Kotch* (1971), *The Sunshine Boys* (1975), *House Calls* (1978), *California Suite* (1978), and *JFK* (1991). He attracted both leading roles and audiences in his 70s, in *Grumpy Old Men* (1993) and its sequel *Grumpier Old Men II* (1995), with onscreen nemesis Jack Lemmon. He co-stars with Ossie Davis in *I'm Not Rappaport* (1996), based on the Tony Award-winning comedy, adapted for the screen and directed by Herb Gardner, with executive producer David Sameth. In 2000, he appears in Diane Keaton's *Hanging Up*, co-starring Diane Keaton, Meg Ryan and Lisa Kudrow. **ACHIEVEMENTS** 1966 Best Supporting Actor Oscar for *The Fortune Cookie*. He served bravely as a radioman-gunner in the Army Air Corps during WWII.

Dave Garroway 📺   6355 Hollywood
See page 255

Charles Ray 🎥   6355 Hollywood
Actor, director

Charles Ray

BORN March 15, 1891, in Jacksonville, IL. **SPOTLIGHTS** Educated at Los Angeles Polytech school, this six-foot tall, 170-pound actor with dark brown hair and brown eyes became an early screen star with Thom. H. Ince Productions. He also directed silents. Later, he returned to his first love, "the speaking stage," Broadway. Films include *A Slave's Devotion* (1913) and *The Clodhopper* (1917). **QUOTE** "Out of any given 10,000 applicants for movie positions here is the result: 93 actually get a chance to appear before the camera; 14 manage to squeeze out a bare existence in the studios; and ONE achieves a place of moderate income. Would any sane person gamble at such odds on any conceivable sport event? Hardly; yet there are tens of thousands every year who stake their lives at those very odds. My advice is this: Search your soul carefully, sound your mind to its depths. If you are then convinced that talent—not vanity—is the urge, make your decision. First, lay aside enough money to keep you—apart from any earnings—for at least six months, a year is better. Then bravely batter your way into every studio in Hollywood and keep sociably assaulting every entrenched performer and studio attache that fate may throw in your way. Never stop, never give up, never quit studying and trying to find out how it is done. Clothe yourself in the hide of a rhinoceros, the better to resist the rebuffs that will be hurled at you. And then, if you are patient, dependable, talented, and accomplished, and can make up, you may get the chance that the law of averages gives you. And where do you go from there? Frankly I do not know. The Three Fates of the motion pictures: Old Man Opportunity, Kind Providence and Lady Luck now take hold of you...Mothers, I beseech you! Fathers, I entreat you! Keep your children out of pictures unless you are very sure of the talent and adaptability and are willing to stand behind them in every way." Died: 1943.

Geraldine Fitzgerald  6353 Hollywood
Actress

BORN Nov. 24, 1914, in Dublin, Ireland. **SPOTLIGHTS** This open-faced, red-headed lass started her career in her hometown, then moved to the London stage. After succeeding in New York she headed to Hollywood. She showed tremendous promise for a stunning career with her sensitive portrayals in *Wuthering Heights* (1939), *Dark Victory* (1939—starring her great gal pal, Bette Davis), *The Gay Sisters* (1942), *Watch on the Rhine* (1943), *Wilson* (1944),

Geraldine Fitzgerald

and *O.S.S.* (1946). Then, she retired. Later, she returned to British films, then took a respite. Re-energized she went back to her first love the stage, then guest-starred in numerous television shows. **QUOTE** "I've spent a lot of my career retiring from it. I've been lucky that I've been able to go back to it. Sometimes the tide goes out so far for an actress that she can't launch her boat again."

Billie Dove 🎥   6351 Hollywood
Actress

BORN Lillian Bohney; May 14, 1903, in New York, NY. **SPOTLIGHTS** As a teenager, the beautiful young woman became an artist's model, who also supplemented her family's income by appearing as an extra in silent movies. The master showman Florenz Ziegfeld spotted her on a magazine cover and scheduled a meeting. When he learned she was only 14 years old, he rejected her. Two years later Dove asked Ziegfeld if she could become a chorus girl. She appeared in the "Follies of 1919," and became a regular cast member and a huge success on Broadway over the next several years. Ready for Hollywood, she appeared as the gorgeous heroine of *Polly of the Follies* (1922). She was a smash in *The Black Pirate* (1926), opposite the dashing Douglas Fairbanks. Dove was signed by First National Studio (later absorbed by Warner Bros.) to star in comedies, melodramas and Westerns. Other movies include

Billie Dove

American Beauty, Notorious Affair, and *The Lady Who Dared.* Her last film was the well-received *Blondie of the Follies* (1932), with Marion Davies. Died at age 97, in 1998.

Gypsy Rose Lee 🎥   6351 Hollywood
Writer, actress, entertainer
BORN Rose Louise Hovick; Feb. 19, 1914, in Seattle, WA. **SPOTLIGHTS** The burlesque queen of the 1930s, uptown New York audiences idolized her stylish performances. Her 12 movies include *Ali Baba Goes to Town* (1937), with Eddie Cantor, *My Lucky Star* (1938), with Sonja Henie, *Belle of the Yukon* (1944), opposite Randolph Scott, and *The Trouble with Angels* (1966), starring Rosalind Russell. Four years earlier, Rosalind Russell starred as Gypsy's mother in the movie based on Lee's 1957 literary striptease, *Gypsy.* It was remade in 1993. **QUOTE** "Royalties are nice and all that, but shaking the beads brings the money quicker." Died: 1970.

Fay Wray 🎥   6349 Hollywood
Actress, writer
BORN Vina Fay Wray; Sept. 15, 1907, in Canada. **SPOTLIGHTS** Youthful and beautiful, she burst into stardom in Erich von Stroheim's *The Wedding March,* an incredibly long (3 hours and 16 minutes) black-and-white silent (1928). Her niche, though, was in 1930s horror films, including the classic thriller, *The Mystery of the Wax Museum.* As the heroine in *King Kong* (1933), she was lifted to new heights and immortalized. Millions of fans crowned the Wray the "Screaming Queen of Monster Movies." She made nearly 100 films, including *The Coast Patrol* (1925), *The Most Dangerous Game* (1932), *One Sunday Afternoon, The Bowery,* (both 1933), *The Richest Girl in the World, Viva Villa!* (both 1934), *Small Town Girl* (1936), *Adam Had Four Sons* (1941), *Tammy and the Bachelor* (1957),

and *Dragstrip Riot* (1958), her last film.

Zachary Scott 🎥   6349 Hollywood
Actor

Zachary Scott

BORN Feb. 24, 1914, in Austin, TX. **SPOTLIGHTS** An extremely talented actor of both the New York and London stages, Scott made his screen debut in the film noir, *The Mask of Dimitrios* (1944), in the ruthless title role. He co-stars in this thriller with Peter Lorre, who plays a writer. This superb movie had been adapted from Eric Ambler's novel, *A Coffin for Dimitrios.* He worked with the great French director, Jean Renoir, in *The Southerner,* and give an evocative, deeply moving performance, then followed up with *Mildred Pierce* (both 1945). This dark-haired, often mustached, smooth leading man was frequently cast as a sleek villain or scoundrel. In *Danger Signal* (1945), he plays a two-timing cad with his fiancee and her sister; in *Her Kind of Man* (1946), he is a gangster gambler. He replaced Bogart on last-minute notice in *Stallion Road,* opposite Ronald Reagan, then stars in *The Unfaithful.* He lends support to Spencer Tracy and Lana Turner in George Sidney's drama *Cass Timberlane* (all 1947). The movie was based on Sinclair Lewis' novel. The Nobel and Pulitzer-prize winner William Faulkner wrote his first Broadway play, "Requiem for a Nun" (1959), specifically for Scott and his actress wife, Ruth Ford. Died: 1965.

Onslow Stevens 🎥   6349 Hollywood
Actor
BORN Onslow Ford Stevenson; March 29, 1902, in Los Angeles, CA. **SPOTLIGHTS** Descended from a creative family, both his parents were stage performers, and his grandfather was a celebrated English composer. His first professional acting job was in "Under the Roof," at the Pasadena Community Theater in 1928. Stevens loved the stage, and happened into movies by serendipity. During one of the hundreds of shows he did in Pasadena, his leading lady was offered a screen test by a Universal talent scout. She asked Stevens to drive her to the studio, and read lines to her. Both won contracts. He made his screen debut in *Heroes of the West* (1932). That same year, he landed his break through role as a harassed author in *Once in a Lifetime.* He specialized in character roles. Movies include *Peg o' My Heart* (1933), *Only Yesterday* (1933), *Counsellor-at-Law* (1933), *The Three Musketeers* (1935—as Aramis), *House of Dracula* (1945), *O.S.S.* (1946), *Angel on My Shoulder* (1946), and *All the Fine Young Cannibals* (1960). In all, he made 55 motion pictures. Died: 1977.

6333 HOLLYWOOD

Bud Abbott
6333 Hollywood

See page 343

Guy Madison
6333 Hollywood

Actor

Guy Madison

BORN Robert Moseley; Jan. 19, 1922, in Bakersfield, CA. **SPOTLIGHTS** He was a real-life 1942 Navy enlistee during WWII. Amazingly, this tall, boyishly handsome, fair-haired gentleman got his break when he was on liberty and an agent spotted him standing in a line at a Hollywood radio station. So instantly likable, David O. Selznick immediately wanted him for a movie. The producer got him a two-week furlough to make his screen debut as a young GI in *Since You Went Away* (1944). His stage name came because he loved to eat lots of Dolly Madison sweets. After his honorable discharge, post-war movies include *Till the End of Time* (1946) opposite Dorothy McGuire, *Honeymoon* (1947) with Shirley Temple, *The Charge at Feather River* (1953) in an original 3-D format, *The Command* (1954) in the first Western shot in CinemaScope, *On the Threshold of Space* (1956), *The Last Frontier* (1956), and *Bullwhip* (1958) with Rhonda Fleming. He gained his greatest fame as TV star of "The Adventures of Wild Bill Hickok" (1951-'58). His blundering sidekick, Jingles (Andy Devine) shrilled, "That's Wild Bill Hickok, mister! The bravest, strongest, fightingest U.S. Marshall in the whole West!" Both the TV and radio programs ran concurrently (1951-'56). The show was based on the real-life Hickok (circa 1880s), who worked as a Pony Express rider, a scout for General Custer, and Marshal of Abilene. Died: 1996.
he became a lifelong vaudeville

Charles Winninger
6333 Hollywood

Actor, singer, dancer

BORN May 26, 1884, in Athens, WI. **SPOTLIGHTS** He dropped out of school at third grade to perform vaudeville across the country with his parents. As a young adult, Winninger sailed the Mississippi river on Captain Adams' *Blossom Time* show boat as a performer at the turn of the century. Then, he landed the role of Captain Andy in Ziegfeld's 1927-'30 Broadway stage extravaganza of "Show Boat." A robust and merry man, he was then cast as Captain Henry for network radio's "Show Boat." It was based on the Broadway production. Listeners were welcomed with the sounds of a cheerful crowd waiting at a dock, the steamboat whistle, the enchanting music of the calliope, the swishing of the paddle wheel, and Winninger's hearty greeting, "Howdy, folks, howdy! It's only the beginnin' folks!" He starred in this musical-variety program from 1932-'35; it was NBC's #1 hit. A real charmer, he made 90 films, including *Show Boat* (1936), *Destry Rides Again* (1939), *The Ziegfeld Girl* (1941) and *Sunday Dinner for a Soldier* (1941). **QUOTE** "Most people have the wrong idea about a show boat. It's just a theater built on a scow. The captain of the show boat in reality knows very little about navigation. He is simply the manager of the theatrical troupe." Died: 1969.

Charles Winninger

Jim Lowe
6333 Hollywood

Songwriter, recording artist, disc jockey

BORN May 7, 1927, in Springfield, MO. **SPOTLIGHT** Hit songs include "The Green Door," "Four Walls," and "Talkin' to the Blues."

Jean Arthur
6333 Hollywood

Actress, comedienne

Jean Arthur

BORN Gladys Greene; Oct. 17, 1905, in New York, NY. **SPOTLIGHTS** A husky-voiced, innocent, peppy blonde, she excelled in 1930s comedies and was director Frank Capra's favorite actress: *Mr. Deeds Goes to Town* (1936), opposite Gary Cooper, *You Can't Take It With You* (1938) with Lionel Barrymore and James Stewart, and *Mr. Smith Goes to Washington* (1939) with Jimmy Stewart. She often played "Miss Average American." Motion pictures include *The Whole Town's Talking* (1935) opposite Edward G. Robinson, her sparkling performance in *The More the Merrier* (1943--in an Oscar-nominated performance), and *Shane* (1953), as the frontier mother. She considered herself "violently shy," and was so nervous that it was not unusual for her to throw up before doing a scene. Capra stated, "Arthur is a cockroach who turns into a butterfly in front of the camera." **HIGHLIGHTS** A high school dropout, she taught drama at Vassar. **QUOTE** She loved acting, but was not thrilled with being a movie star. She stated, "It's a strenuous job to have to live up to the way you look on the screen every day of your life." Died: 1991.

Ed Wynn   6333 Hollywood
See page 328

Paul Winchell   6333 Hollywood
Ventriloquist, host, producer

Paul Winchell and Samantha Hart

BORN Dec. 21, 1924, in New York. **SPOTLIGHTS** A horrible thing happened to Paul Winchell's comedy-variety show. After its successful run, someone destroyed all tapes of it. Although it devastated Winchell, it was a real loss to children who could have enjoyed it in syndication. But, long before fans tuned in to his TV show, Winchell enjoyed popularity with radio's "Paul Winchell-Jerry Mahoney Show." The timing could not have been better. It coincided with the end of WWII, when millions of homecoming soldiers and their eager wives started their families. "The baby boom" generation could not get enough of Winchell's dummies: the precocious Jerry Mahoney, Knucklehead, and Oswald. Greatly admired, he moved his comedy-variety format to TV in 1950. He had an orchestra and lots of entertaining players, such as a young Carol Burnett (at $115. a week on the show). The program aired in prime time until 1954, then switched to daytime from 1954-'61. Later, Winchell did voiceovers on the children's "Smurfs" cartoon show, and became the beloved and original voice of Tigger in *Winnie the Pooh*. **ACHIEVEMENTS** He is medical co-inventor of the world's first artificial heart valve.

Jetta Goudal   6333 Hollywood
Actress
BORN July 18, 1898, in France. **SPOTLIGHTS** *Paris at Midnight* (1926) and *The Cardboard Lover* (1928) were two of her motion pictures. She starred in 69 silent movies. Once talkies arrived, her heavy French accent prevented her from continuing in America. Died: 1985.

Richard Carlson   6333 Hollywood
Actor
BORN April 29, 1912, in Albert Lea, MN. **SPOTLIGHTS** Starred as Herbert Philbrick in the intrigue series, "I Led Three Lives": (1) U.S. citizen, (2) Communist party member, and (3) FBI counterspy. Their Red Scare slogan? "Your best friend might be a traitor." The show fueled public paranoia and panic from 1953-'56. Died: 1977.

Ann Rutherford   6333 Hollywood
See page 469

Tony Martin   6331 Hollywood
See page 399

Otto Kruger   6331 Hollywood
See page 152

Dorothy Kirsten   6331 Hollywood
Opera singer
BORN July 6, 1919, in Montclair, New Jersey. **SPOTLIGHTS** As a child, she studied piano. It was not until her teens that she took up voice where she dreamed of Broadway. While earning money for Juilliard studies, she sang on the radio and was discovered. Even when she became a famous opera star, she said, "I consider myself a singing actor, rather than an opera singer." A glamorous, temperamental lyric soprano, she brought many "firsts" to the art. She was one of the first in the 20th century to bring charm and beauty to the stage, when many of the stars were heavenly to listen to, but not so easy on the eyes. Kirsten reigned at Metropolitan Opera, where she was the first in the Met's history to sing on stage for three consecutive decades. She was the first opera star to appear on the cover of "Life" magazine. And she was the first of this era to be considered the definitive "Madame Butterfly," the disillusioned Japanese bride. Films include *Mr. Music* (1950), co-starring Bing Crosby, and *The Great Caruso* (1951), opposite Mario Lanza. In recital, her trademark blonde tresses and stunning, white gowns gave her an angelic look...Her instructor, Ludwig Fabri, only allowed her to sing exercises—never arias in his class—so her voice would be saved for her performances. Died: 1992.

Kenny Baker   6329 Hollywood
Singer, actor
BORN Kenneth Lawrence Baker, Sept. 30, 1912, in Monrovia, CA. **SPOTLIGHTS** While he attended junior college in Long Beach, California, Baker dreamed of becoming a concert violinist. For fun, he joined the Glee Club where everyone encouraged him to focus on his vocal talents. He quit school to earn money for voice lessons, working as a farm hand in Mexico, a laborer on the Boulder Dam, and a mover for a furniture store. His perseverance paid off when he landed a $19-a-week job singing radio commercials. It was Texaco oil company, though, that launched Baker's career when he won their national singing contest. Baker rose to great fame as radio's popular tenor of the 1930s and '40s. He was a vocalist on "The Jack Benny Program," and "Blue Ribbon Town." Hollywood beckoned: *Metropolitan* (1935), *King of Burlesque* (1935), *A Day at the Races* (1937), *Goldwyn Follies* (1938), *The Mikado* (1939), and *The Harvey Girls* (1946). Died: 1985.

Eve Arden   6329 Hollywood
See page 446

Grace Kelly 🎬 6329 Hollywood

Actress

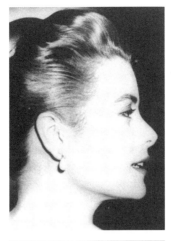

Grace Kelly

BORN Grace Patricia Kelly; Nov. 12, 1928, in Philadelphia, PA. **SPOTLIGHTS** An elegant, graceful, soft-spoken blonde beauty from a privileged family, Kelly was one of Alfred Hitchcock's favorite actresses. He directed her in *Dial M for Murder* and *Rear Window* (both 1954), and *To Catch a Thief* (1955). In the latter, she worked with the handsome Cary Grant on location in Cannes, where she would meet her future husband at his Monaco Palace. Grant, himself, became smitten with the poised young lady. After working with her, he stated, "Whatever Grace does, she does well." And later Grant reflected that Grace Kelly was his favorite leading lady. He revealed, "She was not only astonishingly beautiful, but she also possessed that incredible *serenity*." Kelly delivers a memorable performance in the Western masterpiece, *High Noon* (1952). The following year, she was Oscar-nominated for *Mogambo*. An international legend who was equally loved, she was perfectly suited to play a well-bred lady in *High Society* (1956), with Frank Sinatra and Bing Crosby. **ACHIEVEMENTS** 1954 Best Actress Oscar for *The Country Girl*. **HIGHLIGHTS** Married Prince Rainier III of Monaco in 1956 to become Her Serene Highness Princess Grace of Monaco. In doing so, she not only retired from the screen, but became the most titled woman in the world: twice a Princess, three times a Duchess and six times a Marquise. When reporters asked her father to comment on his daughter marrying into such a regal family, Mr. Kelly declared, "We're not impressed with royalty. We're impressed by the man. Marriage is not a game of musical chairs with us. We play for keeps." The world wept when she died in 1982, of heart failure while in an automobile accident.

C. Aubrey Smith 🎬 6327 Hollywood

Actor

C. Aubrey Smith

BORN Charles Aubrey Smith; July 21, 1863, in England. **SPOTLIGHTS** Educated at Cambridge University, he was an athletic member of England's national cricket team. A tall, imposing, real-life British knight, Sir Charles was a natural to play stately or prominent gentlemen. Films include *Little Lord Fauntleroy* (1936), *The Prisoner of Zenda* (1937) and *Rebecca* (1940). He appears in the very first Agatha Christie novel adapted to the screen, *And Then There Were None* (1945). It is a five-star picture. **QUOTE** Busy in theater for 51 years, he subscribed to the Shakespearean truism: "An actor in his time plays many parts." Died: 1948.

Henry King 🎬 6327 Hollywood

Director

BORN June 24, 1888, in Christianburg, VA. **SPOTLIGHTS** During his 50-year reign, King made 100 films—50 silents and 50 talkies. He was a visual storyteller, direct and down-to-earth. At MGM, he made a movie star out of Ronald Colman with several box-office hits including *The Winning of Barbara Worth* (1926), co-starring Vilma Banky and Gary Cooper. Fox films include *State Fair* (1933), starring Will Rogers, Lew Ayres and Janet Gaynor, *The Country Doctor* (1936), with Jean Hersholt, and the gigantic 1936 hit *Lloyd's of London,* starring Freddie Bartholomew, Tyrone Power, and George Sanders (in his Hollywood debut). A variety of others: *In Old Chicago* (1938), *King Alexander's Ragtime Band* (1938), *Jesse James* (1939), *Stanley and Livingston* (1939), *The Black Swan* (1942), *The Song of Bernadette* (1943), *Wilson* (1944), *Love Is a Many-Splendored Thing* (1955), *Carousel* (1956), and Hemingway's classic tale, *The Sun Also Rises*, in 1957. Died: 1982.

Rosemary Clooney 🎵 6327 Hollywood

Singer, actress

Rosemary Clooney

BORN May 23, 1928, in Maysville, KY. **SPOTLIGHTS** Icon of classical pop and jazz music., she is one of the most important female vocalists—admired for her honesty to whatever she sings and her immaculate phrasing. Clooney has recorded with Duke Ellington, Harry James, and the Benny Goodman Orchestra. She's also a much-admired interpreter of Gershwin, Porter, Kern and Rodgers & Hart with a fascination for the Great American Song. No one can rival her sheer, artful simplicity in pop music. This popular cabaret singer is celebrated for her mellifluous, warm, husky voice, emotional solidity and naturalness. Songs include "Come On-a My House," "Always," "Botch-A-Me," "This Ol' House," and "Tenderly." Movies include her co-starring role in the classic *White Christmas* (1954), with Bing Crosby and Danny Kaye; and *Deep in My Heart* (1955), with her then-husband, actor Jose Ferrer (with whom she had five children—Miguel, Maria, Gabriel, Monsita, Rafael—between Feb. 1955 and Mar. 1960)! Her nephew is actor George Clooney of TV's "ER," and motion picture fame. In 1995 she guest starred in "ER," and earned an Emmy-nomination...The CBS-TV movie "Rosie, The Rosemary Clooney Story" (1982) was based on her autobiography *This For Remembrance*...Director Mike Nichols gave her the ultimate compliment, "She sings like Spencer Tracy acts." Composer/conductor John Williams remarked, "She never sang a word she didn't mean or feel and she made us feel it, too." Clooney celebrated her 55th year in show business in 2000...A collection of her music is available on the Concord Jazz label. **QUOTE** "I'm making a living, and I'm singing well. And I know it. I'm working. That's what I do."

Desi Arnaz 🎥   6327 Hollywood
See page 250

Lawrence Tibbett 🎙   6325 Hollywood
Opera singer

Lawrence Tibbett (left) and Adolph Menjou

BORN Nov. 16, 1896, in Bakersfield, CA. **SPOTLIGHTS** A sheriff's son, he moved to Los Angeles with his mother when his father was killed by cattle thieves. After a performance as Amonasro in *Aida* at the Hollywood Bowl in late 1923, he went to New York to study. Within a year he had his lucky break at the Metropolitan Opera House. In Jan. 1925 while working as an understudy—earning $60 a week—he went on as Ford in *Falstaff*. And then something unheard of happened. The audience gave him 16 minutes of record-shattering applause—the first native-born American to win thunderous bravos and a standing ovation from a critical Met audience. During the 1920s and '30s he reigned in Verdi title roles: Rigoletto, Iago and Simon Boccanegra. Tibbett is considered the finest, most resonant and most vigorous baritone America has produced. In Hollywood, he made *The Rogue Song* (1930), *The New Moon* (1931), and *Cuban Love Song* (1931). In the 1940s he became a national treasure in radio and performing at opera concerts around the country (when there was no official subsidy). Ticket prices ranged from 25 cents to $7 a seat. Tibbett was the country's best-paid singer at $2,500 a performance. An accomplished stage performer, critics thought anything less than opera was a waste of his talents. He rebutted, "I'm doing exactly what I set out to do—to be a versatile

singer." **QUOTE** About his magnificent artistry at his Met breakthrough, Tibbett said, "I let go with all I had. In my second act aria I tore my heart out. Some subconscious force lifted me up." Died: 1960.

Frank Lovejoy 📺   6325 Hollywood
Actor

Frank Lovejoy

BORN March 28, 1914, in Bronx, NY. **SPOTLIGHTS** He starred in two TV detective series: as Mike Barnett in "Man Against Crime" (1956) and *tough guy, but no gun McGraw* in "Meet McGraw" (1957-'59). Formerly, he had been a successful radio and movie performer. Motion pictures include *Home of the Brave* (1949), *In a Lonely Place*, *The Sound of Fury* (both 1950), *I Was a Communist for the FBI*, *I'll See You in My Dreams* (both 1950), *The Hitch-Hiker*, *House of Wax* (both 1953), *The Charge at Feather River* (1953--shot in original 3-D), and *Cole Young--Gunfighter* (1958). Died: 1962.

Gordon MacRae 🎤   6325 Hollywood
Singer, actor

Gordon MacRae

BORN March 12, 1921, in East Orange, NJ. **SPOTLIGHTS** A good-looking, brown-haired, dark-eyed singing talent put under contract by Warner Bros. during the peak of the musical era. His open, trusting looks coupled with his enthusiasm made him ideally cast in films like *The Daughter of Rosie O'Grady* (1950) co-starring June Haver and Debbie Reynolds, *Tea for Two* (1950) with Doris Day, *Carousel* (1955) and *Oklahoma!* (1956), both with Shirley Jones. He was also star of the long-running music radio show, "The Railroad Hour." Also entertainer on TV. Died: 1986.

Lynn Bari 📺   6323 Hollywood
See page 233

Rusty Hamer 📺   6323 Hollywood
Actor

BORN Russell Hamer; Feb. 15, 1947. **SPOTLIGHTS** He played the six-year-old son Rusty Williams on "The Danny Thomas Show" (1953-'64). He grew up on TV. Died: 1990.

June Lockhart 🎥   6321 Hollywood
See page 382

Ann Dvorak 🎥
6321 Hollywood

Actress, dancer

BORN Ann McKim; Aug. 2, 1912, in New York, NY. **SPOTLIGHTS** Dvorak inherited her talent from her silent screen star mother Ann Lehr, and her studio-manager father. She appears as a baby in several silents with her mother. As a four-year-old, she won the title lead in *Ramona* (1916). She grew up at the studio, working in various

Ann Dvorak with Douglas Kennedy

capacities. As a young adult, she was a stand-in for Joan Crawford, and an assistant dance director to choreographer Sammy Lee at MGM. Then, she returned to the silver screen in *The Hollywood Revue of 1929*. She co-stars with Spencer Tracy in *Sky Devils* (1932), plays Paul Muni's sister in *Scarface: Shame of a Nation* (1932), and again works with Muni in *Doctor Socrates* (1935). This feisty talent co-stars with James Cagney in the exciting action picture, *G-Men* (1935). Dvorak was delightful in the enchanting musical, *Thanks a Million* (1935), opposite Dick Powell, Fred Allen, and Patsy Kelly, and brilliant in *Blind Alley* (1939), a *film noir* about a psychologist held hostage by escaped convicts. She co-stars with Randolph Scott in the fast-paced Western *Abilene Town* (1946). She retired in the early 1950s. **ACHIEVEMENTS** She served as a WWII ambulance driver in England. Died: 1979.

Sophie Tucker 🎥
6321 Hollywood

Actress, singer

Sophie Tucker

BORN Sohia Kalish; Jan. 13, 1884, in Russia. (Her father changed their family name to that of a deceased Italian friend. She said, "Papa, who had a terror of the Russian authorities grabbing him and shipping him to Siberia for life, prudently helped himself to the Italian's papers and moniker. I became Sophia Abuza.") **SPOTLIGHTS** Nicknamed "The Last of the Red-Hot Mammas," this bright gem got cut and polished in cabarets a la Gay Nineties. As a cabaret entertainer, she had other singers and an orchestra backing her up while she mingled with the patrons. The queen of the nightclub was rowdy and stirred up wild fun. She bellowed joyously, "Let's raise a little hell around here!" In 1910, the frenzied Chicago police purged the city of this type of decadence and debauchery. Tucker's naughty lyrics brought the men with badges down upon her. They stopped her show when she attempted to sing "Angle Worm Wiggle." One could only imagine what the judge thought when she contested this censorship in court; he ruled in favor of the police. Five years later, she returned triumphantly to the Palace in Chicago, where she broke a performer/audience record by lasting 39 minutes doing a vigorous 16 songs. The next year, in Atlantic City, she was not so lucky. She was barred from singing "Who Paid the Rent for Mrs. Rip Van Winkle, When Rip Van Winkle Was Away?" Disgusted, she quit, but wasn't worried about paying her bills. The outrageous personality was a rage on the New York stage--where she was called "the buxom siren of Broadway," and in London's theatre craze at the Palladium. She offered a saucy rendition of "One of These Days," for her theme song. Films: *Honky Tonk* (1929), *Thoroughbreds Don't Cry* (1937), *Broadway Melody of 1938*, *Follow the Boys* (1944), *Sensations* (1945), and *The Joker Is Wild* (1957). **QUOTE** "From birth to age 18, a girl needs good parents. From 18 to 35, she needs good looks. From 35 to 55, she needs a good personality. From 55 on, she needs cash." This gem died in 1966.

Laurence Olivier 🎥　　　　6321 Hollywood

Actor, director, producer

Laurence Olivier

BORN May 22, 1907, in Surrey, England. **SPOTLIGHTS** Widely acclaimed as the greatest actor of the century, he was a supreme talent. "Whether 'tis nobler in the mind" to be a stage or cinema actor, Olivier dedicated most of his life to the former, but left an indelible treasury of performances in films, too. Olivier, himself, thought little of his early motion picture efforts. He stated, "One film I did was so bad that it had to be retaken before they could put it on the shelf." Then, Greta Garbo personally rejected him for her co-star in *Queen Christina* (1933). Defeated, he returned temporarily to the London stage. In 1935 he alternated with John Gielgud in the lead role in "Romeo and Juliet." Gielgud—a superior theatrical talent in his own right—declared, "Larry had a great advantage over me in his commanding vitality, striking looks, brilliant humor and passionate directness." When Olivier returned to Hollywood, he took the town by storm. He skillfully performed in classical, historical, and modern roles: *Wuthering Heights* (1939); *Rebecca* (1940); *Pride and Prejudice* (1940); *That Hamilton Woman* (1941—Winston Churchill's favorite film); Shakespeare's *Henry V* (1944)—also his directorial debut; *Spartacus* (1960); *The Entertainer* (1960); *Sleuth* (1972); *Marathon Man* (1976); *The Seven Percent Solution* (1976); *Jesus of Nazareth* (1977); and *King Lear* (1983). Asked, in the 1940s, about working in the new medium of TV, he responded, "Television is here to stay." Jeromy Irons and Anthony Andrews shared the honor of working with him in the sumptuous TV series "Brideshead Revisited." He narrated one of the finest motion pictures ever adapted from the Bard's work, Franco Zeffirelli's brilliant *Romeo and Juliet* (1968), starring Olivia Hussey and Leonard Whiting. **ACHIEVEMENTS** 1946 Special Oscar for Shakespearean perfection in *Henry V*; 1944 Best Actor Oscar and Best Picture for *Hamlet*; he also directed both films. 1979 Special Oscar. Appointed director of Britain's National Theatre. Knighted Sir Laurence Olivier (in 1947); in 1960 he received the honor of perage. Died: 1989.

Peggy Lee 🎵   6319 Hollywood
Singer, lyricist, composer

Peggy Lee

BORN Norma Deloris Egstrom; May 27, 1920, in Jamestown, ND. **SPOTLIGHTS** A legendary vocalist. As a teenager she pursued her dreams of heading for "the big time" (in her young mind that was Fargo, North Dakota), where she ended up singing at a prominent radio station. The King of Swing, Benny Goodman, heard her and hired her for his band. With Goodman she had her first big hit, "Why Don't You Do Right?" She immediately had an astonishing following among her peers and fans. Duke Ellington nicknamed her "The Queen" and English jazz critic Peter Clayton wrote, "Miss Peggy Lee is quite simply the finest singer in the history of popular music." Lee's smoldering sensuality, her uniquely husky yet mellow voice, her superb technique, exquisite phrasing, and innate sense of rhythm made her into one of the most famous and popular of all 20th-century singers. She has recorded 630 songs, including a number of her own compositions: "Manana," "It's a Good Day," "Black Coffee," "'S Wonderful," "Lover," "Big Spender," "Johnny Guitar," "Golden Earrings," "I'll Be Seeing You in All the Old Familiar Places," "See See Rider," "Is That All There Is?" and, of course, the sizzling hot number everyone associates with Miss Lee, "Fever." **ACHIEVEMENTS** This Grammy-winner earned an Academy Award nomination for her role of Rosie the alcoholic in *Pete Kelly's Blues* (1955). She collaborated with Sonny Burke in creating the score for *The Lady and the Tramp* (1955), added scenes, and created several voices for the animated film. *Miss Peggy Lee* is the ultimate box set with more than 100 songs of her historic recordings on four compact discs. **QUOTE** "Love is the greatest force in the universe. It's the shining truth."

Bob Crosby 📻   6319 Hollywood
Orchestra leader

Bob Crosby and Marie Wilson

BORN George Robert Crosby; Aug. 23, 1913, in Spokane, WA. **SPOTLIGHTS** Born the youngest of seven children, Bob was inspired to follow in his older brother's footsteps. Unlike Bing Crosby, Bob joked "I'm the only guy in the business who made it without talent." Why it's true he couldn't sing, nor play an instrument, he was gifted as a suave, charming, swinging Big-Band Dixieland sound band leader. On stage, he took special care introducing each member of the orchestra to enable the audience to connect with each one of them personally. The great jazz pianist Joe Sullivan, and singer Doris Day worked with "Bob Crosby and the Bobcats." He had successful runs as a daytime radio (and television) host. Toward the end of his life, Bob revealed his "relationship with Bing was never close." He served the U.S. Marines with distinction during WWII. **QUOTE** Asked by Mike Wallace what advantage he had in being Crosby's brother, Bob responded, "The biggest is that being younger than Bing, I've kept my hair." Died: 1993.

Marjorie Lord 📺   6317 Hollywood
Actress

Marjorie Lord

BORN July 26, 1922, in San Francisco, CA. **SPOTLIGHTS** With some modeling and minor stage experience under her belt, the beauty made her screen debut in *Border Cafe* (1937). A charming talent, she rose to leading lady. Motion pictures include *Shantytown* (1943), *Sherlock Holmes in Washington* (1946), opposite Basil Rathbone, *Johnny Come Lately* (1943), co-starring James Cagney, *New Orleans* (1947), with an all-star cast including Billie Holiday, Woody Herman, and Louis Armstrong, and *Boy, Did I Get a Wrong Number!* (1966), with Bob Hope. She gained widespread fame and became a household name playing Danny Thomas' second wife in "Make Room for Daddy" (1957-'64). The TV show is still seen in syndication. She is the mother of the accomplished and equally beautiful actress, Anne Archer.

Dick Lane 📺   6317 Hollywood

Dick Lane

Sportscaster, TV pioneer, actor
BORN Richard Lane; May 28, 1899, in Rice Lake, WI. **SPOTLIGHTS** His fun, odd-ball career included these movies: *Life of the Party* (1937), *Charlie Chan in Honolulu* (1938), *Union Pacific* (1939), *Meet Boston Blackie* (1941; serial), *Riders of the Purple Sage* (1941), *Wonder Man* (1945), *The Babe Ruth Story* (1948), *Take Me Out to the Ballgame* (1949), and *The Jackie Robinson Story* (1951). He became a fender-bending, fast-talking salesman on TV, and spirited announcer of roller derby and wrestling events. "Whoa, Nellie!" was his popular catchphrase. He covered the first news broadcast of an atomic explosion test in the 1950s. Died: 1982.

Mike Gore 🎞   6315 Hollywood
Pioneer exhibitor, movie magnate
BORN 1876, in Russia. **SPOTLIGHTS** He immigrated to America in 1906. By 1923, he had co-founded West Coast Theaters. Old First National Pictures followed. Died: 1953.

Bill Cunningham 🎙   6315 Hollywood
Newscaster, interviewer
SPOTLIGHTS He was host of the top-notch interview program called "Meet the Boss." The first telecast on June 10, 1952 set into motion a unique format of interviewing executives about their industrious careers. Previously, he had been a highly respected radio newscaster (1944-'52).

Roland Young 📺   6315 Hollywood
See page 96

Jack Holt 🎥   6315 Hollywood

Jack Holt

Actor
BORN Charles J. Holt; May 31, 1888, in Winchester, VA. **SPOTLIGHTS** A tall, dark-haired, mustached leading and supporting actor, he made 150 films between 1914 and 1951. Motion pictures include *North of the Rio Grande* (1922), *Hell's Island* (1930), *The Littlest Rebel* (1935), *Passport to Alcatraz* (1940), *Cat People* (1942), *They Were Expendable* (1945), *My Pal Trigger* (1946), and *The Wild Frontier* (1947). **QUOTE** "Motion picture work is the hardest game I know. I have tried a lot of games. When I left college I was trained for engineering. For several years I fol-lowed that profession in some of the wildest parts of America. Later I went to Alaska where I drove a dog team in weather forty below. After that I ranched in Oregon. All of these were hard but not so hard as the motion picture business. You have to fight desperately hard to gain success and once you have it, you must fight twice as hard to hold it. There are so many struggling to take away your place unless you defend it. Engineer, miner, and rancher but the last, my work in pictures was the hardest test of all." This good gent died in 1951.

W. C. Fields 🎙   6315 Hollywood
See page 505

Hedda Hopper 🎥   6315 Hollywood

Hedda Hopper

Gossip columnist, actress
BORN Elda Furry; June 2, 1890, in Hollidaysburg, PA. **SPOTLIGHTS** Crowned "Hollywood's Gossip Queen," her 35 million+ daily readership wielded her enormous power. Hopper—and arch enemy and rival Louella Parsons—had the ability to make stars, break up marriages, or evaporate careers with their poison pens. Her column's influence on box office receipts by merely hinting a movie was a stinker made even the studio heads fear her. On air, she reached millions more with her successful gossip show all about Hollywood. Before donning the crown of "gossip queen," she acted in movies. Her first was the silent movie *The Battle of the Hearts* (1916), where she plays a sea captain! Others include *The Snob* (1924), *Don Juan* (1926) opposite John Barrymore, *Mona Lisa* (1927--a short color film), *Wings* (1927), *Midnight* (1939), and *Sunset Boulevard* (1950--as herself, gossip queen). She made radio history in 1939 by starring in "Brenthouse." A dramatic serial, it was the first sustained transcontinental radio show to originate in Hollywood. Later, she talked about Tinseltown's hoopla, "You can't fool an old bag like me." Her trademark? A collection of hats. **HIGHLIGHTS** Her son was Dewolf, Jr. (known as William), who was immortalized as an actor in the "Perry Mason" series. He played detective Paul Drake. **QUOTE** Hopper pointed to her house in Beverly Hills, and stated, "That's the house fear built." Died: 1966.

Don Ameche 🎙   6313 Hollywood
Actor
BORN Dominic Felix Amici; May 31, 1908, in Kenosha, WI. **SPOTLIGHTS** A superb actor, blessed with a rich, mellifluous voice, he easily won prominent roles. He played Bob Drake in radio's first network soap opera, "Betty and Bob" (1932-'40). Later, he entertained listeners with his verbal fireworks in "The

Don Ameche

Bickersons" (1946-'48). As the sniping husband against his warring wife (Frances Langford), the two brought new meaning to the word confrontational in this combative comedy. One of their hilarious skits was called *The Honeymoon Is Over;* no domestic bliss here! Ameche's perfect comic timing combined with his natural warmth to create rich characters for more than six decades in all mediums. Motion pictures include *Ramona* (1936), *One in a Million* (1936), *Alexander's Ragtime Band* (1938), *Midnight* (1939), *The Story of Alexander Graham Bell* (1939), *Down Argentine Way* (1940), *Trading Places* (1983), *Harry and the Hendersons* (1987), and *Coming to America* (1988). He was excellent in David Mamet's *Things Change* (1988), an unusual comedy about the mob, co-starring the wonderful Joe Mantegna. His last onscreen appearance was *Folks!* (1992), starring opposite a terrfic Tom Selleck. This clever satire about aging parents was dismissed too quickly. In *Homeward Bound: the Incredible Journey* (1993), he was the soothing voice of the dog...Ameche was adored by his family, friends, colleagues and anyone lucky enough to meet this true-blue, kindly gentleman. **ACHIEVEMENTS** 1985 Best Supporting Actor Award for *Cocoon*. **QUOTE** His favorite movie was *Heaven Can Wait* (not to be confused with the 1978 film of the same title, starring Warren Beatty). In Ernst Lubitsch's 1943 movie, Ameche is cast as an elderly playboy whose death sends him down to Hades. He reviews his peccadilloes to Satan who tosses him Upstairs. Ameche commented, "It was a lovely premise to begin with. It must have been reassuring to a lot of people to think that a man who had lived the life he had could still get into heaven." Died: 1993.

Al St. John 🎥   6313 Hollywood
Comedian

Al "Fuzzy" St. John

BORN Sept. 10, 1893, in Santa Ana, CA. **SPOTLIGHTS** Nicknamed "Fuzzy" due to his light-colored facial hair, this reliable character actor clowned around with the screen's funniest men, including Charlie Chaplin, W. C. Fields, and Roscoe "Fatty" Arbuckle (his real-life uncle) during the silent era. He directed many silents and wrote several screenplays. Often appearing as the violin-playin' sidekick in Westerns, he made the transition to talkies. Movies include *Young and Dumb* (1923), *Stupid but* *Brave* (1924), *Casey Jones* (1927), *The Painted Desert* (1931), *Sing, Cowboy, Sing* (1937) starring Tex Ritter, *The Outcast of Poker Flats* (1937), and *Call of the Yukon* (1938). His nickname made his way into scripts—as Fuzzy Q. Jones—and in 1944 he starred in *Fuzzy Settles Down*. Died: 1963.

Nelson Eddy 🎥   6313 Hollywood
Singer, actor

Nelson Eddy and Jeanette MacDonald

BORN June 29, 1901, in Providence, RI. **SPOTLIGHTS** The 23-year-old handsome baritone won a talent competition to perform with the Philadelphia Civic Opera in *Aida*. He quickly rose to stardom. In Hollywood, his melodic voice perfectly complemented Jeanette MacDonald's in MGM's *Naughty Marietta* (1935), *Rose Marie* (1936), *Rosalie* (1937), and *Sweethearts* (1938). They became *the screen's* favorite romantic singing duo. His popular radio music program was "The Electric Hour" (1944-'46). He closed each show with "May happiness light your home, and more power to you." Classic songs include "Indian Love Call," "Ah! Sweet Mystery of Life," "Rose Marie," "One Kiss," "I Love You Truly," and "Perfect Love." **QUOTE** About his popular movies, Eddy confessed, "I've never seen one of them. Simply because I was too ashamed of them." About his last film with MacDonald, *I Married An Angel* (1942), he declared, "It was a mess." Died: 1967.

Tennessee Ernie Ford 🔴   6311 Hollywood

Tennessee Ernie Ford (center), Don Knotts (left), and Andy Griffith

Singer, songwriter, actor, d.j., comedian

BORN Feb. 13, 1919, in Bristol, TN. **SPOTLIGHTS** A professional Southerner, he was a six-foot tall, mustached performer gifted with a rich bass-baritone voice. Known on radio as the homespun "Hillbilly DJ," he earned $10.00 per week in 1937. He made considerably more when he moved to NBC TV (1956-'61) hosting "The Ford Show," a musical variety program. The show took awhile to pick up steam, but his unhurried and friendly manner appealed to audiences. When "the show caught fire," Ford was "hotter than a bucket of red ants." His show ranked among the top 10, and his catchphrases became part of the national colloquial treasure: "Bless your pea-picken hearts!" and "Nervous as a long-tailed cat in a roomful of rockin' chairs." He recorded 80 albums in a 50-year career. String of hit songs include: "Smokey Mountain Boogie," "Shotgun Boogie," "Mule Train," "River of No Return," and "Ballad of Davy Crockett." He became the first country-music entertainer to perform at the London Palladium in 1953. In 1955, he recorded "Sixteen Tons" selling more than 20 million copies. A song about coal mining--with lyrics"I owe my soul to the company store"--"Sixteen Tons" has been appreciated by generation after generation. Ford commented in 1990, "It's an ever-lasting hit." The lyrics, written by Merle Travis from Kentucky, were a tribute to workers everywhere, who could especially relate to such lines such as "another day older and deeper in debt." He won a 1964 Grammy for Gospel music. Recipient of the Medal of Freedom Award given by President Reagan. **QUOTE** Since his show was a slow starter, an executive recommended he revise its format. Ford refused to change a thing stating, "No use digging bait when you got a boatload of fish." Died: 1991.

Joan Blondell 🎥   6311 Hollywood

Joan Blondell

Actress, singer, dancer

BORN Aug. 30, 1909, in New York, NY. **SPOTLIGHTS** Practically born onstage, both of her parents were vaudeville performers. The Blondell family toured worldwide, before the feisty, large-eyed blonde doll alighted in Texas. This bouncy beauty won the Miss Dallas title. She and James Cagney triumphantly performed in the play *Penny Arcade*. Warner Brothers saw them, signed both actor and actress (her five-year contract started at $200 per week), retitled the play *Sinners' Holiday*, and made a movie (1930). They paired together in later films, including the original gangster movie *The Public*

Enemy (1931), and the musical *Footlight Parade* (1933). The saucy glamour girl appears in the comedy, *The Greeks Had a Word for Them* (1932). By 1935 she was enjoying full-fledged star status. Other movies include the comedy, *The Perfect Speciman* (1937) opposite Errol Flynn; the superb character-driven family drama, *A Tree Grows in Brooklyn* (1945); *The Blue Veil* (1951--in an Oscar-nominated performance); *Will Success Spoil Rock Hunter?* (1958); *The Cincinnati Kid* (1965); *Support Your Local Gunfighter* (1971), and *Grease* (1978). She appears in 100 films. **QUOTE** She described her typical roles as "the happy-go-lucky chorus girl, flip reporter, dumb-blonde waitress, I'll stick-by-you-broad." Died: 1979.

Van Heflin 🎥   6309 Hollywood

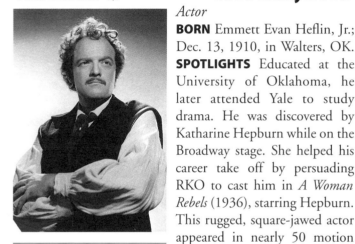

Van Heflin

Actor

BORN Emmett Evan Heflin, Jr.; Dec. 13, 1910, in Walters, OK. **SPOTLIGHTS** Educated at the University of Oklahoma, he later attended Yale to study drama. He was discovered by Katharine Hepburn while on the Broadway stage. She helped his career take off by persuading RKO to cast him in *A Woman Rebels* (1936), starring Hepburn. This rugged, square-jawed actor appeared in nearly 50 motion pictures in both supporting and leading roles. He plays an earth-loving Wyoming homesteader in Paramount's stately and classic Western, *Shane* (1953), with Jean Arthur as his wife. He delivers terrific performances in *Battle Cry* (1955), and Rod Serling's "skyscraper jungle" drama *Patterns* (1956). TV includes "The Dark Side of Earth" (1957), "Rank and File" (1959), and "The Cruel Day" (1960). **ACHIEVEMENTS** 1942 Best Supporting Actor Oscar for his role as an intellectual alcoholic in *Johnny Eager*. Died: 1971.

Hillary Brooke 📺   6307 Hollywood

Hillary Brooke

Actress

BORN Beatrice Peterson; Sept. 8, 1914, in Long Island, NY. **SPOTLIGHTS** A former model and stage actress, she made her screen debut in *New Faces of 1937*, appropriately enough. Elegant, beautiful and capable in both comedy in drama, she kept rose from supporting to leading lady. Movies include *The Adventures of Sherlock Holmes* (1939), *New Moon* (1940), *The Philadelphia Story*

(1942), *Dr. Jekyll and Mr. Hyde* (1941), *Country Fair* (1941), *Sleepytime Gal* (1942), *Ministry of Fear* (1944), *Monsieur Beaucaire* (1946), *Unmasked* (1950), *Insurance Investigator* (1951), *Invaders from Mars* (1953--originally shown in 3-D), and *The Man Who Knew Too Much* (1956). In TV, she was delightful in "The Abbott and Costello Show" (1951-'53), as the girlfriend of comedian Lou Costello. She played the charming love interest Roberta Townsend to the father of "My Little Margie" (1952-'55).

Theda Bara 📽   6307 Hollywood
Actress

Theda Bara

BORN Theodosia Goodman; July 20, 1890, in Cincinnati, OH. **SPOTLIGHTS** *The screen's very first femme fatale.* Her stage name is an anagram; if you rearrange the letters you will discover the hidden message: "Arab Death." She rose to stardom overnight as the dark, heartless, bad girl in the silent film, *A Fool There Was* (1915). Her character was man's downfall; none who could resist her. While "The Vamp" acted out one scene, the movie's subtitle card read: "Kiss me, my fool!" This phrase instantly became popular around the world. The star and the film proved to be a lucky break for Fox studios, as Bara became one of its all-time biggest box office attractions. This picture had been adapted from Rudyard Kipling's poem "The Vampire." Hence, the word "vamp" was added to the English language to describe her, and other dangerously bewitching women like her. Bara made 40 films including *Carmen* (1915),

The Dancer of Paris (1917—as Esmerelda, the dancing gypsy; this was an early version of the classic *The Hunchback of Notre Dame*), *Camille* (1917), *Cleopatra* (1917), *Madame Du Barry* (1918), *When a Woman Sins* (1918), and *Salome* (1918). Most often cast as alluring sirens, occasionally she played against type, such as the sweet *Kathleen Mavourneen* (1919). **HIGHLIGHTS** She was the first star created entirely by publicity. Fox's restrictive contract, which prevented her from a normal life—she could not marry, was forced to wear veils in public like an exotic belly dancer and wear Egyptian snake and silver bracelets, and was always served by oiled, half-naked "Nubian" slaves—provided her with many benefits, including a $4,000-a-week job (at the time income tax free). Onstage she pulled in $6,000-a-week. She retired in 1921 upon becoming happily married. Died: 1955.

Mildred Harris 📽   6305 Hollywood
Actress

BORN Nov. 29, 1901, in Cheyenne, WY. **SPOTLIGHTS** She played Dorothy in *The Wizard of Oz* (1914-'15) silent series. Harris also worked in D.W. Griffith's classic film, *Intolerance* (1916)...Married to Charlie Chaplin (1917-'20). Died: 1944.

Ernie Kovacs 📺   6305 Hollywood
Comedian, actor

BORN Jan. 23, 1919, in Trenton, NJ. **SPOTLIGHTS** A mop-haired, mustached, cigar-chomping, unconventional comedian, he was a complete original. This wacky guy starred in TV's "Ernie in Kovacsland" (1951), but is best remembered for "The Ernie Kovacs Show" (1952-'56). He created zany stunts like putting people in gigantic bottles and turning the sets on an angle. He was inventive with new camera tricks, like shooting under water. He was also a man with many faces and many voices. Oddly enough, this spontaneous personality never could hook prime time spots. It was said of Kovacs that "he was a man with no enemies and no sponsors." He co-hosted "Tonight" (1956-'57), and was a popular quiz show panelist. Movies include *Operation Mad Ball* (1957), *Bell, Book and Candle* (1958), *It Happened to Jane* (1959), *Wake Me When It's Over* (1960), and *North to Alaska* (1960). **HIGHLIGHTS** He

Ernie Kovacs

married one of his regulars on his TV show, the beautiful Edie Adams. (Adams was widely hailed for her impressions of Marilyn Monroe, and the various Gabor sisters—accents and all. She also created the role of Daisy Mae in the Broadway musical "Li'l Abner." They had one daughter.) Adams once said of her husband, "He doesn't like rules, he likes to make them." About Edie, Kovacs said, "The girl is an angel. When I'm away, every time she comes to see me, arriving with a grin from ear to ear, and lugging a suitcaseful of my favorite cigars." His choice smoke at "$2 per cigar," a princely sum at the time, cost him annually the then-astronomical sum of "$13,150" (enough to purchase a large house, paid in full). **QUOTE** "I just like to get through to them out there with whatever comes into my head. Crazy stuff, non-crazy stuff, whatever. I want 'em to get to know me, really me, exactly the kind of clod I am." He received his only Emmy Award after he died in 1962, in an automobile accident.

George Sidney 🎥   6303 Hollywood
Director, producer, writer

George Sidney

BORN Oct. 4, 1916, in Long Island, NY. **SPOTLIGHTS** Born into a show business family, Sidney was a former child actor of stage and screen. At age five, he was starring alongside Tom Mix in Westerns. At age nine, he was making a silent movie with Claudette Colbert in New York. Sidney recalled, "When my big scene was over, I went to Mr. Capra (movie director Frank Capra), and asked him how I did. He grumbled and said, 'Kid, when you grow up, don't be an actor. Get a real job. Become a director. You tell 'em all what to do.'" He got a job as a MGM messenger boy in 1933. By age 18, he was directing *Our Gang* comedies, then rose with panache and style to become one of the studio's favorite musical directors. During his 35 MGM years, Sidney directed many classics. Among his motion pictures are *Thousands Cheer* (1943), a Technicolor extravaganza with an all-star cast including Mickey Rooney, Judy Garland—singing "The Joint Is Really Jumpin'"—and Lena Horne, and *Anchors Aweigh* (1945) starring Gene Kelly and Frank Sinatra. In the latter, Sidney pioneered the technique of combining animation (with Jerry the mouse) and live action (with a dancing Gene Kelly) in a now-classic dance scene. Also at MGM, he made *The Harvey Girls* (1946) starring Judy Garland, and *Annie Get Your Gun* (1950) starring Betty Hutton and Howard Keel. The movie *Show Boat* (1951) starring Kathryn Grayson, Ava Gardner and Howard Keel came about when Sidney and producer Arthur Freed were having drinks. Sidney recalled, "We were a little bored, and he says, 'What's the greatest show tune ever written?' I said, 'Old Man River.' He says, 'Good! Let's re-make Show Boat.'" He also did *Kiss Me Kate* (1953) with Kathryn Grayson, Howard Keel and Ann Miller. In the late 1950s, movie mogul Harry

Cohn finally persuaded Sidney to helm Columbia Studios while producing-directing. There, he made a number of hits, including *Pal Joey* (1957) with Frank Sinatra, Rita Hayworth (doing her famous striptease), and Kim Novak. *Bye Bye Birdie* (1963) starring Ann-Margret, Dick Van Dyke and Janet Leigh, and *Viva Las Vegas* (1964), starring Elvis Presley and Ann-Margret, are considered fun cult classics. Highly skilled with costume pictures, too, he directed the excellent swashbuckler, *Scaramouche* (1952) with Stewart Granger, Eleanor Parker, Janet Leigh and Mel Ferrer; and the royal drama, *Young Bess* (1953), starring Jean Simmons, Stewart Granger, Charles Laughton and Deborah Kerr. **ACHIEVEMENTS** 1940 Oscar for *Quicker 'n a Wink* (one-reel short); 1941 Oscar for *Of Pups and Puzzles* ("Passing Parade" short). In 1950, he received his third Oscar for *The Merry Wives of Windsor*. In 1997, the Producers Guild of America and the Directors Guild of America saluted Sidney for his 75th anniversary in the entertainment industry. Sidney holds the Director Record for having 15 box office hits in a row! In 1998, he received the First International Film Festival Lifetime Achievement Award in his "retirement" hometown of Las Vegas. **HIGHLIGHTS** His wife is Corinne Entratter Sidney, a former model/actress, mother of one son named Ben. A current observer of the Hollywood and Las Vegas scenes, she is a journalist/host. Corinne quips, "It's not who you know in Hollywood, it's who answers your phone calls." **QUOTE** "When I first walked Hollywood Boulevard in 1930 at age 14, I passed movie stars in the streets. I never dreamed that one day I would walk among the legends of filmland and see my name included with the giants of the entertainment world on the Walk of Fame. My thanks and 'Hooray for Hollywood.'"

Gene Lockhart 🎥   6303 Hollywood

Gene Lockhart and wife Kathleen

Actor, singer, dancer
BORN July 18, 1891, in Canada. **SPOTLIGHTS** Of Scotch-Irish-English blood, he was artistically inclined from the get-go. Lockhart began dancing professionally as a six-year-old with the Kilties Band, Scotch Highlander band linked to the 48th Canadian Regiment. As a young adult, he sang in concert billed with the delightful Beatrice Lillie (see her bio in this book). He made his American stage debut in Gilbert and Sullivan's "Ruddigore." On Broadway, in "Ah, Wilderness," starring George M. Cohan, he played the drunkard Uncle Sid, his favorite role (1933-'34). Hollywood beckoned. This versatile, distinguished character actor was extremely good playing a villain or a saint. Offered many choice roles in both comedies and dramas, he never left a director or audience disappointed. He plays Lushin in *Crime*

and Punishment (1935), Bob Crachit in *A Christmas Carol* (1938), the scoundrel Regis in *Algiers* (1938—in an Oscar-nominated performance), Stephen Douglas in *Abe Lincoln in Illinois* (1940), and Monsieur Homais in *Madame Bovary* (1949). A wonderful talent, he made 75 motion pictures, including *Meet John Doe* (1941), *House on 92nd Street* (1945), *Miracle on 34th Street* (1947), *That Wonderful Urge* (1948), *Rhubarb* (1951), *The High and the Mighty* (1954), and *The Man in the Gray Flannel Suit* (1956). **HIGHLIGHTS** Married actress Kathleen Lockhart; father of actress June Lockhart. He co-stars with his wife in *A Christmas Carol*. Their young daughter June made her film debut in it. Both have stars on the Walk of Fame (see their bios in this book). Died: 1959.

Cass Daley 📺   6303 Hollywood
Comedienne, singer, dancer
BORN Katherine Dailey; July 17, 1915, in Philadelphia, PA. **SPOTLIGHTS** ''I said it and I'm glad!'' was her well-loved catchphrase in radio's "Maxwell House Coffee Time," a comedy-variety program (1944-'45). Daley made her film debut in *The Fleet's In* (1941). Others include *Red Garters* (1954). She made countless TV guest appearances; audiences roared at her crazy song-and-dance routines. Died: 1975.

Marie Wilson 🎤   6301 Hollywood
See page 81

George Montgomery 📺 6301 Hollywood

George Montgomery

Actor, director, writer, producer
BORN George M. Letz; Aug. 29, 1916, in Brady, MT. **SPOTLIGHTS** Born one of fourteen children of good, strong Russian peasant stock (although he looked more like a Duke than a farmer), he was raised in Montana with his immigrant parents. He grew into an extremely well-built, six-foot tall champion collegiate boxer who was mesmerized with art and aesthetics. This very masculine athlete studied interior design at the University of Montana. Ruggedly handsome, he was offered a shot at the movies. He made his uncredited screen debut in a Greta Garbo film; he rode alongside her on a horse. He was a bit player in *The Singing Vagabond* (1935), then appears in a number of Westerns, at first using his real name: *The Lone Ranger* (1938--serial), *Billy the Kid Returns* (1938), and *Wall Street Cowboy* (1939). Using his stage name, he made: *The Cisco Kid and the Lady*, *Star Dust* (both 1940), *Young People* (1940), starring Shirley Temple, *Riders of the Purple Sage* (1941), *Roxie Hart* (1954), with Ginger Rogers, *Orchestra Wives* (1942) co-starring Ann Rutherford and the Glenn Miller band, and *China*

Girl (1942), opposite Gene Tierney. After making *Coney Island* in early 1943 (co-starring Betty Grable), he enlisted in the Army Air Corps (Air Force) as a private. He served bravely during WWII. Upon his return to Hollywood, he made *Three Little Girls in Blue* (1946), with June Haver, *The Brasher Doubloon* (1947--as gumshoe Philip Marlowe), *The Girl from Manhattan* (1948), opposite Dorothy Lamour, *Belle Starr's Daughter* (1948), co-starring Ruth Roman, and *Davy Crockett, Indian Scout* (1950--in title lead) with Ellen Drew. He made dozens more pictures while designing and manufacturing furniture. He also rode high in the TV Western, "Cimarron City" (1958-'60). In the 1960s, he wrote, directed and produced several low budget action films in the Philippines. This charming, handsome hunk was engaged to the lovely Ginger Rogers, the stunning Hedy Lamarr, then married Southern belle Dinah Shore (1943-'60). He had two children with the latter. **QUOTE** "I'll take it as it comes. There's no sense in worrying about anything after you've done it."

Constance Binney 🎥   6301 Hollywood
Actress
BORN June 28, 1896; New York, NY. **SPOTLIGHTS** A newcomer on the silent screen, this bit actress was spotted by the keen eye of Adolph Zukor (later president of Paramount), and made into a leading lady. Like a shooting star, her career

Constance Binney

burned brightly and quickly. Movies include *Sporting Life* (1918), *Erstwhile Susan* (1919), *39 East* (1920), *The Magic Cup* (1921), *The Case of Becky* (1921), *Room and Board* (1921), *The Sleepwalker* (1922), *Midnight* (1922), and *Three O'Clock in the Morning* (1923), her last film. Died: 1989.

Matt Moore ♛ 6301 Hollywood
Actor

BORN Jan. 8, 1888, in Ireland. **SPOTLIGHTS** At age nine, he and his family were crossing the Atlanta on a ship out of Ireland bound for America. As a youngster, he tagged along with his two older actor-brothers, Owen and Tom, to Biograph Studios. From silents to talkies, he worked as an extra, did bit parts, supporting roles, then rose to romantic leading man. Later, he worked as a character actor. Films include *Traffic in Souls* (1913), *The Pride of the Clan* (1917), *The Unholy Three* (1925), *His Jazz Bride* (1926), *Coquette* (1929), *The Front Page* (1931), *Rain* (1932), *Anything Goes* (1936), *Wilson* (1944), *The Plymouth Adventure* (1952), *Seven Brides for Seven Brothers* (1954), and *An Affair to Remember* (1957). Died: 1960.

Gloria Swanson ♀ 6301 Hollywood
See page 453

Carmen Cavallaro ● 6301 Hollywood
Pianist, orchestra leader

BORN May 6, 1913, in New York. **SPOTLIGHTS** Known as "the poet of the piano," he was a showy pianist with precise technique. Dance music band leader. Films: *Hollywood Canteen* (1944) and *Diamond Horseshoe* (1945). Soundtrack for movies, radio shows and concerts. Composed songs: "Masquerade Waltz" and "Wanda." Records: "My Silent Love" and "I'm Getting Sentimental Over You." LPs: *The King and I and other Rodgers & Hammerstein Songs*.

Carey Wilson ♛ 6301 Hollywood
Writer, producer

BORN May 10, 1889, in Philadelphia, PA. **SPOTLIGHTS** Wilson wrote stories/screenplays from 1921-'39, and collaborated on *Mutiny on the Bounty* (1935). He produced *The Red Danube* (1949). Died: 1962.

Don McNeill 🎙 6301 Hollywood
Host

BORN Donald T. McNeill; Dec. 23, 1907, in Galena, IL. **SPOTLIGHTS** Told by the station manager he had "NO TALENT," he was fired from his first radio job as an announcer. In 1933 he answered an ad for a nondescript host for "The Pepper Pot." When he surprisingly landed it, McNeill changed the title to something he felt had a homey ring. "I became famous as the host of the most unrehearsed show in radio, 'The Breakfast Club,'" he stated. He put the "corn in the cornflakes" with his spontaneous remarks, soft humor, and silly riddles. An example of a "Breakfast Club" riddle: What's the difference between a tiger and a panther? A tiger is a big cat, but panther what you wear." The show became a phenomenal, award-winning #1 hit. McNeill gave credit to, "old-fashioned friendliness like doing your part in community activities and being cheerful and friendly." His program promoted mid-Western values as "hymn time," "march time," and "memory time. In the full 35 years the vareity show was on air—more than 6,000 broadcasts—he only missed a total of 18 days. He attributed his ability to meet its early schedule to his wife, who awoke every morning at 4:30 and who had placed alarm clocks throughout their house. "I'm the luckiest guy in the world," he said about his wife, family and job. **QUOTE** During WWII, he recited a daily prayer for servicemen: "All over the nation...each in his own words, each in his own way, for a world united in peace, bow your heads, let us pray." 15 seconds of silence followed. The audience enjoyed this segment so much it continued after the war. Died: 1996.

Archie Mayo ♛ 6301 Hollywood
Director

BORN 1891, in NY, NY. **SPOTLIGHTS** At Warner's, he directed James Cagney in *The Mayor of Hell* (1933), and Humphrey Bogart in *Black Legion* (1936). His last film, *A Night in Casablanca* (1946), stars the Marx Brothers. Died: 1968.

Carl Laemmle ♛ Hollywood and Vine
Film pioneer, motion picture tycoon

Carl Laemmle

BORN Jan. 17, 1867, in Germany. **SPOTLIGHTS** He saved every penny he earned from his first job in America, as an errand boy for a drugstore. That was in 1884. He invested his savings in a nickelodeon around 1906 and was amazed by the easy profits. By 1912 his young, start-up picture company, IMP, merged with other small companies to become Universal Studios. An instinctive executive, he proved to the new industry that there was box office gold in feature-length films. His motion picture about white slavery, *Traffic in Souls* (1913), cost $5,000 to make (a lot of money back then), but grossed nearly half a million dollars. A brilliant film pioneer with keen insight and lots of faith, Laemmle purchased the 230-acre parcel of land that Universal Studios Hollywood, in Universal City, sits on in 1915. Affectionately called "Uncle Carl" by employees, he gave many of Hollywood's earliest top executives their start. In 1929 he turned over the reins of production to his son, Carl Laemmle, Jr., commenting, "If Irving Thalberg could run a studio when he was twenty-one years old, my boy can do the same thing." (MGM's "Boy Wonder" Thalberg got his start as Laemmle's personal secretary.) His son did not disappoint him. He produced many classics, including the Academy Award-winning *All Quiet on the Western Front* (1930), *The King of Jazz* (1930), *Dracula* (1931), *Frankenstein* (1931), *Only Yesterday* (1933), and *The Good Fairy* (1935). **HIGHLIGHTS** If you visit Universal Studios Hollywood, survey the property. At first, Laemmle worried about his financial security in the long haul. He asked himself, "What if the picture business goes sour?" He set aside a portion of the land to raise and sell chickens and eggs. This side business went along with his moviemaking. (You can bet Universal's commissary had the freshest chicken dishes in town!)...There is also a Universal Studios in Orlando, Florida, *minus the chicken farm.* Visit Universal's website (www.universalstudios.com). **SIDELIGHTS** Known for his extravagance, Laemmle enjoyed weekly all-night, no-limit poker games. He played alongside other Hollywood powerhouses, with the card games held at various private residences...Born the tenth of 13 children, Laemmle was raised to help care for his family. Once he made it big, he hired around 100 family members, immediate family, cousins, distant relatives and in-laws. Everyone in Hollywood participated in nepotism, but he gave new meaning to the word, and became one for the joke mill. About Laemmle (pronounced lem-lee), Ogden Nash wote this clever-couplet:

"Uncle Carl Laemmle
Has a very large faemmle."

QUOTE "For 20 years some speaker at every motion picture oratorical occasion has unfailingly referred to our art as 'the infant industry.' 20 years hence they will be doing the same thing, and it will be just as true then as it is now. Both as an art and as an industry, motion pictures are in their infancy. Therein, lies the only excuse for their shortcomings of the past and the best promise for the future." Died: 1939.

Neil Armstrong, Buzz Aldrin, Michael Collins ▪ Hollywood and Vine
See page 266

Jo Stafford ▯ Hollywood and Vine
See page 350

Artie Shaw ● Hollywood and Vine
Clarinetist, band leader
BORN Arthur Arshawsky; May 23, 1910, in New York, NY. **SPOTLIGHTS** An exacting perfectionist, Shaw's superior artistic talents made him more than an excellent technical clarinetist. He constantly challenged—and sometimes over took—Benny Goodman for the King of Swing's golden crown. A dedicated and ambitious musician, he formed his band in 1936—a string quartet, clarinet, and three rhythm instruments. The intellectual of the swing band maestros composed and arranged as well as playing and band leading. And when it came time to hire a vocalist Shaw declared, "a singer to me is Billie Holiday," and Lady Day (as she was known) came on board. In 1938 he gave a new interpretation to Cole Porter's "Begin the Beguine." His many hits include "Indian Love Call," "Frenesi," "Summit Ridge Drive," "Dancing In The Dark," and "Concerto For Clarinet." In 1939 when he had the hottest band—and before the world was at war—he said, "Wild dances are reflective of optimism and frenetic happiness." An avid reader, Shaw wrote a book in 1952 entitled *The Trouble with Cinderella.* What was the trouble? *"That the coach always turned back into a pumpkin."* **QUOTE** He was married seven times to real stunners, (Lana Turner, Ava Gardner, Evelyn Keyes...) After his fourth divorce he said, "The only reason I've been married a lot of times is I've wanted to be married a lot of times." After his seventh divorce and years of psychoanalysis he observed, "Show me a guy, who's always out with a beautiful dame and I'll show you a guy who's trying to prove something to himself."

Marilyn Miller 🎥 Hollywood and Vine
Dancer, singer
BORN Mary Ellen Reynolds; Sept 1, around 1898 or 1900 (exact year unknown), in Evansville, IL. **SPOTLIGHTS** Trained as a singer-dancer from age three, she toured America and Europe in her family's vaudeville act. Miller was discovered in London by Lee Shubert at age 15, who cast her in the stage production of "The Passing Show." Showman Flo Ziegfeld put her in his "Follies of 1918," where she rose to "overnight" fame as a musical star. A slender, petite, blue-eyed blonde with plenty of personality, she commanded $5,000 a week onstage, and up to $11,000 per week for film. She made only three movies: *Sally, Sunny* (both 1930); and *Her Majesty Love* (1931). **SIDELIGHTS** Norma Jean Dougherty (Marilyn Monroe) was one of her big biggest fans, and liked the soft sound of Marilyn Miller's double "M" names. This is where she got "Marilyn" for her own stage name. Miller was portrayed by Judy Garland in the film, *Till the Clouds Roll By* (1946), and by June Haver in *Look for the Silver Lining* (1949). Died: 1936.

Marilyn Miller with Ben Lyon

1711 VINE

Jessica Dragonette 🎙   1711 Vine

Singer, hostess

Jessica Dragonette

BORN Born of American parents around the turn of the century in Calcutta, India. **SPOTLIGHTS** Known as "the Angel Voice," she was orphaned as a child. Dragonette grew up nurtured and educated by devoted Catholic nuns in a sheltered convent. As the unseen Angel Voice in Max Reinhardt's stage play *Das Mirakel* (*The Miracle*), she attracted the attention of the blue-eyed giant, Russian operatic bass, Fyodor Chaliapin. During intermission, he asked to meet little Jessica backstage. He bowed to kiss her hand and said, "Allow me to thank you, child, for your exquisite singing." Then smiling from his great height, "But you're only a cherub—half an angel. Maybe some day, if you work hard, you'll be full-fledged." She did work hard, first on Broadway then breaking ground as one of radio's earliest (and youngest) female celebrities. She made her radio debut when NBC was one month old, and before long was attracting more than 35,000,000 listeners weekly. This soprano was known for her pure style of singing "Breath of April," Verdi's "Ave Maria," Mimi's "Addio," "Estrellita," and "Alice Blue Gown." Her repertoire ranged from grand opera to popular songs. Her lifelong motto: "Faith Is a Song." Died: 1980.

George Stevens 🎥   1711 Vine

Director

BORN Dec. 18, 1904, in Oakland, CA. **SPOTLIGHTS** He learned his craft during the silent era while working as a cameraman on Laurel and Hardy shorts. A versatile director, his films include the sparkling, elegant, romantic comedy *Swing Time* (1936), a musical starring Fred Astaire and Ginger Rogers, and the rambunctious adventure *Gunga Din* (1939), starring Cary Grant, Victor McLaglen and Douglas Fairbanks, Jr. When World War II started, he served in real-life as Lieutenant Colonel Stevens. He was part of the military force which liberated Dachau concentration camp and freed its inmates. The horrors he witnessed shocked him,

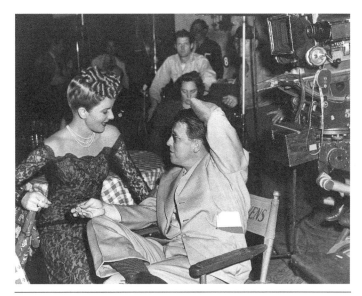

George Stevens and Jean Arthur

permanently altering his creative course. Postwar, his movies showed life's raw edges: untimely death, sacrifice and tragedy. He commented, "It takes a movie just about two hours to give the filmgoer a feeling of emotional fulfillment, to send him out into the street, at the end, so caught up in what he has seen that he does not immediately see the street lights. If he sees those street lights, something's wrong." In 1953 he directed the stately Western *Shane* with Alan Ladd; it's about a noble hero who saves a society which has no place for him. In 1959 he gave us *The Diary of Anne Frank*. He took five years to complete *The Greatest Story Ever Told* (1965). **ACHIEVEMENTS** 1951 Best Director Oscar for *A Place in the Sun*. 1953 Irving G. Thalberg Memorial Award presented "for the most consistent high level of production achievement by an individual producer." 1956 Best Director Oscar for *Giant*. **QUOTE** "Making motion pictures is a time-consuming and exacting job. When the movie industry was young, the filmmaker was its core and the man who handled the business details his partner. When the filmmaker finally looked around, he found his partner's name on the door. Thus the filmmaker became the employee, and the man who had the time to attend to the business details became the head of the studio." Died: 1975.

Miriam Hopkins 🎥   1711 Vine

Actress

BORN Ellen M. Hopkins; Oct. 18, 1902, in Bainbridge, GA. **SPOTLIGHTS** A graduate of Syracuse University, this long-legged beauty got her 1921 break on Broadway as a chorus girl in "Music Box Revue." She landed supporting and starring roles in "Little Jesse James" (1923), "An American Tragedy" (1926), and "The Affairs of Anatole" (1926). An outstanding stage performer, Hopkins' notoriety earned the testy, but chic actress a seven-year Paramount contract

Miriam Hopkins

beginning at $1,000-a-week. The studio put her in sophisticated comedies like Ernest Lubitsch's *The Smiling Lieutenant* (1931), and in the classic *Trouble in Paradise* (1932), where she and Herbert Marshall play two jewel thieves. Several vehicles were fashioned for her: *Design for Living* (1933), *Becky Sharp* (1935), and *These Three* (1936). While she starred in the stage production of "Jezebel" (1933), Bette Davis landed her role in the film version. Supposedly the two were in a 30-year rivalry. Regardless, she and Davis co-star in *The Old Maid* (1939), based on the Edith Wharton novel, and *Old Acquaintance* (1943). Films include *Virginia City* (1949), *The Heiress* (1949), and *Carrie* (1958). She was fascinated with astrology and studied it during her golden years. Died: 1972.

Robert Q. Lewis 📺   1711 Vine

Comedian, host

Robert Q. Lewis

BORN April 5, 1921, in New York. **SPOTLIGHTS** Lewis was an outstanding, energetic, brash comedian with outsized horn-rimmed glasses. At age 11, he began singing as a boy soprano on radio's "Dr. Posner's Kiddie Show." The job ended when his voice changed. After graduating from the University of Michigan, he landed a job at a New York station. He was the only announcer there the day Pearl Harbor was bombed (December 7, 1941). He enlisted in the Army, but was medically discharged due to his poor eyesight. He began doing a weekly morning show, switched to a daily hillbilly show, then a variety show. He hit the network airwaves in 1947 and had gained national fame by 1949. A frequent substitute host on "The Arthur Godfrey Time," Lewis was virtually heard in every radio time slot available during his long career. 1950s - '60s TV: Hosted "The Robert Q. Lewis Show," and "The Show Goes On," talent hunt. Panelist on "What's My Line?" **QUOTE** "Shirts should be full of people and not stuffing."

Deborah Kerr 🎥
1711 Vine

Actress

BORN Deborah Kerr-Trimmer; Sept. 30, 1921, in Helensburgh, Scotland. **SPOTLIGHTS** Kerr typically starred in ladylike roles. Her steamy characterization of an adulteress in *From Here to Eternity* (1953) was a rare and provocative exception, earning her a second Academy Award nomination for best actress. (Her first Oscar nomination was for *Edward and I* in 1949.) She gave a bril-

Deborah Kerr

liant performance as the English governess Anna in *The King and I* (1956). She was immortalized in this role and received her third Oscar nomination. She delivered a divine performance in the classic love story, *An Affair to Remember* (1957). In 1958 she appears opposite Burt Lancaster, Rita Hayworth and David Niven in the character drama, *Separate Tables*. She is also superb in *The Night of the Iguana* (1964). **ACHIEVEMENTS** Oscar-nominated six times, she never won. The Academy awarded her a 1993 Honorary Oscar inscribed with the words: "To Deborah Kerr, In appreciation for a full career's worth of elegant and beautifully crafted performances." **QUOTE** About the "Shall We Dance?" scene in *The King and I*, Kerr reminisced, "A lot of the scene was one long (continuous) shot from a crane. It was hard. The heavy, heavy hoops on my skirt, which were made of metal, swung out at every turn and bruised my legs and waist. And my hip bones—where the top of the metal skirt attached—were black and blue!" *So much for Hollywood glamour.*

Art Acord 🎥   1711 Vine

Actor

BORN April 17, 1890, in Stillwater, OK. **SPOTLIGHTS** A young, rugged rodeo rider, this teen earned a buck-a-day as a movie stuntman. He became Universal's cowboy during the 1920s. Films include *The Oregon Trail* (1923) and *Hard Fists* (1927). Like 99 percent of silent stars, talkies ended it all. His last film *The White Outlaw* (1929) had an ominous title; his next career involved bootlegging and gambling. Died: 1931.

George Eastman 🎥   1711 Vine

Manufacturer

BORN July 13, 1854, in Waterville, NY. **SPOTLIGHTS** Born

George Eastman (left) and Thomas Edison

poverty-stricken, he left school at age 14 to help support his widowed mother and two older sisters, one crippled by polio. His first job as a messenger boy paid $3 per week. He studied accounting and eventually landed a bank clerk job for $800 a year. At 24, he planned his first vacation. An associate suggested he take photographs. The wet-plate photographic equipment he bought rivaled the weight of heavy camping gear, with a cumbersome tripod, big camera, black tent, and chemicals. The mechanically minded Eastman believed taking a photograph should be simple and easy. Inspired, he filed several patents and formed his own company. Eastman changed the world when he pioneered simple photography for the masses. **ACHIEVEMENTS** This genius invented flexible film in 1889, enabling Thomas Edison to develop the motion picture camera (see photo). He invented numerous photographic processes including an emulsion coating machine for dry plates, Eastman film, the Kodak camera, plates and paper for X-rays (1896). The Academy awarded a 1952 Special Oscar (one of several), for Eastman color motion picture film. **HIGHLIGHTS** One of the greatest men of the century, Eastman made more than $100 million. He gave it all away (frequently anonymously) during his lifetime to enable the poor to receive dental treatment, to advance medicine and science, to further education, and to foster the arts. A truly generous employer, Eastman initiated employee profit-sharing. Died: 1932.

John Bowers   1711 Vine

Actor

BORN Dec. 25, 1899, in Garrett, IN. **SPOTLIGHTS** He made his stunning film debut in *Hilda From Holland* (1916), opposite Mary Pickford. A handsome, romantic leading man in many silents, fame's curtain crashed down as movie sound exploded. **LOWLIGHTS** The death scene of the aging, former movie idol in *A Star is Born* (1937) was based on Bowers' own circumstances. Died: 1936, by drowning.

Slim Whitman ● 1711 Vine

Singer, guitarist

BORN Otis Dewey Whitman, Jr.; Jan. 20, 1924, in Tampa, FL. **SPOTLIGHTS** Extremely athletic and gifted in sports, Whitman aspired to be a star pitcher for a professional baseball team. WWII altered that dream. He learned to play guitar on the naval ship *U.S.S. Chilton,* taking to the instrument like a duck to water. Postwar, the tall, slender talent earned money entertaining in local clubs, where he found himself completely at ease. By 1948 Whitman was invited to sing at radio station WDAE in Tampa, where a recording executive offered him a contract. The mustached cowboy, who sang in a high clear tenor, was celebrated for his traditional interpretations of old country standards. A great stylist of older American folk music, he is remembered as one of America's last romantic cowboy singers, and as one of country's last great Western yodelers. Hits include "Love Song of the Waterfall," "Bandera Waltz," "Keep It a Secret," "North Wind," "Secret Love," "China Doll," "Indian Love Song," "Casting My Lasso to the Sky," and "Rainbows Are Back In Style." **ACHIEVEMENTS** In the late 1970s his single "Rose Marie" spent 11 consecutive weeks at #1 on the British Pop Music Charts—not even a Beatles song accomplished that. He sold 55 million records.

Robert Sterling   1711 Vine

Actor

Robert Sterling and Anne Jeffreys

BORN William Hart; Nov. 13, 1917, in New Castle, PA. **SPOTLIGHTS** This handsome actor was immortalized playing the dapper, friendly ghost in TV's situation comedy, "Topper" (1953-'56). As the spirit of George Kirby, he returns to his former earthly home to find the stuffy, uptight banker Cosmo "Topper" living there. He co-starred with his real-life wife, Anne Jeffreys. Jeffreys, a vision of loveliness, played his TV wife Marion Kirby. Together, these fun-loving apparitions try to loosen up Topper to make his life worth living. This top-rated comedy show was based on the hit movie *Topper* (1937).

Rouben Mamoulian   1711 Vine

Director

BORN Oct. 8, 1893, in Tiflis, the Russian province of Georgia. **SPOTLIGHTS** A versatile, inventive *auteur,* Mamoulian directed Gary Cooper and Sylvia Sidney in the gangster melodrama, *City Streets* (1931), with an original screenplay by Dashiell Hammett. The following year, he demonstrated his ingenuity in absolute opposites: the terrifying *Dr. Jekyll and Mr. Hyde,* with Fredric March (the first sound version of the °story), and the enchanting romantic comedy, *Love Me Tonight*, starring Maurice Chevalier and Jeanette MacDonald. In the latter musical are Rodgers' and Hart's charming tunes "Isn't It Romantic," "Lover," and "Mimi." (Offscreen, Chevalier refused to speak to MacDonald, so it was anything but love on the set!) In 1933, Greta Garbo complemented his great style in MGM's *Queen Christina*. Turning to action, Tyrone Power sizzled as the lead in *The Mark of Zorro* (1940), and in *Blood and Sand* (1941), opposite the incandescent Linda Darnell. Mamoulian made only 16 pictures, as his interest in directing Broadway stage plays kept him on the East Coast most of the time. Died: 1987.

Eddie Heywood ● 1711 Vine

Musician, composer, jazz pianist
BORN Dec. 4, 1915 in Atlanta, GA. **SPOTLIGHTS** His father, a graduate of the Boston Conservatory of Music, was a famous band leader-pianist. His uncle, LeRoy Smith, was also a famous band leader, so it was natural that as a child Eddie absorbed jazz almost by osmosis. He played in a crisp, stylized manner. By age 14, he was playing professionally for Atlanta's local 81 Theatre Orchestra. Worked with Wayman Carver's Ramblers, Clarence Love and Benny Carter's Orchestra. He formed his own sextet in 1943 that included trumpeter Doc Cheatham and trombonist Vic Dickenson. They struck gold immediately with instrumental hits: ""Begin the Beguine," and "Please Don't Talk About Me When I'm Gone." He also enjoyed a huge hit with "Featuring Eddie Heywood," and with vocalists Billie Holliday and Ella Fitzgerald. Motion picture appearances include *The Dark Corner* (1946), and *The Junior Prom* (1947). Unfortunately at the peak of his career—in 1947—he suffered from hand paralysis. Unable to perform, he composed and wrote more than 40 songs, including "Land of Dreams," and "Soft Summer Breeze." One of his best-loved compositions—a jazz and pop standard—is "Canadian Sunset." Died: 1989.

Geraldine Farrar ● 1711 Vine

Opera singer, actress
BORN Feb. 28, 1882, in Melrose, MA. **SPOTLIGHTS** Acknowledged internationally as the very finest opera singer of her time, she was a soprano whose lovely timbre and flawless musicality were unmatched. Farrar was the first to take her talents to the screen. Although 1915-'21 pictures were silent, this beauty used her skill as a theatrical performer to win over surprised audiences under the great Cecil B. DeMille's direction. At the Metropolitan Opera House in New York, Farrar's most successful role was Cio-Cio-San ("Butterfly"). Her two other specialties were Carmen and Marguerite. These roles she made uniquely her own, as she declared, "by my slavish prostration to the lyric art." Her reign, from her Berlin debut in 1901, to her Met farewell in 1922, ended when she retired at the top of

her craft. **HIGHLIGHTS** The great Caruso coined her motto, "*Farrar fara*": Farrar will do it. Died: 1967.

George Brent ♛ 1711 Vine

Actor
BORN George B. Nolan; Mar. 15, 1904, in Ireland. **SPOTLIGHTS** A political criminal in his native Ireland, he was smuggled out of the country aboard a freighter bound for Canada. The charming Brent became a reliable lead opposite star actresses, such as Greta Garbo in *The Painted Veil* (1934), but most frequently with Bette Davis in *Jezebel* (1938), *The Old Maid* (1939) and nine others. He is paired with Dorothy McGuire in the spooky suspense thriller *The Spiral Staircase* (1946). **HIGHLIGHTS** Bette Davis commented, "I fell in love with George years before we became an item. He helped me through some difficult personal problems during the making of *Dark Victory* and also fell in love with me. I often hoped he would want to marry me. He never did." Miss Davis saw him again—after a 20-year absence—in San Diego in 1975, while she was on tour with her own show. He sent orchids to her dressing room then came back to visit her. After seeing him, she reminisced, "I might have felt a little cheated except for one rather nice reminder. As he left, George giggled. He still had that same crazy, infectious giggle I remembered so well." Died: 1979.

Elena Verdugo 1711 Vine

Actress
BORN April 20, 1926, in Hollywood, CA. **SPOTLIGHTS** A breakthrough Latino TV star, this very pretty actress played Hispanic secretary Millie Bronson as star of "Meet Millie" (1952-'56). She starred in the radio version (1953-'54). This appealing talent appeared in a variety of situation comedies, and was a regular on the popular medical series, "Marcus Welby, M.D." (1969-'76) as Consuelo Lopez.

Robert Walker ♛ 1711 Vine

Actor
BORN Oct. 13, 1918, in Salt Lake City, UT. **SPOTLIGHTS** After being educated at the San Diego Army and Naval Academy, he attended New York's Academy of Dramatic Arts. With his wavy, brown hair, clear-cut features, and solid body, he could have easily stuck with the boy-next-door roles. He didn't. After the comedy *See Here, Private Hargrove* (1944), he plays opposite his real-life wife Jennifer Jones in *Since You Went Away* (1944). Unfortunately, the film's title proved ominous for their marriage; they were divorced the following year. He co-stars with Judy Garland in the timely WWII drama about falling in love in 24 hours, *The Clock* (1945). He is the compelling, perverted psychopathic killer in *Strangers on a Train* (1951). Died: 1951.

Glen Gray ● 1711 Vine

Band leader, saxes

BORN G. G. Knoblaugh; June 7, 1906, in Roanoke, IL. **SPOT-LIGHTS** Known as "Spike," he studied at Illinois Wesleyan College, then went off to work for the Santa Fe Railroad Company. Off duty, he played local gigs in the sax section. In 1929, together with his Casa Loma Orchestra (in Toronto, Canada), they became the first all-white band to specialize in jazz albums: "Five Feet of Swing." The Casa Loma band appeared in the film, *Girls, Inc.* (1943). Gray's theme songs were "Was I to Blame for Falling in Love With You?" and "Smoke Rings," featuring trombonist Billy Rausch. Died: 1963.

Fred Clark 📽   1711 Vine

Actor

BORN March 9, 1914, in Lincoln, CA. **SPOTLIGHTS** After earning a psychology degree from Stanford University, he won an acting scholarship to the American Academy of Dramatic Arts. An established stage presence on Broadway, he served in WWII, then went to Hollywood. He made his movie debut in the tense film noir, *The Unsuspected* (1947), as a detective. Films include *White Heat* (1949), *Sunset Boulevard* (1950), *The Lemon Drop Kid, A Place in the Sun* (both 1951), *The Caddy, How to Marry a Millionaire* (both 1953), *Abbott and Costello Meet the Keystone Kops, Daddy Long Legs,* and *The Court-Martial of Billy Mitchell* (all 1955). TV: "The George Burns and Gracie Allen Show" (1951-'53), and "Pantomime Quiz" in the 1950s. Died: 1968.

Mauritz Stiller 🎥   1713 Vine

Director

Mauritz Stiller and Greta Garbo

BORN Moshe Stiller; July 17, 1883, in Helsinki. **SPOTLIGHTS** A respected director in early Swedish cinema since 1912, his best silent film is *Sir Arne's Treasure* (1919). Then, Stiller discovered Greta Garbo and cast her in *The Atonement of Gosta Berling* (1924). The following year, Louis B. Mayer (of MGM) lured Stiller to Hollywood. The director accepted with the proviso that Garbo, the actress he had been grooming for stardom, came along, too. Mayer thought she was too fat for American beauty standards, but agreed. When Hollywood moguls saw Garbo's rare, mysterious beauty onscreen, they ousted Stiller instead. He died in 1928; many said of a broken heart from shattered dreams.

Walter Catlett 🎥   1713 Vine

Actor, comic

BORN Feb. 4, 1889, in San Francisco, CA. **SPOTLIGHTS** A former Ziegfeld entertainer, a critic described Catlett as a "low and wonderful American comedian." He was a fidgety, google-eyed performer, whose small, thin frame, and balding pate brought both laughter and tears to comedies and dramas. Movies include *A Tale of Two Cities* (1935), *Mr. Deeds Goes to Town* (1936), *Bringing Up Baby* (1938), and *The Inspector General* (1949). He made 50 motion pictures. Died: 1960.

John Lupton 📽   1713 Vine

Actor

BORN Aug. 22, 1926, in Highland Park, IL. **SPOTLIGHTS** He starred as Native American Indian agent Tom Jeffords on "Broken Arrow" (1956-'60). In the TV series, the Native American Chiricahua Apache Indians and cowboys work together to fight injustice. Paleface peacemaker Jeffords befriends Indian Apache Chief Cochise (Michael Ansara), which results in the two becoming blood brothers. This show, popular in syndication, was based on the Elliott Arnold's novel *Blood Brothers,* and subsequently became the motion picture *Broken Arrow* (1950), starring James Stewart. Historically relevant, it was the first time Hollywood told a Western story from the Native Americans' perspective, helping to change the way they were portrayed, and correcting false cultural stereotypes.

Kim Hunter   1715 Vine

See page 347

Judy Garland 🎥   1715 Vine

Actress, singer

BORN Frances Gumm; June 10, 1922, in Grand Rapids, MI. **SPOTLIGHTS** One of the brightest talents ever, this MGM song-and-dance girl had a marvelous, emotionally charged voice. Immortalized as the little Kansas farm girl Dorothy in *The Wizard of Oz* (1939), she recited the movie's most famous lines, "Oh, Auntie Em, there's no place like home," and sang the movie's most significant song, "Somewhere Over the Rainbow." (One of the most important musical works of the 20th century, the original soundtrack is available on Rhino Movie Music, *The Story & Songs of The Wizard of Oz, Special Edition,* CD R2 75516.) Many critics consider her brilliant work in *A Star is Born* (1954--in an Oscar-nominated performance, where she sang "The Man That Got Away") to be her finest film. Motion pictures include *Broadway Melodies of*

Judy Garland and Mickey Rooney

1938, Thoroughbreds Don't Cry (1937), *Love Finds Andy Hardy* (1938--serial), *Thousands Cheer* (1943), *Meet Me in St. Louis* (1944--with her memorable rendition of "The Trolley Song"), *The Harvey Girls* (1946), *Easter Parade* (1948), and *Judgment at Nuremberg* (1961--in an Oscar-nominated performance). **ACHIEVEMENTS** 1939 Special Oscar for "the best juvenile performer of the year." She displayed energy, vulnerability, and intensity. **HIGHLIGHTS** Her second marriage to director Vincent Minnelli produced daughter-singer Liza Minnelli. With third husband producer Sid Luft, she had two children, singer Lorna and Joseph. **SIDELIGHTS** Onstage since age three, Louis B. Mayer signed her to a contract at age 13. Her stage mother allowed MGM to go beyond their standard grooming of a young charge. The motion picture lot became the teen's home and nursemaid—feeding, comforting and educating the rising talent. Her mother (whom Judy called the "real wicked witch") relinquished discipline and punishment. She constantly threatened, "Judy, if you don't behave, I'll tell the studio!" This legendary talent died in 1969.

Pee Wee King 🎵   1715 Vine

Musician, band leader
BORN Frank Anthony Kuczynski; Feb. 18, 1914, in Abrams, Wisconsin. **SPOTLIGHTS** His father led a local polka band, so it was natural for the tot to play accordion. Later, cowboy great Gene Autry (star of the WLS "National Barn Dance") heard the 20-year-old play on Milwaukee's WRJN "Badger State Barn Dance," and asked the musician to join him. Autry nicknamed the five-foot-seven-inch tall Kuczynski "Pee Wee" because of his size. When Autry rode to Hollywood, Pee Wee formed his own band "The Golden

West Cowboys." By 1937 they had joined the Opry, igniting country entertainment with showy professionalism, and enhancing typical Western music with sophisticated string band sound. Hits include: "Tennessee Polka," "Bonaparte's Retreat," and "Slow Poke." Albums: *Blue Ribbon Country, Vol. 3; Best of Pee Wee King, Stars of the Grand Ole Opry.* He had his own radio and TV musical variety shows (featuring his favorite square dancers). King was a regular cast member in radio's "Grand Ole Opry." His hit "The Tennessee Waltz" became the official state song of Tennessee.

John Bunny 🎥   1715 Vine

Actor, comedian
BORN Sept. 21, 1863, in New York, NY. **SPOTLIGHTS** His mug—open, crumbly and protruding—looked like he was one of the Great Creator's own genial puppets. Although he trained for stage, and had worked in vaudeville, he made motion picture history by becoming the screen's *original* fat funny man. At 295 pounds, his comedy was not crude slapstick, but polished, refined pantomime. In truth, he was a good enough actor to handle dramatic roles with ease, but the public loved him best when he made them laugh. Movies include *Vanity Fair* (1911), *Bachelor Buttons* (1912), *Cure for Pokeritis* (1912), *Bunny Attempts Suicide* (1912), *Polishing Up* (1913), *Pigs Is Pigs* (1914), and *Bunny in Bunnyland* (1915). Died: 1915.

John Nesbitt 🎥   1717 Vine

Narrator, producer
BORN Aug. 23, 1910, in Victoria, B.C., Canada. **SPOTLIGHTS** Called the "top teller of tales" for both his radio and television story telling abilities and beautiful voice, he signed with MGM in 1938 to produce a series of Passing Parade shorts. **ACHIEVEMENTS** Academy Awards for his one-reel shorts: *That Mothers Might Live* (1938); *Pups and Puzzles* and *Main Street on the March* (both 1941); *Stairway to Light* (1945); and *Goodbye Miss Turlock* (1947). **QUOTE** "My distinctive speaking voice is due to the fact I had to talk into my father's close-to-deaf ear." Died: 1960.

Verna Felton 📺   1717 Vine

Actress
BORN July 29, 1890, in Salinas, CA. **SPOTLIGHTS** Her uniquely charming voice was immortalized in a number of Walt Disney's animated classics, including *Dumbo* (1941), *Cinderella* (1950), *Lady and the Tramp* (1955) and *Sleeping Beauty* (1959). Other movies include *Girls of the Big House* (1945), and *Taming Sutton's Gal* (1957). An experienced performer on stage and in radio, in television she played Mrs. Day on "The RCA Victor Show" (1952), and the funny, annoying, busybody friend of the unappreciated wife in "Pete and Gladys" (1960-'61). Died: 1966.

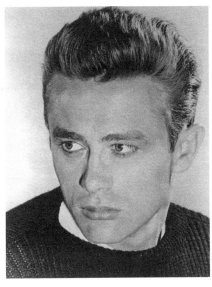

James Dean

James Dean 🎥
1717 Vine

Actor

BORN Feb. 8, 1931, in Marian, NE. **SPOTLIGHTS** Dean remains the handsome sex symbol of rebellious youth. He became a cult hero, then legend. His good friend, actress Shelley Winters said of Dean, "He constantly confused real life with acting, and acting with real life." Dean himself declared, "Acting is the most logical way for people's neuroses to express themselves." He painted portraits of cool anguish. His three acclaimed performances are in *East of Eden* (1955), *Rebel Without a Cause* (1955), and *Giant* (1956). Those were the only major roles in big movies he had, but there were three other films. If you watch the comedy *Has Anybody Seen My Gal?* (1952), with Charles Coburn, Piper Laurie, Rock Hudson, and Gigi Perreau you can spot a brief appearance by Dean. He also had small roles in *Sailor Beware* (1951) and *Fixed Bayonets* (1951). **SIDELIGHTS** His proposal of marriage to the only woman he ever loved, Pier Angeli, was a bitter failure. Her mother wouldn't allow the union because he wasn't Catholic, although Dean wanted to convert. Pier committed suicide 16 years later, stating: "I was only in love once in my life and that was with Jimmy Dean." **QUOTE** The pain and suffering he exuded onscreen gushed from a tormented pool deep within him. Dean said of himself, "I am terribly gauche and so tense I don't see how people stay in the same room with me. I know I wouldn't tolerate myself." Success happened too fast and too soon. He went from fame to death in less than three years, becoming the hero of a generation. He died in 1955, at the wheel of his Porsche Spyder race car in a horrible accident. The distraught speaker at his memorial service mourned, "Few knew him well, none knew him for long." The tag line "Live Fast, Die Young" is part of the James Dean mystique.

César Romero 📺
1719 Vine

See page 78

Mark Sandrich 🎥
1719 Vine

Director

BORN Aug. 26, 1900, in New York. **SPOTLIGHTS** Sandrich's *The Gay Divorcee* (1934) introduced the world to the Rogers-Astaire team, and his brilliant *Top Hat* (1935) linked him forever to great dance numbers in top-rated Hollywood musicals. He directed and produced the yuletide classic *Holiday Inn* (1942) starring Bing Crosby and Fred Astaire. The movie includes Irving Berlin's gem "White Christmas"--the best-selling song of all time. Sandrich shifted gears with the grimly patriotic drama *So Proudly We Hail* (1943) starring Claudette Colbert, Paulette Goddard and Veronica Lake. **ACHIEVEMENTS** 1932-'33 Oscar for *So This is Harris* (short). Died: 1945.

Charlie Murray 🎥
1719 Vine

Comedian, actor

BORN June 22, 1872, in Laurel, IN. **SPOTLIGHTS** A natural born comedian who made 'em laugh for four decades. He was the "Murray" half of the "Murray and Mack" vaudeville team. He joined Biograph Studios in New York in 1912, then moved to "Holly Woods" (as he called the place). Films: *Soldiers of Misfortune* (1914), and *The Cohens and Kellys in Trouble* (1933)--he portrayed Mr. Kelly in this series. **HIGHLIGHTS** In 1924 he wrote: "A Letter from One Irishman to Another: I cannot advise you to adopt the movies as a mode of living. There are enough movie actors out here now to supply all demands. I would advise you to learn a trade and stick to it, and save yourself a lot of grief. I've been working in pictures now for twelve years and the nearest I ever got to being a star was when I played a policeman, and had to wear one. But if you can't find anything to do, you might come here and give the pictures a try. Everybody is doing it, and who knows, you may turn lucky. Must make this message short and send a wreath to my bootlegger, who passed out of my life last Tuesday. He drank some of the oil he had reserved for me. Don't call it fate. It was just bad liquor." Died: 1941.

Victor Fleming 🎥
1719 Vine

Director

BORN Feb. 23, 1883, in Pasadena, CA. **SPOTLIGHTS** A native Southern Californian, Fleming started out as a chauffeur/auto mechanic, but ended up driving home some of the greatest motion pictures in history. During WWI he served in the Army Signal Corps as a photographer. His film work covering the Versailles Peace Conference, in France, on June 28, 1919, remains an historic landmark to the war's end. Upon his return to Hollywood, he signed with Paramount Pictures, where he directed such silent screen stars as Clara Bow in *Mantrap* (1926). *The Virginian* (1929) proved Fleming was equally good working with strong leading men; the film made Gary Cooper a star. Fleming easily made the transition to talkies, and in the early 1930s went to work for MGM. Motion pictures include *Red Dust* (1932), *Bombshell* (1933), *Treasure Island* (1934), *The Farmer Takes a Wife* (1935), *Captains Courageous* (1937), and *Test Pilot* (1938).

ACHIEVEMENTS In 1939 he hit MGM's jackpot! Fleming directed BOTH classics: *The Wizard of Oz*, and *Gone with the Wind*. He won the Best Director Oscar for *Gone with the Wind* (although George Cukor and Sam Wood directed segments as well). Both films were competing for the Best Picture Oscar; *The Wizard of Oz* lost to *Gone with the Wind*. Died: 1949.

Hattie McDaniel 🎥   1719 Vine

Actress, singer

Hattie McDaniel

BORN June 10, 1895, in Wichita, KS. **SPOTLIGHTS** This splendid character actress won a drama award at age 10 in 1905, but decided to first pursue a singing career. As a young adult she became a band vocalist and toured the country. When she arrived in Southern California in 1930, Hollywood embraced her. She was immortalized as Mammy in *Gone with the Wind* (1939)--one of the greatest motion pictures of all time. Movies include *Judge Priest* (1934), *The Little Colonel, China Seas* (both 1935), *Show Boat, Libeled Lady* (both 1936), *Saratoga, Nothing Sacred* (both 1937), *The Shopworn Angel* (1938), *Maryland* (1940), *The Great Lie* (1941) and *Since You Went Away* (1944). **RADIO** As listeners tuned in to hear the blast of the steamboat whistle, the sweet song of the calliope, and the swishing of the paddle wheels, McDaniel's beautiful voice could be heard as a cast member of "Show Boat," starting in 1937. It was a highly successful musical-variety program. Next, she joined radio's incredibly popular, " The Eddie Cantor Show" in 1942. McDaniel became one of the first African-Americans to be a regular in a network show. She became the star of "The Beulah Show" (1947-'52). When the show first was first heard in 1945, a Caucasian male played the part of an African-American female maid! It was considerable progress to cast a real African-American; especially with the sizable paychecks. On air, in film and television, she performed in 500 roles. **ACHIEVEMENTS** 1939 Best Supporting Actress Academy Award for *Gone with the Wind*. She was the first African American to win an Oscar. Died: 1952.

Barbara Britton 📺   1719 Vine

Actress
BORN Barbara Brantingham; Sept. 26, 1919, in Long Beach, CA. **SPOTLIGHTS** An attractive redhead of motion picture fame who played wife-turned-sleuth on TV's "Mr. and Mrs. North" (1952-'54). She also appeared in the soap opera "Date with Life," and spent a decade doing Revlon cosmetics beauty commercials. Died: 1980.

Harold Peary 📺   1719 Vine

See page 355

Thomas Meighan 🎥   1719 Vine

Actor

Thomas Meighan

BORN April 9, 1879, in Pittsburgh, PA. **SPOTLIGHTS** One of Paramount Pictures most popular performers during the silent era, he was as famous as Pola Negri and Harold Lloyd. A tall (six-foot), dark-haired, expressive actor, *The Miracle Man* (1919), was his breakthrough role. Films include *The Forbidden City* (1918), *Male and Female* (1919), *Manslaughter* (1922), *The Admirable Crichton* (1923), and *The Alaskan* (1924). **QUOTE** "Among my faults I admit to being sensitive to nagging criticism. For years the women of America have been slaves to Paris. I know whereof I speak, for during seven years with Poiret and Paquin I myself designed many gowns which became a vogue. Far be it from me to criticize the public, which is the final arbiter of all our fates, and which has been so uniformly kind to me, but I often imagine that certain individuals do not take into consideration the immense detail that is involved in making a picture. Do you wonder I am touchy about unthinking critics who say the movies are careless and superficial?" Died: 1936.

Raymond Massey 🎥   1719 Vine

Actor
BORN Aug. 30, 1896, in Toronto, Canada. **SPOTLIGHTS** A tall, thin, but not particularly handsome man, his lean face and intense glare favored evil-doers. Massey, though, earned cinematic immortality as a hero. He portrayed the highly respectable, sixteenth U.S. President in *Abe Lincoln in Illinois* (1940). Films include *The Scarlet Pimpernel* (1935), *The Prisoner of Zenda* (1937), *Arsenic and Old Lace* (1944), *The Woman in the Window* (1944), *Stairway to Heaven* (1946), *Fountainhead* (1949—as Gail Wynand), *East of Eden* (1955),

Raymond Massey

the WWII action picture *Battle Cry* (1955), *The Naked and the Dead* (1958), and *How the West Was Won* (1962—as Abraham Lincoln). He made 76 pictures, in both leading and supporting roles. Massey played another hero, Dr. Leonard Gillespie on TV's "Dr. Kildare" (1961-'66). **HIGHLIGHTS** While bravely serving in the military, he was wounded during *both* World Wars!...Although intelligent, he was also absent-minded. While paying a bill, he signed the check, "Yours Sincerely, Raymond Massey." Died: 1983.

Charles Christie 🎥   1719 Vine

Executive

BORN April 13, 1880, in Canada. **SPOTLIGHTS** This pioneer filmmaker arrived in Los Angeles in 1915. He did the "Christie Comedies" from his own studio, which he co-owned with his brother Al. (Al handled production; Charles was the administrator). They produced two-reel, 20-minute comedy shorts that were shown along with the main feature, a newsreel and often a travelogue. No one called their comedies great, in fact the opposite was true. Their sets were rundown, the plots were repetitious, and their "clowns" were on the tired side. But their company filled a need at theaters. They managed to be profitable, despite their lack of artistry. **QUOTE** "All the publicity about beauty contest winners to the contrary, I think it is safe to say that 99% of the people who are well known on the screen today have been in pictures from seven to ten years. Now and then we see what we think is a new face prominent on the screen, but it is very likely that that face—not so prominent perhaps—was still in pictures, maybe hovering around the edges of mob scenes, a half dozen years ago. One night I had the pleasure of being at comedian Harold Lloyd's house; Harold asked me if I remembered the days and days that he used to sit on a bench in our outer office and I would never give him a job. That was probably ten or eleven years ago. Harold Lloyd was on the screen for six years before he really achieved prominence with the majority of the fans." Died: 1955.

Agnes Moorehead 🎥   1719 Vine

Actress, singer, dancer

BORN Dec. 6, 1906, in Clinton, MA. **SPOTLIGHTS** Too sensible to try her luck in Hollywood without true career skills, she first earned her Ph.D. in literature. She taught speech and drama in local high schools, and spent her vaca-

tions in summer stock. She ventured onto Broadway, in radio soap operas, and in vaudeville with Phil Baker. By now an extremely skilled stage actress, she joined Orson Welles' Mercury Theatre Company. She made her screen debut in Welles' classic masterpiece, *Citizen Kane* (1941), as the lead character's mother. Her talents shone like a multifaceted diamond in more than 50 films, including Welles' *The Magnificent Ambersons*

Agnes Moorehead

(1942--in an Oscar-nominated performance), *Jane Eyre*, *Mrs. Parkington*, *Since You Went Away* (all 1944), *Our Vines Have Tender Grapes* (1945), *Johnny Belinda* (1948), *Show Boat* (1951), *The Story of Three Loves* (1953), *Pollyanna* (1960), and *Hush...Hush, Sweet Charlotte* (1965). **TV** She was immortalized as Endora—Samantha's witch of a mother—in the sitcom "Bewitched" (1964-'72). Died: 1974.

Conrad Nagel 🎥   1719 Vine

Actor

BORN Mar. 16, 1897, in Keokuk, IA. **SPOTLIGHTS** He made his screen debut in *Little Women* (1918), and ended with *The Man Who Understood Women* (1959). Included in his vast repertoire of 100 films is *The Jazz Singer* (1927)—the first talkie. Ironically, it was the incredible success of this picture that ended his days as a silent screen hero. He still enjoyed top billing, but never regained his enormous "silent" popularity or matinee idol stature. **ACHIEVEMENTS** 1947 Special Academy Award. Died: 1970.

Tony Martin 📺   1719 Vine

See page 399

Wendell Niles 🎙   1719 Vine

Announcer, actor

BORN Dec. 29, 1904, in Livingston, MT. **SPOTLIGHTS** A veteran of radio and television, he was the comedy announcer "for the salesman who keeps getting doors slammed in his face, 'Here Comes Elmer.'" To his credit, Niles announced "The Bob Hope Show," "The Milton Berle Show," "The Tennessee Ernie Ford Show," and the crime drama on "The Adventures of Philip Marlowe." Film work includes the football biopic, *Knute Rockne, All American* (1940) starring the future U.S. President, Ronald Reagan. Died: 1994.

Eddie Foy 🎥   1719 Vine

Singer, dancer, comedian

BORN Edwin Fitzgerald, on March 9, 1856, in New York. **SPOTLIGHTS** This hilarious entertainer began in Chicago revues in the 1880s and 1890s. Perhaps best remembered as one of vaudeville's great acts, Foy was also a success in legit theater. His Broadway shows include "The Earl and the Girl" (1905). By 1907 fans requested his irreverent song, "He Goes to Church on Sundays," a satire about weekday backsliders. His 1910 song-and-dance creation, "Eddie and the Seven Little Foys," showcased his real-life children, and was organized kiddie chaos. The zany family's frenetic routines gave them instant (and long-lasting) fame. In 1912 at the Brighton Beach (N.Y.) Theater the group's comedy routine was stopped by the Gerry Society. When they were finally granted permission to perform, Foy gazed at his children, then convulsed the audience by claiming, "If I lived in Flatbush, it would be a city." Bob Hope stars as Foy in *The Seven Little Foys* (1955). The famed vaudevillian appeared in only one film—with his children in tow—*A Favorite Fool* (1915). **SIDELIGHTS** "Vaudeville" derived from the French *Voix de Ville* (voices of the village/street songs). It was a popular form of variety entertainment from the late 1800s to the 1930s. Foy died before vaudeville did, in 1928.

Pierre Monteux 〇   1719 Vine

Conductor

BORN April 4, 1875, in Paris, France. **SPOTLIGHTS** Renowned for his performance of Stravinsky, Debussy and Ravel's music, his numerous recordings include works from the San Francisco Symphony (1935-'52) and the London Symphony Orchestra (1960-'64). Died: 1964.

Carroll Baker 🎥   1719 Vine

Carroll Baker

Actress

BORN May 28, 1931, in Johnstown, PA. **SPOTLIGHTS** In 1956 Baker joined an all-star cast including Elizabeth Taylor, Rock Hudson, James Dean, Jane Withers, Chill Wills, Mercedes McCambridge, Dennis Hopper and Sal Mineo in the outstanding motion picture, *Giant*. That same year, she broke international barriers and earned an Oscar-nomination playing the erotic, thumb-sucking, girl-wife in *Baby Doll*. (She was 25 years old at the time.) Not wanting to be typecast, she chose her next role carefully, as the spoiled daughter in *The Big Country* (1958), where she gave a wonderful performance. Other films include *The Miracle* (1959), *How the West Was Won* (1962), *The Carpetbaggers* (1964),

Harlow, and *The Greatest Story Ever Told.* (both 1965). If you like oddball black comedy, Baker stars in *Andy Warhol's Bad* (1971). Although not for everyone—some may find it in poor taste—this film achieved cult status. Other films include *The Secret Diary of Sigmund Freud* (1984), *Native Son* (1987), *Ironweed* (1987), *Kindergarten Cop* (1990), and *The Game* (1997). She shines with her poignant performance in Showtime's original movie "North Shore Fish" (1997).

Edmond O'Brien 🎥   1719 Vine

Actor

Edmond O'Brien

BORN Sept. 10, 1915, in New York, NY. **SPOTLIGHTS** O'Brien joined Orson Welles' Mercury Theater group in 1937, and made his screen debut in *The Hunchback of Notre Dame* (1939). This was the first sound version of Victor Hugo's novel, and is a must-see, classic film. A versatile talent in 120 supporting and leading roles, he became one of Hollywood's great character actors. A stocky, hardworking, hard-boiled Irishman, his movies include *The Killers* (1946), *The Web* (1947), *A Double Life* (1947), *An Act of Murder* (1948), *White Heat* (1949), *D.O.A.* (1950—in a brilliant performance), *Warpath* (1951), Ida Lupino's *The Hitch-Hiker* (1953), *Julius Caesar* (1953), Ida Lupino's *The Bigamist* (1953), *The Girl Can't Help It* (1956), *The Rack* (1956—this movie was adapted from Rod Serling's teleplay), *The Man Who Shot Liberty Valance, Birdman of Alcatraz, The Longest Day* (all 1962), *Seven Days in May* (1964--in an Oscar-nominated performance), *The Wild Bunch* (1969), and *Lucky Luciano* (1974). **TV** O'Brien starred in two 1960s series: "Johnny Midnight" and "Sam Benedict." **ACHIEVEMENTS** 1954 Best Supporting Actor Oscar for *The Barefoot Contessa*. His daughter Maria O'Brien is an accomplished actress. Died: 1986.

Marie Doro 🎥   1719 Vine

Actress

BORN Marie Stewart; Feb. 4, 1882, in Duncannon, PA. **SPOTLIGHTS** A popular actress on the Great White Way, she made silent movies only. Films include *Sherlock Holmes, Oliver Twist,* and *The Wood Nymph* (all 1916). Died: 1956.

Nancy Carroll 🎥   1719 Vine

Actress

BORN Ann Lattiff; Nov. 19, 1905, in New York, NY. **SPOTLIGHTS** A dynamic redhead with inviting red lips and a sweet singing voice, she was outrageously popular in the early days of talkies. She was briefly considered the Clara Bow of sound. Oddly, she and Bow worked together in *Paramount on Parade* (1930), as Bow's star was descending and Carroll's ascending. Died: 1965.

Cecil B. DeMille 🎥   1735 Vine

Director, producer, screenwriter

BORN Cecil Blount DeMille; Aug. 12, 1881, in Ashfield, MA. **SPOTLIGHTS** A pioneer filmmaker and creative genius of film spectacular, DeMille was a legendary director. He worked from the silent era through the sound era. Without prior experience, but stating that he thought he could make a picture, he received backing from Samuel Goldwyn and Jesse Lasky. He made *The Squaw Man* (1914) in 18 days, starting with an original budget of $15,000 (the final budget was *triple* that). It was the longest picture ever made at six reels, and was the first Broadway play to be adapted to the screen. It broke new ground by giving credits—listing cast members for the first time. Prior to that, viewers never knew the actors names. The celebrated *Squaw Man* also established Hollywood as the motion picture center of the world and was Hollywood's most important release of the year. It grossed the heady sum of nearly a quarter million dollars within a few short months, taking a baby company into mature growth almost overnight (known today as Paramount Pictures). In his long list of impressive credits stands the epic *The Ten Commandments* (1923, and remake in 1956). DeMille excelled in extravagant biblical and historical pieces with casts of thousands. Motion pictures

Cecil B. DeMille

include *The Virginian* (1914), *Cleopatra* (1934), *The Plainsman* (1936), *Union Pacific* (1939), *Northwest Mounted Police* (1940), *Reap the Wild Wind* (1942), and *Samson and Delilah* (1949). He appears as himself in *Sunset Boulevard* (1950). **ACHIEVEMENTS** 1952 Best Picture Oscar for *The Greatest Show on Earth*. **QUOTE** "An unfortunate idea held by a great many people is that if they individually can only get their feet beyond the door of a motion picture studio, the rest of their progress to fame and fortune will be comparatively easy. Let me take this opportunity to banish that misconception once and for all." Died: 1959.

May McAvoy 🎥   1735 Vine

Actress

May McAvoy

BORN Sept. 18, 1901, in New York, NY. **SPOTLIGHTS** This sweet brunette's first modeling job was for Domino Sugar. She started in silents at age 16 in *Hate* (1917). She stars in *Sentimental Tommy* (1921), and plays Esther in the classic movie, *Ben Hur* (1926). McAvoy gained her foothold in film history by appearing with Al Jolson in Warner Brothers' *The Jazz Singer*, the first talkie (1927). Known as a charmer, she retired to marry in 1930. Later, she enjoyed roles "for the fun of being part of show business." Died: 1984.

Vic Damone 🎵   1735 Vine

Singer, actor

Vic Damone

BORN Vito Farinola; June 12, 1928, in Brooklyn, NY. **SPOTLIGHTS** Like so many other musical talents, his harmonious journey started at home. The youngster was surrounded by tunes; his mother was a piano teacher, his father played guitar. At age two, to his father's accompaniment, he sang "You're Driving Me Crazy." As a teen, Damone dropped out of high school to help support his family after his father became disabled. It was at his first job—working as an usher at the Paramount Theatre in New York—that he received a vote of confidence. He recalled, "Perry Como was starring there one night and I was taking him back up to the dressing room on the fifth floor. He had just finished a show. I said, 'I'm a great fan of yours. Can I ask your advice?' Como said, 'What is it kid?' I told him, 'My mom thinks I can sing. We really can't afford $1 a week for a lesson. Would you listen to me and tell me if I have any talent?' I stopped the elevator between floors. The song was *There Must Be A Way*. I sang four bars and stopped. Perry says, 'Go ahead.' I sang another four bars and stopped. Perry tells me, 'Just finish the song!' I sang the whole song. And Perry says, 'You've really got something kid. Don't stop singing.'" Shortly before his 18th birthday, he broke into show business by winning the Arthur Godfrey Talent Scouts contest on CBS. His first record "I Have But One Heart" hit big, establishing him as a romantic singer. By age 19 he was earning $5,000 a week. He became one of America's most celebrated vocalists. Asked, after 50 years of entertaining, which song—out of the 2,000 he has recorded—was his favorite, he answered, "It has to be 'An Affair to Remember.'" **ACHIEVEMENTS** 1997: Inducted into the Songwriter's Hall of Fame in New York City, and he released *The Greatest Love Songs of the Century*...He beat James Dean in the bid to marry Pier Angeli in 1955.

Marie Dressler 🎞   1735 Vine

Actress, comedienne, singer
BORN Leila Von Koerber; Nov. 9, 1869, in Canada. **SPOTLIGHTS** She described herself as "an overweight, ugly duckling." No matter. This homely woman was one of the few actresses to enjoy a great reputation, tremendous social standing, and endless roles. Considered theatrical royalty, she spent her 1913 summer at the White House as the guest of first lady Mrs. Woodrow Wilson. After years of success on stage, she made her first screen appearance opposite Charlie Chaplin in *Tillie's Punctured Romance* (1914). She gained enormous fame in the *Tugboat Annie* series. She rose to great heights as America's number one box office attraction in the early 1930s when she was in her sixties! Her popularity soared with the introduction of sound. What she lacked in looks, she made up with her strong voice and personality. **ACHIEVEMENTS** 1930 Best Actress Oscar for *Min and Bill*. Died: 1934.

William Wyler 🎞   1735 Vine

Director
BORN July 1, 1902, in Mulhausen, Germany. **SPOTLIGHTS** A perfectionist known as "Ninety-take Wyler—the expensive director," he typically ordered retake after retake because, "a slight movement or the way a word is said makes the difference whether the audience will cry." He often infuriated exhausted actors, but declared, "If there is a choice between making an actor unhappy and doing a good scene, I choose the scene." Of course, when these players won Oscars for their works—in performances exacted by Wyler—they had only the kindest words to say about the notorious director. Wyler had a great ability for creating intense emotionalism that cleverly moved

his audiences in sweeping sentimentality and presentation: *Jezebel* (1938) and *The Letter* (1940), both starring girlfriend Bette Davis. Many of this *auteur's* works reached perfection: *Dodsworth* (1936), *Dead End* (1937), *Wuthering Heights* (1939), and *Roman Holiday* (1953). In 1968 he introduced Barbra Streisand in the sensational musical *Funny Girl*. **ACHIEVEMENTS** 1942 Best Director Oscar for *Mrs. Miniver*; 1946 Academy Award for his socially aware post-war film, *The Best Years of Our Lives*; and 1959 Oscar for *Ben Hur*. During WWII he served in the Army Air Corps and filmed the acclaimed war documentary, *Memphis Belle*. Died: 1981.

Roy Rogers 🎞   1735 Vine

See page 172

Bobby Darin 🎵   1735 Vine

Singer, songwriter, musician, actor

Bobby Darin

BORN Warren Robert Cassotto; May 14, 1936, in Bronx, New York. **SPOTLIGHTS** Born poverty-stricken, he and his mother were welfare recipients. A dark-haired idol of the 1950s, teen girls were attracted by his devilishly cute looks. His songs sold millions. Hits include "Splish Splash" (which he wrote in 12 minutes), "Queen of the Hop," "Dream Lover," and "Mack the Knife." He made his nightclub debut with comedian George Burns, then headlined at the Las Vegas Sahara. In Tinseltown, Darin found both a movie role and a real-life wife in *Come September* (1960). He married co-star Sandra Dee (1960-67). Movies include *Hell Is for Heroes*, and *State Fair* (both 1962), and *Captain Newman, M.D.* (1964--in a Best Supporting Actor Oscar-nominated performance). **ACHIEVEMENTS** He wrote 75 songs. He was inducted into the Rock and Roll Hall of Fame (posthumously) in 1990. Died: 1973 of heart failure.

Jim Backus 📺   1735 Vine

Actor, voiceover artist
BORN Feb. 25, 1913, in Cleveland, OH. **SPOTLIGHTS** A veteran performer of vaudeville, legitimate theatre, radio, and screen, he easily conquered television. This talented actor created the innocent and distinct cartoon voice of the myopic, fumbling "Mr. Magoo." He modeled Magoo's voice after his father. Backus said, "Dad was a wonderful guy and a very successful manufacturer of machinery. But you couldn't tell him a thing that he didn't want to think existed." He was one of Hollywood's most famous voiceover artists. He appeared in

Jim Backus

several successful series. Delightfully played the long-suffering husband in the series "I Married Joan." Backus was immortalized as the spoiled, childlike multimillionaire Thurston Howell III on "Gilligan's Island." This show is seen in worldwide syndication every hour of every day. His TV characters remain some of the most beloved and recognizable personalities. **SIDELIGHTS** Fans of the legendary James Dean recognize Backus in the fatherly role in *Rebel Without a Cause* (1955). In all, Backus made 40 motion pictures. Died: 1989.

Victor McLaglen 🎥   1735 Vine

Actor

Victor McLaglen

BORN Dec. 10, 1886, in England. **SPOTLIGHTS** One of eight boys, his father was a clergyman who had his hands full trying to control his eldest son. At 14, the very large McLaglen lied about his age to enlist in the Life Guards to fight in the Boer War. His father had to drag him out, but his growing son moved alone to Canada to work as a farm laborer. He became the heavyweight boxing champion of Eastern Canada. As he traveled the world, this imposing figure had a succession of jobs related to his physical strength. During WWI, he joined the Irish Fusiliers and served as captain. In the Middle East, he became the provost marshal of Baghdad. Other occupations included gold mining, and performing in Wild West and vaudeville shows. A real-life adventurous tough guy, McLaglen became known as "The Beloved Brute" from his American screen debut in a 1925 silent of the same name. His role as a savage ex-con with a heart of gold, opposite Margerite de la Motte, won him instant fame; fame which would rise and ebb like the tide. Later works include the family film, *Professional Soldier* as the lead, opposite Freddie Bartholomew, *Klondike Annie* co-starring Mae West, and *The Magnificent Brute* (all 1936). Director John Ford, who greatly admired McLaglen's skills in *The Lost Patrol* (1934), cast him as the brawny sergeant opposite Shirley Temple in *Wee Willie Winkie* (1937). The movie, based on a Kipling tale, was the most expensive Temple vehicle ever, at one million dollars production cost. This first-rate family film scored high at the box office. (McLaglen and Temple worked together again in John Ford's 1948 masterpiece, *Fort Apache*, with John Wayne, Henry Fonda, John Agar, Ward Bond and George O'Brien. McLaglen also appears in two other Ford cavalry pictures: *She Wore a Yellow Ribbon* in 1949, and *Rio Grande* in 1950, starring John Wayne.) 1939 was a good year for the actor. He appears in the outstanding action-adventure picture, *Gunga Din* (1939). Director George Stevens took 600 cast and crew on location to India for two and a half months; the total cost of the picture was the astronomical sum (at the time) of $2 million. It was RKO's most expensive film of the decade, costarring Cary Grant and Douglas Fairbanks, Jr., but it was also the second highest grossing feature of the year. The collective talents—both in front of the camera and behind—called it one of their favorite movies of all time. He followed with *Captain Fury* as an ex-con, then, is the *Ex-Champ*. McLaglen was also wonderful in John Ford's *The Quiet Man* (1952). **ACHIEVEMENTS** 1935 Best Actor Oscar in John Ford's *The Informer*. **QUOTE** "I am a very sentimental guy. I'm an Irishman, and there's two things an Irishman can do. He can fight and he can cry." Died: 1959.

Lotte Lehmann ⚫   1735 Vine

Opera singer

BORN Feb. 27, 1888, in Perleberg, Germany. **SPOTLIGHTS** This dramatic soprano sang with the Vienna State Opera (1914 -'38), then fled war torn Europe. A prima donna at Metropolitan Opera (1939-'45), Lehmann was hailed as incomparable in roles such as Marschallin in *Der Rosenkavalier*; Ariadne in *Ariadne auf Naxos*; Leonore in *Fidelio*, and Sieglinde in *Die Walkure*. Richard Strauss wrote the title role of *Arabella* for her. Music critic Neville Cardus called her, "My all-time favorite actress." A skilled interpreter of *lieder*, she devoted much time to singing in concert halls around the globe. Lehmann compared the singing of *lieder* to "a beautiful garden into which one goes, never wishing to return to the world glare." Later, she retired from performing asserting, "My voice is a shadow of itself. I hate to have shadows around me." She became a much sought after vocal coach. Awestruck students claimed to learn just from being near her. **ACHIEVEMENTS** The great conductor, Arturo Toscanini, was infamous for screaming at his singers and musicians. His vicious outbursts made everyone shudder with fear. Lehmann avoided the holy terror until the Salzburg Festival. During a rehearsal, he suddenly stopped the orchestra and squinted his eyes at her. She braced herself for his notorious stinging rages. Toscanini screamed, "You! You are an artist!" She was so shocked with his praise she almost fainted. **QUOTE** "You must *think* what you are doing, *love* what you are doing." Died: 1976.

Barbara Lawrence   1735 Vine

Actress

BORN Feb. 24, 1930, in Carnegie, OK. **SPOTLIGHTS** A former child model, she appears in *Margie* (1946), *Here Come the Nelsons* (1952), and *Oklahoma* (1955). She did countless live TV playhouse performances, and guested on many series.

Dale Evans   1735 Vine

Dale Evans

Actress, singer

BORN Frances Octavia Smith; Oct. 31, 1912, in Uvalde, TX. **SPOTLIGHTS** This pretty, fair-haired lass, and former radio and nightclub singer, made her film debut in *Orchestra Wives* (1942). *Girl Trouble* (1942), *Swing Your Partner* (1943), and two more movies followed before she made the film that would change her life. She met her leading man and future husband, the "King of the Cowboys" Roy Rogers, when they teamed together for *The Cowboy and the Senorita* (1944). Evans made 26 more pictures, including 18 Westerns. **RADIO** She played the female lead on the popular Western variety program opposite her husband on "The Roy Rogers Show" (1944-'54). The *Christian Scientist Monitor* reviewed it as: "a little song, a little riding, a little shooting and a girl to be rescued." Stories revolved around the Golden Rule, high moral standards, and commendable values. Roy Rogers and Dale Evans stood for everything decent. They were true American heroes, who loved God, their country and their family...Her famous horse's name? *Buttermilk.* **TV** The two real-life lovebirds starred together on "The Roy Rogers Show" (1951-'57), making 101 segments. Their young fans were known as Little Buckaroos. In 1962, they starred on the "Roy Rogers & Dale Evans Show." In the 1980s, they moved to the Nashville Network cable where they hosted "Happy Trails Theater." They also had a series of hit records, many with the Sons of the Pioneers. **HIGHLIGHTS** Married Roy Rogers on Dec. 31, 1947 until his death in 1998. Their Roy Rogers-Dale Evans cowboy museum, located in Victorville, California, is open to the public. Their son, Roy Rogers, Jr., oversees the non-profit, educational museum and other family businesses. Evans wrote their signature theme song "Happy Trails to You."

Boris Karloff   1735 Vine

Actor

BORN William Henry Pratt; Nov. 23, 1887, in London, England. **SPOTLIGHTS** During the silent era, Karloff worked as an extra and in bit parts. To supplement his meager income, he drove trucks and was a physical laborer. When sound arrived in the late 1920s, the college-educated talent found himself highly suitable for the microphone with his King's English. After 12 years and making nearly 60 minor movies, he won an important supporting role as the governor's butler in *The Criminal Code* (1931). He had previously appeared in the Los Angeles stage

Boris Karloff

production of the same. The film's director, Howard Hawks, had ten convicts evaluate the story—about an innocent man's wrongful conviction and the system's cruel prison warden. Overflowing with gritty realism, Karloff's key scene reveals a mighty glimpse of his future in horror. Then, after a Universal executive read Mary Shelley's Gothic novel *Frankenstein*, the studio decided to produce the first sound version. Previously, there had been three *Frankenstein* silents. The first *Frankenstein* (1910) was produced by Thomas Edison's company. A second was retitled *Life Without Soul* (1915). The third, *Il Mostro di Frankenstein* (1920) was made in Italy. For the talkie version, Karloff was not director Robert Florey's first choice; Bela Lugosi of *Dracula* fame was. Lugosi ultimately rejected the role as it was a non-speaking part and he had wanted to play the scientist. Then, James Whale (a fellow Englishman) stepped in to direct and cast the film. Whale became interested in the artist after seeing him on stage in "The Criminal Code" and in the gangster flick, *Graft* (1931). Karloff, who was a little-known actor at the time, jumped at Whale's offer. Karloff portrayed the mad doctor's patchwork creation with pain, compassion, and dignity. Through his lucid eyes and clumsy, stiff-jointed body language, he managed to appear completely vulnerable, and after harsh misjudgment, so fearsome. Karloff brought a strange, sad fairy tale beauty to one of the greatest performances in cinema history. This seems all the more remarkable when one realizes he accomplished this through more than 40 pounds of pancake makeup and the monster's characteristic heavy eyelids. (A brilliant makeup job created by Jack Pierce. It was the makeup artist's very first motion picture.) Karloff was immortalized in *Frankenstein* (1931) for the humanity he brought to the role. This horror classic is considered one of the most influential movies of all time. With his sometimes oppressive, sometimes melancholy, sometimes despotic articulation, Karloff scared up a frightful following of loyal fans within the industry as well as the public. Among his 130+ films are: *Five Star Final* (1931), *Scarface* (1932), *The*

Old Dark House (1932), *The Mask of Fu Manchu* (1932), *The Miracle Man* (1932), *The Mummy* (1932), *The Ghoul* (1933), *The Black Cat* (1934), *The Raven* (1935), *The Bride of Frankenstein* (1935), *The Invisible Ray* (1936), *The Walking Dead* (1936), *The Man They Could Not Hang* (1939), *The Son of Frankenstein* (1939), *The Tower of London* (1939), *Before I Hang* (1940), *Devil's Island* (1940), *The Devil Commands* (1941), *The House of Frankenstein* (1944), *The Body Snatcher* (1945), *Isle of the Dead* (1945), *Bedlam* (1946), *The Secret Life of Walter Mitty* (1947—a fantasy comedy), *Tap Roots* (1948), *The Strange Door* (1951), *The Raven* (1962), *The Terror* (1962), *Black Sabbath* (1963), *Comedy of Terrors* (1964), *Die, Monster, Die* (1965), and *Targets* (1968). On Broadway in "Arsenic and Old Lace" in 1941, he cracked audiences up with his line, "I killed him because he said I looked like Boris Karloff." He had the same effect on movie audiences when he reprised his role on film in 1944. His other successful Broadway productions include his role as Captain Hook, opposite Jean Arthur in "Peter Pan" (1951), and as Cauchon in "The Lark" (1955). **TV** Host and frequent star of the suspense series, "Thriller" (NBC, 1960-'62). In a gentler role, he portrayed the good Scotland Yard detective, Colonel March. **RECORDING** Believe it or not, "Mother Goose" (with Celeste Holm) for children. **HIGHLIGHTS** During the shooting of *Frankenstein*, the weight of his costume made it impossible for him to walk any distance; he had to be carried to the commissary to eat lunch. The "electrode screws" applied beneath his ear lobes were put in so deeply they left permanent scars. **ACHIEVEMENTS** Every year during the Christmas holidays, he visited disabled children in hospitals, bringing them baskets of goodies and toys. In real life, Karloff was a kind, considerate gentleman. **QUOTE** "I'm a very lucky man." Died: 1969.

Artur Rubinstein 🎵 1735 Vine

Musician
BORN Jan. 28, 1886, in Lodz, Poland. **SPOTLIGHTS** Powerful, elegant, with stupendous digital dexterity, Rubinstein endured as one of the world's greatest pianists. As a toddler he took to the piano, which his two eldest sisters were learning (to play in part to enhance their marriage prospects). Much to their dismay, he quickly mastered the keyboard and could play any tune he *heard*. Although there were no other musical geniuses in the family, his talents amazed all his relatives. His father, thinking the violin was a more distinguished musical instrument, presented his three-year-old prodigy "with a small fiddle, which I promptly smashed to pieces," he later recalled. His father tried one more time to get him to play "the noble stringed instrument, which I refused." Soon thereafter, his father relinquished. At age five, Artur made his professional debut at a charity event in Warsaw, astounding those present with the lightning speed of his fingers over the keyboard. He quickly grew into a virtuoso. He made his American debut at Carnegie Hall on Jan. 8, 1906, with the Philadelphia Orchestra, conducted by Fritz Scheel. Every major critic wrote

rave reviews of his performance, all calling him "brilliant." Among many great works, Rubinstein is renowned for his interpretation of Chopin. The charmer dazzled international audiences for years with masterpiece after masterpiece. Musical triumphs include *Fantasie-Impromptu in C Sharp Minor*; *Andante Spianato and Grande Polonaise*; *Sonata No. 2 in B Flat Minor*; and *Concerto No. 2 in F Minor, op. 21*, with the NBC Symphony Orchestra under

Artur Rubinstein

William Steinberg. Magnificent pieces include *Schumann: Piano Concerto in A Minor, Chicago Symphony Orchestra, Carlo Maria Giulini, conductor*; *Beethoven: Sonata No. 14 in C Sharp Minor ("Moonlight")*; Tchaikovsky's *Concerto in B Flat Minor*; and *Dvorak: Quintet in A for Piano and Strings with the Guarneri String Quartet*. **FILM** The Academy Award-winning documentary, *Artur Rubinstein—Love of Life* (1975), is a delightful must-see picture for all music lovers. **HIGHLIGHTS** One evening Rubinstein stood in the lobby of the concert hall where he was to perform. The room was packed with a crowd trying to get into the recital. As he gently pushed his way through the throng, an attendant stopped him, assuming he had not seen the "SOLD OUT" sign. The attendant told him, "I'm sorry, mister, but we can't seat you." He inquired patiently, "May I be seated at the piano?" **SIDELIGHTS** The Polish (and Slav) spelling of his first name is "Artur." The musician used that spelling while in those countries. In English-speaking countries he signed his name "Arthur," and in Latin countries, like Spain and Italy, he went by "Arturo." However, his American manager used the *h*-less "Artur" for publicity. Hence the spelling on his Hollywood Walk of Fame star. **QUOTES** "Life can at best be a movement toward perfection." "I accept life unconditionally. Most people ask for happiness on condition." "I talk too much. I would pay people to listen to me." He maintained his youthful vigor till the end. His philosophy for longevity did *not* include vitamins: "Eat four lobsters, eat a pound of caviar—drink fine champagne—live! If you are in love with a beautiful blonde with an empty face and no brains at all, don't be afraid, marry her—live!" Died: 1982, at age 96.

William Boyd 🎥 1735 Vine

Actor, producer
BORN June 5, 1898, in Cambridge, OH. **SPOTLIGHTS** A former silent screen star, he frequently worked with the great director Cecil B. DeMille. Boyd had it all. He began to lose it by boozing, womanizing (married five times), and gambling (away mansions). Then, a freakish twist-of-fate was the final bad luck straw that broke the camel's back. Another actor bearing his same name was arrested for unlawful possession of

William Boyd

whiskey and illegal gambling during the Prohibition. Newspapers rushed to print the scandalous story with accompanying photos. Only they used the wrong photos. The studios did not want any bad press associated with Tinseltown's moral decay, decadence and debauchery. Even though this Boyd was a victim of mistaken identity, his contract was instantly cancelled. All was lost for a handful of years. Through a most unusual comeback, Boyd became a superstar phenomenon. At first, his rise started so slowly that few executives took notice. Boyd rejumped his career in a 1930s B-Western film series. After its initial run, he had a brainstorm. He put everything at stake by borrowing $350,000 to buy up the entire library of 66 films as well as the rights to the character. It took several years, until 1948, to get the deal all sewn up, and still he had a struggle on his hands. He was betting everything that *Hopalong* fit radio's successful model of cowboy greats Gene Autry and Roy Rogers, and even better, would be ideal for the upcoming medium of television. A lot of people disagreed with Boyd's theories, and it was an ongoing battle to find enough money to borrow to produce the radio show. Doors were slammed in his face. Boyd withstood the rejections, and had his first installment of his Western adventure program, "Hopalong Cassidy" on the air in mid-1948. With his unique powerful voice, he was perfectly suited for the medium. Meanwhile, he was pounding the pavement to convince someone to run some of his old films in the new broadcast medium of television. New York bit first in late 1948, then others quickly followed. Every kid under 13 made it an instant hit. *Time* magazine wrote *Hopalong Cassidy* "electrified the junior television slave." In nationwide syndication, he added some new scenes and even shot new TV films. The announcer alerted viewers to: "Hopalong Cassidy, feared, respected, and admired, for this great cowboy rides the trails of adventure and excitement." Foreman of the Bar-20 ranch, and an ace Western detective, Cassidy's trademark black outfit was set off by shiny silver spurs. As every kid in America knew, his horse's name was Topper. A clean living role model, he believed in fairness and justice as he rode "the prairies of the early West." With his terrific, authoritative voice and heroic ways, the master of the frontier was a rootin'-tootin' cowboy idol to every young boy. In fact, offscreen Boyd had long since turned his life around. He had incorporated every good character attribute, forever parting with his old ways. He even remained married to his fifth wife...Whenever he made a public appearance as

Hopalong Cassidy, Boyd was mobbed by upwards of 100,000 children. Licensing on lunch boxes, pajamas, bicycles, roller skates complete with spurs, etc. netted him a fortune. His endorsed products sold out instantly. In total, his investment in *Hopalong Cassidy* paid off handsomely—in excess of $75 million dollars, wealth beyond his wildest imagination. **QUOTE** "It's like a vacation. I ride my horse Topper, chase rustlers and outlaws, shoot my six-shooters, and do the things that every kid—and man, too—in America would want to do." Died: 1972.

Otto Kruger 🎥   1735 Vine

Otto Kruger

Actor
BORN Sept. 6, 1885, in Toledo, OH. **SPOTLIGHTS** Being a dependable, serious actor on the Broadway stage, Kruger—like so many other legitimate talents of the time—thumbed his nose at "photoplays and flicks." However, when William Randolph Hearst, owner of Cosmopolitan Pictures, dangled a larger-than-believable salary carrot in front of his nose, he instantly became ·a "cinemactor." His first silent was *Under the Red Robe* (1920). Sound pictures include *Treasure Island* (1934), and *Dracula's Daughter* (1936). He's must-see in *Dr. Erlich's Magic Bullet* (1940), *High Noon* (1952), and *The Young Philadelphians* (1959). Although he never gained the status of superstardom, with his wit, finesse and skills, he enjoyed a solid reputation among producers and the public. Died: 1974, on his 89th birthday.

Arlene Francis 📺   1735 Vine

See page 398

Groucho Marx 📺   1735 Vine

Comedian, actor
BORN Julius Marx; Oct. 2, 1890, in New York, NY. **SPOTLIGHTS** One of the world's fastest-thinking ad-libbers, he possessed a double-edged razor sharp wit. Marx was a legendary comedian of unsquelchable effrontery. He was also the zany leader of the Marx Brothers comedy team. Son Arthur Marx said, "Dad parlayed a pair of wiggly eyebrows, a fake, painted-on black mustache, and an incomparable wit into the conquest of every entertainment medium from vaudeville to Broadway to motion pictures to television." A nonconformist, Groucho flouted rules, and audiences loved him for it. He stars in many motion pictures with his famous siblings (see below). But, it

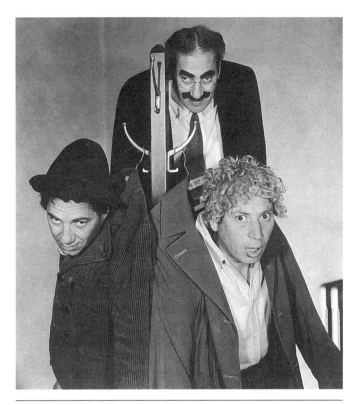

Groucho Marx (upper center), Chico (left), and Harpo

ule. He frequently complained, "How the hell can they expect me to be funny at eight in the morning?" Motion pictures include *Animal Crackers* (1930—with madcap Groucho singing "Hello, I must be going..."), *Horsefeathers* (1932), *Duck Soup* (1933), *A Night at the Opera* (1935), and *A Day at the Races* (1937). Groucho considered the last two movies to be his best. About quitting films in the politically correct environment of his day, he stated, "There are no more Marx Brothers movies because we did satire, and satire today is verboten. The restrictions—political, religious and every other kind—have killed satire." **ACHIEVEMENTS** 1973 Special Oscar. 1950 Emmy for TV's Most Outstanding Personality. 1949 Peabody Award for Radio's Outstanding Comedian. **HIGHLIGHTS** The Marx Brothers included Chico (1886-1961); Harpo (1888-1964); and Zeppo (1901-'79). A fifth brother, Gummo (1897-1977) appeared on stage, but retired from the group in 1934. **QUOTE** He was stopped by a minister, who stated, "Mr. Marx, I want to thank you for all the enjoyment you've given to the world." Marx quickly replied, "And I want to thank you for all the enjoyment you've taken out of the world." The pastor stopped for a moment, then burst into laughter. He then asked for permission to use it in his Sunday sermon. Marx commented, "I spend hours trying to insult people, but they just laugh." Died: 1977.

Dinah Shore 🖋   1749 Vine

See page 490

Ethel Merman 🎤   1749 Vine

Ethel Merman

Singer, actress
BORN Ethel Zimmerman; Jan. 16, 1909, in Astoria, Queens, NY. **SPOTLIGHTS** Her dynamic presence won the hearts of show business insiders and audiences alike. During her lifetime, she was theater's undisputed "Queen of Musical Comedy." After seeing Merman perform in *Annie Get Your Gun,* General Eisenhower remarked, "This is the first time in 30 years that I've seen a Broadway show and it was worth waiting for." Her larger-than-life stage presence was applauded by the greatest showmen around. Irving Berlin said, "You better not write a bad lyric for Merman, because people will hear it in the second balcony." Cole Porter declared, "I'd rather write songs for Ethel Merman than for anyone else in the world. She sounds like a band going by." Hit songs written especially for her include "I Got Rhythm," "You're the Top," and "There's No Business Like Show Business." In Hollywood, she loved working with motion picture director Walter Lang in

was as host of the television's comedy-quiz show "You Bet Your Life," that was "the springboard to more money and fame than he had ever had before," remarked Arthur Marx. The quiz show, which was really a comedy platform for Groucho, included intimate comments that poked fun at the star himself. For example, from a second marriage, he had a child in his later years. He told the audience a story about when his six-year-old daughter Melinda walked up to him, "and said, in all seriousness, 'Daddy, are you dead?'" Groucho responded, "Not that I know of, why do you ask?" Melinda said, "Well, I thought all people died when they got old, and you look very old to me." The audience laughed so hard that Groucho stuck to the opening show format of telling stories that made him the object of ridicule, where he laughed at himself as much as his fans did. A shrewd interviewer, he asked one man what he did for a living. When the contestant replied he sold cars, Groucho asked, "How many times have you been indicted?" A young, pretty student informed him that she was going to "a college for girls." He responded, "That's the reason I'd want to go, too." One woman, a Mrs. Story, revealed to him she had given birth to 22 children. "I really love my husband," she cooed. Groucho replied, "I like my cigar, too, but I take it out once in a while." (This remark was cut from the program before the broadcast. Groucho taped one and one-half hours per show, but only 26 minutes aired. Darn it!) "You Bet Your Life" ran on NBC-TV from 1950-'61. Apparently too much sexual innuendo was left in the show as far as some commentators were concerned. One critic accused him of being obsessed with sex, to which he responded, "It's not an obsession, it's a talent." As a family, the Marx Brothers were famous for their movies. Groucho did *not* like the early movie sched-

Call Me Madam (1953). She said, "Walter won my foolish heart. He told me, 'Get out there and be as brassy and as full of bounce and gusto as you want.'" Died: 1984.

Johnny Carson   1749 Vine

Johnny Carson

Host, comedian, writer
BORN Oct. 23, 1925, in Coring, IA. **SPOTLIGHTS** "The King of Late Night," Carson hosted television's longest running late-night program, "The Tonight Show Starring Johnny Carson." Its genesis was a Steve Allen vehicle called "Tonight: America After Dark" (1954-'57). From 1957-'62 it was renamed "The Jack Paar Tonight Show." In 1962, still based in New York, it became Carson's own show. He was introduced to viewers by Groucho Marx. Carson's smooth, easy-going style, intelligence, and all-American, clean-cut Midwestern good looks gained a wide audience. In 1972 the entertainer moved the show permanently to Burbank, where glamorous Hollywood celebrities lined up to appear on it. But a far more important factor to the show's rating success was Carson's funny opening monologue. This was the beginning of his nightly conversation with the country. The monologues were topical, timely and included anywhere from 15 to 20 gags. When an occasional joke did not work, Carson made a joke about the dud. He was really funny about not being funny. But there was plenty to laugh about. The show lasted through seven different U.S. Presidencies, providing plenty of political grist for his quips. The comic genius delighted in the humor unique to each administration. Another notable Carson feature was his dedication to stand-up comedians; he gave six glorious minutes to each one. If the comic was good, it was the ultimate and immediate breakthrough. From 1962 to 1992, he introduced America to such comedians as Jerry Seinfeld, Roseanne, Drew Carey, Robert Klein, Garry Shandling, Victoria Jackson, Louie Anderson and Rita Rudner, among many others. Carson wrote about half his show's gags, and his hilarious routines included several characters, such as Carnac the Magnificent (the answer-and-question man), the hoary psychic and mentalist El Moldo, *Teatime Movie* host Art Fern, and Aunt Blabby, portrayed by Carson himself in drag. Guests found Carson to be not only quick-witted, but a good listener. There was stiff competition to appear on his show. When Carson decided to call it quits, he selected Bette Midler to be his very last guest. She tearfully performed her #1 song, "Wind Beneath My Wings," in tribute to Carson, who had helped launch her career 22 years earlier. After three decades, and 6,583 "Tonight Shows," he went out at the top of his game. On May 22, 1992, Carson handed over the late-night reins to comedian Jay Leno, who had first appeared on the "TS" on March 2, 1977. (If Leno lasts as long as Carson, he will be on the air until the year 2022.) Johnny Carson closed the show with this simple line, "I bid you a very heartfelt good night." He was one class act. Ed McMahon played Carson's straight man during the entire span of his talk show. (See his bio in this book.)**ACHIEVEMENTS** Emmys: 1976, 1977, 1978, 1979. **SIDELIGHTS** Prior to "The Tonight Show," Carson was the emcee of the daytime show "Who Do You Trust?" (with Ed McMahon as his on-stage announcer) from 1957-62. The title of the evening version: "Do You Trust Your Wife?" **QUOTE** During one show, animal expert Jim Fowler brought a South American monkey onstage. The primate jumped to the top of Carson's head. He deadpanned, "Name me one other place in this entire world of four and a half billion people where a man is sitting with a marmoset on his head."

Barbara Stanwyck   1749 Vine

Barbara Stanwyck

Actress
BORN Ruby Stevens; July 6, 1907, in Brooklyn, NY. **SPOTLIGHTS** Never one to be typecast, this partial listing illustrates Stanwyck's superb and diverse acting range: a repulsed object of intense sexual desire in *The Bitter Tea of General Yen* (1933—it was banned in Great Britain due to its subject matter); a crass vulgarity, yet sympathetic mother in the heartfelt *Stella Dallas* (1937—in an Oscar-nominated performance); a Christmas shoplifter who spends the court's holiday recess in the custody of the prosecutor (Fred MacMurray) in the comedy-drama *Remember the Night* (1940—in one of her best performances); a trampy murderess in *Double Indemnity* (1944—in an Oscar-nominated performance); and the victim in *Sorry, Wrong Number* (1948—in an Oscar-nominated performance). She was a solid, tough, worldly actor. Other motion pictures include *Locked Door* (1930—her first major role), *Banjo on My Knee* (1936), *This is My Affair* (1937), *Breakfast for Two* (1937), *The Mad Miss Manton* (1938), *Union Pacific* (1939), *Golden Boy* (1939), *The Lady Eve* (1941), *Meet John Doe* (1941), *Ball of Fire* (1941—in an Oscar-nominated performance), *Lady of Burlesque* (1943), *Christmas in Connecticut* (1945), *California* (1946), *The Strange Love of Martha Ivers* (1946), *The File on Thelma Jordan* (1949—as a classy lady who sighs, "Maybe I'm just a dame and didn't know it"), *The Furies* (1950), *Clash By Night* (1952), and *Executive Suite* (1953). Professional, luminous, a team player without pretense, this very nice lady was a rarity in town. To newcomers, she was a generous actor, helping them learn the ropes, and never putting on an attitude. Every talent jumped

at the chance to work with her. Kind to the cast and crew alike, she enjoyed Hollywood's most sterling reputation. Her pet name, "Missy," was what her friends and colleagues called her. In 1964 she consented to doing a film, *Roustabout*, with Elvis Presley. Stanwyck was the only major league super talent whom Presley worked with during his entire film career. She also had success as the lead in the action-filled Western adventure television series, "The Big Valley" (1965-'69). She played the concerned matriarch in the acclaimed mini-series "The Thorn Birds." **ACHIEVEMENTS** Nominated four times for an Academy Award. In 1981 she received an Honorary Oscar for lifetime achievement. 1966 Emmy; 1961 Emmy. In 1944 Stanwyck made more money than any other woman in the U.S.—$400,000. (In fact, she made more than the President of the United States.) Second marriage to Robert Taylor (1935-'52). See Taylor's bio, and the bio of Frank Fay in this book. **HIGHLIGHTS** Her good luck charm? She reserved her trademark gift of a gold St. Genesius medal for her favorite cast members in each movie. St. Genesius is the patron saint of actors, and Stanwyck never appeared in front of the camera without wearing it. **QUOTE** While getting ready to shoot a film in the South, Miss Stanwyck was advised that she had been booked into the only nice hotel in town, but that her maid, who was African-American, would have to stay at the other end of town. She cancelled her reservations, instructing her secretary to have her booked into the hotel for African-Americans. "I don't believe they will refuse me a room," she commented. **CLOSING LINE** "I'd like my epitaph to read: 'She never gave a bad performance.'" Died: 1990.

Margaret Sullavan 1749 Vine

Actress
BORN May 19, 1911, in Norfolk, VA. **SPOTLIGHTS** A luminous, fair-haired, oval-faced talent, she sparkles in the must-see romantic comedy, *The Good Fairy* (1935). In it, she plays a good-doer whose good deeds go haywire and wreak havoc. Other films include the drama *Three Comrades* (1930), and *The Moon's Our Home* (1936). She turns in a compelling performance in *The Mortal Storm* (1940), gives another must-see performance in *The Shop Around the Corner* (1940) opposite James Stewart, and stars in the romantic remake of *Back Street* (1941), opposite Charles Boyer. **HIGHLIGHTS** Married to Henry Fonda (1931-'33). A later marriage to top Hollywood agent Leland Hayward stimulated one Hollywood insider to write this humorous note to the newlywed groom: "Congratulations on getting the other 90%." Died: 1960.

Virginia Mayo 1749 Vine

Actress, dancer
BORN Virginia Jones; Nov. 30, 1922, in St. Louis, MO. **SPOTLIGHTS** A gorgeous blonde, her flawless beauty inspired the Sultan of Morocco to describe her "as tangible proof of the existence of God." A dazzling show girl with an hourglass

Virginia Mayo

figure, she made her screen debut in *Jack London* (1943), then quickly became a leading lady in full Technicolor productions. Mayo made dozens of movies, including *The Princess and the Pirate* (1944) with Bob Hope, *Wonder Man* (1945) co-starring Danny Kaye, *The Best Years of Our Lives* (1946), *The Secret Life of Walter Mitty* (1947) with Kaye, *White Heat* (1949) co-starring James Cagney, *Colorado Territory* (1949) opposite Joel McCrea, *West Point Story* (1950) opposite Cagney, *Along the Great Divide* (1951) co-starring Kirk Douglas, *Captain Horatio Hornblower* (1951) with Gregory Peck, the campy cult classic *The Story of Mankind* (1951--as Cleopatra), and *The Proud Ones* (1956).

Betty Compson 1749 Vine

Actress
BORN March 18, 1896, in Beaver, UT. **SPOTLIGHTS** A stunning, bow-lipped, classic beauty, she appeared in countless Al Christie's comedy shorts. Then, she moved into heavy drama with the great Lon Chaney: *The Miracle Man* (1919) and *The Big City* (1928). She made the transition to talkies, including *Hollywood Boulevard* (1936), and appeared in one of director Alfred Hitchcock's most unlikely works, *Mr. and Mrs. Smith* (1941). **QUOTE** "I think that every girl who aspires to be an actress because 'it is an easy life,' should know the truth. The working day of the average actress—and there are six working days in every week, and often seven—begins at 7:30 A.M. By that hour she must be at the studio and in her dressing room, and beginning the long and tedious process of 'making up' with the assortment of creams and cosmetics required for the proper photographic effect. By 9 A.M. she must have reported to her director, and from then until noon she appears steadily before the camera, depicting emotions which, in many cases, are extremely trying. Often during the noon hour she has only a hastily procured sandwich because she must pose for 'still' pictures. From 1 until 5 o'clock she continues to work before the camera, and many times this is prolonged far into the night. On days when she is not appearing before a motion picture camera, every hour is occupied. Scenarios must be studied, gowns fitted, 'still' photographs taken, mail must be answered, besides appearing at necessary social functions. If that constitutes 'a life of ease,' I apologize." Died: 1974.

Elliott Dexter 🎥   1749 Vine

Actor
BORN Sept. 11, 1870, in Galveston, TX. **SPOTLIGHTS** He played romantic leads in silent movies, including *The Heart of Nora Flynn* (1916) and *Adam's Rib* (1923). Died: 1941.

Billy Wilder 🎥   1749 Vine

Director, screenwriter, producer

Billy Wilder

BORN Samuel Wilder; June 22, 1906, in Vienna, Austria. **SPOTLIGHTS** He fled his homeland after the Nazis invaded Austria in the 1930s. His friend, actor Peter Lorre, shared his Los Angeles apartment with him. Wilder, who spoke little English, struggled to learn the language so he would be able to write. While gaining a grasp of the language, Wilder was collaborated with writers who translated his works. In 1937 he landed a job as a screenwriter at Paramount Pictures. Wilder became a director to protect the integrity of *his* scripts! His directorial debut, *The Major and the Minor* (1942), was a smart farce starring Ray Milland and Ginger Rogers. He went on to become one of the most consistent directors of great movies during Hollywood's Golden Era. Motion pictures include *Double Indemnity* (1944), *A Foreign Affair* (1948—inspired by his military service), *The Big Carnival* (1951), *Stalag 17* (1953), *Sabrina* (1954), *The Seven-Year Itch* (1955), *The Spirit of St. Louis* (1957), *Witness for the Prosecution* (1957), and *The Fortune Cookie* (1966). Although considered patient, Wilder became disenchanted with Marilyn Monroe's perpetual lateness to the set during the filming of *Some Like It Hot* (1959). Plus, the insecure actress insisted on going over the dialogue dozens of times before shooting. When a reporter asked Wilder why he put up with her, he replied, "My Aunt Minnie would always be punctual and never hold up production. But who would pay to see my Aunt Minnie?" The film smashed box office records, and was Monroe's all-time biggest hit. **ACHIEVEMENTS** 1945 Best Director and Best Screenplay Oscars (co-written with Charles Brackett) for *The Lost Weekend*. 1950 Best Screenplay Oscars (co-written with Charles Brackett) for *Sunset Boulevard*—"I *am* big, it's the pictures that got small." 1960 Best Picture, Best Director, Best Screenplay Oscars (co-written with Diamond) for *The Apartment*. **QUOTE** "I sleep an awful lot in movie houses and I try to stop others from doing it."

Frankie Carle 🎹   1749 Vine

Composer, pianist, big band leader
BORN Francis Carlone; March 25, 1903, in Providence, RI. **SPOTLIGHTS** A relaxed, self-effacing New Englander, he became a famous big band leader late in his career. Carle started as a professional pianist at age 15, but was 41 when he formed his own band in 1944. His theme song was his huge hit "Sunrise Serenade" which he played in an intense, brittle piano style. While criss-crossing the country on tour, he wrote songs and tuned pianos. He said, "All I did really, was tune certain strings that were out of tune. I just couldn't stand a piano out of tune, and I feel the same way today." One of his gimmicks—which thrilled audiences—was playing piano with his hands behind his back. His most enchanting and romantic waltz numbers were "Shadow Waltz," "Vienna Dreams," "I'm Falling in Love With Someone," and "Kiss Me Again."

Sarah Bernhardt 🎥   1749 Vine

Actress
BORN Henriette-Rosine Bernard on Oct. 25, 1844, in France. **SPOTLIGHTS** Crowned "The Divine Sarah," this legendary French stage star was renowned for her beautiful voice, her interpretation of tragic roles and her startling personality. She also had a reputation for a difficult temperament. No matter, she was a great talent. Her 1911 American road tour was a box office landslide, squashing all other records in the nation. She was so fascinating to the public that 30 days before performing in Chicago newspapers reported, "The theatre she is to play in is being kept secret." She demanded and received her full payment *in gold only* after each performance. Bernhardt made an important historical contribution to motion pictures as the lead in the European-made silent movie *Queen Elizabeth* (1912). As *the* exalted performer—in the first literary work brought to the screen—Bernhardt validated motion pictures as an art form. The film was internationally popular among all classes of people. Her participation was cinema's ultimate stamp of approval...So admired by her Parisian colleagues that the theatre call boy notified her of the first-act curtain call by stating, "Madame, it will be eight o'clock when it suits you." **SIDELIGHTS** Bernhardt still held audiences spellbound with her great emotional power at age 73, after having a leg amputated in 1915. Died: 1923.

Carmel Myers 🎥   1749 Vine

Actress
BORN April 4, 1899, in San Francisco, CA. **SPOTLIGHTS** Romanced by Valentino in sizzling silent screen performances, she stars in *A Society Sensation* (1918), and *The Delicious Little Devil* (1919). Died: 1980.

Virginia Field 🎬   1749 Vine

Actress

BORN Margaret Field; Nov. 4, 1917, in England. **SPOTLIGHTS** A beautiful, blonde, she played leading lady in *Little Lord Fauntleroy* (1936), *The Sun Never Sets* (1939), and dozens more. TV: Guest appearances on "Adam 12" and other series. Died: 1992.

Blanche Sweet 🎥   1749 Vine

Blanche Sweet

Actress

BORN (That was her real name); June 13, 1895, in Chicago, IL. **SPOTLIGHTS** An actress who matched her name as the candied darling of the screen, was not a real-life soft bonbon. Sweet had a determined attitude and a husky, yet attractive hard shell. She became the greatly admired principal character of D.W. Griffith's one-reel pictures including *The Lonedale Operator* (1911), as well as Griffith's first feature and most ambitious project to date, *Judith of Bethulia* (1914). Movies include *The Ragamuffin* (1916), *In the Palace of the King* (1923), *Anna Christie* (1923), and *Tess of the D'Urbervilles* (1924). **QUOTE** "Frequently the impression is given that play-actors have lots of pleasure and little grief. The disappointments, the hard knocks and the hard work is frequently omitted from what the public knows...While essentially, many enter pictures with the idea of making a livelihood it is not long before they become inspired to accomplish something. There is no other business in which even the lowliest is so fired with ambition to get ahead. Even those who from all appearances are in a rut and are satisfied to merely earn a living, are in reality striving, studying and waiting for an opportunity that will lift them out of the ranks. There is no such thing as lack of serious ambition among motion picture players." Died: 1986.

Ray Anthony ⬤   1749 Vine

Orchestra leader, trumpet player

BORN Raymond Antonini; Jan. 20, 1922, in Bentleyville, PA. **SPOTLIGHTS** A musician in several big bands of the swing era, including Glenn Miller's and Jimmy Dorsey's, he was one of the alumni-turned-band leader. Anthony formed an atypical instrumentation band—one trumpet, one French horn, five saxes and three rhythm. His horn, gutty and low-registering, became the feature of the group. He became a valuable Capitol Records artist. Hit: "Dragnet"; co-composer of "The Bunny Hop." Recordings: "Sentimental Me/Spaghetti Rag," "True Blue Lou/They Didn't Believe Me," "The Hokey Pokey." Albums: *Big Band Dixieland*; more.

Stepin Fetchit 🎥   1749 Vine

Stepin Fetchit

Actor, comedian, composer

BORN Lincoln Theodore Monroe Andrew Perry (he was named after four U.S. Presidents); May 30, 1892; Key West, FL. **SPOTLIGHTS** A traveling medicine showman turned vaudevillian, he made he made his screen debut in the silent *Old Kentucky* (1927). A fine performer, he worked for director John Ford in *Salute* (1929), in a degrading role that is considered racist by today's standards. He became a key Fox Studio player in both Will Rogers and Shirley Temple films: *David Harem*, and *Stand Up and Cheer* (both 1934), and *Dimples* (1936). Movies include *Judge Priest* (1934—with Will Rogers, he also appears in the 1953 remake called *The Sun Shines Bright*), *Steamboat 'Round the Bend* (1935—with Rogers again), *Charlie Chan in Egypt* (1935) and *Love is News* (1937). He was the first African American actor to receive feature billing, and the first to earn big money. In the mid-1930s alone, he made two million dollars. Later films include *Miracle in Harlem* (1947), and *Bend of the River* (1952). Slow, lanky and willowy, his stage name had nothing to do with his screen persona. He picked "Stepin Fetchit" from a fast thoroughbred racehorse who was a frequent winner for him during his vaudeville days. He figured it was *the lucky name* and used it as his professional stage name on all screen credits through *Amazing Grace* (1974). He requested it be used on his Walk of Fame star. Neither this appellation, nor his screen characterizations, have gone without controversy. It has been argued that his roles were nothing more than Negro caricatures and that his acceptance of these roles were insulting stereotypes of the African American. Perhaps in hindsight that's easy to state, but during his lifetime the actor himself disagreed. He loved his career and proudly declared that he had opened the door for others with his many firsts...After the enormous success of *Bright Eyes* (1934), starring Shirley Temple, Fox Studios threw a party with required attendance by its top stars. Their set designers created a magical and fancy ambiance for the event, backlit by many candles. Standing near Will Rogers, Fetchit caused a small ripple when he declared it looked like a "swell spot for a craps game." Died: 1985.

Ernest Tubb ⬤   1749 Vine

Singer, guitarist

BORN Feb. 9, 1914, near Crisp, TX. **SPOTLIGHTS** A deep-voiced, drawling singer, he raised honky-tonk's image from hillbilly to country. After his "Grand Ole Opry" debut in 1942 with "I'm Walking the Floor Over You," hits include

"Remember Me, I'm the One Who Loves You," "The Yellow Rose of Texas," "Our Hearts Are Holding Hands," and "Who's Gonna Take The Garbage Out." Promoted electric guitar because it could be heard in noisy honky-tonks. In *Jamboree* (1944), and *Hollywood Barn Dance* (1947). Died: 1984.

James Arness 1749 Vine

James Arness

Actor
BORN May 23, 1923, in Minneapolis, MN. **SPOTLIGHTS** At an impressive height of six-foot-six, this open-faced actor was ideally suited to play a TV cowboy. He did just that as the tough, honest Marshal Matt Dillon on "Gunsmoke" (1955-'75). It was one of the only shows where an actor actually aimed before shooting, and did not always hit his target. He became a hero to millions of children and adults. Director Ted Post said, "When he looks at you with those sad cow eyes of his, a crazy kind of *Weltschmerz* comes from his head through his eyeballs." Earlier John Wayne was originally asked to do the series. Wayne politely declined, but suggested his pal Arness test for it. It just goes to show you, even if you've got the talent, it sure helps to know the right people. Also brother of actor Peter Graves. Movies include *The Thing* (1951--as the alien), *Wagon Master* (1950), *Hondo* (1953), and *Them!* (1954--a classic sci-fi monster movie about giant ants). **HIGHLIGHTS** He enlisted in the Army during WWII, and being the tallest man in his unit, he was ordered by his commanding officer to test the depths of the water at Anzio. Within fourteen days he was wounded in combat and spent the next year in various hospitals. **QUOTE** He was honorably discharged in 1945, then traveled. He ended up in Hollywood. He stated, "I just wanted to see California. I wasn't thinking about acting."

Russ Morgan ● 1749 Vine

Composer, arranger, band leader, musician
BORN April 29, 1904, in Scranton, PA. **SPOTLIGHTS** With Freddy Martin, he created the muted "wah wah" trombone sound. Music in the Morgan manner could be heard in clubs, films, radio, and TV. Wrote songs: "Somebody Else is Taking My Place," and "You're Nobody Till Somebody Loves You." Recordings: "Does Your Heart Beat for Me?" and "Forever and Ever." Died: 1969.

Gene Vincent ● 1749 Vine

Singer, songwriter

BORN Eugene Vincent Craddock; Feb. 11, 1935, in Norfolk, VA. **SPOTLIGHTS** A former choir boy, he became one of America's first rockers. He formed the Blue Caps band in 1955, and recorded their first gigantic hit, "Be-bop-a-lulu" (co-written song with "Sheriff" Tex Davis). Vincent was featured in *The Girl Can't Help It* (1956), along with Little Richard and Fats Domino. Tom Ewell and Jayne Mansfield star in this fun movie. Other hits include: "Lotta Luvin' " and "Dance to the Bop." This pioneer rock 'n' roller was known for his rockabilly stutter. Died: 1971.

Mario Lanza ● 1749 Vine

See page 23

Fred Waring 1749 Vine

See page 413

Rudolf Serkin ● 1749 Vine

Musician
BORN May 28, 1903, in Bohemia. **SPOTLIGHTS** A child prodigy. A musical genius—as well as scholar and poet—his beautiful renderings of Beethoven were peerless. His gave supreme interpretations of Beethoven, Mozart, Brahms, and Bach. Both the purity and the emotional commitments were important to him. Recording: Brahms's *Concerto No. 2 in B-flat Major, op. 83*, with the Philadelphia Orchestra under Eugene Ormandy (Columbia). In 1977 Serkin became the first artist invited to perform at the White House by President Jimmy Carter. By then, he had already played in all the grandiose concerts halls worldwide. **ACHIEVEMENTS** Awarded the Presidential Medal of Freedom on his 100th performance with the New York Philharmonic given by President Lyndon B. Johnson. Recipient of the prestigious Kennedy Center Honor in 1981. His son, Peter, is an accomplished pianist; his son John is an accomplished horn player. **QUOTE** "I believe in a unity in music. I don't believe too much in style. If a performance doesn't move you, it is a bad performance." Died: 1991.

Jan Peerce ● 1749 Vine

Opera singer
BORN Jacob Pinkus Perelmuth; June 3, 1904, in New York. **SPOTLIGHTS** The son of Orthodox Jewish parents, Peerce studied medicine for years to fulfill their dream of seeing their son become a doctor. However love got in the way. He eloped. Taking up work as a violinist and a singer he made enough to support his wife and their three children, and pay for his continuing voice lessons. Discovered at an anniversary dinner, he made his radio debut in 1938 on a symphony broadcast. It was with Arturo Toscanini (see his bio in this book). This dynamic tenor first performed at the

Metropolitan Opera in 1941. Broadway debut as Tevye in "Fiddler on the Roof" (1971). Recordings: *La Boheme*, *La Traviata*, and *Fidelio*. **QUOTE** When friends described his as "a second Enrico Caruso," Peerce replied, "Gee, that's nice, but I'd rather be the first Peerce." Died: 1984.

Freeman Gosden "Amos" 📷   1749 Vine

Comedian, actor
BORN May 5, 1899, in Richmond, VA. **SPOTLIGHTS** "Holy Mackerel, Andy!" He was the Caucasian co-star who performed in "black dialect" on "The Amos 'n' Andy Show," (1926-'60), America's most popular radio show for a time. Amazingly, neither Gosden or Correll rehearsed, because they did not want to lose their spontaneity. Died: 1982.

Earle Williams 🎥   1749 Vine

Actor
BORN Feb. 28, 1880, in Sacramento, CA. **SPOTLIGHTS** A silent screen idol of *Anthony and Cleopatra* (1908), *My Lady's Slipper* (1916), and *Say It with Diamonds* (1927). Died: 1927.

Charles Correll "Andy" 📷   1749 Vine

Comedian, actor
BORN Feb. 1, 1890. **SPOTLIGHTS** Caucasian co-star of "The Amos 'n' Andy Show," he spoke in "black dialect." An officer of the "Mystic Knights of the Sea Lodge," he co-operated the "Fresh Air Taxi Company, Incopolated" [sic]. He gave audiences a long, breezy ride with their comedy--which is now considered racist. The TV series cast Alvin Chidress and Spencer Williams, African Americans. Died: 1972.

John Gilbert 🎥   1749 Vine

John Gilbert and Eleanor Boardman in Bardley's the Magnificent (1925).

Actor
BORN John Pringle; July 10, 1895, in Logan, UT. **SPOTLIGHTS** Gilbert was the reigning romantic lead of the lush romantic films of the 1920s. He became the silent screen's #1 lover in 1927, after melting hearts in *Arabian Love* (1922) and *The Merry Widow* (1925). This classical actor played opposite the one-and-only Greta Garbo in *Flesh and the Devil* (1927), *Love* (1928), and *A Woman of Affairs* (1928). Word about town had it that their award-winning love scenes weren't acted. Gilbert excelled in extravagant romantic pictures and was MGM's premier romantic star. **QUOTE** "In motion pictures you assume new and different personalities continually, and, in fact, you become quite a stranger to your own personality. Then again, there is the congenial company of persons, artistic, dramatic, literary, like yourself, with whom a mutual exchange of views and opinions is always profitable and interesting. Of course, rewards are rewards, but an artistic success is its own reward and, above all, there is no easy road to success, because when it is attained easily or by some fortunate chance, it is seldom, if ever, lasting." Died: 1936.

Jack Perrin 🎥   1749 Vine

Actor
BORN 1896, in Three Rivers, MI. **SPOTLIGHTS** Perrin lucked out with his breakthrough supporting role in Erich von Stroheim's *Blind Husbands* (1919). Later, he utilized his boy scout looks to become king of the cow palace in countless Westerns, including *Ridin' West* (1924). **QUOTE** "If you want to be a cinema-player of the Great Open Spaces, Listen! Health, courage and stick-to-itiveness is what does it. See whether you've got thin lips that can look deadly, a good man's figure and a clean look. Be able to draw a gun and fire it—not like a table fork. Can you wear boots like you didn't have any corns on your feet? Can you fight? Well, just try it. It's not easy, but it has been done." Died: 1967.

Vaughn Monroe 📷   1749 Vine

See page 289

Harry Joe Brown 🎥   1749 Vine

Director, producer
BORN Sept. 22, 1890, in Pittsburgh, PA. **SPOTLIGHTS** An expert lighting technician, Brown directed his first picture in 1925. He specialized in silent Westerns--the most popular movie of the day. Known for impeccable work, he switched to producing in 1933, establishing many stars. Died: 1972.

Edmund Gwenn 🎥   1749 Vine

Actor
BORN Sept. 26, 1875, in Wales. **SPOTLIGHTS** One of the most accomplished character actors of all time, he portrayed saints and sinners with equal aplomb. With his slight English accent, and crinkly eyed stare, his presence enhanced every picture. Gwenn was superb in *Pride and Prejudice* (1940), *Les Miserables* (1952), *Them!* (1954--a classic sci-fi monster movie about giant ants), and Hitchcock's *The Trouble with Harry* (1955). He made more than 100 movies. **ACHIEVEMENTS**

1946 Best Supporting Actor Oscar as Kris Kringle in *Miracle on 34th Street*—a magical Christmas classic shown each yuletide. He was 71 years old at the time. **SIDELIGHTS** Jack Lemmon went to pay his respects to the dying Gwenn. Lemmon asked Gwenn how hard it was to be facing death. "Oh, it's hard," Gween whispered into his ear, "very hard indeed. But not as hard as doing comedy." Died: 1959.

George Jessel 🎥 1751 Vine

George Jessel

Singer, songwriter, actor
BORN April 3, 1898, in New York, NY. **SPOTLIGHTS** Jessel sang and danced professionally at age 11 in the popular vaudeville "School Days" act. Later, after starring in and making *The Jazz Singer* a great success onstage, he assumed that the film role would automatically go to him. He fumed for decades after losing out to competitor Al Jolson. The movie version is considered Hollywood's first talkie (with songs and a few lines of dialog). Jessel made 40 pictures, including *Four Jills in a Jeep* (1944). Crowned America's "Toastmaster General" for his frequent after dinner speech making; he was a compulsive joke and anecdote telling. He served six U.S. Presidents, although President Eisenhower did not like him. 1969 Special Oscar Award. Died: 1981.

Carole Landis 🎥 1777 Vine

Actress, comedienne
BORN Francis Fidste; Jan. 1, 1919, in Fairchild, WI. **SPOTLIGHTS** A child model, she blossomed into a curvaceous pinup girl with curly blonde hair. She made her screen debut in *A Star is Born* (1937). Movies include *A Day at the Races* (1937), and *Topper Returns* (1941). *Four Jills in a Jeep* (1944) was based on her real-life USO experiences entertaining WWII troops, with Martha Raye and Kay Francis. Died: 1948.

William Beaudine 🎥 1777 Vine

Director
BORN Jan. 15, 1892, in New York, NY. **SPOTLIGHTS** He started in show business as a property boy. He directed Mary Pickford in *Little Annie Rooney* (1925) and *Sparrows* (1926), and successfully made the transition to talkies. He also directed TV episodes, including "Lassie." Died: 1970.

John Daly 📺 1777 Vine

Reporter, correspondent
BORN Feb. 20, 1914, in South Africa. **SPOTLIGHTS** As a respected White House correspondent, he logged 150,000 miles traveling with President Franklin Delano Roosevelt. Daly was crucial to CBS news during World War II. On Dec. 7, 1941, he interrupted network programming to announce that the Japanese had bombed Pearl Harbor. He went to Europe in 1943 to report on battle conditions. When Pres. Roosevelt died in 1945, he was the first to broadcast the sad news. He participated in CBS' V-E Day broadcast. He also covered the Nuremberg Trials of Nazi war criminals, in West Germany. The accused were tried for three crimes: Crimes Against Peace, War Crimes, and Crimes Against Humanity. Ultimately new principals were enacted in the law of nations: that every person is responsible for his own acts. Daly was a key reporter in CBS' informative drama "You Were There." He "time traveled" to historic events: to the Civil War to interview soldiers, to the Ford Theatre the night President Lincoln was shot, etc. Audiences enjoyed listening to his rich, resonant voice and intelligent line of questioning. Later, he appeared as the cheerful game show host on "What's My Line?" (1950-'67).

Meiklejohn 🎥 1777 Vine

Vaudeville bookers, exhibitors, agents, mgrs.
BORN Jean (sister), William (brother), Campbell (brother) Meiklejohn, all born in the late 1800s, in California. **SPOTLIGHTS** An early family of show business managers who called their organization "The Meiklejohn Bros." They left off the word "sister" even though Jean was the first female Hollywood-based vaudeville booker, handling such talents as Jack Benny, Judy Garland, Milton Berle and Mickey Rooney. This threesome provided entertainers for every occasion, peaking in the 1920s and 1930s. They were instrumental in getting the talent for such venues as the Orpheum and Pantages circuits. Theater, radio, stage and screen were all served by this powerful association of artists and agents. **QUOTE** In the 1940s William became a producer at Paramount Pictures. He called a character actor into his office to rebuke him, "You state here that your age is 40. I happen to know that you're at least 50." The actor stated, "Oh, no. I simply refuse to count the last ten years in Hollywood as part of my life." Died: Jean (1976), William (1978), Campbell (1979).

Buddy Ebsen 🎥 1777 Vine

Actor, dancer, singer
BORN Christian Rudolph Ebsen, on April 2, 1908, in Belleville, IL. **SPOTLIGHTS** The rubbery-legged, light-on-his-toes Ebsen had learned the athletic art as a child at his father's dancing school. An endearing soul, he was a natural for the screen. He made his screen debut in *Broadway Melody of 1936*. It showcased his impressive dancing skills. He followed up with a beloved Shirley Temple vehicle, *Captain January* (1936), and a rare Barbara Stanwyck musical, *Banjo on My Knee* (1936). Cast as the original Tin Man in the *Wizard of Oz*

Buddy Ebsen

(1939), a makeup and costume-related poisonous illness prevented him from completing the role. He spent painful weeks recuperating in the hospital, while Jack Haley was cast in his place. Ebsen appeared in the Davy Crockett film/TV series of the 1950s, but still had not fully captured superstardom. His acting talents were not in question; he was brilliant in his supporting role in *Breakfast at Tiffany's* (1961), starring Audrey Hepburn and George Peppard. The following year, he gained immortality playing "a man named Jed" on TV's "Beverly Hillbillies" (1962-71). He won legions of fans. The show is still seen daily in syndication. But in the *original* Tin Man's heart of hearts, he would have rather gained his immortality following the yellow brick road...*The Other Side of Oz* is Ebsen's fine autobiography.

June Haver  1777 Vine

Actress, singer, dancer
BORN June Stovenour; June 10, 1926, in Rock Island, IL.
SPOTLIGHTS A delightful 20th Century-Fox blond ingenue of musicals: *Irish Eyes are Smiling* (1944), *The Dolly Sisters* (1945), opposite Betty Grable, and *Three Little Girls in Blue* (1946) co-starring Vivian Blaine and Vera-Ellen. Other movies include *Love Nest* (1951) with Marilyn Monroe. She entered a convent to become a nun in 1953, but was persuaded by lovelorn Fred MacMurray to leave the order to marry him.

Hoot Gibson 1777 Vine

Actor
BORN Edward Gibson; Aug. 6, 1892, in Takamah, NE.
SPOTLIGHTS He had a penchant for spotting owls, hence his nickname, "Hoot." As a teen, he competed in rodeos, and by age 20 had won the title of "World's All-Around Champion Cowboy." After bravely serving in WWI, he had his breakthrough in John Ford's *Action* and *Sure Fire* (both 1921). He become one of the silent screen's most popular stars. Films: *Headin' West* (1922), *The Sawdust Trail* (1924), *The Long, Long Trail* (1929), *The Last Outlaw* (1936), *The Marshal's Daughter* (1953) and *The Horse Soldiers* (1959). **QUOTE** "The Western picture, perhaps, contains something of the elements of a fairy tale—the hero is 100% man, the heroine 100% sweet and pure, and the villain 100% bad. And, contrary to the usually voiced opinion of critics who don't know what they are talking about, it is a good thing that the Western picture is the most popular with the small boys of the land. Because they are a good influence on him. They teach him manliness. They give him, for an example, an all-round he-man who teaches a les-

Hoot Gibson

son of honesty, bravery, and square dealing; and they show him a villain who is everything a boy should not grow up to be, in such a light that the boy will always abhor the qualities the villain stands for. And, you never see sex introduced in a Western play. We Western actors are proud of our work—for we feel that we are leaving something behind us for the good of the nation. We take chances with dangerous horses; we do thrilling stunts—and often get hurt. But we are making the world better for future generations, and that is indeed something to be proud of. Most of us have youngsters of our own—and we'd never think of portraying a role that would set a bad example to children." Died: 1962.

Janet Leigh  1777 Vine

Janet Leigh

Actress
BORN Jeanette Helen Morrison; July 6, 1927, in Merced, CA.
SPOTLIGHTS Leigh was discovered in 1947 by the grande dame actress Norma Shearer (the queen of MGM Studios) at a ski lodge in Soda Springs, California. The fresh-faced, eager youth made her screen debut in *The Romance of Rosy Ridge* (1947), opposite Van Johnson. After making four more films, Leigh delivered an endearing and wholesome performance as Meg in *Little Women* (1949). Her co-stars were June Allyson, Margaret O'Brien and Elizabeth Taylor. She is delightful in *Holiday Affair* (1950), a romantic comedy co-starring Robert Mitchum, and a living doll in *Pete Kelly's Blues* (1955). She co-stars with Dick Van Dyke and Ann-Margret in *Bye Bye Birdie* (1963). Leigh handled comedy with aplomb; she proved solid in drama, action, and Western pictures: *Jet Pilot* (1951), *Scaramouche* (1952), *The Naked Spur* (1953), *Touch of Evil* (1958—re-released with previous cuts restored to Orson Welles' original intentions), *The Manchurian Candidate* (1962), *One Is a Lonely Number* (1972), and *The Fog* (1980). Leigh was immortalized in Hitchcock's classic *Psycho* (1959)—which cured her-of ever taking a shower. The shower scene took seven days to shoot. Leigh lamented, "I felt like a prune!" Hitchcock worried that the film might not be popular. It became the year's second highest grossing movie, and established Leigh as a star. Formerly married to actor Tony Curtis (1959-'62), their daughter, Jamie

Lee Curtis (see their bios in this book).

Marlon Brando 🎥   1777 Vine

Marlon Brando

Actor

BORN April 3, 1924, in Omaha, NE. **SPOTLIGHTS** The original rebel, Brando is one of the finest acting talents of this century, and is one of the greatest actors the screen has ever known. He is a luminous gift to the visual arts. Brando is impossible not to watch. He could brush his teeth in a scene and mesmerize an audience. This magnetic presence is what differentiates those with innate talent from those without. Everything he does is fascinating to watch. Motion pictures include *A Streetcar Named Desire* (1951), *Viva Zapata!* (1952), *Julius Caesar* (1953), *The Wild One* (1954), *Guys and Dolls* (1955), *The Teahouse of the August Moon* (1956), *Sayonara* (1957), *The Young Lions* (1958), *The Fugitive Kind* (1959), *Mutiny on the Bounty* (1962), *Superman—The Movie* (1978), *Apocalypse Now* (1979), *A Dry White Season* (1989), *The Freshman* (1990) and *Don Juan DeMarco* (1995). **SIDELIGHTS** While studying the lives of paraplegic WWII veterans for his screen debut in *The Men* (1950), Brando spent some time in a wheelchair. He took a few disabled men—all legless and in wheelchairs—to a local bar to drink. When a Salvation Army female worker came in and saw this, she lifted her arms skyward and cried out: "Oh, Lord, grant that these men may be able to walk again!" Brando got up and walked out. The paraplegics burst into laughter, but the Salvation Army lady fainted. **ACHIEVEMENTS** Best Actor Oscars in 1954 for *On the Waterfront*—for which he won international acclaim; and 1972 for *The Godfather*...His autobiography, *Brando, Songs My Mother Taught* Me, published by Random House (1994). **QUOTE** About coming to Hollywood from Broadway in 1950, he said, "The only reason I'm here is that I don't yet have the moral courage to turn down the money." In 1954 Brando wryly observed, "The marvelous thing about Hollywood is that these people are recognized as sort of the norm, while I am the flip."

Dom Deluise 🎥   1777 Vine

Dom Deluise

Actor, comedian, author

BORN Aug. 1, 1933, in Brooklyn, NY. **SPOTLIGHTS** A delightful, funny, winsome talent whose screen debut in *Fail Safe* (1964) assured a lasting career as a supporting character actor. For a period of time he worked frequently with Mel Brooks and

Burt Reynolds: *Blazing Saddles* (1974), *The Adventures of Sherlock Holmes' Smarter Brother* (1975), and *Smokey and the Bandit II* (1980). He is a favorite of American audiences. He co-starred in the children's series, "The Charlie Horse Music Pizza," inspiring kids to learn all about music. He has made hundred of guest starring appeareances on TV. He also pens best-selling cookbooks.

Richard Hayman 💿   1779 Vine

Conductor, arranger, composer, musician

BORN Warren Hayman; March 27, 1920, in Cambridge, MA. **SPOTLIGHTS** Orchestrator on MGM musicals: *Girl Crazy* (1943) and *Meet Me in St. Louis* (1944), he was musical director for Bob Hope, Johnny Cash, Olivia-Newton John, among others. The song "Ruby" from *Ruby Gentry* (1953) featured his harmonica playing. Arranger for Boston Pops Orchestra in 1950.

Chuck Berry 💿   1777 Vine

Chuck Berry and Samantha Hart on October 8, 1987.

Musician, songwriter

BORN Charles Edward Anderson Berry; Oct. 18, 1926, in San Jose, CA. **SPOTLIGHTS** Considered the Father of rock 'n' roll, Berry is a charter member of the Rock and Roll Hall of Fame. His great song writing skills both lyrically and musically set the tone for early rock. He blended his witty "pop" lyrics with some rhythm & blues, and country, and took the world by storm. Berry thrilled with having his first hit, "Maybellene," in 1955. Dozens followed, including "School Day," "Rock & Roll Music," "Johnny B. Goode," "Sweet Little Sixteen," "Carol," "Brown-Eyed Handsome Man," "Little Queenie," "Back in the U.S.A.," "Roll Over Beethoven," and "Round and Round." "Nadine," "No Particular Place to Go," and "My Ding-a-Ling" became classics. His unique lyrical, musical formula and youthful, rebellious spirit has influenced every rock musician since his introduction. Films include *Rock, Rock, Rock* (1956), *Mister Rock and Roll* (1957), *Go, Johnny, Go* (1959), and *American Hot Wax* (1979). *Chuck Berry Hail! Hail! Rock 'n' Roll* (1987), is a profile of the legend with a star-studded musical cast including Keith Richards, Roy Orbison, Bruce Springsteen, Eric Clapton, Robert Cray and Etta James. He created his famous "duck walk" in his first national appearance in 1956 at the Brooklyn Paramount Theatre. His trademark signature is his double-string guitar lick.

John Huston 🎥   1779 Vine

John Huston

Director, screenwriter, actor
BORN Aug. 5, 1906, in Nevada, MO. (In a town he claimed was won by his grandfather in a high-stakes poker game.) **SPOTLIGHTS** By the time he could *legally* buy alcohol, Huston had already been a boxer, stage actor, and a cavalryman in the Mexican Army. When he came to Hollywood he brought with him his themes of rugged masculinity: man battling nature, and man battling man. Leaving behind the arty camera angles—that the Germans had created in the 1920s and Hollywood copied—Huston utilized the camera to the physical demands of tense players in action. This director left a treasure trove of interesting motion pictures. The first film he directed became an immediate classic—*The Maltese Falcon* (1941). This is one of the rare occasions where the remake is superior to the original. Many consider Huston's version to be the best detective movie ever made. (The original *The Maltese Falcon*, directed by Roy del Ruth in 1931, is a sexier picture with a more lecherous Sam Spade—terrifically played by Ricardo Cortez.) Motion pictures include *Key Largo* (1948), *The Asphalt Jungle* (1950), *The African Queen* (1950), *Moulin Rouge* (1952), *Moby Dick* (1956), *The Misfits* (1960), *The Unforgiven* (1960), *The Life and Times of Judge Roy Bean* (1973), *The Man Who Would Be King* (1975), and *Prizzi's Honor* (1985). He acted in *Chinatown* (1974), a superb film noir starring Jack Nicholson...He was the son of actor Walter Huston; father of actress Angelica Huston. **ACHIEVEMENTS** 1948 dual Oscars, Best Director and Best Screenplay, *The Treasure of Sierra Madre*. Died: 1987.

Tommy Tune 🎭   1779 Vine

Performer, choreographer, director
BORN February 28, 1939, in Wichita Falls, Texas. **SPOTLIGHTS** Broadway's celebrated song-and-dance man is a lanky, but elegant 6-foot, 6-inch-tall Texan. He first appeared on the New York stage as a chorus dancer in "Baker Street." Since then, he has become known for doing it all and doing it best. Theatrical productions include "Seesaw," "The Best Little Whorehouse in Texas," "My One and Only," "A Day in Hollywood/A Night in the Ukraine," "Stepping Out," "Grand Hotel," and "The Will Roger Follies," to name just a few. When he performs, enthusiastic audiences respond with "Tommy Tune Tonight!" Movies include: *Hello, Dolly* (1968) with Barbra Streisand, and *The Boy Friend* (1972) with model Twiggy, in a British send-up of the 1920s musicals. In 1999 he stepped into the starring role in the Las Vegas extravaganza "EFX." Tune plays himself in this spectacle; it's a dream-like journey through the world. **ACHIEVEMENTS** Recipient of an unprecedented nine Tony Awards. Tune is the only entertainer in theatrical history to win the Tony in four different categories (Direction, Choreography, Lead Actor in a Musical, and Featured Actor in a Musical). He has performed for three U.S. presidents, the Queen of England and the Royal Family of Monaco. **QUOTE** "Everyone dreams. And I've lived all my life in constant pursuit of my dreams."

Tommy Tune

Texas Guinan 🎥   1779 Vine

Texas Guinan

Cabaret hostess, singer, actress
BORN Mary Louise Guinan; Nov. 5, 1903, in Waco, TX. **SPOTLIGHTS** "Hello, Suckers!" was her raucous and famous welcome to patrons during the Roaring '20s. A rough and glamorous character, her career was a direct product of Prohibition laws. (America's prohibiting of the manufacture and sale of alcohol gave birth to "underground" speakeasies funded by beer/whiskey barons, bootleggers and mobsters.) Guinan, hostess of the most popular nightclubs, was the featured celebrity, backed up by dancers. Her fashionable speakeasies attracted high society types, politicians, reporters, show people and gangsters. The glossy Broadway clubs—open from midnight to dawn—were outrageously successful. The firebrand "Queen of the Nightclubs" treated both princes and gangsters alike as she belted out her rowdy tunes. She'd knock the matronly noggins of the social elites with a kleeter-klatter clapper, sending everyone into hysterics. The audience took her treatment and loved it. Nitery's biggest sensation, she belted it out to the tune of $3,000. a bit. One of her "human museums" was the infamous "300 Club." Films include *Fuel of Life* (1917), and *Broadway Thru a Keyhole* (1933)...After her death, her life became the subject of a 1940s Broadway revue, "Billion Dollar Baby." Hollywood went one better: Betty Hutton stars as the rollicking *Incendiary Blonde* (1945), a fantastic biopic of her life. Look for Hutton's rendition of "It Had to be You." Died: 1933.

He is the most tragic and dejected of all monsters.
His leaden gloom and misunderstood humanity pierces the soul.
Boris Karloff stars in the horror classic **Frankenstein** *(1931).*

1770 VINE

Jeff Chandler 🎥   1770 Vine

Jeff Chandler

Actor

BORN Ira Grossell, Dec. 15, 1918, in Brooklyn, NY. **SPOTLIGHTS** One of a rare breed, he emerged more enticing to female fans when his skin glowed under the sweltering studio lights. The camera loved his rugged good looks. The square-jawed, fierce talent utilized his full, clear, radio-trained voice in the crime drama, *Johnny O'Clock* (1947), his screen debut. His breakthrough role in *Broken Arrow* (1949) earned him an Academy Award nomination. The first film to portray Native American Indians objectively, Chandler stars as Cochise, the wise statesman of the Chiracahua Apaches. James Stewart co-stars as the white man coming to terms with the Indians' dignity, respect and code of honor. Chandler played Cochise in two more Westerns. However, he convincingly portrayed a frontier physician in *The Great Sioux Uprising* (1953). The charmer with one slightly raised eyebrow played a softer role in the scandalous melodrama *Return to Peyton Place* (1961). He died that same year of blood poisoning following routine surgery. **QUOTE** "Look, I started in this business because I wanted to make $5,000 a week. I read some place in a movie magazine that that was what stars earned. But I never figured out the rest of it. I don't have anonymity. I can't do anything, go anyplace without being a freak with a sign 'Look at the actor.' I want my anonymity back."

Billy Vera 💿   1770 Vine

Songwriter, musician

BORN May 28, 1944, in Riverside, CA. **SPOTLIGHTS** Inspired, energetic and ambitious, this teen began writing and recording songs in high school. Vera successfully penned hits for Ricky Nelson, Fats Domino, The Shirelles, and George Benson. As a musician, he became guitarist and band leader for such greats as Chuck Berry, Patti La Belle, The Drifters, and The Ronettes. In 1979 he formed his own band, Billy Vera and The Beaters, expertly playing the rhythm and blues his millions of fans demand. He made his acting debut in the 1984 cult-classic *Buckaroo Banzai*, based on the comic book series. **SIDELIGHTS** A musicologist, his record collection contains more than 35,000 discs.

Eddie Cantor 📺   1770 Vine

See page 429

Duran Duran 💿   1770 Vine

Rock musicians, songwriters

BORN Simon Le Bon (vocals) Oct. 27, 1958, Bushey, England. Nick Rhodes (keyboards) born: Nicholas Bates, June 8, 1962, Birmingham; John Taylor (bass), June 20, 1960, Birmingham; Warren Cuccurullo (guitar); Andy Taylor & Roger Taylor (no relation.) **SPOTLIGHTS** A British New Romantic group, their 1981 debut "Duran Duran" went triple-platinum. Premiering on the explosive dawn of the Video Generation—with their New Wave-Disco sound and hip fashions—Simon Le Bon was the first rocker to be labeled *videogenic*. Hit singles include "Hungry Like the Wolf," "Rio," "Union of the Shake," "New Moon on Monday," "The Reflex," "The Wild Boys," "Ordinary World," and "Come Undone." Their theme song for the James Bond film, *A View to a Kill* (1985), went to #1. The group played more than 1,000 sold-out concerts worldwide.

John Lennon 💿   1750 Vine

Singer, songwriter, poet, peace activist

John Lennon

BORN John Winston Lennon, Oct. 9, 1940, in Liverpool, England. **SPOTLIGHTS** Lennon was born during a WWII air raid, while his father, Fred Lennon, was away at sea. When he was two years old, his father deserted both ship and family. In 1945, the elder Lennon returned and tried to persuade his son to move to New Zealand with him. The youngster chose to stay near his mother, and would only see his dad twice in the next 20 years. Yet, it was his mother's sister, Mimi Smith, who took the boy and raised him in the working class neighborhood. In 1955, he heard Elvis Presley's "Heartbreak Hotel." Inspired by the music, Lennon credited the king with influencing him into rock 'n' roll. But it was more than the music. He said, "You know, you went to see those movies with Elvis or somebody in it when we were still in Liverpool. And you'd see everybody waiting to see him. And I'd be waiting there, too. And they'd all scream when he came on the screen. So I thought, 'That's a good job!'" At age 16, he formed his own group, the Quarrymen, which is about the time he met 14-year-old Paul McCartney, who joined the group. In 1958, Lennon wrote his first song, "Hello Little Girl," recorded in

1962 at their audition for Decca Records. In 1960, saying the band needed a catchier name, he renamed them the Silver Beetles. Later that year, the "Silver" was dropped and the spelling of the Beetles was changed to Beatles. It was a pivotal time span for Lennon. He painfully recalled, "When I was 16, I re-established a relationship with my mother for about four years, she taught me about music...And then unfortunately she was run over by an off-duty policeman who was drunk at the time...That was really a hard time for me. And it just absolutely made me very, very bitter." Lennon dedicated himself to the band. The Fab Four, consisting of Paul McCartney, Ringo Starr, George Harrison, and Lennon, made their recording debut on September 11, 1962, with two songs: "Love Me Do," and "P.S. I Love You." The rest, as they say, is history. The team of Lennon-McCartney, with their genius for song writing, profoundly influenced a generation of restless youth and altered the course of the entire music industry. Concerts, albums and singles all went #1. Beatlemania ruled as these prolific talents broke all boundaries. Motion pictures include *A Hard Day's Night* (1964), an immediate worldwide smash, and *Help!* (1965), more box office gold. Lennon gave a singular, wonderful acting performance in *How I Won the War* (1967). Eventually, with the band's breakup, his solo career continued. Among his other works, this "working class hero" released his solo LP *Imagine* which went #1. Working with his second wife, artist Yoko Ono, *Double Fantasy* also topped the charts. **ACHIEVEMENTS** Lennon's first book, *In His Own Write* (1964), became an instant best-seller. In 1965, Lennon was awarded the MBE (Member of the British Empire). **SIDELIGHTS** Not all was "Strawberry Fields Forever." His political viewpoints, speaking out against the Vietnam War, caused him much U.S. governmental grief. Without fear of the Feds, he remained an advocate of peace and led anti-war demonstrations with his wife Yoko Ono. Their famous May 1969 "bed-in" recording of "Give Peace a Chance" was a message heard around the world. **FAMILY** Attempts to start over were successful as he triumphed in court and became a "house-husband" to his wife and newborn son Sean, who was born on Lennon's 35th birthday. Lennon also enjoyed a period of spiritual and creative renewal. Both Sean, and a son from a prior marriage, Julian, (born April 8, 1963 to mother Cynthia Lennon) have followed in their father's footsteps to become singers and songwriters. Died: Dec. 8, 1980; a lone, fanatical gunman assassinated him in front of the Lennon's Dakota apartment on New York City's Upper West Side. His Walk of Fame star was dedicated posthumously on Sept. 30, 1988, in front of the Capitol Records building. Each year on Dec. 8, Lennon fans gather at his Walk of Fame star for a candlelight vigil. This memorial tribute is open to all.

Heinie Conklin 🎞   1750 Vine
Actor, comedian
BORN Charles Conklin; April 2, 1880, in San Francisco, CA. **SPOTLIGHTS** He was a big vaudevillian with a walrus mustache who always got a laugh. Conklin later performed on the

legitimate stage, then in 1915 won his celebrity on the silver screen. He made dozens of comedies, including *Ham and Eggs at the Front* (1927--as Eggs). He also appeared in dramas, such as the classic *All Quiet on the Western Front* (1930). At age 75, he made his last slapstick film, *Abbott and Costello Meet the Keystone Kops* (1955). Conklin died in 1959.

Bob Seger & The Silver Bullet Band 🔊
1750 Vine   *Rock band*

Bob Seger & The Silver Bullet Band

BORN May 6, 1945, in Dearborn, MI. Band: Chris Campbell (bass); Drew Abbott (guitar); Robyn Robbins (keyboards); Alto Reed (sax); Charlie Allen Martin (drums); and Craig Frost. **SPOTLIGHTS** Heavily influenced by the rhythm and blues music of Detroit, Seger went strong with *hard rock and soul*. His first regional hit, "Eastside Story," lead to a contract with Capitol Records in 1967. Later that year, the singer/songwriter issued "2+2+?" He rereleased "Ramblin' Gamblin' Man," which rose to the top of the charts. But his life was not on easy street yet. Regarded as the workingman's rock 'n' roll artist, Seger experienced doubtful times, endured some commercial failures and considered giving up music all together. He even returned to college. As a last ditch effort, he dug in and composed an album's worth of songs he dubbed, *Beautiful Loser*, introducing the Silver Bullet Band. Since then, Seger has produced one superb rock 'n' roll chronicle after another. *Night Moves* sold five million copies, establishing him as a ballad singer, but his song "Rock and Roll Never Forgets" reminded us of his energetic, good-time, hard rock 'n' roll know-how. Platinum and gold albums include *Stranger in Town*, *Against the Wind*, *Like a Rock*, and *Greatest Hits*. Hit songs: "Main Street," "Still the Same," "Hollywood Nights," "We've Got Tonite," "Fire Lake," "Against the Wind," and "Shakedown" (heard in 1987's *Beverly Hills Cop II*). **SIDELIGHTS** One of the happiest song moments in movie history occurs in *Risky Business* (1983). In his breakthrough role, Tom Cruise lip syncs Seger's hit "Old Time Rock & Roll" wearing underwear, socks and dark sunglasses. This famous scene instantly locked into our collective memory and became much-imitated fodder for comedians worldwide. **HIGHLIGHTS** His Walk of Fame star was dedicated on Friday the 13th, of March 1987, in front of Capitol Records. Family, friends, fans, and Don Zimmerman, (president of Capitol Records) congratulated Seger and band members Craig Frost, Chris Campbell and Alto Reed.

Tony Martin 🎞   1750 Vine
See page 399

Buddy DeSylva 🎵   1750 Vine
Songwriter, author, publisher, producer, executive
BORN George Gard De Sylva; Jan. 27, 1895, in New York. **SPOTLIGHTS** He co-founded Capitol Records in 1942 with Johnny Mercer and Glenn Wallichs, although DeSylva single-handedly put up the $10,000 seed money. Not 100% confident of their recording company's future, he held onto his day job as head of Paramount Pictures. The intelligent, creative talent arrived everyday at 10, and went straight to work in his executive suite. DeSylva revived the fifth-placed studio back to its #1 position. He combined that with a second career as a songwriter. The Tin Pan Alley tunesmith—"one of the cleverest fellows in the business"—wrote for Al Jolson ("Sonny Boy"), George Gershwin, Jerome Kern and Victor Herbert. Later, he grew into a powerhouse lyricist in Hollywood and on Broadway. His team created songs for many successful musicals of the 1920s and '30s. He produced five of Shirley Temple's hits, including *Poor Little Rich Girl* (1936). Capitol Records remains the lengthened shadow of this brilliant man. It continues to define music from each generation of listeners—from Nat King Cole to the Beatles to Bonnie Raitt—just as DeSylva planned...Ernest Borgnine portrayed him in *The Best Things In Life Are Free* (1956). Died: 1950.

Lurene Tuttle 🎞   1750 Vine
See page 592

The Steve Miller Band 🎵   1750 Vine
Singer, songwriter, musician
BORN Steve (guitar, vocals) Oct. 5, 1943, Milwaukee, WI. The band: James "Curly" Cooke (guitar, voc.); Lonnie Turner (bass); and Tim Davis (drums). **SPOTLIGHTS** Perhaps proving that talent is learned, and genius is born—and it takes a combination of both—young Stevie was blessed with a father who would bring guests such as T-Bone Walker and Charles Mingus home to enjoy a good meal and jam. He received his first guitar lesson at age four from the legendary Les Paul (another honoree on the Hollywood Walk of Fame). He spent time after school sitting in Paul and Mary Ford's studio recording sessions. By age 12, he formed his first blues band, The Marksmen Combo, and played with Jimmy Reed at age 14. At the University of Wisconsin, his band the Ardels included singer/songwriter Boz Scaggs, who became famous in his own right. As one of the first young Caucasian blues-rockers, he moved to Chicago in 1964, jamming with such greats as Muddy Waters, Howling Wolf, and Paul Butterfield. Miller

journeyed to San Francisco in '66 and the progressive rock scene. Hits include "The Joker," "Fly Like an Eagle," "Rock 'n Me," the classic "Living in the U.S.A.," "Take the Money and Run," "Jet Airliner," "Jungle Love," and "Abracadabra." Five of his albums have gone platinum and he has numerous golds. **QUOTE** Asked about the high point of his career, he responded, "Meeting Les Paul. He was a friend of my father's. As a child he taught me what a career entails, about singles, albums, the electric guitar, how to sing in multiple parts using multi-track recording. Nothing that has happened since would have happened unless I had been exposed to him at such an early age."

Steve Miller

Frank Fay 🎞   1750 Vine
See page 261

Tina Turner 🎵   1750 Vine

Tina Turner

Singer, actress, writer
BORN Anna Mae Bullock; Nov. 25, 1941, in Brownsville, TX. **SPOTLIGHTS** A beautiful, powerful rhythm-and-blues vocalist, she originally became famous for her soul revue. Her 1960 debut single "A Fool in Love" was an accidental hit; she was merely filling in for a singer who failed to show up at the recording session. Because of her instant success, Ike Turner (performer, talent scout, future husband) developed the Ikettes—a trio of sexy backup singers around her, and added nine musicians, culminating in a major soul act. A string of hits on the pop and soul charts followed, including "Come Together," and "I Want to Take You Higher." One classic song from that period opens with Miss Turner's seductive spoken introduction to "Proud Mary," opening with: "We never do anything nice and easy." In 1984 her *Private Dancer* album rocked the Grammy world with "Let's Stay Together," "What's Love Got to Do with It" "Better Be Good to Me," and "Private Dancer." A sensational performer, her concerts are always sold-out. She made her motion picture debut playing the Acid Queen in Ken Russell's version of *Tommy* (1975). This musical includes cast members Roger Daltrey, Ann-Margret, Oliver

Reed, Elton John, Eric Clapton and Jack Nicholson. She plays an evil ruler with panache in *Mad Max Beyond Thunderdome* (1985), opposite Mel Gibson. **ACHIEVEMENTS** Her best-selling autobiography, *I, Tina* (co-written with Kurt Loder) was turned into a triumphant, must-see motion picture. Brian Gibson's *What's Love Got to Do with It* (1993). It stars Angela Bassett and Laurence Fishburne, who give superb performances...Her Walk of Fame dedication ceremony took place on August 28, 1986.

Lowell Thomas 🎤   1750 Vine
Newscaster, narrator, author

Lowell Thomas (right) reporting on starvation conditions abroad.

BORN April 6, 1892, in Woodington, Drake County, OH. **SPOTLIGHTS** Best known as a newscaster, Thomas was equally famous as an adventurer, explorer, foreign correspondent, biographer, lecturer and business executive. He grew up in a booming mine camp where he worked at every job to be had in a mining town. Thomas came to hear the tales the miners told as they prayed and dug for gold from the Klondike to the Transvaal. He later reminisced, "They were a special breed, those men, part dreamer, part cynic, ready to follow their shining vision anywhere, but drawn as much by the quest itself as by any real hope of striking it rich. They held me spellbound with their tales of other lands." Thomas' father, though, was a well-educated, compassionate surgeon, who cared for the miners. Thomas said his dad, "roused in me an abiding curiosity about this planet we live on, and I have spent a lifetime trying to see as much of it as I could." He attended the University of Northern Indiana where he collected both his undergraduate and graduate degrees in two years. That was the beginning of his whirlwind career. Since his first flight (as passenger) in 1917, he logged more miles than any man, visiting every remote corner of the earth. As a WWI foreign correspondent, he eyewitnessed the desert campaigns of Colonel T.E.

Lawrence—Lawrence of Arabia, the legendary guerrilla fighter—learning firsthand of the warrior's desert strategy and personal philosophy. On March 21, 1925, he gave a one-hour impromptu talk on pioneer radio station KDKA, then became a daily news pioneer. He was on the air longer than anyone in radio history (1929-'76). Thomas was also the "Voice" for 20th Century-Fox Movietone News for decades beginning in 1935. As a prolific author, he penned 54 books. **QUOTE** On NBC's "Headline Hunters," his signature closing was, "So long, until tomorrow." But, his best known catchphrase was, "Good evening, everybody." Died: 1981.

Anne Murray 🎵   1750 Vine
Singer

BORN Morna Anne Murray, June 20, 1945, in Springhill, Nova Scotia, Canada. **SPOTLIGHTS** Born and raised in a coal mining town, this vocalist has no fear of combustible heat. She has walked the fiery line between country and pop for two and a half decades without burning a single toosie. The pretty, blonde singer won American country hearts in 1970 with "Snowbird." Her pop debut was a rendition of the Beatles song "You Won't See

Anne Murray

Me." Her string of hits includes "Danny's Song," "You Needed Me," "Could I Have This Dance," "I'll Just Fall in Love Again," "Shadows in the Moonlight," "Broken Hearted Me," "Blessed Are the Believers," "Walk Right Back," "A Little Good News," "Just Another Woman in Love," and "Feed This Fire." **ACHIEVEMENTS** Named Best Country Female Performer, this Grammy-winner has 11 gold, four platinum, one double platinum and two triple platinum albums.

Lee De Forest 🎥   1750 Vine
Inventor

BORN Aug. 26, 1873, in Council Bluffs, IA. **SPOTLIGHTS** A genius whose father encouraged him to go into the ministry, *not* science. The teenage boy respectfully wrote this letter to his father: "Dear Sir: I intend to become a machinist and inventor because I have a great talent in that direction." At age 26, in 1899, he graduated from Yale University with a Ph.D. He went to work in a Western Electric dynamo factory. After hours, the pioneer worked in his home laboratory on a project he described as: "I'll try to send the human voice through the air instead of messages by dots and dashes." In 1907, he invented the audion tube which made both radio and TV possible. Three years later, he set up microphones at the Metropolitan Opera House in New York, and broadcast the great tenor, Enrico Caruso, singing. He devised the first radio station in 1916, produced the first broadcast, and became known as the "Father of Radio." Next, the electronics genius tackled Hollywood's silent pictures by making them talk. Then, he moved into the creation of television. De Forest invented more than 300 complex technical items for motion pictures, radio, and television alone. **QUOTE** In 1958, the elderly inventor required an operation. While lying on the table—before anesthesia—he asked the surgeon what procedure would be used. "Electro-desiccation," the doctor replied. De Forest nodded his head and responded, "Commonly spoken of as a hot wire. I invented it in 1907." The patient recovered nicely. Died: 1961.

Natalie Cole 🔘   1750 Vine
Singer
BORN Stephanie N. Cole; Feb. 6, 1949, in Los Angeles, CA.
SPOTLIGHTS A rare native of Los Angeles, this lithe beauty is the daughter of the legendary singer Nat "King" Cole (see Cole's bio in this book). She earned a degree in child psychology before launching her own musical career with *Inseparable*, which earned two Grammy Awards. Fans of hers—as well as her late father's—were *Thankful* that she had followed in his recording footsteps: "I've Got Love on My Mind," "Jump Start," "Miss You Like Crazy." In 1991, she rocketed to quintuple-platinum #1 album with a loving tribute to her father, *Unforgettable with Love.* This outstanding package equaled her father's romantic standards, surprising listeners with an electronic melding of Nat King Cole's voice (from 1951) with hers, winning seven Grammys. In 1996 the Grammy-winning balladeer performed a duet with her dad again—through the wizardry of sound engineering—"When I Fall in Love Again" on *Stardust.* Her journey back to the standards songbook is a thrill for fans who long for romance. She is versatile in pop, R&B, and jazz. In 1999, she released *The Magic of Christmas.* With techno wizardry she sings one of her dad's best-loved classics "The Christmas Song," with her dad. As an actress, she has appeared in TV's "I'll Fly Away," "Lily in Winter," "Abducted: A Father's Love," "Always Outnumbered," "Socrates," and "Freak City." **QUOTE** "Ballads are soothing music. In a day and age where everything is so crazy and you have to be 'on' all the time, you can mellow out with this."

Conrad Nagel 📺   1750 Vine
See page 145

Beverly Sills 🔘   1750 Vine
Opera singer, Chairman of the Board
BORN Belle Silverman; May 25,1929, in New York.
SPOTLIGHTS Working professionally since age seven, she was known as Belle "Bubbles" Silverman on radio's "Major Bowes' Capitol Family." She had won one of Major Bowes' talent contests in 1936, and sang on his shows regularly for several seasons. Even as a child, she had legions of admirers. Sills advanced from singing commercials to being recognized as one of the greatest and most beloved 20th-century coloratura sopranos. It is a great American success story. She made her

Beverly Sills

debut with the San Francisco Opera in 1953, and with the New York City Opera as Rosalinda in *Die Fledermaus* in 1955. Following her legendary success in the coloratura role of Cleopatra in Handel's *Gulio Cesare* in 1966, Sills began to explore the bel canto repertory in depth and expanded her repertoire to more than 70 operas, including *Manon, Roberto Devereux, Anna Bolena, Maria Stuarda, Traviata, Puritani, Don Pasquale,* and *Barbiere di Siviglia.* Her long-awaited Metropolitan Opera House debut was as Pamira in *The Siege of Corinth* in 1975, to which she received cascades of flowing praise. She has performed in virtually all of the world's leading opera houses. A prolific recording artist, this great diva has recorded 18 full-length operas and several solo reciting discs. After she retired from the opera and concert stage, she was named General Director of the New York City Opera in 1980. Under her intelligent leadership many young singers were discovered and have gone on to international success. She launched the City Opera's first summer season. She also cleverly introduced American audiences to the use of subtitles for all foreign language productions to enhance their opera experience. Her many television appearances include "Live from the Lincoln Center," where she became chairman of the board. **ACHIEVEMENTS** Recipient of the Presidential Medal of Freedom, and Kennedy Center Honors, among dozens of others awards. Sills is the retired national chairman of the March of Dimes Foundation for which she generously helped raise $80,000,000. to prevent birth defects...Kindhearted, Sills once commented that both she and friend Arlene Francis share the same personality trait, "Neither of us could stand it if everybody didn't love us." **QUOTE** "Achieving excellence requires believing in yourself and aiming slightly higher than anyone, perhaps even you, thought you could reach."

Vera Ralston   1750 Vine
Actress
BORN: Vera Hruba; July 12, 1919, in Prague, Czechoslovakia. **SPOTLIGHTS** This 1936 Olympic contender skated through her film debut in *Ice Capades* (1941). In *Dakota* (1945), she weds rugged cowboy John Wayne. Then, the sultry actress portrayed a WWII bride betrayed by her duplicitous husband in *I, Jane Doe* (1948), and stars in *Accused of Murder* (1956).

Helen Reddy ●   1750 Vine
Singer, composer, writer, producer, actress
BORN Oct. 25, 1941, in Melbourne, Australia. **SPOTLIGHTS**: Descended from a show business family, she began performing on stage at age four, and by age 15 had joined a road troupe. This led to her own TV show in Australia, and to her winning a trip to New York. At first she had no luck here. Then, after a key appearance on "The Tonight Show" starring Johnny Carson, doors began opening for her. In 1971, Reddy shot to stardom with her rendition of the song "I Don't Know How to Love Him," from the hit Broadway rock opera musical "Jesus Christ Superstar." The following year, she was immortalized as the composer-singer of the powerful feminist anthem, "I Am Woman." The song opened with this line: "I am woman, watch me roar, in numbers too big to ignore..." It united American women in their march toward equality during that decade. She had succinctly identified their liberating spirit, shooting to #1 and winning a Grammy. Reddy kept hitting the Top Forty with "Delta Dawn," "You and Me Against the World," "Leave Me Alone," "Peaceful," "Angie Baby," "Ain't No Way to Treat a Lady," "I Can't Hear You No More," and "You're My World." As an actress, she appeared in *Airport '75* (1974), Disney's *Pete's Dragon* (1977) and *Sgt. Pepper's Lonely Hearts Club Band* (1978). She toured in the musical stage production of "Blood Brothers," and starred in the one-woman play "Shirley Valentine." In the 1990s she released *Center Stage*, a CD collection of theater songs. **QUOTE** About acting, she stated, "I've gone back to my theatrical roots."

Joe Penner ▯   1750 Vine
Comedian
BORN Joszef Pinta; Nov. 11, 1904, in Budapest, Hungary. **SPOTLIGHTS** An eight-year-old immigrant to America, Penner struggled to learn English with no formal schooling. After toiling in factory jobs, he set his sights on becoming a vaudeville comedy star. Wearing a derby hat popular in its day and chomping on a cheap cigar, he spent his early adulthood learning what made people laugh. Without a pot to spit in, he worked for years in obscurity. That was all to change. Penner struck gold when he ad-libbed the odd question, "Wanna Buy a Duck?" to a bored audience in Birmingham, Alabama. The one-liner got laughs. Penner expanded the silly gag with: "Well, does your brother wanna buy a duck? Well, if you *had* a brother, would he wanna buy a duck?" Audiences loved it. Booked for one night only on NBC's "The Rudy Vallee Hour" in 1933, Penner delivered the duck routine and became an overnight sensation. He immediately got his own radio show at $7,000-a-week. Lighthearted vocalists Ozzie Nelson and Harriet Hilliard provided support, and Penner brought a duck named Goo-Goo on the air. Mel Blanc gave Goo-Goo his funny voice. On this top-rated show, even Goo-Goo became a celebrity. In 1934, voters rated him radio's most outstanding comedian. In addition to his "Wanna Buy a Duck?" catchphrase, millions of listeners imitated his other signature phrases. He exaggerated words with a sarcastic delivery: "Don't ever doooo that!" and "Wo-o-oe is me!" and "You nah-sty man!" Accountants calculated that each word of the silly duck routine made Penner $250,000 richer. Died: 1941.

Bruce Humberstone   1750 Vine
Director
BORN H. Bruce Humberstone; Nov. 18, 1903, in Buffalo, NY. **SPOTLIGHTS** Nicknamed "Lucky," he directed a number of the best Charlie Chan detective films in the series, including *Charlie Chan at the Racetrack* (1936), *Charlie Chan at the Opera* (both 1936), and *Charlie Chan at the Olympics* (1937). Movies include *Time Out for Murder, While New York Sleeps* (both 1938), *Sun Valley Serenade* (1941), *I Wake Up Screaming* (1941—aka *Hot Spot*), *To the Shores of Tripoli* (1942), *Hello Frisco, Hello* (1943), *Pin Up Girl* (1944), *Wonder Man* (1945), *Three Little Girls in Blue* (1946—a musical), *Fury at Furnace Creek* (1948), and *The Desert Song* (1953). Died: 1984.

Beverly Bayne   1750 Vine
Actress
BORN Nov. 11, 1894, in Minneapolis, MN. **SPOTLIGHTS**: This tremendous beauty made movie history when she teamed with Hollywood's very first matinee idol, Francis X. Bushman, to become the silver screen's FIRST romantic couple. She stars as the leading lady in a number of silents opposite Bushman, including *Romeo and Juliet* (1916) and *A Pair of Cupids* (1918). They secretly married, but she later made the mistake of divorcing him. The actor refused to appear with her again. Her movie career abruptly halted. She returned to vaudeville, then, when vaudeville went six feet under, she turned to legitimate theater. Died: 1982.

Joan Crawford   1750 Vine
Actress, dancer
BORN Billie Cassin; changed to Lucille LeSueur; March 23, 1904, in San Antonio, TX. **SPOTLIGHTS** Stunning in her youth, this energetic dancer shimmied her way into Tinseltown's heart. MGM labeled her a "jazz baby" in the mid-1920s, and she came out of *Dancing Daughters* (1928) a star. *Paid* (1930) proved she survived the transition to the 1930s Depression-era talkies, while virtually 98 percent of other

Joan Crawford

female stars dropped out of sight—and *sound.* By *Grand Hotel* (1932), she was the studio's third biggest box office moneymaker, ahead of Greta Garbo by two slots. She surprised everyone when she stormed the next decade with *A Woman's Face* (1941), an Academy Award, and *Possessed* (1947) in another Oscar-nominated performance. Her ability to attract new fans contributed to her miraculous staying power. Her movies *Sudden Fear* (1952) and *Whatever Happened to Baby Jane* (1962) terrified younger audiences. On-screen, she radiated an intense, fiery, dominating presence. Offscreen, she concocted shrewd deals, which allowed her to come out on top in "the old-men's-club of Hollywood." Humphrey Bogart once said: "Joan Crawford, as much as I dislike the lady, is a star." **ACHIEVEMENTS** 1945 Oscar for *Mildred Pierce.* **QUOTE** Offscreen, she always played the dazzling movie star. When asked by a reporter about the new crop of stars, Crawford stated, "You call them stars? I call them personalities. A star will always last, as in the heavens. A personality will go down just as quick as it appears." Died: 1977.

Garth Brooks ●   1750 Vine

Singer, songwriter, musician
BORN Troyal Garth Brooks; February 7, 1962, in Tulsa, OK.
SPOTLIGHTS He is country's top artist and Nashville's shining icon. How did a nice athletic guy, who attended Oklahoma State University on a partial track scholarship and graduated with a degree in marketing (advertising), become the country music superstar of the 1990s? With an electrifying stage-struttin' presence and an immediate connection with audiences, Brooks appears to truly enjoy himself and enjoy the audience more than any other entertainer in recent history. He likes what he is doing and it shows. He became the instrument in expanding country music's potential throughout the world. Brooks' music attracted all sorts of new fans to country music; even those who previously had refused to listen to it. He became a Capitol Nashville Records superstar when his *No Fences* and *Ropin' The Wind* albums broke new ground. *No Fences* sold more than 13 million copies making it the biggest selling country album of all time, and *Ropin' the Wind* was the first album to debut at #1 on Billboard's country and pop charts, selling more than 11 million units. *The Chase*, with his

Garth Brooks

renditions of "Walking After Midnight" and "Dixie Chicken," went straight to the top, to the #1 position, on both pop and country charts in its first week. *The Hits* and *Double Live* are two more titles that sold more than 10 million units in the United States. His concerts, and numerous television specials draw millions of fans. He is adored for his humble manner, his integrity, and decency, exemplifying the best of a gentle soul. Yet his sparkling eyes and good sense of humor remind us all that it's about having a good time, too. He is the consummate showman. Hit songs include "Somewhere Other Than the Night," "Learning to Live Again," "We Shall Be Free," "Ain't Goin' Down (Til the Sun Comes Up)," "American Honky Tonk Bar Association," "Friends In Low Places," "Unanswered Prayers," "The Thunder Rolls," "Much Too Young (To Feel This Damn Old)," "Not Counting You," and "If Tomorrow Never Comes," to name just a few. Brooks' acting credits include guest performances on NBC's "Empty Nest," and ABC's "Muppets Tonight!" as well as a cameo performance on NBC's "Mad About You." He also drew widespread acclaim for the skits he performed as host of "Saturday Night Live" in Feb. 1998. **SIDELIGHTS** He bravely and openly illustrated the dirty little topic of spousal abuse with his video, "The Thunder Rolls." In it, a battered woman shoots and kills her abusive husband. Both TNN and CMT cable stations took what many considered a decidedly un-American censorship stance and banned it from their airwaves. Critics argued that the public would have been better served if the stations had aired "The Thunder Rolls," and used it as an opportunity to launch discussions about domestic violence. Regardless, he won the 1993 CMA Video of the Year Award for it, as well as appreciative letters from female abuse victims. **ACHIEVEMENTS** Brooks was honored with the Artist of the Decade Award presented by the Academy of Country Music in 1999. He won his first Grammy Award for Best Male Vocal Performance—and Country Music Association Album of the Year—in 1992 for *Ropin' The Wind.* He won his second Grammy Award in 1998 for Country Vocal Collaboration with Trisha Yearwood (a duet) for "In Another's Eyes." Brooks is the highest-certified solo artist in U.S. music history. With more than 95 million albums certified since 1989, he is the fastest-selling album artist on record. He is the recipient of more than 75 major industry awards, including the People's Choice Award for Favorite Male Musical Performer (1992-'97), the Academy of

Country Music's Entertainer of the Year for three years and the Country Music Association's Entertainer of the Year for two years in a row. His world tour sold millions of tickets, and his Summer of 1997 free concert in Central Park, New York City attracted 750,000 fans. Taped by HBO, the show was simulcast around the globe...His mother, Colleen Carroll Brooks, recorded for Capitol Records in the 1950s and performed with Red Foley on "The Ozark Jubilee." (Amazingly, her son signed with Capitol nearly three decades later.) **SECRET** Brooks received his Walk of Fame star on June 30, 1995. Hidden beneath it lies a master recording of *The Hits*. (This album was his first greatest hits collection.) It is Brooks' unique Hollywood time capsule. **HIGHLIGHTS** His favorite movies are *To Kill a Mockingbird* (1962), *Forrest Gump* (1994), and *Field of Dreams* (1989). Their mutual theme? How an ordinary man reacts to extraordinary circumstances.

Clarence Brown    1750 Vine
Director

BORN May 10, 1890, in Clinton, MA. **SIDELIGHTS** He directed the stunning Greta Garbo in her most triumphant roles: *Anna Christie* (1930), *Anna Karenina* (1935), and *Conquest* (1937). Brown made one of the most likable motion pictures of all-time, *National Velvet* (1944), starring 12-year-old Elizabeth Taylor. *The Yearling* (1946), based on Marjorie Kinnan Rawling's classic book, stars Gregory Peck and Jane Wyman. An impeccable production, this family drama forever established his pictorial sensitivity. *Intruder in the Dust* (1949), based on William Faulkner's novel and shot in Faulkner's hometown of Oxford, Mississippi, remains one of Brown's most compelling dramatic works. **QUOTE** "Humans cannot stand the strain of long and tragic periods without breaking— and that applies even to the strongest of us. Therefore, in tragedy, humor is necessary. Strange to say, humans cannot stand a long strain of laughing, therefore, tragedy is necessary. It seems to me that dramatic representations of life are made up of, say, three parts of serious effort and one part of humorous effort, and then we have the ideal balance." Died: 1987.

Rory Calhoun   1750 Vine
See page 593

Brian Aherne   1750 Vine
Actor

BORN May 2, 1902, in England. **SPOTLIGHTS** A dignified, pipe-smoking British actor, he symbolized the tweedy upper class. This well-bred talent made his screen debut in *Song of Songs* (1933), opposite Marlene Dietrich. In *My Son, My Son* (1940), he plays a rags-to-riches man who lives to regret spoiling his son. That same year, he plays a gloomy doctor in one of the most interesting nursings stories ever told—about a sickly patient who dies due to (Carole Lombard's) dereliction of duty— in *Vigil in the Night*. He co-stars with the energetic, wisecracking Rosalind Russell in *Hired Wife* (1940), and in the funny, romantic farce *My Sister Eileen* (1942). Other films

include *Titanic* (1953), and *The Swan* (1956). He worked in many early live TV playhouse shows. **HIGHLIGHTS** Married to actress Joan Fontaine (1939-'43). Died: 1986.

George Seaton   1750 Vine
Screenwriter, director, producer

BORN April 17, 1911, in South Bend, IN. **SPOTLIGHTS** He wrote the hilarious Marx Bros. smash picture, *A Day at the Races* (1937). Later, he directed the teenage comedy *Junior Miss* (1945), starring Peggy Ann Garner. He wrote/directed *Airport* (1970), based on Arthur Hailey's best seller. It stars Burt Lancaster, Dean Martin, George Kennedy and Helen Hayes. **ACHIEVEMENTS** 1947 Oscar for writing *Miracle on 34th Street*; he also directed it. 1954 Oscar for *The Country Girl*; which he also directed. **QUOTE** When he paid a hospital visit to the ailing actor Edmund Gwenn (whom he had directed as Santa Claus in *Miracle on 34th Street*), Seaton became depressed. He looked at his deathbed condition and sighed, "It's tough, isn't it?" Gwenn gathered up his breath, tilted his head and whispered, "Yes, it is, but it's not as tough as playing comedy." Died: 1979.

Roy Rogers   1750 Vine
Actor, singer, songwriter, band leader, musician

Roy Rogers and Trigger

BORN Leonard Franklin Slye; Nov. 5, 1911, in Cincinnati, OH. **SPOTLIGHTS** Billed as the "King of the Cowboys," he was a teenager when the Great Depression shattered the economy. His unemployed family headed West to California, joining the migratory workers known as "Okies." While working on farms and ranches, the teen learned to ride and do a variety of gun tricks. The 20-year-old struck the mother lode by landing a singing and guitar playing job for radio's the Rocky Mountaineers. He formed a musical group eventually called The Sons of the Pioneers, becoming successful on air and in concert. When cowboy great Gene Autry volunteered for WWII Army Air Corps duty and left Republic Pictures, Rogers auditioned as an actor. He proudly went in to fill the Western void. His healthy looks, genial manner and pleasant yodeling convinced the studio that he would be big. His first film *as* Roy Rogers was *Under Western Stars* (1938). Soon, the terrific character actor George "Gabby" Hayes saddled up as his sidekick, as did his musical pals The Sons of the Pioneers. The wholesome gent made a slew of musical Westerns, where he yodeled between action sequences. Like a big brother, or father to millions of youngsters, the camera picked up on his compassion, fairness, and honor. This caring, truthful, affable cowboy proudly wore the white hat. Films include *Dark Command* (1940) co-starring John Wayne and Claire Trevor, *Sons of the Pioneers* (1942), *The Yellow Rose of Texas* (1944), *My Pal Trigger* (1946). In all, he made 87 films, and was rated the No. 1 Western Star for 11 consecutive years (1943-'54). His beloved palomino, Trigger, became one of screen's most famous horses. **TV** Rogers and his wife, Dale Evans, shared billing in 101 episodes of "The Roy Rogers Show" between 1951-'57. "Happy Trails To You" was their signature theme song. (See her bio in this book.) **HIGHLIGHTS** He met actress Dale Evans on the set of *The Cowboy and the Senorita* (1944), married her in 1947, and made 26 features with her as the heroine...The Roy Rogers-Dale Evans museum is located in Victorville, California. **SIDELIGHTS** Both Rogers and his wife were devastated by the death of their two-year-old daughter in 1952. He said, "It was like the world had ended all for us. But life goes on—it does, whether you want it to or not, God sees to that—and we went on, too." **QUOTE** A devout Christian, he reconciled his religious beliefs with the sometimes sinful world of Hollywood. Rogers stated, "If the Lord didn't want me in this business, he'd have taken me out. There must be some reason for me being in this cowboy business." Died: 1998.

Donald Meek 🎥   **1750 Vine**
Actor
BORN July 14, 1880, in Glasgow, Scotland. **SPOTLIGHTS** At age 14, he toured America as an acrobat with a professional troupe. An accidental fall ended that career. Four years later, in 1898, Meek was a soldier in the Spanish-American War. Fighting in the tropics, he contracted a rare infectious disease that caused a high fever, and the subsequent lost of his hair. Postwar, he trained in theater. He had a solid Broadway career, before his screen debut in *The Hole in the Wall* (1929). This

Donald Meek

bald, slight, figure specialized in Milquetoast character roles in both dramas and comedies. Meek is best remembered as a quiet, trembling-voiced creature. He performed in a staggering 700 roles throughout six decades. Memorably, he played Mr. Peacock, the shy whiskey drummer in John Ford's landmark Western, *Stagecoach* (1939). Movies include *The Merry Widow* (1934), *Top Hat*, *Barbary Coast*, *China Seas* (all 1935), *You Can't Take It With You* (1938), *Little Miss Broadway* (1938), *Young Mr. Lincoln* (1939), *Star Dust*, *My Little Chickadee* (both 1940), and *Barnacle Bill* (1941). Died: 1946.

Ralph Staub 🎥   **1750 Vine**
Producer, director, cameraman
BORN 1898. **SPOTLIGHTS** He began as cameraman in 1920, then filmed travel shorts in Alaska. He directed a few features before becoming known for the "Screen Snapshots" series at Columbia Pictures. During 20 years there, he made 800 shorts that were shown in between feature films. He won numerous awards, and claimed, "I never had a single flop." Died: 1969.

Madge Evans 🎥   **1750 Vine**
Actress
BORN Margherita Evans; July 1, 1909, in New York. **SPOTLIGHTS** Onscreen since 1915, she matured in front of the cameras. She is fun in the upbeat comedy *The Greeks Had a Word for Them* (1932), with Joan Blondell. She was marvelous in *Dinner at Eight* (1933), with an all-star cast. She retired to marry playwright Sidney Kingsley. Died: 1981.

Lloyd Nolan 📺   **1750 Vine**
Actor
BORN Aug. 11, 1902, in San Francisco, CA. **SPOTLIGHTS** Educated at Stanford University, he joined the prestigious Pasadena Playhouse, in California, when he was 25 years old. For the next few years, he learned his craft in stock and touring companies. He made his Broadway debut at age 29 in "Reunion in Vienna," with the most celebrated couple of American theatre, Alfred Lunt and Lynn Fontanne. He landed the lead in his next play, "One Sunday Afternoon." He made his screen debut in *Stolen Harmony* (1934). A solid, reliable talent, he enjoyed a busy 40-year career. In all, he made 80 movies, including *G-Men* (1935), *Wells Fargo* (1937), *Johnny Apollo* (1940), *Blues in the Night* (1941), *The Man Who Wouldn't Die* (1942), *Bataan* (1943), *Guadalcanal Diary* (1943), *A Tree Grows in Brooklyn* (1945), *House on 92nd Street* (1945), *Lady in the Lake* (1946--with first-person camera work from the point-of-view of detective Philip Marlowe), *The*

Lloyd Nolan

Lemon Drop Kid (1951), *A Hatful of Rain* (1957), *Peyton Place* (1957), and the disaster flicks *Airport* (1970) and *Earthquake* (1974). Nolan was instrumental in helping to break racial stereotypes in the ground breaking TV series "Julia" (1968-'71). In this completely integrated show, he played Dr. Morton Chegley, the employer of nurse Julia Baker (Diahann Carroll). Carroll was the first African American to have a prestige lead in any TV series. (See her bio in this book.) **ACHIEVEMENTS** 1955 Emmy for "The Caine Mutiny Court-Martial," as Captain Queeg. He had played Captain Queeg on Broadway, winning the New York Drama Critics Award and the Donaldson. Critic Brooks Atkinson wrote: "Nolan's portrait of fear, desperation and panic is a stunning piece of work, principally because he has every detail under control." Died: 1985.

Charles Laughton 🎥   1750 Vine

Charles Laughton

Actor, director
BORN July 1, 1899, in England. **SPOTLIGHTS** A thick-lipped, rubbery-faced, round-shouldered, overweight artist, Laughton was brilliant. He delivered bold, vivid characterizations of each individual he portrayed, whether a nobleman or a serf. However, he was notoriously difficult to work with, as he would have to be *in the mood* before he would act. One of motion pictures' greatest talents, in 1935 alone he did: *Ruggles of Red Gap, Les Miserables* and *Mutiny on the Bounty* (as the sadistic Captain Bligh). In *Ruggles of Red Gap,* he plays a straitlaced English butler who recites Lincoln's Gettysburg Address in a Western saloon. That scene alone is worth watching the movie for, but you'll get a whole lot more in this delightful five-star comedy. He stars in the dramatic soap opera, *They Knew What They Wanted* (1940), opposite Carole Lombard. Laughton directed one of the scariest thrillers ever, *The Night of the Hunter* (1955), with a hypnotic Robert Mitchum playing a psychotic preacher. The entire cast is great: Shelley Winters, Lillian Gish, and Peter Graves. In Hollywood social circles, his house served as the intellectual and literary center. A collector of modern French art, Laughton never purchased a painting unless it met two requirements: that it move and bewilder him. The moment he

understood the work, he sold it. **ACHIEVEMENTS** 1932-33 Best Actor Academy Award for *The Private Life of Henry VIII.* In 1958 he won the Best Actor of the Year Award given by the International Cinema Club of Rome for *Witness for the Prosecution*...Stating that radio, film and TV had diminished the importance and joy of reading aloud, Laughton testified "that the **art of reading aloud should be reintroduced to families and in schools.**" Died: 1962.

Ken Murray 📷   1750 Vine

Ken Murray

Actor
BORN Kenneth Abner Doncourt; July 14, 1903, in New York, NY. **SPOTLIGHTS** A straight man and master of ceremonies in vaudeville, his specialty was the revue format. His "Ken Murray's Blackouts," a fabulous, changing revue took place at the El Capitan Theatre, in Hollywood. Cast members came and went while stars such as W.C. Fields, Errol Flynn and Bing Crosby were welcomed at each show. It lasted 3,844 performances, the longest running show in L.A. (1942-'49). "The Ken Murray Show" (CBS-TV, 1950-'53) was a top-rated variety show. **ACHIEVEMENTS** 1947 Special Oscar for *Bill and Coo*, a 91-minute film starring trained birds. Died: 1988.

Conrad Nagel 📷   1750 Vine

See page 145

Jack Mulhall 🎥   1750 Vine

Jack Mulhall and Patsy Ruth Miller

Actor
BORN John Joseph Francis Mulahall; Oct. 7, 1887, in Wappingers Falls, NY. **SPOTLIGHTS** Not many Walk of Fame honorees had the opportunity of working for Thomas Edison— the world's greatest inventor—but Mulhall did. After Edison invented the motion picture camera, he began shooting films in his stark studio called the Black Maria. Mulhall, an art student at the time, needed extra money. Utilizing

abilities he had acquired as a professional child performer, he acted in Edison's first "moving" pictures. When Mulhall relocated to Southern California, he found sunshine, swimming pools, and an abundance of leading roles in the 1920s. Movies include *Molly O'* (1921), *Ladies' Night in a Turkish Bath* (1928), *Twin Beds* (1929), and *Showgirls in Hollywood* (1930). Later, he worked in supporting and character roles, including *Hollywood Boulevard* (1936). He appears in a number of film serials, including *The Three Musketeers* (1933 on), *Buck Rogers* (1939 on), and *Adventures of Captain Marvel* (1941). He made 300 features. Died: 1979.

Shelley Winters 🎥 1750 Vine

Actress

Shelley Winters

BORN Shirley Schrift; Aug. 18, 1922, in St. Louis, MO. **SPOT-LIGHTS** The young Winters was persuaded by a Columbia Pictures talent scout to forsake her successful Broadway career for the silver screen. When she moved into her spacious Hollywood Hills home, she quickly discovered she was terrified of being alone in it. She saved her sanity by calling upon the services of waiters and waitresses of a local restaurant called Googie's, which was open 24 hours a day. They joined her in reading scripts, or sometimes just watched her rehearse until sunrise, when she felt safe to be alone again. She freely admitted her unusual shortcomings. Her refreshing candor surprised Tinseltown, winning over executives and gossip columnists alike. In her unique voice, she good-humoredly declared, "I'm outspoken, but not by many." Winters' earthy sensuality made her a full-fledged movie star in *A Double Life* (1948). This intense, tempestuous, powerful performer is celebrated in dramatic roles. Movies include *Take One False Step* (1949), *Johnny Stool Pigeon* (1949), *Winchester 73* (1950), *A Place in the Sun* (1951), *Phone Call from a Stranger* (1952), *Executive Suite* (1954), *The Night of the Hunter* (1955), *The Big Knife* (1955), *The Young Savages* (1961), *Lolita* (1962), *Bloody Mama* (1970), *What's the Matter with Helen* (1971), *The Poseidon Adventure* (1972—in an Oscar-nominated performance), *Blume in Love* (1973), and *The Portrait of a Lady* (1997). **ACHIEVEMENTS** Best Supporting Academy Awards: 1959 for *The Diary of Anne Frank*, and 1965 for *A Patch of Blue*. **QUOTE** Universal Studios scheduled a meeting between their young starlet and a hot-blooded Italian producer flying into town to meet her. Her publicist warned her, "He's a terrible wolf. He'll tear the clothes off your back." She wisecracked, "So I'll wear an old dress."

Marian Nixon 🎥 1750 Vine

Actress

BORN Oct. 20, 1904, in Superior, WI. **SPOTLIGHTS** A leading lady in hundreds of one-and-two reelers, she appears in a number of films, including *Riders of the Purple Sage* (1925), *Jazz Mad* (1928), and *Silks and Saddles* (1928). Died: 1983.

Alec Templeton 🎙 1750 Vine

Pianist, composer, host

BORN July 4, 1910, in Wales. **SPOTLIGHTS** Born blind, Templeton was a musical prodigy who played his first tune before he was two, and composed before he was four. After studying at London's Royal Academy and playing professionally in several symphonies, he arrived in the United States in 1936. He landed his own radio show "Alec Templeton Time" within three years. This NBC variety treat featured both his music and comedy. A talented mimic and satirist, Templeton humorously played modern popular songs in the manner of the great classics, such as Mozart, Beethoven, Bach and Strauss. He also did comic interpretations of great musical works. **SIDELIGHTS** His radio scripts were not done in Braille. He memorized them by listening to a professional reader go through them 20 times. His radio director communicated to him on air by *touch* cues: a shoulder squeeze meant start to speak or perform, a squeeze with the forefinger meant to speed it up, and a finger across the back meant to slow the tempo. **QUOTE** Because his parents never told him that he lacked sight, young Alec thought "everyone lived in darkness and recognized others by the pitch and tone of their voices." His parents never allowed the word "blind" to be said in their house. It was only at the age of seven, when a visitor accidentally said the word, that Alec learned he was different. An enthusiastic person who loved life, he said: "What I can't have, I don't think about." Died: 1963.

Strongheart 🎥 1750 Vine

German shepherd dog

BORN Etzel von Oeringen in Germany (sired by Nores von der Kriminal Politzei—undefeated champion) in 1918, in Germany. **SPOTLIGHTS** Military trained as a WWI police dog, he was brought as a three-year-old to America by screenwriter Jane Murfin and director Larry Trimble. A magnificent look-

Strongheart, the world's first famous movie dog, was introduced by Paramount Pictures.

Strongheart, as magazine cover dog

ing animal, this 115-pound canine was ferocious in both mood and actions. He literally marched like a soldier, imitating the gait of his original trainers. In Hollywood, he was a fighting machine, formidable in attack or defense. This, however, proved dangerous to his handlers. He flashed his long, sharp fangs many times, and hacked and slashed an equal number of times. This was due to his rigorous and brutal training in Germany. In Hollywood, Trimble took a *gentle* approach to the dog. He stayed with the dog 24 hours a day, seven days a week. They ate together, listened to music together, walked on the beach together, played together and slept together. He gave Strongheart his first box of toys and treats. As the dog began to trust him, some spontaniety appeared. Trimble rewarded and encouraged positive behavior, while *never* hitting or chain-choking bad behavior. He prided himself on his kind system of behavior modification. Over an intense period of many months, he successfully soothed the savage beast. His pet became a blue-ribbon champion, possessing the finest qualities of strength, speed, intelligence, courage, agility and fearlessness. Trimble's love of the dog, and the dog's love of him, made them virtually inseparable. Director-screenwriter William DeMille (Cecil's older brother) launched the dog in movies at Paramount Pictures. He made his screen debut in *The Silent Call* (1921), causing such widespread enthusiasm that he became an overnight sensation. He was the *first* canine hero on screen; another German shepherd dog named Rin-Tin-Tin made his film debut one and a half years later at Warner Bros. Trimble recalled, "His human counterparts on screen were pleased with Strongheart, for even though he tore their clothes

to shreds, he never left a mark of fang or nail on any actor." Amazingly, the dog understood he was just acting. Other films include *Brawn of the North, The Love Master* and London's *White Fang* (1925)...He'd pause every-day to autograph papers by step-ping down on a large ink pad, then pressing down on publicity photographs. **HIGHLIGHT** He had an overpowering instinctual sense of good and bad people. While lounging on his front lawn, he lifted his nose and sniffed the air of pedestrians on the sidewalk. He suddenly bolted after a specific individual. Time again proved Strongheart right in sniffing out the dregs of society. Even so-called important people the dog culled, later proved to be frauds, embezzlers, wife-beaters, etc. To honor him, a plaque was placed over his bed, quoting from the *Book of Job:* "Ask the very beasts, and they will teach you." Died: 1933.

Steve Cochran 📺   1750 Vine
Actor
BORN Robert Cocharan; May 25, 1917, in Eureka, CA. **SPOTLIGHTS** A six-foot tall, 175-pound, dark-haired, green-eyed, rough-and-tough macho guy, he was discovered by sex-pot Mae West. Cast in countless "heavy" villainous roles, he also played the "heel" who loves 'em and leaves 'em." Movies include *White Heat* (1949) opposite James Cagney, Virginia Mayo and Edmond O'Brien, *The Damned Don't Cry* (1950) opposite Joan Crawford, *Highway 301* (1950) with Virginia Grey, *Shark River* (1953) with Carole Matthews, and *Come Next Spring* (1956) co-starring Ann Sheridan. **TV** He starred in and co-produced the "Colonel John Fremont" series. He rejected full-time series work, including the leads in "Mr. Lucky," "Peter Gunn," and "Mike Hammer," preferring to take days off to be "captain of my boat." Died: 1965.

Carter De Haven 🎥   1724 Vine
Actor, director
BORN 1896, in Chicago, IL. **SPOTLIGHTS** An actor in *The College Orphan* (1915), he began directing films the very next year. Movies include *A Gentleman of Nerve* (1916). He brought smart, refined, graceful comedy to the screen. Died: 1977.

Lauren Bacall 🎥   1724 Vine
Actress
BORN Betty Joan Perske; Sept. 16, 1924, in New York, NY. **SPOTLIGHTS** An extraordinarily beautiful model turned actress, she made her stunning film debut opposite Humphrey Bogart in Warner Brothers' 1944 production of *To Have and Have Not*. It was the beginning of a beautiful relationship with

Lauren Bacall

"Bogie." Their chemistry onscreen was magical. She co-stars with Bogart in *The Big Sleep* (1946), *Dark Passage* (1947), and *Key Largo* (1948). Possessing sultry eyes, sensuous full lips, a husky voice, and poise, this tall, lean lady took Hollywood by storm. Other films include *Young Man With a Horn* (1950) opposite Kirk Douglas, *How to Marry a Millionaire* (1953) with Marilyn Monroe and Betty Grable, and *Designing Woman* (1957) with Gregory Peck. She never lost her cinematic touch. She plays Barbra Streisand's mother in *The Mirror Has Two Faces* (1996). That same year, she made *My Fellow American*, and the French film, *Le Jour et La Nuit* (The Day and the Night). She stars opposite Kirk Douglas again in *Diamonds* (1999), as an intriguing madam. An accomplished stage actress, her successful Broadway career includes her own show, "Goodbye Charlie," "Cactus Flower" and "Sweet Bird of Youth." **ACHIEVEMENTS** 1970 Tony Award "Applause"; 1981 Tony Award "Woman of the Year." **SIGNATURE MOVIE LINE** "If you want anything, all you have to do is whistle." **HIGHLIGHTS** She became Bogart's female lead in real life in 1945 as his wife and mother of their two children, Stephen and Leslie. Widowed in 1957, her second marriage to Jason Robards (1961-'73) produced a son, Sam Robards. **QUOTE** "Good taste is a difficult commodity to find in Hollywood."

Eddie Fisher 📺   **1724 Vine**
See page 202

Mary Miles Minter 🎥   **1724 Vine**
Actress
BORN Juliet Riley; April 1, 1902, in Shreveport, LA. **SPOTLIGHTS** A very pretty and precocious child, she was one of the most popular young stars on Broadway. Her determined stage mother pushed her into silent films in *The Nurse* (1912). She blossomed into a romantic leading lady. An apathetic Tinseltown gasped when Paramount studio executive Adolph Zukor signed the teenager to a three-year contract at $1.3 million—in 1919! She was doing swell until 1922 when she became linked to a real life murder mystery involving her sometimes boyfriend, director William Desmond Taylor.

Minter was instantly burdened with guilt by association and the scandal ruined her. (It was later concluded by director King Vidor that Minter's greedy mother had most likely committed the vicious crime.) The aptly entitled *Drums of Fate* (1923) was one of her last films before retirement. In 1981 Minter made the news again, this time as the victim of a home robbery. She was found on the kitchen floor, badly beaten, gagged and left for dead. After she died in 1984, her cremated ashes were scattered over the Pacific Ocean.

Norman Z. McLeod 🎥   **1724 Vine**
Director
BORN Sept. 20, 1898, in Grayling, MI. **SPOTLIGHTS** An assistant director on *Wings* (1927), the first picture to win an Academy Award, he advanced to a director. He specialized in comedies: *Monkey Business* (1931), *It's a Gift* (1934), *Topper* (1937), *The Secret Life of Walter Mitty* (1947), and *The Paleface* (1948). Died: 1964.

Ben Lyon 🎥   **1724 Vine**
Actor

Ben Lyon

BORN Feb. 6, 1901, in Atlanta, GA. **SPOTLIGHTS** *Open Your Eyes* (1919) introduced this genial young actor to the film world, and it liked what it saw. He was his own stunt pilot in his best-remembered film, Howard Hughes' *Hell's Angels* (1930). Versatile and immensely popular in England, he did two radio series there. He also served in England's Royal Air Force during World War II. His career spanned 46 years. **ACHIEVEMENTS** Awarded the Order of the British Empire by Queen Elizabeth II. **QUOTE** "If I say something about how I 'made the grade' it may help others to decide their particular cases. I spent several years on the legitimate stage, both stock and metropolitan productions. I especially value my stock company training, because it is here that an actor is called upon to play a wide range of parts, from juveniles to characters. It gave me that training so necessary to the finished actor. So, therefore, it would seem that my advice would be: Get into a stock company, if possible. Play small 'bits' to begin with. Play any character called upon. Gain all the experience you can in this manner, and that poise, confidence, and dramatic expression so vital to success on the screen will be a part of your repertoire. As a substitute I would advise the amateur stage. Enter enthusiastically into church and social theatricals. Musical comedy, dancing and singing is an asset to getting ahead in motion pictures." Died: 1979.

Lionel Barrymore 🎥   **1724 Vine**
Actor, writer, director, composer

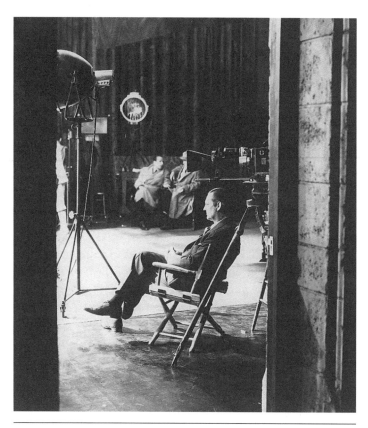

Lionel Barrymore

BORN Lionel Blythe; April 28, 1878, in Philadelphia, PA. **SPOTLIGHTS** As a child, he did not want to follow in his father's footsteps. Although the Barrymores enjoyed distinguished careers in legitimate theater, he detested the family's acting business. Although his parents had introduced him to the stage as a child, he withstood their pressure to follow them into the limelight as he grew. Ultimately, his parents forced the teen onto the stage. Whether he inherited his talent genetically, or learned the art of acting through osmosis, Lionel Barrymore proved to be a brilliant talent of enormous stature, proving sometimes father does know best. A stage success before honoring the silver screen with his presence, he discovered there *were* a few differences between the two mediums. While watching a screening of his second film, *Friends* (1912), with co-star Mary Pickford, he was shocked to see his appearance. He asked the teenager, "Am I really that fat?" America's Sweetheart answered in a soft voice with her eyes cast downward to the floor, "I'm sorry, Mr. Barrymore, but you are." The 33-year-old Barrymore made a resolution that instant: "No more beer for me." He strictly dieted and ran through Central Park with four sweaters on daily. He downsized substantially. He became a dominant, hardworking cinemactor whose vital presence was felt in more than 100 films, including *Mata Hari* (1932) with Greta Garbo, *Dinner at Eight* (1932) with Jean Harlow, *David Copperfield* (1935), *Camille* (1936), *Since You Went Away* (1944), *The Valley of Decision* (1945), *Duel in the Sun* (1946), *Key Largo* (1948), and *Down to the Sea in Ships* (1949). His portrayal of Dr. Gillespie was extremely popular in the MGM series *Dr. Kildare* (15 features starting in the late 1930s) and on radio. He also played Judge Hardy in the first

Andy Hardy movie, *A Family Affair* (1937), starring Mickey Rooney. **RADIO** Among his countless broadcasts, the annual telling of Charles Dickens' classic tale "A Christmas Carol" is considered his finest work. It was stated that Barrymore captured the inherent nature of "that grasping, clutching, conniving, covetous old sinner, Ebenezer Scrooge," as no one else could. These splendid annual broadcasts started in 1934, and continued for two decades. **ACHIEVEMENTS** 1931 Best Actor Oscar for *A Free Soul*. **SIDELIGHTS** In 1938 he was confined to a wheelchair due to crippling arthritis. He chose to ignore his disability and acknowledge his work. He plays the evil Mr. Potter in *It's a Wonderful Life* (1946), whose wicked designs are not diminished by his physical confines. Died: 1954.

Robert Benchley 🎥 1724 Vine
Screenwriter, humorist, actor
BORN Sept. 15, 1889, in Worcester, MA. **SPOTLIGHTS** He wrote (and sometimes appears in) humorous "how to" shorts: *How To Behave* (1936), *How to Become a Detective* (1936), and *How to Figure Income Tax* (1938). All ideal for the Depression-era 1930s-1940s. When he was writing at MGM, he never stepped foot into his office. Thinking that he did not like it, executives ordered a bigger and more luxurious suite. Benchley still did not show. After studio bigwigs begged him to see it, he showed up with maps, charts and blueprints. He walked in, taped all the papers to the walls, stuck push pins in, then never saw the office again. **ACHIEVEMENTS** 1935 Oscar for *How to Sleep*. Died: 1945.

Ida Lupino 📺 1724 Vine
See page 20

William Faversham 🎥 1724 Vine
Actor
BORN Feb. 12, 1868, in England. **SPOTLIGHTS** Born the youngest of 11 sons, Willie ran away from home to become an actor. He started on the London stage in "Swiss Cottage" in 1886. He was an outstanding success in "A Doll's House" and "The Prince and the Pauper." Preferring Shakespeare, he did "Hamlet," "Othella" and "Romeo and Juliet." Onscreen, this six-foot, one-inch tall, 180-pound, black-haired, green-eyed talent became a top matinee idol. Films include *The Man Who Lost Himself* (1920) and *The Sin That Was His* (1921). **QUOTE** "I loved the 50 years of my life I spent onstage." Died: 1940.

Dick Haymes ● 1724 Vine
See page 233

Jon Hall 🎥 1724 Vine
Actor
BORN Charles Hall Locher; Feb. 23, 1913, in Fresno, CA. **SPOTLIGHTS** Hall inherited his good looks and athletic prowess from both his maternal and paternal family sides. His grandmother was Queen of Tahiti; his father was a figure-skating champion in 1910 and 1911. While waiting in a reception

room for his uncle (Norman Hall, co-author of *Mutiny on the Bounty*) to finish a writer's meeting, Sam Goldwyn offered him a $500- a-week contract on the spot. He had no interest in acting, but signed anyway as Goldwyn was a persuasive man. The studio mogul billed him "Goldwyn's Gift to Women" in John Ford's *Hurricane* (1937). In it, the leading man did all his own water stunts, including an amazing 131-foot dive. His eastern/western beefcake good looks enabled him to play roles from Westerns like *Kit Carson* (1940) to exotic fare like *The Tuttles of Tahiti, Arabian Nights* (both 1942) and *Ali Baba and the Forty Thieves* (1943). 1950s TV: Played Dr. Tom Reynolds (Ramar) on "Ramar of the Jungle," a syndicated show. **SIDELIGHTS** His pregnant mother was riding a train when she went into labor. The train made an emergency stop; which is why he was born in Fresno. **QUOTE** "I never liked acting. I don't like to be told what to do and what to say and how to say it. I'm grateful to it as it provided me with the money to do other things, but as a profession, it's a bore." Died: 1979.

Lew Ayres 1724 Vine
See page 113

Deanna Durbin 1724 Vine

Deanna Durbin and Joseph Cotten

Singer, actress
BORN Edna Mae Durbin; Dec. 4, 1921, in Winnipeg, Canada. **SPOTLIGHTS** A sweet, energetic 15-year-old whose box office receipts from her first film *Three Smart Girls* (1936) saved Universal Studios from bankruptcy. Hit musical after hit musical, like *100 Men and a Girl* (1937), and *Mad About You* (1938), were fashioned around her excellent singing voice, charm, and good nature. For a change from her sweet ingenue roles, see *Christmas Holiday* (1944), where her character falls in love with a convict (Gene Kelly). **ACHIEVEMENTS** 1938 Special Oscar for "bringing to the screen the spirit and personification of youth." Actor Mickey Rooney also shared the Academy's honor. She earned all-time top dollar for a leading lady. **SIDELIGHTS** Never comfortable in front of the camera, director Henry Koster had to teach Durbin acting basics at her home during the evening. He instructed her: "The mouth goes up in the corners when you smile and goes down when you cry." Eager to get out of Hollywood, she moved permanently to France with her husband in 1949. *Sacre Bleu!*

Sarah Vaughan 1724 Vine
Singer, pianist
BORN March 27, 1924, in Newark, NJ. **SPOTLIGHTS** The "Divine One" of jazz had a smoky contralto voice of vast range and power. The sheer scope of Miss Vaughan's cords and her musical instincts were first heard at her local church. She hadn't planned on going into show business, but a church friend dared her to try to win the $10 prize money on amateur night at New York's Apollo Theater in 1942. She accompanied herself with grace on the keyboard that night. Billy Eckstine (a vocalist who later formed his own band) and band leader Earl "Fatha" Hines heard that sweet, flexible, richly controlled tone and vibrato. She was hired as a singer/pianist. She toured with Dizzy Gillespie and Charlie Parker training her voice to imitate their trumpet and saxophone. Vaughan did well with the intimacy of clubs and small concert halls, but won a massive international following, singing with major symphony orchestras and for heads of state. Nicknamed "Sassy" for her on stage manner, her favorite hit songs include "Body and Soul," "It's Magic," "The Lord's Prayer," "Sometimes I Feel Like a Motherless Child," "Send in the Clowns," "Once in a While," "Lullaby of Birdland," "Lover Man," "Shulie A Bop," "Say It Isn't So," "I've Got the World on a String," "In a Sentimental Mood," and "I'm Just a Lucky So-And-So." **ACHIEVEMENTS** 1981 Emmy "Rhapsody and Song," a tribute to George Gershwin. Singer Ella Fitzgerald called her, "the greatest singing talent in the world today." **QUOTE** She scoffed at critics who tried to categorize her as a jazz vocalist, as she liked to record popular and standard songs, too. She said, "I just sing. I sing whatever I can." Died: 1990.

Blue Barron 1724 Vine
Musician, band leader
BORN Harry Friedland; Mar. 22, 1911, in Cleveland, OH. **SPOTLIGHTS** As orchestra leader he led Blue Barron on big band remote broadcasts from nightclubs, ballrooms, and hotels throughout the country in the 1930s - '40s. Known as a novelty band that ad-libbed silly jokes and copied one of Kay Kyser's most commercial gimmicks, the singing song titles, Blue Barron was also known as a sweet band featuring syrupy sounding saxes, muted brasses and quiet rhythm sections. With tunes like "Sometimes I'm Happy," they appealed to a large group of fans. They were at the top of the heap with the other types of swing era bands. Harry was a short, pudgy musical trickster with a sense of humor about himself and his melody. He legally changed his name to Blue Barron.

George "Gabby" Hayes   1724 Vine
See page 107

Mr. and Mrs. Sidney Drew 1724 Vine
Actors, producers, directors
BORN Mr.; Aug. 28, 1864, in New York. Mrs.; Jane Morrow; Apr.18, 1890. **SPOTLIGHTS** This very funny couple shared a magical chemistry in the popular "Mr. and Mrs. Sidney Drew" film series (1915-'19). A terrific comedy team, they started the screen's fine tradition of domestic social comedy. Their work was intelligent and refined. One definitive picture is *The*

Professional Patient (1912), where Drew is hired by a dentist to pose as a cheerful, satisfied client to reassure nervous customers. His job forces him to have various painful dental procedures done throughout the day. He must emerge from the dentist's office into the waiting room smiling and happy each time. *The Amateur Liar* (1919) is a classic where he slips out one little white lie which snowballs into a gigantic one...He was one of the Drew-Barrymore theatrical tribe. She was also their screenwriter. Died: Mr. 1919; Mrs. 1925.

Irish McCalla   1724 Vine
Actress, artist
BORN Dec. 25, 1929. **SPOTLIGHTS** She starred as the sexy lead in TV's "Sheena, Queen of the Jungle." The 1950s series was based on the comic. She made 'B' pictures like *She Demons* (1960) before turning to painting, for which she achieved some acceptance in the art world.

Ella Mae Morse ●   1724 Vine
Singer
BORN Sept. 12, 1924, in Mansfield, TX. **SPOTLIGHTS** A charismatic, big band swing singer, she was discovered by Jimmy Dorsey at a jam session--at age 14. He noted her great beat and remarkable sense of phrasing, though it was Dorsey pianist Freddy Slack who starred the teenager on his record. At age 18, Ella Mae Morse became Capitol Records first successful talent discovery. Her and Slack's boogie-woogie novelty number, "Cow Cow Bogie" was a tremendous success. The year was 1942 and her hit provided the struggling record company with plenty of shellac. Other songs include ""The House of Blue Lights," "Pigfoot Pete," "Shoo Shoo Baby," "Patty Cake Man," and "40 Cups of Coffee." Died: 1999.

Paul Henreid   1724 Vine
See page 384

Mark Robson   1724 Vine
Director
BORN Dec. 4, 1913, in Canada. **SPOTLIGHTS** An established editor on Tourneur's hit, *Cat People* (1942), led to his directing a "B" horror flick, *The Seventh Victim* (1943). The nightmarish tale proved he had the right stuff. He made a few films, before boxing his way into fame as a director with *Champion* (1949), starring Kirk Douglas. He showcased actress Susan Hayward in *My Foolish Heart* (1949), and had a huge success with the ultimate soap opera *Peyton Place* (1957), starring Lana Turner, Hope Lange and Arthur Kennedy. Robson earned an Oscar nomation for *Inn of the Sixth Happiness* (1958), based on a true story and starring Ingrid Bergman. He made the all-time trashiest film, *Valley of the Dolls* (1967). Later, he rocked audiences in *Earthquake* (1974), starring Charlton Heston and Ava Gardner. Died: 1978.

Hoagy Carmichael   1724 Vine
Songwriter, pianist, singer, actor

Hoagy Carmichael

BORN Nov. 22, 1899, in Bloomington, IN. **SPOTLIGHTS** A laid-back cat who played hot piano and wrote some cool tunes. In 1927, his original melody for "Stardust" (words by Mitchell Parish) turned into one of the biggest hits of the swing era. Significantly, it became one of America's 20th century's most important musical works; to date, it has been recorded more than 800 times. His exciting version of "Rockin' Chair" featured electrifying trumpeter Roy Eldridge with drummer Gene Krupa. It was Hoagy's song called "Judy" that gave vocalist Ella Fitzgerald her first big break. **SIDELIGHT** His recording debut was set for a tune called "Washboard Blues." While Hoagy was rehearsing, Bing Crosby approached. Bing asked, "Let me see the words, Hoagy." Hoagy responded, "What for?" Bing said tactfully, "I'd just like to learn it." Hoagy questioned, "What for? I'm gonna sing it." Bing stated, "Sure, but it's a swell number and I'd like to learn it." Later, Hoagy wrote, "Dumb? Well, yes. I didn't realize for months that Paul Whiteman wanted some insurance. If I couldn't do it, he wanted somebody there who could. Bing was being kind. He didn't want me to know I might flop. They had a date to make a record whether I was on it or not." Songs include "Lazybones," and "Riverboat Shuffle." Director Hawks cast him as Crickett in *To Have and Have Not* (1944). Next, he made *Johnny Angel* (1945), *The Best Years of Our Lives* (1946), and *Young Man With a Horn* (1950). **ACHIEVEMENTS** 1951 Academy Award for his song "In the Cool Cool Cool of the Evening." Died: 1981.

George Pal   1724 Vine
Special effects man, director
BORN Feb. 1, 1908, in Cegled, Hungary. **SPOTLIGHTS** Crowned Hollywood's "Special Effects Wizard," he was the most creative technical artist during the 1940s - '50s. He made his directorial debut with *Tom Thumb* (1958), and won another Special Effects Oscar. 1943 Special Oscar. Special Effects Awards for *Destination Moon* (1950); *When Worlds Collide* (1951); *War of the Worlds* (1953); and *The Time Machine* (1960). Pal also created the Puppetoon. Died: 1980.

Rod Cameron   1724 Vine
Actor
BORN Nathan Cox; Dec. 7, 1910, in Canada. **SPOTLIGHTS** A real-life construction worker, he spent ten years building houses while trying to open one door in Hollywood. His physical labor paid off with a strong body, an added bonus to his already rugged, dark-haired good looks. At a height of 6' 4" he broke in as a stunt double for cowboy Buck Jones, and later

Rod Cameron

worked as a stand-in for Fred MacMurray. He was disappointed when the scenes he appeared in were left on the editing floor of his very first movie. He fared better with the next couple: *The Quarterback* (1940) and *Christmas in July* (1940),. He rose to leading man. He made about 80 films, including *Belle Starr's Daughter* (1948), *Cavalry Scout* (1951), and *Double Jeopardy* (1955). **TV** He starred as Trooper Rod Blake in the police drama "State Trooper" (1956-'59). **SIDELIGHTS** Offscreen, his unconventional love life led to a strange relationship; he married his third wife's mother and became his own son-in-law. Died: 1983.

Vera Vague  1724 Vine

Actress, comedian

BORN Barbara Jo Allen; Sept. 2, 1905, in New York, NY. **SPOTLIGHTS** Vera Vague was a funny, scatterbrained "man-chasing" old maid character created by Barbara Jo Allen in the 1930s. Allen enjoyed much success as the squeaky Vague on air and in revues, before bringing her to NBC radio's "The Bob Hope Show" in 1943. Her catchphrase was "Yoo-hoo!...oh, Mr.

Vera Vague

Hope!...Yoo-hoo!" She also worked as Vague on radio's "The Edgar Bergen/Charlie McCarthy Show," and "The Signal Carnival." Her movie credits alternated between the Allen and Vague names. Films include: *Melody Ranch* (1940), *The Mad Doctor* (1941), *Larceny, Inc.* (1946), and *The Opposite Sex* (1956). Died: 1974.

Mercedes McCambridge  1722 Vine

Actress

BORN Carlotta Mercedes Agnes McCambridge; March 17, 1918, in Joliet, IL. **SPOTLIGHTS** While attending Mundelein College, this intelligent student began working on the air in radio. A superb talent, her well-trained voice became a much sought-after commodity. Orson Welles declared, "She's the world's greatest living radio actress." This artist brought her considerable gifts to the stage, and the silver screen. Movies include *Johnny Guitar* (1954), where the youthful McCambridge and Joan Crawford engage in a Western cat fight; *Giant* (1956--in an Oscar-nominated performance) with Rock Hudson, Elizabeth Taylor, and James Dean; Orson Welles' *Touch of Evil* (1958); the epic Western *Cimarron*

(1960) with Glenn Ford; and *Angel Baby* (1961--in Burt Reynold's screen debut). Using her power and mastery of language and sound, she scared the hell out of an entire generation of filmgoers. She did the voice-over for Satan in *The Exorcist* (1973--uncredited). **ACHIEVEMENTS** 1949 Best Supporting Actress Oscar for *All the King's Men*; it was her first movie! She penned two autobiographies: *The Two of Us* (1960), and *A Quality of Mercy* (1981).

Mercedes McCambridge

Lillian Gish  1722 Vine

Actress

BORN Lillian De Guiche; Oct. 14, 1896, in Springfield, OH. **SPOTLIGHTS** Miss Gish elegantly wore the crown of "The First Lady of Film," and was, without question, the greatest actress of the silent era. She established the rules for movie acting, paving the way for all future screen actresses. She teamed with "the father of film," director D.W. Griffith (although DeMille claimed this title, too), who among other things developed the close-up, yet it was Miss Gish who decided what to do with it. She had a fragile beauty, a sensitive, delicate look that pleases when her quiet reservoir of inner strength bubbles up. She cleverly played a variety of heroines, including these films (which remain a marvel to watch): *Birth of a Nation* (1915), *Intolerance* (1916), *Hearts of the World* (1916), *Broken Blossoms* (1919), *Way Down East* (1920), *Orphans of the Storm* (1921), *The White Sister* (1923), *Romola* (1924), *The Scarlet Letter* (1926), and the must-see great film, *The Wind* (1928). Gish turned in outstanding performances in the talkies, too:

Lillian Gish

Duel in the Sun (1946), *The Night of the Hunter* (1955), *Orders to Kill* (1958), and *The Whales of August* (1987). **ACHIEVEMENTS** 1970 Special Oscar. Her theatrical and screen career spanned eight decades...Her last wishes stipulated that most of her $10 million estate be used to establish "The Dorothy and Lillian Prize" in memory of her actress sister and herself. This annual award is given to some lucky person in the performing arts. If you're a performer, check it out. She died at the age of 99, months shy of her 100th birthday, in 1993.

Garry Moore   1722 Vine

Garry Moore

Comedian, host
BORN Thomas Garrison Morfit; Jan. 31, 1915, in Baltimore, MD. **SPOTLIGHTS** He started working as a radio announcer at age 24, in 1939. In 1943 he got his big break working on "The Jimmy Durante Show." Audiences roared at his delivery of timely tongue-twisters to Durante. This was an especially impressive feat because he suffered from stuttering. (Previously Moore could not say two consecutive words without stuttering. He said, "I endured a lengthy, arduous study in a special school to overcome this painful problem. It was the most difficult thing I ever suffered.") Ironically, he became one the most popular chatterboxes on television. The happy, perpetually modest fellow initially brought daytime television away from soap operas. Then, he went prime time. His two long-running shows were "The Garry Moore Show," (variety) and "I've Got a Secret" (quiz); the latter successfully competed against the top-rated "What's My Line?" He was known as "the Haircut," with his trademark crew cut and brash bowtie. **QUOTE** Moore's shows were always rating failures at first, then took off strong. About their dismal beginnings, he reflected, "I try too hard." Died: 1993.

Steve Allen   1720 Vine

Actor, composer, writer
BORN Dec. 26, 1921, in New York, NY. **SPOTLIGHTS** A true renaissance genius. A rare thinking man who is also hilarious, he is capable of communicating to the masses as well as the intelligentsia. CBS provided the network air time, he provided the fun on the "Steve Allen Show" (1950-'52). In a moment of foresight, he commented, "I *created* 'The Tonight Show.'" He originally hosted the talk show locally in New York in 1953, then, went with NBC network 1954-'57. In 1955 he made his feature film debut starring in Universal's *The Benny Goodman Story*, with lots of music to swing by. Allen created one of the most original shows ever, "Meeting of Minds" (PBS). This concept took prominent figures in history, such as Cleopatra, Aristotle, Voltaire, Thomas Paine and Gandhi, and put them

in provocative round-table debates; a brilliant way to bring history to life, and life to history. He has a lengthy radio resume in comedy/variety, he wrote the Broadway venture "Sophie" based on the life of Sophie Tucker, and the score for CBS-TV's "Alice in Wonderland." He is married to the beautiful actress Jayne Meadows. **ACHIEVEMENTS** Composer of 6,000 songs, including "This Could Be the Start of Something Big," "South Rampart Street Parade," "Picnic," "Pretend You

Steve Allen

Don't See Her," "With You," and his Grammy Award winning "Gravy Waltz." He has collaborated with such noted composers as George Duning, Neal Hefti, Jimmy McHugh, Pete Rugulo and Erroll Garner and has recorded 52 albums. In 1978 he won the distinguished Peabody Award for "Meeting of Minds," and in 1986 was inducted into the Television Academy Hall of Fame. An inspired and tireless artist, Allen has also written 52 books, including *Dumbth, and 101 Ways to Reason Better & Improve Your Mind, Make 'Em Laugh, The Man Who Turned Back the Clock and Other Short Stories*...With all of his accomplishments, Allen remains a kind gentleman.

Beulah Bondi 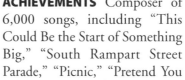   1718 Vine

Actress
BORN Beulah Bondy; May 3, 1892, in Chicago, IL. **SPOTLIGHTS** Her family had no theatrical background, other than the slight connection that her mother—a natural born linguist—had trained young Beulah in elocution. Yet by the time Beulah was nine, she shined in the limelight playing "Little Lord Fauntleroy." Thirteen years later, she played a grandmother onstage, and portrayed an "old lady" in show business ever since. Amazingly, her aged roles in more than 50 films were diversified. Movies include *Arrowsmith* (1931), *Mr. Smith Goes to Washington* (1939), *Our Town* (1940), *One Foot in Heaven* (1941), *Watch on the Rhine* (1943), *The Snake Pit* (1948), and *So Dear to My Heart* (1948). Died: 1981.

Lauritz Melchior ●   1718 Vine

Opera singer
BORN Lebrecht Hommel; March 20, 1890, in Copenhagen, Denmark. **SPOTLIGHTS** This jovial, enormous Dane was originally a baritone who became a tenor—the best *heldentenor*. Siegfried was one of his most famous roles. Melchior made his Metropolitan Opera debut as *Tannhauser* in 1926; in subsequent performances his constant partner was the no-nonsense diva Kirsten Flagstad. Together they created instant classics like *Tristan* under Fritz Reiner. Critics proclaimed it the *Tristan* of the century. The two kept the Met afloat during its dark financial days of the Depression with two sold-out performances a

week (while consciously keeping their salary demands low). He enjoyed tremendous radio play and in the 1940s sold many a platter (record). **SIDELIGHTS** Prior to WWII, he bought a fairy tale estate in Germany. Forced to flee the Nazis in 1939, the Fascists seized his manor, his forest and his lake. They used it for a training camp. Then, after the war, the Communists confiscated it for a workers' vacation home. When East Germany was reunified with West Germany, the solitary government took it. All the while, Melchior's son, Ib, has been battling the German government to return the estate to his family. To date, more than a half a century later, it remains in dispute. **QUOTE** "Don't just be a singer and nothing more, because if you are a one-track person you won't be a good singer! It is not enough to sing with technical skill. There must be feeling as well, and that can be expressed only if one has lived intensely and experienced joy and sorrow." Died: 1973.

Mickey Rooney 🎥   1718 Vine

Mickey Rooney and Judy Garland

Actor, singer, dancer
BORN Joe Yule, Jr.; Sept. 23, 1920, in Brooklyn, NY. **SPOTLIGHTS** The son of vaudevillians, Rooney was a wobbly toddler when he first crawled onstage. He cheered on the orchestra's drummer, the audience went wild, and, at 15 months Rooney had enjoyed his first big laugh. By age two, he was singing "Pal of My Cradle Days" to such enormous applause that his parents decided his career was in show business—*now*—not in the future. He performed in vaudeville for the next two years. Fiercely quick-witted, he made his screen debut in *Not to be Trusted* at age five—appearing as a midget! His screen charisma was undeniable. Rooney became a studio workhorse. As the star in the *Mickey McGuire* series, he made a total of 78 shorts. These two-reel film comedies were based on the derby-hatted comic strip character of the same name. His job ended in 1932 when, at age 12, he had outgrown the part. In 1935 he won acclaim from critics and fans alike for two performances: as the brother in O'Neill's tender coming-of-age comedy, *Ah, Wilderness*, and as the enchanting fairy spirit, Puck, in Shakespeare's *A Midsummer Night's Dream*. Many consider his work in the latter a masterpiece. In 1936 he appeared in the classic family drama *Little Lord Fauntleroy*. At age 16, MGM cast him as Andy Hardy in a low-budget picture entitled *A Family Affair* (1937) co-starring Lionel Barrymore. Although the studio did not expect much out of it, audiences found the look at small-town America charming and loads of fun. He appeared in 15 smash box-office sequels, prompting one accountant to remark: "He makes more money for his employ-

ers than Clark Gable, Greta Garbo and Spencer Tracy combined." That same year, he appears in *Captains Courageous* starring Spencer Tracy in one of Tracy's Academy Award-winning roles. Two of Rooney's close acting associates—Freddie Bartholomew and Lionel Barrymore—also graced this spectacular family adventure. Rooney gave a truly inspired performance in the sentimental classic *Boys' Town* (1938), as a bully who comes clean. Other motion pictures include *Babes in Arms* (1939), *The Human Comedy* (1943) and the exquisite family film, *National Velvet* (1944). Rooney's career was interrupted by World War II. He served in the U.S. Army as a corporal. The war changed everything. He had a tough-go at trying to make a comeback, then settled into character roles: *The Bridges at Toko-Ri* (1954), *Baby Face Nelson* (1957) and *The Last Mile* (1959). In 1998, he co-stars in the wonderful animal comedy, *Babe, Pig in the City*. TV: Star of "The Mickey Rooney Show," situation comedy (1954-'55). Emmy winner for "Bill." **BROADWAY** In 1979 he took to the bright lights with "Sugar Babies" and has toured America with the hit musical show. **ACHIEVEMENTS** 1938 Special Academy Award. The inscription on the Oscar reads for "significant contribution in bringing to the screen the spirit and personification of youth, and as a juvenile player setting a high standard of ability and achievement." From 1938 - '44 he was one of the most popular stars. In 1940 and '41 he was *the* world's biggest star.

Robert Cummings 📺   1718 Vine

See page 65

Donald Cook 📺   1718 Vine
Actor
BORN Sept. 26, 1900, in Portland, OR. **SPOTLIGHTS** A supporting and leading actor rooted in early radio dramas and comedies. Before shifting to television playhouses, anthologies and series ("Too Young To Go Steady"—1959), Cook was a reliable character actor in such great films as *The Public Enemy* (1931), and *Viva Villa!* (1934). Died: 1961.

Laird Cregar 🎥   1718 Vine
Actor
BORN Samuel L. Cregar; July 28, 1916, in Philadelphia, PA. **SPOTLIGHTS** A tall, six-foot, three-inch nightclub bouncer who broke into show business at age 23. An extremely overweight, dark-haired (often seen sporting a goatee), villainous-type character actor, he portrayed the devil with relish in *Heaven Can Wait* (1943), and delivered a powerful performance as Jack the Ripper in *The Lodger* (1944). He was wonderful in comedies, too: *Charley's Aunt* (1941). Died: 1944 of a heart attack while on a crash diet.

Al Jolson 🎵   1718 Vine
See page 423

Lila Lee 🎥   1718 Vine
Actress

*Lila Lee and Lon Chaney in MGM's **The Unholy Three** (1930).*

BORN Augusta Appel; July 25, 1901, in Union Hill, NY. **SPOTLIGHTS** A vaudeville child star of the popular "School Days" (also "School Daze") act in the years before WWI, she blossomed into an elegant, open-faced leading lady in silents. She made her screen debut in *The Cruise of the Make-Believe* (1918), at age 17. Her breakthrough film to international superstardom was *Blood and Sand* (1922), opposite Rudolph Valentino. Movies include *The Ghost Breaker* (1922), and *Woman Proof* (1923). This throaty-voiced, charming beauty worked in talkies in supporting roles: *The Ex-Mrs. Bradford* (1936) and *Two Wise Maids* (1937). Died: 1973.

Bebe Daniels   1718 Vine
Actress

BORN Virginia Daniels; Jan. 14, 1901, in Dallas, TX. **SPOTLIGHTS** The bubbly teenage brunette played opposite comic Harold Lloyd for $10-$100 per week. At Paramount Pictures, Rudolph Valentino romanced "the vamp" (at $1,000 per week). Daniels, one of the studio's warm, beautiful star comediennes, earned $5,000 per week. She appears in talkies in such wonderful works as *Counsellor-at-Law* (1933), with John Barrymore. **QUOTE** In 1924 she wrote, "Is There a Chance for Everyone in Moving Pictures? No, most assuredly there is not. It is worse than folly for persons to imagine that this business is an easy road to money, to contentment or to that strange quality called happiness." She retired in 1955. Died: 1971.

Delbert Mann   1718 Vine
Director

BORN Jan. 30, 1920, in Lawrence, KS. **SPOTLIGHTS** He was educated at the Yale School of Drama before serving in WWII as an Army Air Corp. bomber pilot. He directed television—two of Paddy Chayevsky's works—"Marty" (starring Rod Steiger) and "The Bachelor Party." Hollywood kicked down his door to get him to repeat *Marty* (1955) for the big screen. He won an Academy Award his first crack at the silver screen. (Also see the Ernest Borgnine biography in this book; he

played the lead in the film version.) Movies include *The Bachelor Party* (1957) with Carolyn Jones, *Separate Tables* (1958) with David Niven, Rita Hayworth and Burt Lancaster, *The Outsider* (1961) with Tony Curtis, *Lover Come Back* (1961) starring Doris Day and Rock Hudson, and *That Touch of Mink* (1962) with Doris Day and Cary Grant. He continued to direct TV. He adapted these classics: "Heidi" (1968), "David Copperfield" (1970), and "Jane Eyre" (1971).

Dorothy Malone   1718 Vine
Actress

Dorothy Malone

BORN Dorothy Eloise Maloney; Jan. 30, 1925, in Dallas, TX. **SPOTLIGHTS** A tall, lovely leading lady with large, soulful eyes, porcelain skin and a perfect heart-shaped face, she made her silver screen debut in *Gildersleeve on Broadway* (1943). Her breakthrough was in the film noir *The Big Sleep* (1946). Malone co-stars opposite Humphrey Bogart and Lauren Bacall in this classic crime picture. She was on screen for a dozen years as a brunette, before she blondes really did have more fun. Other motion pictures include *Two Guys from Texas* (1948), *One Sunday Afternoon* (1948), *Scared Stiff* (1953), *Artists and Models* (1955), *Battle Cry* (1955), *The Tarnished Angels* (1957), *Man of a Thousand Faces* (1957), *Too Much, Too Soon* (1958--as Diana Barrymore), *Warlock* (1959—a Western), *Beach Party* (1963), *The Man Who Would Not Die* (1975), *Winter Kills* (1979), *The Day Time Ended* (1980), and *The Being* (1983). She played an ex-con lesbian murderess opposite Sharon Stone in *Basic Instinct* (1992). She appears in more than 60 films. In TV, Malone's credits include the popular "Peyton Place" series, and numerous guest-starring roles. **ACHIEVEMENTS** 1956 Best Supporting Actress Oscar for *Written on the Wind*.

Kay Starr   1708 Vine
Big Band Singer

BORN Katherine Starks; July 31, 1922, in Dougherty, OK. **SPOTLIGHTS** Born on a Native American Indian reservation, she was blessed with golden vocal cords. As a teen, this very attractive brunette was featured on "The Bob Crosby Show" (CBS-Radio, 1939), but as Crosby admitted, "We couldn't hold onto her." This vibrant youth sang with Joe Venuti—truly one of the greatest jazz violinists. Her terrific voice was heard in the 1940s on "The Chesterfield Supper Club" with Sammy Kaye's and Glenn Miller's orchestras. Her extremely popular big band songs include "Baby Me," and "Love, with a Capitol You." She recorded the rare Hoagy Carmichael melody "A Woman Likes to Be Told." In the 1950s, she was a pop star with hits "Wheel of Fortune," and "Rock and Roll Waltz." Other tunes include "Fool, Fool, Fool," and "Noah." She was one of Elvis Presley's two favorite female singers (the other was Patti Page--see her bio in this book).

Dave Brubeck ⦿   1708 Vine
Pianist, composer
BORN Dec. 6, 1920, in Concord, CA. **SPOTLIGHTS** His mother, a pianist, continued to play the keyboard throughout all her pregnancies. Two of her sons became music professors and composers, while Brubeck became a significant innovator in modern jazz. As a child, he officially began piano lessons from his mom at age four. He took cello at age nine. By age 13, he played gigs for Dixieland, swing and local hillbilly tunes. After WWII he formed his own octet, then trio, then quartet, becoming known for his interest in unconventional time (exploring beyond the basic 4/4). In 1954 his jazz combo hit big in San Francisco; they were known as one of the most popular progressive groups. His landmark 1959 album *Time Out* marked a focal point in jazz history—with its *first* million-seller, "Take Five." Hits include "Blue Rondo a La Turk, "Kathy's Waltz," "Unsquare Dance," "In Your Own Sweet Way," "Perdido," "Three to Get Ready," and "How High the Moon." **ACHIEVEMENTS** Recipient of dozens of awards. His family's musical dynasty includes Brubeck's sons—who have all played with him—drummer Danny, keyboardist Darius, bassist and trombonist Chris. He celebrated his 50th wedding anniversary with his wife Iola in 1992. Brubeck and his wife have endowed a program for the study of jazz at the University of the Pacific, in Stockton, California, where they are both alumni. **QUOTE** "First, a jazz group is simply no good unless everyone cooperates." And about those listening to him live in clubs, Brubeck said, "What counts is a genuine attitude of attentiveness and mutual response between players and audience."

Dave Brubeck at piano

Miriam Hopkins 📺   1708 Vine
See page 137

Joan Davis 📺   1708 Vine
See page 324

George Shearing 📺   1708 Vine
Music, composer

George Shearing

BORN Aug. 13, 1919, in Battersea, London, England. **SPOTLIGHTS** Sightless since birth, Shearing attended the Linden Lodge School for the Blind. There, he studied music, and as a youngster was influenced by the recordings of Fats Waller (who later became his friend), Art Tatum and Teddy Wilson. As a young adult he performed in English pubs, then was discovered at a jam session. He landed his first recording contract for Decca at age 20. After WWII, the jazz pianist came to America and joined singer Billy Eckstine. After touring America to packed concert halls, they ended at New York Carnegie's Hall—every ticket had been sold. With his own group, the lush sound of his piano-guitar-vibraphone quintet has stirred up excitement since 1949, yet Shearing shifts between that group, a sextet consisting of vibes, guitar, bass, conga drums, drums and piano, and his solo act. For the latter, he is admired as an inventive soloist of discernment, passion and spontaneity. Collaboration include *Nat King Cole Sings, The George Shearing Quintet Plays*; and look for his work with Mel Torme on the Concord Jazz label. He has taken dozens of pop standards like "Blue Moon," "I'll Remember April," "Moon Over Miami," and "Funny Valentine," and transformed them into jazz classics. Albums include *Alone Together, The Spirit of '76, Cool Canaries, First Edition, Piano,* and *I Hear A Rhapsody.* His signature composition piece is "Lullaby of Birdland." **HIGHLIGHTS** While he was waiting at a busy interaction during rush hour traffic, another blind man tapped him on the shoulder and asked Shearing if he could help him cross the street. "What could I do?" remarked Shearing afterward. "I took him across and it was the biggest thrill of my life." **QUOTE** "Probably the worst advice I've ever been given was to give up the study of classical music. If a jazz musician wants to play a ballad with good taste, he should have a sound knowledge of harmonics. That's something which a pianist can learn from Bach and Schumann."

Rosalind Russell 🎥   1708 Vine
Actress, singer, dancer
BORN June 4, 1912, in Waterbury, CT. **SPOTLIGHTS** Named

Rosalind Russell

after a steamship, the *S.S. Rosalind*, she proved to be just as vigorous in making waves in Hollywood. Russell grew up in a loving home in Connecticut, where her father practiced law and her mother was a fashion editor for *Vogue* magazine. Of her family she declared, "I come from good peasant Irish stock." She attended both Marymount and the American Academy of Dramatic Arts, performed in stock, then headed to the Great White Way. This energetic talent sparkled on Broadway and became one of its biggest stars. Invited to Hollywood to work alongside William Powell and Myrna Loy, she made her screen debut in *Evelyn Prentice* (1934). Within a year she was a movie star. After several successful pictures Russell was cast as a boss lady in *The Women* (1939). It marked the beginning of her playing domineering women whose femininity was buried inside. An intelligent talent with a regal bearing, in 1940 she played fast and funny opposite James Stewart in *No Time for Comedy*, Cary Grant in *His Girl Friday*, and Brian Aherne in *Hired Wife*. In 1942 she plays an executive who orders Fred MacMurray around in *Take a Letter, Darling*. About the frequency in which she was cast as a business professional, Russell remarked, "I've played 23 career women, every kind of executive. Except for different leading men, and a switch in title, they were all stamped out of the same Alice in Careerland." Other motion pictures include *My Sister Eileen* (1942), *Sister Kenny* (1946), *Mourning Becomes Electra* (1947—in an Oscar-nominated performance), *Picnic* (1956), *Gypsy* (1962), and *The Trouble with Angels* (1966). **ACHIEVEMENTS** 1953 Tony Award for *Wonderful Town*. In Hollywood, she was Oscar-nominated four times but never won. The Academy honored her with a special Oscar in 1972...She is closely associated with the flamboyant fictional character, *Auntie Mame* from both her live performance on Broadway, and her repeat performance on film (1958). Auntie Mame's catchphrase is: "Life is a banquet, and most of you poor fools are starving to death." **QUOTE** "People are always asking if I get my energy from yogurt or some secret formula. Ha! My energy is *au naturel*, thank the good Lord...I haven't had a free minute in 20 years. And I'm not complaining. My goal is the same as Auntie Mame's: 'Live! Live! Live!'" She did so fully until she passed away in 1976.

Parkyakarkus ▯   1708 Vine

Comic, actor, writer

BORN Harry Einstein; May 6, 1904, in Boston, MA. **SPOTLIGHTS** As a child with an innate sense of humor, Einstein created the character of "Parkyakarkus" (park your carcass). The boy based the imaginary fellow on the Greek customers who patronized his dad's importing warehouse. As an

Parkyakarkus

adult, Einstein rose to the top as an advertising director, then decided to leave the hype behind for show business. He tested his comedy routines at club functions. Encouraged by the applause, he made his local "on air" radio debut in 1933. He was an instant hit. Playing Parkyakarkus, he made a gag out of running for mayor in Boston. Devoted fans determined he would be the mayor-elect. Not wanting to be in politics, he had to have cards printed containing the line, "Don't vote for Parkyakarkus." Despite this, 1,200 write-in ballots were cast for him, with the winner's plurality being only 1,800! The following year, Eddie Cantor hired him for one Sunday evening to entertain on his *national* NBC radio show. (Cantor was famous for introducing new talent.) Einstein's hilarious Greek impersonations with his funny dialect immediately landed him a contract as an Eddie Cantor regular. With his animated personality, his six-foot-tall frame, black hair and large brown eyes, he turned to motion pictures. Movies include *Strike Me Pink* (1936), *The Life of the Party* (1937), *New Faces of 1937*, *She's Got Everything* (1938), *Glamour Boy* (1941), *The Yanks Are Coming* (1942), *Earl Carroll's Vanities* (1945) and *Out of This World* (1945). From 1945-'47 he created his own comedy radio series, "Meet Me at Parky's." Einstein loved to write, and wrote most of his own shows. For this program, his character Parkyakarkus had become owner of a Greek restaurant, who doubled as chief cook. What listeners did not know about this funny comic was that in real life he suffered from chronic back pain. A spinal operation to alleviate the problem left him partially paralyzed. Because it was radio, fans never saw that he was carried up to the microphone and positioned in front of it to do his show. **ACHIEVEMENTS** He fathered four successful sons. Charles was a well-known sportswriter whose indispensable work, *The Fireside Book of Baseball*, became one the most important reference books on the game. Son Clifford followed in his father's footsteps to become the chairman of Dailey & Associates advertising agency. The third boy, Robert, is television's popular Super Dave Osborne. His fourth son, Albert Brooks, is an actor, screenwriter, and film director whose works include *The Muse* (1999), *Mother* (1996), *Defending Your Life* (1991), *Lost in America* (1985), *Modern Romance* (1981), and *Real Life* (1979). **SIDELIGHTS** Although Parkyakarkus had been ill, he performed at a tribute for Lucille Ball and Desi Arnaz at the Friars Club. Milton Berle said: "He was the smash hit of the evening...he got a standing ovation." After his third bow, he crashed down on Berle's shoulders—dead. Backstage doctors tried to revive him. Desi was crying, Lucy was hysterical. A tearful Desi returned to the microphone, "We're grateful for this wonderful tribute, but we can't go on." He went out too young, but with applause in 1958.

Alfred Newman   1708 Vine
Composer, conductor, music director
BORN March 17, 1901, in New Haven, CT. **ACHIEVEMENTS** A dynamic musical force in more than 200 motion pictures, he created lush, big sounds. His outstanding film scores and orchestration earned the following Academy Awards: 1938 *Alexander's Ragtime Band*; 1940 *Tin Pan Alley*, and *The Song of Bernadette*; 1947 *Mother Wore Tights*; 1952 *With a Song In My Heart*; 1954 *Call Me Madam*; 1955 *Love is a Many Splendored Thing*; 1956 *The King and I*; and 1967 *Camelot*. Died: 1970.

Mantovani   1708 Vine
Band leader
BORN Annunzio Mantovani; Nov. 5, 1905, in Venice, Italy. **SPOTLIGHTS** He formed his orchestra in 1923, and enjoyed hit recordings: "Charmaine," "Dancing with Tears in My Eyes," "It Happened in Monterey," "Mexicali Rose," and "When I Grow Too Old To Dream," his most enchanting and romantic waltz. He was the musical director for Noel Coward in 1945, then turned to TV (1950s-'60s). Died: 1980.

Frazier Hunt   1708 Vine
Newscaster
SPOTLIGHTS He began his radio career in New York in the early 1930s. An intense commentator prior to and during World War II, postwar he delivered conservative viewpoints.

Frank Morgan   1708 Vine
Actor, comic
BORN Francis Wupperman; June 1, 1890, in New York, NY. **SPOTLIGHTS** A well-trained stage and silent screen performer, Morgan easily made the transition to talkies. Under contract for two decades at MGM, Morgan was immortalized in *The Wizard of Oz* (1939). As the wizard, he offered this sage advice to the Tin Man: "A heart is not judged by how much you love, but by how much you are loved by others." His 100 films include his must-see performances in *Tortilla Flat* (1942), *The Shop ARound the Corner* (1940), and *The Human Comedy* (1943). Radio: Star of "The Maxwell House Coffee Time" (1937-'44), where he delighted listeners with his tall-tales monologues. Countless radio broadcasts. His older brother

was actor Ralph Morgan. Died: 1949.

Betty Blythe   1702 Vine

Betty Blythe

Actress
BORN Elizabeth Blythe Slaughter; Sept. 1, 1893, in Los Angeles, CA. **SPOTLIGHTS** Educated at USC, she trained for the stage in London, and appeared on Broadway. A leading lady in silents: *The Queen of Sheeba* (1921--title role), and *She* (1925). Later, she appears in supporting roles: *The Scarlet Letter* (1934) and *Madonna of the Desert* (1948). Her final performance was in *My Fair Lady* (1964). Died: 1972.

Jack Bailey   1706 Vine
See page 110

Perry Como   1706 Vine
See page 71

Raymond Hatton   1706 Vine
Actor
BORN July 7, 1887, in Red, OK. **SPOTLIGHTS** Working in vaudeville since 1891, he was one of the earliest regular performers to move into the pioneer art of cinema. His versatile looks enabled him to play anyone from the menacing villain to the lovable Western comic sidekick to the European aristocrat. Continually busy as a character actor, he was a favorite of director Cecil B. DeMille. He appears in classics: *Oliver Twist* (1916--as the Artful Dodger), *Joan the Woman* (1917--as King Charles VII of France), *The Hunchback of Notre Dame* (as Pierre Gringoire), *The Virginian* (both 1923), *The Squaw Man* (1931--remake), *Alice in Wonderland* (1933--as the mouse), *Steamboat 'Round the Bend* (1935), and *In Cold Blood* (1967). He did more than 500 stage and screen roles. Died: 1971.

Gene Raymond   1704 Vine
See page 595

Teresa Brewer   1704 Vine
Singer
BORN Theresa Breuer; May 7, 1931, in Toledo, OH. **SPOTLIGHTS** She became popular at age two singing "Take Me Out to the Ball Game" on a children's radio show. Three years later, the energetic youngster won a Major Bowes "Amateur Hour" radio talent contest. She toured with the Bowes vaudevillians for seven years, then took a five-year vacation to grow up. By 16, this dynamic singer starred in network radio. A cute, perky, petite talent who belted out tunes, she was nicknamed "the Sophie Tucker of the girl scouts." Brewer also

Teresa Brewer

sang with jazz greats Count Basie and Duke Ellington. Although she admitted she could not read a note of music, she could memorize a tune from hearing one demostration. At 18, she had her first hit song "Music, Music, Music." A 1950s star, other hit tunes include "Baby, Baby, Baby," "Till I Waltz Again with You," "Singin' A Doo Dah Song," "Richochet," and "Pledging My Love." She appears in *Those Redheads from Seattle* (1953), a 3-D musical starring Rhonda Fleming.

Helen Gahagan 1702 Vine
Actress, politician, writer
BORN Nov. 25, 1900, in Boonton, NJ. **SPOTLIGHTS** A Broadway and opera star, she is the only honoree to have only one movie credit! She stars in RKO's *She* (1935), about a 50-year-old woman who cannot die until she falls in love. In real life, she was married to actor Melvyn Douglas (1931 until her death). **HIGHLIGHTS** 1945-'49 Congresswoman, U.S. House of Representatives. She was called: "The Democrat's answer to Clare Boothe Luce" (the first American woman to hold a high diplomatic office). **QUOTE** "I am interested in politics because of a deep conviction that government is just what you make it." Died: 1980.

Howard Hawks 1702 Vine
Director, producer, screenwriter
BORN May 30, 1896, in Goshen, IN. **SPOTLIGHTS** Skilled in virtually all aspects of filmmaking, Hawks was the ultimate Hollywood director. He triumphed in developing relationships of the characters at play. His characters had well-defined emotional personalities that were tightly locked into his extremely cohesive stories. He accomplished this with his own superb style. Motion pictures include *The Criminal Code* (1931—where Hawks paid ten hardened criminals to review it so he could make it authentic), *Scarface* (1932), *Twentieth Century* (1934), *Come and Get It* (1936), *Bringing Up Baby* (1938), *Only Angels Have Wings* (1939), *His Girl Friday* (1940), *Sergeant York* (1941), *To Have and Have Not* (1944), *The Big Sleep* (1946), *Red River* (1948), *Gentlemen Prefer Blondes* (1953—with Marilyn Monroe's song, "Diamonds Are a Girl's Best Friend"), and *Rio Bravo* (1959). **ACHIEVEMENTS** 1975

Honorary Oscar inscribed: "a master American filmmaker whose creative efforts hold a distiguished place in world cinema." His career spanned 50 years. Died: 1977.

Anna May Wong 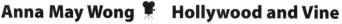 Hollywood and Vine
Actress, singer, correspondent
BORN Wong Lui Tsong; Jan. 3, 1907, in Los Angeles, CA. **SPOTLIGHTS** Wong was plucked from "extra" obscurity while working in the *Red Lantern* (1919). The movie, which was being shot in Chinatown, was an early silent. The 12-year-old's roles grew as she did, from bit to supporting to lead. At age 17, the Asian beauty was immortalized in the masterpiece motion picture, *The Thief of Bagdad* (1924). She plays a slave girl in the Arabian Nights fantasy starring Douglas Fairbanks. In the next decade of talkies, Wong co-stars opposite Marlene Dietrich in the five-star drama *Shanghai Express* (1932). This is the film where Dietrich portrays "the White Flower of the Chinese Coast," delivering the famous line: "It took more than

Anna May Wong

one man to change my name to Shanghai Lily." Wong holds her own, and is exotica personified. Filmed before the Code was enacted, the motion picture offers decadence and international intrigue that the Code would not allow only a short time later. The results at the box office were staggering. The film was Oscar-nominated for Best Picture, and for Best Direction for the great screen stylist, Joseph von Sternberg. It won an Academy Award for Cinematography. Wong was wonderful in *Dangerous to Know* (1938), a story of a loyal mistress to a ganglord, who is ignored for a society lady. She plays opposite Ralph Bellamy in one entry in the crime film series, *Ellery Queen's Penthouse Mystery* (1941). This supremely talented actress co-starred with Laurence Olivier (as Prince Po) on the London stage in *Circle of Chalk* in 1929. The play was "a flop," according to Olivier, and lasted less than one month. Both leads, though, were pleased with what critics wrote about them—it was just the play the reviewers detested. Wong performed on Broadway to rave reviews, and was an accomplished singer of light opera Viennese style. In addition to making films around the world, she was an American correspondent in China, lectured around the globe, and had her own television series "Mme. Liu Tsong." In all, she appeared in more than 40 motion pictures. *Portrait in Black* (1960) was her last film. **HIGHLIGHTS** Hollywood honored her with more than her Walk of Fame star. Her likeness has been immortalized in statue form; see "La Brea Gateway" in this book. Also see the bio of Sid Grauman. Wong died in 1961.

Kay Kyser 🔘 Hollywood and Vine
See page 342

Eleanor Steber 🔘 Hollywood and Vine
Opera singer

BORN July 17, 1916, in Wheeling, WV. **SPOTLIGHTS** One of America's homegrown opera greats, she started singing as a child in the Presbyterian church choir. Later, Steber entered the Metropolitan Opera House radio audition, and beat out 758 candidates. Her prize was $1,000, a polished silver plaque and a chance for a Met debut. In 1940 as Sophie in *Der Rosenkavalier*, she was hailed by critics as "a magnificent find for the Met." She sang in the coloratura, dramatic soprano and lyric soprano repertoires. Indispensable at the Met for a dozen years, she was noted for her exceptional renderings of classic Mozart and Strauss to heavy Wagner, from Puccini and Verdi, to modernists like Berg. Unlike other prima donnas, Steber was cherished worldwide by colleagues for her good cheer, humor, and down-to-earth reliability. Friends adored her warmth and love of life. She avoided the svelte school of thought, candidly remarking, "An opera singer cannot diet and sing well." **ACHIEVEMENTS** In 1952, she astounded everyone by appearing twice in one day, in a matinee performance as Desdemona in *Otello*, and an evening engagement as Fiordiligi in *Cosi Fan Tutte*. One critic likened her Herculean efforts to "Jack Dempsey fighting Gene Tunney in the afternoon and Joe Louis at night." **QUOTE** "All of us Americans have had to fight like hell to get what we get. The Europeans are no better artists. It's just because they are Europeans. Only by ability and integrity have we been able to hold our own and outlast them—plus having to sing immaculately in four different languages if we want to stay in the running."

Tom Mix 🎥 Hollywood and Vine
Actor

BORN Jan. 6, 1880, in Mix Run, PA. **SPOTLIGHTS** Probably the greatest cowboy of the silent era, he was a rugged adventurer, a real colorful cut-up, a prankster, and a hellion by nature. Before pictures, Mix had been employed as sheriff in both Oklahoma and Texas, and as a bodyguard for a Mexican President (a type of soldier of fortune). He made his screen debut in 1909, *On the Little Big Horn or Custard's Last Stand*. He exuded the pep and energy a strong Western hero needed, to which he added his own boyish fun. A natural born showman, Mix rode the dusty, sagebrush trail doing his own stunts

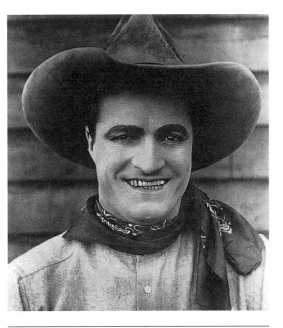

Tom Mix

in close to 150 quickies (one- two- and three-reelers). He always rode his handsome black steed, Tony (the most famous silent movie horse). Then, Mix made more than 60 features films, and some early talkies, including *Just Tony* (1922), *The Lone Star Ranger* (1923), *The Rainbow Trail* (1925), *The Great K. & L. Train Robbery* and *Sky High* (both 1927)...**HIGHLIGHTS** 20th Century-Fox Studios (aka 21st Century-Fox) sits on the land formerly owned by Mix. **QUOTE** "Speaking of horses, I could never determine just how much a horse really reasoned, or how much he reached through an intuitive sense. I do know, if in a moment of crisis, you trust your horse, you cannot go far wrong. Of course, there are dumb horses and smart horses, just like human beings. There are horses that think slowly and act slowly, while others have minds that operate with the rapidity of a machine gun. You usually find cow ponies are mighty smart. Take Tony, for instance. Tony is not, as many seem to think, a trick horse. Tony is just naturally smart. I don't teach Tony. I *quietly* show him what we've got to do to make a scene, and Tony does the rest. He understands." This cowboy died in 1940, when his car overturned in Arizona.

Molly O'Day 🎥 Hollywood and Vine
Actress

BORN Suzanne Noonan; Feb. 11, 1911, in Bayonne, NJ. **SPOTLIGHT** As a young teenager, the appealing brunette started her career in the *Our Gang* comedies. Then, she beat out thousands of competitors for the role of the tough heroine in the prizefighting boxing drama *The Patent Leather Kid* (1927). She was just sweet 16 at the time, but extremely gifted. The starlet was a favorite of George Raft. Alas, according to him, "she's gorgeous, but eats too much." Maybe it was genetic; her mother was Metropolitan Opera singer Hannah Kelly. At age 18, she was threatened with loss of contract unless she loss 20 pounds. The desperate actress paid a "quack" doctor for experimental "fat removal." She also fasted, dieted, and exercised. She dropped from "140 horrible pounds to a more bearable 120, where it remains," according to a reporter. She made dozens of movies until age 24, including *Sea Devils*, *Hard-*

Boiled Hagerty, and *The Lovelorn*. Died: 1998.

Frank Luther 🎤 Hollywood and Vine

Singer, songwriter, announcer

BORN Frank L. Crow; 1900, in Kansas. **SPOTLIGHTS** The announcer on the 1939 radio soap opera "The Life and Love of Dr. Susan," he was also the vocalist on the musical variety-interview show "Luncheon at the Waldorf" (1940-'41). In 1943, "Americans & Their Songs" made him famous. He recorded many popular nursery rhymes and children's song lessons. Died: 1980.

Joanne Dru 📺 Hollywood and Vine

Actress

Joanne Dru

BORN Joan Leticia LaCock; Jan. 31, 1923, in Logan, WV. **SPOTLIGHTS** After the death of her father, she moved to New York with her dress-maker mother, who worked at Macy's department store. Needing to help support the family, and to be able to afford to send for her younger brother, Peter, she set out to find employment. Although petite, this auburn-haired, green-eyed teen beauty found work as a model for the John Robert Powers agency. It was Powers who changed her name from LaCock to Marshall. With the new income, she was able to send for her brother and reunite the family. Enhanced by her hour-glass figure and breathtaking good looks, she easily made the leap to being a chorus girl on the Broadway stage. Her first production was in Al Jolson's last show, "Hold Onto Your Hats." At age 18, she married one of the world's soon-to-be most popular vocalists, Dick Haymes (see his bio in this book). At the time of their wedding, he was making $50-a-week singing with Harry James' Orchestra, and she was making $75-a-week dancing. That would soon change. When her husband received a contract from 20th Century-Fox, they moved to Hollywood. A movie director eyed the beauty sun tanning in Palm Springs, California. Their meeting resulted in her screen debut, *Abie's Irish Rose* (1946), in the leading role. Another bit of good luck happened next. Her

actress girlfriend, Margaret Sheridan, became pregnant and had to pass on a part. Sheridan brought her to meet the director, Howard Hawks. He signed her and changed her name to Dru. She co-stars opposite John Wayne and Montgomery Clift—who would play her love interest—in the classic Western *Red River* (1948). Dru gave a memorable performance as Therissa Mullay "Tess of the River," although Hawks kept changing her role as a gambler with a murky past, and this weakened her work. She gained fame the following year in John Ford's Western *She Wore a Yellow Ribbon* (1949), opposite John Wayne again, in one of his favorite movies. Dru radiated femininity while turning the heads of the United States Calvary in this movie. Typecast in Westerns, she became the heroine of numerous horse operas, but strayed into comedies and dramas. She was excellent in *All the King's Men* (1949), opposite Broderick Crawford, John Ireland and Mercedes McCambridge. (Ireland later became her real-life leading man in wedlock.) This Academy Award-winning Best Picture, adapted from the Pulitzer Prize-winning novel by Robert Penn Warren, was based on the Louisiana governor-turned-senator Huey "Kingfish" Long. It's a must-see political melodrama about corruption. Movies include Ford's *Wagon Master* (1950), *711 Ocean Drive* (1950), *Mr. Belvedere Rings the Bell* (1951), *Return of the Texan* (1952), *The Pride of St. Louis* (1952), *Thunder Bay* (1953), *Outlaw Territory* (1953), *The Siege at Red River* (1954), *Three Ring Circus* (1954), *Durango* (1957) and *The Light in the Forest* (1958). **TV** She starred in the sit-com "Guestward Ho!" as Babs Hooten who flees the skyscraper jungle for a calmer life on a dude ranch. **SIDELIGHTS** The only reason she became an actress, and kept acting, was to feed her children and to pay the bills. Two of her husbands left her with tax problems that the I.R.S. forced her to pay off herself. **HIGHLIGHTS** Her brother is the actor and American game show host, Peter Marshall. Peter described her as "as an angel, for her kindness and sweet disposition." Dru died in 1996.

Wendy Barrie 🎬 Hollywood and Vine

Actress

BORN Margaret Jenkins; April 18, 1912, in Hong Kong. **SPOTLIGHTS** Her most memorable role was that of saucy Jane Seymour opposite Charles Laughton in the British production, *The Private Life of Henry VIII* (1933). She was a leading lady in numerous Hollywood films, including *It's a Small World* (1935), *Dead End* (1937), and *Forever and a Day* (1943). Known for her sparkling ripostes and wordy charm, she became a favorite radio and TV hostess. **QUOTE** "I'm aware some people think I'm a 'gay idiot,' but I doubt they know my background. I'm conversant with international affairs...I've been around the world so many times—I lost count...I can think like a man." Died: 1978.

Neil Armstrong, Buzz Aldrin, Michael Collins
📷 **Hollywood and Vine** *See page 266*

Kirk Douglas 🎥 Hollywood and Vine

Actor, writer, producer

Kirk Douglas

BORN Issur Danielovitch (later Demsky); Sept. 9, 1916, in Amsterdam, NY. **SPOTLIGHTS** A hard-working youngster who put himself through St. Lawrence University and the American Academy of Dramatic Arts, he made his Broadway debut in 1941. When WWII interrupted, he felt compelled to serve in the Navy. After his honorable discharge in 1945, he made his screen debut in *The Strange Love of Martha Ivers* (1946), opposite Barbara Stanwyck and Lizabeth Scott. He delivered a solid performance opposite Robert Mitchum in *Out of the Past* (1947), an excellent film noir. Then, with the searing anger of troubled youth, the powerfully built Douglas punched his way to superstardom in the low-budget film *Champion* (1949--in an Oscar-nominated performance). Directed by Mark Robson and produced by Stanley Kramer, Douglas plays an ambitious, cruel boxer who destroys anyone near him, both in and out of the ring. (Watch for the scene where he collapses, it is gritty realism at its best.) With this classic film, Douglas became a winning prizefighter at the box office, too. A handsome, forceful artist with a trademark dimpled chin and uniquely paced voice, he throws himself fully and passionately into his roles. He was outstanding in *The Glass Menagerie* (1950), *Young Man With a Horn* (1950), *The Big Carnival* (1951), *Detective*

Story (1951), *The Bad and the Beautiful* (1952—his character was based on movie producer David O. Selznick; Douglas received his second Oscar nomination in this role), *The Big Sky* (1952), *20,000 Leagues Under the Sea* (1954), *Man Without a Star* (1955), *Lust for Life* (1956—as Vincent Van Gogh, in which he received his third Oscar nomination; he did win the New York Critics Award for Best Actor), *Gunfight at the O.K Corral* (1957), *Paths of Glory* (1957—also produced), *Spartacus* (1960), *Town Without Pity* (1961), and *The Man from Snowy River* (1982). Remarkably able to land leading roles even into his seventies; he is wry and funny in the comedy *Greedy* (1994). After a real-life disabling stroke, this seemingly indestructible star courageously fought back. He made his highly acclaimed comeback in *Diamonds* (2000), as a retired prizefighter recovering from a stroke. The film also stars Lauren Bacall, Dan Aykroyd and Jenny McCarthy. **ACHIEVEMENTS** 1996 Special Academy Award for Lifetime Achievement. 1985 awarded France's Chevalier of the Legion of Honor. 1981 Presidential Medal of Freedom. He is most proud of his family; he is the loving father of Academy Award-winning producer-actor Michael Douglas...He and his wife are active in many charities, including the hands-on donation of funds and play equipment to improve local schoolyards. Douglas has also penned several best-sellers. **HIGHLIGHTS** Of his 50 years in Hollywood he remarked, "I made 80 films; I like 22 out of them." When asked which picture he liked the best, Douglas replied, "*Lonely Are the Brave* (1962). It's a little film, I play a good guy. It's my favorite." **QUOTE** "You know, acting is a disease. It's the only career I know where nobody is ever forced to do what he's doing. Take a pharmacist; he probably became a pharmacist because his father was a pharmacist, or maybe his mother liked starched white coats."

Edward R. Murrow 🎙 Hollywood and Vine

Reporter, commentator, historian, inquirer

BORN Egbert Roscoe Murrow; April 25, 1908, in Polecat Creek, NC. **SPOTLIGHTS** From humble beginnings as the son of a North Carolina dirt farmer, the tall, lanky youth worked as a lumberjack in the Pacific Northwest. He graduated from Washington State College in 1930 before reinventing himself as a dapper foreign correspondent. Erasing every vestige of his poverty-stricken childhood from his posture, language, clothing, manners, *et al*, he was reborn a magnetic gentleman who wore custom suits and polished shoes. With no real journalistic experience, but an innate genius that one CBS executive recognized, he was hired in 1935. Murrow was dispatched to London as European representative/news producer in 1937. On March 12, 1938, Americans heard him for the first time; he was broadcasting from Vienna, Austria with news of Hitler's invasion. In 1939, the 29-year-old began reporting nightly from England where he opened with his famous intonation: "This is London." Those three words still send chills down the spines of those old enough to recall his dedication to pioneer war reporting from London during the Blitz (starting in September 1940). With his strong voice, he broadcasted to the

THE HOLLYWOOD WALK OF FAME 191

background sounds of bombs, anti-aircraft guns and sirens, often from rooftops during the action. He also flew on two dozen combat missions. He was so brave, so passionate, that it was said of him: "Murrow will fly bombers into hell for what he believes" (1939-'45). After the war, he toured Buchenwald, the hideous German concentration camp. His BBC report made front page news the next day. He became vice president and director of public affairs at CBS (1945-'47); his CBS tenure ended in 1961. He accepted a position as the respected director of the U.S. Information Agency from President John F. Kennedy. **ACHIEVEMENTS** The most famous voice heard during WWII, his name is forver linked with the highest ideals in broadcasting. His innovations in immediate reporting—as opposed to the then-standard debates and speeches of statesmen—gave birth to the era of news radio. It was the golden boy on-the-scene that brought news to the forefront and CBS to the top of the heap for several decades. Emmys: 1953, 1955, 1956, 1957, 1958-'59. **HIGHLIGHTS** The *Saturday Evening Post* described his voice as "a coppery baritone charged with authority." **QUOTE** Murrow's credo: "News programs are broadcast solely for the purpose of enabling the listeners thereto to know the facts. We will endeavor to assist the listener in weighing and judging developments throughout the world, but will refrain—particularly with respect to all controversial, political, social and economic questions—from trying to make up the listener's mind for him." His closing signature was, "Good night, and good luck." Died: 1965.

James Stewart ♥ Hollywood and Vine

Actor, author

BORN May 20, 1908, in Indiana, PA. **SPOTLIGHTS** Gossip columnist Hedda Hopper urged MGM to screen-test Stewart for his "unusually usual" qualities. With his guileless demeanor and slow, endearing drawl, this shy, gawky gentleman became cinema's hesitant hero. Stewart looked liked an average fellow; he was anything but. He exemplified the best in human nature. Possessing high ideals, unwavering principles and being of sound moral character, his passion for veracity restored our faith in mankind. He was strong (in mind), decent, trustworthy, and lovable. His acting technique was subtle, yet honest, and he excelled in all genres. Outstanding films include *You Can't Take It With You* (1938), *Mr. Smith Goes to Washington* (1939), *Destry Rides Again* (1939), *The Shop Around the Corner* (1940), *The Mortal Storm* (1940), *It's a Wonderful Life* (1947), *Harvey* (1950), *Broken Window* (1950), *Winchester '73* (1950), *The Greatest Show on Earth* (1952), *The Naked Spur* (1953), *Rear Window* (1954), *The Far Country* (1955), *The Man Who Knew Too Much* (1956), *The Spirit of St. Louis* (1957—Stewart was thrilled to portray his idol Charles A. Lindbergh), *Vertigo* (1958), *Anatomy of a Murder* (1959), and *The Man Who Shot Liberty Valance* (1962). **ACHIEVEMENTS** 1940 Best Actor Oscar for *The Philadelphia Story*...After the bombing of Pearl Harbor, Stewart immediately tried to enlist in the service. The U.S. military rejected him at first due to his low body weight (139 pounds at a height of 6' 3"). The tall, lean Stewart man-

James Stewart

aged to add 10 pounds by eating fattening foods all day and night long. Accepted into the Army Air Corps (Air Force) as a bomber pilot, he bravely garnered a distinguished service record during WWII. He flew 20 dangerous combat missions over Nazi Germany and rose in military rank from a private to a full colonel. He held the highest rank of any actor *ever* in the U.S. Air Force Reserve--brigadier general--when he retired in 1968. He stated, "I realize a movie actor is an off-beat breed of cat to the military establishment. But there is nothing that says an actor can't be a man who can do an effective job as an officer with duties that normally befall an airman." **HIGHLIGHTS** Stewart earned a degree in architecture from Princeton University in 1932...His real-life hobby was assembling airplanes. **QUOTE** About his characteristic speech pattern of hemming and hawing, he confessed, "I don't know. I just can't get up to speed." About getting older, he said, "After age 70, it's just patch, patch, patch." About the end of the day, Stewart commented, "I kneel down and give thanks." This modest champion of decency died in 1997.

6263 HOLLYWOOD

Mike Wallace   6263 Hollywood

Interviewer, newsman, co-editor

Mike Wallace

BORN Myron Wallace; May 9, 1918, in Brookline, MA. **SPOTLIGHTS** Wallace is known as the most fearless interviewer in the business. A totally unafraid journalist (who else would be brave enough to reveal critical tobacco industry secrets), he'll ask anybody anything—even if it means losing a friend, as it did with Henry Kissinger, or nearly losing one, as it did with Nancy Reagan. Don Hewitt, executive producer of the bold news show "60 Minutes," had this to say about Wallace's interviewing style, "He's like Muhammad Ali. He has a sense of knowing when to lay back, when to dance and when to go in for the kill." Prior to his tenure with America's most interesting news program, Wallace's job resume dates back to the 1940s when he was a radio news writer and broadcaster for the *Chicago Sun*. He became immediately recognizable for his pleasant, yet authoritative voice. He moved to television, where he co-hosted a live interview show, emceed quiz shows, hosted his own show, and anchored the Peabody Award-winning public affairs series "Biography" (1959-'61). After reporting from the bloody rice fields of Vietnam, this no-holds-barred interviewer joined "60 Minutes" as news correspondent and co-editor. The only correspondent who has been with the show since its premiere on Sept. 24, 1968, this distinguished and respected journalist has already celebrated his 30-year anniversary with the program. Ironically, he was not Hewitt's initial choice to anchor—Harry Reasoner was. Wallace has frequently been named the Broadcaster of the Year by various radio and TV organizations. **ACHIEVEMENTS** He is the recipient of countless honors and awards, including 18 Emmys, three George Foster Peabody Awards, numerous Honorary Doctorates, and the prestigious Thomas Paine Award in 1996. This award is presented annually to a journalist whose work reflects Paine's ideals and commitment to free expression. (Born in 1737, Thomas Paine helped to inspire the passion for democracy and free speech.) Upon receiving the bronze award, Wallace said, "If Tom Paine is the father of American journalism, then I'm one of his great, great, great grandchildren. It makes me feel, at 78, young and vital all over again." **QUOTE** "They can melt you down in Madame Toussaud's Wax Museum...but the Walk of Fame is, I guess, forever."

Billy Gilbert   6263 Hollywood

Billy Gilbert

Actor, comedian

BORN Sept. 12, 1894, in Louisville, KY. **SPOTLIGHTS** Known in the business as a second clown, this tall, rotund, jovial talent supported Laurel and Hardy in *The Music Box* (1932), and Charlie Chaplin in *The Great Dictator* (1940). An expert in humor, he appears in 220 comedy shorts and features. Movies include *Destry Rides Again* (1939), *His Girl Friday* (1940), and *Anchors Aweigh* (1945). Gilbert descended from a family of singers—both his parents were stars at the Metropolitan Opera House—and he had a distinct, well-trained voice and tremendous breath control. Walt Disney personally cast him in *Snow White and the Seven Dwarfs* (1938) as Sneezy—his favorite role. It was said that he "made the act of sneezing a true artistic achievement." **QUOTE** "I think we sometimes overlook the chief reason why there are motion pictures. And that is the desire in every human heart for entertainment. That is where the comedy people come in. I think we are inclined to not give due credit for the people who cause the smiles, the chuckles and the hearty laughs. The circus clown usually dies unhonored and unsung, and very likely many of our comedians who are leaping about on the screen today will achieve little lasting recognition for having made millions laugh." Died: 1971.

Ruth Chatterton   6263 Hollywood

Ruth Chatterton

Actress

BORN Dec. 24, 1893, in New York, NY. **SPOTLIGHTS** A former Broadway star, she possessed an endearing heart shaped face. Amazingly, this brunette talent made her screen debut at age 35—late for a woman by Hollywood standards. As a leading lady and in supporting roles, she appeared in *Madame X* (1929--in an Oscar-nominated performance), *Sarah and Son* (1930--in an Oscar-nominated performance), *Dodsworth* (1936), and *Mr. Deeds Goes to Town* (1936). An independent thinker for her times, upon retiring she piloted airplanes and wrote novels. Her first husband declared, "Don't argue with Ruth on any subject. She has the fastest mind in the world—shallow, of course." Book reviewers found her anything but. Died: 1961.

Milton Sills ☕ 6263 Hollywood

Actor

BORN Jan. 12, 1882, in Chicago, IL. **SPOTLIGHTS** A handsome, dark-haired, masculine star of the silent era, he came close to the great John Barrymore's crown. Similar to Barrymore, he had extensive theatrical training. With his finely honed skills, Sills could tackle costume pictures, comedies, action and melodramas. He, though, considered movies more entertainment than dignified art. Motion pictures include *Flaming Youth* (1923), *The Sea Hawk* (1924), *As Man Desires* (1925), and *Valley of the Giants* (1927). He had a good voice but only made one sound picture—the Jack London thriller *The Sea Wolf* (1930). He died right after making it. **QUOTE** "The reason—in my opinion—that the motion picture today is only semi-artistic is the fact that producers have been made to believe that the 20,000,000 people who make up the daily motion picture audience average but 12 years of age in intelligence. Fearing that an adult type of photoplay might be 'over the heads' of the average audience, too many producers have made pictures so silly, so puerile, that a good percentage of the public is cynical in its attitude toward the screen. Recently a thorough analysis of the theater-going public has brought out facts proving that the standards of intelligence accepted during the war (WWI) and before, are not accurate today."

Milton Berle 📺 6263 Hollywood

Comedian, director, producer, author

BORN Milton Berlinger; July 12, 1908, in New York, NY. **SPOTLIGHTS** Called "Mr. Television," and affectionately known as "Uncle Miltie," Berle won his first talent contest at age five impersonating Charlie Chaplin. He quickly went to work in silent comedies. Amazingly, the child ended up working with the great Chaplin, among other superb comedians, in dozens of pictures. Next, he and his sister became vaudeville celebrities with his stage mother managing her children's careers. About his mother, Berle stated, "Her piercing laugh cued audiences in almost every theater in America." Berle became a radio, Broadway, and nightclub entertainer, as well as appearing in dozens of sound motion pictures as an adult. Then, the new medium of television was introduced. In the early days of black-and-white commercial broadcasting few people owned sets. If they did, they could count on curious relatives and neighbors dropping in to view the newfangled thing. Many predicted TV wouldn't last, and stubbornly refused to buy one. It was crazy, slapstick, mugging Berle on "The Texaco Star Theater," and later "The Milton Berle Show" (1948-'56), that sold more TV sets than anyone else. Living his lifelong motto: "Anything for a laugh on stage," the funny guy with the Bugs Bunny smile became a household name. Mr. Television ruled the new medium as its biggest star and its

Milton Berle (left with cigar) and Sir Michael Teilmann

most-talked about comedian. Audiences laughed hysterically at his outrageous vaudevillian-type costumes and spoofing. His onslaught of gags inspired gossip columnist Walter Winchell to dub him the "Thief of Badgags." An active Friars Club member for decades, Berle earned a reputation for his quick wit, ad libs and pithy remarks, as well as his steel-trap mind; he remembers every act in show business that he's ever seen. **ACHIEVEMENTS** 1949 Most Outstanding Kinescope Personality; 1950 Special Emmy to "Mr. Television." Berle celebrated more than 80 years making people laugh. He is also the author of several books. **QUOTE** "There are two kinds of egotists—those who admit it and the rest of us."

Allan Dwan ☕ 6263 Hollywood

Director

BORN Joseph Aloyius Dwan; April 3, 1885, in Toronto, Canada. **SPOTLIGHTS** He played college football while earning an electrical engineering degree at Notre Dame. Later, he coached football for the "Fighting Irish." Dwan parlayed his day job as a lighting engineer to enter Chicago's Essanay motion picture company and moonlight at night as a writer, then story editor. He directed a one-reeler by default; the director who was supposed to work for the American Film Company quit. Dwan stepped into the role and asked the actors: "How do I direct? Tell me what I'm supposed to do." They did, and he went on to make nearly 400 films. Movies include *Robin Hood* (1922) starring Douglas Fairbanks; *Heidi* (1937) starring Shirley Temple; another Temple vehicle, *Rebecca of Sunnybrook Farms* (1938); and *Sands of Iwo Jima* (1949) starring John Wayne, in which Wayne earned his first Oscar nomination. **ACHIEVEMENTS** He showed an uncanny ability for solving technical problems on the set by clever invention. He created the dolly shot (which he shot from a moving Ford automobile to capture actor William H. Crane's stroll) in the folksy comedy *David Harum* (1915). He also invented special equipment (an elevator that goes up and down, as well as forward and backward on a railroad track to be used for the special crane shots in D.W. Griffith's classic *Intolerance* (1916). Died: 1981.

Helen Parrish 🎥   6263 Hollywood

Actress
BORN March 12, 1922, in Columbus, GA. **SPOTLIGHTS** Born with greasepaint in her veins, this child star was a baby-faced joy in the classic *Our Gang* (1927) series. (Seen today in syndication as "The Little Rascals.") She was a supporting actress in Universal's Deanna Durbin vehicle, *Mad About Music* (1938); she played a jealous roommate. Died: 1959.

Helen Twelvetrees 🎥 6263 Hollywood

Actress
BORN Helen Marie Jurgens, on Christmas Day, Dec. 25, 1907, in Brooklyn, NY. **SPOTLIGHTS** An alluring and beautiful blonde, she made her screen debut in *The Ghost Talks* (1929). Appeaing in soap operas and melodramas, she usually played the woeful heroine. Movies include *The Painted Desert* (1931) in Clark Gable's first talkie, *Bad Company* (1931) co-starring Ricardo Cortez, *Unashamed* (1932), *A Bedtime Story* (1933) opposite Maurice Chevalier, *Disgraced* (1933), *She Was a Lady* (1934), and *Now I'll Tell* (1934) co-starring Spencer Tracy. Died: 1958.

Helen Twelvetrees and Ricardo Cortez

Barry Nelson 📺 6263 Hollywood

Barry Nelson and Diane McBain

Actor
BORN Robert Haakon Nielson; April 16, 1920, in Oakland, CA. **SPOTLIGHTS** This handsome, square-jawed actor graced the stage and silver screen, but he became best known in TV. In his first series, "The Hunter" (1952-'54), he played Bart Adams, a wealthy businessman who found himself involved in international intrigue. In the second, he was the successful bank executive George Cooper in "My Favorite Husband" (1953-'55). His lovely scatterbrained wife was played by Joan Caulfield in this popular situation comedy. He made his motion picture debut in *Shadow of the Thin Man* (1941). Other movies include *Johnny Eager* (1941), *Dr. Kildare's Victory* (1942), *Bataan* (1943), *The Human Comedy* (1943), *A Guy Names Joe* (1944), *The Man with My Face* (1951), *Airport* (1970), and *The Shining* (1980). He is the acclaimed star of numerous Broadway hits, including "The Rat Race," "The Moon is Blue," "Mary, Mary," and "Cactus Flower."

Betty Hutton 🎥   6253 Hollywood

Betty Hutton

Singer, actress
BORN Betty Thornburg; Feb. 26, 1921, in Battle Creek, MI. **SPOTLIGHTS** Raised in the depths of poverty, Hutton hungered for a life of fame and fortune. She stated, "I shoved and clawed my way up, through vaudeville, nightclubs, movie show houses and contests into pictures." Known as the blonde bombshell, she won the lead in MGM's *Annie Get Your Gun* (1950) and Paramount's *The Greatest Show on Earth* (1952). She made two dozen movies, including portraying the rollicking nightclub hostess, Texas Guinan, in *Incendiary Blonde* (1945), and the queen of the cliffhangers, Pauline White, in *The Perils of*

Pauline (1947). Other movies include *Happy Go Lucky* (1943), where she delivers a sensational "Murder, He Says." **QUOTE** "If I could just get it across to every audience, if I could explain the thrill I get performing, if I could just look at them out there and tell them: 'There's nothing I wouldn't do for you!'"

Joi Lansing 6253 Hollywood

Actress

BORN Joyce Wassmansdoff; April 6, 1928, in Salt Lake City, Utah. **SPOTLIGHTS** A wonderful character actress, she was busy in all mediums: *Easter Parade* (1948), *Take Me Out to the Ballgame, Neptune's Daughter* (both 1949), *The Merry Widow* (1952), and *Son of Sinbad* (1955). TV: She played Shirley in "The Bob Cummings Show" (1956-'59), and Gladys Flatt (1962-'68) in "The Beverly Hillbillies." Died: 1972.

Howard Keel 6253 Hollywood

Howard Keel

Singer, actor

BORN Harold Leek; April 13, 1917, in Gillespie, IL. **SPOTLIGHTS** As a young, unknown American singer, he nervously walked out before a first night audience in one of London's most famous theatres. In his powerful, rich baritone voice, he deckared, "Oh, what a beautiful morning..." His performance was in the finest tradition of the legitimate stage. The unbelievable number of curtain calls at the end of the Rodgers and Hammerstein's "Oklahoma!" pointed to international fame. Hollywood thought so, too, starring the handsome, strapping talent in several musicals, including *Annie Get Your Gun* (1950), *Showboat* (1951), *Calamity Jane* (1953), *Rose Marie, Seven Brides for Seven Brothers*, and *Kiss Me Kate* (all 1954). Possessing the dramatic punch of Gable, and able to make the leading lady believe he is romantic and gallant with a song, the virile Keel was the all-around cornerstone of those 1950s musicals. He proved to be a capable dramatic actor, too. TV: In the long-running series "Dallas" he portrayed "Clayton Farlow," one of the few men J.R. Ewing respected.

Jerome Cowan 6253 Hollywood

Actor

BORN Oct. 6, 1897, in New York, NY. **SPOTLIGHTS** This dapper character actor appeared in Blondie films (based on the comic strip), as Dagwood's boss. He made more than 100 motion pictures, including *High Sierra, The Maltese Falcon* (both 1941), *Song of Bernadette* (1943), *Mr. Skeffington* (1944), *Miracle on 34th Street* (1947), *The Fountainhead* (1949), *Pocketful of Miracles* (1961), *The Patsy* (1964), and *Frankie and Johnny* (1965). TV: He played company president Herbert Wilson on "The Tycoon" (1964-'65), and appeared in the Western "Alias Smith and Jones." Died: 1972.

Jack Albertson 6253 Hollywood

Actor

BORN June 16, 1910, in Lynn, MA. **SPOTLIGHTS** An extremely versatile veteran of vaudeville, burlesque, the legit stage, and motion pictures, he was also a hit in TV (see below). Movies include *Teacher's Pet* (1958), *Days of Wine and Roses* (1962), *How to Murder Your Wife* (1965), *Willy Wonka in the Chocolate Factory* (1971), and *The Poseidon Adventure* (1972). **ACHIEVEMENTS** 1968 Best Supporting Actor Oscar for *The Subject was Roses*. He also won a Tony Award on Broadway in the same role. Winner of two Emmys; as supporting actor in the "Cher" show, and "Outstanding Lead Actor" in "Chico and the Man," (as "the Man"). Died: 1981.

Robert Casadesus 6251 Hollywood

French pianist, composer

BORN April 7, 1899, in France. **SPOTLIGHTS** He was a magnificent descendant of a well-known musical family. Alongside his pianist wife Gaby, they exquisitely played duets he had composed, including "Concerto for Two Pianos," and "Six Pieces." Recordings: *Ravel Piano Music* and *Saint-Saens Concerto No. 4 in C Minor, op. 44.* After his death in 1972, his wife founded the Robert Casadesus International Piano Competition (Cleveland International Piano Competition).

Anthony Quinn 6251 Hollywood

Anthony Quinn (left), Anna Magnani and Yul Brynner

Actor

BORN Anthony Rudolph Oaxaca Quinn, April 21, 1915, in Chihua-hua, Mexico. **SPOTLIGHTS** In 1936 Mae West gave the 21-year-old "kid" a break by casting him as a 65-year-old man in her play "Clean Beds." Then, in true acting form, he pretended to be a Native Cherokee Indian to land a role in Cecil B. De Mille's *The Plainsman* (1936). It was not the truth; his mother was Mexican, his father Irish. Quinn made more than 100 motion pictures, proving his skill time and again. Movies include *The Ox-Bow Incident* (1943),

Fellini's *La Strada* (1954—as a carnival strongman), *Ulysses* (1955), *The River's Edge* (1957), *The Hunchback of Notre Dame* (1957), *Wild is the Wind* (1957), *The Black Orchid* (1958), *Warlock* (1959—a Western), *Heller in Pink Tights* (1960), *Portrait in Black* (1960), *The Guns of Navarone* (1961), *Requiem for a Heavyweight, Lawrence of Arabia* (both 1962), *Behold a Pale Horse* (1964), *Zorba the Greek* (1964—he was immortalized in the title role), *A High Wind in Jamaica* (1965), *Jungle Fever* (1991), and *Someone to Love* (1996),. **ACHIEVEMENTS** 1952 Best Supporting Actor Oscar for *Viva Zapata!*; and a 1956 Oscar for *Lust for Life*. About this Academy Award he said, "At the risk of being misunderstood I would like to say acting has never been a matter of competition with others. I was only competing with myself—and I thank you for letting me win the fight." **QUOTE** "I've discovered something—the enjoyment of living. Before I thought of life in terms of possessions and accomplishments. I was always in competition with *Somebody*. I read a lot of Thomas Wolfe, and Walt Whitman and Saroyan...Suddenly, I realized I didn't have to prove anything to anybody but myself...To me acting used to be one, two, three. Now it's living. I love to live, so I live. I love to act, so I act. I gotta have vitality. I gotta live."

Dave O'Brien 🎥   6251 Hollywood

Actor, writer
BORN David Barclay; May 31, 1912, in Big Springs, TX. **SPOTLIGHTS** He made the comedy series "Pete Smith" (shorts), then several 'B' vehicles including *The Ghost Creeps* (1940) and *The Spider Returns* (1941). **HIGHLIGHTS** 1960-'61 Emmy for Outstanding Writing Achievement in Comedy: "The Red Skelton Show." Died: 1969.

Laura Hope Crews 🎥   6251 Hollywood

Laura Hope Crews

Actress
BORN Dec. 12, 1879, in San Francisco, CA. **SPOTLIGHTS** After a long, successful Broadway career she retired. It was the late 1920s. Around this time, silent screen stars—terrified of the coming of sound—recruited her as a speech coach. Then, directors called upon her dramatic services. She played the jealous, selfish mother in *The Silver Cord* (1933), with Irene Dunne and Joel McCrea, and broke through the sound barrier. She was immortalized as Scarlett's feebleminded Aunt Pitty-Pat in *Gone with the Wind* (1939). Other movies include *The Age of Innocence* (1934), *Camille* (1937), *Thanks for the Memory* (1938), *The Blue Bird* (1940), *One Foot in Heaven* (1941), and *The Man Who Came to Dinner* (1942). Died: 1942.

Sabu 🎥   6251 Hollywood

Sabu

Actor
BORN Savu Dastagir; Jan. 27, 1924, in India. **SPOTLIGHTS** A British director discovered this mystical-looking boy working in a maharajah's stables. He starred him in *Elephant Boy* (1937). The role was a natural for the teen; Sabu's real-life father was an elephant driver. Sabu possessed enormous charisma, and 22 exotic adventure movies followed. He stars in remake of *The Thief of Bagdad* (1940). Next, he co-stars with Maria Montez and Jon Hall in the fun, campy *Arabian Nights* (1940). Movies include *Jungle Book* (1942)--based on the Nobel Prize-winner Rudyard Kipling's family tale, and the super campy *Cobra Woman* (1944), co-starring Montez and Hall again. Watch for the snake "mating" dance. **ACHIEVEMENTS** A decorated war hero. Died: 1963.

Hugh Herbert 🎥   6251 Hollywood

Actor, playwright, screenwriter
BORN Aug. 10, 1887, in Binghamton, NY. **SPOTLIGHTS** A Broadway playwright and headliner for 25 years, his comic antics—excitedly waving his fidgety hands and giggling "Woo Woo!"—enhanced countless movies. Films include *Million Dollar Legs* (1932), *Traveling Saleslady* (1935), and *Kismet* (1944). **ACHIEVEMENTS** He was co-writer of Hollywood's first *full-length* talkie, *The Lights of New York* (1928). Primitive, but historically important, it was "a 100 percent all-talking film." Died: 1952.

Wayne King 🎥   6251 Hollywood

Composer, conductor, saxophone player
BORN Feb. 16, 1901, in Savannah, IL. **SPOTLIGHTS** During the day he worked as a mechanic for a Chicago insurance company, at night he played music. Ambitious, he was able to quit his day job and support his family with his own dance band in the 1930s. After recording "Josephine" in 1937, he became known for his slow, dreamy style. By the '40s, this popular talent earned $15,000-a-week in radio's "Lady Esther Serenade" show, where he was crowned "The Waltz King." The program featured the marvelous Bess Johnson (1940s). King wrote his own signature tune: "The Waltz You Saved For Me." Songs: "Baby Shoes, " "Blue Hours," "Wabash Moon," "Dream A Little Dream Of Me," "Good Night Sweetheart," and "Maria Elena." He had 30 hit records. Died: 1985.

Susan Hayward 🎥   6251 Hollywood

Susan Hayward

Actress

BORN Edythe Marrener; June 30, 1918, in Brooklyn, NY. **SPOTLIGHTS** A former model, this beautiful redhead became known for her courageous portrayals of strong-willed phoenix-like characters rising from the ashes. Movies include *Smash Up: The Story of a Woman* (1947—in an Oscar-nominated performance), and *With a Song in My Heart* (1952). Others include *Adam Had Four Sons* (1941), *My Foolish Heart* (1949), *Rawhide* (1951), *The Snows of Kilimanjaro* (1953), *Naked Alibi* (1954), and *I'll Cry Tomorrow* (1955—the biopic of Lillian Roth). Director Walter Wanger observed, "She had real fire inside." **ACHIEVEMENTS** 1958 Best Actress Oscar for *I Want to Live*, portraying a vagrant prostitute sentenced to death in the gas chamber. Hayward had chased the Oscar for 20 years. Thrilled to clutch it to her bosom, she commented, "I can finally relax." **QUOTE** "I like people who see life not as a burden to be borne, but as an adventure to be faced with gaiety and spirit. God gave us the grace of laughter. Why shouldn't we use it?" Died: 1975.

William Bendix   6251 Hollywood

See page 274.

Martha Raye 🎥   6251 Hollywood

Actress, singer, entertainer

BORN Margaret O'Reed; Aug. 27, 1916, in Butte, MT. **SPOTLIGHTS** Best known for her boundless, dynamite energy, she was an oversized personality in a small frame of a woman. Raye possessed a wide mouth, a raucous laugh, and could sing her lungs out. A big-hearted clown, she could punch anyone's lights out in the knockabout school of comedy. Her breakthrough film, *Rhythm of the Range* (1936), stars Bing Crosby. But, it was Raye's rendition of "Mr. Paganini" that won hearts worldwide, making her an overnight celebrity. Other films include *Mountain Music* (1937), *The Big Broadcast of 1938*, *The Boys from Syracuse* (1940) and *Hellzapoppin'* (1941). She felt right at home in *Four Jills in a Jeep* (1944), about female entertainers traveling to bases during wartime. Her favorite film was a black comedy directed by Charlie Chaplin, *Monsieur Verdoux* (1947). Chaplin co-stars with Raye, and it is undoubtedly his best sound film. (It was, however, a commercial failure at the time.) In it, Raye portrays a lucky wife whose bigamous husband (Chaplin) satisfies his needs for money by secretly marrying and murdering rich women. Like a good luck charm, she manages not to get murdered. She later revealed, "One thing Chaplin told me was to dress well when

Martha Raye

I do broad comedy, it heightens it." In 1962, she co-stars opposite Jimmy Durante and Doris Day in the circus musical *Jumbo*. **ACHIEVEMENTS** 1969 Jean Hersholt Humanitarian Award for her wartime efforts. As a result of a long-fought campaign led by her husband Mark Harris, close friends Army Reserve Colonel Michael Teilmann and veteran leader Tony Diamond (head of BRAVO— the veteran's group), she was awarded the Presidential Medal of Freedom in 1994. A true patriot, Raye toured hundreds of thousands of miles during WWII, Korea and Vietnam--under very dangerous conditions--to entertain American troops and improve their morale with her merry buffoonery. Known to soldiers worldwide as "Col. Maggie," she was extremely proud of her status as an honorary Lieutenant Colonel of the Army's Special Forces. Her Bel Air home--virtually a military museum--was always open to Vietnam vets. **QUOTE** At the end of her life, she stated: "I thought success in show business was the answer to everything. It isn't. I don't know what is." Died: 1994.

Connie Stevens   6249 Hollywood

Connie Stevens

Actress, singer

BORN Concetta Ann Ingolia; Aug. 8, 1938, in Brooklyn, NY. **SPOTLIGHTS** As Cricket Blake in the mega-hit TV series "Hawaiian Eye" (1959-'63), Connie became the idolized heroine of every adolescent American girl. She had the dreamiest clothes, the coolest blonde hair and the best personality. Connie also had a #1 record "Sixteen Reasons," and was busy making feature films like the comedy *Rock-a-Bye Baby* with Jerry Lewis (1958), *The Party Crashers* (1958) with Frances Farmer in her last screen appearance), the melodrama *Susan Slade* (1961) with Dorothy McGuire, and later *Grease 2* (1982) with Michelle Pfeiffer and Lorna Luft. In addition to her made-for-TV movies, she wows audiences with her revues. **ACHIEVEMENTS** Founder of Project Windfeather, an organization to help the plight of the Native American Indians. Part Native Iroquois Indian herself, Connie speaks with pride of establishing 83 college scholarships for Native Indian youths in medicine, engineering and business...A patriotic citizen, she entertained troops in Korea, Vietnam and the Gulf War. In 1995 she returned to Vietnam with 100 women who had served there to film the fine documentary "A Healing." During its shooting, Connie picked up a rare strain of bacteria somewhere between Hanoi and Saigon. She returned to America deathly ill, where only massive doses of antibiotics and major surgery to remove her her gall bladder saved her life. **HIGHLIGHTS** Her two daughters, Joely Fisher and Tricia Leigh Fisher, are both gifted actresses, and are the source of her greatest pride and joy.

Hedy Lamarr 🎥   6249 Hollywood

Hedy Lamarr

Actress, inventor
BORN Hedwig Eva Marie Kiesler; Nov. 9, 1913, in Vienna, Austria. **SPOTLIGHTS** A determined 19-year-old, the gorgeous teenager snuck into a local studio where she had no trouble getting noticed or nailing a contract. In *Ecstasy* (1933), she bathed in a lake then ran nude through a forest. The shocking film was a hit. When U.S. studio mogul Louis B. Mayer visited London, Lamarr's agent introduced them. Mayer rejected the seductive glamour puss because he felt she might not be able to fit into his respectable MGM family. The headstrong Lamarr refused to take "no" for an answer. Getting a tip as to which vessel Mayer would be returning to America, she "coincidentally" bought a ticket and "bumped" into him on board. As they crossed the Atlantic Ocean, the exotic dark-haired *femme fatale* wooed a long-term contract out of him. Arriving in America in 1938, she was billed as "the most beautiful girl in Hollywood." Her many starring roles include *Algiers* (1938), *Boom Town* (1940), *Comrade X* (1940)--opposite Clark Gable, *Zieglfeld Girl* (1941), co-starring Judy Garland and Lana Turner, *Samson and Delilah* (1949), as Delilah—her most successful dramatic role, and the hilarious Bob Hope vehicle, *My Favorite Spy* (1951). During WWII, she became a popular pin-up model whose photographs sold at the then-hefty price of 50 cents apiece. While she had a near-flawless outer shell, she was not the greatest actress. What she did bring to the screen, though, was the mystery and allure of a great temptress...She invented and obtained a patent for wireless telecommunications. **QUOTE** "Any girl can be glamorous. All you have to do is stand still and look stupid," she once stated. Died: 2000.

June Knight 🎥   6247 Hollywood

Actress, singer, dancer
BORN Margaret Vallikett; 1908, in Los Angeles, CA. **SPOTLIGHTS** A vivacious, charming, pretty blonde with a cute, turned up nose, she rose to prominence in the 1930s under contract to MGM. She melted Robert Taylor's heart in *Broadway Melody of 1936.* She retired too soon (upon first marrying a wealthy oil man, then an industrialist). Died: 1987.

Phil Baker 📻   6247 Hollywood

Comedian, composer, accordionist
BORN Aug. 24, 1898, in Philadelphia, PA. **SPOTLIGHTS** A former accordion-player vaudeville comic, Baker became an innovator in vaudeville. In 1921, he introduced the idea of double acts on the same bill (as opposed to single acts) along with Aileen Stanley. In 1925, at a block party held in Shubert Alley, New York, Baker entertained thousands when he and Eddie Conrad did a "sister act." Other hosts judged a gigantic Charleston contest. **FILMS** He was a pioneer performer in De Forest Phonofilms (1925) which were promoted as "films that actually talk and reproduce music without the use of phonographs." (See bio of Lee De Forest in this book.) **RADIO** "The Phil Baker Show" (1931-39). He was also the funny emcee on the "Take It or Leave It" quiz show (debut on CBS, 1940) which he played heavily for laughs especially during the WWII years. Baker admitted to being terrified of the microphone because he could not see or hear the audience. He thought it was impossible to judge or gauge his own radio performance, since there was no audience rapport. His hands trembled uncontrollably, his stomach flipped-flopped, and he broke out in a scratchy rash before almost every single broadcast! To help alleviate his terrors, Baker created a stooge character named Beetle, who rudely heckled him and chided Baker's routines. The stooge's famous catchphrase was the yell: "Get Off the Air!" Funny as it was, Baker's fear of the microphone never ended. Died: 1963.

Sylvia Sidney 🎥   6245 Hollywood

Actress
BORN Sophia Kosow; Aug. 8, 1910, in Bronx, NY. **SPOTLIGHTS** A Broadway stage star, this very pretty brunette most often played the hysterical, working-class heroine of film noir. She made her silver screen debut in *Through Different Eyes* (1929). Motion pictures include *Street Scene* (1931), *An American Tragedy* (1931), *City Streets* (1931—with an original screenplay by Dashiell Hammett), opposite Gary Cooper, *Jennie Gerhardt* (1933), *Thirty-Day Princess* (1934), co-starring Cary Grant, *Fury* (1936) co-starring Spencer Tracy, and *Dead End* (1937) with Joel McCrea and Humphrey Bogart. She left Hollywood to return to the Great White Way. Later, she

Sylvia Sidney and James Cagney

appeared as a terrific and durable character actress in *Violent Saturday* (1955) and *Behind the High Wall* (1956). She possessed a vulnerable, slightly nervous quality which made her an ideal character in murky, dark films. She returned to the screen again in *Summer Wishes, Winter Dreams* (1973), in an Oscar-nominated performance. Other movies include Tim Burton's *Beetlejuice* (1988; as Juno, the grumpy after death social worker), *Used People* (1992), and Tim Burton's *Mars Attacks!* (1996; as Grandma Norris). **HIGHLIGHTS** After making *Madame Butterfly* (1932), opposite Cary Grant, she became a gigantic star in Japan. Men were particularly fond on her long neck and seductive face. She was so popular in Asia that a beautiful Sidney portrait was used to sell a trademarked brand of Japanese condoms: "the Sylvia Sidney."...One of her three husbands was Bennett A. Cerf. She was honored by the Film Society of Lincoln Center in 1990 for lifetime achievement. Died: 1999.

Randolph Scott 🎥   6245 Hollywood

Randolph Scott

Actor

BORN Randolph Crane Scott; Jan. 23, 1898, in Orange County, VA. **SPOTLIGHTS** A tall, lean, square-jawed, poker-faced hero, he set the standard for Westerns. He played a strong, fearless, yet soft-spoken cowboy. His first big box-office hit was *Badman's Territory* (1946). His 96 movies include *Abilene Town* (1946), *Colt .45* (1950), *The Nevadan* (1950), *Hangman's Knot* (1953), *The Stranger Who Wore a Gun* (1953 —this flick was shot in 3-D, so unless you're wearing 3-D glasses, the action scenes look flat), and *Decision at Sundown* (1957). He was excellent in *Buchanan Rides Alone* (1958). You can see a great cast of characters in *Ride Lonesome* (1959), where a bounty hunter has to bring in his own brother. The movie stars Scott, Karen Steele, Pernell Roberts, Lee Van Cleef, and James Coburn. In *Comanche Station* (1960) he tries to rescue his kidnapped wife (Nancy Gates) who was abducted by the Comanches. He was perfect as the respected former lawman turned greedy by the lust for gold in *Ride the High Country* (1962). This five-star, must-see picture was directed by Sam Peckinpah and is the only film where Scott played against type—down and dirty. Then, he retired. Died: 1987.

Gary Cooper 🎥   6245 Hollywood

Actor

BORN Frank James Cooper; May 7, 1901, in Helena, MT. **SPOTLIGHTS** "That fellow is the world's greatest actor. He can

Gary Cooper

do, with no effort, what the rest of us spend years trying to learn: to be perfectly natural," John Barrymore stated. Humphrey Bogart said, "Coop is a star." The entire industry admired his honest, strong, silent style. He was known as a man of few words: "Yup...nope." His "Yup" from *The Virginian* (1929, Cooper's first all-talkie and breakthrough film) has been imitated countless times by later movie stars. It was ironic he became such a superstar, because his intention in moving to Los Angeles was to draw cartoons. Once here, he could not break in as an illustrator. Instead, the tall (6'3"), handsome fellow obtained extra work in Westerns because he could ride a horse. The year was 1925 and the pay $5-a-day. He only got that job after he had to pay $65 for a screen test. He later recalled, "I was down to the essential starting point for all actors. I was broke." He appeared in a number of films, then landed his first meaningful role opposite Ronald Colman and Vilma Banky in *The Winning of Barbara Worth* (1926). He was paid $50-per-week, double what he had been earning as an extra. In 1927, he co-stars with Clara Bow, Charles "Buddy" Rogers and Richard Arlen in William Wellman's WWI action picture, *Wings*. This was the very first motion picture to win an Academy Award (see Wellman's bio in this book to learn of the film's historical significance). In 1931, he appears opposite Sylvia Sidney in *City Streets*, with an original screenplay by Dashiell Hammett. He gave Oscar-nominated performances in *Mr. Deeds Goes to Town* (1936), and *The Pride of the Yankees* (1942). By 1939 Cooper was the highest paid contract actor at $500,000 per year. **ACHIEVEMENTS** 1941 Best Actor Oscar for *Sergeant York*. (He had turned down this movie three times before finally being persuaded to do it). 1952 Academy Award for *High Noon*. 1960 Honorary Oscar. **QUOTE** When Nunnally Johnson was writing the script for *Along Came Jones* (1945), he lent Cooper the novel on which the movie was to be based. After several weeks, Johnson asked him, "How did you like the book?" "Oh, fine, I'm about halfway through," the actor responded. "I'm reading it word by word." Died: 1961.

Maurice Tourneur 🎥   6243 Hollywood

Director

BORN Maurice Thomas; Feb. 2, 1876, in France. **SPOTLIGHTS** One of the French cinema's preeminent directors, he put on film for the first time the macabre work of Edgar Allan Poe--*Le Systeme du Docteur Goudron et du Professeur Plume* (1912). He brought his great gifts to America in 1913. He made more than 100 motion pictures, both silents and talkies. A strong stylist who captured wondrous depth and beauty in his pictures, Monsieur Tourneur had previously worked as a book illustrator, a decorator, and as an assistant to the master sculptor Auguste Rodin. Previously, he acted. He retired in 1949 after losing a leg in a car accident in his native country. His son, Jacques Tourneur, is a famous director. Died (Maurice): 1961.

Mercedes McCambridge 6243 Hollywood

See page 181

Edward Dmytryk 6241 Hollywood

Director, teacher
BORN Sept 4, 1908, in Grand Forks, British Columbia, Canada. **SPOTLIGHTS** He started at the bottom in the mail room and worked his way up the directorial ladder with such thrillers as *Murder, My Sweet* (1945). This film noir stars Dick Powell as the noble gumshoe Phillip Marlowe, facing off *femme fatale* Claire Trevor. He followed with the revenge picture, *Cornered* (1945), about an ex-serviceman traveling the globe to find the Nazi who killed his wife. He made the landmark crime drama *Crossfire* (1947), starring Robert Young and Robert Mitchum. Dmytryk directed the classic naval courtroom drama, *The Caine Mutiny* (1954), with Humphrey Bogart as the demented Captain Queeg. It was nominated for several Academy Awards, including Best Picture. That same year, he made the Western *Broken Lance* with Spencer Tracy and Jean Peters. His WWII story, *The Young Lions* (1958), stars Marlon Brando, Montgomery Clift, Dean Martin and Hope Lange, and was one of the highest grossing hits of the year. *Warlock* (1959) with Richard Widmark, Henry Fonda, Anthony Quinn and Dorothy Malone, proved to be a tight, exciting Western. In 1965 he did the crime drama, *Mirage*, starring Gregory Peck, Diane Baker and Walter Matthau. Later, he donned Trojan colors and taught. Died: 1999.

Lana Turner 6233 Hollywood

Actress
BORN Julia Jean Mildred Francis Turner; Feb. 8, 1920, in Wallace, ID. **SPOTLIGHTS** Some people have all the luck. One afternoon in Hollywood the 16-year-old redhead decided to ditch high school to hang out at a drugstore at the corner of Sunset and Highland Avenue. There, the nubile teen beauty was discovered by a Tinseltown powerhouse while she was sipping a strawberry malt at the counter. The well-developed "Sweater Girl" made her screen debut with a walk-on part in *They Won't Forget* (1937), and audiences didn't. They immediately fell in love with this diamond-in-the-rough. Although she came out of the picture a winner, when asked what she thought of herself in the movie, she replied disappointedly, "I looked so cheap." Groomed for stardom, she was coached by fashion designer Adrian. He taught her to walk regally and give good pose. She discovered that with excellent posture came the

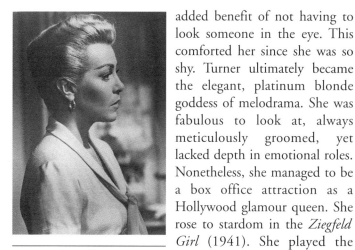

Lana Turner

added benefit of not having to look someone in the eye. This comforted her since she was so shy. Turner ultimately became the elegant, platinum blonde goddess of melodrama. She was fabulous to look at, always meticulously groomed, yet lacked depth in emotional roles. Nonetheless, she managed to be a box office attraction as a Hollywood glamour queen. She rose to stardom in the *Ziegfeld Girl* (1941). She played the murderous adulteress in *The Postman Always Rings Twice* (1946), an actress in the biting drama, *The Bad and the Beautiful* (1952), the mother of an illegitimate daughter in the soapy *Peyton Place* (1957--in an Oscar-nominated performance), and excelled as an ambitious actress in *Imitation of Life* (1959). **SIDELIGHTS** Fans thought Turner's penciled on eyebrows were a fashion statement and copied her. But she was not an intentional trendsetter. Mogul Louis B. Mayer ordered them shaved off for *Adventures of Marco Polo* (1938--her second film), and they never grew back! **QUOTE** "I liked the boys and the boys liked me. I think men are exciting, and the gal who denies that men are exciting is either a lady with no corpuscles, or a saint." Died: 1995.

Henry Winkler 6233 Hollywood

Actor, director, producer, writer
BORN Oct. 30, 1945, in New York, NY. **SPOTLIGHTS** He became an American pop-culture icon as Arthur "Fonzie" Fonzarelli in the nostalgic "Happy Days" television series (1974-'84). Winkler's characterization of the tough, cool, yet vulnerable "Fonz" influenced viewers so greatly that when he signed up for a library card on one show, there was an immediate, real-life 500% increase in library card applications throughout America!

Henry Winkler

Immortalized as the "Fonz," he enjoyed tremendous international appeal, as affirmed by his many global awards, including the *Chevalier de l'Ordre des Arts et Lettres* (the French Ministry of Culture's highest honor). Ironically, the greasy-haired, motorcycle punk he portrayed in the popular sitcom could not have been further from his own roots. His father was president of an international lumber corporation that afforded the young Henry studies in Switzerland, and a lumber mill job in a small

German village. He rejected a family business opportunity to follow his heart's desire to become an actor and study drama at Emerson College. Later, he graduated with a Master's Degree in Fine Arts from Yale University, and acted with the Yale Repertory Theatre. This confirms he could have said "aaayyh!" in several languages. With fame and brains, Winkler ventured behind-the-scenes to executive produce dozens of specials and TV series, including "MacGyver." He produced the outstanding Showtime cable series "Dead Man's Gun." An anthology set in the Old West of 1870, with a twinge of "The Twilight Zone" in it, it is about a unique pistol. Whoever picks it up, his or her life is changed forever. A solid, very capable actor, he excelled onstage in Shakespeare's "Macbeth," made his Broadway stage debut in "42 Seconds from Broadway" in 1973, and performed in the record-breaking run of Neil Simon's "The Dinner Party" in 1999-2000. Motion pictures include *Crazy Joe* (1973), *The Lords of Flatbush* (1974), *The One and Only* (1978), *Night Shift* (1982), *Scream* (1996), *P.U.N.K.S.*, *Ground Control*, *The Waterboy* (all 1998), and *Down to You* (2000). Winkler is also an accomplished film and TV director. **ACHIEVEMENTS** He is a recipient of numerous awards, including a Golden Globe for Best Actor in a Comedy Series, and an Emmy...On Feb. 13, 1980 "Fonzie's" black leather jacket was enshrined in the Smithsonian Museum...This beloved talent received his Walk of Fame star on Feb. 24, 1981...He co-wrote, with singer-songwriter David Capri, the play "Happy Days, The Musical."...Winkler is a tremendous humanitarian, who devotes much personal time and his best efforts to help those in need.

Joel McCrea   6233 Hollywood

See page 14

Eddie Fisher  6233 Hollywood

Eddie Fisher

Singer, actor
BORN Edwin Fisher; Aug. 10, 1928, in Philadelphia, PA. **SPOTLIGHTS** As a skinny, little 12-year-old, he was handpicked from the Thomas Jr. High School by a talent scout to sing "The Army Air Corps Song" on radio. The kid crooner won the "Children's Hour" radio contest, then sang with a couple of bands before heading to the Catskills. It was Labor Day weekend 1949 when comedian Eddie Cantor heard him and booked him for a cross-country tour. Instead of whispering hushed tunes (a popular style at the time), Fisher belted them out with his bold, beautiful, strong voice. The golden-voiced singer became the biggest teen idol of the 1950s—*the pre-Presley obsession*—a full-blown star by 22.

Fisher accurately declared, "Every new song I recorded became an instant best-seller." Hits include: "With These Hands," "I Believe," "How Do You Speak to an Angel?" "Wish You Were Here," "Lady of Spain," "I'm Walking Behind You," and "Oh! My PaPa." He hosted NBC TV's "Coke Time" a top-rated show. Movies include *All About Eve* (1950), and *Butterfield 8* (1960)--with wife Elizabeth Taylor. His four marriages to actresses—Debbie Reynolds (their union produced a daughter Carrie Fisher—an actress/writer, and a son, Todd Fisher, a businessman), Elizabeth Taylor, Connie Stevens (they had two daughters—Joely Fisher and Tricia Leigh Fisher, both actresses), and Terry Richard ended in divorce. He released his memoir, *Been There, Done That*, in 1999.

Carol Channing  6233 Hollywood

Carol Channing

Actress, singer, comedienne
BORN Jan. 31, 1925, in San Francisco, CA. **SPOTLIGHTS** "Aren't I the Luckiest?" A tall, blonde "Kewpie" doll, Channing's trademark is her unique raspy voice, blinking saucer-shaped brown eyes, and gigantic smile. She made her big break by fascinating audiences in a 1948 revue show called "Lend an Ear," in a little theater off Hollywood Boulevard. There, she showed off her comic talents. She has performed in a number of hit stage productions. Channing is a delightful comic creation, ideally suited to play the innocent Lorelei Lee ("the Little Girl from Little Rock") in Anita Loos' stage musical, "Gentlemen Prefer Blondes." Her trademark song became "Diamonds Are a Girl's Best Friend." She has appeared in films, done countless TV guest spots, and was voted a first-rate nightclub entertainer. **SIDELIGHTS** Worried about doing justice to child-genius composer's music for "Hello, Dolly!" (on Broadway), she called "family mentor" George Burns and asked him, "George, do you think I am up to singing this Jerry Herman score?" And George replied, "Carol, what are you worried about? Your voice is as good as mine." **QUOTE** "When you satirize anything, you have to emphasize it by blundering now and then."

Barry Manilow  6233 Hollywood

Singer, songwriter, composer
BORN Barry Pinkus; June 17, 1946, in Brooklyn, NY. **SPOTLIGHTS** Raised by his mother and grandparents, he never knew his father. Young Barry picked up the instrument of the day—the accordion—and, at age seven, dedicated himself to making music. As a teenager, he heard "jazz, big band and Broadway show tunes...I threw out my accordion and knew where my life and music were going." He attended the New

Barry Manilow

York College of Music and the prestigious Juilliard School. At age 18 he found himself in the CBS mail room, free-lanced on an off-Broadway number, then conducted and arranged for Ed Sullivan productions, and worked nights playing a cabaret act duo—where he met Bette Midler. He signed on her team—playing the piano and touring with her—and on the side wrote commercial jingles for giant American corporations. His solo breakthrough tune came in 1973 as "Mandy." Other pop hits and ballads followed, including: "Could It Be Magic," "It's a Miracle," "I Write the Songs," "Hey Mambo," "Even Now," "Copacabana," "Jump Shout Boogie," "Can't Smile Without You," and "Tryin' to Get the Feeling." Although he's ventured into Broadway show tunes and jazz, produced platinum albums for other singers, and scored music to a treasure trove of Johnny Mercer lyrics, he's best known to audiences as a mega-pop star. Ironically he never wanted to be a pop star—never cared about money or fame—he just wanted to write music for musicals. "I was going to be an arranger. I had big aspirations in song writing," Manilow said. **ACHIEVEMENTS** His awards include a Grammy, Tony and Emmy. He has sold 58 million records worldwide and posted a string of 25 consecutive Top 40 hits. *Rolling Stone* magazine anointed him "a giant among entertainers." **QUOTE** "I'm a musician. I'm a creative man. That's all I care about really."

Sir Andrew Lloyd Webber 🎭 6233 Hollywood

Sir Andrew Lloyd Webber

Composer
BORN March 22, 1948, in London, England. **SPOTLIGHTS** He is the world's most successful living musical composer. Continually breaking new records, he became the first person to have three musicals running simultaneously in New York and three in London. In June 1997 "Cats" became the longest-running play in Broadway history, surpassing the previous title holder, "A Chorus Line." His best-loved works are "Joseph and the Amazing Technicolor Dreamcoat" (1968), "Jesus Christ Superstar" (1971), "Evita" (1976), "Cats" (1981), "The Phantom of the Opera" (1988) and "Sunset Boulevard" (1993). Lesser known are some of his film scores, including *Gumshoe* (1971) and *The Odessa File* (1973). In 1996 a reworked *Evita* made its way to the silver screen starring Madonna. **ACHIEVEMENTS** He is the recipient of countless awards, including four Tonys, four Drama Desk Awards, and three Grammys. He was awarded a knighthood in 1992, earning him the title of "Sir." He received his star on the Hollywood Walk of Fame on Feb. 26, 1993. In 1996 Queen Elizabeth II bestowed a barony on Webber.

Mitchell Leisen 🎥 6233 Hollywood

Mitchell Leisen

Director
BORN Oct. 6, 1897, in Menominee, MI. **SPOTLIGHTS** He was educated in both art and architecture at the Art Institute of Chicago and Washington University in St. Louis. With his keen sense of color and design, Leisen stylized his way into show business as a costume designer for the prominent director Cecil B. DeMille. His good fortune of working with *la creme de la creme* continued when he joined Douglas Fairbank's team assembled for *The Thief of Bagdad* (1922). On the United Artists's set, he met and worked with Hollywood's all-time greatest Makeup Master, Max Factor. The resulting motion picture turned out to be a breathtaking triumph. Associated with Paramount for two decades, he directed the must-see *Death Takes a Holiday* (1934), starring Fredric March; *Murder at the Vanities* (1934), a comedy-mystery starring Jack Oakie—with some highly unusual songs; *Hands Across the Table* (1935), a romantic comedy starring Carole Lombard and Fred MacMurray. Leisen's *Easy Living* (1937) is a five-star, classic screwball farce (a definite must-see). It stars Jean Arthur and Edward Arnold in a modern-day Cinderella story, cleverly written by Preston Sturges. You'll get the idea quickly when you see the irate tycoon tossing a sable coat out the window, hitting a working-class Arthur on the head. He switched directions in the romantic drama *Hold Back the Dawn* (1941) starring Charles Boyer, Olivia de Havilland and Paulette Goddard. Boyer plays an unlucky gigolo stuck south of the border, de Havilland plays a spinster teacher (the possible ticket for entry into the U.S.) and Goddard is Boyer's brassy tootsie. When Leisen retired from films, he rediscovered his love for interior design. Died: 1972.

James Nederlander 🎭 6233 Hollywood

Broadway producer
BORN 1922, in Detroit, MI. **SPOTLIGHTS** "There are no bad theaters, just bad plays," he once stated. His productions include *good* works, including "Whose Life Is It Anyway?", "Annie," and "Lena Horne: The Lady and Her Music." He is the owner of seven West Coast theaters, and 11 Broadway the-

aters, and is head of one of the largest chains of legitimate theaters. He is responsible for revivals of such stage winners as "Hello, Dolly!" "Porgy and Bess," and "Fiddler on the Roof."

Marshall Neilan 🎥   6233 Hollywood

Director
BORN April 11, 1891, in San Bernardino, CA. **SPOTLIGHTS** How did he break into show business? He was a chauffeur—when few knew how to drive an automobile—to a great director. Through this contact, he got his chance to act. Neilan found his artistic niche, however, behind the camera. He was at his best directing "America's Sweetheart," Mary Pickford, in *Rebecca of Sunnybrook Farm* (1917) and *A Little Princess* (1917). Died: 1958.

Kathleen Lockhart 🎥   6233 Hollywood

Actress
BORN Kathleen Arthur; 1894, in England. **SPOTLIGHTS** A reliable Bristish-born character actress, she made her screen debut in 1936. She co-stars with her husband, Gene Lockhart, in *A Christmas Carol* (1938). Her daughter, June, also had a role in the classic film. (See the separate bios of Gene Lockhart and June Lockhart in this book). Died: 1978.

Edward G. Robinson 🎥   6233 Hollywood

Actor
BORN Emmanual Goldenberg; Dec. 12, 1893, in Bucharest, Romania. **SPOTLIGHTS** Although short and stocky with a pale, puffy visage, he became a giant playing a vicious, conceited, crime kingpin in the classic gangster film, *Little Caesar* (1931). At the end of the movie, Robinson gasps out his memorable dying line: "Mother of Mercy, is this the end of Rico?" The delivery was made all the more perfect by Robinson's mocking mouth. The movie was one of Warner Bros. biggest hits of the year. Robinson stars in *Five Star Final* (1931), a blistering drama about yellow journalism. As a reformed criminal, he tried to mix with society in the comedy *The Little Giant* (1933). Two years later, he plays a mild-mannered bank clerk mistaken for a gangster in the screwball comedy *The Whole Town's Talking*. He was delightful in the tongue-in-cheek gangster parody, *Brother Orchid* (1940), opposite Ann Southern and Humphrey Bogart. He was also funny spoofing himself in *Larceny, Inc.* (1942). Both were directed by Lloyd Bacon. He plays a cruel captain in the action movie, *Sea Wolf* (1941). Then, Robinson battles George Raft for the affection of Marlene Dietrich in the testosterone-laden, dime-novel melodrama *Manpower* (1941). He made the easy transition to being one of the most powerful players of 1940s film noir genre in *Double Indemnity* (1944), and that same year in the thriller *The Woman in the Window*. As usual, he was brilliant—hypnotic—in *Scarlet Street* (1945) with its surprise ending. He enjoyed working with his pals in the all-star cast of *Key Largo*

Edward G. Robinson

(1948), where he revives his gangster persona and makes everyone sweat. His career suffered during the Communist scare where he was unfairly called before the House Committee on Un-American Activities. He considered himself off the blacklist when cast as a Hebrew leader in DeMille's *The Ten Commandments* (1956--the remake). He appears in the good caper picture *Seven Thieves* (1960), with Joan Collins and Rod Steiger. In 1965 he co-stars with Steve McQueen in *The Cincinnati Kid*. In the early 1970s, Paramount wanted director Francis Ford Coppola to cast Robinson as *The Godfather*. (Coppola won with the actor of his choice, Marlon Brando.) The compelling sci-fi thriller *Soylent Green* (1973), co-starring Charlton Heston, was Robinson's last screen appcarance. **ACHIEVEMENTS** Although never nominated for an Academy Award during his 40-year career, the Academy decided to give him a Special Oscar, marking: "his greatness as a player, a patron of the arts and a dedicated citizen...in sum, a Renaissance man." Unfortunately this giant of talent died before he could receive it in 1973. **QUOTE** "They say imitation is the best form of flattery, but when the imitators start imitating the imitators, it's not good." About enduring as an actor, Robinson observed, "To last you need to be real. And you have to work. I still work as hard, probably harder, at each role I get as I did at the beginning. To my mind, the actor has this great responsibility, you know, it's like taking on another person's life and you have to do it as sincerely and honestly as you can."

Keith Carradine 🦪   6233 Hollywood

Actor, singer, songwriter, musician
BORN Aug. 8, 1949, in San Mateo, CA. **SPOTLIGHTS** A multi-talented performer of stage, screen, and television, Carradine is an all-around versatile talent. He was nominated for a Tony Award for portraying humorist and American icon Will Rogers in the hit show, "The Will Rogers Follies." The show won six Tonys, including Best Musical, and a Grammy for Best Musical Show album. His song "I'm Easy," which he performed in the movie *Nashville* (1975), won an Academy Award and a Golden Globe award for Best Song in a Motion Picture. Motion pictures include *A Gunfight* (1971), *McCabe*

Keith Carradine

and Mrs. Miller (1971), *The Duelists* (1977), *Pretty Baby, Sgt. Pepper's Lonely Hearts Club Band* (both 1978), *The Long Riders* (1980--with David and Robert Carradine, Stacy and James Keach, and Randy and Dennis Quaid), *Southern Comfort* (1981), *Maria's Lover* (1984), *Crisscross* (1992), *Wild Bill* (1995), and *A Thousand Acres* (1997). Television mini-series include "A Rumour of War," "Chiefs," and "Murder Ordained."...He is the son of the late, great actor John Carradine. Just like his father, he has a passion for acting. And he is lanky, just like his father. But he is much better looking. He possesses a natural, easy-going charm with a sparkle in his eyes. His older brother David became star of the hit television series, "Kung Fu." (See both John's and David's bios in this book.) His daughter is the actress Martha Plimpton; he had met her actress mother when both were performing in "Hair" on Broadway...He received his Walk of Fame star on July 15, 1993, in front of the Pantages.

Joshua Logan 🎥 6233 Hollywood
Director, writer, producer
BORN Oct. 5, 1908, in Texarkana, TX. **SPOTLIGHTS** Educated at Princeton University, he was actively involved in both collegiate drama and sports. During the summer, he organized a stock group called the University Players, where James Stewart, Henry Fonda and Margaret Sullavan tested their budding skills. Next, he won a scholarship to study method acting at the Moscow Art Theater under the great Stanislavsky, then returned to New York. He both acted and directed stage plays. With true expertise, he brought "Annie Get Your Gun," "Charley's Aunt," "Mister Roberts," "South Pacific" (also co-author), and "Fanny" to Broadway. Known for his volcanic temperament and flamboyant personality, the whole theater vibrated with energy when Logan was around. He stated, "To me, emotion is the guts of the theater." Turning to film work, he co-wrote the *Mister Roberts* (1955) screenplay with Frank Nugent (from the play he co-wrote years earlier with Thomas Heggen). He directed William Holden and Kim Novak in the must-see Americana drama, *Picnic* (1956). Marilyn Monroe gave one of her best performances in his critically acclaimed *Bus Stop* (1956), a simple story about a saloon singer and a smitten cowboy set in a rodeo town. The Korean War story about forbidden love, *Sayonara* (1957), stars Marlon Brando, Ricardo Montalban, Miko Taka, Miyoshi Umeki, Red Buttons and James Garner. Both Miyoshi Umeki and Red Buttons won Academy Awards for their performances. **SIDELIGHTS** Logan suffered from manic depression throughout his lifetime, staying in psychiatric hospitals during crisis periods. Eventually treated with Lithium, he said it "saved my sanity." With daily

medication, he was able to enjoy a well-earned, 20-year retirement. Died: 1988.

Arthur Godfrey 🎙 6223 Hollywood
See page 419

Bette Davis 📺 6233 Hollywood
See next page, 206

Spring Byington 📺 6233 Hollywood
See page 98

Jane Froman 🎙 6231 Hollywood
Singer

Jane Froman

BORN Ellen J. Froman; Nov. 10, 1917, in University City, MO. **SPOTLIGHTS** Her rich soprano voice won her singing engagements with Benny Goodman, Paul Whiteman, the Dorseys and Charlie Spivak. Next, the dark-haired beauty thrilled audiences on Broadway. When President Roosevelt summoned her to entertain at the first USO show at Camp Belvoir (prior to the Pearl Harbor attack), troops fell in love with her. While en route to Europe for another USO tour in 1943, she was seriously injured when the plane crashed. After a series of painful operations, she bravely volunteered again for the USO, performing for the Allied Forces in 1945. A frequent guest star on "The Andrews Sisters Show," a regular on 1940s records, she starred on radio's "Yours for a Song." Hits include "With a Song in My Heart," "I've Got a Right to Sing the Blues," "Soft Lights and Sweet Music," "I Believe," and "Rocking Chair." In 1952 she was voted "Personality of the Year." TV: "Jane Froman's USA Canteen" (1952-'55). Her remarkable life story was made into the motion picture *With a Song in My Heart*, starring Susan Hayward. **QUOTE** "I get 10 times more kick out of living than I used to. Probably because I'm not scared of very much. I've been through it and I know I can take it." Died: 1980.

Constance Collier 🎥 6231 Hollywood
Actress, dancer, singer
BORN Laura C. Hardie; Jan. 22, 1878, in England. **SPOTLIGHTS** Starting out as a chorus girl in musical revues, she blossomed into an important stage actress. Collier made her silver screen debut in D.W. Griffith's silent classic

Intolerance (1916). An accomplished dramatic talent with an aristocratic bearing, talkies include *Little Lord Fauntleroy* (1936), *Wee Willie Winkie, Stage Door* (both 1937), *Monsieur Beaucatre* (1946), Paramount's biopic *The Perils of Pauline* (1947), and Hitchcock's *Rope* (1948). Died: 1955.

Karl Malden 🎥 6231 Hollywood

Actor

Karl Malden

BORN Mladen Sekulovich (nicknamed "Suki"); March 22, 1914, in Gary, IN. **SPOTLIGHTS** An accomplished Broadway performer since 1937, and one of the most steadily employed, Malden appeared virtually every season in the top plays: "Golden Boy," "Key Largo," "The Gentle People," and "The Desperate Hours," to name just a few. He made his motion picture debut in the top-rated drama, *They Knew What They Wanted* (1940), starring Carole Lombard and Charles Laughton. Although it had been a small role, Malden's capabilities were immediately recognizable. Noted for his realism, he became one of cinema's most distinguished character actors of all time. Motion pictures include *13 rue Madeleine* (1946—told in a semi-documentary style), the terrific crime picture *Boomerang!* (1947), *The Gunfighter* (1950—as a timid bartender), Hitchcock's *I Confess* (as the policeman), *Diplomatic Courier* a Cold War drama, *Ruby Gentry* opposite Jennifer Jones (all 1952), *On the Waterfront* (1954—as the Catholic priest), *Baby Doll* (1956—playing the mixed-up husband), *Fear Strikes Out* (1957—as the domineering father), *The Hanging Tree* (1959—in the role of the villain), *Birdman of Alcatraz* (1962), *Gypsy* (1962—as the hopeful, then disgusted suitor), *Patton* (1970—as General Bradley), and *Nuts* (1987) starring Barbra Streisand and Richard Dreyfuss. TV buffs know him as Detective Lieutenant Mike Stone on "The Streets of San Francisco" (1972-'77), a series co-starring Michael Douglas. **ACHIEVEMENTS** 1951 Best Supporting Actor Oscar for *A Streetcar Named Desire*, in the same role he had played earlier on Broadway. In 1984 he won an Emmy for "Fatal Vision." In 1989 he became president of the Academy of Motion Picture Arts and Sciences. Malden rejuvenated the tired Academy, gave a new face and format to the Oscars presentation, and housed the AMPAS in a world-class facility for year-long studies, training and education. He retired from that post in 1993. **QUOTE** While attending Arkansas State Teachers College he majored in physical education with plans to become an instructor. After a few semesters, he transferred to Chicago's Goodman Theater Dramatic School. He admitted, "I was fooling myself. I knew I'd be an actor. My father was an actor in Yugoslavia."

Jackie Gleason ● 6225 Hollywood

See page 364

Buster Keaton ▄ 6225 Hollywood

See page 76

Anthony Mann 🎥 6225 Hollywood

Director

BORN Emil Anton Bundsmann; June 30, 1906, in San Diego, CA. **SPOTLIGHTS** He started as a production manager at the Theater Guild in the 1930s, then directed stage productions. David O. Selznick discovered his talents and hired him to handle nervous hopefuls for their screen tests. He directed the "B" film noir *Desperate* (1947), an entertaining flick with a capable cast: Steve Brodie, Audrey Long and Raymond Burr. His biggest box office successes were Westerns all starring James Stewart. *Winchester 73* (1950) co-stars Shelley Winters and Dan Duryea; *The Naked Spur* (1953) with Janet Leigh, Ralph Meeker, Robert Ryan and Milliard Mitchell; *The Far Country* (1954) features Ruth Roman, Corinne Calvet and Walter Brennan, and *The Man from Laramie* (1955) co-stars Arthur Kennedy, Donald Crisp and Cathy O'Donnell. In a break from his Westerns, Mann directed the historical epic, *El Cid* (1961), with Charlton Heston and Sophia Loren. It is about at 11th-century warrior. Died: 1967.

Nat "King" Cole 🎤 6225 Hollywood

See page 66

Quentin Reynolds 🎤 6225 Hollywood

Reporter, broadcaster

BORN April 11, 1902, Bronx, New York. **SPOTLIGHTS** An ace reporter, writer and author, Reynolds first observed Adolf Hitler when sent to Germany in 1933. Later, his news coverage of World War II surpassed all other reporters in terms of output and quantity. He wrote scores of books, with the first paragraph of his 1941 book *The Wounded Don't Cry* one of the most memorable book openings: "HITLER MARCHED into Belgium just as I marched into the Ritz bar. The first thing I did was to order a drink. I don't know what Hitler did first." Narrator: *Naked Africa* (1959); *Justice and Caryl Chessman* (1960). Died: 1965.

Bette Davis 🎥 6225 Hollywood

Actress

BORN Ruth Elizabeth Davis; April. 5, 1908, in Lowell, MA. **SPOTLIGHTS** "The First Lady of the Screen" earned that title through sheer determination, talent, and quality. It was a good thing she had more acting ability than Hollywood had ever

Bette Davis

seen, because Davis was competing with the most glamorous women in the world—Greta Garbo, Marlene Dietrich and Hedy Lamarr. Her strong, gutsy personality kept her going, even after she was fired by George Cukor from her first acting job in a stock company. She then "flunked" a screen test; after seeing it Sam Goldwyn remarked, "Who wasted my time?" Next, she was told by an executive at Universal Studios that she had no sex appeal, then was signed by that same studio only to be dropped a year later. With wisdom we can be grateful for, Warner Brothers picked her up, and the rest is history. Her impressive list of fine credits include *Of Human Bondage* (1934), *Bordertown* (1935), *Dark Victory* (1939), *The Old Maid* (1939), *All This and Heaven Too* (1940), *The Letter* (1940), *The Little Foxes* (1941), *Now, Voyager* (1942), *All About Eve* (1950), *Pocketful of Miracles* (1961), *What Ever Happened to Baby Jane?* (1962), and *Hush...Hush, Sweet Charlotte* (1964), among others. During her decades of making films, she went from ingenue, to leading lady, to character actress without breaking her stride. **ACHIEVEMENTS** Best Actress Academy Awards: 1935 for *Dangerous*, and 1938 for *Jezebel*. 1978-'79 Emmy for "Stranger: The Story of a Mother and Daughter." In 1977 Davis became the first woman recipient of the American Film Institute Life Achievement Award. **QUOTE** "I'm a ham. That is, a good ham. A good ham is an actor who really enjoys giving pleasure to people." **SIDELIGHTS** Late in her life, her New York attorney told her a rumor was circulating around town that she was dead. She cocked her head and declared,

"With the newspaper strike on, I wouldn't consider it!" This legendary talent died in 1989.

Eddy Arnold 6225 Hollywood

Eddy Arnold

Singer, musician, composer
BORN Richard Edward Arnold; May 15, 1918, in Henderson, TN. **SPOTLIGHTS** Son of a sharecropper, his devoted mother taught him to play guitar. She also sang sweet, smooth lullabies to him everyday. As a young man, the "Tennessee Plowboy" became one of America's favorite country-western stars. Managed by Colonel Tom Parker (who later handled Elvis Presley), the Plowboy became a gigantic hit maker. His plaintive songs were accented by a rural touch: "Mommy, Please Stay Home With Me," "Rocking Alone in an Old Rocking Chair," "Don't Rob Another Man's Castle," and "I Couldn't Believe It Was True." Starting in the late 1940s and carrying through the 1950s he went big with: "A Heart Full of Love," "Any Time," "Texarkana Baby," "Bouquet of Roses," and the rerelease of "Cattle Call." Other tunes: "I Really Don't Want to Know," "I'll Hold You in My Heart," "It's a Sin," "Just Call Me Lonesome," "Make the World Go Away," "Welcome to My World," and "You Don't Know Me." He enjoyed a huge collection of 1960 hits, but had substituted his cowboy image for that of an urbane crooner. He he was seeking acceptance by the cafe society. He was one of the first C&W singers to cross-over to pop. Arnold's affable personality also proved to be ideal for TV. He continued to chart records into the 1980s. He ranked in the highest caliber of singers, and was the best-selling solo country act of all time *until* Garth Brooks broke his record.

Irene Rich 6225 Hollywood

Irene Rich

Actress, singer
BORN Irene Luther; Oct. 13, 1891, in Buffalo, NY. **SPOTLIGHTS** An extremely busy actress during the silent era, her pictures include *Jes' Call Me Jim* (1920), and *They Had to See Paris* (1929)—both were with Will Rogers. This dignified brunette also played against other giant stars of the day, such as Dustin Farnum and Wallace Beery. When an argument with Warner Bros. in October of 1933 left a sour taste in her mouth, she switched to radio.

She stated, "At three o'clock in the morning I took a plane for New York, and the next day I presented myself at the National Broadcasting Studios." She enjoyed steady employment starring in a variety of radio dramas. **QUOTE** "What is known as 'bluff' is merely self assurance. That is the secret. If you believe you can do things, you will do them. It is faith, hope and self assurance which win." Died: 1988.

Red Foley ⚫   6225 Hollywood

Red Foley

Singer, songwriter

BORN Clyde Julian; June 17, 1910, in Blue Lick, KY. **SPOTLIGHTS** The gentleman of country-western music, this smooth, flexible baritone talent hosted the *National Barn Dance* road shows in the late 1930s and early '40s. His first big record was "Old Shep." Other hit tunes include "Goodnight, Irene" (duet with Ernest Tubb), "Love Bug Itch" (duet with Tubb and Minnie Pearl), "Smoke on the Water" (a World War II song), "New Jole Blon," "Tennessee Saturday Night," "Tennessee Border," "Chattanoogie Shoe Shine Boy," "Birmingham Bounce," "Blues in My Heart," and "(There'll Be) Peace in My Valley (for Me)"—a gospel tune. One of the most versatile C&W performers, he could make the transition from a hymn to a rhythm-and-blues to a novelty tune, without missing a beat or sounding unnatural. In the 1950s, Foley hosted the "Ozark Jubilee"—one of the earliest C&W shows. He also promoted new talent on his own TV show during the 1950s. 1967: Inducted into the Country Music Hall of Fame. **HIGHLIGHTS** Along with pal Ernest Tubb, Foley made a historic contribution to C&W music by establishing the very first recording sessions in Nashville, TN...His daughter, Shirley, married singer-actor Pat Boone (see his bio in this book). **SIDELIGHTS** He was the genial master of ceremonies at the Grand Ole Opry on the historic night of June 11, 1949 when Hank Williams (Sr.) made his memorable debut performance singing "Lovesick Blues." Later, when Williams died, Foley—with his voice breaking—sang "Peace in the Valley" to a crowd of 25,000 mourners. Then, Williams' son, Hank Williams, Jr., was on tour with Foley when Foley died in 1968. Williams recorded "I Was with Red Foley (the Night He Passed Away).

Tod Browning 🎥   6225 Hollywood

Director, screenwriter

BORN Charles Albert; July 12, 1882, in Louisville, KY. **SPOTLIGHTS** After a mysterious and troubled childhood, the teen ran away from home and joined the circus. After learning the tricks of the trade, he performed comedy on the burlesque and vaudeville circuits. He became an actor at Biograph Studios in 1914, and a year later directed his first movie. During the 1920s, he began his long association with Lon Chaney, starting with *Outside the Law* (1921). He shocked audiences—not to mention MGM executives—with *The Unholy Three* (1925), starring Lon Chaney, Harry Earles and Victor McLaglen. His string of motion pictures continued with Chaney. In *East Is East* (1929) Chaney plays a deranged animal trapper who viciously kills his wife by releasing a wild gorilla on her. I'm happy to report that the gorilla eats him, too. Crowned the Horror King of the 1930s, Browning specialized in fear and terror. Universal released Browning's *Dracula* (1931), with the threatening Bela Lugosi in the title role. This brilliant masterpiece was pure box office gold, so Universal gave Browning free rein on his next project. *Freaks* (1932), a circus movie, was the incredible result. It is his most haunting, eccentric, grotesque work, yet beautiful and powerful in essence and meaning. Made decades ahead of its time, *Freaks* remains one of the most unusual, controversial and original films ever made. When it first came out, entire COUNTRIES banned it, and kept it banned for decades. Yet the true "freaks" in the movie are not the disfigured humans born of genetic accidents (and on display at the circus), but those born into lovely shapes and forms. Able to move about freely in their "disguise" of beauty, these greedy, lascivious, selfish, remorseless sociopaths manipulate the weak, the vulnerable, and anyone else who has the misfortune to meet and trust them. It is a burning realization of true ugliness; the freak of nature This thought-provoking movie leaves the viewer analyzing it for a long time, a mark of a real masterpiece. Died: 1962.

Tod Browning

6211 HOLLYWOOD

Sir Cedric Hardwicke 🎬 6211 Hollywood

Sir Cedric Hardwicke

Actor

BORN Feb.19, 1883, in England. **SPOTLIGHTS** "I believe God felt sorry for actors, so He created Hollywood to give them a place in the sun and a swimming pool," he mused. This dark-haired, aristocratic, intelligent, sad looking performer was versatile in villainous or gentle roles. Motion pictures include *Les Miserables* (1935), *The Hunchback of Notre Dame* (1939), *The Moon Is Down* (1940), *Forever and a Day* (1943), *Wilson* (1944), *Keys of the Kingdom* (1945), *Rope* (1948), *I Remember Mama* (1948), *The Winslow Boy* (1950), *Salome* (1953), and *Richard III* (1955). *Newsweek* described him as "stage and screen's veteran Anglo-Saxon archetype...a born actor who knows how to speak an author's lines as if they were new from his own brain." **ACHIEVEMENTS** He trained at the prestigious Royal Academy of Dramatic Arts. Knighted in 1934. **QUOTE** Although he played character comedy for years in England, he rarely got those types of roles in America. He accounted for it by stating, "The average producer feels that if you have a title you must be stuffy, and getting laughs is beneath your dignity." Died: 1964.

Johnnie Ray 💿 6211 Hollywood

Singer

BORN John Alvin Ray; Jan. 10, 1927, in Dallas, OR. **SPOTLIGHTS** Injured when his Boy Scout pals roughly tossed him in a blanket, he became hearing-impaired. Ray did not let his deafness silence his singing. In 1952, after his first gigantic hit "Cry" exposed his fiery emotions, Ray was crowned the "Prince of Wails," "The Nabob of Sob," and "The Weeper." One critic described his voice: " like sandpaper on velvet." Ray was unlike other early 1950s vocal contemporaries, such as Perry Como, whose "coolness" was their trademark. "Cry" was produced by Mitch Miller, with backup by the Four Lads, and sold 25 million copies. It was backed by the #2 "The Little White Cloud That Cried." Pop hits include: "Please Mr. Sun," "Just Walking in the Rain," "Yes Tonight, Josephine," "You Don't Owe Me a Thing," "Satisfied," "Such a Night," "Flip,

Johnnie Ray

Flop and Fly," and "Who's Sorry Now." His lifelong true dream was to be a movie star. He got a shot at the silver screen as a supporting actor—dressed in a priest's frock—in the musical *There's No Business Like Show Business* (1954), starring Ethel Merman, Donald O'Connor and Mitzi Gaynor. Active as a headliner on the international club circuit, Ray was especially loved in England and Australia. **HIGHLIGHTS** After a 1958 surgery restored much of the hearing in his left ear, he heard his voice completely for the first time. Shocked, he commented, "It sounded like the atom bomb exploding in pieces everywhere." Singer Tony Bennett paid him the ultimate compliment when he stated, "Johnnie smashed all the rules. He did something completely different—he became a visual artist. Johnnie charged an audience, he had to rip the curtain down, jump on top of the piano, because he just couldn't stay cool enough not to. And in that sense, I really consider Johnnie Ray to be the father of rock 'n' roll." **ACHIEVEMENTS** He influenced the Beatles, Elton John, Morrissey (who wore a hearing aid on stage in Ray's honor), and Billy Idol. Rocker Billy Joel paid tribute to Ray in the first line of his hit song "We Didn't Start the Fire." **QUOTE** "Above all things a man must be masculine. But when he has to express emotion, he suppresses himself because he doesn't think it's manly. I just show people the emotion they're afraid to show." Died: 1990.

Alice Brady 🎬 6211 Hollywood

Actress, singer

BORN Nov. 2, 1892, in New York, New York. **SPOTLIGHTS** After graduating from a convent, Brady arrived professionally on Broadway with a great theatrical tradition behind her. She first appeared in her father's stage production of *The Balkan Princess*. This accomplished singer became best known for her association in Gilbert and Sullivan musicals. She was rated "the most popular Broadway star" between the years 1909 -

Alice Brady

1917. By World War I, she was one of the highest paid actresses in all of show business. Brady was among the initial group of theatrically trained performers to "pose" for the pictures, beginning with the silent *As Ye Sow* (1914). She would later perform with her father, William A. Brady, at charity events, like the 1921 Friars' Club Social "Insult Night," where the two of them did the wharf scene from *After Dark*—leaping into a stage tank, then emerged dripping while still in character. Good in both comedies and dramas, from silents to talkies: *The Gay Divorcee* (1934); *My Man Godfrey* (1936); and *100 Men and a Girl* (1937). Her last film was *Young Mr. Lincoln* (1939), before she became critically ill. **ACHIEVEMENTS** She won a Best Supporting Actress Oscar for *In Old Chicago* (1938). The following year she died.

Carol Lawrence 🎭   6211 Hollywood

Actress, singer, dancer

Carol Lawrence

BORN Carol Larria; Sept. 5, 1934, in Melrose Park, IL. **SPOTLIGHTS** An exuberant, beautiful, dark-haired talent, her glowing stage performances have culminated in numerous hit Broadway shows. She is the acclaimed, award-winning star of many musicals, including "Guys and Dolls," "South Pacific," "West Side Story," and "Funny Girl." Lawrence is also a popular Casino headliner, club entertainer, and has appeared as a guest on countless TV shows. In 2000, she starred in the successful run of "Over the River and Through the Woods," directed by Asaad Kelada.

Constance Cummings 🎥 6211 Hollywood

Actress

BORN Constance Halverstadt; May 15, 1910, in Seattle, WA. **SPOTLIGHTS** This determined 21-year-old brunette fought back to become a star after being fired from her first film. She turns in an impressive performance in *The Criminal Code*

Constance Cummings with Hugh Sinclair

(1931), and gives it her best in *Movie Crazy* (1932) with comedian Harold Lloyd. The gifted beauty easily kept pace with Spencer Tracy and Jack Oakie in *Looking for Trouble* (1934). She's delightful opposite Robert Montgomery (as his bride) in *Haunted Honeymoon* (1940) where the newlyweds try in vain to enjoy themselves. She's interesting to watch with Peter Sellers in the black comedy, *The Battle of the Sexes* (1960). **ACHIEVEMENTS** She won a 1979 Tony for "Wings."

Joseph L. Mankiewicz 🎥 6211 Hollywood

Director, screenwriter, producer

BORN Feb. 11, 1909, in Wilkes-Barre, PA. **SPOTLIGHTS** After graduating from Columbia University in New York, this very literate talent joined his older brother, Oscar-winning screenwriter Herman J. Mankiewicz, in Hollywood. For 20th Century-Fox he directed the fable *The Ghost and Mrs. Muir* (1947), with the beautiful Gene Tierney and the equally easy-on-the-eyes Rex Harrison. Bernard Herrmann provided the haunting score. Other movies include *No Way Out* (1950) with Sidney Poitier, Linda Darnell and Richard Widmark; *Five Fingers* (1952) --a WWII espionage piece; *The Barefoot Contessa* (1954) with the breathtaking Ava Gardner and Humphrey Bogart (who plays a cynical Hollywood director); and *Guys and Dolls* (1955) a musical with Marlon Brando, Jean Simmons, Frank Sinatra, Vivian Blaine and Stubby Kaye with such classic tunes as "Luck Be a Lady Tonight." In 1959 he directed a movie based on a Tennessee Williams play—*Suddenly, Last Summer*—teaming Elizabeth Taylor, Katherine Hepburn and Montgomery Clift in the gripping drama. He closed his career with his panache by quitting on a high note after receiving an Oscar nomination for the comedy/thriller, murder mystery *Sleuth* (1972), with Laurence Olivier and Michael Caine. **ACHIEVEMENTS** 1949 Best Screenplay and Best Director Oscars for *A Letter to Three Wives* (the first time a director won in both categories). 1950 two Oscars (again!) for Screenwriter and Director for *All About Eve*. Died: 1993.

Frank Faylen   6211 Hollywood

Actor

Frank Faylen

BORN Frank Rufin; Dec. 8, 1909, in St. Louis, MO. **SPOTLIGHTS** His parents were famous vaudevillians—headliners of the team Ruf and Cusik. When Frank was an infant, his father carried the lad onstage with him at the Orpheum Theatre in Denver. By age two, he was on a road tour. As he grew, he became a pantomime artist, then a clown, next an acrobatic song-and-dance man. By age 18, he had graduated from St. Joseph's Preparatory College in Kirkwood, Missouri. By 19 he was making films, and within a year and a half had appeared in 26 pictures, including *The Grapes of Wrath* (1940). In 1943 Paramount Pictures signed this superb character actor. He played the sadistic nurse Bim in *The Lost Weekend* (1945)—his breakthrough role—in an Academy Award-winning picture. Faylen was admired for his great diversification of roles. Films include the dramatic Western, *Blood on the Moon* (1948), and the slapstick Disney comedy, *The Monkey's Uncle* (1965). TV: He played Herbert T. Gillis, contending with his teenage son (played by Dwayne Hickman), in "The Many Loves of Dobie Gillis" (1959-'63). Died: 1985.

Marie Prevost   6211 Hollywood

Actress

Marie Prevost

BORN Mary Dunn; Nov. 8, 1898, in Sarnia, Ontario, Canada. **SPOTLIGHTS** An absolutely lovely 5'4", 123-pound, brunette with large blue eyes. She got her big break in a Mack Sennett's *Her Nature Dance* (1917) as a bathing beauty. After making a handful of films she jumped from the gaggle of gals to become a leading lady. She shot to stardom in the Ernst Lubitsch feature, *The Marriage Circle* (1924). It was her favorite role. Among her 65 films are: *Kiss Me Again* (1925), *The Godless Girl* (1929), *The Party Girl* (1929), *Only Yesterday* (1933), and *Thirteen Hours by Air* (1936). **QUOTE** "What is beauty? I can't define it. I can only be thrilled and wonder at a face that may produce that in me, yet have no regularity of feature. The time, of course, is past in pictures when a girl can get in on looks alone. No one can give anyone else advice how to get into pictures. Each career is a voyage over an uncharted sea. To tell you to get in the way I did, might be just what will keep you out." **LOWLIGHTS** Although she made the difficult transition from talkies to silents, she gained weight in the mid-1930s. Considered too fat for her normal roles, Prevost dieted with all her will power. She ultimately suffered from anorexia. Prevost was found dead due to starvation at the age of 38, in 1937.

Earl Godwin   6207 Hollywood

Correspondent, newscaster

BORN 1881. **SPOTLIGHTS** Nicknamed "the Earl of Godwin," by admirer President Franklin Delano Roosevelt. He received preferential treatment from the White House when assigned a permanent press conference seat close to the presidential desk. President of White House Correspondents Association from 1938-'40, this Washington radio correspondent was also on air during the war and postwar years in "Watch the World Go By" (1942-'49). He wrote for the *Milwaukee Sentinel* and *Montreal Star*. **SIDELIGHTS** His most difficult moment as a newsman came with Pres. FDR's death. Due to his voice cracking with sorrow on April 12, 1945, he was unable to complete the broadcast. An ABC colleague took over for him. **QUOTE** For all his years on the air, his closing line was a sincere "God bless you one and all." Died: 1956.

Ann Harding   6207 Hollywood

Actress

BORN Dorothy Gatley; Aug. 7, 1901, in Houston, TX. **SPOTLIGHTS** Originally a script reader for Famous Players-Lasky (later Paramount), she began training onstage. She made her Broadway debut at age 20. A serene, blue-eyed blonde with an aristocratic voice and style, she was a tremendous asset to the theatre. She worked onstage until she received a movie offer in 1929. By the time she made *Holiday* (1930--in an Oscar-nominated performance), she was a star. Her genteel manner was a natural to portraying long-suffering, teary, noble heroines, but handed the right script this lovely lady could play lighter, happier, more glamorous roles, too. Films include *The Animal Kingdom* (1932), *Double Harness* (1933), *When Ladies Meet* (1933), *Gallant Lady* (1934), *Biography of a Bachelor Girl* (1935), *The North Star* (1943), *It Happened on Fifth Avenue*, *Christmas Eve* (both 1947), *The Magnificent Yankee* (1951), and *The Man in the Gray Flannel Suit* (1956). Died: 1981.

Pinky Lee 📺　　　6207 Hollywood

![Pinky Lee]

Pinky Lee

Vaudevillian, comedian
BORN Pincus Leff; 1916, in St. Paul, MN. **SPOTLIGHTS** He had ambitions to be an attorney, but chucked that notion when classmates laughed at his lisp. "Right then, I decided if I could make them laugh with my lisp, I'd probably do the same thing to a judge and jury in a courtroom. So I turned what might have been considered a liability into an asset and made straight for the entertainment world," Pinky told a reporter for the *L.A. Times* in 1955. His comic lisp became such a valuable asset that to Lloyd's of London it was no laughing matter; they insured it for $50,000.00. "The Pinky Lee Show" (1950) was about a fumbling stagehand in a vaudeville theatre who fills in for absentee singers and comedians. It gave him the opportunity to exhibit his many talents learned from years in musical comedy, burlesque, vaudeville, radio and the movies. The TV program, made in Hollywood, was seen throughout the U.S. by kinescope. Various children shows, including "Those Two" (1951-1953) and his most successful "The Pinky Lee Show," where he wore his trademark baggy pants, bright and busy checkered coat, and rolled-brim hat (1954-'56, NBC) was his claim to fame. His show's time slot could not have been better, it aired right before the extremely popular children's classic "Howdy Doody." Died: 1993.

George O'Brien 🎥　　　6207 Hollywood

Actor
BORN April 19, 1900, in San Francisco, CA. **SPOTLIGHTS** The heavyweight boxing champion of the Pacific Fleet during WWI, he was interested in becoming a cameraman. Postwar, he fell into stunt work, then became a popular leading man. Nicknamed "The Chest" by the studio for his buffed physique, thousands of females wrote fan mail begging for a clipping of his chest hair for a keepsake. He played big, strong cowboys; women melted over his muscles in John Ford's film: *The Iron Horse* (1924). His tour de force occurred early in his career. He stars in the masterpiece, *Sunrise* (1927), opposite Janet Gaynor. This incredible art film has stood the test of time and is definitely worth seeing today. Among his other works: *Riders of the Purple Sage* (1931), *The Painted Desert* (1932—most notable for being Clark Gable's first talkie), *Daniel Boone* (1936), *Hollywood Cowboy* (1937—where O'Brien spoofs himself), *The Fighting Gringo* (1939), and *She Wore a Yellow Ribbon* (1949—starring John Wayne). Died: 1985.

Philip Ahn 🎥　　　6207 Hollywood

Philip Ahn

Actor
BORN March 29, 1911, in Los Angeles, CA. **SPOTLIGHTS** He was one of the most sought after villains for Asian roles. Frequently cast in Japanese or Chinese roles, in actuality he was Korean. He had a smooth, even voice and a mask-like face that remarkably could both disguise and reveal the character's emotions. He appears on the silver screen for three decades. Among his numerous credits are *The General Died at Dawn* (1936), *China Girl* (1943), *The Keys of the Kingdom* (1944), *Blood on the Sun* (1945), *The Cobra Strikes* (1948), *I Was an American Spy* (1951), *Japanese War Bride* (1952), *Macao* (1952), *Battle Zone* (1952), *Fair Wind to Java* (1953), *Love Is a Many Splendored Thing* (1955), *One-Eyed Jacks* (1961), *Confessions of an Opium Eater* (1962), and *Thoroughly Modern Millie* (1967). Handsome in his youth, Ahn aged with dignity. TV fans recall him as the wise, calm Master Kan on the "Kung Fu" series...His real-life father was a Korean revolutionary who died while imprisoned in a Japanese war camp. Died: 1978.

Vincent Price 🎥　　　6207 Hollywood

Actor
BORN May 27, 1911, in St. Louis, MO. **SPOTLIGHTS** A celebrated stage and screen star of oily villains, he was dubbed the "Master of Horror." Tall, well-educated, and articulate, Price elevated the English language; he could make common words sing. He utilized his mellifluous voice to play over-sophisticated horror, such as the wormy gigolo in *Laura* (1944). Motion pictures include *The Private Lives of Elizabeth and Essex* (1939--as Sir Walter Raleigh), *The Invisible Man Returns* (1940--in title role), *The Song of Bernadette* (1943), *Keys of the Kingdom*, *Wilson* (both 1944), *Leave Her to Heaven* (1945), *A Royal Scandal* (1945), *Dragonwyck*, and *Shock* (both 1946). He

appears in the hilarious comedy *Champagne for Caesar* (1950), with Ronald Colman, Celeste Holm and Art Linkletter. Other movies: *The House of Wax* (1953), *The Mad Magician* (1954), *The Ten Commandments* (1956), *While the City Sleeps* (1956), *The Fly* (1958), *House on Haunted Hill, The Bat* (both 1959), *The House of Usher* (1960), and *The Pit and the Pendulum* (1961). At age 70, with his extremely recognizable voice still in top form, he provided the narrative voice-over for singer Michael Jackson's *Thriller* (1982). Fans simply have to close their eyes and listen to his haunting voice to know he was one of the best in the business. On radio, he played "The Saint" (1947-'50), a super detective. He also hosted TV mysteries. He penned several art and cookbooks, as he adored exquisite art and fine dining. **QUOTE** Price, a lifetime lover of fine art, had wanted to become an art professor. He told Edward R. Murrow on "Person to Person": "I have a self-appointed mission to try to tell the American people that art belongs to everybody, not just a special few. And particularly I want to try to tell the American people that they should be enormously proud of their American heritage, because American art is the most exciting thing in the world today. We don't have to look to France anymore for great art. Today, Americans, especially young America, is more art conscious than ever before in history. In the past year, for instance, I was amazed at what I saw while lecturing to over 250,000 young people at various universities. Many of the students brought paintings, water colors and prints they had purchased out of their meager allowances,

Vincent Price

and the results were genuinely impressive. What I saw proved, for anyone who wants to buy a painting, there's an immense and authentic market right here in the United States, irrespective of the buyer's tastes, his ambitions, or his budget." Price's autobiographical book on art is entitled—*I Know What I Like*—where he writes, "Dollar bills make dull decorations." Died: 1993.

Henry B. Walthall 🎥   6207 Hollywood

Actor
BORN March 16, 1878, in Shelby, AL. **SPOTLIGHTS** This wavy-haired leading man with sad eyes was popular during the silent era. Although handsome in his youth, he chose to take on more challenging roles than the romantic hero. Walthall was one of the finest, most memorable dramatic silent screen stars. He showed restraint in his sensitive performances, while others went to the extreme in their pantomime. A handful of his many films are: *The Sorrows of the Unfaithful* (1910), *The God Within* (1912), *The Wedding Gown* (1913), *The Birth of a Nation* (1915—as the Little Colonel—in one of his greatest roles), *The Raven* (1915—as the tortured genius, author Edgar Allen Poe), *Ghosts* (1915), *The Unknown Purple* (1923), *Face on the Barroom Floor* (1923), *The Road to Mandalay* (1926—he played Lon Chaney's brother), and *The Scarlet Letter* (1926—as Roger Prynne). He had no problem making the transition to sound. Walthall's trained voice was rich and flawlessly modulated. Earlier, he had planned on becoming a trial attorney, and used his skilled articulation to full advantage. After attending a school of law in Alabama, he changed his mind and decided to become an actor. Talkies include *Viva Villa!* (1934). **QUOTE** "Emotion should be fostered and developed and lived, and a dramatic artist should court the emotions of life. Certainly, experience is the keynote of dramatic success and the lesson is that when a man or a woman sees the tremendous heights and depths to which the soul's emotions can carry one, then a lesson is taught and, without the lesson, the drama itself becomes infantile." He made more than 100 pictures, working right up until his death. He died—*while preparing for a death scene*—in *China Clipper* in 1936.

Sam Warner 🎥   6207 Hollywood

Film pioneer, producer
BORN Aug. 10, 1888, in Baltimore, MD. **SPOTLIGHTS** Co-founder of Warner Brothers studios, he was considered the brother with foresight. Sam recognized the big business potential of the Edison Kinetoscope motion picture industry. He persuaded his near poverty-stricken family to hock their few prized possessions—their beloved old horse and Pop's gold watch—to buy into show business. Happily, they succeeded in getting their possessions back. Later, when Warner Brothers was already succeeding in the silents—Rin-Tin-Tin and John Barrymore were its biggest stars—Sam's dream was to produce a talking picture. Brother Harry thought it was a lousy idea.

Who'd want to hear actors talk? Others thought it was plain stupid. Sam persuaded Harry it would work and Warner Brothers made history with the first talkie, *The Jazz Singer* (1927). It was also the first musical. **SIDELIGHTS** Also see the bios of Harry Warner and Jack Warner in this book. Died: 1927 from a cerebral hemorrhage the night before *The Jazz Singer* opened. It was a horrible twist of fate that the man who produced the first motion picture with sound did not get to attend its spectacular debut. When Al Jolson opened his mouth on screen to sing, then said, "You ain't heard nothing yet" the audience went wild with joy. Sadly, all the Warners missed that historic evening, as they were mourning the loss of their brother.

Ann Harding

6161 HOLLYWOOD

Jeanette MacDonald 🎥 6161 Hollywood

Singer, actress

Jeanette MacDonald

BORN June 18, 1901, in Philadelphia, PA. **SPOTLIGHTS** Trained in singing and dancing, she made her 1920 New York debut as a chorus girl in "The Demi-Tasse Revue." Within three years she was a leading lady. This red-haired, green-eyed lass landed a contract with the Shuberts, who cast the ingenue in Gershwin's "Tip Toes" in 1925. Paramount Pictures screen tested, then rejected her. Director Ernst Lubitsch disagreed. He cast her as the queen opposite the rakish Maurice Chevalier in *The Love Parade* (1929), where she proved to be a clever comedienne as well. With her lilting soprano voice, ideally suited for light opera, she sweetly sang her way through romantic comedies in period costumes. She and Chevalier appeared in *Love Me Tonight* (1932) and *The Merry Widow* (1934). She was serenaded by newcomer, baritone Nelson Eddy, in *Naughty Marietta* (1935), *Rose Marie* (1936--their best movie), and *Maytime* (1937--her favorite film), *Sweethearts* (1938--MGM's first all-color movie, and one of highest grossing films of the year), among others. Eddy and she were crowned "America's Sweethearts." She co-stars with Clark Gable, Spencer Tracy, and Jack Holt in the Academy Award-nominated picture *San Francisco* (1936). The story is about a Barbary Coast saloon proprietor (Gable), who becomes the Svengali of an opera singer. The finale features special effects of the great earthquake. It proved MacDonald a dramatic actress, capable of holding her own against MGM's biggest male star, Gable. The movie also earned Tracy his first Oscar nomination, and was the studio's most profitable release of the year. MGM's queen was one of their biggest money-makers. Some of her most popular recordings were "Indian Love Call," "Ah! Sweet Mystery of Life," "Rose Marie" and "Lover Come Back to Me." **SIDELIGHTS** Although she aimed to sing grand opera, music snobs, who detested the movies, thought she had cheapened the art. MacDonald was nick-named "The Iron Butterfly" because she withstood the critics' vicious witticisms and goofy wisecracks at her expense. **HIGHLIGHTS** She was married to an early screen idol (and Walk of Famer), Gene Raymond, since 1937. **QUOTE** When asked in the 1950s if she planned a comeback, she replied, "I really don't think so. Movies—why the last movie I think I made, I think I played Lassie's mother. It would be rather difficult to find a vehicle for Nelson and me now." Died: 1965.

Paul Whiteman 🎵 6161 Hollywood

Paul Whiteman and Fanny Brice

Musician, band leader

BORN March 28, 1891, in Denver, CO. **SPOTLIGHTS** A great showman full of heart, he changed popular music entirely in the 1920s. As early as 1918 he pioneered a symphonic approach to dance music and shared his enthusiasm and imagination with others. In 1924 he commissioned a young George Gershwin to write a new piece for his orchestra. The result was the famed "Rhapsody in Blue." By the time of the big band era, "Pops" (as he was affectionately known) had a long, successful history. He decided to feature jazz soloists who could not get a break elsewhere. His varied list of top talent he helped: the Dorsey Brothers, Bix Beiderbecke, Bing Crosby, Johnny Mercer and dozens more. His innovation created a new style of music to which America danced, danced, and danced throughout the 1930s and '40s. Whiteman is generally regarded as the one who brought jazz out of the "immoral" closet and made it respectable. Universal Studios publicized him as "The King of Jazz," releasing a lavish movie of that title showcasing his talents in 1930. It also introduces Bing Crosby to the screen, and has fun with an early cartoon by Walter

Lantz. Recordings include "Whispering," and "Japanese Sandman." Albums include: *Legendary Performer and Composer Paul Whiteman and His Orchestra.* **QUOTE** "You'll never learn to bounce in jazz if you don't know your Bach and Beethoven...You see, jazz is simply a way to play any music." Died: 1967.

House Peters 🎥   6161 Hollywood

Actor
BORN March 28, 1880, in England. **SPOTLIGHTS** A leading man in the silent movies, Peters made 85 pictures, including *In the Bishop's Carriage* (1913). He retired with the advent of sound. Died: 1967.

Herbert Kalmus 🎥   6161 Hollywood

Inventor, scientist
BORN Nov. 9, 1881, in Chelsea, MA. **SPOTLIGHTS** A brilliant scholar and educator, he turned a black-and-white movie world into "living color." Every filmgoer has seen his work: "Color by Technicolor," or "In Technicolor." His daughter appeared in one of the most spectacular Technicolor films, ever, *Gone With the Wind* (1939). She played the Butlers' young daughter who had that tragic riding scene. Kalmus was the dedicated founder of the patented process which took decades to bring to fruition; his Technicolor process reigns supreme. Died: 1963.

Kate Smith 💿 6161 Hollywood

Singer, hostess, commentator

Kate Smith

BORN Kathryn Smith; May 1, 1909, in Greenville, VA. **SPOTLIGHTS** Gifted with a stunning contralto voice, Smith appeared in vaudeville and on the New York stage. All was not happy though. She was the butt of mean-spirited fat jokes that her co-stars ad-libbed with the producers' stamp of approval. Her experience in radio was wholly different. Ted Collins, a former talent scout for Columbia Records, dedicated himself to managing her with integrity. Her first spot was on so late at night that hardly anyone heard the broadcast. Collins persuaded CBS chief William S. Paley to listen to her sing. Impressed, Paley gave Smith a network timeslot opposite the competitors insanely popular "Amos 'n' Andy." Hardly anyone in the business thought she could woo listeners away from the (inane) comedy, but within a few months she had high ratings. Her manager made sure that Smith always enjoyed the dignity she so rightfully deserved. Her musical-

variety program, "The Kate Smith Hour"--with her famous signature song "When the Moon Comes Over the Mountain"--was on air from 1931 - '58. She became known as "The first lady of radio," and was affectionately called the "Songbird of the South." One of radio's biggest stars, only she and Jack Benny had contracts that could not be cancelled. Smith introduced the country to Irving Berlin's song "God Bless America" on Armistice Day, Nov. 11, 1938 (this national holiday is now called Veteran's Day). Berlin had given her exclusive use of the song for two years, and it was her rendition of it that gained her immortality. Americans begged her for more treasures, and she complied by recording the "Star-Spangled Banner," U.S.'s national anthem. TV: "The Kate Smith Show" (1950-'54); it featured Broadway and movie stars, comedians, and jazz greats. Her *This is Christmas* album still sells well. Films include *The Big Broadcast* (1932). **ACHIEVEMENTS** During WWII, she supported the Allied Forces. This champion of freedom sold more than $600 million in war bonds. Died: 1986.

Jay Thomas 🎙   6161 Hollywood

Radio personality, actor

Jay Thomas

BORN July 12, 1948, in Kermit, TX. **SPOTLIGHTS** Raised in New Orleans by his oil man father and tap dancing Southern belle mother (who had won a Shirley Temple look-a-like contest as a child), 16-year-old Thomas secretly began performing as a strip joint comedian. He enjoyed doing stand-up comedy, but a few years later enrolled at Jacksonville University. An athlete, he was plagued by football injuries which led him directly into the radio announcer's booth. He earned his degree in sociology then went to work in a geographical criss-cross of radio stations. His radio career was not without its share of pitfalls. Thomas quipped, "If any candidate were to win all of the states I've been fired in as a disc jockey, he would win the Presidential election by a landslide." He took acting lessons on the side. Finally, Thomas was hailed as one of the country's "shock jocks" of morning radio. Television work in smash comedy series followed, including "Mork and Mindy," "Cheers," "Love and War," and his 1991 Emmy Award winning guest role in "Murphy Brown." Motion pictures include *Mr. Holland's Opus* (1995), *Straight Talk* (1992), and *The Gig* (1985). **QUOTE** "Believe me, I've tried everything. Thank God, I've finally found something that I'm good at."

Jan Murray 💿   6161 Hollywood

Emcee, actor

BORN 1917, in Bronx, New York City, New York. **SPOTLIGHTS** He was a popular, chatty game show host of the 1950s: "Blind Date" (1953); "Dollar a Second" quiz show (1953-'57); and an actor on "Treasure Hunt" (1956-'58). **SIDELIGHTS** Comedian Alan King once quipped, "Jan Murray promises you nothing...and he delivers!"

Helen Ferguson 🎥   6161 Hollywood

Actress
BORN July 23, 1901, in Decatur, IL. **SPOTLIGHTS** This cutie was a capable brown-haired, brown-eyed talent of *The Famous Mrs. Fair* (1923), *Within the Law* (1923), and *The Scarlet West* (1925), among others. **QUOTE** "A girl should realize that a career on the screen demands everything, promising nothing. To the favored few who bask in the glory of Fortune's smile are illimitable gifts thrown, but from thousands who feel the call within them, fewer than a hundred are ever chosen." Died: 1977.

Walter O'Keefe 🎙   6161 Hollywood

Author, actor, producer
BORN Aug. 18, 1900, in Hartford, CO. **SPOTLIGHTS** A vaudeville performer, he personally witnessed its final demise in 1934. He and George Jessel were twin M.C.s at Earl Carroll's Casino Theatre on Broadway. The tickets sold at a scale of 75 cents to $1.50, but the show died within three weeks. O'Keefe switched to radio. He rose to being a quiz show host in the 1940s of "The Battle of the Sexes," and "Double or Nothing," where a contestant had the chance to win as much as "$10 to $40!"

Louis Jordan 🎵   6161 Hollywood

Singer, musician, lyricist, composer
BORN July 8, 1908, in Brinkley, Arkansas. **SPOTLIGHTS** A jazz and blues great with a wonderful wit, he was idolized by all his peers, and loved by all who heard his music. In August 1938, this highly skilled musician with his golden alto sax formed his own group—Louis Jordan and his Tympany Five—one of the most successful small bands in jazz or blues history. Jordan, who sang and played baritone saxophone and clarinet as well, constantly searched for fresh, new material. He mixed witty lyrics with an irresistible rhythm that made both listening to and dancing to his music great fun. He had one of the great jiving jump bands of the 1940s. It was more than that, though. As B.B. King stated, "Louis Jordan made the real marriage between jump-band jazz and barrel-house blues." One of the most important contributors to American music, Jordan blended rhythm & blues with swing for a "jump style" rhythm & blues—the predecessor to modern rock 'n' roll. This likable man with large pop eyes, entertained audiences as he strutted on stage while playing happy music. Among his many hit songs are "Caldonia," "Choo Choo Ch' Boogie," "Five Guys Named Moe," "Is You Is or Is You Ain't My Baby," "Salt Pork, West Virginia," "What's the Use of Gettin' Sober (When You're Gonna Get Drunk Again)," "Knock Me a Kiss," "Buzz Me, Baby," "Somebody Changed the Lock on My Door," "Let the Good Times Roll," "Saturday Night Fish Fry," "Nobody's Here but Us Chickens," "Reet Petite and Gone," "School Days," "I Can't Dance, I Got Ants In My Pants," "Safe, Sane and Single," "I Like 'Em Fat Like That," and "I'm Gonna Move to the Outskirts of Town." He also recorded with music legends such as Ella Fitzgerald, Louis Armstrong, and Bing Crosby. Chuck Berry, B.B. King and Ray Charles are three more of the Walk of Famers who recorded his music. Jordan's movies include *Follow the Boys* (1944), and *Shout Sister Shout* (1949). Died: 1975.

Jester Hairston 📺   6161 Hollywood

Actor, composer, singer

Jester Hairston

BORN July 9, 1901, in North Carolina. **SPOTLIGHTS** A multi-talented musician, conductor, singer, and actor, he graduated from Tufts University and was a Juilliard-trained arranger and composer. His extraordinary gifts came to the attention of President Franklin Roosevelt. For the U.S. State Department, he traveled worldwide as a goodwill ambassador to Europe, Africa, Mexico and South America. He came to Hollywood in 1936 to do the music for the film version *Green Pastures*, after having accomplished the same on Broadway. He caught the ear of the award-winning Russian composer Dimitri Tiomkin. Next, this music lover made choral directions and trained the choir (he had been working with the choir prior to the film) for Tiomkin's Academy Award-winning score in *Lost Horizons* (1937). That encounter was so powerful, that Hairston continued to do the arranging for Tiomkin for the next two decades. And, as long as he was in Hollywood, he appeared in a number of motion pictures, including *The Alamo* (1960), *To Kill a Mockingbird* (1964), *In the Heat of the Night* (1967), *Lady Sings the Blues* (1972), *The Bingo Long Traveling All-Stars & Motor King* (1976), and *The Last Tycoon* (1977). He also dubbed Sidney Poitier's singing voice in *Lilies of the Field* (1963), in which Poitier won a Best Actor Academy Award. **RADIO** He worked for 16 years in network radio. Shows include being a member of the comedy cast of "Amos 'n' Andy" (also TV version) and "Beulah." **TV** Played Wildcat in the situation comedy "That's My Mama," and Rolly Forbes in the comedy series "Amen." About being cast in the latter without ever meeting with the TV writer/producer Ed Weinberger, Hairston said, "I've auditioned for a lot of jobs in the last 50 years, but this one—well, I've never had anyone take me just like that." Awarded four honorary Doctorates of Music and Fine Arts. He received his Hollywood Walk of Fame star on Feb. 12, 1992, at age 90+! Died: 2000.

Gene Kelly 🎥   6161 Hollywood

From left to right: George Murphy, Gene Kelly, Ronald Reagan and William Holden

Dancer, choreographer, actor, singer, director
BORN Eugene Kelly; Aug. 23, 1912, in Pittsburgh, PA.
SPOTLIGHTS One of America's top dancing sensations, he was a cinematic dance genius. Kelly was noted for bringing a magnificent dose of vitality to American dance. This phenomenal MGM musical star often choreographed and co-directed the films he appeared in. Movies include *On the Town* (1949), *An American in Paris* (1951), and *Singin' in the Rain* (1952). He directed Barbra Streisand in *Hello, Dolly!* (1969). Other motion pictures include *For Me and My Gal* (1942), *Thousands Cheer* (1943), *Anchors Aweigh* (1945), *Du Barry Was a Lady* (1943), *Cover Girl* (1944), *Les Girls* (1957), and *Inherit the Wind* (1960), a drama starring Spencer Tracy. **ACHIEVEMENTS** 1951 Special Oscar. 1985 American Film Institute Life Achievement Award. **HIGHLIGHTS** Making an umbrella his dance partner; and turning a swing around the lamppost into a breathtaking, masterful artistic movement. **SIDELIGHTS** A high school star in four sports--baseball, hockey, football and gymnastics-- Kelly discovered that not only did dance "impress girls," but "at that time dancing was the only way you could put your arm around the girl." So he danced.

What did he really want to be? A shortstop for the Pittsburgh Pirates. His love of baseball is evident in *Take Me Out to the Ballgame* (1949). **QUOTE** "My own style of dance is strong, wide open, bravura. I tried to base it all on male movements, athletic movements." Died: 1996.

Bill Williams 📺   6161 Hollywood

Actor
BORN William Herman Katt; 1916, in Brooklyn, NY.
SPOTLIGHTS This rugged, good-looking all-American got his start in show business after serving honorably in the Army Air Corps during World War II. He made his screen debut in *Murder in the Blue Room* (1944), then appeared in 50 more films. Extremely athletic, and a former champion swimmer, he did most of his own stunts. Movies include *Thirty Seconds Over Tokyo* (1944), *Clay Pigeon* (1949—opposite his real life wife, Barbara Hale), *Blue Grass of Kentucky* (1950), *Son of Paleface* (1952), *Gunfight at the O.K. Corral* (1957), *Alaska Passage* (1959), *Rio Lobo* (1970), and *The Giant Spider Invasion* (1975), again opposite his real life wife Hale. Williams gained this greatest fame in television and became a household name as the lead in the Western series, "The Adventures of Kit Carson" (1951-'55). This popular Western series went into worldwide syndication. In 1957 he co-starred with Betty White in the modern situation comedy, "A Date With the

Bill Williams

Angels," where Williams was relieved to be distanced from his previous television character and stated, "I never want to see or hear of Kit Carson again." **HIGHLIGHTS** While shooting the picture *West of the Pecos* (1945) he met actress Barbara Hale. Behind the scenes of the motion picture, *A Likely Story* (1946), the two co-stars fell in love and married that same year. Hale would go on to achieve immortality in the role of Della Street, the sharp-thinking, professional secretary of "Perry Mason." (Also see her bio in this book.) The Williams had three children, one son, a professional actor-director, William Katt, and two daughters. Died: 1992.

Jack Smith    6141 Hollywood

Singer, actor
BORN 1900. **SPOTLIGHTS** This baritone was known as "Whispering Jack Smith" on "The Jack Smith Show" (1946). Singer of popular songs, his best known tune was "Me and My Shadow." Died: 1989.

Stan Freberg   6141 Hollywood

Comedian
BORN Aug. 7, 1926, in Los Angeles, CA. **SPOTLIGHTS** A radio star, his other credits include the *Looney Looney Looney Bugs Bunny Movie* (voice-over), and TV's puppet series "Time for Beany" (1949-'54). He won a 1958 Grammy for spoken word.

Jane Froman   6141 Hollywood

See page 205

Dan Duryea   6141 Hollywood

Dan Duryea

Actor
BORN Jan. 23, 1907, in White Plains, NY. **SPOTLIGHTS** Duryea's pleasant scoutmaster visage worked beautifully on the silver screen, but not as the good guy. Cast opposite of how he looked, Duryea played the sociopathic criminal. His characters extorted, blackmailed, embezzled and murdered their way through 50 films. He also played the tough, two-fisted type in westerns and American period pieces. Motion pictures include *Old Louisiana* (1937), *The Painted Trail* (1938), *The Woman in the Window* (1944-where he slugs Joan Bennett), *Scarlet Street* (1945), *River Lady* (1948), and *Criss Cross* (1949). He made the transition to television for a practical reason. He commented, "I figure my heavy role is wearing

sort of thin. New villains are coming along all the time and I figure most people are beginning to get tired of an old face like mine." TV: On "China Smith" (1952-'55), he played the wisecracking private eye (and sometimes con artist) whose office was a colorful bar in Singapore. He portrayed Eddie Jacks in "Peyton Place" (1967-'68). **QUOTE** "Most actors act for art's sake, and they starve. That's not for me. I can't afford to." Died: 1968.

J. Carrol Naish   6141 Hollywood

J. Carrol Naish

Actor
BORN Joseph C. Naish; Jan. 21, 1897, in New York, NY. **SPOTLIGHTS** The great-great-grandson of a Lord Chancellor of Ireland, and 100% descendent of Irish blood, Naish specialized in almost every type of foreigner, *but* Irish. With his dark eyes, dark hair and expertise with foreign accents, he was considered one of the top Asian villains, and also portrayed Italians, Spaniards, Japanese, Arabs, Jews, Native American Indians, among dozens of other nationalities. With more than 200 films to his credit, movies include *Sahara* (1943—in an Oscar-nominated performance), *A Medal for Benny* (1945—in an Oscar-nominated performance), *The Fugitive* (1947), *That Midnight Kiss* (1949), *Annie Get Your Gun* (1950), *Rio Grande* (1950), and *Violent Saturday* (1955). Naish appears in the first motion picture that combined all its top fiends—Dracula, the Wolf Man, and the Frankenstein Monster—in *The House of Frankenstein* (1944). He plays the hunchback who calls the evil Dr. Gustav Niemann (played by Boris Karloff) "master." TV: Small screen fame for "The New Adventures of Charlie Chan" (1956-'57) as the deadly accurate sleuth. Died: 1973.

Hildegarde   6141 Hollywood

Singer, pianist

BORN Hildegarde Loretta Sell; Feb. 1, 1906, in Adell, Wisconsin. **SPOTLIGHTS** She started on radio at age seven in one of the biggest vogues of vaudeville, the "School Days" act. But it was not until the 1940s that she would find her greatest success as a saucy chanteuse. "The Incomparable Hildegarde" was musical hostess of the quiz show "Beat the Band." Her opening signature line, "Give me a little traveling music, Harry," was much imitated by her listeners. In 1943, while Frank Sinatra belted them out at the Waldorf-Astoria's Wedgwood Room, Hildegarde was the standout attraction at the Persian Room in New York's Hotel Plaza. During WWII, she specialized in melancholy ballads. Internationally celebrated for her glamour, she became the public's symbol of *tomorrow-we-may-die.* This beautiful, elegant misty-eyed chanteuse sang "The Last Time I Saw Paris" in a French accent, while clutching a bouquet of long-stemmed red roses to her bosom, protected by her long, black satin gloves. Another popular song was "When I'm With You." After the war, she switched tunes explaining, "Everything has to pass. I don't want to be associated with the old days." New upbeat songs included light fare like "Eeny Meeny Miney Mo" and "The Purple People Eaters." **VOTED** 1944 and '45 Outstanding Network Radio Talent. **QUOTE** About her 86-city American tour she declared, "I was sensational!" About her upcoming 1960 opening on Broadway, the sophisticate prophesied, "It will be the last word in elegance. I belong to the champagne, not the Coca-Cola set."

Bob Hope 🎞   6141 Hollywood

See page 87

Tallulah Bankhead 🎥   6141 Hollywood

Actress

BORN Jan. 31, 1902, in Huntsville, AL. **SPOTLIGHTS** Bankhead's father, the late Speaker of the House of Representatives, indulged his precocious daughter's every whim. She came from aristocratic lineage; her grandfather was the last surviving Confederate veteran in the Senate, and her uncle was a Senator as well. Her college-educated mother, who died three weeks after she was born, was a stunning Southern belle. One critic wrote "she was a creature right out of *The Arabian Nights.*" Educated in a Catholic convent, at age 15 Tallulah won a *Pictureplay* magazine beauty contest. The prize was a screen contract at $50-per-week in New York. Her startled father frowned at the notion, and her grandmother was less than pleased, after all, "No Southern woman worked unless from necessity." Bucking tradition, she worked on stage and in silent films, in both the U.S. and England. Her *joie de vivre,* quick wit, and remarkable humor made her the toast of the town, wherever she was. When she was 20, she was asked by someone if she were still a virgin. She responded, "I'm as pure as the driven slush." By 1931 her unique, low raspy voice ("Hello, Dahhhling") and throaty laugh were worth $50,000 per talkie

Tallulah Bankhead

film, although most critics considered her style of acting better suited for the stage. She returned to Broadway. This non-conformist was completely fearless, except on opening night. Right before her entrance, she kneeled in front of a photo of her parents, crossed her heart, and prayed, "Dear God, please don't let me make a fool of myself tonight." Then, she picked up her champagne flute and swallowed the bubbly. Eleven years passed without her going in front of a camera. But director Alfred Hitchcock had faith in her, offering Bankhead $75,000 for the lead in *Lifeboat* (1944)--a story written for the screen by John Steinbeck. She dashed to Hollywood. The filming turned into an ordeal, as "Hitchcock flouting the screen's taboos, confined the action of the picture to a claustrophobic forty-foot lifeboat," she recalled. Bankhead was forced to wear a mink coat the entire 15 weeks of shooting under blazing hot studio lamps. Fake oil-based fog engulfed her, and with the constant "cold, wet drenchings of downpours and lurchings followed by rapid drying-outs" she contracted pneumonia. The studio doctor dosed her with sulpha drugs, prescribed whiskey, and returned her to work with a 104 degree temperature. Her resulting performance was outstanding. Critics changed their tune about her and called her the year's best cinema actress. This glamorous talent made only four more films before shunning Hollywood for the theater. Bankhead was also the "mistress of ceremonies" on radio's "The Big Show." She was known for her frankness, unorthodox views on love *and* the seven deadly sins (plus a few of her own added in for good measure). "A high living sinner," she monopolized attention, and overindulged in lovemaking, spending money, drinking alcohol, and consuming drugs. Once told cocaine was addictive, she declared, "It most certainly isn't. I've been using it for fifteen years." About sex, she postulated, "I've had men, and I've had women, there must be something better." Then, to counter rumors about jail time served, she quipped, "Despite all you may have heard to the contrary, I have never had a ride in a patrol wagon." **QUOTE** In her 1952 autobiography, *Tallulah*, she reflected: "I have no formal convictions about religion or life in the hereafter. The miracle of spring, the spectacular display in the heavens on a cold winter's night, for me that is proof of an overall plan...None of us can go through life swindling, lying, and outraging our fellows and escape retribution...'We're all paid off in the end, and the fools first.' Thoreau summed up my pessimism: 'We all lead lives of quiet desperation.'" It was said that "she burned through four lives times in the space of one." Died: 1968.

Lloyd Hamilton 🎥   6141 Hollywood

Actor
BORN Aug. 19, 1891, in Oakland, CA. **SPOTLIGHTS** A busy comedian in one- and two-reelers during the silent era, this zany title hints at his films: *Ham at the Garbage Gentlemen's Ball* (1915). Died: 1935.

W.S. Van Dyke 🎥   6141 Hollywood

Director
BORN Woodbridge Strong Van Dyke III; Mar. 21, 1889, in San Diego, CA. **SPOTLIGHTS** Nicknamed "One Shot Woody" for his efficiency, he thrilled audiences with the exciting jungle picture *Tarzan the Ape Man* (1932). His credits include *The Thin Man* (1934 + sequels) starring William Powell and Myrna Loy; *The Prizefighter and the Lady* (1933) with heavyweight boxing contender Max Baer, Myrna Loy and Walter Huston; *Rose Marie* (1936) an Eddy-MacDonald musical; and *Marie Antoinette* (1938) with Norma Shearer in an epic costume piece. **SIDELIGHTS** Van Dyke contracted malaria on location in Africa while shooting *Trader Horn* (1931), an early talkie starring Harry Carey, and Duncan Renaldo. Died: 1943.

Raoul Walsh 🎥   6141 Hollywood

Director, actor
BORN March 11, 1887, in New York, NY. **SPOTLIGHTS** He played the role of John Wilkes Booth in D.W. Griffith's *The Birth of a Nation* (1915), but preferred being behind the camera. Known for his slick production values in action pictures, he had a keen eye for talent. Walsh gave John Wayne his first leading role *In Old Arizona* (1928), and made a star of Humphrey Bogart in *High Sierra* (1941). His 'A' list of other rugged men include Errol Flynn, Douglas Fairbanks (Sr.), and Gary Cooper. Movie credits include *The Big Trail* (1930), *Dark Command* (1940), *White Heat* (1949), *Blackbeard the Pirate* (1952) and *Battle Cry* (1955). **SIDELIGHTS** He wore a trademark black eye patch after losing his eye in an accident while shooting *In Old Arizona.* (Director John Ford was supposed originally scheduled to do the movie, but he did not like the script.) Amazingly, Walsh did *not* sue. Died: 1981.

Buddy Rogers 🎥   6141 Hollywood

Buddy Rogers and Mary Pickford

Actor, orchestra leader
BORN Charles Rogers; Aug. 13, 1904, in Olathe, KS. **SPOTLIGHTS** A very charming silent screen matinee idol, Rogers initially had no desire to be an actor. Musically inclined, he played the piano, accordion, drums, trumpet, and trombone in school dance bands, and attended the University of Kansas intent on becoming a bandleader. Rogers' father, a publisher of a weekly paper, spotted an open audition for new actors by Paramount Pictures. He urged his tall, handsome son to send a handful of photographs. As luck would have it, Rogers was chosen, and given the most basic of acting lessons. In New York, he made his screen debut in *Fascinating Youth* (1926), then worked with W.C. Fields in *So's Your Old Man* (1926). He was immortalized the very next year in William Wellman's classic WWI motion picture, *Wings* (1927). His co-stars were Richard Arlen, Clara Bow and Gary Cooper. (Also see the bio of William Wellman in this book.) This brilliant movie won the very first Best Picture Academy Award. It also secured Rogers' career as a leading man. *Wings* was re-released in sound in 1929. The future love of his life, Mary Pickford, first caught sight of Rogers in the film. Soon he was cast in her next picture, *My Best Girl* (1927). He did make the transition to sound. Other films include *Paramount on Parade* (1930), *Old Man Rhythm* (1935), *Once in a Million* (1936), *Mexican Spitfire's Baby* and *Sing for Your Supper* (both 1941). He produced his last film, *The Parson and the Outlaw* (1957). In all, he made 60 motion pictures. **HIGHLIGHTS** Married America's Sweetheart, Mary Pickford, in 1937. The gentleman and the lady enjoyed a 42-year marriage. (Also see bio of Mary Pickford in this book.) After Mary's passing, Buddy was fortunate to find happiness once again, through his marriage to the former Beverly Ricono. The elegant, world-famed couple were mainstay of the movie and social set in Beverly Hills and Palm Springs for more than two decades. **ACHIEVEMENTS** In 1985

he was honored with the Academy's Jean Hersholt Humanitarian Award for his charitable contributions and fund-raising efforts for the Motion Picture and Television Fund. **QUOTE** About both his and Mary Pickford's Walk of Fame stars, Rogers graciously commented, "We were both honored by these landmarks. We are in esteemed company, among many friends we have known and loved and worked with. We are thankful to be remembered by the public as well." Died: 1999, at age 94.

Warren Hull ☒ 6141 Hollywood

See page 256

Loretta Young ☒ 6141 Hollywood

See page 232

John Payne ☒ 6125 Hollywood

Actor, singer

BORN May 23, 1912, in Roanoke, VA. **SPOTLIGHTS** A tall, dark-haired and ruggedly handsome leading man, his mother had been an opera sopra-no. His own voice was perfectly suited for light musicals. After performing onstage, he won tough guy roles in action, film noir and Westerns: *Dodsworth* (1936), *Tin Pan Alley* (1940), *To the Shores of Tripoli* (1942), *Hello Frisco Hello* (1943), *The Dolly Sisters* (1945), *The Razor's Edge* (1946), *Miracle on 34th Street*

John Payne

(1947), *Larceny* (1948), *Kansas City Confidential* (1952), *99 River Street* (1953), *Tennessee's Partner* (1955), and *Hidden Fear* (1958). A reliable, solid actor, he made 90 movies. TV: "The Restless Gun" (1957-'59). Died: 1989.,

Virginia Valli ☒ 6125 Hollywood

Actress

BORN Virginia McSweeney; June 10, 1895, in Chicago, IL. **SPOTLIGHTS** Born and educat-ed in Chicago, Valli trained in stock companies. She made her screen debut as a bit player *In the Palace of the King* (1915), then rose to stardom in melodramas. Movies include *The Storm* (1922), *A Lady of Quality* (1924), *K—The Unknown*

Virginia Valli

(1924), and *Ladies Must Dress* (1927). This stunning, elegant leading lady stood 5'3", possessed shiny, dark brown hair and blue eyes, and had a regal bearing. In all, she made 50 pictures. Valli retired in 1932 to marry her true love, actor Charles Farrell. The marriage lasted until her death. **QUOTE** "Hope, determination, trueness, and universal love constitute human personality. When these are intelligently and truly expressed, they are the elemental qualities of success (on screen). Talent is a matter of hard work, self-development and preparation." Died: 1968.

Gene Tierney ☒ 6125 Hollywood

Actress

BORN Nov. 20, 1920, in Brooklyn, NY. **SPOTLIGHTS** Her full lips, lovely blue-green eyes, thick hair, and exquisite heart-shaped face framed with regal high cheek-bones made her one of the Golden Era's greatest beauties. She literally graced the screen in glory. She was utterly breath-taking in *Tobacco Road* (1941), *The Shanghai Gesture*

Gene Tierney

(1941), *Heaven Can Wait* (1943), *Laura* (1944—a classic and irresistible example of film noir), *A Bell for Adano* (1949), *Leave Her to Heaven* (1945—in an Oscar-nominated perfor-mance), *Dragonwyck* (1946), *The Ghost and Mrs. Muir* (1947), *That Wonderful Urge* (1948), *Whirlpool* (1949), *Night and the City* (1950), *Where the Sidewalk Ends* (1950), *The Mating Season* (1951), and *On the Riviera* (1951). **SIDELIGHTS** Her kindness and concern for others backfired. During World War II, she received a call from Bette Davis, who was recruiting entertainers for the Hollywood Canteen (*the* GI hangout). Tierney, who was married to Paramount Pictures costume designer Oleg Cassini, told Bette that she was pregnant (in her first trimester), and extremely tired. Bette excused her, but Tierney felt duty had called. She appeared in the crowded nightclub full of servicemen and women. Two and a half weeks later, she contracted the German measles. In 1943 her daugh-ter Daria was prematurely born, weighing two and a half pounds and requiring eleven blood transfusions. Wanting to be a mother more than anything else, Tierney recalled, "I would not, could not, accept the idea that Daria was retarded or had brain damage." But her daughter was severely retarded, requiring constant medical care. After an anguishing decision to place her baby in an institution, she felt pain down to her very soul. Years of quiet suffering followed. One lovely Sunday afternoon in Los Angeles a young woman approached her at a tennis party. She stated that they had met at the Hollywood Canteen. She asked the star, "Did you happen to catch the German measles after that night? I was in the Marines at the time and the whole camp was infected by the epidemic. I broke quarantine to come to the canteen to meet the stars. Everyone told me I shouldn't, but I just had to go. And you were my favorite," she cheerfully informed the star. Tierney froze in silence. She turned and walked away. "After that," she stated, "I didn't care if I was ever again anyone's favorite actress." Died: 1991.

Smiley Burnette 6125 Hollywood

Actor, songwriter
BORN Lester Burnette; March 18, 1911, in Summum, IL. **SPOTLIGHTS** A chubby, comic Western sidekick for Gene Autry from 1934-'42, he played Frog Milhouse. Frog rode alongside the hero in close to 90 cowboy pictures. In all, made more than 100 oaters. Died: 1967.

Van Heflin 6125 Hollywood

See page 131

William Wellman 6125 Hollywood

Director
BORN Feb. 29, 1896, in Brookline, MA. **SPOTLIGHTS** Nicknamed "Wild Bill" for his toughness, unconventional thinking, and quick temper, he and Paramount Pictures went to battle over *Wings* (1927). Studio executives fought him on his delaying the shooting for weeks while he waited for the weather to change. Wellman insisted on filming the planes with *clouds* in the sky. He was being totally innovative at the time, because with the standard orthochromatic film stock, blue skies were impossible to shoot with any depth or realism, for they faded out completely to a matte-white background. A partially cloudy day could *never* be shot; on screen the clouds blended into the blue-sky-turned-white. This created the same flat, boring white background in all films, which is why Paramount wanted him to go ahead and shoot without regard for the weather. Wellman, however, had his cinematographer switch to the brand new Panchromatic film stock, which depicted a truer relationship to all colors visible to the human eye. It was also sensitive to light and shadow, a significant breakthrough for black-and-white motion pictures, and a superior advantage for his action scenes. Studio executives were also unhappy that Wellman had insisted on shooting accurate

William Wellman (right), Carole Lombard, and Fredric March

flight scenes depicting WWI. He required his actors, such as Buddy Rogers, to learn to fly so the real pilots could duck while the actors took over for the camera shots. The movie became a blockbuster, running for more than two years in theaters. The public went crazy for the realistic air battle scenes. *Wings* became the prototypical military picture, influencing all future aircraft fight shots. Nearly half a century later, similar air scenes thrilled audiences in Tony Scott's *Top Gun* (1986). *Wings* also won the very FIRST Best Picture Academy Award (1927-'28). In addition, some have given Wellman credit as the "father of the wide screen," as his dawn patrol take off scene in *Wings* required a larger screen. When Wellman switched to Warner Bros., producer Darryl Zanuck asked why he wanted to make a gangster picture, after all, he reasoned, so many had already been made like *Doorway to Hell* (1930), and *Little Caesar* (1930), there wasn't anything new to do. Wellman disagreed and replied, "Because I'll make it the toughest damn one of them all!" The studio had hoped to discourage him with a low budget, but *The Public Enemy* (1931) proved Wellman a man of his word, and great instinct—it was the toughest. It also made a star of James Cagney. In 1933 *Wild Boys of the Road* captures the angst of Depression-ravaged hobo kids who strive for a better life. It's one of the finest motion pictures about the bleak era, illustrating the authentic difficulties of surviving dark days, and clearly portraying Wellman's passion for people. Turning on a brighter note, Carole Lombard, Fredric March, and Walter Connolly were brilliant in his screwball comedy, *Nothing Sacred* (1937). He did a spectacular remake of *Beau Geste* (1939) starring Gary Cooper, Ray Milland and Robert Preston as brothers who oppose the cruelty of a French Foreign Legion commander. *The Story of G.I. Joe* (1945) is a superb WWII picture based on the true life story of war correspondent Ernie Pyle. Burgess Meredith gives an extraordinary performance as Pyle, and co-star Robert Mitchum garnered his only Oscar nomination. This was Wellman's personal choice for his best-liked work. He told his children that it was "his absolute favorite," as it was "the most realistic and non-Hollywood picture I ever did." Other splendid works include *Call of the Wild* (1935) an adventure picture with Clark Gable and Loretta Young, *The Ox-Bow Incident* (1943) an outstanding Western starring Henry Fonda, Dana Andrews, Mary Hughes and Anthony Quinn, *Battleground* (1949)--filmed in a semi-documentary war style--with Van Johnson, John Hodiak, and Ricardo Montalban, and *The High and the Mighty* (1954) an action movie starring John Wayne, Claire Trevor, Laraine Day, and Robert Stack that was the forerunner of all air disaster pictures. **ACHIEVEMENTS** 1937 Academy Award for story *A Star is Born*; the original version of the Hollywood melodrama. (It is in Technicolor, although Technicolor had not been perfected yet)...Wellman's composition of shots—his visual framing—was utterly profound, yet he never distracted the audience from the story. He directed 76 motion pictures...Film students and buffs should rent *Wings* to review the cafe scene as the camera moves through couple after couple—each sharing their own brief story seemingly within a frame. What a great picture! **HIGHLIGHTS** His son, William A. Wellman, Jr., is a writer/actor/producer. Wellman, Jr. created and executive produced the acclaimed, award-winning documentary film, *Wild Bill Hollywood Maverick* (1996). **QUOTE** Considered one of the most versatile American directors, he made gangster, romance, comedy, drama, musical, action, and Western movies. At the end of his career, Wellman reflected, "I wanted to make every kind of picture, and I did."

William Wellman

Pauline Starke 🎥   6125 Hollywood

Actress
BORN Jan. 10, 1900, in Joplin, MO. **SPOTLIGHTS** Starke made her screen debut in D. W. Griffith epic, *Intolerance* (1916). She played a dancing girl in this silent motion picture. The lovely teen moved into small roles, then advanced into supporting roles within one year. She stars in *Whom the Gods Destroy* (1918), *The Broken Butterfly* (1919), and a number of others. *Dante's Inferno* (1924), adapted from the great poem, was one of her triumphant works. Although big during the silent era, sound and middle age squashed her career. *$20 a Week* (1935) was her last picture. Died: 1977.

Jane Withers 🎥   6125 Hollywood

Jane Withers

Actress
BORN April 12, 1926, in Atlanta, GA. **SPOTLIGHTS** "Baby W" was in vaudeville virtually from infancy. She quickly expanded to radio, then, at age six, made her screen debut in *Handle With Care*. Withers was perfectly cast as the mean brat who antagonized sweet Shirley Temple in *Bright Eyes* (1934). In it, Withers established herself as the antithesis of childlike innocence. Nicknamed "Dixie's Dainty Dewdrop," she portrayed a feisty, mischievous, assertive, spoiled brat. Years later Shirley Temple would recount: "She was a clever little girl." Withers became one of the top child stars during the 1930s. Other films include *The Holy Terror* (1937), *Always in Trouble* (1938), and *Giant* (1956). In all, she made 40 movies. Later, she worked in TV, making countless guest starring appearances.

John Conte 📺   6125 Hollywood

Host, actor, singer
BORN Sept. 15, 1915, in Palmer, MA. **SPOTLIGHTS** A former actor at the Pasadena Playhouse, he specialized in musicals and comedies, including "Carousel." TV host of "John Conte's Little Show" (1950-'51) and "Montovani Welcomes You" (1958-'59). Later, he went behind the scenes and became a TV executive.

Gale Storm 📺   6125 Hollywood

Actress, singer
BORN Josephine Cottle; April 5, 1922, in Bloomington, TX. **SPOTLIGHTS** This petite, lovely, auburn-haired talent sparkled

Gale Storm

when she worked. She played the lead in the radio comedy "My Little Margie." The show ran simultaneously on TV (1952-'55), but with different episodes! Both the radio and television versions were smash hits. On TV's "The Gale Storm Show" (1956-'60) she played Susanna Pomeroy, who worked on the luxury liner *S.S. Ocean Queen*. This energetic talent also recorded many lively tunes, and appeared in dozens of motion pictures. Extremely well-liked, her adoring fan base included millions of devotees. **QUOTE** Personally involved in all aspects of her program, Storm was always striving for higher production value and new ideas to introduce. She commented, "People aren't dumb. They're just getting more educated all the time out there in Television Land. I say it's wonderful."

Thomas L. Tully 🎥   6125 Hollywood

Actor
BORN Aug. 21, 1896, in Durango, CO. **SPOTLIGHTS** When he was growing up, he dreamed of becoming a Navy officer. That hope was dashed when he fell short by one point on the Naval Academy's entrance exam. He turned to show business for his career—and how he made that leap, we'll *never* know. Tully's early break in radio occurred when it was discovered that he could bark just like a dog for "Renfrew of the Mounted." After playing the dog on numerous episodes, he became a seasoned professional with more than 3,000 *national* radio broadcasts (as a human). An accomplished stage performer, he worked on Broadway before coming to Hollywood. As a character actor, movies include *I'll Be Seeing You* (1944), *June Bride* (1948), *Ruby Gentry* (1952), and *The Caine Mutiny* (1954—in an Oscar-nominated performance). Died: 1982.

Genevieve Tobin 🎥   6125 Hollywood

Genevieve Tobin

Actress
BORN Nov. 29, 1901, in New York, NY. **SPOTLIGHTS** Onstage as a child, and educated in Paris, she made her silent screen debut in *No Mother to Guide Her* (1923). A green-eyed, blonde, she was a vivacious talent. Movies include *Free Love* (1933), Warner's *Goodbye Again* (1933), and *I Loved a Woman* (1933), as the stubborn wife of Edward G.

Robinson. She played perky secretary Della Street in the Perry Mason thriller *The Case of the Lucky Legs* (1935), and was part of all-star cast—Humphrey Bogart, Leslie Howard, and Bette Davis—in *The Petrified Forest* (1936). She was a major Broadway star. Died: 1995.

Sidney Lanfield 🎥   6125 Hollywood

Director
BORN April 20, 1898, in Chicago, IL. **SPOTLIGHTS** His Fox screen debut, *Cheer Up and Smile* (1930--an early talkie), soothed Depression-era audiences. As America moved closer to the war, he entertained fans with the mystery thriller *The Hound of the Baskervilles* (1939). He directed one of Bob Hope's best pictures, *My Favorite Blonde* (1942), and one of Jack Benny's best films, *The Meanest Man in the World* (1943). He worked with Hope again in the comedies *Where There's Life* (1947) and *The Lemon Drop Kid* (1951). He made the Western *Station West* (1948), starring Dick Powell and Jane Greer. He accumulated hundreds of TV show credits. Died: 1972.

Don Ameche 📺   6125 Hollywood

See page 129

George Meeker 🎥   6125 Hollywood

Actor
BORN March 5, 1904, in Brooklyn, NY. **SPOTLIGHTS** A 1921 graduate of the American Academy of Dramatic Arts, this tall, slightly balding character performed frequently in villainous roles. He made his silver screen in *Four Sons* (1928), and was wonderful in *Back Street* (1932), with Irene Dunne. He appeared in MGM's *Marie Antoinette* (1938). Died: 1963.

Johnny Mack Brown 🎥   6125 Hollywood

Johnny Mack Brown

Actor
BORN Sept. 1, 1904, in Dothan, AL. **SPOTLIGHTS** He was a collegiate football hero at the Rose Bowl, in Pasadena, CA. His team, Alabama University—the underdog—narrowly beat the University of Washington when Johnny caught a 59-yard pass. The final score was Alabama 20 to 19 on New Year's Day 1926. A talent scout spotted him at the game and asked him to screen test. He received several offers, but choose to go with MGM. This athletic, square-jawed, dark-haired, handsome hunk was handpicked by Greta Garbo, to play opposite her three times: *The Divine Woman* (1928),

The Single Standard (1929) and *A Woman of Affairs* (1929). *Billy the Kid* (1930) established him in Westerns—he did 70—which he enjoyed the most. Died: 1974.

John Hodiak 📱　　6125 Hollywood

John Hodiak

Actor

BORN April 16, 1914, in Pittsburgh, PA. **SPOTLIGHTS** A movie star first, Hodiak was also a versatile radio actor. He kept busy in a variety of shows playing a wide range of characters, but specialized in villains. This deep, harsh-voiced talent worked in the soap opera "The Guiding Light (1937-1942). He was also the hillbilly with the "mountain kentry" dialect of Dogpatch on "Li'l Abner" (1939-'40)—he used to tell girlfriend Daisy Mae how he loved his "po'k chopsss." He was featured in "Author's Playhouse," a dramatic anthology (1941-'45) that showcased such celebrated writers as William Saroyan. He was also a regular cast member on "The Lone Ranger," "The Romance of Helen Trent," and "Wings of Destiny." Movies include *Lifeboat* (1944), *Sunday Dinner for a Soldier* (1944), *The Harvey Girls* (1946), *Battleground* (1949), *Command Decision* (1949), *The Miniver Story* (1950), and *The On the Threshold of Space* (1956--released after his death). Died: 1955.

William DeMille 🎥　　6125 Hollywood

Director, screenwriter, playwright
BORN July 25, 1878, in Washington, D.C. **SPOTLIGHTS** Before moving West to join his brother Cecil B. DeMille, the elder William had been a celebrated New York playwright. Initially skeptical of the filmmaking business, he foolishly rejected an offer to co-found the Lasky company (now known as Paramount Pictures). He did eventually see the light, and worked in a variety of capacities during the silent era, while acquiring a small fortune. He made dozens of pictures: *The Ragamuffin* (1916), *Miss Lulu Bett* (1921), and *The Splendid Crime* (1925—also story). His biggest contribution was the brilliant launching of the great movie dog, Strongheart, at Paramount. It was the first time an animal was in a leading role as hero. (See "Strongheart" in this book.) Died: 1955.

Danny Kaye 📱　　6125 Hollywood

See page 83

Sonja Henie 🎥　　6125 Hollywood

Actress, ice skater

Sonja Henie

BORN April 8, 1912, in Oslo, Norway. **SPOTLIGHTS** 20th Century-Fox guided this graceful, strong Olympic Woman Figure Skating Champion to the silver screen in lightweight musicals. (From 1927-'36 Henie had been a three-time Olympic gold winner, and a world title winner ten consecutive times.) This pretty, blonde, dimpled athlete made her screen debut in *One in a Million* (1936). Movies include *My Lucky Star* (1938) with Cesar Romero and Buddy Ebsen; *Happy Landing* (1938) with Don Ameche, Cesar Romero, Ethel Merman; and *Second Fiddle* (1939) with Tyrone Power and Rudy Vallee. She was a powerhouse money-maker, too; she earned $75 million in her lifetime. **QUOTE** At age 44, she commented, "I skate because I love it. I'm skating better now than ever. My legs don't get tired and I don't even breathe as heavily after a solo. The day I cease to enjoy my work is the day I quit." Died: 1969.

Ed Sullivan 📺　　6125 Hollywood

Host, columnist
BORN Edward Sullivan; Sept. 28, 1902, in New York, NY. **SPOTLIGHTS** Master of the Big Show, Sullivan was the country's leading television impresario. His show was an American cultural institution. Every Sunday night for 23 years America tuned in to hear, "It's a Reeally Big SHEW Tonight!" Even with his deadpan delivery and cement-faced looks, he became an instant hit from the moment his variety show aired (under the original title "Toast of the Town," in 1948). His specialty was assembling an eclectic group of performers to entertain between the star acts. With fresh faces appearing on each show, his guests ran the gamut from vaudeville type acts to the Bolshoi Ballet. He continually travelled around the world to find talent, and was only disappointed one time when the U.S.

Ed Sullivan

State Department blocked his request for the Chinese Opera to appear. "The Ed Sullivan Show" (the same program with a new title in 1955), introduced this list of top entertainers to the country: Dean Martin and Jerry Lewis (Martin and Lewis premiered the show and each got paid $200), Liza Minnelli, Itzhak Perlman, and the Beatles, among others. One of his oddities was his frequently botched introductions. He greeted one guest by saying, "Please welcome to our stage José Feliciano. He's blind and he's Puerto Rican!" **ACHIEVEMENTS** 1955 Emmy for best variety show...He bravely went against the network tide by showcasing African-Americans, such as Ella Fitzgerald, Duke Ellington and Lena Horne, widely opening television's door. He was criticized for being too liberal and for integrating his show with people of all colors and creeds. Sullivan countered these attacks by remarking, "My Father taught me to respect the rights of all people. He taught me to respect the rights of the underdog. He taught me that all people come from God and are destined to go back to God." **HIGHLIGHTS** Sullivan hyped Elvis' upcoming appearance on his show for many months. When September 9, 1956 finally arrived, Elvis sang "Don't Be Cruel," and was watched by the largest audience in television history to date, a whopping 82.6 percent of the viewing audience! **QUOTE** His successful formula: "Open big, have a good comedy act, put in something for the children, keep the show clean. I believe in getting the best acts I can, introducing them quickly, and getting off!" It all ended in 1971; the master of the big show passed away in 1974.

Marvin Miller   6125 Hollywood

Actor, narrator, writer
BORN Marvin Mueller; July 18, 1913, in St. Louis, MO. **SPOTLIGHTS** Children pushed ABC's button to watch him as Mr. Proteus on "Space Patrol" (1951-'52). As Michael Anthony on "The Millionaire," he led adults to fantasize about money: "What would you do if you had a million dollars?" From 1955-'60 he had the real-life good fortune to find out. His voice was used for various characters in the "Mr. Magoo" cartoon series. Died: 1985.

Bill (William) Boyd   6125 Hollywood

See page 151

Richard Thorpe   6125 Hollywood

Director
BORN Rollo Thorpe; Feb. 24, 1896, in Hutchinson, KS. **SPOTLIGHTS** He holds a near-record at MGM for longevity; he joined in 1935 and stayed until 1968. Movies include the Tarzan series, starting with *Tarzan Escapes!* (1936); dramas like *Barnacle Bill* (1941) with Wallace Beery and Marjorie Main; swashbucklers starring Robert Taylor in *Ivanhoe* and *Knights of the Round Table* (both 1953); and modern rock musicals— *Jailhouse Rock* (1957) starring Elvis Presley. Died: 1991.

Ray Briem   6125 Hollywood

Talk show host

Ray Briem (center), Johnny Grant (left), and Bill Welsh

BORN Leland Ray Briem; Jan. 19, 1930, in Ogden, Utah. **SPOTLIGHTS** A conservative broadcast institution, he began his lengthy career at age 15 by spinning records at his home-town's local radio station. After high school, Briem joined the Army's Information & Education School, then was assigned to Armed Forces Radio where he broadcast to troops worldwide from New York. When the Korean War broke out, he was assigned to AFRTS Far East Network in Tokyo becoming a big hit with GIs. He landed in Los Angeles in 1967 where his mentor, Joe Pine, told Briem to stop spinning records and start talking. Briem had no idea what to talk about, but took on the challenge anyway. He found his voice—and a huge nighttime audience—with the anti-tax movement. Briem was instrumental in bringing information to the masses, along with firebrand activist Howard Jarvis—founder of Proposition 13. When the ballot initiative won by a landslide, Briem became a legendary figure in California political history, and talk radio suddenly became recognized as a powerful communications tool. With his fine conversational skills and dedication to keeping abreast of current happenings around the world, Briem has a loyal group of listeners spanning 30 years. Guests on his programs have included many luminaries, from artists and writers to politicians. **ACHIEVEMENTS** Awarded two Freedom Foundation Awards...His hobbies include piloting his own Piper '59 Tri-Pacer aircraft, or talking with other ham radio operators worldwide. **QUOTE** He has this to say about his job at KIEV 870 AM radio, "Talk radio plays to the extremes. That's stimulating. If you had just moderates on, how dull. This way, you have the listeners in the middle, mostly moderates, being bombarded by all this."

Benny Goodman ● 6125 Hollywood

Musician, band leader

BORN Benjamin David Goodman; May 30, 1909, in Chicago, IL. **SPOTLIGHTS** "The King of Swing" was one of the most famous jazz soloists and band leaders of the 1930s and '40s. A musical prodigy, he began his music studies at age 10 when he picked up the clarinet at the local synagogue. By age 13, this talented youngster joined the musician's union and work part-time jamming in Chicago speakeasies. He also doubled on alto sax, tenor, soprano and baritone saxes. Goodman formed his own band in 1933, and struggled as its leader to gain fans. They performed on broadcast radio from Los Angeles for two years before the mystical night of August 21, 1935, when listeners clicked. Suddenly, he was the first great virtuoso of the swing era. The hot, jazzy period of the '30s and '40s sizzled with his big band sound, as Goodman became the rhythm of a generation. He also broke color barriers by being the first band leader to have both black and white musicians play together on stage. He played ensemble role as well as star leader and surprised audiences with his ability to improvise. Hits include: "Don't Be That Way," "Sing, Sing, Sing," "Stompin' At The Savoy," and "And The Angels Sing." He was extremely popular worldwide in concert. Films featuring Goodman's orchestra: *The Big Broadcast of 1937, Hollywood Hotel* (1937), *Stage Door Canteen* (1943), and *A Song is Born* (1948). Steve Allen stars in the movie based on his life, *The Benny Goodman Story* (1955), while Goodman himself played on the soundtrack. **RECOMMENDED** *Live at Carnegie Hall* (1938), Columbia 450983-2 2CD; *The Birth of Swing* (1935-'36) RCA Bluebird ND 90601 3CD; *After You've Gone* (1935-'37) RCA Bluebird ND 85631 CD; *Solo Flight* (1939-'41) Vintage Jazz Classics VJC-1021-2CD; *Roll 'Em* (1941) Vintage Jazz Classics VJC 1032-2CD; and *B.G.in Hi-Fi* (1954) Capitol B21Y-92684-2 CD. **QUOTE** One of the first to integrate his band, Goodman was questioned by reporters as to why he did it. Although normally shy and reticent, he explained simply, but firmly, "If a guy's got it, let him give it. I'm selling music, not prejudice." The peerless Benny died in 1986.

Benny Goodman, the King of Swing, playing his hot clarinet.

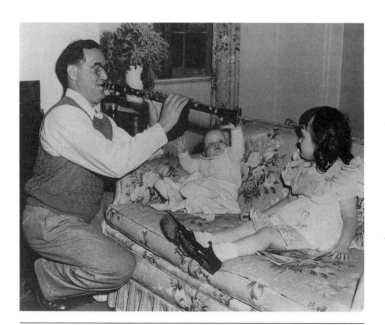

Benny Goodman provided a musical home environment for his daughters, Benjie (left) and Rachel.

6100 HOLLYWOOD

Stanley Kramer   6100 Hollywood

Producer, director

BORN Sept. 29, 1913, in New York, NY. **SPOTLIGHTS** After making World War II training films, Kramer returned to Hollywood and produced *Cyrano de Bergerac* (1950), *Death of a Salesman* (1952), *High Noon* (1952), *The Wild One* (1954) and *The Caine Mutiny* (1954). He directed a number of critically acclaimed motion pictures and/or popular movies, including *The Defiant Ones* (1958), *On the Beach* (1959), *Inherit the Wind* (1960), *Judgment at Nuremberg* (1961), and *It's a Mad Mad Mad Mad World* (1963). Kramer's *Guess Who's Coming to Dinner* (1967), teamed Spencer Tracy and Katherine Hepburn for the last time. It also earned him a third Oscar nomination. **QUOTE** Hailed as the most significant independent producer against the mammoth Hollywood studios, he defined his role as, "a self-styled originator and a quadruple-threat man who can move in several directions at the same time and wind up the day's work by expertly sweeping up the studio after everyone else has gone home."

Gregory Peck   6100 Hollywood

Gregory Peck

Actor

BORN Eldred G. Peck; April 5, 1916, in La Jolla, CA. **SPOTLIGHTS** Extremely well-respected as an actor, Peck maintains absolute integrity with his work. This, in turn, makes him noble, and completely trustworthy to audiences. He is also tall, dark and handsome, with devastating good looks. As an actor, Peck is a tough, but romantic hero, who appeals to both men and women. As a leading man, he has appeared in dramas, comedies, Westerns, war pictures, adventure and action movies. He was nominated for an Oscar for his performance in *The Keys of the Kingdom* (1944), "The role I liked best," he once said. Other Academy Award nominations include *Gentleman's Agreement* (1947), and *Twelve O' Clock High* (1949), for which many thought he should have won a golden boy statuette. Peck has never flinched from the hard work he loved, often making two films at once—*The Yearling* at MGM (in another Oscar-nominated performance)—then driving half a mile down the street to Selznick's for *Duel in the Sun* (1946). He appeared in Hitchcock's *Spellbound* (1945), of which he remarked, "I was lousy." Although others consider this solemn psychological mystery fascinating—especially the Salvador Dali dream sequence—Hitchcock called it, "A manhunt story wrapped in pseudo-psychoanalysis." Among Peck's movies are *Yellow Sky* (1948—a Western), *The Gunfighter* (1950), *Roman Holiday* (1953), and *The Man in the Gray Flannel Suit* (1956). He almost lost his life making John Huston's epic, *Moby Dick* (1956), where rough seas, 16-foot high waves off the coast of Wales and the slippery back of an 80-foot rubbery whale nearly drowned him. Other motion pictures include *The Big Country* (1958), *Pork Chop Hill* (1959), *On the Beach* (1959), *The Guns of Navarone* (1961), *How the West Was Won* (1962), *Cape Fear* (1962; he also appeared in the 1991 remake), *Captain Newman, M.D.* (1963), *The Omen* (1976), *MacArthur* (1977), *Old Gringo* (1989), and *Other People's Money* (1991). Through it all, Peck has remained true-to-his-craft, level-headed, and unspoiled. **ACHIEVEMENTS** 1962 Best Actor Oscar for *To Kill a Mockingbird*. In 1967, the Academy honored him with the Jean Hersholt Humanitarian Award. He is the recipient of the 1989 Life Achievement Award given by the American Film Institute, and the Presidential Medal of Freedom, America's highest civilian award, among countless other honors and tributes. **HIGHLIGHTS** Upon arriving unannounced at a busy restaurant with no available tables, Peck and a friend milled about in the entrance. His companion whispered, "Tell them who you are." Peck responded, "If you have to tell them who you are, you aren't anybody." **QUOTE** His open face photographs with shining virtue and integrity. When asked if this gives him any unfair advantage in real life, Peck commented, "My honest face never impresses anyone, except once when I bluffed in poker and ran a pair of nines over a straight."

Thomas Mitchell   6100 Hollywood

See page 358

Allan Jones   6100 Hollywood

Singer, actor

BORN Oct. 14, 1907, in Scranton, PA. **SPOTLIGHTS** As a supporting actor, he appears in two Marx Brothers comedies: *A Night at the Opera* (1935), and *A Day at the Races* (1937). He stars as the romantic lead in *Show Boat* (1936), opposite Irene Dunne. A terrific singer, his biggest hit was "The Donkey Serenade," which he sang in *The Firefly* (1937), to co-star Jeanette MacDonald. He starred as Sky Masterson in the Chicago company of "Guys and Dolls" for two years. Albums include *Allan Jones Sings Friml Favorites* and *This is the Decade of the 30s*; *World's Greatest Operettas*. His marriage to Irene Hervey produced a son, singer Jack Jones. Died: 1992.

Jack Jones

6100 Hollywood

Singer

BORN Jan. 14, 1938, in Los Angeles, CA. **SPOTLIGHTS** A superb entertainer and classic pop singer, Jones is also celebrated as a leading interpreter of musical theater with acclaimed performances in "Guys and Dolls" and "South Pacific." Raised in Hollywood, he made his singing debut as part of his father's act at the Thunderbird Hotel and Casino in Las Vegas at age 19. Within a few weeks he went out on his own, working

Jack Jones

odd jobs to support himself while pursuing his music career. Inspired by great jazz instrumentalists, such as Gerry Mulligan, Clark Terry, Buddy Rich, and Count Basie, he made a demo album with the song "This Could Be The Start of Something Big." It led to a gig at Fack's night club, in San Francisco. While performing there, he was discovered by Pete King, a producer and artist who quickly signed him to Kapp Records. He did not quit his day job; he was still working as a gas pump jockey when they released his first album. While washing a customer's windshield, he was surprised to hear one of his cuts playing on the car radio. Choosing songs that were both well constructed and emotionally appealing swayed Jones to record works by the greatest balladeers: Sammy Cahn, Jimmy Van Heusen, Cole Porter, the Gershwins, among others. His hit records include "The Race Is On," "Call Me Irresponsible," "Lady," and "What I Did for Love." Other favorites are "Love With The Proper Stranger" (for the film), "Where Love Has Gone," and "The Windmills of Your Mind." In 1971 Jones honored French composer Michel Legrand by recording the French musician's first complete vocal album in English on RCA—*Jack Jones Sings Michel Legrand*. This prompted Mel Torme to say, "Jones is the greatest 'pure' singer in the world." In 1997 Jones recorded *NewJackSwing* for Honest Entertainment, which introduced him to a new generation of fans with hip, swing renditions of "Every Breath You Take," "Have You Ever Loved A Woman," Keb Mo's "Dangerous Mood," "All or Nothing At All," and the classic "Mack the Knife." In 1998 he recorded the Grammy-nominated *Jack Jones Paints A Tribute to Tony Bennett*. This and other Jones recordings are available on Gold Label-Honest Entertainment. To order product call (615) 242-4452 ext. 21, or visit their website at patsgold.com). **SIDELIGHTS** Every single day, somewhere around the world, Jones voice can be heard on television's "The Love Boat" theme song. **HIGHLIGHTS** Part of a "Walk of Fame family," his star is situated next to his father's, singer Allan Jones. His mother, actress Irene Hervey, also has a star on the Walk. He has recorded more than 50 albums (17 of them charting Billboard's Top 20) and consistently enjoys sold-

out world tours. Also an actor with film and TV appearances, he has been a guest performer at Carnegie Hall, the Kennedy Center, and the White House. **ACHIEVEMENTS** Two Grammy Awards for "Best Pop Male Vocal Performance" with his singles "Lollipops and Roses" and "Wives and Lovers." His rendition of "The Impossible Dream" was Grammy-nominated. Jones is an active volunteer and supporter of these charities: Retinitis Pigmentosa, AMC Cancer Research, and Greyhound Pets of America. **QUOTE** His Hollywood Walk of Fame dedication ceremony took place on April 13, 1989. About receiving his star the singer said, "I am honored to be able to join my parents on this very distinguished piece of real estate."

Audrey Meadows

6100 Hollywood

Jayne and Audrey Meadows

Actress, singer

BORN Audrey Cotter; Feb. 8, 1924, in Wu Chang, China. **SPOTLIGHTS** A successful Broadway performer, she became one of the top female comedians during the Golden Age of Live Television. Meadows was immortalized as Alice Kramden in "The Honeymooners." She was the missile-tongued, wisecracking, yet loving wife of Ralph (Jackie Gleason) in the famed 1950s sitcom. Originally, she was rejected for the role because Gleason thought she was too young and pretty. That same day, Audrey scrambled to get a photo made of herself in a drab bargain-basement dress, apron, her hair pulled up like an exhausted *haus frau*, no makeup—all this while holding a frying pan. The next morning she had it delivered to Gleason. When the "Great One" saw it, he roared, "That's Alice!" When advised that was the same girl he had rejected yesterday, Gleason laughed and said, "Hire her. Any dame with a sense of humor like that deserves the job." The rest is television history. "The Honeymooners" went into reruns in 1958, and has never been off the air. Like "I Love Lucy," it is always playing somewhere in the world. Movie roles include the comedies *That Touch of Mink* (1962) with Cary Grant and Doris Day, and *Take Her, She's Mine* (1963) with James Stewart and Sandra Dee. Offscreen, she was known for her warm, funny, engaging personality and razor wit. **ACHIEVEMENTS** 1954-'55 Emmy. **QUOTE** "Talk about Alice in the 'Honeymooners' series, I remember people kept sending me pot-holders, curtains, and aprons by the hundreds. Boy, in the days of the original stage-door-johnnies, the actresses got diamonds and flowers. Meadows got pot-holders." It was suggested, by those that knew her best, to use this line for her epitaph, "Baby, you're the greatest!" *She was.* Died: 1996.

Gregory Ratoff    6100 Hollywood

Gregory Ratoff

Actor, director
BORN April 20, 1897, in St. Petersburg, Russia. **SPOTLIGHTS** Ratoff continued to act sporadically after he had become a director. In *All About Eve* (1950), starring Bette Davis and George Sanders, he works with another supporting player named Marilyn Monroe. During the filming, she revealed to him that this was her first good part, and she hoped it would not be her last. As a director, his most notable movies were *Intermezzo: A Love Story* (1939), which made Ingrid Bergman an international star, *The Corsican Brothers* (1941) starring Douglas Fairbanks Jr. and Ruth Warrick in an exciting swashbuckler, and the backstage musical *Footlight Serenade* (1942) starring Betty Grable, Victor Mature and John Payne, with Phil Silvers providing the comedy. Ratoff's desire to act brought him back in front of the cameras for Hemingway's classic tale, *The Sun Also Rises* (1957), and *Exodus* (1960). Died: 1960.

Montgomery Clift   6100 Hollywood

Montgomery Clift

Actor
BORN Edward M. Clift; Oct. 17, 1920, in Omaha, NE. **SPOTLIGHTS** A thin, dark-haired, brooding leading man, his nervous intensity was apparent in his first role as an American soldier in *The Search* (1948). This powerful postwar drama had audiences weeping, earning Clift an Academy nomination. That same year, he was brilliant in the landmark Western *Red River*, starring John Wayne. He possessed an introspective style that added true psychological dimension to any role he played. Known for his well-crafted performances, films include *A Place in the Sun* (1951), *From Here to Eternity* (1953), *Raintree Country* (1957—with one of his best friends, Elizabeth Taylor), *The Misfits* (1960), *Wild River* (1960), and *Judgment at Nuremberg* (1961). He appears in less than two dozen movies. **QUOTE** "I don't have a big urge to act.

I can't play something I'm not interested in. If I'm not interested, how can I expect the audience to be? Died: 1966.

Lucille Ball   6100 Hollywood

Lucille Ball

Actress, comedienne, producer
BORN Aug. 6, 1911, in Jamestown, NY. **SPOTLIGHTS** Television's queen of comedy and its greatest female star was told she'd never make it in the entertainment business. With aspirations of being an actress, 15-year-old Lucy left home and moved to New York to study drama. Her instructor told her to quit since she did not have any talent. Undeterred, she made up a new background and resume, deciding she was born in "Big Sky" country. As such, the pretty teenager won a year-long contract with Ziegfeld's touring company of "Rio Rita." After only five weeks an assistant told the leggy youth to "Go back to Montana and just be a happy cowgirl." Lucy took a soda fountain job. Determined to get into the movies, she became a part-time model for Broadway's Hattie Carnegie and was cast as a pin-up, poster girl in Goldwyn's *Roman Scandals* (1933). The film, starring Eddie Cantor, was supposed to be a six-week stint in Hollywood. Once Lucy resided in sunny California she remained there. Life was not easy though. She ate at drugstore counters, becoming a saucer-watcher. In other words, she waited for the customer who ordered two doughnuts, or two sandwiches, but ate only one. After he left, she snatched the second one. Goldwyn/20th Century signed her to a very modest contract where she had bit parts in films (unbilled), but dropped her after a handful of pictures. She persuaded RKO to offer her a contract, and, at $50 a week, it was even punier than her previous one. Finally, after five years of hard knocks around Tinseltown she was *Having a Wonderful Time*, with Ginger Rogers and Red Skelton, and continued to enjoy top billing with *The Affairs of Annabel*, and *Room Service* (all 1938). She made 50 motion pictures, including the sentimental drama *The Big Street* (1942—the only one of her films she liked), and the musical *Dubarry Was a Lady* (1943). Yet it would be through the medium of television that Lucy's legendary contributions to show business were made. "I Love Lucy" premiered in October of 1951, and quickly rose straight to the top. With her duck-like voice, she portrayed the feisty, funny, rebellious housewife Lucy Ricardo, whose schemes to get into show business always seemed to backfire and ricochet directly to her husband, Cuban band leader Ricky (played by her real-life spouse, Desi Arnaz). In 1952 the *Time* magazine cover story read: "Lucille belongs to a rare comic aristocracy: the clown with glamour." "I Love Lucy" is the ultimate example of

slapstick situation comedy, where her genuine comedic talents have proved timeless. This classic series is **THE MOST POPU-LAR TELEVISION SHOW OF ALL TIME.** *TV Guide* wrote that Lucy has "a face seen by more people, more often, than the face of any human being who ever lived." Lucy was loved by every-one behind the scenes, too. There was no princess routine for her. She arrived on the set in advance (usually one of the first there), fraternized with cast and crew alike, ate the exact same foods as the lowliest stage worker (and never allowed herself to be served until everyone else had been taken care of). Associates claimed she was a lovely lady, who never brought her personal problems to the set. Zany comedian Phyllis Diller said "She was the pro of all pros." Girlfriends gushed, "You were never sad around Lucy. She was such a cheerful person. Witty, fun, a real hoot!" **ACHIEVEMENTS** "I Love Lucy" was the first sitcom to be a hit, the first show to be No. 1 three years in a row, and the first to be filmed in front of a live audi-ence. She became the highest paid performer at CBS with a lucrative production package deal. When CBS refused to hire a Cuban for "I Love Lucy," Lucy and Desi put up most of the money, created the scripts, began producing—and took the financial risk with their newly formed production company— to make the show. Later when Lucy wanted to produce "Mission Impossible" and the "Star Trek" series under the Desilu Studios banner, executives put their thumbs down. Again Lucy went with her instinct, even though each episode cost Desilu tens of thousands of dollars out-of-pocket. Of course, she was right again, with both shows still succeeding today in some capacity. (See Desi Arnaz's bio in this book.) **QUOTE** "The secret to staying young is to eat sparingly, walk with your shoulders back and lie about your age." Died: 1989.

Loretta Young   6100 Hollywood

Actress
BORN Gretchen Belzer; Jan. 6, 1913, in Salt Lake City, UT. **SPOTLIGHTS** She grew up surrounded by actor hopefuls in the Los Angeles boarding house run singlehandedly by her moth-er. Loretta and her three sisters were sent to "cattle calls" (cast-ing calls for extras in motion pictures) to help supplement the family income so they could afford a formal Catholic educa-tion (convent). In 1927 one of Loretta's sisters, Polly Ann, landed a role in *Naughty but Nice*. She was not able to take it, so director Mervyn Le Roy used pretty Loretta as her replace-ment. She went on to a stellar career. Other motion pictures include *Laugh Clown Laugh* (1928) opposite Lon Chaney. Douglas Fairbanks, Jr. co-stars with her in *The Fast Life* (1929); it was the first in a series of pictures together. She was the essence of 1930s glamour in *The Devil to Pay* (1930). *The Hatchet Man* (1932), co-starring Edward G. Robinson, earned the enchanting brunette a $1,000-a-week salary. She gave one of her best dramatic performances in *A Man's Castle* (1933), opposite Spencer Tracy. In the Christmas classic, *A Bishop's Wife* (1947), her co-stars are David Niven and Cary Grant. She plays opposite William Holden and Robert Mitchum in

Rachel and the Stranger (1948). Her all-time favorite role was in *Come to the Stable* (1948--in an Oscar-nominated performance). The theme reflects her lifetime devotion to Catholicism. She made 98 movies. **TV** Her own two-time Emmy winning show was a dramatic anthology series, 1953-'61. This ultra-feminine creature is best remembered for her sweeping fashion appear-ances. Wearing the finest *haute couture*, her name was rarely absent from the Ten Best

Loretta Young

Dressed Women list. **ACHIEVEMENTS** 1947 Best Actress Oscar for *The Farmer's Daughter*. **QUOTE** "I believe that wear-ing the correct dress for any occasion is good manners."

Will H. Hays 🎥   6100 Hollywood

Business executive
BORN Nov. 5, 1879, in Sullivan, IN. **SPOTLIGHTS** He was head of the Motion Pictures Producers and Distributors of America, Inc., founded in 1922 to keep film executives in line. To placate the American public amid early Hollywood scan-dals, the "Hays Office" enacted strict regulations—the "Hays Code"—to uphold American morals. Its rulings covered sex, violence, language, religion, and racial issues and, because of relentless monitoring, the course of American filmmaking was irrevocably altered. The code was revised in 1966. Film-going audiences entering the third millennium can recognize a con-tinuation of the Hays Office in the motion pictures ratings: G, PG, PG-13, R, NC-17, X. Died: 1954.

Sigmund Lubin 🎥   6100 Hollywood

Producer
BORN 1851, in Breslau, Germany. **SPOTLIGHTS** The early cre-ator of filmed boxing events, his production—*The Battle of Gettysburg* (1912)—simulated an 1897 prizefight, and made a bundle of money. Died: 1923.

Anita Page 🎥   6100 Hollywood

Actress
BORN Anita Pomares; Aug. 4, 1910, in Flushing, NY. **SPOTLIGHTS** A silent screen goddess. While still in New York, the gorgeous teen made her motion picture debut with a small part in the now classic *A Kiss for Cinderella* (1925). Other appearances quickly followed, including *Love 'Em and Leave 'Em* (1926), and her first starring role in *Beach Nuts* (1926). When an executive at MGM studios in Hollywood saw the golden-blonde bombshell, she was offered a long-term contract with that studio. Her first project for MGM, *Telling the World*

Anita Page

*Lynn Bari (right), Lloyd Nolan (left),
and Louis Jean Heydt*

(1927) was a smash hit. Next, she was scheduled to star opposite the studio's leading Latin lover, Ramon Novorro. He romanced her in *Navy Blue* (1927) and *The Flying Fleet* (1928). A breathtaking enchantress, it was her lead role opposite Joan Crawford in *Our Dancing Daughters* (1928), as a jazz-mad flapper, that made her #1 at the box office, and an international superstar. Sound, though, had entered the picture. MGM cast her in their first entry into the talkie era with their musical debut: "All-Talking, All-Dancing, All-Singing" *The Broadway Melody* (1929). It won a Best Picture Oscar, and inspired the studio to launch a stream of outstanding musicals during Hollywood's Golden Era. It also helped Page make the transition to talkies. She made *Free and Easy* (1930) and *Sidewalks of New York* (1931), both with the legendary Buster Keaton. Other movies include *Gentlemen's Fate* (1930) with the great lover John Gilbert, *The Easiest Way* (1931) opposite Clark Gable, and *Night Court* (1932) with Walter Houston. Although cosmetics king Max Factor called her one of the most beautiful women in Hollywood, she retired, still young, in 1933. She surprised devotees when she came out of retirement to co-star in a movie destined to become a cult classic, *Sunset after Dark* (1995), opposite Margaret O'Brien and Randal Malone. This suspense thriller was produced by Wildcat Entertainment and directed by Mark J. Gordon. On the set, Page discussed her career with still photographer/manager Michael Schwibs. She said, "I am thrilled to return to the screen. I always loved being a movie star." **QUOTE** In 1999 she talked about her star on the street of dreams. She said, "It was indeed an honor to appear on the world-famous Hollywood Walk of Fame. I loved being an actress, I loved my career, and that star was my crowning achievement."

Lynn Bari 🎥   6100 Hollywood

Actress
BORN Marjorie Fisher; Dec. 18, 1915, in Roanoke, VA.

SPOTLIGHTS She earned 20th Century-Fox's title "Queen of the B's," although this gifted actress worked in a number of "A" motion pictures. She made her screen debut in *Dancing Lady* (1933), then appears with Shirley Temple in *Stand Up and Cheer* (1934) and *Wee Willie Winkie* (1937). Audiences loved her in the *Mr. Moto* and *Charlie Chan* detective feature film series. Other movies include *The Return of the Cisco Kid* (1939). *Free, Blonde and 21, Lillian Russell,* and *Kit Carson* (all 1940). She appears opposite George Raft in the solid film noir, *Nocturne* (1946). In all, she made 85 films. TV: She played Gwen F. Allen on "Boss Lady" (1952), and did a number of live TV playhouse shows. Died: 1989.

Dick Haymes 🎤   6100 Hollywood

Dick Haymes

Singer, actor
BORN Richard Benjamin Haymes; Sept. 13, 1916, in Buenos Aires, Argentina. **SPOTLIGHTS** A singer and recording artist, he seriously rivaled the world's top male vocalists of the day. He was athletic, charming and multi-lingual. Haymes had enough style, charisma and sophistication to spare. This handsome entertainer became the first to make $50,000-a-week, an unheard of sum at the time, which he made singing in Atlantic City. During WWII, he was the popular radio host of "Everything for the Boys" (servicemen, that is). This musical variety program was broadcast first on NBC, then CBS, from 1944-'48, and was also heard under the name "The Dick Haymes Show." In 1948, he sold seven million records, more than Frank Sinatra, Bing Crosby or Perry Como! Haymes earned a then-astounding annual sum of $230,000 in royalties alone. Hit songs include "You'll Never Know," "Little White Lies," "It Might As Well Be Spring," "Love Letters," "I Only Have Eyes For You," "It's Magic," "The More I See You," "Till the End of Time," "Laura," "Mam'selle," "Daybreak,"

"Moonlight Becomes You," "It Had To Be You" (with Helen Forrest), "How High the Moon," "The Very Thought of You," and "Fools Rush In." His entry into motion pictures came via his big, beautiful baritone voice and his incredible popularity with the ladies. Female fans could not get enough of him. Movies include *Du Barry Was a Lady* (1943), *Four Jills in a Jeep* (1944—his first starring role), *Diamond Horseshoe* (1945), *State Fair* (1945), *Do You Love Me?* (1946), *Carnival in Costa Rica* (1947), *One Touch of Venus* (1948) opposite Ava Gardner, *All Ashore* (1953), and *Cruisin' Down the River* (1953). Crooner Haymes has three stars on the Walk of Fame; another three-star celebrity is Frank Sinatra. **SIDELIGHTS** Reportedly, his father was a diplomat in Argentina. After his parents separated, he moved with his concert-singing mother and was educated in Europe and Canada. Later, Haymes' life revolved around fine wine, beautiful women (he was married *six* times—including to actresses Joanne Dru from 1941-'49— they had three children, and Rita Hayworth from 1953-'55), and song. Eventually he moved to Ireland—which offered big tax breaks to artists—and became an Irish citizen. Died: 1980.

Ralph Edwards   6100 Hollywood

Actor, producer, announcer

Ralph Edwards (left) and Frank Sinatra

BORN June 13, 1913, in Merino, CO. **SPOTLIGHTS** His career began in earnest when Edwards was only 15, but as a child he "made up" and acted in his first play at the age of six in the first grade. Both his mother, Minnie Edwards, and his first grade teacher, Effie Anderson Brown, encouraged him. Their supportive words inspired him for a lifetime. He worked his way through college at radio stations, and earned his degree from the University of California, Berkeley, in 1935. Following his graduation, he hitchhiked across America, intent on getting a radio job in New York City. It was the peak of the Great Depression, and Edwards was on a shoestring budget. He ate nine-cent meals for three months in Bernarr McFadden's Health Food Restaurant. When CBS announced auditions for a staff announcer, he applied and won the position over 60 candidates. Within two years he was announcing as many as 45 *network* shows a week. That staggering amount of work had the opposite effect of slowing him down, it fueled his creative juices. His first success as a creator/producer occurred in 1940 when he produced and starred in "Truth or Consequences," a new kind of show that was to become a landmark in broadcast history. He based it on a game called "Fine or Super-Fine," that he had played as a child on the family farm in Logan County, Colorado. His more complex radio show was known for its endless variety of outrageous stunts, elaborate gags, incredible mischief (Edwards' catchphrase was his sly, "Aren't we devils?"), and weekly happenings. It could also touch the heart. "Truth or Consequences" was described by *Life* magazine as "the nearest thing to insanity in radio today." It was instantly a hit, first on radio—where it was rated the #1 audience participation show for 14 years—and later on television. His other big brain child, "This Is Your Life" became TV's major tearjerker. This human interest show (not a game show) first broadcast in 1948, on radio. The weekly program presented: "the complete life story of a living American." He had crystallized the idea for the show years earlier on a "T or C" show when he connected a wounded, hospitalized, homesick WWII soldier with his hometown via telephone. Everyone from this small locale pitched in to re-create a Saturday night on Main Street. It was a capsulized and interesting version of his life story. Wildly successful, "This Is Your Life," was born. Military heroes made especially good participants, but regular citizens were reunited with an assortment of people who had been instrumental in their lives: the doctor who delivered them, their favorite school teacher, their first love, etc. Occasionally a celebrity was the main guest. The special hook to the show was that the initial set up of each episode was done in total secrecy so that the guest was completely surprised. In 1952 the show made its TV debut. The premise was basically the same: a celebrity or average American was surprised on air by a detailed examination of key areas of their life. He said, "These shows are out of my own head, my own heart. They will hold up as long as there are people on earth." The network run of the TV show ended in 1961, and was followed by three years of first-run syndication, for a total of 503 shows. **ACHIEVEMENTS** In 1950 Edwards pioneered the "live on film" technique still used today. Three Emmy Awards: 1950, 1953, and 1954. Through his various shows, both on radio and TV, Edwards has raised more money for worthy causes than practically anyone else in show business. His efforts on behalf of the March of Dimes (to prevent birth defects), and the Heart Association, have earned him the respect of scores of millions of people. He sold $500,000,000 (that's half a *billion* dollars) worth of U.S. Treasury E. Bonds alone during WWII. He has raised enough money to endow schools for several lifetimes, has helped build hospitals, and with Rear Admiral Samuel G. Fuqua (the last man to walk off the Arizona) organized the fund raising for seed money for the U.S.S. Arizona Memorial, in Pearl Harbor, which was dedicated in 1962...His greatest love was his wife, Barbara Jean Sheldon Edwards (deceased), and their three children, Christine, Gary and Lauren. **QUOTE** "I have always been a big booster of Hollywood and have had my production offices on Hollywood Boulevard for more than 50 years. I am proud of my two stars on the Hollywood Walk of Fame. I am also pleased that my stars are among the first group selected for this honor, and are near Hollywood and Vine, the center of the radio and TV industry at the time the Walk of Fame was created."

Rock Hudson 🎥   6100 Hollywood

Actor

BORN Roy Scherer, Jr.; Nov. 17, 1925, in Winnetka, IL. **SPOTLIGHTS** He was working as a truck driver when an agent discovered him. The young, good-looking man was given dramatic lessons, speech lessons, etiquette lessons, fencing lessons, and singing lessons. His teeth were capped, his hair was dyed, he got a new wardrobe, and his name was changed. *Look* magazine reported that "Rock Hudson is completely an invention of his agent." A publicist hired to promote him said, "His attitude was, 'Well here I am and I guess I'm going to be an actor.'" His dramatic movies include *Fighter Squadron* (1948) starring Edmond O'Brien and Robert Stack, *Magnificent Obsession* (1954) in the film that made him a star playing opposite Jane Wyman (see her bio in this book), and *Giant* (1956) co-starring Elizabeth Taylor and James Dean. When he became a #1 box office attraction, speculation about his popularity became Hollywood fodder around elite power tables. One school of thought was that "the public had tired of spooky actors like James Dean." The huggable, wholesome-looking, beefcake with a soft heart was also an image that played well in comedies. He was at his comic best opposite Doris Day in *Pillow Talk* (1959)...Hudson's co-stars in *Has Anybody Seen My Gal?* (1952) are Charles Coburn and Piper Laurie, with a brief appearance by James Dean. **QUOTE** "Actually I can't say that I do any real acting. I just stand in front of the camera and smile." Died: 1985.

Rock Hudson

William N. Selig 🎥   6100 Hollywood

Pioneer studio head

BORN Mar. 14, 1864, in Chicago, IL. **SPOTLIGHTS** Selig established one of the first studios in Hollywood in 1909.

Films include *The Tramp and the Dog* (1896), and *Dr. Jekyll and Mr. Hyde* (1908). Died: 1948.

Lee Remick 🎥   6104 Hollywood

Lee Remick

Actress

BORN Dec. 14, 1935, in Boston, MA. **SPOTLIGHTS** An alluring beauty, she made her unforgettable screen debut in *A Face in the Crowd* (1957), opposite Andy Griffith. With a reputation for being a lady, she followed up with two amazing dramas, *The Long Hot Summer* (1958), with Paul Newman, and *Anatomy of a Murder* (1959), with James Stewart. Stewart said about his co-star, "She's a lady all right, but a sexy one." After these three films, Hollywood had a new star. She received an Oscar nomination as the dipsomaniac mate of Jack Lemmon in *Days of Wine and Roses* (1962). She made a total of 28 motion pictures, including *Wild River* (1960), *Experiment in Terror* (1962), *No Way to Treat a Lady* (1968), and *The Detective* (1968). She earned Golden Globe Awards for her roles in the TV movie "Jennie, Lady Randolph Churchill" and the series "The Blue Knight." She starred in the outstanding TV movies *Hustling* (1975), about New York City's prostitution industry (based on Gail Sheehy's book), and *The Women's Room* (1980), based on Marilyn French's feminist novel. **HIGHLIGHTS** Her family moved to New York when she was a child, and she began dancing at age eight. Remick recalled that in her youth she had done "itty bitty acting parts when I was not at Miss Hewitt's School. At school, I always kept my acting secret." A natural born talent who was never formally trained in her craft, Remick stated that "everybody thinks I had extensive training, that is because of Kazan." **NOTE** A frail Miss Remick—her appearance distorted by medication and treatment for kidney and lung cancer—appeared on Hollywood Boulevard to receive her star on April 29, 1991. It was her last public appearance, and meant the world to her. Tears streamed down her face when the star was unveiled. Her dear friend, actor Jack Lemmon, was there by her side to cheer her on (see photo on the following page). Three months later, she succumbed to cancer (July 2, 1991). Lemmon remembered the lovely actress saying, "Knowing and working with Lee will always remain one of the most joyous experiences of my life. She was precious, and certainly the embodiment of grace."

Lee Remick and Jack Lemmon at her star ceremony.

Raymond Griffith 🎥 6124 Hollywood

Actor, producer
BORN Jan. 23, 1890, in Boston, MA. **SPOTLIGHTS** A silent screen comedian in both shorts and features, including *Hands Up* (1926). Surprisingly, he gave a powerful dramatic performance as the dying French soldier in the WWI classic *All Quiet on the Western Front* (1930). Later, he produced. Died: 1937.

Edna Best 🎥 6124 Hollywood

Edna Best

Actress, radio director
BORN March 3, 1900, in Sussex, England. **SPOTLIGHTS** At age 17, Best made her London stage debut in "Charley's Aunt." By age 20, she was a star. Thereafter, she lived and worked in three distinct areas: London, New York, and Hollywood. Her important films include *Prison without Bars,* and *Intermezzo* (both 1939), and *The Late George Apley* and *The Ghost and Mrs. Muir* (both 1947). **QUOTE** "During World War II there were a shortage of directors for radio plays. I was happy to do it. But after the war, the boys returned to their jobs, and I returned to domesticity." Died: 1974.

Yvonne De Carlo 🎥 6124 Hollywood

Actress
BORN Peggy Middleton; Sept. 1, 1922, in Canada. **SPOTLIGHTS** Paramount Pictures first put her in *This Gun for Hire* (1942) in a bit part. The studio then decided to cast her in B-horror movies, where she got stuck playing wolf-girl type roles. Director Walter Wanger (who had quite a penchant for brunettes) thought she was being wasted. Wanger said, "I see a certain magic when I look at her." Indeed, for De Carlo was richly-endowed with wondrous, dark beauty. She starred as the glamorous lead of *Salome, Where She Danced* (1945). De Carlo's interpretation of the exotic harem girl—the Arabian night's seductress—was every man's delight. Then, she stars in a series of costume pieces: the Western *Frontier Gal* (1945), the action picture *Buccaneer's Girl* (1950), and the comedy *Hotel Sahara* (1951). During this time she also made the crime picture *Criss Cross* (1949), opposite Burt Lancaster. She combined

Yvonne De Carlo

her abundant charms with humor to result in such classic work as *The Captain's Paradise* (1954). Director Cecil B. DeMille cast her in *The Ten Commandments* (1956). Ironically, when she was in her 40s, she returned to her "horror" roots. Under heavy makeup, she added comic relief to her vampire-like character Lily Munster at 1313 Mockingbird Lane in TV's "The Munsters" (1964-'66).

Art Lund 💿 6126 Hollywood

Singer, actor
BORN Arthur London; April 1, 1920, in Salt Lake City, UT. **SPOTLIGHTS** A former star athlete in football and tennis, he had planned to become a coach. Instead, he became America's popular baritone, whose height of six feet, four inches complemented his rugged good looks. With his well-built physique and thick blonde hair, Lund became a favorite vocalist in Benny Goodman's legendary big band. Starting in the late 1930s, he first got his spit and polish with the swing group, then after a number of years, went solo. Hit recordings include "Blue Skies," "My Blue Heaven," and "Mam'selle." He temporarily retired from show business to join the Navy in 1942. He bravely served during wartime in the South Pacific. When

he returned, he focused on acting. On Broadway, he enjoyed tremendous successes, including a musical adaptation of "Of Mice and Men," and the gigantic hit of 1956, "The Most Happy Fella." He guest starred in TV series: "Gunsmoke," "Police Story," "The Rockford Files," and "Little House on the Prairie." Movies: *The Molly Maguires* (1970), *Bucktown* (1972), and *The Last American Hero* (1973). Died: 1990.

Martha Scott 🎭   6126 Hollywood

Martha Scott

Actress
BORN Sept. 22, 1914, in Jamesport, MO. **SPOTLIGHTS** She majored in drama at the University of Michigan, then acted with the Chicago Shakespearean Company. Scott became an outstanding actress of stage and screen, enduring decades in show business, not as a glamour puss, but as "Miss Average." In 1938 she made her Broadway debut in the Pulitzer Prize-winning play, "Our Town." Two years later, Scott made her screen debut in the movie version of *Our Town* (1940). She was exquisite in both productions. Broadway productions include "Soldier's Wife," "The Male Animal," "Voice of the Turtle," and "The Remarkable Mr. Pennypacker." On the silver screen she starred opposite many greats such as Charlton Heston and Marlon Brando. Films include *Cheers for Miss Bishop* (1941), *The Desperate Hours* (1955—with Humphrey Bogart), *The Ten Commandments* (1956), *Sayonara* (1957), and *Ben-Hur* (1959). TV: Many guest appearances on prime time shows, including "Magnum P.I.," and "Dallas." **QUOTE** "When you've been in the business as long as I have, you learn to live with this thing actors call insecurity. If you become so preoccupied with security that you permit it to dictate your professional future, then you're lost."

John Raitt 🎭   6126 Hollywood

Singer, actor, performer
BORN Jan. 29, 1917, in Santa Ana, CA. **SPOTLIGHTS** This tall, handsome baritone made his theatrical breakthrough on April 19, 1945 as the original Billy Bigelow of Rogers and Hammerstein's "Carousel." His rendition of the famous "Soliloquy" is still considered one of the most memorable moments in American musical theatre. The artist emerged a gigantic star, winning "Best Performance" awards from the New York Drama Critics, Theatre World, and the Donaldson Awards Committee. After Carousel's successful three-year run, Hollywood offered him a $2,000-a-week contract. He commented, "I sat around for three months drawing a salary but never got a camera pointed at me. I decided that I'd have no

more of that, ever." Hollywood, though, did make him an offer he could not refuse. He co-stars with Doris Day in the joyous hit *The Pajama Game* (1957); earlier, he had performed his role in the hit Broadway musical. Other greats are "Annie Get Your Gun," "Kismet," "The Man of La Mancha," "Camelot," and "The Music Man." He has recorded numerous albums. His daughter is singer Bonnie Raitt...Raitt received his Walk of Fame star on his 75th birthday. **QUOTE** "I don't think anybody's ever played more performances of Broadway musicals than I have. I've never stopped."

John Raitt

Gracie Fields 🎤   6126 Hollywood

Comedienne, actress, singer
BORN Gracie Stansfield; Jan. 9, 1898, in Rochdale, Lancashire, England. **SPOTLIGHTS** Great Britain's pride and joy, she tickled funny bones worldwide. The Brits adored her irreverent sense of humor, and its press labeled her "the fireball with English on it." For her film efforts, the *London Times* admired her as "the triumph of the common girl who won't be put upon." Movies include the comedies *Holy Matrimony* (1943) and *Molly and Me* (1945). She enjoyed enormous appeal in radio, concert, recordings, films and TV. She retired to a former Capri prison which she converted to a hotel. She was fond of saying, "We have the most delightful cells for our guests." **QUOTE** Braving life and limb, she entertained the Allied Forces during WWII. She quipped, "I chase defenseless troops halfway around the world singing 'The Biggest Aspidistra' to them." The highest paid comedienne in both Britain and America, she paid enormous taxes. Fields advised soldiers that "it is my income tax that is paying for re-armament. They'll probably name a battleship after me." Died: 1979.

Jimmie Fidler 🎤   6128 Hollywood

Gossip columnist
BORN Aug. 26, 1898, in St. Louis, MO. **SPOTLIGHTS** "Jimmie Fidler in Hollywood" was first broadcast in 1932. Touted as the "reliable, authentic gossip," his reputation suffered greatly in 1941 when *The Hollywood Reporter* ran a front-page story with the headline: "Gossiper admits reviewing pictures he has not seen." Died: 1988.

Don Cornell 💿   6140 Hollywood

Singer
BORN Louis Varlaro; April 21, 1919, in New York. **SPOTLIGHTS** He was a regular vocalist on "The Chesterfield

Supper Club" (radio) to the music of Glenn Miller. Other bands and noted celebrities such as Perry Como also performed on this music show. His theme songs were "A Cigarette, Sweet Music, and You," and "Smoke Dreams."

Mona Barrie 🎥   6140 Hollywood

Mona Barrie

Actress
BORN Mona Smith; Dec. 18, 1909, in London, England. **SPOTLIGHTS** Raised in a convent, Barrie always remained the lady. She trained on the Australian and British stages. A refined actress, her movies include *Charlie Chan in London* (1934), *King of Burlesque* (1935), *I Met Him in Paris* (1937), *Never Give a Sucker an Even Break* (1941), *Cairo* (1942), and *Storm Over Lisbon* (1944). Died: 1964.

Karl Dane 🎥   6140 Hollywood

Actor, comedian
BORN Karl Daen; Oct. 12, 1886, in Denmark. **SPOTLIGHTS** A tall, gangling comic, he was coupled with the tiny George K. Arthur for laughs. Life was *The Big Parade* in 1925 for this rising silent star. It painfully fizzled out by *Whispering Shadows* (1933) because of his thick Danish accent. Died: 1934.

Eileen Heckart 🎥   6140 Hollywood

Actress
BORN Anna Eckart Herbert; March 29, 1919, in Columbus, OH. **SPOTLIGHTS** An award-winning Broadway actress, Heckart brought her artistic gifts to Hollywood. A fine craftswoman, she gave an outstanding performance in *The Bad Seed* (1956) in an Oscar-nominated performance. Other movies include *Bus Stop* (1956) opposite Marilyn Monroe, *Heller in Pink Tights* (1960), *My Six Loves* (1963), *Up the Down Staircase* (1967), *No Way to Treat a Lady* (1968), *The Hiding Place* (1975), *Heartbreak Ridge* and *Seize the Day* (both 1986). She frequently returned to perform on the stage, and appeared in a number of television shows. **ACHIEVEMENTS** 1972 Best Supporting Actress Oscar for *Butterflies Are Free*.

Nazimova 🎥   6140 Hollywood

Actress, violinist, producer
BORN Adelaida (Alla) Leventon; June 4, 1879, in Yalta, Russia. **SPOTLIGHTS** This legendary actress survived a nightmarish childhood of abuse at the hands of her tyrannical father. At age 10, she decided she would act. Nazimova wrote in her diary, "If I have lived not beautifully, I *must* act beautifully." During the

silent era, she was one of the most glamorous, loftiest stars, who seemed to possess a goddess-like quality. Speaking almost no English, she came to America in 1905 on a theatre tour and never looked back. Four years later, the Shuberts named a theater in her honor. She was considered the silent screen's greatest tragedienne. Movies include *War Brides* (1916), *Eye for Eye* (1918), *The Red Lantern* (1919—also produced), *The Brat* (1919), *The Heart of a Child* (1920), *Madame Peacock* (1920—also co-screenplay), *Billions* (1919), *Camille* (1921), *A Doll's House* (1922), *Salome* (1922—based on Oscar Wilde's play; her most famous role), *Madonna of the Streets* (1924), and *My Son* (1925). Later, she returned to the screen as a fine character actress. But it shattered her goddess image with the ravages of time: *Blood and Sand* (1941), and *Since You Went Away* (1944)...She believed in astrology, reincarnation and, as was faddish in the 1920s, held séances at her home that Valentino and June Mathis attended. **HIGHLIGHTS** She was godmother to actress Nancy Reagan (future wife of U.S. President Ronald Reagan)...Nazimova was one of the only Walk of Fame honorees who studied "method" acting with Stanislavsky, the master who started the movement, in Moscow. Died: 1945.

Nazimova

6150 HOLLYWOOD

Roy Del Ruth 🎥

Roy Del Ruth

6150 Hollywood

Director

BORN Oct. 18, 1895, in Philadelphia, PA. **SPOTLIGHTS** Ruth directed Joe E.Brown in the comedy *Hold Everything* (1930). The following year, he switched gears directing the original *Maltese Falcon* (1931), which the *New York Times* claimed "the best mystery thriller of the year." Ricardo Cortez played the lead. (Humphrey Bogart stars in the 1941 remake directed by John Huston.) He hit big with James Cagney in *Blonde Crazy* (1932). *Topper Returns* (1941) is still fun. Died: 1961.

Jerry Lewis 📺

6150 Hollywood

See page 24

George Raft 🎥

George Raft

6150 Hollywood

Actor

BORN George Rauft; Sept. 26, 1903, in Hell's Kitchen, New York City. **SPOTLIGHTS** Born poverty-stricken, he worked odd jobs as a child to help support the family. By age 12 he was on his own, with little education. Almost through osmosis he learned to dance by hanging out at speakeasies. He worked as a dance hall gigolo, then moved up to dinner clubs, "owned by bootleggers and even a few killers," he later remarked. He was a runner for a mobster, and a prize-fighter, before appearing on the Broadway stage as a dancer. This slick, tough guy was immortalized as a criminal in *Scarface* (1932). Director/producer Howard Hawks had the steely-eyed Raft flip a coin, which Raft did with such a menacing style that he became a superstar overnight. Even now, that powerful image lingers in filmgoers' minds. As a villain, he could be pure evil, as in *Taxi* and *Dancers in the Dark* (both 1932). The public crowned him "Mr. Cool," and Raft's pearl-gray hat and red handkerchief in his breast pocket became his masculine trademarks. Raft appears in *Bolero* (1934), with Carole Lombard, the musical *Every Night at Eight* (1935), the crime picture *The Glass Key* (1935), *You and Me* (1938) co-starring Slyvia Sidney, *I Stole a Million* (1939) with Claire Trevor, *They Drive By Night* (1940) co-starring Humphrey Bogart and Ann Sheridan, *House Across the Bay* (1940) opposite Joan Bennett, *Manpower* (1941) with Edward G. Robinson, and *Nocturne* (1946) opposite Lynn Bari. In the latter, he plays a police detective. He is gangster Spats Colombo in Billy Wilder's *Some Like It Hot* (1959), with Marilyn Monroe, Jack Lemmon and Tony Curtis. He played himself in *Casino Royale* (1967), a disastrous James Bond spoof, then became a professional greeter for the Riviera Hotel, in Las Vegas...Raft turned down: *High Sierra* (1941), *The Maltese Falcon* (1941) and *Casablanca* (1942); all were snapped up by Humphrey Bogart. He became owner of "George Raft's Colony Club," London's most successful gambling casino and "in" club. While visiting Hollywood in Jan. 1967, United Kingdom officials declared him an "undesirable alien." **QUOTE** "I was barred from England from guilt by association. Sure I knew Benny Siegel; he was a guy who tried to imitate me. He dressed like me and tried to copy my style. I met Meyer Lansky, Al Capone, Frank Costello, Vito Genovese, Dutch Schultz, Machinegun Jack McGurn, Lucky Luciano. (I'll tell you the truth: I admired them.) I knew lots of people. In London, a guy from Bobby Kennedy's office came into the club and gave me a PT 109 tie clip. He said that when Bobby Kennedy became President this was my ticket to the inauguration." Time proved British officials right. In 1972, U.S. Feds disclosed that the club's silent majority owner was Mafia chieftain Meyer Lansky. Died: 1980.

Irene Rich 📱

6150 Hollywood

See page 207

Art Mooney 💿

6150 Hollywood

Band leader

SPOTLIGHTS The friendly Mooney started with a small band, but switched to big band swing music. Albums include *This Is the Decade of the 30s* and *Decade of the 40s*. His biggest 1950s hit was "I'm looking Over a Four-Leaf Clover." He toured in "The Big Band Calvacade."

Anna Q. Nilsson 🎥

6150 Hollywood

Actress

BORN March 30, 1890, in Ystad, Sweden. **SPOTLIGHTS** While in her teens, she visited a neighbor who had just returned from a vacation. The woman was wearing a hat made of ostrich plumes that she had purchased in New York City. That hat convinced young Anna to cross the Atlantic Ocean. She recalled, "I'd never seen anything so beautiful in my life as that hat. I decided America was the place for me!" In America, she took a job as a nursemaid and studied English. The artist Carol Bickwith spotted her in front of Carnegie Hall (where she was searching for an address). She became the Stanlow Poster Girl. Nilsson made her screen debut in *Molly Pitcher* (1911). An immediate success, she worked steadily until a 1925 horseback riding accident ended her career. She recovered after many surgeries, but, by then, pictures were talkies. She made a cameo appearance in *Sunset Boulevard* (1950), playing cards with old pals Gloria Swanson, Buster Keaton and H.B. Warner. Died: 1974.

Mary Boland 🎥   6150 Hollywood

Actress

Mary Boland

BORN Jan. 28, 1880, in Philadelphia, PA. **SPOTLIGHTS** A seasoned stage performer, she made her silent screen debut in *The Edge of Abyss* (1915). But it was in talkies where her funny comedic skills came to play. She appeared in a series of fluttery, dimwitted roles. She was delightful in *Trouble in Paradise*, *If I Had a Million* (both 1932), *Ruggles of Red Gap* and *People Will Talk* (both 1935). Died: 1965.

Jeanie MacPherson 🎥   6150 Hollywood

Screenwriter

BORN 1884, in Boston, MA. **SPOTLIGHTS** A lovely, brunette actress, she turned to writing for her creative freedom and ultimate calling. For director Cecil B. DeMille, her hit scripts include *The Affairs of Anatol* (1921), *Adam's Rib* (1923), *The Ten Commandments* (1923), and *The King of Kings* (1927), among many others. **QUOTE** "The trouble with ninety-nine out of one hundred stories is that they lack the cement of perspective...A story is a unit and not a conglomeration, but this is a fact that few who desire to write ever learn." Died: 1946.

Herbert Rawlinson 🎥 6150 Hollywood

Actor

BORN Oct. 13, 1885, in England. **SPOTLIGHTS** He made his screen debut--accurately enough--in *The Novice* (1911). He stars in 80 silents, including *Playthings of Destiny* (1921). In talkies, he was a fine actor, often cast as distin-

Herbert Rawlinson

guished characters, including his work in *Hollywood Boulevard* (1936), *That Certain Woman* (1937), *Marie Antoinette* (1938), *Dark Victory* (1939), *Swiss Family Robinson* (1940), *Seven Sinners* (1940), *Joan of Arc* (1948), and *Gene Autry and the Mounties* (1951). Died: 1953.

Bud Collyer 📻   6150 Hollywood

Actor, TV host

BORN Clayton "Bud" Collyer; June 18, 1908, in N.Y. **SPOTLIGHTS** Collyer made history as the first actor to portray Superman. The radio show was based on the DC Comics book character. Collyer was cast as the man "more powerful than a speeding bullet" who "moonlighted" as the Daily Planet's reporter, Clark Kent in "The Adventures of Superman" (1940-1950). Collyer gave Superman's character many of the traits that have lasted to this day, including the micro-second ability to go from the mild-mannered Clark, "This looks like a job..." to the hero, "SUPERMAN!" Collyer did not initially get famous in the role, as his contract stipulated that he *not* reveal he played the man of steel. Finally in 1946, *the series made history* when it tackled for the first time on network air, hot button subjects of racial and religious intolerance. Due to these broadcasts, Collyer was permitted to disclose it was he who played Superman in *Time* magazine. Others include "Break the Bank," "The Guiding Light," and "Truth of Consequences."

Ina Claire 🎥   6160 Hollywood

Comedienne, actress, dancer

Ina Claire

BORN Ina Fagan; Oct. 15, 1895, in Washington, DC. **SPOTLIGHTS** After performing in amateur productions, Claire joined vaudeville at age 10 as a singing mimic. By age 16, she had the lead in "The Quaker Girl." Three years later, she starred on the London stage in "The Girl from Utah." At 20, she worked for Flo Ziegfeld in the "Follies" and "Midnight Frolic," doing her hilarious impersonations and earning a whopping $1,000-a-week. In 1917, she appeared in her first serious dramatic work, "Polly with a Past," which critics thought superb. She was not only Broadway's top comedienne during the 1920s, but also one of the favorite stars in serious theater!

She made her silent screen debut in 1915, then made a handful of talkies. Movies include *The Greeks Had a Word for Them* (1932), opposite Joan Blondell; and Lubitsch's *Ninotchka* (1939) with Greta Garbo, Melvyn Douglas, and Bela Lugosi. **ACHIEVEMENTS** She was awarded a medal from the American Academy of Arts and Letters. **HIGHLIGHTS** Claire was briefly married to the dashing, dark-haired romantic leading man, John Gilbert (1929-'31). A hint on the brevity of the pairing may be linked to the battle of their egos. A reporter asked her, "How does it feel to be married to a great star?" She sniffed, "I don't know, why don't you ask Mr. Gilbert?" Died: 1985.

Barry Sullivan 🎥   6160 Hollywood

Actor

Barry Sullivan

BORN Patrick Barry; Aug. 29, 1912, in New York, NY. **SPOTLIGHTS** A rugged actor, Sullivan made his 1936 stage debut in "Brother Rat." This solid talent worked many years on Broadway before venturing to Hollywood, making his screen debut in *We Refuse to Die* (1943). Motion pictures include *The Gangster* (1947), *Mr. Imperium* (1951) with Ezio Pinza, Lana Turner, Debbie Reynolds, and Marjorie Main, the biting drama *The Bad and the Beautiful* (1952) opposite Kirk Douglas and Lana Turner, *Ship Ahoy!* (1952), *The Miami Story* (1954), his must-see performance in *Tell Them Willie Boy Is Here* (1969), and *Oh, God!* (1977). TV: He played Deputy Sheriff Pat Garrett on "The Tall Man" (1960-'62). He enjoyed the unique privilege of starring in Steven Spielberg's 1969 directorial debut in TV's "Night Gallery," as a fugitive war criminal. Died: 1994.

Yul Brynner 🎥   6160 Hollywood

Actor, director

Yul Brynner

BORN Youl Bryner; July 11, 1915 (or 1920), in Russia. **SPOTLIGHTS** Born of gypsy blood, he was a teenage trapeze artist with a French circus. A near-crippling fall ended that high flying career. After working as a stagehand, the intelligent youth, who was fluent in several languages, studied at the University of Sorbonne, in Paris. He arrived in America in 1940 with a Shakespeare company. When WWII broke out, the U.S. Office of War Information asked the linguist to be a French radio commentator. Postwar, he made his stage debut on Broadway in "Lute Song," opposite Mary Martin. Brynner made his screen debut in *Port of New York* (1949). He stars in 1958's #1 box office motion picture: *The Brothers Karamazov.* Frequently cast as a "heavy," he played a fearless gunslinger in *The Magnificent Seven* (1960); and as a deadly malfunctioning robot in *Westworld* (1973). Movies include *The Ten Commandments* (1956), *Anastasia* (1956), *The Journey* (1959), *Invitation to a Gunfighter* (1964), and *Futureworld* (1973). **ACHIEVEMENTS** 1956 Best Actor Oscar for *The King and I*. He was immortalized as the King of Siam. In 1977, he revived this role on Broadway and enjoyed enormous success...Brynner became the screen's most famous bald-headed leading man...During his last years he spoke out against cigarettes, which had caused his lung cancer. In one of TV's most powerful and chilling moments, a public service announcement aired after his death, where Brynner states he has died from smoking. Died: 1985.

Gower Champion 📺   6162 Hollywood

Dancer, choreographer

Gower and Marge Champion

BORN June 21, 1921, in Geneva, IL. **SPOTLIGHTS** An exquisite dancer, he enjoyed great success as half of the husband and wife team (with Marge) on Broadway and in films. TV includes "Admiral Broadway Revue" (1949), a variety show starring Sid Caesar and Imogene Coca. They also had their own sit-com, "The Marge and Gower Champion Show" (1957). Married to Marge Champion from 1947-'73; see her bio in this book. Died: 1980.

Tommy Riggs and Betty Lou 🎤   6166 Hollywood

Voice specialist

BORN Oct. 21, 1908, in Pittsburgh, PA. **SPOTLIGHTS** Tommy Riggs was a comedian. Due to a rare medical condition diagnosed as "bi-vocalism," he could speak in his own baritone voice as easily as the high-pitched, sweet voice of a female child. Some thought he was a ventriloquist, but he *never* threw his voice. His alter ego was a little girl named Betty Lou, but she was not a dummy. With his incredibly flexible voice, he conjured up an act as a student at Brown University. Riggs caused a few minutes of collegiate mayhem when he "brought up her voice" in the men's locker room. He could barely hold back his laugher as he watched his teammates leap for their clothes. He also used her voice to talk like a drill sergeant, sing funny tunes, etc. During the Great Depression, he landed a job as a singer-pianist at a local radio station. When the station manager heard what Riggs could do, he gave him his own late night radio show called "The Tom and Betty Program." Her voice sounded so real that the FCC and the Child Labor Board demanded the little girl not work such late hours, and be sent home to bed! Riggs and the lovable Betty Lou were first introduced to the national audience on Rudy Vallee's show in 1937. He was offered the longest, on-going contract with Vallee, for 49 weeks. Then, he hit gold with his own network show, "Tommy Riggs and Betty Lou" (1938-'43), as star(s). He joined the U.S. Navy, where he entertained the Allied Forces. By the time he returned, he was all but forgotten as the new medium of TV dawned. Died: 1967.

Rudolph Valentino 🎥   6166 Hollywood

Rudolph Valentino and Wanda Hawley

Rudolph Valentino and Vilma Banky

Actor
BORN Rodolfo Alfonzo Raffaele Pierre Guglielmi (di Valentina d'Antonguolla); May 6, 1895, in Castellaneta, Italy.
SPOTLIGHTS This Italian-born actor became the top romantic star during the silent era. Known as "the screen's greatest lover," the darkly handsome Valentino specialized in exotic roles. His smoldering sex appeal and glamorous characterizations made him the idol of millions. In *The Four Horsemen of the Apocalypse* (1921), the Latin archetype captured the world's attention with his amorous interpretation of the tango. Most had never seen the tango performed, and this act of love that sizzled for minutes onscreen introduced the dance of romance to audiences everywhere. It inspired countless lessons and sold as many copies of "Lacumparsita," history's most popular tango. In *The Sheik* (1921), he unleashed a flood of sensuous fantasies that Victorian women did not even realize they had. Although the actor once stated he hated the film, the audience loved it and it grossed two million dollars, as astronomical sum at the time. Suddenly, everything Arabesque was in vogue, and "the Arab" was the hottest star in Hollywood's heaven. He liked the sequel, *The Son of the Sheik* (1926), which followed

years later. In between, he made a variety of movies, although none placed emphasis on his fine qualities of humor, sensitivity and athletic prowess. He stars in *Beyond the Rocks* (1922), where he caused a global sensation by romantically kissing the open palm of his leading lady's hand. He co-stars with Nita Naldi in *Blood and Sand* (1922), a bull-fighting story. Next, Valentino stars in *The Young Rajah* (1922), a disastrous film that made male viewers dislike him even more. A costume picture, female filmgoers fainted at the erotic sight of his bejeweled bare chest. He fared better with *Monsieur Beaucaire* (1924), as a barber who parades as a nobleman, opposite Bebe Daniels...Offscreen, he gardened, his favorite hobby. **HIGHLIGHTS** Elvis Presley was inspired to grow his own sideburns long after seeing Valentino's movies...Stricken with a perforated ulcer, Valentino received his final curtain call from the Great Director in 1926. His death caused riots in the streets of New York, and profound sorrow and grief to an entire world.

Theodore Roberts 🎥   6166 Hollywood

Actor
BORN Oct. 2, 1861, in San Francisco, CA. **SPOTLIGHTS** A distinguished gentleman, he was nicknamed the "grand duke of Hollywood." An outstanding stage performer, he entered the fledgling film industry when he was in his fifties. He made his screen debut as Simon Legree in *Uncle Tom* (1910). Within two decades, he made 200 films. His most important role was portraying Moses in De Mille's *The Ten Commandments* (1923). Silents: *Arizona* (1913), *The Call of the North* (1914), *The Arab* (1915), *The Trail of the Lonesome Pine* (1915), *Joan the Woman* (1917--as Bishop Peter Cauchon), *The Affairs of Anatol* (1921), and *Noisy Neighbors* and *Ned McCobb's Daughter* (both 1929--released after his death). Died: 1928, at the dawn of sound.

6200 HOLLYWOOD

Jan Clayton 📺   6200 Hollywood
Actress
BORN Aug. 26, 1917, in Tularosa, NM. **SPOTLIGHTS** She played the widowed mother Ellen Miller (1954-'57) on "Lassie," and was a regular on "Pantomime Quiz" (1953-'54; 1962-'63). Mini-series "Scruples" (1980).

Leonard Bernstein 🎧   6200 Hollywood
Conductor, composer, pianist

Leonard Bernstein

BORN Aug. 25, 1918, in Lawrence, MA. **SPOTLIGHTS** A free spirit. A musical phenomenon. A brilliant artist. However, Bernstein's early years were not happy. He stated he was, "a scared, sickly, skinny kid." At age 10, his family inherited an upright piano. Bernstein took to it instantly, insisting on dollar-an-hour piano lessons. His parents had no interest in their son acquiring musical skills, but eventually gave in to his demands. With music in his life, Bernstein thrived physically (becoming husky), emotionally (gaining friends and popularity), and mentally (improving his grades to become a top-notch academic). Still, his musical talents were not encouraged. His father, a beauty shop supplier, later commented, "How was I suppose to know he would grow up to be Leonard Bernstein?" He was raised in a middle-class neighborhood in Boston, was educated at Harvard, and served an apprenticeship to conductor Serge Koussevitzky. In 1943 he made the dramatic substitution for conductor Bruno Walter in Carnegie Hall. Hailed by critics and public alike, the 25-year-old met fame with complete acceptance. He possessed a tremendous versatility that baffled critics, but made fans from audiences of every musical taste. He had an intense drive and stated, "what never gets mentioned is that I work hard." His string of Broadway musicals include "West Side Story," and "Candide." His compositions include the symphony "Jeremiah," and his ballet with Jerome Robbins "Fancy Free" blossomed into the Broadway musical "On the Town." He was Oscar-nominated for his music to *On the Waterfront* (1954), but was immortalized with his musical score for *West Side Story* (1961). He became the assistant conductor for the New York Philharmonic (1943-'44), then conducted the New York Symphony (1945-'48). He ascended to conductor of the New York Philharmonic Orchestra (1958-'69)—at age 40. Bernstein became the *first* native-born American to hold the coveted position, and one of the youngest ever to reign over its podium. The flamboyant, well-built Bernstein later became a guest conductor to leading orchestras around the globe. Pristine works include: *Bernstein: Overture to Candide*, and *Symphonic Dances from West Side Story*, among many others. He was the pianist and conductor on *Gershwin: Rhapsody in Blue*. Other favorites: *Beethoven: Symphony No. 9* recorded live on Christmas Day 1989 at the Berlin Wall; *Barber: Adagio for Strings*; *Schubert: Symphony No. 8 ("Unfinished")*. His brother, Elmer, became a Hollywood composer. **ACHIEVEMENTS** Tonys: 1953 and 1959. Emmys: 1956, 1957, 1960, 1961, 1965, 1972, 1976. Grammys: 1961 (9 awards), 1962, 1963, 1964, 1967, and 1977. **QUOTE** An admirer of composer John Philip Sousa's "The Stars and Stripes Forever," Bernstein declared, "I would have given ten years of my creative life to have written it." (See Sousa's bio in this book.) Died: 1990.

Tex Beneke 🎧   6200 Hollywood
Band leader, musician, singer

Tex Beneke

BORN Gordon Beneke; Feb. 12, 1914, in Fort Worth, Texas. **SPOTLIGHTS** This wonderful band leader became a professional musician as a teen while still in high school. Performing as a saxophonist and vocalist for the legendary Glenn Miller (who had discovered Beneke), the band made numerous hit records and were also featured in a number of motion pictures. With the tragic death of Miller in 1944, the attractive, gifted Beneke took over leadership, and changed the name to the "The Glenn Miller Band with Tex Beneke." His music "helps keep memories alive." Known as a gentleman, and popular with peers and the public, his hits include "Give Me Five Minutes More," and "Chattanooga Choo Choo." The latter was RCA Victor's very first gold record.

Gordon Hollingshead 🎥 6200 Hollywood
Actor, director
BORN Jan. 8, 1892, in Garfield, NJ. **SPOTLIGHTS** An actor in the pioneer business, he later directed silents. Died: 1952.

John Nesbitt 🎙   6200 Hollywood
See page 142

Rochelle Hudson 🎥   6200 Hollywood

20th Century-Fox contract players, from left to right: Iris Shunn, Elsie Larson, Nadine Dore, Anne Nagel, Rochelle Hudson (center), Dorothy Dearing, "Pat" Paterson, Rosemary Ames and Drue Leyton.

Actress

BORN March 6, 1914, in Oklahoma City, OK. **SPOTLIGHTS** Due to her open, heart-shaped face and doe eyes, this American beauty was initially cast in sweet ingenue roles. Later, she was allowed to sink her teeth into darker roles. Films include *She Done Him Wrong* (1933), *Imitation of Life* (1934), *Curly Top* (1935), *Les Miserables* (1935), *Meet Boston Blackie* (1941), and *Rebel Without a Cause* (1955). Hudson worked with one of America's top wits, the homespun humorist Will Rogers in *Mr. Skitch* (1933), *Judge Priest* (1934), and *Life Begins at Forty* (1935). The latter is a gentle comedy that offers witty comments of human nature. In the 1960s, she made "B" horror pictures. In all, she made 50 pictures. When she retired from show business, Hudson became a prominent real estate broker. **HIGHLIGHTS** She was one of Max Factor's favorites. Hudson dedicated the "Brunette Room" at his world famous beauty salon in Hollywood. **ACHIEVEMENTS** During World War II, she took a break from her busy motion picture career to join her husband and serve in Naval Intelligence in Mexico and Central America. Died: 1972.

Herbert Marshall 🎥   6200 Hollywood

Actor

BORN May 23, 1890, in London, England. **SPOTLIGHTS** Known for his suave English style, his performance in *The Letter* (1929) delivered newsworthy mail across America. This veteran stage actor was 40 years old for this cinematic break-through. Instead of casting him solely the grand lover, Paramount Pictures decided to focus him in roles which were

more character in nature. Their decision was due to a slight, permanent limp Marshall had. Yet the attractive, intelligent, well-mannered talent could have remained the romantic lead, as he was adored by all his female co-stars—Garbo, Dietrich, Davis, Colbert, and Hepburn. And female fans either did not notice the limp, or were simply not bothered by it. His impressive list of global credits includes the masterpiece of light comedy, *Trouble in Paradise* (1932). Among his other fine works: *The Lady Consents* (1936), *Forgotten Faces* (1936), *Angel* (1937), *A Bill of Divorcement* (1940), *The Letter* (1940), *Foreign Correspondent* (1940), *The Little Foxes* (1941), *Forever and a Day* (1943), *The Enchanted Cottage* (1945), *The Razor's Edge* (1946), *Duel in the Sun* (1946), and *The Secret Garden* (1949). **HIGHLIGHTS** He lost his right leg during World War I while serving in the British Merchant Marine, but trained himself to walk with only the slightest stiffness. He always wore long pants so the public wouldn't know. Died: 1966.

Pat Sajak 📺   6200 Hollywood

Host, broadcaster

BORN Oct. 26, 1946, in Chicago, IL. **SPOTLIGHTS** Sajak is the world's most popular game show host. Prior to coming to Hollywood, Sajak roared, "Goood morrrning, Vietnaaam," into the microphone while serving on duty as a morning disc jockey in Saigon with Armed Forces Radio Vietnam. Soldiers enthusiastically applauded Sajak's wit and spontaneity, winning him a huge audience before being discharged in 1972. Once back in the States, Sajak landed a rock 'n' roll radio slot,

Pat Sajak and Vanna White

then his first television job as a local weatherman in Nashville, Tennessee. Scrambling up the TV ladder, he added public affairs programs and a talk show to his daily schedule. With his all-American boy good looks and friendly demeanor, he was picked up by the NBC affiliate in Los Angeles as the nightly weatherman and the weekend host of "The Sunday Show." It was in Los Angeles in 1981 that Merv Griffin—creator of the game show "WHEEL OF FORTUNE"—selected Sajak to host the then-daytime network version of "WHEEL." Syndicated in 1983, it quickly became the nation's highest-rated game show. It virtually rules the airwaves in its time slot. He has maintained his gigantic hit status for nearly two decades. Sajak entertains with a personable, easy-going style and a wry wit. *TV Guide* declared "WHEEL OF FORTUNE" as "unquestionably the most popular television game show on earth." **ACHIEVEMENTS** In his long list of honors are numerous Emmy nominations, three Emmys Awards and a People's Choice Award. **SIDELIGHTS** The Emmy Award-winning producer, Harry Friedman, produces both of America's top shows: "WHEEL OF FORTUNE," and "Jeopardy!" (Also see the separate bios of Merv Griffin and Alex Trebek in this book.) **HIGHLIGHTS** Sajak remembers sneaking out of bed as an 11-year-old to watch the great Jack Paar host "The Tonight Show." Inspired by this legendary master of the early tube, Sajak decided at that time to have a broadcasting career. It's fitting, then, that 38 years later—on Feb. 10, 1994—his star on Hollywood Boulevard would be dedicated next to his idol Jack Paar's star. Sajak also hosted his own late-night "The Pat Sajak Show," on CBS. **QUOTE** "When I was a kid, I used to write my name in chalk on our sidewalk and pretend it was the Hollywood Walk of Fame. Now I've got the real thing, and, best of all I don't have to rewrite it after it rains."

Jack Paar 📺   6200 Hollywood

TV host, comic

BORN May 1, 1918, in Canton, OH. **SPOTLIGHTS** A TV critic once called him: "the man who never had an unspoken thought." Paar stated that he was: "always fascinated by people." His early years in radio offered the high school dropout both the opportunity to perfect his comic timing, and to talk to and about people. Drafted in 1942, he did his military stint on the Special Services vaudeville circuit entertaining thousands of troops. In the South Pacific, his goal was to get the GIs to temporarily forget about their bouts with dysentery, battle fatigue, etc., so he felt he had to be as funny as possible. Under wartime conditions he developed combustible dialogue that usually targeted superior officers. This incendiary technique later carried over to the more intimate setting of his talk show. After the war, he enjoyed a brief period in Hollywood working with such stars as Marilyn Monroe in the film *Love Nest* (1951), then

Jack Paar

turned to the small screen. Paar's best-remembered television work is as the unpredictable personality and host of "The Tonight Show" (1957-'62). During his late-night reign, Paar recalled, "that America either loved or loathed me five nights a week, five years running." Each show ran 1.8 hours for a total of 36 hours a month. NBC paid the kingly sum of $10,000,000 annually to him for his 432 hours work. "The Tonight Show" featured the chatty star introducing new talents, reviving old ones, or talking with interesting guests. The midnight master created fresh gags, staged skits and unusual stunts. He had a unique approach to storytelling. It was gentle, employing a humorous zing at the end. But with conversation he could be controversial. He was called "Little Lord Fauntleroy with a switchblade knife," "A bull in *his own* china shop," as well as "A minister after four martinis." He may have been a little of all those things. Paar was particularly temperamental, and one night he got fed up, said his peace, and walked off the show. After his abrupt departure, Johnny Carson succeeded him in 1962. Paar later stated, "I quit when I got even. TV got in the way of living." **QUOTE** He was the subject of much research early in his TV career. Paar recalled, "A man who was paid several thousand dollars by a sponsor to analyze my character reported that I didn't have any. This so wounded me that I made my own report. I was, I said, 'complicated, sentimental, lovable, honest, loyal, decent, generous, likable, lonely.'"

Jean Negulesco 🎥   6200 Hollywood

Director

BORN Feb. 29, 1900, in Romania. **SPOTLIGHTS** A Parisian painter-turned-director, Negulesco was brilliant at reinventing himself, and brilliant at reinventing his film speciality. First known in Hollywood for his 1940s film noir, the next decade he specialized in romantic comedies. Works include *The Mask of Dimitrios* (1944) with Peter Lorre and Sidney Greenstreet, *Road House* (1948) starring Ida Lupino, *How to Marry a Millionaire* (1953) starring Marilyn Monroe, Betty Grable and Lauren Bacall, and *Three Coins in the Fountain* (1954), with Clifton Webb and Dorothy McGuire. One of his best remembered dramas is *Johnny Belinda* (1948), starring Jane Wyman and Lew Ayres. Died: 1993.

Gigi Perreau 📺   6200 Hollywood

Gigi Perreau

Actress

BORN Ghislaine Perreau-Saussine; Feb. 6, 1941, in Los Angeles, CA. **SPOTLIGHTS** This precious bundle of joy was born six weeks after her mother and father escaped from Nazi-occupied Paris, France. Once in Southern California, Madame Perreau quickly fell in love with all things Hollywood. A gentle and refined stage mother, she took her son, Gerald, to MGM studios in an attempt to get him cast in a film. The toddler Gigi accompanied them in a perambulator. As luck would have it, MGM was looking for a petite one for their upcoming film, *Madame Curie* (1943), starring Greer Garson and Walter Pidgeon. Director Mervyn LeRoy instantly cast her as Eve Curie. She was just two years old. With her open heart-shaped face, button nose, brown hair and brown eyes, Perreau was the perfectly photogenic, perfectly adorable and perfectly charming child. As she grew in *The Master Race* (1944), *Mr. Skeffington* (1944), *Yolanda and the Thief* (1945), *Song of Love* and *Green Dolphin Street* (both 1947), her acting abilities grew, too. Her first important role was in *Enchantment* (1949) opposite her brother. She appears in a number of motion pictures and won the Critics Award for the comedy *Has Anybody Seen My Gal?* (1952). Her co-stars are Charles Coburn, Piper Laurie and Rock Hudson, with a brief appearance by James Dean. Other honors include *Parents* magazine Juvenile Acting Award and the Screen Children's Guild Small Fry Award. Movies include *Weekend With Father* (1951), *Bonzo Goes to College* (1952), *The Man in the Gray Flannel Suit* (1956), *Tammy Tell Me True* (1961), and *Journey to the Center of Time* (1967). TV: She appeared in live dramatic playhouse shows, and in many several guest starring roles. Series work includes "The Betty Hutton Show" (1959-'60) and Katharine Ann Richards on "Follow the Sun" (1961-'62).

Jean Renoir 🎥   6200 Hollywood

Jean Renoir (standing)

Actor, director, screenwriter

BORN Sept. 15, 1894, in Paris, France. **SPOTLIGHTS** Born the second son of the famous French Impressionist painter, Pierre-Auguste Renoir (1841-1919), the darling, curly-haired little boy frequently modeled for portraits by his father. He was raised in an atmosphere where *creativity ranked superior* to all else—even above intelligence—and where the circle of artistic friends were part of the household. Bathed in his father's pristine love of nature, Jean was acutely perceptive of its beauty; its exquisite life force becoming a trademark in his films. He valued the absolute truth. He was utterly fascinated by the role that social setting plays with us mere mortals, locking in our destiny, as we flounder about. Monsieur Renoir had no difficulty making the leap from silents to talkies—he welcomed the added dimension to the art of motion pictures. His first successful talkie, a melodrama entitled *La Chienne* (1931), examined Montmartre (Paris) life. His first international success, *Grand Illusion* (1937), is brilliant. Renoir made dozens of features, including the memorable tragedy, *La Bete Humaine/The Human Beast* (1938), but *La Regle du Jeu/The Rules of the Game* (1939), is his masterpiece. It was originally a box office bomb. The following year, he fled Nazi-invaded France and emigrated to the U.S. He settled in Beverly Hills, California. **ACHIEVEMENTS** 1975 Honorary Oscar. He wrote a biography of his famous father entitled *Renoir* (the original French title). He quotes his father as saying, "I work with my hands. I am therefore a manual laborer. A laborer of paint." **HIGHLIGHTS** His first wife, Catherine Hessling, was his father's beautiful model. She was also the star of the first movie he financed, *Vie sans Joie/Catherine* (*Life Without Joy/Catherine*, 1924--he also wrote the screenplay). **QUOTE** When asked why he did not follow in his father's footsteps to become a painter, Renoir answered, "How could I? Having seen my father made me understand that painting is something beyond representation of nature. I still don't believe I'd have the spiritual strength to paint, after my father." Died: 1979.

Dorothy Lamour 🎤   6200 Hollywood

See page 374

William Seiter 🎥   6240 Hollywood

Director

BORN June 10, 1892, in New York. **SPOTLIGHTS** After graduating from the Hudson Military Academy, he diametrically opposed the direction of his formal education by joining Mack Sennett's hilarious, slapstick, frenzied Keystone Kops. He wrote screenplays, then graduated to assistant director. Seiter directed countless silents and 70 sound pictures, many for Warner Brothers: *The Truth About Youth* (1930) with Myrna Loy, *Going Wild* (1931) starring Joe E. Brown, and *Big Business Girl* (1931) starring Loretta Young, and Ricardo Cortez. He did one of the best—if not *the* best—Laurel and Hardy feature, *Sons of the Desert* (1933). Curly Top cutie Shirley Temple stars in *Dimples* and *Stowaway* (both 1936), while the Marx Brothers, Lucille Ball and Ann Miller went crazy in the farce *Room Service* (1938). His popular wartime work was the musical *You Were Never Lovelier* (1942). Died: 1964.

John Carradine 🎥   6240 Hollywood

John Carradine

Actor
B O R N Richmond Carradine; Feb. 5, 1906, in Greenwich Village, NY. **SPOTLIGHTS** His deep, resonant voice and gaunt, morose face enabled him to be one of cinema's most versatile character actors. He appears in 220 films—from Westerns to horror, and from drama to comedy—including *The Invisible Man* (1933), *Cleopatra* (1933), *Cardinal Richelieu* (1935), *White Fang* (1936), John Ford's *The Prisoner of Shark Island* (1936), *Captains Courageous* (1937), Ford's *Stagecoach* and *Drums Along the Mohawk* (both 1939), Ford's *The Grapes of Wrath* (1940), *House of Dracula* (1945), *Johnny Guitar* (1954), *The Ten Commandments* (1956), *The Man Who Shot Liberty Valance* (1962), and *Peggy Sue Got Married* (1986). **HIGHLIGHTS** Carradine's lifelong love affair with the works of Shakespeare began in his childhood. Later, he recited Shakespeare *while* strolling down Hollywood Boulevard on the Walk of Fame stars. In his magnificent, cultured voice he could be heard clearly for some distance:

> "O! what a rogue and peasant slave am I:
> Is it not monstrous that this player here,
> But in fiction, in a dream of passion,
> Could force his soul so to his own conceit
> ...and all for nothing!" —Shakespeare,
>   *Hamlet*, Act II, Scene II

Greatly admired, he earned the affectionate nickname "the 'Bard of the Boulevard." He was also an accomplished stage star. Three of his sons—David, Keith, and Robert—are talented actors. Died: 1988.

Celia Cruz 💿   6240 Hollywood

Celia Cruz

Singer
BORN Oct. 21, 1929, in El Barrio de Santos Suarez, Havana, Cuba. **SPOTLIGHTS** The foremost female vocalist in the world of hot Cuban music, Cruz has been crowned "The Queen of Salsa." She grew up in what she describes as "the poor part" of the city, in a household of 14 children including nieces, nephews and cousins. As a child, she sang lullabies to other children, and the adult neighbors would gather to listen. Although she had a beautiful voice, her father did not want her to become a singer as he thought it was not respectable. Her mother, though, encouraged her and said, "Go ahead, I'll back you up." She immigrated to America in the 1950s, where her driving energy and penetrating, gutsy voice created a vast global audience. With her lively lyrical, scat-like improvisations, Cruz is considered the most recognizable Cuban singer in the world. Her trademark dancing style—with traditional fast hip and feet movement—combines mambo and rumba. She is a fun entertainer to watch, and has used her fame to help introduce mainstream listeners to salsa. She appears in *The Mambo Kings* (1992) **ACHIEVEMENTS** 1990 Grammy for "Ritmo En El Corazon" (recorded with Latin jazz star Ray Barretto). Her two LP's on Santero Music (Afro-Cuban religious) remain collector's items. Internationally renowned, she has 20 gold records and more than 100 awards from various countries. Her career has spanned 50 years as a defining force in Latin music. She broke the all-time concert attendance record, in Tenerife, Spain, with 240,000 fans attending. **QUOTE** Known for her sparkling, rapid-fire improvisation Cruz stated, "It's something you're born with. You can't practice ahead of time because it won't come out right. I never know what I'm going to say and the same thing never comes out twice." About recording in Spanish, instead of English, she said, "When there's good music, language is the least of the barriers. Good music is good music."

Robert Mitchum 🎥   6240 Hollywood

Actor
BORN Aug. 6, 1917, in Bridgeport, CO. **SPOTLIGHTS** A legendary talent and Hollywood's archetypal bad boy, he once declared, "I guess my ambition has always been to be a bum."

Robert Mitchum

He was a myth of a man whose mere walk into a room spoke volumes about his character. (Nobody could swagger like Robert Mitchum.) This tall, barrel-chested, ruggedly handsome actor appeared in the gritty war film, *Thirty Seconds Over Tokyo* (1944), before his portrayal of an Army Captain in *The Story of G.I. Joe* (1945) earned him his first and only Oscar nomination. A solid performer, he stars as a private eye with a dark history in the sultry film noir *Out of the Past* (1947) with frequent co-star Jane Greer. It is a brilliant picture. Mitchum made 125 movies, including the excellent, tense film noir *The Big Steal* (1949) with Greer, *River of No Return* (1954) with Marilyn Monroe, *The Night of the Hunter* (1955—as the psychotic preacher in a thrilling performance), *Heaven Knows, Mr. Allison* (1957—he plays a macho Marine), *The Enemy Below* (1957—he portrays a ship's commander in a dramatic game of death—U-boat vs. destroyer), *Thunder Road* (1958—about Kentucky moonshiners, gangsters and the law; Mitchum's older son, Jim, made his screen debut in this film), *Cape Fear* (1961—as the menacing ex-con), *Ryan's Daughter* (1970—as a genteel schoolteacher), and *Farewell, My Lovely* (1975—as the hard-boiled private eye, Philip Marlowe). When asked how it was possible he made so many films, Mitchum quipped, "I work cheap." Then he added, "Making movies keeps me away from harder work." **TV** In 1983, Mitchum starred in Herman Wouk's *The Winds of War*. Both men believed that television was capable of doing projects of substance. **QUOTE** About receiving his long overdue star on Jan. 25, 1984, Mitchum commented, "I never looked forward so much as to seeing that precious star on Hollywood Boulevard. Unless there's a catastrophe, or some demented person digs it up for one reason or another, at least people will know I was here." This tough guy then wiped a tear rolling down his cheek. Died: 1997.

Cecil B. DeMille 🔖   6240 Hollywood

See page 147

Pat O'Brien 📺   6240 Hollywood

See page 325

Loretta Swit 📺   6240 Hollywood

Actress, singer, dancer
BORN Nov. 4, 1937, in Passaic, NJ. **SPOTLIGHTS** This blonde beauty began her stage career with the National Touring Company as the lead in "Any Wednesday." She subsequently

starred in "The Odd Couple," "Mame," "I Do, I Do," and in 1976-77 was a huge success on Broadway in "Same Time, Next Year." Swit, though, became best known for her as Major "Hot Lips" Houlihan in the smash hit TV series "M*A*S*H." This Emmy-winning talent has also appeared in numerous dramatic made-for-TV movies, including "The Execution," "Miracle at Moreaux," "Friendship, Secrets and Lies," and "Games Mother Never Taught You." Her

Loretta Swit

numerous TV guest appearances on major musical variety shows--"The Perry Como Special," and "The Bob Hope Christmas"--have highlighted her singing, dancing and comedy skills. Winner of several People's Choice Awards, her lifelong passion is protection of animals.

Nunnally Johnson 🎥   6240 Hollywood

Screenwriter, producer, director
BORN Dec. 5, 1897, in Columbus, GA. **SPOTLIGHTS** A former newspaper and magazine short stories writer, Johnson was asked how he would adjust writing for the wide screen. He commented, "Very simple. I'll just put the paper in sideways." A brilliant screenwriter whose shining intelligence became his trademark, including 20th Century-Fox's *The House of Rothschild* (1934), starring George Arliss, a truly devious Boris Karloff, and Loretta Young. The next year, he began producing. For the same studio, he superbly adapted John Steinbeck's book *The Grapes of Wrath* (1940). Directed by John Ford, this Academy Award winning film is a masterpiece. He wrote/produced *The Desert Fox* (1951), an historical WWII picture starring James Mason and Jessica Tandy. On the lighter side, he wrote *How to Marry a Millionaire* (1953) starring Marilyn Monroe, Betty Grable and Lauren Bacall. He became a director with *Night People* (1954), starring Gregory Peck. Joanne Woodward won her Best Actress Oscar under his direction: *The Three Faces of Eve* (1957). In 1959 he received the Laurel Award for the writer who had contributed most to the literature of the screen. His last screenplay is another must-see: *The Dirty Dozen* (1967). About his 25 years of writing for the screen, Johnson stated his scripts were "as clean of unnecessary material as possible." **QUOTE** About studio executives interfering with a writer's work he mocked, "They are geniuses in high places who, though they are unable to write anything that makes sense or even spell are continually becoming inspired. They'll shout, 'somebody sharp me a pencil,' and then they'll slit hell out of a script that a competent writer has worked on for weeks." Died: 1977.

6250 HOLLYWOOD

Lena Horne 6250 Hollywood
See page 260

Ona Munson 6250 Hollywood
Actress, singer

Ona Munson

BORN June 16, 1906, in Portland, OR. **SPOTLIGHTS** Immortalized as the scandalous Belle Watling in *Gone With the Wind* (1939), she glowed in the role of the wanton madam. Her scarlet sinner exuded both sympathy and humor, while running Atlanta's biggest house of ill repute. Perhaps no other actress has so succinctly conveyed the cheerful whore who possessed a heart of gold. Other movies include *Five Star Final* (1931), *The Shanghai Gesture* (1941), *Idaho* (1943), *The Cheaters* (1945), and *The Red House* (1947). Earlier, she performed in comic musical revues. By her 20s, she was starring on Broadway, then made her screen debut in *Going Wild* (1931). Died: 1955.

Arlene Harris 6250 Hollywood
Actress

BORN 1899, in Toronto, Canada. **SPOTLIGHTS** She was known as "The Human Chatterbox," for her mile-a-minute funny telephone monologues on "Al Pearce and His Gang." (The bashful door-to-door salesman and his gang first aired on NBC in 1933; the show ended after WWII.) Harris was a delightful comedienne who was clocked speaking 240 words a minute, and gave audiences as many chuckles. She played "The puny Plaza Hotel's switchboard operator" on "Here Comes Elmer" (1944). Postwar, Harris landed the plum role of Mommy/Mrs. Higgins on Fanny Brice's "The Baby Snooks Show." Died: 1976.

Constance Bennett 6250 Hollywood
Actress
BORN Oct. 22, 1904, in New York, NY. **SPOTLIGHTS** She was known as being as difficult as her father—matinee idol Richard Bennett—and equally as aggressive and stubborn. Yet, she was one of the few who made the transition from silents to talkies. Known for her facile elegance, she was a witty, glamorous, sophisticated blonde with a husky voice and an oversized personality. Films include *Sin Takes a Holiday* (1930), *What Price Hollywood?* (1932), *Bed of Roses* (1933), *Topper* (1937) with Cary Grant, and *Topper Takes a Trip* (1939), to

name a few in her long list of credits. Director George Cukor said, "she had a kind of romantic, F. Scott Fitzgerald look about her. It was the look of the 1930s—or perhaps the 1930s looked like her." She married and divorced industrial magnates and royalty alike, and whipped around the world in only the best *haute couture* style. **SIDELIGHTS** Her favorite pastime was poker, at which she was an exceptional player. The games would start at her palatial Holmby Hills mansion on a

Constance Bennett

Friday evening and end Monday morning. Studio heads, executives and celebrities were her gambling guests, who barely bothered to sleep. Major studios nearly changed hands at those high-stakes poker games. **QUOTE** Bennett was making $30,000-a-week when new income tax laws were first put in place. Studio accountants informed her that she could potentially have a serious IRS problem. With her typical cavalier attitude, she advised them, "Oh, then you will have to pay the tax, for I must have $30,000 clear." Died: 1965.

Bob Crosby 6252 Hollywood
See page 128

Barry Fitzgerald 6252 Hollywood
Actor

Barry Fitzgerald

BORN William Shields; March 10, 1888, in Ireland. **SPOTLIGHTS** An Irishman with bright, blue eyes, he was known as a "scene stealer" for his great skill and charms. A versatile talent, he played rogues, near-saints and villains with equal aplomb. Movies include *Bringing Up Baby* (1938), and *How Green Was My Valley* (1941). He appeared in the very first Agatha Christie novel brought to the screen, the excellent thriller, *And Then There Were None* (1945). He was perfect in *The Naked City* (1948), and *The Quiet Man* (1952). **ACHIEVEMENTS** 1944 Best Supporting Actor Oscar in *Going My Way*. Ironically, he played a Irish Catholic priest; in real-life he was a Irish

Protestant. Died: 1961.

Everett Sloane 🖤 6252 Hollywood

Actor

BORN Oct 1, 1909, in New York, NY. **SPOTLIGHTS** He planned a Wall Street career until the stock market crash of 1929. His gambling persona persisted, for he pursued an acting career. He worked in radio dramas, then hit the jackpot in Orson Welles' classic movie—*Citizen Kane* (1941). He usually played tough characters, which was odd because he was small, almost bald, and wore round, wire-rimmed glasses. TV includes "The Loretta Young Show" (1953-'61). Died: 1965.

Everett Mitchell 🎙 6254 Hollywood

Host

SPOTLIGHTS Mitchell was rural America's red, white and blue flag-waver on "The National Farm and Home Hour" (1928-58). For three decades, the variety program was made with approval of the U.S. Department of Agriculture and the Farmers Union. Known as "the farmer's bulletin board," it provided farm tips, expert growing advice from a number of excellent sources, music, news, political debates, support contacts with governmental agencies, and dramatizations (where Don Ameche played a forest ranger). The show also carried live coverage from important agricultural events around the country. Mitchell, who created the show, stayed with the program for decades, and, in doing so, improved farmers lives. He is an important part of American family farming history that has been lost forever. **QUOTE** No matter what the weather, the cheerful Mitchell opened each broadcast with the catchphrase: "It's a bee-eeu-ti-ful day in Chicago!"

Sammy Davis, Jr. ⏺ 6254 Hollywood

Singer, dancer, actor

BORN Dec. 8, 1925, in New York, NY. **SPOTLIGHTS** At age four, the diminutive one began performing in the Will Mastin Trio act alongside his father and uncle Will. Tutored by Bill (Bojangles) Robinson, this natural born talent developed his lightning-speed dance technique. A pure joy to watch, one reviewer observed, "his feet remind me of *liquid rhythm.*" Davis temporarily quit show business to enlist in the Army during WWII. After his honorable discharge in 1945, he rejoined the Trio and made his breakthrough at Slapsie Maxie's, in Hollywood. The group broke every club record, with Davis's talents as a comedian, showman, impersonator, and vocalist making him the star of the show. This world-class talent glided with graceful, catlike swift movement. He was a vital, energetic, fresh tap dancing phenomenon; a complete entertainer in every sense of the word. Al Jolson declared: "he's the world's greatest entertainer." When he opened on Broadway in the musical comedy "Mr. Wonderful," both audiences and critics rejoiced. One critic wrote: "He dances as well as Bill Robinson, he sings like a lark and can flatten you with

Sammy Davis, Jr.

his imitations." Another praised: "Davis does just about everything, and everything he does is right." Films include *The Benny Goodman Story* (1956), *Anna Lucasta* (1958), *Porgy and Bess* (1959—as Sportin' Life), *Ocean's Eleven* (1960—with his Las Vegas "Rat Pack" buddies: Frank Sinatra, Dean Martin and Peter Lawford), *Johnny Cool* (1963), *Robin and the Seven Hoods* (1964—with his "Rat Pack" buddies), *Sweet Charity* (1968), *That's Dancing* (1985), and *Tap* (1989). Hit singles include "Candy Man" and "People Tree." His spectacular rendition of "Mr. Bo Jangles" has become a treasured American classic. **SIDELIGHTS** He lost his left eye in a 1954 automobile accident, and wore a glass eye thereafter. **ACHIEVEMENTS** President Reagan presented him with the Kennedy Center Award in a special 1987 ceremony. In 1989, he was Grand Marshal of the 58th Hollywood Christmas Parade. He died shortly thereafter in 1990.

Desi Arnaz 🖤 6254 Hollywood

Actor, singer, musician, band leader

BORN Desiderio Alberto Arnaz y de Acha, III; Mar. 2, 1917, in Cuba. **SPOTLIGHTS** His father, a politician and ranch owner, was exiled after the 1933 Cuban revolution. At age 16, the handsome, young aristocrat émigrated to the United States. Arnaz's fun rumba music and conga drums delighted audiences, making him a popular act. From nightclubs and cabarets, he cha-cha-cha'd his way onto the silver screen and into co-star (and future wife) Lucille Ball's heart. They made

Desi Arnaz

their film debit in RKO's *Too Many Girls* (1940). It was not their most memorable film together (*The Long, Long Trailer* made in 1954 is their funniest), but it united a couple who would make important television contributions. Their history-making show was initially rejected, as CBS executives unanimously stated, "it would never work." To prove these businessmen wrong, Lucy and Desi took their act on the road, winning audiences throughout America. CBS network heads still refused the racially mixed couple. Lucy and Desi formed their own production company, wrote their own scripts (loosely based on their lives), and assumed most of the show's financial burden. When CBS held a private showing of "I Love Lucy" to its executives, one company man viewed it, then declared it: "unfunny, silly and totally boring." Still, the network did not have much to lose. "I Love Lucy" premiered on Oct. 15, 1951. It shocked the so-called TV experts with its astounding success. Within four months, it rated #1. Desilu productions had created television's all-time most popular series "I Love Lucy." They "babalued" all the way to the bank. **ACHIEVEMENTS** Arnaz's business innovations include the pioneering of television's: three-camera technique, syndication, and establishment of the sit-com as a genre. "I Love Lucy" was the first show to be filmed live before a studio audience, and the first sit-com to be a hit. It firmly remains the most popular show in history, and is being watched every minute of every day somewhere around the world. Died: 1986.

Imogene Coca   6256 Hollywood

Imogene Coca

Comedienne, actress
BORN Nov. 18, 1908, in Philadelphia, PA. **SPOTLIGHTS** Paired with Sid Caesar, this tiny, big-eyed, and large-mouthed funny lady made the Saturday night live comedy series "Your Show of Shows" (1949-'54) a huge hit. By appearance, she could have been a skinny librarian, but her quick wit and clownish mugging brought the house down. This outstanding, Emmy Award-winning talent is best remembered for her zany skits and wacky take-offs of ballerinas, opera stars, wives and strays. She was also an accomplished Broadway performer, and nightclub entertainer. Films include *National Lampoon's Vacation* (1983), and *Nothing Lasts Forever* (1984).

Henry Wilcoxon   6256 Hollywood

Actor, producer
BORN Sept. 8, 1905, in the West Indies. **SPOTLIGHTS** This dark-haired British stage and screen star made his American debut as Marc Antony in DeMille's *Cleopatra* (1934), and became one of DeMille's favorite actors. He played Sir Lancelot in *A Connecticut Yankee in King Arthur's Court* (1949) with Bing Crosby and Rhonda Fleming. Films include *The Greatest Show on Earth* (1952), *Scaramouche* (1952), *The Ten Commandments* (1956), and *F.I.S.T.* (1978). Died: 1984.

Fulton Lewis   6258 Hollywood

Commentator, columnist
BORN F. Lewis. Jr.; April 30, 1903, in Washington, D.C. **SPOTLIGHTS** A fifth-generation Washingtonian on his mother's side, he was immersed in politics. After graduating from the University of Virginia in 1924, he took a position as a newspaper reporter with the Washington *Herald*. Within three brief years, he had been promoted to its editor. In 1928, he joined the Hearst news service, writing a column entitled "The Washington Side Show." Outspoken against liberal causes, Lewis was known for his ultra-conservative policies and ties to right-wing politicians. He targeted people and organizations; he constantly berated the Ford Foundation. Worshipped by a large percentage of his listeners, he was equally hated. His 7 P.M. radio show, "Top of the News from Washington," started in 1937 and lasted for 20 years. He was instrumental in securing a radio gallery in the U.S. Senate and House. A no-nonsense commentator, he often broke stories which had been leaked to him. Lewis also insulted many well-respected journalists by claiming on air that they gave "so-called facts." But, in all honesty, Lewis reported "the truth" as *he* perceived it; *not* in an unbiased manner. Suffice it to say, news' giant Edward R. Murrow was *not* a fan. **QUOTE** His signature line: "...and that's the top of the news as it looks from here." Died: 1966.

Andy Devine   6258 Hollywood

See page 384

Helen Hayes   6258 Hollywood

Actress
BORN Helen H. Brown; Oct. 10, 1900, in Washington, D.C. **SPOTLIGHTS** Crowned the "First Lady of the American Theater," Hayes appeared under the bright lights of Broadway, and on stages across the U.S. At five feet tall she was petite in

Helen Hayes

size, but a grand actress with a commanding presence. Known for her wistful beauty, grace, and brisk, humorous style, she was an actress of phenomenal skill. Films include *Arrowsmith* (1931), *A Farewell to Arms* (1932), *Another Language* (1933), *Crime Without Passion, What Every Woman Knows* (both 1934), and *Anastasia* (1956). **ACHIEVEMENTS** 1931 Best Actress Academy Award for *The Sin of Madelon Claudet;* 1970 Best Supporting Oscar for *Airport.* 1988 National Medal of Arts awarded by President Reagan. **QUOTE** "Always I gazed outward at the world, not inward upon myself." Died: 1993. For her eulogy, a dear Catholic friend, the Rev. Jerome Vereb, recited a line from one of Hayes' long-running plays, and the one that is considered her most remarkable and significant performance. The record-breaking show was called "Victoria Regina" (spanning 80 years of Queen Victoria's life), and Hayes toured with it to 43 cities. The Reverend glanced at the script and said, "Go to it, old girl. You've done very well."

Ozzie and Harriet Nelson 🎙 6260 Hollywood

Actor, band leader, writer, producer; singer, actress
BORN Oswald George Nelson; March 20,1906, in Jersey City, NJ. Harriet Louise Snyder; July 18, 1909, in Des Moines, IA (also professionally known as Harriet Hilliard). **SPOTLIGHTS** "America's favorite young couple" started their professional relationship in 1931 when band leader Ozzie hired Harriet as vocalist for his band. They were perfectly suited for the time as the country sank into the dark years of the Great Depression. Americans were searching for security, and his orchestra offered sweetness, light and comfort. Both Ozzie and Harriet were very good musically, as well as being attractive. They often sang boy-girl duets sprinkled with good-natured humor. The band featured two pianos, a warm brass section, and a full-bodied sax. They married on October 8, 1935. Five years later, Harriet was hired by Red Skelton for his new radio program in Hollywood, then in 1944 Ozzie and Harriet won their own show. "The Adventures of Ozzie and Harriet" about an average, happy middle-class family handling the mundane decisions of daily life turned into the hit TV show watched by millions. The cast included their two real-life sons, David and Ricky, who together with their Mom and Pop became "America's favorite family, the Nelsons." Ozzie played the befuddled, stubborn man of the house to Harriet's forbearing spouse, who never argued but proved her point one way or the other. Ozzie invented this style and genre of family situation comedy; it became an American staple. **ACHIEVEMENTS** At age 13, Ozzie became the nation's youngest Eagle Scout. Later,

The Nelson Family (from left to right): Ricky, David, Harriet and Ozzie

an honor student at Rutgers University, he excelled in football and lacrosse, and played on both teams...The close-knit Nelsons' love and devotion to one another was sincere. The phrase "Ozzie and Harriet" has come to mean an idyllic family life. (See the bios of David and Rick Nelson in this book.) Died: Ozzie in 1975; Harriet in 1994; Rick in 1985.

Donald Woods 📺 6260 Hollywood

Actor
BORN Ralph L. Zink; Dec. 1, 1904, in Brandon, Canada. **SPOTLIGHTS** Known as a "B" picture star, he offers terrific support in "A" movies, including *Mexican Spitfire* (1939), *Watch on the Rhine* (1943), and *Wonder Man* (1945). He jumped to TV and alternated with then-emcee Ronald Reagan in "The Orchid Award" (1953-'54), a musical variety program. On "Tammy" (1965-'66) he was the sophisticated, but good-humored boss. His last film was *True Grit* (1969). Died: 1998.

Ruth Roland 🎥 6260 Hollywood

Actress
BORN Aug. 26, 1892, in San Francisco, CA. **SPOTLIGHTS** She blossomed from "Baby Ruth" to being crowned the "Queen of silent serials." This hard-working, busy, athletic leading lady appears in 12 Western *serials,* often doing her own stunts. **QUOTE** "Often I am asked what I consider the real secret of success. My answer can be given in two words—personality and concentration—the real secret of success in any line of endeavor. Once you choose what you want to be, concentrate on this thought day and night, work for it always, and never lose sight of the goal, for who knows, it may be just around the

corner where you can't see it. Don't give up after a short time and change—stick to it no matter how dark the way. Make every thought you think, everything you do, bring you that much nearer, and whatever you may do, concentrate on it—give it your whole, undivided attention. Remember, gold seldom lies on the surface of the ground. To get to the pure gold—the real success of life—one must dig, and dig deep and continuously, for nothing can be obtained without labor in any field of endeavor." Died: 1937.

Thelma Todd 🎥   6262 Hollywood
Actress

Thelma Todd

BORN July 29, 1905, in Lawrence, MA. **SPOTLIGHTS** Nicknamed "Hot Toddy," she was a luscious peaches-and-cream blond sexpot with penciled eyebrows and a contagious smile. Motion pictures include *Maltese Falcon* (1931—the original version which is *sexier* than the 1941 remake with Bogart), *Horse Feathers* (1932) with the Marx Brothers, *Speak Easily* (1932) with Buster Keaton, *The Devil's Brother* (1933) with Laurel and Hardy, *Counsellor-at-Law* (1933) with John Barrymore, *Son of a Sailor* (1933) co-starring Joe E. Brown, and *Palooka* (1934) with Jimmy Durante. Died: 1935, under mysterious circumstances (suspected mob ties).

Ralph Edwards 📺   6262 Hollywood
See page 234

Marian Anderson 🎵   6262 Hollywood
Singer

BORN Feb. 17, 1897, in Philadelphia, PA. **SPOTLIGHTS** The greatest contralto of the 20th century was born in a ghetto to a deeply religious, hardworking family. Her love affair with music started at the nearby Baptist church. She had no formal singing lessons until she was 15, when a small scholarship was set up for her by church members to help fund her education. When her father died, she scrubbed porch stoops at five cents apiece to help support the family and her lessons. Finally, with cash in hand, she applied to a Philadelphia music school. She was turned down flat with this statement: "We don't take colored people." Years later, she discussed that rejection, "It was as if a cold, horrifying hand had been laid on me. My skin was different but not my feelings." She persevered with self-taught lessons, becoming proficient with music by Handel, Italian

Marian Anderson

opera, and German *lieder*, but she never forgot her roots in black spirituals either. Critics attribute Miss Anderson's broad repertoire and her impassioned, dark velvet, hypnotizing voice to this period of her life. With bookings in America few and far between, she traveled to Europe giving her first performance in Berlin in 1930. Five years later, at the Salzburg Festival in Austria, she was introduced to the great conductor Arturo Toscanini. He proclaimed, "A voice like yours is heard once in 100 years." She returned to America triumphant, performing at a state dinner for President Franklin D. Roosevelt in honor of Britain's King George VI and his queen in 1938. In doing so, she was the first African American to perform at the White House. Next, she broke all records by doing 70 recitals in the United States—more than any singer had ever done. The next year would not be so carefree. She was refused permission to sing at Constitution Hall in Washington, D.C. by the all-white Daughters of the American Revolution. Eleanor Roosevelt resigned from the organization within days of this news, whereupon the Secretary of the Interior asked Miss Anderson to perform at the Lincoln Memorial. 75,000 people showed up demonstrating their support of her, including members of the Supreme Court. Years later she reminisced, "My heart leaped wildly and I could not talk." This singular event catapulted her into the history books as the quiet, dignified crusader of civil rights. Yet, her most glorious day would occur on January 7, 1955, when she appeared on the stage of the Metropolitan Opera as the sorceress Ulrica in Verdi's "Un Ballo in Maschera" ("A Masked Ball"). This was not only the day she broke the Met's color barrier, it was the culmination of her childhood dreams, and the realizaiton of her heart's passion. **ACHIEVEMENTS** One of the greatest singers of the 20th century, she was a recipient of countless honors, including honorary degrees, White House performances, appointments as a U.S. delegate to the United Nations in 1958 and to the National Council of Arts in 1966. She won a lifetime achievement Grammy Award in 1991. She overcame every obstacle of racism, poverty, and elusive happiness to prevail as an American legend. **QUOTE** She rose above repression, as she commented, "leading by example, not words." Died: 1993.

Carmen Miranda

did not want to lose Miranda's unique appeal, so the studio hired an Italian gentleman to teach her English. (This explains her darling, foreign accent.) A fun, warm, and exotic personality, she charmed audience with her colorful costumes and wild foot-high headdresses. Next, she performed a spicy rendition of "Chica, Chica, Boom, Chic" in *That Night in Rio* (1940), with Don Ameche. By 1943 she provided the craziest entertainment as "The Lady in the Tutti-Fruiti Hat." In *The Gangs All Here,* 30 feet of bananas topped her head! Her influence in the 1940s fashion world included platform shoes, bare midriffs, turbans, and brightly colorful, long-sleeved ruffled shirts. Even women in America's heartland could be seen sporting this attire off the farm. The American song closely associated with her is: "I'm Chiquita Banana and I've come to say, bananas have to ripen in a certain way..." Died: 1955.

Una Merkel 🎥   6262 Hollywood

Actress

BORN Dec. 10, 1903, in Covington, KY. **SPOTLIGHTS** A smart-aleck, pert character actress with red-gold hair, her busy career spanned four decades and 125 movies. Pictures include *Blonde Bombshell* (1933), *Cat's Paw* (1934), and *Saratoga* (1937). In *Destry Rides Again* (1939), she gets into a rough and tumble catfight with Marlene Dietrich. She was Oscar-nominated for her role as the menacingly addled mother in *Summer and Smoke* (1961). Died: 1971.

Carmen Miranda 🎥   6262 Hollywood

Singer, dancer, actress

BORN Maria de Carmo de Cunha; Feb. 9, 1909, in Portugal. **SPOTLIGHTS** The daughter of a successful wholesale fruit vendor in Rio de Janeiro, she became an accomplished radio, recording and film star in her native country. This energetic beauty conquered Broadway, and excited sold-out audiences at the Waldorf-Astoria, then landed a 20th Century-Fox contract. Billed as the "Brazilian Bombshell," she made her U.S. screen debut in *Down Argentine Way* (1940). Interestingly, Fox

Peggy Knudsen   6262 Hollywood

Actress

BORN April 27, 1923, in Duluth, MN. **SPOTLIGHTS** A pretty blonde, she played April Adam in the sit-coms "So This is Hollywood" (1955). Previously, she appeared in Warner Brothers films. Died: 1980.

Ogden Nash ☒   6262 Hollywood

Panelist, author, poet

BORN Frederic O. Nash; Aug. 19, 1902, in Rye, NY. **SPOTLIGHTS** A master of humorous verse, and a celebrated poet, Nash was known for his sage and sparkling distortions to the English language. "The great worsifier" (as he called himself), claimed that his "verse came hard." He added, "my style is my individual method for concealing my illiteracy." Of the 20 volumes of his unique work, some were for children, including *The Bad Parents' Garden of Verse* (1936). **TV** Nash queried disguised celebrity contestants in the madly successful quiz show "Masquerade Party" (1953-'57). His wit was one of the true stars. **RADIO** He was a clever panelist on "Author, Author" (1939-'40), and the resident wit on Guy Lombardo's show (1943). **RECOMMENDED** *In Their Own Voices, A Century of*

Recorded Poetry (A four-CD box set available on Rhino Records/RhinoWord, R2 72408. Website: www.rhino.com). **QUOTE** Radio director Tom Carlson's dog chewed up an autographed copy of one of Nash's books. Upset, he sent a note to the author explaining what had happened, and requesting that he autograph the replacement copy. Nash returned the book penned with this inscription, "To Tom Carlson or his dog—depending on whose taste it best suits." Died: 1971.

Charles Ruggles 🎥   6262 Hollywood

Actor

Charles Ruggles

BORN Feb. 8, 1886, in Los Angeles, CA. **SPOTLIGHTS** In 1905 he made his acting debut in a stock company production in San Francisco, California. Gaining theatrical experience, he traveled with stock companies from 1914 to 1929 throughout the nation. He performed on virtually every stage in the country. With his impressive resume, Paramount Pictures recruited him. This dapper, but meek Casper Milquetoast was both a leading and supporting actor. Movies include *Charley's Aunt* (1930), *Ruggles of Red Gap* (1935), *Anything Goes* (1936), *Early to Bed* (1936), and *It Happened on Fifth Avenue* (1947—as Michael O'Connor, his favorite role). He is remembered in four distinct character categories: as a drunk, as a bumbling, good-natured comic-type, as a hen-pecked husband, and/or the kindly, endearing father and grandfather. He returned to the Great White Way and earned a 1958 Tony Award. **TV** His was the voice of Aesop on "The Bullwinkle Show" (1960s cartoon series). **QUOTE** Asked how he liked working in movies, Ruggles smiled and responded, "How can you help but feel affectionate toward an institution that puts so much money into your pocket?" Died: 1970.

Dave Garroway 📺   6262 Hollywood

Radio and TV personality

BORN July 13, 1913, in Schenectady, NY. **SPOTLIGHTS** This tall, large-framed former radio host pioneered the *first* morning television program—the "Today" show. On January 14, 1952, at 7 A.M., he opened with, "Well here we are, and good morning to you. The very first good morning of what I hope and suspect will be a great many good mornings between you and me. Here it is...when NBC begins a new program called *Today* and, if it doesn't sound too revolutionary, I really believe this begins a new kind of television." Viewers enjoyed his bland, yet direct presence. His was a cozy approach to an interview, and he was an eager listener. He said, "I'm curious about people. I talk as if there were just two or three friends out there. I think you have to be pretty easygoing." Garroway wore a bow tie, a tweed jacket, and possessed a sense of humor that seemed to comfort viewers with what the day had in store for them. *He closed each show with one quiet word: "Peace."* Died: 1982.

Peggie Castle 📺   6262 Hollywood

Actress, singer

Peggie Castle

BORN Dec. 22, 1927, in Appalachia, VA. **SPOTLIGHTS** She modeled for a soap company, then became a "B" movie actress: *Hell's Crossroads*, and *Begining of the End* (both 1957). She found fame and fortune in TV as the Birdcage saloon keeper Lily Merril in "The Lawman" (1959-'62). A regular in "The Outlaws," she also guest-starred in many other shows. Died: 1973.

Charles Coburn 🎥   6262 Hollywood

Actor

Charles Coburn

BORN June 19, 1877, in Savannah, GA. **SPOTLIGHTS** Nearly 60 years old when he entered films (!), this aristocratic, cigar smoking, thick-lipped character actor delighted audiences with his old-school gentlemanly manners. He wore his monocle as if it were part of his face. Before coming to pictures, this authoritative actor ran his own Shakespeare company and was an accomplished Broadway performer. He resisted Hollywood's offers until *Of Human Hearts* (1938). After that, he became part of the movie diet as the dignified, pompous or callous figure with a soft underbelly and heart of gold. He was excellent in so many films: *The Devil and Miss Jones* (1941--in an Oscar-nominated performance), *King's Row* (1941), *Heaven Can Wait* and *The Constant Nymph* (both 1943), *Wilson* (1944), *The Green Years* (1946--in an Oscar-nominated performance), *Has Anybody Seen My Gal?* (1952), *Gentlemen Prefer Blondes* (1953), and *Around the World in 80 Days* (1957). In all, he made 68 pictures. **ACHIEVEMENTS** 1944 Best Supporting Actor for *The More the Merrier*. **QUOTE** "I can never remember when I did not want to be an actor." Died: 1961.

Pat Boone   6262 Hollywood

See page 352

Mitzi Gaynor 🎥   6262 Hollywood

Actress, singer, dancer

Mitzi Gaynor

BORN Francesca M. von Gerber; Sept. 4, 1930, in Chicago, IL. **SPOTLIGHTS** Born into a show business family, both Gaynor's mother and aunt were ex-hoofers who began to teach her to dance as soon as she could walk. Then, the three "girls" moved to Hollywood where the bright 12-year-old performed in USO shows. By age 14, she was appearing in the Civic Light Opera Company of Los Angeles. She made her silver screen debut in a Betty Grable vehicle, the musical *My Blue Heaven* (1950). Gaynor appeared in a number of other movies, including *There's No Business Like Show Business* (1954) with Ethel Merman, Dan Dailey, Donald O'Connor, Marilyn Monroe and Johnny Ray. A leggy, perky, pixie-faced blonde with plenty of screen personality, studios initially considered her a dancer first and foremost. Gaynor responded, "I'd like to be known as an actress who can dance, rather than the other way around." Finally recognized as an actress, she starred with the biggest leading men: Bing Crosby in *Anything Goes* (1956), Frank Sinatra in *The Joker Is Wild* (1957), Gene Kelly in *Les Girls* (1957), David Niven in *Happy Anniversary* (1959), Yul Brynner in *Surprise Package* (1960), and Kirk Douglas and Gig Young in *For Love or Money* (1963). Gaynor was immortalized in Rodgers and Hammerstein's classic musical *South Pacific* (1958). The motion picture was adapted from the smash Broadway play directed by Joshua Logan, and co-written by Logan, for which he won a Pulitzer Prize. Gaynor plays Nellie Forbush, an American Navy nurse serving on a South Pacific island during World War II. She becomes romantically involved with a French planter, played by Rossano Brazzi. Unexpectedly, she finds herself forced to deal with the ugly issues of prejudice, interracial marriages and their mixed offspring. In addition to the lush photography, terrific action sequences and all-star luminous cast, Gaynor steals the show with her spirited rendition of "I'm Gonna Wash That Man Right Out of My Hair." The songs and movie score are truly enchanting. Logan declared, "Mitzi is probably the most talented girl—in all directions—of anyone around."

Mel Ferrer 🎥   6262 Hollywood

Actor, director, producer

BORN Aug. 25, 1917, in Elberton, NJ. **SPOTLIGHTS** While attending Princeton University, he dropped out of his sophomore year to become an actor. His Cuban-born surgeon father and Manhattan socialite mother were less than impressed with his career choice. Nonetheless, he persevered, working in publishing while polishing his dramatic skills. He first appeared on Broadway as a dancer in 1938. In Hollywood, his breakthrough was in a film entitled *Lost Boundaries* (1949). He plays a light-skinned African-American doctor forced to pass as a Caucasian to practice medicine in a conservative New England town. *Scaramouche* (1952) is an entertaining 18th-century action picture. Next, he appeared in the French-themed movie, *Lili* (1953). It is a magical musical co-starring Leslie Caron. He portrays the disabled puppeteer; this is the role in which he is best remembered. Ferrer, though, had no designs on acting forever. "I've acted only to get to directing," he stated. Ferrer directed Audrey Hepburn in *Green Mansions* (1950) and, again when she was his wife in *Wait Until Dark* (1967). About the former film he said, "Some of my current delight over directing *Green Mansions* may be coming from my being on one side of the camera, and Audrey on the other." Ferrer acted in the spectacular *War and Peace* (1956) with Audrey Hepburn and Henry Fonda. That same year, he returned to France to work for director Jean Renoir (see Renoir's bio in this book). The film, *Elena et les Hommes* (*Elena and her Men*), stars Ingrid Bergman. Ferrer's elegance and air of nobility were two of his notable personality traits. In 1957 he appeared in Hemingway's classic tale, *The Sun Also Rises*. He was wonderful in *Fall of the Roman Empire* (1964).

Jo Stafford 📺   6270 Hollywood

See page 350

Constance Moore 🎥   6270 Hollywood

Actress, singer

BORN Jan. 18, 1909, in Sioux City, IA. **SPOTLIGHTS** A pretty five-foot, four-inch Columbia Broadcasting staff singer, who worked with Universal Studios, then Paramount Pictures for more than three decades. Films include *You Can't Cheat an Honest Man*, *Charlie Chan Detective* (both 1939), *Argentine Nights* (1940), and *Earl Carroll Vanities* (1945).

Warren Hull 🎤   6270 Hollywood

Actor, singer

BORN Jan. 17, 1903, in Gasport, NY. **SPOTLIGHTS** He was host of radio's popular quiz/audience participation show, "Strike It Rich" (first broadcast in 1947). Needy people were the only contestants allowed on air. These long-suffering destitutes told their woeful stories, and then were asked simple questions. Whoever was chosen "the winner" was helped with medical expenses, or whatever else he or she was in dire need of. "The losers" had a chance to be helped when Hull asked the listening audience to chip in "some charity." This was the basis for the equally successful TV series (1951-'55). Died: 1974.

Ernest Schoedsach 🎥   6270 Hollywood

Director

BORN June 8, 1893, in Council Bluffs, IA. **SPOTLIGHTS** He specialized in fantasy, and directed--with Merian C. Cooper--one of the greatest monster movies of them all, the classic—*King Kong* (1933)—starring Fay Wray. Schoedsach took a risk with *Dr. Cyclops* (1940), Hollywood's first grade-A crack at the Technicolor beast. The science fiction thriller had an exotic South American setting and an outstanding mad scientist (played by Albert Dekker). Died: 1979.

Grace Moore 🎥   6274 Hollywood

Opera singer, actress

BORN Dec. 5, 1901, in Slabtown, TN. **SPOTLIGHTS** When young Moore arrived in New York, she sang in musical comedies. This soprano singing sensation made her Metropolitan Opera debut in 1928. Even during the depths of the Great Depression, the highly priced prima donna commanded $2,500 to $3,000 for each concert performance. The Met was less than pleased when Hollywood called upon the diva's services to fill the lush market for musicals. Seven films to her credit—including *New Moon* (1931) and *One Night of Love* (1934)—all showcased her prestigious talents in the grand opera selections. In 1953, Kathryn Grayson and Merv Griffin star in the story of her life in *So This is Love*. **LOWLIGHTS** In 1933, Moore was scheduled to sing at the Capitol in New York. Upset about some recent entertainers who had performed there, she demanded a special clause be written into her contract stipulating "no-colored-acts" while she was there. Loews Management told her to take a flying leap and called off the deal. Died: 1947, in a plane crash.

Stu Erwin 📺   6274 Hollywood

Stu Erwin

Actor

BORN Stuart Erwin; St. Valentine's Day, Feb. 14, 1902, in Squaw Valley, CA. **SPOTLIGHTS** Trained in the theater, he enjoyed a successful and versatile career in motion pictures, radio and television. A character actor with a somewhat cherubic looking face. Erwin, known for his light comedies, was also adept in dramas. He appeared in nearly 100 films, including *Palooka* (1934—playing the lead role as the cartoon character), *Viva Villa!* (1934), *Pigskin Parade* (1936—in an Oscar-nominated performance), *Our Town* (1940), and *The Son of Flubber* (1963). His radio career spanned the 1930s and '40s, where he worked as a regular cast member on such comedy shows as "Jack Oakie's College," as well as his own situation comedy, "Phone Again, Finnegan." He starred as a dimwitted, but sweet manager of an apartment complex whose tenants were an endless source of problems. **TV** He played the bumbling, folksy, innocent lead in the situation comedy "The Stu Erwin Show" aka "The Trouble with Father" (1950-55). He played opposite his real-life wife, June Collyer. Erwin was a frequent guest star in "Perry Mason," and "Playhouse" dramas. His son Stu Erwin, Jr. is a studio executive. Died: 1967.

Merle Oberon 🎥   6274 Hollywood

Merle Oberon and Joseph Cotten

Actress

BORN Estelle M. Thompson; Feb. 19, 1911, in Tasmania. **SPOTLIGHTS** Her career existed because of her regal beauty. She captivated great men with her astounding brunette tresses, oval face and brown eyes. She is best remembered for her performance as Cathy in *Wuthering Heights* (1939), co-starring Laurence Olivier and David Niven. Films include *The Private Life of Henry VIII* (1933) with Charles Laughton, Binnie Barnes and Robert Donat and Elsa Lanchester, *The Scarlet Pimpernel* (1935) opposite Leslie Howard and Raymond Massey, *The Dark Angel* (1935—in an Oscar-nominated performance), *Lydia* (1941) with Joseph Cotten, and *Forever and a Day* (1943) with an all-star cast. In private life, she amassed an impressive collection of emeralds that insurers speculated came in only second to Queen Elizabeth's in value...Nicknamed "Queenie" as a child in Calcutta because of her regal bearing, in Hollywood colleagues dubbed her "the Princess." Later, her husband's nephew, writer Michael Korda, reportedly based his novel *Queenie* on her. Died: 1979.

Arthur Treacher 🎥   6274 Hollywood

Actor

BORN Arthur Veary; July 23, 1894, in Brighton, Sussex, England. **SPOTLIGHTS** Filmland's most formidable majordomo was a tall (6'4"), distinguished gentleman. He played the

Arthur Treacher

well-bred, bored, dour-faced, superior domestic with such aplomb that the mere recitation of his traditional line, "You rang, sir?" alerted viewers to who was *really* in charge of the household. Always impeccably dressed and nearly always perfect (although occasionally haughty), he played the role of a butler in so many films throughout the 1930s and 1940s that offscreen he was named Honorary President of the Butler's Club. In Hollywood, he was nicknamed "Pip." Films include *Madame Du Barry* (1934), *Bordertown, David Copperfield, Curly Top, A Midsummer Night's Dream* (all 1935), *Magnificent Obsession* (1936), *Thank you, Jeeves* (1936), *The Little Princess* (1939), *Forever and a Day* (1943), and *National Velvet* (1944). Treacher was "supercalifragilisticexpealedocious" in Disney's *Mary Poppins* (1964), his last film. Died: 1975.

Lou Costello ⅄   6278 Hollywood

See page 399

Richard Basehart ⅄   6278 Hollywood

Actor

Richard Basehart

BORN Aug. 31, 1915, in Zanesville, OH. **SPOTLIGHTS** He followed in his father's journalistic footsteps before opting for the bright lights of Broadway at age 24. Hollywood called when he won the 1945 New York Drama Critics Award, and welcomed his *Repeat Performance* (1947), as a gently insane poet. This ruggedly handsome actor split his time between the Broadway stage and Hollywood. Movies include *He Walked by Night* (1948), *Fourteen Hours* (1951--in which Grace Kelly made her debut, *Fixed Bayonets* (1951), *Titanic* (1953), *La Strada* (1954), *Moby Dick* (1956—as Ishmael), and *Time Limit* (1957). Died: 1984.

Jack Webb ⅄   6278 Hollywood

Actor, director, producer
BORN April 2, 1920, in Santa Monica, CA. **SPOTLIGHTS** "DUM-DE-DUM-DUM." Opening; "Ladies and gentlemen...the story you are about to hear is true. Only the names

Jack Webb

have been changed to protect the innocent." Webb created the police drama "Dragnet" and was also its star. Quiet, conservative, with a cold, impassive face, he captured the imaginations of viewers with his depiction of a dedicated Los Angeles police officer. Pitching his dialogue to one side of his mouth, Webb used his matter-of-fact manner to portray Sergeant Joe Friday on the long-running weekly series "Dragnet" (1951-'59; 1967-'70). He played a cop's cop, who was tough, but caring. The show's stories were based on actual crime files from the Los Angeles Police Department. "Dragnet" aired in a semi-documentary dramatic style. His staccato speech clipped words like an automatic pistol, with his familiar dialogue imitated by fans around the country: "Name's Friday, Ma'am. I'm a cop," and "Just the facts, only the facts, Ma'am." Previously, Webb had his breakthrough on radio playing the hard-nosed waterfront private eye for the thriller "Pat Novak for Hire." Then, at the peak of the show's success, Webb left for Hollywood. There, he worked with a Los Angeles police sergeant who shared Webb's belief that police work possessed its own dramatic merits; a private eye character was not necessary. *Realism was.* After a year in research and development, Webb broached NBC radio. The executives had little interest in the project. With the cooperation of the police force, Webb was able to convince the network to give it a green light. The show made its quiet debut on June 3, 1949; it was *not* an instant success. Word-of-mouth, weekly tweaking and perfecting, and the absolute realism (down to the exact number of steps in the staircases between floors in Los Angeles police headquarters) made it more popular. When Webb spoke of the acting technique utilized on the show to *Time* magazine, he said, "Underplaying is still acting. We try to make it as *real* as a guy pouring a cup of coffee." Within two years, the show was on television. A workaholic, Webb also created the children's series, "Noah's Ark." **QUOTE** "The public dictates and you listen to them. You give them, not approximately, but *exactly* what they want." Webb died Dec. 23, 1982. Out of respect, the LAPD lowered their flags to half-mast.

Doris Day ◑   6278 Hollywood

Actress, singer
BORN Doris Von Kappelhoff; April 3, 1924, in Cincinnati, OH. **SPOTLIGHTS** As a child, she had dreams of becoming a dancer. When an auto accident injured one of her legs, she spent her recovery time learning how to sing. The lessons paid off quickly. By age 16, she was a professional singer. Soon she was earning $300 a week with Les Brown's orchestra, then toured with Jimmy Dorsey's swing-era band. Audiences fre-

Doris Day

quently requested that she sing a ballad called "Day After Day." Her rendition was so popular that she changed her last name to Day. The bubbly singer sold five million records annually, and Hollywood called. A blonde, fresh-faced beauty with twinkling eyes, she has a matching sparkling, toothpaste smile with a sugar candy voice. She's the girl-next-door (in your dreams). Day made her screen debut in Warner's *Romance on the High Seas,* with the song "It's Magic" (1948). She appears with Kirk Douglas in *Young Man With a Horn* (1950). The actress delivered a brilliant performance as the 1920s torch singer Ruth Etting in *Love Me or Leave Me* (1955), co-starring James Cagney. The film's new song "I'll Never Stop Loving You" became a hit. Next, Day turns in a fine dramatic performance in Hitchcock's *The Man Who Knew Too Much,* with the song "Que Sera Sera" (1956). The following year, she stars in Warner's romantic musical comedy *The Pajama Game* (1957), opposite John Raitt. The comedy, *Teacher's Pet* (1958), followed with Clark Gable and Gig Young. She teamed with Rock Hudson in *Pillow Talk* (1959), in a classic battle-of-the-sexes comedy. In 1962, she co-stars opposite Jimmy Durante and Martha Raye in the circus musical *Jumbo.* Day was one of the world's biggest box office stars. **QUOTE** A devout Christian Scientist, she is faithful to a healthy lifestyle; she neither drinks nor smokes. She commented, "I believe that happiness has to be made—and can be made—by the individual." She retired to Carmel, California, and is dedicated to the prevention of cruelty to animals. **RECOMMENDED** *It's Magic: Doris Day's Early Years at Warner Bros.* Available on Rhino, CD 75543-2.

Jean Muir 🎥   6280 Hollywood

Actress

BORN J.M. Fullarton; Feb. 13, 1911, in New York, NY. **SPOTLIGHTS** Starting in her late teens, Jean performed on the Broadway stage until she reached stardom at age 22 in "Saint Wench." A Warner's talent scout saw her and signed her. She made her screen debut in *The World Changes* (1933). Warner's *A Midsummer Night's Dream* (1935) with James Cagney was probably one of her top pictures. Other movies include *Stars Over Broadway* (1935), *White Fang* (1936), and *The Constant Nymph* (1943). Feeling that she was not getting "A" scripts, and that her talents were under utilized, she returned to the theater. Then, signed to work in a comedy series in the new medium of television, her name was unfairly dragged through the mud in the 1950s Communist witch hunt. Muir was blacklisted. Extremely depressed and distressed, she became an alcoholic for several years. Eventually, Muir triumphed over

Jean Muir with her Scottish terrier puppy on the set

the addiction, and in the next decade returned to the Great White Way to perform, worked in TV, and traveled to the London stage. Next, she taught drama at Stephens College, in Columbia, Missouri (1968-'76). Died: 1996.

Mary Pickford

Mary Pickford 🎥 6280 Hollywood

Actress, executive

BORN Gladys Smith; April 8, 1892, in Canada. **SPOTLIGHTS** The world's first real movie star. On stage at age five as Baby Gladys Smith, this impoverished child developed a shrewdness that made her one of the keenest financial minds the industry has ever confronted. An example of this trait in early childhood was seen when she approached Biograph Studios in 1909. Director D.W. Griffith thought she was "too little and too fat," but had her work on a film that day, anyway. When he asked the curly-haired child to return the next day for $5, she insisted on $10, and got it! In the pioneer film days, actors did not receive credit. In *The Little Teacher* (1910), the subtitle "Little Mary" finally identified her. "Little Mary, The Girl with the Curls" became a household name and the first famous movie performer. Soon, she was known worldwide as "America's Sweetheart," enchanting viewers with her purity as she smiled through the darkest hour to prevail a winner. She used her popularity to drive her salary up past $500,000 a year, plus percentages, and extensive creative control. Then, when she found out Charlie Chaplin was paid more, she insisted on another raise to top him—and got it! In Hollywood, her excellent money sense earned her the nickname "Bank America's Sweetheart." In 1919 *Pollyanna* was shot in Pasadena, California. The story about a saintly little girl was a commercial success. It stars the 27-year old Pickford, who apparently convinced audiences that she was a 12-year old. Ticket buyers worldwide--especially in Russia, loved the movie. Pickford was typecast in little girl roles. When talkies arrived, her two attempts to perform in adult roles failed. She retired a happy lady, worth more than $50 million. **ACHIEVEMENTS** In 1919 she, Charlie Chaplin, D.W. Griffith, and Douglas Fairbanks formed their own studio. Pickford remarked, "I saw one of my dearest dreams fulfilled--the formation of United Artists." She added that when news leaked out prematurely, someone observed, 'The asylum is now in the hands of the maniacs.'" In 1929 she won the Academy Award for *Coquette*. 1975 Special Oscar. Married to Owen Moore (1911-'19), Douglas Fairbanks (1920-'36), and Charles "Buddy" Rogers (1937 on). Died: 1979.

Marge Champion 📺   6280 Hollywood

Dancer, actress

Gower and Marge Champion

BORN Marjorie Celeste Belcher; Sept. 2, 1923, in Hollywood, CA. **SPOTLIGHTS** A very attractive, charming dancing sensation, she, along with her dance partner-husband, Gower Champion, were known as "America's Dancing Sweethearts." They were hits in both 1950s television (the pair were the first dancing stars in this medium), and movie musicals. Champion's father had been a ballet coach-instructor to the stars, so her own leap into fame was not far. Walt Disney chose her as model for the "fairest of them all," *Snow White and the Seven Dwarfs* (1937). She proved to be the ideal pattern for the Blue Fairy in Disney's *Pinocchio* (1940). After breaking her toe in the Broadway production of "The Little Dog Laughed," she spent her recuperation learning to sing and act. (She had been forbidden to dance for two years for proper healing.) She appeared as an ingenue in *Portrait of a Lady* (1942), starring Ruth Gordon. Motion pictures include *Show Boat* (1951), *Lovely to Look At* (1952), *Everything I Have is Yours* (1952), *Three for the Show* (1954), and *The Party* (1968). **ACHIEVEMENTS** 1975 Emmy as choreographer of "Queen of the Stardust Ballroom." **HIGHLIGHTS**

Married to Gower Champion from 1947-'73. Their marriage produced a son, Gregg Ernest. Died: 1980.

Ben Bernie 🎙   6280 Hollywood

Composer, violinist, orchestra conductor

BORN May 30, 1891, in New York, NY. **SPOTLIGHTS** This flamboyant showman was given the moniker "The Old Maestro" in conjunction with his skill in handling a band, not due to his age. He was one of the earliest on air, starting in 1923, nearly at the birth of commercial broadcasting. This charmer honeyed his speech with such trademark comments as "yowsah, yowsah, yowsah," which the whole nation embraced and imitated. "Yowsah," meaning something hot or exciting, is still heard occasionally in the new millennium. His lovely theme was "It's a Lonesome Old Town." By 1926, Bernie's orchestra was hand-picked by NBC radio to perform live in the Grand Ballroom at the Waldorf for a staggering $25,000. That same year, he was denied a work permit in England, as the xenophobic nation rallied in opposition to American music. No matter, he was continually one of the most popular stars. "The Ben Bernie Show" provided CBS listeners with relaxing music and light comedy. Songs include "Who's Your Little Whoosis?" and "Sweet Georgia Brown." **QUOTE** For 20 years, he signed off with: "Au revoir, a fond cheerio, a bit of toodle-oo, God bless you and pleasant dreams." "The Old Maestro" joined *the* heavenly orchestra upstairs in 1943.

Lena Horne 🎥   6280 Hollywood

Singer, actress, entertainer

Lena Horne

BORN June 30, 1917, in Brooklyn, NY. **SPOTLIGHTS** Drama critic Richard Watts declared Miss Horne "the most beautiful girl in the world." While her tremendous beauty was of some help, she still suffered from racial prejudice during America's segregation of the 1940s and '50s. She kept her dignity throughout her ordeal of climbing to the top and, in doing so, helped break the color barrier. Her ambitious mother pushed the 16-year-old Lena into dancing as a chorus girl in the floor show at Harlem's Cotton Club, where it was apparent even then she was destined for fame. In her remarkable voice, she sang both blues and ballads at trendy nightclubs: Cafe Society, Little Troc, and the Savoy-Plaza Hotel. She was the first African

American woman to sign a long-term, seven-year contract with a major studio (MGM). Because those movies would be shown in the Deep South, Miss Horne commented, "Can you believe this? I can't even be shown talking to white people in pictures that are shown in the South. So, I can only be cast as a non-talking-to-white-people singer!" The studio initially limited her to cameo appearances as a singer of glossy allure. Motion pictures include *The Duke is Tops* (1938), *Panama Hattie* (1942), *Cabin in the Sky, Stormy Weather, I Dood It, Thousands Cheer, Swing Fever* (all 1943), *Broadway Rhythm, Two Girls and a Sailor* (both 1944), *Ziegfeld Follies, Till the Clouds Roll By* (both 1946), *Duchess of Idaho* (1950), *Meet Me in Las Vegas* (1956), *Death of a Gunfighter* (1969), and *The Wiz* (1978--as Glinda). Hit Broadway shows include "Jamaica," "Blackbirds," "Lena Horne—the Lady and Her Music." Recordings include "Stormy Weather," "The Lady Is a Tramp," "Just One of Those Things," "Ain't It the Truth," "Paper Doll," "Come Rain or Come Shine," and "Yesterday, When I Was Young." **ACHIEVEMENTS** She is the 1984 recipient of a Lifetime Achievement Award bestowed upon her at the Kennedy Center. Her 1981 Broadway show, "Lena Horne: The Lady and Her Music," won two Grammys, a Tony and the prestigious New York Drama Critics Circle Award. 1995 Grammy for Best Jazz Performance for *An Evening with Lena Horne*. Her "Lena Horne at the Waldorf-Astoria" became RCA Victor's biggest-selling album by a female vocalist. This elegant American legend has two Walk of Fame stars; the other is for Recording and is located at the front of this block.

Frank Fay    6280 Hollywood
Comic, actor
BORN Nov. 17, 1894, in Ireland. **SPOTLIGHTS** Fay was the first vaudevillian to entertain using a conversational style, as opposed to slapstick gags, magic tricks or corny costumes. His method influenced comic greats such as Jack Benny. Although his professional life may have inspired others, his negative, inhumane, fault-finding personality grated on all. Milton Berle once stated, "Fay's friends could be counted on the missing arm of a one-armed man." When comic Jackie Gleason reviewed Humphrey Bogart's characterization of the vicious brute Duke Mantee in *The Petrified Forest*, Gleason said, "Bogart played a real creep. He must have studied Frank Fay for weeks!" But it was Bogart himself who launched the heat-seeking missile. Gathered together for a big dinner—at which Fay was being his normal bitter, cruel self—Bogart told him, "Frank, if you were doing a one-man show, I bet you'd quit because you couldn't stand the cast." He was a hopeless alcoholic. His motion picture credits include David O. Selznick's comedy *Nothing Sacred* (1937), starring Carole Lombard and Fredric March. In 1940 he appeared in the dramatic soap opera, *They Knew What They Wanted*, starring Carole Lombard and Charles Laughton. Radio: "The Frank Fay Show" was an effort of the meglomaniac to be it all: a star comedian, emcee, writer, director, and producer. It collapsed within three

months. He returned to Broadway, starring in "Harvey" (1944). In real life, Fay was such a disgusting, cruel rat that when he was married to Barbara Stanwyck he not only beat her, but in a fit of rage once threw their infant baby into the swimming pool. Stanwyck saved their baby and fled. The next day, she filed for divorce with the support of the Hollywood community. When he died in 1961, show folks lifted champagne flutes in a unanimous toast: "Good Riddance!"

Janet Gaynor    6280 Hollywood
Actress

Janet Gaynor

BORN Laura Gainer; Oct. 6, 1906, in Philadelphia, PA. **SPOTLIGHTS** She was immortalized in her "three" Academy Award-winning performances (see below). A wholesome sweetheart, her optimistic characterizations appealed to Depression-era audiences: *Lucky Star* and *Sunny Side Up* (both 1929), *Happy Days* and *High Society Blues* (both 1930), *Daddy Long Legs* and *Merrily Mary Ann* (both 1931), and *State Fair* (1933), opposite Will Rogers. This baby-faced, little girl-voiced cutie was the top ranking female star and the fairer sex's biggest box office draw until Shirley Temple snatched the title from her. She gave a commanding performance in David O. Selznick's original *A Star is Born* (1937), opposite Fredric March, in one of her last screen appearances. The following year, she stars in another film that made "the ten best pictures of the year list," the comedy *The Young in Heart*. **ACHIEVEMENTS** She won the first-ever Academy Award presented to Best Actress, 1927-'28 for *Seventh Heaven, Street Angel* and *Sunrise*. (At that time, the Academy presented one award for an entertainer's performances in several films.) If you choose to see any of these, select *Sunrise*. It is a true masterpiece and her performance as a loving wife (whose husband plots to murder her) is more than glorious. Without question, it is one of the finest art pictures ever made. Died: 1984.

Paderewski    6280 Hollywood
Composer, musician, statesman
BORN Ignace Jan Paderewski; Nov. 6, 1860, in Poland. **SPOTLIGHTS** World famous for the virtuosity of his playing, this eminent concert pianist and composer became radio's second biggest cultural event in 1937 (after Toscanini). A true musical triumph, he possessed an air of restrained charm and an excessive amount of dignity. **ACHIEVEMENTS** He was the first Prime Minister of the Polish republic in 1919. During WWI, Charlie Chaplin bumped into Paderewski in New York at the Ritz Hotel. Chaplin inquired if he were to give a con-

cert. Paderewski somberly responded, "I do not give concerts when I am in the service of my country." Chaplin wanted to repeat the French statesman Georges Clemenceau's famous question, "How is it that a gifted artist like you would stoop so low as to become a politician?" Paderewski never loss sight of politics; in 1940-'41 he led the Polish government in exile. **QUOTE** After a royal engagement, Queen Victoria exclaimed, "Mr. Paderewski, you are a genius." Paderewski who spent hours each day practicing responded, "Perhaps, Your Majesty, but before that I was a drudge." Died: 1941.

Monte Blue 🎥   6280 Hollywood

Actor

BORN Jan. 11, 1890, in Indianapolis, IN. **SPOTLIGHTS** Descended from Native American Indian, his handsome facial features were complemented by his strong body. Blue worked in D.W. Griffith's classics: *The Birth of a Nation* (1915) and *Intolerance* (1916). This extremely popular talent made 200 movies--as star, a supporting and character actor--during four decades. His last film was *Apache* (1954).

Monte Blue

QUOTE "I was flung into the movies through a turn of the wheel of Fate. Frankly, I was hungry and found it necessary to eat. I had been a soldier, sailor, cowboy, railroader, even shoveled the street. I was always searching for something and found it on the screen, not when I was a success and made money, but in the dark of poverty and obscurity. 'This is your medium of expression,' and it was my own soul which spoke, so I stuck to it through the years of purgatory and, as I said, it isn't Heaven even now and never will be." Died: 1963.

Katharine Hepburn 🎥 6280 Hollywood

Actress

BORN Nov. 9, 1907, in Hartford, CT. **SPOTLIGHTS** A fiercely independent, private, intelligent heroine, she made her brilliant screen debut in *A Bill of Divorcement* (1932), opposite John Barrymore. Hepburn gave exalted performances in *Little Woman* (1933), *Alice Adams* (1935—in an Oscar-nominated performance), *Bringing Up Baby* (1938), *The Philadelphia Story* (1940—in an Oscar-nominated performance), *Adam's Rib* (1949), *The African Queen* (1951—in an Oscar-nominated performance), *Pat and Mike* (1952), *Summertime* (1955—in an Oscar-nominated performance), *The Rainmaker* (1956—in an Oscar-nominated performance), Suddenly Last Summer (1959—in an Oscar-nominated performance), and *The Long Day's Journey Into Night* (1962—in an Oscar-nomi-

nated performance). After working with her in *Bringing Up Baby*, Cary Grant said Hepburn was his "best co-star because of her professionalism, her courage, and because she was foolish enough to trust me." **ACHIEVEMENTS** She is the record breaker for both the number of Oscar nominations and recipient of the coveted statues. She won Best Actress Academy Awards for *Morning Glory* (1933), *Guess Who's Coming to Dinner* (1967), *The Lion in Winter* (1969), and *On*

Katharine Hepburn

Golden Pond (1981). To date, she has been Oscar-nominated 12 times and won four; Meryl Streep (see her bio in this book) has been Oscar-nominated 12 times, and won two, and Bette Davis (see her bio) garnered 10 Oscar nominations, and took home two...She met her lifelong love match, Spencer Tracy, on the set of *Woman of the Year* (1942—in an Oscar-nominated performance). "I'm afraid I'm a little tall for you, Mr. Tracy," Hepburn remarked. Tracy responded "Don't worry, Miss Hepburn, I'll soon cut you down to my size." **QUOTE** During the filming of *The Lion in Winter*, a reporter spied Hepburn wearing tennis shoes under her 12th-century robes. The actress declared, "I play Eleanor of Aquitaine, Queen of England— and also a practical woman who believed in comfort."

Jim Davis 📺   6280 Hollywood

Actor

BORN Aug. 26, 1915, in Edgerton, MO. **SPOTLIGHTS** Husky, rugged and slow-speaking, he was born to play John Ross "Jock" Ewing on TV's popular series "Dallas." Before he struck oil in Texas, he had appeared in a couple of short-lived series, and dozens of motion pictures, including *The Maverick Queen* (1955) starring Barbara Stanwyck. Died: 1981.

Clifton Fadiman ✒   6280 Hollywood

Literary critic, editor, host

BORN May 15, 1904, in Brooklyn, NY. **SPOTLIGHTS** Graduated Phi Beta Kappa in 1925, Fadiman wrote book reviews, taught high school English, became an editor at Simon and Schuster, then by 1929, became book editor of the *New Yorker* magazine. As author, editor, critic and moderator of radio's quiz show "Information Please" (NBC, 1938-'52), he was praised for bringing intellectualism to the masses. Each show started with the announcement, "Wake up, America! It's time to stump the experts!" Contestants who did stump the experts won a set of *Encyclopedia Britannica*. He was quiz master and emcee on: "Quiz Kids," "Mathematics," and "Alumni Fun." Died: 1999.

Jonathan Winters    6280 Hollywood

Actor, comedian

Jonathan Winters

BORN Nov. 11, 1925, in Dayton, OH. **SPOTLIGHTS** The funny, moon-faced Winters hosted several television shows before his first big hit, "The Jonathan Winters Show" (1967-'69). Then, his show kept popping up in different incarnations. It came around again when the quick-witted comedian amused audiences on "The Wacky World of Jonathan Winters" (1972-'74). A brilliant comedian, he is famous for his impromptu jokes. Adored by millions for his hilarious comic style, his range of funny characters includes everyone's favorite: old Maude Frickert. From 1981-'82, he gained a younger generation of new fans in the role of Mearth, the 225-pound baby of "Mork and Mindy." Movies include *It's a Mad Mad Mad Mad World* (1963), *The Russians Are Coming! The Russians Are Coming!* (1966), *Moon Over Parador* (1988), and *The Flintstones* (1994). **ACHIEVEMENTS** In 2000, he received the second annual Mark Twain Prize at the Kennedy Center. This prestigious award is given to those who "create humor from their uniquely American experiences." Winters is credited with being the father of modern comedy and altering the "nature of comedy," according to Twain Prize organizers.

Warner Baxter   6280 Hollywood

Actor

BORN March 29, 1889, in Columbus, OH. **SPOTLIGHTS** His father died when he was six months old, forcing his mother to relocate to San Francisco. It was an untimely move; they lost all their possessions in the 1906 earthquake. He helped support his mom by working odd jobs, until making his first picture in 1914. Baxter matured into a handsome, mustachioed solid actor, and a tremendously popular leading man. One of his best-remembered roles is in the title role of *The Cisco Kid* (1931). He brilliantly portrays the real-life Dr. Samuel Mudd—the physician who innocently treated the injured assassin John Wilkes Booth after President Lincoln's murder (and ends up in prison for it)—in *The Prisoner of Shark Island* (1936). John Carradine is scary as the cruel prison guard. Motion pictures include *First Love* (1921), *The Squaw Man* (1931, the remake), *Stand Up and Cheer* (1934), *King of Burlesque* (1935), *Robin Hood of El Dorado* (1936), *Adam Had Four Sons* (1941), and *Crime Doctor* (1943). **ACHIEVEMENTS** 1928-'29 Best Actor Academy Award for *Old Arizona* (Fox's first outdoor all-Talkie). He starred as the bandit Cisco Kid; it was his breakthrough role. Baxter was Hollywood's top moneymaker in 1936. Died: 1951 of pneumonia contracted after a hideous lobotomy performed to relieve his arthritis.

Tom Breneman   6280 Hollywood

Emcee, producer

BORN 1902. **SPOTLIGHTS** A silver-tongued, yet sentimental host, he pried the most interesting anecdotes out of audience members. Breneman was the creator and host of "Breakfast at Sardi's." With a radio remote situated in the center of Sardi's restaurant on Hollywood Boulevard, this live, audience participation show, offered no music or established comedy routines. From 1941 (until his sudden death) it was successful on its own as a daily morning breakfast program that perked the day up for listeners and for its live audience. It did not hurt that he was the heartthrob of middle-aged housewives. Although occasionally a celebrity would show up, such as Orson Welles, the ladies in the audience were the real stars. Each day the show was fresh and unrehearsed. Breneman stated, "We start from scratch every morning." The ladies sat in rows of booths, while Breneman asked them questions that seemingly came out of the blue. During one show he asked the younger women: "Who gets up for the midnight feedings, you or your husband?" After several responses, he turned to an older woman who blurted out: "It certainly wasn't him. We didn't have bottles in those days." "Breakfast at Sardi's" was the highest-rated morning show of all breakfast programs with 10,000,000 radio listeners. In 1942 a reporter for *Newsweek* magazine wrote that the enormous secret of Breneman's success was he had "the magic of making women feel young." In 1943 the show's name was changed to "Breakfast in Hollywood," so not be confused with Sardi's restaurant in New York. **HIGHLIGHTS** His popular "wishing ring ceremony" segment gave one selected audience member a designer ring. Then, she acknowledged the wish she held dearest to her heart, and the audience was asked to wish along with her. (Often the wish would come true after it had been broadcast, via a listener's—or corporation's—generosity.) Died: 1948.

Jessica Tandy   6280 Hollywood

Actress

BORN June 7, 1909, in London, England. **SPOTLIGHTS** In her youth, she joined her two older brothers in "home dramatics." A natural born talent, she was mesmerized by acting, which, she recalled, "overbalanced all other interests, including orthodox education." She made her professional stage debut at age 18 in "The Manderson Girls." In 1930 she crossed the Atlanta

Jessica Tandy

with a troupe performing "The Matriarch and the Last Enemy." After the run, she returned to England. There, she made her screen debut in *The Indiscretions of Eve* (1932). Extremely versatile and accomplished, she played these Shakespearean roles onstage: Titania, Ophelia, Viola and Cordelia. Then, the Nazis and their bombings (the start of WWII) convinced her to leave. She arrived in America in 1938. Working onstage steadily in a wide variety of roles and genres, she experimented in all forms of theatre. In Los Angeles, she starred in Tennessee Williams' one-act play, "Portrait of a Madonna," at the Actor's Lab Theatre. Producer Irene Selznick and director Eliz Kazan were in the audience. They selected her to introduce the role of Blanche du Bois on Broadway (see below), for which she won numerous awards. Her well-crafted performances made her a master of the arts, and earned her the crown "The First Lady of Broadway" from Helen Hayes. With her beloved second husband, actor Hume Cronyn, the twosome worked together in live theatre throughout the world. She co-starred with Cronyn on Broadway in "The Fourposter," "Madame, Will You Walk," "The Honeys," "A Day By the Sea," "The Man in the Dog Suit," and "Triple Play." He directed her in "Hilda Crane." They also appear in numerous films together. Serene, ladylike, and poised, she graced the American screen with her presence during five decades. Among her many fine motion pictures are: *The Seventh Cross* (1944), *The Green Years*, *Dragonwyck* (both 1946), *Forever Amber* (1947), *September Affair* (1950), *The Desert Fox* (1951), *The Birds* (1963), *The World According to Garp* (1982), *Cocoon* (1985), *Fried Green Tomatoes* (1991—in an Oscar-nominated performance), *Used People* (1992), *To Dance with the White Dog* (1993), and *Nobody's Fool* (1994), in her final performance. She also worked in radio and television. **ACHIEVEMENTS** Tony Awards for "A Streetcar Named Desire" (1948), as Blanche de Bois, opposite Marlon Brando; "The Gin Game" (1978); and "Foxfire" (1982). 1989 Best Actress Academy Award for *Driving Miss Daisy*...Her marriage match to actor Hume Cronyn lasted 62 years, onstage and off. This exceptional and beloved actress died in 1994.

Spike Jones   6280 Hollywood
See page 313

Marquerite Chapman   6280 Hollywood
Actress

BORN March 9, 1920, in Chatham, NY. **SPOTLIGHTS** A former artist and magazine model, she had a regal bearing and elegance. She studied acting and acquired some minor stage experience. In television, she was seen in live dramatic anthology playhouse works and guest-starred in a number of series, both dramas and comedies. This tremendous dark-haired beauty appears in mainly "B" dramatic pictures from 1940 to 1960 as leading lady and second actress. Movies include *Charlie Chan at the Wax Museum* (1940), *Navy Blues*, *The Body Disappears* (both 1941), *Spy Smasher* (1942--serial), *Submarine Raider*, *Parachute Nurse*, *A Man's World* (all 1942), *Murder in Times Square* (1943), *Pardon My Past* (1945), *Mr. District Attorney* (1947), *The Green Promise* (1949), *Kansas Raiders* (1950), *Flight to Mars* (1951), *Bloodhounds of Broadway* (1952), and *The Seven Year Itch* (1955), starring Marilyn Monroe. Her last film was *The Amazing Transparent Man* (1960). Died: 1999.

Marquerite Chapman

1680 VINE

Gladys Swarthout 🔴   1680 Vine

Gladys Swarthout

Opera singer

BORN Christmas morning, Dec. 25, 1904, in Deepwater, MO. **SPOTLIGHTS** Called "the precious gift" due to her notable birthday, as a child she was so serious about her singing that she blew soap-bubbles as a daily dozen to develop and exercise her lungs. She sang in church, for her parent's friends and relatives, and daily around the family home. A *bel canto*, critics widely praised her Metropolitan Opera debut in *La Gioconda* in 1929. Audiences rejoiced hearing her rich, colorful mezzo-soprano in a variety of roles, although they admired her most as *Carmen*, the fiery gypsy girl. A gigantic success in radio, recording, and concerts, she commanded between $1,500 and $2,000 a performance and could afford to be quite a fashion plate. Paramount stars the lovely brunette in movies featuring opera selections like *Champagne Waltz* (1937). **QUOTE** When asked why she had agreed to appear in a movie where the script called for her to be smacked in the face with a ripe tomato, she answered, "I felt that if it were necessary to throw tomatoes at me in order to have the American public listen to good music, then let them throw." Died: 1969.

Donald O'Connor 🎥   1680 Vine

Actor, dancer, singer

BORN Aug. 28, 1925, in Chicago, IL. **SPOTLIGHTS** An American legend. Agile, noble, fast, a master of dance and film, a dancer's dancer, singer, and comedian. Amazingly, he never had formal dance lessons, but this natural born talent did have some instruction at age 15. Prior to that, he was known as "young Mr. Show Business." He began in vaudeville at the age of three days when he was brought onstage in a bundle, and shown to the audience for applause. He was just starting to crawl when his father died. He automatically became a part of "The O'Connor Family: The Greatest Act in Vaudeville." At six months old, he earned $25-a-week doing headstands on his brother Jack's hands. His mother built her son into the act, and by four he was a versatile performer helping to support the family. At age 13, he made his screen debut in *Sing You Sinners,* starring Bing Crosby. (He's the child listening to Crosby sing "Small Fry.") The following year, Paramount

Donald O'Connor

Pictures rushed him into films before he grew. He made 11 movies, including *Tom Sawyer—Detective* (1938—as Huck Finn). By the time he reached age 30, he was a veteran of 50 motion pictures, with more to come. He is wonderful in all these: *Beau Geste* (1939), *The Merry Monahans* (1944), *Feudin', Fussin' and A-Fightin'* (1948), *Singin' in the Rain*

Donald O'Connor and Samantha Hart

(1952), *Call Me Madam* (1953), *I Love Melvyn* (1953), *The Buster Keaton Story* (1957—title role), *That's Entertainment* (1974 + sequels through 1994), and *Ragtime* (1981). He also did the *Francis the Talking Mule* series (from 1950-'55). About the four-legged animal pictures, O'Connor remarked, "The animal stole every scene. I got so I couldn't act with real people. It was tough being upstaged by a jackass!" Later works include *Out to Sea* (1997), and many guest appearances on TV and concerts. In all, he made more than 100 movies. **ACHIEVEMENTS** 1953 Emmy for "The Donald O'Connor Show." He has won virtually every single theatrical award and honor, including the prestigious Peabody, Golden Globe, and Slyvania, except the Oscar. **WALK OF FAME QUOTE** "Cement is better than the sands of time. Make 'em laugh, make 'em cry, what more is there?"

Neil Armstrong, Buzz Aldrin, Michael Collins 🎬 *Astronauts* **Hollywood and Vine**

BORN Neil Alden Armstrong, Aug. 5, 1930 on a farm near Wapakoneta, Ohio; Buzz Aldrin on Jan. 20, 1930, in Montclair, New Jersey (born Edwin Eugene Aldrin, Jr., he was nicknamed Buzz by his sister, called Buzz throughout his life, and universally known as Buzz. Aldrin had his name legally changed in 1984); Collins, Oct. 31, 1930, in Rome, Italy. **SPOTLIGHTS** Armstrong, Aldrin and Collins participated in that historic Apollo XI mission to the moon (July 20, 1969). When the lunar module Eagle descended to within 50,000 feet of the moon, its descent rocket fired to slow the spacecraft. As the landing pads' wire probes neared the surface of the moon, Aldrin exclaimed, "Contact, light!" When it touched down, Aldrin declared, "Okay. Engine stop. ACA out of detent." Armstrong injected, "Got it." Aldrin continued, "Mode controls both auto, descent engine command override off. Engine arm off. 413 is in." They had accomplished what no one else had ever done, as Armstrong spoke to NASA in Texas, stating, "Houston, Tranquility base here. The Eagle has landed." Hours later, as hundreds of millions of TV viewers watched around the globe, Armstrong stepped his foot on the moon and uttered these famous words, "That's one small step for man, one giant leap for mankind." When Aldrin stepped down the ladder, he exclaimed, "Magnificent destination." Collins' important job kept him in lunar orbit aboard the command module Columbia. He was not able to join the moonwalkers, who made U.S. citizens feel a patriotic swell as they spiked an American flag into the moon's dusty surface. Then, they read these words off a plaque mounted on the Eagle: "Here men from the planet Earth first step foot upon the Moon, July, 1969 A.D. We came in peace for all mankind." The Eagle would not return to Earth, it had found a permanent new home in a very exclusive neighborhood, on the Sea of Tranquility. This was the single most important live TV broadcast ever. So many people watched this event, that the streets throughout the entire country were empty—and it was quiet elsewhere in the world. This was the longest continuous live

NASA astronauts (from left): Collins, Armstrong and Aldrin

TV coverage in history (31 hours). **HIGHLIGHTS** The astronauts were honored with uniquely designed "stars" on the four corners of Hollywood and Vine to represent their reach to the four corners of the earth. On July 20, 1999, these stars were rededicated in honor of the 30th anniversary of landing on the moon. **QUOTE** About his four Walk of Fame stars, Aldrin quipped, "Not stars, but four moons." Then, his beautiful wife Lois added, "My husband has made famous footprints on the moon, it's just that nobody will see them."

Julius La Rosa 🎬 **Hollywood and Vine**

Singer

BORN Jan. 2, 1930 in Brooklyn, NY. **SPOTLIGHTS** After joining the U.S. Navy in 1947, he realized he could escape tedious military tasks by singing in Navy clubs. In 1950, Arthur Godfrey heard him in Pensacola, Florida, and hired him for his radio show. Later, he joined "Arthur Godfrey and His Friends" TV musical variety show (1952-'53). His light baritone and youthful charm won him thousands of weekly fan letters. Considered a part of the "Sinatra School" for the quality of his intonation and respect for lyrics, he had a number of hits, including "Anywhere I Wander," used in *Hans Christian Andersen* (1952). La Rosa hit high stakes in Las Vegas during the 1960s. Then, he became a popular DJ at WNEW in New York City until 1977. **SIDELIGHTS** One of TV's most infamous moments was when Arthur Godfrey fired him on the air for "lacking humility." Afterwards, the press criticized Godfrey, and La Rosa became a "folk hero." Network executives awarded him "The Julius La Rosa Show" (1956-'57).

Maria Callas 🎙 **Hollywood and Vine**

Opera singer

BORN Maria Anna Sofia Cecilia Calogeropoulous; Dec. 3, 1923, in NY, NY. **SPOTLIGHTS** The fiery diva. *Diva divina*. Callas was a temperamental prima donna with an animal intensity. Dramatically powerful onstage, she was devoted to text and character. The beautiful, dark-haired soprano was

Maria Callas

famous for her expressive phrasing. Her voice was flawed, but spectacular. It was extremely flexible, full of accent and color. She was a tireless rehearser, always begging the maestro for another run through, determined to be the best. She was *the complete singer.* Callas attracted the most passionate of admirers, one of whom commented that she was "the only creature who has ever deserved to stand on the opera stage." She was without peer. She appeared in a variety of roles through four decades; her most celebrated in Bellini's "Norma," Verdi's "La Traviata, Puccini's "Tosca," and Donizetti's "Lucia di Lammermoor." Two great plays, "Lisbon Traviata" and "Master Class," were written around her. **SIDELIGHTS** She enjoyed many triumphs, but suffered an equal number of disasters. She shared an ill-fated relationship with the Greek shipping tycoon, Aristotle Onassis. **QUOTE** Even early in her career, she refused to start in supporting roles and follow the traditional struggle to the top. Callas declared, "Either you've got the voice or you haven't. And if you've got it, you begin singing the lead parts right away." This grand legend sang her last note in 1977.

Gale Storm 🎞

1680 Vine

See page 224

Vladimir Horowitz 🎞

1680 Vine

Virtuoso pianist
BORN Oct. 1, 1904, in Kiev, Russia. **SPOTLIGHTS** The "tornado from the steppes" began playing piano at age six in the Ukraine. At age 12, he attended the Kiev Conservatory of Music. Within five years he was performing. His successful concert debut in 1922 enabled him to obtain a visa to get out of Russia. He did not return home from his six-month study in Germany. His first American concert was a great 1928 event, and the beginning of a long list of classical recordings, sold-out concerts, White House invitations, and enrichment of radio programming. His "heaven-storming octaves" include *Rachmaninoff: Piano Concerto No. 3 New York Philharmonic, Eugene Ormandy, conductor; Debussy: Preludes, Book II, Nos. 4, 5 and 6;* and *Schubert: Impromptu in G Flat.* **ACHIEVEMENTS**

He collected an impressive 18 Grammy awards. Horowitz became a U.S. citizen in 1944, then returned to his homeland in 1987 after his long, self-imposed exodus. His concerts in Moscow and Leningrad were well-received. **QUOTE** In 1936 at the height of his career, he suddenly secluded himself in Paris, France, and Zurich, Switzerland. He returned to America in 1940, stating, "I think I really began to live then. For years I had been playing constantly. I played certain works so often that I couldn't hear them any more. I think I have found new things in my music. I know that I have learned more than I could have possibly learned if I had been continuing the exhausting round of practicing, rushing for trains, and giving concerts month after month." Indeed, critics found a new richness in his music. Died: 1989.

Joe E. Brown 🎥

1680 Vine

Joe E. Brown

Actor, comedian
BORN July 28, 1892, in Holgate, OH. **SPOTLIGHTS** Brown's trademark 1,000-watt grin was attributed to his having the widest mouth in show business. At age 10, he ran away from home to join the circus. Under the big tent he made audiences laugh by inserting a regular sized cup and saucer into his wide oversized, elastic mouth. He was just clowning around in those days, but by the time he made his film debut in *Hit the Show* (1927), he scored so heavily he belonged to Hollywood from then on. Although everyone was an immediate fan of the lovable mug, Joe E. Brown was shocked at his own screen appearance. He declared, "When I first saw my face on the screen, in a closeup six feet high, I jumped up and yelled, 'It's a lie!'" His many hilarious pictures include *Son of a Sailor* (1933) with Thelma Todd, *Shut My Big Mouth* (1942), *Chatterbox* (1943), and *Around the World in 80 Days* (1956— a star-studded adventure). But it was in the classic comedy *Some Like It Hot* (1959) where he was immortalized. This comedy stars Marilyn Monroe, Jack Lemmon and Tony Curtis. He occasionally appeared in dramas, such as *Show Boat* (1951—as Captain Andy). **ACHIEVEMENTS** Brown bravely and continually entertained troops on the front line in the Pacific during WWII. He put on a happy face even though his own son had been killed in that same war. He was presented with the Bronze Star for his tireless work. Died: 1973.

Duncan Renaldo 📺

1680 Vine

Actor
BORN Abandoned by both parents, his birth date and place remain a mystery. Renaldo guessed he was born between 1903

Duncan Renaldo

and 1906, in Spain. **SPOTLIGHTS** He became an American resident in 1921 by accident when the ship he was a seaman on caught fire in the port of Baltimore. While the vessel was being repaired, he busied himself with sketching—his life-long hobby. Renaldo sketched the Havana docks for a movie director and was hired on the spot as a set designer for $15-a-week. His dashing style, perfectly suited for silents, earned him many film roles. He appears in Van Dyke's *Trader Horn* (1931), an early talkie shot in Africa. His greatest claim to fame was as the dashing Mexican adventurer in the Western "The Cisco Kid" (1950-'56). He did 164 "Cisco" full-length features and 156 half-hour television shows. His character would sweep his sombrero, a lovely senorita would swoon, and then the bad guys got Cisco's quick draw. He'd shoot their guns out of their hands before harm struck. His sidekick was Leo Carillo, and his horse's name was Diablo. **ACHIEVEMENTS** "The Cisco Kid" was the first ever syndicated show; it never ran on network. The successful show also made history by being the first filmed program—*not* shown live. Amazingly, it was filmed in color, but only seen in black & white because TV broadcast in black & white during this time. Died: 1980.

Ted Weems ●   1680 Vine
Band leader
BORN Sept. 26, 1901, in Pitcairn, PA. **SPOTLIGHTS** A one-hit wonder, Weems gained famed recording the song "Heartaches." It was a gigantic hit each of the three times he recorded it over a 20 year period. His 14-piece orchestra featured Elmo "the Whistling Troubadour" Tanner, and singer Perry Como. An orchestra leader for two decades, Weems was also radio's famed musical director on "Beat the Band" quiz show, first broadcast in 1940 from Chicago with a young, hilarious Garry Moore as master of ceremonies. "The incomparable Hildegarde" took over the show in New York and delighted listeners with her catchphrase "Give me a little traveling music, Harry." (Jackie Gleason borrowed that phrase and made it his own in television.) The show ended in 1944 in New York after a successful run. Died: 1963.

Garry Moore 📺 1680 Vine
See page 182

Teresa Wright 🎥   1680 Vine
Actress

Teresa Wright

BORN Muriel T. Wright; Oct. 27, 1918, in New York, NY. **SPOTLIGHTS** She was spotted by Samuel Goldwyn while performing in the stage production of "Life with Father." The mogul offered her an unusually restrictive contract that prevented her from doing cheesecake pinups, glamorizing herself as a movie star, or having a public romance for seven years. She agreed. This petite, earthy beauty with reddish-brown hair possessed the sweet, girl-next-door good looks. She made her silver screen debut as the timid daughter in *The Little Foxes* (1941--in an Oscar-nominated performance; a rarity for a first film role). The post-Civil War drama, starring Bette Davis, was based on Lillian Hellman's brilliant play, with Hellman's superb screenplay. Next, she won an Academy Award (see below). She followed with *The Pride of the Yankees* (1942), opposite Gary Cooper. This is the beloved baseball story of Yankee first baseman Lou Gehrig—universally referred to as the Iron Man—who contracted a rare muscle-wasting disease. Other movies include Hitchcock's suspenseful thriller, *Shadow of a Doubt* (1943), co-starring Joseph Cotten, the Academy Award-winning *The Best Years of Our Lives* (1946), *Enchantment* (1948), with David Niven, *The Steel Trap* (1952), again with Cotten, *The Actress* (1953), starring Spencer Tracy and Jean Simmons, *The Search for Bridey Murphy* (1956), *Somewhere in Time* (1979) and *The Good Mother* (1988). **ACHIEVEMENTS** 1942 Best Supporting Actress Oscar for *Mrs. Miniver*.

Michael O'Shea 📺 1680 Vine
Actor
BORN Edward O'Shea; March 17, 1906, in Hartford, CT. **SPOTLIGHTS** A red-haired, friendly "straight man" in the circus, vaudeville and radio, his unique crackling voice carried a touch of the Irish brogue. On screen, he went against his humorous nature. Movies include such classic film noir thrillers as *The Threat* (1949) where he plays a kidnapped cop being held by a vindictive killer. Other movies include *Jack London* (1943—in the title role), *Mr. District Attorney* (1947), *Parole, Inc.* (1948), and *It Should Happen to You* (1954). **TV** He appeared in numerous live dramatic performances. He also starred in the popular sit-com "It's a Great Life" (1954-'56), as a recently discharged soldier who was adjusting to civilian life in sunny Southern California. Died: 1973.

Jimmy Wakely ●   1680 Vine
Singer, actor
BORN James Wakely; Feb. 16, 1914, in Mineola, Arkansas.

SPOTLIGHTS A country and western singer, he easily made the transition to radio celebrity via an invitation from cowboy great Gene Autry. Autry made Wakely a regular member of his cast on his "Melody Ranch" show, and put him in some of his films. Wakely made his film debut in *Saga of Death Valley* (1939). A natural rhinestone cowboy, he made 50 motion pictures, becoming the third most popular screen cowboy (Gene Autry and Roy Rogers were #1 and #2). The Jimmy Wakely Trio (Wakely, Johnny Bond and Dick Reinhart) had several hit recordings. His all-time chart-topping country classics include "I'm Sending You Red Roses," "One Has My Name, The Other Has My Heart," and "Slippin' Around" (duet with Margaret Whiting). He recorded four songs in tribute to actor James Dean: "Giant," "His Name Was Dean," "James Dean," and "Jimmy, Jimmy." Died: 1982.

Louis Hayward 📺   1680 Vine

See page 306

Arthur Spiegel 🎥   1680 Vine

Pioneer producer

BORN Nov. 11, 1903, in Jaroslau, Austria (now Poland). **SPOTLIGHTS** Oops! His first name on the star should read "Sam." (This was a Chamber spelling mistake made in 1960 when it was installed. Although he also called himelf S.P. Eagle, for prestige purposes, he is known to the film world as Sam Spiegel.) One of the globe's very best independent producers, he worked in Berlin, Vienna, London, Paris and Hollywood. Spiegel had numerous successes. In Europe, productions include *The Unlucky Five, Invisible Enemies,* and *The Invader,* starring Buster Keaton. Hollywood movies include *On the Waterfront* (1954; Academy Award "best picture" winner), *The Bridge on the River Kwai* (1957; Academy Award "best picture" winner), and *Lawrence of Arabia* (1962; Academy Award "best picture" winner). **ACHIEVEMENTS** 1963 Irving G. Thalberg Memorial Award. Died: 1985.

Jack Pearl 🎙   1680 Vine

Comedian, actor, quiz show host

BORN Jack Pearlman; Oct. 29, 1895, in New York. **SPOTLIGHTS** Raised in the lower East Side ghetto, Pearl was a product of the region that produced Fanny Brice and Al Jolson. He got his professional start at age 15 in a vaudeville, then gradually advanced through burlesque and legit theatre to become a Ziegfeld headliner. One of radio's earliest actors, he was radio's first expert with dialects. He is best remembered for his comic portrayal of the German Baron von Munchhausen, the wild teller of tales: "Oh shure, l vass in a much bigger vun"—on "The Jack Pearl Show." (It first aired on NBC, 1933.) He was great with verbal dexterity. Another favorite character was that of Peter Pfeiffer in his Frigidaire series. Later, hosted "The Baron and the Bee" spelling bee (NBC, 1953). Died: Christmas Day, 1982.

Morton Downey 🎙   1656 Vine

Composer, singer

BORN Nov. 14, 1902, in Wallingford, CO. **SPOTLIGHTS** Gifted with an exquisite tenor voice, he was nicknamed "the Irish Thrush," and "the Irish Troubadour." As a child, he sang in the church choir and performed at the Elks Lodge. At age 17, he was discovered by band leader Paul Whitman—the self-styled "king of jazz." Downey became a top-billed vocalist with the Paul Whiteman Orchestra. In the late 1920s he enjoyed a sold-out European tour, then won his own radio show in 1928 (BBC, London). He stars in four early musicals, from 1929-'30, just as sound was being introduced and experimented with in movies. This featured tenor with a "romantic voice" switched to CBS radio in 1930, and by 1932 was voted "America's best male vocalist." By 1936 he was one of radio's highest paid stars, pulling in a cool quarter of a million dollars annual salary, plus recording fees and royalties. Downey remained on air through various incarnations through 1951. He enjoyed a longstanding relationship with sponsor Coca-Cola ("The Coke Club"). Songs include "Wabash Moon" and "Now You're in My Arms," to name a couple of his 1,000+ recordings. **SIDELIGHTS** Opened his own New York nightclub—The Delmonico—in 1930 and broadcast from its elegant bandstand. **HIGHLIGHT** His early radio trademark was his distinct whistle before each song. Died: 1985.

Jackie Coogan 🎥   1654 Vine

Jackie Coogan and Betty Grable

Actor

BORN Oct. 24, 1914, in Los Angeles, CA. **SPOTLIGHTS** The all-time most successful one and one-half-year-old to enter films, he made his silent screen debut in *Skinners Baby* (released 1917). This round-faced, wide-eyed kid was cast by director/star Charlie Chaplin in *A Days Pleasure* (1919), and liked him so much he cast him in another film. A problem arose when Chaplin could not persuade the sweet youngster to smack him—as required in a scene—for *The Kid* (1920). Chaplin tricked him into thinking that hitting was a game. Convinced, gentle Jackie finally cuffed him. Much later in Coogan's career, TV buffs recall him as Uncle Fester in "The Addams Family" (1964-'66). **ACHIEVEMENTS** His financial suffering paved ground for the California Child Actors Bill. The "Coogan Act" was passed to protect children (it was already too late for him) from having their earnings stolen by greedy parents, abusive guardians, etc. Unfortunately, Coogan's court battle to recover $4 million yielded him only $125,000. **HIGHLIGHTS** Married to *Million Dollar Legs*

(1939) co-star Betty Grable (1937-'39). The photo shows one of their happier moments. Money problems were cited in divorce proceedings. Died: 1984.

Hal Roach 🎥   1654 Vine

Movie pioneer, screenwriter, director, producer

Hal Roach

BORN Jan. 14, 1892, in Elmira, NY. **SPOTLIGHTS** "When I first came to L.A. in 1912, I read an ad in the paper: 'Men wanted in Western costume. Be in front of the post office at 7 a.m.' A dollar, carfare and lunch was the pay." Later, behind-the-scenes, Roach was crowned the Comedy King by making Harold Lloyd a star, and by pairing Laurel and Hardy, film history's most successful comedy team. He also masterminded the *Our Gang* (1922) film series. The Little Rascals had one funny, brief adventure after another. Roach was a pioneer in every sense of the word. He manufactured the Little Rascals by the seat-of-his-pants, with half planned plots and sketchy scripts. Gags came to him while they were shooting. This was the free-wheeling way of Old Hollywood. Founder of Hal Roach Studios, he made more than 300 movies. Films include the classic screwball comedy about ghosts, *Topper* (1937—series), and the extraordinary dramatic adaptation of John Steinbeck's *Of Mice and Men* (1939). In 1967, he released the compilation film *The Crazy World of Laurel and Hardy.* **ACHIEVEMENTS** 1932 Academy Award for *The Music Box* (Laurel and Hardy classic short); 1936 Academy Award for *Bored of Education* (Our Gang); 1983 Special Oscar. **QUOTE** Asked if laughter is the key to longevity, Roach mused, "Oh, I don't know, why not ask George Burns or Bob Hope if there's any truth to that." Died: Weeks short of his 101th birthday, in 1992.

Paulette Goddard 🎥   1650 Vine

Actress

BORN Pauline Marion Levee; June 3, 1911, in Long Island, NY. **SPOTLIGHTS** A former Ziegfeld showgirl, Goddard was a saucy, mischievous beauty nicknamed "Peaches." This striking brunette became a movie star in *Modern Times* (1936). She co-stars opposite her real-life, then-secret fiance, Charlie Chaplin, who also directed her. Then, Goddard appears in a funny comedy that would make the ten best pictures of the year list, *The Young in Heart* (1938). The stunning actress co-stars opposite her then-husband Charlie Chaplin in *The Great Dictator* (1940). Other motion pictures include Cecil B. DeMille's *Northwest Mounted Police* (1940), *Hold Back the Dawn* (1941), *Nothing but the Truth* (1941), *Second Chorus* (1941), *Diary of a Chambermaid* (1941) with then-husband

Burgess Meredith, *Hold Back the Dawn* (1941), *Star Spangled Rhythm* (1942), *So Proudly We Hail* (1943—in an Oscar-nominated performance), *Kitty* (1945), *The Diary of a Chambermaid* (1946), and *Unconquered* (1947). **HIGHLIGHTS** She had a notorious first marriage when she was just 14 years old to timber magnate Edgar James. He had spotted her in the Ziegfeld Follies. She tem-

Paulette Goddard and Charlie Chaplin

porarily retired upon marrying him. Her second marriage was to Charlie Chaplin (1936-'42). Her third of four husbands was Burgess Meredith (1944-'49). Her fourth husband was writer Erich Maria Remarque (1958 until his death in 1970)...The men in her life showered her with a fabulous collection of jewels and an outstanding collection of art masterpieces by Cezanne, Renoir and Monet. **QUOTE** Throughout her life, she worked at staying, fit, trim and beautiful. She coyly remarked, "If you don't watch your figure, the boys won't." Died: 1990.

Vera Miles 📺   1650 Vine

Actress

Vera Miles

BORN Vera Ralston; Aug. 23, 1929, in Boise City, OK. **SPOTLIGHTS** After winning a beauty contest, this shapely, green-eyed blonde appeared in the new medium of television in countless live performances. Programs included the "Pepsi-Cola Playhouse" (early 1950s) and "Twilight Theatre" (late 1950s). An extremely gifted actress, Miles was rated among the best. She made dozens of movies, both as leading lady and supporting actress. Films include *The Charge at Feather River* (1953--shot in original 3-D), *Wichita* (1955), *The Searchers* (1956), *Beau James* (1957), Hitchcock's *The Wrong Man* (1957), *The FBI Story* (1959), *A Touch of Larceny* (1959), Hitchcock's *Psycho* (1960), *Back Street* (1961), *The Man Who Shot Liberty Valance* (1962), *The Wild Country* (1970), *One Little Indian* (1973), and *Into the Night* (1985). She also acted in TV movies: "The Case Against Paul Ryker," "The Hanged Man," "In Search of America," "Jigsaw," "Runaway," and "The Underground Man." **HIGHLIGHTS**

Director Alfred Hitchcock cast Miles to star in his masterpiece *Vertigo* (1958), but her pregnancy prevented that. Kim Novak replaced her.

Audrey Hepburn 1650 Vine

Actress

Audrey Hepburn

BORN Edda van Heemstra Hepburn-Ruston; May 4, 1929, in Brussels, Belgium. **SPOTLIGHTS** Considering that her father was an English banker, and her mother a Dutch baroness, she should have led a life of privilege. WWII obliterated that entitlement. During the five years the Nazis occupied the Netherlands, the young Hepburn suffered from severe malnutrition. "There was always a cloud of fear and repression," she said about those horrible years. When Holland was liberated, Red Cross relief trucks flooded the city with food, and saved her and thousands others. The slender, long-legged beauty traveled to London on a ballet scholarship, where she began modeling and doing bit roles in films. While making *Monte Carlo Baby* (1951) on the French Riviera, she was picked out of a crowd by the famed French author Colette. The writer had spotted Hepburn's ravishing smile, huge eyes—that both sparkled with amusement and sincere warmth—as well as her matchless visage. Colette declared, "I could not take my eyes away. 'There,' I said to myself incredulously, 'is Gigi.' That afternoon I offered her the part in the Broadway play, and she accepted my offer." A slender, doe-eyed, long-necked brunette, her aristocratic European background and delightful waif-like innocence combined with stunning results onstage. With the freshest face in New York, audiences and critics loved her. She was a resounding success. A star was born. The elegant talent was immediately spotted for films by director William Wyler. She delivers a regal performance in her first U.S. film, Wyler's romantic comedy *Roman Holiday* (1953), where she plays an incognito princess being wooed by Gregory Peck. The wistful beauty exuded a shining purity, and true charm, and the film was nominated for 10 Academy Awards (see below). She plays a Cinderella-type role in *Sabrina* (1954--in an Oscar-nominated performance) as the chauffeur's engaging daughter who attracts two bachelor heirs of the family fortune after she undergoes a European makeover. It co-stars William Holden and Humphrey Bogart. She plays Natasha in *War and Peace* (1956); a long three and a half-hour movie. She co-stars with Gary Cooper and Maurice Chevalier in *Love in the Afternoon* (1957). Hepburn appears opposite Fred Astaire in *Funny Face* (1957). With its spectacular cinematography of Paris, and Gershwin tunes ("S'Wonderful," and "How Long Has This Been Going On"), it is a stylish musical. She received an Academy Award nomination for her performance in the thoughtful drama that studies religious life in The *Nun's Story* (1959). She was described as having "an indestructible frailness." Hepburn was fluid as the free-spirited gigolo Holly Golightly in *Breakfast at Tiffany's* (1961--in an Oscar-nominated performance). Cary Grant is her co-star in the suspense comedy *Charade* (1963), also with Walter Matthau, James Coburn and George Kennedy. She stars as the Cockney flower girl Eliza Doolittle in George Cukor's *My Fair Lady* (1964), who turns into a sophisticate under the supervision of Professor Henry Higgins (Rex Harrison). The memorable scene where she walks down the stairs in her ball gown defines and captures Hepburn's spirit. She is breathtaking, graceful, and divine. The movie won the Academy Award for Best Picture. She convincingly plays a blind housewife terrorized by drug smugglers in the thriller *Wait Until Dark* (1967--in an Oscar-nominated performance). **ACHIEVEMENTS** 1953 Best Actress Oscar for *Roman Holiday*. The next year, she returned to Broadway and won a Tony Award for "Ondine," playing opposite Mel Ferrer. She was honored posthumously with the 1993 Jean Hersholt Humanitarian Academy Award. Hepburn remained humble, kind and gracious through it all. She was a tremendous humanitarian who campaigned tirelessly against world hunger. She dedicated herself to United Nations International Children's Emergency Fund (UNICEF). As its goodwill ambassador, she traveled to Ethiopia, Sudan, Guatemala, Bangladesh, Vietnam and Somalia. She raised funds for UNICEF as well as personally distributing food and medicine to needy children. **SIDELIGHTS** One of her marriages was to actor and fellow Walk of Fame honoree Mel Ferrer. **QUOTE** In her typical, sincere, self-effacing style, Hepburn was asked if she felt like a movie star after winning her Oscar and becoming the second highest paid actress in Hollywood (the highest paid was Elizabeth Taylor). She politely stated, "When I've made about 70 films and the public still wants to see me, then I shall think of myself as a star." The world wept when it lost this earth angel in 1993.

Scott Forbes 1650 Vine

Actor

BORN 1920. **SPOTLIGHTS** The rugged Western leading man made a number of movies in the 1950s, including *Rocky Mountain, Raton Pass,* and *Inside the Walls of Folsom Prison.* He starred in the TV series, "The Seeking Heart" (1954), and "The Adventures of Jim Bowie" (1956-'58).

Al Hibbler 🎙️   1650 Vine

Singer

BORN Aug. 16, 1915, in Little Rock, AR. **SPOTLIGHTS** Born blind and raised in Philadelphia, his deep baritone made him the most popular singer with the giant of jazz and soul, Duke Ellington (1943-'51). Classic hits include "Don't You Know Me?" "I'm Just A Lucky So And So," "I Ain't Got Nothin' But The Blues," and "Don't Get Around Much Anymore." His biggest hit was "Unchained Melody." He also recorded with Count Basie. Onstage, Duke Ellington walked with him—their shoulders touching—thereby guiding Hibbler to the microphone. The audience did not know he was blind.

Jimmy Durante 🎥   1650 Vine

See page 286

Tom Brown 🎥   1648 Vine

Actor

BORN Jan. 6, 1913, in New York, NY. **SPOTLIGHTS** Typecast in innocent, boy-next-door roles, he appears in the silent, *The Hoosier Schoolmaster* (1924). He changed his tune to play a villainous convict on a chain gang in *Hell's Highway* (1932). Then, he appears in the charming *Anne of Green Gables* (1934), and is an Annapolis cadet in *Navy Blue and Gold* (1937). He co-stars with Wallace Beery in *Sergeant Madden* (1939), about a criminally minded son who breaks his policeman father's heart. Other movies include *Operation Haylift* (1950), and *The Quiet Gun* (1957). He gained new fame in TV's long-running Western series, "Gunsmoke," as Ed O'Connor. Died: 1990.

Paul Douglas 🎥   1648 Vine

*Paul Douglas
and Ruth Roman*

Actor

BORN Nov. 4, 1907, in Philadelphia, PA. **SPOTLIGHTS** Raised in the city of brotherly love, and educated at Yale, this burly, hulking, athletic student first became a professional football player. He followed his pro career with various radio jobs. As an announcer, he worked on the "Chesterfield Time" starring "the king of jazz" Paul Whiteman, and later for the sensational Glenn Miller. It was in this show that listeners could her Douglas' voice soothingly praise the virtues of "the cigarette that satisfies." He was also a radio announcer on the wildly popular juvenile science fiction serial, "Buck Rogers in the 25th Century," and the comedy show "Burns and Allen" (The ditzy Gracie Allen flirted with Douglas as a running gag). He was also a sportscaster, and boisterous commentator. He made his Broadway debut in "Double Dummy" (1935), and starred in Garson Kanin's "Born Yesterday." Starting in 1945, this was one of Broadway's most successful and longest-running hits. Douglas said, "They wanted a big loudmouth like Paul Douglas. Well, they found one--me!" After more than 1,000 successful performances as the quick-tempered Harry Brock, he made the mistake of rejecting the film version, which turned out to be a smash hit. He made his screen debut in *A Letter to Three Wives* (1948), a splendid drama. Movies include *It Happens Every Spring* (1949), *Everybody Does It* (1949), *Panic in the Streets*, *Love That Brute* (both 1950), *Angels in the Outfield* (1951), *Fourteen Hours* (1951; Grace Kelly in her screen debut), *Clash by Night* (1952), *High and Dry* (1954--aka *The Maggie*) and *Joe Macbeth* (1955). He is funny in *The Mating Game* (1959) as the father of Debbie Reynolds—who's fallen for I.R.S. man Tony Randall. Through a comedy of errors, he attempts to get his farm tax records out of his future son-in-law's hands. Later, when he worked in the new medium of TV, he declared, "Trouble with TV is not so much scaling down entertainment to the adult mind of 13, it's the problem of the 11-year-old mind on Madison Avenue trying to catch up with the 13-year-old adult." **ACHIEVEMENTS** Douglas donated his time and talent to "Command Performance," a stupendous wartime variety show that *Time* magazine called "the best wartime program in America." It was produced by the U.S. War Department, and heard by WWII troops fighting overseas via direct shortwave transmission...Two of his marriages were to actresses: Virginia Field (they had a daughter named Margaret), and Jan Sterling (they had a son named Adam). **QUOTE** "I'm a conscientious ham." Died: 1959.

Richard Crooks 🎙️   1648 Vine

Opera singer

BORN June 26, 1900, in Trenton, NJ. **SPOTLIGHTS** This powerful tenor made his Metropolitan Opera debut in 1933. He became one of the alternating soloists on "The Voice of Firestone" (1932-'34) with another opera great, Lawrence Tibbett. This program, which started by featuring popular music, switched its format to showcase opera's finest talents. It ran for 24 years (1928-54). He made numerous recordings.

Rosemary De Camp   1642 Vine

Actress

BORN Nov. 14, 1910, in Prescott, AZ. **SPOTLIGHTS** Following in the footsteps of performers before her, De Camp cut her teeth on stage and radio before becoming a motion picture actress. With her sweet, non-threatening, compassionate looks, she was often cast as the well-meaning or goodly sister, aunt or mother. Her 18 movies include the entertaining *Yankee Doodle Dandy* (1942) about the life of singer, dancer, composer George M. Cohan, and *Rhapsody in Blue* (1945) about the life of composer George Gershwin. Switching to TV, she played the confused sister, Margaret McDonald, of bachelor

Bob on "The Bob Cummings Show" (1955-'59); and mother Helen Marie (1967-'70) on "That Girl." She made commercials for 20-Mule Team Borax on "Death Valley Days," some were hosted by the future U.S. President, Ronald Reagan.

John Ford 🎥   1642 Vine

John Ford

Director

BORN Sean O'Feeney; Feb. 1, 1895, in Cape Elizabeth, ME. **SPOTLIGHTS** Ford was one of America's greatest directors, if not *the* greatest. Inspired by his Irish heritage, his work was an eclectic mix of poetry and raucousness, of masculinity and honor, of patriotism and family. His favorite story to tell, though, was that of the morally uncomplicated American West. Ford created masterpiece after masterpiece. Motion pictures include *Wee Willie Winkie* (1937), a Shirley Temple vehicle which Ford moves at a brisk pace, and *Stagecoach* (1939), John Wayne's breakthrough movie. A landmark Western, *Stagecoach* was made for adults, not for the kids. It was partially shot in the spectacular Monument Valley which found its way into many Ford movies. Other remarkable works include *Arrowsmith* (1940), *Young Mr. Lincoln* (1939), *The Long Voyage Home* (1940), *They Were Expendable* (1945), *My Darling Clementine* (1946), *The Fugitive* (1947) this is a gripping tale of commitment, based on Graham Greene's novel *The Power and the Glory*; it is *not* about a murder involving Dr. Richard Kimball, *Fort Apache* (1948), *She Wore a Yellow Ribbon* (1949), *Wagon Master* (1950), *Rio Grande* (1950), *Mogambo* (1953), *The Long Gray Line* (1955), *Mister Roberts* (1955), *The Last Hurrah* (1958), and *The Man Who Shot Liberty Valance* (1962), where a newspaper editor recites this classic line: "This is the West, sir. When the legend becomes fact, print the legend." **SIDELIGHTS** *The Sun Shines Bright* (1953) is a remake of Ford's early talkie, *Judge Priest* (1934). *Judge Priest* is based on humorist/actor Irvin Cobb's collection of short stories, and stars Will Rogers and Stepin Fetchit. Ford's 1953 cast includes Charles Winninger, Stepin Fetchit (again), Milburn Stone, Mae Marsh, and Jane Darwell. The movie deals with small town prejudice and was Ford's favorite film. **ACHIEVEMENTS** He won more Academy Awards than any other director (yet none were for a Western—his special craft). Oscars: 1935 for *The Informer.* Ford said, "I made *The Informer* in three weeks after dreaming about it for five years." The film's small, limited budget did not affect its brilliant outcome. Other Oscars: 1940 *The Grapes of Wrath*; 1941 *How Green Was My Valley*; and 1952 *The Quiet Man*, which he also co-produced—as well as two for war documentaries. He had enlisted in the Navy during World War II. In 1942 he filmed the famous 20-minute documentary, *The Battle of Midway.* It was the first WWII documentary shot during combat and won an Oscar. His rank was Lieutenant Commander. **NICKNAME** Cast and crew affectionately called him "Pappy." That is, everyone except John Wayne (a former USC football player), who called him "Coach," and Jimmy Stewart, who called him "Boss." **HIGHLIGHTS** Hollywood nicknamed the scenic Monument Valley (Arizona/Utah border) "Ford Country" because he shot so many epics there, capturing the phenomenal beauty of the territory. **QUOTE** Ford wanted his epitaph to read: "He made Westerns." Died: 1973.

Tom Moore 🎥   1642 Vine

Actor

BORN Nov. 14, 1884. **SPOTLIGHTS** Big and handsome, he melted many hearts in silent films: *The Cinderella Man* (1917) and *A Man and His Money* (1919). Successful in horror films and Westerns, too. Died: 1955.

Portland Hoffa 🎤   1642 Vine

Portland Hoffa (left) and Helen Jepson

Actress, comedienne

BORN in Portland, Oregon (for which she was named). **SPOTLIGHTS** A former chorus girl, she used her comical voice as co-star on "The Fred Allen Show." It was one of radio's wittiest, longest-running comedy programs (1932-'49). She played Allen's naive second banana, an airhead whose perpetual questions gave life to his jokes. Earlier shows include "Town Hall Tonight" and "The Texaco Star Theatre." She was married to Fred Allen from 1927 until his death. In real life, her husband was known for being decent and gentle. When they went out, he always carried a row of bills to hand out to the needy. For all their wealth, they made few household acquisitions. Hoffa and her devoted spouse lived in a New York apartment uncluttered by possessions. Her husband had stated, "I don't want to own anything that won't fit in my coffin." Died: 1990.

Hanley Stafford 🎤   1640 Vine

Actor

BORN Sept. 22, 1898, in England. **SPOTLIGHTS** He played Mr. Lancelot "Daddy" Higgens on "The Baby Snooks Show." The singer-comedienne Fanny Brice was 46 years old when she went on air as the super brat, Baby Snooks. Of her "father" on the show, Brice declared, "Stafford was perfect!" He was the great stack-blower. He blew his temper at his mischievous daughter at least once per show. This popular sitcom first aired in 1936, and through various incarnations lasted through 1951. He also played J.C. Dithers (Dagwood's boss) on radio's "Blondie" show (1939-'50). Other roles included "Snapper Snitch the Crocodile" on the children's fantasy show "The Cinnamon Bear." Died: 1968.

Henry Hathaway 🎥   1640 Vine

Director

BORN March 13, 1898, in Sacramento, CA. **SPOTLIGHTS** A Universal Studios messenger boy during the silent era, he became a propman for Frank Lloyd before moving up to assistant director. Hathaway was all over the map; he directed action, Westerns, comedy, drama, and romance throughout his long 40-year career. Motion pictures include *The Trail of the Lonesome Pine* (1936), *Go West, Young Man* (1936), *Johnny Apollo* (1940), *Wing and a Prayer* (1944), and *The House on 92nd Street* (1945—an influential picture made in a semi-documentary style). He directed *Kiss of Death* (1947), where Richard Widmark's evil character pushes a lady in a wheelchair down a flight of stairs. He was skillful in eliciting Marilyn Monroe's strengths as a *femme fatale* in her first big role—the thriller *Niagara* (1952). Other movies include *13 rue Madeleine* (1946), *O.S.S.* (1947), *Fourteen Hours* (1951—which introduced Grace Kelly), *Seven Thieves* (1960), *North to Alaska* (1960), *How the West Was Won* (1962—he co-directed with John Ford and George Marshall), and *The Sons of Katie Elder* (1965). He directed John Wayne in his only Academy Award-winning performance, *True Grit* (1969). Died: 1985.

Lee Tracy 🎥   1638 Vine

Actor

BORN William L. Tracy; April 14, 1898, in Atlanta, GA. **SPOTLIGHTS** A laborer on the railroad, he found happiness acting in stock companies. From there, he moved to Broadway, then Hollywood. A fair-haired, fast-talking, dynamic actor, he was often cast as a wise guy reporter. Films include *Advice to the Lovelorn* (1933), *Dinner at Eight* (1933), *The Lemon Drop Kid* (1951), and *The Best Man* (1964). Died: 1968.

William Bendix ⬛   1638 Vine

Actor

BORN Jan. 4, 1906, in New York, NY. **SPOTLIGHTS** A big, barrel-chested performer, he was initially cast as a rugged, dim-witted thug, or the likable, burly guy. Motion pictures include *Wake Island* (1942--in an Oscar-nominated performance), *The Hairy Ape* (1944), *Lifeboat* (1944), *A Bell for Adano* (1945), and the title role in *The Babe Ruth Story* (1948). The baseball picture had his heart; he had wanted to be a professional baseball player for the New York Giants, not an actor. He found tremendous fame on radio with his 1940s series "The Life of

Riley." He starred as Chester A. Riley, a bumbling, wide-eyed optimist, whose life is perpetually complicated by minor crises that grow into potential catastrophes. His long-suffering wife is the only one who can save the day. Riley's catchphrase—"What a revoltin' development this is!"—became part of the American diet. He also stars in *The Life of Riley* (1948), and in the TV show (1953-'58). Died: 1964.

William Bendix

William Powell 🎥   1636 Vine

William Powell

Actor

BORN July 29, 1892, in Pittsburgh, PA. **SPOTLIGHTS** The son of a public accountant, Powell was raised in Kansas City. As a student, he performed in a Christmas play and fell in love with acting. His father, who had wanted him to be an attorney, was especially disappointed when his son went off to study at the American Academy of Dramatic Arts, in New York. After one year, he did some "one night stands," then in 1912 landed a bit part on Broadway in "The Ne'er Do Well." His talents were recognized almost immediately, and by 1913 he had an important role with a touring company as Eddie Griggs in "Within the Law." His Broadway stage role in "Spanish Love" (1922) brought him to the attention of movie producers. Cast in an evil supporting role, Powell made his screen debut in the silent *Sherlock Holmes* (1922), starring John Barrymore. For the next six years, he was cast as a treacherous villain or scoundrel in both dramas and comedy melodramas. In the silent movie, *Romola* (1924), he plays a distinguished-looking, but dastardly Italian count who wrongs both Gish sisters. In Josef von Sternberg's *The Last Demand* (1928), he plays a cruel film director. He appears in Paramount Pictures' first all-talkie *Interference* (1929). He plays Philo Vance, detective, in his second talkie *The Canary Murder Case* (1929). There, he realized that "my voice suited a suave, sophisticated character." His career skyrocketed as the good guy. He became best known as the debonair, wisecracking detective Nick Charles in *The Thin Man*, co-starring Myrna Loy, for which he also received his first Academy Award nomination. Breathing the air of refined superiority into Dashiell Hammett's character, this tremendously successful MGM movie series started in 1934 and ended in 1947. Powell plays the butler Godfrey opposite Carole Lombard (his real-life, friendly ex-wife) in the quintessential screwball comedy *My Man Godfrey* (1936--in an Academy Award-nominated performance). With a vain imperiousness, he stars in the title role as impresario, *The Great Ziegfeld* (1936). This extravagant MGM musical won the Best Picture Academy Award. That same year, he appears in the outstanding screwball comedy, *Libelled Lady*, with Jean Harlow (who would have been his real-life wife had she not died suddenly), Myrna Loy and Spencer Tracy--a perfect foursome. He was Oscar-nominated as the irascible father in the delightful comedy, *Life with Father* (1947). Later films include *How to Marry a Millionaire* (1953) with Marilyn Monroe, Betty Grable and Lauren Bacall, and his last, *Mr. Roberts* (1955--as Doc) with Henry Fonda, James Cagney and Jack Lemmon. In all, he made 96 films. Dressed to the nines, this gentleman remained poised and polished, both on-screen and off. He was always a welcome party guest due to his sparkling, lofty, witty conversation. **HIGHLIGHTS** So skilled at his craft, this artist was known as "a scene stealer." Yet, he remained popular among his colleagues because everyone liked him too much to be jealous. **QUOTE** "An actor must act to live." He took his final curtain call in 1984.

George Sanders 🎥 1636 Vine

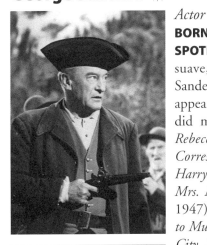

George Sanders

Actor

BORN July 3, 1906, in Russia. **SPOTLIGHTS** Worldly, dry wit, suave, and cynical describe Sanders on-screen and off. He appeared in a number of splendid motion pictures, including *Rebecca* (1940), *Foreign Correspondent* (1940), *Uncle Harry* (1945), *The Ghost and Mrs. Muir*, *Forever Amber* (both 1947), *Ivanhoe* (1952), *Witness to Murder* (1954), and *While the City Sleeps* (1956). He played *The Saint*, detective Simon Templar, in five of the adventure-mystery movie series from 1939 - '41. His last film was ominously titled *Psychomania* (1972)...The second of his five wives was Zsa Zsa Gabor (1949-'57). She had to deal a contemptuous, chauvinist, sneering husband. His acid-tongued views on women ranged from "little beasts" to "almost human." **ACHIEVEMENTS** 1950 Best Supporting Oscar for *All About Eve*. **QUOTE** "I have solved the secret of longevity in show business. It is to be consistently mediocre, like me, tottering as it were, from one lousy film to another. That way, you see, you can never get worse." Died: 1972.

Ann Sothern 📺 1634 Vine

See page 283

Ezra Stone 🎙 1634 Vine

Actor, director

BORN Dec. 2, 1917, in New Bedford, MA. **SPOTLIGHTS** He starred as the chaos-causing teenage son Henry Aldrich on "The Aldrich Family." The situation comedy started in 1939, with Stone's character causing mayhem. In each episode his long-suffering mother (Lea Penman) called out: "Hen-reeee! Henry Aldrich!" His plaintive cry of "Coming, Mother!" became a popular catchphrase for American youths. Because he delivered "Coming, Mother!" with a cacophonous, "up," cracking wail, listeners burst into robust laughter, inevitably splitting their sides so long they could not catch the next few lines of dialogue. He played the 16-year-old Henry during the show's entire 14-year run, with the exception of when he served in the Army during WWII. From 1942 - '45 there were three other actors who tried to fill his shoes, but they got drafted, too. During the war, he assisted staging Irving Berlin's "This Is the Army" musical revue with 300 soldiers. After his honorable discharge, he returned to playing the teenage student at Central High School, in the town of Centerville, until the show ended in 1953. Stone became a TV director of such noted comedy series as "I Love Lucy." Also director of the David Library of the American Revolution. Died: 1994.

Delmer L. Daves 🎥 1634 Vine

Director, screenwriter

BORN July 24, 1904, in San Francisco, CA. **SPOTLIGHTS** His *Broken Arrow* (1950) broke new ground by presenting the film from the Native Americans perspective—changing the way Hollywood portrayed "Indians." He wrote and directed *The Red House* (1947), a suspense thriller starring Edward G. Robinson. *The Hanging Tree* (1959) stars Gary Cooper, but has an incredible performance by George C. Scott in his screen debut. Died: 1977.

Fred Stone 🎥 1634 Vine

Actor

BORN Aug. 19, 1893, in Denver, CO. **SPOTLIGHTS** Known as the "grand old man of the American theater," he started in show business as a circus/vaudeville tight-rope performer. Later, he created the original scarecrow in the stage version of "The Wizard of Oz." On Broadway he became the pillar of American musical comedy. Stone made a dozen films, including *Alice Adams* (1935), *Trail of the Lonesome Pine* (1936), and *Life Begins in College* (1937). Died: 1959.

Akim Tamiroff 🎥 1634 Vine

Actor

BORN Oct. 29, 1899, in the Russian Caucasus. **SPOTLIGHTS** A round, slightly bald, mustached, distrustful-looking character, he frequently played scoundrels. Director Cecil B. DeMille

Akim Tamiroff

considered Tamiroff: "one of the finest workmen as an actor." In *The General Died at Dawn* (1936), he appears as a Chinese warlord. He portrays Dominique You, Napoleon's famous gunner who became pirate Jean Lafitte's chief lieutenant in *The Buccaneer* (1938). He is must-see in the Western *Union Pacific* (1939), Hemingway's adventure tale *For Whom the Bell Tolls* (1943), and *Topkapi* (1964), a caper about a group of thieves plotting to rob an Istanbul museum. He made hundreds of movies. Died: 1972.

Jane Greer   1634 Vine

Jane Greer

Actress, singer

BORN Bettejane Greer; Sept. 9, 1924, in Washington, D.C. **SPOTLIGHTS** A former child model, this striking, dark-haired, deep-voiced, young adult beauty was hired by Uncle Sam to model in a WAC uniform on a recruitment poster. Spotted by Hollywood, she was offered a contract by Howard Hughes. Although that relationship did not work out, she made her screen debut in *Two O'Clock Courage* (1945). Motion pictures include *George White's Scandals*, *Dick Tracy* (both 1945), *The Falcon's Alibi* (1946), *Sinbad the Sailor* (1947—co-starring Douglas Fairbanks, Jr.), *Station West* (1948), *The Prisoner of Zenda* (1952), *The Clown* (1953), *Man of a Thousand Faces* (1957), *The Outfit* (1974), *Against All Odds* (1984), *Just Between Friends* (1986), and *Immediate Family* (1989). A versatile and gifted artist, Greer played the sweet girl, but she excelled in cold and calculating roles as well. In film noir, she is most outstanding paired with Robert Mitchum in *Out of the Past* (1947) and *The Big Steal* (1949).

Ray Milland   1634 Vine
See page 347

Margaret O'Brien   1628 Vine
See page 416

Charlie Ruggles   1628 Vine
See page 255

Rudy Vallee   1628 Vine

Singer, saxophone player, actor, band leader

Rudy Vallee

BORN Hubert Vallee; July 28, 1901, in Island Point, VT. **SPOTLIGHTS** One of the three saxophonists with the Yale Collegians, Vallee paid his university tuition by playing with the orchestra. Graduating in 1927, he rose with the speed of a rocket. In network radio, he became a vastly popular personality. His voice was as familiar to Americans as the 31st President of the United States, Herbert Hoover. Vallee was the first of the legendary singers to bear the title "the crooner." (Bing Crosby and Frank Sinatra followed.) In his youth, he was a cute, wavy-haired, droopy-eyed singing idol. Female fans of all ages swooned to his tunes. He held his megaphone in one hand, and voiced his well-loved catchphrase, "Heigh ho, everybody." A gigantic recording star of the late 1920s-'30s, the title of his hit song "The Vagabond Lover" became the title of his debut film (1929). He appears in 33 pictures, including *Happy Go Lucky* (1943). Much of his film work consisted of light, romantic musical comedies using his trademark megaphone. He sang the salute 'There's a New Star in Heaven Tonight, R-u-d-y V-a-l-e-n-t-i-n-o," after the silent star's sudden death. **QUOTE** So thrifty he made Lincoln scream (on the head of a penny), Vallee brought his own wine to restaurants. He declared, "Most restaurants don't have the wine I prefer—an Ohio state wine." Died: 1986.

Grantland Rice   1628 Vine

Sportscaster, journalist, author

BORN Nov. 1, 1880, in Murfreesboro, TN. **SPOTLIGHTS** A newspaper reporter in 1909, he started in radio during its earliest hours and became one of the first great sportscasters. He announced the first four innings of the World Series in 1923, but experienced difficulty with the play-by-play. Rice did not give up. He is best remembered for his original gems, which are still repeated today to every kid engaged in sports: *"It's not whether you win or lose, it's how you play the game."* He covered the World Series and other major sports events, including football on "The Cities Service Concert" (NBC, late 1920s). He was also a commentator on short subjects. Rice was well-known for his stories and syndicated column "The Sportlight." Author of *Only the Brave* (1941). Died: 1954.

Joe Kirkwood, Jr. 📺   1628 Vine

Actor

BORN May 30, 1920, in Melbourne Australia. **SPOTLIGHTS** Blond, handsome, and muscular, he starred as a comic strip character in the successful *Joe Palooka* movie series. Films include *Joe Palooka—Champ* (1946), *Joe Palooka in the Big Fight* (1949), and six others. This was the basis for his 1954 syndicated TV show, co-starring Cathy Downs. He became a wealthy man as owner/operator of a L.A. sports center.

Emil Jannings 🎥   1628 Vine

Actor

BORN Theodor E. Janenz; July 22, 1884, in Switzerland. **SPOTLIGHTS** He gave powerful, tragic characterizations of historical rulers in *Anne Boleyn* (1920), and *Peter the Great* (1922). He moved to Hollywood in 1927, but two years later sound pictures ended his career. He went to Germany where he was "Falling in Love Again" with Marlene Dietrich in *Der blaue Engel/ The Blue Angel* (1930). **ACHIEVEMENTS** 1927-'28 Academy Award, first ever presented to a Best Actor for two films, *The Last Command* and *The Way of All Flesh*. **THE FALL OF JANNINGS** Raised in a German village, he was recruited by the Third Reich. With Hitler's backing, movies glorifying Nazi hatred were made under Janning's guidance. After the fall of the Third Reich, and detested by the worldwide film community, he never worked again. Died: 1950.

Dolores del Rio 🎥   1628 Vine

Dolores del Rio

Actress

BORN Lolita Dolores Martinez Asunsolo Lopez Negrette; Aug. 3, 1905, in Durango, Mexico. **SPOTLIGHTS** It was said of del Rio that she was so beautiful she did not have to act. Critic Harriet Van Horne wrote: "... her magnificent white marble face with its flashing black eyes was spectacle enough...Miss del Rio is as indifferent to time as the Mona Lisa." Discovered at a tea party in Mexico City by a director struck by her breathtaking looks—her big eyes, bow lips, and an oval face. She stunned audiences in *Joanna* (1925). Motion pictures include *What Price Glory* (1926), *No Other Woman* (1928), *Madame DuBarry* (1934), *In Caliente* (1935) and *Journey into Fear* (1942). Her legendary glamour sparkled during Hollywood's Golden Era. She stars in the musical *Flying Down to Rio* (1933), in which Fred Astaire and Ginger Rogers made their joint screen debut as supporting actors. About her work in *The Fugitive* (1947), director John Ford paid her his highest compliment. He said, "Amazing! She's not a beauty, she's an actress." **HIGHLIGHTS** She was married to MGM art director Cedric Gibbons in 1930...In addition to her Walk of Fame star, her likeness has been immortalized in a statue (see "La Brea Gateway" in this book). **QUOTE** "Hollywood has a way of grabbing you and wrapping you up." Died: 1983.

Jeanette MacDonald 🎵   1628 Vine

See page 215

Donald Crisp 🎥   1628 Vine

Actor, director

BORN July 27, 1880, in Scotland. **SPOTLIGHTS** One of the founding fathers of the motion picture industry, he was a top director as well as character actor. Initially, he honed his craft while working with D.W. Griffith in *The Birth of a Nation* (1915). He enjoyed working with Buster Keaton in *The Navigator* (1924). Movies include *Mutiny on the Bounty* (1935), *The Life of Emile Zola* (1937), *Jezebel* (1938), *National Velvet* (1944), and *The Long Gray Line* (1955). **ACHIEVEMENTS** 1941 Best Supporting Actor Academy Award for *How Green Was My Valley*. Died: 1974.

Tex McCrary 📺   1628 Vine

Journalist, TV and radio personality

BORN John Reagan; Oct. 13, 1910, in Calvert, TX. **SPOTLIGHTS** After working as a copy boy, reporter, then chief editorial writer, this 1932 Yale graduate abruptly quit with this stinging rebuke: "I was tired of writing for people who move their lips when they read." He went into broadcasting, headed his own public relations firm, had a radio show, and with his wife, Jinx Falkenburg, hosted one of the early TV talk shows. When a critic complained that McCrary brought his own PR clients on his show to promote them (while cuing them with what to say), he lashed out, "It's not a conflict of interest. I'd rather call it a double interest." "Tex and Jinx" (1947-'49) was the forerunner of the TV magazine format talk show. On the air and off, he was the exact opposite of his wife (see Jinx Falkenburg's bio in this book). He had a tense personality, talked in a monotonous tone, and when something pleased him, he only offered a wary *half*-smile. He was known for his bleak, morose outlook on life. **QUOTE** "I have a genius for antagonizing people in positions of command. I don't know how to make friends except by starting a fight. People who dislike me do so instantly and I always manage to make it worse."

Robert Edeson    1628 Vine

Actor
BORN Jan. 23, 1868, in New Orleans, LA. **SPOTLIGHTS** He learned his craft from his well-known comedian father, George R. Edeson. A veteran stage actor of 30 years, his silent movie career was impressive. He appears in *The Masqueraders, Under the Red Robe, The Little Minister* and other hits. He stars in *Soldiers of Fortune, Ransom's Folly* and *Strongheart.* Died: 1931.

Barbara Hale   1628 Vine

Barbara Hale

Actress
BORN April 18, 1921, in DeKalb, IL. **SPOTLIGHTS** Hale achieved immortality in the role of Della Street, in the law drama "Perry Mason" from 1957-'66. She had been the personal choice of the producer of the series, Gail Patrick Jackson, who no doubt agreed with one leading television critic that "no leading lady blushes quite as prettily as Barbara Hale." And no one was more qualified than Hale to assume this major assignment which would require her to be alert, pert, self-sufficient--but not too hardboiled--as the right arm to master lawyer-sleuth Perry Mason. This incredibly popular television show is still seen daily in syndication, where fresh admirers of Hale's sincere, warm performances come with each new generation. As Raymond Burr recounted, "Barbara, without being ostentatious about it, is a remarkably intuitive actress. She has an instinct for doing exactly the right thing at the right time." Previously, she had been both a top model (she always kept her excellent posture), and a motion picture actress. She graced the sound stages of famed RKO pictures, alongside Katharine Hepburn, Irene Dunne, Ginger Rogers, Lucille Ball, Joan Fontaine and Jane Russell. This beautiful brunette made her screen debut in the silly comedy *Gildersleeve's Bad Day* (1943), then followed up in the nightmarish horror picture, *The Seventh Victim* (1943). Hale became a popular leading lady playing opposite all the grand Golden Era male movie stars, such as James Stewart, Frank Sinatra, James Cagney, Robert Mitchum, Rock Hudson, Anthony Quinn, Charlton Heston, and Fred MacMurray. Other motion pictures include *The Boy With the Green Hair* (1948), *The Clay Pigeon* (1949) opposite her real life husband Bill Williams, *Jolson Sings Again* (1949), *The Window* (1949), *The Jackpot* (1950), *Lorne Doone* (1951), *Unchained* (1955), *Seventh Calvary* (1956), *Airport* (1970), and *The Giant Spider Invasion* (1975), again opposite her real life husband Williams. **ACHIEVEMENTS** 1959 Emmy for her role in "Perry Mason."

HIGHLIGHTS While shooting the picture *West of the Pecos* (1945) she met actor Bill Williams. Behind the scenes of *A Likely Story* (1946), the two co-stars fell in love and married that same year. Williams would later become a household name on the Western TV series, "The Adventures of Kit Carson." (Also see his bio in this book.) They had three children, one son, a professional actor-director, William Katt (who made his 1976 screen debut in the classic horror picture *Carrie*, as Sissy Spacek's prom date), and two daughters. Hale appeared in all 30, two-hour color special "Perry Mason" television movies made during the 1980s and 1990s. She played opposite her real-life talented son, who also directed her. The shows were well-received by the public and critics alike. **QUOTE** "My Hollywood Walk of Fame star used to be in front of the world-famous Brown Derby restaurant. Now, it's in front of a parking lot! Well, as everyone knows, into each life a little rain must fall."

Ted Malone   1628 Vine
Host
BORN Alden Russell; May 18, 1908, in Colorado Springs, CO. **SPOTLIGHTS** Radio's top poetry reader of "poems that are famous and poems that are unknown." A program executive, he landed on air by default in 1929. When an act failed to show up, he was pushed in front of a microphone and told to fill air time. With nothing but a book of poetry near him, he grabbed it and improvised. In doing so, he unwittingly created a new show that would endure for 25 years (he was on it for 15 of those years). Ironically, as the first show neared the end of the broadcast, he was too embarrassed to use his real name "because I thought poetry was sissy stuff." He ad-libbed, "Ladies and gentlemen, you have been visiting with 'Between the Bookends' with Ted Malone." Balding and chubby, the "cupid of romance" united couples with his wonderful readings, and won a huge following of female fans who worshipped him. In 1935 he revealed to *Newsweek* magazine, "Sometimes I play games with them. Sometimes I make love. If I blow softly across the microphone, their eardrums will vibrate just as though I'd blown in their ears." In 1939 *Time* magazine wrote, "Malone is Prince Charming, Don Juan, and Galahad in one." Two years later, he admitted to the press that he had fallen in love with verse, and had amassed a huge home library. He was off the air for one year starting in 1944, to report as a war correspondent from Italy. As D-Day approached, he reported from London. Postwar, he was also a moderator on "Leave It to the Girls," and enjoyed another long-running series, "The Ted Malone Show." It featured news, edgy political editorials, stories, humor and travel reports. Died: 1989.

Johnny Mercer   1628 Vine
Composer, lyricist, vocalist
BORN Nov. 18, 1909, in Savannah, GA. **SPOTLIGHTS** One of the finest American lyricists of the 20th century. At age 15,

Johnny Mercer (left)

Charlton Heston and Sophia Loren

Mercer wrote his first number, "Sister Susie, Strut Your Stuff," and rarely put down his pen thereafter. He wrote and/or co-wrote 1,000 songs in his lifetime. Mercer was also a singer, and enjoyed great success as a vocalist in radio. His legacy, though, as a tunesmith started in the 1930s with "Lazy Bones," "Here Come the British with a Bang, Bang, Bang," and "Goody Goody." He became one of America's most prolific songwriters. His timeless classics include "That Old Black Magic," "Midnight Sun," "When the World Was Young," "Autumn Leaves," "Charade," "Fools Rush In," "One for My Baby," and "Come Rain or Come Shine." His upbeat, whimsical, light-hearted songs include "You Must Have Been a Beautiful Baby," "Ac-cen-tchu-ate the Positive," "Lazybones," "G.I. Jive," and "Jeepers Creepers." Singer Billie Holiday gave vibrant life to: "If You Were Mine," "Too Marvelous for Words," and "Sentimental and Melancholy." He co-founded Capitol Records with Los Angeles record shop owner Glenn Wallichs and movie producer Buddy DeSylva. They turned the company into a mega-recording success. **ACHIEVEMENTS** Oscars for: "On the Atcheson, Topeka and Santa Fe" (1946); "In the Cool Cool Cool of the Evening" (1951); "Moon River" (1961); and "Days of Wine and Roses" (1962). He celebrated his heritage in many tunes, but this Georgia boy's signature tune was "Pardon My Southern Accent." In his song, "One for My Baby," he wrote, "You'd never know it, but, buddy, I'm a kind of poet." Indeed. Died: 1976.

Charlton Heston 🎥   1626 Vine

Actor, spokesman, public servant
BORN John C. Carter; Oct. 4, 1923, in Evanston, IL.
SPOTLIGHTS A Hollywood legend and powerhouse, Heston is a tall, strong, sculptured Adonis with piercing gray-blue eyes. Heston came to America's attention in Cecil B. De Mille's classic five-star picture, *The Greatest Show on Earth* (1952), as the tough circus owner. One fan offered him high praise when she wrote a letter to the studio stating that the movie had truly captured the essence of a circus, and how Betty Hutton,

Cornel Wilde and Jimmy Stewart performed well in their parts, then closed with "I was also amazed at how well the circus manager fitted in with the real actors." *The Greatest Show on Earth* instantly made him a superstar. Heston plays a man raised by an Native American Indian tribe in *The Savage* (1952). It is one of the earliest pictures to show an Indian story from their (Sioux) point-of-view. Heston stars as Buffalo Bill in the Western *Pony Express* (1952), opposite Rhonda Fleming, Jan Sterling, and Forrest Tucker. While it seemed he might be forever typecast in rugged parts, he surprised everyone by convincingly playing a sexier role in *Ruby Gentry* (1952). He gives an exciting performance in *The Naked Jungle* (1954), opposite Eleanor Parker. Like a multi-faceted diamond, Heston shines from each cutting angle, although he would become best known for his dynamic portrayals of heroic figures in epic films: as Moses in *The Ten Commandments* (1956), the title role in *Ben-Hur* (1959—see Oscar info. below), and Michelangelo in *The Agony and the Ecstasy* (1965). About his title role in the spectacular historical drama, *Ben-Hur*, Heston remarked, "I happen to be one of two men in Hollywood who can drive a chariot. Francis X. Bushman is the other, but he's over 70." He took on a Mexican persona in Orson Welles' *Touch of Evil* (1958); make sure to see the director's cut. That same year, he plays the ranch foreman in *The Big Country* (1958). In the next decade, Heston plays the legendary Spanish warrior *El Cid* (1961). He is utterly fantastic in the shocking, sci-fi picture *The Planet of the Apes* (1967 and sequel). Next, Heston plays an illiterate, middle-aged cowpuncher in the fine Western drama, *Will Penny* (1968). In 1970, he stars in the adaptation of novelist James Michener's work, *The Hawaiians*, with Geraldine Chaplin, Mako, Tina Chen, Keye Luke and John Phillip Law. He offers a grim depiction of the future if the current population explosion continues, in *Soylent Green* (1973), opposite Edward G. Robinson. In 1975, he joins the all-star cast of the swashbuckler, *The Four Musketeers*. In 2000, he appears in Oliver Stone's *Any Given Sunday* with Al Pacino, Cameron Diaz, Dennis Quaid, James Woods, Jamie Foxx, LL Cool J, and Matthew Modine. It is no exaggeration to state that Heston attained legendary star status in the 1950s and has only gained in stature since. He has starred in more than 70 motion pictures, nearly as many theater productions, and innumerable television shows and appearances. His performance documentary, *Charlton Heston Presents the Bible*, received wide acclaim from both scholars and the public. **ACHIEVEMENTS** 1959 Best Actor Academy Award for *Ben Hur*. 1977 Jean Hersholt Humanitarian Award. 1997 recipient of the prestigious Kennedy Center Honors for lifetime achievement in the performing arts, one of just 105 individuals ever to receive, as the national cultural center describes it, "America's equivalent of a knighthood in Britain, or the French Legion of Honor, the quintessential reward for a lifetime's endeavor." The recipient of countless international citations and honors, Heston was elected six times as president of the Screen Actors Guild, served as the first Chairman of the American Film Institute and has authored five books. He served three years in the Army Air Corps (11th Air Force) during World War II, achieving the rank of Staff Sergeant, and spent two years in the Pacific Theatre. Since his honorable discharge, he has continued to serve both the U.S. government and public in a multitude of capacities throughout his duty-conscious life. Heston was one of the first major stars to campaign for racial equality during the early 1960s, well *before* it was a popular stance. In 1963, the noted performer headed a contingent from the arts community for Dr. Martin Luther King, Jr.'s march on Washington, D.C., an event that led to the passage of the Civil Rights Act in 1965. Later, as president of the Screen Actors Guild, Heston worked once again with Dr. King, helping African-Americans gain entry into the Hollywood technical work force. He has done chores for every branch of the armed services, films for a variety of governmental departments and, in 1982, traveled to India, Pakistan and Bangladesh to film a documentary designed to wage war against agricultural failure and the resulting famine. In 1984, the tireless activist went to Ethiopia on behalf of the Red Cross, followed by countless acts and efforts to aid humankind. Heston has one of Hollywood's most enduring marriages, to the former Lydia Clark since 1944. They have one son, Fraser Clarke, who is a writer-director, and one daughter, Holly Ann—who is a special events coordinator, plus their treasured grandchildren. **SIDELIGHTS** While shooting *The Greatest Story Ever Told* (1965), John the Baptist (Charlton Heston) stood in the freezing Colorado River baptizing scores of converts (extras). The converts were supposed to appear ecstatic after having their heads dipped into the water, but the water was so cold many came up semi-conscious. Afterwards, Heston looked at director George Stevens and commented, "If the Jordan had been as cold as the Colorado, Christianity would never have gotten off the ground." **QUOTE** "The Hollywood Walk of Fame is unique. As one of the early inductees, I'm glad to be part of so popular an attraction (though it's odd to realize people are walking on your face everyday)."

Arthur Fiedler 🎵   1624 Vine

Conductor, violinist
BORN Dec. 17, 1894, in Boston, MA. **SPOTLIGHTS** A first-rate musician and conductor, the debonair Fiedler possessed flair, humor and poise. Although famous for his innovative light interpretations, his repertoire included classical, light classical, jazz and other contemporary works. A musician for 15 years with the Boston Symphony Orchestra, he became conductor of the Boston Pops Orchestra in 1930, and presid-

Arthur Fiedler

ed over it until 1979, exactly 50 seasons. Considered one of the finest orchestras, its leader became affectionately known as "Mr. Pops." A lifelong Bostonian, Fiedler conducted huge patriotic spectacles celebrating America. His annual Fourth of July celebration was televised around the world. In addition to the May-July season, Fiedler put on Christmas and New Year's Eve concerts every year. **HIGHLIGHTS** He played the violin, viola, piano, and a few percussion instruments. **RECOMMENDED** Fiedler and his Orchestra issued a number of albums—some with odd titles—*Classical Music for People Who Hate Classical Music*, *Slaughter on Tenth Avenue*, *Boston Tea Party*, *In the Latin Flavor*, *Boston Pops Orchestra*, *Fiedler & Friends* (Special Guests: Chet Atkins, Duke Ellington, Stan Getz, Leontyne Price, and Kate Smith), and *Music for a Summer Night*. His best-loved, romantic waltz was "Wunderbar." **QUOTE** This distinguished conductor was famous for his informal indoor and outdoor concerts, mingling everything from Bach to Boogie Woogie in one show. About his musical presentation he stated, "It's like mixing a salad." Died: 1979.

Arlene Dahl 🎬   1624 Vine

Arlene Dahl

Actress
BORN Aug. 11, 1924, in Minneapolis, MN. **SPOTLIGHTS** A luscious, green-eyed redhead, she made her screen debut in the delightful comedy, *Life With Father* (1947), starring Irene Dunne, William Powell, and Elizabeth Taylor. Dahl's light comedy talent graced *A Southern Yankee* (1940), co-starring Red Skelton and Brian Donlevy. This ultra-feminine, ravishing and glamorous doll appears in the all-star cast of *Three Little Words* (1950)—a bright

MGM musical with some terrific tunes. She stars with Bob Hope in a charming fare, *Here Come the Girls* (1954). She gives another wonderful performance in the sci-fi family adventure *Journey to the Center of the Earth* (1959). Dahl had a supporting role in *Kisses for the President* (1964) a fantasy—oops, I mean comedy—about the first female president. She has made more than 30 movies...Her marriage to Fernando Lamas (1954-'60) produced Lorenzo Lamas, a handsome, dark-haired son. He is an actor. In 1991 she appeared with him in *Night of the Warrior*.

Alice Lake 🎥   1624 Vine

Actress
BORN March 23, 1897, in Brooklyn, NY. **SPOTLIGHTS** *The Infamous Miss Revell* (1921) and *The Price of Success* (1925) were two of the 50 pictures she appeared in; almost all were silents. Her career ended in 1934. Died: 1967.

Lizabeth Scott 🎥   1624 Vine

Lizabeth Scott

Actress
BORN Emma Matzo; Sept. 29, 1922, in Scranton, PA. **SPOTLIGHTS** A former *Harper Bazaar*'s model, she was seen as a hot, blonde defying "threat." With her sexy, husky voice, Scott was often cast as a cruel, deceiving woman in thrillers, like *Dead Reckoning* (1947) with Humphrey Bogart. The alluring siren delivers an interesting *film noir* performance in *Too Late for Tears* (1949), where she reveals her character's true nature after finding a bag of stolen loot. She is gritty in the melodrama *The Company She Keeps* (1950). In *Dark City* (1950) she helps Charlton Heston cuts his teeth in his first motion picture. Other movies include *The Strange Love of Martha Ivers* (1946), *Desert Fury* (1947), *Easy Living* (1949), *The Racket* (1951), *Red Mountain*, *Stolen Face* (both 1952), *Scared Stiff* (1953--a comedy with Martin and Lewis), and *Silver Lode* (1954). In the crime satire, *Pulp* (1972), she plays opposite Michael Caine. **QUOTE** "Nothing made me happier than to do things for the camera. It was as if I were mesmerized by that lens. In actuality I was performing for it. I was interested in pleasing it to the ultimate."

Arthur Kennedy 📺   1624 Vine

See page 57

Roy Rogers 📺   1620 Vine

See page 172

Jane Wyman 📺   1620 Vine

Jane Wyman

Actress
BORN Sarah Jane Fulks; Jan. 4, 1914, in St. Joseph, MO. **SPOTLIGHTS** A natural born talent, her mother hoped she would be a "Shirley Temple." By the time Wyman broke into films, she was a young woman. "I posed in bathing suits with Santa Claus, the Easter Bunny and the Thanksgiving Turkey," she said of studio publicity shots. After playing the chorus girl in a few bit roles, she landed a larger role in *My Man Godfrey* (1936), but had to wait until the 1940s to really come into her dramatic own. She gave a must-see brilliant performance in *The Lost Weekend* (1945), and was excellent in *The Yearling* (1946). Other films include *Larceny, Inc* (1942), *Stage Fright* (1950), *Here Comes the Groom* (1951), *The Blue Veil* (1951), *The Glass Menagerie* (1950), *The Story of Will Rogers* (1952), *Lucy Gallant* (1955), *All That Heaven Allows* (1955), and *Pollyanna* (1960). **TV** She starred as Angela Channing on the long-running evening soap opera, "Falcon Crest" (1980s). **ACHIEVEMENTS** 1948 Best Actress Oscar for *Johnny Belinda*.

SIDELIGHTS During the shooting of *Magnificent Obsession* (1954), Rock Hudson was so nervous that he made continuous mistakes with the dialogue. Each scene took thirty to forty takes! Hudson was blowing his lines because he was afraid of acting with Jane Wyman—an Academy Award winning actress, as well as it being his first dramatic performance. She never lost her cool during the lengthy and painful process. After it was completed, Hudson thanked her and commented, "You really went out of your way to be nice to me. I appreciate it." She responded graciously, "It was handed to me by somebody, and I handed it to you. Now, it's your turn." **QUOTE** Her second husband was actor Ronald Reagan (1940-'48), who became President of the U.S. (See his bio in this book.) After her third marriage-divorce, Wyman quipped, "I recommend marriage highly for everyone, but me."

Estelle Taylor 🎥   1620 Vine

Actress

BORN Estelle Boylan; May 20, 1899, in Wilmington, DE. **SPOTLIGHTS** A fabulous looking brunette, she stars in DeMille's religious epic *The Ten Commandments* (1923--as Miriam, sister of Moses). The heavyweight boxer, Jack Dempsey, was her co-star in *Manhattan Madness* (1925). In no time, the world champion became her real-life future husband. Her last film was *The Southerner* (1945). **QUOTE** "Years of training and experience are necessary before one can make a good actor or actress. It takes longer to reach fame on the stage than in the motion pictures because of the comparatively small audiences played to each night. When one has once learned the lessons and obtained a start in pictures, fame and success are meteoric." Died: 1958.

Fredric March 🎥   1616 Vine

Fredric March

Actor

BORN Frederick Ernest McIntyre Bickel; Aug. 31, 1897, in Racine, WI. **SPOTLIGHTS** After serving as an artillery lieutenant during WWI, he studied collegiate drama. He appeared in hundreds of stage and film roles, including *Anna Karenina*, and *The Dark Angel* (both 1935), *Nothing Sacred* (1937), *A Star is Born* (1937), *Bedtime Story* and *I Married a Witch* (both 1942), *Death of a Salesman* (1951--as Willy Loman), *Executive Suite* (1954), *The Desperate Hours* (1955), *The Man in the Gray Flannel Suit* (1956), *Inherit the Wind* (1960), and *The Iceman Cometh* (1973). **ACHIEVEMENTS** 1931 Best Actor Academy Award for his dual performance in *Dr. Jekyll and Mr. Hyde* (his interpretation is considered superior to all others to date); and a 1946 Best Actor Academy Award for *The Best Years of Our Lives*. "I'm just a ham," he said. **HIGHLIGHTS** In 1933 Samuel Goldwyn cast Fredric March and Anna Sten in an adaptation of Leo Tolstoy's novel entitled *Resurrection*. Goldwyn retitled it *We Live Again*. During a script meeting, the actor bemoaned his little part. Goldwyn patted him on the back and soothingly said, "Freddie, you got the best part in the picture." Then, Goldwyn saw Anna Sten frowning at this comment. He proclaimed, "And, Anna, you got the best part, too." **QUOTE** In 1920 he worked as a teller at the National City Bank, in New York. He said, "Inside me there was a bursting love of the theater, but I never had the nerve to do anything about it. Then one day I went straight from the bank to the hospital with acute appendicitis. While there, flat on my back, I began to think about my future. My mind drifted dreamily from a teller's cage to the Broadway stage...Stage versus Cage...After that, it wasn't really much of a contest." Died: 1975.

Robert Young 📺   1616 Vine

See page 601

Charles Bickford 📺   1616 Vine

See page 461

Leroy Anderson 💿   1616 Vine

Composer, conductor, arranger, organist

BORN June 29, 1909, in Cambridge, MA. **SPOTLIGHTS** The maestro of sweet-styled, uncomplicated music, he was initially taught music by his mother. This 1929 Harvard University graduate (magna cum laude) pursued higher degrees in both musical theory and foreign languages. From 1932-'35, he held the position of director of the Harvard University Band. Anderson's arrangements are still used at the school today. He came to the attention of Arthur Fiedler of the Boston Pops Orchestra, who invited Anderson to conduct and orchestrate. His career was interrupted by WWII. He enlisted in the Army in 1942, where his knowledge of Scandinavian languages made him one of the top translators. Postwar, he teamed with Fiedler again and signed a recording deal with Decca Records. He specialized in light classical music, and his instrumental combos were favorite dance rhythms. Recordings include "The Typewriter," "Jazz Legato," "Jazz Pizzicato," "The Irish Suite," and "Belle of the Ball," his romantic, enchanting waltz. In 1951 his "Blue Tango" was the first purely instrumental tune to reach the top of the charts on *Hit Parade*. **SIDELIGHTS** Anderson's "The Syncopated Clock" became familiar to viewers of TV's "Late Show." Died: 1975.

Geraldine Farrar 🎥   1616 Vine

See page 140

Eugene O'Brien 🎥   1616 Vine

Actor

BORN Nov. 14, 1882, in Boulder, CO. **SPOTLIGHTS** He quit his medical practice to act. On stage and the silent screen from 1917- '28, he thrilled female fans as *The Perfect Lover* (1919). He was frequently paired with Norma Talmadge: *The Only Woman* (1924). Died: 1966.

Norman Luboff 💿   1616 Vine

Musician, choir

BORN May 14, 1917, in Chicago, IL. **SPOTLIGHTS** A Grammy Award- winning composer-conductor under contract to Warner Brothers. Songs include "It's Some Spring" and "Warm." He also received choir credits on radio's popular musical drama "The Railroad Hour" (1948-'54).

George Brent 📺   1612 Vine

See page 140

Adrienne Ames 🎥   1612 Vine

Adrienne Ames

Actress

BORN Adrienne McClure; Aug. 3, 1907, in Fort Worth, TX. **SPOTLIGHTS** A charming, elegant lead, she appears in both A and Bs during her eight-year (1931-'39) motion picture career. Movies include include *A Bedtime Story*, *The Avenger* (both 1933) and George White's *Scandals* (1934). Died: 1947.

Ann Sothern 🎥   1612 Vine

Ann Sothern

Actress, singer

BORN Harriette Lake; Jan. 22, 1909, in Valley City, ND. **SPOTLIGHTS** A high-spirited blonde beauty, she enchanted audiences with her lovely voice. Possessing an attitude, she was terrific playing wisecracking dames with the heart of gold. It was made all the more striking by her arched eyebrows and pouty lower lip. Sothern appears in more than four dozen movies. She sparkles in both drama and comedy. She stars in *Maisie* (1934). It turned into an incredibly popular comedy series; she made in ten of them. She cast her real-life Scottie dog, Doonie, in a walk-on part in *Maisie Goes to Reno* (1944). Other movies include *Kid Millions* (1934), *Trade Winds* (1938), *Lady Be Good* (1941), the Cole Porter musical *Panama Hattie* (1942), the drama *Cry Havoc* (1943), *A Letter to Three Wives* (1949—a must-see performance), *Crazy Mama* (1975), and *The Whales of August* (1987—in an Oscar-nominated role). **TV** Her own shows aired from 1953-'61. **SIDELIGHTS** Her real-life grandfather pioneered a submarine design.

Donna Reed 🎥   1612 Vine

Donna Reed and Carl Betz

Actress

BORN Donna Mullenger; Jan. 27, 1921, in Denison, IA. **SPOTLIGHTS** A fresh-faced, quiet leading lady of wholesome roles, she was immortalized in Frank Capra's *It's a Wonderful Life* (1946), opposite James Stewart. Capra said of her, "Just perfect as Mary Bailey, her greatest role." The movie became a Christmas evergreen. Motion pictures include *Shadow of a Thin Man* (1941), *The Human Comedy* (1943), *See Here, Private Hargrove* (1944), *They Were Expendable* (1945), *The Last Time I Saw Paris* (1954) with Elizabeth Taylor, and *The Benny Goodman Story* (1955). **TV** She became a household name on "The Donna Reed Show" (1958-'66). Millions of children fantasized about having her as their mother. **ACHIEVEMENTS** 1953 Best Supporting Actress Oscar for *From Here to Eternity*—the one time she did not play a good girl. Reed stated that she viewed *most* of her parts before her 1953 role as Alma to be "namby-pamby parts with one emotion, one mood." Died: 1986.

Julia Sanderson 🎙   1610 Vine

Actress

BORN Aug. 20, 1887, in Springfield, MA. **SPOTLIGHTS** A personality from the first days of network radio, she formed one of the earliest husband-wife teams with her real-life spouse, Frank Crumit. They became famous in a series "designed to prove once and for all" whether men or women were smarter. Sanderson, captain of the female team, played against Crumit, captain of the male team. With questions written by editors of *Quiz Digest* magazine, Sanderson interrogated the male team, while her husband queried the women. The obvious name of this spirited quiz game show, "The Battles of the Sexes," ran on NBC with Sanderson and Crumit from 1938-'42, but it was never determined which sex was smarter. The pair had hosted numerous shows together. When he died in 1942, she hosted, "Let's Be Charming." Died: 1975.

Cary Grant 🎥   1610 Vine

Actor, singer, dancer

Cary Grant

BORN Archibald Leach; Jan. 18, 1904, in Bristol, England. **SPOTLIGHTS** One of cinema's all-time greatest actors, filmgoers came to know and love Grant as a sophisticated and debonair leading man with a sense of humor. Yet, his life started out as anything but charmed. Grant came from a troubled, poverty-stricken background. His parents did not get along; his father, who was barely home due to long work hours and hanging out at the local pub, had his depressed wife institutionalized when Grant was only nine years old. She had absolutely loved and cherished her son, and when he arrived home one day after school, his father simply told Grant that his mother had gone away, not telling him the truth. The child felt lonely and resented her abandonment. When his father and he moved in with his indifferent, cold grandmother, Grant's life became more miserable. Then, he discovered the Bristol Hippodrome, its entertainers, and a reason for living. Later he recalled, "I found myself in a dazzling land of smiling, jostling people. They were wearing all sorts of costumes and doing all sorts of clever things. And that's when I knew. What other life could there be, but that of an actor?" At age 13, the youngster ran away from home to join a traveling troupe of boys who performed comic skits and acrobatics in Pender's Knockabout Comedians. His father retrieved him, but relented the following year in 1918 and let the teen rejoin the organization. The 14-year-old thrived in the regimented schedule, and was trained in the art of mime, acrobatics, dancing and acting. There, Grant learned the necessary discipline to succeed in life. In 1920 the group boarded the British Olympic ocean liner (the ill-fated Titanic's sister ship) for the United States. He was 16 years old, and had been invited with his associates to perform at New York's Globe Theater. Next, they trav-

eled America's vaudeville circuit. After their engagement, the 19-year-old stayed behind, finding employment on Coney Island as a walking advertisement who drew attention to his sandwich boards by getting around on stilts. His biggest problem was the children who tried to get him to fall by tripping him. Grant earned $5-a-day during the week, and $10 daily on the weekends. He wanted an onstage speaking part. He landed a Broadway contract with the Hammersteins, then worked with the Shuberts in musical theater. In 1931, with encouragement from actress Fay Wray—with whom he had appeared in the production of "Nikki," where he played the character Cary Lockwood—he headed to Hollywood. Within one month, at age 28, he had a contract from Paramount Pictures at $450-a-week and his new name, which he had picked himself. He made eight films before his breakthrough in *She Done Him Wrong* (1933), opposite Mae West. West had seen him walking on the back lot and told her producer, "He's gorgeous. If this one can talk, I'll take him." It was in *She Done Him Wrong* that West delivered her famous line to Grant, "Why don't you come up sometime and see me?" (That is the actual wording. It has been altered through popular culture as "why don't you come up and see me sometime?") The movie was a gigantic hit for Paramount Pictures which re-teamed the two in *I'm No Angel* (1933), an even bigger hit. The sexpot dispensed this celebrated remark to Grant, "When I'm good, I'm very good..but when I'm bad, I'm better." The tall, dark and handsome leading man would go on to rule the box office for three decades. He excelled in light comedy and romance, but was wonderful in dramas and thrillers, too. Quite simply, he could do it all. Amazingly enough, Grant was a chronic worrier on the set, but you'd never know it by the screen result. Motion pictures include *Topper* (1937), *The Awful Truth* (1938), *Bringing Up Baby* (1938), *Holiday* (1938), *Gunga Din* (1939), *The Philadelphia Story* (1940), *Suspicion* (1941), *Penny Serenade* (1941—in an Oscar-nominated performance), *Mr. Lucky* (1943), *Arsenic and Old Lace* (1944), *None But the Lonely Heart* (1944—again nominated for an Academy Award), *Notorious* (1946) opposite Ingrid Bergman with one of screen's most memorable kisses, *The Bishop's Wife* (1947), *Mr. Blandings Builds His Dream House* (1948), *To Catch a Thief* (1955), *An Affair to Remember* (1957), *Indiscreet* (1958), *North by Northwest* (1959), *Operation Petticoat* (1959), *That Touch of Mink* (1962), *Charade* (1963) and *Father Goose* (1964). **HIGHLIGHTS** Many have imitated Grant's voice, but his grace, charm and style have not been equalled. When asked how he had reinvented himself after his childhood, Grant answered, "I pretended to be somebody I wanted to be until finally I became that person. Or, rather, he became me." About his debonair ways, Grant commented, "I'm a pseudo-sophisticate. But I play my idea of a sophisticate. Really, I play myself to perfection." **REGRETS** He rued the day he turned down the original role of James Bond (it was later given to Sean Connery). **ACHIEVEMENTS** 1969 Special Oscar "for his unique mastery of the art of screen acting." Married to two Walk of Fame honorees, first wife Virginia Cherrill (1933-'35) and fourth wife (of five) Dyan Cannon (1965-'68), 35 years his junior. They had one daughter, Jennifer, who is an actress. Grant was ecstatic with the arrival of his daughter. He adored her. He told friends, "She's probably the only perfect baby in the world." **SIDELIGHTS** With one of his best friends—former record executive turned movie producer, Gray Jones—Grant enjoyed his favorite recreation--watching boxing. Jones commented, "He was absolutely passionate about boxing. He would tape hours of the sport, then would tell me, 'You have to watch this fight.' When I went over to his house, I learned he had taped enough boxing to last two days!" **FAME** While filming *Houseboat* (1958) in Paris, France, Grant suggested to his co-star Sophia Loren that they take a stroll on their free afternoon. Worried about being mobbed by fans, Grant said they should disguise themselves. Loren, though, stated she did not think it necessary for her since nobody outside of Italy really knew her. When she arrived at Grant's hotel, she barely recognized him. He had donned a cap, dark glasses, and a shawl hiding his face. They began down the boulevard, where fans immediately sighted Loren. Grant was totally ignored. As they continued their promenade, autograph-seekers excitedly circled around Loren, again no one paid any attention to Grant. Slowly, on their walk, Grant's glasses came off, then the shawl, etc. Later, Loren giggled, "the only thing missing from Cary was a flashing, red neon sign pointing to him!" **ABOUT HIS HOLLYWOOD WALK OF FAME STAR** "I'm just so lucky. It's incredible to be this fortunate." **QUOTE** "I take good care of myself because it pleases me to stay handsome at a mature age. And it pleases the people who have to observe me. I've given up smoking and I've given up drinking. Now I can devote all my energy to the only vice I've got left—lovemaking." He remained handsome and charming to the very end; this legendary talent died in 1986.

Henry Rene ● 1610 Vine

Arranger, conductor

BORN Henre Rene; Dec. 29, 1906, in New York, NY. **SPOTLIGHTS** Called an "A & R" man (Artist and Repertoire), his recording and music for movies and TV from 1925-'75 brought him acclaim. He worked with such musical giants as Artur Rubenstein, to contemporary talents as Dinah Shore. His best-loved, romantic and enchanting waltz was "Always."

Richard Dix 🎥 1610 Vine

Actor

BORN Ernest Brimmer; July 8, 1894, in St. Paul, MN. **SPOTLIGHTS** Dix studied to be a doctor, but removed his lab coat for a university play and never donned it again. Hollywood screen tests showed his potential as the strong, silent he-man. His best 1920s work includes *The Christian, The Ten Commandments, Nothing But the Truth,* and Zane Grey's *The Vanishing American.* In the latter, he plays a Native American Indian hero returning from the battlefields of World War I to

Richard Dix

find his people being persecuted by self-serving white politicians and slick, greedy con men. He stars with newcomer Irene Dunne in *Cimarron* (1931)— the first Western to win Best Picture Oscar. **QUOTE** "'A clear brain can live only in a clean body,' says an old proverb. I heard it first when I was a child. It was good advice and I am passing it on to other young men—no matter what their chosen profession. Keep your body in the finest trim. Swimming, boating, horseback riding, tennis, golf, motoring, mountain climbing—all will help the actor. If the actor cannot find opportunities for these sports— let him join a gymnasium. When the blood tingles, when the muscles throb, when the skin feels alive and the head feels clear, the player is ready to perform any kind of role—rugged Western type or sophisticated evening dress character. I never begin a day's work without beginning with a regular physical tuning up. It adds the joy of good health to the pleasure of playing a good role." Died: 1949.

Clark Gable 🎥 1610 Vine

Actor

BORN William Clark Gable; Feb. 1, 1901, in Cadiz, OH. **SPOTLIGHTS** A legendary talent, and one of the most famous movie stars of all time, he was a man's man. He manufactured box office magic for so many years, that around Hollywood he was simply referred to as the King. Although he made more than 75 motion pictures, Gable was immortalized as Rhett Butler in *Gone with the Wind* (1939). About his

Clark Gable

charming, virile, devil-may-care portrayal of the dashing gent in that picture, Gable said, "The high spot in my career was Rhett Butler, and it has been pretty difficult to live up to it since." Gable was admired by all around the globe. Films include *A Free Soul* (1931), *Red Dust* (1932), *Mutiny on the Bounty* (1935), *China Seas* (1935), *Too Hot to Handle* (1938), *Boom Town* (1940), *Honky Tonk* (1941), *Mogambo* (1953), and *The Misfits* (1961—released after his death). **WORKING**

HABITS Clark Gable felt such an affinity for the working man that he carefully constructed his work day to run from 9 sharp to 5. Even if he was in a middle of a take, toward the end of the day he'd announce to the crew, "Five more minutes, boys!" At precisely 5 o'clock he got up and left. This ensured that all other workers on the movies—contract players, as well as behind-the-scenes staff—earned another day's pay. **ACHIEVEMENTS** 1934 Best Actor Academy Award for the comedy *It Happened One Night*...Married to witty beauty Carole Lombard (from 1939 to her death in 1942). **SIDELIGHTS** Even studio heads can be wrong about star potential. MGM said of Gable's screen test, "Awful, take it away." and Warners asked, "What can you do with a guy with ears like that?" Died: 1960.

John Ireland 　　　1610 Vine

John Ireland

Actor
BORN Jan. 30, 1914, in Canada. **SPOTLIGHTS** This entertainer originally swam in a water carnival. His career spanned 40 years and 100 pictures, covering Westerns, comedies and dramas: *My Darling Clementine* (1946), *A Southern Yankee* (1948), and *Red River* (1948). He was nominated for an Oscar for supporting role in *All the King's Men* (1949), and excellent in *Gunfight at the O.K. Corral* (1957) with Burt Lancaster and Kirk Douglas. His performances remained strong to the end: *Farewell, My Lovely* (1975). He played tough guy Jed Colby on TV's Western "Rawhide." Died: 1991.

Mae Marsh 🎥　　　1606 Vine

Mae Marsh

Actress
BORN Mary Marsh; Nov. 9, 1895, in Madrid, NM. **SPOTLIGHTS** One of the finest actresses of the silent screen, her theatrical craftsmanship equaled Lillian Gish. As a young beauty, D.W. Griffith captured her spirit in two classics: *The Birth of a Nation* (1915) and *Intolerance* (1916). She was unbelievably moving in *The White Rose* (1923), portraying an innocent girl who falls in love with a minister. After he seduces her, the coward disappears. As an unmarried, pregnant woman, she is fired from her job and thrown out of her lodgings. Throughout the ordeal she exudes inner strength, yet the audience sees the abject helplessness of her situation. Shot

in bayou country and directed by her favorite, D.W. Griffith, this is one of the most moving love stories ever told about that period of history. She worked sporadically for several decades. Other movies include *Hollywood Boulevard* (1936), and *Jane Eyre* (1944). Died: 1968.

Jimmy Durante 🎥　　　1606 Vine

Jimmy Durante (left) and Garry Moore

Comedian, singer, pianist
BORN Feb. 10, 1893, in New York, NY. **SPOTLIGHTS** Nicknamed "Schnozzola" and "the Schnozz" for his huge nose, this gravel-voiced singer-comedian is fondly remembered shaking his head and saying, "It's da condishuns dat prevail!" Along with his nose--which he had insured with Lloyd's of London for one million dollars--he possessed a unique, ungrammatical speech pattern and cheerful sense of humor that made him more than a novelty. He became a top paid entertainer with his famous nightclub act during the Prohibition era (1919 - '33 with the 18th Amendment to the Constitution which outlawed liquor), and went on to star on Broadway in "Jumbo," Cole Porter's "Red, Hot, and Blue" with Ethel Merman and Bob Hope, "The New Yorkers," and other hits. Amazingly, he was virtually a self-taught musician of ragtime piano, song writing and performing. His theme song? Why, it's "Inka-Dinka-doo." He wrote it himself. He also wrote tunes "Unbriago," and "The Lost Chord." Durante also favored the tune, "You Gotta Start Off Each Day with a Song." His film career spanned three decades (1930-'63). He made dozens of pictures, including *The New Adventures of Get-Rich Quick Wallingford* (1931), *Palooka* (1934)—where he is at his best; and *The Man Who Came to Dinner* (1941). In 1962 he co-stars opposite Doris Day and Martha Raye in the circus musical *Jumbo.* NBC radio: "The Jimmy Durante Show" was a musical comedy program which registered high ratings. Audiences loved both Durante's warmth, and how he butchered the language. He became known for his mispronunciation of malapropisms. His television show, which first aired in 1950, won the 1951 Peabody Award. His famous closing line was: "Good night Mrs. Calabash, wherever you are." (It remained a mystery who Mrs. Calabash was, but many speculated it was his late wife, Jeanne Olson, who died in 1943.) **HIGHLIGHTS** His friend, stage and screen star John Barrymore, once said to him, "You know, Jimmy, some day you should play 'Hamlet.'" Durante responded, "The hell with them small towns, New York is the only place for me." **SIDELIGHTS** Durante was always surrounded by friends and flunkies. He commented, "Everybodee wants tuh get inta da act." **QUOTE** "Dere's a million good lookin' guys, but I'm a novelty." Died: 1980.

Norman Taurog 🎥   1606 Vine

Director

BORN Feb. 23, 1899, in Chicago, IL. **SPOTLIGHTS** Onstage as a cute child actor, he began in films as a teenager, then by age 20 directed two-reeler comedy shorts. In this capacity, he moved audiences from laughter to tears in *Skippy* (1931). It stars his real-life nephew Jackie Coogan as a kid trying to raise a few bucks to get his pooch out of the dog pound. He directed an episode of the wonderful anthology *If I Had a Million* (1932). His funny plot is about an anonymous millionaire who picks names out of a telephone book to leave his fortune to. Other big movies include *The Adventures of Tom Sawyer; Boys Town* with Spencer Tracy and Mickey Rooney; and *Mad about Music* starring Deanna Durbin and Herbert Marshall (all 1938). In 1940: *Young Tom Edison,* starring Mickey Rooney; and *Broadway Melody of 1940* starring Fred Astaire and Eleanor Powell with a top Cole Porter score. *Girl Crazy* (1943) was the last teaming of Judy Garland and Mickey Rooney in a musical. It has outstanding Gershwin songs: "But Not for Me," and "Embraceable You." Dean Martin and Jerry Lewis star in these Taurog comedies: *Jumping Jacks* and *The Stooge* (both 1952), *The Caddy* (1953), *Living It Up* (1954), *You're Never Too Young* (1955), and Don't Give *Up the Ship* (1959; Lewis solo). He switched to Elvis Presley, and how could he do anything but succeed with the handsome, charismatic singer? Even if the critics poo-pooed the pictures, Presley fans loved them (and still do): *G.I. Blues* (1960), *Blue Hawaii* (1961) including the smash song "Can't Help Falling in Love with You," and the motion picture *Girls, Girls, Girls* (1962) had Elvis' tune "Return to Sender." In 1966 *Spinout* had weaker songs, but Elvis still gets the checkered flag. *Speedway* (1968) has "The King" falling for Nancy Sinatra. **ACHIEVEMENTS** 1931 Academy Award for *Skippy*. Died: 1981.

Leopold Stokowski 🎵   1606 Vine

Leopold Stokowski

Conductor

BORN April 18, 1882, in England. **SPOTLIGHTS** In addition to being a brilliant, flamboyant, innovative conductor, he played the violin, piano and organ. This British conductor became a U.S. citizen in 1915, and led the Philadelphia Orchestra (1912-'38), and the New York Philharmonic Symphony Orchestra. Recordings include *Tchaikovsky Symphony No. 5 in E Minor, op. 64;* and *Beethoven (Leonora Overture No. 3).* **ACHIEVEMENTS** 1941 Oscar "for unique achievement in visualized music" in Walt Disney's *Fantasia.* **QUOTE** Irritated by people coughing during his a series of his concerts, he told his Philadelphia audience that he would be leaving for a six month tour of the Far East. He added, "Goodbye for a long time. I hope when I come back your colds will all be better." Died: 1977.

Dick Foran 📺   1600 Vine

Actor

BORN John Foran; June 18, 1910, in Flemington, NJ. **SPOTLIGHTS** A tall, kind, fair-haired singing cowboy on the Warners lot. As Slim in the situation comedy "O.K. Crackerby" (1965-'66), he was an associate of the richest man in the world; a person who also happened to be extremely uncivilized. Died: 1979.

Webb Pierce 🎵   1600 Vine

Singer, musician

BORN Aug. 8, 1921, in West Monroe, Louisiana. **SPOTLIGHTS** A good ol' Honky-Tonk boy, he altered his vocal style to suit the song. He was cocky for upbeat tunes, but achingly expressive on ballads. Hits: "Wondering," "That Heart Belongs to Me," "Back Street Affair," "I Ain't Never," "Good Lord Giveth," "It's Been So Long," "There Stands the Glass," "I'm Walkin' the Dog," "Slowly" (the first song to feature the pedal steel guitar), and "In the Jailhouse Now." His trademarks were his silver dollar-inlaid Pontiac automobile and guitar-shaped swimming pool (it cost him $35,000 to build in 1960). Died: 1991.

Tim McCoy 🎥   1600 Vine

Actor, technical advisor

BORN April 19, 1891, in Saginaw, MI. **SPOTLIGHTS** He lived for many years on a ranch that bordered a Sioux Indian reservation to gain more expertise on Native Americans. After serving in WWI as a lieutenant colonel, he became a film advisor on Native Indian issues: customs, dialects, eating habits and costumes. He worked behind-the-scenes on James Cruze's *The Covered Wagon* (1923). Two years later, MGM signed him as a star. McCoy cared about authenticity and his work in Westerns is still acclaimed. Movies include *Winners of the Wilderness* (1927), opposite a young Joan Crawford, and *The Indians Are Coming* (1930), Universal Studios first sound serial. Died: 1978.

Orson Welles 🎥   1600 Vine

Actor, screenwriter, director, producer

BORN George Orson Welles; May 15, 1915, in Kenosha, WI.

SPOTLIGHTS *Enfant terrible.* Boy genius. *Wunderkind.* A gifted child, his mother was a concert pianist, and his father was both an inventor and factory owner. A precocious boy, he played the piano, painted, wrote verse, recited Shakespeare, was an expert magician and put on neighborhood plays. His mother died when he was only eight. His father and he took .off for a worldwide excursion that lasted several years. At age 11, he entered the exclusive Todd School, in Woodstock, Illinois. (His father would die one year later. A kindly gentleman, Dr. Maurice Bernstein of Chicago, became his guardian.) Progressive teachers neglected one of the basics, arithmetic, to encourage his theatrical growth. Ivy League colleges offered him scholarships, but after graduation—at barely age 16—Welles took off for Dublin, Ireland. Using his persuasive speaking powers, he convinced the Gate Theatre management that he was an established New York director and actor. After his acting debut there, Welles received shining reviews in the local paper and landed a one-year contract. (What the Gate Theatre did not know was that Welles also had a part-time job as a newspaper reporter and *had written his own review.* Which might account for all the outstanding adjectives he used to describe his performance.) By age 17, he won the role of Tybalt in "Romeo and Juliet" on Broadway. In 1937 he teamed with John Houseman to form The Mercury Theatre Group. The Group produced an avant-garde production of "Macbeth" with an all African American cast, in Harlem. He won acclaim from the theatre world for its fresh presentation. Welles' bigger-than-life showman personality expanded into radio with The Mercury Theatre on Air. He stunned audiences with the shocking October 30, 1938 radio broadcast of H.G. Wells' "The War of the Worlds." With Orson Welles' feverish delivery, the fictional drama of an alien invasion in New Jersey struck panic in the hearts of thousands of listeners not aware it was a play intended for Halloween. The narrator's powerful voice—used in a documentary type style—frightened some into evacuating their homes, causing national media coverage. Tinseltown called. This prompted him to remark, "Hollywood

Orson Welles

is just a small town main street filled with gossips. The only difference is that the gossips are syndicated." One studio made him an offer he could not refuse. RKO extended full discretionary power to the 23-year-old to make any film of his liking. This deal resulted with one of the finest—if not the greatest—motion picture ever made. In fact, in 1998 the American Film Institute voted it *the* best film out of the top 100 made since the beginning of motion pictures. The dynamic Welles co-scripted, directed, produced and starred in the masterpiece, *Citizen Kane* (1941). It was an astounding tour de force. He was showered with superlatives, invitations, and offers. One Hollywood insider quipped, "Orson at 26 is overshadowed by the glorious memory of Orson at six." Regardless of the brilliance of *Citizen Kane*, Welles was never given free rein at any studio again; his work was tampered with, edited improperly, or halted. Accountants were especially upset with his lack of financial savvy; Welles did not have the necessary math skills—or the desire—to stay on budget. In all, he directed less than a dozen feature films and a few shorts, including *The Magnificent Ambersons* (1942), *The Lady from Shanghai* (1948), *Touch of Evil* (1958)—make sure to see the director's cut, not the edited version—and *Chimes at Midnight* (1966). As an actor, he appeared in *Follow the Boys* and *Jane Eyre* (both 1944), *The Third Man* (1949), *Compulsion* (1959), and *The V.I.P.s* (1963). **ACHIEVEMENTS** 1941 Best Screenplay Oscar for *Citizen Kane.* 1970 Special Oscar. 1975 Recipient of the American Film Institute's Life Achievement Award. In 1984, he was bestowed the highest honor by the Director's Guild of America...He was known in Hollywood as a "triple threat; he could write, direct and produce." He could also act...He was married to Rita Hayworth (1943-'47). **QUOTE** A sometimes contradictory individual, his moods greatly fluctuated. Once he stated, "If there's one thing that I loathe, it's an exhibitionist." Later he declared, "I have no more dignity than a nude at noon on Fifth Avenue. Get this straight—I am a lurid character." To sum up his theatre, radio and motion picture career, Welles stated, "My only crime was youth." Died: 1985.

Fritz Lang 🎥   1600 Vine

Director

BORN Dec. 5, 1890, in Vienna, Austria. **SPOTLIGHTS** "Every picture has a certain rhythm which only one man can give it; that man is the director. He is the captain of the ship," Lang declared. There was no mistaking who was the boss on a Lang picture. He told the actors precisely what he expected from them in each scene by describing it in elaborate detail. He demanded technical precision from the stage crew with drill sergeant tactics. Lang was so disliked by his workers that many threatened to drop sandbags or heavy arc lamps on him. This negativity was not far from his art. His art tended to be more pessimistic than typical Tinseltown lore. He projected a horrifying glimpse into the future in *Metropolis* (1926), a standard for all history of motion picture college classes. *Fury* (1936) a searing, unforgiving story is about mob mentality and lynching. *You Only Live Once* (1937) stars Henry Fonda (as a hard-luck ex-con) and Slyvia Sidney as young lovers on the run from the law. His violent film noir, *The Woman in the Window* (1944) employs Edward G. Robinson as a married college professor who inadvertently gets involved with Joan Bennett; she misleads him down a miserable, sinking spiral. That same year, *The Ministry of Fear,* adapted from a Graham Greene thriller, has Ray Milland unjustly locked up in an insane asylum, eventually released, then caught up in a dangerous assortment of spies and double agents. *The Big Heat* (1953) stars Glenn Ford and Gloria Grahame in a story about police corruption and the mob. *While the City Sleeps* (1956), a nightmarish crime picture, has an all-star cast including Dana Andrews, Ida Lupino, Rhonda Fleming, George Sanders, and Vincent Price. These works illustrate his internal struggle with life's inexplicable inhumanity. Known as the master of (expressionistic) suspense, Lang plays himself in Jean-Luc Godard's scathing assessment of the movie business in *Contempt* (1963). Definitely put this on a "must see" list. **HIGHLIGHTS** He bravely made an anti-Nazi film, *Das Testament von Dr. Mabuse* (1932), before fleeing to America. He was forced to leave everything behind, including his bank accounts, and wife Thea. His wife supported Hitler, and she remained in Germany to write-direct many of the Reich's propaganda films. He became an American citizen in 1935. Died: 1976.

Kathryn Grayson   1600 Vine

Kathryn Grayson and Ricardo Montalban

Singer, actress
BORN Zelma K. Hedrick; Feb. 9, 1922, in Winston-Salem, NC. **SPOTLIGHTS** This dark-haired beauty with a curvaceous figure was an extremely talented coloratura soprano. While working in radio, she was offered a MGM contract. She made her film debut in the fun, corny *Andy Hardy's Private Secretary* (1941). She co-stars with Gene Kelly in the musical extravaganza *Thousands Cheer* (1943). The all-star cast also showcases Judy Garland, Mickey Rooney, Red Skelton, Eleanor Powell, Lena Horne, and Frank Morgan. In 1949 she appears opposite handsome tenor Mario Lanza in *That Midnight Kiss.* Her key song: "Celeste Aida." She was wonderful in *Show Boat* (1950), and *Kiss Me, Kate!* (1953), opposite Howard Keel. She stars in *The Vagabond King* (1956). In all, she made 20 films.

Tennessee Ernie Ford   1600 Vine

See page 130

Vaughn Monroe   1600 Vine

Singer, orchestra leader
BORN Oct. 7, 1911, in Akron, OH. **SPOTLIGHTS** Known as "the baritone with muscles," he was one of the most romantic looking band leaders of the swing era. He had a strong body, sculptured face and great smile. So dynamic a personality, the band could have succeeded solely on his sex appeal to the ladies. As radio host, he had a huge hit with "Camel Caravan," a musical variety show (1945 - early '50s). He recorded prosperously on Victor/RCA with such hits as "My Devotion." **TV** Fans adored "The Vaughn Monroe Show." Their favorite tunes were "There I've Said It Again," "Racing with the Moon," and "Ghost Riders in the Sky." Died: 1973.

Madge Kennedy   1600 Vine

Actress
BORN Aug. 1, 1892, in Chicago, IL. **SPOTLIGHTS** She made dozens of silent pictures between 1917 and 1926 before retiring, among them *Nearly Married* (1917) and *The Girl with a Jazz Heart* (1921). She came out of retirement and made a a few screen appearances from the 1950s-'70s. Died: 1987.

Frank Sinatra   1600 Vine

Frank Sinatra

Singer, actor
BORN Francis Albert Sinatra, Dec. 12, 1915, in Hoboken, NJ. **SPOTLIGHTS** Nicknamed "the Voice," called "Ol' Blue Eyes," and known as "the Chairman of the Board," Sinatra is recognized as the greatest singer of popular music of the 20th century. His massive collection of hits includes "Young at Heart," "Night and Day," "You'd Be So Nice to Come Home To," "Dancing in the Dark," "All the Way," "Strangers in the Night," "That's Life," "My Way," "New York, New York," "I've Got the World on a String," "One for My Baby," "You Make Me Feel So Young," "My Kind of Town (Chicago Is)," "Angel Eyes," "What Is This Thing Called Love," "The Lady Is a Tramp," "Mood Indigo," "In the Wee Small Hours," "I Get a Kick Out of You," "Here Goes," "Come Fly With Me," and "I've Got a Crush on You," among countless others. His mellow baritone, elegance and warmth, and natural rhythmic swing made lyrics seem like personal statements from him. He sang with great nuance, shading and inflection, and performed with a cool, tough guy persona which women found irre-

Frank Sinatra's star

sistible. Sinatra became both the romantic "Sultan of Swoon," as well as America's first boy baritone pop idol. He made his motion picture debut as the vocalist with Tommy Dorsey's band in *Las Vegas Nights* (1941); later, he practically owned the town as a Las Vegas headliner. In his first real acting job, he played himself in the musical *Higher and Higher* (1943). He sang the tunes: "A Lovely Way to Spend An Evening," and "I Couldn't Sleep A Wink Last Night." His first acting-only role earned him an Oscar (see below). Next, he earned critical acclaim for his dramatic performance in *The Man with the Golden Arm* (1955). Sinatra also showed equal ability in light musicals and sophisticated comedies. Films include *Suddenly* (1954), *Guys and Dolls* (1955), *The Tender Trap* (1955), *High Society* (1956), *Pal Joey* (1957), *The Joker is Wild* (1957), *The Manchurian Candidate* (1962), *Come Blow Your Horn* (1963), *Robin and the 7 Hoods* (1964--also produced), *Von Ryan's Express* (1965), *Marriage on the Rocks* (1965),*Tony Rome* (1967), *The Detective* (1968), and *Who Framed Roger Rabbit?* (1988--voiceover). He recorded about 200 albums, and made 63 movies. Stanley Kramer, who directed Sinatra in *Not as a Stranger* (1955) and *The Pride and the Passion* (1957), stated, "If Sinatra really wanted to prepare for a role, research it, he'd be the greatest actor in the world. He's darn near being that right now." In 1968, he stars as *The Detective*, as a New York City cop dealing with sleazy subject matter. The actor also appeared in numerous TV specials, shows and tributes. **ACHIEVEMENTS** Advertisements in the trades touted Sinatra's performance of Private Maggio in *From Here to Eternity*, as "the hottest thing in show business." He was. Sinatra won the 1953 Best Supporting Actor Oscar for the tragic role in *From Here to Eternity*. In a self-effacing manner, Sinatra stated, "I'm no actor, but I know this guy. I went to school with him. I've been beaten up by him. I might have been Maggio." Later, in 1970, he was honored with the Jean Hersholt Humanitarian Award. He was also the recipient of numerous Grammys, and countless music awards. During his lifetime, Sinatra quietly and generously raised more than $1 billion for charities...All his children are artistically inclined. His daughter Nancy Sinatra produced *Sinatra* (1992), an excellent television drama, starring

Philip Casnoff, Marcia Gay Harden, Olympia Dukakis, Joe Santos and Rod Steiger. **SIDELIGHTS** In his younger years, Sinatra was very skinny and suffered from fainting spells. He went to his doctor, who asked him, "Mr. Sinatra, how much money do you earn?" The singer replied, "Somewhere between four hundred thousand and a million dollars a year." The doctor stated, "In that case, I suggest you go right out and buy yourself some red meat. You're suffering from malnutrition." **QUOTE** When I asked Mr. Sinatra what he thought about his *three* stars on the Hollywood Walk of Fame, he answered, "That's not bad real estate for a saloon singer." This legendary talent died in 1998.

Frank Sinatra (center) receives an award from the President of the International Association of Chiefs of Police John Norton (left), and Arthur M. Kassel (right).

Hugo Winterhalter 🎵   1600 Vine

Arranger, band leader, musician
BORN Aug. 15, 1909, in Wilkes-Barre, PA. **SPOTLIGHTS** A former school teacher, he arranged for such great bands as Count Basie in the early 1940s. Singer Kate Smith adored Winterhalter's creative talents. He composed "How Do I Love Thee?" and "Far Away Blues." He favored large string orchestras, but enjoyed huge successes as recorder-arranger for jazz pianist Eddie Heywood with the instrumental compositions "Canadian Sunset," "Soft Summer Breeze," and "Land of Dreams." Records include: "Blue Violins/Fandango." His most enchanting and romantic waltz was "Around the World." He occasionally played sax in bands. Died: 1973.

1560 VINE

Art Linkletter

TV and radio host, author

1560 Vine

Art Linkletter

BORN Arthur Gordon Kelley, July 17, 1912, in Moosejaw, Saskatchewn, Canada. **SPOTLIGHTS** Adopted when he was one month old, he was blessed with a warm, loving family. The evangelical Baptist minister, the Reverend Fulton John Linkletter, and his wife Mary, moved their family to California when Linkletter was three. Raised around large crowds of religious folks preaching the Gospel, he grew into an eloquent speaker. Gifted with strong language skills, he could discuss any topic at length while fascinating the listener. In 1934, Linkletter graduated from San Diego State College with a B.A. degree in English and psychology, intent on becoming a professor. His scholarly path, though, changed when a CBS affiliate offered him a job as a radio announcer. With his quick wit, madcap sense of humor, and enthusiasm, his career took off and never stopped soaring. A television and radio star for more than 60 years, Linkletter has starred in two of the longest running shows in broadcast history. "House Party" featured unrehearsed and spontaneous interviews with children. It aired on daytime CBS-TV and radio for 25 years. A master of the double entendre, and a natural with facial expressions, he transformed innocent remarks into seemingly ribald (but harmless) plays on words. On one show, he asked a little girl what her mother had told her not to talk about. The girl leaned into the microphone and said, "Mommy told me not to tell you she's pregnant." Linkletter raised his eyebrows and dead panned to the audience's howls. "People Are Funny," a stunt show, ran on prime time NBC-TV and radio for 19 years. He appears in the hilarious comedy *Champagne for Caesar* (1950), with Ronald Colman, Celeste Holm and Vincent Price. **ACHIEVEMENTS** Among his countless awards are two Emmys, one Grammy, and 10 honorary doctorate degrees. He wrote one of the top 14 best sellers in American publishing history, *Kids Say the Darndest Things.* He penned 23 books including, *Old Age Is Not For Sissies*...Married since 1935, he holds a Hollywood record. With their children and grandchildren, the Linkletters enjoy the great American outdoors—mountain backpacking, swimming, surfing, scuba diving, and skiing. He walks the walk as a board member of the National Committee on Physical Education, and as Vice Chairman of the Center for Aging at UCLA.

Ava Gardner

Actress

1560 Vine

Ava Gardner

BORN Jan. 24, 1922, in Smithfield, NC. **SPOTLIGHTS** She was one of cinema's most alluring actresses and one of its greatest beauties. She of the high cheekbones was so stunning to look at in person that many people lost their breath upon first glance! When MGM signed this green-eyed, brunette love goddess, they lifted her from a horrible existence. Raised in a poor, strict farming family, she grew up shy, depressed, and unpopular. "I never had any ambitions to be anything but dead in those days," Gardner painfully recalled. Her rise was not meteoric, but once in Hollywood the actress had a variety of small film roles. The husky-voiced, sensual talent did not immediately click with audiences. Postwar, however, she broke through to stardom. Motion pictures include *Whistle Stop* (1946), *The Killers* (1946), *Pandora and the Flying Dutchman* (1951), *Show Boat* (1951), *Mogambo* (1953), *The Barefoot Contessa* (1954), *The Sun Also Rises* (1957), *On the Beach* (1959), *The Night of the Iguana* (1964), and *The Long Hot Summer* (1985). **SIDELIGHTS** She was married and divorced to Mickey Rooney, Artie Shaw, and Frank Sinatra. About these men, she lamented, "I found the one love in my life three times. The pity is my husbands didn't also find it." **PERSONAL NOTE** I spoke with Miss Gardner during a three-year period of researching and writing Max Factor at the Max Factor Museum, in Hollywood. (In addition to the archives, the outstanding art deco building housed a cosmetics gift shop, and fully stocked perfume and makeup warehouse; it was *heavenly to write there*). Gardner had become dependent on Factor's pan-stik makeup during her studio days and remained loyal to MF makeup throughout her life. There were several other MF items she could not find in England, where she was residing. Of course, boxes of cosmetics were shipped to her without charge. (Movie stars can always get products free.) Conversations with the grand movie star have been incorporated into my book, *Max Factor: Hollywood's 100 Greatest Beauty Secrets and Celebrity Stories*. (See my website at www.hollywoodfame.com for information.) **QUOTE** Gardner exuded a sinful sensuousness in her roles, although she stated, "Acting bores me. I have no need for money. This movie thing is not the end. I don't enjoy being a star...I am much better equipped for having babies. I wish I were Queen of England. She has a husband and two children and all the people love her. She has the respect of everyone." This spectacular creature died in 1990.

Tommy Sands   1560 Vine

Singer, actor

Tommy Sands

BORN Thomas Adrian Sands; Aug. 27, 1937, in Chicago, IL. **SPOTLIGHTS** A lively rock 'n' roll guitarist, he gained overnight fame in a TV drama called "The Singin' Idol" playing an Elvis Presley-type character. He appears in *Sing Boy Sing* (1958), and co-stars with Ray Bolger, Annette Funicello, and Ed Wynn in Disney's *Babes in Toyland* (1961). He appears with a young Jack Nicholson in *Ensign Pulver* (1964), and with Frank Sinatra in *None But The Brave* (1965). He is an acclaimed singer and nightclub/concert personality. He was married to Frank Sinatra's daughter, Nancy, for five years. **QUOTE** About being compared to Elvis Presley during the late 1950s through early '60s, Sands remarked, "I stand still when I sing. I like rock 'n' roll, but I don't want to be classified."

Dorothy Dalton   1560 Vine

Actress

BORN May 4, 1894, in Chicago, IL. **SPOTLIGHTS** A gorgeous brunette with dimples, she was an early silent star (1915-'24). Movies: *The Disciple*, and *The Mortal Sinner.* Died: 1972.

Ruth Ashton Taylor   1560 Vine

Broadcaster

Ruth Ashton Taylor

BORN August 27, 1937, in Chicago, IL. **SPOTLIGHTS** The first woman broadcast journalist in Los Angeles television got her start in 1949 as a producer in Edward R. Murrow's original documentary unit. Then, she became anchor of the CBS Saturday News; she was the first woman to hold that lofty position. She landed her own radio show, "The Ruth Ashton News Program." She also did feature reporting for "Ralph Story's

Storyline." **ACHIEVEMENTS** The recipient of broadcasting's top awards, her honors include the Television Academy of Arts and Sciences "Governors Award" Emmy, an Emmy for "Best Live Coverage of Breaking News," and a Golden Mike Award. **QUOTE** "Journalism awards don't mean anything to others. But the Hollywood Walk of Fame is a glamour thing. It's the only award that gets a 'Wow!' out of anybody. Even kids think you're somebody."

Mervyn LeRoy   1560 Vine

Director, producer, writer

General Patton (left), Mervyn LeRoy (center) and General Doolittle

BORN Oct. 15, 1900, in San Francisco, CA. **SPOTLIGHTS** The cousin of film pioneer/producer Jesse Lasky (see his bio in this book), LeRoy rose through the ranks behind-the-scenes. He started in 1917 as a wardrobe office boy folding costumes. He advanced to gag-writer status for one and two-reel silent comedies. He became a director in the next decade with his breakthrough film *No Place to Go* (1927). A top director during the 1930s, LeRoy's golden touch made a bundle for Warners. (He was so well-liked he married Harry Warner's daughter, Doris.) In 1931 he catapulted Edward G. Robinson to superstardom as a vicious crime kingpin in the classic gangster film, *Little Caesar.* At the end of the movie, Robinson gasps out his memorable dying line: "Mother of Mercy, is this the end of Rico?" The delivery was made all the more perfect by Robinson's mocking mouth. LeRoy's brutal realism and blistering depiction of a Southern prison camp in *I Am a Fugitive from a Chain Gang* (1932) remains shocking and socially compelling today. It stars Paul Muni, who gives a powerful performance as an innocent man who is falsely convicted, viciously treated, and tries to escape it all. Muni delivers this line after learning his pardon is refused: "The state's promise didn't mean anything. It was all lies. They just wanted to get me back so they can have their revenge, to keep me here nine more years. Why their crimes are worse than mine, worse than anybody's here. They're the ones who should be in jail, not me." The movie was Oscar-nominated for best picture, and best actor, but most importantly, it had a profound real-life affect on prisons. It reformed Georgia's penal system. During the Great Depression, audiences forgot their financial woes with *The Gold Diggers of 1933*. Its catchy tune "We're in the Money" remains a Depression-era classic today. There was nothing depressing about the Depression for him. In 1935 he was one of Hollywood's highest paid directors with an annual salary of $198,583. For MGM, he produced *The Wizard of Oz* (1939). *Random Harvest* (1942) earned LeRoy his only Academy Award nomination for best director. Greer Garson is stunning as the leading lady, as her shell-shocked WWI vet husband (Ronald Colman) suffers from amnesia. (Even after 45 years, and seeing the movie 50 times, Garson revealed at a USA Film Festival: "it still makes me cry!") *Madame Curie* (1943) was nominated for Best Picture, and he remade *Little Women* (1949) with Janet Leigh, Elizabeth Taylor, June Allyson and Margaret O'Brien. This Hollywood icon did a picture diametrically opposed to the sweetness of childhood, *The Bad Seed* (1956). It remains a gripping and suspenseful horror picture starring Nancy Kelly, Eileen Heckart and child actress Patty McCormack—all Oscar-nominated by the Academy. In it, Henry Jones taunts the murderous McCormack with this line about electric chairs: "They got a little blue chair for little boys and a little pink chair for little girls." Movies include *Five Star Final* (1931), *They Won't Forget* (1937--in Lana Turner's breakthrough role), *Thirty Seconds Over Tokyo*, *Johnny Eager* (both 1942), *Mister Roberts* (1955), and *The FBI Story* (1959). **ACHIEVEMENTS** 1945 Special Oscar for *The House I Live In*, a documentary short about racial intolerance. LeRoy directed and co-produced it, and Frank Sinatra drove the message home. In 1975 he was honored with the Irving G. Thalberg Memorial Award "for the most consistent high level of production achievement by an individual producer." **QUOTE** Slightly superstitious, he said, "I put the number 62 somewhere in each movie." Well, it worked for him. Died: 1987.

Billie Holiday 🎵　　　　　1560 Vine

Singer

Billie Holiday

BORN Eleanora McKay; April 15, 1915, in Baltimore, MD. **SPOTLIGHTS** Holiday was immortalized as the foremost female singer in jazz history. She first recorded with Benny Goodman in 1933, then sang with Count Basie in 1937, and Artie Shaw in 1938. Holiday was pegged a "Master of the Blues," which she rarely sang, but when she did, it was from her heart and soul. She co-wrote the song "God Bless the Child." Other exquisite songs include "Strange Fruit" (about lynching), "Gloomy Sunday," "Lover Man," "Did I Remember?" and "Fine and Mellow." She appears in the movie *New Orleans* (1947). Overlook the plot; there's great music: Louis Armstrong, Woody Herman, and Holiday. Plus, this is her *only* motion picture. **ACHIEVEMENTS** Grammy, Lifetime Achievement Award (presented posthumously). **HIGHLIGHTS** She was nicknamed "Lady Day" when she refused to accept tips without using her hands in a Harlem adult club. Diana Ross portrays her in *Lady Sings the Blues* (1972). **QUOTE** Known as a jazz instrument soloist, she explained, "I don't think I'm singing. I feel like I'm playing a horn. I try to improvise like Lester Young, Louis Armstrong, or someone else I admire. I have to change a tune to my own way of doing it." Died: 1959.

Mischa Elman 🎵　　　　　1560 Vine

Violinist

BORN Jan. 20, 1891, in Stalnoje, Russia. **SPOTLIGHTS** This child prodigy made his first public performance at age five. The virtuoso traveled throughout Europe, playing to sold out halls everywhere. By age 14 the great violinist had an audience with the British Royal Family in Buckingham Palace. He introduced Tchaikovsky's "Violin Concerto" at his 1908 U.S. debut performance. (He was naturalized in 1923.) Following World War I, he became one of the most recognized soloists of the 1920s and '30s, playing more concerts than any of his contemporaries. In December of 1958 he celebrated the 50th anniversary of his American debut in Carnegie Hall. Recordings include Mendelssohn's *Concerto in E Minor, op. 64*, and Tchaikovsky's *Concerto in D Major, op. 35*. **QUOTE** Feisty rather than temperamental, he once lashed out at critics who proclaimed his approach to Bach sentimental. He demanded, "How do they know how Bach wanted his music played? Were they there?" Died: 1967.

The Three Stooges 🎥　　　　　1560 Vine

Comedy team, slapstick artists

BORN Brothers: Morris (Moe Howard) Horowitz on June 19, 1897, Samuel (Shemp) on Mar. 17, 1895, and Jerome (Curly) on Oct. 22, 1903 (all born in Brooklyn, NY). Larry Fineberg (a.k.a. Fine) on Oct. 5, 1902, in Philadelphia, PA. **SPOTLIGHTS** The sultans of slapstick, they collectively redefined American humor. They started in vaudeville in 1922, then moved to Depression-era Hollywood in 1931 muckling and yukkling while they punched out 190 18-minute comedy shorts for Columbia Pictures and 14 feature films. The knuckleheads were famous for their use of nose-tweaking, head-thumping, eye-poking, face-slapping and hair-pulling antics. Moe was the pie-throwing ringleader of the bunch, but it was the original Curly who became the biggest star—called the Superstooge—of all the Stooges. Favorite catchphrases: "Why, Soitenly!" "Why, yooouuuu...I'll moida ya!" "Nyuk-nyuk-nkuk," and "Woo-woo-woo." Note: Six men played the role of

The Three Stooges

a Stooge during its nearly 50-year-run. Here's a brief history. Curly *reluctantly* replaced Shemp in 1931, unhappy about being forced to shave his thick, wavy brown hair for the role. As Curly himself put it, "I'm a victim of coi-coum-stance!" In 1946 Curly suffered a stroke, and Shemp came back to replace him. After Shemp passed on, Joe Besser replaced him (1955 - '58) until Joe DeRita took over the role in 1959. Died: Curly 1952; Shemp, 1955; Joe Besser, 1972; Larry, 1974; Moe, 1975; Joe De Rita, 1993.

Chester Conklin 🎥   1560 Vine

Chester Conklin (center), Charles Dale (left) and Joe Smith

Comedian
BORN Jules Cowles; Jan. 11, 1888, in Oskaloosa, IA. **SPOTLIGHTS** Trained as a circus clown, Mack Sennett cast Conklin as a Keystone Kop in zany, silent comedies. Known in the business as a "secondary clown," he supported the stars. His crotchety squint under his trademark walrus mustache and exaggerated body language complemented Charlie Chaplin in *Cruel, Cruel Love* (1914), and W. C. Fields in the feature-length

Tillie's Punctual Romance (1928). After making countless two-reel shorts, talkies came. Charlie Chaplin never forgot him; he cast him in two great films: *Modern Times* (1936), and *The Great Dictator* (1940). Died: 1971.

Al Lohman & Roger Barkley 🎙   1560 Vine

Radio personalities
BORN Lohman, January 15, 1935, in Sioux City, IA; Barkley, September 11, 1936, in Odebolt, IA. **SPOTLIGHTS** Teamed together in 1963, this duo became comedy kings of Los Angeles radio for 24 years. Lohman was known for his hilarious range of funny voices, while Barkley played the witty, straight man. The Emmy Award-winning team also performed in nightclubs like the Playboy Club and Coconut Grove. They both hosted and appeared as guests on many TV variety shows (such as "The Ed Sullivan Show"). They dissolved their relationship in 1986. Both continued with successful broadcasting careers. Died: Barkley, 1997.

Bobby Driscoll 🎥   1560 Vine

Actor
BORN May 3, 1937, in Cedar Rapids, IA. **SPOTLIGHTS** A sparkling gem of a youngster with dark-blonde hair and blue eyes, he exuded a natural sincerity. After making one film, Fox tested him for the key role of Al Sullivan in *The Sullivans* (1944). Director Lloyd Bacon said, "Bobby is the greatest child find since Jackie Cooper played *Skippy.*" Movies include *Song of the South* (1946), *So Dear to My Heart* (1948), *Treasure Island* (1950), and *The Happy Time* (1952). **ACHIEVEMENTS** 1949 Special Oscar for *The Window* as "outstanding juvenile actor." Died: 1968.

Charlie Tuna 🎙   1560 Vine

Radio personality, host, announcer

Charlie Tuna

BORN Art Ferguson; Apr. 18, in Kearney, NE. **SPOTLIGHTS** A legendary radio man, he is praised for his light humorous style and quick wit. The lively talent with the great voice has worked as morning drive personality for more stations and formats than anyone in Los Angeles radio history: Top 40, AC, Hot AC, Oldies, Talk, Sports Talk, and Country. Simultaneously, Tuna entertained millions daily on 400 stations worldwide on the Armed Forces Radio Network. From 1970 - 1995 he broadcast more than 6,000 popular music shows to American servicemen and women overseas. He is also heard on nationally syndicated radio shows, and is seen in three different internationally syndicated television shows. He is a TV game show announcer, and voice-over expert. **ACHIEVEMENTS** Rated one of the Top 10 disc jockeys through 1997, he is also winner of Billboard's "Personality of the Year" award. **QUOTE** "When I was growing up in Nebraska I remember listening to radio shows like 'People Are Funny.' They used to take their broadcast out on the street for an occasional skit. Radio being a theatre of the mind, all sorts of neon images would flash through my mind what that famous intersection must look like. Years later when I arrived in Hollywood I stayed just up the street from Sunset and Vine. In 1968 my parents visited me from Nebraska and spent their entire first day in Hollywood walking all the streets just to see the stars on the world-famous boulevard. There is no more significant honor that brings my life and radio career full circle than my Hollywood Walk of Fame star right near Sunset and Vine. It's a small town Nebraska boy's 'Impossible Dream.'"

Mae West 🎥   1560 Vine

Actress, writer, singer, author

Mae West

BORN Aug. 17, 1892, in Brooklyn, NY. **SPOTLIGHTS** A voluptuous platinum blonde goddess, she sashayed about in glitter, sequins, jewels and feathers of the gay 1890s, and ruled the stage and screen. She wrote many of her own scripts and was known for such witticism as: "Opportunity knocks for every man, but give a woman a ring," "It's better to be looked over than over looked," and the much-imitated (but not verbatim) "come up and see me some time." (See Cary Grant's bio in this book for exact wording.) The sexually provocative West became the world's most quoted entertainer. To the public at large, who held puritanical views, she was controversial. This did not hurt her career. While she maintained herself as a romantic lady, many newspaper critics called her "obscene," "immoral," and "filthy." West responded, "I'm never vulgar...I kid sex. I take it out in the open and laugh at it. I'm a healthy influence." Throughout her career she was known for her verbal dexterity. On love: "The best way to hold a man is in your arms." On herself: "I used to be Snow White but I drifted." On the opposite sex: "It's not the men in my life, it's the life in my men that counts." These fresh, fast, burlesque-style one-liners saved Paramount from bankruptcy. This former vaudeville star, and established Broadway star, made her screen debut at the unlikely age of 40 in a George Raft vehicle *Night After Night* (1932). Movies include *She Done Him Wrong*, and *I'm No Angel* (both 1933); *Belle of the Nineties, Klondike Annie*

(1935), *Go West Young Man* (1936), and *My Little Chickadee* (1940). **ACHIEVEMENTS** In 1935, she was the highest paid woman in the U.S. with an annual salary of $480,000...During her lifetime, the Royal Air Force named their inflatable life-saving vest after the buxom, shapely legend. She responded: "I've been in 'Who's Who,' and I know what's what, but it's the first time I've been in a dictionary." When George Bush's plane was shot down during WWII, the "Mae West" helped saved the future U.S. President...A true icon, she has been immortalized twice on the Walk of Fame. You can also see her likeness in beautiful stainless steel at the southeast corner of Hollywood and La Brea. (See "La Brea Gateway" in this book.) Praised with how good she was West quipped, "Goodness has nothing to do with it." That line became the title of her 1959 autobiography. Died: 1980.

Rick Dees 🎤   1560 Vine

Radio Personality, TV host, recording artist

Superstar Rick Dees with Jody Tults (from the Hollywood Chamber of Commerce)

BORN Rigdon Osmond Dees III; March 14, in Greensboro, NC. **SPOTLIGHTS** A terrific radio personality and prankster, this hilarious talent plays jokes on all sorts of people, no matter who they are. An example is his famous, crazy-making April Fools' Day in 1996 at Mayor Riordan's office in Los Angeles. Dees broadcast from City Hall, exchanging traffic tickets for concert tickets, among instituting other zany new city policies. While he was busy controlling the city, he had the honorable Mayor spin records. Besides his top-rated morning show on KIIS-FM, Dees is the very funny, quick-witted, knowledgeable host of one of the highest rated syndicated radio shows, "The Rick Dees Weekly Top 40." It is heard internationally with a large, devoted audience of 50 million people in more than 70 countries. His warm, friendly voice has made him one of America's most popular celebrities. He writes his own clever material, and smoothly slips in statements like: "Comedy is the most important facet of my career. But it's not the money, it's the amount!" Listeners tune in to hear his humorous take about topical issues of the day, which include, but extend beyond rock 'n' roll legends and trivia. He is also a capable interviewer of rock 'n' roll and pop singers, musicians, actors and sports figures. More than 35 million people tune in to KIIS FM/AM weekly. This attractive, affable performer appears in motion pictures, including including *La Bamba* (1987) and *Jetsons: The Movie* (1990). TV work varies from acting in prime time sit-coms to hosting "The Late

Show" and "The Grammy Awards." In the animated "Flintstones" children program, he does the voice-over for a character called "Rock Dees." **ACHIEVEMENTS** People's Choice Award for his parody of the disco craze with his platinum spoof, "Disco Duck." Received a Grammy Governor's Award and a nomination for his comedy album, "Hurt Me Baby, Make Me Write Bad Checks." He has received ten consecutive "Number One Radio Personality of America" Billboard Awards, and has interviewed virtually every major celebrity from the world of entertainment. He is married to the talented voice-over artist, Julie Dees. **QUOTE** On Jan. 17, 1984, Hollywood police were forced to close the streets for his star dedication ceremony so that the cheering throng of Dees' fans could see their idol *without causing auto accidents.* About his star Dees said, "Academy Awards are awesome, Grammys are great—but being part of the most famous sidewalk in the world—not even my Mother can believe it!"

Richard Wallace 🎥   1560 Vine

Director

BORN Aug. 26, 1894, in Sacramento, CA. **SPOTLIGHTS** Wallace was attending Chicago's Rush Medical College to become a surgeon, when he was forced to leave school for lack of tuition. He traveled with a circus as a merry-go-round operator and got off in L.A., where he decided to join a bigger circus—Tinseltown. He edited during the silent era. Later, he became known as a "lady's director." He brilliantly guided Tallulah Bankhead, Loretta Young, and others (1925-'50) through dramas and romantic comedies. *The Young in Heart* (1938) was listed one of the ten best films of the year and has an outstanding all-star cast. It remains a funny and entertaining comedy. Movies include *Captain Caution* (1940), *A Girl, a Guy, and a Gob* (1941), *Because of Him* (1946). Died: 1954.

Humberto Luna 📻   1540 Vine

Humberto Luna

Personality, host, broadcaster, actor **BORN** Zacatecas, Mexico. **SPOTLIGHTS** He is America's best known and most celebrated Latino radio personality. The popular host of "Luna & His Lunatic Listeners" morning show wakes up his audience with crazy humor and jovial chatter. "I think the people in the morning want entertainment. I talk about things in the news, jokes, gossip. I try to have a complete variety, but funny. To help people wake up with a smile," Luna stated. And if imitation is a form of flattery, Luna has received much adoration. His "zoo morning format" style has been copied by English language stations around North America. He, though, has maintained his top-rated status on station KTNQ/Los Angeles 21 years. Fans—who phone-in—love his lighthearted touch, but can also discuss serious issues. Luna has been known to make up zany characters, then make prank calls disguising his voice. One of his favorites is Dona Kika, a racy old lady. Can be heard via satellite across the nation and in much of Latin America. He also has a daily television show on the Telemundo network entitled "*La Hora Lunatica,*" which airs in the U.S., Mexico and Central America. In January of 1999, his radio station went all-talk so Luna went elsewhere. He signed with radio station KLAX-FM (97.9). He commented, "I'm very happy because I wanted a show with music. I didn't feel comfortable in talk radio." He plans to make it the top-rated station, even if it takes awhile. Luna stated, "I know radio and I know what people want, especially the Mexicans." Previously, he co-hosted TV's weekly series "*Hablamos de Cine*" (Let's Talk Movies), which was syndicated nationwide on Spanish television. Luna, a handsome man with thick, dark hair and a million dollar smile, has acted in 25 Spanish language films. On October 12, 1990, he became the first Spanish language radio personality to be honored on the Hollywood Walk of Fame.

Joan Leslie 📺   1560 Vine

Actress

BORN Joan Brodel; Jan. 26, 1925, in Detroit, MI. **SPOTLIGHTS** A fresh, pert, wholesome Warner Bros. talent, her auburn hair reflected her warm, radiating screen persona. She was often cast as the girl-next-door. In 1941 she offered support to an all-star cast in *High Sierra*. She was a joy to behold in *Yankee Doodle Dandy* (1942), and patriotic to the WWII boys in *Hollywood Canteen* (1944). Other pictures include *Cinderella Jones* (1946), *Born to be Bad* (1950), and *Hellgate* (1952). Leslie did a lot of live TV in the 1950s. Later works include "Smoke Jumpers," and "The Keegans."

Richard Farnsworth   1560 Vine

Richard Farnsworth

Actor, stuntman **BORN** Sept. 1, 1920, in Los Angeles, CA. **SPOTLIGHTS** For the first four decades of his long professional life, he worked as a stuntman. Since his screen debut in *The Adventures of Marco Polo* (1937), starring Gary Cooper, he has appeared in 300 motion pictures and TV movies, including acting as Roy Rogers' stunt double in countless movies. In *Comes a Horseman* (1977), with Jane Fonda and James Caan, he earned an Oscar nomination, and his career took a new turn. This talent earned Canada's best actor award and worldwide fame for *The Grey Fox* (1982), as an aging outlaw. Other movies include *Spartacus* (1960), *The Life and Times of Judge Roy Bean* (1972), *Resurrection* (1980), *Tom Horn* (1980), *The Natural* (1984), *Misery* (1990), and *The Getaway* (1994). He gives an outstanding Oscar-nominated performance in *The Straight Story* (1999), opposite Sissy Spacek. This sweet, simple, deeply moving movie, directed by David Lynch and presented by Walt Disney Pictures, received rave reviews by critics and the public alike. He received his Walk of Fame star on Aug. 17, 1992. **QUOTE** Throughout his wild riding, fist fighting, gun fighting, sword fighting and chariot driving, he claims his most spectacular stunt was: "Trying to get paid!"

Isabel Jewell 🎥   1560 Vine

Actress
BORN July 10, 1910, in Shoshone, WY. **SPOTLIGHTS** A gem of an actress, she co-stars with John Barrymore in *Counsellor-at Law* (1933), and Ronald Colman in *A Tale of Two Cities* (1935) and *Lost Horizon* (1937). Other movies include *The Crowd Roars* (1938), *Northwest Passage* (1940), *High Sierra* (1941), *The Seventh Victim* (1943), *Unfaithfully Yours* and *The Snake Pit* (1948). Died: 1972.

Hal Fishman 📺   1560 Vine

Broadcast journalist, news anchor

Hal Fishman

BORN Jan. 21, in Barcelona, Spain. **SPOTLIGHTS** A multi-award winning newscaster, Fishman began his television career in 1960, while he was an assistant professor of government at California State College, in Los Angeles. In June 1960, the scholarly, but videogenic gentleman was asked to conduct a course before one of the largest classrooms ever assembled. State-sponsored for college credit, Professor Fishman's course was "American Political Parties and Politics." His rostrum was located on a television sound stage and his students were located in their home living rooms, monitoring the class on TV. Both the class and Fishman were so well received that the station persuaded him to become a permanent part of their daily news program. A second career had blossomed. He joined KTLA-TV (Los Angeles) in 1965, the year of the bloody Watts Riots. His live coverage as a field reporter on the fiery streets contributed to the station winning both an Emmy and the Peabody award. He catapulted the station into the #1 ratings position for 264 consecutive months. Known as a news purist,

the venerable Fishman strives to keep his stories news worthy, as opposed to following an ever growing, popular trend of non-news. The fluff-puff pieces have slowly eaten away at the hard news stories, but *not* with Fishman's news. **ACHIEVEMENTS** He is the recipient of the 1987 Governor's Award Emmy, the first Amendment Award by the Anti-Defamation League, among many other honors. A licensed pilot, he holds twelve world speed records in prop, turbo prop and jet planes. **QUOTE** "I share this star with all those people who made it possible for me to broadcast from our studios in Hollywood and bring the news to our viewers for almost half a century."

Hal March 🎙   1560 Vine

Actor, comic
BORN Harold Mendelson; April 22, 1920, in San Francisco, CA. **SPOTLIGHTS** A busy radio performer, he worked in countless shows, including "The Alan Young Show," "My Favorite Husband" (starring Lucille Ball), "Burns and Allen," "December Bride," "Too Many Cooks" and "The Hoagy Carmichael Show" (he was part of the comic duo with Bob Sweeney). He teamed again with his comedy partner in "Sweeney and March" doing hilarious skits, then was part of TV history as host of the scandal-plagued "$64,000 Question" (1955-'58). Died: 1970.

Rod La Rocque 🎥   1560 Vine

Rod La Rocque and Marcelene Day

Actor
BORN Roderick la Rocque de la Rour; Nov. 29, 1896, in Chicago, IL. **SPOTLIGHTS** A handsome, dashing lady's man, he was an extremely popular matinee idol. Movies include *Stolen Kiss* (1920) and *Jazz Mania* (1923). He is superb in *The Hunchback of Notre Dame* (1939), starring Charles Laughton, Cedric Hardwicke, and Maureen O'Hara. His last film was *Meet John Doe* (1941). Later, he became a successful real estate broker. **QUOTE** Before

the age of big studio budgets, the chore of choosing the right costume fell on the actor's shoulders and the cost came out of his personal pocket. La Rocque said, "Few people outside the profession realize the really hard work which falls upon an actor in picking out the clothes he is to wear on the screen. Buying clothes for photoplays is a hard problem. Regardless of the shades you personally like in cloth—you must get colors that photograph well. Hence that it is often necessary for us to wear things that we would not select for street wear. For instance, the fad of colored shirts with collars of the same shade—came from a motion picture necessity. Motion picture actors found that light blue collars photographed better than white, and for that reason only began to wear them. Now the vogue is international. And leading actors must have dozens of suits. We cannot wear the same suit in successive pictures—and we must have several changes for each picture."...His marriage to actresss Vilma Banky (1927 until his death), was one of Hollywood's best love stories. Died: 1969.

Jack Carson 📺   1560 Vine

Actor, comedian, singer

BORN John Carson; Oct. 27, 1910, in Carmen, Canada. **SPOTLIGHTS** He usually portrayed one of three types: the backslapping pest, the bumbling, dumb guy, or the cowardly bully. Carson also typified the guy who never got the gal. This expressive talent stars in *Romance on the High Seas* (1948), in Doris Day's screen debut. Both appear in *My Dream Is Yours* (1949). Radio: He was on air in many shows, including "The Gulf Screen Guild Theatre" with James Cagney and Olivia de Havilland, and his own "The Jack Carson Show" (1943-'47; 1948-'49, and 1955-'56). TV: Hosted the "All Star Revue," and "Live, from New York, it's the U.S. Royal Showcase." **QUOTE** "A fan club is a group of people who tell an actor he's not alone in the way he feels about himself." Died: 1963.

Esther Williams 🎥   1560 Vine

Actress, champion swimmer

BORN Aug. 8, 1923, in Los Angeles, CA. **SPOTLIGHTS** Raised in Los Angeles, Esther's sister Maureen taught her to swim in the nearby Pacific Ocean. A natural born athlete, she won the Women's Outdoor Nationals in the 100 meter freestyle, with further crowns in the 50 and 100 meter breaststroke. An almost certain candidate for the 1940 Olympic Games, her dreams of gold were sunk with the explosions of World War II. She was appearing with Olympian Johnny Weismuller in a Billy Rose Aquacade spectacular, when discovered by MGM talent scouts. The beauty was offered a screen test that included kissing Clark Gable. Asked how she handled her nerves testing with the superstar, Williams responded, "Life is full of missed opportunities, and I decided that would not be my fate." Asked if Gable was a good kisser, she mused, "He'd better be, after all the experience he's had." She added, "Though for me, it was like kissing an uncle, I was 17 and he was in his 50s." MGM offered the beauty a contract, and she made her screen debut opposite Mickey Rooney in *Andy Hardy's Double Life* (1942). But it was in *Bathing Beauty* (1944) that she splashed colorful waves. She was spectacular in Busby's Berkeley's timeless motion pictures: *Neptune's Daughter* (1949) and *Million Dollar Mermaid* (1952). This world-class swimmer/entertainer became known as the "Million Dollar Mermaid" for her visionary water ballet sequences and for her top ten box-office clout. She swam approximately 1,250 miles during the 25 aqua-musicals she made for MGM. The perky mermaid possessed the quintessential combination of glamour

Esther Williams

and athleticism, setting an excellent example of well-being and beauty for women everywhere. With a lifetime devoted to the sport of swimming, as well as the health and recreational benefits of swimming, she created the Esther Williams Swimwear collection to bring women of all ages back into the water with their sun-sational fabrics and comfortable, swimmable fit. **RECOMMENDED** Her 1999 autobiography entitled, *Million Dollar Mermaid*, published by Simon & Schuster.

Tony Bennett 💿   1560 Vine

Singer

BORN Antonio Dominick Benedetto, Aug. 3, 1926, in Queens, New York. **SPOTLIGHTS** The essence of cool, and one of the greatest interpreters of American song of the 20th and 21st centuries. A grocer's son, he grew up poor in the Astoria section of Queens during the Depression. In World War II, Bennett served almost three years as a front-line infantryman in Germany. Postwar, he established his singing career spending many years in small cabarets and clubs. His first break came via singer Pearl Bailey who insisted he sing at the same New York City nightclub where she performed. Bailey advised him, "It takes 10 years to learn what to do and what not to do on stage. You can look awful good at the beginning, but that doesn't mean you can sustain." His big break happened at that same club where Bailey had gotten him the job. At the time—in 1949—he was performing under the stage name of "Joe Bari." Comedian Bob Hope discovered him, then changed the

Tony Bennett

young singer's name. "Bob Hope even taught me how to walk on stage," Bennett said. "He told me, 'Come out smiling. Show the people you like them.' To this day, I still follow those rules." This lyric baritone with a pleasing throaty edge employs utter sincerity in his vocals. The romantic troubadour is loved for his emotional and moving ballads, and is one of the top interpreters of classic jazz-inflected American song. With his innate sense of swing, and his obvious pleasure in performing, he has won over devoted audiences scaling generations. Hits include: "I Left My Heart in San Francisco," "Who Can I Turn To?" "Because of You," "Body and Soul," "One for My Baby," and "Stranger in Paradise." **ACHIEVEMENTS** The recipient of eight Grammys Awards, he has released more than 90 albums. Bennett has entertained fans of all ages during the past five decades. When he's not singing, he enjoys painting. Frank Sinatra declared, "Tony Bennett is the best singer in the business, the best exponent of a song. He excites me whenever I watch him—he moves me." Bing Crosby stated, "Tony Bennett is the best singer I've ever heard." *Tony Bennett on Holiday* pays tribute to the woman he describes as "a great influence on every singer" and "the goddess of style," Billie Holiday. **QUOTE** Early in his career he stated, "I mean I love nightclubs and TV and all that, but this concert work—now that's really something. Look at Liberace and Belafonte. I tell you if you do it right, you can't beat it. A few more years, and I'll get into it all the way."

Jeannie Carson 　　　　1560 Vine

Actress
BORN Jean Shufflebottom; May 28, 1929, in England. **SPOTLIGHTS** She played a Scottish lass surviving in New York in the late 1950s TV sitcom "Hey Jeannie!"

Corinne Griffith 　　　　1560 Vine

Corinne Griffith

Actress, writer, producer
BORN Nov. 24, 1896, in Texarkana, TX. **SPOTLIGHTS** One of the beautiful women who graced the silent screen, this dark-haired, oval-faced gem lit up *Miss Ambition* (1916). But in *Lilies of the Field* (1924), in which she starred and was the executive producer, she proved there were brains, too. She made

a few talkies before bowing out gracefully. **QUOTE** "There is no more fascinating 'game' in the world than the motion picture—and none more fickle or difficult to 'break into.' The novice must be ready to face its many ups and downs if success may ever be attained." Died: 1979.

Helen Vinson 　　　　1560 Vine

Actress
BORN Sept. 17, 1907, in Beaumont, TX. **SPOTLIGHTS** Broadway-trained, this New York socialite's 17-year screen career included wonderful supporting and leading roles in *I Am a Fugitive from a Chain Gang* (1932), *Broadway Bill* (1934), and *The Thin Man Goes Home* (1945).

Kurt Kreuger 　　　　1560 Vine

Actor
BORN July 23, 1916, in Michenberg, Germany. **SPOTLIGHTS** Exceedingly well-educated and multi-lingual, he was raised in Switzerland. He attended London's School of Economics, then Columbia University in N.Y. He was frightfully believable as a Nazi officer and soldier: *The Strange Death of Adolf Hitler* (1943), *Hotel Berlin* (1945), and *Paris Underground* (1945). In real life, he pledged his allegiance to the United States.

Jean Hagen 　　　　1560 Vine

Actress
BORN Jean Verhagen, Aug. 3, 1923, in Chicago, IL. **SPOTLIGHTS** This perky talent was wonderful in *Adam's Ribs* (1949) with Spencer Tracy, Katherine Hepburn and Judy Holliday; moving in *The Asphalt Jungle* (1950), and chirpy in *Singin' in the Rain* (1952). As Mrs. Margaret Williams (1953-'56) she was the happy, loving mother and wife on "The Danny Thomas Show." Died: 1977.

Marvin Gaye 　　　　1500 Vine

Marvin Gaye

Singer, songwriter, composer
BORN Marvin Pentz Gaye, Jr.; April 2, 1939, in Washington, D.C. **SPOTLIGHTS** A legendary Motown artist, his musical gifts were apparent from age three, when Gaye began singing in the church where his father was a minister. By age five, he was playing the organ and piano on the Sabbath. As he absorbed the abundant imprint of gospel—that would later manifest in his exquisite solos—his talent grew as he did. After serving in the Air Force, he sang in street-cor-

ner doo-wop groups, where his mellifluous tenor and three-octave range brought recognition from such greats as Bo Diddley. In 1961, while singing at a party in Detroit, he was heard and signed by Berry Gordy, Jr., of Motown Records. Although Gaye wanted to do ballads, Gordy convinced him to record "Stubborn Kind of Fellow" (1962), which topped the R&B charts. This handsome, charismatic vocalist specialized in mid-tempo ballads. His classic collection of hits includes "I'll Be Doggone," "Ain't That Peculiar," "Pride and Joy," and "How Sweet It Is to Be Loved by You." He became Motown's "sweetheart" and their grittiest male singer. Gaye sang duet with Tammi Terrell (while Ashford and Simpson wrote and produced): "Ain't No Mountain High Enough," "Your Precious Love" and "Ain't Nothing Like the Real Thing." He continued through the 1970s with his Grammy-winning album, *What's Going On*, which he also co-produced. This was the first Motown album shaped away from the hit production line, with the songs more expansive both lyrically and musically. Others include *Let's Get It On; Diana and Marvin (with Diana Ross)*, and *The Best of Marvin Gaye*. He enjoyed many hit singles, including the #1 hit, "Got to Give It Up, Pt. 1." He continued into his third decade—the 1980s—as the most memorable pop artist with "Sexual Healing." A revered genius, his sensual, spiritual music combined with haunting, poetic lyrics to form true works of pop beauty. **ACHIEVEMENTS** 1982 Grammy Award for his album *Midnight Love*. He was inducted into the Rock and Roll Hall of Fame posthumously in 1987. His friends—Berry Gordy, Suzanne DePasse, Smokey Robinson and Eddie Murphy— nominated and petitioned the Hollywood Walk of Fame committee to get Gaye a star. Murphy wrote: "My work causes me to spend a great deal of time in Los Angeles and so I have on a number of occasions walked parts of the Walk of Fame. Most of the greats of our business have been given their rightful due. An important quality of each of those that you have honored is that they had a special niche that was their kingdom. I will assure you that Marvin Gaye is no different: he established an immense artistic kingdom which is still expanding. I know that you would be doing his millions of fans a special honor by including him, and indirectly them, in your Walk of Fame." With dozens of celebrities in attendance and Gaye's three children—Marvin III, Frankie and Nona—his shining Hollywood Walk of Fame star was dedicated on Sept. 27, 1990. This gleaming terrazzo and bronze monument is a testament to his artistry. **QUOTE** "I think music is God. It's one of the closest kinships with God we can possibly experience. I think it's a common vibrating tone of musical notes that holds all life together." Died: 1984.

Mary Martin 🔘   1560 Vine

Actress, singer, dancer

BORN Virginia Martin; Dec. 1, 1913, in Weatherford, TX. **SPOTLIGHTS** Blessed with all-American, girl-next-door looks and a clear soprano voice, she earned recognition with "My Heart Belongs to Daddy" in the Cole Porter story "Leave It to

Me" (aka "Night and Day"). But it was "One Touch of Venus" in 1943 that established Martin as a Broadway musical star. Her next hit was "Annie Get Your Gun" in the touring company; a part in which she wowed audiences. In 1949 she dazzled audiences in the role of a lifetime, that of the unsophisticated army nurse, in "South Pacific." It seemed as if she had been born to play the role. She was

Mary Martin (right) as Peter Pan

paired with opera basso Ezio Pinza in perfect casting. Rogers & Hammerstein's "I'm Gonna Wash That Man Right Out of My Hair," "A Wonderful Guy," "A Cockeyed Optimist" and "Honey-Bun" became Martin's signature songs. With the perfect complement of romance, verve and style, she exemplified musical theater at its most accomplished level. The show, an historic high-mark for the bright lights of Broadway, ran for an impressive 1925 performances. Martin also played "Peter Pan" on Broadway. About the musical she said, "It took me 13 years to do it, but our motto is, 'Once You Have Dreamed It, Never Let It Go.'" (In 1960 she starred in the enchanting TV version.) She was the female lead in the hugely successful von Trapp story, "The Sound of Music." The musical opened in the 1959-'60 season, preceding the movie by five years. Her warmth and energy are conveyed in her many splendid recordings. Movies include *Happy Go Lucky* (1943), and *Night and Day* (1946). **ACHIEVEMENTS** Her son is actor Larry Hagman...The recipient of two Tonys for "South Pacific," and "The Sound of Music," she won a Peabody Award for the 1979 telefilm "Valentine." In 1989 she proudly accepted the prestigious Kennedy Center Honor. Died: 1990.

Larry Hagman 🎥   1560 Vine

Actor, producer, director

BORN Sept. 21, 1931, in Fort Worth, TX. **SPOTLIGHTS** He is the son of the gifted Broadway actress-singer, Mary Martin, and attorney Ben Hagman. As the United States does not need another lawyer, we are all grateful that Hagman decided to follow in his mother's theatrical footsteps. He trained in Theatre-in-the-Round, in Dallas, and regional theater in New York, before moving to England. There, he joined his mother's big stage hit, "South Pacific" for five years, before enlisting in the U.S. Air Force, where he produced and directed shows for ser-

Larry Hagman

vicemen. After his honorable discharge, Hagman returned to a series of Broadway and off-Broadway plays. He landed a gig in the daytime soap opera "The Edge of Night," but found his greatest success in prime time shows, starting with the comedy series "I Dream of Jeannie" (1965-'70). He played the amiable astronaut Captain (later Major) Tony Nelson, whose life is complicated by a well-meaning, devoted, beautiful blonde genie (Barbara Eden). It was not until 1978, when the dramatic series "Dallas" premiered, that Hagman became a worldwide celebrity. He played the larger-than-life oil tycoon John Ross (J.R.) Ewing, Jr., a despicable, corrupt, merciless, lying, cheating (and loving every minute of it) S.O.B. Hagman was the star of the show, the man everyone loved to hate, and the reason that on March 21, 1980 more than 350 million fans in 57 countries tuned in to find out "Who shot J.R.?" The series—which Hagman occasionally directed—ran for an unprecedented 13 seasons, with additional movies, like "Dallas: JR Returns," another ratings blockbuster for CBS. Motion pictures include *Ensign Pulver* (1964), *The Group* (1966), *No Place to Run* (1972), *Harry and Tonto* (1974), *The Eagle Has Landed* (1977), *Superman* (1978), Oliver Stone's *Nixon* (1995) and *Primary Colors* (1998). **ACHIEVEMENTS** In addition to critical acclaim for his work, Hagman is an adamant non-smoker. He chaired the American Cancer Society's "Great American Smokeout" from 1981 to 1992...After having received a liver transplant in 1995, he serves as an advocate of organ donation and transplantation.

Dick Powell 🎙   1560 Vine

See page 4

John Philip Sousa 💿   1500 Vine

Composer, band leader
BORN Nov. 6, 1854, in Washington, D.C. **SPOTLIGHTS** Musical spokesman of a proud, young country, Sousa composed America's national march—the big, beautiful, brassy "The Stars and Stripes Forever." It had been inspired by God and the American flag, the composer was fond of saying. He was traveling on a steamship voyage from Europe to America, when he learned his dear friend and manager had died. Sousa felt particularly at odds, as well as extremely homesick. In his autobiography, *Marching Along*, Sousa wrote, "As the vessel steamed out of the harbor, I was pacing the deck, absorbed in the thoughts of my manager's death...Suddenly I began to sense the rhythmic beat of a band playing within my brain. It

John Philip Sousa

kept on ceaselessly, playing, playing, playing. Throughout the whole tense voyage, that imaginary band continued to unfold the same themes, echoing and re-echoing the most distinct melody. I did not transfer a note of that music to paper while I was on the steamer, but when we reached shore, I set down the measures that my brain-band had been playing for me, and not a note of it has ever been changed." Sousa composed entire works *in his mind* with great speed. The first performance of "The Stars and Stripes Forever" took place on May 14, 1897, at Philadelphia's Academy of Music, with U.S. President William McKinley in attendance. The enthusiastic audience demanded two encores before Sousa could leave the stage. This beloved march—with its florid brass and piccolo—lasts three minutes and 45 seconds when played at march tempo. The three parts of the piece represent three areas of the United States; the main melody is the North, the South is represented by the piccolo obbligato, and the daring West by the trombone counter melody. "The Stars and Stripes Forever" is universally agreed to be the finest march ever composed, a true masterpiece. Music critic Harold Schonberg declared that it was, "the most perfect piece of American music ever written." Sousa told a reporter for the *Washington Times* that it, "...is intended to convey the feeling of the homeward-bound Americans. Most Americans are more strongly impressed with the grandeur of their native country when they return from a ramble in some strange land than when they are at home. It is on the return voyage that the patriotism swells, under the rapture of the moment, and 'The Stars and Stripes Forever' was written under the press of such feelings." He also arranged for piano, guitar, mandolin, zither, mixed chorus, the popular male quartet of the time, and wrote comic operettas, suites, waltzes, songs, and more. Marches include "The Salvation Army" and "Semper Fidelis" (which is traditionally known as the march of the U.S. Marine Corps). In all, he wrote 136 marches. Other Sousa works include "El Capitan," "Hands Across the Sea," "Liberty Bell," and "The Thunderer." His father had been in the U.S. Marine Band, and Sousa himself joined as an apprentice musician in his youth. He accepted leadership of the "The President's Own" United States Marine Band in 1880, becoming its 17th leader. Nine years later, he wrote the splendid march called, "The Washington Post." Slightly adapted, it rode the wave of popularity with the new "two-step" dance, becoming America and Europe's most requested tune. It was then that a British journalist called Sousa "The March King," a name that has remained to this day. When he left the U.S. Marine Corps in 1892—after 12 years of service—he formed the Sousa Band, a civilian concert band, which he would lead for 39 years. This extremely polished showman traveled the globe four times to bring American band music to Europe and Asia. Conscious of never wanting to bore his audience, his concerts were entertaining as well as musically inspiring. During 40 years of concert tours, there was never a concert that did not play the "The Stars and Stripes Forever." **HIGHLIGHTS** His early training was in classical violin. As an adult, he frequently took an imaginary violin and played it, while fingering the imaginary strings. He could hear the violin music in his head. He had the Sousaphone built for his musical requirements with the "bell-up" in the early 1890s....His bandsman's jacket included 36 yards of fine braid. It can be viewed at the Sousa Archives, Univ. of Illinois, in Urbana. Its capable curator is Phyllis Danner. Website: www.library.uiuc.edu/sousa. "THE PRESIDENT'S OWN" U.S. Marine Band: Thanks to LtCol Timothy W. Foley, director, and MGySgt Mike Ressler, chief librarian, in Washington, DC for their assistance in supplying historical research and photograph. **FILM** *Stars and Stripes Forever* (1952) is a movie based on his life—using ample poetic license—starring Clifton Webb, Robert Wagner and Ruth Hussey. There's plenty of music; it gives a rousing imitation of his symphony orchestra in brass. **ACHIEVEMENTS** Director of the United States Marine Band under five U.S. Presidents...Internationally recognized as one of America's greatest composers and showmen...He helped Victor Herbert establish the American Society of Composers, Authors, and Publishers (ASCAP)...The House and Senate passed legislation to officially designate Sousa's "The Stars and Stripes Forever" the national march, and on Dec. 11, 1987 President Reagan signed the bill...Sousa died in 1932 and was one of only 99 citizens enshrined in the Hall of Fame for Great Americans. The enshrinement occurred during the country's Bicentennial celebration with the U.S. Marine Band playing his beloved march. Sousa's Hollywood Walk of Fame star was awarded posthumously on Flag Day, June 14, 1990.

Evelyn Venable and Phil Regan

Evelyn Venable
1500 Vine

Actress

BORN Oct. 18, 1913, in Cincinnati, OH. **SPOTLIGHTS** Raised a vegetarian, Evelyn never tasted meat or fish in her life. "I don't eat any organism with a conscious life," was her quiet motto. This demure, intelligent beauty came from a family of writers and teachers, so it's little surprise she won a four-year scholarship to Vassar. She also studied at the University of Cincinnati, although she never enrolled in a drama class. Later, she toured with Hampden's road company, then was spotted by a Paramount Pictures talent scout. Films include *Mrs. Wiggs of the Cabbage Patch* (1934), *Death Takes a Holiday* (1934), *David Harum* (1934), and *Alice Adams* (1935). She was married to Oscar-winning cinematographer Hal Mohr, and retired to raise their family. Later, she taught at UCLA. Died: 1993.

Yakima Canutt   1500 Vine

Stuntman, supporting actor

Yakima "Yak" Canutt

BORN Enos Canut; Nov. 29, 1895, in Colfax, WA. **SPOTLIGHTS** Fellow Hollywood Walk of Fame honoree, actor Charlton Heston, wrote this in honor of the legendary Yak: "The first and perhaps the best of the great stunt men, he transformed a suicidal gamble into a modern profession." Previously, Canutt had been a world champion rodeo cowboy (twice) who made an easy transition to the silver screen during the silent era. This was a wild ride in the movie business, when a stuntman was basically an untrained fool willing to take a risk--without any safety precautions. A fellow stuntman once admitted, "I get $22-a-week, and they've broken 22 of my bones. That's a dollar a bone." Canutt made stunts a serious business, work to be accomplished with safety in mind. He took these cautionary skills into the sound era. Every superstar director used him to design and direct dangerous action sequences. He worked in hundreds of motion pictures, including *Stagecoach*, and *Gone with the Wind* (both 1939). He was the second-unit director on *Ben Hur* (1959). **ACHIEVEMENTS** 1966 Special Oscar for "achievement as a stuntman and for the development of safety devices used by stuntmen everywhere." His son, Joe, has followed in his father's tricky footsteps. **QUOTE** While doubling for John Wayne in a fight sequence against beefy, bull-like Noah Beery, the latter got into a nasty argument with the producer. Noah vilely cussed the producer out in front of the entire crew. The humiliated producer secretly pulled Yak aside and asked him for a favor. He wanted Yak to really rough Noah up during the fight scene. Yak responded, "Sure, I'd be happy to beat the living daylights out of him on one condition." The producer asked what that was. Yak declared, "That you get Noah to call me the same names he's been calling you." Died: 1986 (he had been the longest-living stuntman).

Jinx Falkenburg 🎥   1500 Vine

Jinx Falkenburg

Performer

BORN Eugenia Falkenburg, Jan. 21, 1919, in Barcelona, Spain. **SPOTLIGHTS** The top outdoor-type, all-American magazine "Cover Girl," she graced more than 200 magazine covers. Falkenburg began her screen career in 1939 with the serial *The Lone Ranger Rides Again*. About her movie roles, she stated, "I spent six years trying to get into pictures, and even *I* wasn't very impressed with the end results." She appeared in *Song of the Buckaroo* and *Professional Model*, to boost soldiers' morale during World War II. The leggy beauty was one of the hottest cheesecake pinups around, complementing those of Betty Grable, Dorothy Lamour and Lana Turner. Along with the legendary Bob Hope, Jinx logged some 60,000 miles of wartime travels to entertain the American troops for Christmas. On the homefront, she and Eddie Cantor did the "Purple Heart Circuit" supporting Veterans Hospital Camp Shows. Movies include *Two Latins from Manhattan* (1941), *Sweetheart of the Fleet* (1942), and *Cover Girl* (1944). Radio: She co-starred with her husband, Tex McCrary, on the "Tex and Jinx" talk show. The same chatty format was successfully copied later for television. The pair were known as "Mr. Brains and Mrs. Beauty." Her Yale-graduate husband defended her by stating, "She's the most intelligent uneducated person I know." What made Falkenburg unique was that no subject was off-limits. Nor did she shy away from talking to the scholars of the world. Her interviewing technique was to continually ask questions until she understood what the experts were talking about. Listeners felt they learned more this way and could understand the complicated subject matter better. **QUOTE** Asked to word her own epitaph, she wrote, "She died trying."

Janet Jackson 💿   1500 Vine

Singer, performer, actress, songwriter

Janet Jackson

BORN Janet Damita Jackson, May 16, 1966, in Gary, Indiana. **SPOTLIGHTS** The ninth child of a musical dynasty, her multi-faceted career began at age seven with her famous family. She began performing as part of the Jackson Five, then sequed into TV. She became a well-known actress on the sitcoms "Good Times," "Diff'rent Strokes," and "Fame." Her solo recording career took shape in 1982 with her debut album, and hit rhythm & blues song "Young Love." She had her breakthrough in 1986, working with Jimmy Jam and Terry Lewis (songwriters/musicians/producers). With her high energy and dazzling choreography, the Grammy-award winning pop singer took *Control*. She paved the way for hard-hitting dance music—choreographed by Paula Abdul—for her innovative, streetwise videos. *Control* sharply enhanced her exceptional pop-funk diva appeal. Hit songs from the album include "What Have You Done For Me Lately?" "Nasty," "When I Think of You," "Control," "Let's Wait Awhile," and "The Pleasure Principal." Working with Jam and Lewis again, her album *Rhythm Nation 1814*, topped the charts with her mega-million sales. When she performed during her first major tour, fans were thrilled to see Jackson was as good "live" as on her fabulous videos. Hit songs include "Escapade," "Miss You Much," "Rhythm Nation," "Come Back to Me," "Black Cat," and "Love Will Never Do Without You." The *Janet* album, released in 1993, sold more than 12 million copies worldwide and featured five top ten hits. In 1997 she released *The Velvet Rope* collection on Virgin Records, considered to be her most creative, elaborate and daring work to date. It received rave reviews for its style, honesty, and ingenuity. When she went on the opulent, high-tech Velvet Rope tour in 1998, Jackson's dedication to entertaining, her precision production, and her warm rapport with the audience, brought her close to Broadway standards. She has also received rave reviews for her performances on American Music Awards and Grammy Awards telecasts. Nominated for several Grammys and nine American Music Awards. Sister of singer Michael Jackson, the "King of Pop," she's been dubbed the "Rhythm Queen." **ACHIEVEMENTS** First female artist to land five Top 5 pop hits from a single album on the Billboard charts. She received her Walk of Fame star on April 2, 1990.

Xavier Cugat 🔘   1500 Vine

Band leader, actor, musician, cartoonist

Xavier Cugat

BORN New Year's Day, Jan. 1, 1900, in Barcelona, Spain. **SPOTLIGHTS** A student of the violin since age five, Cugat arrived in America as the violin accompanist to the tenor, Enrico Caruso. The great opera star, who had a penchant for drawing caricatures, discovered Cugat's talent in the graphic arts. Cugat left the musical world behind for his new occupation as a cartoonist for *The Los Angeles Times* daily newspaper. Not too much time passed before he quit. He said, "When the *Times* tells you to be funny at 10:30 in the morning—I can't do it." In 1928 Cugie (the name he preferred to be called by) formed his own "little band of six men" to play Latin tunes in nightclubs. Originally, Latin music was considered "gigolo" music (it was that unflattering of a spin). Cugie—more than any other Latin American envoy—made it not only acceptable to listen to rumba, cha-cha, conga, tango, and merengue in good clubs, but nurtured it into a respected art form. Cugie's "South-of-the-Border" tunes found their way into the big bands of the swing era. Often "stationed" at New York's Waldorf Astoria Hotel, he played all the top club and hotel venues across America, colleges and theatres. America fell in love with him and crowned him "Cugie, the undisputed Rumba King." About latin music, he declared, "More than just a fad or fancy, it's here to stay!" Cugie and his orchestra appeared in many Hollywood motion pictures starting in 1936 with *Go West Young Man*. MGM musicals with Esther Williams include *Bathing Beauty, Neptune's Daughter,* and *Stage Door Canteen*. Others include the family musical *A Date with Judy* (1948), and *Holiday in Mexico* (1946), where you can glimpse Cuban Premier Fidel Castro. Cugie also had his own 1950s TV show. He formed a new band, The Rumba King, at age 87. **QUOTE** "This music is folk music, all of it has been passed down for hundreds of years...A feeling of freedom and flowing smoothness comes from it that allows people to release their tensions and emotions." The unofficial Ambassador of Latin American Arts died peacefully of old age in 1990.

Martin Sheen 🎥   1500 Vine

Martin Sheen and Samantha Hart

Actor
BORN Ramon Estevez, Aug. 3, 1940, in Dayton, OH. **SPOTLIGHTS** Of Spanish-Irish descent, and coming from an extremely poor family, this attractive brown-haired, blue-eyed talent went straight to New York after graduating from high school. The hardworking youth toiled as a dishwasher, messenger boy and janitor while performing in off-Broadway shows. In 1964 Sheen landed his breakthrough role on Broadway in "The Subject Was Roses." (He would repeat this role in a 1968 film of the same name.) He expanded to Shakespearean repertoire in Joseph Papp's rock version of "Hamlet," and the New York Shakespeare Festival's "Romeo and Juliet." Sheen also played opposite George C. Scott in the Broadway revival of "Death of a Salesman." He earned critical acclaim on Broadway before turning to television and film. For television, Sheen has given exceptional portrayals of several contemporary political figures, including Robert Kennedy in the "Missiles of October" (1974), and John F. Kennedy in the mini-series "Kennedy" (1983). In 1981, he received an Emmy for his role in "The Long Road Home." His production, "Babies Having Babies," marked Sheen's directorial debut for which he won an Emmy Award, as well as his daughter Renee's acting debut. He worked with actor son, Emilio Estevez, in "The Custody of Strangers." He is star of NBC's "West Wing" (1999-), playing the U.S. President in this behind-the-scenes drama. A versatile actor, movies include *Catch-22* (1970), *Badlands* (1973), *Apocalypse Now* (1979), *Gandhi* (1982), *Firestarter* (1984), *Broken Rainbow* (1985—narrator of Oscar-winning documentary about the Native American Navajo Indians), *State of Emergency* (1986—which allowed him to work with his son, Ramon), *Wall Street* (1987—which featured his son, Charlie, who also

has a star on this famous Walk), *JFK* (1991—narrator), *The American President* (1995), *Entertaining Angels* (1996), and *Spawn* (1997). **ACHIEVEMENTS** In 1999 he became the proud recipient of the Hispanic Award. He received his Walk of Fame star on Aug. 25, 1989. Known for his charitable efforts, he is devoted to doing his part to improving humankind's plight through social causes, environmental and health-related issues.

George Raft 📺   1500 Vine

See page 239

Bill Stout 📺   1500 Vine

Broadcaster
BORN Los Angeles, CA. **SPOTLIGHTS** He began as a print reporter in 1947, then moved into Los Angeles broadcasting in 1950. He became a researcher, writer and reporter of the investigative series "Special Assignment." Later, he advanced to the anchor slot. Stout created "Perspective" (1978), a daily commentary on topical issues that encouraged in-depth analysis. He was a frequent speaker on journalistic ethics, and regularly served as moderator for political, civic and professional panel discussions. **ACHIEVEMENTS** He received numerous broadcasting awards, including the 1986 Governors Award Emmy, the top honor for career excellence from the Academy of Television Arts and Sciences. Died: 1989.

Celeste Holm 📺   1500 Vine

Celeste Holm

Actress, singer
BORN April 29, 1919, in New York, NY. **SPOTLIGHTS** Born into an affluent, artistic household, Holm enjoyed a world-class European education. As a youth, she excelled in academics, ballet and acting. Later, she studied drama at the University of Chicago. The lovely, poised, blue-eyed blonde made her 1938 Broadway debut in "Gloriana." She enjoyed her grand breakthrough in the musical "Oklahoma!" in 1943. Holm stopped the show with her delightful performance as Ado Annie who sings "I'm Just a Girl Who Can't Say No." One of her shining qualities was her genuine sense of humor. She starred in "Bloomer Girl," then hit the big screen in the lavish musical, *Three Little Girls in Blue* (1946). She was Oscar-nominated for her performances in *Come to the Stable* (1949) and *All About Eve* (1950). Holm brings intelligence to her roles. Other movies include *The Snake Pit* (1949), *Everybody Does It* (1949), *A Letter to Three Wives* (1949—voice only), *Champagne for Caesar* (1950), *The*

Tender Trap (1955), *High Society* (1956—in a wisecracking role), *Tom Sawyer* (1973—as Aunt Polly), *Three Men and a Baby* (1987), and *Still Breathing* (1996). **TV** She appeared in a number of dramatic and situation comedy shows. Her miniseries work includes "Backstairs at the White House" (1969). **ACHIEVEMENTS** 1947 Best Supporting Actress Oscar for *Gentleman's Agreement*. In 1979 she was knighted by King Olva V of Norway (her father was a Norwegian-born executive). In 1982 President Reagan appointed her to the National Council for the Arts. **QUOTE** A star of stage, movies, television and nightclubs, Holm has been described as versatile. To which she responded, "Versatile? Who's versatile? Not me. I'm limited. I guess people have gotten the idea I'm versatile because I do whatever I do in lots of different kinds of places."

The Lennon Sisters 📺   1500 Vine

The Lennon Sisters

Singing group
BORN Dianne, Peggy, Kathy and Janet Lenin in Los Angeles, CA. **SPOTLIGHTS** America's singing sweethearts, known for their unique blend of voices, talent, and friendship, began their career singing in church. They were discovered by Lawrence Welk's son (Diane's classmate) who, after hearing them sing, insisted they audition for his father. The result was an immediate invitation to appear on Welk's TV Christmas special in 1955. The public response was so great that within a month they were signed as regulars. For the next 12 years, they were for 12 years a part of the professional Welk family. Regular guest appearances on all major network shows followed, as well as their own show. Sparkling, fun and professional, they co-headline in Las Vegas, Reno, Lake Tahoe and Atlantic City. They appear with such stars as Don Rickles and Eddie Arnold. **HIGHLIGHTS** They raise money for many charitable causes, including St. Joseph's Center for the Needy, The Boy Scouts of America, The Salvation Army, and Nosotros...Their Hollywood Walk of Fame star was dedicated on Dec. 15, 1987...Their autobiography is entitled *Same Song, Separate Voices.*

Jack Conway 🎥   1500 Vine

Director
BORN July 17, 1887, in Graceville, MN. **SPOTLIGHTS**

Conway never worried about where his next paycheck would be coming from, he was the house director for MGM from 1925 until his retirement in 1948. He directed Lon Chaney in his only talkie, the remake of *The Unholy Three* (1930). It is about a ventriloquist on a crime spree with circus cohorts. Conway's *Redheaded Woman* (1932) catapulted Jean Harlow into superstardom. *The Girl from Missouri* (1934) also stars Jean Harlow with sidekick Patsy Kelly. He made Pancho Villa's story *Viva Villa!* (1934) with Wallace Beery, Leo Carrillo and Fay Wray, *A Tale of Two Cities* (1935), and one of the decade's best comedies, *Libeled Lady* (1936), starring Jean Harlow, Spencer Tracy, William Powell and Myrna Loy. He directed Clark Gable in *Too Hot to Handle* (1938) and *Boom Town* (1940). *Love Crazy* (1941) is a deft comedy, where a husband pretends he is insane to delay divorce proceedings. Died: 1952.

Klaus Landsberg   1500 Vine

Executive, technician
BORN July 7, 1916, in Germany. **SPOTLIGHTS** One of TV's earliest and most innovative technicians, he worked in the experimental TV bureaus in 1934. In 1941, he pioneered KTLA-TV. He produced and directed 3,500 telecasts.

Louis Hayward   1500 Vine

Actor
BORN Seafield Grant; March 19, 1909, in South Africa. **SPOTLIGHTS** A former London and Broadway performer, the suave, dark-haired leading talent possessed a mocking smile. Hayward was perfectly cast as *The Saint in New York* (1938); the first to be cast as detective Simon Templar. His work is usually considered the best out of the entire series. This talented actor was excellent in the absorbing dramatic saga, *My Son, My Son* (1940). In 1941 he stars opposite his real-life wife, Ida Lupino, in the gripping thriller, *Ladies in Retirement*. It also features Evelyn Keyes and Elsa Lanchester. In 1945 he appears in the very first Agatha Christie novel brought to the screen, *And Then There Were None*. It is excellent. Hayward also appears in swashbuckling dramas, including *The Man in the Iron Mask* (1939). In all, he made 40 films. His last movie was *Terror in the Wax Museum* (1973). **ACHIEVEMENTS** He was awarded a Bronze Star for his WWII heroism in the U.S. Marine Corps. Died: 1985.

Dorothy Arzner   1500 Vine

Director, screenwriter, editor
BORN Jan. 3, 1900, in San Francisco, CA. **SPOTLIGHTS** She was a pioneer female editor, screenwriter, and director. Women writers wrote more than half of all movies during the silent era, only their names rarely appeared on the screen. No matter, these women were highly compensated and often did not put up a fight to get screen credits. In 1922 she impressed colleagues with her brilliant editing of the bullfight scenes in

Blood and Sand, starring Rudolph Valentino. The next year she was offered the editing job on the famous Western, *The Covered Wagon*. She was involved in the making of dozens of films in various capacities. Paramount Pictures provided her first directing job, *Fashions for Women* (1927). She made other silents, then Paramount entrusted her to make their first talkie, *The Wild Party* (1929). Other pictures include *Merrily We Go to Hell* (1932), *Christopher Strong* (1933), *Dance, Girl Dance* (1940), and *First Comes Courage* (1943). Postwar she retired. She returned to teach at the prestigious Pasadena Playhouse, and UCLA. She also produced plays and directed TV commercials. She was the first female member of the Director's Guild of America...Arzner was an ambulance driver during World War I. She also served the country during World War II making military training films (WAC). Died: 1979.

William K. Howard   1500 Vine

Director
BORN June 16, 1899, in St. Mary's, OH. **SPOTLIGHTS** After doing silents for 11 years, he broke through the sound barrier with *Sherlock Holmes* (1932), then directed *The Power and the Glory* (1933), the predecessor to Orson Welles' *Citizen Kane*. Carole Lombard stars in his mystery-comedy *The Princess Comes Across* (1936). Died: 1954.

Michael Landon   1500 Vine

Michael Landon

Actor, writer, director, producer
BORN Eugene Orowitz, Oct. 31, 1937, in Forest Hills, NY. **SPOTLIGHTS** One of TV's most endearing stars rose from a childhood fraught with physical and mental abuse by a suicidal mother who often "wished him dead." But even in his youth, he was determined to succeed. Being of slight build in high school, Landon dedicated himself to countless hours on the athletic field. He set a national high school record in javelin hurling with a successful throw of 211 feet, 7 inches. He revealed to a reporter for *TV Guide* in 1969 that had been his first taste of public admiration and he immediately got addicted to it. Landon recalled, "I delighted in seeing the shock on people's faces when they saw such a scrawny guy get such distance." After attending USC briefly on scholarship, he auditioned for Warner Bros. acting school. After only four months of acting lessons, he won his first role in TV's "Telephone Time." He picked his stage name out of a telephone book. Landon's rugged good looks and sensitive acting have never lost their appeal to viewers. He was first immortalized as Little Joe Cartwright on the long-running Western

series, "Bonanza" (1959-'73). He gained a new generation of fans in "Little House on the Prairie" (1974-'82). He wore many hats on the show; he frequently wrote and directed, as well as produced and starred. In 1984 he became the angel Jonathan Smith on "Highway to Heaven," and executive producer and writer. Previously, Landon made his silver screen debut in *These Wilder Years* (1956) starring Barbara Stanwyck and James Cagney (look for Landon in the pool room). The following year, he stars in the campy B classic horror flick, *I Was a Teenage Werewolf.* Other films include *God's Little Acre* (1958), and *The Errand Boy* (1961)...He received his Walk of Fame star on August 15, 1984. Died: 1991.

Shirley Temple 🎥   1500 Vine

Actress

BORN April 23, 1928, in Santa Monica, CA. **SPOTLIGHTS** The most famous child actor of all time, she was set apart from the start. Shirley was such a beautiful baby that neighbors talked about her to their friends. Strangers, hearing about this remarkably breathtaking infant, came uninvited to the Temple house, asking permission to see her. But the precious one was so painfully shy that she did not want to see anyone but her own family. As a toddler, her mother brought her to dance lessons in hopes of helping her. Maternal instinct proved right. Just two years old, little Shirley really enjoyed learning different dance steps to the music. It slowly aided her in overcoming her timidness. She began in show business with a few bit parts in small films. At age six, she shot to superstardom in *Stand Up and Cheer* (1934), with her song-and-dance routine "Baby Take a Bow." Other 1934 motion pictures include *Little Miss Marker* with Adolphe Menjou, and *Baby Take a Bow*, in her first starring feature. Next, she co-stars with Gary Cooper and Carole Lombard in the family drama *Now and Forever.* She plays an orphan in *Bright Eyes*, singing the sweet tune "On the Good Ship Lollipop." She could do it all. Her superior acting range--from the highest highs to emotional lows--even amazed her adult co-stars. This kid could pull the heart strings with such sweetness that the world became her stage. The public rejoiced when the Academy of Motion Picture Arts and Sciences honored the little darling. They presented her with a diminutive Oscar (half its normal size) in a Special Academy Award category for "outstanding contribution to screen entertainment." Not expecting to win anything, her acceptance speech was brief. She tilted her head upward to the microphone and politely said, "Thank you all very much. Mommy, can we go home now?" In 1935, she stars in *The Little Colonel, The Littlest Rebel,* and *Curly Top* (the moppet's nickname due to her fifty-four curls). A natural born talent, and smart as a whip, she instinctively knew how to deliver lines for maximum comic (or dramatic) effect. For example, after asking John Boles in *Curly Top* what a lawyer is, Boles answers: "Well, a lawyer is a person who gets you out of trouble." Temple shoots back: "Oh, my! I could use one almost every day!" By now, the eight-year-old was the world's #1 box office

Shirley Temple, the greatest child star of all time.

draw, and, according to the Internal Revenue Service, she earned a whopping $307,014 in 1936 alone. (To put this in perspective: In 1941--a full five years later--two-thirds of all American families earned $1,000 to $3,000 annually. They were the middle class. Another 27% of workers' income was between $500 to $1,000 annually.) The studio also paid her mother Gertrude--as Shirley's coach and governess--her own 1936 salary of $68,500+. Amazingly, the child star was worth half the bank's assets at the same financial institution where her father was bank manager. Films that year include *Poor Little Rich Girl*, *Dimples*, and *Stowaway*. In 1937, little Shirley was the most photographed person in the world. During this year and the next, she enjoyed the pinnacle of success in such features as *Wee Willie Winkie, Rebecca of Sunnybrook Farm, Little Miss Broadway* and *Heidi*. She was so far ahead of all other movie talents, and infinitely more popular, that the polls were abandoned. Her weekly fan mail was more than all the top female leading ladies combined. Congress declared: "Shirley Temple is the most beloved individual in the world." J. Edgar Hoover, the director of the F.B.I., personally supervised the installation of a top-notch electronic security system at her home to help protect this American treasure. She was superb in *The Little Princess* (1939). Inevitably, she began growing up, which resulted in fewer good film roles. Later motion pictures include *Since You Went Away* (1944), *I'll Be Seeing You* (1944), *The Bachelor and the Bobby Soxer* (1947), *Honeymoon* (1947), *That Hagen Girl* (1947) opposite future President of the U.S. Ronald Reagan (who stated he regretted making this film), and *Fort Apache* (1948). **ACHIEVEMENTS** 1934 Special

*Ambassador Shirley Temple
and security expert
Arthur M. Kassel*

Oscar. 1968 U.S. representative at the U.N. 1974-'76, U.S. Ambassador to Ghana; promoted to U.S. Chief of Protocol. In 1989 President Bush appointed her to U.S. Ambassador to Czechoslovakia. Her wonderful autobiography, *Child Star*, was published in 1988 by McGraw Hill. She is the recipient of hundreds of awards and honors...Right before she stepped onto the set, her beloved mother chirped three inspirational words: "Sparkle, Shirley, sparkle!" Her mother's nickname for the precious one? "Presh." **HIGHLIGHTS** How popular was she? She recalled that at age six, "Mother took me to see Santa Claus in a department store, and he asked me for my autograph." **QUOTE** Shirley Temple became an American institution during the Great Depression. Reflecting on her career, she commented, "People were looking for something to cheer them up. They fell in love with a little girl."

Ricardo Cortez 🎥   1500 Vine

Actor

BORN Jacob Krantz; Sept. 19, 1899, in Alsace-Lorraine, France. **SPOTLIGHTS** Paramount signed this tall, dark-haired, handsome talent for *Sixty Cents an Hour* (1923). A debonair gent, he possessed luxurious black hair and soulful, large brown eyes. MGM cast him as the great Latin lover opposite Greta Garbo in her U.S. screen debut, *The Torrent* (1926). In 1931, he stars as private eye Sam Spade in *The Maltese Falcon* at Warner Bros. (This is the original sexier version; ten years later it was remade starring Bogart.) Later, he specialized in villainous character roles. Among his 200 movies are *Bad*

Ricardo Cortez

Company (1931), *13 Women* (1932), *Wonder Bar* (1934), *The Man With Two Faces* (1934), *I Am a Thief* (1935), and *The Case of the Black Cat* (1935--a Perry Mason murder investigation). **QUOTE** "The motion picture game is one of the hardest in the world. At the very outset is tremendous competition. Everywhere young people believe they have the gift of acting before the camera and, as a result, the producers and directors have been compelled to raise barriers to eliminate the unfit." Died: 1977.

Robert Taylor 🎥   1500 Vine

Actor

BORN Spangler Arlington Brugh; Aug. 5, 1911, in Filley, NE. **SPOTLIGHTS** Taylor rivaled screen idol Clark Gable for the number of love letters received from fans. Then, he beat Gable's 22-year record of remaining at one studio, MGM. The two pals shared similar interests in outdoor sports. Both of their dressing rooms were in a masculine decor in knotty pine, with overstuffed leather furniture, and were adorned with hunting rifles and prints. Taylor stayed at

Robert Taylor

MGM for 24 years, then regretted his decision. In 1958, he discussed his relationship with the studio. He stated, "I'd have been wise to have have left Metro six years ago. I was hotter than a pistol then with *Knights of the Round Table* and *Quo Vadis*." Earlier in his career, he was cast in romantic, pretty boy leads. In fact, he was considered too "powder puff pretty" to get serious roles. Makeup king Max Factor suggested Taylor grow a tidy mustache to be more handsome—and less beautiful. That did the trick. By 1936 he became America's "most admired matinee idol since the late Rudolph Valentino." Amazingly, he never rejected a role. In the 1950s, he revived his box office glory with a series of medieval swashbucklers. Films include *Magnificent Obsession* (1935), *Camille* (1936), *Yank at Oxford* (1938), *Three Comrades* (1938), *Billy the Kid* (1941--his favorite role), *Ivanhoe* (1953), and *Quentin Durward* (1955). **ACHIEVEMENTS** Even though he had legally adopted his stage name, he enlisted in the Navy in 1942 using his birth name. He bravely served as Lieutenant S.A. Brugh during WWII and saw combat. After his tour of duty, he was honorably discharged in 1945. **HIGHLIGHTS** He married Barbara Stanwyck, his co-star in *This is My Affair* (1937). The union lasted from 1939-'52. He died in 1969. Ronald Reagan, former actor and then-Governor of California, eulogized at his funeral, "He was more than a pretty boy, an image that embarrassed him because he was a man who respected his profession and was a master of it."

Clara Bow 🎥   1500 Vine

Clara Bow

Actress

BORN Aug. 15, 1905, in Brooklyn, NY. **SPOTLIGHTS** The bees-knees! Razz-ma-tazz! The ideal flapper of the Jazz Age. With her bobbed red hair, cupid bee-stung lips, large eyes, and hip-thrusting walk, this darling talent personified the essence of the Roaring Twenties. She was *the* flaming youth—vivacious and emancipated. Bow began her career in 1922, but "The Hottest Jazz Baby" didn't become super hot until 1926, with *Mantrap* and *Kid Boots*. These successes led her to the phenomenal box office smash *It* (1927)—in which she was immortalized as the "It" girl. Millions of women worldwide flattened their bosoms to achieve her flat-chested flapper look. (Bow's chest had been wrapped tightly with adhesive tape.) She stars in *Wings*, the very first film to win a Best Picture Academy Award, and rose to the #1 favorite actress. A few years later, with the coming of sound, she quit acting due to her nasal voice, as well as the new type of leading lady in demand. **HIGHLIGHTS** The flamboyant Bow loved to drive down Hollywood Boulevard in her flame red Kissel convertible (painted to match her hair color), with her two chow dogs whose fur had been dyed in the same red tint. But, in private, she felt so inept socially. Rather than attend parties and hazard a potential faux pas, she quietly stayed home and played cards with her servants. **SIDELIGHTS** Born into a poverty-stricken home, she came from a dysfunctional family, run by a manipulative, controlling, selfish mother. When her mom learned that daughter Clara had won a *Fame and Fortune* fan magazine contest, her borderline personality snapped into temporary insanity. Furious over her 16-year-old daughter's chosen career, she waited until nighttime to take action. She creeped into her bedroom, stood over her sleeping daughter, and attempted to slit her throat with a butcher knife. Clara woke up in the nick of time to defend herself and halt the attack. She left her miserable family behind, and accepted the contest's first prize. It was a bit role in *Beyond the Rainbow* (1922)--her screen debut. **QUOTE** "No one who complains, moans and pities herself ever succeeded. We realize outwardly, just exactly what we realize inwardly. It is an infallible law. Success does not depend on others. It depends on yourself. Success is a matter of concentration and of knowledge, and, having acquired these wonderful attributes, you will find that obstacles will remove themselves almost automatically. Life is not nearly so hard as men and women are fond of imagining it to be. They make it hard by their thought." Died: 1965.

Don Wilson 🎙   1500 Vine

Announcer, actor

BORN Sept. 1, 1900, in Lincoln, NE. **SPOTLIGHTS** He was the most popular announcer on the air, according to countless polls conducted from the 1930s through the 1950s. This robust, beaming sidekick knew how to warm up studio audiences and keep the folks at home laughing, too. on Blessed with a mellifluous voice and a hearty laugh, Wilson started as a radio announcer and friend to Benny on "The Jack Benny Show" in 1934. The perfect sidekick to Benny's underplayed comedy, Wilson continued with the program when it moved to television ("The Jack Benny Show"—1950-'77). As Benny's foil, Wilson protest catchphrase was: "But Jack." When Benny was asked how he had cast the show, he declared, "Of course, we must have at least one nice character. That's Don Wilson." Wilson also served as an announcer and/or host on a number of top-rated radio programs like "The Baby Snooks Show" and "Hollywood Theatre." He was a beloved and trusted figure to tens of millions of listeners over many decades. Died: 1982.

Frances Langford 🎥   1500 Vine

Actress, singer, comedienne

BORN April 4, 1913, in Lakeland, FL. **SPOTLIGHTS** With romantic love songs like "Harbor Lights," Langford was voted "radio's most popular singer in nationwide polls." She began as a lyric soprano, but her voice changed to a deep, smooth contralto after a tonsillectomy at age 16. First hired by Rudy Vallee in 1932, she had her own radio show by 1933. Then, she joined "The Bob Hope Show" in 1938 and stayed for much of its long run. Next, utilizing her fast verbal dexterity, she played the argumentative wife—Blanche Bickerson—on radio's hit show "The Bickersons," opposite Don Ameche (1946-'51). Pretty and petite at five-feet, three-inches tall, she possessed a fine hourglass figure and weighed in at 108-pounds. This blonde-haired, brown-eyed talent oozed Southern charm, and was a natural for musical motion pictures. Movies include *Broadway Melody of 1936*, *Born to Dance* (1936), *The Hit Parade* (1937), *Yankee Doodle Dandy* (1942), *This is the Army* and *Follow the Band* (both 1943). She played herself in *The Glenn Miller Story* (1954). **ACHIEVEMENTS** A true patriot, she bravely and continually risked her life to entertain troops during World War II. Given only a 24-notice, she "hopped a bomber" with Bob Hope to travel to distant and dangerous outposts. They covered every camp, every base and every hospital doing three to five shows a day, plus their weekly radio show. (Only twice during this period did they go on air from the studio.) Sometimes they performed during attacks from enemy artillery. (To which Hope and she made many immediate jokes about how their "fans" were showing their love and affection for their comedy, how their last show bombed, too, etc.) She continued to support American servicemen and women when she toured Vietnam with her own troupe.

Norma Talmadge 🎥   1500 Vine

Norma Talmadge

Actress

BORN May 26, 1897, in Niagara Falls, NY. **SPOTLIGHTS** A ravishing brunette with large, beautiful brown eyes, full lips and creamy white skin, she entered films at age 14. With no prior stage experience, the youthful beauty landed the lead in *A Tale of Two Cities* (1911), and became a permanent movie fixture. Although she made comedies, this petite, 110-pound actress was most often cast as the noble sufferer. She portrayed strong-willed, spirited women, courageous types who battled the odds for love, and smiled bravely through their tears. Talmadge was the Bette Davis of the silent era. Films include *The Sacrifice of Kathleen* (1914), *Children in the House* (1916), *The Forbidden City* (1918), *Love's Redemption* (1921), and *Camille* (1927). Talmadge made more than 300 feature-length pictures and shorts before sound forced her retirement—but neither her English nor her voice were her problems. She articulated properly and eloquently. Approaching her 40s, Talmadge would have been obliged to take *supporting* roles. And she was too grand a silent star to agree to being downgraded in the new medium of talkies. She was married to producer Joseph Schenck (1917-'26). **QUOTE** "On every train that comes to California from the East—and I am told that each month about 15,000 persons arrive in Southern California—there are scores of girls whose principal purpose in coming to the coast is to make a place for themselves in motion pictures. What chances of success have these girls? Some girls have nothing but good looks to recommend them. The fact that they have not learned to dance, that their general education has been neglected, and that many of them do not respond quickly to suggestions from the director—all mitigates against their success. If after preliminary training in dance, musical education, theatrical experience in stock, stage, vaudeville or opera, and Nature has been kind in her awards of good looks, then let the aspirant come to Los Angeles. But let him or her come prepared for the worst. The girl will find it a hard 'game.' She will wait many, many weary hours in theatrical placement bureaus. She will tramp around from studio to studio meeting with nothing but discouragement. She will find her funds growing lower and lower, day by day. There will be times when she will despair. She may find work at last as 'an extra girl'—work that may last for only a few days. Then will come more long weeks of idleness, followed perhaps by several more days or nights of work. Then, perhaps, again, some director may 'discover' her. He will call her from the back ranks into the foreground close to the camera. Then will come her opportunity. If she has been well-trained, if she uses her brains; if she rises to the occasion, success will follow. And now that I have finished, let me add a little postscript. It has been my experience that it is 'the girl with the eyes' who wins out in motion pictures. Eyes that are quick to fill with tears, eyes that sparkle with laughter at the slightest suggestion, eyes that can glint with anger, and eyes that mirror passing moods even without accompanying facial expressions. But, of course, that's just my own private opinion." Died: 1957.

Bob Keeshan/Capt. Kangaroo 📺   1500 Vine

Bob Keeshan

Performer, creator, producer

BORN June 27, 1927, in Lynbrook, NY. **SPOTLIGHTS** Keeshan landed his first show business job—near the bottom of the ladder—as a network page at NBC Radio. He resigned to join the U.S. Marine Corps. Following his honorable discharge, he returned to his job, where he met Bob Smith, originator of TV's long-running "Howdy Doody Show." Keeshan became Smith's assistant, and from their association the character Clarabelle the Clown was created. A classic clown, Clarabelle never spoke, but communicated through mugging, honking the horn and squirting everyone with seltzer. Keeshan discovered his special gift in relating to children, and his second character Corny the Clown ("Time for Fun"), made young ones laugh. He earned his greatest fame as the beloved title character in "Captain Kangaroo." For millions of youngsters, the grandfatherly Captain Kangaroo, his sidekick, Mr. Green Jeans, along with Dancing Bear, Bunny Rabbit, Mister Moose and Grandfather Clock was required daily viewing. Children delighted in the safe, gentle place Keeshan had created for them. The CBS show premiered on Oct. 3, 1955, and continued nearly 30 years, making "Captain Kangaroo" the longest-running children's program in network television. He hosted the CBS Radio Network Program "The Subject Is Young People," and appeared on the CBS news program "Up to the Minute." As host of "Storybreak," he presented original adaptations of literature for young people. In 1996 he wrote *Good Morning, Captain* and penned children's books for Fairview Press. Call 800.544.8207, or e-mail: jmeyer2@fairview.org **ACHIEVEMENTS** "Captain Kangaroo" won several Emmys and the prestigious Peabody. During his 50 show business years, Keeshan was named "Broadcaster of the Year," "Television Father of the Year," and is the recipient of numerous honorary degrees. He is co-founder—with former Tennessee Gov. Lamar Alexander—of Corporate Child Care Inc., an on-site child care business program.

Mack Swain 1500 Vine

Comedian

BORN Feb. 16, 1876, in Salt Lake City, UT. **SPOTLIGHTS** A big, burly Keystone Kop—built like a brick wall—he worked with Mack Sennett. Swain had a bushy mustache and pinwheel eyes. He was an all-around, talented funnyman. He felt best playing the straight man to Charlie Chaplin, who he supported in many pictures. His roles consisted of either taking a spiked club in the chops for laughs, or playing a buffoon authority figure. In *The Knockout* (1914), he plays the Sheriff, who supervises a boxing match. He must ensure that the two squirrley characters are fighting fair and square. As the bossy, demanding construction foreman in *Pay Day* (1922), he forces his second story scaffold laborers to work faster. Perched like a bird, Chaplin must catch bricks quickly being thrown up at him. He collects them beneath his chin, between his knees, etc. (Chaplin experimented with trick photography with this gag.) In *The Pilgrim* (1923), Swain plays the church deacon with the obvious collection plate. He was "Big Jim" McKay in Chaplin's classic *The Gold Rush* (1925). Died: 1935.

Fibber McGee and Molly 1500 Vine

Comedy team, voice specialists

BORN Jim Jordan (Fibber); Nov. 16, 1896, in Peoria, IL. Marian Driscoll (Molly); April 15, 1897, also in Peoria, IL. **SPOTLIGHTS** They were the hilarious stars of NBC's popular Tuesday night situation comedy "Fibber McGee and Molly." As all of America knew, the fictional couple lived at 79 Wistful Vista, and Fibber's trademark gag was opening a messy closet which was jam-packed with everything but the kitchen sink. Radio listeners roared as the closet's contents dumped noisily onto the floor. Golf clubs, musical instruments, roller skates, a sword, a pith helmet, a broken clock, etc, dropped. The final fall would be the gentle tinker of a bell, and deafening applause. The stars were married to each other in real life. So closely associated with their radio characters, the husband-and-wife comedy team of Jim and Marian Jordan were often called Mr. and Mrs. Fibber when they were in public. But, if truth be known, during the show's long-run (1935-'57), Marian played a dazzling array of 69 different characters, including the young girl Teeny whose famous catchphrase was "Whatcha doin', huh mister, whatcha?" Jim played 71 different characters. Motion pictures include: *This Way Please* (1938), *Look Who's Laughing* (1941), *Here We Go Again* (1942) and *Heavenly Days* (1944). Died: Marian Jordan in 1961; Jim Jordan died in 1988.

Joan Caulfield

Joan Caulfield 1500 Vine

Actress

BORN Beatrice J. Caulfield, June 1, 1922, in Orange, NJ. **SPOTLIGHTS** From wholesome modeling, she was Paramount's demure feminine beauty. With milk-white skin and shiny blonde hair, WWII soldiers were fond of her great Technicolor looks. Movies include *Duffy's Tavern* (1945), *Blue Skies* (1946), *Monsieur Beaucaire* (1946), *Welcome Stranger* (1947), and *Dear Wife* (1950). TV: She played the harebrained wife, Liz Cooper, in "My Favorite Husband." Died: 1991.

Smokey Robinson 1500 Vine

Singer, songwriter, producer

BORN William "Smokey" Robinson, Feb. 19, 1940, in Detroit, MI. **SPOTLIGHTS** "Everything's good in the world tonight/when Smokey sings." Robinson is the premier writer of love songs and the ultimate singer of romantic, poetic and soul ballads. Songs include "My Girl," "You've Really Got a Hold on Me," "Ooo Baby Baby," "The Tracks of My Tears," and "The Tears of a Clown." Anyone who's anyone has recorded his songs, including "Don't Mess with Bill" (the Marvelettes), "I'll Be Doggone" (Marvin Gaye), "My Guy" (Mary Wells), "You've Really Got a Hold on Me" (the Beatles), "Going a Go-Go" (the Rolling Stones), and "The Hunter Gets Captured by the Game" (Blondie). He founded the Miracles in Detroit in 1957: Ronnie White (b: Apr. 5, 1939) baritone voc.; Bobby Rogers (b. Feb. 19,1940) tenor voc.; Warren "Pete" Moore (b. Nov. 19, 1939) bass voc.; Claudette Rogers (Bobby's younger sister, and Smokey's wife—now divorced) voc. **ACHIEVEMENTS** The recipient of many awards, including two Grammys (one Legend Award), he is a beloved musical figure and a great American artist.

Fanny Brice 1500 Vine

See page 109

The Jacksons 1500 Vine

Pop Soul Vocal Musical group

BORN Sigmund Esco (Jackie), May 4,1951; Toriano Aldryll (Tito), Oct. 15, 1953; Marlon David, Mar. 12,1957; Jermaine La Jaune, Dec.11, 1954; Michael Joe, Aug. 29,1958—all born in Gary, Indiana. Also known as The Jackson 5 and The Jackson Family. **SPOTLIGHTS** They hit #1 with "I Want You Back," "ABC," "The Love You Save," and "I'll Be There" during the 1970s. The group became the basis for a Saturday morning children's cartoon series in 1971. In 1976 their own TV show "The Jacksons" had all nine siblings in the act. Many other hits include: "Shake Your Body (Down to the Ground)." Their records have sold more than 100 million copies.

Leo McCarey 1500 Vine

Director, screenwriter, producer

BORN Oct. 3, 1898, in Los Angeles, CA. **SPOTLIGHTS** He excelled in French farce, wacky slapstick, and the great 1930s sophisticated comedies, where his wit sparkled like a multi-faceted diamond. McCarey was also capable of doing good religious drama, but humorous works were his forte. For starters, he supervised, wrote the story and/or directed some of the funniest Laurel and Hardy movies, including *Two Tars* (1928), *Liberty* (1929), *Big Business* (1929), and *Hog Wild* (1930). In 1933 he directed the Marx Brothers' gag-filled romp, *Duck Soup*. It is generally considered their greatest movie (with the famous mirror sequence). McCarey worked with the screen's premier comics: *Belle of the Nineties* (1934) starring Mae West as a New Orleans singer doing what she does best with double entendres (the picture is enhanced with an early screen appearance by Duke Ellington and his orchestra), *Six of a Kind* (1934) a road picture starring W.C. Fields, and the riotous boxing comedy *The Milky Way* (1936), starring Harold Lloyd in his best sound picture (with Lloyd's classic ducks punches scene). Other films include a fish-out-of-water comedy featuring Charles Laughton as the uptight English butler who is sold in a poker game and is forced to face the Wild West in *Ruggles of Red Gap* (1935), *Love Affair* (1939--a drama), *The Bells of St. Mary* (1945--religious story), *An Affair to Remember* (1957--a remake of *Love Affair*), and *Rally 'Round the Flag, Boys!* (1958). **ACHIEVEMENTS** 1937 Best Director Oscar for *The Awful Truth,* starring Cary Grant and Irene Dunne. 1944 two Oscars: Best Director and Best Screenplay for *Going My Way*. **QUOTE** "I like my characters to walk in clouds, I like a little bit of the fairy tale. As long as I'm there behind the camera lens, I'll let somebody else photograph the ugliness of the world." Died: 1969.

Dick Clark

Dick Clark ▄ Sunset and Vine

Personality, host, executive, producer

BORN Nov. 30, 1929, in Mt. Vernon, NY. **SPOTLIGHTS** He is the epitome of the clean-cut master of ceremonies. This pop music host started a cultural revolution on TV's "American Bandstand" in the 1950s. He was panned by critics for the type of music he played, and the type of dancing the audience did. Clark responded, "The critics don't understand what kids like. I take them seriously and they take me seriously too." Through the 1960s, 1970s, and 1980s, Clark's show appealed to one generation after another. Decade after decade, millions watched him introduce new up-and-comers, such as Madonna. He has hosted "The $10,000 Pyramid," and "Bloopers and Practical Jokes." He heads his own production company. With his eternally youthful looks, he has ironically become Father Time, ringing in the spirit of each new year in Times Square, New York City. He hosts the annual countdown and the dropping of the ball, including the one-of-a-kind Waterford crystal ball uniquely made for 2000's special millennium celebration. Mr. Eternal Youth was clearly America's identifiable choice to welcome the next 1,000 years. **QUOTE** "There's only one person who makes a record a hit, and that's the guy who buys it."

B.P. Schulberg 🎥 Sunset and Vine

Producer, motion picture pioneer

BORN Benjamin Percival Schulberg; on Jan 19, 1892, in Bridgeport, CT. **SPOTLIGHTS** A former screenwriter and publicity man, it was his phenomenal discovery of actress Clara Bow that made him a permanent Hollywood fixture. Producer Schulberg brought Bow, "The Hottest Jazz Baby in Films," first to a small, independent company called Arrow, then to Paramount in 1926 at $50 a week. They put her in snazzy films, with the top leading men and best directors. This Roaring Twenties flapper rose to #1. Films include *Rough House Rosie, Red Hair* and *The Wild Party*, and, of most importantly, *It* (1927). And, because of "It," Schulberg became Paramount's chief of production. **QUOTE** A tough producer, one evening B.P. Schulberg came home and was prodded by his wife to read "little Budd's first poem." He loudly complained, "Damn it all, I spend all day with thousand-dollar-a-week writers, and now I have to spend the evening listening to a kid on a four-bit allowance!" (His son, Budd Schulberg, later became the acclaimed novelist/screenwriter of *What Makes Sammy Run?* and the Academy Award-winning screenwriter of *On the Waterfront.* Budd attributed his sometime speech stammer to his father's abruptness.) B.P. died in 1957.

Beach Boys 🔘 Sunset and Vine

Musicians, singers, songwriters

BORN Brian Wilson, June 20,1942, in Hawthorne, CA (voc., bass, piano); Carl Wilson, Dec.21,1946, in Hawthorne, CA (voc., guitar); Dennis Wilson, Dec.4,1944, in Hawthorne, CA (voc., drums); Al (Alan) Jardine, Sept 3,1942, in Lima, Ohio, (voc., guitar); and Mike Love, March 15,1941, in L.A., CA (voc., perc.). **SPOTLIGHTS** Girls. Sunshine. Surf. Fast Cars. The Beach Boys are the inventors of California rock and the foremost vocal harmony group in good time rock 'n' roll, and pop music. The group formed in a suburb of Los Angeles in 1961. Within a year of signing with Capitol Records, they made a splash. Their hits, "Surfin' Safari," "Surfin' U.S.A.," and "Surfer Girl," all idealized the easy, sunny California lifestyle. Another day in paradise for teens in love with dating, driving and surfing: "I Get Around," "Fun, Fun, Fun," "Help Me Rhonda," "Wouldn't It Be Nice," and "California Girls." No doubt about it, they've got those "Good Vibrations." In 1988 they launched a comeback with "Kokomo," which topped the charts. **ACHIEVEMENTS** More than 75 million records sold. 15 top 10 singles (including four that reached the

#1 position), and 16 gold or platinum albums. **SIDELIGHTS** Partially deaf Brian Wilson never surfed. Mike Love is the Wilson's first cousin. Paul McCartney of the Beatles was inspired by the Beach Boys' 1966 album, *Pet Sounds*, including the song "Wouldn't It Be Nice" resulting in *Sergeant Pepper's Lonely Heart Club Band*. **DIED** Dennis Wilson, 1983 (ironically by drowning). He was buried at sea with special permission granted by President Reagan. Died: Carl Wilson, 1998.

Spike Jones 🔊   Sunset and Vine

Musical satirist, radio actor, band leader
BORN Lindley Armstrong Jones; Dec.14, 1911, in Long Beach, CA. **SPOTLIGHTS** Known as "the man who murdered music!" Jones was a strange-looking fellow, extremely thin, with a big head, and big talent. He called himself, "a satirist who records fruitcake music that is zany as well as refreshingly danceable." Still funny are his outrageous song ditties: "Dinner Music for People Who Aren't Very Hungry," "Der Fuehrer's Face" (an anti-Nazi war tune), "Cocktails for Two," "I Wuv a Wabbit," "Gesundheit Polka," "Holiday for Strings," "Chloe," and "Hawaiian War Chant." The master of musical mayhem made his screen debut in the all-star musical where the entertainers poked fun at themselves in *Thank Your Lucky Stars* (1943). Other movies followed, including *Fireman Save My Child* (1954), with Buddy Hackett, Hugh O' Brian and Adele

Jergens. **RADIO** "The Spike Jones Show," a musical madness and comedy variety program featured Jones' irreverent style, vocalist Dorothy Shay "the Park Avenue Hillbilly," and his wild ensemble novelty band, the City Slickers. The band was known as "the craziest band in the land," for their loud use of unconventional instruments like cowbells, foghorns, automobile horns and common household kitchen utensils. Their special sound effects included sneezes, hissing and gun shots. The bands motto? "The band that plays for fun." Believe it or not, one of the show's announcers was Myron "Mike" Wallace. (That's right, later of "60 Minutes" fame.) **TV** "The Spike Jones Show" featured wife Helen Grayco, as vocalist on straight songs, and his band, the City Slickers. Jones also had the "Club Oasis" show; these shows aired during the mid-1950s through early '60s. **SIDELIGHTS** His father worked as a railroad agent. When Jones was a child, a railroad telegraph operator said the boy was as skinny as a railroad "spike." The nickname stuck. **QUOTE** About his TV shows he said, "Now we have a chance to prove it takes a better band to play crazy music occasionally than straight music all the time. When the audience knows you know better, it is satire, but when they think you can't do any better, it's corn." Died: 1965.

Quincy Jones 🔊   Sunset and Vine

Quincy Jones and friend

Musician, composer, conductor, arranger, producer, executive
BORN March 14, 1933, in Chicago, IL. **SPOTLIGHTS** One of the most charismatic and successful figures in pop, rock 'n' roll, rhythm and blues, and jazz, Jones began his musical legacy in his childhood. As a youngster, he studied trumpet in Seattle. When Jones was 14, he met Ray Charles and the two formed a soul band. The following year, he joined Lionel Hampton's band. His dreams of going to Europe with the vibraphonist-virtuoso were foiled by Hampton's wife who insisted the highly intelligent and quick-witted teen stay home and go to school. It turned out to be good advice as he won a scholarship to Boston's Berklee School of Music. He carried a full load of classes and worked nights in seedy, burlesque joints. Much to the "entertainers'" dismay, Jones's trumpet playing was the hottest thing going. Word spread to New York and he was hired to do arrangements there for less than $20 a pop. The city was alive with some of jazz's greatest talents—such as Thelonious Monk and Miles Davis—

Spike Jones

and they became his friends. His jump to Europe came in the 1950s in the blues and jazz friendly city of Paris, France. He became an award-winning conductor-arranger. He returned to America in the early 1960s, landing a groundbreaking job as vice president for Mercury Records—one of the first African Americans to do so. That was the beginning of his history-making, hit-making career in the record, television and motion picture business that has spanned many decades. He has guided dozens of careers. Among his countless gigantic hits are items like his producing and arranging Michael Jackson's album *Off the Wall,* which sold into the multi-millions. Then, Jones produced *Thriller*—the best-selling album in history. He collaborated with Ella Fitzgerald, Count Basie, Peggy Lee, Frank Sinatra, Sarah Vaughn, Ray Charles, Leslie Gore, George Benson, Chaka Khan and Rufus, to name a few. Among the numerous movies he has scored are: *The Pawnbroker, Banning, The Deadly Affair,* and *In Cold Blood.* Jones co-produced the feature film *The Color Purple* starring Danny Glover, Whoopi Goldberg, and Oprah Winfrey in her screen debut. He produced TV theme music "Ironside," and "The Bill Cosby Show" to name a couple. In 1991 he became executive producer of the TV series "The Fresh Prince of Bel Air." **ACHIEVEMENTS** The media mogul is the recipient of hundreds of honors. He is very proud of his eldest daughter, Jolie (her name means "pretty" in French). She is an accomplished jazz-styled singer...Jones has been nominated for 76 Grammys and has won 27 Grammys to date. His numerous Emmys include his 1977 award for the "Roots" soundtrack. 1967 Academy Award for his score *In the Heat of the Night.* Then, more than 30 years later, he produced the show, the 68th Annual Academy Awards. **VIEWING** "Quincy Jones...The First 50 Years" (1997) is an interesting tribute and overview of this enormous talent.

Barry Sullivan 📺 Sunset and Vine

See page 241

Neil Sedaka 💿 Sunset and Vine

Songwriter, singer, pianist
BORN March 13, 1939, in Brooklyn, NY. **SPOTLIGHTS** A child prodigy, he played the great classical works of Chopin, Bach, Beethoven, Ravel, Tchaikovsky, Rachmaninoff and Schumann. At age nine, he won a scholarship at the Juilliard School of Music in New York City. He attended both Juilliard and public school for the next eight years. As a youngster, Sedaka was slight for his age, wore glasses and braces, had a high-pitched voice and felt unpopular. At age 13, he discovered pop music and that he "had the gift of song writing." It made him instantly popular with the public school kids. The pianist-singer reflected, "Not only was I invited to every party, but I was the excitement, the life of every party I attended." Meanwhile, his serious classmates at Julliard were horrified with Sedaka's outside musical interests. The 13-year-old

Sedaka and another boy named Howard Greenfield, who lived in the same apartment building, began collaborating on songs. They worked mostly on ballads—"one a day for three years"—then were inspired to change to rock after hearing "Earth Angel." In 1958 singer Connie Francis recorded their "Stupid Cupid." The record sold like red roses on Valentine's Day; it was their first hit. At age 19, the tenor landed a contract with RCA/Victor as a singer-composer. During the next five years, he sold more than 25 million records. Hits include: "Where the Boys Are" "Calendar Girl," "Happy Birthday, Sweet Sixteen," "Oh! Carol," "Stairway to Heaven," "Little Devil," "Next Door to an Angel," and "Breaking Up Is Hard To Do." When Beatle-mania introduced a new era of rock 'n' roll to America, Sedaka faded temporarily into the background. He composed hit tunes for stars such as Tom Jones ("Puppet Man"). He moved to England in 1970, and hooked up with Elton John, whose training is also in classical music. John helped jump-start his career again. Hits include "Laughter In The Rain," "That's When The Music Takes Me," "Love Will Keep Us Together," "Bad Blood" and "New York City Blues." **HIGHLIGHTS** A devoted family man, Sedaka married childhood sweetheart, the former Leba Margaret Strassberg. They have two children, Dara Felice, who is also a singer-composer and who has recorded duets with her father, and a son, Marc Charles. **ACHIEVEMENTS** This Grammy-winning artist was inducted into the Songwriters Hall of Fame in 1983. **QUOTE** "I've written over 1,000 songs, and each one has its own life."

Helene Costello 🎥 Sunset and Vine

Actress, dancer
BORN June 21, 1903, in New York, NY. **SPOTLIGHTS** The daughter of actor Maurice Costello, and sister of actress Dolores Costello, she made her screen debut as a child in *The Geranium* (1911). She worked in silent films, then switched to modeling and, as a young adult danced on stage in "George White's Scandals." She returned to the screen at age 23. Movies include *The Love Toy* (1926), and *Good Time Charley* (1927). The advent of sound destroyed her career. Died: 1957.

George Fenneman 📺 🎙 Sunset and Vine

Host, announcer
BORN Nov. 10, 1919, in Peking, China. **SPOTLIGHTS** He was Groucho Marx's foil on "You Bet Your Life," in both the radio and TV versions (1947-'62). According to Marx, Fenneman was the "perfect straight man. In fact, he's straight on all six sides." He was "the Secret Word" man, instructing contestants that they would receive a cash

George Fenneman

bonus if they said "the secret word—it's a common word, something you see every day" (like fence, gate, milk, etc.). Other TV credits include the famous voice-over at the beginning of each "Dragnet" show, "The story you're about to hear is true. Only the names have been changed to protect the innocent." Also: The "Jim Nabors Show"(1969-'71); and the "Donny and Marie Osmond Show" (1976-1979). This extremely likable gent died in 1997.

Oliver Hardy (left) and Stan Laurel

Oliver Hardy 🎥   Sunset and Vine

Comedian, film director
BORN Norvell Hardy, Jan. 18, 1892, in Harlem, GA. **SPOT-LIGHTS** This lovable, short-tempered comedian with the funny little mustache (almost nonexistent on his round, chubby face with the trademark double chin) first crossed paths with thin, clownish Stan Laurel in *Lucky Dog* (1917). But, it wasn't until 1927 that they teamed together for comedy shorts/features and made their mark in motion picture history. Ollie (his preferred name) played the older, smarter brother-type. He was always trying to thwart a calamity from befalling his best friend, yet inevitably found himself dragged into the shenanigans. Roly-poly Hardy nervously twiddled his necktie, gave his long-suffering look, or cheated to the camera in disgust after reprimanding the cry-baby Laurel with "Another fine mess you've gotten me into this time!" Yet Hardy figured out a tender way of extracting themselves from the unfortunate situation. One unique aspect of his character was that even when he was outraged, Ollie kept his gentility. And the two really were the best of friends onscreen and off. (See the bio of "Stan Laurel" in this book.) His affectionate nickname was "Babe." **QUOTE** "As a child I got into a habit that I still have. I sit in the lobby of any hotel where I stay and I just watch people. Once in a while someone will ask me where Stan and I dreamed up the characters we play in the movies. They seem to think that these fellows aren't like anybody else. I know they're *dumber* than anyone else, but there are plenty of Laurels and Hardys in the world. Whenever I travel, I still am in the habit of sitting in the lobby and watching the people walk by—and I can tell you I see many Laurels and Hardys. I used to see them in my mother's hotel when I was a kid: the dumb, dumb guy who never has anything bad happen to him—and the smart, smart guy who's dumber than the dumb guy only he doesn't know it." Died: 1957.

David Wolper 📺   Sunset and Vine

Producer
BORN Jan. 11, 1928, in New York, NY. **SPOTLIGHTS** With an astounding 500 films to his credit, Wolper is one of the most prolific and successful producers in history. His work has garnered more than 150 awards, including two Oscars, 50 Emmys, seven Golden Globes, five Peabody Awards, and France's highest civilian distinction, the French National Order of the Legion of Honor. He has shaped the medium of television with his innovations and creations. First, Wolper challenged the networks restriction of never airing independent producers products. His historic acquisition of original Russian space program footage could not be ignored. This controversial, official Soviet documentation became Wolper's "The Race for Space" (1960). Narrated by his good friend Mike Wallace, the show became the first television program to be Oscar-nominated. Next, he adapted Theodore H. White's Pulitzer Prize-winning book on the Kennedy-Nixon presidential contest, "The Making of the President." It aired in 1963; Wolper received an Emmy for "Outstanding Program of the Year." Four Emmy statuettes were also given for the program's outstanding achievement in documentary production, music, editing and writing. Two presidential sequels followed. Shows include "D-Day," "The Rise and Fall of the Third Reich," "The Legend of Marilyn Monroe," "October Madness: The World Series," "A Nation of Immigrants," "A Thousand Days" (his tribute to John F. Kennedy), and "Monsters! Mysteries or Myths?" (with the Smithsonian Institute). He was: the first to bring nature to prime time network with his "National Geographic Specials," and the first to take viewers underwater by convincing French explorer/filmmaker Jacques Cousteau to take an expedition around the world for a series of American television specials. Wolper created the concept of the docudrama, re-enacting events in "They've Killed President Lincoln!" He devised the idea of having an international collection of famous directors shooting 10 to 12 minutes on any aspect of the 1972 Munich Olympic Games. The resulting film "Visions of Eight," was honored at film festivals from

David Wolper (left) and Jacques Cousteau

Cannes to Moscow. In 1974 he met the then-unknown author, Alex Haley, and acquired the rights to "Roots." It became the most-watched mini-series in TV history and won an unprecedented nine Emmy Awards. "The Thorn Birds" is his award-winning mini-series. It ranks in the top-ten viewed TV programs of all time. Wolper made the popular 24-hour mini-series, "North and South," (1985-'86), based on John Jakes' best-selling novels. TV series include "Welcome Back, Kotter" (1975-'79), introducing John Travolta to America. His love of Hollywood inspired him to create another genre; he's the originator behind compiling Tinseltown's history for the small screen. Features include *If It's Tuesday, This Must Be Belgium* (1969), *Willy Wonka and the Chocolate Factory* (1971—a children's favorite), *Imagine: John Lennon* (1988), *Surviving Picasso* (1996), and *L.A. Confidential* (1997). **QUOTE** "My definition of a producer is 'A Man with the Dream.' I don't write, act, direct, compose, so what do I do? I make it happen—I make dreams come true. That's what a producer does."

Franklin Pangborn 🎥 Sunset and Vine

Actor

BORN Jan. 23, 1893, in Newark, NJ. **SPOTLIGHTS** An accomplished dramatic Broadway talent, he became one of Hollywood's most popular funny men. *Exit Smiling* (1926) was an appropriate title for this character actor with an uppity manner. As a hotel or bank manager, a dress designer, a store manager, or department store floorwalker, he superciliously raised his eyebrow, sniffed at his employees, and haughtily turned his back on them. Pangborn did not become a full-time comedian until *My Man Godfrey* (1936), starring William Powell. His characterization of an overwrought tabulator of a high society scavenger hunt brought endless kudos. Within one year, he appeared in 27 other Golden Era pictures! He was wonderful in Frank Capra's *Mr. Deeds Goes to Town* (1936) with Gary Cooper, *The Bank Dick* (1940) starring W. C. Fields, *Never Give a Sucker an Even Break* (1941) also starring Fields, and *George Washington Slept Here* (1942). Died: 1958.

1501 VINE

Edward Small ⬛   Sunset and Vine

Producer
BORN Feb. 1, 1891, in Brooklyn, NY. **SPOTLIGHTS** A jack-of-all-trades, he went from actor to agent to producer and executive producer. Productions include *Kit Carson* (1940), and *Witness for the Prosecution* (1958). Died: 1977.

Anne Jeffreys ⬛   Sunset and Vine

Actress, singer

Anne Jeffreys

BORN Anne Carmichael; Jan. 26, 1923, in Goldsboro, NC. **SPOTLIGHTS** Known to hundreds of millions worldwide as Captain Mitch Buchannon's (David Hasselhoff) mother in TV's "Baywatch" series, Miss Jeffreys had enchanted a different generation of fans during the 1950s. The beautiful blonde delightfully haunted the set as Marion Kirby's ghost on "Topper" (1953-'56), where her co-star was her real-life husband, Robert Sterling. Destined to entertain, she began singing at age one and one-half, and sang publicly at five. Eventually she sang opera, where she was applauded for her voice, stage presence, grace and charm. She exudes class with a capitol C. Starring motion picture roles include the original *Dick Tracy* (1945), and *Return of the Badmen* (1948), among others. **QUOTE** "I am very grateful and I owe it all to my Mother. She encouraged and guided me in show business. It never occurred to me to question her, I loved her completely. And it's the best thing that happened."

Johnny Mathis 🔴   Sunset and Vine

Singer, entertainer
BORN John Royce Mathis; Sept. 30, 1935, in San Francisco, CA. **SPOTLIGHTS** He grew up in a basement apartment on Post Street, where his father—a former vaudevillian—scraped together $25 to purchase a used upright piano. He taught little Johnny his first songs and routines. The child loved to perform for visiting guests, who identified his tremendous talent even back then. At age 13, his dad bartered professional singing lessons for his son in exchange for doing odd jobs around the instructor's house. Mathis studied for six years while performing in church, school functions, and amateur shows. Meanwhile, he was a star athlete on his school's track and field team, specializing in the high jump and hurdles. He also played basketball. Sports reporters referred to him as "the

best all-around athlete to come out of the San Francisco Bay Area." While attending San Francisco State College, he landed a weekend singing job at Ann Dee's 440 Club. A devoted fan and club owner, Helen Nogo, repeatedly urged the head of Columbia Record's Jazz A & R "to come hear Johnny sing." When the executive finally did, he sent a telegram back to his company: "Have found phenomenal 19-year-old boy who could go all the way. Send

Johnny Mathis

blank contracts." The superb athlete had also been invited to attend the trials for the 1956 Olympic team, but chose his recording career instead. Columbia put him under the expert direction of Mitch Miller, who favored Mathis' voice to sing soft, romantic ballads, creating the hits "Wonderful Wonderful," and "It's Not for Me to Say." This velvety-voiced tenor soon had his #1 hit with "Chances Are." Mathis Magic has made such favorites as "The Twelfth of Never," and "Misty." His duet with Deniece Williams "Too Much, Too Little, Too Late," rocketed to #1 on both the pop and R&B charts in 1978. The good looking entertainer is also a popular Las Vegas and Atlantic City headliner. A shrewd businessman and deal maker, he has amassed millions of dollars. **ACHIEVEMENTS** A living legend, his *Greatest Hits* album spent nine and 1/2 years on the charts! (This accomplishment was duly noted in the *Guinness Book of World Records*.) His recordings have hit the Billboard charts in five consecutive decades (1950s, '60s, '70s, '80s, '90s). Amazingly enough, a Mathis release originally recorded from 1964-'66 entered the Billboard charts in April of 1997! He has sung at the White House numerous times in honor of visiting Heads of State. In 1978, he sang for the British Royal Family at a Command Performance held at the famed London Palladium. In 2000, he celebrates his 45th year as a recording artist.

Binnie Barnes 🎥   Sunset and Vine

Actress
BORN Gitelle Gertrude Maude Barnes; March 25, 1905, in London, England. **SPOTLIGHTS** Disguising her elegant British accent and billing herself as "Texas Binnie," she lassoed her way into vaudeville. From there, bit parts in film shorts blossomed into greater things. Her first big break was an important role starring opposite Charles Laughton in *The Private Life of Henry VIII* (1933). She turned in a brilliant portrayal of Catherine Howard and was beckoned by Hollywood. Motion pictures include *Diamond Jim* (1935--as Lillian

Binnie Barnes

Russell), *The Last of the Mohicans* (1936), *The Magnificent Brute* (1936), *Three Smart Girls* (1937), *Three Blind Mice* (1938), *Holiday* (1938), *The Three Musketeers* (1939), and *In Old California* (1942). Barnes played leading ladies, second lead, and character roles. Often cast as the sophisticated, wise-cracking, caustic blonde during her peak years, she went against type and turned religious in one of her last roles, *The Trouble With Angels* (1966 + two sequels), about Catholic nuns at a girls academy. Died: 1998.

Clive Davis ● 1501 Vine

Executive

Clive Davis and Janis Joplin

BORN Clive Jay Davis; April 4, 1934, in Brooklyn, NY. **SPOTLIGHTS** Known as the "king of the record business," and the man with the golden ear. After graduating at the top of his class at Harvard School of Law, he started as a business-minded attorney working for Columbia Records in 1960. Then, with no formal music background, he became president of that label in 1966. With a unique combination of creative perception, business acumen and the keen ability to recognize a commercial sound, he was the first president of a large record company to assume the personal point of view and active role of the small company head and apply these perspectives to a major label. And although corporate heads rarely double as talent scout, or have artistic inclinations, Davis' breakthrough was hearing Janis Joplin sing at the Monterey Pop Festival in 1967. About watching Joplin perform, he said, "It changed my life. I realized this was my moment and I seized it." Relying on his gut instinct, he signed her on the spot, as well as Laura Nyro and the Electric Flag. Davis discovered his burning passion for music, and personally participated in the acquisition of talent. Thus began a new era for Columbia, and Davis brought in such stellar rock 'n' roll acts as Blood, Sweat & Tears, Santana, Bruce Springsteen, Billy Joel, and Earth, Wind & Fire. He brought jazz great Miles Davis to the world's attention. He formed Arista Records in 1975 and launched the careers of such varied and vital artists as Barry Manilow, Patti Smith, The

Outlaws, Ray Parker, Jr., Whitney Houston, Kenny G, Monica, Next, and Deborah Cox. The label has also attracted such important artists as the great Aretha Franklin, the Grateful Dead, Eurythmics and Carly Simon. Arista's impressive accumulation of platinum and gold records, a chart success ratio that became the envy of the industry, and rising revenues led *Newsweek* magazine to praise Davis' "Midas touch."

Clive Davis and Aretha Franklin

He loves all types of music from R&B to pop to jazz, with everything in between. A workaholic, he also meets with songwriters, producers and potential new talents while keeping an eye on innovative trends. One of Davis' great gifts is his ability to know a hit when he hears it. He also believes in a hands-on approach to his artists, "finding hit songs and matching them with producers, who can deliver both the arrangement and production to an artist who has a God-given voice." He keeps up with the times. Davis stated that he "listens to every record that comes out that hits the charts." When working with Babyface, who is a self-contained writer/producer, Davis offers gives wide-ranging artistic freedom. That effort resulted in Whitney Houston's #1 hit, "I'm Your Baby Tonight." Davis made his agreement with L.A. Reid and Babyface to form LaFace Records in October 1989. LaFace has an incredible roster of hit making artists such as TLC, Toni Braxton, the Tony Rich Project, Usher, OutKast and The Goodie Mob, plus the double-platinum *Soul Food* motion picture soundtrack. In 1994 Davis and producer-songwriter-entrepreneur Sean "Puffy" Combs entered into a 50/50 joint venture that resulted in the creation of Bad Boy Records with an artist roster that includes Notorious B.I.G., Faith Evans, Total, 112, Mase and others. He was instrumental in Santana's Grammy Award-winning comeback in 2000. Davis reflected, "I've been fortunate to work with many creative geniuses, and I am very proud of it." **ACHIEVEMENTS** Davis' deep passion for music is matched only by his passion for helping his fellow man. Among his many honors are several Humanitarian of the Year awards given by various organizations including the Anti-Defamation League, the T.J. Martell Foundation for Leukemia and Cancer Research, and by the Black Music Association. He is also actively involved in the fight against AIDS. In March of 1990 at New York's famed Radio City Music Hall, Davis was responsible for turning Arista's 15th anniversary concert into the "That's What Friends Are For" benefit, which raised more than $2 million in one evening to help in the battle against the disease. His Walk of Fame star was dedicated on Jan. 28, 1997. **QUOTE** "Music has been the soul of my life, and has taken a kid from P.S. 161 and Erasmus Hall High School in Brooklyn on a wonderful and rewarding ride. The Hollywood Walk of Fame star is a genuine thrill for its lasting tangible expression of what the music of the artists I've discovered and worked with has meant to others."

Percy Faith ●   1501 Vine

Composer, band leader, pianist

BORN April 7, 1908, in Toronto, Canada. **SPOTLIGHTS** From the 1930s - '50s Faith and his orchestra were regulars on radio's "The Carnation Contented Hour (Carnation's milk comes from contented cows)," "The Woolworth Hour," and "The Pause that Refreshes on the Air (the Coca-Cola Hour)." Songs include "Buy a Bond for Victory," "My Heart Cries for You," the 1952 song from *Moulin Rouge,* and his most enchanting and romantic waltz, "Beautiful Ohio." His movie theme song, *A Summer Place* (1959), became a major pop hit. Died: 1976.

Cliffie Stone ▮   1501 Vine

Musician, producer, DJ, songwriter, host, personality

Cliffie Stone

BORN Clifford Gilpin Snyder; March 1, 1917, in Stockton, CA. **SPOTLIGHTS** "Mr. Country Music" did it all in country music. As a boy, he played bass in his father's band. Later, he became a studio musician, a big band player, then celebrity disc jockey. He was also a singer, songwriter, comedian, band leader, music publisher and talent manager. This energetic man admitted, "I love life! I just love life!" He produced hits for Tex Williams, Tennessee Ernie Ford, and Tex Ritter. Together with Merle Travis, the duo co-wrote these classic hits: "No Vacancy," "Steel Guitar Rag," & "Divorce Me C.O.D." His hits with Capitol Records include "Silver Stars, Purple Sage, Eyes of Blue," "Peepin' Through the Keyhole," and "When My Blue Moon Turns to Gold Again." He hosted both radio's and TV's "Hometown Jamboree" for more than two decades. Inducted into the Disc Jockey Country Music Hall of Fame in Nashville, Tennessee. His son, Curtis, is a bass player with the group Highway 101. **QUOTE** "I happen to have been very lucky. I think luck and persistence—the more persistent you are the luckier you get—is the answer to the entertainment world. It's not talent. That sounds weird, but I know a lot of talented people that are starving." Died: 1998.

James Brown ●   1501 Vine

Singer, musician

James Brown

BORN May 3, 1933, in Barnwell, SC. **SPOTLIGHTS** He is known as Soul Brother #1, and the Godfather of Soul. Gospel-influenced with heavy rhythm & blues style, Brown had his first hit, "Please, Please, Please," with the Famous Flames group. He created the James Brown Revue with the James Brown Band and toured the country. Mr. Dynamite is celebrated for his funk, Brown's choreographed dance moves, and raw, powerful voice won him ecstatic fans in African-American venues. His jump-and-shout recordings hit big one after the other. Some of his hit rhythm songs include "I Don't Mind," "Lost Someone," "Out of Sight," "Papa's Got a Brand New Bag," "I Got You (I Feel Good)," and "It's a Man's, Man's, Man's World." Movie appearances include *The Blues Brothers* (1980 + sequel). His "Living in America" was the theme song to *Rocky IV.* More than a showman, and proud of his heritage, he inspired others to triumph over hardship. Socially conscious songs are: "Say It Loud," "Don't Be a Drop-Out," and "I Don't Want Nobody to Give Me Nothing (Open Up the Door I'll Get It Myself)." When not on tour, his social reform efforts include helping inner city youths with special programs, and investing in African American owned businesses. **ACHIEVEMENTS** He bravely entertained troops during the Vietnam war...He publicly pleaded for peace after the brutal assassination of Martin Luther King...He was inducted into the Rock and Roll Hall of Fame as a charter member in 1986...He received his Walk of Fame star on Jan. 10, 1997, in celebration of his 40th anniversary in show business. Fans will enjoy his autobiography, *James Brown: The Godfather of Soul.*

Harold Lloyd 🎥   1501 Vine

Actor, writer

BORN April 20, 1893, in Burchard, NE. **SPOTLIGHTS** One of the great silent stars, Lloyd was called "The King of Daredevil Comedy." A fit performer with athletic prowess, his antics differed from Chaplin's or Keaton's. Fans roared at the "glasses character"—a neatly dressed young man with black horn-rimmed glasses and a straw hat, who was an innocent but ambitious gent, thinking up zany ways to get out of difficult dilemmas (which he constantly found himself in). He originated his "glasses character" in 1917, and made his first full-length comedy, *Grandma's Boy,* in 1922. His clean-cut, wholesome character who teetered on the brink of disaster struck the funny bone in *Safety Last* (1923); *Girl Shy* (1924); *The Freshman* (1925); and *The Kid Brother* (1927). In *Speedy* (1928), Lloyd uses New York City as the urban backdrop to show the world a hilarious side to "the crush" of life in the Big

Harold Lloyd

Rick Nelson

Apple. It's a story about the last horse-drawn trolley in the frantic city but it stills gets slugger Babe Ruth from an orphanage to the stadium. His funniest sound picture is *The Milky Way* (1936), where he plays a meek milkman who accidentally KOs a prize-fighter, and then is relentlessly pursued by a boxing promoter (Adolphe Menjou). Watch for Lloyd's classic ducks punches scene. A compilation of his comic climaxes is *Harold Lloyd's World of Comedy* (1962). **ACHIEVEMENTS** 1952 Oscar: "Master comedian and good citizen." **SIDELIGHTS** Lloyd acted out all of his own stunts; in *Haunted Spooks* (1920) a bomb explosion cost him his right thumb and forefinger. (He often wore gloves after the accident.) **QUOTE** "It has been our observation that in any audience there are a certain number of persons who will demand the slapstick type of comedy. But audiences are appreciating more than ever the comedy which has a fairly well-defined plot, with action that is not as rough as the old slapstick, and still not too genteel, which is about the best way I know to express it. We have noted that audiences are drawing closer to an appreciation of comedy wherein the gags are mingled with story than in just straight gag comedies—pictures built entirely for laughs. Natural gags, laughs that are obtained in legitimate situations and by legitimate means, are always more valued by audiences than are incidents thrown in purely for a laugh. Not that the audience will not laugh at a forced situation, but you obtain a more wholesome, and frequently a more sustained, laugh through the natural gag in a legitimate situation." Died: 1971.

Rick Nelson 🎵   1501 Vine

Singer, songwriter, musician, actor
BORN Eric Hilliard Nelson; May 8, 1940, in Teaneck, NJ. **SPOTLIGHTS** A former American teen idol. As a teenager, Nelson had not planned on a singing career, but when a girlfriend told him she loved Elvis, he broke the spell by telling her he was cutting a record, too. Getting a song recorded was easy for him. Prior to the family's hit television (and radio) show "The Adventures of Ozzie and Harriet," his father had been a famous big band leader, his mother a talented singer. Rick had spent hours as a child stretched out on the floor of his family's living room listening to all styles of music, ranging from classical to swing, on the radio. He always loved music. His first record, "I'm Walkin'/Teenager's Romance" was initially presented on the family's television show. It sold more than one million copies, and made him as big a seller as Elvis. Other 1950s hit songs include "Be-Bop Baby," "It's Late," "Stood Up," and "Believe What You Say." His pure voice and meticulous phrasing is evident on his ballads "Lonesome Town," "Poor Little Fool," and "Sweeter Than You," which also rated in the Top Ten. This rock 'n' roll recording artist took a break from music to make two movies: *Rio Bravo* (1959) with John Wayne, and *The Wackiest Ship in the Army* (1960). In the 1960s he hit big with "Teenage Idol," "Young World," "It's Up to You," and "Hello, Mary Lou." His 1961 "Travelin' Man" not only topped the charts, but was the *first* music video as well. Work in the 1970s include Bob Dylan's "She Belongs To Me," and "Garden Party." Rick sought acceptance by his peers for his talents as a rock 'n' roll musician with his Stone Canyon Band. He was invited to perform at an oldies show at New York's Madison Square Garden. He did not want to do the gig, as recollections of TV's "Ricky" were strongly etched in the memories of fans and he did not want to reinforce it, but he had a new album to promote. When he arrived, he did not resemble his teen image. The fans at the event wanted to see and hear the "teeny-bopper Ricky," and literally booed the long-haired, rock 'n' roll Rick off the stage. He defined this dilemma in the lyrics of a song he wrote after the show. Working quickly, with no hesitations, he wrote "Garden Party" in one straight draft on a single sheet of yellow-lined legal paper. (It is currently on loan to the Rock and Roll Hall of Fame, in Cleveland, Ohio.) The revealing lyrics: "If you gotta play at garden parties, I wish you a lot of luck, but if memories were all I sang, I'd rather drive a truck." Rick's recording of his song became critically acclaimed, went to the Top Ten on the charts, and turned Gold. It was to be his last hit. In retrospect, accomplished musicians and recording artists in the music industry now officially recognize Rick's exceptional talent and subtlety as a vocalist. Most consider the recordings of Elvis Presley and Rick Nelson to be the two influential cornerstones of the early rock 'n' roll era. **HIGHLIGHTS** Marriage to Kristin Harmon (now Kristin Nelson Tinker), a renowned primitive-style artist and author of *Out of My Mind: A Painted Journal*. Published by Harry Abrams, this art/autobiographical book is available by calling (800) 288-2131. The marriage continued the talent line: their daughter Tracy is an actress, their identical twin sons Gunnar and Matthew lead the

rock group "Nelson," and their youngest, Sam, has completed studies in art and filmmaking at Boston University. **SIDELIGHTS** His TV catchphrase: "I don't mess around, boy" was imitated by millions of American youngsters. His older brother David, who co-starred on the family's TV and radio shows, became a film and TV director/producer. (See "David Nelson" and "Ozzie and Harriet Nelson" biographies in this book.) **QUOTE** In 1977 Rick was interviewed saying, "I don't see myself growing older. Now, whatever that means, I don't know what that means, but I can't... (sigh) I don't know." Died: On New Year's Eve 1985, en route to a performance, in the crash of a chartered DC-3 airplane. Ironically, Rick had just completed recording Buddy Holly's "True Love Weighs." (Holly also died in a small airplane crash.) In 1988 the National Transportation Safety Board determined the crash had been caused by a fire started by a malfunctioning, old-style gasoline-powered heater in the airplane.

Jack Benny 🎭   1501 Vine

See page 432

Clint Walker 📺   1501 Vine

Clint Walker

Actor
BORN Norman Walker; May 30, 1927, in Hartford, IL. **SPOTLIGHTS** This vital, tall (6'6"), muscular, dark-haired, handsome hunk starred in TV's top-rated "Cheyenne" (1955-'63). He played a Western adventurer who, following the days after the Civil War, drifted from one interesting job to another. In one episode he was a trail scout on a wagon train; in the next a recently deputized lawman; then, in another he was a foreman on a ranch. Along the way, the husky-voiced, brooding champion of freedom and justice fought bad guys, and met up with beautiful women. He also starred in the short-lived television drama "Kodiak," as an Alaska State Patrol policeman. Walker made his movie debut in DeMille's religious epic, *The Ten Commandments* (1956). Other films include *Yellowstone Kelly* (1959), *Send Me No Flowers* (1964), *None but the Brave* (1965), *The Dirty Dozen* (1967), *The Great Bank Robbery* (1969), *Pancho Villa* (1974), and *Serpent Warriors* (1986).

Jackie Cooper 🎥   1501 Vine

Actor, director, executive producer
BORN John Cooper, Jr., Sept. 15, 1921, in Los Angeles, CA. **SPOTLIGHTS** The sensitive, snub-nosed child began acting at

age three in comedies, and was quickly on his way to becoming America's favorite boy tot. The youngster played one of the kids in eight episodes of the classic *Our Gang* film series. At age seven, he signed a long-term contract with MGM Studios, witnessed by mogul Louis B. Mayer. He was not without family on the lot; his uncle was MGM director Norman Taurog. This endearing, extraordinary, natural born talent was a box office Pied Piper. Fans were

Jack(ie) Cooper

moved to joy and sorrow by him throughout the Great Depression. He received a 1931 Academy Award nomination for best actor in Taurog's *Skippy*. Other movies from that period include *The Champ* (1931), *The Bowery* (1933), *Treasure Island* (1934), and *Peck's Bad Boy* (1935). As he grew, his roles explored teen life in *What a Life* (1939), *Seventeen* (1940), and *Her First Beau* (1941). This young star had earned more than $1.5 million dollars before enlisting in the Navy. He served bravely during World War II. Upon his honorable discharge, Hollywood executives had prefixed notions about him. Cooper stated, "They wanted me to play a grown up Skippy. But I was tired of sticking out my lower lip." And like his predecessor, Jackie Coogan, Cooper found childhood stardom not all it was cracked up to be. He reflected, "I lived in an all-adult world, studied at the studio and seldom met kids my own age. I wasn't given an ounce of responsibility or taught the value of money. It makes you emotionally ill to be treated like an enlarged infant." Postwar, Cooper moved to New York, dropped the "ie" from his first name, and took stock of himself. As an actor, he worked in theater and TV. Later films include *Stand Up and Be Counted* (1972--his directorial film debut), *Superman* (1978), *Superman II* (1980), *Superman III* (1983), and *Superman IV: The Quest for Peace* (1987). He is an Emmy Award-winning TV director of "M*A*S*H."

Alice White 🎥   1501 Vine

Actress
BORN Alva White, Aug. 28, 1907, in Patterson, NJ. **SPOTLIGHTS** This woman's career went full circle; from an office job to lofty screen position then back to the office. She was a real-life secretary turned silent star, turned real-life-secretary. At the top in *Naughty Boy* and *Hot Stuff* (both 1929), she was favorably compared with the "It" girl, superstar Clara Bow. She co-stars with James Cagney and Bette Davis in *Jimmy the Gent* (1934), but could not keep it going. Died: 1983.

Belle Bennett 🎥   1501 Vine

Actress

BORN Oct. 21, 1892, in Milaca, MN. **SPOTLIGHTS** This leading lady's ethereal looks melted hearts in a number of silents: *Flesh and Spirit* (1922), *Stella Dallas* (1925), and *Playing with Souls* (1925). She worked with director John Ford *in Mother Machree* (1928). Died: 1932.

Major Bowes    1501 Vine

Actor, composer

BORN Major Edward Bowes; June 14, 1874, in San Francisco, CA. **SPOTLIGHTS** He was a great showman in the same league as Phineas T. Barnum. Bowes ran the talent contest of all talent contests. And, at times, ran it just like the big top. "Major Bowes and His Original Amateur Hour" contest excited radio listeners with human interest stories and hopefuls competing against one another at a shot of the brass ring. He opened each show with: "A spinning goes our weekly wheel of fortune, around and around she goes, and where she stops nobody knows." A handful of true talents were discovered: soprano Beverly Sills when she was seven years old, Frank Sinatra in 1937, and Robert Merrill—all Walk of Fame honorees—sang their way into superstardom. The show ended in 1945. Ted Mack, who been a master of ceremonies for Bowes, brought back the show (see his bio in this book). Died: 1946.

The Wynns with Keenan (left), Tracy (center), and Ed (right)

Keenan Wynn   1501 Vine

Actor

BORN Francis Wynn, July 27, 1916, in New York, NY. **SPOTLIGHTS** One of Hollywood's most reliable character actors, he appeared in more than 100 motion pictures. He worked equally well in comedies or dramas, and spent a good deal of his career with MGM. He is the grandson of stage and silent screen star Frank Keenan, and son of "The Perfect Fool," character actor Ed Wynn (another Walk of Famer). Keenan made his screen debut in a Busby Berkeley musical, *For Me and My Gal* (1942), starring Judy Garland, George Murphy, and introducing Gene Kelly. He made waves with a good supporting role in his very next picture, *See Here, Private Hargrove* (1944), a military comedy about a bunch of green recruits. It stars Robert Walker and Donna Reed. Movies include *Since You Went Away* (1944), *Weekend at the Waldorf* (1945), *The Hucksters* (1947), *Annie Get Your Gun* (1950), *Angels in the Outfield* (1951), *Kiss Me, Kate!* (1953), *The Man in the Gray Flannel Suit* (1956), *The Great Man* (1956), *Don't Go Near the Water* (1957), *The Absent-Minded Professor* (1961), *The Great Race* (1965), *Pretty Maids all in a Row* (1971), and *The Shaggy D.A.* (1976). He appeared in countless live TV playhouse specials, including the dramatic production of "Requiem for a Heavyweight." Later, he played Willard (Digger) Barnes in TV's "Dallas" (1979-'80). In all, Wynn appeared in 250 TV shows. He was also an accomplished stage and radio performer. His son, Tracy Keenan Wynn, is the family's fourth generation to go into show business; he is a screenwriter. **QUOTE** Asked why he became a character actor, he replied, "Let the stars take the blame, I had the fun." Died: 1986.

Loretta Lynn   1501 Vine

Singer, performer, songwriter

BORN Loretta Webb, April 14, 1936 (or so) in Butchers Hollow, KY. **SPOTLIGHTS** The most successful and beloved female country star of all time. A coal miner's daughter, born poverty-stricken in the backwoods South during the Great Depression, she wed at barely age 14 to Oliver V. "Mooney" Lynn. She began writing songs on her Sears Roebuck guitar and helped support her own growing family by taking in other

Loretta Lynn

people's laundry and picking strawberries with migrant workers. Although she sang for her children (at age 18 she was already the mother of four) and husband, she did not dream of becoming a professionally. Later, Lynn recalled, "My husband was the one that wanted me to start singing. I really wouldn't have started if he hadn't pushed me, because I was kind of bashful and backward." She began performing in local honkytonks, then won a talent contest hosted by Buck Owens. She worked with him on his local TV show, landed a recording contract, and after a struggle promoting her record "I'm a Honky Tonk Girl," launched her career when it went to #15 on the charts. In 1960 she received an invitation to perform at the Grand Ole Opry. Two years later, she had her first bit hit aptly titled "Success." That same year, she became a member of the Grand Ole Opry. She followed up with more winners: "Before I'm over You," "Wine, Women and Song," "Happy Birthday," and her personal favorite, "Blue Kentucky Girl." With Ernest Tubb she had big winners with "Mr. and Mrs.

Used-To-Be," "Sweet Thang," "Our Hearts Are Holding Hands," and "Who's Gonna Take the Garbage Out." Her hit songs--original, gutsy, expressive with their rural Southern roots--have flowed year after year: "Don't Come Home A-Drinkin' (With Lovin' on Your Mind)," "Your Squaw Is on the Warpath," "Fist City," "You Ain't Woman Enough," and "Woman of the World (Leave My World Alone)." Her collaborations with Conway Twitty were also hits: "After the Fire Is Gone," "Louisiana Woman--Mississippi Man," "Lead Me On," "As Soon As I Hang Up the Phone," and "Feelins'." During the women's liberation era of the 1970s, she recorded "The Pill" and "Rated X." Working with Shel Silverstein she did "One's on the Way." Lynn revolutionized country western music by being its first female solo artist to represent women's changing attitudes as they strove for equality. She is one of America's most popular, friendly and lovable entertainers. In 1970, she wrote and sang one of the century's most significant songs, "Coal Miner's Daughter." From that sprang her courageous and inspirational life story—and best-selling book. Adapted into the five-star motion picture, *Coal Miner's Daughter* (1979), it stars Sissy Spacek and Tommy Lee Jones. **ACHIEVEMENTS** 1971 Grammy, country vocal. 1972, *the first woman ever* to win the Entertainer of the Year Award from the Country Music Association. She is the recipient of countless other honors.

Carl Smith ◉   1501 Vine

Singer, guitarist
BORN March 15, 1927, in Maynardsville, TN. **SPOTLIGHTS** This energetic 1950s honky-tonk giant had five #1 records, 30 Top Tens, and 93 on the charts. His robust, full-throated vocal style and instrumental accompaniment produced hit after hit: "Let's Live a Little," "Mr. Moon," "If Teardrops Were Pennies," "Let Old Mother Nature Have Her Way," "(When You Feel Like You're in Love) Don't Just Stand There," "Are You Teasing Me," "It's a Lovely, Lovely World," "Our Honeymoon," "This Orchid Means Goodbye," "Just Wait Till I Get You Alone," "Hey, Joe!" "Go Boy Go," and "You Are the One." This country music legend retired in 1984 to become a gentleman farmer in Tennessee. His daughter, Charlene, is a singer.

Leo Carrillo 📺   1501 Vine

See page 354

Gale Storm ◉   1501 Vine

See page 224

Harry Carey 🎥   1501 Vine

Actor
BORN Jan. 16, 1878, in the Bronx, NY. **SPOTLIGHTS** On-screen from 1909, this early silent Western star made a smooth transition to the talkies. He appears in Van Dyke's *Trader Horn* (1931), an early talkie shot in Africa. In *The Last Outlaw* (1936), he gives a must-see performance as a gunslinger out of jail after a 25-year-term. He tries to cope in a Wild West he no longer recognizes. He delivers another outstanding performance in *Mr. Smith Goes to Washington* (1939). He appears in the dramatic soap opera, *They Knew What They Wanted* (1940), starring Carole Lombard and Charles Laughton. *Angel and the Badman* (1947) is about the redemption of a wounded gunslinger (John Wayne). *Red River* was released after his death. Died: 1947. Director John Ford dedicated *The Three God-fathers* (1948) *"to the memory of Harry Carey—bright star of the early Western sky."*

Billy Dee Williams 🎥   1501 Vine

Billy Dee Williams

Actor
BORN April 6, 1937, in New York, NY. **SPOTLIGHTS** Williams possesses ample magnetism, charm and talent. He gave a powerful, moving performance as a Chicago Bears football player in *Brian's Song* (1970—in one of the finest television movies of all time), opposite James Caan. This handsome, debonair leading man gave an outstanding performance in the biopic of jazz great Billie Holiday, in *Lady Sings the Blues* (1972). He stars in a movie—that possibly has the longest title ever—*The Bingo Long Traveling All-Stars and Motor Kings* (1976). An offbeat, but absorbing comedy about baseball, its exuberant cast also features James Earl Jones and Richard Pryor. In 1979 Williams plays a soldier returning to visit a group of nuns in *Christmas Lilies of the Field*. (This is the sequel to *Lilies of the Field*, for which Sydney Poitier won an Oscar.) Williams was immortalized in his important supporting role in *The Empire Strikes Back, Star Wars II* (1980), and in the conclusion of the *Star Wars* trilogy, *The Return of the Jedi* (1983). He co-stars with Sylvester Stallone, Lindsay Wagner and Rutger Hauer in the crime drama *Nighthawks* (1981). He appears in Tim Burton's dark vision of *Batman* (1989), then in Stuart Gordon's *The Pit and the Pendulum* (1991). The following year, Williams made *Driving Me Crazy*. He gives a choice performance in another sports picture—this time boxing—in *Percy and Thunder* (1993), opposite James Earl Jones. Earlier, Williams conquered the stage at age seven, and as an adult has appeared in a variety of productions since 1961. **TV** In addition to guest starring roles, he co-starred in a thriller with Oscar nominees Burt Reynolds, Robert Duvall and Charles Durning in Turner network's highly rated "Hard Time."

Joan Davis

Joan Davis 🎥 1501 Vine

Actress, comedienne

BORN Madonna Josephine Davis, June 29, 1907, in St. Paul, MN. **SPOTLIGHTS** An absolute crackup, her madcap abandon and wisecracking wit appealed to the intelligentsia and the masses. This top-notch comedienne possessed expressive eyes, a wide mouth, a modulated voice, and rubbery legged wizardry. She employed perfect and sometimes sophisticated facial twinges reacting to each comedy circumstance. She plays a professional radio screamer in the hilarious comedy *Hold That Ghost* (1941), starring funny men Abbott and Costello--in one of their best pictures. Look for the side-splitting dance scene. (Plus the Andrew Sisters make an appearance singing, "Aurora.") Motion pictures include *On the Avenue* (1937), *She Wrote the Book* (1946), *If You Knew Susie* (1948), and *Love That Brute* (1950). **TV** Starred in "I Married Joan" (NBC, 1952-'55), with Jim Backus as her husband. **TRADEMARK GAG** Her famous falling dishes routine. **QUOTE** In the late 1940s, comedienne-singer Fanny Brice stated, "There's one dame that could play me, that's Joan Davis." Davis did not live long enough to portray the Ziegfeld Follies star in the movie based on her life. *Funny Girl* (1968) stars Barbra Streisand. **LOWLIGHTS** In 1961, at age 54, Davis complained to her mother of aches and pains she was suffering in her back. She was rushed to the local hospital, but died of a heart attack a few hours later.

Edith Storey 🎥 1501 Vine

Actress

BORN March 18, 1892. **SPOTLIGHTS** An accomplished stage actress with athletic prowess, she was popular in silents from 1908. Movies include *Lincoln's Gettysburg Address* (1912), and *The Dust of Egypt* (1915). She retired in 1921. Died: 1967.

Angela Lansbury 📺 1501 Vine

See page 75

Jack Pickford 🎥 1501 Vine

Actor, director

BORN Jack Smith, Aug. 18, 1896, in Canada. **SPOTLIGHTS** His older, incredibly famous sister Mary had proven the Pickford name as good as gold at the box office. Silent movies include *Poor Little Peppina* (1916), *Tom Sawyer* (1917), and *The Hill Billy* (1924)...When his sister co-founded United Artists, he became a director...He was married to Olive

Thomas, "the most beautiful girl in the world." She was a Ziegfeld Follies star and Alberto Vargas model until her sudden death in 1920. **QUOTE** "It is frequently said—too frequently, in fact—that all you need to achieve fame is 'a drag.' If you only know the manager. Or if you only have influence with the owner. Or if you are rich. All a matter of 'if'—and 'drag.' With persons who hold these views, I beg to differ. Incredible though it may seem to some, 'pull' is more apt to be a liability than as asset." Died: 1933.

John Ericson 📺 1501 Vine

John Ericson

Actor

BORN Joseph Meibes, Sept. 25, 1926, in Dusseldorf, Germany. **SPOTLIGHTS** In 1930, at age four, he was brought to the U.S. to escape the Nazis. After graduating from the American Academy of Dramatic Arts, the tall, attractive 25-year-old made his 1951 Broadway stage debut in "Stalag 17," and screen debut in *Teresa*. MGM signed him in 1954. Motion pictures include *Rhapsody* (1954--opposite Elizabeth Taylor), *The Student Prince* (1954--with Ann Blyth), *Bad Day at Black Rock* (1955--starring Spencer Tracy), *Forty Guns* (1957), and *Pretty Boy Floyd* (1960--in title role). He played detective Sam Bolt in TV's "Honey West" (1965-66).

Marjorie Reynolds 📺 1501 Vine

Actress, dancer

BORN Marjorie Goodspeed, Aug. 12, 1921, in Buhl, ID. **SPOTLIGHTS** A child actor in silent pictures, she advanced to Westerns. Her crowning glory was appearing in the Irving Berlin musical, *Holiday Inn* (1942). She plays the love interest between rivals Bing Crosby and Fred Astaire. She sings with Crosby, and dances the minuet with Astaire. Films include *Up in Mabel's Room* (1944), *Duffy's Tavern* (1945), *Monsieur Beaucaire* (1946) and *That Midnight Kiss* (1949). TV: Reynolds endeared herself to audiences as the long-suffering wife, Peg, in the situation comedy, "The Life of Riley" (1953-'58), opposite William Bendix. Died: 1997.

Frances Langford 🎙️ 1501 Vine

See page 309

Louis Lumière 🎥 1533 Vine

Inventor, producer, director

BORN Oct. 5, 1864, in France. **SPOTLIGHTS** Called "the father of cinema," in 1895 he co-invented the Cinématographe with his brother Auguste Lumière. Their invention was a combination camera-projector (based on Thomas Edison's kinetoscope). Whereby Edison had invented an early type of motion picture camera, it could not project images. A person viewed Edison's moving pictures through an individual device which provided a light source and rapidly rotating shutters. The historic birth of world cinema occurred on Dec. 13, 1895, when a paying audience watched the Lumières' films projected on a "screen," at Le Grand Café on the Boulevard des Capucines, in Paris, France. By 1900, the Lumières had produced 2,000 pictures and newscasts, and Louis had directed 60 films. Died: 1948.

Lina Basquette 🎥   1533 Vine

Dancer, actress
BORN Lina Baskette, April 19, 1907, in San Mateo, CA. **SPOTLIGHTS** A black-haired beauty of the Ziegfeld Follies, she basked in her celebrity. Movies include *Juvenile Dancer* (1916), and *The Godless Girl* (1929). She endured lengthy court battles over the estate of her late husband, Sam Warner (of Warner Bros.) and over their daughter, of whom she lost custody to the surviving brother, Harry. An animal lover, she moved to Pennsylvania to breed champion Great Danes. Died: 1994.

Perez Prado 🔘   1533 Vine

Pianist, band leader
BORN Dec. 11, 1922, in Matanas, Cuba. **SPOTLIGHTS** This outstanding Latin talent toured America with his phenomenal band. Albums include *Grandes Exitos De*, *This Is the Decade of the 30s*, and *Decade of the 50s*. Singles include "Cherry Pink and Apple Blossom White." Died: 1989.

Pat O'Brien 🎥 🎥   1533 Vine

Pat O'Brien

Actor
BORN William Joseph Patrick O'Brien, Nov. 11, 1899, in Milwaukee, WI. **SPOTLIGHTS** An easy-going, but tough-looking Irish-American, he was reliable in both gentle and villainous roles. In the 1930s he made *The Front Page* (1931) co-starring Adolphe Menjou and Mary Brian, *Bombshell* (1933) with Jean Harlow, *Here Comes the Navy* (1934) opposite James Cagney, *In Caliente* (1935) with love interest Dolores del Rio, and *Angels with Dirty Faces* (1938--as the priest) with James Cagney and Humphrey Bogart. He was excellent in *Knute Rockne-All American* (1940)- -which set the standard for Hollywood sports biographies. When then-actor Ronald Reagan learned Warner Bros. had cast O'Brien in the lead, he asked him for help getting cast as George Gipp, the Notre Dame football star. O'Brien persuaded Jack Warner in the front office to give Reagan the green light. Later, as the real-life President of the United States, Reagan recited the famous line from the film's pep talk: "Go out and win one for the Gipper." Other movies include *Crack-Up* (1946) co-starring Claire Trevor, *The Boy with Green Hair* (1948) with Dean Stockwell and Robert Ryan, *The People Against O'Hara* (1951) with Spencer Tracy, *The Last Hurrah* (1958) co-starring Spencer Tracy and Jeffrey Hunter, *Some Like it Hot* (1959) starring Marilyn Monroe, and *The End* (1978) with Burt Reynolds. His last film was *Ragtime* (1981), starring his old pal, James Cagney. **ACHIEVEMENTS** He joined the Navy with childhood pal Spencer Tracy during WWI. **HIGHLIGHTS** A devoted family man, he created an international scandal when he refused to be presented to King George VI and Queen Elizabeth without his wife Eloise at his side. Amazingly, the Royal family altered their protocol. Both Mr. and Mrs. O' Brien were presented to His and Her Highnesses. Died: 1983.

Betty Furness 🎥   1533 Vine

See page 59
See page 59

Roger Williams 🔘   1533 Vine

Pianist, composer, arranger
BORN Louis Weertz, Oct. 1, 1926, in Omaha, NE. **SPOTLIGHTS** The son of a music teacher, he began playing the piano at age three. Williams was a winner on the "Arthur Godfrey Talent Scouts," and attended the Juilliard School of Music. Albums include *Music of the 1940s*, *Music of the 1950s*, *Music of the 1970s*, *To Amadeus with Love*, and *The Way We Were*. Singles include: "Almost Paradise," "Born Free," "Impossible Dream," and "Autumn Leaves" (1955).

Paul Weston 🔘   1533 Vine

Conductor, composer, author
BORN P. Wetstein, March 12, 1912, in Springfield, MA. **SPOTLIGHTS** The Music Maker works in mysterious ways. Weston was a graduate student at Columbia University when a 1933 train wreck injury caused him a long period of convalescence. To pass the time in bed, he wrote musical arrangements. The Joe Haymes Orchestra bought a few of his arrangements, then Rudy Vallee heard them. Vallee signed the kid as an arranger on his radio show, "The Fleischman Hour." By 1940 he had Hollywood in the palms of his hands, not only by his talent, but by his sweet personality which accompanied it. He arranged the score for the perennial Christmas special *Holiday Inn* (1942), starring Bing Crosby and Fred Astaire. He conducted and arranged for such greats as Rudy Vallee,

Tommy Dorsey, Bing Crosby, Ella Fitzgerald, Kate Smith, Sarah Vaughan, Judy Garland, Doris Day, Jim Nabors, Dinah Shore, and Rosemary Clooney. His favorite singer, though, was his wife, Jo Stafford. He composed pop hits: "Day by Day," "I Should Care," "Shrimp Boats," and "Autumn in Rome." Albums: *Cinema Cameos, Easy Jazz*. His son is jazz guitarist Tim Weston; his daughter Amy, a singer. **ACHIEVEMENTS** A founder of the National Academy of Recording Arts and Sciences. 1960 Grammy. Died: 1996.

June Allyson 🎥   1533 Vine

June Allyson

Actress, singer
BORN Ella Geisman, Oct. 7, 1917, in Bronx, NY. **SPOTLIGHTS** Allyson's husky voice, toothpaste smile and sense of humor helped her land a job as a chorus girl in the 1938 Broadway production of "Sing Out the News." She reminisced, "The only honest way to describe it is to say that they hired me for laughs." Nonetheless, the vivacious talent parlayed the opportunity. She became a feature player in George Abbott's 1941 musical, "Best Foot Forward." She followed the same part to Hollywood. Lucille Ball landed the 1943 lead and Allyson the supporting role. Her warm, cheerful, personable on-screen appearances endeared her in "the girl next door" roles throughout the 1940s. Films include Norman Taurog's *Girl Crazy* (1943), and George Sidney's *Thousands Cheer* (1943). One of her most memorable films was the classic, *Little Women* (1949--as Jo). With her charming personality and sunny disposition, she played the perfectly devoted and dutiful wife throughout the 1950s. Films include *The Glenn Miller Story* (1953), *The McConnell Story* (1955), and *The Shrike* (1955—where she plays against type as the nastiest, cruel hearted spouse). She was married to Dick Powell (1945-'63) until his death. In 2000, she starred in a celebration of the "Classic Hollywood Musicals" at the Pasadena Civic.

Mel Torme 💿   1541 Vine

Singer, songwriter, arranger, musician, actor
BORN Sept. 13, 1925, in Chicago, IL. **SPOTLIGHTS** Nicknamed "The Velvet Fog," he was a honey-smooth, romantic jazz singer. His assured phrasing and rhythmic panache created a unique lightness and tenderness. As a dynamic jazz spirit, he really cooked. He set the drums on fire with Woody Herman, or "Sing, Sing, Sing" when he performed live. The supreme Torme made many fine recordings. Not to be missed are "Mel Torme Swings Shubert Alley" and "The Ellington and

Basie Songbooks." Included are the classics: "Too Darn Hot," "Just in Time," "A Sleeping' Bee" "Reminiscing In Tempo," and "I'm Gonna Go Fishin'." Earlier, at age 15, he wrote his first hit song "Lament to Love." This Grammy-winner never stopped making hits during his lengthy career. As an actor, he made his screen debut in *Higher and Higher* (1943), with Frank Sinatra in a musical Cinderella-type story. The following year,

Mel Torme

he appeared in *Pardon My Rhythm*, and *Let's Go Steady*. TV: He hosted his own show, as well as guest starring in a number of programs. His most famous composition was "The Christmas Song," with the familiar opening lyrics, "Chestnuts roasting on an open fire..." *An Evening with George Shearing & Mel Torme*; *Nothing Without You*; *Mel Torme/Rob McConnell and the Boss Brass*; *Top Drawer*; and *A&E: An Evening With Mel Torme — Live from the Disney Institute* are available on the Concord Jazz Label. Call (925) 682-6770; (800)-551-5299; or website: www.aent.com/concord Died: 1999.

Steve Allen 📺   1541 Vine

See page 182

Steve Lawrence and Eydie Gorme 💿
Singers, actors   **1541 Vine**

Steve Lawrence and Eydie Gorme

BORN Lawrence: Sidney Liebowitz; July 8,1935; Eydie: Aug. 16, 1931; both in NY. **SPOTLIGHTS** In 1960 the pair stepped on the stage for the first time as "Steve and Eydie." In 2000 they celebrated their 37th anniversary as one of America's most popular singing duos. Lawrence commented, "Eydie and I have been singing together all these years and still nothing gives us greater joy than performing for an audience." Perennially known as Steve and Eydie, a cool, hep cat and his tigress, they have kept audiences cheering with a collection of pop standards throughout four decades. National columnist and talk show host Larry King wrote, "If Steve Lawrence and Eydie Gorme don't entertain you, then no one can entertain you." All-around performers, Lawrence earned the New York Drama Critics Award and a Tony nomination for his Broadway debut in "What Makes Sammy Run." Next, the couple shared the bright lights on stage in the musical comedy-drama "Golden Rainbow." Their TV specials saluting the great American songwriters are high quality, stylish and delivered with expert showmanship. After their sold-out Diamond Jubilee world tour with Frank Sinatra, Sinatra declared, "Steve and Eydie represent all that is good about performers and the interpretation of a song. They're the best." **ACHIEVEMENTS** Winner of seven Emmy Awards for "Steve and Eydie Celebrate Irving Berlin." Winner of two Emmys for their TV tribute to George and Ira Gershwin, "Our Love is Here to Stay." 1995 Recipients of the Society of Singers prestigious "Ella" Lifetime Achievement Award. 1966 Grammy for Gorme for her solo recording of "If He Walked Into My Life." 1960 Grammy for their album *We've Got Us*.

John Wayne (left), Frank Sinatra (center), and Monty Hall

John Wayne 🎥　　　　　1541 Vine

John Wayne

Actor, producer, director

BORN Marion Michael Morrison; May 26,1907, in Winterset, IA. **S P O T L I G H T S** Nicknamed the "Duke," he was a strong, charismatic, quiet craftsman with a magnetic, bigger-than-life presence. A man's man and a woman's man, his hallmark was integrity and that translated worldwide. He became a hero as the romantic and touching Ringo Kid in John Ford's landmark Western, *Stagecoach* (1939)-- his breakthrough film. But, *She Wore a Yellow Ribbon* (1949), a Technicolor tribute to the U.S. Calvary was his personal favorite. Other motion pictures include *Dark Command* (1940), *The Long Voyage Home* (1940), *Seven Sinners* (all 1940), *Shepherd of the Hills* (1941--his first color picture), *Reap the Wild Wind*, *The Spoilers* (both 1942), *A Lady Takes a Chance* (1943), *They Were Expendable* (1945), *Fort Apache* (1948), *Red River* (1948), *The Horse Soldiers* (1949), *The Quiet Man* (1952), *Hondo* (1954), *The Searchers* (1959), and *North to Alaska* (1960). **HIGHLIGHTS** He said he liked working: "in Westerns because in a Western there's no phoniness. Cowboys—and soldiers—have simple basic reactions. They look at somebody they love like they love 'em and somebody they hate like they hate 'em, and people with normal healthy reactions can feel that." When asked about his acting technique, Wayne roared, "How often do I gotta tell you that I don't act at all—I re-act." Of his 50-year career, he once said, "I can't remember if I've made 200 or 400 films." About his characters, he declared, "I play John Wayne in every picture regardless of the character. I've been doing okay, haven't I? I'd be a fool to change even if I could." Amazingly, after being so closely associated with Westerns, he received an Academy Award nomination for the *Sands of Iwo Jima* (1949), a war film. In 1956 he was the highest paid actor in the world. *Time* magazine said he was—for the studios—"the biggest money-maker in movie history." In 1974 he went to Cambridge to be roasted by the Harvard Lampoon. A student in the audience asked, "Do you look at yourself as an American Legend?" The Duke furrowed his brow and drawled, "Well, not being a Harvard man, I don't look at myself anymore than necessary." **NICKNAME** Growing up, he had a favorite Airedale terrier named Duke. The boy and his dog were inseparable as they walked around town. The firemen at the local station started calling him Duke (after his dog), and the nickname stuck. **ACHIEVEMENTS** 1969 Best Actor Oscar for *True Grit*. As he accepted the award, Wayne said, "Wow! If I'd known, I'd have put on that eye patch 35 years earlier." **RECOMMENDED** *John Wayne's America* by Garry Wills, published by Simon & Schuster. **SIDELIGHTS** He rued the day he rejected Don Siegel's *Dirty Harry* (1971); he stated the title role would have kept him #1 at the box office. Clint Eastwood appears in the crime series. **QUOTE** Asked how he would like his tombstone to read, Wayne stated, "I would like to be remembered—well, the Mexicans have a phrase, *'Feo, fuerte y formal'* which means: he was ugly, was strong, and had dignity." Died: 1979.

Merv Griffin 📺　　　　　1541 Vine

Host, singer, producer

BORN Mervyn Griffin; June 6, 1925, in San Mateo, CA. **SPOTLIGHTS** A show business tycoon, he has been called "the total performer," an "entrepreneurial powerhouse," and "friend and confidant." Griffin, who grew up in the depths of the Great Depression, literally built the ladder of his success step by step. He first entered talent contests, wrote songs, and sang on the local radio station KFRC in San Francisco—billed as

Merv Griffin

"America's Romantic Singing Star." In the 1940s, Griffin became a top vocalist with the big band, "Freddy Martin and His Orchestra," specializing in love ballads. As a romantic nightclub singer, he struck gold in 1950 with the #1 song "I've Got a Lovely Bunch of Coconuts." It sold more than three million copies. He continued to record hit songs "Wilhelmina," and "Never Been Kissed," until actress-singer Doris Day watched him perform in a trendy club. She was so impressed that she arranged for Warner Bros.' to screen-test him. As an actor, he appears in the musical biopic *So This is Love* (1953), opposite opera star Kathryn Grayson, the Western *The Boy from Oklahoma* (1954), with Will Rogers, Jr. and Lon Chaney, Jr., and *By the Light of the Silvery Moon*, a nostalgic, happy American family musical, co-starring Doris Day and Gordon MacRae. Griffin, an all-around superb entertainer, became a popular headliner in Las Vegas during this time. Yet, the medium in which he would obtain his greatest fame was television. Griffin became a regular performer on "The Arthur Murray Show," and "The Jack Paar Show." In 1958, he hosted "Play Your Hunch." Its success led to his hosting/producing "Word for Word," five years later. Simultaneously in 1963, Griffin conceived the idea for what was to become one of the most successful quiz shows in TV history, "Jeopardy!" which first aired in 1964. He also created TV's most popular game show ever, "Wheel of Fortune." (Also see the bios of Pat Sajak and Alex Trebek in this book.) However, it was in 1962 that his career took an even more interesting turn. He became a regular guest host of Jack Paar's "The Tonight Show," and the "Merv-phenomenon" swept the late night audience, scoring some of the highest ratings the show had ever seen. NBC gave him his own hour-long talk show program. Griffin set new standards for TV talk when he created "The Merv Griffin Show" (1963-'86). Over the years, the intelligent host pioneered a talk show format that has become the model for every successful talk show aired since. His relaxed, but probing style of interviewing celebrities received the highest praise when Peter Ustinov stated that he enjoyed being on "The Merv Griffin Show as I find out what I think about things." Griffin also delved into serious subjects such as nuclear disarmament, Vietnam, and civil rights with his now-famous interview with Dr. Martin Luther King, Jr. He traveled the globe interviewing world leaders, and broadcast from the White House. **ACHIEVEMENTS** Winner of 15 Emmy Awards, he was honored with the prestigious 1994 Broadcasting and Cable "Hall of Fame" Award, alongside honorees Diane Sawyer and Dan Rather. He hosts a variety of charity events, including the annual "Christmas Tree Lane"

benefitting "City Hearts, Kids Say Yes to the Arts." **HIGHLIGHTS** Some of his enterprises are: "Merv Griffin Entertainment" (TV), Liberty (Radio) Broadcasting Group, "Merv Griffin Hotels," including the Beverly Hilton Hotel, in Beverly Hills, California, and Merv Griffin's Resorts Casino Hotel in Atlantic City.

Ed Wynn 🎥   1541 Vine

Actor, clown, singer, writer
BORN Issiah Edwin Leopold; Nov. 9, 1886, in Philadelphia, PA. (His stage name was a simple split of his middle name.) **SPOTLIGHTS** Wynn was a big, cuddly bear of a man with an uncommonly squeaky, sweet and silly voice. A former vaudeville clown known for his collection of funny and outrageous hats and bell-bottomed coats, he commented, "Clown clothes make me feel funny, and if I felt funny I hoped I would sound funny." In 1914, he was employed as a Ziegfeld Follies entertainer. One year after joining the Follies, he shared billing with W.C. Fields. Wynn rose to stardom as a kind, daffy "Perfect Fool" of Broadway musicals. Under contract to the Shuberts, he was earning $1,700-a-week at the time, an astronomical sum. For added comic effect, and due to his stage fright nervousness, he added an hysterical, falsetto shriek to his dialogue, and became one of America's most beloved entertainers. For 25 years he enjoyed hit after hit on Broadway—many shows he wrote himself, including the music, songs, and jokes—and Wynn never received a bad stage review! Then, he experimented with the new medium of television (see below). Wynn pulled a rabbit out of the hat when he switched to serious, dramatic roles. It was totally unexpected of him, but he excelled in Rod Serling's TV work, "Requiem for a Heavyweight." Dramatic movies followed, including *The Great Man* (1956), *Marjorie Morningstar* (1958), and *The Diary of Anne Frank* (1959--in an Oscar-nominated performance). In Disney's masterpiece, *Mary Poppins* (1964), he loved to laugh. **ACHIEVEMENTS** In 1949 he won *the first ever Emmy* for "The Ed Wynn Show."...His son Keenan Wynn said, "father was a supreme clown, he could make you laugh, or cry." **QUOTE** "I doubt if there is any great dramatic actor who could change to comedy and become a great comedian. Because the greatest art of the two, by far, is comedy. For me, the greatest achievement is making people laugh." Died: 1966.

Shirley Jones 🎥   1541 Vine

Singer, actress
BORN March 31, 1934, in Smithston, PA. **SPOTLIGHTS** At age 17, this wholesome, dignified blonde left her hometown (population 812) for the bright lights of Broadway. Her first professional audition was for the chorus of *South Pacific* at New York's St. James Theater. What happened next sounds as if it came right out of a movie script. On that very same day, the legendary team of Richard Rodgers and Oscar Hammerstein made a rare visit to the audition. It was then and

Shirley Jones

there that Shirley Jones was discovered, and what a way to get a break! It was said of her that: "she struggled to become a star for about 20 minutes." She appeared on stage in *South Pacific*, then *Me and Juliet*, before winning the film role in the now-classic musical *Oklahoma!* (1955). It was the first role in which she would be immortalized. Movie fans wanted more of America's new sweetheart and Hollywood responded. She co-stars opposite Gordon MacRae in *Carousel* (1956), with Pat Boone in the musical *April Love* (1957), and with James Cagney in *Never Steal Anything Small* (1959). Jones was immortalized again in the timeless Americana family musical, *The Music Man* (1962), co-starring Robert Preston and "Ronny" Howard. Other movies include *The Courtship of Eddie's Father* (1963), opposite Glenn Ford and Ron Howard, *Bedtime Story* (1963) with Marlon Brando and David Niven, and *The Secret of My Success* (1965). **TV** She starred in the hit series "The Partridge Family" with stepson David Cassidy (1970-'74). She has made numerous specials and has guest starred in many top shows, including playing the sexy, older girlfriend to a much-younger Drew Carey on the situation comedy "The Drew Carey Show" (1998-'99). **ACHIEVEMENTS** 1960 Best Supporting Actress Oscar for *Elmer Gantry*. She went against type to portray the salvation-seeking hooker, in this film adaptation of Sinclair Lewis' cynical novel...Her first marriage was to actor-singer-dancer Jack Cassidy, with whom she had two sons; Shaun Cassidy, is an actor-singer-producer.

Roy Acuff 🎸   1541 Vine

Singer, musician (fiddler), composer
BORN Sept. 15, 1903, in Maynardsville, TN. **SPOTLIGHTS** The Grand Ole Opry recognized they had a new star when, in 1938, Acuff and his band auditioned with "Great Speckled Bird." He explored and promoted more of an acoustic "mountain sound," as opposed to standard country and western, or country with pop. He was also a man of strong convictions; studios called upon him to change his image to Hollywood's version of a "cowboy band," but he refused, turning down seven big offers. His fans approved of his "ain't gonna betray myself or my music" decision, and repaid him by buying millions of his excellent sentimental hits: "Low and Lonely," "Beneath That Lonely Mound of Clay," "The Precious Jewel," "Fire Ball Mail," "Wreck on the Highway," and "Wabash Country." He became known as the "King of Country Music." Albums include *Backstage at the Grand Ole Opry*, and *I Wonder if God Likes Country Music*. **ACHIEVEMENTS** Being his own

man, the Opry star did not want Hollywood and New York publishers buying up the copyrights to his originals songs. So, on Oct. 13, 1942, with $25,000 seed money and a gentleman's handshake with partner Fred Rose (the prolific Tin Pan Alley songwriter), the Acuff-Rose Publishing Company opened for business in Nashville. It was the first modern music publishing company to locate there. It became a multi-million dollar conglomerate and was eventually purchased by the Opryland Music Group. He was the first living artist to be inducted into the Country Music Hall of Fame in 1962. **HIGHLIGHTS** In an effort to wreak havoc on the morale of the U.S. Marines during WWII, the enemy shouted through loudspeakers: "To Hell with Franklin Roosevelt! To Hell with Babe Ruth! To Hell with Roy Acuff!" The American government countered by supplying Acuff music on V-discs so the troops' spirits would remain high. Died: 1992.

Eleanor Powell 🎥   1541 Vine

Eleanor Powell and Fred Astaire

Actress
BORN Nov. 21, 1912, in Springfield, MA. **SPOTLIGHTS** MGM created a string of musicals around "The World's Greatest Tap Dancer." She made her silver screen debut in *George White's Scandals*, and followed with *Broadway Melody of 1936* (both 1935). This leggy, vivacious hoofer was a terrifc entertainer. She "put 'em down like a man," according to the king himself, Fred Astaire, who co-stars with her in *Broadway Melody of 1940*. Other movies include *Born to Dance* (1936), *Rosalie* (1937), *Honolulu* (1939), *Lady Be Good* (1941), *Ship Ahoy!* (1942), *Thousands Cheer* (1943), and *I Dood It* (1943). After marrying actor Glenn Ford (1943-'59), she made only a few more pictures. **HIGHLIGHTS** Ordained a minister of the Unity Church, this charitable, kindhearted soul spent much of her life doing Good Works for others. Died: 1982.

Les Paul and Mary Ford 🎸   1541 Vine

Musician, singer, inventor
BORN Lester William Polfus; June 9, 1915 in Waukesha, WI.; Colleen Summers; July 7, 1928, in Pasadena, CA.

SPOTLIGHTS Les Paul: An American original. A guitar legend. A virtuoso. As a young teen—strongly encouraged by his mother—he could play harmonica, guitar and banjo. He lived in a rural area and occasionally performed in local country & western bands. His hobby, though, was electronics. He tinkered with a crystal radio set and anything else he could get his hands on. Completely curious about how things worked, he was determined to find fame and fortune. Even in his teens, he knew that some day he'd string his two loves together—music and electronics. (He amplified his first guitar by sticking an old record-player needle into the wood.) Using the stage name of Red Hot Red, he played hillbilly guitar-harmonica songs on street corners. After a couple of years he became very popular. With his newfound celebrity he quit high school and took to the road. Joe Wolverton, an older guitarist who taught Paul many guitar lick tricks, dubbed him Rhubard Red for their many radio shows. In 1934 he built his first guitar pickup using ham radio headphones parts. In 1936 he formed the Les Paul Trio; the next year, the band moved to New York and worked with Fred Waring's NBC radio show. On the East Coast, Paul's musical inclinations moved toward jazz. He now used the name Les Paul. On one radio station he would perform C&W, then go to a sister station to perform jazz. When not working, he returned to his electronics hobby. In 1941 he built the remarkable prototype of the solid-body electric guitar (he nicknamed it "the Log.") He married singer-guitarist Mary Ford. In the 1950s, they recorded using their ingenious and revolutionary techniques—called the New Sound on their mellow ballads: "Mockin' Bird Hill," "How High the Moon," and "Vaya Con Dios" (May God Be With You). **ACHIEVEMENTS** Inventor Paul created over-dubbing (known as sound-on-sound—which first brought him international fame), the solid-body electric guitar; 8-track tape recorder; techniques such as electronic echo, as well as other electronic musical devices. Paul brought the guitar out of the background rhythm section to a lead position. Recipient of countless honors and awards including the Grammy. Inducted into the Rock and Roll Hall of Fame in 1988. Died: Mary Ford, 1977.

Michael Jackson 🖋   1541 Vine

Broadcaster
BORN April 16, 1934, in London, England. **SPOTLIGHTS** August 22, 1984 was one of the most significant events in a stellar broadcasting career for Los Angeles radio talk show host Michael Jackson. It was the day on which he received his star on the Hollywood Walk of Fame. Coincidentally, it is placed between the stars of both his in-laws, Alan Ladd and Sue Carol Ladd, whose motion picture stars line Vine street. Jackson has been married to their daughter, Alana, for more than 34 years. He is, very possibly, the most honored of radio talk show hosts. Following in the footsteps of Edward R. Murrow and Alistair Cooke, he is the recipient of the M.B.E. (the Most Honorable Order of The British Empire) from her majesty Queen Elizabeth. President Mitterand of France presented him with

Michael Jackson

the distinguished Legion of Merit. For his work in television, he is the recipient of seven Emmys (and thirteen nominations). In radio broadcasting, Jackson has been honored with four Golden Mikes. For the years 1997 and '98, he was voted #1 in the nation from among more than 4000 hosts as "Radio Talk show Host of the Year." Although born in England, at age 11 he emigrated with his parents to South Africa. His radio career began at age 16 (he had claimed he was 22 years old), with the South African Broadcasting Corporation. Extremely successful as a disc jockey and producer, at the real age of 22 he returned to England and joined the BBC. He worked, simultaneously, in radio and television, as well as Radio Luxembourg. In 1959, when he felt he was ready to fulfill his dream, he emigrated to the United Sates. Feeling that he had much to learn about his adopted country, he began in a small market, in Springfield, Massachusetts (at WHYN radio and TV). From there, he moved to San Francisco working all night at KYA as a rock disc jockey. He later quipped, "I was so bad...I was good." Then, at KEWB where he almost invented controversial talk radio. From midnight to dawn, he discussed everything and the ratings went through the roof. That landed him offers from Los Angeles, and he has been entertaining here ever since. First with KHJ, then KNX, followed by 32 years at KABC. In 1989, his career took another leap: he was wooed away by CBS. Their affiliate KRLA decided to change their format and build a talk station around Jackson. It is now "The New LATALK, 1110." **HIGHLIGHTS** Jackson has three children: Alan Ladd Jackson, Alisa Sue Jackson and Devon Michael Jackson. **QUOTE** "I'm loving what I do more and more with the passage of time. Day in and day out I meet the most diverse group of guests from every walk of life; politicians and authors, scientists, stars, educators, world leaders, and the public at large. I believe that the purpose of language is communication, no people do it better than the citizens of this country. Whatever their background or experience, whatever their level of education, whatever their racial and ethnic heritage, when an American speaks, you know what they mean!"

Richard Rowland 🎥   1541 Vine

Pioneer producer
BORN 1881, in New York. **SPOTLIGHTS** Fascinated with the new business of moving pictures, he became a pioneer film distributor at the age of 18. By age 23 he founded a film company; and by 31 was a millionaire. He is credited with bringing many stage celebrities to the screen. Died: 1947.

Dick Van Patten    1541 Vine

Actor

BORN Dec. 9, 1928, in Kew Gardens, NY. **SPOTLIGHTS** His remarkable career includes 600 radio shows, two dozen feature films, seven television series and impressive stage work. A one-time child actor billed as Dickie Van Patten, he first performed on Broadway at the Shubert Theater in 1935 when he was seven years old. He played the son of Elissa Landi and Melvyn Douglas in "Tapestry and Gray."

Dick Van Patten

Thereafter, he appeared in a continuous stream of Broadway shows—27 in all—including three Pulitzer Prize winners: "On Borrowed Time," "The Skin of Our Teeth" (starring Tallulah Bankhead and Fredric March), and he played Ensign Pulver opposite Henry Fonda's "Mister Roberts." This all-American, affable actor has worked with many of the great directors in American theater: Max Reinhardt, Josh Logan, Moss Hart, George Abbott, Elia Kazan and Elaine May. He is most proud of his association with Alfred Lunt and Lynn Fontaine, with whom he worked with for four years, in Terrace Rattigan's smash hit "Oh Mistress Mine." Van Patten made the transition from stage to the small screen in the award-winning, "I Remember Mama." He played Mama's son Nels, in this warm-hearted, comedy-drama (1949-'56). It was one of TV's earliest and best-loved shows. Since then, he has made numerous guest starring appearances in almost every major TV series. His motion picture credits include *Charly* (1968), *Westworld* (1973), *Soylent Green* (1973), *The Shaggy D.A.* (1976—Van Patten co-stars in seven Disney movies), *High Anxiety* (1977; he has made several films with director/actor/writer, Mel Brooks), and Brooks' *Robin Hood: Men in Tights* (1993). Another family series attracted a new generation of fans. In TV's "Eight is Enough" he starred as the father, Tom Bradford (1977-'81), of eight very independent children. In 1997 he co-starred for one year with his younger sister, actress Joyce Van Patten, in the Chicago company production of "Show Boat," directed and choreographed by Hal Prince. This is the first stage show that starred a brother-sister act since John, Lionel and Ethel Barrymore worked together. **HIGHLIGHTS** He met his wife Pat when they were in the seventh and eighth grades together. The beauty became one of the June Taylor dancers on "The Jackie Gleason Show." Other than dancing, her main job was to look glamorous. They have one of Hollywood's fairy-tale marriages—already having celebrated their 45th wedding anniversary, and having produced three sons: Nels (named after his character above), James and Vincent. They are a tennis family. Their youngest son, Vincent, a former and busy child actor gave up acting at age 18 to go on the tour as one of the world's top ranking tennis players. **SIDELIGHTS** One of his other passions is thoroughbred horse racing. Like other horse owners, he dreams of having a Kentucky Derby contender one day. **QUOTE** On Feb. 25, 1993, Van Patten's Walk of Fame star was unveiled. He quipped, "Please curb your dog." Later he commented, "As a kid growing up in New York City, I was always in awe of Hollywood. When I came here in 1970, I walked up and down the Walk of Fame just to look at it in person. Receiving my star was the one thing that excited me the most in my career."

Virginia Cherrill    1541 Vine

Actress

BORN April 12, 1908, in Carthage, IL. **SPOTLIGHTS** Cherrill made her film debut in Charlie Chaplin's sentimental and heart wrenching silent classic *City Lights* (1931). She stars as the blind flower girl who regains her sight thanks to the love and financial support of "the Tramp." It instantly made her a movie star, which came as a big surprise to the lovely 23-year-old. She had zero desire to be an actress and absolutely no prior experience. A chance meeting with the artistic genius Chaplin, with his keen eye for talent, altered her life forever. He instructed her to look at him, but "to look inwardly and not to see me." She became an accomplished actress after three years spent under the master's meticulous direction, which included months of painful retakes. The one scene where the little tramp falls in love with the flower girl was reshot 300 times before Chaplin was happy with it. The final scene is called one of the greatest scenes ever shot, with some of the greatest acting ever seen. Other movies include *Delicious* (1931), and *Charlie Chan's Greatest Case* (1933). By another bit of luck, she met and married Cary Grant (1933-'35), then married the ninth Earl of Jersey, in England (1937-'46). Died: 1996.

Joe Pasternak   1541 Vine

Producer

BORN Sept. 19, 1901, in Szilagy-Somlyo (then a village in Austria-Hungary). **SPOTLIGHTS** Reflecting back on his long, illustrious career, Pasternak stated, "To me, the writer was always the most important thing." He was specific in the types of films he would direct. He said, "No doubt the world is full of stinkers and misery and ugliness and hatred. I decided my pictures would show clean-looking people; they would be full of

Joe Pasternak

fun, filled with the joy of life, fun, lovemaking, singing and dancing." It was just this theory, too, that helped saved

Universal Studios from bankruptcy. Pasternak produced the profitable Deanna Durbin series of musical films that kept that studio afloat during tough times. (Their first film together—*Three Smart Girls* in 1937 cost about $300,000 and grossed two million.) Pasternak also relied on gut instinct. When Marlene Dietrich was considered box office poison, and "couldn't get arrested," Pasternak cast her as a sultry dance hall girl in *Destry Rides Again* (1939). She co-stars opposite James Stewart as a shy sheriff, in box office gold. Other films include *It Started with Eve* (1941), *Music for Millions* (1945), *The Merry Widow* (1952), and *The Courtship of Eddie's Father* (1963). He produced more than 85 motion pictures, many of them winning awards in Berlin, Vienna, Budapest, and Hollywood. **HIGHLIGHTS** Ever grateful for being allowed to become an American citizen in 1926, he dedicated his autobiography in part: "to my adopted country, which took in a stranger and made it all possible." **QUOTE** "A good producer has to be a psychiatrist and a chiseler; you have to know when to tell the truth, and when to lie, when to be kind and when to insist," he philosophized. Died: 1991.

Frederick Stock   1541 Vine

Musician
BORN Nov. 11, 1872, in Germany. **SPOTLIGHTS** Master of the baton, he brilliantly conducted the Chicago Symphony for 35 years starting in 1905. Died: 1942.

Jamie Farr   1541 Vine

Jamie Farr

Actor, singer, dancer
BORN Jameel Joseph Farah; July 1, 1934, in Toledo, OH. **SPOTLIGHTS** Best known for his role as Klinger on TV's "M*A*S*H," he was originally hired for only one day's work on the show. The situation comedy involved the medical team of the 4077th Mobile Army Surgical Hospital, stationed in Korea. His hilarious characterization of a fake transvestite attempting to get thrown out for a "Section Eight" (a mentally unbalanced discharge) delighted viewers.

Fans loved his hairy legs under a flowing skirt and his chomping cigar antics. He was immediately hired as a regular (1973-83). Also an experienced stage performer, he has excelled in such musicals as *Oklahoma!* Renowned choreographer Agnes de Mille stated that Farr was the best Hakim she had ever seen. His film debut as the mentally retarded student Santini in *The Blackboard Jungle* (1955) is classic. **ACHIEVEMENTS** While in the U.S. Army, Farr served in Korea (two years). Farr was the *only* cast member of "M*A*S*H" *to have actually served there.*

Andrea King   1541 Vine

Actress
BORN Georgette Barry; Feb. 7, 1915, in Paris, France. **SPOTLIGHTS** Educated in America, she had no problem with the language. She made her screen debut in *The Very Thought of You* (1944). Other movies include *Hollywood Canteen* (1944), *God Is My Co-Pilot* (1945), *My Wild Irish Rose* (1947), *Mr. Peabody and the Mermaid* (1948), *The Lemon Drop Kid* (1951), *Red Planet Mars* (1952), and *Blackenstein* (1973). TV She was a frequent talent on many top shows, including "Maverick" "Perry Mason," and "The Days of Our Lives."

Bill Keene    1541 Vine

Weatherman, reporter
BORN 1927. **SPOTLIGHTS** A fixture on the L.A. airwaves, he reported on weather and traffic conditions six times hourly during morning and rush hours for KNX News. He monitored 50 government and private radio frequencies during the peak commute hours to better serve the public. With the often unbearable travel conditions in the city, Keene's quick wit, humor and outrageous puns helped keep drivers chuckling instead of fuming. He described an auto accident as "chrome crusher," "cattywampus," and "paint peeler." He also hosted his own TV variety show, and served as a weather consultant for film companies and private industries. Died: 2000.

Colleen Moore   1549 Vine

Colleen Moore

Actress
BORN Kathleen Morrison; Aug. 19, 1900, in Port Huron, MI. **SPOTLIGHTS** A vivacious, large-eyed, bow-lipped Irish-American beauty, she captured the fun and female independence of the spirited Roaring Twenties. Audiences loved her, but critics assailed her with reproaches. They detested her characterization "of the free-thinking wanton woman." Movies include *Flaming Youth* (1923), *The Perfect Flapper* (1924), *Twinkletoes* (1926), and *Naughty but Nice* (1927). She co-stars opposite Spencer Tracy in *The Power and the Glory* (1933). She told friends she would quit show business when she had earned one million dollars. She did just that, at the top. **HIGHLIGHTS** She donated her priceless doll house, replete with minatures made of gold, silver and precious gems to the Museum of Science and Industry in Chicago. The chandelier in the grand hall sparkles with diamonds and emeralds that once had been her grandmother's necklace. She penned a book

about her prized Fairy Princess Castle entitled *Colleen Moore's Doll House*. **QUOTE** In 1923, she defended herself against critics. She stated, "All movie fans—among the ladies—are not flappers, but all flappers are movie fans. In characterizing the flapper on the screen I have always endeavored to show that underneath the ultra-modern veneer of the flapper there beats a heart as stout, as sympathetic and as human as in the bosom of the quaint old-fashioned maid of our grandmother's time...There is nothing unhealthy or off-color in the flapper's attitude. The fire of youth, the natural beauties and the romance of the movies gives the flapper the entertainment that appeals to her age. Our grandmothers when they were girls would have thrilled at motion pictures in their day had they had them, just as the flappers enjoy them today. The following of the modern girl—and the modern girl happens to be the flapper—is a great goal of any enterprise." Died: 1988.

Brian Donlevy 📺 1549 Vine

Brian Donlevy

Actor
BORN Grosson B. Donlevy; Feb. 9, 1899, in Ireland. **SPOTLIGHTS** A tough action man, he had an extensive career in "B" pictures. (The "B" stands for "Budget." These flicks were a studio device to utilize studio space and acting talent in between major motion pictures. "B" flicks also supplied theatre chains with a steady flow of product. Typically, "B" picture took only 12 to 18 days to film.) Although a resume of "B's" could jeopardize a career, in Donlevy's case these slumming years enhanced his reputation and got him better, and higher paying roles. In "A" pictures, he occasionally won the lead, but was often a supporting talent. Films include *Beau Geste* (as a sadistic officer), and *Destry Rides Again* (both 1939). He stars as a hobo who is catapulted into the governor's mansion in the political satire *The Great McGinty* (1940). He delivers another outstanding performance in the WWII action picture *Wake Island* (1942), plays a cutthroat gambler in *Heaven Only Knows* (1947), appears in the crime drama *Kiss of Death* (1947), and works with Jerry Lewis in the hilarious comedy *The Errand Boy* (1961). 1950s TV series: "Dangerous Assignment," as Steve Mitchell, the hero. **ACHIEVEMENTS** He visited military camps, performed in USO shows, and participated in fund-raising drives to aid the WWII effort. Died: 1972.

Ruth Hussey 🎥 1549 Vine

Actress
BORN Oct. 30, 1911, in Providence, RI. **SPOTLIGHTS**

Rejected for a role in a high school play during her senior year, this intelligent, brunette beauty would go on to achieve great stardom. Before coming to Hollywood, she enrolled in Pembroke College (now part of Brown University), and tackled the very difficult subject matter of philosophy, in which she earned her degree. Still wanting to act, she did one year of graduate work in drama at the University of Michigan, then tested the waters via summer stock in regional theaters. She

Ruth Hussey

returned to her hometown, where she was hired as a radio fashion commentator. Confident with her skills, Hussey made the leap to New York City, signing with producer Jules Leventhal for several road show productions. When the company was organizing the Sidney Kingsley play, "Dead End," for a transcontinental tour, the actress won the desirable role of Kay, and that led her to Hollywood. In the summer of 1937, while doing this show at the Biltmore Theater in Los Angeles, she received a backstage note after the first act. It was from MGM talent scout Billy Grady, who requested she screen-test for that studio. She did, was awarded a seven-year contract, and made her film debut in *The Big City* (1937), a drama starring Spencer Tracy. Other films quickly followed, including *Judge Hardy's Children* (1938), *Marie Antoinette* (1938), *Another Thin Man* (1939), *Northwest Passage* (1940), and *Susan and God* (1940). Like many of the top stars of the day, she modeled for Max Factor, who showcased her lovely high cheekbones, large blue eyes and perfect lips. Sophisticated, ladylike, and with stunning good looks, she was cast in George Cukor's *The Philadelphia Story* (1940), starring Katharine Hepburn and Cary Grant. She received an Oscar nomination for best supporting actress for her role as the photographer-sidekick of James Stewart. Her next film was the Navy drama, *Flight Command* (1940), co-starring Robert Taylor and Walter Pidgeon, with superb performances by all. Hussey was absolutely endearing in the romantic light comedy, *Married Bachelor* (1941), opposite Robert Young. Later motion pictures include *The Uninvited* (1944), *The Great Gatsby* (1949), and *Louisa* (1950). She made 40 films during her career, and was an accomplished stage actress. She starred on Broadway in the 1946 Pulitzer Prize-winning "State of the Union." She was also a frequent TV guest star. **SIDELIGHTS** The Hussey family name dates back to 17th-century Nantucket Island. **HIGHLIGHTS** At the original Brown Derby, located at 1628 North Vine Street, she was having lunch with some show business friends, who introduced her to talent agent Robert Longenecker. The two were married seven weeks later in 1942. They are one of Hollywood's romantic success stories, having celebrated their 57th wedding anniversary in 1999. Their union produced three children: Rob Longenecker, a former Navy pilot, Mary Elizabeth Hendrix, a fine artist in oil, water colors, and pastels, and John Longenecker, an Academy Award-winning producer for *The Resurrection of Broncho Billy* (1970). The sepia-toned tribute to the old West and Western films stars Johnny Crawford and Kristin Nelson. John Longenecker is also a gifted director/cinematographer of films and popular music videos. Visit www.IndieFilmsOnline.com for information on compelling short films and features.

Farley Granger   1549 Vine

Actor

BORN July 1, 1925, in San Jose, CA. **SPOTLIGHTS** Discovered by Samuel Goldwyn while performing in the play, "The Wookey," the mogul signed the 17-year-old Hollywood High School senior on the spot. Granger made his film debut as a young Russian soldier in *The North Star* (1943), then followed up with another war picture *The Purple Heart* (1944). In real life, he took time off to serve in World War II,

Farley Granger and Leslie Caron

then excelled in the crime drama *They Live By Night* (1948). That same year, Hitchcock directed him in *Rope*, where Granger plays a sociopathic killer, opposite James Stewart. With his curly, dark hair, liquid brown eyes, and brooding good looks, he was perfectly cast as a disturbed youth, or as a vulnerable romantic lead. He was frightfully brittle in Hitchcock's *Strangers on a Train* (1951), as the disagreeable hero. He is spellbinding to watch in the suspenseful thriller. After working in 20 films, he left Hollywood for New York in 1955. He stated, "I wanted to be, for this short time on earth, a creative being." He loved the freedom of the stage, as opposed to the constant re-takes required in filmmaking by a demanding director. Instead of heading straight to the bright lights of the Great White Way, he worked in small theater. Granger waited four years before making his Broadway debut in the musical version of "Pride and Prejudice." Critics celebrated his performance. He also enjoyed doing live TV, performing in many playhouse shows, including "The U. S. Steel Hour." Specials include "The Lives of Jenny Dolan." In 1976 he originated the role of Dr. Will Vernon in the soap opera, "One Life to Live." **QUOTE** "You see something on the stage and think that it's being thought or said or done for absolutely the first time. Now that's great acting."

Warren William   1549 Vine

Actor

BORN Warren W. Krech; Dec. 2, 1895, in Aitkin, MN. **SPOTLIGHTS** A dark-haired, mustached leading man of the 1920s, director Cecil B. DeMille cast him as Julius Caesar to Claudette Colbert's *Cleopatra* (1934). The young Britisher Henry Wilcoxon was cast as Marc Antony. This was one of DeMille's most extravagant ventures, where he reveled in exotic costuming, sets, and action montages. William earned much acclaim and widespread popularity as the intelligent sleuth in the *Lone Wolf* series (1939-'43). Died: 1948.

Arthur Godfrey   1549 Vine

See page 419

Lorne Greene and Betty White

Lorne Greene
1555 Vine

Actor

BORN Feb. 12, 1915, in Canada. **SPOTLIGHTS** A barrel-chested man, Greene's speaking voice was a deep, rich baritone. His voice was praised by a critic as "surely one of the finest ever wrought by nature." He put it to good use in TV's Western series "Bonanza." His character, Ben Cartwright, was the stern, but compassionate widower father of three strong-willed sons, and owner of the 1,000-square mile Ponderosa Ranch. He operated from a point of complete integrity and honor. "Bonanza" was the first Western to be telecast in color, and was unusual as it focused more on relationships, and less on shoot-'em-up violence. The series made its mark in TV history as the second longest-running Western (1959-'73)—second only to "Gunsmoke." Immortalized in this role, Greene played the patriarch of the interesting clan for 14 seasons. The show's catchy theme song, "A gun and a rope and a hat full of hope, Bonanza," was written by Jay Livingston and Ray Evans, and made the hit parade. In his next series, Greene's real-life love of the great outdoors was apparent: "Lorne Green's Last of the Wild" (1974-'79). This fascinating nature program inspired environmental concern, preservation action and "green" laws. Other TV series include "Battlestar: Galactica." He starred in the excellent 1971 TV movie "The Harness," adapted from John Steinbeck's story. TV mini-series include "The Bastard," based on John Jakes' novel. Motion pictures include *Autumn Leaves* (1956), *The The Gift of Love* (1958), *Earthquake* (1974), and *The Alamo--13 Days to Glory* (1987). Greene served as an important role model for boys and young men. As a father figure, he was ethical, honest, loving and held high moral standards. Died: 1987.

Mary Brian 🎥   1555 Vine

Actress

BORN Louise Dantzler; Feb. 17, 1908, in Coriscana, TX. **SPOTLIGHTS** After winning a "Miss Personality" contest, the studio's front gate opened. The petite brunette made her movie debut as Wendy in *Peter Pan* (1924), and was typecast in sweet roles. Her 60 films include *The Virginian* (1929), *The Front Page* (1931), *College Rhythm* (1934), *Charlie Chan at Paris*, and *The Man on the Flying Trapeze* (both 1935).

Marie Windsor 🎥   1555 Vine

Marie Windsor

Actress

BORN Emily M. Bertelson; Dec. 11, 1922, in Marysvale, VT. **SPOTLIGHTS** The ultimate film noir heroine, Windsor was a former beauty contest winner, was very good at being very bad. The glamorous and dangerous leading lady made "B" movies watchable, but excelled in "A" pictures, too. She gives a convincing performance in *Force of Evil* (1948), a film noir crime story about values and corruption. In a lesser movie, she co-stars with Jon Hall in *Hurricane Island* (1951), a plot involving evil spirits and women pirates. She is wonderful in the Western, *Little Big Horn* (1951) co-starring Lloyd Bridges and John Ireland. It is about General Custard's rush to attack the Sioux and Cheyenne nations. She gives an outstanding performance as a tough broad in *The Narrow Margin* (1952), a thriller-on-a-train classic. She struts her funny stuff in the comedy *Abbott and Costello Meet the Mummy* (1955), and shines in *Support Your Local Gunfighter* (1971), a Western spoof. She guest starred in hundreds of TV series, including "Perry Mason."

Alec Guinness 🎥   1555 Vine

Actor, writer

BORN Alec Guinness de Cuffe; April 2, 1914, in London, England. **SPOTLIGHTS** He studied acting with the renowned instructor Martita Hunt, who proclaimed to Guinness: "You have no talent." Undaunted, he auditioned for John Gielgud's Old Vic Company and was rewarded with a Shakespearean role. He played 34 roles in 23 of the Bard's great works within the next 60 months. This accomplished stage actor entered films after WWII. He showed his incredible versatility playing eight brothers and sisters in *Kind Hearts and Coronets* (1949), and amazed colleagues with his makeup artistry and character distinction. Hilarious in *The Lavender Hill Mob* (1951), he was Oscar-nominated for best actor. In the 20th Century-Fox production of *The Mudlark* (1951), Guinness plays the famous British prime minister Benjamin Disraeli. The highlight of the film was a speech given by Guinness, punctuated by a long pause halfway through it. Producer Darryl Zanuck said, "it was one of the most effective moments of *silence* in film history." Since the script didn't call for it, Zanuck asked Guinness how he had thought of it. "I didn't," replied the British actor, "In the

Alec Guinness

middle of my speech, I forgot my lines—dried up." He was fabulous in the wry comedy *The Captain's Paradise* (1954), where he plays an affable sea captain with a wife in each port—Tangier and Gibraltar. He is delightful, as is co-star Katie Johnson, in *The Lady Killers* (1955). In his private life, he studied and converted to Catholicism in 1956. He was Oscar-nominated for best screenplay for *The Horse's Mouth* (1958), and also stars in this wry comedy. In the spectacular epic *Lawrence of Arabia* (1962), he plays His Royal Highness Prince Faisal. He is superb in *Tunes of Glory* (1960), adapted from James Kennaway's novel. Guinness is haunting as Yevgraf Zhivago in *Doctor Zhivago* (1965). In all, he made more than 50 splendid motion pictures, but found immortality as the spiritual warrior Obi-wan Kenobi, in George Lucas' fantastic *Star Wars* (1977) sci-fi trilogy. He also appears in *The Empire Strikes Back* (1980) and *Return of the Jedi* (1983). **ACHIEVEMENTS** 1950 New York Drama Critics Award for his portrayal of a prosaic psychiatrist in "The Cocktail Party." 1957 Best Actor Oscar for *The Bridge on the River Kwai*. (He referred to his role as "the dotty colonel.") Knighted by Queen Elizabeth in 1959 for achievements on stage and screen. 1980 Honorary Oscar "for advancing the art of screen acting through a host of memorable and distinguished performances." **QUOTE** "When I was younger, I didn't like my face or personality and I tried to get away from it. I still don't like me, but I'm getting more used to myself."

Max Steiner 🎥   1555 Vine

Composer

BORN Maxmilian Raoul Steiner; May 10, 1888, in Vienna, Austria. **SPOTLIGHTS** His "Tara" music in "The Most Magnificent Picture Ever," *Gone with the Wind* (1939), is one of America's most significant musical works. A prolific genius, he was nominated for an Academy Award for the Civil War epic. *Gone With the Wind* won 10, but he did not receive one himself. Also Oscar-nominated for *Casablanca* (1942), *he lost to himself for his work in another film!* (See below.) Don't miss

Dark Victory (1939) for Steiner's throbbing background music (with the added benefit of the classic film and its stars). He started out in the early days of talkies, and helped developed music into its full-blown status in movies today. When he was initially assigned head of the RKO music department, he recalled, "A constant fear prevailed among producers, directors and musicians that they would be asked, 'Where does the music come from?' Therefore, they never used music unless it could be explained by the presence of a source like an orchestra, piano player, phonograph, or radio, which was specified in the script." Steiner's first original score was for *Cimarron* (1931). It was the first Western to win an Oscar for best picture, but his name never made it to the credits. He scored big with the music for *King Kong* (1933). Oscar Levant stated it was "the kind of music no one had ever heard before--or since. Full of weird chords, strident background noises, rumblings and heavings." He spent much of his career at Warner Bros. **ACHIEVEMENTS** Academy Awards for the following scores: 1935 *The Informer*; 1942 *Now, Voyager*; and 1944 *Since You Went Away*. Steiner is the one who advanced the synchronization of note and image by separating film footage into its smallest time components and adapting the music functionally beat by beat. "Music by Max Steiner" was shorthand for "excellence." **QUOTE** "When the dreaded release date is upon us, sleep is a thing unknown. I have had stretches of work for 56 consecutive hours without sleep, in order to complete a picture for the booking date." Died: 1971.

Jules White 🎥   1555 Vine

Director, producer
BORN 1900, in Budapest, Hungary. **SPOTLIGHTS** He was the executive in charge of Columbia Pictures' short films unit from 1933-'59, and the zany hand behind the Three Stooges comedies in 136 comedy shorts. In 1929, he created talking dog comedies at MGM called *The Barkies*. Died: 1985.

George Carlin 🎭   1555 Vine

Comedian, actor
BORN May 12, 1938, in the Bronx, NY. **SPOTLIGHTS** Cranky and insightful, Carlin rose to national prominence as the irreverent comic who shook up the country for reciting his now-classic routine, "Seven Words You Can Never Use on Television." His 1972 arrest at the Milwaukee summer fest for repeating these "Seven Words," made the daring comedian even more popular for his stance on Freedom of Speech. He's a whiz at using the English language in groundbreaking acts, while adding his personal flavor of pessimism about society-at-large. In 1975 he was the first guest host of "Saturday Night Live." About his screen work—*With Six You Get Egg Roll* (1967), *Car Wash* (1978), *Outrageous Fortune* (1987), and *The Prince of Tides* (1991)—he said, "I try to do a film every ten years." **SIDELIGHTS** He broke into show business while serving in the U.S. Air Force. Although his primary job was to do

electronic maintenance on B-47s, he worked as a radio DJ at Shreveport, Louisiana's KJOE. **ACHIEVEMENTS** One of the funniest and most provocative comedians of the last four decades, Carlin has released 20 albums (four Golds), won two Grammys, two Cable Ace Awards, and has made more HBO specials than anyone else. He penned an outrageously funny book, *Braindroppings*, published by Hyperion in 1997. On "Celebrity Do-Gooders."

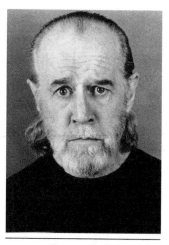

George Carlin

Don't you get tired of celebrities who explain their charity work by saying they feel they have to 'give something back?' You celebrity people want to give something back? How about giving back half the money? Or a couple of those houses? Or maybe, if you people really want to give something back, you could let go of a little of that arrogance." **QUOTE** About receiving his Hollywood Walk of Fame star on Jan. 21, 1987, he said: "At least they've moved me ten feet from the gutter."

Robert Shaw 💿   1559 Vine

Conductor
BORN April 30, 1916, in Red Bluff, CA. **SPOTLIGHTS** A music pioneer and master musician, Shaw was the dean of American choral conducting. He established chorale singing as an American tradition. Experts agree that all of his recordings are good and many are absolutely inspired. Named "America's greatest chorale conductor" by the National Association of Composers and Conductors in 1943, Shaw became director of the choral department of the Juilliard School from 1945-'48. This intense and gifted gentleman created the legendary Robert Shaw Chorale in 1948, and toured internationally through 1966. On air, he was choral director, leader and coach of "the glee club" on "The Fred Waring Show," a popular, long-running musical variety radio show. Recordings include *Dvorak: Stabat Mater*, *America the Beautiful*, *Christmas Hymns and Carols*, and *Sea Shanties*. **ACHIEVEMENTS** Recipient of 14 Grammy Awards, the 1991 Kennedy Center Honor, the 1992 National Medal of Arts, and an inductee into the American Classical Music Hall of Fame in Cincinnati, Ohio, in 1998...He was known for his exceptional control over the balance of tone, phrasing and diction of his singers. **QUOTE** "We believe that music is more a necessity than a luxury. Music is a doer's art, and that the choral art offers the most immediate and accessible avenue of participation." Died: 1999.

David Nelson ▼   1501 Vine

Actor, director, producer

David Nelson

BORN October 24, 1936, in Doctors Hospital, New York City, New York. **SPOTLIGHTS** David began his show business career with the family's popular radio show, "The Adventures of Ozzie and Harriet." Although the show made its radio debut on October 8, 1944, he was not the original "David," there were two other actors who played him. When his father, Ozzie, agreed in 1947 to put his sons on the air, it quickly became clear that his eldest son David was the best "David" in this situation comedy (and the younger Ricky the best "Ricky"). The program became one of CBS's all-time, longest running hits. The show moved to ABC television in October 1952. It was the first family situation comedy on the small screen, a concept invented by David's father. It depicted the real-life Nelsons as a pleasant, middle-class family dealing with the routines of daily life and small moral issues. David and Ricky were the two stars of the show, and viewers faithfully watched the handsome boys grow up. Their caring parents treated their children with respect and kindness. But one of the family's most endearing qualities was their obvious, true love for one another. Corny? Nope. There's nothing trite about devoted family love, even in today's jaded society. David commented that he admired his father so much that he never wanted to do anything that would disappoint him in real life, and never did. He did, however, get a chance to stretch his wings behind-the-scenes, successfully directing numerous episodes. In doing so, he became the youngest member of the Directors Guild of America. (This was, in a sense, following in his father's early achievement footsteps—Ozzie had become the nation's youngest Eagle Scout at age 13.) The show ended in 1966, but remains in syndication. He went on to direct both feature films and television shows, and owns a production company for sales films and commercials. In 1998 the Arts & Entertainment network earned their highest ratings ever for their biography of "Ozzie & Harriet." (Also see the biographies of "Rick Nelson" and "Ozzie and Harriet Nelson" in this book.) **QUOTE** Reflecting upon the loss of his brother, and of being the sole survivor of the family, David stated, "I think it's the Lord's time we're here on, and it's his clock. When He decides it's up, it's up. And I think if you learn one thing, it's you have to live life to the fullest. You have to get the most out of life."

John Wayne

Colleen Moore

1601 VINE

Bob Burns 🎥

1601 Vine

Actor

Bob Burns

BORN Aug. 2, 1893, in Van Buren, AR. **SPOTLIGHTS** He made his screen debut in *Quick Millions* (1931), a solid crime film about a blue collar worker who becomes a gangster. The fast-paced drama stars Spencer Tracy, with support from George Raft. Movies include *Rhythm on the Range* (1936--in Martha Raye's screen debut), *The Big Broadcast of 1937* (1936), *Wells Fargo* (1937), *Waikiki Wedding* (1937), *The Arkansas Traveler* (1938), and *Belle of the Yukon* (1944). Still, Burns was most famous for his outstanding radio career. Known as the Arkansas Traveler (also his theme song), he played the hillbilly-in-residence in "The Bob Burns Show" (1941-'49). Although he amused audiences with his hillbilly twang, he did not play a dumb hick. Burns was educated, intuitive and bright. In fact, he got his first big break as a political country wit in Rudy Vallee's show. *Newsweek* wrote: "in appearance Burns resembles Gene Tunney, (but) sounds like Will Rogers." Burns was a beloved American figure, admired for his humor and good, backwoods common sense. The zany Spike Jones and his novelty band accompanied him. (See Jones' bio in this book.) **ACHIEVEMENTS** At age 15, Burns assembled two pieces of a gas pipe with a whiskey funnel at the end, "where the music comes out." He called his creation the "bazooka." During WWII, the Army named the "bazooka" weapon after Burns' musical instrument. **QUOTE** He often spoke of retiring, stating, "A feller gets kinda tired workin' 30 minutes every week." Died: 1956.

Frank Crumit 🎤

1601 Vine

Host, author, composer, singer, musician

BORN Sept. 26, 1889, in Jackson, OH. **SPOTLIGHTS** His vaudeville act emphasized his breezy personality and informal talk over the footlights. He signed up with his wife, Julia Sanderson, for radio; they formed an ideal combination. He had the good-natured personality and she, the tinkling laugh on "The Battle of the Sexes" (1938-'44). They also hosted "Mr. Adams and Mrs. Eve," again pitting the sexes against one another in a quiz show format (1942-'43). His song "The Buckeye Battle Cry" became Ohio State University's football tune. Other songs include his home run hits "Gay Caballero" and "Abdul Abulbul Amir." When he died in 1943, radio lost one of its "Sweethearts of the Air."

Alan Ladd 🎥

1601 Vine

Actor

Alan Ladd and Veronica Lake

BORN Sept. 3, 1913, in Hot Springs, AR. **SPOTLIGHTS** A movie tough guy, he became a legendary leading man. This light-haired, poker-faced talent shot to stardom in *This Gun for Hire* (1942). He played the ferocious hired gun opposite the very blonde, seductive Veronica Lake. The belted trench coat—with upturned collar—that he wore in this thriller became his trademark, while the peek-a-boo hair became hers. His teaming with Veronica Lake was box-office magic and produced the same screen chemistry as Bogie and Bacall—only *they* were first. Ladd, unsmiling and cool, and Lake, silky and sultry. Before becoming one of the best known—and in his time the highest paid—and most popular of screen actors, he started his Hollywood saga by holding a series of odd jobs in the industry; Ladd was a "grip" at Warner Brothers. His big break came after he met, and eventually married, his agent (former silent and early talkie favorite, Sue Carol). They were a dynamic team. In 1942 the Ladd-Lake team were featured in another excellent crime picture, *The Glass Key*. Ladd gave another excellent performance. However, their next film together, *Star Spangled Rhythm*, was a Paramount musical with an ensemble cast. It was not was the public had come to expect from the pair, although music fans enjoyed it. He made a number of films before joining the U.S. Army Air Corps during World War II. Ladd proved to be one of the studio's biggest money-makers. His memorable postwar films include *Salty O'Rourke* (1945), *O.S.S.* (1946), *The Blue Dahlia* (1946), *Two Years Before the Mast* (1946), *Whispering Smith* (1948), and *Chicago Deadline* (1949). Ladd was immortalized in *Shane* (1953), one of the finest Westerns ever made, with Ladd at his most stellar. Directed by George Stevens, *Shane* rated number 69 in American Film Institute's list of the 100 greatest films of all time. In 1956 the actor turned down the role of Jett Rink in *Giant*; James Dean—the studio's second choice—was thilled to accept it. **HIGHLIGHTS** He married agent Sue Carol in 1942 (see her bio in this book). Their union produced four children. Son Alan Ladd Junior (Laddie) has had a distinguished career as a producer, heading "The Ladd Company," as C.E.O. and Chairman of MGM and President of 20th Century-Fox. He received the Best Picture Oscar for *Braveheart* (1995), starring Mel Gibson. Daughter Carol Lee was married to the late John Veitch, longtime production chief of Columbia Pictures. Daughter Alana Ladd married radio broadcaster Michael Jackson (see his bio in this book). As a child, son David Ladd stars with his father in *The Proud Rebel* (1958). This wonderful family drama is set in the Civil War era. Ladd's ten-year-old son modestly said, "I'll never be a big star...because I'm no good...that's why." Well he was good in it, but he preferred working behind-the-scenes. He became MGM's senior vice president of production. **QUOTE** "TV is where the big money is. I'll be making TV films, but not appearing in them. I'm not building an empire for myself. Sue and I have enjoyed the greatest of everything. There's nothing we lack. Nothing we want...guess you could say it's for love of my family." Died: 1964.

Audie Murphy 🎥　　　　　　1601 Vine

Actor

Audie Murphy

BORN June 20, 1924, in Kingston, TX. **SPOTLIGHTS** America's most decorated soldier of World War II was a true American hero, who came from the humblest of beginnings. He was born dirt-poor—the seventh out of twelve children—to cotton sharecropper parents. With his Texan family too poor to buy groceries, Murphy hunted for their food. Bullets were very expensive, so he learned from boyhood to make every shot count. The only way to do that, was with precision marksmanship. He readily became a sharpshooter. When he was age 16, his father deserted the family. The next year, his mother died. Broke and orphaned, he tried to enlist in the U. S. Marine Corps. They rejected him because he was "too skinny." He was accepted into the U.S. Army infantry at age 18 in Dallas, Texas. Almost immediately this GI saw WWII combat action in Italy, then France, and finally Germany. Although teased by his comrades for his "baby face," Murphy proved to be one of the greatest and bravest soldiers America has ever produced. Postwar, this "boy soldier" landed the cover of *Life* magazine as the country's patriot. Actor James Cagney saw it and invited him to Hollywood. The young-looking 24-year-old made his screen debut in *Beyond Glory* (1948), starring Alan Ladd and Donna Reed. Murphy received bursts of publicity, yet good roles were few and far between. He once joked, "As an actor, I'd make a very good stunt man." The redheaded Murphy got a break from his good guy image when cast as the villain Billy the Kid in *The Kid from Texas*, and Jesse James in *Kansas Raiders* (both 1950). He made 40 pictures, including starring in John Huston's legendary *The Red Badge of Courage* (1951), which had been adapted from Stephen Crane's classic Civil War drama, and *To Hell and Back* (1955), adapted from his own autobiography, where he plays himself. Frequently cast as the good guy in Westerns, he said, "The scripts are the same, only the horses have changed." **ACHIEVEMENTS** The most decorated GI of WWII, Murphy earned every medal—24 in all—that the U.S. military awards, including the Congressional Medal of Honor, which is awarded to one: "who shall, in action involving actual conflict with the enemy, distinguish himself conspicuously by gallantry and intrepidity at the risk of his life, above and beyond the call of duty." President Harry Truman declared that Murphy really knew how "to give 'em hell," and that Murphy was "the greatest soldier since George Washington." **QUOTES** "Bravery in battle is often the fallout of anger, hunger, wet and cold, and wanting to be home." "War is like a giant pack rat. It takes something from you, and it leaves something behind in its stead." Died: 1971, in a plane crash.

Preston Sturges 🎥　　　　　　1601 Vine

Director, screenwriter

BORN Edmond P. Biden; Aug. 29, 1898, in Chicago, IL. **SPOTLIGHTS** The maestro of screwball comedy and wit during the Golden Era, he scripted *Easy Living* (1937), a wacky comedy starring Jean Arthur and Ray Milland. His *Christmas in July* (1940) is a zany picture about a clerk (Dick Powell) who goes on a shopping spree after he mistakenly thinks he's won $25,000. *The Lady Eve* (1941) turns the tables on a con artist (Barbara Stanwyck). Many critics consider *Sullivan's Travels* (1941) his masterpiece. It is a tragi-comedy combining slapstick farce and human misery. Others declare *Hail the Conquering Hero* (1944)—a brilliant satirical comedy—his trademark work. *Unfaithfully Yours* (1948), a dark comedy starring Rex Harrison and Linda Darnell, is another five-star Sturges picture. Films that he either wrote or directed or both include *The Power and the Glory* (1933—his successful screenplay uses an elaborate flashback structure comparable to *Citizen Kane*), *The Good Fairy* (1935), *Remember the Night* (1940), and the romantic comedy, *The Palm Beach Story* (1942). **ACHIEVEMENTS** 1940 Academy Award for Best Screenplay, *The Great McGinty* (he also directed). Died: 1959.

Paul Whiteman 🎤　　　　　　1601 Vine

See page 215

Henry Fonda 🎥　　　　　　1601 Vine

Actor

BORN May 16, 1905, in Grand Island, NE. **SPOTLIGHTS** He was quiet, spoke with a definite Midwestern drawl, and surprised himself with his long film career, which he expected would last only two years. Fonda possessed all-American farm boy looks and a shy demeanor. He seemed the unlikely hero. But hero he did become. Riding a successful Broadway career, Fonda went the distance in Hollywood from 1935-'81 with 100 films. He proved adept in drama and comedy, and made

Henry Fonda (right) with Ed Sullivan

out the 1950s and crossed over to the new medium of the little screen. 1950s TV: She hit big with "Your Hit Parade," and followed with her own "The Gisele Mackenzie Show." A superb entertainer, she continues to perform onstage and nightclubs, with an easy style and a lot of fun. **QUOTE** "I learned to sing when fate stepped in and my beloved violin was stolen out of the car."

Gisele MacKenzie

Lawrence Welk
1601 Vine

See page 78

Renee Adoree and Lew Cody

his craft look easy. Motion pictures include *The Trail of the Lonesome Pine* (1936—his first epic), *Jezebel* (1938), *Jesse James* (1939), *Young Mr. Lincoln* (1939—as Abe in this inspirational family pic), *Drums Along the Mohawk* (1939), *Grapes of Wrath* (1940—as Tom Joad), *The Lady Eve* (1941), *The Male Animal* (1942), *The Ox-Bow Incident* (1943), *My Darling Clementine* (1946—as Wyatt Earp), *The Fugitive* (1947), *Fort Apache* (1948), Hitchcock's *The Wrong Man* (1957), *12 Angry Men* (1957—also co-produced), *Warlock* (1959), *Advise and Consent* (1962), and *How the West Was Won* (1962). Fonda never left theatrical work behind him. He returned to the Great White Way for the title role in "Mister Roberts." After this triumph, he remained onstage for "Point of No Return," and "The Caine Mutiny Court-Martial." Hollywood persuaded Fonda to reprise his role of *Mister Roberts* in 1955. He appears with James Cagney, William Powell, Jack Lemmon and Ward Bond. In *War and Peace* (1956--as Pierre), Fonda experienced problems with lines his character was to say. He told director King Vidor, "Gee, I can't say that." When Vidor asked him why not, Fonda replied, "Because it doesn't feel real." Vidor responded, "Of course it isn't real, it's a movie!" **ACHIEVEMENTS** 1980 Honorary Oscar; 1981 Best Actor for *On Golden Pond*; 1948 and 1979 Tonys. With his second wife, Frances Brokaw, they had Jane and Peter Fonda. (Later, Peter fathered Bridget Fonda.) **QUOTE** "Audiences like real people. I don't like artificiality under any circumstances...I believe in naturalness." Died: 1982.

Gisele MacKenzie   1601 Vine

Singer, actress, violinist, pianist
BORN Marie Gisele La Fleche; Jan. 10, 1927, in Winnipeg, Canada. **SPOTLIGHTS** She studied at Toronto's prestigious Royal Conservatory of Music to be a concert violinist. After graduation, she was hired by a Canadian dance band as both a musician and vocalist. A radio talent scout caught her act and featured her on Bob Crosby's "Club Fifteen." She also was the popular vocalist on "The Mario Lanza Show" (1951-'52). She was one of the regular vocalists on "Your Hit Parade" through-

Renee Adoree   1601 Vine

Actress
BORN Jeanne de La Fonte; Sept. 30, 1898, in Lille, France. **SPOTLIGHTS** A kewpie doll-faced daughter of the Big Top, she began performing at age five as an acrobat. As she blossomed into a brunette beauty, she left the circus to join the Parisian Folies Bergere as a chorus girl. She had a stunning oval-shaped face with large, dramatic eyes, a darling nose, and a flawless porcelain complexion. In Hollywood, *The Big Parade* (1925) boosted her to superstardom, playing opposite John Gilbert. **QUOTE** "There is one grave danger that every aspirant to movie fame must, sooner or later, encounter. And because it lacks the glamour of romance, and because it offers no possibilities of salacious entertainment, it is rarely, if ever, mentioned. It is the danger of slow starvation...From every corner of the earth they come, on their tireless wings of youthful optimism. Pathetic pilgrims these, struggling on to ultimate disillusion. In most cases their assets, amount to a one-way ticket to Hollywood, an inadequate wardrobe, a still less adequate bankroll, a terrifying determination to break into the

movies, and (most disastrous) the rather appalling knowledge that in the old home town they were considered to be good looking." Died: 1933, from tuberculosis.

Cyd Charisse 🎥   1601 Vine

Cyd Charisse

Actress, dancer
BORN Tula Ellice Finklea; March 8, 1921, in Amarillo, TX. **SPOTLIGHTS** Born of some Native American Indian blood, Charisse is a former member of the *Ballet Russe*. This sultry, glamorous brunette possesses beautiful legs and tremendous grace. Her appearance in *Singing in the Rain* (1952), starring Gene Kelly, proved she was an entertaining actress, too. The following year, she stars opposite Fred Astaire in *The Band Wagon*.

Motion pictures include *Brigadoon* (1954) with Frank Sinatra, *Meet Me in Las Vegas* (1956) with Dan Dailey, *Silk Stockings* (1957), *Twilight for the Gods* (1958) with Rock Hudson, and *Party Girl* (1958) opposite Robert Taylor. Her stage name came from childhood; Cyd was her younger brother's mispronunciation of "Sis." Her marriage to singer Tony Martin (1948 on) produced Tony Jr. In 2000, she co-starred with her husband in a celebration of the "Classic Hollywood Musicals" at the Pasadena Civic.

Kay Kyser 🎙   1601 Vine

Kay Kyser (left) during WWII.

Band leader, humorist
BORN James Kyser; June 18, 1905, in Chapel Hill, NC. **SPOTLIGHTS** He was radio's humorous quiz master, the Dean of "Kay Kyser's Kollege of Musical Knowledge." Kyser, costumed in collegiate cap and gown, "lectured" to his amateur contestants: "*That's right, you're wrong!*" Played heavily for laughs, Kyser employed smart musical gimmicks, lots of gags, and funny regular cast members, such as "dumb" comedian Ish Kabbible. He captured a gigantic, loyal following. This immensely popular radio program moved to TV in 1949-'54. His theme song was the ballad "Thinking of You." Kyser's novelty band recorded: "Three Little Fishes," "Who Wouldn't Love You," and "Don't Sit Under the Apple Tree." With Harry Babbitt, he had the WWII hit ("There'll Be Bluebirds Over) The White Cliffs of Dover."

ACHIEVEMENTS/QUOTE The band's most famous recording was the wartime song "Praise the Lord and Pass the Ammunition." A big supporter of American troops during World War II, Kyser performed a record 1,700 shows at military bases. When praised for his patriotism, Kyser quipped, "It's not only fun, but where else can I get meat?" Died: 1985.

Xavier Cugat 🎵   1601 Vine

See page 304

Charlotte Greenwood 🎙   1605 Vine

Charlotte Greenwood

Actress, dancer
BORN Frances C. Greenwood; June 25, 1893, in Philadelphia, PA. **SPOTLIGHTS** This tall, lithe talent used kooky body language as her greatest comedy tool. Her trademark gag was her high kick, with a twist. She extended her heel flat out, instead of pointing her toe. In 1912—around the same time the Titanic sank—she performed at The Winter Garden in the musical comedy "Passing Show." The horrible news about the sinking ship killed box office sales for weeks. Greenwood persevered through good and bad times, wisely deserting a dying vaudeville for revues. She became a beloved stage actress, then the lack of male talent during World War II encouraged the networks to give women a shot at the airwaves. In 1944, NBC aired "The Charlotte Greenwood Show." One of the top female radio stars, along with Dinah Shore, Judy Canova, Kate Smith, the Andrew Sisters, Hildegarde and Fanny Brice. These women collectively accounted for much of the $46,865,000 talent cost in 1945, but they brought in many times that amount. Under movie contract to Fox, her movies include *Down Argentine Way* (1940), *Moon Over Miami* (1941), and *Up in Mabel's Room* (1944). Died: 1978.

Susan Peters 🎥   1605 Vine

Actress
BORN Suzanne Carnahan; July 3, 1921, in Spokane, WA. **SPOTLIGHTS** A beautiful brunette with classic bone structure and full lips, she was groomed for stardom by MGM. Films include *Santa Fe Trail* (1940), and *Dr. Gillespie's New Assistant* (1942). A hunting accident resulted in permanent spinal cord injury, paralyzing her from the waist down. Died: 1952.

Ezio Pinza   1605 Vine

Opera singer, actor

BORN Fortunato E. Pinza; May 18, 1892, in Rome, Italy. **SPOTLIGHTS** Pinza was an outstanding basso with a rich, powerful voice. He was first the adored star of Milan's La Scala, then with the Metropolitan Opera from 1926. In the 1930s Pinza inspired the Mozart revivals at the Met. He was most loved for his roles as Don Giovanni, Boris, and in Verdi roles. Recorded on Columbia before being lured away by RCA. A versatile performer, he appears in *Carnegie Hall* (1947), with a stellar musical cast), *Strictly Dishonorable* (1951) opposite Janet Leigh, *Mr. Imperium* (1951) co-starring Lana Turner, Debbie Reynolds, Marjorie Main, and Barry Sullivan, and *Tonight We Sing* (1953) with Anne Bancroft, Isaac Stern and Jan Peerce. **QUOTE** After one Broadway performance of "South Pacific" (co-starring Mary Martin), he went to his favorite Italian restaurant. Upon ordering his standard *12-course* dinner, Pinza noticed the waiter's flabbergasted face. Pinza sternly demanded, "What's the matter with you? I may be singing musical comedy these days, but I still *eat* grand opera!" Died: 1957.

Willard Waterman   1605 Vine

Actor

BORN Aug. 29, 1914 in Madison, WI. **SPOTLIGHTS** He began in radio serials in Chicago in 1936. Waterman worked in comedy, drama and horror productions for more than two decades. In the mid-1940s, he played Roger Barton in the soap opera "The Guiding Light." His most famous role was as Throckmorton P. Gildersleeve, bachelor father and water commissioner in the town of Summerfield, USA, in "The Great Gildersleeve" (1950-'57). Also: "Those Websters," "Lights Out," "The Halls of Ivy," and "Stepmother." Died: 1995.

George Murphy

George Murphy   1605 Vine

Dancer, actor

BORN July 4, 1902, in New Haven, CO. **SPOTLIGHTS** Murphy's many supreme years of "putting 'em down" on Broadway enhanced Goldwyn's *Kid Millions* (1935), starring Eddie Cantor, and *Broadway Melody of 1938*, co-starring the excellent tap dancer Eleanor Powell. Movies include *Little Miss Broadway* (1938), *Little Nellie Kelly* (1940), *A Girl, a Guy and a Gob*, and *Rise and Shine* (both 1941), and *For Me and My Gal* (1942). **ACHIEVEMENTS** 1950 Special Oscar...He left his position as president of the Screen Actors Guild for actor Ronald Reagan (1947). Elected to the U.S. Senate from California (he defeated Pierre Salinger)...His father was a professional track coach, who trained Jim Thorpe. Died: 1992.

John B. Kennedy   1615 Vine

Newscaster, commentator

Born: Jan. 16, 1894, in Quebec, Canada. **SPOTLIGHTS** After working at various newspapers and at *Colliers* magazine for a decade, he turned to radio in 1933. *Colliers* magazine brought life to his pre-Depression variety program, "The Collier Hour" (NBC, 1927)—the first important network dramatic anthology. He was commentator on RCA's musical program, "The Magic Key" (1935-'39). He remained on the air as news commentator, and announcer, through 1951. Died: 1963.

Victor Schertzinger   1615 Vine

Director

BORN April 8, 1880, in Mahonoy City, PA. **SPOTLIGHTS** He directed the very first "road" picture, *Road to Singapore* (1940), co-starring Bob Hope, Bing Crosby, and Dorothy Lamour. He also did *Road to Zanzibar* (1941). Died: 1941.

Bud Abbott   1615 Vine

Comedian

BORN William Abbott; Oct. 2, 1895, in Asbury Park, NJ. **SPOTLIGHTS** He started as a cashier in a Brooklyn burlesque club. In 1931, headliner Lou Costello was minus his partner at showtime and asked Abbott to fill in as the straight man. The team was formed, with Abbott receiving 40 percent of the take. Although they painstakingly worked out all their gags, their performances led audiences to believe they were spontaneous. Radio: They came to America's attention on Kate Smith's show, where they revealed their brazen comedy routines. They also had their own, "The Abbott and Costello Show." In 1940, Universal Studios put the duo in the musical *One Night in the Tropics*. Abbott's slender build, towering over roly-poly Costello, combined with their quick cross-talk and slapstick routines to make them hot Top 10 box office material for nearly a decade. Baseball's *"Who's on first?"* was their greatest routine, which clearly stood the test of time. Their own daytime

Bud Abbott (right) and Lou Costello

syndicated and network TV series ran successfully on bad puns and rowdy slapstick from 1951-'53. The team split in 1957. (See the bio of Lou Costello in this book.) Died: 1974.

Bing Crosby   1615 Vine

Singer, actor

Bing Crosby

BORN Harry Lillis Crosby; May 2, 1901, in Tacoma, WA. He took his name "Bing" from a cartoon strip. **SPOTLIGHTS** At his 1930 wedding to Dixie Lee, his father-in-law said of the groom, "He's a useless good-for-nothing type." Then, after Crosby's first radio appearance on Sept. 2, 1931, the performer himself wrote to his older brother/manager: "Dear Ev, Cancel all contracts. I gave all I had and it's no good." Dixie Lee's father felt vindicated, warning his daughter to leave her "talentless husband." A Paramount Pictures talent scout heard the broadcast and thought otherwise. The studio cast the smooth-voiced crooner in *The Big Broadcast* (1932), with husband-and-wife team George Burns and Gracie Allen. In the next decade, he was earning $175,000 per picture and co-starring with Bob Hope in the "Road" film series. The two men proved they were masters of the gag. Four favorites of these funny "anything goes" movies are: *Road to Morocco* (1942--with Bing singing "Moonlight Becomes You"), *Road to Utopia* (1945--playing gold miners), *Road to Rio* (1947--with the Andrew Sisters singing "You Don't Have to Know the

Language"), and *Road to Bali* (1952--in Technicolor, with a cameo appearance by Humphrey Bogart). Other Crosby motion pictures, *Holiday Inn* (1942--it includes the all-time best-selling song "White Christmas") and *The Bells of St. Mary* (1945) are Hollywood evergreens. While busy making films, doing radio programs and concerts, his recording career was simultaneously soaring with such hits as "Mexicali Rose," and "Now Is The Hour." The most amazing aspect of his radio shows, performances and TV work was the fact that he always looked so relaxed that the public thought he *ad-libbed*, when in fact he was well-rehearsed. One TV host asked the star how he managed to have such an unruffled air about him. Crosby reached into his pocket and pulled out an enormous roll of cash. "That helps!" he remarked. **ACHIEVEMENTS** Best Actor Oscar for *Going My Way* (1944--with the Oscar-winning song, "Swinging on a Star." **QUOTE** After recording million-seller platters including "Pennies from Heaven," and "When the Blue of the Night Meets the Gold of the Day," the crooner was asked if he was worried about straining his voice. He modestly responded, "Oh the kinda singing I do, you can't hurt your voice." Died: 1977, on a golf course in Spain.

Bea Benaderet    1615 Vine

Actress

BORN April 4, 1906, in New York. **SPOTLIGHTS** A huge radio star, she fared equally well on TV. She played neighbor Blanche Morton on "The George Burns and Gracie Allen Show" (1950-'58). From 1962-'63, she played Cousin Pearl Bodine, a colorful addition to "The Beverly Hillbillies." Then, the network offered her the role of Kate Bradley in her own situation comedy series, "Petticoat Junction" (1963-'68). Cartoon fans recognize her as the voice of Betty Rubble, of "The Flintstones" (1960-'66), America's first prime time animated series. Died: 1968.

James A. Fitzpatrick   1615 Vine

Producer

BORN Feb. 26, 1902 in Shelton, CO. **SPOTLIGHTS** Starting in 1925, he wrote, narrated, directed, and produced travel shorts (*Fitzpatrick Travel Talks),* that were distributed through MGM. Also did film shorts for Paramount. Died: 1980.

Elissa Landi   1615 Vine

Actress

BORN Elisabeth Kuehnelt; Dec. 6, 1904, in Italy. **SPOTLIGHTS** She was brilliant in Cecil B. DeMille's *The Sign of the Cross* (1932). Other movies include *Body and Soul* (1931), *The Count of Monte Crisco* (1934), *After the Thin Man* (1936), and *The Thirteenth Chair* (1937). Thereafter, she mixed her passion for writing novels with her acting career. **HIGHLIGHTS** Descended from royalty (emperor of Austria), Kuehnelt changed her last name to that of her nobleman stepfather, Count Zanardi-Landi. Died: 1944.

Shirley MacLaine 🎥   1615 Vine

Actress, dancer, author

Shirley MacLaine

BORN Shirley MacLean Beaty; April 24, 1934, in Richmond, VA. **SPOTLIGHTS** A sparkling, long-legged freckle-faced entertainer, her enchanting screen debut in Hitchcock's *The Trouble with Harry* (1955) led to an illustrious career. She followed with the Dean Martin-Jerry Lewis comedy vehicle *Artists and Models* (1955). Next, she appears in an all-star cast in *Around the World in 80 Days* (1957), with David Niven, and Cantinflas. Based on the Jules Verne tale, it won the Best Picture Oscar. Other motion pictures include *Some Came Running* (1959—in an Oscar-nominated performance), *The Apartment* (1960—in an Oscar-nominated performance), *Irma La Douce* (1963—in an Oscar-nominated performance), *Sweet Charity* (1969), *Two Mules for Sister Sara* (1970), *The Year of the Woman* (1973—documentary), *The Turning Point* (1977—in an Oscar-nominated performance), *Madame Sousatzka* (1988—for which she won the best actress prize at the Venice Festival), *Guarding Tess* (1994), *The Celluloid Closet* (1995), and *Mrs. Winterbourne* (1996). MacLaine co-stars opposite Peter Sellers with hilarious results in *Being There* (1979), a must-see comedy adapted from Jerry Kosinki's novel. In *Steel Magnolias* (1989), MacLaine works with an all-star female cast: Sally Field, Dolly Parton, Daryl Hannah, Olympia Dukakis, and Julia Roberts. It is a sentimental, but moving tearjerker perfect for rainy day viewing. The enduring actress plays a competitive mother in a work adapted from Carrie Fisher's clever novel, *Postcards from the Edge* (1990), opposite Meryl Streep. The following year, she portrays herself in Albert Brooks' outstanding comedy, *Defending Your Life.* **ACHIEVEMENTS** 1983 Best Actress Oscar for *Terms of Endearment*. She wrote, produced and co-directed (with Claudia Weill) a feature-length documentary entitled, *The Other Half of the Sky: A China Memoir* (1975). 1976 Emmy. **ACTING** About her approach to the art of acting, MacLaine said, "I don't think 'the method' would be good for me. I just keep my eyes and ears open and if I can use anything in a scene I do." **ABOUT LIFE** "I used to be addicted to overcoming things. Now, my goal is to get out of my own way." **HIGHLIGHTS** She is the older sister of actor-producer-director Warren Beatty, but they have never teamed together on-screen. Her daughter is actress Stephanie Sachiko (her stage name is Sachi Parker—a woman MacLaine believes was her mother in a past lifetime). Author of several best-selling books, including some which delve into her belief in reincarnation. **QUOTE** For her movie *Evening Star* (1996), she successfully petitioned the Motion Picture Assn. of America's ratings board to change the film from an "R" rating to "PG-13." She told them, "After all, I have never been in an 'R' rated film, at least not in this life!"

Anne Francis

Anne Francis 📺   1615 Vine

Actress

BORN Sept. 16, 1930, in Ossining, NY. **SPOTLIGHTS** A child darling of radio shows since age five, Francis became known as "the Little Queen of Soap Opera." She blossomed into a stunning blonde beauty with acting ability to match. She stars in the gritty *Blackboard Jungle* (1955) opposite Glenn Ford, with a compelling performance that has survived the test of time. Motion pictures include *Portrait of Jennie* (1948), *Bad Day at Black Rock* (1954), the WWII action picture *Battle Cry* (1955), *The Rack* (1956—this movie was adapted from Rod Serling's teleplay), and the five-star motion picture *Forbidden Planet* (1956—considered the finest sci-fi movie until the release of *2001*). Francis also appears in comedies and musicals—*Don't Go Near the Water* (1957), and *Funny Girl* (1968), and *Little Vegas.* (1990). Although she made more films than TV series, she earned a "TV" star on the Walk of Fame because it was so rare back in the 1960s to have a full-fledged movie star do television. Francis played the light dramatic lead detective in "Honey West" (1965-'66); Terri Dowling (1971-72) in "My Three Sons"; and Arliss Cooper in "Dallas" (1981).

Theodore Kosloff 🎥   1615 Vine

Dancer, actor

BORN April 5, 1882, in Moscow, Russia. **SPOTLIGHTS** An extraordinary ballet dancer, he quickly embraced the flapper style in *Children of Jazz* (1923). He had anything but *Feet of Clay* (1924). He appeared in numerous silents. **QUOTE** "The art of dancing is essential to life itself. It is the universal mode of rhythmic expression. It is the soul in action. It is grace, exercise and the poetry of thought. Dancing is an obsession and, in this obsession, one finds a never ending interest. Dancing is a stimulation, a recreation, a mode of thought." Died: 1956.

Ralph Morgan 1615 Vine

Actor

BORN Raphael Wupperman; July 6, 1882, in New York, NY. **SPOTLIGHTS** A superb character actor, Morgan was educated at Trinity School and Columbia University, where he earned his law degree in 1904. The 22-year-old decided to bypass a legal career, in favor of following in his brother, Frank's, show business footsteps. He had watched Frank become a huge star of both stage and silent screen. Ralph began acting in regional theater, stock, and touring the country in both Shakespearean plays and lesser works. Where his brother specialized in comedy, Ralph had a natural ability for drama, including villainous roles. He honed his craft on stage for nearly two decades before he made his impressive screen debut in the *lead* role in *Penny Philanthropist* (1923). He possessed a wide, open face and strength of character. One of Morgan's most important roles was portraying the last Russian Czar, Nicholas II, in the cinematic event of the year, MGM's *Rasputin and the Empress* (1932). It co-stars the Barrymore trio—John, Ethel, and Lionel—in the only motion picture they ever made together. This teaming and extravagant "photoplay" were so important that MGM "introduced a new sound-camera." MGM also had to keep the screenwriter, Charles MacArthur, on the set to rewrite scenes from hour to hour. This was to placate the clashing of the colossal Barrymore egos, as there was much bickering and sibling jealousy over who had the best dialogue. Morgan, a fine actor in his own right, later reflected that their arguing had produced a better script. He made more than 70 movies, including *Magnificent Obsession* (1936), *The Life of Emile Zola* (1937), *Wells Fargo* (1937) and *Geronimo* (1940). He appears in several police serials, including the popular *Dick Tracy vs. Crime, Inc.* (starting in 1941). **HIGHLIGHTS** He combined both his expertise in law and show business to become founder/president of the Screen Actors Guild. Died: 1956.

Charlie Farrell 1615 Vine

See page 572

Adolph Zukor 1615 Vine

Executive

BORN Jan. 7, 1873, in Hungary. **SPOTLIGHTS** He became rich distributing *Queen Elizabeth* (1912), starring Sarah Bernhardt. It introduced the theatrical experience to the masses. This single film legitimized the art of motion pictures for all classes of people. His company, Famous Players (later Paramount Pictures), was a motion picture company par excellence. Going against the filmmaking tide of one and two reelers based on a story line or a gag, he produced films of five to six thousand feet, based on the world's

Adolph Zukor

finest plays and stories, and with premier cinemactors. America's Sweetheart, Mary Pickford, recalled her five and one-half years with Zukor's company, "the happiest years of my screen life. I became one of his children." Zukor found filmmaking to be a roller coaster ride. He borrowed on his life insurance and pawned his wife's diamond necklace to meet the payroll of $10,000 for *Tess of the Storm Country* (1914). The film, though, saved Zukor from bankruptcy, and he was back on top. In 1921 alone, the company made more than 100 films. **ACHIEVEMENTS** 1949 Special Academy Award...He lived the Horatio Alger story; Zukor arrived in the U.S. penniless and unable to speak English. **SIDELIGHTS** This comment has been attributed to his business sense: "Never let that bastard back in here--unless we need him." (Reportedly other tycoons used the line, so it is not definite if he originated it.) **QUOTE** "Those of us who became film producers hailed from all sorts of occupations—furriers, magicians, butchers, boilermakers—and for this reason highbrows have often poked fun at us. Yet one thing is certain: every man who succeeded was a born showman. And once in the show business, he was never happy out of it." Died: 1976.

Tom Conway 1615 Vine

Actor

BORN Thomas Charles Sanders; Sept. 15, 1904, in St. Petersburg, Russia, to British parents. **SPOTLIGHTS** A suave, handsome, mustached leading man, he often played the hero in black-and-white thrillers. In 1939 he tagged along with older brother-actor, George Sanders, to Hollywood. He made his screen debut the very next year in *Sky Murder*. Conway appeared in close to 150 movies, including *The People vs. Dr. Kildare* (1941), *Tarzan's Secret Treasure* (1941), *Mrs. Miniver* (1942), and *Cat People* (1942). He was excellent in *The Seventh Victim* (1943), a nightmarish, horror film. He is probably best remembered for *The Falcon* film series, a role he inherited from his brother, including *The Falcon's Brother* (1942), *The Falcon Strikes Back* (1943), and *The Falcon in San Francisco* (1946). One of his last motion pictures was Disney's classic *101 Dalmatians* (1961—voice only). **TV** He starred as "Inspector Mark Saber," a dapper British detective with a pencil-thin mustache and pinstriped suits who solved big city crimes postwar America. **RADIO** After Vincent Price stepped down in 1951, Conway took the lead role of Simon Templar, a.k.a. "The Saint," a.k.a. "the Robin Hood of modern crime." He learned Price was a hard act to follow. Died: 1967.

Dean Martin ☉   1615 Vine

See page 96

Kim Hunter ☗   1615 Vine

Actress
BORN Janet Cole; Nov. 12, 1922, in Detroit, MI. **SPOTLIGHTS** Trained at the Actors Studio, this performer received rave reviews for her terrific screen debut in *The Seventh Victim* (1943). This nightmarish, horror picture proved her a superb new Hollywood talent. Hunter became known as an actor's actor. Other movies include *Tender Comrade* and *A Canterbury Tale* (both 1944), and *You Came Along* (1945). She displays superior motion picture acting in the outstanding fantasy about life and death in *Stairway to Heaven* (1946), opposite David Niven, and was equally brilliant in *A Streetcar Named Desire* (1951), as Stella Kowalski opposite Marlon Brando. She followed up with a drama—*Deadline U.S.A.* (1952)—about a newspaper's integrity. It co-stars Humphrey Bogart and Ethel Barrymore. Unfortunately, Hunter became entangled offscreen with the nasty red politics purge. She was blacklisted for seven years. Later, she delivered excellent performances in the fantastic sci-fi serial *Planet of the Apes* (1967), *Beneath the Planet of the Apes* (1970), and *Escape from the Planet of the Apes* (1971). She is also a cookbook author. **ACHIEVEMENTS** 1951 Best Supporting Actress Oscar for *A Streetcar Named Desire*.

Marcus Loew ☗   1615 Vine

Executive
BORN May 7, 1870, in New York, NY. **SPOTLIGHTS** Loew lived the American dream. Born of penniless, immigrant parents, he was basically self-educated, and only had attended a few years of grade school. He worked hard and followed his gut instinct on show business, owning a chain of 400 theaters by his 40th birthday! Before he was 50, he owned Metro Pictures, and a few years later (1924) corporately controlled Metro-Goldwyn-Mayer (MGM). Died: 1927.

Ray Milland ☗   1627 Vine

Actor, director
BORN Reginald Truscott-Jones; Jan. 3, 1905, in Neath, Wales. **SPOTLIGHTS** A cool, suave, dark-haired leading man with a subtle edge, he was educated for a brief time at Kings College.

He then served as a royal guardsman with the Household Cavalry of the British Royal Family from 1926-'29. Suffering an economic loss by the lofty lifestyle of the Cavalry, Milland turned to show business. He performed as one-half of a dance team opposite Anna Neagle, toured with the play "The Woman in Room 13," and was a walk-on extra in some British films, which led to bit roles. Anita Loos told MGM about him, and Milland came to Hollywood. He made his

Ray Milland

American screen debut in *Polly of the Circus* (1929)—a star vehicle for Marion Davies. He also worked with Davies in *The Bachelor Father* (1931). He made a number of films learning his craft, then Milland appears in *The Gilded Lily* (1935) opposite Claudette Colbert and Fred MacMurray. It was this film that Hollywood took serious notice of him. In the romantic comedy *Easy Living* (1937—scripted by Preston Sturges), and opposite Jean Arthur, Milland delivers a sterling performance. He came out of it a movie star. When it was learned by directors that he could project shallowness, he moved from light comedies to heavy dramas. In all, he made more than 100 movies, including *Charlie Chan in London* (1934), *Three Smart Girls* (1937), *Beau Geste* (1939), *The Doctor Takes a Wife* (1940), *Skylark* (1941), *The Major and the Minor* (1942), *Forever and a Day* (1943), *The Uninvited* (1944—a bloodcurdling ghost story), *Ministry of Fear* (1944), *Kitty* (1945), *Golden Earrings* (1947), *The Big Clock* (1948), *Alias Nick Beale* (1949), *Rhubarb* (1951), *Dial M for Murder* (1954), *The Girl in the Red Velvet Swing* (1955), and *The Last Tycoon* (1977). **ACHIEVEMENTS** 1945 Best Actor Oscar for *The Lost Weekend*. He also won top prize at the Cannes Film Festival, and the New York Critics' award for his portrayal of the tortured alcoholic. This film performance remains one of his best. Offscreen, Milland commented, "One cocktail is enough for me. I get my pleasure out of mixing the things. Sort of a hobby of mine. Did all my drinking in *Lost Weekend*, you know..." **HIGHLIGHTS** About *Reap the Wild Wind* (1942)--a smash hit--and notable for the fight scene where he battles an enormous squid, Milland stated, "I thought it was horrible." About the Western *Copper Canyon* (1950), the actor declared, "I loathed it. I hated working with Hedy Lamarr." He plays Ryan O' Neal's wealthy father in the romantic melodrama *Love Story* (1970), co-starring Ali MacGraw. The tearjerker was one of the biggest box office hits of the year. In it, Milland is seen bald. He commented, "the first time since 1948 without a toupee." **QUOTE** "Learning to act at all is hard. In one picture, I spent two full working days trying to walk naturally through a door." Died: 1986.

Vanessa Brown

Vanessa Brown 🎥
1627 Vine

Actress, writer

BORN Smylla Brind; March 24, 1928, in Vienna, Austria. **SPOTLIGHTS** A gifted youngster with a high IQ, both her parents possessed doctorate degrees. Her father was language teacher, Nah Brind, who had taught her several languages, including German, Italian, French and English. Her mother was the acclaimed psychologist Anna Brind. In 1937, the family fled their native country to France, then made their way to America to escape the Nazis. While attending school in Manhattan, New York, she heard there was a theatrical opening for a girl who spoke English with a German accent. On her own, she borrowed the money to ride the subway, then met with playwright Lillian Hellman. She became an understudy in the Broadway play "Watch on the Rhine," then throughout its run became a regular cast member. She was 13 years old. Next, this poised, humble and gracious genius wowed radio listeners on the incredibly popular quiz show "The Quiz Kids." She was paid a $100 Liberty or War Bond for each broadcast. On the air for years, she became a major celebrity. It was movie producer David O. Selznick (of *Gone with the Wind* fame), who called her to Hollywood. She made her silver screen debut at age 16 in *Youth Runs Wild* (1944—billed as Tessa Brind). Other movies include *Margie* (1946), *The Late George Apley* (1947), *The Ghost and Mrs. Muir* (1947), *The Heiress* (1949), *Tarzan and the Slave Girl*, and *Three Husbands* (both 1950), *The Bad and the Beautiful* (1952), *Bless the Beasts and the Children* (1972), and *The Witch Who Came from the Sea* (1976). An accomplished Broadway stage actress, she enjoyed a 1952 hit show with the "Seven Year Itch." She played the leading female role that Marilyn Monroe did in the film version. Brown continued to star in a number of radio shows, including "The Song of Bernadette," and was voted one of radio's most outstanding personalities. She was also a panelist on TV's "Leave It to the Girls" (1949-'54)...She married her second husband, director Mark Sandrich Jr. in 1959. They had two children, David and Cathy Sandrich. Died: 1999.

Richard Cromwell 🎥   1627 Vine

Actor

BORN Roy Radabaugh; Jan. 8, 1910, in Los Angeles, CA. **SPOTLIGHTS** A boyish-looking, mild-mannered supporting actor, he joined Will Rogers in the fine comedy *Life Begins at Forty* (1935). For Paramount, he works with W. C. Fields in *Poppy* (1936). He was excellent in Warner's *Jezebel* (1938), a stylistic pre-Civil War melodrama starring Bette Davis and his

friend, Henry Fonda. The next year, he worked in another period piece, *Young Mr. Lincoln* (1939), starring Fonda again. He joined the Coast Guard during WWII, and postwar made only one movie. Died: 1960.

Barbara Lamarr 🎥   1627 Vine

Actress

BORN Rheatha Watson; July 28, 1896, in Richmond, VA. **SPOTLIGHTS** A breathtaking silent screen beauty queen, she played an erotic part in *Arabian Love* (1922), and exuded sensuality in *Heart of a Siren* (1925). Died: 1926.

Pete Smith 🎥   1627 Vine

Publicist, writer, narrator, producer

BORN Pete Schmidt; Sept. 4, 1892, in New York, NY. **SPOTLIGHTS** A master publicist in Hollywood's early days, he wielded enormous power. Smith could make the earth shake for moguls and movie stars alike. He left his lucrative private practice to work at Metro-Goldwyn, and succeeded in getting Louis B. Mayer's name added to the studio (much to the displeasure of Loew's). He earned $1,000-a-week at a time most Americans earned $1,000 annually. His famous stunts included having MGM's Leo the Lion travel from Los Angeles to New York. To attract major press, he flew the lion in a plane-- as any aircraft flight during the 1920s was news. He hired the famous aviator, Martin Jensen, as its pilot. Smith underestimated how big the news would be when the pilot was forced to crash land in Arizona. The story reached around the globe. He handled fresh talent such as Greta Garbo, right off the boat from Sweden. In 1931, he decided to write and narate his own shorts. These were shown alongwith MGM feature films. **ACHIEVEMENTS** 1937 Academy Award for *Penny Wisdom*; 1940 for *Quicker 'n a Wink*. 1955 special Oscar. Died: 1979.

Rin-Tin-Tin 🎥   1627 Vine

German shepherd

BORN Rintintin (original spelling; the dog was named after a French war orphan), in 1916, in France. **SPOTLIGHTS** Found in a trench during World War I, he was brought as a puppy to America by U.S. Army lieutenant Lee Duncan. Duncan used his own special training technique to produce one of the finest police and Red Cross rescue dogs ever recorded. After Rin-Tin-Tin *broke all records* at a champion dog show held at the Ambassador Hotel, in Los Angeles, California, Duncan decided to film "Rinty" (as he was affectionately known) doing tricks, stunts, and winning agility competitions. At a Red Cross benefit, the reel was shown to an audience including Rin-Tin-Tin himself. Duncan commented, "At first the dog did not know he was watching pictures of himself, but when it dawned on him his tail wagged ferociously. It was then that Rintintin aspired to motion picture stardom." Rin-Tin-Tin was introduced in Warner Bros.' *Where the North Begins*

Warner Bros. created the most famous movie dog star of all time, Rin-Tin-Tin (original movie photo for fans).

(1923), breaking all box office records. This beautiful, massive, muscular, dark-colored canine was an overnight superstar. Critics argued that the dog was more intelligent and delivered a more sensitive performance than many of his leading human counterparts. Even studio boss Jack Warner praised the dog for "a gallant heart." Loved by virtually every child in the world and a hero to most everyone else, Rinty became *the globe's most popular actor* in 1926. His remarkable films that year include *The Night Cry*, where one scene is played entirely in close up and you could swear the dog was really acting. This power pooch got top billing and earned $1,000 a week, while his leading men and women earned a lesser $150 - $250. Many of his conceited human co-stars flew into jealous rages around him. They felt humiliated that a four-legged creature with fleas earned more than they did *and* received better reviews. Yet, they soon learned to conceal their hostility for fear of being attacked. *This incredibly sensitive K-9 could smell anger. Those who did not like him, and advanced toward him were bit!* If the bite didn't hurt enough, anyone who was bitten might be thrown off the picture so as not to further antagonize its star! Actors who wanted to keep their paychecks learned these rules: "Don't challenge the dog by looking into his eyes. Freeze if he comes near you when he's roaming about the set. Learn to admire him so your scent doesn't set him off. Avoid him if his trainer is not around." (Rinty was fiercely devoted to Duncan.) Abusive-type actors, who were on the set for the first time, were instructed in how to be humane. (They were they types that thought it was okay to kick dogs, pull tails, wack noses, etc.) Of course, if they behaved cruelly, that was a mistake they only made once. Punishment from the dog, Duncan and Warner Bros. was swift and final. *Interestingly enough, the actors*

who loved the dog experienced no problems whatsoever. Around them, Rin-Tin-Tin behaved like a gentle pet, who wagged his tail, played with them, and kissed them! **HIGHLIGHTS** The arrival of sound in motion pictures caused no problems for the dog. He could do a variety of different sounding growls and barks on cue. In 1930, he landed his own radio show. It was originally called "The Wonder Dog," and later "Rin-Tin-Tin." It was a dog adventure drama. Rinty did his own sound effects. **ACHIEVEMENTS** In making 19 features, Rinty saved Warners from bankruptcy several times. The canine was such a valuable studio asset that there were 18 trained look-alike doubles, and the studio used every one. Owner-trainer Lee Duncan made $5 million on Rin-Tin-Tin's films! That ain't just puppy love, that's what *I* call *Man's Best Friend.* **HIGHLIGHTS** During his first film, he was fed hamburger. After the movie proved to be a blockbuster, his mega-celebrity studio perks included a private chef who prepared Rinty's daily lunch of large tenderloin steak, and a live combo who performed classical music during his meals to soothe his digestion. As a gift, Rinty received a spectacular diamond-studded collar that turned many eyes emerald green with envy. Set with approximately 100 high quality gems, weighing three to four carats each, the necklace in the year 2000 would be worth anywhere from $2 - $3 million dollars! **QUOTE** Duncan proudly declared, "Rintintin has never been whipped and the wonderful things this dog accomplishes on the screen are accomplished through kindness and instructions—but never with the whip. Even in scenes where Rintintin is supposed to be beaten, I never permit a whip to touch the dog." On one sad afternoon at their home in 1932, the dog could no longer muster the strength to lie next to Duncan's side. Completely distraught, Duncan telephoned his neighbor across the street, the captivating platinum bombshell,

Paying his respects to Rin-Tin-Tin is Doc Holliday.*

*Doc Holliday is an International Superdog, and is the #1 Boston Terrier in North America. He is the first to receive Flyball Dog Champion and Flyball Master titles.
E-mail usagility@funtv.com or visit the websites:
w.usagility.webprovider.com
www.brandybostons.webprovider.com

Jean Harlow. She was a compassionate, caring individual in real life, and immediately ran to help them. As mogul Jack Warner recalled, "And she cradled the great furry head in her lap, and there he died."

Ronald Colman   1627 Vine

See page 29

Gordon Jones   1627 Vine

Actor, comic

Gordon Jones

BORN April 5, 1911, in Alden, IA. **SPOTLIGHTS** He teamed up with two of his former vaudeville pals in TV's "The Abbott and Costello Show" (1951-'53), as Mike the Cop. From 1953-'54, he played Pete, Ray Milland's bachelor friend, on radio and TV's "Meet Mr. McNutley." He was also a familiar face on one of America's original family series, "The Adventures of Ozzie and Harriet," from 1958-'60. Motion pictures include *I Stand Accused* (1938), *Pride of the Navy* (1939), *The Arizona Cowboy, Sunset in the West*, and *North of the Great Divide* (all 1950). Died: 1963.

Dean Jagger   1627 Vine

Actor
BORN Dean Jeffries; Nov. 7, 1903, in Lima, OH. **SPOTLIGHTS** This veteran character actor appeared in 150 motion pictures. Movies include Zane Grey's adapted novel, *Western Union* (1941) with Randolph Scott and Robert Young, the tense drama *Bad Day at Black Rock* (1954) starring Spencer Tracy, the classic *White Christmas* (1954) with Bing Crosby and Danny Kaye, and the excellent *Elmer Gantry* (1960). Jagger's personal favorite was *Brigham Young—Frontiersman* (1940), in which he stars in the title role. **ACHIEVEMENTS** 1949 Best Supporting Actor for *12 O'Clock High*. Died: 1991.

Ilona Massey   1627 Vine

Actress, singer
BORN Ilona Hajmassy; June 16, 1910, in Hungary. **SPOTLIGHTS** A beautiful blonde soprano with a real beauty mark, she plays opposite Nelson Eddy in *Rosalie* (1938), and *Balalaika* (1939). Massey hit big on Broadway in the "Ziegfeld Follies" in 1943, opposite Milton Berle. Died: 1974.

Melachrino   1627 Vine

Composer, arranger, orchestra leader

BORN George Melachrino; May 1, 1909, in England. **SPOTLIGHTS** He organized the Melachrino Strings and created joyous, light, sweet "Music for Relaxation," and "Reverie"--ideal music for a world recovering from WWII. His fans often requested he play the enchanting and famous waltz, "Blue Danube." Died: 1965.

Edna May Oliver   1627 Vine

Actress, comedienne
BORN Ida May Nutter; Nov. 9, 1883, in Malden, MA. **SPOTLIGHTS** Edna May was a descendent of John Quincy Adams (the sixth President of the United States between 1825 - 1829, he was the first to follow his dad into the Presidency; his father John Adams had been America's second President). Oliver's expansive and cultured upbringing made her one of the most versatile actresses on stage and screen. In her childhood she studied voice culture, which was a tremendous advantage in front of audiences. She also studied piano and dance, and performed in local amateur productions. At the turn of the century she joined a light opera company. An established stage actress, in both drama and comedy, of two decades on Broadway, she made her screen debut in 1923. Oliver headed to the West Coast to make talkies in 1930. Her voice, appearance and experience made her an ideal character actress who was always in demand. She delivered perfect characterizations of disapproving relatives, most frequently seen as a spinster or widow or eccentric nurse-figure. Films include *Cimarron* (1931)—the first Western to win Best Picture Oscar, *Only Yesterday, Little Women* (as Aunt March), *Alice in Wonderland* (all 1933), *David Copperfield* (1935—as Aunt Betsy Trotwood), *A Tale of Two Cities* (1935), *Romeo and Juliet* (1936—as the Nurse), *Drums Along the Mohawk* (1939—in an Academy Award-nominated performance), and *Pride and Prejudice* (1940). Died: 1942 (on her birthday).

Bobby Sherwood   1627 Vine

Band leader, trumpeter, host
BORN Robert Sherwood, Jr.; May 30, 1914, in Indianapolis, IN. **SPOTLIGHTS** A regular on "The Milton Berle Show," and a humorist panelist on "Masquerade Party." Died: 1981.

David Niven   1627 Vine

See page 390

Jo Stafford   1627 Vine

Singer
BORN Nov. 12, 1918, in Coalinga, CA. **SPOTLIGHTS** She was a vocalist with the Tommy Dorsey Orchestra until going solo in 1943. Hit recordings include "I'll Be Seeing You," "I'll Never Smile Again," "Street of Dreams" (with the Pied Pipers), "You Belong to Me," and "Tumbling Tumbleweeds." Radio

Jo Stafford

shows include "The Al Jolson Show" (the theme song was "April Showers"), "The Chesterfield Supper Club" (she was the featured singer on Tuesdays and Thursdays), and "Johnny Mercer's Music Shop" with the Pied Pipers. Her husband Paul Weston and his orchestra played in TV's 1950 "The Jo Stafford Show." **ACHIEVEMENTS** 1960 Grammy...During WWII, she was America's favorite female singer. The enemy attempted to destroy morale by playing her records on loudspeakers so that the American soldiers would get homesick and surrender!

Milton Cross 1627 Vine

Narrator, singer, actor

BORN April 16, 1897, in New York. **SPOTLIGHTS** Radio broadcasting began in 1920. Cross worked as an announcer on station WJZ in 1921. His clear, strong voice could be heard on the "A & P Gypsies," a musical program that first aired in 1923, thus making him one of the earliest persons to gain radio fame. He became the long running host of the successful "Metropolitan Opera Broadcasts" from New York. Cross was renowned for his solemn introduction of singers and became known as "the pontiff of radio music." First broadcast on NBC, starting in 1931, he only missed two performances (due to his wife's death) in the 43 years of announcing for the Met. He was known for his near-flawless diction. *Time* magazine described Cross as a: "huge, humble, bespectacled music-charmed announcer, whose cultured genuflecting voice seems to come straight from NBC's artistic soul." Cross worked right up until his death in 1975.

Diana Lynn 1627 Vine

Actress, musician

BORN Dolores Loehr; Oct. 7, 1926, in Los Angeles, CA. **SPOTLIGHTS** *They Shall Have Music* (1939) showcased a young, gifted Lynn as a pianist. Movies include *The Major and the Minor* (1942) and *The Miracle of Morgan's Creek* (1944). **TV** Numerous live roles in "The U.S. Steel Hour." Died: 1971.

Howard Duff 1627 Vine

Actor

BORN Nov. 24. 1917, in Bremerton, WA. **SPOTLIGHTS** A big, tough, action guy with a distinctive, resonant voice, he earned his stripes with the Armed Forces Radio Service. After his discharge, Duff was ideally cast as the title character in radio's

Howard Duff

"The Adventures of Sam Spade, Detective" (1946-'50). This detective drama, based on the gritty character created by writer Dashiell Hammett, had Duff playing the role most closely associated with Humphrey Bogart onscreen. Duff brought his own style to Sam Spade, he was sarcastic where Bogie had been stern. He also brought a quirky edge of humor to Spade, as well as a fast wit and charm. Highly rated, network executives reluctantly let Duff go, due to government pressure from the Communist witch hunt days. Dashiell Hammett's name showed up on one of the red lists, as did Duff's around November of 1950. After the show's cancellation, NBC (who had taken the show from CBS in Sept. 1949) was barraged with hundreds of thousands of protest letters from fans. NBC put the show back on without Duff, and it failed miserably. The original broadcasts with Duff are timeless classics in the realm of the private eye stories; if you get a chance to hear them, don't miss the opportunity. Duff also made more than 25 motion pictures. Movies include *The Naked City* (1948), *All My Sons* (1948) with Edward G. Robinson, *Johnny Stool Pigeon* (1949) co-starring Shelley Winters and Dan Duryea, *Woman in Hiding* (1949) opposite Ida Lupino, *While the City Sleeps* (1956) with Ida Lupino, *Boys' Night Out* (1962) with Kim Novak, James Gardner, Tony Randall, Patti Page and Zsa Zsa Gabor, *Panic in the City* (1968), and *Kramer vs. Kramer* (1979). **TV** "Mr. Adams and Eve" (1957-'58) opposite his real-life wife, Ida Lupino (they divorced in 1973); "Felony Squad" (1966-'69); and Sheriff Titus Sample in "Flamingo Road" (1981-'82). Also in the 1980s, he played Senator Henry Harrison O'Dell in "Dallas." Died: 1990.

Sidney Blackmer 1627 Vine

Actor

BORN July 13, 1895, in Salisbury, NC. **SPOTLIGHTS** A villainous actor in early silents since 1914, when Blackmer narrowed his dark eyes, audiences hissed. His criminals were classy, aristocratic nasties. Yet, he aspired to make good on the Great White Way. His dream came true when he won the Tony Award for his Broadway performance as Doc in "Come Back, Little Sheba." Thereafter, he alternated between both coasts. Talkies include *The Count of Monte Cristo* (1934), *The Little Colonel* (1935), *Trade Winds* (1939), *Wilson* (1944), *Duel in the Sun* (1948), *High Society* (1957), and *Sweet Bird of Youth* (1959). His last film was *Rosemary's Baby* (1968). Died: 1973.

Horace Heidt 1633 Vine

Host, orchestra leader

BORN May 21, 1901, in Oakland, CA. **SPOTLIGHTS** Heidt was a true showman with a winning personality, but moved in a somewhat clumsy manner. His band provided dancing music, and was one of the most popular to tour the United States. Horace Heidt & His Musical Knights were featured in NBC's radio show "Pot o' Gold," where a $1,000 prize drew a large listening audience. It was America's first big money give-away show. The prize money was so large at the time, that it could pay off a *mortgage*. Needless to say, the show was a gigantic hit. Heidt flipped through telephone directories, randomly made a selection, announced their name, street, and city on the air, and then called. "Hold it, Horace, stop the music!" his announcer enthusiastically declared when a listener answered the telephone. As long as it was the party Horace wanted to reach, the person instantly won the money. No questions asked. The money was immediately wired to them. If the person was not home, their listening friends, family, co-workers and neighbors never let them forget about their bad luck in missing the "gold." The accumulated money was added to the "Pot o' Gold." He closed each show with his sleepy theme ballad, "I'll Love You in My Dreams." Died: 1986.

Pat Boone 🎵   1633 Vine

Singer, actor, composer, lyricist, writer

BORN Charles Eugene Boone; June 1, 1934, in Jacksonville, FL. **SPOTLIGHTS** He is a descendent of early American frontier hero Daniel Boone. Pat Boone, like his ancestor, is a man of high moral standards, and in a town where contracts can be as thick as telephone directories, he is a man of his word. Boone was raised, from the age of one, in Nashville, Tennessee—a state he still considers to be his home. With his all-American boy good looks, and his nice, easy, soft-spoken style, Boone was voted the "Most Popular Boy" at David Lipscomb High School. At age 17, the student sang on his own radio show at a local station. The following year Boone was a national winner on television's "Ted Mack Amateur Hour." It was the country's most important talent show, with Mack also having discovered Frank Sinatra and Gladys Knight. The win led to guest stints on "The Arthur Godfrey Talent Scouts Show." Boone took a job singing at WBAP-TV in Ft. Worth, Texas, while attending North Texas Teachers College in 1954. Around this time, he signed an exclusive contract with the Dot label, recording his first hit "Two Hearts, Two Kisses, One Love." Then, on the air after one of Boone's appearances, Godfrey invited him to come back any time: "You don't have to call or check with anybody—just show up. Any time!" With those encouraging words, Boone—now a husband and a father—moved his family to New York. He enrolled as a student at Columbia University, and became a regular on Godfrey's show. Fans loved his deep, rich voice, and his star rose fast. "Ain't That A Shame," his second recording and first #1 hit followed, then his own network TV show, movies and more top-charting tunes. On the side, he earned his college

degree with honors. His hit songs include "Love Letters in the Sand," "I'll Be Home," "A Wonderful Time Up There," "I Almost Lost My Mind," "Friendly Persuasion," "Speedy Gonzales," "Tutti Frutti," and "Why Baby Why." He made his motion picture debut in *Bernardine* (1957), and sang the hit theme song of the same name. Movies include *April Love* (1957) with his hit song of the same name, the sensational family sci-fi picture *Journey to the Center of the Earth* (1959), *State*

Pat Boone

Fair (1962), *Goodbye Charlie* (1964), *The Greatest Story Ever Told* (1965), *The Cross and the Switchblade* (1970), and *Roger and Me* (1988—documentary). Boone is an accomplished stage actor, too. His 40th anniversary tour in 1995 came on the heels of his performing in the title role of the musical comedy, "The Will Rogers Follies," in Branson, Missouri. **TV** "The Pat Boone, Chevy Showroom," musical variety program (ABC, 1957-'60). Since then, the entertainer has been a frequent guest star on countless shows. **RADIO** Since 1983 "The Pat Boone Show," classified as a "Contemporary Christian" program, is heard worldwide. **RECORDING** Chairman of Gold Label record company, Boone said, "Gold Label will provide a home for artists with gold record status to continue their record careers. Legendary artists who have been ignored by the major labels, have *not* been neglected by their fans. In my experience, the fans have embraced new recordings, attended concerts, and requested more from their favorite artists." Their roster includes Jack Jones, Toni Tennille, Irish duo Foster & Allen, among others. Call 615.242.4452 ext. 21 (or website: patsgold.com). **HIGHLIGHTS** He is one of Hollywood's success stories as a husband and father. He married his high school sweetheart, Shirley Foley (daughter of the legendary country music singer, Red Foley), when they were both age 19. The union produced four children: Cherry, Lindy, Debby (another celebrated pop singer), and Laury, and 15 grandchildren. **ACHIEVEMENTS** Boone holds *Billboard's* all-time record of 200 consecutive weeks on the charts with more than one song. Of the top 40 solo recording artists of the rock 'n' roll era, Boone is among the top three. He has sold more than 50 million records. His many charitable works include the Easter Seals Society Telethon, where he has helped raise more than a half-billion dollars to treat the disabled. He is co-founder of Mercy Corps, a world hunger organization which addresses all the crisis spots globally. **QUOTE** "I'm thinking of hiring a detective and finding out what happened to my third star. When they first put the list together, they had me down for three stars: television, movies and records. I once knew where the three stars were. But I think Hollywood Boulevard caved in and now there's only two stars left, one in television, and the other in records. People are telling me they only have a record of these two stars. I'm thinking of hiring a detective to find my third star. I know it was there once."

Robert Montgomery   1633 Vine

See page 401

Floyd Gibbons 1635 Vine

Newscaster

SPOTLIGHTS Gibbons made radio history by being the first newscaster to broadcast on network air. First heard across the country on Christmas 1925, he was celebrated for his interesting reports which he delivered in a fast-paced style (clocked at 217 words a minute), often using conversational slang in a dramatic articulation. A renowned journalist, he had worked for the *Minneapolis Daily News* and the *Chicago Tribune*. He sought danger and adventure wherever it could be found. He interviewed the Mexican bandit, revolutionary leader and hero, Francisco Villa (better known as "Pancho Villa"), rode a camel across the Sahara desert, braved battle fronts in Africa, Russia and China, explored jungles, and survived the sinking of the *Laconia*. In 1929, he became host of NBC's "Headline Hunters." With his swashbuckling personality, he collected a vast array of fascinating stories, which radio audiences found riveting. Americans listening to NBC heard him broadcast from Ethiopia in 1935, and the following year from Spain. **ACHIEVEMENTS** He pioneered the use of the portable microphone in 1929. Decorated for his valor by the French during World War I, he was wounded three times in Beleau Arbres. One injury cost him his left eye. Afterwards, he wore a crisp, white linen eye patch that became his closely identifiable trademark. Died: 1939.

Samuel Goldwyn 1635 Vine

Motion picture pioneer, producer

BORN Schmuel Gelbfisz; July 1879 (was his most likely birth date), in Warsaw, Poland. **SPOTLIGHTS** Born into poverty, the eldest of six children, the boy was fatherless by age 15. With no good prospects for a Jewish person to be had in Russian Poland, and with dreams of coming to America, he struck out on his own at age 16. Gelbfisz walked for nearly 300 miles, then crossed the Oder River, and was smuggled into Germany in 1895. Then, he walked another 200 miles to arrive in Hamburg, to connect with someone his mother had known. There, the teen learned glove making. In about a month he went to London, England alone, eating scraps from trash cans, and sleeping in the thick shrubbery around Hyde Park. When the thin youth went to stay with his mother's sister in nearby Birmingham, he found another crowded ghetto. Too weak to work at backbreaking jobs--the only kind of labor available--he was continuously fired. He found himself openly crying, and would remain emotional for the rest of his life. He began

Samuel Goldwyn (center) with Bob Hope and Virginia Mayo

studying English, and in 1898 set sail for North America. Records do not exist of him entering the country; it is believed he was an illegal alien who got into New York via Canada. Just as he had imagined, his hard work and efforts paid off in his new country. In 1913, and now known as Goldfish, he co-founded the Jesse L. Lasky Feature Players Company with his brother-in law. Lasky and he teamed with a man named Cecil B. DeMille, who had never made a film, but said he thought he could. The producer raised money and the production started. In 18 days, with DeMille directing, they made Hollywood's first feature-length film, *The Squaw Man* (1914). The original budget of $15,000 had tripled, and that was twice what the company was worth. It was the longest picture ever made at six reels, and was the first Broadway play to be adapted to the screen. It broke new ground by grossing the heady sum of a quarter of a million dollars within a few months. The celebrated *Squaw Man* also established Hollywood as the motion picture center of the world and was Hollywood's most important release of the year. It took their baby company into mature growth almost overnight (Paramount Pictures). They were able to make 21 movies from the proceeds. In 1916, the company merged with Adolph Zukor's Famous Players. After a buy-out of almost one million dollars, he co-founded the Goldwyn Company. When he wanted to legally change his name to Goldwyn, his partner tried to stop him in court. The judge ruled in Goldwyn's favor, stating: "A self-made man may prefer a self-made name." The company later merged to become Metro-Goldwyn-Mayer, better known as MGM. He and another partner, Louis B. Mayer, were in a constant power struggle. They got into a noisy scuffle at the Hillcrest Country Club, in Los Angeles, with Mayer pushing him into the locker room's laundry hamper. When asked about the fight, Goldwyn acted shocked. He answered, "What? We're like friends, we're like brothers. We love each other. We'd do anything for each other. We'd even cut each other's throats for each other!" By 1923 he decided he had enough with partners and formed Samuel Goldwyn Productions. His productions were of the highest quality. Movies include *Ben Hur* (1925), *The Greeks Had a Word for Them* (1932), *Roman Scandals* (1933), *Wuthering Heights* (1939), *The Pride of the Yankees* (1942), *The Secret Life of Walter Mitty* (1947), *Guys and Dolls* (1955), and *Porgy and Bess* (1959). A tough taskmaster of many award-winning motion pictures, he once said: "A producer shouldn't get ulcers, he should give them." **MOTTO** "I am willing to admit that I may not always be right, but I am never wrong." **ACHIEVEMENTS** 1946 Special Oscar. 1946 Best Picture Oscar for *The Best Years of Our Lives*. Goldwyn spoke to a gathering of reporters. "I don't care if it doesn't make a nickel. I just want every man, woman and child in America to see it!" This sensitive, classic post-war study of soldiers adjusting to civilian life won eight Oscars...1957 Jean Hersholt Humanitarian Award. Father of independent producer-director Samuel Goldwyn, Jr. (born 1926), and grandfather of actor-director Tony Goldwyn (born 1960). **QUOTE** Polish-born, he was never able to fully master English. Known for his "Goldwynisms," he coined a number of classic Hollywood phrases. Goldwyn declared: "In two words, impossible!" "A verbal agreement isn't worth the paper it's written on." "Include me out." "Tell me, how did you love the picture?" And, "Any man who goes to a psychiatrist should have his head examined." Died: 1974.

Linda Darnell 🎥   1635 Vine

Linda Darnell visits convalescing WWII GIs at a VA hospital.

Actress

BORN Monetta Eloyse Darnell; Oct. 16, 1921, in Dallas, TX. **SPOTLIGHTS** A brunette dynamo at Fox Studios in the 1940s, Darnell made her screen debut in *Hotel for Women* (1939). Many pictures quickly followed. Initially, she started in sugary ingenue roles, but reached her limit when she felt it was "hitting me at the box office." She said, "After three years, people just got tired of seeing the sweet, young things I was playing and wham, one morning I found myself at the bottom of the heap." She convinced the studio to launch a massive campaign building up her sex appeal. Her first "sultry siren" role was in *Summer Storm* (1944). Darnell was absolutely perfect in John Ford's Western *My Darling Clementine* (1946), co-starring Henry Fonda. She was wonderful in *Forever Amber* (1947) in the title role, and Preston Sturges' *Unfaithfully Yours* (1948), a dark comedy co-starring Rex Harrison. Movies include *Star Dust*, *Brigham Young*, *The Mark of Zorro* (all 1940), Mamoulian's *Blood and Sand* (1941), co-starring Tyrone Power and Rita Hayworth, *The Loves of Edgar Allen Poe* (1942), *The Song of Bernadette* (1943—as the Virgin Mary), *Fallen Angel* (1945), *A Letter to Three Wives* (1948), *No Way Out* (1950), *The 13th Letter* (1951), and *This Is My Love* (1954). Died: 1965.

Leo Carrillo 🎥   1635 Vine

Leo Carrillo

Actor

BORN Aug. 6, 1880, in Los Angeles, CA. **SPOTLIGHTS** One of Hollywood's busiest character actors, he specialized in dialects. His "put-on" accents (Spanish, Greek, Chinese, American Southern, etc.) and appropriately matching body language fooled millions of people. He made his screen debut in *Mister Antonio* (1929). Carrillo appears in more than 60 movies, including *Viva Villa!* (1934), *In Caliente* (1935), *The Gay Desperado* (1936), *City Streets* (1938), *Too Hot to Handle* (1938), and *Barnacle Bill* (1941). **TV** At age 70, he started working on the series "The Cisco Kid" (1950-'56). He played Pancho, loyal sidekick of Cisco. He would warn his pal, "Ceesco, the shereef and hees posse, ees getting closer!" Amazingly, this senior citizen rode his own horse, Loco, and performed his own stunts! **HIGHLIGHTS** Carrillo is one of California's original families. **QUOTE** "I don't believe in old age." Died: 1961.

Don Fedderson   1635 Vine

Executive producer, host

BORN April 16, 1913, in Beresford, SD. **SPOTLIGHTS** He attended the Kansas City School of Law before selling newspaper advertising. He switched to radio and developed the nation's first all-disc jockey format. He also introduced TV viewers to the "Liberace Show," "Life with Elizabeth" starring Betty White, "Do You Trust Your Wife?" with Edgar Bergen, and "Who Do You Trust" with a young Johnny Carson. He executive produced "My Three Sons" and "Family Affair." Lawrence Welk treasured him. Died: 1994.

Cornel Wilde 🎥 1637 Vine

Cornel Wilde

Actor, director

BORN Cornelius Wilde; Oct. 13, 1915, in New York, NY. **SPOTLIGHTS** He plays a sensational Chopin in *A Song to Remember* (1945), and co-stars with the beautiful Gene Tierney in the suspenseful melodrama *Leave Her to Heaven* (1945). He plays opposite Jeanne Crain and Linda Darnell in *Centennial Summer* (1946), and was superb in *Forever Amber* (1947). Movies include *The Homestretch* (1947), and *The Greatest Show on Earth* (1952). He stars in the campy *Omar Khayyam* (1957). Wilde added directing to his credits with *Storm Fear* (1956), *Sword of Lancelot* (1962), *The Naked Prey* (1965), and *Beach Red* (1967). Died: 1989.

Frank Sinatra 🎙   1637 Vine

See page 289

Louis B. Mayer 🎥   1637 Vine

Executive, producer

Louis B. Mayer

BORN Eliezer Meyer; July 4, 1885 (estimated—he could have been born a few years earlier), in Russia. **SPOTLIGHTS** A successful junk dealer in 1904, who became partners with Samuel Goldwyn in 1924 to form Metro-Goldwyn-Mayer (MGM). A few years later, he helped formed the Academy of Motion Picture Arts and Sciences, and many of MGM's pictures deservedly earned Academy Awards in the coming years. In 1937, he was the highest paid executive in the nation, with an annual salary of $1,161,753. Mayer had a keen eye for future stars. From Europe, he imported Greta Garbo (as part of a package deal with director Mauritz Stiller), Hedy Lamarr, and Greer Garson. Mayer was also credited with producing some of the most spectacular movies ever, including *Gone With the Wind* and *The Wizard of Oz* (both 1939). A gifted, but quick-tempered taskmaker, he bitterly relinquished his executive position at MGM in 1951. (See the bio of Samuel Goldwyn in this book.) **HIGHLIGHTS** Mayer believed in "The Chicken Soup Cure." Using a recipe provided by his wife, Mayer had a company edict that this penicillin-in-a-pot be made daily in the studio commissary. He believed chicken soup would help cut down on sick time, and help keep the staff healthy. Any employee could buy a delicious bowl of soup for 35 cents. The paternal Mayer had a bowl everyday, and greatly believed he benefited from its medicinal properties. Nearly a half a centu-

ry later, high-tech medical research studies proved Mayer right...Around town, he was the one-punch artist. He powerfully slugged any man who dared denigrate the sanctity of women or motherhood. **QUOTE** An astute businessman, Mayer once lamented, "We are the only company whose assets all walk out the gates at night." Died: 1957.

George Burns 🎥   1637 Vine

See page 438

Vera Vague 🎙   1637 Vine

See page 181

Sue Carol Ladd 🎥   1637 Vine

Actress, agent

Alan Ladd and Sue Carol Ladd

BORN Evelyn Lederer; Oct. 30, 1907, in Chicago, IL. **SIDELIGHTS** Under contract to Fox, she was an ingenue in *Slaves of Beauty* (1927) and other silents. In talkies, she stars in *The Golden Calf* (1930), then decided herself to go behind-the-scenes. She became one of Hollywood's first female theatrical agents, paving the way for future generations of women. Able to access the studios' most powerful executives, this energetic woman launched the stellar career of Alan Ladd (her future husband), among others. Sue Carol had brains, guts, and charm. (Also see Alan Ladd's bio in this book.) Died: 1982.

Nelson Eddy 🎙   1637 Vine

See page 130

Harold Peary 🎙   1637 Vine

Actor, singer

BORN Harrold Jose de Faria; July 25, 1908, in San Leandro, CA. **SPOTLIGHTS** The son of a Portuguese immigrant, he began entertaining in radio's early days in 1923. By the late 1920s he sang and acted in "The Spanish Serenader," then headed to Chicago in the late 1930s. He became a steadily employed radio insider, busy in comedy and drama serials, and specializing in dialects. Peary's claim to fame came from "The Great Gildersleeve" series, on both radio and film. According to a publicity release from RKO, "The man who parlayed a sinister laugh into a million-dollar asset and became The Great Gildersleeve." That is, Throckmorton P. Gildersleeve, water commissioner in the town of Summerfield, USA. With a height of 5-foot, 9-inches, this 210-pound, black-haired character had a deep, booming voice. He played a pompous windbag, with a kind heart, disguised behind the barrier of a bully for nearly a decade, before he tired of it and quit. Died: 1985.

Dolores Costello 🎵   1645 Vine

Actress
BORN Sept. 17, 1905, in Pittsburgh, PA. **SPOTLIGHTS** Her matinee idol father, Maurice Costello, placed his large-eyed, angelic, oval-faced, blonde, curly-haired daughter in his Vitagraph pictures before she was six. She became a popular silent screen ingenue. She appeared in several talkies. Costello played the mother in *Little Lord Fauntleroy* (1936). **HIGHLIGHTS** Married co-star (*The Sea Beast*, 1926) John Barrymore (through 1955). Died: 1979.

Joan Fontaine 🎥   1645 Vine

Actress
BORN Joan de Beauvoir de Havilland; Oct. 22, 1917, in Tokyo, Japan (to British parents). **SPOTLIGHTS** After appearing in mostly B flicks without progressing further, Fontaine was ready to throw in the towel. At a dinner party she sat next to movie producer David O. Selznick. He discussed with her his upcoming feature, the screen adaptation of Daphne du Maurier's bestselling gothic mystery novel, *Rebecca*. He had acquired the property at a great expense, to be his follow-up success to his previous year's *Gone with the Wind*. He suggested she test for the part, and director Alfred Hitchcock approved. In her breakthrough role she plays a mousy wife opposite Laurence Olivier, creating tremendous tension. The genteel, exquisite talent received her first Academy Award nomination for best actress, and Hitchcock received his first Oscar nomination for best direction. The film won a Best Picture Academy Award. A fetching performer, her movies

The lovely Joan Fontaine and Mark Stevens

include *Gunga Din* (1939), *This Above All* (1942), *The Constant Nymph* (1943--in an Oscar-nominated performance), *Jane Eyre* (1944), *Letter from an Unknown Woman* (1948), *Frenchman's Creek* (1944), *Flight to Tangiers* (1953), and *September Affair* (1950). She is the younger sister of Olivia de Havilland (of *Gone with the Wind* fame). **ACHIEVEMENTS** 1941 Best Actress Oscar for *Suspicion*. Fontaine became a licensed pilot, a licensed interior decorator, graduated from France's Cordon Bleu cooking school, became a champion balloonist, expert golfer, and prize-winning fisherman!

Frankie Laine 📺   1645 Vine

See page 113

Walter Winchell 📺   1645 Vine

See page 447

William Steinberg 🎵   1645 Vine

Musician
BORN Hans Wilhelm Steinberg; Aug. 1, 1899, in Cologne, Germany. **SPOTLIGHTS** Steinberg's remarkable talent for interpreting musical compositions established him as a "Conductor of Eminence." He recorded Beethoven's *Symphony No. 6 in F Major, op. 68*, the "Pastoral," with Pittsburgh Symphony Symphony; among others. Died: 1978.

Jerry Colonna 🎤   1645 Vine

Actor, musician, singer, comedian
BORN Gerald Colonna; Sept. 17, 1904, in Boston, MA.

Jerry Colonna

SPOTLIGHTS He was America's #1 madcap comic sidekick on the top rated radio show of the 1940s. A former professional trombonist, the wild Colonna had played with the Big Bands of the Swing Era, including Benny Goodman's, Artie Shaw's and Jimmy Dorsey's. But, it would be on air where he would find great fame and fortune with "The Bob Hope Show." Colonna worked on the comedy show from 1938-'48. Known as "the Professor," he was the glib foil to the celebrated Hope, causing havoc with his outrageous and ridiculous schemes. *Newsweek* magazine wrote he was "tearing up straight songs in a voice that begins in a mousy whisper and reaches a roaring crescendo. He can--and usually does--hold a note longer than most opera singers, an attribute ordinarily found only in hog callers." Colonna played fun-crazy as no other singer-comic had done before. Hope wrote about the Professor's two-dimensional character, "One is the zany, silly moron, and the other is the deep-thinking serious moron." With his trademark four-inch walrus moustache, rolling eyes, and characteristic bellow-like voice, Colonna also appeared in movies and television, where his mere presence caused volcanic laughter to erupt. **ACHIEVEMENTS** During WWII, he traveled with Bob Hope to distant and dangerous battlegournd outposts, entertaining servicemen and women. They visited every camp, every base and every hospital. Died: 1986.

Jane Froman ■ 1645 Vine

See page 205

Mary Anderson 🎥 1645 Vine

Actress
BORN April 3, 1924, in Birmingham, AL. **SPOTLIGHTS** Her Southern accent was a natural in her screen debut, *Gone with the Wind* (1939). (Not bad!) She appears as a leading lady or in strong supporting roles in 17 movies, including her must-see performance in *Lifeboat* and *Wilson* (both 1944)

Michele Morgan 🎥 1645 Vine

Actress
BORN Simone Roussel; Feb. 29, 1920, in Nueilly, France. **SPOTLIGHTS** An ash-blonde, serene, graceful beauty with high cheekbones and large eyes, this international star was known as the "Venus of Paris." A superstar in France since she was 17, in America her chiselled features were compared to Dietrich's, Del Rio's and Garbo's. During WWII she worked in Hollywood, staying only for about five years. U.S. pictures include *Higher and Higher* (1943) starring Frank Sinatra, *Passage to Marseille* (1944), and *The Chase* (1946). **QUOTE** "To succeed in films you must burst through the screen. Above everything else, you must have an intangible quality, a certain presence which is better than all the experience in the world."

Sessue Hayakawa 🎥 1645 Vine

Actor
BORN Kintaro Hayakawa; June 10, 1889, in Chiba, Japan. **SPOTLIGHTS** He was an ordained Buddhist priest who applied the enlightened Zen teachings to Hollywood. He was discovered in 1913 by producer Thomas Ince when his Japanese Imperial Company troupe was touring the American West. Ince offered him a contract, and the following year he enjoyed enormous success in *Typhoon* (1914). He became the dean of scoundrels, appearing in dozens of silents. The actor explained, "My villain represents, in rapid punishment, the eventual execution of effect of evil...my villain gives a valuable lesson." A silent screen superstar with all the trappings, he lived in a castle in Laurel Canyon (Hollywood), and kept a stable of thor-

Sessue Hayakawa

oughbred horses on the property. Dinner parties for 900 guests were not uncommon, and they dined to the music of three different orchestras. He rode around town in a gold-plated Pierce Arrow until comedian Fatty Arbuckle bought a duplicate automobile. Hayakawa donated his to the fire department. He commented, "Carbon copies are for typewriters." He left the United States in the mid-1920s to do European and Asian films. Hayakawa proved as brilliant in later American films. He received an Oscar nomination for his intensely crafted Colonel Saito, in *The Bridge on the River Kwai* (1957). Movies include *Geisha Boy* (1958) starring Jerry Lewis, and *The Swiss Family Robinson* (1960). **QUOTE** "Everyday I meditate for one or two hours. In both TV and movies I use these powers of concentration. I completely transform myself. Then, I don't exist. I'm just noneness...Now, it takes me only 20 seconds to lose myself before going before the camera...You must submit to complete self-denial. It takes many years of suffering." Died: 1973.

Kent Taylor 🎥 1645 Vine

See page 466

Rita Hayworth 🎥 1645 Vine

Actress, dancer
BORN Margarita Cansino; Oct. 17, 1918, in Brooklyn, NY. **SPOTLIGHTS** Born into a family of dancers, she began performing professionally as a young teen with her father. They danced in nightclubs in Los Angeles and in Tijuana, Mexico. A talent scout from Fox spotted her and signed her to a contract, but she was assigned to low-budget pictures. After a makeover, Hayworth became A-list material, and known as the Love Goddess. This voluptuous, glamorous beauty made 60 motion pictures, including *Blood and Sand* (1941) co-starring Tyrone Power, *You Were Never Lovelier* (1942) with Fred Astaire, *Cover*

Rita Hayworth

Girl (1944) co-starring Gene Kelly, and "There never was a woman like" *Gilda* (1946). Her sizzling rendition of "Put the Blame on Mame" caused such a sensation that her photograph decorated that atom bomb (Gilda) that was dropped on the Bikini Islands. During WWII, she entertained soldiers in USO performances, and as a pinup, lifted their spirits. Movies include *The Loves of Carmen* (1948), *The Lady from Shanghai* (1948), *Salome* (1953), *Fire Down Below* (1957), *Pal Joey* (1957), and *Separate Tables* (1958). Her second marriage was to Orson Welles (1943-'47). During their divorce, she declared, "I just can't stand his genius anymore." **QUOTE** "A girl is, well, a girl. It's nice to know that one is good at it." Died: 1987.

Lionel Barrymore   1645 Vine

See page 177

Thomas Mitchell   1645 Vine

Actor, playwright
BORN July 11, 1892, in Elizabeth, NJ. **SPOTLIGHTS** This Irish-American landed great roles: *Mr. Smith Goes to Washington* and *Gone with the Wind* (both 1939). Considered one of the finest dramatic talents on Broadway and on-screen, his films include *Theodora Goes Wild* (1936--a madcap comedy), *Lost Horizon* (1937), *Swiss Family Robinson* (the original), and *Our Town* (both 1940), *Wilson* (1944), *It's a Wonderful Life* (1946), *High Noon* (1952), and *While the City Sleeps* (1956). **ACHIEVEMENTS** 1939 Best Supporting Actor Oscar for *Stagecoach*. **QUOTE** "Being an actor is a necessity with me. It never was a matter of choice or a career consciously and deliberately chosen. It was as inevitable as gravity, as compelling as drink. I couldn't have avoided it if I had wanted to." Died: 1962.

David Powell   1645 Vine

Actor

BORN Around 1870, in England. **SPOTLIGHTS** A handsome, dashing leading man of the silent era, he appears opposite Mary Pickford in *Less Than the Dust* (1916). One of Paramount's shining attractions in the 1920s, he stars in *Glimpse of the Moon* (1923), with Bebe Daniels. Died: 1925.

Ben Turpin   1645 Vine

Ben Turpin

Comedian
BORN Sept. 17, 1874, in New Orleans, LA. **SPOTLIGHTS** A great silent screen comedian, his comic device was that he played opposite his appearance. Instead of playing the bumbling, hen-pecked husband (which is what the tiny, cross-eyed actor looked like), he starred as the romantic lover, the superb athlete, the dashing man-about-town. Movies include *A Small Town Idol* (1921), *Bright Eyes Daredevil* (1922), and *When a Man's a Prince* (1926). He was also famous for lampooning. He successfully poked satirical fun at superstars such as Valentino in *The Sheik of Araby* (1923), and at movie stuntmen in *The Daredevil* (1923). His eyes were insured by Lloyd's of London against *uncrossing* for $100,000. Died: 1940.

Katrina Paxinou   1645 Vine

Actress
BORN Katrinas Constantopoulous; Dec. 17, 1900, in Piraeus, Greece. **SPOTLIGHTS** An exotic, dramatic international talent, she made only six American films while she was "visiting." **ACHIEVEMENTS** 1943 Best Supporting Actress Academy Award *For Whom the Bell Tolls*. Died: 1973.

Eddie Bracken   1645 Vine

See page 42

Francis X. Bushman   1645 Vine

Actor
BORN Jan. 12, 1882, in Baltimore, MD. **SPOTLIGHTS** *The first movie matinee idol*. Although Bushman was a star of the stage when he arrived at Metro, he had no concept of the global fame movies would bring. Handsome, with a strong, stunning physique (he had been a former model for a famous sculptor), this "Greek god of love" became a superstar. As a leading man, Bushman appears in 424 movies. His salary stunned Hollywood when he earned $6 million in just five years. He plays opposite fiancée Beverly Bayne in *Every Inch a King* (1914) and *Romeo and Juliet* (1916). Bushman co-stars

Francis X. Bushman

with Mae Murray and Basil Rathbone in *The Masked Bride* (1925). He gained immortality in the classic *Ben-Hur* (1926), as the Roman Messala opposite the great Ramon Navorro. Amazingly, he refused a stunt driver and drove his own chariot in the climactic race scene. (Also see Charlton Heston's bio in this book.) **HIGHLIGHTS** His studio devised an early publicity stunt for him. They sent him down the boulevard, with his pockets filled with shiny nickles, and poked full of thin holes. The coins trickled to the ground. In those days, a nickle bought a lunch, so pedestrians quickly gathered around him. Newspapers carried photographs of the mob circling "Bushman, star of screen." **QUOTE** "*Ben-Hur* was a great joke on Mussolini. When we went to Italy to shoot the picture, he was most hospitable. He thought we were about to recreate the grandeur that was Rome. He couldn't do too much for us. Then, when we were done and had gone home, and he saw the film, he almost had a stroke. The hero was a young Jewish follower of Christ, and a Roman was the villain of the picture." Died: 1966.

William Holden 🎥   **1645 Vine**

William Holden

Actor

BORN William Franklin Beedle, Jr.; April 17, 1918, in O'Fallen, IL. **SPOTLIGHTS** A clean-cut, divinely handsome, dark-haired leading man, he grew up in Pasadena, California. Discovered at the Pasadena Playhouse by a Paramount Pictures talent scout, Holden landed a contract with that studio in 1937. His first important role, though, was in Columbia's *The Golden Boy* (1939), opposite Barbara Stanwyck. He delivers a great performance as a poor boy torn between the violin and prizefighting. The next year, he stars in Thornton Wilder's stylized story, *Our Town* (1940). Adapted from Wilder's Pulitzer Prize-winning play, and directed by Sam Wood, this is classic Americana at its finest. Holden gives a must-see wonderful performance. Also apparent was his obvious movie magic. He made a number of films, including the excellent action picture *Texas* (1941), then struck gold in *Sunset Boulevard* (1950). He plays sleazy, out-of-luck screenwriter Joe Gillis, who agrees to be kept by a has-been—former

silent screen goddess Norma Desmond (Gloria Swanson). His expressive pain illustrates his weak-willed character's self-hatred. Directed by Billy Wilder, this is a must-see classic film. Next, the charming Holden sparkles in George Cukor's award-winning comedy *Born Yesterday* (1950). One Hollywood director assessed Holden as, "the typical American boy who wanted to become a slob, but couldn't make the grade." In 1956, he sizzles on-screen in *Picnic* opposite Kim Novak (watch for the dance scene). Another must-see performance is in David Lean's epic *The Bridge on the River Kwai* (1957), where his strength as a P.O.W. in a Japanese labor camp is truly admirable. His gritty performance of a long-in-the-tooth Texan outlaw who crosses over into Mexico in 1913 with his gang in *The Wild Bunch* (1969), introduced to audiences a new genre of violent, macho Westerns. Director Sam Peckinpah made the stylistic breakthrough a bloodbath, shooting much of it as it could have truly happened during those times. Holden gives one of his finest performances in the Western *Wild Rovers* (1971). Holden was absolutely brilliant in Sidney Lumet's *Network* (1976), opposite Faye Dunaway, Peter Finch, Robert Duvall and Ned Beatty. He made nearly 80 films and retained his position as the number one box office star for many years. **ACHIEVEMENTS** 1953 Best Actor Oscar for *Stalag 17*, in his role as a cynical sergeant. Yet, he considered his most important role as a real-life conservationist and founder of the Mt. Kenya Game Ranch. Actress Stefanie Powers has continued the work in his memory. If you're interested in the preservation of wildlife, please contact the William Holden Wildlife Foundation, P.O. Box 67981, L.A., CA 90067 U.S.A. (www.allmediapr.com/whwf. *E-mail*: whwildlife@aol.com). **QUOTE** For years, Hollywood cast him as the "All-American boy-next-door" claiming "he'd be big if only he had sex appeal." After his Oscar-nominated performance in *Sunset Boulevard*, he was seen in a new light. Holden wryly observed, "Producers now say I have sex appeal. Honest, I had it all the time...well, for years." Died: 1981.

Maurice Chevalier 🎥   **1645 Vine**

Maurice Chevalier

Actor, singer

BORN Sept. 12, 1888, in France. **SPOTLIGHTS** An international stage star at age 20, he was a cinema star by 40. This charming Frenchman exuded *joie de vivre* in *Love Me Tonight* (1932). Chevalier possessed a jaunty, buoyant style and was known for his trademark jutting lower lip, straw hat and crisp bow tie. He stars as Audrey Hepburn's father in *Love in the Afternoon* (1957), then was immortalized in *Gigi* (1958), with his twinkling eyes and roguish smile singing "I'm

Glad I'm Not Young Anymore." Two songs remain uniquely his own: "Every Little Breeze Seems to Whisper Louise" and "Thank Heaven for Little Girls." **ACHIEVEMENTS** 1958 Special Oscar. **QUOTE** "Your age is only bothersome when you stop to coddle it, or try to ignore it...I'm at a time of life when I can delight in just admiring beautiful women. Old age isn't so bad when you consider the alternative." Died: 1972.

Red Buttons   1645 Vine

Red Buttons

Actor, comedian, singer
BORN Aaron Chwatt; Feb. 5, 1919, in New York, NY. **SPOTLIGHTS** He grew up on the Lower East Side in an area he stated "was a pretty tough block." At age 12 he won an amateur night contest, and four years later a job as a bellboy-singer at Dinty Moore's Tavern in the Bronx. There, he got his stage name from the bright red bellboy uniform and his matching red hair. While still in his teens, he began on the Borscht Circuit as a Catskill comedian. By 1942 he made his Broadway debut in "Vickie," starring Jose Ferrer. His career was interrupted by World War II when he served in the Army. During his military service and after his honorable discharge he continued to do plays. He gingerly made the leap into "The Red Buttons Show" a comedy-variety television program (1952-'55). Watching his show became a national fad with everybody imitating his catchy "Ho Ho" theme. About TV, he quipped, "Every comedian should have a medal just for showing up." Among his dozens of motion pictures are *Imitation General* (1958), *They Shoot Horses, Don't They?* (1969--in an Oscar-nominated performance), and *Poseidon Adventure* (1972). **ACHIEVEMENTS** In 1957 he won a Best Supporting Actor Academy Award for his role as Sergeant Joe Kelly in *Sayonara*. **QUOTE** About the momentous Oscar event, he commented, "They tell me my feet never touched the ground after my name was called."

Greer Garson 🎥
1645 Vine

Greer Garson

Actress
BORN Sept. 29, 1903, in County Down, Northern Ireland. **SPOTLIGHTS** A titian-haired beauty with blue-green eyes and alabaster skin, Garson was known for her grace and charm. When her father died when she was four months old, her mother fell on hard times.

The two relocated to London, England, in hopes of a better life. It was not to be. She later reflected on her childhood: "I was ill for six months out of every year and unpopular at school." Somehow she managed to reinvent herself. She blossomed into an elegant lady. Discovered by Louis B. Mayer, he put her under contract to MGM, where she was known for her cleverness. She epitomized nobility, wisdom and courage. Movies include *Goodbye Mr. Chips* (1939), *Madame Curie* (1942), and *Mrs. Parkington* (1944). She was often paired with Walter Pidgeon. **ACHIEVEMENTS** 1942 Best Actress Oscar for *Mrs. Miniver*. Died: 1996.

Broncho Billy Anderson 🎥   1645 Vine

Actor, director, producer
BORN Max Aronson; March 21, 1882, in Little Rock, AR. **SPOTLIGHTS** Prolific star and director of the "Broncho Billy" silent Westerns; made more than 400 one-and two-reelers between 1907 and 1918. The *first* Western star, Anderson set the pace for all the followers. The only mistake he made was not moving into features soon enough. Cowboy Tom Mix moved right on in this opening. Anderson retired in the early 1920s. **ACHIEVEMENTS** 1957 Special Oscar "for the contributions to the development of motion pictures as entertainment." **RECOMMENDED** The Academy Award-winning film, *The Resurrection of Broncho Billy* (1970), produced by John Longenecker, is a tribute to the old West and Western movies. (www.bronchobilly.com or www.IndieFilmsOnline.com). **QUOTE** When asked by a reporter what he had been up to some 40 years since retiring, he replied, "Just driftin' along with the breeze." Died: 1971.

Alistair Cooke 📺   1645 Vine

Journalist, broadcaster
BORN Alfred Alistair Cooke; Nov. 20, 1908, in Manchester, England. **SPOTLIGHTS** Educated at Cambridge University, this shy, creative, very literate student received his degree in 1930. He came to America to study at Harvard (one year), and Yale (one year), then returned to England. He acquired the position of film critic for the BBC, and became the London correspondent for NBC in America. In 1938 Cooke flip-flopped his roles; he came to the United States as the American correspondent for the BBC, and special journalist and essayist for the London *Times*. Three years later, he became an American citizen. In 1947 he was BBC radio's esteemed commentator for "A Letter from America." Not the typical host, he spoke in undertones, and very softly. His florid observations of America and her people won him the prestigious Peabody Award. Cooke switched gears when he covered the two hotly debated, controversial Alger Hiss spy trials (June and November 1949). Many legal scholars did (and still do) *not* consider "the pumpkin papers"—discovered by finger-pointing Whittaker Chambers—to be proof of Hiss' guilt. Half of the attorneys and half of the public argued that Hiss' convic-

tion was a grave judicial travesty perpetrated against an inno-cent man—a scapegoat—and was one of America's darkest moments. Countless have likened the political inquest with the notorious and scandalous French Dreyfus Affair. Cooke's 1950 book on the subject, *A Generation on Trial*, brought him inter-national acclaim. The reader was presented with all the court-room facts in a clear, interesting and unbiased manner, but never knew if Cooke personally believed in Hiss' innocence or guilt, or what he thought of Chambers. His next book, *One Man's America*, published in 1952 was praised by a New York *Herald Tribune* reporter as more constructive to British-American relations than "most of the work of embassies." The reserved-looking Cooke became the Emmy Award-winning host of TV's cultural/educational "Omnibus" (1952-'61). It was unique in commercial TV broadcasting as there were no commercial interruptions! (Ford Foundation financed it.) He hosted TV's acclaimed "Masterpiece Theatre."

Blanche Thebom 🔴   Hollywood and Vine

Opera singer
BORN Sept. 19, 1918, in Monessen, PA. **SPOTLIGHTS** A beau-tiful, sleek, dark mezzo-soprano, she made her 1944 Metropolitan Opera debut singing the role of Fricka in *Die Walkure*. Recordings include Igor Stravinsky's *The Rakes Progress* (complete opera in English) with the Metropolitan Opera, conducted by the composer himself for Columbia Records; and Bach's *St. John Passion* (RCA Victor Symphony Orchestra under Robert Shaw). There were no draperies or rugs in her apartment because she said, "They eat up too much sound." She was the first American prima donna to tour behind the Iron Curtain in 1955. She said, "I felt I represent-ed all American singers, even the whole country. I wanted des-perately to succeed." **QUOTE** About her sexy performance in *Carmen*, she stated, "When I actually kissed Don José—a real kiss, not the old Italian style—there was an uproar. I lost count of the ovations."

Neil Armstrong, Buzz Aldrin, Michael Collins
📺 **Hollywood and Vine**   *See page 266*

Constance Talmadge 🎥 Hollywood and Vine
Actress

BORN April 19, 1898, in Brooklyn, NY. **SPOTLIGHTS** Called a "demi clown" in show business, *she had to be funny* and *pret-ty*. Her first important role came as the mountain girl in the Babylonian sequence in the D.W. Griffith's classic *Intolerance* (1916). She had a peppy personality, and excelled in sophisti-cated pieces. Movies include *A Virtual Vamp* (1919), *The Primitive Lover* (1922), *Dulcy* (1923), *Her Night of Romance* (1924), and *Her Sister from Paris* (1925). She retired in 1929, with the onset of sound. **HIGHLIGHTS** The older sister of Norma Talmadge, the two *tied* for second place as the most

Constance Talmadge

popular actress of 1921! **QUOTE** "Don't try for fame before the camera! First, get an old-fash-ioned job—behind the camera. That's my advice to the girls who soon will be flocking toward Hollywood and New York seeking fame on the screen. To those girls who come to Hollywood, I would suggest that they first take a look around stu-dio-land and investi-gate the many lucrative capacities "off the screen" in which they might make a good living, before they try for success in the heartbreaking calling of an actress. For instance, studios need artists for designing sets, and advertising lithographs. There's costume departments, laboratory jobs in splicing, edit-ing, accounting, and all the stars have highly paid secretaries. Plus, there are girls who have become writers and directors. There are many women who are casting directors. And so, when I consider the innumerable profitable vocations which a girl can follow in Hollywood, I often wonder why it is that so many girls come to Hollywood each year and live three or four in a room merely for the privilege working now and then in a picture. The extra girls make only a precarious living. They spend many weary, discouraging days trampling around from one studio and one employment office to another when they might be making a comfortable living in some specialized branch of studio technical work. My advice to the thousands of girls who come to Hollywood is to seek, first, a plain, ordi-nary, every-day 'job' around the studios. The opportunity to become a star may come later." Died: 1973.

Rex Ingram 🎥   Hollywood and Vine

Actor
BORN Oct. 20, 1895; born on the floating riverboat *Robert E. Lee* near Cairo, IL. **SPOTLIGHTS** He graduated from a military

Rex Ingram

school in Chicago, then from the Medical School of Northwestern University. At age 23, the huge, muscular doctor dumped his physicianship to appear in the silent version of *Tarzan of the Apes*. After a handful of years on the west coast, working both in silents and in stage productions, he was cast in prominent roles on Broadway. His breakthrough screen role, as Marc Connelly in *The Green Pastures* (1936) was utterly brilliant. Because of prejudice, stereotype, and limited script possibilities, the need for African American leading actors was slim. Ingram often agreed to supporting roles. He is best remembered as the slave Jim in *The Adventures of Huckleberry Finn* (1939), as the giant genie who laughed uproariously in *The Thief of Bagdad* (1940), for his work in George Stevens' intelligent comedy *The Talk of the Town* (1942), as Lucifer in *Cabin in the Sky* (1943), and for his solid performance in *Sahara* (1943), a fine WWII drama. He appears with an all-star African American cast in the drama *Anna Lucasta* (1958). Other motion pictures include *God's*

Little Acre (1958), *Elmer Gantry* (1960), *Your Cheatin' Heart* (1964), and *Journey to Shiloh* (1968), his last film. Died: 1969.

Hank Mann 🎥   Hollywood and Vine

Comedian

BORN David Liebermann; 1888, in New York, NY.
SPOTLIGHTS A secondary clown, he had a big, walrus-moustache, "bowl" haircut, with dark, thick bangs down to his eyebrows. He used this haircut to feature his eyes, often uplifted, to suggest he might just be a man of style if he was not being chased, stretched, or punched. He was a slapstick clown in Sennett's *Keystone Kops* (1912-'14 series), very good in *City Lights* with Charlie Chaplin, and brought back memories in *Abbott and Costello Meet the Keystone Kops* (1955). Died: 1971.

Broncho Billy Anderson (center)

6302 HOLLYWOOD

Fred Waring 🎙️   6302 Hollywood

See page 413

Polly Moran 🎥   6302 Hollywood

Polly Moran

Comedienne
BORN June 28, 1884, in Chicago, IL. **SPOTLIGHTS** Moran was known as one of moviedom's most rollicking comics. At age 12, this buck-toothed gal started in vaudeville, and was a seasoned performer by the time Mack Sennett discovered her on the Orpheum stage in Los Angeles. She romped through the silents in Sennett comedies, including her stand-out hilarious Western role in *Sheriff Nell*. The carefree spirit reached the peak of her popularity playing opposite Marie Dressler—where the duo were quite a team! Talkies include *Bringing Up Father* (1928), and *Alice in Wonderland* (1933--as the Dodo Bird). Her last notable film was a classic Tracy-Hepburn vehicle, *Adam's Rib* (1949). Died: 1952.

Louella O. Parsons 🖊️   6302 Hollywood

See page 395

Red Foley 📺   6302 Hollywood

See page 208

Luise Rainer 🎥   6302 Hollywood

Luise Rainer

Actress
BORN Jan. 12, 1912, in Vienna, Austria. **SPOTLIGHTS** A Hollywood enigma. A wide-eyed brunette, she came to town in 1935, too easily reached the very top (see below), and left a few years later for married life in England. She appears in *Hostages* (1943), retired from the screen when she found the scripts "idiotic," then waited 55 years before making another movie, *The Gambler*, based on Feodor Dostoevsky's 19th-century story. **ACHIEVEMENTS** She won back-to-back Academy Awards. She took home Oscars for Best Actress in 1936 for *The Great Ziegfeld,* and in 1937 for *The Good Earth*. Critics and audiences alike were shocked that she won over Greta Garbo (Garbo's first nomination and possibly her best work) in *Camille* (1936) **QUOTE** "I was born with talent that God gave to me. If He puts it in your cradle, it remains always."

Marguerite Clark 🎥   6304 Hollywood

Actress
BORN Feb. 22, 1884, in Avondale, OH. **SPOTLIGHTS** Her very successful career in silents made this delicate beauty rich: *Wildflower* (1914) to *Scrambled Wives* (1921). Died: 1940.

John Farrow 🎥   6304 Hollywood

Director, writer
BORN Feb. 10, 1904, in Australia. **SPOTLIGHTS** A marine research specialist in the Royal Naval Academy, he wrote plays for a hobby. Farrow came to Hollywood as a technical advisor/screenwriter for sea pictures. He advanced to directing: *A Bill of Divorcement* (1940) with Adolph Menjou and Maureen O'Hara; the WWII drama *Wake Island* (1942); *The Big Clock* (1945)—a suspenseful *film noir* with wife Maureen O'Sullivan, Ray Milland and Charles Laughton; and *Hondo* (1953) with John Wayne...He met his future wife, Maureen O'Sullivan, as screenwriter of *Tarzan Escapes* (1936). He married the dark-haired Irish beauty that same year. The union produced dughters-actresses Mia and Tisa Farrow. Died: 1963.

Charles Boyer 📺   6304 Hollywood

See page 364

Frank Borzage 🎥   6306 Hollywood

Director
BORN April 23, 1893, in Salt Lake City, UT. **SPOTLIGHTS** Labeled "a romantic sentimentalist" due to his many tearjerkers, critics consider his trademark work *A Farewell to Arms* (1932). It stars Gary Cooper in Ernest Hemingway's tale of romance and sacrifice. (Hemingway was furious when Hollywood predictably altered his tragic ending, but producers knew it would help the box office, and it did.) Cooper co-stars with Marlene Dietrich in the wonderful romantic comedy about a European jewel thief in *Desire* (1936). *The Mortal Storm* (1940) is his compelling drama about a 1930s family split by Nazism. **ACHIEVEMENTS** 1927 Best Director Oscar (the FIRST EVER presented) for *Seventh Heaven*. 1931 Best Director Oscar for *Bad Girl*. He is a rarity; having received a golden statuette in *both silents and talkies*. Died: 1962.

Ted Mack 📺   6306 Hollywood

Emcee, Host

Ted Mack

BORN William Maguiness; Feb. 12, 1904, in Greenley, CO. **SPOTLIGHTS** Called "the Master Master-of-Ceremonies," he was a former assistant to Major Bowes (the talent scoutmaster). He inherited the reins of Bowes popular talent show in 1946. This included 37,000,000 loyal viewers and the show's Wheel of Fortune. Fans eagerly awaited his exciting line, "Around and around she goes, and where she stops nobody knows." Popular in both radio and television, "The Original Amateur Hour" was the ultimate talent search contest. More than 725,000 amateurs were given the platform to perform in this variety program through the years. The ultra cordial host had a soothing personality which calmed nervous hopefuls. He was always encouraging. At least 500 giant stars were discovered on this show, among those: Frank Sinatra, Pat Boone, and Gladys Knight. A celebrity himself, Mack successfully had three different shows running simultaneously on each one of the three big networks. Died: 1976.

James Melton 🎙   6306 Hollywood

Singer, actor

BORN Jan. 2, 1904, in Moultrie, GA. **SPOTLIGHTS** This engaging personality toured the concert circuit with pianist George Gershwin, then became a popular singing sensation in radio during the 1930s and '40s. His repertoire ranged from popular romantic ballads to *lieder* to African-American spirituals. Though his biggest musical ambition was to sing grand opera. Melton made his Metropolitan Opera debut in 1942 in the light tenor role of Tamino in Mozart's *The Magic Flute.* He received good reviews from tough critics. He also hosted his own radio and television shows...His hobby was collecting antique automobiles. Among his 60 automobiles, he had electric, steamers and gas—*all in running condition.* Died: 1961.

Charles Boyer 🎥   6306 Hollywood

Actor

BORN Aug. 28, 1899, in Figeac, France. **SPOTLIGHTS** Although tall, dark and handsome in his youth, his face always looked as though it had been mapped out by painful memories. His large, sensuous eyes were telling. His elegant accent emphasized his sexiness or cruelty, depending on the role. He portrayed Emperor Napoleon in *Conquest* (1938), while Greta Garbo stars as the Polish countess Walewska. He was the desperate fugitive in *Algiers* (1938), while the beautiful Hedy Lamarr was the smoldering romantic interest in this glamorous Hollywood production. Boyer was thought to have recited this famous line in *Algiers*: "Comm wiz me to ze Casbah." It's a much-parodied line, but he never said it. Boyer declared, "In 1938 the year *Algiers* came out, studio publicity invented that line, and it's been plaguing me ever since." (Warner Bros.' cartoon skunk, Pepe Le Pew, is

Charles Boyer

based on this Charles Boyer character.) He is a married industrialist with a secret mistress in *Back Street* (1941). Boyer co-stars opposite Paulette Goddard in *Hold Back the Dawn* (1941). He is devilish in the suspense thriller *Gaslight* (1944). He is superb in *The Happy Time* (1952). **ACHIEVEMENTS** 1942 Special Oscar. Died: 1978.

Jackie Gleason 📺   6310 Hollywood

Jackie Gleason

Actor, comedian, composer, conductor

BORN Herbert John Gleason; Feb. 26, 1916, in Brooklyn, NY. **SPOTLIGHTS** "How sweet it is!" How true that rang for a grown-up Jackie after a horrible childhood. His father abandoned him when he was a boy. (He'd later quip, "He was as good a father as I've ever known.") His mother earned her lowly living as a ticket clerk in the subway. At night, she numbed the pain with liquor. Panic attacks crashed down on Jackie; a fear placated only by eating. But the kid was gifted with a sparkling sense of humor that enabled him to work comedy in the local pool halls of Brooklyn's tough Bushwick section. Realizing he was the funniest guy in town, he dropped out of school after the 8th grade to emcee, comic in burlesque clubs/intimate bistros and compete in "amateur-night contests." Not deep below the teen's laughter were tears. His mother died, and with no home to return to, he headed to the Big Apple with 36 cents in his threadbare pocket. There, he survived on "free tomato soup"— hot water, ketchup, and Tabasco for flavoring. With a booming voice—and laughter to match—he landed a gig in a New Jersey club at $114 a week. This comic perfectionist created such a buzz that network flies dive-bombed. In 1949 his swift, non-stop elevator ride from a walk-up to the penthouse started with "The Life of Riley." After a mere year, he rocketed to his own variety show, "Cavalcade of Stars." He reigned as Mr. Saturday Night during the Golden Age of Live Television, when Orson Welles dubbed him "The Great One." He was 36 years old when CBS catapulted him to the top floor with "The Jackie Gleason Show." The deal was sealed with $11 million (a phenomenal sum of money at the time) for three years. Unbelievably inventive, he created a funny skit called "The Honeymooners," which spun off to its own series. As opposed to the middle-class niceness of "Ozzie and Harriet," it featured poor, lower-class folks struggling to make ends meet. He played the portly bus driver Ralph Kramden, a lovable loser who schemes to get rich quick. His wife, Alice, was the wise-cracking Audrey Meadows, who wore bargain basement dresses. Their devoted neighbors were Ed Norton (Art Carney), who described himself as "an engineer of subterranean station" (he worked in New York city sewers), and wife Trixie (Joyce Randolph). Gleason's comedy was instinctive, spontaneous, and smart. About "The Honeymooners," Groucho Marx said it was: "TV's only real classic." Movies include *The Hustler* (1961)—in which he played a pool shark; *Gigot* (1962)—his favorite film role where he plays a penniless Parisian deaf mute (this character most honestly represents the real-life Gleason); *Requiem for a Heavyweight* (1962); *Smokey and the Bandit* (1977); and *Nothing In Common* (1986—his last film). With his orchestra he released 64 albums. **ACHIEVEMENTS** 1960 Tony for "Take Me Along." He left the world a legacy of laughter and happiness. "The Honeymooners" went into reruns in 1958, and has never been off the air. It is always playing somewhere in the world. Ralph's catchphrase? "One of these days, Alice. Pow! Right in the Kisser!" **QUOTE** "I have a terrific ego. I always think I give a great performance or I wouldn't put on a show."...In the end, the comedian sensed the final curtain was dropping. He told family and friends at his bedside, "If God wants another joke man, I'm ready." Mr. Gleason died peacefully moments later. The year was 1987.

Nanette Fabray 6310 Hollywood

Comedienne, singer, actress
BORN Ruby Bernadette Nanette Theresa Fabares; Oct. 27, 1920, in San Diego, CA. **SPOTLIGHTS** Fabray made her vaudeville debut at age three as Baby Nan, and was a film star of *Our Gang* (1927) by age seven. By age 19, she joined the dramatic cast of *A Child is Born,* with great character actors Geraldine Fitzgerald, Gladys George, Spring Byington and Eve Arden. She did not disappoint fans when she appeared in the sophisticated MGM musical, *The Band Wagon* (1953). She co-

Nanette Fabray

starred with Barbara Eden in the comedy about female liberation in *"Harper Valley, P.T.A."* It was based on the popular country song. This energetic entertainer with a button nose has appeared in countless variety guest spots as well as her own TV series in the '60s. Live Theatre: An accomplished stage performer, she starred in "No, No, Nanette" (1996-'97). **ACHIEVEMENTS** 1949 Tony; three Emmy Awards.

Joan Bennett 6310 Hollywood

Joan Bennett

Actress
BORN Feb. 27, 1910, in Palisades, NJ. **SPOTLIGHTS** No stranger to the marquee, her ancestors were in the theatre since eighteenth-century England (they were strolling players). Trained in NY theatre, this petite beauty with soft, petulant lips and a provocative deep voice was recruited for sound. She feared working with the great silent screen lover Ronald Colman in *Bulldog Drummond* (1929)—his first talkier. Bennett commented, "I had a crush on him when I was in school, so I was scared. But he was very kind." The dewy-eyed, demure young lady joined Katharine Hepburn in the original *Little Women* (1933). After years of playing the sweet heroine, she swtiched to being a brunette and got to play a *femme fatale* in *Trade Winds* (1939). This started the second phase of her acting career. She and Edward G. Robinson excelled in the crime thriller *The Woman in the Window* (1944). She was fun in *Father of the Bride* (1950), with Spencer Tracy and Elizabeth Taylor. Died: 1990.

Al Goodman 6310 Hollywood

Pianist, composer, musicologist, band leader
BORN Alfred Goodman; Aug. 12, 1890, in Nikopol, Russia. **SPOTLIGHTS** A leading studio musician during the big band era, he was also a conductor in several radio shows, and was a skilled arranger for Broadway musicals. His most enchanting and romantic waltz was "A Wonderful Guy." Died: 1972.

Basil Rathbone 6312 Hollywood

See page 86

Heather Angel 6312 Hollywood

Actress

BORN Feb. 9, 1909, in England. **SPOTLIGHTS** A graduate of London Polytechnic of Dramatic Arts, this delicate British lady made her 1926 stage debut at the Old Vic. In Hollywood, her movies include *Charlie Chan's Greatest Case, Berkeley Square* (both 1933), *Orient Express* (1934), *The Mystery of Edwin Drood, The Informer* (both 1935), *Bulldog Drummond* (1937- '39 film serial), and *Pride and Prejudice* (1940). She delivers a moving performance as a desperate mother who drowns herself after her baby dies in Hitchcock's *Lifeboat* (1944). For Disney, she provided delightful voice-overs in *Alice in Wonderland* (1951), and *Peter Pan* (1953). Died: 1986.

Helen Mack 🎥   6312 Hollywood

Actress

BORN Helen McDougall; Nov. 13, 1913, in Rock Island, IL. **SPOTLIGHTS** Educated at New York's Professional Children's School, she was a successful child actress on the Broadway stage. She did some bit parts in silent movies, then returned to the screen as an adult. Sound motion pictures include *Melody Cruise, Son of Kong* (both 1933), *All of Me, The Lemon Drop Kid* (both 1934), *She* (1935), *The Milky Way* (1936), and *Strange Holiday* (1945). Died: 1986.

Patty McCormack 🎥   6312 Hollywood

Actress, singer

BORN Patricia McCormack; Aug. 21, 1945, in Brooklyn, NY. **SPOTLIGHTS** A beautiful baby girl with angelic blonde tresses and sparkling sapphire blue eyes, she was a professional model by age four. Three years later, she landed her first television role. Next, this natural born talent passed her Broadway audition with flying colors. She made her intense, dramatic stage debut in "Touchstone." McCormack's striking gifts earned her the plum role of the lying, manipulative eight-year-old murderess in *The Bad Seed* (1956). She was actually ten at the time of filming, an early age to receive immortality in a Hollywood classic. She was so very, very, very good at being so very very,

*As **The Bad Seed** (left), and Patty McCormack in 2000*

very bad that the Academy nominated her for an Oscar. In 1958 she appeared in the comedy *Kathy O'*, where she plays a spoiled Hollywood child star. Other movies include *Huckleberry Finn* (1960), *The Explosive Generation* (1961), *Maryjane* (1962), *Bug* (1975), and the horror spoof *Saturday the 14th* (1981). A recipient of numerous acting awards, this talented actress continues to garner credits, rave reviews and popularity in TV, film and on the stage.

King Baggot 🎥   6314 Hollywood

Actor, director, writer

BORN Nov. 7, 1879, in St. Louis, MO. **SPOTLIGHTS** This handsome, popular stage actor made his silver screen debut in *The Scarlet Letter* (1911). He appears in hundreds of profitable silents for IMP, Universal, and other studios, including the pioneer *Dr. Jekyll and Mr. Hyde* (1913--in the title role). He made his directorial debut with *Crime's Triangle* (1915), in which he also wrote the screenplay and directed himself. He also directed *The Kentucky Derby* (1922), *Tumbleweeds* (1925), and *Lovey Mary* (1926). **QUOTE** "If you were an employer in any big industry and a man came to you looking for a job, would you ask him if he had any experience in your line? If he answered 'No' you might start him in a very humble position where experience was not necessary, but if he said 'Yes' and could prove it, then you have found your man and you employ him. All industries are alike in certain respects." Died: 1948.

Les Baxter 💿   6314 Hollywood

Arranger, composer

BORN March 14, 1922, in Mexia, TX. **SPOTLIGHTS** Extremely creative with an endless flow of energy, this musical giant composed more than 250 scores. He pioneered orchestral lounge music in the 1950s, after having worked in radio as a music arranger for Bob Hope, and for Abbott and Costello. His scary music is heard in *The Pit and the Pendulum* (1961), and his cheerful sounds in the best of the "beach party" series, *Beach Blanket Bingo* (1965). Top hits: "Unchained Melody," "Lisbon Antigua," "Poor People of Paris," and "Quiet Village." Albums: *Music Out of the Moon* and *African Jazz*. Died: 1996.

George Hicks 🎙   6314 Hollywood

Announcer, war correspondent, special events announcer

SPOTLIGHTS His diction was well suited for radio's Western adventure anthology "Death Valley Days" (first heard in 1930, it ran for 15 years). Future President Reagan, another Walk of Fame honoree, hosted the TV version. Hicks became a feature reporter for NBC, then when WWII broke out, he did a daily show on men at war for the Blue Network. He became a top war correspondent when he bravely traveled to the dangerous battle fronts line to report. Often, he was the only newsman there to record historic battle moments. As the war came to a close, Hicks reported from London. On D-Day, he gave his classic 10-minute report that immortalized him.

Rowland Lee 🎥   6314 Hollywood

Director

BORN Sept. 6, 1891, in Findlay, OH. **SPOTLIGHTS** Best remembered for his visually stimulating work in the fantasy-horror genre: *Son of Frankenstein* (1939), starring Basil Rathbone, Boris Karloff, and Bela Lugosi; *Tower of London* (1939), starring Basil Rathbone, Boris Karloff, and Vincent Price; and *The Son of Monte Cristo* (1940), starring Louis Hayward and Joan Bennett. Died: 1975.

Nita Naldi 🎥   6314 Hollywood

Actress

Nita Naldi in costume as a vamp.

BORN Anita Dooley; April 1, 1899, in New York, NY. **SPOTLIGHTS** A beautiful Ziegfeld Follies seductress, her exotic passion heated up the screen. Films include *Midsummer Madness* (1920) and *The Ten Commandments* (1923), but her most famous role occurred in 1922 when Rudolph Valentino made love to this temptress in *Blood and Sand* (1922). **SIDELIGHTS** Artist Alberto Vargas captured her essence in a painting in which a Greek god admires her. Died: 1961.

Douglas Fairbanks, Jr. 🎥 6318 Hollywood

Actor, executive producer

BORN Douglas Elton Fairbanks, Jr., Dec. 9, 1909, in New York, NY. **SPOTLIGHTS** The gorgeous Fairbanks family looks were apparent from his earliest days. He was a sweet bundle of photogenic joy at his christening at Trinity Church, in Lower Manhattan, with age enhancing the growing lad. The privileged, well-mannered youngster grew up to be a handsome, *bon vivant* during Hollywood's Golden Era. Educated at the Knickerbocker Greys in New York City, Polytechnic School in Pasadena, and Harvard Military School in

Douglas Fairbanks, Jr. (left), with his equally famous father, Douglas Fairbanks

Los Angeles, by age 12, he had memorized Shakespeare's *Richard III.* The following year, movie mogul Jesse. L. Lasky signed him to a $1,000-a-week contract. He made his silver screen debut at age 13 for Paramount Pictures in *Stephen Steps Out* (1923). The star of 80 motion pictures, he gave superb performances in *Little Caesar* (1931), *Catherine the Great* (1934), *Accused* (1936), *Having Wonderful Time* (1938), *The Rage of Paris* (1938), *Gunga Din* (1939), and *The Corsican Brothers* (1941). Critics universally agree he gave the performance of his life in *The Prisoner of Zenda* (1937). Fairbanks is absolutely dashing in this classic role, and it was one of the best pictures made that year. The following year, he stars in *The Young in Heart*, a funny and entertaining comedy that made the top ten best pictures list that year. He followed in his famous father's footsteps—as a dashing swashbuckler in *Sinbad the Sailor* (1947), and as a ladies' man both on and off-screen—with such glamour queens as Marlene Dietrich and Rita Hayworth. He did work in TV, his father had not explored, bringing class with programming in "Douglas Fairbanks Presents." Filmed in England during 1952-'57, it was a first rate show. An accomplished stage and radio performer, Fairbanks, Jr. also served on the Board of The Royal Shakespeare Company and The Pilgrims Society. **ACHIEVEMENTS** During WWII, he served as a Lieutenant in the U.S. Naval Reserve. This brave soul earned a British D.S.C. as the only U.S. Naval officer to command a flotilla of raiding craft for supreme allied commander, British Admiral Mountbatten's Commandos. He received the Distinguished Service Cross from England. In America, his military awards include the Silver Star Medal and the Legion of Merit with a "V" for valor. He is also recipient of the French and Italian governments highest honors for gallantry in action. He was made a Knight of the British Empire in 1949 by King George VI for "furthering Anglo-American Amity." His charity involvements include CARE, United Nations work, and a number of institutions of higher learning...He was married to Joan Crawford (1929-'33), first of two. His second wife is the former Vera Shelton. A tall, thin dark-haired beauty, she was formerly a fashion industry executive and worked for the QVC. **HIGHLIGHTS** He selected his autobiography's title, *Salad Days,* from Shakespeare's *Antony and Cleopatra*: "My salad days, When I was green in judgment." **QUOTE** "I was born with too many vitamins and more energy than I have a right to have. I believe in many things, but am quite prepared to be disillusioned and go on optimistically hoping. That is part of the American breed, the belief in the happy ending, it is a national rather than a personal trait." **WALK OF FAME QUOTE** "I am here today, and hope to be here tomorrow."

Margaret Lindsay 🎥   6318 Hollywood

Actress
BORN Margaret Kies; Sept. 19, 1910, in Dubuque, IA. **SPOTLIGHTS** Mystery fans recall the pleasant brunette in a number of the Ellery Queen detective series, including *Ellery Queen, Master Detective* (1940), *Ellery Queen and the Murder Ring* (1941), *Ellery Queen's Penthouse Mystery* (1941), *Ellery Queen and the Perfect Crime* (1941). Died: 1981.

Mae Murray 🎥   6318 Hollywood

Mae Murray

Actress, dancer
BORN Marie Koenig; May 10, 1889, in Portsmouth, VA. **SPOTLIGHTS** She made her Broadway debut in "About Town" in 1906. Then, this charming show girl dazzled theatergoers, including President Theodore (Teddy) Roosevelt, on opening night of the lavish Ziegfeld Follies of 1908. Tremendously graceful and possessing serenity, Murray was made famous by the Follies. Love struck admirers threw diamond bracelets to her onstage. When she arrived via train in Los Angeles to start her movie career, her delicate wrists were weighed down by the gems. After appearing as a featured dancer in *Watch Your Step* (1914), she returned to the East Coast. Adolph Zukor saw her in the Follies of 1915 and offered her a movie contract. He stars her in *Dream Girl* (1916). Silents include *Modern Love, Body in Bond, & The Delicious Little Devil* (all 1918), *The Masked Bride* and *The Merry Widow* (both 1925). With her beautiful mouth highlighted by the lipstick style of the era, she was nicknamed "The Girl with the Bee-Stung Lips," and was also known as America's "Number One Glamour Girl." She worked with the top leading men, including John Gilbert and Francis X. Bushman. She earned the then-staggering amount of $3 million dollars making films. **QUOTE** "I have often been asked is dancing essential to a motion picture aspirant? The correct answer, it seems to me, is very simple. If one has com-

plete and graceful control of his or her body, it follows that he or she has also a complete and graceful control of his or her mind. Certainly I would advise everyone to acquire a knowledge of dancing. It may be said that the success of many of our stars has come from just that poise, self-control and natural grace which are a part of the art of dancing and a knowledge of that free movement and lack of self-consciousness, which is dancing's ultimate expression." Died: 1965.

August Lumière 🎥   6318 Hollywood

Inventor, producer, director
BORN Oct. 19, 1862, in France. **SPOTLIGHTS** See the bio of "Louis Lumière" in this book. This star is misspelled; his first name was "Auguste." Died: 1954.

Tab Hunter 🔘   6320 Hollywood

Tab Hunter

Singer, actor
BORN Arthur Kelm (or Gelien); July 11, 1931, in New York, NY. **SPOTLIGHTS** A 1950s teen idol, his big recording hits include "Young Love" and "There's No Fool Like A Young Fool." He delivers a fine performance in the WWII action picture *Battle Cry* (1955), then co-stars with Natalie Wood in the boy-coming-to-age comedy *The Girl He Left Behind* (1956). As a new Army recruit, he receives support from the likable actor James Garner. He did not fare so well in the military film, *Lafayette Escadrille* (1958), a confused WWI drama. However, that same year, Hunter is wonderful as the lead in a terrific musical, *Damn Yankees*. It includes the sizzling tune "What Lola Wants." Hunter made 24 films while recording and making TV appearances, but *The Fickle Finger of Fate* (1967) aptly describes the fall of his star from the screen. No problem, he changed to theatrical stage work. **QUOTE** Because he was a teen idol, he landed movie roles quickly. About his work in *Island of Desire* (1952), opposite Linda Darnell, he stated: "I was so bad, I still hate thinking about it...if I had it to do all over again, I think I'd work my way up slowly from the bottom instead of starting big and scrambling to stay with it."

Johnny Cash 🔘   6320 Hollywood

Singer, songwriter, actor
BORN John Ray Cash; Feb. 26, 1932, in Kingsland, AR. **SPOTLIGHTS** A legendary singer, he is nicknamed the "Man in Black." Born to desperately poor cotton farmers during the Great Depression, his family managed to improve their lot in

Johnny Cash

life through the federal government's resettlement program and hard work. As a youngster he loved listening to music on their battery-operated radio--they were without electricity until 1946). His father encouraged the whole family to listen carefully to the wonderful variety of music on the radio. Both sides of Cash's family were musical—his mother's father was a singing instructor—and they all enjoyed singing. Cash grew into a gutsy baritone with rockabilly sound and raw power. His first regional success was "Cry, Cry, Cry" in 1955. Soon thereafter, he had his first enduring hit, another Cash original, "I Walk the Line." With this song, it was evident that the singer had put his emphasis on lyric content. His trademark deep, brooding growl possesses a bluesy edge, and accompanied by his simple, rhythmic acoustic guitar, the song crossed over to the pop market. It gave the artist broad appeal and made him immediately recognizable. It sold more than a million copies in 1956. Cash became a regular member of the Grand Ole Opry that same year. His two other signature songs are "Folsom Prison Blues," and "Man in Black." Successful in both country and pop, his collection of hits includes "Ring of Fire," "Get Rhythm," "There You Go," "So Doggone Lonesome," "Don't Take Your Guns to Town," "I Heard That Lonesome Whistle," "Train of Love," "A Boy Named Sue," "A Thing Called Love," and "One Piece at a Time." Many of his tunes share a theme—the work of the common man. **TV** "The Johnny Cash Show" (1969-'71, ABC) showcased diverse musical talents from Louis Armstrong to Bob Dylan. He has appeared in a number of TV specials including "Johnny Cash, Cowboy Heroes." Films include *A Gunfight* (1970), starring Kirk Douglas. **RELATED READING** *Little Labels—Big Sound*, by Rick Kennedy and Randy McNutt, trace the early recording days at Sun Records, in Memphis, of Johnny Cash, Elvis Presley, and Jerry Lee Lewis. Published by Indiana University Press, call 1-800-842-6796 (from inside the U.S.). **ACHIEVEMENTS** The recipient of virtually every important music award, he won seven Grammys. He was inducted into the Nashville Songwriter's Hall of Fame with 400 songs to his credit, and inducted into the Country Music Hall of Fame, as well as the Rock and Roll Hall of Fame. 1996 received the Kennedy Center Honor for lifetime contribution to our nation's culture. Married to the celebrated singer June Carter Cash, with whom he received the Grammy Award for their duet of "Jackson" in 1967. His daughter is the gifted singer Rosanne Cash. **QUOTE** "I got this idea of singin' for a livin' because I was starvin' to death."

Humphrey Bogart ✪ 6320 Hollywood

Actor
BORN On Christmas Day, Dec. 25, 1899, in New York, NY. **SPOTLIGHTS** A legendary superstar talent from Hollywood's Golden Era, and one of the all-time most important movie stars, he grew up in a wealthy, privileged, but not affectionate household. His father was a prominent Manhattan surgeon, his mother, Maud Humphrey, a celebrated illustrator who had studied art in Paris taught by the exquisite

Humphrey Bogart

American painter and etcher, James Whistler. She had drawn sketches of Bogart as a child for children's books, and advertisements in *The Dilineator* magazine. After Bogart failed to achieve the high grades needed to attend Yale University, and caused enough problems to get expelled from the Phillips Academy in Andover, Massachusetts, he enlisted in the Navy. World War I was raging. He was assigned as the helmsman on a troop transport ship. An injury from a shelling resulted in his partially paralyzed upper lip and his characteristic lisp. After the war ended, he received an honorable discharge. Bogart, extremely disciplined with a strong work ethic, started his professional career in 1920. He initially had two lines in a stage play as well as managing the theatrical company. Then, like an automatic pistol, he performed in a dizzying number of roles, one right after the other. He usually played the delinquent, and in private life he always ignored his bad reviews. Bogart made his screen debut in *Broadway's Like That* (1930—a film short), then landed a studio contract with Fox, who loaned him out to Universal. Who nicknamed him Bogie? Actor Spencer Tracy did during the filming of John Ford's *Up the River* (1930)--in the only picture the two friends ever made together. He appeared in several stinkers, then went back to Broadway stating, "I wasn't Gable and I flopped." In 1935 he was cast as Duke Mantee, a psychopathic gangster in Robert Sherwood's production of "The Petrified Forest," starring Leslie Howard. He received outstanding reviews for every aspect of his portrayal of a convict. Warner Bros. bought the rights, and wanted to use Edward G. Robinson— the big name who they had under contract—*not* Bogart reprising his role. Howard insisted that Warner's hire Bogart. In fact, he refused to do the movie without him. Bogie did make *The Petrified Forest* (1936), and was superb in it, though it did not make him a star. He got top billing in *Dead End* (1937), the first in the notable B film series, and soon followed up with *Swing Your Lady* (1938), to which he declared, "was the worst film I ever did." By now, he had made dozens of pictures as a villain. Later, in an interview with George Frazier, he stated, "I was shot in twelve, electrocuted or hanged in eight, and was a jailbird in nine. I played more scenes writhing around on the floor than I did standing up." It would take 11 years from his first film for his breakthrough in *High Sierra* (1941), in a role of an aging gangster. George Raft, James Cagney and Edward G. Robinson had all first rejected the role that Bogie had to go after with determination. He had to fight to get the part, and was brilliant in the crime classic. He also went after the detective role in *The Maltese Falcon* (1941), after George Raft had rejected it. Bogie was immortalized as Sam Spade, private eye. About the role, he said, "I had a lot going for me in that one. First, there was Huston. He made the Dashiell Hammett novel into something you don't come across too often. It was practically a masterpiece. I don't have many things I'm proud of...but that's one." In regard to the classic *Casablanca* (1942), future President Ronald Reagan, and beauty Ann Sheridan were the original choices for the leads, but they were not interested. The movie, slated somewhere between an A and B picture, did not even have an acceptable finished script. Director Michael Curtiz wanted tough guy George Raft to play opposite Ingrid Bergman. Raft refused the role, declaring, "Who ever heard of Casablanca? Besides I'm not starring opposite some unknown Swedish broad." (Later Raft admitted it was the single biggest mistake of his life.) Bogart was the *seventh* choice for the part of Rick! At the end of the film when Bogart delivers the now-famous line to Claude Rains, "...the beginning of a beautiful friendship," the director knew he had a perfect and magical movie. It earned Bogie an Oscar nomination and won a Best Picture Oscar. Bogie became America's existential hero, a sex symbol, and king of the Warner's lot...finally, after 45 motion pictures! Movies include *King of the Underworld* (1939), *Dead Reckoning* (1947), *Dark Passage* (1947—opposite wife Lauren Bacall), *Sirocco* (1951), *Deadline U.S.A.* (1952), and *Beat the Devil* (1954). A man of solid integrity, a soul that could not be bought, was captured by the camera. He remains one of the world's all-time most fascinating stars. Masterpieces include *Angels with Dirty Faces* (1938), *To Have and Have Not* (1944—where he met and fell in love with his future wife, Lauren Bacall), *The Big Sleep* (1946—opposite Bacall), *The Treasure of the Sierra Madre* (1948), *Key Largo* (1948—opposite Bacall), *In a Lonely Place* (1950), *The Enforcer* (1951), *The Caine Mutiny* (1954—in an Oscar-nominated performance), *Sabrina* (1954—in an unusual role), and *The Barefoot Contessa* (1954). Four times Oscar-nominated, Bogie stated that any competition between actors "is meaningless unless they play the same part." An island of unimpeachable integrity, his off-screen personality was not much different than on-screen. He declared, "The only reason to make a million dollars in this business is to tell some fat producer to go to hell." **ACHIEVEMENTS** 1951 Best Actor Oscar for *The African Queen*. After winning, Bogie commented, "The way to survive an Oscar is never to try to win another one. You've seen what happened to some Oscar winners. They spend the rest of their lives turning down scripts while searching for the great role to win another one. Hell, I hope I'm never nominated again. It's meat-and-potatoes roles for me from now on." **HIGHLIGHTS** Married to Lauren Bacall (fourth wife) from 1945 until his death. A marriage made in heaven, they had two children: a

son Stephen, and daughter, Leslie. **QUOTE** In a 1954 *Time* magazine portrait, Bogart stated, "There's an awful lot of bunk written about acting. But it isn't easy. You can't just make faces." This legendary talent died in 1957.

William Frawley 🎥   6320 Hollywood

William Frawley

Actor
BORN Feb. 26, 1887, in Burlington, IA. **SPOTLIGHTS** This bald, cigar-chewing gent specialized in playing tough-on-the-outside, soft-on-the-inside characters. The cauliflower-faced Frawley had a long entertainment history in show business doing comedy on the vaudeville circuit, then moved to the silent screen. An experienced and reliable talent, this gruff, irascible character actor went on to make 125 films. His movie career spanned six decades, including *Cupid Beats Father* (1915), *Lord Loveland Discovers America* (1916), *The Lemon Drop Kid* (1934), *Huckleberry Finn* (1939), *Ziegfeld Follies* (1946), *Miracle on 34th Street* (1947), *Mother Wore Tights* (1947), *The Babe Ruth Story* (1948), and *Rhubarb* (1951). **ACHIEVEMENTS** He was immortalized in TV's "I Love Lucy" as the cranky neighbor, best friend and landlord Fred Mertz. **SIDELIGHTS** Later, he played father-in-law, Michael Francis "Bub" O'Casey (a lovable old coot), in TV's family sit-com "My Three Sons" (1960-'64). Died: 1966.

Nina Foch 🎥   6324 Hollywood

Nina Foch

Actor, director, professor
BORN Nina Consuelo Maude Fock; April 20, 1924, in Leydon, Holland. **SPOTLIGHTS** An accomplished actress of stage, screen and television, Foch carries an aristocratic, cool air about her and speaks in a crisp, exacting tone. Somehow she also manages to appear fragile and doll-like and glamorous. The blonde daughter of Dutch composer-conductor Dirk Fock, and the gorgeous American show girl/actress Consuelo Flowerton, she was raised in a privileged atmosphere in Manhattan. Her early days included performances as a pianist; she also dabbled in oil painting. Foch switched gears, training at the American Academy of Dramatic Arts, then working in small theater and stock. In

1943 she landed a contract with Columbia Studios appearing on the silver screen in the horror film, *The Return of the Vampire* (1943). Other motion pictures include the gothic noir *My Name is Julia Ross* (1945), *Johnny O'Clock* (1947), the thrilling psychological drama, *The Dark Past* (1949), opposite William Holden, MGM's Academy Award-winning musical, *An American in Paris* (1951), opposite Gene Kelly, *Executive Suite* (1953), *The Ten Commandments* (1956), *Spartacus* (1960), *Till There Was You* (1997), *Hush* (1998) and *Shadow of Doubt* (1998), to name a few in her long list of impressive credits. This worldly talent graced the Broadway stage in several of Shakespeare's works, including "Taming of the Shrew" (as Kate), for which she received rave reviews. Her TV specials and movies are too numerous to mention. **HIGHLIGHTS** She worked on *The Diary of Anne Frank* (1959), not as an actress, but as the superior acting coach on hand. She explained her duties as, "trying to give actors enough of a concept of the part so they will be able to be directed. I'm trying this kind of position out for size." The size suited her fine—Foch became one of the premier acting instructors in Los Angeles (310.553.5805). **HIGHLIGHTS** From 1974-77, she held the post of senior faculty of the American Film Institute Center for Advanced Film Studies. Since 1987 she has been Adjunct Professor at USC's Graduate Film School teaching directing. **QUOTES** "I prepare films with directors, that what I do for a living. I'm the secret ingredient to a lot of filmmakers. Usually we sit in my house working on every single beat of the script. I ask all sorts of questions about scenes: about how they're going to shoot the scenes, about the kind of music they want, and even during the rewrite I discuss how they're going to talk to writers. That's what I do. It's very rewarding." And, "When friends or colleagues tell me they saw my star on the Hollywood Walk of Fame, it's fun to ask, 'Which one?'"

William Farnum 🎥   6324 Hollywood

William Farnum

Actor
BORN July 4, 1876, in Boston, MA. **SPOTLIGHTS** He worked the vaudeville circuit with his brother, Dustin, then soared to stardom in his first movie, *The Spoilers* (1914). Films include *Samson* (1915), *Les Miserables*— as Jean Valjean (1917), *A Tale of Two Cities* (1917), and *Riders of the Purple Sage* (1918). After sustaining a serious injury during the filming of *A Man Who Fights Alone* (1925), he turned to character roles: *Kit Carson* (1940).
QUOTE "It has been my experience that there is no easy road to permanent fame on the screen. Some fortunate persons, born with great talent and distinctive personalities, have achieved early recognition and a measure of fame in moving

pictures. In some cases the fame has been lasting; in others they have flashed meteor-like across the sky and then descended quickly into oblivion. Any number of reasons could be given to account for the permanence of one artist and the decline of another. Some would be right, of course, some would be wrong. But I think there is one reason which we can all agree, and that is that, in the one case the person has merited the favor of the public, and in the other, that he has failed to strike the chord of popular response. The actor has only one mission: it is for him to accurately visualize the part he is to portray. The degree of truthfulness of the portrayal is the degree of his success as an actor." Died: 1953.

Sherry Jackson 📺   6324 Hollywood

Actress
BORN Feb. 15, 1942, in Wendell, Idaho. **SPOTLIGHTS** Discovered by a (legitimate!) agent at a restaurant on the Sunset Strip in Hollywood, he thought her cherubic looks and dark-haired pigtails were perfectly suited for pictures. This little lass was signed to a movie contract at age five. (Prior to that she had been a child model.) After taking drama, singing and dancing lessons she made her screen debut with a small role in *You're My Everything* (1949). Movies include *The Breaking Point* (1950), *Where Danger Lives* (1950), *The Great Caruso* (1950), *When I Grow Up* (1951), and *Come Next Spring* (1955). TV: She played Terry Williams on "The Danny Thomas Show" (1953-'58; also known as "Make Room for Daddy"). **ACHIEVEMENTS** 1952 Parents Gold Medal Award as Best Child Star, and the Box Office Blue Ribbon Award for her role in *The Miracle of Our Lady of Fatima*.

Ernest Borgnine 🎥   6324 Hollywood

Ernest Borgnine

Actor
BORN Ermes Effron Borgnino; Jan. 24, 1917, in Hamden, CT. **SPOTLIGHTS** Borgnine, who was raised in Milan, Italy, returned to the United States in 1924. At age 18, he enlisted in the Navy and served honorably for ten years; he saw combat duty during World War II. After the war, he was discharged and used the GI bill to study acting at the Randall School of Dramatic Art. He joined Virginia's Barter Theater in 1946, and performed with the company for four years. Borgnine made his Broadway debut in "Harvey" in 1950, then toured the country in "Hamlet." He made his screen debut in *China Corsair* (1951), then followed up that same year with other small roles in *The Whistle at Eaton Falls* and *The Mob*. He was becoming known for his work as the heavy-set, scowling,

brutal villain, but was still not under contract, and was basically starving like countless other actors. After Borgnine read the book, *From Here to Eternity*, he said to himself, "Oh, man, I know I will play the part of Fatso Judson. Why? I have no idea. But I said, 'I know there is a God above and I am going to play that part.'" Meanwhile, Borgnine worked with the superb actress, Helen Hayes, in television's "Mrs. McThing" (1952) out of New York, then again searched for work. Nearly two years after reading the *Eternity* book, Borgnine was preparing to go to the local post office and apply for a job when he got a call from Hollywood. Back to the silver screen, he played the cruel Sergeant "Fatso" Judson in the all-star production of *From Here to Eternity* (1953). It was his breakthrough film. Other movies include *Johnny Guitar* (1954), *Vera Cruz* (1954), *Bad Day at Black Rock* (1954), *Violent Saturday* (1955), *Jubal* (1956), *The Catered Affair* (1956, also by Paddy Chayefsky, creator of *Marty*—see below), *The Best Things in Life Are Free* (1956), *Three Brave Men* (1957), *The Badlanders* (1958), *The Vikings* (1958), *The Rabbit Trap* (1959), and *Pay or Die* (1960). A versatile actor, Borgnine did not always play the bad guy, he has also been the victim, the average working man, and the hero. Borgnine was superb in the WWII action adventure, *The Dirty Dozen* (1967). His performance as an over-the-hill, Texan bandit who crosses over into 1913 Mexico in the bloody *The Wild Bunch* (1969) is truly inspired. His facial expressions light up key scenes—he is that good in it. Later films include *The Poseidon Adventure* (1972), *Escape From New York* (1981), and *All Dogs Go to Heaven* (1996—voiceover). Borgnine also appeared in the lead role in the wacky television situation comedy, "McHale's Navy" (1962-'66), stars in the feature *McHale's Navy* (1964), and appears in the 1997 remake. His beautiful wife, Tova Borgnine, is CEO of Tova Corp. **ACHIEVEMENTS** 1955 Best Actor Oscar for *Marty*. He plays a gentle, lonely Italian-American butcher. (Paddy Chayefsky's *Marty* was the FIRST *TV* drama adapted to the silver screen.) The picture took only 18 days to shoot. Borgnine earned $5,000 for the part. Years later, and still closely identified with the part, he chose to distance himself by stating, "I'm no playboy, but I'm not a dumb slob either. Marty was just a role."

Henry Morgan   6328 Hollywood

Comedian, writer, host, actor
BORN Henry Lerner Van Ost; March 31, 1915, in Detroit, MI. Or, as Morgan put it, "I was born at an early age—of mixed parentage—man and woman, on the day before April Fool's Day, 1915, in New York City." **SPOTLIGHTS** This very funny, gutsy man's own radio program "The Henry Morgan Show" (1940-'50) opened with the theme song, "For He's A Jolly Good Fellow." King of the sharp-tongued heckles, Morgan held no subject sacred, especially sponsor patronage. He was one of the first to do "kidding radio commercials" winning the public's admiration. Totally irreverent, his delivery was a refreshingly brash style. And when radio network and advertising executives pulled him aside off the air, and tried to

Henry Morgan

intimidate him into behaving, Morgan's audience heard all the gruesome details the next show. He *named* names. Audiences, of course, hated commercial interruptions so they loved his badgering, while manufacturers often threatened to sue. It proved difficult to pursue legal action, because the sales of their products skyrocketed after Morgan's ridicule. Morgan told listeners that Life Savers candy was a fraud, as the hole in the middle cheated consumers. When describing Life Savers six delicious flavors, he announced: "...cement, asphalt, and asbestos." Life Savers canceled their advertisements. One reviewer for *Liberty* magazine wrote a profile of his listeners: "an astonishing collection ranging from professional humorists, and show people to clergymen, children, taxi drivers, and an admiring clique in an insane asylum." His comedy show also entertained the vast audience with an eclectic mix of records—some odd novelty, and others pushing the edge of the envelope. An example would be the ghoulish tune about King Henry VIII's second wife, Anne Boleyn, "with 'er 'ead tucked underneath 'er arm..." Morgan himself used a variety of dialects to humorous effect. Even his weather reports were funny: "High winds, followed by high skirts, followed by men." He closed his show with: "Morgan'll be on this same corner in front of the cigar stand next week at this same time." **QUOTE** TV was not the best medium for his special talent. He woefully observed, "Malice is missing from television, you have to be lovable." Died: 1994.

Marion Davies   6328 Hollywood

Marion Davies

Actress, singer
BORN Marion Douras; Jan. 3, 1897, in Brooklyn, NY. **SPOTLIGHTS** After being educated in a convent school, Davies studied ballet, tap and acting. This pretty, saucy blonde made her Broadway debut at age 16 in a chorus line. While performing in the Ziegfeld "Follies" in 1916 and 1917, she met her future lifelong companion and patron, William Randolph Hearst, a publishing tycoon of a vast newspaper empire. Madly in love with the young actress, Hearst was resolute on making her a movie star. He managed and controlled her career. He envisioned her in virginal, inno-

cent and dramatic roles; but Davies, a natural born mimic was best in fun-loving comedies, which he rarely let her do. MGM paid her $10,000 a week, but she was wealthy by affiliation, hardly needing the paycheck. When sound arrived, Davies faced another problem, she stuttered. Due to her speech impediment, she was bypassed for many good roles. Motion pictures include *Little Old New York* (1923), *Tillie the Toiler* (1926), *The Cardboard Lover* (1928), *The Patsy* (1928), *Show People* (1928), *Marianne* (1929—her first talkie), *Going Hollywood* and *Operation Thirteen* (both 1934). She later moved to Warner Bros. where she made *Hearts Divided* (1936), and *Ever Since Eve* (1937—her last picture). Davies co-stars with Robert Montgomery, Billie Dove, Jimmy Durante and Zasu Pitts in *Blondie of the Follies* (1932), a cheerful little comedy with a capable cast. She is also delightful in the charming comedy, *Peg o' My Heart* (1933), opposite Onslow Stevens. Movie friends called her by her pet name, Daisy (from the character she played in *The Floradora Girl*). She called W.R. Hearst "Pappy." By a Hearst company edict, Davies' name appeared daily in 22 newspapers (all owned by Hearst). **HIGHLIGHTS** She created the stand-in system when she hired a real-life woman named Vera Bennett to stand in so she could relax between takes, as well as for lighting purposes. Previously, stand-ins were wooden dummies. Died: 1961.

Wendell Corey 📺   6328 Hollywood

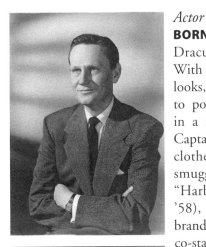
Wendell Corey

Actor
BORN March 20, 1914, in Dracut, MA. **SPOTLIGHTS** With his square, solemn-faced looks, Corey was perfectly suited to portray serious professionals in a number of TV series. As Captain Ralph Baxter, the plain-clothes officer battling drug smugglers and murderers on "Harbor Command" (1957-'58), he brought his special brand of cynicism to the role. He co-starred with Nanette Fabray in "Westinghouse Playhouse," then played psychiatrist Dr. Theodore Bassett on "The Eleventh Hour" (1962-'63). Formerly, this dark-haired, brooding talent was a Broadway star of "Dream Girl" in 1945. He made his silver screen debut in *Desert Fury* (1947). Corey appears in nearly 40 motion pictures, including *Sorry, Wrong Number* (1948), *The Furies* (1950), *Rear Window* (1954), *The Rack* (1956—this movie was adapted from Rod Serling's brilliant TV play), and *The Rainmaker* (1956). **HIGHLIGHTS** Politically inclined, he served as director of the Screen Actors Guild, and as president of the Academy of Motion Picture Arts and Sciences. Corey was elected to the Santa Monica city council in 1965. Died: 1968.

Jayne Mansfield 🎥 6328 Hollywood

Jayne Mansfield

Actress
BORN Vera J. Palmer; April 19, 1933, in Bryn Mawr, PA. **SPOTLIGHTS** Like bosomy, blonde Marilyn Monroe, sex symbol Mansfield married at 16, had the keen sense of a publicity hound, and was picked up by 20th Century-Fox. She was kind-hearted and very much like the little girl whose voice she used. Yet she was more athletic and animated than the breathy Marilyn Monroe. She was wonderful in the rock 'n' roll comedy, *The Girl Can't Help It* (1956) with Tom Ewell, Fats Domino, Little Richard and The Platters. She was hilarious in *Will Success Spoil Rock Hunter?* (1957), in a role she had originally done on Broadway in 1955. She appears in the movie adaptation of John Steinbeck's novel, *The Wayward Bus* (1957) opposite Joan Collins, and *Kiss Them for Me* (1957) opposite Cary Grant. **QUOTES** "I do bathe in pink champagne. I do it. I definitely do it. I've got a champagne man. It takes bottles and bottles. I do it all the time about twice a week because I think it's terribly exciting. I do all sorts of weird things. I sun bathe in the nude outside. I just feel I have to. I don't know why." And: "All my life I wanted to be a Hollywood movie star." Determined to get to the top,

Jayne Mansfield in **Promises! Promises!** *(1963)*

Mansfield called her press agent every morning asking, "What kind of pictures are we going to take of me today?" Tinseltown publicists agreed that Jayne Mansfield herself orchestrated the best self-promotion, and achieved the premiere buildup job ever done on any star during her lifetime. Once she was famous, she admitted, "Whenever I get depressed, I read my clippings." Died: 1967, in a freak car accident, where it was falsely rumored that she had been decapitated. It made gruesome and ghoulish reading, but it was *not* true. Her (bloodied) wig flew off her head and led to inaccurate reports.

Henry Rowland 6328 Hollywood

Actor
BORN 1913, in Omaha, NE. **SPOTLIGHTS** Live dramas include "Johnny Guitar," among others. Died: 1984.

Al Pearce 6330 Hollywood

Actor, comedian
BORN 1899, in New York, NY. **SPOTLIGHTS** He was the comedy star of "Al Pearce and His Gang" (1928-'47). Hilarious characters on the show included the Human Chatterbox (Arlene Harris, clocked at 240 words a minute), the Laughing Lady, Tizzie Lish (a female impersonator), Yahbut, Lord Bilegwater, Ed and Zeb (two geezers), and Yogi Yorgeson (a Swede who sang "Yingle Bells" and "I Yust Go Nuts at Christmas," among many other popular songs). Pierce's most famous character was as Elmer Blurt, the shy door-to-door salesman. His distinctive knock on a door was "bump-bump-abump-bump...bump-bump." His catchphrase was: "Nobody home, I-hope, I-hope, I-hope." Died: 1961.

Gene Austin 6332 Hollywood

Actor, singer, composer
BORN June 24, 1900, in Gainesville, TX. **SPOTLIGHTS** "The Whispering Tenor" was a frequent guest on the "Sing It Again" CBS music quiz radio show (1948-'51), and vocalist on "The Joe Penner Show." In the latter, Ozzie Nelson was the orchestra leader-vocalist and Harriet Hilliard was the regular vocalist. Films include *My Little Chickadee* (1940). Died: 1972.

Lillian Roth and Skeets Gallagher

Lillian Roth 6332 Hollywood

Singer, actress
BORN Lillian Rutstein; Dec. 13, 1910, in New York City. **SPOTLIGHTS** A vivacious, singing sensation on Broadway, in radio and films, she got her first job posing "as a living statue" for the Educational Pictures' trademark. Movies include

Animal Crackers (1930), with the Marx Brothers and Margaret Dumont, and *Paramount on Parade* (1930). The legendary gal sizzled with the number that helped win so many fans "Sing, You Sinners." Other favorite songs: "When the Red, Red, Robin Comes Bob, Bob, Bobbin' Along," and "I'd Climb the Highest Mountain." When her best-selling autobiography *I'll Cry Tomorrow* (1955) was adapted as a film, she chose Susan Hayward for the lead. Hayward used her own singing voice; her portrayal inspired Roth to state, "It was almost like looking in a mirror." Died: 1980.

Dorothy Lamour 6332 Hollywood

Dorothy Lamour

Actress, singer
BORN Mary D. Kaumeyer; Dec. 10, 1914, in New Orleans, LA. **SPOTLIGHTS** The sultry, dark-haired beauty was crowned *Miss New Orleans* at age 17. Next, she joined the competition for the Miss Universe contest. Inspired by the legendary beauties Max Factor created for the screen, Lamour applied some of his fabulous soft, subtle red lipstick. Instead of being kissable, she was disqualified for breaking a contest rule by wearing lipstick! She seriously pursued her career from this point on. Radio experience with band leader Herbie Kay (husband, 1935-'39) landed her own NBC show. In 1936, Paramount signed her as *The Jungle Princess*. She gained notoriety for wearing exotic silk sarongs, but gained fame as the love interest in the "road" pictures, co-starring Bing Crosby and Bob Hope. Out of the seven "road" films—where she always played the straight-faced foil to the boys—these were her favorites: *The Road to Morocco* (1942), *The Road to Utopia* (1945), and *The Road to Rio* (1947). She admitted that it was useless to memorize the scripts word-for-word, because both Bob and Bing loved to ad-lib. This always confused her as to her cue to deliver a line. But, she said, "I was the happiest and highest paid straight woman."...She was a WWII favorite pinup model. **QUOTE** "Sometimes show business can be very cruel. It suddenly got difficult for me to reach certain Hollywood people by phone. These were the same people I had done so many favors when I was box office magic." Died: 1996.

Kim Novak 6336 Hollywood

Actress
BORN Marilyn Pauline Novak; Feb. 13, 1933, in Chicago, IL. **SPOTLIGHTS** The reluctant blonde goddess, who at a height of 5' 7", 125 pounds, and measurements of 37-23-37, made strong men weak. Her breakthrough role in *Phffft!* (1954)

Kim Novak

Darryl Zanuck

insisting that Al Jolson's lines be left in the first sound picture (Jack Warner only wanted the song "Dirty Hands, Dirty Feet" in it). He ordered Darryl to cut the scene with "the talking tricks." Darryl fought back in lengthy discussions. Harry Warner worried people might "laugh when they hear that guy talking. We'll be ruined!" Zanuck thought otherwise, realizing the era of silents was over. The night of the premiere proved him right. Audiences shouted their approval when they heard Jolson cry, "Mammy!" One phenomenal success followed another like *The Public Enemy* (1931), starring his discovery James Cagney. He was a true trailblazer who did not take kindly to fools. Zanuck was known to tell brown-nosing underlings, "For God's sake, don't say 'yes' until I'm finished talking!" In 1933, he co-founded 20th Century Pictures (a year later it merged with Fox to become 20th Century-Fox), where he dominated production. His tiny darling of the screen— Shirley Temple—helped bankroll the studio. *Stand Up and Cheer* (1934) proved a worldwide box office smash, causing Zanuck to gush, " she's the world's eighth wonder." Among Zanuck's many classics: John Steinbeck's *The Grapes of Wrath* (1940)...His son, Richard D. Zanuck, is a successful producer. **QUOTE** Early on, Zanuck commented, "Television doesn't mean a damn thing. It's just a passing fad." Well, you can't be right about everything. The great producer died in 1979.

made Novak virtually recognizable everywhere. Immediately, studio chief Harry Cohn ordered the director to make *Five Against the House* (1955) "a Kim Novak picture." In *Man with the Golden Arm* (1955) starring Frank Sinatra, she turned in a compelling piece of dramatic work. The difficult subject matter of heroin addiction and withdrawal was handled exquisitely by Sinatra. Novak is must-see in *Picnic* (1956) with William Holden (watch for the dance scene). She co-stars with Sinatra again in George Sidney's musical, *Pal Joey* (1957) Bewitchingly beautiful in Columbia's *Bell, Book and Candle* (1958), co-starring James Stewart and Jack Lemmon. She is exceptional in Alfred Hitchcock's *Vertigo* (1958), co-starring James Stewart. This movie is generally considered Hitchcock's masterpiece. About Novak, cameraman James Wong Howe said, "What makes her interesting is the combination of her classical beauty with a sensual lush quality." *Middle of the Night* (1959) was one of the entries at the Cannes Film Festival, with a moving dramatic script written by Paddy Chayevsky (based on his teleplay), and directed by Delbert Mann. She was delightful in the sex comedy *Boys' Night Out* (1962) with James Garner, Tony Randall and Howard Duff. Other films include *Kiss Me, Stupid* (1964), and *The Amorous Adventures of Moll Flanders* (1965). Her strong comeback in *The Mirror Crack'd* (1980), opposite Elizabeth Taylor, portended future projects, but Novak prefers the solitude of country life, spending much of her time riding horses, tending ranch animals, and painting.

Darryl Zanuck 🎥   6336 Hollywood

Studio executive, producer
BORN Sept. 5, 1902 in Wahoo, NE. **SPOTLIGHTS** He started out in the cutting room at Warner Bros. studios, learning the craft of editing. Then, he wrote the screenplay *Find Your Man* (1924) for movieland's biggest star Rin-Tin-Tin. His great scripts and the superb canine saved Warner's from bankruptcy. Promoted to co-producer, Zanuck altered film history by

Elizabeth Taylor 🎥   6336 Hollywood

Actress
BORN Feb. 27, 1932, in North London, England. **HIGHLIGHTS** This precious talent was raised according to her parents' credo: "We believe that children should be allowed

Elizabeth Taylor

and encouraged to develop on their natural lines." As soon as she could walk, she took dance lessons. At the age of three, Taylor gave a ballet recital with her class before King George V and the rest of the Royal Family. By age 10, the violet-eyed, raven-haired angel was a star in Hollywood. This gorgeous creature inherited her flair for theatrics from her actress-mother, although it was her art dealer father who brought her to the studio. Her classmates at MGM's Little Red School

House included co-star Roddy McDowall in *Lassie Come Home* (1943), Mickey Rooney in *National Velvet* (1944), and Judy Garland. By the time she appeared in *Little Women* (1949—as Meg), she had blossomed into a breathtaking beauty. In 1949 *Time* magazine wrote: "Eye-filling Elizabeth Taylor...pretends to no more learning than she needs, reads little besides movie magazines, hates school, loves ice cream sodas, convertibles and swimming pools, and admires big, strong men." It seemed the whole world had fallen for the spectacular, glamorous creature. Taylor was delightful in the comedy *Father of the Bride* (1950) starring Spencer Tracy, and its sequel *Father's Little Dividend* (1951). A solid actress, she was Oscar-nominated in *Raintree Country* (1957), *Cat on a Hot Tin Roof* (1958), and *Suddenly Last Summer* (1959). Motion pictures include *A Place in the Sun* (1951), *Ivanhoe* (1952), *The Last Time I Saw Paris* (1954), *Beau Brummel* (1954), *Giant* (1956), *Cleopatra* (1963—in title role), *The V.I.P.s* (1963), *The Taming of the Shrew* (1967), *Hammersmith Is Out* (1972), *The Mirror Crack'd* (1980), and *The Flintstones* (1994). **ACHIEVEMENTS** Best Actress Oscars: *Butterfield 8* (1960), and *Who's Afraid of Virginia Woolf?* (1966). In 2000, she was designated Dame Elizabeth by Queen Elizabeth. She quipped, "Well, I've always been a broad, now it's a great honor to be a dame."...Her tireless and generous charitable efforts on behalf of AIDS has helped tens of thousands of sick people...Her love life has been as spectacular as a Hollywood movie; she has been married eight times (twice to Richard Burton) with the latest divorce occurring in 1996. When asked in 1999 if she would marry again, she stated emphatically, "NEVER! NEVER! *EVER*!" **QUOTE** Why do we love her? For a million reasons, plus this: At one event, Great Britain's Princess Margaret noticed Taylor's spectacularly large diamond ring and commented, "That's a bit vulgar." Taylor asked her if she would like to try it on. Once on her Royal Highness' digit, Taylor asked, "There, it's not so vulgar now, is it?"

Marjorie Rambeau 🎥 6336 Hollywood

Actress

BORN July 15, 1889, in San Francisco, CA. **SPOTLIGHTS** A character actress, she typically played middle-aged harlots. She was frantic, funny and fast in *Palooka* (1934), with Jimmy Durante, Stu Erwin, Lupe Velez, and Thelma Todd. Adept in drama, she appears opposite Gene Tierney in *Tobacco Road* (1941). She earned an Oscar nomination for Best Supporting Actress in *Primrose Path* (1940). Died: 1970.

Arturo Toscanini 🎙 6336 Hollywood

The Maestro

BORN March 25, 1867, in Parma, Italy. **SPOTLIGHTS** One of the greatest conductors who ever lived, he was, without question, the most famous conductor of the 20th century. Called the "supreme master of all conductors," by colleague Leopold Stokowski, Toscanini was widely acclaimed for his work of the old masters. He meticulously held true to each composer's spirit: Beethoven, Mozart, Verdi, Brahms and Wagner. Praised with cascading superlatives, it was said that his interpretations were "the purest and noblest of all time." He

Arturo Toscanini

became La Scala's brilliant musical director at age 31, and conducted the New York Metropolitan Opera from 1908 - '14. He headed the New York Philharmonic from 1926 - '36, bringing classical music to the masses in NBC's early radio years. It was the first time many Americans had heard classical music. He brought dignity, respect and ratings to NBC (although millions still had not heard "serious mucic" yet), then retired to Italy in 1936. To get him to return to America, NBC's David Sarnoff offered him a deal he could not refuse. The unprecedented package included an annual salary of $40,000 tax-free (NBC paid all taxes), for ten broadcasts. The maestro had complete freedom in hiring world-class musicians to create the finest orchestra, and with all musical programming. NBC did not interfere with the show's budget, or his personal expense account. And, since Toscanini detested studio clocks, not only did Sarnoff have them pulled off the walls, but he let Toscanini decide how long to play. The extraordinary network policy was to let him run free with time. The only other person the network would let run long--without cutting him off--was President Roosevelt. "The NBC Symphony Orchestra" instantly became the world's greatest. The broadcasts originated from studio 8-H. It was one of NBC's larger auditoriums, that seated 1,200 people. Many of the free tickets were scalped for upwards of $50, $75 and $100. Each week, hundreds more begged to be seated. Each show was an astonishing experience. This superb 90-piece orchestra received so much press that everyone with a radio tuned in to hear what the fuss was all about. Finally, even isolated people in the heartland heard the beautiful music and discovered an innate love for it. He stayed with NBC radio for 17 seasons, until 1954. Recordings include *Beethoven: Symphony No. 5*; *Rossini: William Tell Overture, II Signor Bruschino Overture*; *Brahms: Symphony No. 1, Hungarian Dance No. 1*; *Verdi: Prelude to La Traviata, Overture to La Forza del Destino*; *Respighi: The Pines of Rome*; *Wagner: Lohengrin: Prelude to Act III, Die Meistersinger von Nuernberg*. **HIGHLIGHTS** Many musicians walked away with unpleasant memories of the demanding, petulant maestro, who more often than not, flew into a rage. If Toscanini felt the musicians were not performing their best during rehearsal sessions, he gave them a dose of his hot-fired temper spiked with burning-ear language. He also broke batons (going through half a dozen per rehearsal), and threw valuable scores at them.

QUOTE During one rehearsal, a trumpet player irritated him. Toscanini angrily shouted at him, "God tells me how the music should sound, but *you* stand in the way!" On another occasion, Toscanini ordered a musician off the stage. When the bassist reached the exit, he turned toward the conductor and yelled, "Nuts to you! You're a no-good son-of-a-bitch!" Toscanini shouted back, "It's too late to apologize." Died: 1957.

Laurence Trimble 🎥   6338 Hollywood

Director

BORN April 1, 1885, in Robbinston, ME. **SPOTLIGHTS** He wins hands down for the most unusual way to get a job in show business; in 1910 his pooch was signed by the studio to become Jean, the Vitagraph Dog. Whoever hired him had good instincts, because Trimble's most remarkable feat was creating the first hero dog for the silver screen. He went to Germany in search of the perfect German shepherd and picked one dog out of hundreds of contenders. (See the bio of "Strongheart" in this book.) Died: 1954.

Irene Hervey 🎥   6338 Hollywood

Actress

Irene Hervey

BORN Irene Herwick; July 11, 1910, in Los Angeles, CA. **SPOTLIGHTS** A beautiful talent of some 50 motion pictures, she was both leading lady and supporting actress. With her wavy brunette hair, perfect heart-shaped face, large eyes and flashing smile, Hervey made her breakthrough in *The Girl Who Said No* (1937—her first starring role) playing against her sweet ingenue type. She was absolutely glorious in Universal's classic Western *Destry Rides Again* (1939), starring James Stewart and Marlene Dietrich. Among her many fine works are: *The Count of Monte Crisco* (1934), *Charlie Chan in Shanghai* (1935), *Three Godfathers* (1936), *House of Fear* (1939), *The Boys from Syracuse* (1940), *Mr. Peabody and the Mermaid* (1948), *Cactus Flower* (1969), and *Play Misty for Me* (1971). She was also an accomplished stage actress, and guest starred in various TV shows. **HIGHLIGHTS** Her marriage to the actor-singer Allan Jones produced a son, singer Jack Jones. (See their respective bios in this book.) Died: 1998.

Stan Kenton 🔴   6338 Hollywood

Composer, conductor, piano, vocals

BORN Stanley Newcomb Kenton; on Feb. 19, 1911, in Wichita, KS. **SPOTLIGHTS** This proponent of progressive jazz created some of the biggest sounds and sights that had ever been heard or seen. Kenton's new ideas and exhilarating showmanship brought him admiring fans, and vocal enemies--for his controversial approach was not approved by all. He recorded many fine works on Capitol Records, including "Retrospective," "Summer of '51," "New Concepts of Artistry in Rhythm" (with top-flight musicians), "The Concerts in Miniature Broadcasts 1952-53," "Festival of Modern American Jazz," "At Ukiah," "In New Jersey," "Mellophonium Magic," and "Mellophonium Moods." **QUOTE** "If you can really swing, somehow you're never real broke. If you become a professional musician and you're good, your wife won't be weighted down with minks—but there'll always be a place for you somewhere." About rock 'n' roll, Kenton stated, "It's the kindergarten of jazz." Died: 1979.

Robert Wise 🎥   6338 Hollywood

Director, producer

BORN Sept. 10, 1914, in Winchester, IN. **SPOTLIGHTS** Wise landed a job as an assistant editor, then worked his way up to a full-fledged film editor. To write that he was excellent in the position would be an understatement. He worked on: *Bachelor Mother* (1939), starring Ginger Rogers and David Niven, the must-see *The Hunchback of Notre Dame* (1939), starring Charles Laughton, Maureen O'Hara and Cedric Hardwicke, *My Favorite Wife* (1940), starring Cary Grant and Irene Dunne, the flawless *Citizen Kane* (1941), starring Orson Welles and Joseph Cotten, and *The Magnificent Ambersons* (1942), starring Tim Holt, Joseph Cotten, Dolores Costello and Anne Baxter. Wise made his directorial debut in 1944 with the psychological thriller, *The Curse of the Cat People*. Other films include one of the best boxing films ever made, *The Set-Up* (1949). This intelligent director proved versatile in horror, sports, musicals, film noir, science fiction, war dramas, Westerns and romance. Wise directed the five-star extraterrestrial production *The Day the Earth Stood Still* (1951); a depiction of life in the old West, *Tribute to a Bad Man* (1956), with a fine performance by James Cagney; *Somebody Up There Likes Me* (1957), another excellent boxing picture about the life of middleweight champion Rocky Graziano, and starring Paul Newman. Motion pictures include *Born to Kill* (1947), with Claire Trevor and Lawrence Tierney, *Run Silent, Run Deep* (1958), with Burt Lancaster and Clark Gable, *I Want to Live* (1958), starring Susan Hayward, *Sand Pebbles* (1966—also produced), starring Steve McQueen, and *Star Trek—The Motion Picture* (1979), reuniting the TV cast. **ACHIEVEMENTS** 1961 Best Picture and Best Director Oscars for *West Side Story* (he co-directed, and produced); 1965 Best Picture and Best Director Oscars for *The Sound of Music* (also produced); 1966 Irving G. Thalberg Memorial Award for "the most consistent high level of production achievement by an individual producer." He became President of the Academy of Motion Picture Arts and Sciences. **HIGHLIGHTS** Why did he come to Hollywood? He ran out of funds for college, so he decided to visit his brother, who was an accountant at RKO studios.

William Collier 🎥   6338 Hollywood

Actor, singer, writer
BORN Nov. 6, 1866, in New York. NY. **SPOTLIGHTS** At age 11, he ran away from home to join the touring company of Gilbert and Sullivan's "Pinafore." By 23, he was a Broadway star. He was 49 when he made his first film, *Fatty and the Broadway Stars* (1915), the worked in countless silents. When sound arrived, he became a dialogue writer/director, and character actor: *Thanks for the Memory* (1938). Died: 1944.

Paul Gilbert 📺   6340 Hollywood

Comedian, dancer, actor
BORN Paul MacMahon; 1917. **SPOTLIGHTS** He clowned around as a circus performer, before becoming a vaudeville celebrity and film star. Movies include *The Second Greatest Sex* (1955). He played the lead in "The Duke" (1954), a TV sitcom about a heavyweight fighter who slips into society life via his love for painting. Died: 1976.

Carlyle Blackwell 🎥   6340 Hollywood

Actor
BORN April 21, 1888, in Troy, PA. **SPOTLIGHTS** A successful Broadway actor, Blackwell made his silent screen debut in *A Dixie Mother* (1909). The handsome, tough guy quickly became a leading man in *Uncle Tom's Cabin* (1909), *Such a Little Queen* (1914) opposite Mary Pickford, and *His Brother's Wife* (1916). His last film was *The Hound of the Baskervilles* (1931). Died: 1955.

Igor Stravinsky 🎤   6340 Hollywood

Composer, conductor
BORN June 17, 1882, in Russia. **SPOTLIGHTS** A musical genius and the most famous composer of the 20th century, this prolific artist gave the world many moving compositions, and sometimes stirred up a controversy while doing so. His ballet scores, *The Firebird* in 1910, *Petrouchka* in 1911, and *The Rite of Spring* in 1913, were masterpieces. For the latter, he premiered the wild, primitive music in Paris. With its clashing cords, chaotic rhythms and sensual melody, the work was greeted by an immediate riot—complete with fist fights—to which Stravinsky responded by coolly leaving the concert hall. He ignored criticism calling him a "musical traitor." Later, he explained how the piece came to him in a daydream. He stated, "I saw in imagination a solemn pagen rite. Sage elders, seated in a circle, watched a young girl dance herself to death. They were sacrificing her to propitiate the god of spring." His brilliant 1918 musical-theatre piece (a folk tale for an a seven-piece orchestra) is about a soldier and the devil, "L'Histoire du Soldat." He intended it as "a living work." Stravinsky wrote: "I

Igor Stravinsky

still encourage producers to localize the play and to dress the soldier in a uniform sympathetic to the audience." (Following the 1992 Los Angeles riots, a young African American actor named Seth Gilliam played the soldier, and African American actor Harold Perrineau Jr. portrayed the devil. Dressed in blue jeans and shockingly bright tee-shirts. their stage was the back of a flatbed truck. The story's narrator was a female rap duo from South Central, L.A., named T-Love and Suggah-B.) In the 1920s, Stravinsky's neoclassicism had more to do with Russian stylistic changes than with influences by fashionable Paris. While some considered his work "reactionary," others praised him for being a "courageous explorer." Significant works include *Symphonies of Wind Instruments* in 1920—one of his most spiritual works, his 1922 opera "Marva," the opera-oratorio *Oedipus Rex* (1927), the ballet of *Apollo* (1927), *Symphony of Psalms* in 1930, *Symphony in Three Movements* in 1942, 1943, 1944, and 1945, and *Threni* in 1958. **ACHIEVEMENTS** He provided hundreds of new ideas about music, virtuosity and beauty. In 1939-'40, he lectured at Harvard University, stating, "Tradition is a living force that animates and informs the present." **QUOTE** "The trouble with music appreciation in general is that people are taught to have too much respect for music. They should be taught to love it instead."...He wrote the very Russian-sounding "Requiem Canticles," for his funeral; it played in 1971.

Gale Gordon 🎤   6340 Hollywood

Actor
BORN Charles T. Aldrich, Jr.; Feb. 2, 1906, in New York City, NY. **SPOTLIGHTS** A blustery character, he played a stuffy foil whose bark was worse than his bite. This radio star worked in "The Burns and Allen Show," "Fibber McGee and Molly," and Granby's Green Acres" (forerunner to "Green Acres"). **TV** Played the crusty principal in "Our Miss Brooks" (1952-'56), and Mooney/Carter in "The Lucy Show" (1963-'74). Died: 1995.

William Holden and Eleanor Parker

Bela Lugosi and Lia Tora

Eleanor Parker 🎥   6340 Hollywood

Actress

BORN June 26, 1922, in Cedarville, OH. **SPOTLIGHTS** A strong-willed, beautiful redhead, and gifted actress, Parker brings a fascinating intensity to her many diverse roles. She co-stars with Agnes Moorehead in possibly the first (and best) women-behind-bars melodrama, *Caged* (1950). Playing an increasingly bitter prisoner, she earned her first Oscar nomination. Her more than 50 motion pictures include *Never Say Goodbye* (1946), *Of Human Bondage* (1946), *Three Secrets* (1950), *Detective Story* (1951—in an Oscar-nominated performance), *Scaramouche* (1952), *The Naked Jungle* (1954), *Interrupted Melody* (1955—in an Oscar-nominated performance), *The Man with the Golden Arm* (1955), *A Hole in the Head* (1959), *Return to Peyton Place* (1961), *The Sound of Music* (1965), *An American Dream* (1966), *Dressed to Kill* (1979), and *Madame X* (1981).

Bela Lugosi 🎥   6340 Hollywood

Actor

BORN B. Blasko; Oct. 20, 1882, in Hungary. **SPOTLIGHTS** "I...am Dra-cu-la. I bid you welcome." Lugosi perfected his characterization of the bloodthirsty vampire on Broadway in 1927, then was immortalized as the pale-faced, Transylvanian count in Universal's first sound horror movie, *Dracula* (1931). Depression-era audiences hungered for this evil monster, as the terror they watched onscreen surpassed their own poverty-stricken, hopeless lives. When fans left the theatre, they were relieved that no matter how bad their own lives were, at least they were safe from becoming "children of the night." Movies include *The Veiled Woman* (1929), *Murders in Rue Morgue,*

White Zombie (both 1932), *Night of Terror* (1933), *The Invisible Ray* (1936), and *The Wolf Man* (1941). He stars in a number of film serials. He was buried wearing in his Dracula cape in 1956.

Gale Gordon

Gypsy Rose Lee and Randolph Scott

Fay Wray (Notice how the trunk of Wray's body commingles with the shape of the tree's roots.)

6350 HOLLYWOOD

Bill Haley   6350 Hollywood

Singer, songwriter, guitarist

Bill Haley

BORN William Haley, Jr.; July 6, 1925, in Highland Park, MI. **SPOTLIGHTS** Called the "Father of Rock 'n' Roll," he was originally a country artist. His first non-country recording was the rhythm-and-blues tune "Rocket '88." Many music historians consider this the first rock 'n' roll song done by a white artist. The year was 1951. In 1953, Bill Haley and His Comets made the *Billboard* charts at #12 with "Crazy Man, Crazy." Other hits include "Shake, Rattle and Roll," "See You Later, Aligator," and "Rip It Up." The term "rock 'n' roll" was coined from his song "Rock Rock, Rock Everybody, Roll, Roll, Roll, Everybody." Even more significant was his 1954 recording "(We're Gonna) Rock Around the Clock." Interestingly, the song did not take off until a year later as the theme song for the movie *Blackboard Jungle*. "Rock Around the Clock" went to #1 on *Billboard* charts on July 9, 1955. That date became the official birthday of the Rock Era. The song became one of rock 'n' rolls greatest sellers. Ironically, Haley was a conservative-type who felt he had created "a monster." Died: 1981.

Ramon Novarro 🎥   6350 Hollywood

Actor

BORN Ramon Samaniegas; Feb. 6, 1899, in Mexico. **SPOTLIGHTS** The top Chicano star during the silent era entered movies two years after Rudolph Valentino. Unfortunately, he found himself labeled "a second Valentino." Yet, this Latin lover had a stronger physique than Valentino and was considerably more virile. As the global marketplace gobbled up the lush, romantic pictures of the 1920s, there was plenty of room at the top. Feminine hearts were set ablaze during his love scenes. It was reported that "his passionate, amorous ways makes the weaker sex swoon." One of the most popular movie idols, this handsome, dark-haired talent rose to superstardom as the charming scoundrel Rupert of Hentzau in *The Prisoner of Zenda* (1923). Movies include *Where the Pavement Ends* (1923), *The Arab* (1924), the classic *Ben Hur* (1926—in the title role—it was his biggest hit), *The Student Prince* (1927), *Mata Hari* (1932), co-starring Greta Garbo. and *Heller in Pink Tights* (1960), a Western spoof adapted from Louis L'Amour's novel, starring Sophia Loren and

Ramon Novarro

Anthony Quinn. Died: 1968.

Diana Lynn 📺   6350 Hollywood

See page 351

Jane Wyatt 📺   6352 Hollywood

Jane Wyatt

Actress

BORN Aug. 12, 1911, in New York, NY. **SPOTLIGHTS** Millions of American children dreamed that the TV character, Margaret Anderson (sweetly played by Wyatt) was their second mommy. This serene lady was pretty, kind-hearted, and understanding. When she smiled, her eyes twinkled with an inner peacefulness. She and her husband (played by Robert Young), knew how to lovingly care for their family in "Father Knows Best" (1954-'63). This Emmy-winner set American family standards, even if they were idealized. Before TV, Wyatt appears in such exquisite films as *Lost Horizon* (1937), and *Gentleman's Agreement* (1947), and the terrific crime picture, *Boomerang!* (1947).

Dorothy Phillips 🎥   6358 Hollywood

Actress, producer
BORN Dorothy Strible; Dec. 23, 1892, in Baltimore, MD.
SPOTLIGHTS A pioneer silent screen star and one of the earliest female producers. She exuded great depths of pain and occasionally humor in *The Rosary* (1911), *The Adventures of a Sea-Going Hack* (1915), *A Soul for Sale* (1918). Her last film was *The Man Who Shot Liberty Valance* (1962). Died: 1980.

Dave Willock 📺   6358 Hollywood

Actor, comic

Dave Willock

BORN 1905, in Chicago, IL. **SPOTLIGHTS** He became a teen idol after his film debut in *Legion of Lost Flyers* (1939). Later, he was a regular guest in TV's "Pantomime Quiz." In 1955, he parlayed his real-life home hobby into a humorous, but informative TV show called "Do It Yourself." He was also a regular on "The Beautiful Phyllis Diller Show." Died: 1990.

George Kennedy 🎥 6356 Hollywood

Actor
BORN Feb. 18, 1925, in New York, NY. **SPOTLIGHTS** His father was a composer-conductor, his mother a dancer. Kennedy made his professional stage debut at age two, traveling with a touring company of "Bringing Up Father." He spent 15 years in the Army during and post-World War II, serving considerable time with the Armed Forces Radio and Television Service in Europe and the Far East. In his first civilian stint, he was military advisor, stand-in, gopher and assistant on the "Sergeant Bilko" show. It starred comic legend Phil Silvers. Although he never took any acting lessons, Kennedy stated, "I learned more about timing from Phil Silvers in four years than if I'd studied with Stanislovsky himself." Neither Hollywood nor his fans disagreed. This natural born talent has been a dynamo in more than 100 motion pictures. A giant of a man—built like a solid brick wall—he possesses rugged looks and is frequently cast as the "heavy." Movies include *Lonely Are*

the Brave (1962), *Charade* (1963—his favorite film role), *The Dirty Dozen* (1967), *Airport* (1970), *Cahill—U.S. Marshall* (1973), *Earthquake* (1974), *Death on the Nile* (1978), *Modern Romance* (1981), and *The Naked Gun* (1988 + sequels). **ACHIEVEMENTS** 1968 Oscar for Best Supporting Actor in *Cool Hand Luke*. He earned two Bronze Star Medals as a combat infantryman in WWII...His Hollywood Walk of Fame star was dedicated on Oct.

George Kennedy

17, 1991. **QUOTE** Dinner in his household starts with a simple prayer, "Dear Lord, please help us try and remember to give something back."

Robert Young 📺   6358 Hollywood

See page 601

Mala Powers 📺   6360 Hollywood

Actress

Mala Powers

BORN Mary Ellen Powers; Dec. 29, 1931, in San Francisco, CA. **SPOTLIGHTS** Since childhood she pursued her dream of acting and made her screen debut in *Tough as They Come* (1942), at age 11. By 18, she had starred as the unattainable love Roxanne in *Cyrano de Bergerac* (1950). Educated at UCLA, other movies include *City Beneath the Sea* (1953) opposite Robert Ryan and Anthony Quinn, *City That Never Sleeps* (1953) co-starring Gig Young, *Rage at Dawn* (1955), and *Tammy and the Bachelor* (1957) with Debbie Reynolds, Walter Brennan and Leslie Nielsen. She played Mona Williams (1965-'66) in TV's sitcom "Hazel." She also played secretary Marian Crane to Anthony Quinn's "The Man and the City" (1971-'72).

June Lockhart   6362 Hollywood

Actress
BORN June 25, 1925, in New York, NY. **SPOTLIGHTS** The daughter of actors Gene and Kathleen Lockhart, she made her screen debut in *A Christmas Carol* (1938), starring her parents (see their respective bios in this book). Lockhart was wonderful in *Sergeant York* (1941), a true story about an unassuming

June Lockhart

farmer who becomes a war hero. Movies include the outstanding, elegant drama *Forever and a Day* (1943), the family musical *Meet Me in St. Louis* (1944), the tear-jerker *The Yearling* (1946), and the comedy *The Big Picture* (1989). She stars in the 1945 motion picture *Son of Lassie*, then won the role of the nurturing mother Ruth Martin in TV's "Lassie" (1958-'64). It was this series that captured the imagination of millions of youngsters. who became her devoted fans. Still seen in syndication, genera-

tion after generation have watched this adventure series, learning about family values and appreciation of animals (especially collies). Next, this versatile, affable talent moved into deep space as mother Maureen Robinson in the popular, campy sci-fi series "Lost in Space" (1965-'68). She worked in the New Line movie of the same name in 1998.

Bill Welsh 📺   6362 Hollywood

Bill Welsh

Radio sportscaster, TV pioneer
BORN William H. Welsh; April 25, 1912, in Greeley, CO. **SPOTLIGHTS** His perfect pronunciation and stylish delivery made him an early radio broadcaster in Colorado, where he covered sports and did live interviews by remotes (with people such as Eleanor Roosevelt). By his early 30s, he moved to California, where he soon won an invitation to cover USC and UCLA football and basketball games. Reporting over the roar of the crowd, Welsh could wring

every drop of drama from an event. His vivid coverage and robust play-by-play descriptions were sometimes more exciting than the game itself. From this success, he became a pioneer in the new medium of television. In 1946, his first assignment was to cover ice hockey. Compared to his phenomenal base of radio listeners, there were only about 300 TV sets in Southern California. Radio colleagues warned Welsh, "You're making a terrible mistake. This television thing is never going to happen." Welsh ignored them. He later stated, "I saw television as the future." When he and newscaster Stan Chambers telecast the Kathy Fiscus story (a little girl had fallen into a well and was trapped) in 1949, for a live, continuous 27 1/2 hours, they "shut down the town. Nobody went out to restaurants or the theatres. They all stayed home." This helped establish TV news

as a viable source. **ACHIEVEMENTS** Welsh hosted the spectacular FIRST telecast of the Annual Tournament of Roses Parade, in Pasadena, California, and continued for nearly half a century. He telecast the FIRST Rose Bowl football game on Jan. 1, 1948. Nicknamed "Mr. Hollywood," he also served as president of the Hollywood Chamber of Commerce for many decades, leading the city into renewal and revitalization. **QUOTE** "I had the good fortune to get into television in 1946. I grew up with the industry. "I've had a wonderful life, all because of Hollywood." Died: 2000.

Phil Spitalny 🎙   6364 Hollywood

Orchestra leader, composer, clarinetist

Phil Spitalny

BORN Nov. 7, 1890, in Russia. **SPOTLIGHTS** A child prodigy, his family moved to America when he was a boy. Before this genius musician reached age 30, he had toured the world successfully, played professionally on radio and, as Maestro, led a 50-piece symphony orchestra in Boston. Going against the wishes of his parents, and fighting the rampant tide of sexism, Spitalny became one of the modern world's earliest feminists. When the serious music community dismissed the idea of professional female musicians--choosing to propagate the ridiculous notion that women lacked the ability to focus--he argued otherwise. After being exhilarated upon hearing one outstanding female violinist in concert, he decided "to assemble an all-girl band." He criss-crossed the country auditioning female musicians. At New York's prestigious Juilliard School of Music, he heard the brilliant playing of Evelyn Kaye Klein. She became his first violinist (playing on a 1756 Bergonzi), concert mistress, and in 1946, his wife. Spitalny formed a 27-piece all-girl orchestra. When critics noted that all the women were very attractive, Spitalny defended his hiring, stating, "No performer is hired who can't give a firsthand rendition of two sonatas and two concerti, who hasn't the individual gifts of rhythm and melodic perception, who can't read music fluently, and who hasn't had a good deal of experience." He forced the group to have higher standards than male musicians, observing, "If a man makes a mistake, no one cares. But if a woman does, they'll say: 'Well, what can you expect?'" The "girls" were expected to be sweet and charming not only on stage, but at all times, and to one another. Their off-hours were strictly regulated; no liquor was allowed. Dating was nearly impossible unless the prospective gent could pass the requirements of the appointed five-girl committee, and all participants had to sign an agreement not to marry for at least two years. Their appearance, hair ("long, soft bobs"), clothes, weight (which could never rise above 122 pounds) was closely monitored. Still, when Spitalny tried to book the act, he met with prejudice. There was blanket discrimination against women in hiring practices. Finally, the maestro kept the orchestra hidden, and had them play by remote to land their first radio contract. The executive who signed them in 1935 did not realize they were women. But the 13-week contract was extended to six months, then General Electric picked the show up for another 10 years. Called "The Hour of Charm," it was radio's "most celebrated all-girl orchestra." They played everything from symphonic to hymns to pop music. Songs include "Madeleine," "The American Hymn of Liberty," "We Must Be Vigilant," and "It's You, No One But You." **HIGHLIGHTS** Director Billy Wilder co-wrote one the movieland's best comedies, *Some Like It Hot* (1959), starring Marilyn Monroe, Jack Lemmon, Tony Curtis, and Joe E. Brown. The film was inspired and loosely based on Spitalny's all-girl band. Died: 1970.

Jack White 🎥   6364 Hollywood

Actor
BORN 1865. **SPOTLIGHTS** Trained onstage, he came to Hollywood for *The Spoilers* and *Girl of the Golden West* (both 1930). He appears in both the 1932 and '44 versions of *Sign of the Cross*. Died: 1949.

Andy Devine 📺   6366 Hollywood

Actor
BORN Oct. 7, 1905, in Flagstaff, AZ. **SPOTLIGHTS** Devine's strange, crackly and high-pitched voice resulted from a childhood injury. Dreaming of a Hollywood career, agents advised "the hick" that he did not have a shot in Hades of succeeding onscreen. He refused to give up, and lived to see those so-called experts proved wrong. Movie audiences liked him a lot, in 100+ pictures. Often cast as the Western comic sidekick to cowboys such as Roy Rogers, his acting ability extended beyond light oaters. Movies include *A Star Is Born* (1937),

Stagecoach (1939), *The Red Badge of Courage* (1951), *Pete Kelly's Blues* (1955), *Around the World in 80 Days* (1956), *The Adventures of Huckleberry Finn* (1960), *The Man Who Shot Liberty Valance* (1962), and *How the West Was Won* (1962). In TV, he played the roly-poly sidekick, Jingles B. Jones, in "The Adventures of Wild Bill Hickok" (1951-'58). He enthusiastically called his boss: "the bravest, strongest, fightingest U.S. Marshal in the whole West!" He also portrayed the same character in the juvenile radio adventure show. Died: 1977.

Andy Devine

Paul Henreid 🎥   6366 Hollywood

Paul Henreid

Actor, director
BORN Paul George Julius von Henreid; Jan. 10, 1908, in Trieste, Austria. (Trieste is now officially part of Italy.) **SPOTLIGHTS** The son of Baron Carl Alphons von Henreid, he is one of the titled actors on the Walk of Fame. 1942 was a grand year for this fair-haired, debonair talent when Warners developed his elegant, soft-spoken European qualities in *Now Voyager*, opposite Bette Davis. That same year, he played Victor Laszlo, the WWII Resistance Fighter, in the must-see classic *Casablanca*, opposite Ingrid Bergman and Humphrey Bogart. He made dozens of films, and directed six "Bs." Died: 1992.

6370 HOLLYWOOD

Anne Bancroft 📺   6370 Hollywood

Actress, director

Anne Bancroft

BORN Anna Maria Luise Italiano; Sept. 17, 1932, in Bronx, NY. **SPOTLIGHTS** Although she had already changed her name from Anna Italiano to Anne Marno, producer Darryl Zanuck did not like either. He drew up a list of names, and told her to pick one. She remarked, "Bancroft was the only name that didn't make me sound like a bubble dancer." A few of her many fine films include *Tonight We Sing* (1953) with Ezio Pinza, Isaac Stern and Jan Peerce, *The Pumpkin Eater* (1964—for which she won the Golden Globe and Cannes Film Festival Awards, and an Academy Award nomination), *Seven Women* (1966—director John Ford's last film), and *The Turning Point* (1977—in an Oscar-nominated performance). A vibrant talent, she is capable of playing roles of incredible depth, as witnessed in *The Miracle Worker* (1962), and *The Graduate* (1967). She gave a brilliant performance in *The Elephant Man* (1980), and was superb in *Agnes of God* (1985), in which she was Oscar-nominated. Bancroft made her directorial debut with the comedy, *Fatso* (1980); she also co-stars with Dom DeLuise and earned a screenplay credit. She co-stars with her real-life husband, Mel Brooks, in the hilarious comedy *To Be or Not To Be* (1983). Always the consummate actress, she is spellbinding to watch in *84 Charing Cross Road* (1987) and *The Oldest Living Confederate Tells All* (1994). She received both thumbs up for her 1997 performance in *G.I. Jane*. In 1998 she co-stars with Gwyneth Paltrow in the remake of *Great Expectations*. TV: She plays Mary Magdalene in Zeffirelli's "Jesus of Nazareth" (1976), this annual Easter telecast has become a classic. Bancroft has a Walk of Fame star in the television category because early in her career she had leads in 100 teleplays. Her star was dedicated before her immense body of important film work. In all, she has made more than 40 motion pictures. **ACHIEVEMENTS** 1962 Best Actress Oscar for *The Miracle Worker*. **QUOTE** About her early show business ambitions, and she started in show business at age four, this natural born talent said, "When I was age two, I could sing 'Under a Blanket of Blue.' I was so willing to perform that nobody had to coax me."

Lassie 🎥   6370 Hollywood

Canine star
BORN 1941. The original Lassie was a male collie named Pal.

Lassie

SPOTLIGHTS Lassie, the wonder dog of MGM motion pictures, followed the lead of such great movie dogs as Strongheart and Rin-Tin-Tin (see their separate bios in this book). Although those two powerful, fierce dogs were military-trained German shepherds, Lassie was a fluffy, sweet-looking collie. This canine was an endearing family pet who performed heroic deeds with loyalty and courage, protecting its master's family and defending its turf. The animal appeared for the first time in *Lassie Come Home* (1943). This sentimental story about a poor family forced to sell their cherished collie, starring Roddy McDowell and Elizabeth Taylor, was a huge commercial success for MGM. Sequels followed, including *Son of Lassie* (1945) starring June Lockhart—who would later star in the extremely popular long-running TV series (1954-'71)—and *Courage of Lassie* (1946). The dog became a big star in film, radio and television. The protective Lassie was, at times, seemingly more intelligent than his human counterparts. A common line that was heard in nearly every television episode was: "I think that dog is tryin' to tell us somethin'." And Lassie always was. **HIGHLIGHTS** Rudd Weatherwax, owner of the millionaire pooch and his offspring, also trained the dogs. When radio executives decided to create a juvenile adventure show starring Lassie, they did not want to use the dog—who they feared would be unreliable. But Weatherwax insisted Lassie do all his own sound effects *live*. Behind-the-scenes radio personnel were surprised to hear Lassie pant, whine, snarl, bark and growl (in varying degrees) on cue. *Time* magazine wrote Lassie did so with "exquisite nuance." However, a *human* named Earl Keen (a superb animal imitator), played all the *other dog and creature* roles on the radio show! It aired from 1947-'50. **GENDER-BENDER** It was thought the lovable and good-tempered Lassie would be better received by audiences if the dog were a female. However due to female hormonal shifts and the shedding caused by it, the director discovered that a female's fur did not look consistently plush week after week. It was also learned that males were more attractive (although slightly less intelligent than females), so a male was finally cast in the lead of the female. Yet, even into the 1990s, the controversy rages on about that canine's gender. Nationally syndicated newspaper advice columnist "Dear Abby" has even gotten involved in this debate more than once. Died: 1953.

Robert Goulet ●   6370 Hollywood

Singer, actor
BORN Nov. 26, 1933, in Lawrence, MA. **SPOTLIGHTS** A

Robert Goulet

handsome, dark-haired performer whose break came in 1960 when he landed the role of Sir Lancelot in the Lerner and Lowe Broadway musical, "Camelot." He played Sir Lancelot to Richard Burton's King Arthur and Julie Andrews' Guenevere. He was musical star of Rodgers and Hammerstein's "Carousel," Cole Porter's "Kiss Me Kate," as well as "South Pacific," "On a Clear Day You Can See Forever," "I Do, I Do," and the 1990s revival of the classic "Camelot" (this time in the role of King Arthur). In all, he has given more than 2200 performances of Camelot. When asked how does he keep it fresh, Goulet answered, "I am just getting it down. I will never be satisfied with my performance." The vibrant, big baritone has recorded 40 albums, and appears in *I'd Rather Be Rich* (1964), *Atlantic City* (1980), *Beetlejuice* (1988) and *The Naked Gun 2 1/2* (1991). **ACHIEVEMENTS** 1962 Grammy. 1968 Tony.

Robert Z. Leonard 🎥   6370 Hollywood

Director
BORN Oct. 7, 1889, in Chicago, IL. **SPOTLIGHTS** One of MGM's premier directors for more than three decades, gloss, beauty, and harmony were his trademarks. *The Divorcee* (1930) was his first Oscar-nominated work. Other hits include *The Dancing Lady* (1933), starring Joan Crawford; the flamboyant biopic *The Great Ziegfeld* (1936), starring William Powell and

Myrna Loy; *Maytime* (1937), starring Jeanette MacDonald (her favorite film); *Pride and Prejudice* (1940), starring Laurence Olivier and Greer Garson; *Ziegfeld Girl* (1941), starring Judy Garland; and *The King's Thief* (1955), with David Niven. Died: 1968.

Jack Benny 📺   6370 Hollywood

See page 432

Rich Little 📺   6372 Hollywood

Impressionist, comedian, actor
BORN Richard Caruthers Little; Nov. 26, 1938, in Ottawa,

Rich Little

Canada. **SPOTLIGHTS** The master of mimicry, he has been described as "the most accurate, original, daring, and dependable impressionist this side of Xerox." As an entertainer, he combines his genius for imitating voices, with comedy and song. He is famous worldwide for his vast repertoire, including impersonations of President Bill Clinton, to Kermit the Frog. He is a popular TV star, and a top Las Vegas/Atlantic City headliner for four decades. One of his earliest TV specials, "Liberace in Wonderland" (1965), stars Kirk Douglas (as the Cheshire Cat), Jack Lemmon (as the March Hare), and Jack Benny (as the Queen of Hearts)—had Little playing all of the roles. It showcased his hilarious versatility and superb comic timing. His celebrity impersonations include Cary Grant's, James Stewart's, W.C. Fields', Johnny Carson's, Richard Nixon's, and many others. He has produced nine comedy recordings, including his million-selling "The First Family Rides Again." **ACHIEVEMENTS** When David Niven's illness (Lou Gehrig's disease) prevented him from working, Little dubbed his voice in *The Trail of the Pink Panther* and *The Curse of the Pink Panther*. He is the recipient of numerous comedy awards and honors...He walked the Walk of Fame imitating each person as he stepped on their star. He always thought that would make a great skit. **QUOTE** "I can't imitate Bob Hope, because of his unique vocal rhythms, the timing is hard to get down."

Mickey Rooney 🎙   6372 Hollywood

See page 183

George Putnam 📺   6372 Hollywood

Newsman, anchor, talk show host
BORN July 14, in Breckenridge, MN. **SPOTLIGHTS** Putnam

George Putnam

began the news business when he was nine years old delivering newspapers. As a child, he also milked a dozen cows every morning before school and evenings before dinner. On weekends and summer holidays, he hayed, harvested and threshed from five in the morning until the chores were finished around eight in the evening. During high school he excelled in leadership and sports, then became a cub reporter for the St.Paul Dispatch. His collegiate pursuits were abruptly halted when his family suffered severe financial setbacks during the Great Depression. Forced to leave the academic life, Putnam became a janitor at WDGY in Minneapolis. He pleaded with management to give him a shot at going on the air. For his 20th birthday present they granted his wish and he's been a broadcaster ever since. Five years later, NBC in New York hired him, where he maintained the highest ratings as a reporter both in TV and radio. Putnam commented, "Walter Winchell made my career. The thing that gave me attention was he said, 'George Putnam's voice is the greatest in American radio and television.' I went from $190-a-month to better than $200,000-a- year, which was much too much for a 24-year-old kid out of Minnesota." A reporter for *Time* magazine wrote that Putnam's voice was "silvery, melodious and super smooth." With these accolades, the journalist signed with KTTV in Los Angeles in 1951. On tough assignments, he disrupted City Hall and dug up dirt and corruption where he could find it. Putnam is one of a select few newsmen in the history of electronic journalism who has spoken out, putting his job—even his life—on the line for the peoples' causes. It has cost him dearly, but it has never deterred him from championing free speech and justice for all, regardless of the personal cost. Now in his 62nd year of writing and reporting, he's on KIEV 870 AM Talk Radio. His "Talk Back" program is a blend of two-way conversation with in-studio guests, newsmakers across the nation and his listeners. His show is different as he will talk to any listener who wants to speak with him and the calls are not screened for age, occupation, subject mater, point of view or for any other purpose. **ACHIEVEMENTS** Recipient of more than 300 awards including four Emmys, and two citations for his service as an officer in the U.S. Marine Corps during WWII. He has ridden horseback in 38 Hollywood Christmas Parades, and 41 consecutive years in the world-famous Pasadena Tournament of Roses Parade on New Years Day. Actively involved in Thoroughbred horse racing, he owns a large stable of winners. The Putnam Coat of Arms appears on his racing colors. It read, "*DEUM NON ALIUM TIMEO*" (I fear God and none other).

Ronald Reagan   6374 Hollywood

Actor, former President of the U.S.A.

President Ronald Reagan

BORN Feb. 6, 1911, in Tampico, IL. **SPOTLIGHTS** A charismatic talent, he signed with Warner Brothers in 1937 as a contract player. Among his earliest pictures are *Sergeant Murphy* (1938) which was based on a true story, *Hollywood Hotel* (1938), an opulent Busby Berkeley musical with an all-star cast and a great collection of Johnny Mercer-Richard Whiting songs, and *Code of the Secret Service* (1939), an action film, where Reagan plays Lt. "Brass" Bancroft. This handsome, reliable actor, known for his good sense of humor, made more than 50 motion pictures, including the well-loved sports movie, *Knute Rockne, All American* (1940), with his famous scene as "The Gipper." His sensitive work in *King's Row* (1942) is considered one of his best performances; it inspired members of the Academy of Motion Picture Arts and Sciences to write-in his name on Oscar ballots. He came out of it a movie star. He was excellent in *The Hasty Heart*. He presented a strong dramatic grasp of the role. In *King's Row*, he plays a man whose legs are amputated by a sadistic doctor. After the operation he regains consciousness. He delivers the haunting question, "Where's the rest of me?" This line became the title of Ronald Reagan's autobiography published in 1965. He stars in the classic *Bedtime for Bonzo* (1951), where a professor tries to prove character is determined by environment (versus genetics), using a chimpanzee in the experiment. He appears with his wife Nancy Davis in *Hellcats of the Navy* (1957); this action movie is their only screen appearance together. **TV** Hosted-starred in "General Electric Theater" (1954-'61), and "Death Valley Days" (1965-'66). **CASTING** A featured leading man, he was most often cast as the hero's buddy (who did not get the girl, or win at the end). "The Great Loser" was a staple character during Hollywood's Golden Era. When his former, longtime boss Jack Warner (of Warner Bros.) returned from Europe and learned Reagan had been nominated for Republican candidate for Governor of California, the mogul protested, "No, no, no, Jimmy Stewart for Governor. Ronald Reagan for best friend." **ACHIEVEMENTS** He was the first actor to be elected to America's highest office when he became the 40th President of the United States (1980-'84). He received two thumbs up from the public at large when he was voted to a Presidential second term (1984-'88). Previously, he was elected Governor of California (1967-'75), and was president of the Screen Actors Guild (1947-'52). **NICKNAME** "Ever since my birth, my nickname has been 'Dutch,' President Reagan stated. **HIGHLIGHTS** Married actress Jane Wyman (1940-'48); married actress and true love Nancy Davis in 1952. **QUOTE** "...Strangely enough, the word 'liberty' traced back to its roots means 'growing up' or 'maturing' or 'taking responsibility.' And therein lies the whole story—we can have peace and brotherly love by accepting our responsibility to preserve freedom here where it has known its longest run in six thousand years of recorded history."

Mark Goodson 6374 Hollywood

Producer, writer
BORN Jan. 24, 1915, in Sacramento, CA. **SPOTLIGHTS** "Will the Mystery Guest enter and sign in please!" Goodson and his associate Bill Todman co-produced America's most popular, most prestigious TV quiz show, "What's My Line?" This unique, long-running game show was like a magnet to thousands of the most interesting personalities of the day—movie stars, film and Broadway directors, opera stars, high-ranking politicians and lawyers (senators, governors, Supreme Court justices, *et al*), high-ranking military personnel, athletes, comedians, TV hosts, motion picture tycoons, artists (such as Salvador Dali), writers, composers, *et al*—as well as the infamous. The panelists were some of the most intelligent, quick-witted and entertaining profilers assembled, and included Steve Allen, Arlene Francis, Bennett Cerf, Dorothy Kilgallen, and Fred Allen, to name a few (see their respective bios in this book). "What's My Line?" was broadcast live at the same time weekly. It ran year-round on CBS for 17 years. There were no repeats. "What's My Line?" made a very wealthy man out of Goodson (along with his partner, and CBS). This high-caliber show was so much fun to watch (with no "dumbing down" for the television viewers) that President Eisenhower rarely missed a show. Even royalty, such as the Duke and Duchess of Windsor, visited the set when they were in town. "What's My Line?" ran from 1950 - '67. Goodson also co-produced other popular, long-running quiz shows including "Beat the Clock" (1950-'58), and "To Tell the Truth" (1956-'67). He also created "The Price is Right," hosted by the legendary Bob Barker. It first aired in 1957 and as of 1999 it is still on the air with new shows. In 1991 Goodson estimated "The Price is Right" had given away $100 million dollar in prizes. He observed, "You can measure time in many ways. One of them is to look at the price of things when we began—including a car valued at $2,600." **QUOTE** When he was unhappy about some aspect of his television production, Goodson's standard line to his subordinates was: "I guess you haven't had the time to think this through properly, but..." Died: 1992.

Perry Como 6376 Hollywood

See page 71

Laura La Plante 6376 Hollywood

Actress

Laura La Plante

BORN Nov. 1, 1904, in St. Louis, MO. **SPOTLIGHTS** One of silent movies original damsels in distress, she was also delightful in comedies. Full of pep and personality, La Plante appears in countless shorts and features. Movies include *Shooting for Love* (1923), and *The Beautiful Cheat* (1926). A Universal Studios headliner, her best film is generally considered to be *The Cat and the Canary* (1927), an English manor house thriller. Died: 1996.

George Cukor 6378 Hollywood

Director
BORN July 7, 1899, in New York, NY. **SPOTLIGHTS** Cukor was a Broadway director scooped up by Hollywood after the introduction of sound. He did a few movies before locking in with friend David O. Selznick, who had just moved to RKO. *What Price Hollywood?* (1932)—the precursor to *A Star is Born*—is a fine blend of drama and comedy. He followed with *A Bill of Divorcement* (1932), a very good melodrama starring John Barrymore and introducing Katharine Hepburn. The next year—at MGM—he brilliantly directed the all-star production of *Dinner at Eight* (1933). *Little Women* (1933) starring Katherine Hepburn was a major box office success; it also earned him his first Academy Award nomination. *David Copperfield* (1935) became an instant classic, and remains one of the definitive Charles Dickens works translated to screen. It was nominated for Best Picture. Working with friend Greta Garbo, he created magic with her fantastic performance in *Camille* (1937). In 1937 he began pre-production for *Gone with the Wind*. As a close pal of Selznick's, as well as being a fine director in his own right, Cukor began shooting the picture. Star Clark Gable complained about Selznick's choice because Cukor was "a ladies director." He was fired. But, *The Philadelphia Story* (1940), starring Katharine Hepburn proved he still had confidence. It earned him a Best Director Oscar nomination. *Gaslight* (1944), a suspenseful drama, introduces Angela Lansbury in her screen debut (in an Oscar-nominated performance). Other films include *A Double Life* (1947), *Adam's Rib* (1947), *Born Yesterday* (1950); and *A Star Is Born* (1954)—his first Technicolor picture. **ACHIEVEMENTS** 1964 Academy Award for *My Fair Lady* (1964). **HIGHLIGHTS** Actor

Jack Lemmon made his film debut in Cukor's *It Should Happen to You* (1954). Lemmon said: "Every time I'd deliver my lines, he'd say, 'Less.' After several times of hearing him say 'Less,' I said, 'Mr. Cukor, if you keep it up, I won't be acting at all.' And Cukor said, 'You're beginning to get it, my boy.'" **QUOTE** Although deeply wounded by being removed from one of the greatest pictures of all time, Cukor learned to live with it. Decades after the incident, he called to offer support to another director who was forced off a film. He stated: "I'm phoning to tell you not to worry. It's not going to make the slightest difference to your career. And I should know, because I was the man that was taken off *Gone With the Wind*." Died: 1983.

Rex Harrison 〓 6380 Hollywood

See page 483

Joseph Cotten 🎥 6382 Hollywood

Joseph Cotten

Actor
BORN May 15, 1905, in Petersburg, VA. **SPOTLIGHTS** Cotten made his screen debut in Orson Welles' *Citizen Kane* (1941), the greatest motion picture ever made. He had this to say about it, "Mine was a heady beginning in the movies. We made a classic without knowing it." The tall, thin, curly haired talent was the most enduring, debonair actor of Hollywood's Golden Era. Cotten excelled in work of unobtrusive craftsmanship. He submerged himself into the characters so thoroughly and convincingly that he could play a full range of roles, running the gamut from very good to evil, and make himself completely believable to audiences. His favorite film was Hitchcock's *Shadow of a Doubt* (1943). In the leading role, Cotten gives the performance of his career as the charming, murderous Uncle Charlie, and Hitchcock was extraordinarily gratified by it. Filmed entirely on location in Northern California, with a screenplay co-scripted by Thorton Wilder, Sally Benson and Alma Reville, and based on a true story, this remarkable film is one of the best thrillers of the 1940s. *Shadow of a Doubt* is Hitchcock's quiet film and remains a suspense classic. Cotten's role as the Merry Widow murderer is flawless. Other masterpieces include *The Magnificent Ambersons* (1942), *Duel in the Sun* (1946), *The Farmer's Daughter* (1947), *Portrait of Jenny* (1948), *The Third Man* (1949), and *Touch of Evil* (1958—uncredited as the drunken coroner; see the director's cut which was re-mastered in the late 1990s). Splendid works include *Lydia* (1941), *Gaslight* (1944), *Since You Went Away* (1944), *I'll Be Seeing You* (1944), *Love Letters* (1945), *September Affair* (1950), *The Steel Trap* (1952),

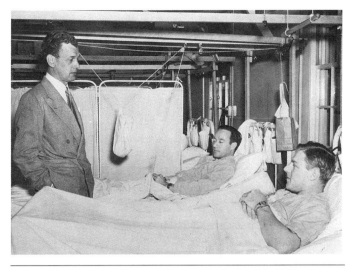

Joseph Cotten visits convalescing GIs during World War II.

Blueprint for Murder (1953), *Hush...Hush, Sweet Charlotte* (1964), and *Soylent Green* (1973). In 1953, he plays Marilyn Monroe's jealous, murderous husband in *Niagara*. His resonant voice and diffident, low-key charm were his trademarks. **HIGHLIGHTS** As a former stage actor, Cotten had been a player in Orson Welles' Mercury Theatre Group since 1937. When Welles landed a contract with RKO studios, to direct, produce, star in and co-script *Citizen Kane*, he reassembled many actors from his Mercury Theatre days, including Cotten, his good friend. The two worked together in several films. **QUOTE** "The whole story's fantastic. Here I am a Virginia ham from little old Petersburg, where I was torn between dramatics and a football career. The ham won out." He loved to travel via his Rolls Royce visiting spots like San Francisco, Palm Springs and even Mexico City. Cotten said, "It's absolutely the cheapest way to get across the country in first-class comfort." Died: 1994.

Pat Buttram 〓 6382 Hollywood

Pat Buttram (center) Johnny Grant (lower left) and Bill Welsh (right) with pals Iron Eyes Cody (upper left), and Gene Autry (standing, with cowboy hat)

Actor, comedian, writer

BORN June 19, 1917, in Addison, AL. **SPOTLIGHTS** One of America's favorite Western sidekicks, he had a unique voice that had been likened to a "angry jackass with a bad sore throat." Buttram was fortunate to appear with his real-life best friend—Gene Autry—in some 40 films. The son of a circuit-riding minister, he started his career in radio's "National Barn Dance," sharing the microphone with Homer & Jethro, Andy Williams, and Red Foley. With his twangy Southern accent, gentle sarcasm and Will Rogers wit, his reputation as a humorist and writer soared. His zany one-liners and funny anecdotes received rave reviews and plenty of laughs. He played the shrew, irritating deal maker, Mr. Haney, in TV's rural comedy "Green Acres." (1965-'71). Died: 1994.

David Niven 🎥   6384 Hollywood

Actor, writer

BORN James David Graham Niven; March 1, 1910, in Kirriemuir, Scotland. **SPOTLIGHTS** A descendent of two generations of professional soldiers, Niven broke the mold. As an actor, he was the world's sophisticated, eloquent, mustached wit. Motion pictures include *Thank You Jeeves* (1936), *Dodsworth* (1936), *The Prisoner of Zenda* (1937), *Bachelor Mother* (1939), *Wuthering Heights* (1939), *Stairway to Heaven* (1946), *The Bishop's Wife* (1947), *Around the World in 80 Days* (1956), *My Man Godfrey* (1957), *Happy Anniversary* (1959), *The Pink Panther* (1964—film series), *The Guns of Navarone* (1961), and *Murder By Death* (1976). This debonair gentleman's trademark was his great style and tongue-in-cheek humor. This urbane talent penned several books, including *The Moon's a Balloon* (1971). (Also see the bio of Greta Garbo in this book.) **ACHIEVEMENTS** 1958 Best Actor Oscar for *Separate Tables*. With delightfully refreshing candor, Niven stated, "I must say I wanted to win and I'm happy I did." His son, David Niven, Jr. is a motion picture and TV producer. **QUOTE** A classic Oscar moment occurred when David Niven was standing at the Academy's podium in 1974. While he was speaking, a male streaker (an entirely nude man) interrupted the ceremony by running across the stage. Nothing could be done to stop the show as it was being telecast live. Niven quickly responded with his usual wit: "Just think, probably the only laugh that man will ever get is for stripping and showing his shortcomings." Died: 1983.

Dick Whittinghill 🎤   6384 Hollywood

Disc jockey, singer

BORN Mar. 5, 1913, in Helena, MT. **SPOTLIGHTS** Formerly one of the Pied Pipers, he became a successful disc jockey in 1950. His quirky sense of humor won him millions of daily listeners, as he instructed them with gems like this: "Everyone on the Hollywood freeway, let's play musical cars. White cars stop. Green cars move a lane right. Japanese cars face the rising sun on the count of three." Nicknamed "sweet Dick," his pen-

chant for practical jokes extended to the former Soviet Union where he tricked authorities into giving him a live, satellite telephone hookup with Alexie Golyenko. Even though he was working at station KIEV, Whittinghill restrained himself from making Chicken Kiev jokes, but got the laughs anyway. His station general manager said, "Nothing of great substance was settled with the Soviets, but we had fun." He gladly paid the $7,000 phone bill when he realized the audience was increased by 25 million. Soviet officials would not have wasted their time had they known his reputation. Riding in a helicopter, he dropped a giant Alka-Seltzer into the Atlantic Ocean after a nerve-gas spill, and placed bagfuls of human hair onto Mount Baldy. His pranks, skits, and interviews made him legendary.

Gene Autry 🎙   6384 Hollywood

See page 428

Jerry Fairbanks 🎥   6384 Hollywood

Producer, director, cameraman

BORN Nov. 1, 1904, in San Francisco, CA. **SPOTLIGHTS** He started as a projectionist in 1919; then became a cameraman in 1924. He won fame for his Universal Studios and Paramount Pictures film shorts. He developed new techniques and equipment, including the dual plane process by which live animals "were made to talk." **ACHIEVEMENTS** 1942 Academy Award for *Unusual Occupations*; 1944 Oscar for *Speaking of Animals*. Died: 1989.

Greta Garbo and Robert Taylor

6400 HOLLYWOOD

Claude Rains 🎥

Actor

Claude Rains

6400 Hollywood

BORN William C. Rains; Nov. 10, 1889, in England. **SPOTLIGHTS** An actor's actor, he was immortalized in *Casablanca* (1942), opposite Humphrey Bogart. This fair-haired, stocky thespian had extensive stage experience and was a highly respected instructor at the Royal Academy of Dramatic Arts. In fact, Charles Laughton was one of his students. In Hollywood, he became one of the cinema's best character actors. His memorable facial features include his perfect mustache and arched eyebrow. The artist's superbly trained voice implemented a clipped accent that littered words with sardonic inflections. Rains excelled in sinister roles. When he played the bad guy, it was the most likable, charming villain the screen had ever seen. He played such a suave scoundrel that he inspired fan mail from the great playwright George Bernard Shaw. Rains received a postcard from him reading: "Dear Mr. Rains: Must you be so so cha-a-rming? G.B.S." Motion pictures include *Mr. Smith Goes to Washington* (1939), *Here Comes Mr. Jordan* (1941), *The Phantom of the Opera* (1943), *Mr. Skeffington* (1944—"no woman is truly beautiful until she is loved"), *Notorious* (1946), *Angel on My Shoulder* (1946), and *Lawrence of Arabia* (1962). Rains never won an Oscar, but he should have. Died: 1967.

Hank Williams 🎵

Singer, guitarist, songwriter

6400 Hollywood

BORN Hiriam Hank Williams; Sept. 17, 1923, in Georgiana, AL. **SPOTLIGHTS** One of the greatest figures in country western music had a rough and rural beginning. His father entered a Veterans Administration Hospital when little Hank was seven years old and basically disappeared from his life. His mother was overbearing and far from feminine. An elderly African-American nicknamed Tee-Tot (real name Rufe Payne) became the boy's unlikely mentor and the one who shaped Williams musical life. Tee-Tot, a singer and musician, taught the youngster chord progression

Hank Williams

on the guitar, bass runs and other fundamentals. Tee-Tot's background was in blues and some light jazz, and he taught the boy phrasing and timing thoroughly. Williams felt so accomplished by their lessons that he never took musical instruction from anyone else. Although rejected the first go-around at the Grand Ole Opry, the sad-looking young Williams would soon enough prove his stuff. At station WSM—and under Wesley Rose's outstanding handling—Williams' wide vocal range, strong, steady singing style, straightforward lyrics, and beautiful melodies changed the country-western music world. When he finally made his Opry debut in June 1949, it was his total conquest. He received half a dozen standing ovations, and immediately became sought-after. Onstage, he exuded warmth and a genuine nature, off-stage, he was shy and moody. And although the artist was bone skinny, while performing he possessed an animal magnetism that women found irresistible. He quickly put together a band—"The Drifting Cowboys"—and the band became an overnight success. He could sing honky-tonk to the blues and make any city slicker enjoy it, but more important than that he was recognized as highly gifted by his own peers and considered a genius songwriter of world-class caliber. His brief career spanned only six years (1946-'52), but left a legacy of great songs—hymns, love ballads, bouncy honky-tonk and novelty—including "Six More Miles To the Graveyard," "When God Comes and Gathers His Jewels," "I Saw the Light," "Mansion On the Hill," "Move It On Over," "Love Sick Blues," "I Can't Help It (If I'm Still in Love With You)" "Your Cheatin' Heart," "I'm So Lonesome I Could Cry," "Hey, Good Lookin'," "Why Don't You Love Me (Like You Used to Do)," "Kaw-Liga," and "Jambalaya (on the Bayou)." **ACHIEVEMENTS** Country's all-time preeminent songwriter. Contemplate his brilliant lyrics that open "I'm So Lonesome I Could Cry": "Hear that lonesome whippoorwill, he sounds too blue to fly...That means he's lost the will to live, I'm so lonesome I could cry." Also Williams was the first to close the gap and effectively link country and pop worlds. His song "Cold, Cold Heart" was purchased by Mitch Miller and recorded by an aspiring pop singer named Tony Bennett. It sold more than a million copies and reached #1 on the pop charts. This forever tore down the barriers between country and pop. He recorded numerous platinum and double platinum albums; these still sell like hot cakes in the new millennium. 1999 Grammy for Best Boxed Recording Package: "The Complete Hank Williams," Jim Kemp and Virginia Team, art directors. 1999 Grammy for Best Historical Album: "The Complete Hank Williams" Colin Escott and Kira Florita, producers. **HIGHLIGHTS** His marriage to Audrey Williams produced one son, singer Hank Williams, Jr. He also had one daughter, singer Jett Williams. She was born on Jan. 6, 1953, five days after her daddy died, but she is the living spitting image of him. On Feb. 8, 1999, Cecil Jackson, a longtime family friend realized his lifelong ambition and opened the Hank Williams Museum, in Montgomery, Alabama. Williams Jr. donated his pop's 1952 blue Cadillac convertible to the collection. The museum's telephone number is (334) 262-3600. E-mail: hankwilliams.museum@cwix.com. **QUOTE** During one recording session Rose suggested that Williams forget about guitar playing and just concentrate on singing. The star responded, "I paid good money for this old box, and I ain't gonna lay it down now." Williams died on New Year's Day, 1953. 25,000 people turned out for his funeral on a cold winter's day.

Marlene Dietrich ♟ 6400 Hollywood

Actress, singer, entertainer

Marlene Dietrich

BORN Maria Magdelene Dietrich; Dec. 27, 1901, in Berlin, Germany. **SPOTLIGHTS** She was the screen's greatest femme fatale. Earlier, when director Josef von Sternberg ordered the well-bred Dietrich to "learn a vulgar song" for her role in *The Blue Angel* (1930), she thought it would destroy her career. Her character was the cheap, tawdry Lola Lola, who strides across a cabaret stage reciting "They call me naughty Lola." She seduces and uses the aging Emil Jannings, then tosses him aside. Her husky, sordid rendition of "Falling in Love Again" is a classic. Contrary to what she feared, the movie made her an international celebrity. Paramount Pictures immediately signed her. She was their competition against MGM's Greta Garbo. That same year, she made *Morocco*, a story about a bewitching chanteuse and the French Foreign Legion, co-starring Adolph Menjou and Gary Cooper. Next she played a Mata-Hari-type spy in *Dishonoured* (1931). For a while, she was cast in those dirty roles which the public loved. One of her more famous bad girl lines is: "It took more than one man to change my name to Shanghai Lily." Her character unashamedly admits this in *Shanghai Express* (1932). *The Devil Is a Woman* (1935) was her personal favorite because she felt she was more beautiful: "than in any other of my whole career." In 1936 *Time* magazine wrote: "she is—the ultimate refinement of a rare and delicate artifact, the distilled essence of a movie actress." Motion pictures include *Blonde Venus* (1932), *Destry Rides Again* (1939), *Seven Sinners* (1940), *Kismet* (1944), *Golden Earrings* (1947), *A Foreign Affair* (1948), *Stage Fright* (1950), *No Highway* (1951), *Witness for the Prosecution* (1958), and *Judgment at Nuremberg* (1961). She narrated the exquisite Oscar-nominated documentary based on her life, Maximilian Schell's *Marlene* (1984). She was also a world-class entertainer in concert and cabarets. **TRENDSETTER** Her gorgeous legs were the shapeliest in the business (although Greta Garbo disputed this, stating she had prettier legs). Yet Dietrich often covered them with slacks—at a time when it simply was not permissible for women to wear slacks. She started a rage that changed American fashion. **ACHIEVEMENTS** The Nazis attempted to recruit her for their propaganda films; she publicly insulted Hitler by refusing. Dietrich became an American citizen and made countless anti-Nazi speeches. She traveled tirelessly to the front to entertain U.S. troops. A war hero, she was awarded the Medal of Freedom for her patriotic service to America. **HIGHLIGHTS** Writer-friend Ernest Hemingway said of her, "Brave, beautiful, loyal, generous...She knows about love and knows that it is a thing which exists or does not exist. I value her opinion more than the professors." Hemingway added, "If she only had her voice, she would break your heart." **QUOTE** During one of her radio shows, listeners tuned in to find out Dietrich's elixir of love. One housewife called in, questioning Dietrich about how to hold onto her man. To that woman and millions of other female listeners, she ordered, "Stop complaining, and do your duty!" This legendary love goddess died in 1992.

Robert Ripley ⌧ 6400 Hollywood

Actor, author, cartoonist, creator

Robert Ripley

BORN LeRoy Ripley; Dec. 25, 1893, in Santa Rosa, CA. **SPOTLIGHTS** Ripley created the newspaper column, "Believe It or Not" in 1918. The popularity of these freakish and fantastic true stories fascinated all of America and led to a dramatic NBC radio show, first heard in 1930. The show flourished with Ripley's abilities to combine statistics with historical and new topical facts to make an interesting story. During WWII, he came up with daily gems about Allied Forces movement. For example, he revealed that a British patrol found themselves trapped in the same valley where the Israelites were surrounded by Philistines 3,000 years ago, and escaped using the same hidden route. Another day Ripley informed the country about an American soldier fighting in the Pacific who just missed being mortally wounded by enemy shrapnel. When the soldier examined the piece of jagged metal, he saw his father's name etched into it! (His father, an airline mechanic at Boeing, had cut his name into his automobile engine in 1929, then later scrapped the car for the war effort. No one ever learned how the Japanese acquired the scrap metal.) Amazing stories like these kept America tuned into his fascinating show. And when our troops stormed North African beaches, "Believe it or not" became one of the GIs' passwords. The program, "Believe It or Not," moved to NBC-TV in 1949, with Ripley as the host. The series had a successful run again from 1982-'86. There are numerous Ripley's "Believe It or Not! odditoriums" worldwide which testify to Ripley's sense of how to entertain us. **STRANGE, BUT TRUE** He collected cars for a hobby, but did not drive...Women desperate to bear children have gone to Ripley's to rub their imported fertility statues made by African witch doctors. Many infertile couples *have* become pregnant after rubbing these primitive "dolls," where expensive, high tech American reproductive medicine had previously failed them—*Believe It or Not!* **SIDELIGHTS** In Hollywood, *Ripley's Believe It of Not!* is located at 6780 Hollywood Boulevard; telephone (323) 466-6335. Ripley died in 1949.

Charles Walters 🎥   6402 Hollywood

Director

BORN Nov. 17, 1911, in Brooklyn, NY. **SPOTLIGHTS** An energetic former dancer and choreographer, he naturally complemented the Rogers-Astaire team, Judy Garland, and Leslie Caron. Movies include *Easter Parade* (1948), *Lili* (1953), and *High Society* (1956). Died: 1982.

John Reed King 🎙   6402 Hollywood

Actor, producer, newscaster

BORN Oct. 25. 1914, in Wilmington, DE. **SPOTLIGHTS** He was radio's glib king of game show hosts. Known for his ability to fast talk with contestants, his popular 1940s-50s quiz shows included "Double or Nothing" with winnings up to $40! "Break the Bank" with $5+ winnings per question, with good contestants breaking the bank with winnings up to $9,000, and "Chance of a Lifetime," a game of probability. King also hosted many playhouse dramatic shows, "Death Valley Days," and narrated Paramount newsreels. **HIGHLIGHTS** Here's one show I think we'd all like to see come back, King's "Go for the House." Winners received household furnishings complete *with* a small house! Died: 1979.

Beatrice Lillie 🎥   6404 Hollywood

Comedienne, vocalist

BORN Also known as "Bea" Lillie. May 29, 1895, in Toronto, Canada. **SPOTLIGHTS** Lillie fell in love with the stage at an early age and set her heart on show business. She took regular singing and "gesture" lessons. Lillie explained, "Through 'gestures,' I learned to express sorrow and joy, birds flying, a bunch of grapes, and farewell to summer." While singing a solo in the church choir, Lillie dramatically used the gestures she had so carefully studied. She had meant her performance to be somber, but the whole congregation burst into convulsions. Lillie grew into an elegant clown of enormous talent. She made her New York stage debut in "Charlot's Revue of 1924," and

Beatrice Lillie with Charles Bickford

was an overnight sensation. Critics heaped praise on her: "I can think of no clown more comical!" And, "she is slim, beautiful, and enormously funny, all at once." Known as "the funniest woman in the world," she made her motion picture debut in *Exit Smiling* (1926). Other movies include *Dr. Rhythm* (1938), *Around the World in 80 Days* (1956), and *Thoroughly Modern Millie* (1967). None of those movies were specifically built around her genius—in that regard she was a little before her time. However, her radiance shines through in glimpses. Affectionately nicknamed "The Toast of Two Continents," she was an adored jet-setter, loved equally by the British— Winston Churchill, Sir Noel Coward, Charlie Chaplin—and the Americans. Lucky theatergoers had a chance to watch her in action throughout several decades, as she appeared in a series of hit Broadway and London shows. In 1952 she starred on Broadway in "An Evening With Beatrice Lillie" to rave reviews. She brought the house down with her singing *There are fairies at the bottom of my garden. Guess who their Queen is? (This will slay you...) It's ME!* Audiences howled at her facial contortions, wild gags, and rowdiness. Amazingly, Lillie handled her comedy with the finesse of a headmistress and that of a witty, elegant sophisticate, which made her all the more funny. She was so popular, in fact, that other actors got jobs impersonating her. In 1957 she appeared—with star billing—in a special 50th anniversary edition of Ziegfeld Follies (for the Shuberts). The following year, she took over the role of "Auntie Mame" from Greer Garson. **RADIO** Crooner Rudy Vallee, who loved to showcase new talent, exposed this bright comic to American radio audiences around 1928. Lillie joined forces with the great Lionel Barrymore for the annual broadcast of Charles Dickens' classic story, "A Christmas Carol." It first aired during three hours in the afternoon on Dec. 25, 1934, and became the all-time favorite Yuletide show. Her own network radio show, was heard first on NBC, then CBS, and was called "The Beatrice Lillie Show" (1935-'37). In 1936, she also worked in two other musical variety shows, "The Flying Red Horse Tavern," and "Folies de Paris." Her autobiography, *Every Other Inch a Lady*, was published in 1972. Died: 1989.

Georgia Gibbs ●   6406 Hollywood

Vocalist, actress

BORN Fredda Gipson; Aug.17,1926, in Worcester, MA. **SPOTLIGHTS** "Her singing nibs, sweet Georgia Gibbs" performed in a fast, up-beat style. She commented, "Down beneath the outer shell, I was terribly unsure of myself, a frightened kid. It was to disguise this that I began to sing loud and with a great deal of energy...these things became associated with me, and when rock 'n' roll came along, I had no trouble at all adjusting to it." She had good reason to be unsure of herself. After her father died when she was one, she was placed in an orphanage. Nobody adopted her, but at age eight she was returned to her mother. Three years later, she was singing for money (she earned $2.35 a session), and at age 13 she began touring the country with bands. "It was tough," she said, "but good training. Above all it gave me confidence. That's something I needed." By her late teens, she had fine-tuned her vocal instrument. She sang with various bands including Tommy Dorsey (at the same time Bing Crosby was the male vocalist), the Hudson-DeLange Orchestra, and with Artie Shaw's swing-era band. In 1945, she landed a radio job as a vocalist on "The Jimmy Durante Show," then became a recording star. She became a frequent guest on radio, TV and clubs. Among her hits are "Tweedle-Dee," "Kiss of Fire," "If We Never Meet Again," and "The Hula Hoop Song." She also successful covered Etta James' hit, "Dance with Me, Henry."

Ginny Simms 📻   6408 Hollywood

Singer, actress

Ginny Simms

BORN Virginia Simms, May 25, 1916, in San Antonio, TX. **SPOTLIGHTS** A popular vocalist of the late 1930s and 1940s, at age 21 the gorgeous brunette joined Kay Kyser's popular big band, gaining immediate fame as his lead singer. A true stunner, she followed Kyser to Hollywood and easily made the transition to film: *That's Right, You're Wrong* (1939), *Playmates* (1941), *Here We Go Again* (1942), *Shady Lady* (1945), and *Night and Day* (1946). Her Hit Parade songs, such as "Don't Ever Change" established her network radio program, "The Ginny Sims Show" variety (CBS, 1945). Other hits: "What Is This Thing Called Love?" and "Just One of Those Things." **ACHIEVEMENTS** With Kyser's orchestra, she sang in 580 service installations at military camps and hospitals during WWII. Died: 1994.

Alma Rubens 🎥   6408 Hollywood

Actress

BORN Alma Smith; Feb. 8, 1897, in San Francisco, CA. **SPOTLIGHTS** Immortalized in D.W. Griffith's *Intolerance* (1916), the beauty appears in dozens of silents: *The Price She Paid* (1924), *The Heart of Salome* (1927), *The Masks of the Devil* (1928), and *Show Boat* (1928). Died: 1931.

Cecil Brown 📻   6410 Hollywood

Commentator, newscaster

Cecil Brown

BORN Sept. 14, 1907, in New Brighton, PA. **SPOTLIGHTS** A noted war correspondent, he began free-lancing in Europe in 1937. Then, he was hired by CBS in Jan. 1940. Renowned for his brash, anti-Fascist stance before WWII's outbreak, his radio comments from Rome characterized the buildup of troops as "a comic-opera army preparing for slaughter under orders of a *Duce* with a titanic contempt for his own people." Brown was promptly banned from the country's airwaves, then expelled by Benito Mussolini's Italian government. Brown's boss, Edward R. Murrow, headed up CBS' European bureau during WWII, where they broadcast from London, England. Like Murrow, Brown was incredibly brave. He went directly into combat action to report. One day after the bombing of Pearl Harbor (Dec. 8, 1941), he boarded the Repulse to check out rumors of supplies being run to Japan by way of Malaya. The ship was bombed in the South China Sea. Only Brown and a few crewmen survived the sinking. He filed a graphic account of the sinking of the British battle cruiser. This dedicated newsman and patriotic American continued to put his life at great personal risk—including being captured by the Germans—to report key military moves from various fronts from Yugoslavia to North Africa. On Java, he described an unrelenting Japanese bomb attack as "glistening like raindrops in the sun." After the war, he worked a CBS post in Washington. During the 1950s, Brown served as president of the Overseas Press Club, and covered the Korean War. He was also a news commentator in radio's Mutual network. He switched to NBC in 1958 to become their Far East Bureau Chief. The following decade, he worked as the highly respected, critical commentator and director of news and public affairs at KCET, the public broadcasting station in Los Angeles, California. As a scholar, he taught English at California State Polytechnic University. In 1980, he was named outstanding professor of the year. **ACHIEVEMENTS** Brown was honored with the prestigious George Foster Peabody Award for journalistic excellence. He was the recipient of countless broadcasting awards and "best reporter" tributes. His adventures were detailed in his book, *Suez to Singapore* (1942). Died: 1987.

Edwin F. Goldman 6410 Hollywood

Composer, band leader, author

BORN Edwin Franko Goldman; Jan. 1, 1878, in Louisville, KY. **SPOTLIGHTS** At age 17, he joined the Metropolitan Opera orchestra. Considered the successor to John Philip Sousa (see his bio in this book), Goldman was both enthusiastic and very talented. The Edwin Franko Goldman Band was a lively, big brass band renowned for its musicianship. Praised as "a symphony orchestra in brass," it also had a lot of heart. With the assist of a Guggenheim grant, he provided free summer concerts in New York's Central Park. These performances, and others in the surrounding area, were broadcast on network radio throughout America. He also became musical director of radio's "Cities Service Concerts" in 1927. Goldman wrote the book, *The Foundation to Cornet Playing*. He recorded many instrumental works, including *Sans Souci* and *The Chimes of Liberty*. Goldman combined his work ethic with his passion for music. He never missed a summer performance in Central Park, from 1918 until 1955, when he fell ill. Died: 1956.

Tex Williams 6412 Hollywood

Actor, singer, songwriter

BORN Sol Williams; Aug. 23, 1917, in Fayette County, IL. **SPOTLIGHTS** A country-and-western recording star, he played guitar, banjo, and harmonica, with his band, the Western Caravan. Featured prominently on "The Grand Ole Opry," he was extremely popular in radio and TV from 1950-'65. His hit singles include "The Rose of the Alamo," "California Polka," and "Texas in My Soul." Died: 1985.

Lewis J. Selznick 6412 Hollywood

Film mogul

BORN L. Zeleznik; May 2, 1870, in Russia. **SPOTLIGHTS** Born poverty-stricken, one of 18 children, he apprenticed in his youth, then worked in a factory in England. He saved enough to sail to the U.S., in steerage. But once here, he began to fulfill the American dream. Eventually, he founded the Selznick Company with the slogan: "Selznick Pictures Make Happy Hours." He became one of Hollywood's earliest motion picture tycoons and was a key figure in the early Twenties. **HIGHLIGHTS** Father of three sons--Myron, David, and Howard--he taught his children everything he knew about the movie business, from basics to editing, from marketing to selling. Myron became Hollywood's first fierce powerhouse theatrical agent; his motto was: "Stars should get as much money as they can, while they can. They don't last long." Son David produced *Gone With the Wind*. **QUOTE** Lewis J. Selznick once testified before Congress, "Less brains are necessary in the motion picture business than in any other." Died: 1933.

Walter Pidgeon 6412 Hollywood

Walter Pidgeon

Actor, singer

BORN Sept. 23, 1897, in East St. John, New Brunswick, Canada. **SPOTLIGHTS** A deep-voiced baritone, he attended the New England Conservatory of Music. While singing at a friend's elegant party, another guest named Fred Astaire asked him, "Why don't you get on the stage?" Pidgeon responded, "Why don't you put me on the stage?" Astaire did, which led to his first contract. After he appeared at the Palace Theater in the revue "Puzzles of 1925," the *Daily Variety* (the industry trade paper) wrote a scathing review of his performance: "Walter Pidgeon looks like an old and stale Abe Lincoln and sings like the graduate of a southern Iowa correspondence school. Who wants vaudeville—when it involves that?" Pidgeon persevered, ignoring the devastating criticism. The tall, blue-eyed, dark-haired Pidgeon made his screen debut in *The Mannequin* (1926). He became one of Hollywood's most reliable actors in nearly 100 films. Movies include *Saratoga* (1937—Jean Harlow's last film), *The Shopworn Angel* (1938), *Too Hot to Handle* (1938), *Dark Command* (1940), *Blossoms in the Dust* (1941), *Man Hunt* (1941), *How Green Was My Valley* (1941), *Mrs. Miniver* (1942, opposite Greer Garson—he played her husband in a number of MGM hits), *Madame Curie* (1943), *Command Decision* (1948), *The Bad and the Beautiful* (1952), *Executive Suite* (1954), *The Rack* (1956—adapted from Rod Serling's TV play), *Voyage to the Bottom of the Sea* (1961), *Advise and Consent* (1962), and *Funny Girl* (1968—as Florenz Ziegfeld). He scored many triumphs on Broadway, including "The Happiest Millionaire," and "Take Me Along." **SIDELIGHTS** When he discussed getting a stage name, he was discouraged to do so by vaudeville star Elsie Janis. About his real name, she said, "It's so funny, people will remember it." Died: 1984.

Edward R. Murrow 6412 Hollywood

See page 191

Louella O. Parsons 6418 Hollywood

Columnist

BORN Louella Oettinger; Aug. 6, 1881, in Freeport, IL. **SPOTLIGHTS** She was known as the most celebrated writer of "the long parade of Movie Stars." She was called "the most powerful woman in Hollywood." Celebrities courted her, studio giants befriended her, all respected and feared her. Personalities spoke cautiously around her lest she decide to turn her poison

Louella O. Parsons

pen on them. Although she once confessed that she had buried more scandals than printed, she could just as easily turn an aspiring actor/actress into a superstar, or destroy a full-fledged star overnight with her acid-tainted comments. About her writing style, which tended to be "chatty," Parsons declared, "I have been too busy to build any false illusions about my literary talents. If I have any particular style, it is a form of 'chatting' with my readers about the best-known glamour personalities in the world." The people loved her style. More than 37 million readers of William Randolph Hearst's 22 daily newspapers relished her Tinseltown scoops. Parsons also had tens of millions of devoted listeners tuning into her daily network radio show: "Hollywood Reporter" (1945-'51). Prior to that, she had the first coast-to-coast entertainment news program to originate from Hollywood; she started hosting the show in 1928. She dished exclusives; if a star was pregnant, Parsons usually heard from the doctor's office *before* the star herself knew. If an actor threw a temper tantrum on the set, the phone lines were burning simultaneously. If a marriage was in trouble, she added gasoline to the flames. Overall, most stars were grateful for the tremendous boost she gave to their careers. **SIDELIGHTS** Her arch enemy was gossip columnist, Hedda Hopper, who fought her everyday for the inside skinny—the latest scoop—on each juicy Tinseltown morsel. **HIGHLIGHTS** Parsons has two stars on the Walk of Fame; the other is in radio. She founded the Hollywood Women's Press Club in 1928. This is one of the oldest and most respected organizations in Hollywood. Friends called her "Lolly." **QUOTE** "The first person I ever cared deeply and sincerely about was--myself." Died: 1972.

Andy Griffith 📺   6418 Hollywood

Actor, singer

BORN June 1, 1926, in Mount Airy, NC. **SPOTLIGHTS** America's homespun hero was a former music teacher, who performed in civic clubs on the side. Doing a church act, he played a preacher who delighted audiences with such gems as: "The person putting frogs in the baptismal font ought to cut it out 'cause everybody is gettin' warts!" Griffith recorded "What It Was—Was Football," which sold well regionally. He progressed to a nightclub act, then made his TV debut in the "The Ed Sullivan Show." With his wry wit, Southern twang, and easy delivery he was a natural for celebrity. In 1955 Griffith made his Broadway debut in "No Time for Sergeants," playing an illiterate hillbilly inductee. Seeing his stunning performance, Hollywood called. He made his silver screen debut in Elia Kazan's drama, *A Face in the Crowd* (1957). Griffith's

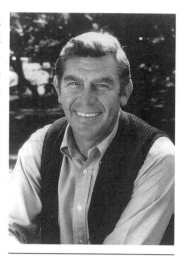

Andy Griffith

remarkable performance as a country bumpkin handpicked to rise to fame, impressed critics and fans alike. Next, he reprised his excellent stage role for film in *No Time for Sergeants* (1958). Griffith headed back to the Great White Way for the musical comedy "Destry." He was hilarious in the show, which also marked his 33rd birthday. When asked what he wanted for a present, Griffith offered an un-celebrity response: "A tractor." He received the rather large gift. Hollywood called again. Other motion pictures include *Onionhead* (1958), *The Second Time Around* (1961), *Angel in My Pocket* (1969), and *Spy Hard* (1996). Even with these spectacular achievements, he was immortalized as Mayberry's Sheriff Andy Taylor in TV's "The Andy Griffith Show" (1960-'68). What made the show so special was Griffith's insistence that each episode have a moral or spiritual lesson to it. *Never* preachy, the messages were cloaked in Southern humor and good ol' American common sense. With its folksy philosophy, homespun wit, and kindhearted people, the gentle sheriff guided the way. This clever, funny series is a national treasure and is still seen daily in syndication. As a bonus, viewers can enjoy watching a young Ron Howard play Opie Taylor; the fine character actress Frances Bavier play the lovable Aunt Bee Taylor; and Don Knotts play the skittish, inept deputy sheriff Barney Fife; among a cast of other accomplished veteran actors. "The Andy Griffith Show" remains one of the few acceptable, decent family shows in television. It is a time capsule of American family, moral and cultural values from the 1930s up to the Vietnam War. Griffith made many other popular television works, including the legal drama "Matlock" (1986-'95). Griffith is an icon of unbelievable stature and respect. His album of gospel songs, *I Love to Tell the Story*, was rated one of the nation's 200 top-selling albums of 1996. A few years later, he was nominated for a Grammy for *Just As I Am.*

Robert Donat 🎥   6418 Hollywood

Actor

BORN March 18, 1905, in England. **SPOTLIGHTS** In order to correct his stuttering, Donat read Shakespeare aloud *everyday* as a child. Not only did these efforts turn him into an eloquent speaker with a beautiful speaking voice, but they also led to a role in "Julius Caesar." Other distinguished classical parts followed, as he learned his craft and became a polished actor. Tall, handsome and possessing a quiet charm, the somewhat shy Donat was never really comfortable with being a movie star. He preferred acting on the stage, but left a legacy of wonderful movies. Donat was excellent in the original version of Hitchcock's *The 39 Steps* (1935). Other motion pictures include *The Private Life of Henry VIII* (1933), *The Count of Monte Cristo* (1934), *The Ghost Goes West* (1935), *The Young Mr. Pitt* (1942), *Perfect Strangers* (1945), *The Winslow Boy* (1949), and *Lease of Life* (1954). He co-stars with Ingrid Bergman in inspiring drama, *The Inn of the Sixth Happiness* (1958), in his final film appearance. Even though he had been hampered by ill health (he suffered throughout his life from chronic asthma), he gave an impeccable performance as a Chinese Mandarin. His last words on-screen were uttered truthfully: "We shall not see each other again, I think. Farewell." He died shortly thereafter. Actor Charles Laughton praised Donat as, "the most graceful actor of our time." **ACHIEVEMENTS** 1939 Best Actor Oscar for *Goodbye Mr. Chips*. Died: 1958.

Helen Traubel 🎙 6420 Hollywood

Opera singer, actress
BORN June 20, 1899, in St. Louis, MO. **SPOTLIGHTS** A powerful dramatic, queen-sized soprano, Traubel made her Metropolitan Opera debut in 1937. When she and Rudolf Bing, general manager of the Met, disagreed over the prima

Helen Traubel

donna's extracurricular nightclub appearances in 1953, she left the Met. Traubel stated, "Mr. Bing and I parted gentle enemies." A fine Wagnerian soprano, she contributed many excellent recordings: *Gotterdammerung* (Victor) and *Die Walkure* (Columbia). Her two most unusual recordings: "A Real Piano Player," and "The Song's Gotta Come from the Heart," a duet with Jimmy Durante! **SIDELIGHTS** Her hobby? She wrote detective stories: *The Metropolitan Opera Murders*. Died: 1972.

Richard Brooks 🎥 6422 Hollywood

Screenwriter, director
BORN May 18, 1912, in Philadelphia, PA. **SPOTLIGHTS** He excelled in adapting great literary works for the screen, and was equally talented with directing them. *The Blackboard Jungle* (1955--adapted from Evan Hunter's book), is a tale of hoodlum students, and featured the first rock 'n' roll music in a motion picture (Bill Haley's "Rock Around the Clock"). It is generally considered his breakthrough film, in which he was Oscar-nominated as the writer. Other fine pictures include *Cat on a Hot Tin Roof* (1958--based on the original Tennessee Williams' play; he was Oscar-nominated as director and co-

writer); *The Brothers Karamazov* (1958--from Fyodor Dostpyevsky's work); *Sweet Bird of Youth* (1962--based on Tennessee Williams' classic play); *The Professionals* (1966--he was Oscar-nominated as director and writer); and *In Cold Blood* (1967--adapted from Truman Capote's book; he was Oscar-nominated as director and writer). **ACHIEVEMENTS** 1960 Academy Award, Best Screenplay for *Elmer Gantry* (adapted from a Sinclair Lewis novel). Died: 1992.

Adela Rogers St. John 🎥 6424 Hollywood

Journalist, author, screenwriter
BORN May 20, 1894, in Los Angeles, CA. **SPOTLIGHTS** She was a pioneer writer in films, sports and news. Since filmmaking was not deemed a serious business when it started, women writers were welcomed with open doors—and no glass ceilings. In fact, half of all movies made up to 1925 were written by women—and a number of them were by the highly paid, highly respected St. John herself. With her clever screenplays, St. John made movie stars out of ordinary mortals. Clark Gable sang her praises with her brilliant script, *A Free Soul* (1931), in which he stars. She co-wrote "What Price Hollywood" with David O. Selznick. Selznick's movie, *A Star is Born* (1937), was based partly on that story. She was the first woman sportswriter, with gems like: "Babe Ruth punted it over the fence." She also covered the Dempsey-Tunney boxing match. She retired from Hollywood to concentrate on plays and novels. Her 1962 best-seller, *Final Verdict*, was about about her father. **ACHIEVEMENTS** Called the "First Lady of American Letters," she was awarded the Medal of Freedom. She received her Hollywood High School diploma in 1951 (41 years after her class had graduated). The principal took into account her many literary accomplishments to make up for the few credits she lacked (she had flunked math). She later taught journalism at UCLA. Died: 1988.

Wesley Ruggles 🎥 6424 Hollywood

Director
BORN June 11, 1889, in Los Angeles, CA. **SPOTLIGHTS** He joined his brother Charles Ruggles as a comedy player in early silents. He became a Keystone Kop, then got work with the brilliant Charlie Chaplin. He directed Mae West, who got away with some of her best lines in Ruggles' *I'm No Angel* (1933). It took the devil's debt off Paramount's back, too. In 1934 he directed George Raft, Carole Lombard and fan dancer Sally Rand in *Bolero*. In 1935 Ruggles showed he knew a thing or two about romance in *The Gilded Lily*. In 1940 he directed Jean Arthur and Fred MacMurray in the comedy *Too Many Husbands*. **ACHIEVEMENTS** His early work *Cimarron* (1931) was the first Western to win a Best Picture Oscar. It would take Clint Eastwood's *Unforgiven* (1992) for a Western to win that honor again. Died: 1972.

Clyde McCoy 🎙 6428 Hollywood

Musician
BORN Dec. 29, 1903, in Ashland, KY. **SPOTLIGHTS** As a youth, he performed on river boats. He formed own band at age 16, and audiences loved his Dixieland style. Hit recordings include "Sugar Blues" and "Way Down Yonder in New Orleans." His career spanned decades.

Ed Wynn   6428 Hollywood

See page 328

George O'Hanlon   6428 Hollywood

Actor, writer
BORN Nov. 23, 1917, in Brooklyn, NY. **SPOTLIGHTS** He started in the 1930s as a chorus boy in Warner Bros. musicals. Star of 60 comedy shorts and dozens of TV roles. Died: 1989.

Mitzi Green   6430 Hollywood

Actress
BORN Elizabeth Keno; Oct. 22, 1920, in Bronx, NY. **SPOTLIGHTS** With golden brown hair and large, green eyes she first appeared on stage in her parents' vaudeville act. She imitated popular celebrities of the day, and within one year was working at the Palace on Broadway—the best venue of them all. The darling girl with a "Buster Brown bowl" haircut was discovered by a movie scout while visiting fellow child actor, Jackie Coogan, in Los Angeles. "Little Mitzi" was cast as a holy terror, and played such a terrific brat that Paramount Pictures signed her to a contract—their first multi-picture deal *ever* for a child. From age nine to 13, she appears in *Santa Fe Trail* and *Tom Sawyer* (both 1930), *Skippy*, and *Huckleberry Finn* (both 1931), and *Little Orphan Annie* (1932). Died: 1969.

Arlene Francis   6434 Hollywood

Actress
BORN Arline Francis Kazanjian; Oct. 20, 1912, in Boston, MA. **SPOTLIGHTS** For years, Francis worked in a number of small radio roles. She commented, "There isn't a soap opera on that at one time or another I wasn't in." She gained nationwide fame as the ad-lib hostess of her interview show "Blind Date." First heard via radio, it sold to television. Her tremendous quick wit and humor in that program led to her getting hired in the job of a lifetime that same year. Francis became a panelist on "What's My Line?" (1950-'65), TV's most famous, prestigious, and popular panel

Arlene Francis

show. She once let slip, "Oh, my God!" Then quickly covered herself by adding, "Oh, my God, I can't say 'Oh, my God' over the air!" (Also see the bio of Beverly Sills in this book.) **QUOTE** "Work is the only thing that replenishes me. Vacations mean nothing. If I have four days when I'm not doing anything I always think I'd better scrub the floors."

John Hart   6434 Hollywood

Actor, producer, director
BORN Los Angeles, CA. **SPOTLIGHTS** He made his silver screen debut in *Buccaneer* (1937). Then, in "Hawkeye and the Last of the Mohicans" Hart had TV's starring role as frontier scout Nat Cutler. Lon Chaney, Jr. was his sidekick, Chingachgook. He moved behind the scenes to shoot Celebrity International Tours. **SIDELIGHTS** He studied drama at Pasadena High with William Holden.

Ernest Gold   6434 Hollywood

Composer, conductor
BORN July 13, 1921, in Vienna. **SPOTLIGHTS** Film scores include *Judgment at Nuremberg* (1961) and *Fun with Dick and Jane* (1976). **ACHIEVEMENTS** 1960 Oscar for *Exodus*; 1960 two Grammys for "It's a Mad Mad Mad Mad World" (song of the year and soundtrack).

Ben Alexander   6434 Hollywood

Actor

Ben Alexander

BORN Nicholas Alexander; May 26, 1911, in Goldfield, NV. **SPOTLIGHTS** His long and illustrious career began as a child actor working with two giant directors of the silent era: D.W. Griffith and Cecil B. DeMille. He made dozens of films, including co-starring with Lillian Gish in *Hearts of the World* (1918). Other movies include *All Quiet on the Western Front* (1930), and *Dragnet* (1954). He co-starred in the TV series "Dragnet" (1953-59) as the heavy, Officer Frank Smith. "The stories you are about to hear are true...Dum-de-dum-dum." He starred in TV's "Felony Squad." Died: 1969.

Lucille Ball   6438 Hollywood

See page 231

Cantinflas   6438 Hollywood

Actor
BORN Mario Moreno Reyes; Aug. 12, 1911, in Mexico City, Mexico. **SPOTLIGHTS** Born during the height of the Mexican Revolution into utter poverty, this beloved comedian became Latin America's most celebrated actor. He made only two movies in the U.S., one is the must-see *Around the World in 80 Days* (1956) in the role of Passepartout, the bumbling, hapless valet of Phineas Fogg (played by David Niven). An

Cantinflas

all-star cameo cast of 44 joined them on their hilarious journey. He also stars as *Pepe* (1960)—a dud that unfortunately had him running south of the border for more reliable scripts. In his native country, he made scores of hilarious movies. His films are still seen daily in international syndication. Each generation who sees his work admires this incredible and funny talent. **ACHIEVEMENTS** Charlie Chaplin called him "the world's greatest comedian." His favorite thing to do with his abundance of money was to build houses for the underprivileged. Throughout his professional life he helped the poor. **SIDELIGHTS** The name "Cantinflas" was invented. This beloved talent died: 1993.

Tony Martin 🎥 6438 Hollywood

Singer, actor, musician
BORN Alvin Morris; Dec. 25, 1913, in San Francisco, CA. **SPOTLIGHTS** *Sing Baby Sing* (1936), and boy, could he! Singing in the popular styles of Bing Crosby and Perry Como, Martin became famous on radio, recording, television and motion pictures. Other films

Tony Martin

include *Ziegfeld Girl* (1941), *Till the Clouds Roll By* (1947), *Casbah* (1948), and *Hit the Deck* (1955), among others. Previously he had been discovered while playing—clarinet and saxophone—and singing at the Chicago World's Fair. Hit songs include "I'll See You in My Dreams," "I Get Ideas," and "There's No Tomorrow." Albums: *Tony Martin at the Plaza*, *This Is the Decade of the 30s*. He's married to the beautiful actress-dancer Cyd Charisse. **QUOTE** About his million-selling records he said, "They helped build my swimming pool."

Chicago 💿 6438 Hollywood

Chicago

Rock band
FORMED 1967, Chicago, Illinois. Terry Kath (born: Jan. 31, 1946, Chicago/died: 1978) guitar. voc.; Peter Cetera (Sept. 13, 1944) bass, voc; Robert Lamm (Oct. 13, 1944, Brooklyn, NY) keyboards, voc.; Walter Parazaider (Mar. 14, 1945, Chicago) saxes, clarinet; Danny Seraphine (Aug. 28, 1948, Chicago) drums; James Pankow (Aug. 20, 1947, Chicago) trombone; Lee Loughnane (Oct. 21, 1946, Chicago) trumpet. Also Donnie Dacus, Jason Scheff—son of longtime Elvis Presley bassist Jerry Scheff, Bill Champlin, Dawayne Bailey, and Tris Imboden. **SPOTLIGHTS** This legendary Windy City band blew in big time with a blazing horn section going on to record more than 20 albums. The group's members come from all musical backgrounds, and are well versed in classical and jazz. They blended a fusion of rock, jazz, R&B and horns, with great song writing. It was a milestone in music. 1970s and '80s hits include "Saturday in the Park," "Feeling Stronger Every Day," "Wishing You Were Here." "Hard to Say I'm Sorry," "You're the Inspiration," "Hard Habit to Break," and "Look Away." In 1998 Chicago released two hit albums: *The Heart of Chicago 1967-1998 Volume II*, and their first holiday collection, *Chicago 25—The Christmas Album*. Still rockin' together more than 33 years down the road, they have had 20 Top Ten hits, 20 gold and platinum albums., and sold 120 million albums. Their Hollywood Walk of Fame star was dedicated on July 23, 1992.

Lou Costello 🎥 6438 Hollywood

Comedian
BORN Louis Cristillo; March 6, 1906, in Patterson, NJ. **SPOTLIGHTS** A huge film star who, along with his sidekick Bud Abbott, personified the last surviving breath of the glory that was vaudeville. The fact that this great vaudeville talent successfully translated his theatrical antics to radio, film and television is magic in itself. In 1931 the short, cherubic comic Costello teamed with the tall, lean, stony Bud Abbott, who played the straight man. Known as Abbott and Costello they

Lou Costello (right) & Bud Abbott

achieved top billing in vaudeville and burlesque, then got their first break on Kate Smith's radio show. After an initial ho-hum film *One Night in the Tropics* (1940), they hit gold with *Buck Privates* (1941). They shined with scripts that incorporated their stage routines. Abbott and Costello were Universal Studio's biggest moneymaking comedy team during the 1940s and early '50s. Although the team admitted that "no joke we use is less than 10 years old" (and they were referring to vaudeville!), their pantomime, horseplay, spoofing, and funny slapstick kept audiences in stitches. The double-talking comedy team kept their tried-and-true acts in a number of formula films—which is what the audience wanted. It kept them in the top-ten box-office winners for more than a decade. Motion pictures include *Keep 'em Flying* (1941), *Pardon My Sarong* (1942), *Who Done It?* (1942), *Abbott and Costello Meet Frankenstein* (1948), *Mexican Hayride* (1948), and *Abbott and Costello Meet The Invisible Man* (1951). **HIGHLIGHTS** Their famous, hilarious baseball routine, "Who's on First?" always brought the house down. The gold recording of it has been placed in a position of honor—on permanent display—in the National Baseball Hall of Fame, in Cooperstown, New York...An energized spark plug, the chubby comedian's antics made him the favorite of the team. He received a 60-percent split of the cut. Abbott and Costello had a successful TV series from 1951-'53. The two split—after years of escalating friction—in July 1957. About their breakup Costello said, "I was tired of being slapped." Abbott remarked, "The comedian always wants to go alone, not the straight man." **FOR ABBOTT & COSTELLO GIFT INFO** visit the website: www.city-net.com/abbottandcostellofc. This talented comedian died in 1959, of a heart attack just a few days shy of his 51st birthday.

Richard Pryor   6438 Hollywood

Actor, comedian, writer

BORN Dec. 1, 1940, in Peoria, IL. **SPOTLIGHTS** This worldly-wise observer of social and ethnic divisions is universally recognized as the man who revolutionized stand-up comedy. He grew up in the '40s around his grandfather's billiard parlor, an endless source of inspiration for his amazing cast of characters.

Richard Pryor

With his bold, acerbic wit, he burst on the national scene in the 1960s with his great talent and unique point of view. His film career took off after playing the piano player in *Lady Sings The Blues* (1972), starring Diana Ross. Dozens of dramatic and comedic roles followed. Motion pictures include *Uptown Saturday Night* (1974) starring Sidney Poitier and Bill Cosby, *The Bingo Long Traveling All-Stars and Motor Kings*, *Car Wash* with George Carlin, *Silver Streak* opposite Gene Wilder (all 1976), *Blue Collar* with Harvey Keitel, *The Wiz*, *California Suite* (all 1978), *The Muppet Movie* (1979), *Bustin' Loose* (1981--also co-prod. and story), *Some Kind of Hero*, *The Toy* (both 1982), *Brewster's Millions* (1985), *Jo Jo Dancer—Your Life Is Calling* (1986) opposite Debbie Allen (he also co-wrote, directed and produced the picture), *Harlem Nights* (1987), *Look Who's Talking Two* (1990--voiceover) and *Another You* (1991). He co-wrote the hilarious Western spoof, *Blazing Saddles* (1974) with Mel Brooks. He wrote TV comedy scripts for "Sanford and Son" and "The Flip Wilson Show." Major concert appearances. **ACHIEVEMENTS** Three Grammys; seven platinum albums; an Emmy; and a Lifetime Achievement Honor by the American Comedy Awards.

Irene Dunne   6440 Hollywood

Actress, singer

Irene Dunne and Charles Coburn

BORN Dec. 20, 1898, in Louisville, KY. **SPOTLIGHTS** Dubbed "Dunne the Duchess" for her regal bearing and her ladylike manners, she started her career with hopes of singing at the Metropolitan Opera. Instead, all she was offered was a chorus girl job in the "Ziegfeld Follies." That job came about when showman Florenz Ziegfeld discovered her in an elevator. Dunne remarked, "I was wearing this floppy blue hat. It was kind of a picture hat and the inside brim was hand-painted. After Mr. Ziegfeld offered me a job in the chorus line, I politely declined. I told him I was a serious singer. He remembered me, and later offered me the role of Magnolia in the road company stage production of 'Show Boat.'" RKO spotted Dunne in it. The studio signed the lovely enchantress and cast her in their military musical, *Leathernecking* (1930). She followed with *Cimarron* (1931), in her first starring role and received an Oscar nomination. She was spectacularly good in weepies, including *Back Street* (1932), *Magnificent Obsession* (1935) and *Love Affair* (1939--in an Oscar-nominated performance). While proving herself a capable actress in tearjerkers, she did the same in comedies: *Theodora Goes Wild* (1936--in an Oscar-nominated performance), *The Awful Truth* (1937), and *My Favorite Wife* (1940). Among her 48 fine motion pictures credits are *Show Boat* (1936) and *The White Cliffs of Dover* (1937). Dunne appears in the original, non-musical version of *Anna and the King of Siam* (1946) opposite Rex Harrison. She gave luminous performances in *Life with Father* (1947) and *I Remember Mama* (1948--in an Oscar-nominated performance). She enjoyed a sparkling reputation as the most charming, unaffected, best-rehearsed Hollywood actress. **QUOTE** "I guess I'll go on acting until I'm old and feeble and nobody wants to look at me anymore." But Dunne changed her mind and retired from films to work in the United Nations General Assembly. She observed, "No play or motion picture I was ever in had as much drama." Died: 1990.

Robert Montgomery 🎥 6440 Hollywood

Actor, producer, director
BORN Henry Montgomery, Jr.; May 21, 1904, in Beacon, NY.
SPOTLIGHTS A suave, handsome, leading man of the 1930s and '40s, he was equally convincing in light comedies, or heavy dramas--when allowed to do so by his studio, MGM. Movies include *The Big House* (1930), *Inspiration* (1931), *The Mystery of Mr. X* (1934), *Vanessa: Her Love Story* (1935), *Night Must Fall* (1937--in an Oscar-nominated performance), *Earl of Chicago* (1940), *Mr. and Mrs. Smith* (1941), *Here Comes Mr. Jordan* (1941--in an Oscar-nominated performance), *They Were Expendable* (1945--he also filled in as director when John Ford fell ill), and *June Bride* (1948). Using an innovative approach, his first

Robert Montgomery

credited directorial effort was *The Lady in the Lake* (1949--also acted), which he successfully adapted from a Raymond Chandler mystery thriller and uniquely told in first person. As director-actor he did: *Ride the Pink Horse* (1947), *Once More My Darling* (1949), *Your Witness* (1950), and *The Gallant Hours* (1960). **TV** He was the father of actress Elizabeth Montgomery (born April 15, 1933) who played Samantha on "Bewitched." The two earlier appeared on "Robert Montgomery Presents" dramatic anthology (1950-'57). **ACHIEVEMENTS** He was first elected to the Screen Actors Guild's president in 1935, then served four terms...He had a distinguished military record. During World War II, he was commissioned a lieutenant in the U.S. Naval Reserve. He served as an attaché at the Embassy in London, set up naval operations in the White House, served on Guadalcanal, commanded a PT boat in the Pacific, and was an operations officer on a destroyer during the D-Day invasion of France. Awarded the Bronze Star, he was also decorated as a Chevalier of the French Legion of Honor. He was honorably discharged with the rank of commander...As a Broadway director, he won a Tony Award for "The Desperate Hours." **QUOTE** When his actress-daughter Elizabeth was just starting out in the business, he said, "If you achieve success, you will get applause, and if you get applause, you will hear it. My advice to you concerning applause is this: Enjoy it, but never quite believe it." Robert died in 1981; daughter Elizabeth died in 1995.

Ginger Rogers lends a hand to the war effort in 1944.

Walk of Fame Honorees (from left to right):

Virginia Field, Mitchell Leisen, Betty Hutton and Edith Head

6500 HOLLYWOOD

Dale Robertson 🎥   6500 Hollywood

Dale Robertson

Actor

BORN Dayle Robertson; July 14, 1923, in Oklahoma City, OK. **SPOTLIGHTS** Born and bred in the heartland, this tall, dark and handsome former schoolteacher filled the bill of popular Westerns. He usually depicted—in both motion pictures and TV—the moral pacing of a bygone era, portraying the slice of Americana many dream of recapturing. Robertson appears in *City of Bad Men* (1953), an unusual Western with a boxing twist. He is excellent in *A Day of Fury* (1956)—an oater with a psychological twist. As Jim Hardie, he was the faithful employee and adventurer on TV's "Tales of Wells Fargo" (1957-'62). He played Ben Calhoun, owner of a railroad, in TV's "The Iron Horse" (1966-'68), which captured the spirit of Western expansion in the United States.

Jack Lescoulie 📺   6500 Hollywood

Announcer, host

BORN Nov. 17, 1912, in Sacramento. CA. **SPOTLIGHTS** He was a breakthrough announcer during the Golden Era of Live Television. A "Today" show pioneer, he played second banana to Dave Garroway. He stated, "Since 'Today' was designed to be a television 'newspaper,' I went to the city room of a New York newspaper to observe. While there, I found a young man who used to just kid everybody and no one seemed to resent it. When I tried that on the set it worked beautifully, and did for many years." "Today" show host Garroway nicknamed him "the saver," for his skill in salvaging interviews that were going badly. He also worked with "The Jackie Gleason Show" and "Meet the Champions." Died: 1987.

Josephine Hull 🎥   6500 Hollywood

Actress

BORN Josephine Sherwood; May 30, 1884, in Newton, MA. **SPOTLIGHTS** This sweet, tottering, funny old lady only graced five films, including *Arsenic and Old Lace* (1944), and *Lady from Texas* (1951). A versatile character actress, she was a lifelong Broadway star. **ACHIEVEMENTS** 1950 Best Supporting Actress Oscar for *Harvey*. Died: 1957.

Edith Head 🎥   6500 Hollywood

Edith Head

Costume designer

BORN Oct. 28, 1907, in Los Angeles, CA. **SPOTLIGHTS** The first woman to hold such a high position in any major studio, Head was *the* chief dress designer for Paramount Pictures. And she was absolutely brilliant at it. Prior to coming to the studios, she had spent most of her childhood divided between Native American Indian reservations of the Southwest, and Mexico. She received her B.A. degree at UCLA, and her M.A. at Stanford University, where her major was languages. She taught Spanish by day at two schools in Los Angeles, then studied at the Otis Art Institute and Chouinard Art School at night, where she concentrated on design. Eventually she stopped teaching and devoted herself to the art of design. Hired by Paramount as a sketch artist in 1936, her first assignment was reportedly designing a waistband for an elephant. By 1938, she had been promoted to head designer. When asked where her ideas came from, she stated: "The script. It tells you exactly the kind of persons, their status, their social background, their locale. When you read a script, it tells you pretty much how the people should look." She worked several decades at Paramount, and stated: "I have the most exciting job in the world." She also said: "I had the most fun dressing Mae West in her comedies, and Charles Laughton, for his role as Nero." The petite Edith Head was the most successful Hollywood designer ever, working on more than 1,000 pictures during her career. She designed most of the fabrics too, traveling worldwide for ideas. Offscreen, she was a personal designer for many celebrities. **ACHIEVEMENTS** Oscar-nominated 35 times between 1948 and 1977, she is the all-time most winning female. Head collected eight Academy Awards: 1949 *The Heiress*; 1950 *Samson and Delilah* and *All About Eve*; 1951 *A Place in the Sun*; 1953 *Roman Holiday*; 1954 *Sabrina*; 1960 *The Facts of Life*; and 1973 *The Sting*. Many of her creations have found permanent homes in museums and collections throughout the world. The exotic silk sarong she created for Dorothy Lamour remains in the Smithsonian Institute. **QUOTE** "Good clothes are not good luck. They are the result of a pretty thorough-going knowledge of the people you are dressing." Died: 1981.

James Cagney 🎥   6502 Hollywood

Actor

BORN July 17, 1899, on New York's lower East Side, NY. **SPOTLIGHTS** He was a light-footed hoofer who danced on the

James Cagney

balls of his feet before becoming *The Public Enemy* (1931). His powerful, smug, snarling persona of a murderous thug captured the imagination of America. Cagney seized immortality in one of the most memorable movie scenes of all-time when he angrily smashes a grapefruit into gang moll Mae Clarke's face—a first in motion picture history. The New York Critics voted him the year's best actor for his portrayal of a hood in *Angels with Dirty Faces* (1938), with Humphrey Bogart. One of Warner Bros.' last gangster pictures, *The Roaring Twenties* (1939), is a tale of bootleggers, where the beautiful Gladys George recites his epitaph: "He was a big shot." Indeed, Cagney was the best gangster there ever was. But he was much more than that. His dynamic energy and finely tuned skills greatly enhanced every movie he did. His portrayal of Bottom in *A Midsummer Night's Dream* makes the inconsistent film almost worth watching, and the blame for its failure could not be pinned on Shakespeare nor Cagney. Without doubt, Cagney was one of America's best-loved and talented actors. Motion pictures include *Smart Money*, *Blonde Crazy* (both 1931), *Taxi!* (1932), *Hard to Handle*, *The Mayor of Hell*, *Picture Snatcher*, *Footlight Parade*, *Lady Killer* (all 1933), *Jimmy the Gent* (1934), *Frisco Kid*, *Ceiling Zero* (both 1935), *Boy Meets Girl* (1938), *White Heat* (1949), *The West Point Story* (1950), *Mister Roberts*, *Love Me or Leave Me* (both 1955), and *Ragtime* (1981). **ACHIEVEMENTS** 1942 Best Actor Oscar for his portrayal of George M. Cohan, a song-and-dance man, in *Yankee Doodle Dandy*. 1982 recipient of the Presidential Medal of Freedom. Married Billie Vernon in 1922; it was a great love

match. Offscreen, he was quiet and charming. **QUOTE** "There's not much to tell you about acting but this: never settle back on your heels. Never relax. If you relax, the audience relaxes. And always mean everything you say." Died: 1986, on Easter Sunday. He just closed his eyes and went to sleep.

Don Alvarado 🎥   6504 Hollywood

Actor
BORN Jose Paige; Nov. 5, 1904, in Albuquerque, NM. **SPOTLIGHTS** Known as "the Latin Lover," he was a romantic, suave leading man in *Loves of Carmen* (1927). As he aged, he turned to character roles. He has great fun in the comedy *Cafe Society* (1939), starring Madeleine Carroll and Fred MacMurray, and is must-see in RKO's vigorous crime story, *The Big Steal* (1949--in which William Faulkner has a screenwriting credit), starring Robert Mitchum. Died: 1967.

Agnes Ayres 🎥   6504 Hollywood

Agnes Ayres

Actress
BORN Agnes Hinkle; Sept. 4, 1896, in Carbondale, IL. **SPOTLIGHTS** Kissing the dreamy, divinely handsome, mysterious Rudolph Valentino in *The Sheik* (1921) shot her glamorous image into the stratosphere. His passionate kiss was considered so shocking at the time that women fainted in the aisles of the movie theatre. Millions worldwide worshiped the dark-haired idol. Understandably, Ayres almost broke her legs leaping at the chance to be with the handsome star again in *Son of the Sheik* (1926). It proved to be Valentino's last film; he died that same year of a perforated ulcer. Her career didn't last much longer; her voice was improperly pitched for sound. She didn't mind though, she had been forever immortalized with Rudolph Valentino. Died: 1940.

Alfred Hitchcock 🎥   6506 Hollywood

See page 589

Maurice Jarre 🎥   6506 Hollywood

Composer, Conductor
BORN Sept. 13, 1924, in Lyons, France. **SPOTLIGHTS** Without former musical training, he declared to his parents at age 16 that he would be going to Paris to study music, to become a composer and conductor. "I didn't know one note on the keyboard," says Jarre, "and all my family laughed at me.

Maurice Jarre

But something told me that I had to become a composer." He began studying solfeggio, harmony and percussion at the Paris Conservatory of Music. After three years, he was one of the principal timpanists of the major Paris orchestras, then studied counterpoint, fugue, orchestration and conducting. He also learned electronic music and *musique concrete*. Jarre rose to become musical director of the French National Theater for 12 years. In that position he wrote and conducted nearly sixty scores for important plays. He began his film work in France, and has worked with the greatest directors in the world, including Alfred Hitchcock, William Wyler, John Houston, Fred Zinnemann, and Franco Zeffirelli, among many others. He scored more than 40 pictures, including *Lawrence of Arabia, Doctor Zhivago, Passage to India, Gorillas in the Mist, Dead Poet's Society, Fatal Attraction*; more. Worldwide acclaim for his concert works and ballets. **ACHIEVEMENTS** Three Oscars, three Golden Globe Awards. One of the world's most prolific and versatile composers, he is the recipient of numerous international awards and the highest French honors in recognition of his contributions to music.

Florian Zabach 📺   6508 Hollywood

Composer, violinist
BORN Aug. 15, 1921, in Chicago, IL. **SPOTLIGHTS** A concert artist by age 12, he was a master of classical music before turning to pop. A soloist on the radio with Percy Faith, he became known for his tasteful use of harmonic. Well known for "The Hot Canary" tune, Zabach was a violinist on the musical variety show "Club Embassy" (1952-'53). Many records including "This Dream I Have" and "The Funny Fiddle." He is most identifiable with his wonderful version of the traditional "Turkey in the Straw." A marvelous technician and showman, he sometimes whistled while performing in concert.

Joe Williams 💿   6508 Hollywood

Singer
BORN Joseph Goreed; Dec. 12, 1918, in Cordele, GA. **SPOTLIGHTS** A jazz giant, Williams brought a new sophistication to the microphone. He first became famous singing blues in Count Basie's big band with songs such as "Alright, Okay,

You Win," "Ev'ry Day I Have the Blues" "The Comeback," "Teach Me Tonight," "Roll 'em Pete," and "In The Evenin'." Ironically, when he had previously worked in Lionel Hampton's band, they had pejoratively nicknamed him "the shouter." He was told his big-voiced style would not cut it, and Williams was axed from the band. He ignored Hampton's criticism. A tall, mellifluous baritone, he sang in a rich-toned smoothness combined with a vigorous enthusiasm. Count Basie commented, "J.W. (Joe Williams) is the only man who could really do it." He worked with Basie—who also called him "my son"— from 1954-61, then emerged a star in a solo career. Subsequently, Williams recorded with many jazz leaders and musical partners. Voted "Best Singer with a Band" by the musicians' union, he was a Grammy Award-winner, and a regular at the Playboy Jazz Festival. About racism he had encountered on the road, especially early in his career, Williams stated, "Hate is too important an emotion to waste on someone you don't like. I believe that if someone comes after you, defend yourself by all means, by any means possible. But I don't have time to go around hating people." **RECOMMENDED** *The Overwhelming Joe Williams*, Bluebird Label ND86464 CD; *Count Basie Swings, Joe Williams Sings* Verve Label 519852-2 CD—for which he was named "Top Male Singer of 1955." **QUOTE** "There've been tough times, sure, and I've some of the same problems other artists have had. I understand a level playing field. You start out as a kid playing sports and learning how to play fair. The bursting of the bubble comes when you grow up and find out it's all a bunch of malarkey, that it's dog-eat-dog out there." Died: 1999.

Gale Robbins 📺   6508 Hollywood

Actress, singer
BORN May 7, 1924, in Chicago, IL. **SPOTLIGHTS** A ravishing redhead who entered TV after making many movies, including *Oh You Beautiful Doll* (1949). Star o TV's variety show "Hollywood House." Died: 1980.

Count Basie 💿   6508 Hollywood

Count Basie

Jazz pianist, composer, band leader
BORN William "Count" Basie; Aug. 21, 1904, in Red Bank, NJ. **SPOTLIGHTS** Crowned "The Jump King," Basie was a premier jazz pianist, composer and band leader. In the early 1920s, Basie earned a living playing piano in Harlem clubs, and doing gigs playing the organ at a string of silent movie theaters. He fondly remembered, "It was Fats Waller who showed me how to play the piano."

Throughout his career, he resisted musical fads, remaining faithful to his beloved Fats Waller and the hopping Kansas City roots. He joined the Bennie Moten band in 1928, and became band leader at age 31 when Moten died suddenly in 1934. As a band leader, Basie conceived his own school of jazz. He erased the formerly jagged edges of rhythm and jazz improvisation, but kept the large, robust enthusiasm in jazz. Though he always maintained the ability to play softly yet still hop. Basie utilized his strong rhythm section and outstanding jazz musicians to bring about a smooth swing era into the big band music of the 1930s and '40s. Under encouragement from Benny Goodman, the Count Basie Orchestra surprised New York audiences, including a number of radio network executives, when Basie opened at a small club called the Famous Door. The year was 1938 and he was an immediate success; his music was coined "Jump Rhythm." In 1939 after jazzing Carnegie Hall, his original composition, "One O'Clock Jump" gained national popularity and became the band's celebrated theme song. "Jumpin' at the Woodside" and "April in Paris" were two other hits he composed, and "Every Day" "Sent For You Yesterday," "John's Idea," and "Every Tub," were other smash hits. In 1941 he recorded "Big Joe" sung by America's great basso vocalists, Paul Robeson. By 1944 Count Basie had become a household name in America, selling more than three million albums a year on the Columbia label. Count Basie led the band with his refined, yet exuberant piano playing; he "built from the rhythm section to the tenors, and then on to the rest." The Count had many of the finest singers assembled, for starters, Billie Holiday (about her he said, "She was our first girl vocalist and she was beautiful to work with. I was just as thrilled to hear her as the audience was"), Ella Fitzgerald, Frank

Count Basie and Dorothy Dandridge

Sinatra and Tony Bennett. Later, the Count's music bridged the swing era with the tonal dynamics of the cooler more progressive jazz techniques. The top musical talents in the country—Louis Armstrong, Nat "King" Cole, the Dorsey Brothers, Andre Previn, Bill Harris, Dizzy Gillespie, Woody Herman, Stan Getz, and countless others—voted the Count Basie Band "*The Greatest Ever*." Movie appearances include *Stage Door Canteen* (1943), *Cinderfella* (1950), *Jamboree* (1957), *Sex and the Single Girl* (1964), and *Blazing Saddles* (1974). **ACHIEVEMENTS** One of the most swinging bands in music history, Basie is the recipient of conceivably every music honor in existence, including countless "Best Big Band" wins. He was inducted into the *Playboy* Music Hall of Fame in 1967, in a ceremony also honoring Duke Ellington and Ella Fitzgerald. Died: 1984.

Phil Harris   6508 Hollywood
See page 68

George Burns   6510 Hollywood
See page 438

Nelson Eddy   6512 Hollywood
See page 130

David Rose   6512 Hollywood
Composer, conductor, pianist, arranger
BORN June 24, 1910, in England. **SPOTLIGHTS** He formed his first orchestra in 1936. Later, he scored numerous films, and was guest conductor of symphony orchestras. Songs and instrumentals include "Holiday for Strings," "Our Waltz," and "Never Too Late." **ACHIEVEMENTS** 1959 Emmy; 1971 Emmy for "Bonanza"; 1979 and 1982 Emmys for "Little House on the Prairie." Died: 1990.

Marlin Hurt   6512 Hollywood
Actor
BORN 1906. **SPOTLIGHTS** In the early 1940s, he played Dick on "The Affairs of Tom, Dick and Harry" variety show. Then, he specialized in playing Beulah, a black maid on the comedy show "Beulah." Hurt was a Caucasian male using a black dialect to play an African-American female. He also played Beulah's lazy boyfriend Bill Jackson. (CBS, 1945 - until his sudden death. After he died, Hattie McDaniel took over the role--see her bio in this book.) Supporting cast members over the years included Butterfly McQueen, Louise Beavers, and Vivian and Dorothy Dandridge. Hurt died in 1946.

Maurice Costello 🎥   6516 Hollywood

Actor
BORN Feb. 2, 1877, in Pittsburgh, PA. **SPOTLIGHTS** A Shakespearean silent screen star—*The Merchant of Venice* (1908) and *King Lear* (1909)—he traveled the distance to *Hollywood Boulevard* (1936). He was *one of the first* important stage stars to agree to appear in "moving pictures," a form of entertainment many artists first thought degrading. Died: 1950.

Lois Weber 🎥   6518 Hollywood

Director, actress, producer
BORN June 13, 1881, in Allegheny, PA. **SPOTLIGHTS** Weber takes a first in many categories: she was Universal Studio's first ranked woman producer, who at the time was also "the highest-salaried woman director in the world." She seriously dealt with women's issues on film, as early as 1916. Pictures include *The Angel of Broadway* (1927). Died: 1939.

Gene Autry 🎤   6520 Hollywood

See page 428

Walter Lang 🎥   6520 Hollywood

Director
BORN Aug. 10, 1898, in Memphis, TN. **SPOTLIGHTS** A former men's fashion illustrator, he enjoyed a quarter-century career at Fox Studios. Riding the wave of popularity of biopics (biography pictures), Lang ideally cast Wallace Beery as the legendary circus showman, *The Mighty Barnum* (1934). He gave Depression-era audiences what they wanted—entertaining fables. Viewers found relief in *I'll Give a Million* (1938), starring Warner Baxter as a weary millionaire. He pretends to be a hobo to see if anyone likes him for himself. The next year, Lang directed Shirley Temple in *The Little Princess*. (This is the movie that Fox insisted Shirley Temple do, instead of loaning her out to MGM to star in *The Wizard of Oz*.) He scored in the next decade with *Tin Pan Alley* (1940), and even bigger with *Moon over Miami* (1941), starring Don Ameche, Betty Grable and Robert Cummings. He had a huge hit with *Sitting Pretty* (1948), about a writer who becomes a baby-sitter to learn about life in suburbia, starring Clifton Webb, Robert Young and Maureen O'Hara. He directed a real-life, turn-of-the-century family comedy, *Cheaper by the Dozen* (1950), about an efficiency expert raising 12 children. Ethel Merman called Lang her favorite director for *Call Me Madam* (1953), and *There's No Business like Show Business* (1954). A thousand times better was *The King and I* (1956), starring Yul Brynner and Deborah Kerr, with the Rodgers and Hammerstein music. The world left the theatre singing "Getting to Know You," and Lang was nominated for his only Oscar. Died: 1972.

Gloria Grahame 🎥   6522 Hollywood

Actress, singer
BORN Gloria G. Hallward; Nov. 28, 1925, in Los Angeles, CA. **SPOTLIGHTS** Driven since childhood to be an actress, by age nine she was performing professionally at the Pasadena Playhouse, in California. As an adult, the green-eyed beauty specialized in the sultry blonde. Effective in tough roles, movies include *In a Lonely Place* (1950) opposite Humphrey Bogart; Josef Von Sternberg's drama set in Hong Kong, *Macao* (1952--in a supporting role to Jane Russell); *Sudden Fear* (1952--in a supporting role to Joan Crawford); *The Bad and the Beautiful* (1952) with Kirk Douglas, Lana Turner, Dick Powell, Barry Sullivan, Walter Pidgeon and Gilbert Roland; *The Big Heat* (1953) opposite Glenn Ford; and *Human Desire* (1954--based on the famed French novelist Émile Zola's *La Bete Humaine*) co-starring Glenn Ford. Going against type, she plays a boy-crazy girl in the musical *Oklahoma!* (1955). With her unique slight lisp, and endearing charms, she is an absolute delight to watch. She also appears in *It's a Wonderful Life* (1946). **ACHIEVEMENTS** Oscar-nominated for *Crossfire* (1947), she won a 1952 Best Supporting Actress Academy Award for *The Bad and the Beautiful*. **SIDELIGHTS** An alluring siren in real life, she was married and divorced four times. One husband was her *former step-son*, actor-producer Tony Ray, the son of second husband Nick Ray! Died: 1981.

E. Power Biggs 🎵   6522 Hollywood

Musician
BORN Edward George Power Biggs; March 29, 1906, in Westcliff, England. **SPOTLIGHTS** After studying electrical engineering for two years, the 18-year-old won the Thomas Threlfall Organ Scholarship to the Royal Academy of Music. The recipient of the school's highest honors, Biggs reflected, "It's practically impossible to be an infant prodigy on the organ. The pedals are so low, a tot can't reach 'em. Mozart did it at six, but he had to walk up and down on tiptoe, reaching above his head all the time." He graduated at age 23 and was asked to present a program at Queen's Hall in London--on a two-day notice. It was a brilliant start to an equally stunning career. It was said of Biggs that his music "blew clear the cathedral dust off the majestic organ." This esteemed musician played to packed concert halls around the globe, had a lengthy run with CBS Radio with his Sunday morning broadcasts (1942-'58), and a successful recording career. He was known for his bright interpretations of Bach. Recordings include *Toccata*, and *Fugue in D Minor*. He was the official organist with the Boston Symphony Orchestra. The treasured Baroque Organ in the Germanic Museum at Harvard was his all-time favorite instrument. **QUOTE** "Organists are often considered to be on the lunatic fringe of musicians, probably because they hang around churches all the time. I advise my pupils to mix with other sorts of musicians, never with organists...Nero played it...he had a public-be-damned attitude, but so do most organists." Died: 1977.

Hobart Bosworth 🎥   6522 Hollywood

Actor

BORN Aug. 10, 1865, in Marietta, OH. **SPOTLIGHTS** One of the earliest stage stars to work in "moving pictures," he appears *In the Sultan's Power* (1909), an early silent and *the first movie to made in Los Angeles*. He became a busy leading and character actor in 100 films--both silents and talkies--including portraying General Lee in *Abraham Lincoln* (1930). He occasionally directed, wrote, and produced. **QUOTE** "There is a careless condescension to this 'funny, new little business' that offers stage actors such huge sums for making a picture or two during the summer when theatres were closed. The thespians failed to take us seriously, laughed at us, said we were merely canned drama people, not artists at all, and were quite scathing in their criticisms of our methods, our stories, our results generally. I know this to be true from my first picture. I fell for the temptation because I needed the money, and many a time since I have seen stage actors go through that experience. I found the work tremendously interesting, and the actors who saw it as I did are still making pictures, and are the backbone of the profession, making traditions, helping to carry on the big work." Died: 1943.

Glenda Farrell 🎥   6524 Hollywood

Actress

BORN June 30, 1904, in Enid, OK. **SPOTLIGHTS** Gangsters loved her as a girlfriend, but Hollywood enjoyed her best as a wisecracking blonde. Movies include *Lady for a Day* (1933) and *Gold Diggers of 1937*, where she played off Joan Blondell. She is remembered as the reporter in the *Torchy Blane* film series. She won a 1963 Emmy. Died: 1971.

Lewis Stone 🎥   6524 Hollywood

Actor

BORN Nov. 15. 1879, in Worcester, MA. **SPOTLIGHTS** A thin, distinguished, mustached leading man, Stone was not handsome enough to be the romantic hero, but he excelled as the gentleman-hero. Chivalrous, loyal and well-mannered, Stone looked like the type most comfortable at home in his drawing room. He appears in countless silent movies. Middle-aged by the time sound arrived—and possessing a perfectly modulated voice—he became a steadily employed character actor. Films include MGM's *Mata Hari* (1932) and *Queen Christina* (1933), both with the enchanting Greta Garbo, *Treasure Island* (1934), and *The Prisoner of Zenda* (1952; he was also in the 1922 version). Stone played All-American as the distinguished, affable Judge Hardy in the *Andy Hardy* series, starring Mickey Rooney. In all he made close to 200 films. Died: 1953.

Vanessa Brown 📺   6528 Hollywood

See page 348

John Boles 🎥   6530 Hollywood

Actor, singer

BORN Oct. 27, 1895, in Greenville, TX. **SPOTLIGHTS** A handsome, reliable leading man, he played opposite high-powered actresses. Movies include *The Desert Song* (1929), and two Shirley Temple vehicles, *Stand Up and Cheer* (1934) and *Curly Top* (1935). **SIDELIGHTS** He engaged in successful espionage activities against the Germans during WWI. Died: 1969.

Alan Hale 🎥   6530 Hollywood

Actor, director, writer, inventor
BORN Rufus A. McKahan; Feb. 10, 1892, in Washington, DC. **SPOTLIGHTS** Hale appears in nearly 200 films, from 1911-'50. He was a big, reliable supporting actor. Movies include *Of Human Bondage, Imitation of Life* (both 1934), *The Good Fairy* (1935), *The Prince and the Pauper* (1937), *Stella Dallas* (1937), *The Adventures of Robin Hood* (as Little John), *Algiers* (both 1938), *The Man in the Iron Mask* (1939), and

Alan Hale

Manpower (1941). **HIGHLIGHTS** Father of Alan Hale, Jr. of TV's "Gilligan's Island" fame...He invented movable theatre seats and a fire extinguisher. Died: 1950.

Freddy Martin 🎵   6536 Hollywood

Band leader, musician

BORN Dec. 9, 1906, in Cleveland, OH. **SPOTLIGHTS** The famed alto tenor saxist was peerless. He was recognized as the greatest player of the instrument. Called "Mr. Silvertone" for his smooth, sweet music, the maestro had one of the Swing Era's most relaxed dance bands. He formed his first band while in high school, and got his big break "when Guy Lombardo asked us to fill in his regular spot." Merv Griffin was a vocalist with Martin and had the 1948 hit "I've Got a Lovely Bunch of Coconuts." At the immensely popular night spot, the Cocoanut Grove, in the Ambassador Hotel, Martin became known as "the voice of the Grove." A record executive at MCA said, "Freddy Martin is such a nice man; he's almost too nice for his own good." Recordings include "Paris in Spring/Bonjour Mam'selle," "I Should Have Known You Years Ago," "All or Nothing at All," "Everything I've Got," "The Hut Sut Song," "Why Don't We Do This More Often?" "I Look at Heaven," and "Intermezzo." His enchanting melodies of the romantic waltz include "Let Me Call You Sweetheart," "Girl of My Dreams," "Sweetheart of Sigma Chi," and "Will You Remember?" His radio tagline was "Music in the Martin manner" (1933-'56). His theme song was his 1941 hit

"Tonight We Love," based on "Tchaikovsky's Piano Concerto No. 1." **QUOTE** "My pal Larry Barnett kept telling me to invest a little bit of my money each week into IBM stock. The only trouble was I wasn't making as much as Larry was. That's why *he* is now a millionaire." Died: 1983.

Hal March   6538 Hollywood

See page 297

MacDonald Carey   6538 Hollywood

MacDonald Carey

Actor

BORN March 15, 1913, in Sioux City, IA. **SPOTLIGHTS** He played a good-guy lawyer, Herbert Maris, who defended the wrongly accused in TV's "Lock Up" (1959-'61), before becoming a household name to millions of homemakers in the soap opera "Days of Our Lives" (starting in 1965). His voice-over can be heard: "Like the sands through the hourglass, so these are the days of our lives." Carey was the first movie star—with excellent credits like *Wake Island* (1942), Hitchcock's *Shadow of a Doubt* (1943) and the Western *Copper Canyon* (1950), to become a cast member in a daytime series. It seemed only fitting, though, his career started in New York's Radio Row in the soap opera "Stella Davis." Broadcast from 1937-'55, he played Dick Grosvenor, a young, wealthy, upper class banker. Died: 1994.

Jay Silverheels   6540 Hollywood

Actor

BORN Harold Jay Smith; May 26, 1919, on Six Nations Indian Reservation, Ontario, Canada. **SPOTLIGHTS** The son of a full-blooded North American Mohawk chief, the athletic Silverheels portrayed his real-life people from the Indian Nation with strength, intelligence and kindness. An amateur boxer, he made his silver screen debut in *Too Many Girls* (1940). Then, he appears in the Western *Valley of the Sun* (1942) with Lucille Ball. Silverheels made dozens of movies, including *Key Largo* (1948), with Humphrey Bogart and Edward G. Robinson, and the wonderful family drama *Sand* (1949), about a horse's freedom. He stars as Geronimo—the greatest war leader of the Apache Indians of Arizona—in the breakthrough Western, *Broken Arrow* (1950). The unique story is told from the Apaches' perspective. This outstanding motion picture also stars James Stewart, Jeff Chandler and Debra Paget. Two years later, he stars as Geronimo again in *The Battle at Apache Pass* (1952). He plays opposite Alan Ladd in

Clayton Moore and Jay Silverheels (right)

Saskatchewan (1954). This Western drama made movie history with a story that actually distinguishes—for the first time—the differences of various Indian tribes—such as the peaceful Cree and warlike Sioux. Silverheels stars opposite Audie Murphy and Anne Bancroft in the intelligent Western, *Walk the Proud Land* (1956), where he again plays Geronimo. Other movies include *Alias Jesse James* (1959) with Bob Hope and Rhonda Fleming, *Indian Paint* (1964) with Johnny Crawford, *Smith!* (1969) with Glenn Ford, *The Man Who Loved Cat Dancing*, *One Little Indian*, and *Santee* (all 1973). **TV** Silverheels played Tonto, the hero's faithful companion on the wildly popular, long-running series, "The Lone Ranger" (1949-'57). The premise: A long time past, the Lone Ranger saved Tonto's life. Then, through the passage of time and many years of separation, Tonto saved the Lone Ranger's life. The two made a solemn pact: "As long as you live, as long as I live, I will ride with you." Tonto called his companion, "Kemo sabe, it mean 'faithful friend'" and "trusty scout." He appears as Tonto in the related feature films: *The Lone Ranger* (1956), and *The Lone Ranger and the Lost City of Gold* (1958). **HIGHLIGHTS** Tonto supposedly came from the Potawatomi tribe of Michigan. When real-life linguists and academic scholars tried to trace the words "kemo sabe," they could find no Native Indian dialects anywhere in North America that contained them. It was later learned that radio director, James

Sammy Cahn (center holding star plaque), Dudley Moore (left), and Jack Jones (right)

Jewell, coined it for an early 1938 broadcast. He got the idea from a relative, who managed a kids' summer camp in Northern Michigan called "Ke-Mo-Sah-Bee." Died: 1980.

Frank Sinatra 📺   6540 Hollywood

See page 289

Sammy Cahn ⏺   6540 Hollywood

Lyricist, songwriter
BORN June 18, 1913, Lower East Side, Manhattan, NY. **SPOTLIGHTS** Cahn received more Best Song Oscar nominations than other person. Nominated 26 times, he won four Academy Awards as songwriter and legendary lyricist. His countless #1 Hit Parade songs include the international smash hit "Bei Mir Bist Du Schon," "Rhythm Is Our Business," and "You're My Girl," among many others. He wrote numerous hits for Frank Sinatra, such as "Three Coins in a Fountain" (Academy Award-winner), "Call Me Irresponsible," and "Fly Me to the Moon." In the film *The Joker is Wild* (1957), Sinatra sings the Oscar-winning "All the Way." His renowned musical partnerships with Jules Styne and James Van Heusen resulted in dozens of hits, including "Let It Snow! Let It Snow! Let It Snow!" "I'll Walk Alone," "It's Magic," "The Second Time Around," "My Kind of Town (Chicago Is)," and "Come Fly With Me." He conquered movies and Broadway with his

exceptional talent and prolific output. **ACHIEVEMENTS** He won the only Emmy ever given for a song, namely "Love and Marriage." Another of his Academy Award-winning songs is "High Hopes." President of the Songwriters Hall of Fame. Published his autobiography, "I Should Care." On Feb. 2, 1990, Cahn asked that his Hollywood Walk of Fame monument be placed next to Frank Sinatra's star. Died: 1994.

Louise Dresser 🎥   6540 Hollywood

Actress
BORN Louise Kerlin; Oct. 5, 1878, in Evansville, IN. **SPOTLIGHTS** A former vaudeville actress, she advanced to the Broadway stage. She was 44 years old when she made her screen debut. Dresser was a splendid character actress. She appears opposite Rudolph Valentino in The Eagle (1925--as Catherine the Great), proves *Mother Knows Best* (1928), and knows how to make her sonny boy sing *Mammy* (1930), in an early Al Jolson musical. She was very good in the original *State Fair* (1933), starring Will Rogers. Died: 1965.

Isaac Stern ⏺   6540 Hollywood

Violinist
BORN July 21, 1920, in Kreminiecz, Russia. **SPOTLIGHTS** At age one, Stern was brought to America to escape Bolshevism. He began playing piano at age four, but switched to violin at age six. This gifted youngster studied at the San Francisco Conservatory and made his professional debut in that city in 1931—at 11 years old. Following his bow, he toured the country and made his New York appearance in 1937. Stern later recalled that the critics noted his potential, but "were of the 'yes-but' variety." He firmly responded, "I don't want to take any excuses for my youth—or for anything else. I'm willing to put it on the line." On Jan. 12, 1943 he performed at Carnegie Hall in New York City, with one critic declaring, "Stern rocketed into the sparsely populated heaven of first-rate violinists." One of the world's top violinists, and one of the rare breed to have come out of America's training. His range is from classical to romantic to modern composers such as Hindemith and Bartok. He said, "I don't tire of such old war horses as Mendelssohn and Tchaikovsky anymore than audiences do." He dubbed the violin solos for John Garfield in *Humoresque* (1946), and worked on other movie soundtracks, including *Fiddler on the Roof* (1971). He appears in *Tonight We Sing* (1953). **ACHIEVEMENTS** Grammys, solo, 1961, 1962, 1964, 1981; chamber performances, 1970; classical album of the year, 1977. **QUOTE** "We have to get more qualified people and better paid and trained people for the job—to begin the idea that music is not an acquired culture. It's *not* something you learn instead of something else. It's *not* a sissy part of living, but an active part of natural life. That which we love and cherish. I would like to see more understanding of that in this country."

6542 HOLLYWOOD

Monty Woolley   6542 Hollywood

Monty Woolley

Actor

BORN Edgar Montillion Woolley; Aug. 17, 1888, in New York, NY. **SPOTLIGHTS** An articulate English and graduate dramatics professor at Yale University, Woolley's students included Thornton Wilder and Stephen Vincent Benet. A late bloomer by Hollywood standards, Woolley was 52 when his sparkling characterization of Sheridan Whiteside, in the comedy *The Man Who Came to Dinner* (1941), won him international acclaim. He gave wonderful performances in *The Pied Piper* (1942), *Holy Matrimony* (1943) with Gracie Fields, *Since You Went Away* (1944) with Claudette Colbert, and *The Bishop's Wife* (1947) starring Cary Grant, Loretta Young and David Niven. He made dozens of pictures, but when he was not working, he resided year-round at his family-owned Saratoga Springs resort (his grandfather was proprietor of the Grand Union Hotel). He loathed possessions, lived for solitude, preferred wining and dining alone, and, when his privacy was interrupted was known to speak only in Elizabethan language. **QUOTE** Nicknamed "the Beard" by Yale classmate, Cole Porter, Woolley had one of Hollywood's most distinguishable. He remarked, "I regard the beard as an accolade. It is an economic asset. It enhances my beauty. What does one remember of Michelangelo's Moses? The great curling beard. The fringe of Abe Lincoln's face is as familiar as the Statue of Liberty (who is beardless, I admit). Take the beard off Santa Claus and Bluebeard and what have you? A pair of overstuffed bores. To top it all off, what beard is more famous than the billy goat appendage of Uncle Sam? Long may it wave. The offense rests." Died: 1963.

Ralph Bellamy   ◼   6542 Hollywood

Actor

BORN June 17, 1904, in Chicago, IL. **SPOTLIGHTS** His career in film, TV, stage and radio spanned six decades. He lost his gal, Irene Dunne, to Cary Grant in *The Awful Truth* (1937), but won an Academy Award nomination for his performance in this screwball comedy. He paired again with Cary Grant in *His Girl Friday* (1940), with Rosalind Russell. (Guess who won the girl in the end?) Bellamy became a favorite in comedies as a pushover artist—a moneyed, but confused hick; a charming goof. He triumphed on Broadway with his *tour-de-force* portrayal of Franklin Delano Roosevelt in "Sunrise at

Campobello" (Broadway 1958-'59)—"the highlight of my career," he stated—which won him a Tony Award. When Hollywood produced the picture (1960), he again played FDR. Bellamy was utterly frightful in the diabolical *Rosemary's Baby* (1968). A versatile actor, movie fans revere him as Mr. Duke, the older eccentric, scheming billionaire in the very clever comedy, *Trading Places* (1983). His character

Ralph Bellamy

uses a snooty preppie employee-executive (Dan Aykroyd) and a down-and-out soul (Eddie Murphy) as guinea pigs in a heredity versus environment experiment, with hilarious results. He made close to 100 films. Died: 1991.

André Kostelanetz   ◉   6542 Hollywood

Conductor

BORN Dec. 22, 1901, in St. Petersburg, Russia. **SPOTLIGHTS** A great Russian talent, he arrived in America in 1920, and was one of the earliest conductors to perform on the air. Starting in 1924, he enjoyed a 20-year relationship with CBS radio. He worked with a 65-piece orchestra (at its largest), a 16-member choir, and various opera soloists. Kostelanetz did not restrict his shows to "serious music," he appealed to the masses by playing popular music. His best-loved, romantic and enchanting waltz numbers: "Danube Waves," and "Dark Eyes." Recordings include *Andre Kostelanetz Plays the World's Greatest Love Songs*, and *Oscar Levant playing George Gershwin's Piano Concerto in F with the New York Philharmonic Symphony Orchestra under Kostelanetz.* **QUOTE** "We will win music lovers by the hundreds when we expose them to good music by degrees, not drag them to tedious performances where they'll develop a life-long antagonism to classical music." Died: 1980.

Patric Knowles   ◼   6542 Hollywood

Actor

BORN Reginald Knowles; Nov. 11, 1911, in Horsforth, England. **SPOTLIGHTS** A debonair, light-haired, romantic leading man, Knowles was a contemporary of Errol Flynn. He starred in Ibsen's *A Doll's House*, hosted by (future President) Ronald Reagan for TV's "General Electric Theater." Previously, he enjoyed a busy film career. Movies include *The Adventures of Robin Hood* (1938), *Another Thin Man* (1939), *O.S.S.* (1946), and *Monsieur Beaucaire* (1946). Died: 1995.

John Stahl 🎥   6546 Hollywood

Director, producer

BORN Jan. 21, 1886, in New York, NY. **SPOTLIGHTS** Through four decades and 41 pictures—silents through talkies—Stahl kept his finger on the pulse and sentiment of the times. In *Back Street* (1932), Irene Dunne stars as a mistress pining away for the unattainable John Boles. It is a landmark melodrama and still holds up today. In *Imitation of Life* (1934), Stahl questions the fine line between black and white, and mother and daughter relationships. This tearjerker has an extremely capable cast of Claudette Colbert, Louise Beavers, and Rochelle Hudson. More tears flowed with *Magnificent Obsession* (1935), with Irene Dunne and Robert Taylor. Gene Tierney was radiant in the suspenseful Technicolor production of *Leave Her to Heaven* (1945), co-starring Cornel Wilde, Vincent Price and Jeanne Crain. Died: 1950.

Evelyn Brent 🎥   6548 Hollywood

Actress

BORN Oct. 20, 1899, in Tampa, FL. **SPOTLIGHTS** She was an extra who landed the lead in Paramount's *Underworld* (1927), a silent directed by Josef von Sternberg. She stars in von Sternberg's *The Last Command* (1928)—an exceptional film—portraying the most dangerous revolutionary in Russia. The next year, she was *Slightly Scarlet*. Died: 1975.

Leslie Howard 🎥   6550 Hollywood

Leslie Howard

Actor, producer

BORN Leslie H. Stainer; April 24, 1893, in London, England. **SPOTLIGHTS** The real-life nightmarish hell of unrelenting attacks on the Western Front during World War I caused Howard to suffer from shell shock. His parents, Hungarian immigrants, encouraged him to take up acting lessons as therapy. He was a natural born actor, who became known for his elegance and grace, often as the well-bred gentleman. Motion pictures include *The Scarlet Pimpernel* (1934), and *The Petrified Forest* (1936). In the latter he insisted on working with stage colleague Humphrey Bogart and put up quite a fight to get him introduced to the silver screen. Howard was excellent as Henry Higgins in *Pygmalion* (1938), the non-musical basis for *My Fair Lady*. Yet, he was forever immortalized as Ashley Wilkes in *Gone with the Wind* (1939). That same year, he stars in and co-produced *Intermezzo: A Love Story* (1939), in which Ingrid Bergman comes to attention of American filmmakers and and shot to international stardom. Died: 1943, in a plane shot down during WWII by Nazis who mistakenly thought Winston Churchill was on board. Ironically, WWI thrust him into the limelight, the second dropped the curtain.

Orson Welles 🎤   6552 Hollywood

See page 287

Zasu Pitts 🎥   6554 Hollywood

Zasu Pitts

Actress, comedienne

BORN Jan. 3, 1898, in Parsons, KS. (Named after her two aunts: Liza and Susan.) **SPOTLIGHTS** "Oh dear me!...my gracious—oh me, oh my!" was the trademark catchphrase of this funny talent. A thin, dark-haired lass whose fretful look crossed her wide brown-eyed face, she enhanced portrayals of nervous ladies by fluttering her hands. One of the all-time most successful actresses, Pitts remarkably appears in 500 films from 1917 to 1963. In silents, she worked in both leading lady roles and character parts. One of her greatest silents is Erich von Stroheim's masterpiece, *Greed* (1924). She plays a money-loving, penny-pinching wife. An unusual role for Pitts, it was a dramatic tour-de-force. Later, when she appears in *All Quiet on the Western Front* (1930), she ended up on the cutting room floor because it was thought audiences would not accept this superb comedian in a serious work. Pictures include *Blondie of the Follies* (1932), *Mr. Skitch* (1933—opposite America's homespun wit, Will Rogers), *Mrs. Wiggs of the Cabbage Patch* (1934), *Ruggles of Red Gap* (1935), *Miss Polly* (1941), and *Life with Father* (1947). **TV** She appeared in "The Gale Storm Show" (1956-'60). She was also an accomplished Broadway actress. **QUOTE** "Beauty is only skin deep. Expression is much deeper than that. Expression is life and there can be as much youth in the soul of a girl who scrubs a kitchen floor as there is in the heart of a butterfly. Nearly all girls seek the boudoir. I love to seek the difficult character without artificial aids. I love to strip emotion bare and enter a field which is, practically, undiscovered. I love to prove that youth is eternal, and that, beneath the unattractive exterior, there is the attractive interior and that, from the label, one cannot tell what might be on the inside. There is a great field in youthful character work. It is undeveloped and undiscovered. Experiment in this field. It may be worthwhile." Died: 1963.

Ed Gardner 🎤   6554 Hollywood

Actor

BORN Eddie Poggenburg; June 29, 1901, in Astoria, NY. **SPOTLIGHTS** On radio from 1940-'52, he played Archie, the man who made insult an art form, as manager of "Duffy's Tavern." The saloon was the "eyesore of the East Side" where the Irish "elite meet to eat." The food was lousy--corned beef, cabbage, and pickled pigs feet--but the service was worse. The important guests could count on one thing--Archie's verbal stingers. His then-wife Shirley Booth, co-starred as Duffy's gum-chewing, dim-witted, chatty daughter. (After Booth and Gardner divorced in 1942, Florence Halop took the role.) It was one of the most popular comedies of the decade, a favorite among prisoners--San Quentin's inmates voted it #1--who probably loved the fact that the *New York World-Telegram* wrote the show "drips with grammatical gore." The theme song was "When Irish Eyes are Smiling," and allowed for the only people spared from Archie's tongue, Irish Tenors. He made one film, *Duffy's Tavern* (1945). He moved to Puerto Rico in 1949 for tax purposes. Died: 1963.

Fred Waring 🎤   6560 Hollywood

Composer, conductor, publisher

Fred Waring

BORN June 9, 1900, in Tyrone, PA. **SPOTLIGHTS** A conservative showman, Waring formed his first small "banjazztra" when he was 17 years old. Although only playing local dates at the time, he had already established a reputation as a pro, requiring band members to spend several hours each day in rehearsals. The Pennsylvanians was formed after he graduated from college. He hit the national music scene with the best staged show. The "fast-paced, curtain-to-curtain nonstop act with no talk and no encores left the audience breathless and applauding," one observer wrote. It came into age in the 1920s with their two hits "Sleep" and "Collegiate." They were the first big band to do both vaudeville and stage. They made their radio debut in 1933, where Waring's elaborate musical shows became an American institution. "The Fred Waring Show" featured his enlarged band, billed as "more than half a hundred Pennsylvanians." His later radio shows featured Robert Shaw leading a large glee club in perfect harmony. Songs include "I Hear Music" and "Fouled Up in Love." His band lasted into the 1970s...President of Waring Corporation (Waring Blender). **QUOTE** "I'm a perfectionist." Died: 1984.

Tay Garnett 🎥   6560 Hollywood

Director, screenwriter

Tay Garnett

BORN William Taylor Garnett; June 13, 1894, in Los Angeles, CA. **SPOTLIGHTS** Garnett started out as a screenwriter during the silent era, and ended up directing 40 sound pictures. He lit box office dynamite with *China Seas* (MGM, 1935), starring Clark Gable and Jean Harlow. *She Couldn't Take It* (1935) starring George Raft and Joan Bennett was his entry into screwball crime comedy. Joan Bennett sizzled across the seven seas in *Trade Winds* (1938). He gave audiences the ultimate sentimental school teacher story about true sacrifice in *Cheers for Miss Bishop* (1941). *Seven Sinners* (1940) stars Marlene Dietrich and John Wayne in a romantic comedy. Garnett compelled viewers with the ultimate tale of guilt and retribution in *The Postman Always Rings Twice* (1946), with Lana Turner and John Garfield. It was his best film noir. Died: 1977.

Franchot Tone 🎥   6560 Hollywood

Actor

BORN Stanislas F. Tone; Feb. 27, 1906, in Niagara Falls, NY. **SPOTLIGHTS** This quiet, charming, sometimes callow leading man frequently depicted a successful businessman. He was first and foremost a Broadway star. He came to Hollywood in the 1930s and married his co-star Joan Crawford from *Today We Live* (1933). (Crawford later divorced him after she caught his personal act with a starlet in his dressing room.) Tone was delightful with Jean Harlow in *The Girl from Missouri* (1934). He gave a superb, must-see performance in *Mutiny on the Bounty* (1935) as Roger Byam, in the role Robert Montgomery rejected. He was also brilliant in *Phantom Lady* (1944), an exciting, must-see psychological thriller. Died: 1968.

Olga Petrova 🎥   6562 Hollywood

Actress, writer

BORN Muriel Harding; Feb. 19, 1886, in England. **SPOTLIGHTS** She changed her name to the more exotic Olga Petrova in order to compete with the screen's first vamp, Theda Bara: "Kiss me, my fool!" She never acquired Bara's notoriety, but did exert some executive control over her own projects, and in doing so, helped pave the star-studded boulevard for other women producers, directors, and writers. *Daughters of Destiny* (1917). Died: 1977.

Pee-Wee Herman

Pee-Wee Herman 🎥
6562 Hollywood

Actor

BORN Paul Rubenfeld; August 27, 1952 in Peekskill, FL. (His professional stage name is Paul Reubens.) **SPOTLIGHTS** He captured the hearts of children with his popular TV series "Pee-Wee's Playhouse," winning six Emmys in its first year—more nominations than any other daytime series. In his trademark tight suit, bow tie and white shoes his mischievous character could radiate a gentle innocence, a furious glare, or a shriek of delight with a dazzling smile, all of which he did in his two hit movies, *Pee-wee's Big Adventure* (1985) and (1988) *Big Top Pee-wee*. After he ended his series in 1991, he sought temporarily refuge from a suddenly harsh spotlight. When he returned to show business, Herman (who also uses the name Reubens) moved to prime time TV, using his comedic gifts in situation comedies, and began appearing in a number of motion pictures: *Batman Returns* (1992), *Buffy the Vampire Slayer* (1992), and *Buddy* (1997). His star dedication ceremony took place on July 20, 1988. Appropriately, his star lies in front of the Hollywood Toys and Costumes store on the famous Walk of Fame.

James Melton 🎙   6562 Hollywood

See page 364

David Torrence 🎥   6562 Hollywood

Actor

BORN April 23, 1880, in Scotland. **SPOTLIGHTS** A former stage performer, he was busy on screen during the 1920s and '30s. Movies include *Sherlock Holmes* (1922); and *Queen Christina* (1933), starring the one-and-only Greta Garbo. Died: 1942.

Sidney Franklin 🎥   6562 Hollywood

Director, producer

BORN May 21, 1893, in San Francisco, CA. **SPOTLIGHTS** Called "a woman's director," he directed such top talent as Greta Garbo, Norma Shearer (Franklin was a favorite of her husband, MGM's "boy wonder," Irving Thalberg), and Mary Pickford. He worked non-stop in silents before moving easily into talkies. *The Good Earth* (1937) is one of his finest pictures, after which he switched to producing only. **ACHIEVEMENTS** 1942 Best Picture Academy Award for *Mrs. Miniver*; 1942 Irving G. Thalberg Memorial Award. Died: 1972.

Jamie Lee Curtis 🎥   6600 Hollywood

Actress

BORN Nov. 22, 1958, in Los Angeles, CA. **SPOTLIGHTS** This child of Hollywood grew up surrounded by celebrated talents as well as behind the scenes people. Curtis, though, is definitely of her own making. At age 19, this strong-willed, intelligent actress landed a contract with Universal Studios, and immediately went to work in television. She played a Navy nurse in the military situation comedy, "Operation Petticoat" (1977-'78). This series was based on the 1959

Jamie Lee Curtis (right) and Janet Leigh

motion picture starring Cary Grant, and her father Tony Curtis. While working in TV, she was cast in John Carpenter's low-budget horror flick *Halloween* (1978). Curtis delivered an awesome, spine chilling performance. She shot to international screen fame in the role, and the scary movie became a classic. Other menacing features followed: *The Fog, Prom Night*, and *Terror Train* (all 1980), *Road Games* and *Halloween II* (1981). Her next work was her tour-de-force. Revealing herself like in no other role, Curtis slowly peels back the psychological layers in Amy Jones' superb drama, *Love Letters* (1983). Audiences witnessed the sensitive transformation of her character. It was superior motion picture acting. That same year, she teams with Dan Aykroyd and Eddie Murphy in John Landis' hilarious comedy *Trading Places* (1983), in which she earned a British Film Academy award for Best Supporting Actress. By now, Curtis had established her tremendous versatility and range. She returned to England to make *A Fish Called Wanda* (1988). Curtis co-stars opposite John Cleese in this farcical black comedy about greed and sex. She was terrific in it. She also appears in the sequel to it, *Fierce Creatures* (1997). Other motion pictures include *Dominick and Eugene* (1988), *My Girl* and *Queens Logic* (both 1991), *Forever Young* (1992), *Mother's Boys, My Girl 2*, and *True Lies* (all 1994), and *Drowning Mona* (2000). In *True Lies*, she earned a Golden Globe Award. She also appears in *Halloween '98*. Although it is rare of stars of her stature to do television, she is not afraid of the medium. She made the touching story "Nicholas' Gift" for CBS, starred in the sitcom "Anything But Love," was striking in "Death of a Centerfold: The Dorothy Stratten Story," and worked with the legendary Bette Davis in "As Summer Dies." **SIDELIGHTS** She pens children's books, including *Today I Feel Silly: And Other Moods That Make My Day, When I Was Little*, and *Tell Me Again About the Night I Was Born*. **HIGHLIGHTS** Her mother is actress Janet Leigh, and her father is actor Tony Curtis. (See their bios in this book.) She is married to actor-director Christopher Guest, since 1984. They have two children. **QUOTE** Her star was unveiled on August 3, 1998. She said, "I am so thrilled to join my parents on the Walk of Fame. I am especially pleased to have been placed between Frederick's of Hollywood and Hollywood Toys and Costumes. It's the perfect pairing to represent my biggest successes."

H. B. Warner 🎥 6602 Hollywood

Actor

H. B. Warner

BORN Henry Bryon Charles Stewart Warner; Oct. 26, 1876, in England. **SPOTLIGHTS** His impressive career spanned half a century (1914-'57) with leading and supporting roles in both silents and talkies. The son of a famous 19th-century actor, he descended from three generations of actors on the English stage. He began his career as a child in one of his father's productions. After a number of important theatrical roles, he immigrated to America in 1905. He would duplicate many of his stage performances on film. Tall and thin, with a regal bearing that spoke volumes about his personal integrity, Warner possessed soulful eyes capable of communicating love, pain, and compassion. He was a favorite of director Cecil B. DeMille, and portrays Jesus Christ in *The King of Kings* (1927). It was a triumphant success and one of his favorite roles. He later played Amminadab in DeMille's religious epic, *The Ten Commandments* (1956). H.B. was wonderful in Frank Capra's *Lost Horizon* (1937). In all, he made 200 pictures, including *Five Star Final* (1931), *A Tale of Two Cities* (1935), *The Garden Murder* and *Mr. Deeds Goes to Town* (both 1936), *Bulldog Drummond in Africa* (1938—as Col. Nielson in the film series), *The Gracie Allen Murder Case* and *Mr. Smith Goes to Washington* (both 1939), *The Rains Came* (1940—as the Maharajah), *It's A Wonderful Life* (1946), and *Sunset Boulevard* (1950—as himself). Died: 1958.

Van Johnson 🎥 6602 Hollywood

Actor

Van Johnson

BORN Charles V. Johnson; Aug. 25, 1916, in Newport, RI. **SPOTLIGHTS** This blue-eyed performer with reddish-gold hair rose to stardom at MGM during WWII: *Murder in the Big House* (1941), *The War Against Mrs.*

Hadley (1942), and *Thirty Seconds Over Tokyo* (1944). He remained big after the war, starring in William Wellman's *Battleground* (1949), with John Hodiak and Ricardo Montalban. **SIDELIGHTS** American military authorities did not consider Johnson fit for WWII service because of a head injury he sustained. After a near-fatal automobile accident, a metal plate was inserted into his head.

Joseph Szigeti 🎥 6602 Hollywood

Violinist

BORN Sept. 5, 1892, in Hungary. **SPOTLIGHTS** This child prodigy played professionally at age 10, then toured successfully in Europe, America and the Far East. He was renowned for his performances of virtuoso contemporary works, and performed in the Library of Congress in Washington, D.C. in 1940. **QUOTE** "The artist should constantly set himself new tasks and perform them to the best of his ability. By doing this he is always renewing himself; he keeps within himself a sense of freshness and thrill, which is impossible if he falls into a routine." Died: 1973.

Ella Raines 📺 6602 Hollywood

See page 588

Sir Cedric Hardwicke 📺 6602 Hollywood

See page 209

Burton Holmes 🎥 6602 Hollywood

Actor, producer

BORN Jan. 8, 1870, in Chicago, IL. **SPOTLIGHTS** "The Father of Travelogues" loved vacationing and sharing his travel information with others. Using the new medium of film, he found a way to channel both into fun and profit. Holmes made travel shorts and features. **ACHIEVEMENTS** He was the first to show *Italy* (1897), and *Hawaii* (1898), as well as other exotic locations. Died: 1958.

Peggy Ann Garner 🎥 6608 Hollywood

Actress

BORN Feb. 3, 1932, in Canton, OH. **SPOTLIGHTS** A plain child, her average looks her realistic looks propelled her modeling career. New York agencies employed her in ads as the devoted daughter or kid sister. Her stage mother pushed little Peggy Ann upon Hollywood producers. She made her screen debut as a child in *Little Miss Thoroughbred* (1938). Four years later, she earned star billing in the *Pied Piper* (1942). She gave a sensitive portrayal in *Jane Eyre* (1944), and was charming in *Junior Miss* (1945). A quick study, she never forgot a line. **ACHIEVEMENTS** 1945 Special Oscar for "outstanding child performer" in *A Tree Grows in Brooklyn.*

Tom Jones

Tom Jones ●
6608 Hollywood

Singer, entertainer

BORN Thomas Jones Woodward; June 7, 1940, in Pontypridd, South Wales. **SPOTLIGHTS** This international superstar started out by singing in local pubs as a lad. Known as "Jones the Voice" in his native Wales, he has covered all styles from gospel to pop, rock to light jazz, rhythm-and-blues to rockabilly and country. Jones possesses a deep, weighty voice with a baritone to tenor range. He is a powerhouse of tempos and dynamics, and has the physical prowess to give his audience every ounce of his energy and enthusiasm. He is also known for his openly sensuous style. He hit big with "It's Not Unusual" (1965), followed by "What's New Pussycat" and "Thunderball." When "Green, Green Grass of Home" hit for Jones in 1966, Elvis Presley called radio stations repeatedly to request the song. Paul McCartney is also one of his fans. In fact, McCartney wrote "The Long and Winding Road" especially for Jones. Jones' avalanche of golden sellers include "Delilah," "Help Yourself," "Love Me Tonight," "I'll Never Fall in Love Again," "I (Who Have Nothing)," and "She's A Lady," to name just a few. In the 1990s, this singer enjoys newfound popularity with Generation X. He appeared in a Jack Nicholson vehicle, the sci-fi spoof, *Mars Attacks!* (1996) testing his comedic acting skills. He passed with flying colors. As of 2000, his nickname "the hunk" still fits. **SIDELIGHTS** His father was a poverty-stricken, hard working coal miner. **HIGHLIGHTS** Jones' star was unveiled on the Hollywood Walk of Fame on June 29, 1989. About this dedication ceremony, he said, "I am proud of my star. I love having the recognition amongst my peers and the greats of Hollywood. It means a lot to me to have my name 'carved in stone' for everybody to see for a long time to come."

Annette Kellerman 🎥 6608 Hollywood

Swimmer, actress

BORN Dec. 1, 1887, in Australia. **SPOTLIGHTS** She was arrested at age 19 for *wearing the first one-piece swim suit!* With her magnificent body clad in this same one-piece bathing suit she became a headliner in vaudeville. By 1910 this mermaid was making $2,000.00 a week tax-free plunging into stage tanks in San Francisco, Chicago and New York. Dove into films like a duck to water in *Neptune's Daughter* (1914) and *Queen of the Sea* (1918) making box-office gold. Annette was the beautiful forerunner of swimmer Esther Williams. And, in fact, Williams would later star in the movie, *Million Dollar*

Annette Kellerman

Mermaid (1952), based on Annette's life. The two stars would meet at the time of the filming. The spectacular Busby Berkeley water ballets are an exceptional treat to see. **QUOTE** "Every woman's greatest assets are health and personality. Only in rare instances has extreme beauty without personality brought success to its owner. My first lesson has also been one that taught faith. Faith in God, faith in yourself and faith in your body mean success because health is happiness and happiness is life—real life. Therefore, it is essential you cultivate health. It means strength, a clear mind and your character, combined with your personality will make you an outstanding figure which will attract attention." Died: 1975.

Robert Fuller 📺 6608 Hollywood

Actor

BORN July 29, 1934, in Troy, NY. **SPOTLIGHTS** He gained TV fame as the Wyoming drifter Jess Harper in "Laramie" (1959-'63), and as Cooper Smith in another Western, "Wagon Train" (1963-'65). He rushed to the "Emergency," as Dr. Kelly Brackett (1972-'77).

Margaret O'Brien 🎥 6608 Hollywood

Actress

BORN Angela Maxine O'Brien; Jan. 15, 1937, in Los Angeles, CA. **SPOTLIGHTS** Dubbed the "child wonder" and the greatest "little" actress, her powerful screen impact had critics call-

Margaret O'Brien

ing her a true Hollywood darling at age four. She had a pixie face, a whispery voice and an impetuous personality. As a child, Margaret possessed a remarkable *full* acting range from drama to comedy, as well as the ability to cry or laugh hypnotically at the drop of a hat. She started modeling for photographer Paul Hesse as a "cover baby" at age three. Spotted by a talent scout from her magazine cover, O'Brien was signed by MGM for two lines in Busby Berkeley's *Babes on Broadway* (1941). With the subtlety and naturalness that would become her hallmark, she delivered her lines, "Don't send my brother to the chair. Don't let him burn." That was the beginning of her extraordinary decade-long career at that studio. She took her stage name from her next film, a wartime drama starring Robert Young, *Journey for Margaret* (1942), and legally had it changed. The six-year-old was outstanding in *Lost Angel* (1943), where she plays a child genius named Alpha whose every move is monitored by scientists. A kindly newspaperman helps her learn about being a happy child. It is a wonderful family picture. She appears in the fun comedy *The Canterbury Ghost* (1944) with Charles Laughton and Robert Young. It is about a cowardly ghost who is forced to haunt his castle until one of his descendants performs an act of bravery. Movies include *Jane Eyre* (1944) opposite Orson Welles and Joan Fontaine, *Music for Millions* (1944) with June Allyson and Jimmy Durante, *Our Vines Have Tender Grapes* (1945) co-starring Edward G. Robinson, *The Unfinished Dance* (1947) with Cyd Charisse, *Big City* (1948) with Robert Preston and Danny Thomas, *Tenth Avenue Angel* (1948) opposite Angela Lansbury, *The Secret Garden* (1949) co-starring Herbert Marshall and Dean Stockwell, and *Her First Romance* (1951). As a young adult, she appears in *Glory* (1955), *Heller in Pink Tights* (1960), *Diabolic Wedding* (1971), *Annabelle Lee* (1972), and *Amy* (1981). Under her new management of Michael Schwibs, she co-stars in *Sunset After Dark* (1995) with Anita Page and Randal Malone, and *Hollywood Mortuary* (1999), also co-starring Page and Malone. **ACHIEVEMENTS** 1944 Special Oscar for the Most Outstanding Child Actress for her glorious role as "Tootie Smith" in *Meet Me in St. Louis*. She was seven years old. Although she made a number of splendid films, O'Brien was immortalized as Beth March in *Little Women* (1949)...She was given the highest praise by actor Lionel Barrymore, who worked with her in *Dr. Gillespie's Criminal Case* (1943), and *Three Wise Fools* (1946). Barrymore said, "She's the only actress besides Ethel who's made me take out my handkerchief in thirty years." **QUOTE** "Things are here today and gone tomorrow, but the Hollywood Walk of Fame remains forever. And to be a part of that is wonderful."

Dyan Cannon 🎥
6608 Hollywood

Dyan Cannon

Actress, singer
BORN Samille Diane Friesen; Jan. 4, 1940, in Tacoma, WA. **SPOTLIGHTS** A heady blonde with effervescent eyes, who "Believe it or Not," was discovered on Sunset Boulevard while having lunch with friends. An agent (a real one, not a fake) approached her at a restaurant and asked her to screen-test at Fox studios. This extremely likable, open-faced doll has a spectacular smile, and her unique, unforgettable laugh is Hollywood's *best*. Cannon excels in comedies, where she frequently receives rave reviews for her work, but is adept in drama, too. Motion pictures include *The Rise and Fall of Legs Diamond* (1960—a fast-moving crime drama, in which she made her screen debut), *Bob & Ted & Carol & Alice* (1969—in an Oscar-nominated performance), *The Anderson Tapes* (1971—an action film), *Heaven Can Wait* (1978—in an Oscar-nominated performance), *Author! Author!* (1982), *Out to Sea* (1997), and *That Darn Cat* (1997). Cannon was absolutely hysterical in the dark comedy *8 Heads in a Duffel Bag* (1997), where she gives a laugh out loud performance. The entire cast is very good and features Joe Pesci and George Hamilton. She appears as a duplicitous sexpot in the campy melodrama, *The Love Machine* (1972), co-starring John Phillip Law. Directed by Jack Haley, Jr., this time capsule was adapted from a trashy Jacqueline Susann novel, and became a cult classic. Cannon directed, produced and wrote the screenplay for *End of Innocence* (1990). She is also the star of this drama-comedy dealing with a troubled woman on the edge, due to family demands. Arnold Schwarzenegger cast her in the lead for his directorial debut, *Christmas in Connecticut* (1992). **ACHIEVEMENTS** 1969 Winner of the Best Supporting Actress Award given by the New York Film Critics for *Bob & Ted & Carol & Alice*. Nominated for an Academy Award for her 1976 film *Number One*; she wrote, produced, directed and co-edited it...Married to Cary Grant (1965-'68); she temporarily retired from the screen upon marrying him. Their union produced his only child, a daughter, Jennifer, in 1966. **QUOTE** Asked her beauty tip, she responded, "Prayer."

Will Rogers 🎤 6608 Hollywood

See page 111

Fleetwood Mac 💿   6608 Hollywood

Singers, musicians
SINGERS British blues band formed in 1967, London,

England. Mick Fleetwood (June 24, 1947, Redruth, Eng.) drums; John McVie (Nov. 26, 1945, London) bass; Jeremy Spencer (July 4, 1948, West Hartlepool, Eng.) guitar, voc.; Stevie Nicks (Stephanie Nicks, May 26,1948, Phoenix, Ariz.) voc.; Christine McVie (July 12, 1944) keyboard, voc.; Lindsey Buckingham (Oct. 3, 1947, Palo Alto, CA) lead guitar. **SPOTLIGHTS** They hit big in Great Britain with "Black Magic Woman," and the instrumental "Albatross." When the U.S.A. fell in love with singer Stevie Nicks, the band *Fleetwood Mac* raced up the charts. They soared to having the second best-selling pop album of all time entitled *Rumours*. It sold more than 17 million copies with such popular tunes as: "Go Your Own Way," "Dreams," "Don't Stop," and "You Make Loving Fun." Winner of numerous Grammys. Past members: Peter Green (a founding member—born Peter Greenbaum, Oct. 29, 1946, London) guitar, voc.; Bob Welch (July 31, 1946, in Los Angeles, CA) guitar, voc.; Daniel Kirwan (May 13, 1950, London) guitar, voc.; Bob Weston, guitar; Dave Walker, voc., guitar; Billy Burnette (May 8, 1953, Memphis, Tenn) guitar, voc.; Rick Vito (Oct. 13, 1949, Darby, Penn.) guitar, voc.; Bekka Bramlett (Apr. 19, 1968, Westwood, CA) voc.; Dave Mason (May 10, 1946, Worcester, Eng.) guitar, voc.

Jack Palance   6608 Hollywood

Jack Palance

Actor
BORN Vladmir (changed to Walter) J. Palahnuik; Feb. 18, 1920, in Lattimer, PA. **SPOTLIGHTS** The son of Russian immigrants, he suffered burn injuries during WWII and had reconstructive plastic surgery. Palance successfully auditioned for *Star of Tomorrow* (1950). TV series include "Ripley's Believe It or Not" (1982-'86), and "The Greatest Show on Earth" (1963-'64). Although very good in TV--he won a well-deserved 1956 Emmy for "Requiem for a Heavyweight"--film is a better medium for this artist, as it shows off his massive, charismatic on-screen presence. So adept at facial expressions is Palance that we sense he is hiding a fiery personality beneath his calm surface, like a smoldering volcano that may—or, may not—blow. Closely associated with the great outdoors, it might surprise you that in the classic Western *Shane* (1953), Palance's grim expressions were not due to acting, but due to his FEAR of horses. Audiences weren't the wiser and he was nominated for an Oscar. His filmography includes *The Halls of Montezuma* (1950), *The Big Knife* (1955), *The Lonely Man* (1957), *Contempt* (1963), *Bagdad Cafe* (1988), *Young Guns* (1988), *Batman* (1989), and *The Swan Princess* (1994—voiceover). **ACHIEVEMENTS** 1991 Academy Award for Best

Supporting Actor for *City Slickers*. He is the father of two actors: Holly and Cody Palance. **QUOTE** After making his screen debut in Elia Kazan's *Panic in the Streets* (1950—for which he was nominated for a "Best Supporting Actor" Oscar), and the clever crime picture *Sudden Fear* (1952), Palance commented, "Before going to Hollywood I was on Broadway four years. And I starved for most of that period. I've been eating pretty good since the movies came into my life."

Ken Minyard and Bob Arthur 🎙
Broadcasters   **6608 Hollywood**

Ken Minyard (right) and son Rick Minyard

BORN Kenny Haskell Minyard; Feb. 9, 1939, in McAlester, OK; Arthur, 1922 in Kansas. **SPOTLIGHTS** Minyard holds the record for the top-rated radio show in Los Angeles for the longest period of time. From 1977 until 1991, his morning show, first as "Ken & Bob," (with Bob Arthur), then as "Ken & Barkley (with Roger Barkley, another Walk of Famer), was ranked #1 for virtually the entire period. Minyard spent 29 years at KABC Radio, in Los Angeles. In January of 1999, he moved to KRLA, where he currently hosts an afternoon show called "Minyard & Minyard" with his new (and he says, "his last") partner, his son Rick. His radio career dates back to his freshman year in McAlester High School in the early 1950s, when he hosted a weekend record show called "Teenage Platter Party." That led to a full-time radio job at KTMC in his hometown during his junior and senior years—heady stuff for a young student. It set the course for his future career. After high school he attended San Francisco State College where he continued his interest in broadcasting. That was followed by radio stops across the country, and finally to Southern California in November of 1969. While he has done TV work over the years, Minyard's first love remains radio. He observed, "Radio, done properly, is the only arena where the performer is in complete control. After having that kind of freedom, I shudder to think what it'd be like to hold down a real job!" Arthur was a reporter for Los Angeles station KNX and a distinguished interviewer of such political notables as President John F. Kennedy and the Rev. Martin Luther King, Jr. Their diversified backgrounds merged to form an irreverent mix of entertainment and news. Their catchphrase was "EGBOK" ("Everything's Gonna Be O-K"). **ACHIEVEMENTS** Recipients of numerous honors, including Golden Mikes and Press Club Awards. **QUOTE** Minyard said, "It's pretty cool to know that your children and their children and the Minyard children of future generations can come to Hollywood and spot my name on that famous Walk of Fame. They'll know the old guy must have done something right!" Died: Arthur, 1997.

Ford Sterling 🎥　　　6608 Hollywood

Comedian

Ford Sterling (far left)

BORN George F. Stitch; Nov. 3, 1883, in LaCrosse, WI. **SPOTLIGHTS** At first, all comics imitated him. Then, when he was age 40, Charlie Chaplin rolled into town. Before long, Sterling was a celebrated secondary clown who supported the great Chaplin, among others. A big slapstick star with Mack Sennett's Keystone Kops, he was always at his comic best. Films include *The Knockout* (1914), *The Adventurer* (1914), *Court House Crook* (1915) and *He Who Gets Slapped* (1924). Due to a 1931 accident his leg was amputated. He became incapacitated. **HIGHLIGHTS** Part of Charlie Chaplin's famous "Tramp" costume came from Sterling. He gave Chaplin his used, black flapping shoes which Chaplin used through all of his films, and are now enshrined. **QUOTE** "The world of make believe pays in satisfaction, the achievement of something one has set out to achieve. It pays in money, which is the legitimate and very necessary reward for achievement, and it pays, above all, if one can make the world laugh, smile, grin or even giggle." Died: 1939.

Eva Gabor 📺　　　6614 Hollywood

Actress
BORN Feb. 11, 1924, in Budapest, Hungary. **SPOTLIGHTS** The younger sister of actress Zsa Zsa Gabor (all the Gabors went to finishing school), Eva was a former cafe singer who emerged a stage actress and a Broadway performer. The stage was her true passion; she declared, "Eet ees een my blood. I luff it weeth my whole soul!" Known primarily for her beauty,

grace, charm and endearing Hungarian accent, she appears in such motion pictures as *The Last Time I Saw Paris* (1954), *Artists and Models* (1955), and *Gigi* (1958). Television: Gabor had her own talk-interview show, and guest-starred in many shows. But she was immortalized as Lisa Douglas, the silly, sexy, scatterbrained blonde socialite on "Green Acres" (1965-'71). Gabor showcased her talents as a light comedienne. Married numerous times, she commented, "Acting ees less disappointing than marriage. At least een acting you can look forward to ze next show, no?" **QUOTE** "Glamour ees a part of edducation." Died: 1995.

Frank Capra 🎥🎥　　　6614 Hollywood

Director, writer, producer
BORN May 18, 1897, in Bisacquino, Sicily. **SPOTLIGHTS** Capra started directing during the silent era, but with sound quickly delivered the fast paced, clever comedy *Platinum Blonde* (1931). It stars the effervescent Jean Harlow and not only made gigantic box office waves, it started a new trend with hair color. The director switched gears with *The Bitter Tea of General Yen* (1933). This hypnotic, erotic, lush drama stars Barbara Stanwyck, and is the most unlike "Capraesque" film. That same year he directed *Lady for a Day* (he remade it as *Pocketful of Miracles* in 1961—his last film). In 1937 Capra made the fine fantasy film, *Lost Horizon* (1937). Then he became known as the champion behind "the regular Joe." He embraced the common man, putting forth the populace message with humor, wit and imagination: *Mr. Smith Goes to Washington* (1939), and *Meet Joe Doe* (1941). One of his most profound works, the now-classic Christmas tale, *It's a Wonderful Life* (1946), stars James Stewart. He plays a down-on-his-luck average fellow, who gets to see what life would have been like had he never been born. It's a wonderful twist of fate that Capra lived long enough to see this picture become an American evergreen—when it was originally released, nobody liked it, and it was a bomb. Viewers found the realism of everyday cruelty too cutting and ignored the heart-warming overtones and message of hope. **ACHIEVEMENTS** Oscars: 1934 *It Happened One Night*; 1936 *Mr. Deed Goes to Town*; and 1938 *You Can't Take It with You*. Also 1934 and 1938 Oscars for Best Picture. **QUOTE** "There are no rules in film making, only sins. And the cardinal sin is dullness." Died: 1991.

Arthur Godfrey 🎙　　　6616 Hollywood

Radio and TV personality
BORN Aug. 31, 1903, in New York City. **SPOTLIGHTS** An enigma. "The barefoot boy of broadcasting" was one of the giants in the industry, but his meager beginnings were anything but great. In fact, he grew up in miserable conditions. His family was too poor to buy groceries on a regular basis, so as a child he often went hungry. Godfrey took to stealing milk bottles, eggs and cheese off other people's porches. At age 10 he got a part-time job, but still managed to get good grades in

school. His excellent speaking abilities got him got elected to captain of the high school debating team at age 14. He also had to take a full-time job, missing weeks upon weeks of school. Then, things got really tough for the family. Godfrey was kicked off the team for missing too much school. The bank evicted the family from their house. The family split up, with siblings paired up with neighbors and relatives. Unable to take anymore heartache, he dropped out of school and ran away from home. He was all of 15. Life on the streets was rough-and-tumble, but he scrambled to make something of himself. Traversing America, meeting all kinds of people and taking all kinds of jobs, he was, at times, a dishwasher, lumberjack, miner, vaudeville trouper and taxi cab driver. He considered himself a failure until he joined the Navy in 1920 and was sent to radio school. Finally, he began to feel that something was right in his life. When he was discharged from the Navy in 1924, he sold cemetery plots door-to-door. Although the product was morbid, he enjoyed sales. In the late 1920s, he joined the Coast Guard, becoming a radio technician, and again things began to click for him. In 1929 he appeared on a radio talent show, and two weeks later had his own show, where he was billed as "Red Godfrey, the Warbling Banjoist." His easy, low-pressure approach to advertising was discovered and he won announcer duties as well. After being an announcer in Washington, he became popular in 1937 as the man-on-the-street. This radio format combined questions to create his show "Professor Quiz." His first national job came in 1945 when—in his honest heartfelt manner—he reported President Franklin Roosevelt's funeral, clearly emotional while describing the horse-drawn procession. America wept along with him and CBS offered him the nation. Postwar fans liked his relaxed, reassuring delivery both on radio and television. By the early 1950s, he was the most popular man in America. Critic John Crosby referred to Godfrey as "the small boy of radio who grew up to be the high priest of television." Godfrey's style was friendly, rambling and casual, like a next-door neighbor. He was a super-salesman of items he believed in, and audiences

Arthur Godfrey

trusted him implicitly. When he said a product was good, people bought it in droves. Day and night he was heard or seen by 80,000,000 devoted fans monthly. Comedian Fred Allen quipped, "The only thing I can turn on in my house *without* getting Arthur Godfrey is the cold water." Shows include "Arthur Godfrey Time," "Arthur Godfrey's Digest," "Arthur Godfrey's Talent Scouts," and "Arthur Godfrey and His Friends." He discovered many celebrities along the way, inspired others, and was the innovator of talk shows. Radio and television host Larry King remarked, "Arthur Godfrey was our uncle, he was our friend, he was my father, he was Arthur." Former Godfrey staff writer and "60 Minutes" commentator Andy Rooney observed, "Arthur Godfrey is the single most forgotten man in television. I don't think that there was anyone ever as important to the medium as he was." **HIGHLIGHTS** Godfrey has two more stars on the Walk of Fame, one is in "radio," the other in "TV." Died: 1983. **NOTE** One of America's most treasured entertainers is virtually unknown to those born after the 1950s since his shows were done live. After they aired, they were gone forever.

Larry King 📺 6616 Hollywood

Broadcaster

BORN Lawrence Harvey Zeiger; November 19, 1933, in Brooklyn, New York. **SPOTLIGHTS** A natural born story teller with a gift of gab, this smart, baseball loving kid from Brooklyn decided at his bar mitzvah to pursue his dream of public speaking. In King's best-selling book, *When You're From Brooklyn, Everything Else Is Tokyo*, he wrote: "At 13, standing there winning over an audience with my voice, I took myself seriously, and the people in the synagogue took me seriously. I never had a doubt from that day forward that I would be on the radio someday. I never entertained a day's thought about any other profession." At age 17, he was selected from the audience to be a contestant on the radio show "Quick as a Flash," hosted by Bud Collier. He reveled in his appearance, won $15 and a bagful of goodies. It was a windfall for a child of the Great Depression, plus it reinforced his self-visualization of being on air. After graduating from high school, he skipped college and got a job. He needed to support his widowed mother, besides he was not academically inclined. His strength lie in being a keen observer of human nature and his ability to

Arthur Godfrey having fun on the ice .

Larry King

be an interesting, quick-witted conversationalist. While working for U.P.S. delivery service he focused his thoughts on radio broadcasting, imagining what he would say if he were to take over sports announcing duties for the Brooklyn Dodgers, or picturing himself as a mirror image of his idol Arthur Godfrey. Then, came his call to arms, which quickly went South when he was rejected by the U.S. Navy with a 4F classification due to his poor eyesight. (It was a good thing, too, considering King did not know how to swim, isn't fond of large bodies of water, and still today won't dip his toes into his own backyard swimming pool.) Later, he switched jobs to deliver Borden's milk. He spent as much time as possible hanging around the CBS building hoping to meet his favorite celebrities. As destiny would have it, one day he met James Sirmons, the chief staff announcer whose voice could be heard saying, "*This* is the CBS Radio Network." The gregarious youth approached him with enthusiasm, catching his attention. He told him, "I'd really like to get into radio. Do you have any suggestions?" "Try Miami," Sirmons remarked. "It's a big, growing market, there are no unions, they have big stations, small stations, guys on the way up, guys on the way down, a lot of good people to meet, a lot of opportunities." In 1957 in Miami, the 24-year-old landed a morning disc jockey job at a small AM station, WAHR. The general manager told him that his name was not show business enough so he suggested King. In Miami, King perfected his interview style on both radio and TV. From 1978 to 1994, his was the familiar voice heard by millions across the nation on Mutual Radio's "The Larry King Show." Yet it is television that brought him global recognition. Since its 1985 debut, "Larry King Live," has delivered headline-making, news-breaking interviews to CNN's global audience. King's trademark look includes spiffy suspenders, an elegant silk tie and glasses. But never a jacket. His appearance, reminiscent of the old school of broadcasting, gives him a hands-on, rolled-up sleeves approach to a topic. His show is the only worldwide, live television viewer call-in program. Which suits King fine since he treats his viewers as friends, and is truly interested in what his live phone-in callers interject. In doing so, he has won the loyalty of viewers everywhere. He is highly respected for his unique manner of mediating a panel of experts on a specialized topic in any given field. He controls the environment, and with his built-in radar, probes his guests with insightful questions. All the while the trustworthy King gleans delicious nuggets for his audience to savor. Each show is really a meeting of the minds—whether a famous person is examined, a lively exchange about the crime *du jour* is debated, or politicians come to express opinions or declare positions, utilizing the show as the new, high-tech town hall, a forum for statesmen to voice their convictions to the American people. The award-winning "Larry King Live" is watched in 175 million households in 210 countries and territories. He singlehandedly revolutionized the medium, capturing the attention of people in all walks of life. Joe Hooper, A.S.I.D.—interior designer to celebrities and royalty alike—commented, "It's nice to see Larry wherever I am in the world and keep abreast of the hot topics in the United States. Especially with his excellent choice of guests and panelists; these people mean business." **HIGHLIGHTS** When his star was unveiled on May 1, 1997, it celebrated his 40th anniversary in broadcasting. The placement of his star is significant, too; he is next to the star of radio's and television's legendary Arthur Godfrey. King declared, "What a radio genius Arthur Godfrey was. He remains my inspiration on the air. He took chances. He wasn't afraid. Sometimes they worked, and when they didn't, he was still on top." **ACHIEVEMENTS** Recipient of five broadcasting Hall of Fames and two Peabody Awards, he has received countless other awards and honors. King has conducted more than 30,000 live interviews since he signed on in 1957, including Eleanor Roosevelt, Martin Luther King, Jr., Lucille Ball, Malcolm X, Jackie Robinson, Jackie Gleason, Elizabeth Taylor, Mohammed Ali, Barbra Streisand, Al Pacino, Mikhail Gorbachev, Margaret Thatcher, Yasser Arafat, First Lady Barbara Bush, and First Lady Hillary Clinton. In 1992 he conceived a new kind of televised political forum for presidential candidates, giving voters an opportunity to get a clearer picture of the men and women working Washington's machinery...He chairs the Larry King Cardiac Foundation which awards grants to individuals suffering from heart disease, and gives generously to the Save the Children Foundation. **QUOTE** "The only secret in this business is there's no secret. Be yourself. The minute you're not, you're in trouble."

Fats Domino 🔴   6616 Hollywood

Singer, pianist, songwriter
BORN Antoine Domino; May 10, 1929, in New Orleans, LA. **SPOTLIGHTS** He is a legendary boogie-woogie, rock 'n' roller who tickles the ivories with a dynamic, rolling, pounding energy. Domino began playing the piano at age 10; by age 11 he was playing for pennies in honky-tonks with heavy emphasis on the New Orleans music sound. His first record, "The Fat Man" sold one million copies in 1949, and he continued cutting rhythm & blues tunes "Goin' Home" and "Going to the River" before the rock 'n' roll revolution. When he performs, he is a powerhouse entertainer. Audiences really connect to him and his music. A number of solid gold tunes made him a superstar. Songs include "Ain't that a Shame," "Blueberry Hill," "I'm Walkin'," "I'm In Love Again," and "Blue

Monday." His holiday album, *Christmas Is A Special Day* (1993), received top-notch critical acclaim. **ACHIEVEMENTS** Fats outsold every 1950s rock 'n' roller except Elvis Presley; selling more than 65 million records. He has 23 gold records, and is no shrinking violet when it comes to his livelihood. Blessed with a down-to-earth business and marketing skills, as well as good common sense, he has lived by a set of rules that include "Keep your standards up." He is widely admired by his colleagues and the public. **HIGHLIGHTS** He returned to his hometown with his wife to raise their eight children, who all have names starting with the letter "A."

June Havoc 🎥   6618 Hollywood

June Havoc

Actress, writer
BORN June Hovick; Nov. 8, 1916, in Seattle, WA. **SPOTLIGHTS**: Baby June's stage mother pushed her to perform as soon as she could place one foot in front of the other. You might remember seeing the movie *Gypsy* (original version 1962, with a superior remake in 1993) based on her family. Her older sister was the real-life stripper Gypsy Rose Lee. Little June appeared in front of the cameras when she was only two with comedian Harold Lloyd, then Hal Roach hired her for his comedies (1918-'24). Among her grown up credits are *Four Jacks and a Jill* (1941), *My Sister Eileen* (1942) and *Brewster's Millions* (1945).

Little Jack Little 🎤   6618 Hollywood

Composer, singer, pianist
BORN May 28, 1900, in London, England. **SPOTLIGHTS** Known as "Radio's Cheerful Little Earful." His 1930s music show, "Little Jack Little" was well-received by listening audiences. He sang in a friendly now-I'm-singing, now I'm talking style. His band's popularity soared in the years before the Big Bands. Leader Little Jack played the piano part time in his band. Songs: "A Shanty in Old Shanty Town," and "You're a Heavenly Thing." Died: 1956.

Albert Dekker 📺   6620 Hollywood

Actor
BORN Dec. 20, 1904, in New York, NY. **SPOTLIGHTS** A tall, sturdy, mustached character actor, he convincingly played villainous roles. Her stars in the title role *Dr. Cyclops* (1940), as the mad scientist. This was the first sci-fi film to be made in Technicolor, and remains a cult classic. He made 80 films, including *Wake Island* (1942), *Seven Sinners* (1940), *The Killers* (1946), *Fury at Furnace Creek* (1948), *Kiss Me Deadly* (1955), *East of Eden* (1955) and *The Wild Bunch* (released 1969). He worked in live TV. **ACHIEVEMENTS** Served in the California Legislature, as a Democrat representing the Hollywood district. **QUOTE** Upon entering the California State House, Dekker stated, "Occasionally, an innocent man is sent to the legislature." Died: 1968.

Gilda Gray 🎥   6620 Hollywood

Actress, dancer
BORN Marianna Michalska; Oct. 24, 1901, in Poland. **SPOTLIGHTS** While in her teens, she was more than provocative--she was outrageous--dancing a shoulder-moving, chest-shaking dance in a Milwaukee saloon. When a wealthy Italian-American from Chicago asked her what she was doing, she described her unique upper body movement as "I'm shaking my little shimmy." (Hence the phrase: "shake that little moneymaker.") Billed as the "The Queen of Jazz," she introduced the shimmy in New York in late 1918. It was considered "indecent" by lawmakers and enraged police, who threatened to shut down any cabarets allowing the dance. A duplicate warning in the 1920s did not stop Sophie Tucker, who showcased

Gilda Gray

Gilda doing the "Shimmy Shewabble" on Broadway. This "vulgar cooch dance" grew in its popularity for both sexes, vibrating to super fame with the jazz tune "Indianola." It seemed that everyone was doing it, including Mae West in her 1921 show *Mimic World*, but it was Gilda Gray who shook her way to fame and fortune. Impresario Flo Ziegfeld hired "the Golden Girl" at $3,500-a-week; she enjoyed working for him for three years. Gilda was the first to "shimmy" on-screen. Ads promoting her films read, *"When Gilda Gray shakes, San Francisco quakes."* She made $6,000 a picture, plus 20% of the gross over $250,000. Not a bad deal for a shimmy virtuoso, but then again she set a record in 1925 for box office grosses. Movies include *Lawful Larceny* (1923), *Aloma of the South Seas*, *Cabaret* (both 1926), *The Devil Dancer* (1928), and *Piccadilly* (1929). The famous Roaring Twenties dance—the Charleston—swept the nation and her career stalled. Later, she appears in *The Great Ziegfeld* (1936), starring William Powell. **HIGHLIGHTS** Col. Parker told Elvis Presley to watch Gray's old movies and study her dance technique. Parker wanted Presley to improve his moves and dance like her. Presley did watch and he did pick up a few new tricks that drove the fans wild. Died: 1959.

Al Jolson 🎥   6622 Hollywood

Singer, actor
BORN Asa Yoelson; May 26, 1886, in Russia. **SPOTLIGHTS** An entertainer bursting with vitality and self-confidence, he initially gained fame for his minstrel-show routines and singing "Mammy" in blackface. (Popular at the time and historically relevant, this would not be considered acceptable entertainment in today's blended, more enlightened, and more progressive society.) Then, Jolson made movie history for speaking in the first talkie—*The Jazz Singer* (1927). During the shooting of the film—which originally just had songs, but no dialogue—Jolson cried out to the technicians, "Wait a minute!

Al Jolson in now-controversial (racist) blackface.

Wait a minute! You ain't heard nothin' yet." Although these lines were unscripted, they ended up in the film when co-producer Darryl Zanuck decided the audience would like hearing them. But Zanuck's boss, Harry Warner (of Warner Bros.) worried that "people might laugh when they hear that guy talkin'." Zanuck argued to keep the very first movie dialogue in place. A last minute decision by Warner favored Zanuck's position. Audiences went wild when they heard Jolson speak. Paid $75,000 for his role, the studio grossed $3.5 million, and ushered in the age of sound. His next film, *The Singing Fool* (1928), held one of the highest box office records for 11 years. Died: 1950.

Eva Marie Saint 🎥   6624 Hollywood

Eva Marie Saint

Actress
BORN On Independence Day, July 4, 1924, in Newark, NJ. **SPOTLIGHTS** A sensitive, blonde beauty with delicate features, she got an unusually late start in motion pictures—at 30 years old. She immediately received an invitation to that rarified party of actresses who win an Academy Award on their first movie date. By her choice, she has participated in less than two dozen pictures. Never driven by the desire for money, Saint choose quality over quantity. She wanted to do works that both she and her family could be proud of. Films include *That Certain Feeling* (1956) with Bob Hope, *Raintree Country* (1957) with Elizabeth Taylor, *A Hatful of Rain* (1957—a story about a junkie and how addiction affects others), and Hitchcock's *North by Northwest* (1959) with Cary Grant, to mention a few of her films. Saint was delightful in the madcap comedy *The Russians Are Coming! The Russians Are Coming!* (1966) with the funny Carl Reiner and ruggedly handsome co-star John Phillip Law. Later movies include *Nothing in Common* (1986) with Jackie Gleason and Tom Hanks. Previously, Saint, an accomplished stage actress, was discovered by motion picture director Elia Kazan in 1953 while performing in "A Trip to Bountiful." Her many very good television roles include "Middle of the Night," "Our Town," and "My Antonia." She also played Cybill Shepherd's mother on the television series "Moonlighting." **ACHIEVEMENTS** 1954 Best Supporting Actress Oscar for *On the Waterfront*, her first film role ("it takes periods of loneliness of defeat, and the winter of the spirit to make us capable of appreciating times of happiness and contentment"). She married director Jeffrey Hayden and had two children, Darrell and Laurette. About her children Saint remarked, "It's selfish to center all the love on one, and we have so much love to give."

Otto Preminger 🎥
6624 Hollywood

Otto Preminger

Director, producer, actor
BORN Dec. 5, 1906, in Vienna, Austria. **SPOTLIGHTS** He left a legacy of provocative work. His murder mystery, *Laura* (1941), has an outstanding cast, haunting music and a brilliant twist. It is a "must-see" movie, and earned Preminger his first Oscar nomination. His historical *Forever Amber* (1947) captures the naughtiness of Charles II's court. He remade the French picture, *Le Corbeau*, into *The 13th Letter* (1951), a drama about poison pen letters. In 1953, he became an independent producer; he declared, "the emphasis on independent." Movies during this time include *Stalag 17* (also actor), the thriller *Angel Face* (both 1953), *River of No Return* (1954), and *Carmen Jones* (1954). The latter was with an all-black cast; singer-actress Dorothy Dandridge received a best actress Oscar nomination. Frank Sinatra was nominated for his first Oscar in Preminger's *The Man with the Golden Arm* (1955). *The Court-Martial of Billy Mitchell* is a compelling, true-life drama about a military man who accurately predicted the Pearl Harbor attack 16 years before it happened. Films include *Porgy and Bess* (1959) starring Sidney Poitier, Dorothy Dandridge, and Pearl Bailey, *Anatomy of a Murder* (1959), with James Stewart and Lee Remick, and *Hurry Sundown* (1966) starring Faye Dunaway and John Phillip Law. **QUOTE** He caused a stir when he released *The Moon Is Blue* (1953) without code approval. Preminger stated, "I never wanted to start a fight on censorship, but I felt I had the right to turn out movies without censorship, whether by the industry or by the critics." The debate helped to create a box office smash. Died: 1986.

Janis Paige 🎥
6624 Hollywood

Actress, singer
BORN Donna Mae Jaden; Sept. 16, 1923, in Tacoma, WA. **SPOTLIGHTS** A girlish redhead gifted with a golden throat, she was somewhat under used in musicals. Paige was extremely good in MGM's *Silk Stockings* (1957), starring Fred Astaire, Cyd Charisse and Peter Lorre. *Follow the Boys* (1963) provided the lush scenery of the French Rivera with Connie Francis and Paula Prentiss. She appears in the remake of the bad guy-makes-a-deal-with-the-devil story, *Angel on My Shoulder* (1980)—but the original version (1946) is twice as good. She's fun to watch as a Broadway diva in *Please Don't Eat the Daisies* (1960), starring Doris Day and David Niven. Versatile on stage and in television, too.

Walter Huston 🎥
6626 Hollywood

Actor
BORN Walter Houghston; April 6, 1884, in Toronto, Canada. **SPOTLIGHTS** A great stage actor who—fortunately for movie buffs—liked the weather in California and left an extremely talented bloodline to

Walter Huston with Noel Francis

follow in his footsteps. He played a mustache-twirling villain in *The Virginian* (1929), in the film that made Gary Cooper a star. He portrays Honest Abe in *Abraham Lincoln* (1930), in D.W. Griffith's first talkie. Huston is wonderful in *Rain* (1932), and *Dodsworth* (1936). He plays the smooth talking Mr. Scratch in *All That Money Can Buy* (1941—also known as *The Devil and Daniel Webster*). This talented actor is terrific in *The Shanghai Gesture* (1941), and *Yankee Doodle Dandy* (1942). In 1945 he appears in *the very first* Agatha Christie novel brought to screen, *And Then There Were None*, a five-star picture. **ACHIEVEMENTS** 1948 Best Supporting Actor Oscar for *The Treasure of the Sierra Madre*, written and directed by his famous son, John Huston, who also won two awards! Grandfather of Academy Award-winning actress, Angelica Huston. Died: 1950.

Rip Taylor
6626 Hollywood

Rip Taylor

Comedian, singer, actor
BORN Charles Elmer Taylor; 1930, in Washington, D.C. **SPOTLIGHTS** A brilliant comic genius and master of "razzle-dazzle" comic showmanship, Taylor began performing when he was a page in the U.S. Senate (proving Washington is a circus). A singer and lip-syncer, he changed his name to "Rip" because, he explained, "it sounded like a guy who kept people in stitches!" He experimented with pantomime (the key to all great comedians), and gradually eased into stand up comedy. The latter led to his introduction of "prop comedy." Even in his early days of entertainment, Rip's repertoire was eclectic enough to include everything from the zany novelty music of Spike Jones (see his bio in this book), to Yiddish folk songs. A tireless performer, he sobbed buckets and shed torrents of tears with delirious results. As he traveled the country with his act, he became known as "The Crying Comedian."

This title led to his bigger-than-life props. Every performance was like a parade. His confetti-throwing antics became his comedic trademark, and took on dozens of forms: multi-colored paper, sequin, popcorn, sparklers and publicity photos. A continuous round of nightclub and showroom appearances earned him the names "The Prince of Pandemonium" and "The Count of Chaos." His TV appearance on "The Ed Sullivan Show" was seen by a Las Vegas Show producer and landed him his first casino job at the Dunes Hotel. He was an instant favorite. Stage shows include "The Student Prince," "Oliver" (he played Fagan), "Peter Pan" (as Captain Hook), and on Broadway with Ann Miller in "Sugar Babies." He followed that hit with a national tour of the Lincoln Center's production of "Anything Goes." **TV:** One of the most recognizable faces in all of show business, he has had hundreds of guest-starring roles in series, appeared in several music-variety Specials, and had his own "$1.98 Beauty Show." He does voiceovers for cartoon series, including being the voice of Uncle Fester in Hanna-Barbera's "The Addams Family." Movies include *Home Alone II* (1992), and *Indecent Proposal* (1993) as Demi Moore's bald-headed boss (no wig for this one). Believe it or not, he has also performed Shakespeare. A generous soul, he entertains at countless charity events. **ACHIEVEMENTS** He celebrated his 25th anniversary in show business with his star dedication ceremony on Oct. 15, 1992. Taylor's star was appropriately located in front of the Outfitter's Wig Shop (and yes, he did flip his wig with all the wacky and wild excitement of the day). **QUOTE** About getting his star, he said, "It's the highlight of my career. From now until the 'big one' hits, people will be dropping garbage and stepping on my name, I love it!"

Gordon Jenkins ● 6626 Hollywood

Pianist, composer, arranger
BORN May 12, 1910, in Webster Groves, MO. **SPOTLIGHTS** In his youth, Jenkins played the organ at a movie palace. He began playing in clubs, and wouldn't be convinced to keep away from St. Louis speakeasies during the Prohibition. His experience paid off when he was hired as a big band arranger-conductor for Isham Jones, among others. Jenkins said about working for Jones, "I went to bed and lay for some time thinking about the 'good old days' and the Old Jones band. That, gents, was a band...writing for that band was fun, not work...It was the greatest sweet ensemble of that time or any other time." He also became the musical director at Paramount in 1938, then established himself at NBC (1939-'44). Popular from Las Vegas to New York, he frequently collaborated with Johnny Mercer. Songs: "I Want to Be Loved," 'When a Woman Loves A Man," "Bewitched." His theme song was the mournful ballad "Goodbye." Died: 1984.

Alice Terry ♥ 6628 Hollywood

Actress
BORN Alice Taafe; July 24, 1899, in Vicennes, IN.

SPOTLIGHTS A graceful, alluring, blue-eyed blonde, she was considered tall at 5'6" and weighed a perfect 130 pounds. This poised beauty wore her costumes with elegance, and starred with the leading men of the day. It did not hurt her career any to marry director Rex Ingram. Her top movies include *The Four Horsemen of the Apocalypse* (1921), *The Prisoner of Zenda* (1922), *Scaramouche* (1923), *The Arab* (1924), and *The Three Passions* (1929). Died: 1987.

Alice Terry

Renata Tebaldi ● 6628 Hollywood

Opera singer
BORN Feb. 1, 1922, in Pesaro, Italy. **SPOTLIGHTS** She was dubbed "La Superba" by admirers. This tall (5'10"), perpetually youthful-looking soprano of Puccini's operas had a powerful voice was well suited for the whole Italian repertoire up to the grand Verdis. Postwar, the adored diva was selected by Toscanini to perform at the 1946 reopening ceremony of the rebuilt La Scala, the world famous Milan opera house. Tebaldi's U.S. debut in San Francisco in 1950 as Aida brought praise to her as the finest *lirico spinto*—a classification between the lyric and the dramatic that enables exploitation of both. Her vocal range stretched from low F to D over high C. It took almost five years for her general manager, Rudolf Bing, to get her to sign a contract with the Metropolitan Opera. And when he did, it was on her terms. For this stubborn streak, she was labeled "Dimples of Steel." Metropolitan Opera debut in 1955 as Desdemona in *Othello*. After her performances, fans threw so many flowers that the stage took on the appearance of carpeting. Although she pretended not to be a *bellicose prima donna*, she went about absolutely getting her own way—always! She was well worth the pampering, she became the greatest box office draw since Flagstad. Recordings: Puccini's *Madame Butterfly*, *Manon Lescaut*, *Tosca*, *Aida*; more. **SIDELIGHTS** Her French poodle was named "New." **QUOTE** From the old school of thought, Tebaldi stated, "I think that a singer should have a beautiful, *even* voice. If I want to see good acting, I go to the play, not the opera."

Horace Heidt ☆ 6630 Hollywood

See page 351

Charley Chase ♥ 6630 Hollywood

Actor, director, comedian
BORN Charles Parrot; Oct. 20, 1893, in Baltimore, MD. **SPOTLIGHTS** Chase had the good fortune to work for the early

masters of comedy, such as Mack Sennett and Charlie Chaplin. The polished, wealthy householder fussed his way through a number of funny silent one and two-reelers, with a fancy pompadour. He joined the Hal Roach studios, and with his excellent sense of timing, directed comedians such as Stan Laurel. Later, he acted in sound pictures. Died: 1940.

Sonny James   6630 Hollywood

Singer, guitarist, songwriter
BORN Jimmie Loden; May 1, 1929, in Hackleburg, Alabama. **SPOTLIGHTS** He knew what he was going to be at age four after winning a folk talent contest. In the 1950s he played country-and-western, pop, and rock. A string of hit singles includes: "Young Love," "Behind the Tear," "I'll Keep Holding On," "Only Love Can Break a Heart" and "Don't Keep Me Hangin On." James also uses alternating Spanish-English lyrics in his country music. His music crosses over to the pop music world. Albums: *True Love's a Blessing*, and *World of Our Own*.

Roddy McDowall 6630 Hollywood

Roddy McDowall

Actor, photographer
BORN Roderick Andrew Anthony Jude McDowall; Sept. 17, 1928, in London, England. **SPOTLIGHTS** A natural born talent, he studied diction and dramatics while most children played knights in shining armor. Blessed with angelic looks and an innate understanding of timing, he worked onstage before winning his first screen role at age eight in the feature *Murder in the Family*. Other British film roles followed, but when Germany's bombing raids in London hit dangerously close to their home during WWII, his mother fled with him and his younger sister to America. With the equivalent of only $42. in cash, it was imperative that the youngster find work fast in Hollywood to support his family. Discovered by director William Wyler—who had viewed Roddy's screen test with keen interest—the child made his U.S. debut in the excellent WWII thriller *Man Hunt* (1941). At age 13, he won American audiences' hearts with his brilliant performance in the five-star production of *How Green Was My Valley*. Critically acclaimed box office hits *The Pied Piper* (1942), *My Friend Flicka* and *Lassie Come Home* (both 1943) followed. Meanwhile, his new school was the sunny back lot at 20th Century-Fox Studio School, a far cry from the strict St. Joseph's Academy in rainy ol' England. The teenager did not seem to mind, especially as he was cast in important Shakespeare works such as the tragedy *Macbeth* (1948), directed by Orson Welles. And as he grew up he would not experience the conundrum in which most child

actors find themselves—plenty of experience and previous stardom, but no job offers. Though convincing his studio to let him mature was a struggle. Reflecting on those times he stated, "There was an unspoken conspiracy against my ever growing up." He left Hollywood for New York to study drama commenting, "Acting is a serious endeavor and profession." He made his 1953 Broadway debut in Shaw's "Misalliance." As an adult, he proved extremely adept with dry comedy, drama, TV work, stage and film. Although he made about 70 motion pictures, science fiction buffs are devoted to his craftsmanship in *Planet of the Apes* (1967), and its sequels including *Escape from the Planet of the Apes* (1971). Even in full makeup and costume, he brought a unique intelligence and vital presence to his roles. His charisma cannot be overestimated. Other motion pictures include *The Greatest Story Ever Told* (1965), *The Poseidon Adventure* (1972), *The Life and Times of Judge Roy Bean* (1972), *Fright Night* (1985), *Overboard* (1987), and *The Big Picture* (1989). TV work includes mini-series, specials and movies of the week: "An Inconvenient Woman," "Hollywood Wives," "Hart to Hart" "The Tempest," "The Martian Chronicles" and "The Memory of Eva Ryker." **ACHIEVEMENTS** 1961 Emmy for "Not Without Honor." 1960 Tony for "The Fighting Cock." Died: 1998.

Vaughn De Leath 6630 Hollywood

Singer, composer, pianist
BORN Sept. 26, 1896, in Mt. Pulaski, IL. **SPOTLIGHTS** Known as "The Original Radio Girl," she was thought to be the first woman to sing on the air in 1920, as soon as radio production began. (Actually an opera singer worked in experimental radio around 1907.) This large woman sang in a smooth, throaty voice that became known as crooning. It's a style she initiated. Her theme song was "Red Sails in the Sunset," and the soloist remained on the radio for two decades, almost until her death. De Leath was also the composer of more than 500 songs, including: "Hi Yo Silver" and "Madonna's Lullaby." Died: 1943.

Neil Hamilton 6636 Hollywood

Actor
BORN Sept. 9, 1899, in Lynn, MA. **SPOTLIGHTS** He got his break in D.W. Griffith's silent *White Rose* (1923). Talkies include *Tarzan the Ape Man* (1932) and *What Price Hollywood?* (1932)—the forerunner to *A Star is Born*. But, he was immortalized in television as Police Commissioner Gordon on "Batman" (1966-'68). Whenever evil-doers waged war on Gotham City, the Commissioner would pick up the special Bat phone, or summon Batman and Robin with a searchlight Bat signal. Died: 1984.

Norma Shearer 6638 Hollywood

Actress

Norma Shearer

BORN Edith N. Shearer; Aug. 10, 1900, in Canada. **SPOTLIGHTS** She was one of MGM's biggest international stars during the 1930s. Not particularly beautiful by Hollywood standards, she stated that she felt beautiful inside. She was always impeccably dressed, and made millions of people think she was gorgeous. Movies include *A Lady by Chance* (1928); *A Free Soul* (1931), and *Marie Antoinette* (1938). **ACHIEVEMENTS** 1930 Best Actress Oscar for *The Divorcee*. **HIGHLIGHTS** Married to "The Boy Wonder of Hollywood," Irving Thalberg (from 1927 to his death in 1936), who wisely guided her career. **QUOTE** Without her brilliant husband's advice, she made the two biggest mistakes of her career. First, she turned down the role of Scarlett O'Hara in *Gone with the Wind,* because she said, "My fans didn't want me to play a bad woman." Second, she rejected the lead in *Mrs. Miniver* because she explained, "I would have had to play a mother with a grown son." Oops. Died: 1983.

Dale Evans 🎤   6638 1/2 Hollywood

See page 150

Billy Eckstine ●   6640 Hollywood

Singer, band leader, musician
BORN William Eckstein; July 8, 1914, in Pittsburgh, PA. **SPOTLIGHTS** "The Ecstatic Mr. B" was a strong, silky baritone. As an entertainer, his assets included his good looks—he was *very* handsome. Eckstine possessed a charming manner, and his snazzy way of putting himself together included him dressing to the nines and his perfectly coiffed hair. These qual-

ities appealed to the ladies with whom he was *extremely popular*. He worked with Charlie Parker, Miles Davis, Dexter Gordon and Sarah Vaughan (a timid girl at the time). This giant of a talent formed his first big band with Dizzy Gillespie in 1944, then went solo in 1947. Two years later, he was idolized by millions of bobby-soxers. In fact, he broke attendance records and sold more tickets than the previously held position by Frank Sinatra! He was one of the first—if not *the* first—to erase color lines in entertainment. Universally known both as "Mr. B," and "The Vibrato," he was too cool. Among his musical peers, he was widely admired, and many tried to emulate him. Hits include "Jelly, Jelly," "Stormy Monday Blues," "My Foolish Heart" "No Orchids for My Lady," "Fools Rush In," "Skylark," "Prisoner of Love," "Everything I Have Is Yours," and "My Destiny." Elvis Presley said "Mr. B" was influencial in his music development. Died: 1993.

Schumann-Heink ●   6640 Hollywood

Opera singer
BORN Ernestine Rossler; June 15, 1861, in Lieben, Germany. **SPOTLIGHTS** A gifted German contralto at Metropolitan Opera (1899, 1903), she was celebrated for her interpretations of Wagnerian works. This phenomenal talent had a repertoire of 150 roles. **QUOTE** One evening, the portly singer—who loved good food—was dining at a gourmet restaurant. The great opera singer Enrico Caruso entered the restaurant and saw she was about to dig into a *gigantic*, juicy steak. He went to her table and asked her, "Stina, surely you are not going to eat that alone?" She shook her head and replied, "No, no, not alone. Mit potatoes." Died: 1936.

Michael Curtiz 🎥   6640 Hollywood

Director
BORN Mihaly Kertesz; Dec. 24, 1888, in Budapest, Hungary. **SPOTLIGHTS** In 1933 he concentrated on crime themes:

"Mr. B." (right) with Johnny Grant on KMPC radio.

Michael Curtiz with Joan Crawford

20,000 Years in Sing Sing, *The Mystery of the Wax Museum*, and *The Kennel Murder Case*. In 1934 he surprised everyone with the gangster comedy about a con man called *Jimmy the Gent*. In 1935 audiences thrilled at newcomer Errol Flynn in *Captain Blood*. In 1938 *Angels with Dirty Faces* became an Academy Award-nominee. *Dodge City* (1939) and *The Sea Hawk* (1940) proved smashing successes both starring Errol Flynn. Perhaps he dipped into the memory of his own refugee status (during World War I), to make the classic *Casablanca* (1942). That same year, he directed the musical biography of George M. Cohan in *Yankee Doodle Dandy*; it's an Americana feel-good movie. *Mildred Pierce* (1945) scrutinized money and its effects, and stunned middle America. He directed the all-star cast of Kirk Douglas, Lauren Bacall, Doris Day and Hoagy Carmichael in *Young Man With a Horn* (1950). In *King Creole* (1958), Elvis Presley stars as a New Orleans nightclub singer. He also directed *The Adventures of Huckleberry Finn* (1960). **ACHIEVEMENTS** 1942 Oscar for *Casablanca*. Died: 1962.

Gene Autry 🎥   6644 Hollywood

Gene Autry

Singer, song writer, guitarist, actor

BORN Sept. 29, 1907, in Tioga, TX. **SPOTLIGHTS** America's favorite singing cowboy. As an 18-year-old railroad telegrapher in Oklahoma, he bought a guitar and taught himself to play it to pass the night. Between trains, he would sing his heart out. Will Rogers came in to send a telegram, and heard young Autry sing. He said, "Stick to it, young fella, and you'll make something of yourself." By 1927 he was a radio celebrity, by 1929, a recording star. Eventually he recorded 2,000 songs—300 of which he wrote or co-wrote—including, "That Silver Haired Daddy of Mine," and "The Yellow Rose of Texas." His film debut was in *Old Santa Fe* (1934), then he stars in *Tumblin' Tumbleweeds* (1935) and 91 more movies, always playing himself. He was the top box office Western star for a record-breaking six years (1936-'42), when he absented himself to volunteer for WWII combat duty as a pilot in the Army Air Corps. Autry served with distinction. Radio: "Gene Autry's Melody Ranch" (first aired in 1940). TV: "The Gene Autry Show" (CBS, 1950-56). An unprecedented career that incorporated radio, motion pictures, television, recording and live theater combined to make Gene Autry the only person on the Hollywood Walk of Fame to earn one star in each of the five categories. **SIDELIGHTS** The song "Here Comes Santa Claus" crystallized while he was riding as Grand Marshal in the Hollywood Santa Claus Lane parade and heard children excitedly scream, "Here comes Santa Claus!" Owned the California Angels baseball team for many years then sold to Disney. **CODE OF HONOR** Gene Autry helped establish the "Cowboy Code of Honor" and is most closely associated with its merits. As such, it is that an honorable man would never slug anyone smaller than himself or take unfair advantage, nobody gets shot in the back, a leading lady is treated like *a lady*, there's no lying, stealing or cheating, and it incorporates many other noble behaviors. Inspired by these values, actor Chuck Norris said, "I'll never play a drug addict or an alcoholic. Whatever role I'm playing, in the kids' eyes it's Chuck Norris up there on the screen." **VISIT** The outstanding museum Autry founded: The Autry Museum of Western Heritage. The address is: 4700 Western Heritage Way, Los Angeles (near Griffith Park). Telephone (323) 667-2000 (website: www.Autry-Museum.org). The world mourned when this legendary cowboy died in 1998.

Arthur Lake 🎙   6644 Hollywood

Actor

BORN Arthur Silverlake; April 17, 1905, in Corbin, KY. **SPOTLIGHTS** Born to a circus family, he played his first clown at age three. He was a veteran comedian by the time he was cast as the rattled husband Dagwood Bumstead on "Blondie" (CBS-Radio 1939-'50). His much-imitated call was "BLONNNNNNNNNDIE! Rushing in where angels fear to tread, he also starred in the film

Arthur Lake

series (1938-50), and the TV version of the 1950s. Other movies include *Exile to Shanghai* (1937), and *The Big Show-Off* (1945). Died: 1987.

Dennis Day 📺   6646 Hollywood

Dennis Day (right) and Don Wilson

Singer, actor

BORN May 21, 1917, in New York, NY. **SPOTLIGHTS** When he joined "The Jack Benny Show" in 1939, he was a nervous kid straight out of college. Lucky for him he had such a great boss. The antithesis of Benny's cranky, stingy show business character, the cheerful Day was treated like a favorite son. A tenor vocalist, he moved with the cast to the TV show (CBS, 1950-'60), still playing a lamebrained kid when he was middle aged. Died: 1988.

Cathy Downs 📺   6648 Hollywood

Actress

BORN March 3, 1924, in Port Jefferson, NY. **SPOTLIGHTS** At a height of five feet, 6 inches, 122 pounds, with a 24-inch waist, Downs existed as the perfect "Sweater Girl." She modeled for "Vogue" and "Mademoiselle" magazines, among others. Additionally, her blue eyes, brown hair, and a beautiful face encouraged 20th Century-Fox to sign her. She co-stars with Henry Fonda in John Ford's *My Darling Clementine* (1946). In all, she made 24 movies. She appeared in the "Joe Palooka" TV series. Died: 1976.

Eddie Cantor 🎥   6648 Hollywood

Actor, singer

Eddie Cantor

BORN Edward Iskowitz; Jan. 31, 1892, in New York, NY. **SPOTLIGHTS** His life started out as anything but a song. Born in the ghetto, he lost both parents early in his childhood. He quit school to work days as a singing waiter at Coney Island, and perform (amateur) nights in his teens at a burlesque show. He learned his theatrical ropes in vaudeville with one-liners. By 1917 he was winning audiences' hearts in the Ziegfeld Follies. His first movie, Paramount's *Kid Boots* (1926), co-stars Clara Bow and was a smash. Affectionately known as "Banjo Eyes" due to his rolling of his "large pop eyes" when he mugged, he earned $5,000 a week from radio fees. By 1931, he was rolling in the dough from stage, recording and motion picture salaries. Eddie Fisher commented, "Because of his great influence as a singer, every young singer dreamed of being discovered by Cantor." The approval came when Cantor said, "Believe me, ladies and gentlemen, this boy (girl) is really going to be something." TV: Two popular shows, "The Colgate Comedy Hour" and "Eddie Cantor Comedy Theater," gave audiences the opportunity to watch this energetic, legendary talent croon "If You Knew Susie," "Tomatoes Are Cheaper, Potatoes Are Cheaper/Now's the time to fall in loooove!" and "Ma!" **ACHIEVEMENTS** 1956 Special Academy Award. During WWII, he entertained U.S. and Allied Forces overseas. **QUOTE** After a battle with sponsors over the contents of his radio show, he refused to be dictated to by Madison Avenue. He said, "Long after I'm through as a comedian, I'll still be a man." Died: 1964.

James Caan 🎥   6648 Hollywood

Actor

BORN March 26, 1939, in New York, NY. **SPOTLIGHTS** This ruggedly handsome, tough leading man made his screen debut in *Irma La Douce* (1963—unbilled), starring Shirley MacLaine and Jack Lemmon. He followed up with a number of films—including the top notch cowboy picture, *El Dorado* (1967) with John Wayne and Robert Mitchum, and as the feebleminded ex-football player in *The Rain People* (1969), to name a couple—before coming to America's attention in the perfect TV movie "Brian's Song" (1970). Based on the true story

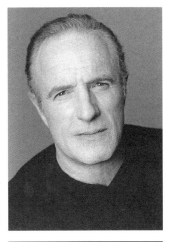
James Caan

of the friendship of two Chicago Bears football teammates, Caan portrays the dying athlete, Brian Piccolo, with sublime timing, delivery and emotional output. Co-star Billy Dee Williams was excellent as well. He was brilliant in *The Godfather* (1972) as mobster Sonny Corleone—the role that brought him worldwide acclaim, as well as an Academy nomination for Best Supporting Actor. He was excellent in Stephen King's *Misery* (1990), as a sympathetic writer cruelly held hostage by a demented fan. His co-star was Oscar-winning actress Kathy Bates. Caan's talents extend beyond drama; his charisma can light up a screen in more cheerful fare, like in *Honeymoon in Vegas* (1992), with Nicolas Cage and Sarah Jessica Parker. This was one of his rare films with room for his unique comedic gifts to shine. Motion pictures include *The Gambler* (1974), *The Godfather Part II* (1974—cameo), *Rollerball* (1975), *Chapter Two* (1979), *Thief* (1981), *For the Boys* (1991), *Flesh and Bone* (1993), and *Eraser* (1996). In 1999, he stars in the highly acclaimed romantic drama, *This is My Father*, with Aidan Quinn, Stephen Rea and John Cusack, and *Mickey Blue Eyes*, co-starring Hugh Grant and Jeanne Tripplehorn.

George Arliss 🎥   6648 Hollywood

Actor

BORN George Andrews; April 10, 1868, in England. **SPOTLIGHTS** Known as "The Gentleman of the Screen," this upper crust Englishman made his American stage debut at age 33. He made his screen debut 19 years later in *The Devil* (1921). Frequently cast in period pieces, he portrayed important historical figures. Movies include *Disraeli* (1921 silent and 1929 talkie), *Voltaire* (1933), *The House of Rothschild* (1934), and

George Arliss

Cardinal Richelieu (1935--in title role, see photo). His notable quality embodied the best of aristocracy; reportedly he behaved nobly off the set as well. A devoted husband, he retired after *Dr. Syn* (1937), to care for his ailing wife. **ACHIEVEMENTS** 1929 Best Actor Academy Award for *Disraeli.* Died: 1946.

Mister Rogers 🖵   6600 Hollywood

Host, producer, writer, composer

BORN Fred McFeely Rogers; Mar. 20, 1928, in Latrobe, PA. **SPOTLIGHTS** A national treasure. An American institution. America's favorite neighbor. After earning a degree in musical composition at Rollins College, in Florida, he landed a job at NBC-TV in New York. While serving as a floor manager for the 1950s Saturday morning cowboy Gabby Hayes, Rogers learned show business's most valuable tip. He asked Gabby Hayes, "What do you think about when you look into the camera knowing that hundreds of thousands of children are watching?" The "old Codger" replied, "Freddie, you just think of one little buckaroo." In November 1953, he moved back to Pittsburgh at the request of WQED—the nation's first community-supported television station. Rogers developed "The Children's Corner," with the perky singer-host, Josie Carey. He supplied the puppets and their voices, but his face was never seen. During its seven-year run, Rogers began studying child development and attending the Pittsburgh Theological Seminary during his off-duty hours. He was ordained a Presbyterian minister in 1962 with the charge to continue his work with children and families through the media. In 1968 the Public Broadcasting Service took his creation, "Mister Rogers' Neighborhood" nationwide, with Rogers as host. Children think of Mister Rogers as their good neighbor, and think of the "Neighborhood" as a place where they feel accepted, safe and understood. With his serene, slow-cadenced voice and easy conservational style he paces each program like a visit between two friends who have important things to discuss. The conversation *is* about important things: love, fear, sadness, jealousy, anger, friendship, trust, joy and satisfaction. Working from a strong and consistent developmental framework, Rogers talks candidly about childhood anxieties, like separation anxiety, among hundreds of other topics. He observed, "Whatever is mentionable can be manageable." *The Village Voice* cited him as the only valid father figure on television. **SIDELIGHTS** Of all Rogers' creative alliances, his most valued in the series' growth was his 30-year association with the late Dr. Margaret B. McFarland, an internationally respected clinical psychologist and child-development specialist who died in 1988. From Dr. McFarland's lifework came many of the insights and anecdotes that, through Rogers' interpretation have emerged as "Neighborhood" episodes. Daily programs explore topics for a whole week, like "What Do You Do with the Mad That You Feel?" Rogers stated, "Children can't be expected to leave the unhappy or angry parts of themselves at the door before coming in. We all need to feel that we can bring the whole of our-

selves to the people who care about us." "Mister Rogers' Neighborhood" is the longest-running children's program on public television. This award-winning program supports the emotional, social and intellectual growth of children. "Mister Rogers' Neighborhood" has been clinically proven to encourage the development of skills such as cooperation, sharing, persistence, and self-control while it enhances and nurtures self-esteem, healthy curiosity, and imaginative play. **HIGHLIGHTS** The third most requested exhibit in the Smithsonian Museum of American History in its popular culture area is Mister Rogers' red sweater! The Smithsonian installed the trademark sweater in a 1984 ceremony. **ACHIEVEMENTS** The recipient of hundreds of awards, including the prestigious Peabody Award, 30 honorary doctorate degrees, two 1997 Emmys—one for Lifetime Achievement, and an Honorary Knight for Life Award—*he who seeks to serve another, best serves himself.* **PERSONAL** A health-minded and compassionate vegetarian, he swims laps daily. In 1952 Rogers married college sweetheart, Joanne Byrd, and had two sons. Many people have wondered if Fred Rogers was for real, or an act. Rogers' colleague, David Newell stated, "Rogers soothing and caring personality is real." For more information, write to: Family Comm., Dept. CC, 4802 Fifth Ave., Pittsburgh, PA 15213 (website: http://www.misterrogers.org). **QUOTE** His Hollywood Walk of Fame star was unveiled on Jan. 8, 1998. Mr. Rogers appropriately sang, "It's a beautiful day in the neighborhood," along with hundreds of well-wishers who attended the happy ceremony, many of them small children. He also recited "Twinkle, twinkle little star" to the enthusiastic crowd, and closed by declaring, "The children who watched the program for 30 years will be represented by this star, and they are far, far greater than any star in the sky."

Mister Rogers

6650 HOLLYWOOD

Red Skelton ⌐📺

Actor, comedian, singer

Red Skelton (right) and Johnny Grant

6650 Hollywood

BORN Richard Bernard Skelton; July 18, 1906, in Vicennes, IN. **SPOTLIGHTS** Skelton was a superb craftsman, who played a wide variety of hilarious characters and brought laughter to millions. He accomplished greatness by overcoming a poverty-stricken, fatherless childhood. His father, a professional clown, had died before he was born, and his mother could not earn enough to keep them fed. When both he and his mother found themselves desperately hungry, at age seven he began singing for pennies on street corners. Three years later, he left home to join a traveling medicine show. Through his teen years, Skelton performed in a circus (the same one that his father had joined at the turn of the century), on showboats, in burlesque, and on the vaudeville circuit. While working at the Pantages Theater in Kansas City in 1930, he met his future wife, Edna Stillwell, who was the undertaker's daughter. Although Skelton was instantly smitten by her, Stillwell, who was working as an usherette, thought his "routine was terrible." He kept improving his jokes on return engagements. When he finally gave her a big enough laugh, they got married (June 1931). She became part of his act, playing the stooge. Offstage, she had a keen eye for what was funny in life. Once, while sitting in a cafe, she noticed a man dunking his doughnut into his coffee in a stealthy manner. He tried not to let anyone see him doing it. She developed a funny doughnut-dunking routine for her husband. It lifted him into the big time and became his trademark. After a successful date at New York's Paramount Theater, Skelton moved into network radio on Rudy Vallee's show in 1937. With his wife writing many of the gags, Skelton had his own radio show from 1939-'52, mainly on NBC. Hollywood called. He made his screen debut in *Having Wonderful Time* (1938), opposite Ginger Rogers, where he performs his famous doughnut-dunking routine. Other motion pictures include *Flight Command* (1941), *The People vs. Dr. Kildare* (1941), *Du Barry Was a Lady* (1943), *Thousands Cheer* (1943), *I Dood It* (1943), *A Southern Yankee* (1948), *Neptune's Daughter* (1949), *Three Little Words* (1950), *Lovely to Look At* (1952), and *The Clown* (1953, playing in a rare dramatic role). In all, he made 40 films. In television, he brought his unique gift of pantomime to his own comedy-variety show. He portrayed Junior, the Mean Widdle Kid who bragged, "I dood it!" when he did something naughty. He was also Clem Kadiddlehopper—the singing cab driver with the goofy teeth, Sheriff Deadeye—the blight of the West, Freddie the Freeloader, and the habitual inebriate, Willie Lump-Lump whose line was, "bwess his widdle heart." He commented, "People think my characters are funny because they remind them of someone they know." "The Red Skelton Show," with its hundreds of funny routines, continuously rated high in radio and TV from 1941 through 1971. He closed each show with a sincere, "God Bless." **ACHIEVEMENTS** 1951 Emmy, Best Comedy Show. 1960-'61 Emmy, Outstanding Writing...Bravery is not readily associated with funny guys, but in private life Skelton reacted quickly in a crisis. He was flying to Europe in 1951, where he was to perform at the London Palladium. *Three* of the airplane's four engines *failed* while flying over the Swiss Alps. As the plane perilously approached the mountaintop, some passengers screamed, while others prayed. All were hysterical. Skelton grabbed the microphone and broke into one of his best comedy routines. Finally, the pilot spied an open field and miraculously landed the plane. Still in shock, everyone remained in a hushed silence. Skelton returned to the microphone and declared, *"Now, ladies and gentlemen, you may return to all the evil habits you gave up twenty minutes ago."* **QUOTE** "I've often been asked, 'Just what is it you do when you get out in front of an audience?' My answer is always the the same--I don't know, because when I'm on, or out there, I'm somebody else." This prince of a man died in 1997.

Norm Crosby ⌐📺

Norm Crosby

6650 Hollywood

Comedian

BORN Sept. 15, 1927, in Boston, MA. **SPOTLIGHTS** The Master Comic of the Malaprop, he misuses a word that sounds similar to the correct word that was intended. For example, a woman told the doctor that she couldn't have a sexually transmitted disease because although there were problems in her marriage, she and her husband were absolutely "monotonous." Crosby is the most recognized and widely quoted performer of these gems: "Women need tenderness and affliction." "We are a nation of adults and adulteresses." "Chastity begins at home." Born and raised in the Boston area, he served in the U.S. Coast Guard as a radar operator in the North Atlantic on Anti-Submarine patrol, where he developed a hearing problem caused by concussions from the depth charges. After being discharged, Crosby entered the advertising business. Everyone noticed his funny flair and he was encouraged to dip his toes into local show business. The adman began his comedy campaign in small New England clubs, perfected his style, and after five years decided to try entertaining professionally. He readily headlined Casino showrooms, the nation's best resorts and the banquet circuit. He also became a regular on such TV programs as "The Beautiful Phyllis Diller Show," "Liar's Club," as well as his own series "Norm Crosby's Comedy Shop." Anheuser-Busch signed "the likable guy who talks funny" as a spokesman for Budweiser beer. **ACHIEVEMENTS** President Ronald Reagan appointed him Special Ambassador for better Hearing and Speech. Crosby is a major fund-raiser and tireless worker for the City of Hope and Childhelp, USA. ...He received his Hollywood Walk of Fame star on February 24, 1982. Overheard at the party: "Hey, could you pour me a cup of that decapitated coffee?"

Jack Benny 🎥   6650 Hollywood

Jack Benny with Marilyn Monroe

Comedian

BORN Benjamin Kubelsky; Feb. 14, 1894, in Waukegan, IL. **SPOTLIGHTS** The Master of Comic timing. Benny triumphed in vaudeville, radio and television. His persona as a miser was adored by audiences. Generous in real life, for shows he painted a self-portrait of a man so tight with money that he squeaked when he walked. Too cheap to buy a modern vehicle, his chauffeur/valet Rochester was forced to drive an old, dilapidated Maxwell automobile. He had a running gag about the money vault in his basement. It was guarded by a security man who had not seen the light of day for years. He owned a polar bear named Carmichael who ate the utilities man so Benny could not be billed. His intentionally squeaky violin playing inspired much laughter, while his hillbilly sketch remains one of his most popular comic classics—both in radio and televi-

sion. His radio show first aired in 1932 and was an instant hit. Listeners loved to imitate Benny's catchphrases: "Wait a minute. Wait a minute. Wait a minute," and "Now cut that out." When the show moved to TV in 1950, Benny remained loyal to his co-workers, bringing the entire cast with him to the network for a decade-long run. Benny became even more famous on the small screen to a whole new generation of fans. His unique brand of humor centered around making fun of Jack Benny himself—not others. He never used his comedy to insult others. His jesting represented all the faults and frailties (stinginess, vanity, conceit, etc.) of the average man, which is what the audience connected with. That, and his *absolutely perfect* comic timing. Benny specialized in long silent pauses—which were hilarious—and he took his time with story telling, getting laughs even with the story's tiny details, not just with the punch line (which usually a co-star would deliver). He stars in numerous motion pictures including *Charley's Aunt* (1941). He is must-see in *To Be or Not to Be* (1942). **QUOTE** In real life, the comic became frustrated because he could never make his best friend George Burns laugh. Once when Benny was staying at a hotel in Milwaukee, Burns telephoned his room to say he was coming up. Benny said, "I got undressed and stood naked on a table posing like a statue holding a rose in my hand. I figured when he came in the door, he'd have to laugh." What happened? "He sent the maid in first," Benny lamented...In later years he said, "With Bob Hope imitating my walk and Rich Little doing my voice, I can do nothing and be a star." Died: 1974.

Smilin' Ed McConnell 🎙   6650 Hollywood

Host, actor, singer, musician

BORN James Ed McConnell; 1892. **SPOTLIGHTS** On air since 1922, this cheerful, gravel-voiced talent gained national fame as host/actor in "Smiling' Ed's Buster Brown Gang" (NBC radio, 1944-'53). This Saturday morning potpourri show appealed to children under age 12. Buster Brown's famous dog was named Tige: "Buster Brown lives in a shoe (bark bark), and my dog Tige lives in there too." This oldtime variety show was acclaimed for its adventurous tales and delightful characters: "Squeeky the Mouse," "Midnight the Cat," "Grandie the Piano," and mischievous "Froggy the Gremlin," all performed by the McConnell. NBC-TV picked the popular show up in 1950. Died: 1955.

Bessie Barriscale 🎥   6652 Hollywood

Actress

BORN 1884, in New York, NY. **SPOTLIGHTS** This lovely, dark-haired vaudeville performer starred in more than 25 silent movies, including *A Painted Soul* (1915), and *Wooden Shoes* (1917). Died: 1965.

Errol Flynn 🎥   6654 Hollywood

Errol Flynn

Actor

BORN June 20, 1909, in Tasmania. **SPOTLIGHTS** A charming, devilishly handsome leading man, Flynn was the screen's magnificent swashbuckler. He got his big break in show business when actor Robert Donat did not show up for the lead in *Captain Blood* (1935). He seized the part, opposite the beautiful Olivia de Havilland, and their chemistry sizzled on-screen. A natural born athlete, he easily handled the rigors of action-adventure movies, and look great in period costumes. Flynn could gracefully wave a heavy sword about with the greatest of ease, while jumping down a flight of stairs, *without* a stunt double. The movie was a smash hit. He teams with Olivia de Havilland in eight more films, including *The Adventures of Robin Hood* (1938). He plays opposite Bette Davis in *The Private Lives of Elizabeth and Essex* (1939), in a role Davis had wanted to go to Laurence Olivier. Flynn also made Westerns, including *Virginia City* (1940). *Adventures of Don Juan* (1949) was his last epic. He appears in Hemingway's classic tale, *The Sun Also Rises* (1957). **QUOTES** "They've great respect for the dead in Hollywood, but none for the living." And, "I never worry about money so long as I can reconcile my net income with my gross habits." Died: 1959.

Debbie Reynolds 🎥   6654 Hollywood

Actress, singer, dancer

BORN Mary Frances Reynolds; April 1, 1932, in El Paso, TX. **SPOTLIGHTS** "America's Sweetheart" won this crowning title during her jubilant film work of the 1950s and '60s. Idolized by millions of blue jeans and bobbie-soxers, this pretty girl-next-door radiated perkiness and cheerfulness. These positive

attributes do not diminish her other considerable talents. Reynolds started her musical life playing the French horn and bassoon in the Burbank Youth Symphony Orchestra. She was an accomplished dancer as well. At age 16, she claimed top prize in the "Miss Burbank" beauty contest. Two of the judges were talent scouts from the local neighborhood studio. Warner Bros. put her in *June Bride* (1948) as an extra, and changed her name.

*Debbie Reynolds
and Sir Michael Teilmann*

She moved into a supporting role in *The Daughter of Rosie O'Grady* (1950). MGM liked her so much they quickly signed her to a contract, developing her "wholesome" image in starring roles in both musicals and light comedies. When directors allowed her to go full tilt, Reynolds exuded dynamite energy singing and dancing. In calmer roles, she was soothing to watch and fun to spend time with—like a best friend. Motion pictures include *Three Little Words* (1950), *Two Weeks with Love* (1950—in which she sings "Aba Daba Honeymoon," one of her signature songs), *Singin' in the Rain* (1952—a terrific movie musical), *Susan Slept Here* (1954), *Tammy and the Bachelor* (1957—where her gigantic hit song "Tammy" topped record charts), *The Mating Game* (1959), *How the West Was Won* (1962), *The Unsinkable Molly Brown* (1964—in an Oscar-nominated performance), *Goodbye, Charlie* (1964), *The Singing Nun* (1966), *How Sweet It Is!* (1968), *What's the Matter with Helen?* (1971), *Charlotte's Web* (1973—voiceover as Charlotte), *The Bodyguard* (1992), *Heaven and Earth* (1993), *That's Entertainment! III* (1994), *Mother* (1996), *In and Out*, and *Wedding Bell Blues* (both 1997). **BROADWAY** She broke box office records in the musical revival of "Irene," and starred in the hit revival of Irving Berlin's "Annie Get Your Gun," and "Woman of the Year." In 1989, she toured nationally with "The Unsinkable Molly Brown." **HIGHLIGHTS** Married to Eddie Fisher (1955-'59), the union produced one daughter, actress-writer Carrie Fisher, of *Star Wars* fame, and a son, Todd, who manages the family's business affairs. She is involved with the Girl Scouts of America and was a founder and president of the Thalians, an entertainment organization devoted to helping emotionally disturbed children and adults. **QUOTE** "I feel that any experience in life, be it good or bad, must have some worthwhile value. I've got exactly what I need to keep me happy. I've got my children and I've got my work."

Raymond Burr 📺   6656 Hollywood

Raymond Burr (center) and the "Perry Mason" cast: Barbara Hale (left), and William Hopper (right, the real-life son of gossip queen Hedda Hopper), Ray Collins (upper left) and William Talman

Actor, singer

BORN May 21, 1917, in New Westminster, British Columbia. **SPOTLIGHTS** Educated at Stanford University, University of California, and Columbia University, Burr became an accomplished director at the prestigious Pasadena Playhouse, in California. He was also an experienced stage actor. In radio, Burr's authoritative, but pleasant voice was heard on "Dragnet" (1949-'57), starring Jack Webb. He played Ed Backstrand, chief of detectives on this pioneering hard-edged police drama. Burr was also a regular supporting talent on "The Lineup," a radio police drama on air from 1950-'53. Though, he did *not* participate in the earlier "Perry Mason" radio crime serial. The actor made his silver screen debut in *San Quentin* (1946), as a malicious villain, where he utilized his despondent facial features to emote without overacting. Other movies include the tense, B-movie *Desperate* (1947), the tight film noir *Pitfall* (1948) with Dick Powell, Lizabeth Scott and Jane Wyatt, the melodrama *Ruthless* (1948) opposite Zachary Scott, Sidney Greenstreet, Diana Lynn and Louis Hayward, *Sleep, My Love* (1948), a drama starring Claudette Colbert, Robert Cummings and Don Ameche, and the violent crime melodrama *Raw Deal* (1948), where he plays a gangster who frames another. He is the fascinating archetypal heavy in a baby adoption tale, *Abandoned* (1949), appears in the *Adventures of Don Juan* (1949) in Errol Flynn's last swashbuckling epic, *Key to the City* (1950) with Clark Gable, *His Kind of Woman* (1951) with Robert Mitchum and Jane Russell, *A Place in the Sun* (1951) with Montgomery Clift, Elizabeth Taylor and Shelley Winters, *Meet Danny Wilson* (1952) with Frank Sinatra and Shelley Winters, *Gorilla at Large* (1954), a splendid amusement park

mystery, and *You're Never Too Young* (1955), as a jewel thief chasing Jerry Lewis. He stars in the Japanese-made monster movie *Godzilla, King of the Monsters* (1956--a gigantic cult classic). At Paramount Pictures, Burr plays a troubled, murderous husband in Hitchcock's *Rear Window* (1954). James Stewart plays the wheelchair-bound voyeur, and Grace Kelly is his slinky girlfriend. The pair observe (along with the audience) Burr's flawless performance as the killer across the courtyard. This is one of Hitchcock's finest works. Burr also made Westerns, *New Mexico* and *Horizons West* (both 1952). Still, the actor bypassed superstar fame until the age of 40. Burr became a household name and was immortalized as "Perry Mason," the most successful defense attorney in television history. Virtually unbeatable, the lawyer-sleuth lost only one criminal case from 1957-'66. The series also made TV history as it was the first ever 60-minute mystery drama series. It made its debut on CBS-TV, September 21, 1957, with the episode "The Case of the Reckless Redhead." The distinguished star once reflected, "'Perry Mason' went on the air when people were first buying television sets. A lot of people in this country didn't know what their legal system was all about...They found out the system of justice." The tall, dark-haired Burr had the most beautiful, large eyes of any actor in show business. Fans knew to watch his orbs for clues to when he thought something important, relevant, or ironic. With his diplomatic and intelligent presence, certainty of law, and power in the courtroom, "Perry Mason" rose to one of the highest rated shows with 30 million+ viewers tuning in every Saturday night. Initially, critics did *not* like it, predicting the show would have a quick death sentence. In fact, the show only ended when Burr quit. (Also see the bio of Barbara Hale in this book.) Later, he starred in "Ironside" (1967-'75), as Chief Robert T. Ironside, a wheelchair-bound crime solver whose disability did not stop him from tracking felons. **ACHIEVEMENTS** Burr had a distinguished Naval career during WWII...Recipient of two Emmy Awards for best actor in a dramatic series for "Perry Mason."...Raised prize-winning orchids on his own private 3,000-acre South Pacific island, and was a winegrower in Northern California. **SIDELIGHTS** Actor William Holden was the producer's first choice to play Perry Mason. After Holden rejected the role, it was offered to the six-foot, one-inch tall Burr *providing* he lose weight. Burr, who weighed in at a hefty 340 pounds, had to drop to 210 pounds in order to land the role. **QUOTE** "Acting is what I do for a living. I'm not a workaholic, but I do like to keep busy. I doubt very much if you'll ever hear a retirement speech from Raymond Burr." He had just completed the "Perry Mason" television movie, "The Case of the Killer Kiss," one month before he died in 1993.

Eartha Kitt 🔊   6656 Hollywood

Singer, actress, dancer

BORN Jan. 26, 1928, in North, SC. **SPOTLIGHTS** After a devastatingly abusive childhood in the cotton fields of South Carolina, then in Harlem, "sweet 16" really was for Eartha

Eartha Kitt

when she won a scholarship to study dance with Katherine Dunham. She became a member of the famous Katherine Dunham troupe of dancers on Broadway and toured throughout the United States and Mexico. She began a different phase of her career as a successful nightclub singer in Paris. Her sensuous voice and sultry looks played well to full houses in Europe; she won hearts with her multilingual repertoire: "*C'est Si Bon,*" "Monotonous," "Santa Baby," "I Want to be Evil," "*Uska Dara.*" This adored darling returned to America as a mature artist, conquering Broadway stage and film. Albums include *Fabulous Eartha Kitt, That Bad Eartha, New Faces of 1952.* Motion pictures include *Anna Lucasta* (1949), *St. Louis Blues* (1958), *Mark of the Hawk* (1958), *Friday Foster* (1975), and *Boomerang* (1992). Her two autobiographies, *Thursday's Child* (1956), and decades later, *Alone with Me*, impressed critics and fans.

Paul Robeson 🎥   6658 Hollywood

Actor, singer
BORN April 9, 1898, in Princeton, NJ. **SPOTLIGHTS** The son of a former slave, his voice, intellence, presence and physical prowess were his supreme gifts. Robeson was an all-American football player at Rutgers University. A brilliant scholar, he was valedictorian of his graduating class in 1919. He then earned a law degree. He made his New York concert debut in 1925 singing spirituals. Robeson enjoyed a successful stage

Paul Robeson

career including, "All God's Chillun Got Wings" (an Eugene O'Neill play), "Show Boat" (originally based on an Edna Ferber novel), and as Porgy in "Porgy and Bess." He was the first African American to play Othello in the United States, which he played magnificently. The American production of "Othello" started in 1946 and ran longer than any other previous Shakespeare play. For his many outstanding stage appearances, Robeson received the Actors Equity Award for exemplifying "the ideals of true broth-

Paul Robeson

erhood of all mankind and the dignity of the individual." In motion pictures, he stars in the dramatic *Emperor Jones* (1933), an inadequate adaptation of an Eugene O'Neill play that did not highlight his spectacular voice. His powerful, moving rendition of "Ol' Man River," in the superb musical *Show Boat* (1936) immortalized him. That classic landmark performance is one of screen's greatest scenes. Other movies include *Song of Freedom* (1936), *King Solomon's Mines* (1937), *Jericho* (1938), and *Big Fella* (1938). On Nov. 5, 1939, Robeson made radio history on CBS' "The Pursuit of Happiness." He sang the 11-minute "Ballad for Americans," written by Earl Robinson. It greatly embodied all the struggle, promise and hope of Amerca. When he finished, 600 audience members jumped to their feet in thunderous applaud. They were so moved by his performance that they kept applauding for 15 minutes after the show ended. CBS was flooded with telephone calls, telegrams, and letters congratualing the network and Robeson. *The Proud Valley* (1940—the one motion picture considered completely worthy of his enormous talents), and *Native Land* (1942). Actor James Earl Jones is wonderful in *Paul Robeson* (1977), a one-man show chronicling the singer's life. Robeson was one of America's greatest artists of the 20th century. Died: 1976.

Marsha Hunt 📺   6658 Hollywood

Actress, civic leader
BORN Marcia Virginia Hunt; Oct. 17, 1917, in Chicago, IL. **SPOTLIGHTS** She inherited her talent from her mother, an operatic soprano who taught her daughter to speak impeccably. Raised in New York, she trained at the Theodore Irving School of Dramatics. She worked as Powers model, then made her silver screen debut in *The Virginia Judge* (1935). She co-

Marsha Hunt

stars in *Hollywood Boulevard* (1936), her second film. This clever talent appears in 50 films, including *Pride and Prejudice* (1940), *The Trial of Mary Dugan* (1941), *Unholy Partners* (1941), *Panama Hattie* (1942), *The Human Comedy* (1943), *Thousands Cheer* (1943), *Music for Millions* (1944), *Carnegie Hall* (1947), *The Happy Time* (1952), *Blue Denim* (1959), and *Johnny Got His Gun* (1971). She starred in TV's 1950s sitcom "Peck's Bad Girl," appeared live in "Playhouse Theater," and guest starred on "Perry Mason," "Barnaby Jones" among countless other series.

Rhonda Fleming 🎥   6660 Hollywood

Actress

BORN Marilyn Louis; Aug. 10, 1923, in Los Angeles, CA. **SPOTLIGHTS** With show business parents, and major studios nearby, Fleming grew up in the industry town. When this fresh faced teenager appeared on the cover of a Beverly Hills High School student magazine, an agent offered her a screen test. She worked as an extra and did bit parts in films of 1943 and 1944. Her breakthough role was in Hitchcock's thriller *Spellbound* (1945), starring Ingrid Bergman and Gregory Peck. She followed with another excellent thriller, *The Spiral Staircase* (1946), starring Dorothy McGuire, George Brent and

Rhonda Fleming

Ethel Barrymore. A ravishing redhead with large green eyes and an hourglass figure, she seemed born to dazzle Technicolor movies. This elegant, intelligent talent gracefully moved into leading lady roles, proving she was more than beauty--she possessed impressive talent and sensitivity. She is outstanding in *A Connecticut Yankee in King Arthur's Court* (1949), opposite Bing Crosby. That same year, she co-stars in the marvelous comedy *The Great Lover*, opposite Bob Hope. Fleming co-stars with Charlton Heston in the Western *Pony Express* (1952); the film also has fine performances by Jan Sterling and Forrest Tucker. She turns in a compelling performance in *Inferno* (1953), as a murderous wife bent on taking her husband's money. Next, the charmer appears in *Those Three Redheads from Seattle* (1953), with Gene Barry, Agnes Moorehead and Theresa Brewer. She is excellent in *While the City Sleeps* (1956), *Gunfight at the O.K. Corral* (1957), *Bullwhip* (1958), *Home Before Dark* (1958), and *The Big Circus* (1959). Later movies include *The Patsy* (1964), *Won Ton Ton—The Dog Who Saved Hollywood* (1976—cameo), and the spoof, *The Nude Bomb* (1980). In addition to her acting legacy, she is a tremendous humanitarian. Fleming actively participates in numerous charities, including providing scholarship funds for foster children.

James Wallington   6660 Hollywood

Announcer

BORN 1907. **SPOTLIGHTS** Known as Jimmy, he was one of the highest-paid and busiest network announcers for more than three decades. Shows include "Ben Bernie, The Old Maestro," "The Adventures of the Thin Man," "The Big Show," "Duffy's Tavern," "The Doctor Fights," "The Eddie Cantor Show" (he and Cantor created audience participation when the two rushed into the audience with a gag and the audience burst into laughter), "The Fred Allen Show," and "Burns and Allen." These shows made him almost as famous as the personalities who starred in them. Died: 1972.

Hans Conreid 📺   6664 Hollywood

Hans Conreid

Actor, comic

BORN April 15, 1917, in Baltimore, MD. **SPOTLIGHTS** This popular character actor looked like a mad professor, and was a tremendous talent. From 1938-'80, he 150 movies: *The Senator Was Indiscreet* (1947), *The 5,000 Fingers of Dr. T.* (1953), *Davy Crockett, King of the Wild Frontier* (1955), *Bus Stop* (1956), *Rock-a-Bye Baby* (1958), *The Patsy* (1964), and *American Dream* (1981). **TV** Co-starred in the long-running, popular sitcom, "The Danny Thomas Show" (1958-'71), as Uncle Tonoose. Died: 1982.

Boris Karloff   6664 Hollywood

See page 150

Esther Ralston   6664 Hollywood

Actress

Esther Ralston (left) and Laura La Plante

BORN Sept. 17, 1902, in Bar Harbor, ME. **SPOTLIGHTS** A blue-eyed, blonde beauty, she became the highly paid, glamorous star of silents, including *Huckleberry Finn* (1920), *Oliver Twist* (1922), *The Little French Girl* (1925), *A Kiss for Cinderella* (1925--as the Fairy Godmother), and *The American Venus* (1926), which became her nickname. In talkies, she played supporting roles: *Tin Pan Alley* (1940). Died: 1994.

Michael Ansara   6666 Hollywood

Actor
BORN April 15, 1922, in Lowell, MA. **SPOTLIGHTS** Of Lebanese descent, he was cast as Native American Indian, Apache Chief Cochise, in "Broken Arrow" (1956-'60). He played Lame Beaver in the historical drama "Centennial" (1978-'80)...Married to actress Barbara Eden (1958-'73).

Kenny Rogers   6666 Hollywood

Singer, songwriter, guitarist
BORN Aug. 21, 1938, in Crockett, TX. **SPOTLIGHTS** Born with a tin spoon in his mouth, he grew up in the housing projects in Houston, Texas with his seven brothers and sisters. Although the family were welfare recipients, Rogers said, "I was never hungry. And, you know, I didn't know any difference." At 17 years old, he found his way out of the projects by singing with the Scholars, a local group who enjoyed their 15 minutes of fame with a tune called "Crazy Feeling." It earned them a desirable spot on TV's "American Bandstand." As a musician playing bass he became a member of various groups.

At age 29 he formed his own band, The First Edition. The pop-country-rock band produced eight Gold singles and four Gold albums from around 1967-76. After two decades of pursuing the ultimate solo platinum ring, "(You Picked a Fine Time to Leave Me) Lucille" in 1977 became a mega-hit. At long last his distinctive vocal style had won him a legion of devoted fans in both country and pop. Dozens of #1 songs followed, bringing him international recognition, and more

Kenny Rogers

money from royalties than he could ever spend. His list of hit songs includes "The Gambler" "She Believes in Me," "Lady" "You Decorated My Life," "Love Will Turn You Around," "Coward of the County," "Islands in the Stream" (a Dolly Parton-Kenny Rogers duet), "Real Love," "Tomb of the Unknown Love," and "Every Time Two Fools Collide." They topped the pop and country charts. As an entertainer, he has done several high-rated television specials. As an actor, he has appeared in both TV and feature films, including "The Gambler" (mini-series), and *Six Pack*. **ACHIEVEMENTS** Winner of numerous Grammy Awards and Country Music Association Awards. Known for his keen business acumen, his vast holdings include real estate, and a restaurant chain (Kenny Rogers Roasters). **QUOTE** "A friend once told me that to have a happy and successful life, you need to have someone to love, something to do and something to look forward to. I believe that with all my heart."

Marty Robbins   6666 Hollywood

Singer, songwriter, guitarist, pianist
BORN Sept. 26, 1925, in Glendale, AZ. **SPOTLIGHTS** Known as "*the* cowboy's cowboy," Robbins learned to play guitar with Hawaiian tunes in the Pacific while serving in the Navy. He became a popular Nashville singer of country-and-western music, with a strong following in rockabilly and pop. He was a prominent figure on the Grand Ole Opry from 1953 to his death. Hits include "Singing the Blues," "Stairway of Love," "El Paso," "Beggin' to You," and "My Woman, My Woman, My Wife." **ACHIEVEMENTS** 1960 and 1970 Grammy Awards. Recorded 60 albums. **SIDELIGHTS** Chose the hobby of stock car racing, and learned how unforgiving walls are at 150 m.p.h. in a serous, near-fatal collision. Died: 1982.

Crosby, Stills & Nash 6666 Hollywood

Recording artists
BORN David Crosby, born David Van Cortland, Aug. 14, 1941 in Los Angeles, CA (guitar, vocals); Stephen Stills, Jan. 3,

Crosby, Stills & Nash

1945, in Dallas, TX (guitar, keyboards, bass, vocals); Graham Nash (guitar, keyboards, vocals), Feb. 2, 1942, in Blackpool, England (guitar, keyboards, vocals). Starting in the summer of 1969, they were sometimes joined by Neil Young, Nov. 12, 1945, Toronto, Canada (guitar, vocals), and were then called "Crosby, Stills, Nash and Young." **SPOTLIGHTS** The members were formerly associated with other successful groups—The Byrds, Buffalo Springfield, and The Hollies, before forming their own group in 1968, in Los Angeles, California. Crosby, Stills & Nash first recorded in 1969, and enjoyed immediate success with Nash's "Marrakesh Express," and Stills' "Suite: Judy Blue Eyes." With Young, the four headed out on tour. Amazingly, their second live performance was at the historic Woodstock Festival in August 1969, with 500,000 people. With their close, high harmonies, fresh approach to music, and strong writing skills, the group immediately established themselves as the leader in soft rock songs during the 1970s. Their album *Deja Vu*, was a gigantic seller, with unheard of advance orders of two million copies. It sprouted these top hits: "Teach Your Children," "Woodstock," and "Our House." Yet, these rockers suffered from interpersonal conflicts—they just could not get along well enough to stay together. Subsequently, they disbanded and re-banded several times, with some of the members cutting hit solo albums. In 1977, the original trio reunited and released the album, *CSN*, which went quadruple-platinum. The group received their Hollywood Walk of Fame star on June 21, 1978. Then, in 1982, they released the Top Ten album, *Daylight*. Other songs include "Ohio" (about the tragic abuse of police power at a Kent State University protest), "Wasted on the Way," and "Southern Cross." **SOLO** Stills' "Love the One You're With" benefitted from guest guitarists Jimi Hendrix and Eric Clapton. It rose to #4 on the charts. **LOWLIGHTS** Crosby battled drug addiction and alcohol abuse, for which he served time in prison. His book, *Long Time Gone* (1990), chronicles his ordeal. In 1994, he received a liver transplant. **HIGHLIGHTS** As a youngster, Nash's father introduced him to the camera. The art of photography has remained Nash's lifelong joy and passion. An accomplished photographer, the British-born Nash became an American citizen in 1980. In May of 1999, he appeared in "Jeopardy!" To the surprise of millions of TV viewers, who assumed rock 'n' rollers were uneducated oafs, Nash conquered his competitors with his quick thinking and vast scope of knowledge.

Guy Lombardo 🎵   6666 Hollywood

See page 58

Jean Parker   6670 Hollywood

Actress

BORN Luisa-Stephanie Zelinska; Aug. 11, 1912, in Butte, MT. **SPOTLIGHTS** Immortalized as Beth in Selznick's original production of *Little Women* (1933), she was also wonderful in *The Gunfighter* (1950), starring Gregory Peck, and *Black Tuesday* (1954) with Edward G. Robinson and Peter Graves.

William Lundigan 📺   6670 Hollywood

Actor

BORN June 12, 1914, in Syracuse, NY. **SPOTLIGHTS** Veteran of radio and films, he hosted two Chrysler Corporation shows (1954-'58): "Climax" (dramatic anthology) and "Shower of Stars" (musical variety). Died: 1975.

George Burns 🎭   6670 Hollywood

Norm Crosby, Phyllis McGuire and George Burns (right)

Comedian, actor, dancer, executive

BORN Nathan Birnbaum; Jan. 20, 1896, in New York, NY. **SPOTLIGHTS** Burns sang for pennies on street corners when he was a child. He was frequently fired in vaudeville for being so bad, but he'd change his name, wear a disguise and show up the next week on stage as a different act. It was that determination that made him an American institution. Motion pictures include *Here Comes Cookie* (1935) co-starring his chirpy, malaprop innocent wife Gracie Allen, and *A Damsel in Distress* (1937) co-starring Fred Astaire and Gracie Allen. He stopped making movies (in 1939) for 36 years. Then, when Jack Benny fell out of the lead for *The Sunshine Boys* (1975), Burns stepped in and resumed his career. He followed up with the wildly successful *Oh God!* (1977), in the title role. In TV and radio, he was the very funny straight man to his wife's scatterbrained antics on "The George Burns and Gracie Allen Show" (1950-

'58). Burns' closing line was: "Say good night, Gracie." Allen's was: "Good night, Gracie." One of their most recited jokes was: Burns: "Did the nurse ever drop you on your head when you were a baby?" Allen: "Oh, we couldn't afford a nurse. My mother had to do it." He was rarely seen without his trademark cigar and horn-rimmed glasses. **ACHIEVEMENTS** 1975 Best Supporting Actor Oscar for *The Sunshine Boys*—he was the oldest actor to win an Oscar. Married Gracie Allen (1926 until her death in 1964; see her bio). Died: 1996.

Gracie Allen 📺 6672 Hollywood

Gracie Allen, George Burns (right) and Guy Lombardo (left)

Actress, comedienne
BORN Grace Ethel Cecile Rosalie Allen; July 26, 1906, in San Francisco, CA. (Born months after San Francisco's earthquake.) **SPOTLIGHTS** This natural born talent had greasepaint in her veins; both her parents were vaudevillians. She met future husband George Burns when she was 20, and to their mutual delight, they discovered a comic electricity running between them. The Burns and Allen team was formed. Originally, Burns had the comedy lines, and Allen was the "straight girl." But she got all the laughs. So they switched roles—Allen played the "Dumb Dora" type, he the straight man. It was the beginning of a happy relationship, both in business (stage, radio, films and TV) and marriage (since 1926 until death). The dainty, ladylike Allen specialized in "illogical logic," and quick delivery. She always appeared utterly sincere. She even incorporated her persona into commercials for sponsors. Allen: "This Carnation Evaporated Milk is wonderful. But you know, there's one thing that puzzles me. How do they get milk from carnations?" On one show, Allen consulted the doctor about Burns' sneezing attacks. Allen: "What causes sneezing?" Doctor: "Well sneezing is usually merely symptomatic of an underlying cause. It may be a momentary irritation of the mucous membrane, it could be a psychosomatic

manifestation, or it may be due to an infection in the respiratory system." Gracie: "My goodness!" Doctor: "I'm afraid that's a little difficult to understand." Gracie: "Well, say it again slowly and I'll try to explain it to you." Allen portrayed a scatterbrained wife on their long-running hit TV program, "The George Burns and Gracie Allen Show" (1950-58). As the fuzzy-headed imp, who had a flair for being wrong at the right time, she had her own train of thought—and America rode along for the laughs. Died: 1964.

Ruth Roman 📺 6672 Hollywood

Actress
BORN Dec. 22, 1924, in Boston, MA. **SPOTLIGHTS** She was a dark-haired, sultry, cool, strong-willed mistress. She played Minnie Littlejohn in TV's "The Long, Hot Summer." Roman also acted in a number of live playhouse dramas during TV's early days. Previously, she had been a successful stage and motion picture actress. Her first important movie role was in *Champion* (1949), opposite Kirk Douglas. Warner Bros. quickly signed her to a contract. She turned in a brilliant, must-see performance in Hitchcock's *Strangers on a Train*

Ruth Roman

(1951). Movies include *The Jungle Queen* (1945—serial), *Beyond the Forest* (1949) with Bette Davis, *The Window* (1949), Robert Wise's *Three Secrets* (1950), *Maru Maru* (1952), *The Far Country* (1955) co-starring James Stewart, *Bitter Victory* (1958) opposite Richard Burton, and *Day of the Animals* (1977). This glamorous actress made more than 50 feature films. **HIGHLIGHTS** Like the unsinkable Molly Brown (but on a different ship), Ruth Roman survived the horrendous sinking of the Italian luxury liner named the Andrea Doria. The ship collided with a Swedish vessel called the Stockholm, about 45 miles south of Nantucket Island, and sank on July 26, 1956. 51 persons perished in the frigid, treacherous waters of the Atlantic Ocean. **QUOTE** "Acting is my life. The profession can break my heart. In fact, it already has several times. But I love it." Died: 1999.

Ed Gardner 📺 6674 Hollywood

See page 412

Laraine Day 🎥 6674 Hollywood

Actress, writer
BORN Laraine Johnson; Oct. 13, 1917, in Roosevelt, UT. **SPOTLIGHTS** Born in the heart of Mormon country, Day's grandfather was a Brigham Young elder who had 52 children. When her father, a building contractor, moved his family of 10

Laraine Day

to Long Beach, California, she joined a theater group called the Players Guild. There, she met a young Robert Mitchum, her future co-star in *The Locket* (1946), though her first break was a small role in *Stella Dallas* (1937), starring Barbara Stanwyck. Day gained fame in MGM's Dr. Kildaire film series, portraying the kindly, antiseptic Nurse Mary Lamont in her crisp, white uniform. She assisted Dr. Kildaire (Lew Ayres), and the duo became one of the screen's most popular teams in seven *Dr. Kildare* films between 1939-'42. Movies include *Sergeant Madden* (1939), Hitchcock's thriller *Foreign Correspondent* (1940), *My Son, My Son* (1940), *Unholy Partners* (1941), *Kathleen* (1941), *Mr. Lucky* (1943), and *The High and the Mighty* (1954).

Charles Vidor 🎥   6674 Hollywood

Director

BORN July 27, 1900, in Budapest, Hungary. **SPOTLIGHTS** A Wagnerian opera singer, he turned to filmmaking with the advent of sound. Motion pictures include *The Tuttles of Tahiti* (1942—a comedy with Charles Laughton), and the action packed Western, *The Desperadoes* (1943). He made some spectacular works, among them, *Cover Girl* (1944) and *Gilda* (1946) both starring Rita Hayworth. Fans of musicals enjoy his *Hans Christian Anderson* (1952) with Danny Kaye. James Cagney plays Doris Day's gangster boyfriend in *Love Me or Leave Me* (1955), based on Ruth Etting's life. Died: 1959.

Vincente Minnelli 🎥   6674 Hollywood

Director

BORN Feb. 28, 1910, in Chicago, IL. **SPOTLIGHTS** He was part of the Minnelli brothers' family act at age, performing in the circus and on stage. Later, he became a Broadway art director, then went to Hollywood. This talent became best known for his highly stylized musicals. Minnelli, though, deftly handled his dramatic directorial debut with *The Clock* (1945), and later proved as brilliant with *Madame Bovary* (1949), *The Bad and the Beautiful* (1952), and *Lust for Life* (1956). A partial listing of some of his fabulous musicals include *Meet Me in St. Louis* (1944), *An American in Paris* (1951), *The Band Wagon* (1953), and *The Bells Are Ringing* (1960). He also made the comedy, *The Long, Long Trailer* (1953), starring Lucille Ball and Desi Arnaz. **ACHIEVEMENTS** 1958 Oscar for *Gigi*.

Vincente and Liza Minnelli

HIGHLIGHTS Married to Judy Garland (1945-'50); father of Liza Minnelli. **QUOTE** "You see, the search for an appropriate style is as valid for musicals as it is for drama. One has to tell a story in as mannered a way as possible to create a little magic. It is not always easy to catch each delicate nuance, to be able to allow the characters to reveal themselves incongruously." Died: 1986.

Glenn Miller

6700 HOLLYWOOD

Thomas A. Edison 🎥   6700 Hollywood

Inventor

BORN Thomas Alva Edison; Feb. 11, 1847, in Milan, OH.

Thomas A. Edison

SPOTLIGHTS The world's all-time greatest inventor, Edison was born hearing-impaired, and felt uncomfortable in school. His mother home-schooled him, where she encouraged his curiosity, experimentation, persistence and creativity. Edison told her he was "interested in learning about everything," and his mother did an excellent full-time job of educating and inspiring him. In 1879 his carbon filament light bulb lit up the world—just one of his *more than 1,000 patents*. He became known as the "Wizard of Menlo Park." When a reporter mentioned to Edison that he had failed tens of thousands of times in his search for a new storage battery—before obtaining results—the inventor responded, "Results? Why I have gotten a lot of results. I know 50,000 things that won't work." After inventing the phonograph, he decided to enhance its enjoyment by visual, moving effects, giving birth to the motion picture camera in 1887. In 1889 the Kinetograph camera combined with his Kinetoscope viewer. Edison's inventions of electric lighting, the phonograph and the motion picture camera altered the arts more than anything else in history, and changed human existence. The photo below is from his film, *The Kiss* (1900). **QUOTE** "I consider the greatest mission of the motion picture is first to make people happy...to bring more joy and cheer and wholesome good will into this world of ours. And God knows we need it." Died: 1931.

Frank Morgan 🖊   6700 Hollywood

See page 187.

Eugene Pallette 🎥   6702 Hollywood

Actor

BORN July 8, 1889, in Winfield, KS. **SPOTLIGHTS** A rotund, frog-voiced, dark-haired character actor, he had formerly been a streetcar conductor. Both of his parents were in show business and had toured the country for years. When he finally followed in their footsteps, he appeared in theater for six years, then became a film extra in 1910. His face and body were unique enough to distinguish him from

Eugene Pallette

the herd—he was thinner and more handsome then—and within a month he was featured in one-reelers. Toward the end of the decade ,he was co-starring with beauties such as Norma Talmadge. He enlisted in the military to serve in World War I, and upon his return discovered his career as a leading man had vanished. After gaining weight, he found his career had returned, this time in supporting roles. Pallette was capable of exuding great gentleness or cruelty. This roly-poly artist, who tipped the scales at 300 pounds at his heaviest—became one of Hollywood's favorites. He made some 150 films at all the major studios. Motion pictures include *The Tattooed Arm* (1913), *The Three Musketeers* (1921—as Aramis), *The Adventures of Huckleberry Finn* (1931), *Steamboat 'Round the Bend* (1935), *My Man Godfrey* (1936), *Topper* (1937), *The Adventures of Robin Hood* (1938—as Friar Tuck), *The Mark of Zorro* (1940), *Heaven Can Wait* (1943), and *The Cheaters* (1945). Died: 1954.

Morris Stoloff 🎵   6702 Hollywood

Music director, conductor, musician

BORN Aug. 1, 1898, in Philadelphia, PA. **SPOTLIGHTS** This musical talent began playing the violin as a child, was on the professional concert tour by age 16, and became the youngest member of Los Angeles Philharmonic. In 1936, he became music director for Columbia Pictures He was 38 years old. Scores for movies include *From Here to Eternity* (1953). This Academy Award-winner (see below) also released popular albums. Recordings include *Soundtracks, Voices and Themes* by Morris Stoloff and Stars Orchestra. **ACHIEVEMENTS** Academy Awards: 1944 *Cover Girl*; 1946 *The Jolson Story*; and 1960 *Song Without End*. Died: 1980.

Zino Francescatti 6704 Hollywood

Violinist

BORN Aug. 9, 1905, in France. **SPOTLIGHTS** A virtuoso at age five, his violin-playing father actually *discouraged* his son from following in his footsteps. Pop, who had had enough with the instrument, suddenly stopped playing on his 40th birthday. He counseled his son Zino to become an attorney. Zino did. When his father died in 1927, he returned to the violin which he loved so much. Francescatti exemplified the ultra-refined French style of violin playing. His brilliant recordings are considered great musical feats—not simply technical accomlishments, including Paganini *Concerto No. 1 in D Major* (Columbia). He made his U.S. debut in 1939 with the New York Philharmonic. He performed encores of fiddle repertoire with precision and esprit. **QUOTE** "Before the public you put in more scratching, more fire, more sweat. But when you record, the 'micro' is so near, if you do the same thing it sounds coarse. You must play *little*, for you. You do not play for an audience, for 'micro,' you play for yourself, *very small* and *very perfect*." Died: 1991.

Ford Bond 6706 Hollywood

Announcer

BORN David Bond; 1905. **SPOTLIGHTS** A former baseball sports figure, Bond became a steadily employed actor from radio's early years through its Golden Era. For years, Bond worked on the serial drama: "And now Stella Dallas, a continuation on the air of the true-to-life story of mother love and sacrifice in which Stella Dallas saw her own beloved daughter Laurel marry into wealth and society, and realizing the differences in their tastes and worlds, went out of Laurel's life..." (first broadcast NBC, 1937, the show lasted almost two decades with several different announcers). He was the familiar announcer on "Highway in Melody," a musical variety program (NBC, first aired 1944). Other shows include "Easy Aces," "Backstage Wife," "David Harum," and "Manhattan Merry-Go-Round," a popular music program. Died: 1962.

Ken Carpenter 6706 Hollywood

Sportscaster, announcer

BORN Aug. 21, 1900, in Avon, IL. **SPOTLIGHTS** He was an ace announcer on "The Edgar Bergen and Charlie McCarthy Show" (first broadcast in 1936), the "Kraft Music Hall" hosted by Bing Crosby (1936-'46), and "One Man's Family," the great American serial during the 1940s. Other programs include "Truth or Consequences," "Three Sheets to the Wind" (a comedy-mystery with John Wayne playing a lush), and "The Halls of Ivy," a situation comedy of the early 1950s starring Ronald Colman. He was also a sportscaster for Santa Anita Handicaps, the Rose Bowl football games (he broadcast the first one between Stanford and Columbia in 1934), and other

sports events. **ACHIEVEMENTS** Carpenter donated his time and talent to "Command Performance," a stupendous wartime variety show that *Time* magazine called "the best wartime program in America." It was produced by the United States War Department, and heard by WWII troops fighting overseas via direct shortwave transmission.

Bernadette Peters 6706 Hollywood

Singer, actress, comedienne

BORN Bernadette Lazzara; Feb. 28, 1948, in Ozone Park Queens, New York, NY. **SPOTLIGHTS** An American Broadway treasure, this musical diva is a gifted actress. When her Italian immigrant mother (who formerly had aspirations of being in show business) spotted her daughter performing in front of the family room's TV set, she knew little Bernadette could be a star. By age five, she was professionally employed—a *paid* actress—on TV's "Horn and Hardart Children's Hour." When she was nine years old, director Otto Preminger cast her in the play "This Is Goggle." At age 13, she toured with the road show of "Gypsy." After virtually spending her entire youth performing, she finally made her Broadway debut in "Johnny No Trump," a 1967 show which opened and closed in one night. She kept at it and landed another role that same season in "George M!" starring Joel Gray. Her big break though came in 1969 in an off-Broadway production, "Dames at Sea." Called the "New-thirties' musical," it was a big hit. Peters left the show an established New York theater actress. In 1974 she starred as silent screen actress-comedienne Mabel Normand in "Mack and Mabel." The brilliant Jerry Herman did the score. She sang the now-classic "Time Heals Everything." The *New York Times* wrote that Peters emerged "a major Broadway star."

Bernadette Peters

She possesses an enchanting voice and immaculate porcelain-like skin. She is petite, beautiful, warm and sweet and has been said to resemble a precious Kewpie doll. Others have likened her to a beautiful 19th-century painting come to glorious life, which made her ideal for the lead in the 1984 award-winning Broadway hit, "Sunday in the Park with George." Stephen Sondheim wrote the score for the show. He said, "Like very few others, she sings and acts at the same time. Most performers act then sing. Bernadette is flawless as far as I'm concerned." Other outstanding plays that this Tony Award-winning actress has starred in include "Song and Dance," and "Into the Woods," to mention a couple. In 1999, she starred in the revival of that theatrical evergreen "Annie Get Your Gun." (The show's original star was Ethel Merman.) Motion pictures include *The Longest Yard* (1974), *Silent Movie* (1976), *Slaves of New York* (1989), *Pink Cadillac* (1989), *Alice* (1990), *Impromptu* (1992), and *Snow Days* (1999). She made *The Jerk* (1979), and *Pennies From Heaven* (1981), co-starring her then-boyfriend Steve Martin. **QUOTE** Her Hollywood Walk of Fame star dedication ceremony took place on April 23, 1987. Asked what she would do if she did not act, she replied, "I don't know how to do anything else."

Raymond Massey   6706 Hollywood

See page 144

Dolly Parton 🎵   6712 Hollywood

Singer, songwriter, musician, actress

Dolly Parton

BORN Jan. 19, 1946, in Locust Ridge, Sevier County, TN. **SPOTLIGHTS** Country's most pervasive queen was born the fourth of 12 children to poor sharecropper parents. Descended from Dutch, Irish and Native American Cherokee Indian, she was raised in a crowded one-room cabin in east Tennessee. Her musical gifts were apparent almost from the start. By age five, this little farm girl composed before she could write, and by age six, she sang in the Church of God in the foothills of the Smoky Mountains. As a child, she constructed her first guitar out of an old mandolin and two bass guitar strings. She performed professionally on local television and radio by age 10, and by age 13 had cut her first record, "Puppy Love." Determined to make it as a country singer, Parton moved to Nashville the day after she graduated from high school in 1964. Her featured spot on Porter Wagoner's syndicated TV series (1967-'74)—along with her blonde, bosomy good looks—and her album, *Hello, I'm Dolly*, brought her national

attention. Her intelligent bright eyes and wide smile complement her voluptuous figure. Audiences fell in love with the singer, who they quickly discovered had a heart of gold, and a terrific sense of humor. Her former *big* hairdo attracted much attention. She once told a Las Vegas audience, "You'd be amazed how expensive it is to make a wig look this cheap." In 1969, she became a member of the Grand Ole Opry. Her countless musical treasures include: "Coat of Many Colors" (in which she wrote about the poverty of her youth), "Jolene," "My Tennessee Mountain Home," "We'll Get Ahead Someday," "If Teardrops Were Pennies," "Please Don't Stop Loving Me," "I Will Always Love You," and "Here You Come Again." Parton made her screen debut in *9 to 5* (1980), playing a slightly naive working woman who couldn't help being sexy. She delighted fans in with her natural acting ability. The Academy was impressed with her music and lyrics, including the title song, for which she was Oscar-nominated. Next, she appeared in *The Best Little Whorehouse in Texas* (1982—also some songs), with Burt Reynolds. Later, she surprised critics with her outstanding dramatic performance in the weepy *Steel Magnolias* (1989). She followed with a starring role as a radio advice host in *Straight Talk* (1992--also songs), opposite James Woods. She appears in *Beverly Hillbillies* (1993). Hit recordings include *Here You Come Again*, *The Great Pretender*, *Trio*, *White Limozeen*, *Eagle When She Flies*, *Honky Tonk Angels*, *I Believe*, *Hungry Again* and *Trio II*. Her album, *Treasures*, captures an eclectic collection of songs and musicians with 11 country, pop, folk and rock gems. *The Grass Is Blue* is pure, fun American bluegrass. Parton stated, "No electric, all acoustic and always an upright bass and no piano." In addition to musical variety TV, she has starred and guest starred in a number of movies made for TV and series. Shows include "Wild Texas Wind," "The Dottie West Story," "Unlikely Angel," "Mindin' My Own Business," and "Blue Valley Songbird." **ACHIEVEMENTS** An American treasure, she is the recipient of virtually every important music award and honor, including four Grammys, and seven Country Music Association Awards. Parton is a prolific songwriter with more than 3,000 songs to her credit. A shrewd businesswoman, *Ms.* magazine named her "Woman of the Year" in 1986. Charity involvements include Dollywood Foundation, a non-profit organization that supports education and helps to reduce school dropout rate. Parton opened Eagle Mountain Sanctuary in 1991 to protect majestic American eagles. In Sept. 1999 she was inducted into the Country Music Hall of Fame. **HIGHLIGHTS** Her Smoky Mountain theme park, Dollywood, is located in Pigeon Forge, Tennessee. Dollywood enjoyed its 15th season in 2000. It is the biggest, most popular theme park in that part of the land, drawing millions of visitors each summer. She said, "I joke that we drove Opryland out of business." **QUOTE** Her Hollywood Walk of Fame star was unveiled in a rare double ceremony with Sylvester Stallone on June 14, 1984. It coincided with the debut of their joint movie, *Rhinestone*. Instilled with good, solid values and a strong faith in God, Parton commented, "I believe God is right here and He keeps me strong. I lean on

Him all the time."

Douglas Fairbanks, Jr. 🎤 6712 Hollywood

See page 367

Scatman Crothers 🎥 6712 Hollywood

Scatman Crothers (second from left)

Actor, comedian, singer, musician
BORN Benjamin Sherman Crothers; May 23, 1910, in Terre Haute, IN. **SPOTLIGHTS** A self-taught jazz musician who, at age 14 played drums, guitar, and sang at a speakeasy. "I entertained for all the gangsters," he said with his trademark grin. It was during this time that he earned his nickname "Scatman" for singing scat. He was wonderfully talented at improvisational singing of nonsense syllables to an instrumental accompaniment. A career in radio followed, then the tall, thin actor made his silver screen debut in *Yes Sir, Mr. Bones* (1951). Other movies include *The Patsy* (1964), *The Aristocats* (1970--voiceover), *Lady Sings the Blues* (1972), *One Flew Over the Cuckoo's Nest* (1975), *The Shootist* (1976), *Silver Streak* (1976), *The Shining* (1980), *Broncho Billy* (1980), *Twilight Zone: The Movie* (1983), and *The Journey of Natty Gann* (1985). **TV** He

NOTE TO READERS WALKING THE WALK You are standing in front of the world famous Egyptian Theatre which now houses the American Cinematheque: "a non-profit, viewer-supported film exhibition and cultural organization dedicated to the celebration of the Moving Picture in all of its art forms...Programs range from in-person tributes to filmmakers and actors, screenings of classics, independents, new and retrospective foreign films. The Egyptian Theatre boasts state-of-the-art technology at work within an historic shell." Of interest is "Hollywood Forever"—a documentary which screens daily. Call their 24-hour info line: 323. 466.3456, or visit www.egyptiantheatre.com

gained national fame playing the comic character Louie the garbage man on "Chico and the Man" (1974-'78). He played Mingo in the historic mini-series "Roots" (1977). Died: 1986.

Cass Daley 🎤 6712 Hollywood

See page 134

Diana Ross 💿 6712 Hollywood

Diana Ross

Singer, actress
BORN March 26, 1944, in Detroit, MI. **SPOTLIGHTS** Known as the "first lady of Motown," this beautiful talent enjoyed a string of hits as a member of the Supremes. When Miss Ross turned solo artist, she created dazzling musical triumphs. She had a huge hit with her first single "Reach Out and Touch Somebody's Hand" in 1970. It hit on both pop and R&B charts, but "Ain't No Love High Enough" went to #1. She sang a duet with Lionel Ritchie for the theme of the movie *Endless Love*; her cooing voice was perfectly romantic on it. As an actress, she stars in *Lady Sings the Blues* (1972), in an Oscar-nominated performance. The *Lady* is singer Billie Holiday (see her bio in this book). Other movies include *The Wiz* (1978). A phenomenal entertainer, a pop-music legend, she is a superstar worshipped by millions. She has made countless TV and live concert appearances. For an extraordinary collection of her music, the 4-CD Box Set *Forever Diana*, covers her 30-year musical odyssey (available on Motown Master Series). **RECOMMENDED** *Diana Ross Memoirs: Secrets of a Sparrow*, published 1993 by Villard Books. **QUOTES** "Life is a process of moving forward, sometimes stumbling, sometimes soaring. I have discovered that life is not the arrival at a particular destination, but rather it is a journey itself, the odyssey."...Her Walk of Fame dedication ceremony took place on May 6, 1982. She said, "I'm proud of what I've achieved. It reminds me of how blessed I am and that I want to give more of myself to others."

Mack Sennett 🎥 6712 Hollywood

Director, producer, actor
BORN Mikall (Michael) Sinnott; Jan. 17, 1884, outside of Quebec, Canada. **SPOTLIGHTS** Born in Canada, of working-class Irish descent, he became America's pioneer of slapstick humor. Sennett formed the Keystone Company in 1912, with his Keystone Kops, and invented for the screen a wild and free form of humor with broad action comedy. There was pie throwing, people dangling off flag poles, crazy car chases,

Mack Sennett

police being tricked by scamps and scoundrels, a romantic suitor sitting down on a large pin cushion, a blindfolded circus man who high dives into a supposed tank of water that an elephant just drank from and left empty, so he crashes through and ends up coming through the earth a few yards away, etc.—as opposed to the restrained French-type of comedy that the movies had utilized up to this time. Nicknamed the "fun factory," virtually every significant comedy star performed under his comic bossiness, among them W.C. Fields, Mabel Normand, Ford Sterling, Charlie Chaplin, Gloria Swanson, Fatty Arbuckle and Louise Fazenda. Those artists, along with his zany Keystone Kops, and many other silent screen greats appeared in more than 1,000 Sennett comic "shorts." In 1917, he headed up Mack Sennett Comedies Company. His name was known throughout the world for madcap fun, but his glory years ended with the approach of sound in the late 1920s. **ACHIEVEMENTS** 1937 Special Oscar. Died: 1960.

Sylvester Stallone 🎥   6712 Hollywood

Sylvester Stallone

Actor, screenwriter, director
BORN July 6, 1946, in New York, NY. **SPOTLIGHTS** Boxing films historically do well with ticket sales, and the muscular Stallone had the savvy to know it. After writing the script for *Rocky* over a long weekend, he sold it on the condition that he star in it. Much like the dark-haired character's rise to glory—against all odds—Stallone had his breakthrough with *Rocky* (1976). This sympathetic underdog became was a champ at the box office, and the movie won Academy Awards for best picture, best director and best editing. A number of *Rocky* sequels followed—some good, some not—and were spread out from 1979-'90. A partial listing of his other film credits includes *Bananas* (1971), *The Lords of Flatbush* (1974), *Capone* (1975), *Farewell My Lovely* (1975), *No Place to Hide* (1977), *F.I.S.T.* (1978), *Paradise Alley* (1978), the macho *Rambo* series (starting with *First Blood*, 1982), *Tango and Cash* (1989), *Cliffhanger* (1993—he is very good in it), and *Demolition Man* (1993). In *Cop Land* (1997), he delivers a superior dramatic performance using brains, not brawn.

Sylvester Stallone with Dolly Parton (behind his right shoulder)

It was a refreshing and interesting change that both the critics and audiences loved. Offscreen, Stallone discovered his love of painting, and has successfully exhibited his art.

Yehudi Menuhin 🎙   6712 Hollywood

Violinist, conductor
BORN April 22, 1916, in New York, NY. **SPOTLIGHTS** One of the century's greatest musicians, Menuhin was a child prodigy. He began taking violin lessons at age three, and his elegant concert debut at the San Francisco Symphony Orchestra at age seven. After the eminent scientist Albert Einstein heard the spectacular 12-year-old perform, Einstein leaned toward the boy and commented, "Today, Yehudi, you have once again proved to me that there is a God in heaven." This internationally acclaimed violinist sparked much attention by reviving old masterpieces and creating renewed interest in these exquisite works. He was a master instructor at schools he founded in England and Switzerland for gifted children. He released 100 fine recordings—many of them considered classics—in the span of his 75-year career. **ACHIEVEMENTS** In 1986 Menuhin was awarded a Kennedy Center Honor by President Ronald Reagan. During WWII, he played more than 500 live concerts to U.S. troops and Allied Forces to boost their spirits. Afterwards his charity efforts to raise cash for war victims helped save thousands of lives. He devoted his life to bringing peace through global cultural cooperation. He fought diligently for human rights internationally. **HIGHLIGHTS** He was home-schooled by his Russian immigrant parents, who found California's public school system too laxed...He devoted 20 minutes daily to the practice of yoga. He was a lifelong vegetarian. **QUOTE** "The artist alone gives reality to the dreams of mankind." Died: 1999, at age 82.

Bob Barker 📺   6714 Hollywood

Emcee, host, television personality
BORN Robert Barker; Dec. 12, in Darrington, WA.

Bob Barker and Federico

SPOTLIGHTS The likable, youthful looking, all-American TV personality has entertained audiences since the 1950s. With his cheerful banter, Barker won millions of devoted game show fans. Shows include "Truth or Consequences," and "The Price Is Right." He signed with the latter in 1972, and his familiar calling to audience contestants, "Come on down!" rings in every show. "The Price Is Right" is the longest-running game show in television history. To commemorate the taping of the show's 5000th episode and celebrate its 25th season, CBS rededicated Studio 33--where the show had been taped--as Bob Barker Studios. He is the first performer to whom CBS has ever dedicated a stage. CBS statistics show Barker has made more TV appearances than any other person in the history of the medium. He has been hugged and kissed by more contestants than anyone else. The *Guinness Book of World Records* has named him twice as TV's "most durable performer," and "most generous host in television history." He hosted of the Miss U.S.A. and Miss Universe beauty pageants for 21 years. **ACHIEVEMENTS** Barker has won ten Emmy Awards as TV host, more than any other performer, and two more as executive producer of "The Price Is Right." He is the recipient of the coveted Carbon Mike Award of the Pioneer Broadcasters. Barker was honored with an Emmy Award for "Lifetime Achievement" at the 26th annual Daytime Awards in 1999. His acceptance speech referenced his many years of giving away household goods for prizes. He said, "I wish I had a refrigerator for every one of you." Barker has become the most visible figure in the animal rights movement. He has established the DJ&T Foundation to help control the dog and cat population by funding low-cost or free spay/neuter clinics. The foundation is named in memory of his wife Dorothy Jo, and his mother Matilda (Tilly) Valandra, both of whom loved animals. **QUOTE** "A tourist summed it up for me. He said, 'Bob, you should be proud of your star on Hollywood Boulevard. Nothing says Hollywood quite like the Walk of Fame.'"

Eve Arden 📺   6714 Hollywood

Actress, comedian
BORN Eunice Quedens; April 12, 1912, in Mill Valley, CA. **SPOTLIGHTS** A blonde show girl with large knowing eyes, she entertained at the Ziegfeld Follies, then became a household name for her wisecracking ways. Arden was the comedy queen of ego-deflating lines and fast double-edged zingers. Audiences loved her. Motion pictures include *Oh, Doctor!* (1937), *Stage Door* (1937), *Slightly Honorable* (1939), *Cover Girl* (1944),

Mildred Pierce (1945), *Earl Carroll's Vanities* (1945), *The Kid from Brooklyn* (1946), *Night and Day* (1946), *The Unfaithful* (1947), *One Touch of Venus* (1948), *Three Husbands* (1950), *Anatomy of a Murder* (1959), and *Grease* (1978, as the principal). Arden made her radio debut on "The Danny Kaye Show" as a regular from 1945-'46. Several programs followed, then she starred as Connie Brooks, the testy English teacher at Madison High School in the

Eve Arden

comedy series, "Our Miss Brooks" (1948 - 1957). Arden possessed flawless comic timing. With her sarcastic wit, she was the called the female counterpart to Groucho Marx. With her devilish, lively and snappy comebacks, the show was a huge immediate success. In 1952, the program became hit TV—for which she won an Emmy—until she called it quits four years later. But before it was all over, she did the movie version *Our Miss Brooks* (1956). She ventured to TV again in the sitcom, "The Mothers-in-Law" (1967-'69). Died: 1990.

Richard Crenna 🎥   6714 Hollywood

Richard Crenna

Actor, director, writer, producer
BORN November 30, 1926, in Los Angeles, CA. **SPOTLIGHTS** A native Californian, Crenna grew up in the hotel his parents owned. He amused himself and guests by mimicking the colorful characters who lived in and passed through the hotel. Hollywood, only a bus ride away, was then the center of West Coast radio broadcasting. At age 11 Crenna auditioned for the "Boy Scout Jamboree." He won the role of a perpetual foul-up named Herman. With the encouragement of his loving parents, he became one of the most-heard voices on radio. On air in such series as "Dr. Christian," and "Amos 'n' Andy," at one point in his teens he had continuing parts in eight radio serials, including "Burns and Allen," and "Gunsmoke." Later, he landed the TV role of Luke McCoy, the hillbilly grandson of Walter Brennan on "The Real McCoys" (1957-'63). During the fifth and sixth seasons of that show, and to date, he has directed more than 200 episodes, pilots and movies of the week. He appears in the motion picture *Our Miss Brooks* (1956), starring Eve Arden and Gale Gordon (he also appeared in the TV show of the

same name). He gave a powerful dramatic performance as the gunboat captain in *The Sand Pebbles* (1966), opposite Steve McQueen. He was outstanding in the spine tingler *Wait Until Dark* (1967) with Audrey Hepburn, and *Red Sky at Morning* (1970). He plays a rich, older husband that sexy Kathleen Turner wants dead in *Body Heat* (1981). Crenna gained a new generation of fans playing the macho Colonel Trautman in the *Rambo* series, starring Sylvester Stallone, and beginning with *First Blood* (1982). He is delightful to watch in the *Flamingo Kid* (1984), and *Hot Shots! Part Deux* (1993). In 1996 he appeared in the remake of *Sabrina*. Earnest, friendly, and warm, Crenna is a man with firm opinions and enthusiasm for his career. He manages to be funny, charming and look elegant all at the same time. This affable, handsome, mellow-voiced star is well-loved by audiences.

Walter Winchell 📺   6714 Hollywood

Walter Winchell

Journalist, columnist
BORN Walter Winchel (with one "l"); April 7, 1897, in New York, NY. **SPOTLIGHTS** "Good evening, Mr. and Mrs. North America, and all the ships at sea. Let's go to press!" was the familiar opening to Sunday evening's Walter Winchell gossip and commentary. This long-running show, first aired in 1930, was listened to faithfully by millions of Americans. "Flash! This is hot off the wires!" exclaimed Winchell for "Hollywood Reporters" (1945-'51). His brash, rapid-fire delivery was punctuated by a telegraph key which he used aggressively to dramatize gossip items. He was the most controversial columnist of his day. TV: Narrator of "The Untouchables" (1959-'63). **QUOTE** "As you may have heard, I'm supposed to be an S.O.B. Well, maybe I am." Died: 1972.

Sam Wood 🎥   6718 Hollywood

Director
BORN July 18, 1883, in Philadelphia, PA. **SPOTLIGHTS** A gold miner who only struck fool's gold in Nevada, Wood tried his luck in Tinseltown. His talent made him lucky. First, he was a bit actor in silent movies. Next, he became an assistant director to Cecil B. DeMille. After directing a number of films starring Gloria Swanson, he successfully moved into talkies. He enjoyed huge hits with the Marx Brothers in *A Night at the Opera* (1935) and *A Day at the Races* (1937). Other motion pictures include *Goodbye Mr. Chips* (1939), starring Robert Donat. (Donat won the Best Actor Oscar that year over Clark Gable in *Gone with the Wind* .) Ironically, Wood had directed a considerable percentage of scenes in that Civil War epic, too, when Victor Fleming fell ill. (Then, in another twist of fate,

Sam Wood instructing subordinates on a Marx Brothers set.

Victor Fleming took home the Best Director Academy Award.) Wood did an excellent job with the adaptation of Thornton Wilder's Pulitzer Prize-winning play, *Our Town* (1940). William Holden and Martha Scott star in this bit of Americana. He also directed *Kitty Foyle* (1940), *The Devil and Miss Jones* (1941), *King's Row* (1942), *The Pride of the Yankees* (1942), and *For Whom the Bell Tolls* (1943). Died: 1949.

Kate Smith 📺   6720 Hollywood

See page 216

Cliff Arquette 📺   6720 Hollywood

Comedian, actor
BORN Dec. 28, 1905, in Toledo, OH. **SPOTLIGHTS** A comic actor with an expert sense of timing and delivery, this talent was more than steadily employed, he was busy running from one radio broadcast to another. He starred as Sheriff Luke Ferguson on "Edgar A. Guest," a variety program that included elements of drama, homespun philosophy and rustic poetry (1932-'38). In 1936 he played Wallingford Tuttle Gildersleeve on "Fibber McGee and Molly," and enjoyed being an initial part of one of radio's most popular sit-coms. From Hollywood, Arquette worked in the extremely successful adventure-mystery serial drama, "I Love a Mystery" (1939-'44). In "Point Sublime" (1940-'48), he starred in "the human story of a fella named Ben Willet," as town philosopher and mayor, who owned the general store, and pumped gas. In the comedy/musical variety/audience interview show, *Glamour Manor* (1944-'47), he starred as the hotel's manager. On that same show, he played the elderly Mrs. Wilson (a female impersonation he had been doing for years). Then, he put his dialects to good use in the backwoods community of "Lum and Abner." **HIGHLIGHTS** His granddaughters are actresses:

Rosanna Arquette (of *Desperately Seeking Susan* fame); and Patricia Arquette (of *Ed Wood* fame). His grandson is actor David Arquette...He played a folksy character named Charley Weaver (many fans thought that was his real name) as a regular cast member in TV's "The Tonight Show," starring Jack Paar. **QUOTE** "I've butted my head against the great wall of stardom for 30 years, and it took Jack to give it to me. I owe everything to him." Died: 1974.

Mabel Taliaferro 🎥   6720 Hollywood

Actress

BORN May 21, 1887, in New York, NY. **SPOTLIGHTS** Her engaging smile took her from *Cinderella* (1911) to *The Rich Slave* (1921). Died: 1979.

*Sam Wood and Joan Fontaine on the set of **Ivy** (1947). Wood is pointing to the word ivy, in the ivy.*

6724 HOLLYWOOD

Norman Kerry    6724 Hollywood

Actor

BORN Arnold Kaiser; June 16, 1889, in Rochester, NY. **SPOT-LIGHTS** A dashing silent screen star with a waxed mustache, he was Universal Studios' big box office draw. Desperately wanting to be named "the most popular film performer of 1926," he rivaled for the top dog position. Although handsome, debonair and romantic in *The Love Thief,* he could not compete against the Warner Bros. star who won the "world's most popular" title through his sheer animal magnetism. That star's name? Rin-

Norman Kerry

Tin-Tin. Embarrassed to be rated beneath man's best friend, Kerry just put the proverbial tail between his legs to star in *The Irresistible Lover* (1927). **QUOTE** "A leading man is one who, through the force of his own personality and appearance, has battled his way through many obstacles until he occupies the spotlight in the picture. I have never seen a business in which success was so instantaneous at times, provided one has the material. It holds greater rewards than any business I know and there is a pleasure and a fascination in the work which is undeniable. There are plenty at the bottom, but the top is always a little bare." Died: 1956.

Eddy Howard ●   6724 Hollywood

Singer, band leader

BORN Sept. 12, 1914, in Woodland, CA. **SPOTLIGHTS** With the clean-cut good looks of a youthful, polite country clerk, Howard performed in a relaxed, pleasant style. His soft, intimate manner helped create big hits, including the 1950s romantic love song "Sin (It's No Sin)," "To Each His Own," "Something Old-Something New," "Lonesome Tonight," and "The Girl That I Marry," his most enchanting and romantic waltz. Albums include *Eddy Howard and His Orchestra Play 22 Original Big Band Recordings* and *Happy Birthday/Anniversary Waltz.* Died: 1963.

Anita Stewart    6724 Hollywood

Actress

BORN Anna Stewart; Feb. 7, 1895, in Brooklyn, NY. **SPOT-LIGHTS** A beautiful actress, she rose to the top five box office draw in the early 1920s. She made her film debut in *The Wood Violet* (1912). In all, she made 90 silents, including *Her Mad Bargain* (1921), and *A Question of Honor* (1922). Died: 1961.

Nelson Riddle ●   6724 Hollywood

Conductor, composer, arranger

BORN June 1, 1921, in Oradell, NJ. **SPOTLIGHTS** A master of simplicity, he arranged for big bands like Tommy Dorsey in the 1940s, and was arranger and conductor for Judy Garland, Frank Sinatra (Riddle figured strongly in Sinatra's comeback), and other superstars. His music of the 1950s defined the decade. Singer Linda Ronstadt worked with the legend on her 1983 hit album, *What's New.* Motion picture/TV scores include *Paint Your Wagon,* and "Cagney and Lacey." Music lovers and critics alike praised the outstanding 1996 CD *Rosemary Clooney Dedicated to Nelson,* available on the Concord Jazz Label. **ACHIEVEMENTS** 1975 Oscar for *The Great Gatsby.* 1958 Grammy. He was in charge of White House inauguration ceremonies for President John F. Kennedy in 1961, and President Ronald Reagan in 1985. Died: 1985.

Oscar Levant ●   6724 Hollywood

Pianist, writer, host, composer

BORN Dec. 27, 1906, in Pittsburgh, PA. **SPOTLIGHTS** Incomparable pianist and wit whose life motto was "I am an open-minded man. All I want is my own way." He usually got it. Devotee and real-life pal of George Gershwin, Levant became the premier pianist-interpreter of Gershwin's music. Once, he paid a visit to the Gershwins and stayed for two years. He entertained them with such witticism as: "Tell me, George, if you had to do it all over again, would you fall in

Oscar Levant

love with yourself?" In their circle, Levant was known as the "wit's wit." When required to appear before the WWII draft-board examiner, he was asked by a military man, "Do you think you can kill?" Levant paused, "I don't know about strangers, but friends, yes." His first break came when the scheduled pianist became ill, and Levant was substituted in for a recording of "Rhapsody in Blue." Regarding his work in a number of films he said, "I played an unsympathetic character—myself." Regarding his work on the small box, his self-description was "the verbal vampire of television," He once interviewed Zsa Zsa Gabor on the "Secret of Staying Perpetually Middle-Aged." He was utterly bombastic to everyone—no matter who they were or what lofty position they held in society. One critic wrote: "Levant has raised disrespect to the level of high art." His concert recitals were extremely popular; he was also a smash on radio. Known to be somewhat of a hypochondriac, he saw a psychiatrist daily. "It gives me something to do," he commented. "There is a thin line between genius and insanity. I have erased that line." His must-see films include *Rhythm on the River* (1940), *Rhapsody in Blue* (1945), and *O'Henry's Full House* (1952). Recordings include Gershwin's *Concerto in F* with the New York Philharmonic under Andre Kostelanetz. A prolific composer in his own right, he composed two string quartets, a nocturne for symphony orchestra, a piano concerto, music for two big motion pictures, several hit songs and more—in 18 months alone. **SIDELIGHTS** At a dinner party, Levant was introduced to the famous poet Wallace Stevens (whose beautiful wife modeled for the face of the Liberty Dime). Oscar's opening line to Stevens was, "Why shouldn't you be a great poet? I'd be inspired too if my wife had little wings where her ears should be." **QUOTE** Looking back at his career he stated, "In some situations I was difficult, in odd moments impossible, in rare moments loathsome, but, at my best, unapproachably great." Died: 1972.

Gilbert Roland 🎥   6724 Hollywood

Actor

BORN Luis Antonio Damaso de Alanso; Dec. 11, 1905, in Chihuahua, Mexico. **SPOTLIGHTS** The handsome, muscular youth was determined to follow in his father's footsteps as a bullfighter. Then, Pancho Villa attacked the city of Juarez, Mexico, during the Mexican Revolutionary War. This battle forced the family to flee to the Texas, U.S.A. Correctly figuring that Hollywood was about as risky as facing an angry bull, Roland got his start as an extra in the early silent classic, *The Hunchback of Notre Dame* (1923), starring Lon Chaney. He earned $3 a day plus a box lunch. His good looks won him the role of Armand opposite Norma Talmadge in *Camille* (1927). The affable actor was one of the few who made the transition from silents to talkies. A mixture of glamour and swashbuckler made him a dashing Cisco Kid in 11 pictures. As the hero of the under class, he showed the Kid reading Shakespeare. *The Bullfighter and the Lady* (1951) is one of his finest works. He co-stars opposite Kirk Douglas and Lana Turner in the biting Hollywood drama, *The Bad and the Beautiful* (1952). He appears in the action-packed Western, *Three Violent People* (1956), opposite Charlton Heston, and Anne Baxter. **QUOTE** "My Cisco Kid might have been a bandit, but he fought for the poor and was a civilized man in the true sense of the word. I wanted to be sure the Mexicano was not portrayed as an unwashed, uneducated, savage clown." Died: 1994.

Eva Marie Saint 🎥   6724 Hollywood

See page 423

Ruby Keeler 🎥   6724 Hollywood

Actress, dancer

Ruby Keeler and Dick Powell

BORN Ethel Keeler; Aug. 25, 1909, in Canada. **SPOTLIGHTS** While in her teens, she was a tap dancing chorus girl in a George M. Cohan Broadway musical. Within a few years, she was a featured player. She made her screen debut in a bit part in *Show Girl in Hollywood* (1930). She had her wonderful breakthrough paired with Dick Powell in Busby Berkeley's *42nd Street* (1933). Berkeley's *Gold Diggers of 1933* was another extravagant musical and box office hit. In all, she stars in 12 motion pictures...In private life, she was a low handicap golfer, good enough to go on professional tour. She was married to entertainer Al Jolson (1928-'40). **QUOTE** Her own toughest critic, she reflected on her career and moaned, "I couldn't act. I had that terrible singing voice, and now I can see I wasn't the greatest tap dancer in the world either." Died: 1993.

George M. Cohan 💿   6724 Hollywood

Actor, songwriter, dancer, comedian, playwright, producer

BORN George Michael Cohan; July 4, 1878, in Providence, RI. **SPOTLIGHTS** A child hoofer, he grew up to become one of the great American legends. In 1893 at age 15, as the junior member of the Four Cohans (his family's theatrical group), he wrote songs as quickly as they were rejected. Never stopping, he wrote half a dozen a week. This production speed was rooted in his temperament. He had an innate sense of melody and rhythm, a spontaneity, and he brought something of his own inventiveness to each tune. Cohan proved to be in advance of the ragtime craze, and the hot-tempered urchin would have the biggest stars singing his material in just a few years. In 1897, when publishers told him his kind of music—"I Guess I'll Have to Telegraph My Baby"— was dead, he shook his head "no." He told them, "It hasn't even started yet, boys," then tap-danced out of the room with all the whimsy and idiosyncrasies that became his identifiable trademarks. That same year, he produced "The Warmest Baby in the Bunch," and he wasn't quite 20 years old! This tremendous talent was one of America's most successful playwrights, producers, songwriters and yes, even, actors, during the Tin Pan Alley days (c.1900-'35). It was a time when no respectable home would be without a piano and a pretty embroidered picture hanging over the family sofa. His *self-described* traits: "arrogant, impatient, swell-headed, ambitious, adaptive, a torrential speaker." Supremely confidant, he claimed to be "no more pompous than George V of England." He was one of the best verse writers of the era with hits: "Give My Regards to Broadway," I'm A Yankee Doodle Dandy," "You're a Grand Old Flag," "Mary's A Grand

The Four Cohans in "The Yankee Prince"
George M. Cohan (bottom left), with sister Josephine (bottom right)
his father and mother

Old Name," and the peppy WWI military march song "Over There," for which he won a Congressional medal. He was a one-key player; his acquaintance with four chords in the black key of F-sharp were enough to equip him for a quarter century of song. The patriotic Cohan was one of the U.S.'s biggest WWI flag wavers, and not just with his inspirational tunes. He organized the "Over There Theatre League" to entertain American troops overseas in England and France. In 1937 Cohan *set a precedent when his name was above the production title* in "I'd Rather Be Right." Broadway audiences paid top dollar to see him impersonate President Franklin Delano Roosevelt (F.D.R.). When he took the show on the road, he smashed his own box office records. **RECOMMENDED** Warners' musical biopic, *Yankee Doodle Dandy* (1942). This four-star patriotic profile of Cohan, includes an Oscar-winning performance by James Cagney. **QUOTE** He gave the most famous curtain speech in show business, "My Father thanks you, my Mother thanks you, my sister thanks you, and I thank you." Died: 1942.

Broderick Crawford ⛏ 6724 Hollywood

Actor
BORN Dec. 9, 1911, in Philadelphia, PA. **SPOTLIGHTS** The son of vaudevillians, he began working onstage as a child. As an adult, he earned money as a heavyweight boxer, and worked for awhile as a seaman. By 23, he made his legitimate stage debut in "She Loves Me Not," in London. He made his 1935 New York stage debut in "Point Valaine." In 1937, he returned to Broadway for his greatest stage role--the gentle half-wit Lennie in John Steinbeck's "Of Mice and Men." He received rave reviews. This accomplished actor possessed a large body

and gruff voice that suited Hollywood's image of a tough guy. Repeatedly cast in Westerns and gangster stories, he occasionally made comedies. Movies include *Beau Geste* (1939), *When the Daltons Rode* (1940), *Larceny Inc*, *Sin Town* (both 1942), *Seven Sinners* (1940), *Born Yesterday* (1950), *The Mob* (1951), *The Last Posse* (1953), and *Night People* (1954). In all, he made nearly 100 motion pictures. **TV** He played Chief Dan Matthews

Broderick Crawford (r) and Chill Wills

in the popular syndicated crime series "Highway Patrol" (1957-'67). As a hardened, but solid cop, he delivered police-speak: "Ten-four, ten-four." **ACHIEVEMENTS** 1949 Best Actor Academy Award for *All the King's Men*. Adapted from Robert Penn Warren's Pulitzer Prize-winning novel, this American political story was loosely based on Louisiana Senator Huey Long. It is a parable of how absolute power corrupts absolutely. (In a case of life imitating art imitating life, director Robert Rossen pulled a truly demonic performance out of Crawford by telling him to base his character on Columbia Picture's notoriously ruthless studio mogul, Harry Cohn.) Died: 1986.

Ella Fitzgerald ⏺ 6740 Hollywood

Singer, composer
BORN April 25, 1918, in Newport News, VA. **SPOTLIGHTS** Jazz's First Lady of Song, and one of America's greatest artists of the 20th century. This outstanding jazz singer possessed remarkable and complete vocal control. She kicked off her career as a teenager by winning a prize at the Apollo Theatre amateur night, in Harlem. The shy youngster won a second contest at Harlem Opera House. She made her professional debut Feb.16, 1935 as the featured singer with the Chick Webb band; she was 16. Especially noted for her scat singing ("Take the A Train"). Albums include *Best is Yet to Come, Billie, Ella, Lena, Sarah, Dream Dancing, Fine and Mellow, Jazz Heritage, Ella Swings the Band* (1936-'39), and *Song Book* series (her tribute to the Gershwins, Ellington, Porter, Rodgers & Hart, Berlin and Arlen, Kern and Mercer). She made a total of 200 recordings which captured her exceptional skill and purity of voice. Movies include include *Pete Kelly's Blues* (1955—a must-see for jazz fanatics), and the incredible musical *St. Louis Blues* (1958), featuring vintage songs with an all-star cast: Nat "King" Cole, Eartha Kitt, Pearl Bailey, Ruby Dee, Cab Calloway, Ella Fitzgerald and Mahalia Jackson. **ACHIEVEMENTS** Winner of 13 Grammys. The quintessential jazz singer, she was awarded the 1987 National Medal of Art by President Ronald Reagan...She co-wrote one of America's favorite songs "A-Tisket A-Tasket," with band arranger Van

Alexander. It was based on the nursery rhyme. **QUOTE** "I sing swing, bop, soul, blues, Broadway show tunes, bossa nova, and even rock 'n' roll and hillbilly music...Anything if it's played well." Died: 1996.

Jim Healy   6740 Hollywood

Jim Healy (left) and Babe Ruth

Sportscaster
BORN Sept. 14, 1923, in Spokane, WA. **SPOTLIGHTS** A great Los Angeles legend and the longest-running, on-air sports personality in the United States, he began his career in 1946 as writer and pinch-hit announcer on Dick Fishell's nightly sportscast. During the '60s Healy inaugurated prime time sports as an ABC anchor for the City of Angels. Although a versatile play-by-play man, he was best known for his sportscasting on boxing, thoroughbred racing, and football. His nightly radio commentaries featured exclusive scoops and tapes, punctuated by humorous sound effects. Justin Dedeaux, of the prominent Southern California baseball family recalled, "From 5:30 to 6:00 PM every sports fan hurried to the radio for the Jim Healy Show. His fun filled program featured a Walter Winchell-type format complete with a telegraph clicker between each juicy morsel of sports gossip: 'Extremely confidential, but is it true... It ain't my (bleep bleep) fault Campanis is the (bleep) guy... This athlete just set the all-time 'you know' record with 16 'you knows' in a two-minute interview.' He poked fun at everyone. Howard Cosell was his favorite target, along with 'Dan Dear Dork' or the 'Dorkster' (Dan Dierdorf of Monday Night Football). His following was so loyal that listeners taped his shows when they were out of town."

Jim Healy in his office with his Golden Mikes and winning Thoroughbred racehorse friend.

ACHIEVEMENTS Four Golden Mikes, five Associated Press Awards. The continuous winner of a poll picking L.A.'s favorite and most hated sportscasters (taking first place in both categories). His son, Patrick Healy, is an established and respected news reporter for NBC Channel 4. **HIGHLIGHTS** Dubbed "the Lord of Discord" and "Radio's Raging Bull" for his controversial, off-the-wall style, he played himself in many movies. Died: 1994.

Jack Douglas   6740 Hollywood

Producer, narrator, host
BORN April 26, 1927, in Newcastle-upon-Tyne, England. **SPOTLIGHTS** Host of the high-quality travelogue show, "Golden Voyage" (1954-'66).

Tim Conway   6740 Hollywood

Comedian, actor, writer

Tim Conway

BORN Tom Conway; Dec. 15, 1933, in Willoughby, OH. **SPOTLIGHTS** Where other actors have struggled to reach the top, this quick-witted humorist moved effortlessly from a behind-the-scenes staff member position at a Cleveland television station to one of its guests. "The Steve Allen Show" picked him up as a regular, then he won the role of Ensign Charles Parker on the sitcom "McHale's Navy" (1962-'66). This cherubic talent had his own show briefly before joining "The Carol Burnett Show" (1975-'79). In an on-going popular sketch he played Mr. Tudball, a frustrated, ever-suffering boss to Burnett's Mrs. Wiggins, an incompetent, blonde office worker. Enjoying the heck out of himself in this marvelous comedy-variety show with its outstanding cast, Conway won four Emmys. Movies include *The World's Greatest Athlete* (1973) and *The Apple Dumpling Gang* (1975 + sequel). Known to his peers as "the comedian's comedian," Conway also wrote and starred in a series of home videos: "Dorf on Golf," "Dorf and the First Games of Mt. Olympus," and "Dorf's Golf Bible." And this should crack you up, he is a diligent do-it-yourselfer at home. His Walk of Fame star was unveiled on Feb. 21, 1989. His son, Tim Conway, Jr. is a broadcaster on KLSX-FM (97.1) talk radio.

Bud Abbott 📺   6740 Hollywood

See page 343

Al Jolson 🎙   6752 Hollywood

See page 423

Rev. James Cleveland 💿   6752 Hollywood

The Rev. Cleveland

Singer, composer, pianist
BORN Dec. 5, 1932, in Chicago, IL. **SPOTLIGHTS** Known as the "King of Gospel," he made his solo debut at age eight at a Baptist Church in Chicago. At age 16, he composed his first hit, "Grace is Sufficient." The Reverend performed all over the world spreading the word of God to enthusiastic crowds. His religious hits include "Peace Be Still," "Walk on by Faith," "Lord, Help Me to Hold Out," "Ain't That Good News," "As Long as There's God," "The Love of God," "It's My Lord." A partial listing of his albums: *Angelic Choir, Cleveland Singers, Down Memory Lane, Everything Will Be All Right, God's Promises, I Walk with God,* and *Songs of Dedication.* He was also a brilliant conductor. **ACHIEVEMENTS** Two Grammy Awards; six gold and platinum records. Organized the Gospel Music Workshop of America in 1968. In 1971, he became Pastor of the Cornerstone Institutional Baptist Church, located at 4626 W. Washington Blvd. in the heart of Los Angeles: "We are the church where everybody is somebody and Jesus is the Chief Cornerstone." The church welcomes all. **HIGHLIGHTS** On Aretha Franklin's pure gospel recording of *Amazing Grace,* the Reverend James Cleveland played the piano and conducted the choir, and her own father, the Reverend C. L. Franklin officiated. He was chosen to join *the Man's* choir Upstairs in 1991.

Gloria Swanson 🎥   6752 Hollywood

Actress, singer
BORN March 27, 1897, in Chicago, IL. **SPOTLIGHTS** Queen of the Silent Screen. She made her movie debut in *The End of a Perfect Day* (1914), and within one year, enjoyed top billing in *The Fable of Elvira.* It was not until she teamed with the great director, Cecil B. DeMille, that she obtained superstardom: *Male and Female* (1919); *Don't Change Your Husband* (1919). By 1921 *The Affairs of Anatol* and *The Great Moment* ensured her status on the world's stage. At Paramount, the

flamboyant Swanson stated, "I have decided when I am a star, I will be every inch and every moment the star! Everybody from the studio gate man to the highest executive will know it." This glamour puss was a queen off the set, and, by always dressing the part (she never wore the same dress twice), she won women's admiration everywhere. In Europe in 1925 she married the Marquis de la Falaise de la Coudraye; she was the first movie star to marry an aristocrat. This legitimized the whole

Gloria Swanson

"sordid movie business" to those who previously had felt it was scandalous. Now even the best bred of American society could feel comfortable inside a theater—*before the lights went down!* When the newlyweds arrived in New York, the studio threw a gala ball in the Crystal Room at the Ritz—and the whole world knew about it. For the long five-day train trip to Los Angeles, the studio sent her cross country in a private train—not car—*train.* Thousands of fans waited at the station, thrilled to see Hollywood's royalty. Paramount's *Sadie Thompson* (1928) peaked her international popularity. She was one of only a handful of silent screen stars who could speak properly for the talkies, but *The Trespasser*'s (1929) horrible reception had her tiptoeing "stage left to the 'EXIT' sign." Around this time, she made the classic Hollywood remark, "We didn't need dialogue...We had faces!" Her comeback as the aging, eccentric recluse, Norma Desmond, in Billy Wilder's *Sunset Boulevard* (1950), was all the more remarkable since she had been Wilder's fifth choice for the role. The film was a revelation. It was as if Wilder had the camera dissect her character, peeling away raw, bitter nerves, and leaving us with a spooky, fascinating study of human nature. Swanson consciously delivered an over-the-top performance, winning an Academy Award nomination. Cecil B. DeMille appears as himself in the film, and Gloria Swanson said for the record that she hoped the audience would realize this was just *a* story, *not the* story based on her life. Two memorable lines from the movie are: "I *am* big, it's the pictures that got small," and "I'm ready for my closeup, Mr. DeMille." After she received resounding critical acclaim, Swanson found herself again in the limelight. She segued into revivals, her own radio and television shows, and a fashion line. **HIGHLIGHTS** As a lark, during the height of her career, Miss Swanson donned a blonde wig, changed her make-up and used a fake name at a screen test. She flunked it! **QUOTE** She attributed her energy and health to her diet. She ate organically grown vegetables (decades before it was popular), whole wheat grains, natural rice, and only small portions of meat on occasion. Her beverage of choice was fruit juice, *not* champagne. She stated, "I fight for pure food, preventive medicine and things like that." Died: 1983.

Harold Russell   6752 Hollywood

Actor, hero, ex-paratrooper

BORN Jan 14, 1914, in Nova Scotia, Canada. **SPOTLIGHTS** An authentic veteran actor. In real life, Sergeant Russell's hands were blown off by a grenade explosion during World War II. He woke up to find himself in an Army hospital bed in 1944. He made heroic efforts on the path to his recovery. This led to a role in Goldwyn's provocative and important story of three soldiers who experience difficulty adjusting to their small town lives in America's heartland after WWII, *The Best Years of Our Lives* (1946). Russell, who had no previous acting experience gave a compelling performance. The film was superbly directed by William Wyler, and became one of the highest grossing films of the decade. Russell retired after winning his Oscars, then returned to the silver screen to appear in Richard Donner's *Inside Moves* (1980) about the difficulties faced by the disabled, and in George Hickenlooper's *Dogtown* (1996), where he plays a disabled veteran in a small town in Missouri. **ACHIEVEMENTS** 1946 Best Supporting Actor Oscar, and a 1946 Special Oscar ("bringing hope and courage to fellow veterans" for his portrayal of Homer Parrish). Russell made Oscar history; he is the only performer ever to win two Academy Awards for the same role. After winning, he did something unheard of, he left Southern California. He returned to Boston University under the GI Bill to earn a college degree in public relations. He became the 1964 Chair of the President's Committee on Hiring the Handicapped, where he served for 25 years. He dedicated his life to being an advocate for the disabled. **QUOTE** "The war's been over for 54 years, but *The Best Years of Our Lives* is a gauge of what happened. It's the story of 17 million guys who came back from World War II."

Jack Oakie   6752 Hollywood

Actor

Jack Oakie

BORN Lewis Offield; Nov. 12, 1903, in Sedalia, MO. **SPOTLIGHTS** You can tell he had a great sense of humor from his stage name; this cheerful fellow chose "Oakie" from the State of Oklahoma where he was raised. He was also inventive with comic routines; he's the one who pushed the double-take into a comic triple take. He played Tweedledum in *Alice in Wonderland* (1933), and a foil to Lucille Ball in *The Affairs of Annabel* (1938). This portly, dark-haired actor considered his greatest role as that of supporting Charlie Chaplin in *The Great Dictator* (1940--in an Oscar-nominated performance). He steals the limelight in *Tin Pan Alley*, and *Little Men* (both 1940). Died: 1978.

Frank Albertson   6752 Hollywood

Actor

BORN Feb. 2, 1909, in Fergus Falls, MN. **SPOTLIGHTS** He worked in prop departments for six years before getting a shot in front of the cameras in *The Farmer's Daughter* (1928). For 35 years, his all-American looks characters enhanced such films as *Fury* (1936), *Bachelor Mother* (1939), *Wake Island* (1942), *It's a Wonderful Life* (1946), *Psycho* (1960), and *Bye-Bye Birdie* (1963). Died: 1964.

Fred Astaire   6756 Hollywood

Actor, dancer, singer

Fred Astaire

BORN Frederick Austerlitz; May 10, 1899, in Omaha, NE. **SPOTLIGHTS** "Can't act. Can't sing. Balding. Can dance a little," wrote an executive upon viewing Astaire's screen test in 1928. Producer David O. Selznick disagreed. He thought Astaire had charm, "in spite of his enormous ears and bad chin line." He made his screen debut in *Dancing Lady* (1933), opposite Joan Crawford at MGM. One critic described the actor as having "the face of a comedian and the figure of a jockey." While MGM stalled momentarily, RKO leaped to sign him. The studio teamed him with Ginger Rogers for his second film, *Flying Down to Rio* (1933). Audiences went wild, clamoring for more of the glamorous dancing pair. In 1934, *The Gay Divorcee* established Fred Astaire and Ginger Rogers as the screen's hottest dancing properties. The twosome became the biggest money-making team in motion picture history. RKO insured his and her legs for a million dollars per pair. Eight pictures followed including *Roberta* and *Top Hat* (both 1935). He retired in 1945, but Gene Kelly broke his ankle and could not make *Easter Parade* (1946). Kelly asked Astaire to come out of retirement as a special favor to him. Astaire appeared opposite Judy Garland in the smash hit musical. Other films followed, including *Three Little Words* (1950), *Silk Stockings*, and *Funny Face* (both 1957), and the end-of-the-world drama, *On the Beach* (1959). In all, he appeared in 42 motion pictures. **ACHIEVEMENTS** 1949 Special Oscar inscribed: "For his unique artistry and his contribution to the technique of musical pictures." At the post-Awards party, Astaire did *not* dance. That was not out of real-life character for him. He almost never danced socially...Emmy 1959 for "Best Actor on TV." He was also an accomplished choreographer. **SIDELIGHTS** His sister Adele nicknamed her perfectionist brother "Moaning

Minnie." They began dancing together professionally as children and went from vaudeville to Broadway superstardom. When his sister left the team to get married, she thought he'd never find another good partner again. Why? Because he was painfully shy. **RECOMMENDED** The soundtrack anthology entitled, *Fred Astaire & Ginger Rogers at RKO* (available on Rhino Movie Music--Turner Classic Movies; website: www.rhino.com). This legendary talent died in 1987.

The Ritz Brothers 🎥 6756 Hollywood

Dance, comedy team

The Ritz Brothers

BORN Al Joachim, Aug. 27, 1901; Jimmy Joachim, Oct. 23, 1904; Harry Joachim, May 28, 1907; all in Newark, NJ. **SPOTLIGHTS** Three talented brothers, one solid team. Vaudeville first saw their appearance in 1925. All natural dancers, they brought a satirical and wacky humor to their routines. They could mug, mimic, and move like no one else, influencing the great performers who came after them. Spotted by producer Darryl Zanuck in a Hollywood nightclub, the producer signed them for a part in *Sing Baby, Sing*. The trio appeared in 15 more movies. With boundless energy they played only the best nightclubs in the country, several TV All Star Revues and "The Ed Sullivan Show." **HIGHLIGHTS** Offers to work separately were never accepted by the three brothers. Died: Al (1965); Jimmy (1985); Harry (1986).

Bob Hope 📺 6756 Hollywood

See page 87

Andy Clyde 🎥 6758 Hollywood

Actor

BORN March 23, 1891, in Scotland. **SPOTLIGHTS** *Annie Oakley* (1935), *It's a Wonderful World* (1939) and *Abe Lincoln in Illinois* (1940) were a few of his films. He was William Boyd's sidekick in many of the 1940s *Hopalong Cassidy* film series. During the 1950s, these Westerns were shown on TV. This popular actor also appeared as a regular in TV's "The Real McCoys" (1957-'63), and "Lassie" (1958-'64). Died: 1967.

Patti Page 💿 6760 Hollywood

Singer, actress

BORN Clara Ann Fowler; Nov. 8, 1927, in Muskogee, OK. **SPOTLIGHTS** Dubbed "The Singing Rage," this gifted talent started singing in the late 1940s (after World War II). Her pop song "Money, Marbles and Chalk" crossed over to the country charts. The fair-skinned, blonde beauty made history by being one of the first singers to harmonize with herself on records. The resulting song "Confess" was a hit. Known for her honey-tanged voice accented

Patti Page

with a slight hint of Oklahoma twang, her exquisite rendition of Pee Wee King's folk tune "Tennessee Waltz" was so popular it became the official state song. It still ranks as one of the best-selling recordings in music history. She had fun with the song "How Much Is That Doggie in the Window," which became an American classic. She has 15 gold singles, including "Old Cape Cod," "With My Eyes Wide Open," "Allegheny Moon," "You Belong to Me," "Mocking Bird Hill," and "Hello, We're Lonely." With more than 100 million record sales in both country and pop, and three gold albums including *Say Wonderful Things* and *Country Hits*, Page is one of *the* all-time best-selling female soloists. She has been successful for five decades. Her appearance on television's "The Ed Sullivan Show" led to her hostessing "The Big Record," and to her own "The Patti Page Olds Show" (1958-'59). Her motion picture performances as a supporting actress include the must-see drama, *Elmer Gantry* (1960), and the hilarious comedy, *Boys' Night Out* (1962). Page was wonderful in both. In the 1990s she headlined in Las Vegas and other grand venues, and celebrity hosted a nationwide radio show, "The Music of Your Life." **HIGHLIGHTS** From a large family; she has seven sisters and three brothers. **ACHIEVEMENTS** Among her many honors, she is the recipient of the Pioneer Award from the Academy of Country Music. 1999 Grammy "Best Traditional Pop Vocal Performance" for *Live at Carnegie Hall—The 50th Anniversary Concert*.

Henry Koster 🎥 6760 Hollywood

Director

BORN Hermann Kosterlitz; May 1, 1905, in Berlin, Germany. **SPOTLIGHTS** The then-financially strapped Universal Studios desperately needed to compete with Fox's sensational talent Shirley Temple. Deanna Durbin was just the ticket. Universal brought Koster in specifically to work on her films. The plan worked, starting with the popular *Three Smart Girls* (1936—bringing in a ton of much-needed revenue for Universal), *One Hundred Men and a Girl* (1937) and *Three Smart Girls Grow Up* (1939). Koster enjoyed fantasy themes: *Spring Parade*

(1940), where a lowly baker's assistant falls in love with a member of the Austrian royal family; *The Bishop's Wife* (1947), where an urbane angel takes human form (Cary Grant) to help a bishop (David Niven) get back in touch with his wife (Loretta Young) and parishioners; and the brilliant comedy *Harvey* (1950), where Elwood P. Dowd (played by James Stewart) is a souse whose imaginary pal turns out to be an invisible, six-foot-tall white rabbit named Harvey. This causes a well-meaning family member to try to have Stewart certified. Koster directed Richard Burton in his first Hollywood film, *My Cousin Rachel* (1952). His historical pic, *A Man Called Peter* (1955), was a smash. Koster closed with a wholesome, albeit campy, true-life story of *The Singing Nun* (1966), starring Debbie Reynolds, and Greer Garson. **QUOTE** A sentimental guy, he was saddened on the last day shooting. Koster bemoaned, "That seems to be the tragedy of Hollywood friendship, it dies after working together finishes." Died: 1988.

Olivia de Havilland 🎥 6764 Hollywood

Actress

Olivia de Havilland and John Payne

BORN July 1, 1916, in Tokyo, Japan. **SPOTLIGHTS** After being spotted in a college production of *A Midsummer's Night Dream*, she was signed for the film of the same title at the tender age of 19. At Warners, she became the pretty leading lady opposite such greats as James Cagney, Errol Flynn, and Leslie Howard. James Cagney said about his talented co-star, "That girl can play any part ever written." Miss de Havilland was delightful in the exciting swashbuckler *Captain Blood* (1935). This elegant, serene beauty was immortalized in one of her toughest roles, as Melanie in *Gone with the Wind* (1939). She stars opposite the romantic Frenchman Charles Boyer in the must-see *Hold Back the Dawn* (1941). She was *brilliant* as an insane asylum inmate in *The Snake Pit* (1948). Richard Burton falls in love with her while trying to prove she's a murderess in *My Cousin Rachel* (1952). She quit Hollywood and moved to France to be with her husband. She commented, "Hollywood is primitive. All women are regarded physically with no respect for dignity." But De Havilland could not resist the script for *The Proud Rebel* (1958), and returned to appear opposite Alan Ladd in this wonderful film. Worked with her best friend Bette Davis in the psychological drama *Hush...Hush, Sweet Charlotte* (1964). Both extremely talented women were ranked One-Two among Hollywood insiders as Best Actresses. Her estranged sister is actress Joan Fontaine. **ACHIEVEMENTS** 1946 Best Actress Oscar *To Each His Own*. 1949 Best Actress Oscar for *The*

Heiress. Remarkably she was never cursed by typecasting. **QUOTES** She attributed her ever-youthful looks to yoga. She said, "I can stand on my head in the middle of the room. Yoga exercises every muscle in my body. My husband lured me into it."...During Hollywood's 1960s sex goddess exploitation films, she predicted, "With the aggressive bosom, American women risk losing their femininity."

Judy Garland 🎙 6764 Hollywood

See page 141

Arnold Schwarzenegger 🎥 6764 Hollywood

Actor, director

Arnold Schwarzenegger

BORN July 30, 1947, in Graz, Austria. **SPOTLIGHTS** The son of a police chief, he chose the sport of bodybuilding over soccer—going against his father's wishes. Schwarzenegger's instincts proved right. He became a star in the world of bodybuilding, holding the Mr. Olympia title seven times. The film, *Pumping Iron* (1975), documented the rippling muscles of his royal hulkiness. After making a handful of movies, he had his breakthrough role in the violent, but successful *Conan The Barbarian* (1982). He became a naturalized American citizen in 1983. Then, in 1984 he became a full-fledged movie star in *The Terminator*, doing the near-impossible by bringing pathos to a robotic role. Bringing his faint but familiar Austrian accent to his roles, his signature movie lines became: "I'll be back" and "*Hasta la vista, baby.*" No one can forget his presence and power in *Total Recall* (1990), *Terminator 2* (1991), and *True Lies* (1994). He proved adept in comedy, too. In *Twins* (1988), he was Danny De Vito's good brother; in *Kindergarten Cop,* he played an undercover teacher (1990); in *Junior* (1994), he starred as a scientist who becomes the first pregnant man. Other movies include *Jingle All the Way* (1996), *Batman & Robin* (1997—as Mr. Freeze), and *End of Days* (1999). In 1992 he directed the remake of *Christmas in Connecticut*, starring Dyan Cannon, Kris Kristofferson and Tony Curtis. **ACHIEVEMENTS** Author of four best-selling books on fitness and bodybuilding. Credited with bringing the sport into the American mainstream. Devotes much time and energy to supporting the Special Olympics, and Los Angeles' Inner City Games for Youths. A staunch Republican, he is married to Maria Shriver (of the Democratic Kennedy clan)...He exudes confidence, and believes daily workouts help to build not only muscles, but self-esteem.

Kay Francis 🎥 6764 Hollywood

Kay Francis

Actress

BORN Katherine Gibbs; Jan. 13, 1903, in Oklahoma City, OK. **SPOTLIGHTS** Educated in a convent, Francis appeared onstage in 1925, then made her silver screen debut in *Gentlemen of the Press* (1929). She was a lovely, graceful, very feminine brunette—with an endearing lisp—whose face belonged to Warner Bros. This gifted actress made 60 movies, including *Strangers in Love* (1932), *I Found Stella Parrish* (1935), *Confession* (1937), *When the Daltons Rode* (1940), *Four Jills in a Jeep* (1944), and *Wife Wanted* (1946). She periodically returned to the Great White Way, and worked in small theaters across the land. During WWII, she bravely went to the front to entertain troops in Europe, India and China. Died: 1968.

Ray Bolger 🎥   6764 Hollywood

Actor, singer, dancer, comedian

BORN Raymond Bolger; Jan. 10, 1904, in Dorchester, MA. **SPOTLIGHTS** Bolger was immortalized in *The Wizard of Oz* (1939), as the floppy, rubbery-legged, under stuffed scarecrow ("If I only had a brain..."). As that collection of straw, he projected love, warmth and jumbled charm along the Yellow Brick Road. About the role, Bolger stated, "I belong to an American classic." Among his other movies, he stars in Warner's *Where's Charley?* (1952), and was an absolute delight. He had earlier appeared in the musical stage production of the same, for which he won a Tony Award in 1951. Bolger also liked his work in *Rosalie* (1937), *Sweethearts* (1938), *The Harvey Girls* (1946), and *The Entertainer* (1975). **TV** "The Ray Bolger Show" (1953-'55); "Where's Raymond"; and "Washington Square." **HIGHLIGHTS** He started out in show business as a gofer (go for coffee, go for a sandwich...) in vaudeville. The 5-foot, 10-inch, 135-pound song-and-dance man achieved Broadway stardom in "On Your Toes" in 1936, with his show stopper number—performing George Balanchine's fabulous dance "Slaughter on Tenth Avenue." **QUOTE** "I'm still a comedian. I became a dancer in self-defense. I was doing a comedy monologue and didn't know how else to get off the stage, so I danced off. I've been dancing ever since, but I'm still a comedian." Died: 1987.

Elsie Janis 🎥   6776 Hollywood

Actress

BORN Elsie Bierbauer; March 16, 1889, in Columbus, OH. **SPOTLIGHTS** Not lacking in talent, she was a stage, screen, and vaudeville celebrity, as well as a busy composer, author and screenwriter. She faced the cameras in *The Caprices of Kitty* (1915). Other movies include *Betty in Search of a Thrill* (1919). She "discovered" a young, virile Walter Pidgeon at a Hammerstein musical audition and guided his career. Romantically linked offstage, too, she cast him in her revues in 1924 and 1925. A wonderful impersonator (she did a great John Barrymore), her career was buried in the same box as vaudeville. Simultaneously, the advent of sound destroyed her career. Died: 1956.

Feodor Chaliapin 🔴   6776 Hollywood

Opera singer

BORN Fyodor Chalyapin; Feb. 11, 1873, in Kazan, Russia. **SPOTLIGHTS** A formidable performer notorious for his grandiose manner, he was born with a bossy temperament. Chaliapin even took charge of the orchestra, *while performing on stage,* if he felt the conductor did not have the tempo to his liking. How did he do this while maintaining character? He was a giant of a man who used his massive girth to stamp out the correct rhythm. Although no stranger to Mozart or Salieri, the singer, a bass, was immortalized as the greatest Boris ever, in Musorgsky's *Boris Godunov*. This Russian opera, a standard in that country, is rarely heard elsewhere as finding a cast capable of handling the language is nearly impossible. The British Royal family in 1912 requested him to sing it in a special performance, which, of course, was awe-inspiring *to them*. On stage Chaliapin remained unrivaled as a singing actor. He was larger-than-life offstage, too—gesturing, dancing, miming, roaring, lunging, whispering, and posing through life. The majestic one died in 1938.

Ginger Rogers 🎥   6776 Hollywood

Actress, dancer, singer

BORN Virginia Katherine McMath; July 16, 1911, in Independence, MO. **SPOTLIGHTS** At age 14, Ginger kicked open the door of show business by winning a Charleston contest in Texas. The exuberant youth then toured the vaudeville circuit with other teenagers in "Ginger and her Redheads" revue. Four years later, she hit Broadway and easily sequed to movies. Her devoted mother, Lela, gave up her career as a news reporter to chaperone and guide her daughter. Ginger would later comment, "She had a lot of horse sense." Even when Ginger became Queen of RKO studios, she remained a regular Midwestern Gal, a good sport who never pulled any star punches. She made 73 motion pictures, but is best known for the ten she made with Fred Astaire. The dynamic teaming was launched when the duo were featured in *Flying Down to Rio* (1933). Their magical screen chemistry inspired audiences worldwide to kick off their shoes and dance the Continental. This gigantic dance craze demanded the duo repeat it in *The Gay Divorcee* (1934), *Top Hat* (1935), *Swing Time* (1936), *Shall We Dance* (1937), and *Carefree*. All enjoyed huge international success and they became the #1 dance team in the

Ginger Rogers

Stefanie Powers

Actress, dancer, singer
BORN Stefania Federkiewicz; Nov. 2, 1947, in Hollywood, CA. **SPOTLIGHTS** Smart, charismatic and sexy, Powers exemplifies the "new Hollywood." Yet her grace, beauty and sophistication harken back to Hollywood's Golden Era. She recalled, "I feel very privileged to have been on the tail end of the star system. I began to work at 15, and when I was put under contract to Columbia Pictures, they still believed in 'grooming' their young hopefuls. That process allowed me to learn how movies were made since the studio was my playground. In many ways, the experience of working with such movie greats as John Wayne, Lana Turner, Maureen O'Hara, Glenn Ford, Cliff Robertson and David Niven helped to give me a sense of the importance of balancing career and life. Roddy McDowall, Tallulah Bankhead, Helen Hayes and Ava Gardner became friends after our work together and gave me a sense of appreciation and respect for all those greats who set such a high standard for all of us to follow. But they all said the same thing— 'When the makeup comes off you still have to go home and face your life; make sure it is as satisfying as the one you left at the dressing table.' I think I have." She has made 27 feature films including the superb thriller *Experiment in Terror* (1962), *The Interns* (1962), *Die! Die! My Darling* (1965), and *Stagecoach* (1966). **TV** A veteran of countless shows and miniseries, her first starring role in a series was "The Girl from U.N.C.L.E.," followed by "The Feather & Father Gang." Powers, though, is best known for her portrayal of the writer Jennifer Hart in "Hart to Hart," with Robert Wagner. The extremely fit beauty has also appeared on stage in many musical and dramatic productions. **ACHIEVEMENTS** She has achieved an award-winning acting career, a life of heartfelt philanthropic work, with dedication and active participation in the preservation of African wildlife. To get involved, contact the William Holden Wildlife Foundation, P.O. Box 67981, L.A., CA 90067, USA. *Web site:* www.allmediapr.com/whwf. *E-mail:* whwildlife@aol.com. **SIDELIGHTS** Those interested in joining her fan club can write to: Stefanie Power's Official Fan Club, P.O. Box 5087, Sherman Oaks, CA 91403. Website: www.fansource.com (or e-mail: stefanie@fansource.com). **QUOTE** Powers' Hollywood Walk of Fame star was unveiled on Nov. 25, 1992. About the landmark tribute, she said, "When I attended Hollywood High School, there was a hangout on "the Boulevard" called Coffee Dan's. We would all go there after school and terrorize the patrons and the waitresses. I was thrilled that my star was placed in front of the former site of Coffee Dan's, it sort of completes the circle for me."

world. Rogers typically played a sassy, intelligent, independent gal, while Astaire played classy, suave, and debonair. *Time* magazine wrote: "Ginger Rogers has glamour, acting ability and a pair of lyric legs...she represents the American Girl, 1939 model—alert, friendly, energetic, elusive." Rogers and Astaire were reunited after a 10-year separation in *The Barkleys of Broadway* (1949). Contrary to rumors, Rogers stated that the two got along "swell." Other movies include *I'll Be Seeing You* (1944), a touching love story with Joseph Cotten. **ACHIEVEMENTS** 1940 Best Actress Oscar for *Kitty Foyle*...As a dancer, she had to do everything Fred Astaire did, but backwards and in high heels!...Costume designers loved Rogers' svelte figure. It was said of her: "she can wear a chiffon dress better than any woman alive." Rogers did not attribute her stunning figure--and 19-inch waistline--to dancing. She said, "I play tennis like a champion, and that's what did it."..Her mother was Lucille Ball's drama coach...Rogers' beautiful costumes were often made with thousands of decorative bugle beads. When she was swirling, the beads lifted up and smacked Astaire in the face! Talk about dancing "Cheek to Cheek!" **QUOTE** When asked about her days in those #1 musicals, she responded, "I really have no nostalgia about them. I live for today. But maybe that's why people think I'm strange, I don't even have a psychiatrist!" Died: 1995.

Stefanie Powers 📺   **6776 Hollywood**

Marilyn Monroe 🎥   6776 Hollywood

Marilyn Monroe

Actress

BORN Norma Jean Mortensen; June 1, 1926, in Los Angeles, CA. **SPOTLIGHTS** The world's most famous sex symbol. Her soft, husky voice, delicious pout, bottom wiggle, and aura of vulnerability made her 20th Century-Fox's biggest attraction. Probably more has been written about her than any other movie star. The myth, or the legend, remains a powerful fixture in movie fans' imaginations. Two things are for certain: the camera loved her and the world felt great affection for her. After years of modeling and bit parts, Monroe appeared in a fleeting moment in John Houston's ground breaking *The Asphalt Jungle*, and in a small role in *All About Eve* (both 1950). Then the nude calendar scandal broke. She had posed *au naturel* previously, and now it had come back to haunt her. When a few nasty reporters tried to rip her to shreds, their stories had the reverse effect. Monroe answered their questions honestly. She said that she was broke at the time and had needed the $50. The public admired Monroe for her forthrightness. When prodded by one journalist and asked, "You mean you had *nothing* on at the time?" She replied softly, "Oh yes, I had the radio on." The publicity was of some help to her career. In 1953 she played a *femme fatale* in *Niagara*; the sexy entertainer Lorelei in the musical *Gentlemen Prefer Blondes* co-starring Jane Russell; and a bachelorette in *How to Marry a Millionaire* with Lauren Bacall and Betty Grable. Other movies include *River of No Return* (1954), *There's No Business Like Show Business* (1954), Billy Wilder's *The Seven Year Itch* (1955), and *Bus Stop* (1956). She worked with director Wilder again in *Some Like It Hot* (1959), with co-stars Jack Lemmon and Tony Curtis. *Some Like It Hot* proved to be a dazzling, hilarious sex farce. She was difficult to work with on this picture, and perpetually late to the set, but she was also *pregnant*. Regardless, she was electrifying in the role and appeared luminous on screen. The film smashed box office records, and turned out to be Monroe's all-time biggest hit. It is a comedy classic. Unfortunately, she suffered a miscarriage. Her last film was *The Misfits* (1961), co-starring her idol Clark Gable. It was written by her third husband, Arthur Miller. Clark Gable, who gave one of his best performances, did not live to see his reviews. **SIDELIGHTS** With her mentally ill mother institutionalized, Monroe's difficult childhood was spent in foster homes. She had a strong craving and need for love and attention, which she partially—and superficially—obtained from her movie fans. Although she loved them, sometimes it overwhelmed her. On the verge of an emotional collapse, she stated, "Everybody is always tugging at you. They'd all like sort of a chunk of you. They kind of like to take pieces out of you." **BEAUTY SECRET** Monroe's famous figure measuring 37-23-37 was kept that way by her special exercise routine of rowing. Whenever she was near a body of water, she put on a dark wig and scarf, get into a boat, and row and row and row. It was her favorite sport. Her second favorite form of exercise was swimming. Her voluptuous figure was not a tiny size. Monroe's ample curves took a size 12 to 16 dress, depending on her weight at any given time—with her average dress size of 14. **HIGHLIGHTS** Married to baseball legend Joe DiMaggio (1954-'55), and playwright Arthur Miller (1956-'61). **THE PRESS** An astronomical number of reporters and photographers, 800 in all, showed up at the Savoy Hotel in London, England, to hear the announcement that Marilyn Monroe and Laurence Olivier would team together for the upcoming movie *The Prince and the Show girl* (1957). Monroe's husband was sitting at her side for the press conference. One British journalist asked Marilyn, "What do you wear when you go to bed?" She glanced playfully at her hubby, and replied, "Chanel No. 5." **QUOTE** About his wife, Miller observed, "Everything she does is 'herself,' whether playing with the dog, redoing the cleaning woman's hair, emerging from the ocean after a swim, or bursting into the house full of news. Her beauty shines because her spirit is forever showing itself." **FINAL NOTE** Amazingly she never won an Academy Award (nor was she ever nominated), but Monroe was excited beyond belief to receive her Hollywood Walk of Fame star in 1960. She felt she had finally been recognized by her peers in the Hollywood community. This legendary movie star died in 1962.

Arsenio Hall 📺   6776 Hollywood

Talk show host, comic, actor

BORN February 12, 1955, in Cleveland, OH. **SPOTLIGHTS** He grew up dirt poor in a troubled household in the ghetto. While his friends watched cartoons, Hall found himself obsessed with Dinah Shore, Merv Griffin and Johnny Carson during summer vacations. He told himself, "I think I could do that when I grow up!" After graduating from Kent State

Arsenio Hall

University, he moved to Chicago and began his stand-up comedy career. Soon, he was opening for many top name performers. In 1983, he took his act to television as co-host of "The 1/2 Hour Comedy Hour." Hall became a regular on "Thicke of the Night," co-hosted the music/variety series "Solid Gold," and was an interim guest on "The Late Show" (1987). He made his motion picture debut in Dante's, Gottlieb's, Horton's and Landis' *Amazon Women on the Moon* (1986). Yes, there were four directors who worked on this misguided patchwork collection of comedy spoofs and sketches. Hall fared much better when he played the second lead to pal/star Eddie Murphy in *Coming To America* (1988--Hall was also one of the four writers of the film). Hall delivers a hilarious performance as Semmi, the mischievous friend of an African Prince. He also plays a Baptist Preacher, Barber, and "an extremely ugly girl in drag." In January 1989, Paramount announced the debut of "The Arsenio Hall Show." A young hipster with a dazzling smile and cutting edge, he appealed as a pop icon to the MTV pop-culture crowd—the teens and trend setters—of TV viewing. But what surprised advertisers was Hall's crossover to white audiences. When questioned about this, Arsenio replied: "To be successful and a black man in this country, you have to be bi-cultural. White people can concern themselves with white things, but a black man has to know it all." Then, as the country began its steep nose dive into one of its worst economic recessions in history, Hall had one goal as a late night TV host and entertainer, "What I do every night is important to bring a smile to your face...I know some of the people sitting at home laughing have to go out and look for a job the next day. I'll give them his hour, because we *need* laughter. *Laughter heals*." The great comedian Bob Hope agreed wholeheartedly with Hall's statement. It also became obvious to viewers what a truly funny, witty, and kindhearted person he was, and that brought him ample audience loyalty. Later, during the L.A. riots, *Newsweek* magazine praised Hall's "healing

presence." After a five-year run, Hall opted not to re-sign with Paramount Television in order to aggressively pursue his acting career. In 1998, he teamed up with Sammo Hung to star in the CBS-TV action series, "Martial Law." **QUOTE** "I love that my star is next to Marilyn Monroe's star...and late at night...when everyone is asleep, our *stars* actually make out."

Edward Arnold 🎥 6776 Hollywood

Edward Arnold

Actor
BORN Gunther E. A. Schneider; Feb. 18, 1890, in New York, NY. **SPOTLIGHTS** This incredibly versatile talent came late to films. He did not arrive in Hollywood until his 40s. A superb character actor, he was frequently cast as a statesman, judge, or others in powerful positions, such as the political administrator, Jim Taylor, in *Mr. Smith Goes to Washington* (1939). Among his fine credits are *Come and Get It* (1936), *Easy Living* (1937), *Idiot's Delight* (1939), *Johnny Apollo* (1940), and *Meet John Doe* (1941). Arnold appeared in more than 100 films from 1932-'56. In 1935 alone, he portrayed "Diamond" Jim Brady in *Lillian Russell*, Louis XIII in *Cardinal Richelieu*, and the policeman after Peter Lorre in *Crime and Punishment*. He deserved an Oscar, but never got one. Died: 1956.

Victor Mature 🎥 6780 Hollywood

Victor Mature & Maureen O'Hara

Actor
BORN Jan. 29, 1915, in Louisville, KY. **SPOTLIGHTS** This craggy, dark-haired, sleepy-eyed actor ushered in the dawn of a new type of leading man. Although powerful, this wonderful talent—who was trained at the famed Pasadena Playhouse— could deliver sensitive characterizations. He made all types of movies, but specialized in action-adventure due to his strength and size (six-foot-two, 200 pounds). During World War II, Mature put his career on hold and served honorably in the U.S. Coast Guard. Movies include *One Million B.C.* (1940), *I Wake Up Screaming* (1941), *The Shanghai Gesture* (1941), *My Darling Clementine* (1946), *Kiss of Death* (1947), *Fury at Furnace Creek* (1948), *Cry of the City* (1948), *Easy Living* (1949), *Wabash Avenue*

(1950), *Stella* (1950), *Million Dollar Mermaid* (1952), *Violent Saturday* (1955), and *Every Little Crook* and *Nanny* (1975). **SIDELIGHTS** He stars as Samson in *Samson and Delilah* (1949), with Hedy Lamarr as the famous temptress, Delilah. Mature sent an invitation to the premiere to his pal Groucho Marx. The comedian sent back a note declining the offer. He wrote, "No picture can hold my interest where the leading man's bust is larger than the leading lady's." **QUOTE** Known as the "Beautiful Hunk of a Man," he was somewhat puzzled by the label. He confessed, "Honestly, sometimes I can't see what the girls see in me. I'm revolting." Died: 1994.

Dorothy Kilgallen   6780 Hollywood

Columnist, reporter, panelist
BORN July 3, 1913, in Chicago, IL. **SPOTLIGHTS** She was a humorous gossip columnist with television's most famous panel show, "What's My Line?" She premiered with the show's debut on Feb. 2, 1950. As an extremely witty panelist she enjoyed the long stretch and stayed through 1965. Her job was to find out the occupation of the contestant, or identify the Mystery Guest—someone either famous or of important stature in business or the community—by asking questions which could be answered with a "yes" or "no." She was known for her amusing, sometimes feline, cool, crisp, gossipy ways on both television and radio, as well as print. About the nupitals of Grace Kelly and Prince Rainier of Monaco, she said, "I have eleven pieces of luggage, but there's just no way of covering a royal wedding without the proper equipment...a sapphire mink stole...an ermine wrap...a little chinchilla wrap...a white cashmere coat and a gold brocade evening raincoat." **QUOTE** A reporter of serious material, too, she covered Dr. Sam Sheppard's trial. She wrote: "Astounding is the word for the verdict. I heard the same evidence the jury heard. I could not have convicted him of anything except possible negligence in not locking his front door. I have covered a score or more of murder trials. It is the first time I have ever been scared by the jury system, and I mean scared." (Both a television series and feature film were based on the crime and conviction. Then, in 1997, due to his son's insistence and belief in his father, DNA tests proved that Sheppard was innocent. A 1998 mini-series based on his son's struggle to vindicate his father received high ratings.) Died: 1965.

Jay Leno   6780 Hollywood

Comedian, host, writer, actor
BORN April 28, 1950, in New Rochelle, NY.   **SPOTLIGHTS** Considered the "Most Popular Regular Guy in America," he is one of the country's top stand-up comedians, and unquestionably its #1 host. Leno took over the throne of America's favorite late-night program, NBC's "The Tonight Show," on May 25, 1992. He is the fourth in a supreme dynasty to wear the crown of host since 1954, following in the legendary footsteps of Steve Allen, Jack Paar and Johnny Carson (see their

Jay Leno

respectives bios in this book). Leno's "everyman" quality and his personable style have helped him earn millions of fans around the world. He has been touted as one of the nicest people in show business as well as the hardest working, a winning combination for the man who says, "anyone can have a life, careers are hard to come by." Comedy is a serious business, and he puts in long hours, rarely hitting the sheets until 4 a.m.. He said, "I feel like a good-for-nothing if I sleep past 9." For the past 20 years, he has appeared in hundreds of comedy shows across the United States, sometimes traveling up to 300 nights a year. He still appears in intimate clubs, college campuses, as well as the big-time Las Vegas casinos and concert venues. In TV, he has guest-starred in a number of popular sitcoms, including the critically acclaimed "Seinfeld," "The Simpsons," "Home Improvement," "South Park" (voiceover), and "The Larry Sanders Show." Movies include *Fun With Dick and Jane* (1977), *American Hot Wax* (1978), *Silver Bears* (1978), *Americathon* (1979), and *Collision Course* (1987). Recent motion pictures include *Contact, EdTV, Dave, In & Out,* and *Wag the Dog.* A born entertainer, he loves to make people laugh, and is completely natural onstage...His life philosophy follows basically what his mother taught him as a child: "One day at a time. It may take you a little longer, but you'll get there, you 'll do just fine."...He has assembled an exquisite automobile and motorcycle collection, which he is passionate about. He quipped, "Yeah, that's why I do the show, to afford the cars." **HIGHLIGHTS** Married to the former Mavis Nicholson since 1980...His best-seller was entitled *Leading With My Chin,* published by HarperCollins. He has also compiled four *Headlines* books, and *Police Blotter.* All book proceeds go to charities...He is also patriotic, performing for military troops abroad. **QUOTE** "Funny is funny."

Charles Bickford   6780 Hollywood

Actor
BORN Jan. 1, 1889, in Cambridge, MA. **SPOTLIGHTS** Educated at MIT, Bickford first became a civil engineer. He

Charles Bickford with Beatrice Lillie

bravely served in the Navy during WWI. After his honorable discharge, he turned to vaudeville for a few laughs. That's where the acting bug bit. After spending a decade on the Broadway stage, he came to Hollywood at the advent of sound. A hardy, dark-haired actor, he skillfully handled romance, drama, and comedy. Movies include *Anna Christie* (1930) opposite Greta Garbo, *Little Miss Marker* (1934--as a mean hood), starring Shirley Temple, *Of Mice and Men* (1939) with Lon Chaney, Jr., Burgess Meredith, and Betty Field, *The Song of Bernadette* (1944) opposite Jennifer Jones, *The Farmer's Daughter* (1947) with Loretta Young, Joseph Cotten and Ethel Barrymore, and *Johnny Belinda* (1948), starring Jane Wyman. **ACHIEVEMENTS** 1944, 1947, and 1948 Academy Award nominations. Died: 1967.

Joseph Schildkraut 🎥   6780 Hollywood

Actor
BORN March 22, 1896, in Vienna, Austria. **SPOTLIGHTS** The son of a famous stage actor, in his youth Schildkraut was billed as "the handsomest man since Rudolph Valentino." He succeeded as one of the rare talents who excelled in both disciplines of silents and talkies. This versatile, distinguished, and poised actor appeared in close to 100 films. He co-stars with the Gish sisters in *Orphans of the Storm* (1922)—a classic silent motion picture. Other pictures include *Show Boat* (1929), *Viva Villa!* (1934), *The Garden of Allah* (1936), *Marie Antoinette* (1938—as the Duke d'Orleans), *The Three Musketeers* (1939—as Louis XIII), *The Man in the Iron Mask* (1939—as Fouquet), *Mr. Moto Takes a Vacastion* (1939—in the last of the detective series), *The Shop Around the Corner* (1940),

The Cheaters (1945--a charming comedy), and *Monsieur Beaucaire* (1946). This dark-haired character actor was frequently cast in evil roles, but was superb as the hero, too. A man of all faces, his chameleon-like talents were rewarded with terrific roles. He was outstanding in *The Diary of Anne Frank* (1959), and as Nicodemus, in *The Greatest Story Ever Told*

Joseph Schildkraut

(released in 1965). **ACHIEVEMENTS** 1937 Best Supporting Actor Oscar for his role of Capt. Alfred Dreyfus in *The Life of Emile Zola*. 1942 Special Oscar for MGM's *Tell-Tale Heart*. Died: 1964.

Lou Costello 🎙   6780 Hollywood

See page 399

Fanny Brice as radio's "Baby Snooks."

6800 HOLLYWOOD

Art Laboe 📻   6800 Hollywood

Radio and music personality
BORN Aug. 7, 1925, in Salt Lake City, UT. **SPOTLIGHTS** The classic 1950s D.J. , he was the first to play rock 'n' roll on the West Coast. He broadcast live from Scrivner's drive-in restaurant on Sunset and Cahuenga, in Hollywood. Rick Nelson and other kids from Hollywood High came by faithfully to place their song requests. "Earth Angel" and a variety of other songs inspired Laboe to assemble the first *Oldies but Goodies* album, combining a variety of artists. Founded the Original Sound Entertainment (Record) Company, in Hollywood.

Evelyn Rudie 📺   6800 Hollywood

Actress
BORN Evelyn R. Bernauer; March 28, in Hollywood, CA. **SPOTLIGHTS** A multi-talented child star of the 1950s, she played the adopted child in the sentimental tearjerker *The Gift of Love* (1958), with Lauren Bacall, Robert Stack and Lorne Greene. She worked in the very early days of live television, then won critical acclaim and audiences' hearts with "Eloise." TV appearances include "Wagon Train," "Perry Mason, and "77 Sunset Strip." Later, she became the artistic director and producer at Santa Monica Playhouse, in California.

Richard Widmark 🎥   6800 Hollywood

Richard Widmark

Actor
BORN Dec. 26, 1914, in Sunrise, MN. **SPOTLIGHTS** A handsome, light-haired, gray-eyed talent, his breakthrough came in his screen debut. His demented performance as a depraved, pyschopathic gangster in *Kiss of Death* (1947), earned him an Oscar nomination. This film contains the memorable scene where he pushes a disabled lady in a wheelchair down the stairs. His cruel smirk and evil, chilling laugh perfectly suited villainous characters. Hollywood latched onto him, putting him in a number of blood-curdling supporting, then starring roles: *Cry of the City* (1948), *Road House* (1948), *Street with No Name* (1948), and *Night and the City* (1950). In 1950, he convinced the studio to let him play the hero occasionally. Thereafter, throughout his career, this durable actor alternated between the good guy and the bad guy, as well as in a light comedy every now and then. He stars in the *Halls of Montezuma* (1950), where his metallic voice served his characterization of an unpopular WWII commander. Motion pictures include *No Way Out* (1950), *Broken Lance* (1954), *Tunnel of Love* (1958), *Warlock* (1959—a Western), *Judgment at Nuremberg* (1961), *The Bedford Incident* (1965), *Murder on the Orient Express* (1974), *Coma* (1978), and *True Colors* (1991). **HIGHLIGHTS** His son-in-law is former star pitcher and baseball hero, Sandy Koufax.

Buddy Clark 💿   6800 Hollywood

Vocalist
BORN Samuel Goldberg; July 26, 1912, in Dorchester, MA. **SPOTLIGHTS** He was a vocalist on the Old Maestro's "Ben Bernie" music radio show during the 1930s, and the "Let's Dance" radio show (1934-'36) with Benny Goodman. Clark made a handful of records with Freddy Martin, who played music with warmth and sweetness. Later, he was with big band leader Wayne King, whose dance orchestra was known *not* for King's swing, but for his waltz. Clark was a superior ballad singer. His hit records include "Isn't It a Shame?" "I Married an Angel," "Linda," "It Had to Be You," and "Let's Do It" (with Dinah Shore). Died: 1949, when he was thrown from a small plane which crash-landed.

Elia Kazan 🎥   6800 Hollywood

Director
BORN Elia Kazanjoglov; Sept. 7, 1909, in Instanbul (once Constantinople), Turkey. **SPOTLIGHTS** *A Tree Grows in Brooklyn* (1945)—his first for Fox—secured his career. He scored with the taut thriller *Boomerang!* (1947), and a touching racial drama *Pinky* (1949). By the 1950s, his ability to capture human frailty and neurosis reflected a mirror image of what Kazan said he felt about himself. He confessed he felt like an anguished soul with a social responsibility. He directed Marlon Brando's animal rage in *A Streetcar Named Desire* (1951), and opened the violent life rising to power in *Viva Zapata!* (1952). James Dean is rebellious confusion in *East of Eden* (1954). Montgomery Clift is outstanding in the 1930s Tennessee drama *Wild River* (1960). In *Splendor in the Grass* (1961), Natalie Wood readily communicates neurotic teenage longings. Adapting F. Scott Fitzgerald's novel to the screen, *The Last Tycoon* (1976) pulls remarkable performances from Robert De Niro, Tony Curtis, Robert Mitchum, Jeanne Moreau and Jack Nicholson. It is a story of a Hollywood mogul in ill health, who desperately tries to hold onto his empire. **ACHIEVEMENTS** Best Director Oscars: 1947 Academy Award for *Gentleman's Agreement*, and 1954 Academy Award for *On the Waterfront*. Amid much controversy regarding his activities during the bleak days of the McCarthy era, Kazan received the Academy's prestigious

Irving Thalberg Award in 1999. **QUOTE** Co-founder of the Actors Studio (with Lee Strasberg) in New York, Kazan wanted actors to be immersed in "The Method" (an acting technique/style). He stated, "All that matters is the actor. That little human thing you want to get at—that little moisture in the girl's eyes, the way she lifts her hand, or the funny kind of laugh she's got in her throat."

Spade Cooley 6800 Hollywood

Singer, fiddler, band leader
BORN Donnell Clyde Cooley; Dec. 17, 1910, in Pack Saddle Creek, OK. **SPOTLIGHTS** He was born dirt poor—literally—in a storm cellar under a shack. Cooley's break in show business came because, on-screen, he looked like a dead ringer for Roy Rogers. He doubled for him in films. On the side, he hired the smooth vocalist Tex Williams and gifted steel guitarist Earl

Spade Cooley

"Joaquin" Murphey to join his group. They were signed to Columbia in 1945—and enjoyed a phenomenal breakthrough recording year: "Shame, Shame on You," "A Pair of Broken Hearts," "I've Taken All I'm Gonna Take from You," and "Detour." 1946 and '47 hits include "You Can't Break My Heart," and "Crazy Cause I Love You." He landed his own Saturday night show called "The Hoffman Hayride" on Los Angeles TV station KTLA, where he was dubbed the "King of Western Swing." **SIDELIGHTS** His nickname "Spade" came from his terrific poker playing. Died: 1969.

Don De Fore 6800 Hollywood

Actor
BORN Aug. 25, 1917, in Cedar Rapids, IA. **SPOTLIGHTS** A movie actor, this genial talent became known as Thorney Thornberry (1952-'58), the knowledgeable, funny neighbor in "The Adventures of Ozzie and Harriet." In another successful series called "Hazel," the maid (Shirley Booth) never thought her employer George Baxter (De Fore) was king of his castle. She ruled the roost from 1961-

Don De Fore

'65. Films include *The Human Comedy* (1943), *The Stork Club* (1945), *It Happened on Fifth Avenue* (1947), and *My Friend Irma* (1949). Offscreen, President Reagan named him "goodwill ambassador" to

Swaziland in 1981. Died: 1993.

Woody Herman 6806 Hollywood

Band leader, clarinetist, singer
BORN Woodrow Charles Herman; May 16, 1913, in Milwaukee, WI. **SPOTLIGHTS** As a vaudeville trouper, he was billed as the "Boy Wonder of the Clarinet." All of nine years old, the young musician (who also played alto saxophone), and singer worked to support his family. In 1936 he entered the first phase of his adult musical life. The 23-year-old became the leader of a band loosely formed by Isham Jones Orchestra members and renamed it "The Band

Woody Herman

That Plays the Blues." Three years later, they had a huge hit with "Woodchoppers Ball." This afforded Herman fame and opportunity. In the 1940s he changed his musical direction to swing for the second phase of his career. Herman's new, spirited, exuberant band during this period was "The First Herd." (Also known as "The Thundering Herd.") The theme song was "Blue Flame." The public wanted him, and Hollywood responded. He appears with his band in several films. The postwar period of 1945-'47 was the high point of his career with a perfectly cohesive band. The rhythm section was dazzling. About the trumpet section, he said, "When those guys blow, I duck." About his trombonist, Bill Harris, the band leader stated "He was so powerful he used to pull the whole section with him." The third phase of his musical life started in the 1950s with what he dubbed "America's greatest entertaining unit, the band that brought back dancing." Songs throughout his diversified career include "Hot Numbers," "Bijou," "Northwest Passage," "Happiness Is Just a Thing Called Joe," "Blues in the Night," "Apple Honey," and The Good Earth." **ACHIEVEMENTS** 1963, 1973, 1974 Grammys. **QUOTE** "The spirit of jazz is abandon. When you present it too grimly serious, you lose naturalness." Died: 1987.

Bill Goodwin 6808 Hollywood

Announcer, entertainer
BORN July 19, 1910, in San Francisco, CA. **SPOTLIGHTS** His fantastic voice landed him all the top 1930s and '40s radio shows, including "The George Burns and Gracie Allen Show," "The Bob Hope Show," and "Blondie" with his famous "Uh-uh-uh, don't touch that dial!" Goodwin totaled thousands of exciting hours in broadcasting. Died: 1958.

Claudette Colbert 6810 Hollywood

Actress

Claudette Colbert

BORN Lily Claudette Chauchoin; Sept. 13, 1905, in Paris, France. **SPOTLIGHTS** Her signature was her velvety, full-throated, creamy voice. This leading lady's other assets did not hurt, either. She was leggy, doe-eyed with a heart-shaped face, and ample mouth. The glamorous Colbert possessed an air of refined sex appeal and an acerbic wit. She used it to chuckle through movies and life. When columnist Hy Gardner asked her if she were bitter about anything, she responded, "No, but I'm open to suggestions." Although most fans think of her in sophisticated comedies, this beauty was sensual as Poppaea in Cecil B. DeMille's Roman Empire epic, *The Sign of the Cross* (1932), and was splendid as the Queen of the Nile in Cecil B. DeMille's *Cleopatra* (1934). She was superb in one of the best films ever about early Colonial life in Revolutionary America: *Drums along the Mohawk* (1939). Like a multifaceted diamond, Colbert sparkled in madcap comedies and dramas: *It's a Wonderful World* (1939), *Midnight* (1939), *The Palm Beach Story* (1942), and *Since You Went Away* (1944), among others. She was absolutely stoic in Dominick Dunne's TV movie, *The Two Mrs. Grenvilles* (1987), opposite Ann-Margret. **ACHIEVEMENTS** 1934 Best Actress Academy Award for *It Happened One Night*. Honored by the Kennedy Center for the Performing Arts in 1989. **SIDELIGHTS** She never allowed the right side of her face to be photographed, because she believed her left side to be much prettier. **QUOTE** Her secret for a long life: "One vitamin and one vodka a day. Plus a dose of laughter." Died: 1996.

Joni James 🎵 6814 Hollywood

Singer

BORN Joan Carmella Babbo; Sept. 22, 1930, in Chicago, IL. **SPOTLIGHTS** A darling, petite singer, she could belt out romantic ballads loud and clear. This sweet vocalist was admired for her wholesomeness. She was crowned "Miss America of Music." James became wildly popular with the jukebox set in 1952 for her recording "Why Don't You Believe Me?" Young Barb(a)ra Streisand soaked up James' hits. Then, the nine-year-old sat on the stairway in her apartment building: "with its great halls with these brass railings, and the ceilings were very high and there was this echo." Reaping the acoustical benefits of the space, Streisand—in her little-girl voice—imitated Joni James tunes like "Have You Heard?" Other hits: "Your Cheatin' Heart," "Let There Be Love," "You Belong to Me," "Is it Any Wonder?" and "My Love, My Love."

Spencer Tracy 🎥 6814 Hollywood

Actor

BORN April 5, 1900, in Milwaukee, WI. **SPOTLIGHTS** Cinema's #1 actor's actor. He had originally been trained for the theater. "Spence," as his co-workers called him, had a penchant for drinking and fighting. But he was also a natural, powerful actor, widely admired by his colleagues, except for those *he* did not like. Spence did not like his co-star, Joan Crawford, who

Spencer Tracy and Ruth Hussey

was his love interest in *Mannequin* (1938). He chewed raw cloves of garlic before kissing her. She was not amused. Tracy was brilliant in the comedy *Woman of the Year* (1942), which paired him for the first time with his Katherine Hepburn (who proved to be the great love of his private life). Both he and Hepburn turned in sparkling performances in *Adam's Rib* (1949). He worked with Hepburn again in *Pat and Mike* (1952). Tracy always insisted on top billing over Hepburn. When asked why he did not put the lady first, he gruffly stated, "This is a movie, not a lifeboat." Tracy was charming as Elizabeth Taylor's daffy dad in *Father of the Bride* (1950), and *Father's Little Dividend* (1951). Watch the master at work in *Fury* (1936), opposite Sylvia Sidney, *The Actress* (1953), with Jean Simmons, *Bad Day at Black Rock* (1954), with Robert Ryan, *Broken Lance* (1954), with Jean Peters, *The Last Hurrah* (1958), with Jeffrey Hunter and Dianne Foster, *The Old Man and the Sea* (1958), *Inherit the Wind* (1960), with Fredric March and Gene Kelly, Stanley Kramer's *Judgment at Nuremburg* (1961), with Marlene Dietrich, as well as his Oscar winners (see below). These are just a few of his great pictures. Tracy discovered and possessed the great truth inherent in each role. This trait made him such an exceptional player of intense and interesting characters. His last film was *Guess Who's Coming to Dinner* (1967), with Hepburn. **ACHIEVEMENTS** Best Actor Oscar: 1937 *Captains Courageous*—where he played an old sea-dog. When he received his Academy Award, it was incorrectly engraved to "Dick Tracy." In 1938 his elegant tribute to crusading Father Flanagan in *Boys Town* garnered another Best Actor Oscar. Only Spencer Tracy (1937 & 1938) and Tom Hanks (1994 & 1995) have won Best Actor Oscars back-to-back. **HIGHLIGHTS** The film he had the most fun making? John Ford's gangster movie, *Up the River* (1930). During the shooting, he nicknamed pal and supporting actor Humphrey Bogart, "Bogie." **ACTING ADVICE** When asked by an aspiring thespian his acting secret, Tracy remarked, "Just know your lines and don't bump into the furniture." **QUOTE** When asked what he looked for in a movie script, Tracy quipped, "Days off." This master craftsman died in 1967.

Irving Cummings 🎥 6816 Hollywood

Irving Cummings with Clara Kimball Young

Director, actor, writer, producer
BORN Oct. 9, 1888, in New York, NY. **SPOTLIGHTS** He was an actor in *Uncle Tom's Cabin* (1914). Later, he earned an Academy Award nomination for directing *The Cisco Kid* (1931), starring Warner Baxter. He stuck with directing thereafter. The public fell in love with his Shirley Temple classics: *Curly Top* (1935) with the popular song "Animal Crackers in My Soup," and *Poor Little Rich Girl* (1936). He wowed international audiences, media, and celebrities alike with the perfect Technicolor production, *Vogues of 1938* (1937). This picture introduced Max Factor's Pancake Make-up; film's cosmetic savior. Cummings made the splashy Technicolor musical comedy *Down Argentine Way* (1940), starring Betty Grable and Don Ameche with a sensational Carmen Miranda doing "South American Way." *My Gal Sal* (1942) is a love story set in the Gay Nighties with gorgeous Rita Hayworth and Victor Mature. Died: 1959.

Kent Taylor 📺 6818 Hollywood

Actor
BORN Louis Weiss; May 11, 1907, in Nashau, LA. **SPOTLIGHTS** He made his screen debut in *Road to Reno* (1931), and quickly followed with two other "B" pictures: *The Devil in the Deep* and *Merrily We Go to Hell* (both 1932). He proved to be a fine supporting talent when Cecil B. DeMille cast him in his Roman Empire epic, *The Sign of the Cross* (1932). Taylor was also a reliable second-feature hero. Movies include *Death Takes a Holiday, David Harum, Mrs. Wiggs of the Cabbage Patch* (all 1934), *The Gracie Allen Murder Case* (1939), *Tombstone* (1942), *The Daltons Ride Again* (1945), and *Hell's Bloody Devils* (1970). **TV:** Star of "Boston Blackie" (1951-'53), and "The Rough Rider" (1958-'59). Died: 1987.

Jane Powell 🎥 6818 Hollywood

Singer, actress

BORN Suzanne Burce; April 1, 1929, in Portland, OR. **SPOTLIGHTS** A teenage singing sensation, she was signed by MGM. The studio hoped they had a second Judy Garland. In fact, when Garland failed to show up for rehearsal for *Royal Wedding* (1951) ,co-starring Fred Astaire, the studio substituted the lively Powell in her place. Her large, innocent blue eyes, exquisite voice, and winsome girlishness enhanced many light musicals. She enjoyed All-American, girl-

Jane Powell

next-door admiration and popularity. One of her most beloved and endearing roles is Milly in the beautifully scored *Seven Brides for Seven Brothers* (1954), opposite Howard Keel. Other movies include *Holiday in Mexico* (1946), *Three Daring Daughters* (1948), *A Date with Judy* (1948), *Rich, Young and Pretty* (1951), *Athena* (1954), and *Hit the Deck* (1957). In 1957, after making 20 films, she terminated her exclusive contract with MGM, hit Las Vegas as a headliner, and worked in TV...She has been married five times.

Spike Jones 📺 6818 Hollywood

See page 313

Erich Von Stroheim 🎥 6820 Hollywood

Erich Von Stroheim

Director, actor, writer
BORN Sept. 22, 1885, in Austria. **SPOTLIGHTS** He was the mastermind of extravagant silent movies. Von Stroheim's *Foolish Wives* (1922) was billed as "The First Million-Dollar Movie." It shocked Universal Studios with its outrageous cost. The film, though, proved to be their biggest box-office hit to date. Others include *The Merry Widow* (1925), where he made all the soldiers wear real silk underwear under their costumes to inspire realism. On that same film, he got into a fight with Louis B. Mayer, when he told the mogul that the film's heroine was a whore. Mayer retorted, "We don't make films about whores." Von Stroheim fired back, "All women are whores." To which Louis B. Mayer, propenent of the sanctity of womenhood, promptly K.O'd him with one punch, then barred him from the lot. Von Stroheim became known as the *homme terrible*. Movies include *Merry-Go-Round* (1923), and *The*

Wedding March (1927). The director's extravagant, psychological themes, lurid passages, and opulent spending of the studio's money were his trademarks, along with his unique attire. This former Austro-Hungarian Army officer wore black boots, and had a sword (he had a penchant for fencing). His masterpiece is *Greed* (1923-25), and is a must-see picture for cinema buffs and historians. He never directed a sound picture, but returned to acting. Talkies include Jean Renoir's *La Grande Illusion/Grand Illusion* (1937). He was later nominated for an Academy Award as best supporting actor in *Sunset Boulevard* (1950). Died: 1957.

Adolphe Menjou 🎞   6822 Hollywood

Adolphe Menjou

Actor

BORN Feb. 18, 1890, in Pittsburgh, PA. **SPOTLIGHTS** Exceedingly well educated at the Culver Military Academy, in Indiana, and Cornell University, he was an engineer by degree. This dark-haired brainpower tried acting as a lark. Menjou was sleek, exuded finesse and shined with a *gentleman's* inner strength. His career began on stage, then he worked in silents in New York, starting with *The Blue Envelope Mystery* (1916). After making a handful of pictures, he headed to Southern California, where work was more plentiful due to its agreeable weather. His stock-in-trade was his black waxed mustache. It allowed him to play villains and foreigners, both of whom were synonymous in countless silents. Menjou also made his clothes a priority. In those early film making days, the actors had to provide their own wardrobe, on their own budgets. About it he said, "I started this best-dressed man business as a deliberate stunt when I first came to Hollywood in 1920. In those days, everyone was typed. Bill Hart was the big, Western he-man, Rudolph Valentino was the handsome sheik. The only type I could fill was the debonair habitué of the drawing rooms." His exquisite wardrobe cost so much he was forced to drive an old automobile for several years. (In 1948 his autobiography was appropriately entitled, *It Took Nine Tailors*.) He used his sophisticated, worldly looks and regal bearing to play King Louis XIII in *The Three Musketeers* (1921). As a dapper gent, he provided wonderful support to Rudolph Valentino in the classic *The Sheik* (1921). He played the dastardly rich fellow in Charlie Chaplin's *A Woman of Paris* (1923—it was his first starring role). He soared to stardom. When talkies made sound waves in the late 1920s, he was temporarily reduced to independent film companies. His charming, devilish ways soon led to juicy roles. Movies include *Morocco* (1930) opposite Marlene Dietrich, *The Front Page* (1931—in an Oscar-nominated per-

formance), *A Farewell to Arms* (1932), *Little Miss Marker* (1934), *A Star is Born* (1937), *Cafe Metropole* (1937), *Stage Door* (1937), *The Goldwyn Follies* (1938), *Golden Boy* (1939), *A Bill of Divorcement* (1940), *The Hucksters* (1947), *State of the Union* (1948), *The Ambassador's Daughter* (1956), *Paths of Glory* (1957), and *Pollyanna* (1960). **QUOTE** "Hollywood is the workshop from which the world gets the most of its entertainment and pictorial art. Within its walls live men and women of culture from all parts of the world...I have seen much of the world. I have heard the praises sung of the Mediterranean. Even those beautiful sunny lands have failed in comparison with the wonders of Hollywood. Its wonderful climate has made it the land of magnificent homes and gardens as well as of studios." Died: 1963.

Bill Hay 🎙   6822 Hollywood

Announcer

BORN William G. Hay; 1887, in Scotland. **SPOTLIGHTS** As announcer on the immensely popular, long-running "Amos 'n' Andy," he became oddly historic. Called "the all-time favorite radio show," the comedy program had an incredible 34-year run with several networks. Hay joined the show in 1928, in radio's early days. Soon though, 40 million Americans tuned in nightly to hear the program. That was fully one-third of radio's entire listening population. Hay's familiar low-key voice was comforting to the financially decimated nation. The show was full of silly calamities, and provided free comic relief to listeners. Many of whom were bankrupt or unemployed, surviving day to day. If a person did not have a radio, he or she could hear it at a neighbor's, a local bar (without buying a drink), a store, or stand near any open window. It would certainly be playing on a nearby radio. Played by two Caucasians, Freeman Gosden and Charles Correll, the African American characters were sympathetic common folk, broke, with no job, and no prospects. In that sense--during the Great Depression--everybody could relate to them. By 1943, the show had lost its grip. When a new team was hired to invigorate the show, Hay received a dreaded pink slip. After 15 years he was heartbroken. The show finally ended in 1960. "Amos 'n' Andy" remains a controversial slice of racism to this day. Died: 1978.

Louise Glaum

Louise Glaum 🎞 6834 Hollywood

Actress, comedienne

BORN 1900, in Baltimore, MD. **SPOTLIGHTS** With a fetching face for silent movies, this dark-haired funny gal made her screen debut in Mack Sennett slapstick comedies. She appears in hundreds of silents, including *Hell's Hinges* (1916), and *I Am Guilty* (1921). **QUOTE**

"Amusing moving pictures will last forever. I love them. I cherish my work and Hollywood." Died: 1970.

Roy O. Disney 🎥   6838 Hollywood

Executive

Roy O. Disney

BORN Roy Oliver Disney, June 24, 1893, in Chicago, IL. **SPOTLIGHTS** About eight and one half years older than his baby brother Walt Disney, Roy and Walt formed a lifelong bond in childhood. Walt commented, "It was Roy's job to push me around. He started to do it, and he's been doing it ever since (laugh). Roy was always the one brother I remembered. He was always close. He always seemed like a brother. The others went away from home so they were more or less strangers to me all my life." Roy admired his sibling's artistic abilities, and helped Walt land his first job in a commercial studio. Then, when Walt's first attempt at running his own business failed, he came to California to be with Roy. Roy, the consummate businessman, perfectly complemented Walt, the ideas man. They formed their lasting partnership in 1923, with Roy being the financial brains of the operation. Roy, co-founder of the Walt Disney Studios, worked side by side with his sibling. He commented, "Walt puts up a mild front, but underneath it there's drive, drive, drive." Incredibly savvy with finances and merchandising, Roy was instrumental in the growth and management of the Disney empire. And, by relieving his younger brother from the strains of money management, Roy freed Walt's creative energies. Mickey Mouse *et al* were in Roy's capable, trustworthy hands. As the company became more and more successful, the modest Roy was content to stay in the background taking care of business. One of the highest compliments given to Roy was by his son, Roy Edward Disney, current Vice Chairman of The Walt Disney Co. He observed, "Everyone who did business with him always talked about knowing where you stood, a deal was a deal, and a handshake was as good as a contract. He meant what he said and said what he meant." After Walt's death in 1966, Roy cancelled his plans to retire. During the next five years, he accomplished what was one of the greatest achievements of his career, the construction of Walt Disney World, in Florida. When the $400-million park opened in 1971, it was completely debt-free and destined to be an enormous success. Walt Disney World was the ultimate tribute to his beloved brother Walt, and, of course, to himself. Three months later, due to the strain of the work, Roy died of a massive brain hemorrhage at age 78. His brilliant son, Roy E. Disney, was present at the July 24, 1998 Walk of Fame star dedication celebration...In 2000, Walt Disney Companies employ in excess of 115,000 people world-

wide. It is an astonishing figure and further proof of Roy's business acumen. Also see the bios in this book of: Walt Disney, Mickey Mouse, Snow White, Robert B. and Richard M. Sherman, Annette Funicello and Jimmie Dodd. **READ** *Building a Company: Roy O. Disney and the Creation of an Entertainment Empire*, by Bob Thomas, published by Hyperion. It is a superb book on the subject.

Roy E. Disney, Vice Chairman of the Walt Disney Company

Buck Jones 🎥   6834 Hollywood

Actor, director

BORN Charles Gebhart; Dec. 4, 1889, in Vincennes, IN. **SPOTLIGHTS** A former member of the U.S. Calvary, Jones became a popular stunt rider in Wild West shows. This rugged talent made his screen debut in *Blood Will Tell* (1917). This real-life cowboy emulated on-screen what he thought a cowboy stood for: a man of action, fairness and justice. He stars in more than 100 movies, including *The Fighting Buckaroo* (1926), *Black Jack* (1927), *Red Ryder* (1934—serial), and *Law*

Buck Jones

for Tombstone (1937—which he also directed). By 1936, his annual salary had risen to $143,000. **QUOTE** "It seems the world will always like a hard rider. It seems that it will always love the West. Maybe, they like it because we like it so much, this country where you can ride and breathe deeply and—be yourself. In becoming a cowboy, just bury your dress suit and quit eating mayonnaise and lose your stomach. Get yourself a horse for hard riding, buy a Colt "45" with a silver butt and practice twirling it on your fingers, cultivate a bad look at times, have lots of courage, and be popular with the ladies, because the ladies always count." The world lost quite a cowboy in 1942, when Buck—who was on a patriotic campaign tour selling U.S. War Bonds—died a hero's death rescuing victims of a fire in Boston.

Annette Funicello 🎥   6834 Hollywood

Annette Funicello and Frankie Avalon

Actress, dancer, singer
BORN Oct. 22, 1942, in Utica, NY. **SPOTLIGHTS** As a child, she was known as "shy, little dolly" because she would hide in closets when the doorbell rang. Her mother started Annette in dance lessons to help her overcome her bashfulness. At age 12, while dancing the lead in the ballet "Swan Lake," she was discovered by Walt Disney himself. Unannounced, he had been in the audience. Annette said, "The next thing I knew, I was called into Disney Studios to audition for a new show called, 'The Mickey Mouse Club.'" After rehearsals one day, Annette went to see Mr. Disney and stated, "I want to change my last name because everyone mispronounces it. I prefer Annette Turner to Annette Funicello. He looked at me and said, 'You have a beautiful Italian name, and once people learn how to pronounce it, they will never forget it.'" From the moment it aired on television on Oct. 3, 1955, Annette was the #1 Mouseketeer. Her popularity had a lot to do with her wholesome looks and personality. She was the perfect, girl-next-door. America had a new sweetheart. When she grew into a teen idol, it was with purity of spirit. Her romances were completely innocent. She became a symbol of a kinder time, when kids stayed kids longer. Annette remained under contract to Disney appearing in episodic TV and films: *The Shaggy Dog* (1959) and *Babes in Toyland* (1961). Disney signed her to a recording contract as well. "How Will I Know My Love," "Tall Paul," "First Name Initial," and "Pineapple Princess" topped the charts. Annette described what happened next. "I was on loan-out from Disney Studios. Mr. Disney came to me one day and said, 'Annette, I have a favor to ask of you. I know all the girls in the film will be bikini-clad, but you have an image to uphold and I would appreciate it if you would wear a one-piece suit.' I did," she remarked, "and never regretted it." *Beach Party* (1963) made Annette and Frankie the most popular couple since Fred and Ginger. It also spawned six fun, campy sequels, and a 1987 spoof. (Look for a young Stevie Wonder in *Bikini Beach*—1964). In 1992 she publicly announced her battle with multiple sclerosis (MS) and set up The Annette Funicello Research Fund for Neurological

Diseases. A courageous and graceful lady, she remarked, "Even sitting in my wheelchair, life doesn't have to be perfect to be wonderful." **QUOTE** On September 14, 1993, her Walk of Fame star was unveiled. She said, "Oh you know, they even were able to fit my whole last name on there! Thank you, thank you."

Ann Rutherford 🎥   6834 Hollywood

Actress
BORN Nov. 2, 1917, in Canada. **SPOTLIGHTS** This pretty brunette began in low-budget Westerns with John Wayne and Gene Autry. She gained national fame as Polly Benedict—Mickey Rooney's special friend—in MGM's *Andy Hardy* series. 16 pictures as "Polly" include *Andy Hardy Meets Debutante* (1940), co-starring a young Judy Garland singing "I'm Nobody's Baby." She was wonderful in *A Christmas Carol* (1938), then immortalized in one of the *Gone With the Wind* (1939). She gives a fun, showy performance in the *Adventures of Don Juan* (1949)—Errol Flynn's last swashbuckling epic.

The Andrews Sisters 💿   6834 Hollywood

Singing group
BORN July 6, 1915 (LaVerne); Jan. 3, 1918 (Maxene); Feb. 16, 1920 (Patty), all three were born in Minneapolis, MN. **SPOTLIGHTS** Raised in the depths of the Great Depression, they were all junior high school dropouts. They were so poor they had to stretch one chicken for an entire week's worth of meals. Struggling to support their family, they sang with a small band at roadhouses in the South and the Midwest. Since there were no vocal teachers to train them to stand still—which was standard at the time—the Andrew Sisters simply

The Andrews Sisters: Maxene, Patty and LaVerne

felt the music in their bodies and got into the swing. Without realizing it, they had created an act. Still, after half a dozen years, they were discouraged and about to call it quits. A music promoter (who later married Maxene) introduced them to Sammy Cahn in 1937. Cahn suggested they sing the Yiddish Folk Song "Bei Mir Bist Du Schoen" in English. Decca paid them a flat $50 to record it. It hit the top of the charts, and was the first song by a "girl group" to rise above the one-million mark in sales. Known for their close harmony, they became popular recording stars of the 1940s Swing Era. Patty sang lead, Maxene soprano and LaVerne alto. They became frequest guests on the air, and had their own radio show. They recorded some 900 records. Their songs were woven into the fabric of the culture: "Boogie Woogie Bugle Boy," "Rum and Coca-Cola," "Roll Out the Barrel," "Don't Sit Under the Apple Tree," "Rhumboogie," "Beer Barrel Polka," and "Straighten Up and Fly Right." They worked with Bing Crosby recording "Jingle Bells" as a jazz thing—"We were really hip in our day, you know," Patty remarked slyly. They appear in more than 20 feature films, many with Abbott and Costello. They dissolved their act after the war. **HIGHLIGHTS** During WWII, they toured extensively with the U.S.O. throughout war torn Europe. The Andrew Sisters were a phenomenal boost to GIs morale. Countless men and women in uniform recalled that watching them perform gave them the will to continue. Their most memorable wartime concert appearance was in a dirigible hangar in Naples, Italy, in 1945. The commanding officer asked the Andrew Sisters to stop singing and read a note he had passed to them. It read: "the war in Japan is over." **ACHIEVEMENTS** *They were the most successful female recording group in pop history.* Awarded the Medal for Distinguished Public Service (1987)—the highest civilian honor given by the military. **QUOTE** About their incomparable harmony, Maxine said, "We hear it in our minds. You see, musically educated vocalists sing what they read. We sing what we *feel*, from the *heart*." Died: LaVerne, 1967; Patty, 1995.

Buddy Hackett   6834 Hollywood

Comedian, actor, writer
BORN Leonard Hacker; Aug. 31, 1924, in Brooklyn, NY. **SPOTLIGHTS** An intuitive comedian, he can walk into a room, say "hello," and make people laugh. "I'm very funny," Hackett said. "I look at people, and they're laughing is how I know." Life was not always so cheerful. Hackett avoided following in his father's footsteps as an upholsterer. He had a hard childhood, with a lot of sacrifice. As a young man, he recalled, "We didn't have the material things." By age 16, he was a hotel waiter in the Catskill Mountains, as well as the substitute for another comedian on that same "Borscht circuit." How did he get started in comedy? "I was fat and I was from Brooklyn. That made me a funny man," Hackett commented. Fast on his feet, and quick with a joke, the chubby babbler landed a job in a road company production, then concentrated on being one of the best nightclub comics in the business. About his profes-

sion, he said, "I found out that if you make most people laugh, they like you. Most people got to like me because I made them laugh. When they didn't, I hit them." Hollywood called. He made a number of films, then in 1954 jumped to Broadway. His performance in "Lunatics and Lovers" won the Donaldson Award. Returning to features, he made the worthwhile drama, *God's Little Acre*

Buddy Hackett and Johnny Grant

(1958) where he portrays Pluto, the loveless rube. Hackett is delightful in *The Music Man* (1962), campy in *Muscle Beach Party* (1964), fantastic in *The Wonderful World of the Brothers Grimm* (1966), and funny in the slapstick, family comedy *The Love Bug* (1969). Later, he appeared in the modernized comedy *Scrooged* (1988—based on *A Christmas Carol*) starring Bill Murray. His voice-over work includes his top-flight performance as Scuttle, the silly sea gull, in Disney's 28th animated movie, *The Little Mermaid* (1989). Hackett has also made countless television appearances in his 50-year entertainment career. **SIDELIGHTS** One day while lunching with colleagues at Columbia Pictures, the talk turned to the topic of Elizabeth Taylor breaking the bank (and new Hollywood ground) by getting the then-unheard of one million dollars in salary to play *Cleopatra* (1963). At the time, it was the most extravagant, expensive picture ever made. One producer commented, "It's a helluva lot of money." Then, he asked, "Buddy, would you give Liz Taylor a million for a picture?" Hackett responded, "Nan, I'd probably offer her $35,000." The shocked executive asked, "Only $35,000?" Hackett said, "Yeah, and she'd say to me, 'Kiss my ass,' and that's all I want from her anyway!" Hackett's star was unveiled on March 31, 1998. It rained; a rarity for a ceremony date. **QUOTE** When asked by his hometown congregation to participate in a funeral plot for church members, he remarked, "To tell you the truth, fellas, I'm not too thrilled spending time with you when we're alive!"

José Iturbi   6834 Hollywood

Jose Iturbi

Steve McQueen

Pianist, conductor, composer **BORN** Nov. 28, 1895, in Valencia, Spain. **SPOTLIGHTS** A musical prodigy of Basque ancestry, he *taught* piano when he was seven years old. Educated at the Paris Conservatory, he toured internationally before signing on as conductor of the Philadelphia Symphony Orchestra. Known for his bravura temperament, in 1941 he withdrew from conducting a program when he learned Benny Goodman was the featured soloist and he planned to play jazz. Iturbi commented, "You can arrange for a picnic with hamburger, but when you have a stiff shirt and white tie dinner you serve caviar." He further elaborated he would not do the concert, because he announced, "It is beneath my dignity." He did bend his own rules a couple of years later by performing in MGM's *Thousands Cheer* (1943). Judy Garland sang "The Joint is Really Jumpin' Down at Carnegie Hall" accompanied by Iturbi. He played light classical selections in MGM's *Music for Millions* (1944), with stars June Allyson, Margaret O'Brien, and Jimmy Durante (who is wild with "Umbriago"). His playing of "Polanaise in A Flat" in Chopin's biopic—*A Song to Remember* (1945)— helped push record sales of it into the millions. In *Holiday in Mexico* (1946), the plot revolves around the American ambassador's daughter (Jane Powell) falling in love with the eminent pianist Jose Iturbi. Also featured is a young Roddy McDowell and Iturbi's pianist sister, Amparo. In motion pictures, Iturbi always played himself. Died: 1980.

Sarah Vaughan   6834 Hollywood

See page 179

Danny Kaye   6834 Hollywood

See page 83

Steve McQueen   6834 Hollywood

Actor
BORN Steven Terrence McQueen; March 24, 1930, in Beech Grove, IN. **SPOTLIGHTS** Deserted by his father when he was a baby, McQueen spent most of his angry youth in a California reform school, the Boys Republic. It was not a happy experience for him. When he was still in his teens, he joined the Merchant Marine, then became a deck hand on a Greek oil tanker. He worked as a California lumberjack, an oil rigger in Texas, and a barker in a traveling carnival. His show business success first came in the TV Western series, "Wanted, Dead or Alive." In 1958, he made the classic 'B' horror picture *The Blob*. In it, his screen charisma is apparent. Rebellious and oozing with testosterone, McQueen became the 1960s symbol of nonconformity. A handsome, rugged, free spirited actor, his aggressive virility appealed to female fans. Men liked his machismo. Motion pictures include *Never So Few* (1959), *The Magnificent Seven* (1960), *The Great Escape* (1963), *Love with the Proper Stranger* (1963), *Baby, the Rain Must Fall* (1964), *The Cincinnati Kid* (1965), *Sand Pebbles* (1966—in one of his best performances), *The Thomas Crown Affair* (1968), *Bullitt* (1968), for Grand Prix race fans only—*Le Mans* (1971), *Papillon* (1973), *The Towering Inferno* (1974), and *Tom Horn* (1980). **QUOTE** Although a writer labeled McQueen "the reluctant star," the opposite was true. He loved being *a movie star*. He enjoyed being the center of attention, as well as being the recipient of the endless perks and pleasures that go with celebrity. He likened being a superstar to having magical powers. McQueen stated, "Snap your fingers and your wish is granted!" Died: 1980.

Ray Bolger   6834 Hollywood

See page 457

Linda Evans   6834 Hollywood

Actress
BORN Nov. 18, 1942, in Hartford, CT. **SPOTLIGHTS** A quiet beauty, she created her own fairy tale existence. Her family moved to Southern California when she was a child. Linda commented, "They made me take drama at school because I was so shy and to bring me out." While attending Hollywood High School, she signed to do several commercials. After graduation she was placed under contract by MGM. She made her screen debut with Richard Chamberlain in *Twilight of Honor* (1963). Other motion pictures include *The Klansman* (1974), *Avalanche Express* (1979), and *Tom Horn* (1980). In 1965 she landed her breakthrough TV role as Audra Barkley in "The Big Valley," starring Barbara Stanwyck. The popular action-filled Western adventure series ended in 1969. Evans had learned

Linda Evans

plenty about the actor's craft from one of the best, Stanwyck. In 1977 she appeared in "Hunter." From 1981-'89 she played Krystle Carrington in the prime time drama "Dynasty." This immensely trendy program was perfectly suited for the excessive 1980s. Evans played the good, devoted wife to John Forsythe, who was forced to stand up to the manipulative Joan Collins. It was one of the most popular TV series ever. She occasionally makes TV movies, like "The Reunion," and "The Stepsister," but acting takes second place to her health and fitness program, and her boyfriend, recording star Yanni. She is the owner of a chain of 15 health clubs, and travels the globe with Yanni when he is on tour. **ACHIEVEMENTS** Four People's Choice Awards for favorite female performer. Golden Globe for best actress in a dramatic television series.

Victor Moore 🎥   6838 Hollywood

Actor, comic

BORN Feb. 24, 1876, in Hammonton, NJ. **SPOTLIGHTS** This funny character actor gained fame for impersonating the shy, gentle, confused little man. At age 17 he started in vaudeville, then struck gold on Broadway in the musical revue, *Of Thee I Sing*. Playing a fuzzy-headed Vice President of the United States, he sits on a park bench and reads a Washington telephone directory, saying: "...Hmm, Vice Admiral, Viceroy, Viscount—there *isn't* any Vice President!" Audiences roared. Although he performed in countless plays, celluloid captured his hilarious befuddlement: *Louisiana Purchase* (1941), *Star-Spangled Rhythm* (1942), *Ziegfeld Follies* (1946), and *It Happened on Fifth Avenue* (1947). He went out with a bang, *The Seven Year Itch* (1955), sharing laughter with stars Tom Ewell and Marilyn Monroe. He played the plumber in Marilyn Monroe's bathtub scene. Censors prevented him from speaking what was on his mind. Died: 1962.

Garry Marshall 📺   6838 Hollywood

Writer, actor, director, producer

BORN Nov. 13, 1934, in New York, NY. Grew up in the Bronx. **SPOTLIGHTS** Nostalgia. Nepotism. Nasal Bronx Accent. Nice guy. Best known for creating both a hoodlum and a hooker with hearts of gold that launched the careers of Henry Winkler on the TV series "Happy Days," and Julia Roberts in the film *Pretty Woman*. Marshall is a former sitcom king turned movie director who has produced and created 14 prime time television series, including "The Odd Couple" (1970-'75),

"Happy Days" (1974-'84), "Laverne & Shirley" (1976-'83—starring his sister, actress-director Penny Marshall as Laverne), and "Mork and Mindy" (1978-'82). Marshall has excelled on the silver screen—directing more than nine features—including the funny coming-of-age story, *The Flamingo Kid* (1984—also co-screenplay), starring Matt Dillon, and *Nothing in Common* (1986), starring Tom Hanks and Jackie Gleason--in his last

Garry Marshall

film appearance. *Overboard* (1987) is about a snob with amnesia and a blue-collar worker who find opposites attract. It stars the real-life romantic duo of Goldie Hawn and Kurt Russell. Women everywhere fell in love with *Beaches* (1988), starring Bette Midler and Barbara Hershey. Watching *Beaches* requires a box of Kleenex, but it's full of bite, too. *Pretty Woman* (1990), a fantasy Cinderella-type story with a controversial twist, proved a box-office bonanza. The poignant *Frankie and Johnny* (1991) stars Al Pacino and Michelle Pfeiffer. Every aspect of this picture is beautifully done; it is destined to be a classic. When not directing, Marshall takes his turn in front of the camera; he had a recurring role as the tempcramcntal network exec Stan Lansing on the 1990s TV series "Murphy Brown." He played the casino boss in the cult film *Lost in America* (1985). Other feature film roles include *Soapdish* (1991), *A League of Their Own* (1992—directed by his sister Penny Marshall), *Hocus-Pocus* (1993), and *Dear God* (1996). **ACHIEVEMENTS** During the week of January 28, 1979, "Laverne & Shirley," "Happy Days," and "Mork and Mindy" were the number one, two and three Nielsen-rated TV shows in the country. In 1991, *Pretty Woman* became the highest grossing film in the history of Walt Disney Studios. The movie cost $14 million to produce and grossed more than $450 million worldwide. **HIGHLIGHTS** His star, dedicated on Nov. 23, 1983, is located near the star of former "Happy Days" pal Ron Howard.

Pee Wee Hunt 🎵   6838 Hollywood

Vocalist, jazz trombonist

BORN Walter Hunt; May 10, 1907, in Mt. Healthy, OH. **SPOTLIGHTS** He had been inspired by the music he heard daily in his home; Hunt's father was a violinist, his mother a guitarist. Pee Wee, a natural born talent, first earned his nickname when he was just a wee thing playing the banjo. Later, he graduated from the Cincinnati Conservatory, and by the time he was age 22 had become a founder-member of Casa Loma Band, with Glen Gray. The big band trombone player/band leader did duets with greats such as Louis Armstrong.

Recordings: *On the Sunny Side of the Street.* He was also a featured jazz musician on radio's musical variety program, "The Hoagy Carmichael Show" (1944-'45). Single: "Twelfth Street Rag" (tongue-in-cheek) sold more than three million copies—the biggest selling ragtime record ever; another hit "Oh!" Died: 1979.

Burt Reynolds 🎥   6838 Hollywood

Burt Reynolds

Actor, director, producer
BORN Feb. 11, 1936, in Waycross, GA. **SPOTLIGHTS** Reynolds' paternal grandmother was a full-blooded Native American Cherokee Indian. His father was first a cowboy, then a police chief in Palm Beach, Florida. Somewhat despondent in his youth, Reynolds once recalled, "Money is everything (in Palm Beach). If you're not rich, you're nothing. We were very poor." The restless teenager ran away from home, but later returned to his family. A superb athlete, Reynolds aspired to a career in professional sports. He won a football scholarship to Florida State University, where he became an All-Star Southern Conference halfback. A knee injury put an end to his shot with the Baltimore Colts. He left college in 1955, before finishing his studies, to pursue an acting career. After struggling in New York working as a dishwasher and a bouncer, he won a role in "Mr. Roberts." It was the 1956 New York City Center revival, which starred Charlton Heston in this John Forsythe directed production. This led to a Universal Studios contract, where he acted in small roles and did stunts with panther-like agility. As a tough, macho man, he worked in several television series. He played Ben Frazer in the 1840s adventure show "Riverboat" (1959-60), Quint Asper in the Western "Gunsmoke" (1962-'65), Lt. John Hawk in the police drama "Hawk" (1966), and Deputy Lt. Dan August in the police drama "Dan August" (1970-'71). The handsome, dark-haired actor, who exudes charm and sex appeal, made his silver screen debut in *Angel Baby* (1961). Other movies followed, including a starring role in the early Vietnam action picture, *Operation C.I.A.* (1965), a Western called *Sam Whiskey* (1968) opposite Angie Dickinson and Clint Walker, the gold treasure hunt called *Impasse* (1968) with Anne Francis, *100 Rifles* (1969), a Western co-starring football hero Jim Brown and sex goddess Raquel Welch, and *Skullduggery* (1970). After some stage work, four TV series and seven motion pictures, Reynolds finally broke through in John Boorman's stylish backwoods drama *Deliverance* (1972). He gave a critically acclaimed performance that should have earned him an Oscar nomination. Although he was not, the film was nominated in two categories, for best picture and best direction. The screenplay, written by James Dickey, had been adapted from Dickey's own novel. The adult adventure story is about four businessman who spend a holiday weekend on a canoeing trip, and who are transported into a whirling abomination. As they descend farther down the river located in the deep South, they travel the passage of man's inhumanity to man. *Deliverance* co-stars Jon Voight, Ned Beatty and Ronny Cox were all wonderful. A dramatic triumph, and masterfully paced, it was a gigantic box office success. *Time* magazine hailed Reynolds' portrayal of Lewis as exceptional. The film made the actor an international superstar. Could a sequel be made that equals the excellence of the original? To date, that oft-repeated Hollywood question remains unanswered. Among Reynolds' other personal favorites are *The Longest Yard* (1974), an edgy football-prison inmate comedy with Eddie Albert, Michael Conrad and Bernadette Peters, *Smokey and the Bandit* (1977) as a poker-faced, good ol' boy beer runner in a fun comedy which sparked two sequels and co-stars Sally Field and Jackie Gleason, the black comedy *The End* (1978--also directed), *Starting Over* (1979), a romantic comedy with Jill Clayburgh, Candice Bergen and Charles Durning, and the crime drama *Sharkey's Machine* (1981) co-starring Rachel Ward and Vittorio Gassman, which Reynolds also directed. The great Orson Welles once said of him, "Success is Burt Reynolds' only handicap. Some of our finest actors have survived the stigma of being Number One at the box-office." In all, he has made more than 50 motion pictures, including *Everything You Always Wanted to Know About Sex but Were Afraid to Ask* (1972), *The Man Who Loved Cat Dancing* (1973), *White Lightning* (1973), *Lucky Lady* (1975), *Hustle* (1975), *Silent Movie* (1976—unbilled cameo in one of the best scenes), *Gator* (1976—his directorial debut), *Semi-Tough* (1977), *Hooper* (1978), *The Best Little Whorehouse in Texas* (1982), *Best Friends* (1982), *Stroker Ace* (1983), the animated *All Dogs Go to Heaven* (1989—voice-over), and *The Player* (1992—cameo). In 1996, he joined the terrific cast of the comedy movie *Citizen Ruth*, starring the tremendous talent, Laura Dern. The following year Reynolds appeared in the comedy *Bean* with Rowan Atkinson, then enjoyed a phenomenal motion picture comeback in *Boogie Nights*. He co-stars with Mark Wahlberg and Julianne Moore in this critically acclaimed film. Reynolds won a Golden Globe Award for his outstanding performance. The New York Film Critics, The Los Angeles Times Film Critics, The Chicago Film Critics and the National Society of Film Critics all named him best supporting actor in their 1998 awards list. Reynolds also received his first Oscar nomination for *Boogie Nights*. In 1999, he appears in Disney's *Mystery Alaska*. **OTHER TV** Reynolds did his "B.L. Stryker"

series out of his native Florida. His warm-hearted comedy series, "Evening Shade," earned him his ninth People's Choice Award, a 1991 Emmy Award for "Best Performance in a Comedy," and a Golden Globe. He starred in and directed "Hard Time" (1999), a six-hour thriller trilogy for the Turner Network. **ACHIEVEMENTS** The world's #1 box office star *for five straight years* (1978-'82), a record which remains unbeaten. Also named America's "Favorite All Around Motion Picture Actor" (People's Choice Award) for a record six consecutive years. His best-selling 1994 autobiography, entitled *My Life*, was published by Hyperion. **SIDELIGHTS** While Reynolds longs for his golden boy statuette, he ironically turned down one role that could have possibly earned it for him. After Reynolds' rejection, Jack Nicholson accepted the part and appeared in *Terms of Endearment* (1983). It garnered a best supporting Academy Award for Nicholson. **QUOTE** His Hollywood Walk of Fame star was unveiled on March 16, 1978. About the famed landmark, Reynolds stated, "An award set in stone seems so permanent. This is especially attractive in a town where so much is based on illusion. The business of Hollywood is to entertain, inspire, or horrify. Dreamy or crisp images of the world, or from out of this world, are evoked by the actors who—when a film works—whisk you away to their make-believe lives. Sometimes my whole career seems like a dream. I still can't believe it all happened."

Jan Sterling 🎥   6838 Hollywood

Actress

BORN Jane Sterling Adriance; April 3, 1923, New York, NY. **SPOTLIGHTS** A blonde double threat, she held Hollywood hostage as the Tramp, but played the Lady on Broadway for 20 years. This dramatic talent is must-see in Warner's *Johnny Belinda* (1948), her screen debut. She supports Jane Wyman's Oscar-winning performance, and works brilliantly with the gifted Agnes Moorehead. She appears opposite Moorehead again in *Caged* (1950), the best of the women-in-prison pictures, and quickly became known as Tinseltown's hard-boiled blonde. Sterling's sharp with the shears in the drama, *The Big Carnival* (1951), where she is not above plunging a pair into Kirk Douglas' chest. She plays the sexpot tantalizing Tony Curtis in *Flesh and Fu*ry (1952). She also appears in the Western *Pony Express* (1952), opposite Charlton Heston, Rhonda Fleming, and Forrest Tucker. She appears in the farce *Rhubarb* (1951), where an eccentric man leaves his fortune—including his baseball team—to a cat. Sterling plays opposite Ray Milland, Gene Lockhart, William Frawley, and Leonard Nimoy. John Wayne flew the floozy in *The High and the Mighty* (1954). That same year, she appears in the sci-fi movie *1984*, based on George Orwell's prophetic book. Later films include *The Angry Breed* (1968), *The Minx* (1969), *Sammy Somebody* (1976) and *First Monday in October* (1981). She played First Lady, Lou Hoover, in the TV documentary/drama "Backstage at the White House" (1979).

Ron Howard   6838 Hollywood

Actor, writer, director, producer

Ron Howard

BORN March 1, 1953, in Duncan, OK. **SPOTLIGHTS** The son of theatrical parents, Rance and Jean Howard, the diapered toddler made his show business debut at age 18 months. He appeared with them in a Baltimore stage production of "The Seven Year Itch." Soon thereafter, the enchanting boy with shiny gold-red hair made his motion picture debut in *Frontier Woman* (1956). Several other movies followed, including the classic American musical, *The Music Man* (1962), co-starring Robert Preston, Shirley Jones, and Buddy Hackett. The period film had been adapted from Meredith Willson's best-selling book and Broadway hit. The freckled-face tyke mesmerized audiences with his uniquely endearing speech pattern and outstanding performance. When the youthful innocent steals every scene from Glenn Ford in *The Courtship of Eddie's Father* (1963), one thinks of W.C. Fields' rule never to work "with small children or animals." Even the female leads—Shirley Jones, Stella Stevens and Dina Merrill—were not immune to his childlike charisma and skillful command of the screen. Howard's first television series, "The Andy Griffith Show" (1960-'68), remains a true classic. He literally grew up as Opie Taylor, emerging into his teen years guided by the fatherly wisdom and common sense of Southerner Andy Griffith. (Also see the bio of Andy Griffith in this book.) Still seen in worldwide syndication, Howard was immortalized in this TV role. Fans wanted him to stay young forever. He changed their minds in George Lucas' coming-of-age movie *American Graffiti* (1973). Set in the early 1960s, this hot-rodding comedy also features Richard Dreyfuss, Paul Le Mat, Cindy Williams, Charles Martin Smith, Harrison Ford, and Suzanne Somers. Director Lucas shot it in less than a month, at a cost under $1 million dollars. Initially, Universal Studios did not want to release it. Lucas' mentor at the time, director Francis Ford Coppola, who was also executive producer of the film, went to bat to get it distributed. It was one of the year's biggest box office hits and grossed more than $100 million dollars. Then, Howard returned to television in the situation comedy "Happy Days" (1974-'80). The show was set in the nostalgic 1950s, when America was riding high on victory from World War II, a booming economy and population, and a general innocence about life. He played teenager Richie Cunningham, and worked with Henry Winkler, Tom Bosley and Marion Ross, among many other fine actors. Howard proved to be a talent behind the camera as well. He made his motion picture directorial debut with *Grand Theft Auto*

(1977). He co-wrote the screenplay with his father. His next directing effort was a funny, offbeat comedy called *Night Shift* (1982). It co-stars Henry Winkler, Michael Keaton, and Shelley Long. Along with Tom Hanks, we all fell in love with a quirky mermaid (Daryl Hannah) in *Splash* (1984). Howard had proven himself a sensitive, intelligent *auteur* with a keen eye for what works. Many critical and commercial successes have followed: *Cocoon* (1985), *Gung Ho* (1986—also exec. prod.), *Clean and Sober* (1988), *Parenthood* (1989—also co-story), *Backdraft* (1991), *Far and Away* (1992), *Apollo 13* (1995), *Ransom* (1996), and *Ed TV* (1999). In 1999, he produced the highly acclaimed, emotional, behind-the-scenes wrestling documentary, *Beyond the Mat*...He teamed with Brian Grazer to form Imagine Entertainment. (See Grazer's bio in this book.)...Howard is the recipient of countless awards, including being honored with an Entertainment Industry Salute by The March of Dimes. His Hollywood Walk of Fame dedication ceremony took place on June 3, 1981.

Pearl White   6838 Hollywood

Pearl White

Actress

BORN March 4, 1889, in Green Ridge, MO. **SPOTLIGHTS** A silent star with a sparkling and stupendous personality, White was immortalized in *The Perils of Pauline* (1914-'19), a melodramatic film serial. She played the heroine who was always in imminent danger in the last scene of each picture. These suspenseful non-endings—known as cliff-hangers—captivated audiences. Audiences were forced to attend the next weekly show if they wanted to find out how White had escaped her dire predicament. The actress performed many of her own stunts, even though she had a previous spinal injury from a horseback riding accident. She preferred mystery stories to straight adventures, and made most of her films in Ithaca, upstate New York, and Fort Lee, New Jersey. She did appear in a handful of dramas. In all, she appeared in more than 150 movies. Her autobiography, *Just Me* (1919), illustrates to readers how far back celebrity life stories date. In 1947, George Marshall directed the story of her life, *The Perils of Pauline*, starring an exuberant Betty Hutton, with cameos from silent giants Chester Conklin, William Farnum and Creighton Hale. A re-make was made in 1967. The heroine died in 1938.

Chuck Connors   6840 Hollywood

Actor

BORN Kevin Joseph Connors; April 10, 1921, in Brooklyn,

NY. **SPOTLIGHTS** A former professional baseball player for the New York Yankees, the Brooklyn Dodgers, the Chicago Cubs and the Los Angeles Angels, he switched to acting. A tall (6-foot, 5-inch), strapping, fairheaded fellow, his success in *Pat and Mike* (1952), starring Spencer Tracy and Katharine Hepburn, permanently altered the course of his life to show business. Other motion pictures include *Naked Alibi* (1954), *Hold Back the Night* (1956), *The Hired Gun* (1957), *The Big*

Chuck Connors

Country (1958), *Geronimo* (1962), *Flipper* (1963), *Captain Nemo and the Underwater City* (1970), *Support Your Local Gunfighter* (1971), *Pancho Villa* (1972), *Soylent Green* (1973), and *Last Flight to Hell* (1991). His claim to TV fame was as the tough Lucas McCain in the Western series "The Rifleman" (1958-'63). His modified trick Winchester rifle enabled him to fire off his first round in three-tenths of a second, keeping North Fork, New Mexico safe. Unlike many TV actors, he was a real natural on a horse. In keeping with his cowboy character, in real life Connors believed in being tough and straightforward. He was a loving father to his four sons, as well as a hero to his TV son, Crawford. He earned an Emmy nomination playing the lustful slave owner Tom Moore in Alex Hailey's breakthrough mini-series "Roots" (1977). **ACHIEVEMENTS** He was a professional basketball player for the Boston Celtics (1946-'48). Connors decided he was a better first baseman than forward, so he switched sports! When he left pro baseball for acting, his retirement letter read in part: "Baseball owes me nothing. I owe it all that I have and much of what I hope to have. Baseball made my entrance to the film industry immeasurably easier than I could have made it alone. To the greatest game in the world I shall be eternally in debt." Died: 1992.

George Gobel   6840 Hollywood

Comedian, actor, singer

BORN May 20, 1919, in Chicago, IL. **SPOTLIGHTS** He was a former choir boy whose grown-up looks remained perpetually bewildered, a little vulnerable and slightly naughty. Gobel tickled audiences with his catchphrase: "Well, I'll be a dirty bird!" He hosted his Emmy-winning comedy variety "The George Gobel Show" (1954-'60). During his debut year on television, this short, cherubic comic became the recipient of the Peabody Award for "the best comedian of the year." He also took this honor at the Sylvania Awards, where he quipped, "If it weren't for electricity, we'd all be watching television by candlelight." Prior to his own show, he was in the Army Air Corps (Air Force), did stand-up comedy at nightclubs for nine years, sang on radio, and was a regular guest on the "Garry Moore Show." He shared a show with singer Eddie Fisher during the late 1950s. **SIDELIGHTS** A stable of talented writers/directors came out of his show, including Norman Lear. Died: 1991.

Ann Harding 📺   6840 Hollywood

See page 211

A.C. Lyles 🎥   6840 Hollywood

*John Wayne, Barbara Stanwyck
and A.C. Lyles (right)*

Producer

BORN May 17, 1918, in Jacksonville, FL. **SPOTLIGHTS** As a child, Lyles was devoted to Saturday matinees. After watching the exciting WWI drama *Wings* (1927; it was the first picture to win an Academy Award), the youngster asked the theater manager for a job. Lyles recalled, "He told me, 'I could use you, kid. Take these circulars and pass them out at the main corner.' I was doing that on Saturdays, after school and putting bumper stickers on cars." So, at age nine, he found himself in show business distributing hand bills for his hometown Florida Theater—part of the Paramount public chain. Within three months, he had talked the theater manager into adding a page boy to ushers' staff. By age 14, he had been promoted to usher. He had the good fortune of meeting Adolph Zukor, founder and head of Paramount Pictures. Lyles took it upon himself to make his own introduction to Zukor. The teenager brazenly asked, "Mr. Zukor, would you take me to Hollywood? I want to learn about making movies." Zukor told A.C. to complete high school and keep in touch. To Lyles, "keeping in touch" meant just that and he wrote to Zukor every Sunday for the next four years. After graduation he convinced the local newspaper and the theater to send him to Hollywood to do a column on Shirley Temple. Arriving at the world-famous Paramount gate, he confidently announced, "Mr. Zukor is expecting me." Zukor saw him and assigned him to a mail room job. The dedicated and energetic youth also doubled as a personal assistant to the chief. Within a few weeks he met James Cagney, who would become one of his best friends. Through Cagney, he was introduced to an upcoming actor named Ronald Reagan. (He would work closely on and off the lot for many decades with the future President.) Still in his late teens, Lyles was quickly promoted to the publicity department, and by age 19 was named head of a PR unit for young contract players. Friendly, tall, and enthusiastic, Lyles conversed with everyone on the lot. He was thrilled when he met the various actors in *Wings*, telling Richard Arlen, Clara Bow, Charles "Buddy" Rogers and Gary Cooper, how they had changed his life. The dapper gent established permanent friendships with those stars, as well as John Wayne, Barbara Stanwyck, and Frank Sinatra. Later, he was promoted to associate producer for a Spencer Tracy film. In 1956 he formed his own production company in association with Paramount, gaining a reputation of making successful films on budget and on schedule. He was introduced to the Western series as associate producer on TV's "Rawhide," which made Clint Eastwood a star. Lyles produced scores of action-adventure Westerns with many popular stars. **ACHIEVEMENTS** Awarded the Golden Spurs Award, along with John Wayne, for "keeping alive the spirit and tradition of the old West" in his movies. His 70-year association with Paramount Pictures earned him the title of "Ambassador of Good Will." Lyles received the coveted Valley Forge Freedom Foundation Award from his friend, President Ronald Reagan, during ceremonies in the oval office. **SIDELIGHTS** Lyles has never revealed his first name. Speculation abounds in Hollywood that A.C. was possibly named something unique like Augustus Chauncy. But others joke it stands for Awfully Charming.

Shirley Booth 🎥   6840 Hollywood

Shirley Booth and Prego

Actress

BORN Thelma Booth Ford; Aug. 30, 1898, in New York, NY. **SPOTLIGHTS** Her Broadway debut was in a supporting role in "Hell's Angels," alongside another newcomer, Humphrey Bogart. The year was 1925 and thereafter she was an extremely busy stage actress. After being widowed in 1951, while starring in "A Tree Grows in Brooklyn," she left New York and her successful theatrical life behind her. In Hollywood, Booth gave an outstanding performance in her first picture, *Come Back Little Sheba* (1952). She won an Oscar for her role as the slovenly Lola Delaney, the tortured wife of an alcoholic. Her film legacy includes a treasury of only six films including *The Matchmaker* (1958). About her fame, she said in her uniquely crackly voice, "I feel a little like a movie star, but a movie star would look like one and I never have." She gained admiration from another generation of fans in the title role of her television series "Hazel" (1961-'66). She played the pleasantly domineering live-in maid who *ran* the household. **ACHIEVEMENTS** 1952 Academy Award for Best Actress. Multiple recipient of the Tony and Emmy awards, too. **QUOTE** "I'd be perfectly content to live in Cape Cod with my poodle, Prego, and memories of my late husband." In regard to a public life, she stated, "I'm devoted to privacy. On stage you give so much energy you need to recharge." Regarding her thoughts on money, she admitted that the TV series had made her rich. She said, "Money gives the power of choice. Now I choose a role the way I'd choose a friend." About life, she declared, "As my mother used to say, 'Enjoy yourself; it's already too late.'" Died: 1992.

Rod Serling 📺　　　6840 Hollywood

Writer, producer, playwright, author

Rod Serling

BORN Rodman Edward Serling; Christmas Day, Dec. 25, 1924, in Syracuse, NY. **SPOTLIGHTS** A legendary master of his craft, he was a true writing talent for the television age. Serling's background included his World War II duty as an Army paratrooper. He served three years in the Pacific with a demolition-assault platoon of the 511th Parachute Infantry. He was also a runner-up for the Featherweight Divisional Boxing Championship. He ruefully remembered, "It left me with a three-day pass, a twice-broken nose and eight stitches over my left eye." After his honorable discharge, he attended Antioch College on the GI bill. He came to television only after being fired from a Midwest family radio program. The program director who dismissed him stated: "Serling, it's this way. Your stuff's too stilted. You seem to be missing the common touch." He spent some hungry years trying to peddle his free-lance scripts. Then, he sold a big one. Serling recalled, "On January 13, 1955, the *Kraft Television Theatre* presented 'Patterns.' One minute after the show went off the air my phone started to ring. It has been ringing ever since." Regarding the new literary arena of teleplays during the 1950s, Serling observed, "The TV writer is never trained to be a TV writer." This prolific contributor of fine dramas saw more than 500 of his TV plays produced. It was not all sweet though. Serling was forced to take on some unpleasant battles with the networks, ad agencies and sponsors who wanted his scripts dealing with racial issues toned down. He also fought with directors who tried to change his biting dialogue. Serling lost on "Noon on Doomsday" where his bitter study of regional bigotry proved "too hot to leave in its original form," according to network sponsors. Serling was disgusted with the censoring deletions. Admonishing its final form he said, "It's been diluted and my characters had mounted a soap box to shout something that had become too vague to warrant any shouting." He won the battle with executives with "A Town Has Turned to Dust" about the lynching of an innocent Mexican boy in a small American southwest town. *Time* magazine described Serling as "a man who had served TV with some of the most tightly constructed, trenchant lines it has ever spoken." He was critically lauded for his outstanding teleplays, including "Requiem For A Heavyweight" (1959). A show about boxing, it was a subject matter close to his heart. He remarked, "I'd left a helluva lot of my blood in several rings." That same year, Serling achieved immortality by creating and executive producing "The Twilight Zone" (1959-'64). He wrote many of the shows and served as series host. The somewhat spooky, offbeat show opened with: **"THERE IS A FIFTH DIMENSION** beyond that which is known to man. It is a dimension as vast as space and as timeless as infinity. It is the middle ground between light and shadow, between science and superstition, and it lies between the pit of man's fears and the summit of his knowledge. This is the dimension of imagination. It is an area we call *The Twilight Zone.*" **ACHIEVEMENTS** A man of character and quality, his work embodied his ironic insights into the human condition. Six Emmys for Best Dramatic Writing, the first Peabody Award ever given a writer in its history, four Writers Guild Awards, and three honorary doctorates...Married to the former Carolyn Kramer of Coumbus, Ohio since 1948 to his death. They had two daughters, Jodi and Nan...Serling's posthumous dedication ceremony on the Hollywood Walk of Fame was held on Oct. 6, 1988 at 6:31 p.m., *the exact moment of twilight for that day.* The close of "The Twilight Zone" posed the question, "...and you, have you ever been there?" Serling went somewhere mysterious—that man has never been able to unlock or understand—when he died in 1975, leaving us to ponder the infinite possibilities of his spirit.

Clifton Webb 🎥　　　6840 Hollywood

Actor

BORN Webb Parmallee Hollenbeck; Nov. 19, 1893, in Grossville, TN. **SPOTLIGHTS** An incredibly talented stage actor, he spent most of his life in the theater—in both London and on Broadway—but made the world take notice whenever he graced the screen. He did not enter films until he was 50 years old. It was stated about the impeccably dressed sophisticate that he was the only man in Southern California who knew how to use a fish fork. Webb was so elegant it was thought he was British, when, in fact, he was an All-American Hoosier. He was nominated for an Oscar in *Laura* (1944), starring Gene Tierney. It was his debut film and a classic performance. Webb received another Academy Award nomination

Clifton Webb and Gene Tierney

for *The Razor's Edge* (1946). This fair-haired, mustached, persnickety character became known as the wry, chic, caustic baby-sitter, Mr. Belvedere, in the hilarious comedy *Sitting Pretty* (1948)—the first in the series. He officially became a movie star with this film. Other films include *Cheaper by the Dozen* (1950), *Stars and Stripes Forever* (1952), *Three Coins in the Fountain* (1954) and *The Man Who Never Was* (1956). **QUOTE** When asked if he was surprised to learn of his Academy Award nomination for his first film, Webb responded, "Certainly not. The word 'mediocrity' has never been in my vocabulary." Died: 1966.

Harold Lloyd 🎥   6840 Hollywood

See page 319

Jane Russell 🎥   6840 Hollywood

Actress

BORN Ernestine J. Russell; June 21, 1921, in Bemidji, MN. **SPOTLIGHTS** A big, beautiful brunette, her voluptuous hourglass figure held back her career at the onset. If you want to see what all the fuss was about, see the close-ups of Jane stretching in the hay in *The Outlaw* (1943). Billionaire producer Howard Hughes found her to be in all her seductive glory with her ample 38-inch bust. It took three years to win approval by the Hays censors, but still, the film had problems being released. It was banned entirely in the state of Maryland. The judge declared Russell's breasts "hung over the picture like a summer thunderstorm spread out over a landscape." This reluctant sex goddess seemed amused by all the commotion. She successfully moved into comedy in *The Paleface* (1948). She plays Calamity Jane to Bob Hope's Painless Potter, D.D.S.; the fun sets in when timid Hope is mistaken for scout and U.S. marshal, Wild Bill Hickok. She also co-stars with Hope in the sequel, *Son of Paleface* (1952). She had a good time with co-star Marilyn Monroe in the classic musical, *Gentlemen Prefer Blondes* (1953), where Monroe really enjoyed Russell's terrific sense of humor. They made a permanent impression as a team in the world-famous courtyard at the Grauman's Chinese Theatre, in Hollywood. At the ceremony, Russell teased Monroe, "Instead of putting our hand and footprints in the cement, we should put what we're best known for—your bottom and my bosom!" In 1955 she co-stars with Clark Gable in the Western *The Tall Men*. She stars as a bleached blonde movie star in *The Fuzzy Pink Nightgown* (1957). This comedy is about how kidnappers cannot convince anyone that their

Jane Russell

crime was not a publicity stunt. In all, she made 24 films. **ACHIEVEMENTS** Miss Russell started the WAIFS foundation, which has placed more than 45,000 orphans in loving homes. Although she recently retired from her post, the organization continues her good works to date. She personally considers this her greatest accomplishment in life. **QUOTE** "When I was 12 years old, me and my friend Pat Alexander went to Grauman's Chinese Theatre and tried to fit our feet in Gloria Swanson's and Jean Harlow's. They wouldn't fit. And you can bet Marilyn (Monroe) and mine *still* wouldn't fit. But, we were thrilled!"

Paul Anka

Paul Anka ⬤   6840 Hollywood

Singer, composer

BORN July 30, 1941, in Ottawa, Canada. **SPOTLIGHTS** His father was a Lebanese restaurateur who encouraged his 10-year-old son to start performing with songs and impressions. When he was 14 years old, his dad paid for a trip to Hollywood, and by 1956 the teenager had cut his first record "I Confess." The following year, he won a contest for saving the most soup-can labels; his prize was a trip to New York City. When the average 16-year-old simply had a girl like "Diana" on his mind, this gifted teen had written about her. He auditioned for ABC with it, and rose to stardom. This 1950s teen idol had girls screaming in the aisles of his concerts. He is considered an early rock 'n' roll stylist, who has worked through four decades. Highly prolific, he has composed more than 900 songs including Frank Sinatra's theme song "My Way" (Anka wrote the English lyrics; the original is French), "You Are My Destiny," "All of a Sudden My Heart Sings," "Crazy Love," "Lonely Boy," "Hello, Young Lovers," "Little Girl," "Love Me Warm and Tender," and "Feelings." Anka has often been inspired by the women in his life. His romantic hits "Put Your Head on My Shoulder" and "Puppy Love" were written about then-girlfriend Annette Funicello (see her bio in this book). In 1972, he wrote "(You're) Having My Baby" for his wife. The controversial song was released two years later to protests about sexist lyrics, but still went to #1 on the charts. In concert Anka substitutes "our baby" for "my baby." His 123rd album, *A Body of Work*, includes vocals by Anka's daughter, Anthea. There is also a "My Way" duet with Frank Sinatra where Anka took the 1967 eight-track tape with Sinatra on it, removed all the noise, then Anka sang with the orchestra and blended the vocals together. TV: Anka composed the theme song for "The Tonight Show" starring Johnny Carson. Film work includes *The Longest Day* (1962). **HIGHLIGHTS** Married since 1963 to Anne de Zogheb, they have five daughters. Anka quipped, "There's a lot of PMS in my house—that means Paul Must Suffer." **QUOTE** When he was 18 years old, he received an offer to appear on the "Ed Sullivan Show." After he agreed, he learned the venue had been changed from the small studio to the gigantic Madison Square Gardens--telecast live. How did the young Canadian feel about making his American television debut? Anka confessed, "I was scared to death."

Fred Thomson 🎥 6840 Hollywood

Actor

BORN Feb. 26, 1890, in Pasadena CA. **SPOTLIGHTS** This rugged cowboy star rode his horse, Silver King, throughout silent movies of the 1920s. Among his Westerns are *Galloping Gallagher* (1924), and *The Wild Bull's Lair* (1925). **SIDELIGHTS** He broke his leg while serving as a chaplain during World War I. The injury proved to be a blessing in disguise, as he met Mary Pickford and his future wife, screenwriter Frances Marion, while they were making goodwill hospital rounds. After the war, the women convinced him to move to Hollywood. A top-notch horseback rider, and good looking to the hilt, he became an instant hit in Westerns. Died: 1928, on Christmas day, from pneumonia.

Mahalia Jackson 💿 6840 Hollywood

Singer

Mahalia Jackson

BORN Oct. 26, 1911, in New Orleans, LA. **SPOTLIGHTS** The legendary Queen of Gospel Music. Her grandparents were slaves on a rice plantation, but her father, a free man, earned his living as a dock worker. On Sundays, he relished his role as a clergyman. Jackson was first heard at age five in her father's church. At age 16, she became the featured vocalist at Chicago's South Side Greater Salem Baptist Church. As you might imagine when Mahalia Jackson sang, the pews were never empty. Her serene and golden voice rose on celestial wings. It was as if heaven had descended to earth. Jackson observed, "Gospel music is nothing but singing of good tidings." She toured with "the father of Gospel music," Thomas A. Dorsey, during the Great Depression. During this period of high unemployment and business/bank failures, Jackson created her own breadline. She supplied and fed people from her own kitchen whenever she was home. Her string of hit singles include "Dig a Little Deeper," "Just Over the Hill," "Walk in Jerusalem," "He's Got the Whole World in His Hands," and "I Want My Crown," to name just a few. Jackson wrote and sang her platinum-seller, "I Will Move On Up a Little Higher." She gave sold-out recitals at Carnegie Hall, and all the important European venues. Television appearances included "The Ed Sullivan Show," "The Dinah Shore Show," and "Your Hit Parade," where she sang her beloved spiritual "Didn't It Rain." Her thrilling deep, rich contralto voice had a spellbinding quality to it which has proved timeless. She continues to win fans with each new generation who find her singing truly inspired. Religion was her hallmark, and spreading good tidings her reason for being. She refused, on principle, to sell out her talent to sing jazz—for jazz's sake—or the blues. She stated, "Anybody singing the blues is in a deep pit yelling for help, and I'm not simply in that kind of position." Although she did record religious tunes with Duke Ellington in a jazz vein, it was with a *spiritual* fervor. **ACHIEVEMENTS** She brought international recognition to the art form; her three world tours included important performances for heads of state. After facing discrimination and prejudice at the highest levels in Washington, D.C., she became a key figure of the Civil Rights Movement in the 1960s. **QUOTE** "I sing God's music because it gives me hope." This legendary talent died in 1972.

Morey Amsterdam 📺 6840 Hollywood

Comedian, actor

BORN Dec. 14, 1914, in Chicago, IL. **SPOTLIGHTS** The

From left: Red Skelton, Johnny Grant, Morey Amsterdam (center), Dick Martin, Bob Hope and Dan Rowan

Little Richard

"Human Joke Machine" could make up jokes on a moment's notice. The former vaudevillian was immortalized as Maurice "Buddy" Sorrell in TV's classic comedy "The Dick Van Dyke Show" (1961-'66). His partner in rhyme was the hilarious Rose Marie, and together with Dick Van Dyke and Mary Tyler Moore they made TV history in one of the best shows of all time. Prior to that, the wisecracker was a seasoned veteran of radio humor. He hosted "The Laugh and Swing Club," a song-and-sketch variety show, and was a funny panelist on Milton Berle's "Stop Me If You've Heard This One." Films include *It Came From Outer Space* (1953), originally shown in 3-D; *Machine Gun Kelly* (1958), with Charles Bronson; and *Sandman* (1992). His career spanned seven decades. **SIDELIGHTS** After his first season on "The Dick Van Dyke Show," he lost 55 pounds and had plastic surgery to remove sagging skin under his chin. About his youthful appearance, he said, "Everyone who can afford to change his appearance for the better should do so. It can alter a person's outlook on life and improve his personality." **QUOTE** "Hollywood is the kind of place where the skeletons in the closet are ashamed of the people who live in the house." Died: 1996.

Little Richard ●   6840 Hollywood

Singer, songwriter

BORN Richard Wayne Penniman; Dec. 5, 1932, in Macon, GA. **SPOTLIGHTS** The Quasar of Rock is also known as the King of Rock 'n' Roll. "I was always singing even as a little boy, and I'd beat on the steps in front of the house and sing to that," he described in his best-selling biography, *The Life and Times of Little Richard* (written by Charles White, published by Harmony Books in 1984). The third-born of thirteen children, as a child he sang gospel in a group called the Tiny Tots at old folks' homes and at the Seventh Day Adventist Church. By age 19, he had recorded with RCA, with little interest. That same year, his father passed away; he took a job as a dishwasher in a Greyhound bus station to help support his family. Then, after

many false starts, he burst out as the "originator, emancipator and architect" of rock 'n' roll. His electrifying high-energy, raw, primitive talent and stage antics of pounding the piano and whooping, shouting his vocals in a wild falsetto rocked the music world. This flamboyant artist exploded on the scene in 1955 with his first hit, "Tutti Frutti." Using his hard-edged voice with this opening: "Womp-Bomp-a-Loo-Momp Alop-Bomp-Bomp. Tutti Frutti, Aw-Rootie (5 times)...," and his frenzied style, Little Richard seized audiences and brought them to their feet. Other gold smashes include "Lucille," "Ready Teddy," "Long Tall Sally," "Rip It Up," "Slippin' and Slidin'," "Jenny, Jenny," "Keep a Knockin'" "Ooh! My Soul," and, of course, "Good Golly Miss Molly." Fans loved everything about this controversial figure, from his trademark pompadour, mirrored suit, Max Factor pancake makeup to his mascara-laden eyelashes. Audiences ached to see him in motion pictures, including *Don't Knock the Rock* (1956), *The Girl Can't Help It* (1956), *Mister Rock 'n' Roll* (1957), and *Down and Out in Beverly Hills* (1986). He has also appeared in a variety of TV shows and specials. After three decades of rock 'n' roll, Little Richard had a change of heart and life strategy. He began performing for children, singing a rock-rap version of "Itsy Bitsy Spider," "Shake It All About," "On Top of Old Smokey," and "Keep a Knockin'." **ACHIEVEMENTS** One of the first ten inductees into the Rock and Roll Hall of Fame (1986). Performed at President Clinton's inaugural ball in 1993. Featured on the 60th Annual Academy Awards telecast. Paul McCartney said about his friend: "Richard is one of the greatest kings of rock 'n' roll." Smokey Robinson declared: "Little Richard is the beginning of rock 'n' roll." Elvis Presley stated: "Your music has inspired me—you're the greatest." Bo Diddley commented: "Little Richard is one of a kind, a show-business genius. I was afraid to follow him on stage."

Francis Lederer 🎥   6904 Hollywood

Actor

BORN Frantisek "Franz" Lederer; Nov. 6, 1906, in Prague, Czechoslovakia. **SPOTLIGHTS** A dark, handsome, square-jawed heartthrob, he was star of stage and screen in both Europe and America. Movies include *A Man of Two Worlds* (1934), *The Pursuit of Happiness* (1934), *One Rainy Afternoon* (1936—where he passionately kisses Ida Lupino in one scene, and caused a real-life national scandal), *My American Wife* (1936), *Confessions of a Nazi Spy* (1939), *Puddin' Head* (1941), *The Diary of a Chambermaid* (1946), *Million Dollar Weekend*

(1948), and *Lisbon* (1956). He was both a leading man and supporting talent. A shrew businessman, he invested wisely in Southern California real estate and retired from the screen a wealthy man. Fluent in four languages, Lederer remained active in both the Hollywood and world community promoting all the arts until his death. Died: 1988.

Marlo Thomas   6904 Hollywood

Marlo Thomas

Actress, producer

BORN Nov. 21, in Detroit, MI. **SPOTLIGHTS** The beautiful daughter of famed entertainer Danny Thomas, Marlo began her career by performing in regional theaters around the country. With her unique voice and exquisite sense of comic timing, director Mike Nichols cast her in the London production of Neil Simon's "Barefoot in the Park." The show was a smash hit and made Thomas an international stage star. When she returned to the U.S., she ventured into television where she made her indelible mark as an innovator. Thomas conceived of a entirely new way to look at women. "That Girl" (1966-'71) was an absolute breakthrough. She stars as the delightfully determined Ann Marie, who sets out on her own to pursue her dreams of becoming an actress in New York City. It was the first series to portray an independent single woman living alone. It inspired millions of women to believe in themselves, and was entertaining to watch. Thomas excelled as the good-natured and spirited Ann Marie. This incredibly popular program would become the prototype for all future female-oriented situation comedies, including "The Mary Tyler Moore Show." Behind the scenes, Thomas produced the show. On Broadway, she has appeared in Herb Gardner's "Thieves," brilliantly directed by Charles Grodin, Andrew Bergman's "Social Security," directed by her friend Mike Nichols, and the Pulitzer-Prized winning play written by Michael Cristofer and directed by Jack Hofsiss, "The Shadow Box." She has a number of other important theater credits; among them "Who's Afraid of Virginia Woolf?" at the Hartford Stage, Alan Ayckbourn's "Woman in Mind" directed by Gordon Edelstein, and the national tour of "Six Degrees of Separation," directed by Jerry Zaks. Thomas stunned audiences when she returned to television. She gave fine performances, consistently interesting, in a variety of highly dramatic roles. It was discovered she could play the tragic heroine with angst, and millions of fans fell in love with her all over again. Movies for television include "The Lost Honor of Kathryn Beck" opposite Kris Kristofferson, "Consenting Adults" co-starring Martin Sheen, and "Nobody's Child" directed by Lee Grant. The latter brought Thomas her fourth Emmy Award.

The category for this TV movie was Best Dramatic Actress. Others: "It Happened One Christmas," "Ultimate Betrayal" with Ally Sheedy and Eileen Heckart, and "Reunion" co-starring Peter Strauss and Frances Sternhagen. With her winning verve, Thomas dipped her toes back in situation comedy by playing Jennifer Aniston's mother on the hit show "Friends." For children's television, Thomas created, produced and co-hosted the landmark specials "Free To Be...You and Me" which received the Emmy, Peabody, Christopher and Maxi Awards and became a best-selling children's book as well as a Gold Record. "Free To Be...A Family" also won an Emmy Award and became a best-selling book and record. **ACHIEVEMENTS** Thomas is a social activist, and has been honored by her peers in all those areas of endeavors. Awards include four Emmys, nine Emmy nominations, a Golden Globe, the George Foster Peabody Award, the Helen Caldicott Award for Nuclear Disarmament, the Thomas Paine Award from the A.C.L.U., the American Women in Radio and Television Satellite Award, and induction into the Broadcasting and Cable Hall of Fame. With her family, she carries on her father's life work for St. Jude Children's Research Hospital, the institution he founded which specializes in catastrophic children's diseases and spearheaded the conquest of childhood leukemia. (Also see bio of Danny Thomas in this book.) She is also a member of the Actor's Studio. Thomas received her star on the Walk of Fame on Dec. 18, 1992. She is married to former TV talk show host, Phil Donahue. Her brother is producer Tony Thomas.

Marguerite De La Motte ♟ 6904 Hollywood

Actress, dancer

BORN June 22, 1902, in Duluth, MN. **SPOTLIGHTS** Trained under the legendary Russian ballet dancer, Anna Pavlova, De La Motte moved with impeccable grace and beauty. She co-stars with Douglas Fairbanks in *Arizona* (1918), *The Mark of Zorro* (1920), and *The Three Musketeers* (1921), playing his love interest. She made 60 silents and talkies. Died: 1950.

Debbie Allen ♟   6904 Hollywood

Actress, dancer, singer, choreographer

BORN Jan. 16, 1950, in Houston, TX. **SPOTLIGHTS** Dubbed "Miss Versatile" by her high school classmates, the teenager excelled in academics, sports and the arts. Educated at Howard University School of Fine Arts, with emphasis on speech and drama, the supremely focused Allen earned her BA degree and graduated with honors. She headed straight to the bright lights of Broadway. Extremely athletic, with a feminine yet fit body, a beautiful face with large eyes and flashing smile, she gracefully made her Broadway debut in the chorus of the show "Purlie" in 1972. Even then she stood out from the crowd. Cast in a supporting role in "Raisin" in 1973, other important productions followed: "Ain't Misbehavin'" and "The Short-Lived Alice" By 1979 she played the coveted role of Anita in "West Side Story," for which she garnered the prestigious

Debbie Allen

Drama Desk Award and her first Tony nomination. Next, she took the film world by storm. Allen captured the imagination of the public in the motion picture, *Fame*, as dance teacher Lydia Grant, instructor at New York High School of Performing Arts. The following year, Allen was a revelation in the TV series "Fame." Luminous in her role, smart and vigorous, with a sharp, but caring attitude, she became an inspiration to millions of youths, and adored by a loyal international audience. Allen was also the respected choreographer for the show, and directed numerous episodes. She directed other TV shows, then became director and producer of TV's "A Different World." By steering the creative thinking toward pertinent and topical issues on a college campus, Allen's leadership helped the NBC show place in the top five consistently. She has received several Emmy nominations for her directorial efforts. This hard-working dynamo generated much excitement when she triumphantly returned to the Great White Way in Bob Fosse's "Sweet Charity," for which she received another Tony nomination. The revival enjoyed a record-breaking run on Broadway. Motion pictures include *Ragtime* (1981), *Jo Jo Dancer, Your Life is Calling* (1986—she plays Richard Pryor's feisty wife in this semi-autobiographical film), and *Blank Check* (1994). Steven Spielberg's *Amistad* (1997) was the first feature film Allen produced. It was the realization of one of her dreams. She had been dedicated to developing the story for more than 15 years. She also directed the feature film *Out of Sync*, and directed "The Fresh Prince of Bel Air" television pilot, Showtime's "Lync's Place," and the Martin Luther King television special entitled, "One Day," for the Disney Channel. Like a multifaceted diamond, Allen is one of entertainment's true gems. **ACHIEVEMENTS** Two Emmys and a Golden Globe Award for Best Actress in a Television Series, for "Fame." She is the acclaimed choreographer for the Academy Awards, serving at the helm for five consecutive years. Her segments for the 1999 Oscar ceremony received worldwide accolades. She is the recipient of two Honorary Doctorate degrees from the North Carolina School of the Arts, as well as from her alma mater Howard University. Her star dedication ceremony took place on Oct. 11, 1991, while thousands of cheering fans shared in her joy. **HIGHLIGHTS** Questioned about her remarkable powers, Allen observed, "I've always been accustomed to doing a lot of things. *I've never put any limitations on myself.*"

Bruno Walter ●   6904 Hollywood

Bruno Walter

Conductor
BORN Bruno Schlesinger; Sept. 15, 1876, in Berlin, Germany. **SPOTLIGHTS** His mother had been a pianist-singer before retiring to become a full-time *hausfrau*. She focused her musical abilities on her talented son, who soon became the protégé of Austrian composer-conductor, Gustav Mahler. Mahler familiarized Walter with philosophers and writers, Schopenhauer, Nietzsche, and Dostoyevsky, making him aware of the ponderous, impassioned, romantic pessimism of the 19th-century, and the beginnings of modern existentialism (man is what he makes himself and is also responsible for what he makes of himself). Mahler's original symphonies, a realization of 19th-century Romanticism, are linked to the early 20th-century with their astonishing harmonic and orchestral effects. Inspired by Mahler's genius, Walter viewed the music world differently. This young musician who, at age 23, was a pianist with the Berlin Philharmonic decided to become a conductor while watching Hans von Bulow conduct. Walter said he witnessed, "the glow of inspiration and the concentration of energy. I felt the compelling force of his gestures, noticed the attention and devotion of the players, and was conscious of the expressiveness and precision of their playing. It became at once clear to me that it was one man who was producing music, that he had transformed those hundred performers into his instrument, and that he was playing it as a pianist plays a piano." In 1913 he was appointed the Royal Music Director at Bavaria. In 1925, at age 49, he landed the prestigious post as director of the Berlin Municipal Opera. On the precipice of World War II, Walter was forced to flee the Nazis. In the United States he became best known for his remarkable renderings of Viennese symphonic music. During his lifetime he was the undisputed interpreter of Mahler, Beethoven, Schubert, Wagner, Schumann and Brahms, and therefore some of the world's greatest musical works. **QUOTES** He triumphantly conducted "The Magic Flute" at the Metropolitan Opera House. Walter declared, "Truth can be repulsive, but Mozart has the power to speak truth with beauty. He was born with heavenly harmony in his soul. Everything he touched has beauty." On his 80th birthday he said, "Music means more to me the longer I live. I cannot imagine what it would be like when I am 100." Died: 1962.

Burgess Meredith 🎥   6904 Hollywood

Actor, director
BORN George Burgess; Nov. 16, 1908, in Cleveland, OH.

Burgess Meredith

SPOTLIGHTS An actor's actor. For six decades, Meredith excelled in every facet of theatrical entertainment. A veteran of Broadway since 1936, this artist skillfully handled such difficult Shakespearean works as "Hamlet" and "Macbeth." On Broadway, he was also a Tony-nominated director. In Hollywood, he proved to be an ideal character actor. A diminutive, raspy-voiced talent, he appeared in 50 films, including *Winterset* (1936), *Star Wagon* (1937), *Five Kings* (1938), *Of Mice and Men* (1939--as George), *Castle on the Hudson* (1940), *That Uncertain Feeling* (1941), *Tom, Dick and Harry* (1941), Renoir's *The Diary of a Chambermaid* (1946—which critics found too surrealistic, but remained one of Meredith's favorite films), *Rocky* (I/1976 & II/1979), *True Confessions* (1980), and *Grumpy Old Men* (I/1993 & II/1995). He plays WWII correspondent Ernie Pyle in *The Story of G.I. Joe* (1945), the real-life Pyle had personally selected him to play the part. Twice nominated for an Academy Award—*The Day of the Locust* (1975), and for *Rocky* (1976)—he won neither time. In the latter, he plays Mickey, the aging boxing manager. Nicknamed Buzz, he had a sometimes explosive personality onscreen and off, and felt perfectly suited for the *Rocky* part. **TV** Numerous roles include his memorable role as the fiendish, scheming Penguin in the 1960s "Batman" series. His characterization of the last man to be left alive on earth ranks as one of the best in "The Twilight Zone." He guest starred on countless Westerns like "Bonanza," and "Rawhide," and appeared in TV movies: "The Last Hurrah." One of his four wives—and onscreen partner—was actress Paulette Goddard. **ACHIEVEMENTS** 1977 Emmy for "Tail Gunner Joe," as attorney Joseph Welch in a story about Sen. Joseph McCarthy. 1960 Special Tony Award for his staging of "A Thurber Carnival." **QUOTE** "I don't know what tomorrow will bring—but so far, so good." Died: 1997.

Rex Harrison 🎥   6904 Hollywood

Actor

BORN Reginald Carey Harrison; March 5, 1908, in Huyton, England. **SPOTLIGHTS** He was an adroit master of sophisticated, black tie comedy. A veteran of both stage and screen, this handsome, elegant gentleman handled comedy and drama with equal aplomb. In films, he left an indelible memory. He is delightful, as is his co-star Wendy Hiller, in the witty British comedy *Major Barbara* (1941). The sparkling piece had been adapted from a George Bernard Shaw play. Harrison appears in the original, non-musical version of *Anna and the King of Siam* (1946), opposite Irene Dunne. Exceedingly versatile, he played the crusty sea captain in the romance *The Ghost and*

Rex Harrison

Mrs. Muir (1947), then switched to the compulsively jealous conductor in *Unfaithfully Yours* (1948). He stars as a bigamist in the comedy, *The Constant Husband* (1954). In *The Agony and the Ecstasy* (1963), he played his Holiness Pope Julius II. Harrison appears in one of Vicente Minnelli's best comedies, *The Reluctant Debutante* (1958). Later, he earned an Oscar nomination as Julius Caesar in *Cleopatra* (1963). **HIGHLIGHTS** The press labeled him "Sexy Rexy," and the name stuck throughout his career. **ACHIEVEMENTS** 1964 Best Actor Oscar for *My Fair Lady*, as Professor Henry Higgins. Reportedly, this character was close to his own true nature. (It also marked the second work that Harrison had starred in which had been adapted from a George Bernard Shaw vehicle. Harrison seemed born to play both Shaw's and playwright Noel Coward's characters.) Recipient of three Tony Awards. Knighted in 1989 by Queen Elizabeth II. Died: 1990.

Harold Greene 📺   6908 Hollywood

News anchor, producer, writer

BORN June 1, in San Francisco. **SPOTLIGHTS** After serving in

From left: Johnny Grant, Honorary Mayor of Hollywood; "Shotgun" Tom Kelly, Radio D.J. Legend; Harold Greene (holding star plaque); and Lou Walters, CNN Anchor man.

the United States Army with Armed Forces Radio during the Vietnam War, Greene became a street reporter/news camera-man covering passionate anti-war protests in America. The year was 1968 and the demonstrations were growing louder and stronger each day. As tensions mounted and tempers flared, he captured a heated moment in history. A violent riot erupted when then-President Richard Nixon appeared at the Century Plaza Hotel (in Century City, Los Angeles). News of this bloody event raced throughout the world. In the 1970s, he covered the both the Chicano rights and feminist rights move-ments in the Southland. He produced and anchored a weekly TV news magazine, and an annual TV musical variety show, garnering both the coveted Iris award and the local Emmy. In the '80s, he became L.A.'s top-rated morning man, then enter-tained the country with his "Hollywood Closeup," a weekend show. When he returned to news broadcasting, he was award-ed a Golden Mike for his outstanding coverage of the Cerritos mid-air disaster. He is recognized for his high journalistic stan-dards. He has also become a fixture on Academy Awards night as he broadcasts the arrival of Hollywood's biggest names to millions of fans around the country and the world. **QUOTE** Receiving a star on the Hollywood Walk of Fame is a dream come true. As one of the few television news journalists hon-ored with his own star, I belive it represents the old adage that dreams do come true in Tinsel Town. By the way, when look-ing at my star on Hollywood Boulevard, please curb your dog.

Dane Clark 📺   6908 Hollywood

Actor
BORN Bernard Zanville; Feb. 18, 1913, in Brooklyn, NY. **SPOTLIGHTS** TV's version of the movie tough guy, Clark played a brooding heel throughout much of his 50-year career. Ironically, he never wanted to be in show business, but turned to acting to help pay his way through law school. Films include *Action in the North Atlantic* (1943) with Humphrey Bogart, *Destination Tokyo* (1944) with Cary Grant and pal John Garfield, *Hollywood Canteen* (1944), *The Very Thought of You* (1944), *God Is My Co-Pilot* (1945), *A Stolen Life* (1946) with Bette Davis, *Highly Dangerous* (1951), and *Last Rites* (1988) with Tom Berenger. **TV** He starred in a number of series including "Wire Service." Although in real life he never fin-ished law school, he got close to his chosen profession when he portrayed Lieutenant Arthur Tragg on the law drama "The New Perry Mason." Clark guest starred on such popular series as "The Twilight Zone." He appeared in numerous plays, which were telecast live, and numerous movies of the week including "The Jimmy Dean Story," and "Murder on Flight 502." **QUOTE** When asked about his show "Bold Adventure," Clark declared, "Eugene O'Neill this ain't. It's television, but I think it's pretty exciting." Died: 1998.

Blake Edwards 🎥   6908 Hollywood

Director, writer, producer

Blake Edwards

BORN William Blake McEdwards; July 26, 1922, in Tulsa, OK. **SPOTLIGHTS** Descended from a show busi-ness family, his grandfather had been a leading director during the silent era and had directed actress Theda Bara—Fox's biggest property—in 12 films, including *Cleopatra* (1917). His father had been one of the top assistant directors and pro-duction managers during the Golden Era. Raised in Los Angeles, Edwards decided to pursue a career in acting. He made his screen debut in *Ten Gentlemen from West Point* (1942). Within the next six years he appeared in 27 films, wrote screenplays and radio series. For early television, he cre-ated "Mr. Lucky" and "Peter Gunn." He worked steadily behind the camera at motion picture studios as writer, produc-er and director. His first big hit as a director was the military comedy, *Operation Petticoat* (1959), starring Cary Grant and Tony Curtis. Two years later he directed *Breakfast at Tiffany's*, starring Audrey Hepburn as the free-spirited Holly Golightly. This critically acclaimed film proved to be his breakthrough, bringing the admiration of worldwide audiences. He followed with the suspenseful crime drama, *Experiment in Terror* (1962) with Glenn Ford, Lee Remick and Stefanie Powers. His out-standing drama, *Days of Wine and Roses* (1962), stars Jack Lemmon and Lee Remick in a heartbreaking story of alco-holism. He obtained brilliant Academy Award-nominated per-formances from both lead actors. Edwards exploded on the opposite end of the movie spectrum with the highly colorful comedy, *The Pink Panther* (1964). This absurd farce starred Peter Sellers as the inept, insipid Inspector Clouseau, who was absolutely splendid in the role. The charming and sophisticat-ed supporting cast included David Niven, Capucine, Robert Wagner, and Claudia Cardinale. Wildly popular and full of surprise, Edwards rushed its sequel into production that same year. *A Shot in the Dark* again starred Sellers, with support from Elke Sommer, Herbert Lom, and George Sanders. It was a gigantic hit, and sparkled as brightly as the first. *The Pink Panther* (and its numerous sequels) became the most successful comedy film series of all time. Edwards commented, "I had decided at one point in my career that I would not go on being a director unless I had creative freedom. I was lucky enough to have directed a series of films that made a lot of money, which is what the Hollywood establishment understands." Edwards was given carte blanche. Other motion pictures include *The Great Race* (1965) with Jack Lemmon, Tony Curtis and Natalie Wood; *The Party* (1968) starring Peter Sellers; *Wild Rovers* (1971) starring William Holden and Ryan O'Neal; *10* (1979) with Dudley Moore, Julie Andrews and Bo Derek; *S.O.B.* (1981) with William Holden and Julie Andrews;

Victor/Victoria (1982) starring Julie Andrews, James Garner, Robert Preston, and Lesley Ann Warren; *Micki & Maude* (1984) with Dudley Moore, Amy Irving and Ann Reinking; *Blind Date* (1987) featuring Bruce Willis and Kim Basinger; and *Switch* (1991) with Ellen Barkin and Jimmy Smits. In 1995 Edwards successfully brought "Victor/Victoria" to Broadway, with Julie Andrews reprising her Academy-nominated film role. **ACHIEVEMENTS** Recipient of dozens of awards and honors, including the Preston Sturges Award by the Directors Guild of America and the Writers Guild of America, the French *Cesar*, the French Legion of Honor, the French Commander of the Arts and Letters, the Italian *David di Donatello* Award, the Italian Premio Filmcritica *Maestri del Cinema Campidoglio* Award. His Hollywood Walk of Fame dedication ceremony on April 3, 1991 was commemorated by dozens of celebrities, hundreds of well-wishers, and a throng of international media. **HIGHLIGHTS** On Nov. 12, 1969 he married singer/actress Julie Andrews. (See her bio in this book.) He and his wife contribute to various charities and are on the board of Operation USA, an international relief agency which rushes help to disaster areas worldwide. They are also on the board of the Foundation for Hereditary Disease.

Gregory La Cava 🎥   6908 Hollywood

Director

BORN March 10, 1892, in Towanda, PA. **SPOTLIGHTS** Born with a flair for illustration, La Cava attended the acclaimed Chicago Institute of Art and New York's Academy of Design. After graduation, he landed a cartoonist job for a New York paper. By age 25 he had been hired to run the brand new animated cartoon division for Hearst Enterprises. After seven years he made the leap to Paramount Pictures, writing and directing comedy shorts and features. This temperamental director is best known for his classic screwball comedies. *The Half-Naked Truth* (1932) starring exotic Mexican spitfire Lupe Velez as a scheming actress and Lee Tracy as a carnival shill/publicity whiz really put La Cava on the map. He directed Claudette Colbert and Melvyn Douglas in the light romantic comedy, *She Married Her Boss* (1935); Carole Lombard and William Powell in *My Man Godfrey* (1936); and Katharine Hepburn and Ginger Rogers in the comic melodrama, *Stage Door* (1937). Died: 1952.

Cubby Broccoli 🎥   6910 Hollywood

Producer

BORN Albert Romolo Broccoli; April 5, 1909, in Long Island, NY. **SPOTLIGHTS** Titillated by Tinseltown's glamour, he began at the bottom of movieland's ladder, waking up extras for the Western *Outlaw* (1943). As his tasks grew in importance, Cubby (as he liked to be called) waited for his big break producing. He spent his days at the studio, and nights socializing with starlets on the nightclub circuit. He lived to be seen in such hot spots as Ciro's on the Sunset Strip. His first attempt

at producing brought Alan Ladd and Susan Stephen together in a Technicolor production entitled *The Red Beret* (1953). It's a routine war pic, but the battle scenes showed good action promise. He co-founded Warwick Pictures in England (with Irving Allen) and soon after adapted the novel by author Ian Fleming into the first James Bond film. The lead role of Agent 007 was originally offered to actor Cary Grant, who turned it down, and lived to regret it. When

Cubby Broccoli

Mrs. Broccoli saw a screen test of Sean Connery, she exclaimed, "Take that one! He's gorgeous!" *Dr. No* (1963) was the spectacular result. The rest is cinematic history, with Cubby creating the longest-running film series ever. James Bond films include *From Russia With Love* (1963), *Goldfinger* (1964), *Thunderball* (1965), *You Only Live Twice* (1967), *The Spy Who Loved Me* (1977), *Moonraker* (1979), *For Your Eyes Only* (1981), *Octopussy* (1983), *A View to Kill* (1985), *Goldeneye* (1995), and *Tomorrow Never Dies* (1997). In 1999, Pierce Brosnan stars in *The World is Not Enough*, the 19th entry in the 007 franchise. **ACHIEVEMENTS** Received the Academy's prestigious Irving G. Thalberg Memorial Award, The Order Of The British Empire, and the French *Commandeur Des Arts Et Des Lettres*. **HIGHLIGHTS** After Disney's spectacular success with *Mary Poppins* (1965), Broccoli discovered that he owned the rights to a children's book entitled *Chitty Chitty Bang Bang*. It was the one children's book that author Ian Fleming had written and had included in his sale of the James Bond library. Broccoli approached Disney to do a joint venture musical fantasy. Disney, who never split creative control, politely declined. The producer quickly set about to reassemble as many members of the original *Mary Poppins* team. While Dick Van Dyke signed on, Julie Andrews was not available. Broccoli cast Sally Ann Howes in the female lead. Although Howes is a blonde, the producer was pleased that she resembled Andrews in the right light. Died: 1996.

Phillips Holmes 🎥   6910 Hollywood

Actor

BORN July 22, 1907, in Grand Rapids, MI. **SPOTLIGHTS** The son of veteran character actor, Taylor Holmes, the youngster enjoyed a privileged upbringing and the finest education money could buy. He attended Princeton University and studied at L'Université de Sorbonne, in Paris, France. He made his screen debut in *Varsity* (1928). His breakthrough role, as the ambitious, treacherous lover in Josef Von Sternberg's *An American Tragedy* (1931), made national headlines. Holmes came out of the Paramout film a star. He made dozens of films during the 1930s. He was brilliant in the WWI drama about killing, remorse and redemptive love in *Broken Lullaby* (1932). Other motion pictures include the all-star comedy/drama *Dinner at Eight* (1933), the tragic love story *Nana* (1934), and an early screen version of Dicken's classic tale *Great Expectations* (1934—as the orphan Pip). Died: 1942, in a midair military collision plane crash while serving in WWII.

Snow White ✿   6910 Hollywood

Cartoon character

Snow White and the Seven Dwarfs, with the Prince

CREATED Dec. 21, 1937, by Walt Disney. **SPOTLIGHTS** "Magic mirror on the wall, who is the fairest one of all?" Fifty years after that question was posed by the wicked queen, the darling princess with "hair black as ebony, skin white like snow, her name—Snow White!" continues to reign in the imaginations of tens of millions of devotees. *Snow White and the Seven Dwarfs* (1937) was Walt Disney's first feature-length film. Since no one had ever attempted a seven-reel cartoon before, and because it took three years on the drawing boards, entertainment insiders believed it would be a dismal failure. The industry tagged the production "Disney's Folly." Because of escalating costs—it went *ten times* over budget—both Walt Disney and his brother Roy were forced to put up everything they owned for collateral. Intelligent enough to be worried, but with enough faith to believe in the project, the two signed away $1.5 million in property. For the Disneys, fairy tales did come true; *Snow White and the Seven Dwarfs* was the top film of the year. The story, adapted from Grimm's Fairy Tales, brought animation to the highest technical level. Artists produced a beautifully detailed background and perfect character development. For the first time an animated, two-dimensional character seemed human. Audiences identified with Snow White. She had come alive for them, with a personality, real dangers and romantic adventures. The human model for Snow White was another Walk of Fame honoree, dancer-actress Marge Champion. Champion acted out the scenes for the animators to base Snow White's movements on. Snow White's

voice was that of a young singer with an opera background, Adriana Caselotti. **ACHIEVEMENTS** In 1939 Shirley Temple presented Disney with his Oscar and seven dwarf-sized Oscars (for Doc, Bashful, Dopey, Sleepy, Happy, Grumpy and Sneezy). *Snow White* became Hollywood's highest grossing film until 1939, when *Gone with the Wind* knocked it out of its place! **SPOTLIGHTS** The star was dedicated on *Snow White*'s 50th Anniversary in 1987. On its Golden Anniversary, it became the first movie to be exhibited simultaneously in more than 60 countries—including America, Russia and China—in more than ten languages.

Jean Harlow ✿   6912 Hollywood

Jean Harlow

Actress
BORN Harlean Carpentier; March 3, 1911, in Kansas City, MO. **SPOTLIGHTS** The Platinum Bombshell. After advancing from bit parts, like in Laurel and Hardy's comedy *Double Whopee* (1928), billionaire movie producer Howard Hughes put her in the sound version of the WWI saga *Hell's Angels* (1930). Harlow did not immediately capture the public's attention. She played tough and vulgar in the sensational gangster story, *The Public Enemy* (1931), and received her best reviews to date. With the massive publicity campaign and release of *Platinum Blonde* (1931), Harlow complained, "If it hadn't been for the color of my hair, Hollywood wouldn't even know I was alive." This smart, sexy broad really broke through to stardom when she appeared opposite Clark Gable in *Red Dust* (1932)—in a role originally cast for Greta Garbo. This jungle romance movie was so steamy at the time, many didn't think it would pass the censors. Her co-star Gable had this to say about her, "I'm nuts about the Baby. She's the real thing." Next, she wisecracked her way into fame. Director George Cukor said, "She played comedy as naturally as a hen lays eggs." His *Dinner at Eight* (1933) was something to cluck about, Harlow shined like a Fabergé egg. That same year, she was exquisite in *Bombshell*—one of her best performances. She worked with Gable again in the action picture, *China Seas* (1935). When several reviewers focused on her cleavage, rather than her great performance, Harlow responded, "My God, must I always wear a low-cut dress to be important?" *Libeled Lady* (1936) afforded her the opportunity to perform with fiance William Powell. **QUOTE** When she took a liking to a person, she'd tell him or her, "Call me 'Baby,' that's what my friends call me." Baby died too young in 1937.

Tom Cruise ✿   6912 Hollywood

Tom Cruise

Actor

BORN Thomas Cruise Mapother IV; July 3, 1962, in Syracuse, NY. **SPOTLIGHTS** This handsome leading actor used to be considered *the* golden boy in Hollywood; it is a title now held by Leonardo DiCaprio. That, though, is of little concern to Cruise, who has established himself as a fine dramatic and comedic talent. His feet are firmly planted on the summit of his fame. Yet life has not always been so kind. Abandoned by his father, Cruise was raised by his devoted mother. Too proud to take government assistance, she worked two to three jobs to provide for her brood (Cruise and his three sisters). The *all-female* clan doted on him, and he returned the favor by joyfully participating in their sweet traditions. When, on holidays like Christmas, there was no money for presents, the family ingeniously wrote poems for one another. They also gave "work" gifts, like making beds for a week, or doing the other's housekeeping chores. Cruise's problems arose outside the house. The family moved around a lot so it was difficult to make and keep friends. Born with an innate sense of style, but unable to afford new clothes, he often wore ill-fitting hand-me-downs from relatives. As a teenager, he found himself shy, lonely and withdrawn. To top it off, he was born with the learning disability dyslexia, which went undiagnosed during most of his education. Subsequently, he was mistakenly placed in lower-level classes for "slow" students, where he grew up feeling ashamed of himself. (Although a high percentage of people who have dyslexia are intelligent, it affects their brain in a way that makes reading and other tasks difficult. For example, Cruise could not tell which was his right or left hand.) His direction for what to do with his life happened by accident; while training for senior wrestling he tore a tendon in his leg. This gave him the time to try out for the musical "Guys and Dolls." He won the starring role. About the experience, he said, "All of a sudden you're up there, and you're doing something you really enjoy...And I said to myself, 'This is it!'" Cruise launched his career on high school graduation day, skipping the ceremony to head off to New York. He gave himself three years to find work acting; within five months he made his screen debut with a bit role in *Endless Love* (1981). He is only on screen for seven minutes in this embarrassingly bad picture (although this is no fault of his). That same year, he played a supporting role as the psychotic cadet, David Shawn, in *Taps*. He made a couple more films, then with his boy-next-door looks and his trademark grin, won his breakthrough role as a suburban teenager who grows up suddenly in *Risky Business* (1983). He came out of it a major star. His two hit movies of 1986, *Top Gun* and *The Color of Money*, contrast flash with class. The former was a mega-hit with hollow char- acters, romance and fun adventure. The latter shows Cruise's psychologically complex character in perfect sync with the legendary Paul Newman (who won the Oscar for his role as pool shark Fast Eddie Felson). Cruise was equally strong playing opposite Dustin Hoffman in *Rain Man* (1988—in which Hoffman won the Oscar for his role as an autistic idiot-savant). The next year, this hardworking actor should have won an Academy Award for his brilliant characterization of an All-American patriot, who becomes an embittered paraplegic Vietnam vet in *Born on the Fourth of July.* After working with his co-star Nicole Kidman in *Days of Thunder* (1990), he married her on Christmas Eve. Next, the couple co-star in the epic *Far and Away* (1992), about Irish immigrants coming to America for the land rush. There is splendid acting, a romantic chemistry between the stars, sweeping cinematography and a fascinating old-fashioned story in *Far and Away*. It is a wonderful motion picture, directed by Ron Howard. Cruise played the vampire Lestat in the stylish adaptation of Anne Rice's book, *Interview with a Vampire* (1994). Rice first battled publicly against having Cruise in the lead, then after having seen the movie reversed her stance. In 1996 he gave an outstanding performance, and one of his best ever, as *Jerry Maguire* in the romantic comedy of the year. His character evolves from a supreme blow hard to finding the better man inside himself. He co-stars with his wife Nicole Kidman in their third film together, and the most erotic to date, in Stanley Kubrick's last motion picture, *Eyes Wide Shut* (1999). He earned an Oscar nomination for best supporting actor in *Magnolia* (1999). **QUOTE** While waiting for his star to be unveiled on October 16, 1986, Cruise stood at the podium with a good-hearted smile on his face and admitted, "Since I learned that they wanted to give me this gracious gift, I've been having nightmares that no one would show up except my parents and my girlfriend."

Phillips Lord 🎙️   6914 Hollywood

Actor, producer

BORN Phillips H. Lord; Oct. 1, 1903, in Chicago, IL. **SPOTLIGHTS** He created and starred in one of radio's earliest successes, "Seth Parker." This program, which started in 1929, featured Lord as an elderly New England gentleman. (When audience members were in tow he applied Max Factor's white whiskers for his aged role since he was only in his 20s at the time.) Singing old-fashioned hymns, praising the virtues of Mother Nature, talking about peaceful, cozy home environments, and having family members treat one another in "their very nice and restrained manner" won the show millions of listeners. Hundreds of "Seth Parker" clubs formed throughout North America to practice altruism. Lord, though, had tired of the show by 1935 and literally took to the sea. When he returned to radio, it was in an entirely different vein. Lord wore three hats, as narrator, producer and director, on the highly successful, "Gang Busters" (1935-'57). He announced to listeners know that his hard-hitting dramatic crime anthology was based on true crime stories, was made "in cooperation with police and federal law enforcement departments throughout the United States...the only national program that brings you authentic police case histories." The noisy sound effects were fast, frequent and loud: gunshots, screaming, broken windows, a policeman's whistle, sirens, etc. This most popular of all police shows added a new phrase to the English language: "to come on like gangbusters." Defined in the *Dictionary of American Slang*: "to enter, arrive, perform...in a sensational, loud, active, or striking manner." He also produced "We the People" for NBC starting in 1936, and "By Popular Demand" book review for CBS in 1938. In addition, Lord enjoyed another huge hit producing "Counterspy," an espionage adventure drama (1942-'57). To learn more about classic radio shows and broadcasting achievements, contact Pacific Pioneer Broadcasters, P.O. Box 4866, North Hollywood, CA 91617, or telephone (323) 462-9606. Lord died: 1968.

Roy Clark 📺   6914 Hollywood

Musician, singer, songwriter

Roy Clark

BORN Roy Linwood Clark; April 15, 1933, in Meherrin, VA. **SPOTLIGHTS** The son of a tobacco farmer, Clark's first musical instrument was a cigar box with a ukulele neck and four strings that his daddy had rigged up for him to play in an elementary school band. On Christmas he received a Silvertone guitar model from Sears; he was 14 years old. At age 15, he gave his first public performance with his father's square dance band at a military service club. The following year, he got his first paid job in music; he received $2 for one night's work. By the time he was in his late teens, he had learned to play banjo and guitar and was known for his lightning fast fingers. Clark said, "Music was my salvation, the thing I loved most and did best." After winning the national banjo championship competition in 1950, Clark received an invitation to perform at the Grand Ole Opry, which led to shows with Red Foley and Ernest Tubb. Enthusiastic for all types of music, this versatile, energetic talent also plays jazz, pop and rock 'n' roll. In 1954 he joined Jimmy Dean and the Texas Wildcats, appearing in clubs and on radio and TV, and even backing up Elvis Presley. At age 27 Clark, still scrambling, received an invitation to perform at the Golden Nugget in Las Vegas. It proved to be the mesmerizing musician's breakthrough. He hit the road on his own tour, for 345 straight nights at one stretch. Upon his return to Las Vegas in 1962 he had become a headliner. He signed with Capitol Records releasing "The Tips of My Fingers" which became a 1963 top ten single and his first

hit. In 1969 he gained international recognition as host of TV's "Hee Haw" (along with co-host Buck Owens). He spent 24 years doing hillbilly cornball with America's finest country talent. With his quick wit, homespun humor and sincere warmth, Clark led "Hee Haw" to the longest-running syndicated television series in history. It has been estimated—with no exaggeration—that Clark has inspired more people around the globe to learn how to play the guitar than any other musician in history. Hits include: "Thank God and Greyhound You're Gone," "I Never Picked Cotton," "Come Live with Me," "Yesterday, When I Was Young," "Somewhere Between Love and Tomorrow," "If I Had It To Do All Over Again," and "The Lawrence Welk-Hee Haw Counter Revolution Polka." Clark's 12-string guitar rendition of *Malaguena* is a classic. Also: *Guitar Spectacular, The Best of Roy Clark, Superpicker* and *Greatest Hits*. **ACHIEVEMENTS** The recipient of many honors, including the 1997 Pioneer Award from the Academy of Country Music; 1982 Grammy (Best Country Instrumental) for *Alabama Jubilee*; 1972 & 1973 Country Music Entertainer of the Year; 1987 the Grand Ole Opry's 63rd member. About the Roy Clark Music Scholarship Fund for Longwood College, in Farmville, Virginia, he said, "I was blessed with wonderful parents who were a huge part of who I am today. To carry forward their generous spirit and their support of musical talent into future generations through the scholarship is the perfect tribute to their memory." **SIDELIGHTS** At age 16, Clark was offered a tryout with the then-St. Louis Browns baseball team. But in those days the applicant had to pay his own way to training camp, and Clark had to decline because he could not afford the fare. **QUOTE** "What an honor it is to have a star that's associated with all of my heroes. The first time I walked down this street, the furthest thing from my mind was that someday I would have a star here. Dreams are dreams, but this is *dreamland!*"

Irving Reis 🎥   6914 Hollywood

Director, screenwriter

BORN May 7, 1906, in New York, NY. **SPOTLIGHTS** As founder and director of CBS Radio's Columbia Workshop, Reis recognized and developed talent. He gave first breaks to a number of great entertainers, including Orson Welles, who won his first radio job from Reis. He moved into writing, then became a "B" movie director. A brave and patriotic soul, he bravely served in WWII, where he witnessed too many horrors. The experience altered his sense of self. He came back a changed man, directing a much higher caliber of film in both drama and comedy. Pictures include *Crack-Up* (1946), a clever, suspenseful *film noir* about art forgery starring Pat O'Brien, Claire Trevor, and Herbert Marshall. Next, he directed the all-star cast of Shirley Temple, Cary Grant and Myrna Loy in *The Bachelor and the Bobbysoxer* (1947). This is one of Temple's best post-adolescent films. Grant and Loy are snappy with the sharp dialogue from this Sidney Sheldon script, for which he won an Oscar for best screenplay. In 1948, Reis directed *All*

My Sons, a painful story about the loss of a son during WWII, and a father's unscrupulous part in selling defective airplane parts to the military. This powerful drama, adapted from Arthur Miller's play, stars Edward G. Robinson and Burt Lancaster. He followed up with a wartime tearjerker, *Enchantment* (1948), starring David Niven, Teresa Wright Evelyn Keyes, and Farley Granger. Died: 1953.

Clayton Moore   The Lone Ranger

Actor   **6914 Hollywood**

Clayton Moore

BORN John Carlton Moore; Sept. 14, 1914, in Chicago, IL. **SPOTLIGHTS** A Saturday morning hero, he taught the principles of fairness and honesty to the first generation of children television viewers. Immortalized in the title role of "The Lone Ranger," Moore felt it had been his destiny to play "the masked man." He achieved his lifelong goal of being a media cowboy after studying and working as a stuntman, actor, and rider. In 1948, he heard of a talent search to find TV's "Lone Ranger." With his resonant voice, upright posture and true belief that good ultimately triumphs over evil, Moore beat out 75 actors to land the plum role. As the champion of justice, he made 169 half-hour "Lone Ranger" thrilling dramatic episodes. As the show opened, he rode to the music of Rossini's "William Tell Overture," on "his fiery horse with the speed of light." It was the first Western juvenile series made for television. Children viewers were delighted that "The Lone Ranger" had the blacksmith install silver shoes for his white stallion named Silver. The horseshoes matched both the Ranger's silver bullets and pair of silver six-guns (twin Colt .45s). His catchphrase quickly captured the imaginations of America's youth: "Hi-Yo, Silver!" Moore also made two feature films: *The Lone Ranger* (1956), and *The Lone Ranger and the Lost City of Gold* (1958). His co-star, Jay Silverheels, played his faithful Native American Indian sidekick, Tonto. (See the bio of Silverheels in this book.) **HIGHLIGHTS** "The Lone Ranger Creed" includes these clearly formulated principles:
"I BELIEVE:
That to have a friend, a man must be one.
That all men are created equal and that everyone has with in himself the power to make this a better world.
That God put the firewood there, but every man must gather and light it himself.
That sooner or later, somewhere, somehow, we must settle with the world and make payment for what we have taken.
That all things change but truth, and that truth alone lives on forever." Offscreen, Moore pledged, "I believe truly and always in the Lone Ranger's Creed." **QUOTE** "When I take off to that Big Ranch in the sky, I still want to have my white hat on my head." Died: 1999.

Ann Miller   **6914 Hollywood**

Actress, dancer, singer

Ann Miller

BORN Lucille Ann Collier; April 12, 1919, in Chireno, TX. **SPOTLIGHTS** At age 12, this talented girl began dancing professionally in vaudeville to help support her family. She blossomed into a devastatingly fast tap dancer whose lovely dark-haired looks helped propel her into pictures. She made her screen debut in *New Faces of 1937*. With her high cheekbones, flashing smile, long legs that never end, and a sassy sweetness, this energetic lady quickly began a star. A partial listing of her films includes *Stage Door* (1937), *Having Wonderful Time* (1938), *Too Many Girls* (1940), *Time Out for Rhythm* (1941), *Hit Parade of 1941*, *Reveille with Beverly* (1943) with cameo roles of Frank Sinatra, Count Basie, Duke Ellington, and the Mills Brothers, *Jam Session* (1944—a jazz fan's must-see film), *Easter Parade* (1948), *On the Town* (1949), *Lovely to Look At* (1952), *Kiss Me, Kate!* (1953), *Deep in My Heart* (1954), *Hit the Deck* (1955), and *That's Entertainment! III* (1994). This super friendly, well-loved talent spent many happy years with MGM, under the leadership of Louis B. Mayer, when that studio was turning out top notch musical extravaganzas. Miller is a dynamo who has continued performing on stage and touring extensively. Stage shows include revivals of "Mame," "Sugar Babies," and "Follies." She also keeps busy working in television throughout the 1990s. **ACHIEVEMENTS** Miller earned her rightful spot in television history as being the FIRST tap dancer to perform in that new medium. **QUOTE** Asked how it felt to be rated the #1 tap dancer, Miller replied, "It's great, except people are apt to overlook my face for my feet."

Charles Fries   **6916 Hollywood**

Producer, executive
BORN Sept. 30, 1928, in Cincinnati, OH. **SPOTLIGHTS** A graduate of Ohio State University, Fries became one of the most prolific independent producers of quality movies for theatrical television. He began his behind-the-scenes show business career and served in various production and administrative capacities in the entertainment industry. Fries became vice-president in charge of production at Screen Gems, the Columbia Pictures Television arm, and subsequently became v.p. in charge of feature film production/administration for the

Aaron Spelling (left), Peter Chernin, and Charles Fries (right)

parent company where he worked with the top producers and directors in the industry. Then as executive v.p. in charge of production for Metromedia, Fries produced and/or supervised some 30 movies for television, nine television series and five theatrical films. He is known for producing issue-oriented movies for TV: "Small Sacrifices" starring Farrah Fawcett and Ryan O'Neal, "The Neon Empire" starring Ray Sharkey, Martin Landau and Gary Busey, "Leona Helmsley: The Queen of Mean," starring Suzanne Pleshette and Lloyd Bridges, "The Martian Chronicles" by Ray Bradbury starring Rock Hudson (six-hour mini-series), "Blood Vows: Mafia Wife" starring Melissa Gilbert, "Rosie—The Rosemary Clooney Story" starring Sandra Locke, and "Woman on the Ledge" with Deidre Hall. Motion pictures include *Tales From the Crypt* (1972), *The Cat People* (1982), *Flowers in the Attic* (1987), and *Troop Beverly Hills* (1989). **ACHIEVEMENTS** Recipient of numerous awards, Fries is a member of the Board of Trustees and Executive Committee at the American Film Institute, where he established the Charles W. Fries Producer of the Year Award to encourage quality programming. He is a member of the Academy of Television Arts and Sciences, the Academy of Motion Pictures Arts and Sciences, and the Producer's Guild of America. **QUOTE** "I came to Hollywood at the beginning of the 'miracle of television.' I learned a philosophy that has helped me gain success. Have *passion* for what you want to achieve. Have *perseverance* and never give up on something you are passionate about. Have *patience* in case it does not happen 'today.' With passion, perseverance and patience you can be 'king of the world.'"

Dinah Shore 📺   6916 Hollywood

Singer, hostess, TV personality
BORN Frances (Fanny) Rose Shore; March 1, 1917, in Winchester, TN. **SPOTLIGHTS** An elegant Southern belle who attended Vanderbilt University, she was proud as punch when she first landed a vocalist job on a radio show. Then, she "was promptly fired for not singing fast or loud enough." Not giving up hope, Shore became one of America's most beloved entertainers—*without changing her style*. In 1938 she paired with Frank Sinatra (who was also an unknown at the time) for a New York radio program. Xavier Cugat heard them and offered *Shore* a deal. She made her debut album with him. Billed as a star vocalist on radio's "The Eddie Cantor Show," she sang on the air for three and a half years. In 1942 this lovely lady was considered the most popular recording artist since

the rise of the big-voiced Kate Smith in the early 1930s. Shore's popular 1940s songs include "Miss You," "Something to Remember You By," and "You'd Be So Nice to Come Home To." Hollywood called. After making several good films—*Thank Your Lucky Stars* (1943), *Follow the Boys* (1944), *Belle of the Yukon* (1944), and *Up in Arms* (1944)—Shore felt her career was not moving fast enough and declared, "I bombed as a movie star." She found her

Dinah Shore

nitch in the medium of television where her videogenic personality captured millions of fans immediately. This dynamo became widely admired as "Miss Television." "The Dinah Shore Show," a musical variety program (1956-'63) attracted the highest caliber of guest stars, top ratings and garnered a number of Emmys. **HIGHLIGHTS** Shore told dinner partner Sir Michael Teilmann that the most exciting moment in her life was when she was invited to perform at New York's famed Carnegie Hall. It was a thrill that remained with her until the end. **SIDELIGHTS** Married to handsome cowboy star George Montgomery whose own television show battled hers for ratings in the same time slot on a rival network. **QUOTE** "Basically I'm a blues singer. There are beat pop singers and lyric pop singers. A lyric pop singer is one who tells a story. When he sings, he thinks about and cares about the words. I interpret both ways: lyric pop and beat." Died: 1994.

Bobby Vinton 🎙   6916 Hollywood

Singer
BORN April 16, 1935, in Canonsburg, PA. **SPOTLIGHTS** Known as the Polish Prince, he was considered the #1 love song singer. Vinton revealed, "I learned how to break into show business by watching the Elvis Presley movie *Jailhouse Rock* (1957). Anyone can watch it and learn how to press your own records, promote it, and get friendly with the disc jockeys." It worked for him; he sold millions of records. In 1962 he organized the four-piece band, the Bachelors. Female fans swooned over his romantic, entertaining style. Hit songs include: "Take Good Care of My Baby," "Roses Are Red (My Love)," and "No Arms Can Ever Hold You."

Veronica Lake 🎥   6916 Hollywood

Actress
BORN Constance Ocklem; Nov. 14, 1919, in Brooklyn, NY. **SPOTLIGHTS** She arrived in Los Angeles via the beauty contest circuit, and began performing in local plays. By 1939 she was doing bit parts in movies for RKO, MGM, and Paramount

Veronica Lake

Pictures. Her breakthrough role quickly followed in *I Wanted Wings* (1941), with Ray Milland and William Holden. After this film, Paramount signed the petite, husky-voiced blonde to a seven-year contract at $75-a-week. Lake was wonderful in Preston Sturges' savvy comedy, *Sullivan's Travels* (1941), opposite Joel McCrea. She was divine in the clever comedy *I Married a Witch* (1942) opposite Fredric March. The story is about a victim of the Salem witch hunts who comes back to haunt the descendants of those who burned her at the stake. Lake, though, was paired most successfully with Alan Ladd in *This Gun for Hire* and *The Glass Key* (both 1942), and *The Blue Dahlia* (1946). Lake was *the* 1940s screen vamp. **SIDELIGHTS** Her long, peek-a-boo hair style was copied by women across America, which caused unsightly accidents for female machinists in World War II defense factories. Because of these work injuries, the U.S. government asked Paramount to alter her hair style. In *So Proudly We Hail* (1943) she wore her hair in a tight bun. She was never truly popular after that. Died: 1973, from acute hepatitis.

Richard & Robert Sherman 🎥

Composers, lyricists   **6916 Hollywood**

BORN Richard M.; June 12,1928; Robert B.; Dec.19,1925, both in New York, NY. **SPOTLIGHTS** Hollywood's greatest and most dynamic brother song writing team. Talent runs in the family; they are the grandsons of Samuel Sherman, a concert master and first violinist in the Royal Court of the Emperor of Austria-Hungary. When Sherman immigrated to America, he discovered a country immersed in jazz and ragtime, not classical—his singular specialty. Disappointed in the music world, he did not want his son, Albert, to follow in his footsteps. Al, though, bought *Beyers Book for Beginners* and taught himself how to play the piano. By 1918, he had his own trio and was working alongside a young George Gershwin. Al Sherman became the noted Tin Pan Alley songwriter, who specialized in fun "word play songs." Sherman's hits include the songs, "(Ho Ho, Ha Ha) Me Too!" "On A Dew-Dew-Dewy Day," "On the Beach at Bali-Bali," "Pretending," and "(Five, Six, Seven, Eight) Nine Little Miles from Ten Ten Tennessee" which was one of Duke Ellington's first recordings. His happy 1930s novelty hit, "(Potatoes Are Cheaper - Tomatoes Are Cheaper) Now's the Time To Fall In Love" was made famous by Eddie Cantor, while a march called "Lindbergh, Eagle of the U.S.A." was played by John Philip Sousa. His "You've Gotta Be A Football Hero" has become a time-honored American sports tune. His sons, Richard and Robert Sherman,

Robert B. Sherman (left), Walt Disney and Richard M. Sherman

would soar to their own new musical heights. First, though, Robert enlisted in the Army and served bravely during WWII. He received the Purple Heart, the Combat Infantry Badge, and two battle stars. After his honorable discharge, he attended Bard College, in New York, in 1946 on the GI bill, and his younger brother Richard joined him there. They both graduated in 1949, and by 1951 were challenged by their father to write songs together. Five months later they sold their first popular song "Gold Can Buy Anything (But Love)." It was a country tune recorded by Gene Autry. Soon thereafter, during the Korean conflict, Richard enlisted in the Army. They reteamed in 1958. Richard and Robert Sherman wrote several Top Ten pop and rock 'n' roll hits, including Annette Funicello's "Tall Paul," and "Pineapple Princess," and Johnny Burnette's smash "You're Sixteen" (later recorded by Ringo Starr). Their work with Funicello brought them to the attention of Walt Disney. Disney himself appointed them his *only* full-time staff songwriters in 1960. Their work together was nothing short of magical. They created more than 150 splendid songs featured in 27 Disney films, two dozen TV productions, and Disney's theme parks worldwide. Their impressive and well-loved collection includes classic songs from Disney's masterpiece, *Mary Poppins* (1964): "Feed the Birds" (Walt Disney's favorite song), "A Spoonful of Sugar," "Let's Go Fly A Kite," "I Love to Laugh," and "Supercalifragilisticexpialidocious," among others. About their work, they said, "This is what we like to do—give people a chance to escape and forget their cares." Other motion picture scores—for Disney—include *The Parent Trap* (1961), *Summer Magic* (1963), *Jungle Book* (1967), *The Happiest Millionaire* (1967), *The Family Band* (1968), *The Aristocats* (1970), *Bedknobs and Broomsticks* (1971), and five *Winnie the Pooh* films (1966-2000). For a variety of studios, their movie musicals include *Chitty Chitty Bang Bang* (1968), *Snoopy Come Home* (1972), and *Charlotte's Web* (1973). They have also written the screenplays and scores for several films including *Tom Sawyer* (1973—the first American film to win the Best Music

Score at the Moscow Film Festival), *Huckleberry Finn* (1974), *The Slipper and the Rose* (1976—the Royal Command performance film in England), and *The Magic of Lassie* (1978). In all, they have more than 500 published and recorded songs, two Grammys, and 21 gold and platinum albums. **ACHIEVEMENTS** Nominated for nine Academy Awards, Richard M. and Robert B. Sherman have won two Oscars, for *Mary Poppins* Best Score, and Best Song: "Chim Chim Cheree." For their acceptance speech, they said, "There are no words. All we can say is supercalifragelisticexpialidocious." Since their song "It's A Small World (After All)" was introduced at the New York World's Fair in 1964-65 in a tribute to the children of the world for UNICEF (the United Nations Charity Organization), *it has become the most translated and performed song on earth.* (Also see the bios in this book of: Walt Disney, Roy O. Disney, Mickey Mouse, Snow White, and Annette Funicello.) Their spectacular autobiography, *Walt's Time* is a lavish, full-color memoir with 900 illustrations, never-before-seen photos, original Disney artwork and the lyrics to more than 75 Sherman Brothers hit songs. Write to: Camphor Tree Publishers, P.O. Box 800088, Santa Clarita, CA 91380-0088, or E-mail: info@camphortree.com **HIGHLIGHTS** The only brother song writing team to have a star on the Hollywood Walk of Fame, their dedication ceremony took place on Nov. 17, 1976. **QUOTE** "In our song score for *Mary Poppins*, we have a favorite line which is said by Mr. Banks in an unguarded and honest moment: 'A man has dreams of walking with giants, to carve his niche in the edifice of time.' We think that sums up the way we feel. We treasure our star on the Hollywood Walk of Fame."

Jeffrey Hunter ⚊ 6916 Hollywood

Jeffrey Hunter

Actor
BORN Henry McKinnies, Jr.; Nov. 25, 1925, in New Orleans, LA. **SPOTLIGHTS** A tall, dark-haired, handsome talent with All-American boy-next-door good looks, Hunter studied drama at UCLA's graduate level. He made his screen debut in *Call Me Mister* (1951), and was signed by 20th Century-Fox. During his busy movie career, he made more than 60 pictures, including *The Proud Ones* (1956), *King of Kings* (1961--as Jesus Christ), *The Last Hurrah* (1958), *Sergeant Rutledge* (1960), and *A Guide for the Married Man* (1967). TV movies: "The Empty Room," "The Secret Mission," and "The Man From Galveston." He starred in TV's Western series "Temple Houston" (1963-'64). Died: 1969, from complications stemming from brain surgery (brought on by an accidental fall).

Gary Collins ⚊ 6916 Hollywood

Gary Collins (left) with Ted Knight

Actor, host, singer
BORN April 30, 1938, in Los Angeles, CA. **SPOTLIGHTS** He played WWII Lieutenant Richard (Rip) Riddle in "The Wackiest Ship in the Army" (1965-'66). "The Iron Horse" put him in the Wild West of the 1880s as Dave Tarrant (1966-'68). He played Grill on the outstanding "Roots" mini-series (1977). He hosted daytime's "Hour Magazine" in the 1980s, and is also an accomplished lyric baritone. Married to a former Miss America, Mary Ann Mobley.

Sonny Burke ⚊ 6916 Hollywood

Band leader, composer
BORN March 22, 1914, in Scranton, PA. **SPOTLIGHTS** A graduate of Duke University, Burke first began playing the piano and violin at age five. He was arranger-conductor for Jimmy Dorsey and Charlie Spivak. He became an important figure in the recording and television fields. After he put his band leading days behind him, he switched to writing songs for singers such as Mel Torme. He produced for Frank Sinatra, including his challenging 1980 release *Trilogy: Past, Present, and Future.* (Released after his death.) His most popular tune was "Mambo Jambo." Died: 1979.

Ray Rennahan 🎥 6916 Hollywood

Cinematographer
BORN May 1, 1896, in Las Vegas, NV. **ACHIEVEMENTS** 1939 Academy Award for *Gone with the Wind*; 1941 Academy Award for *Blood and Sand* (shared). He was known for his brilliant composition. Died: 1980.

Peter Lawford ⚊ 6916 Hollywood

Actor
BORN Sept. 7, 1923, in England. **SPOTLIGHTS** He was a busy contract player with bobby sox appeal at MGM (1942-'52). But Lawford also possessed a poised elegance that enhanced such films as *Mrs. Miniver, Random Harvest* (both 1942), *The White Cliffs of Dover, The Canterville Ghost,* and *Mrs. Parkington* (all 1944), *Easter Parade* (1948), *Little Women* (1949), and *Ocean's 11* (1960--with Frank Sinatra's "Rat Pack Gang). He joined the ranks of other screen actors on "the boob tube" in "Dear Phoebe" (1954-'56), where he impersonates a

"female" columnist, and "The Thin Man" (1957-'59). **HIGHLIGHTS** Married Patricia Kennedy, sister of President JFK. Son of Lady May Somerville Lawford. Died: 1984.

Dionne Warwick 6920 Hollywood

Dionne Warwick

Singer
BORN Dec. 12, 1941, in East Orange, NJ. **SPOTLIGHTS** "I Say a Little Prayer for You," might have been inspired by her upbringing in a gospel-singing family. She grew into a tremendous singer, and teamed with composer Burt Bacharach and lyricist Hal David, the trio had a string of hits starting in 1962: "Don't Make Me Over," "Anyone Who Had a Heart," "Walk On By," and "You'll Never Get to Heaven." **ACHIEVEMENTS** 1969 Grammy, "Do You Know the Way to San Jose?"; 1979 "I'll Never Love This Way Again," and "Deja Vu"; the first woman to win awards simultaneously in both pop and rhythm-and-blues.

Tennessee Ernie Ford 6920 Hollywood

See page 130

Aretha Franklin 6920 Hollywood

Aretha Franklin

Singer
BORN March 25, 1942, in Memphis, TN. **SPOTLIGHTS** Called the "Queen of Soul," and "Lady Soul," she is one of America's greatest singers. As a child, she sang gospel with her parents. Her father, the Reverend C. L. Franklin (pastor of Detroit's New Bethel Baptist Church) was known as "the Man with the Million-Dollar Voice." Aretha's duets with her mother, Barbara, abruptly ended when Barbara abandoned her husband, her children, and six-year-old Aretha. The family found strength in the church; eight years later, the teen would record her first album there. By the mid-Sixties Aretha had come into her own. Blending the gospel music on which she was weaned with the inventiveness of jazz, the sensuality of Rhythm & Blues and the energy of pop, she recorded such spectacular songs as: "Respect," "Baby I Love You," "Chain of Fools," and "Since You've Been Gone." In the 1970s: "Bridge Over Troubled Waters," "Spanish Harlem," "Day Dreaming," and "Until You Come Back to me (That's What I'm Gonna Do)." She made a cameo appearance in *The Blues Brothers* (1980), where she performed two of her songs, along with appearances made by James Brown and Cab Calloway. 1980s albums include *Jump to It, Who's Zoomin' Who,* and *Aretha.* Her gospel roots blossomed into *One Lord, One Faith, One Baptism.* **ACHIEVEMENTS** 15 Grammys. In 1987 Miss Franklin became the First Woman to be inducted into the Rock and Roll Hall of Fame. She has had more million-sellers than any woman in recording history.

James Cruze 6922 Hollywood

Director, producer
BORN March 27, 1884, in Ogden, UT. **SPOTLIGHTS** Born to Mormon parents, as a child actor he traveled far and wide with David Belasco's theatrical company. In 1908 he opted for a film career in acting, when movies were considered a passing fad. Within ten years he became a giant directing silents at Paramount Pictures, working with comedian Fatty Arbuckle. Next, Cruze succeeded with an important historical Western, *The Covered Wagon* (1923). It influenced all future Westerns. He made such major productions as *Merton of the Movies* (1924), and *The Pony Express* (1925). Yet due to a poor business decision on his part, he left Paramount to form his own company. Without the huge resources behind him, he never could sink his teeth big time into talkies. He managed to team up with the major studios for a couple of movies, including Fox's *Mr. Skitch* (1933) and *David Harum* (1934), both starring Will Rogers. Died: 1942.

The Harlem Globetrotters 6922 Hollywood

Basketball team
SPOTLIGHTS Known as the "Clown Princes" of basketball—although the team does have female members—their TV break came on "The Ed Sullivan Show" in 1954. The sports drama *Go, Man, Go!* (1954), starring Sidney Poitier and Dane Clark, is a wonderful story of the beginnings of this African-American comic sports team. Poitier also co-produced the movie. Their "live" appearances in 150 countries have been seen by more than 250 million spectators. There have been dozens of team players during the last four decades. They are always a terrific crack up and can entertain with a basketball, even if you don't like the sport.

Eugene Ormandy 6922 Hollywood

Conductor, violinist
BORN Eugene Blau; Nov. 18, 1899, in Budapest, Hungary. **SPOTLIGHTS** A child prodigy who, by age three, was already an accomplished violinist. When asked by his dentist father what he wanted to be when he grew up, the youngster replied,

Eugene Ormandy

"To be a *Wundermann*." He arrived in America in 1920 with plenty of talent, but no money. He found a position with a theatre orchestra in New York, and scored success as a radio conductor. To those who were aghast that a man of his great talent would work in radio, he replied, "Don't be superior about radio. Be thankful down on your knees that it has brought a whole new audience to music." He enjoyed a brilliant conducting career with various organizations. Ormandy became a conductor of the Philadelphia Orchestra in 1936 and remained a force for nearly 50 years. He was well-known as an interpreter of Romantic works, and for his variety of music in program balance. **ACHIEVEMENTS** 1967 Grammy, classic performance. **QUOTE** "A program must be made up of important and significant music, but there has to be in every program something an audience can hum on its way home." Died: 1985.

Max Factor 🎥   6922 Hollywood

Cosmetician, makeup artist, manufacturer

Max Factor and Carole Lombard

BORN Max Faktor; Aug. 5, 1877, in Poland. **SPOTLIGHTS** A brilliant pioneer in the beauty industry, he coined the word "makeup." Early Hollywood film stars flocked to Factor for special makeup techniques and improved cosmetics. Factor created, for the first time, thin greasepaint in 12 different shades, followed by "sanitary" greasepaint in a tube (not a jar). He also created color harmony, a principle that established for the first time that certain combinations of a woman's complexion, hair, and eye coloring were most effectively complemented by specific makeup shades. Other products include "pancake makeup" for color motion pictures, which worked so well it quickly became the standard. He personally made up the most beautiful faces in Hollywood. Name any great beauty; Max Factor created her look! After his death, his son--MF, Jr.--who had worked at his side his entire life assumed his father's position. Today, Procter & Gamble carries on the tradition of excellence in beauty products bearing the creator's name. **RECOMMENDED** *Max Factor: Hollywood's 100 Greatest Beauty Secrets and Celebrity Stories* by Samantha Hart. Regarding the world as a stage, this indispensable book documents how the heroes and villains, and the winners and losers were created by the legendary Max Factor, Makeup King to the Stars. From Hollywood's earliest accounts of the stars through the Golden Era, from its black and white silent days to its stunning Technicolor glory, each chapter reflects not only a great deal about the growing entertainment industry, but how entertainment has evolved. The world's biggest stars--from Valentino to Jean Harlow, Clark Gable to Rita Hayworth--the moguls and their studios, all turned to Max Factor to set the standard of appearance, as did the world at large. One of the most powerful men in Hollywood, this book reveals original makeup recipes, Max Factor's theories on color, beauty, behind-the-scenes revelations, and more (visit the website: www.hollywoodfame.com). The beloved makeup genius died in 1938.

Eleanor Boardman 🎥   6922 Hollywood

Actress

BORN Aug. 19, 1898, in Philadelphia, PA. **SPOTLIGHTS** This beauty first came to the public's attention as the Eastman Kodak's "Kodak Girl." The popular poster girl was seen everywhere. She stars in one of the first realistic screen dramas, MGM's *The Crowd* (1928). It was co-written and directed by future husband King Vidor. She was one of MGM's top leading women in movie's early days. Died: 1991.

Billy Barty 📺   6922 Hollywood

Actor

BORN Oct. 25, 1924, in Millsboro, PA. **SPOTLIGHTS** Barty began in show business at age three portraying Mickey Rooney's baby brother in the "Mickey McGuire" comedy film shorts (2-reelers). He worked in the series for a number of years, then made his feature film debut in *Gold Diggers of 1933*. He appears in 200 films, including *A Midsummer's Night Dream* (1935), *Nothing Sacred* (1937), *The Clown* (1957), *Billy Rose's Jumbo* (1962), *The Day of the Locust* (1975), *Foul Play* (1978), Ridley Scott's *Legend* (1986), *Rumpelstiltskin* (1987—title role), and Mel Brooks' *Life Stinks* (1991). Of his more recent works, Barty liked making the fast-paced, sci-fi fantasy picture, *Willow* (1988). In it, he plays the leader of the village. He remarked, "It was not a large part, but it was an important role, and I enjoyed working with director Ron Howard and producer George Lucas." **TV** This gifted actor entered television in its early years of development dating back to 1948. From 1950 to '52 he appeared in such programs as "James Melton's Ford Festival" and "Milton Berle's Texaco Star Theater." Barty stated that "one of my all-time favorite television roles was in Alfred Hitchcock's 'The Glass Eye.' I co-star with Jessica Tandy and Tom Conway. Conway plays the ventriloquist, and I play the dummy. In the end, it is revealed that I am really the ventriloquist and he is the dummy." Barty has appeared regularly in a number of television variety shows as well as in hundreds of guest spots. He starred or appeared in

Billy Barty

feature roles in several series, including his popular role as Little Tom, on "Circus Boy" (1956-'58) and Inch, owner of the shanty bar, on "Ace Crawford, Private Eye" (1983). This "little giant," a 3-foot 9-inch, 80-pound talent, is a beloved and world-renowned activist on behalf of the world's "little people." **ACHIEVEMENTS** In 1957 he founded of Little People of America. In 1975 he established The Billy Barty Foundation. During the past 42 years, his efforts have helped more than 1.5 million educationally, vocationally and psychologically. In the 1990s, Los Angeles Mayor Richard Riordan appointed Billy Barty to the City Commission on Disability; County Supervisor Mike Antonovich to the county commission on disability. **QUOTE** "After 70 years in the motion picture industry, it is an honor to be recognized with a star on Hollywood's Walk of Fame."

Alice Faye 🎥   6922 Hollywood

Actress, singer, dancer

BORN Alice Jeanne Leppert; May 5, 1912, in Hell's Kitchen, NY. **SPOTLIGHTS** A friendly, sentimental girl, she was discovered by crooner Rudy Vallee while singing at a party. He launched this luscious cutie-beauty in her musical film career by demanding that she get the lead in George White's *Scandals* (1934). With her blonde hair that turned a glistening pale by the hot, bright klieg lights, and her navy blue eyes that sparkled and radiated pure joy, Faye became "Queen of 20th Century-Fox musicals" during the 1930s and '40s. Faye sang in a silky, deep-throated style, and introduced to America the romantic love tunes "You'll Never Know," "I've Got My Love to Keep Me Warm," and "This Year's Kisses." An accomplished

Alice Faye

dancer, as well as a notorious giggler when the cameras were not rolling, Faye got along famously with her frequent co-star—the world's biggest movie star—Shirley Temple. Hits they made together include *Poor Little Rich Girl* (1936—with the delightful, precision tap number "I Love a Military Man" with Temple dancing between Faye and Jack Haley), and *Stowaway* (1936). Other co-stars also found Faye to have a pleasant personality and be completely professional when it was time to work. Among her

many credits are *Sing, Baby, Sing* (1936), *Alexander's Ragtime Band* (1938), *In Old Chicago* (1938), *Sally, Irene and Mary* (1938), *Tin Pan Alley* (1940), *Lillian Russell* (1940), and *That Night in Rio* (1941). She retired, for the most part, after her marriage to band leader Phil Harris in 1941, although they did do a radio show together. Occasionally, she returned to Fox Studios do make a movie, including *State Fair* (1962). Died: 1998.

Bill Cosby 📺   6922 Hollywood

Actor, comedian, author, producer

Bill Cosby

BORN July 12, 1938, in Philadelphia, PA. **SPOTLIGHTS** An American treasure. A legendary storyteller. One of America's great humorists. Blessed with the gift of comedy, in his youth Cosby practiced routines on his encouraging and appreciative mother. The jokes and gags revolved around everyday household happenings—a recurring theme that would appear in his later career. He grew up in the projects in Philadelphia, with pals Fat Albert, Old Weird Harold, Dumb Donald, and Weasel—friends who would be immortalized in Cosby's hilarious comedy routines. A natural born athlete, he pursued sports over academics. Still, Cosby's sixth grade teacher must have sensed his genius when she wrote in his report card, "Williams is a boy's boy, an all-around fellow, and he should grow up to do great things." He left his junior year at high school to join the Navy. During the service, he earned his degree via a correspondence course. After his honorable discharge, he attended Temple University on an athletic scholarship, this time also earning academic honors. A superb football player who could have possibly gone pro, Cosby originally planned to become a physical education teacher. To support himself during his college days, he tended bar at night, where he found a primed audience for his brand of home-grown humor. His customers convinced him to give stand-up comedy a try. His first stage appearance was at a night spot called "The Underground" in a small room named "the Cellar." It did not have a stage, so he sat on a chair that had been placed on top of a table. He could not stand up because of his height, so it was joked he was the world's first "sit-down" comedian. Cosby's urban act elaborated on his youth in Philly, where "two guys on the block shared one broken-down auto, crashed parties, cowered from trouble, and constantly scrimped around to raise the 19 cents they needed for gas for their car and the 14 dollars they needed for oil." Instead of using vulgarity to get a laugh, Cosby's wry wit, storytelling skills and great comic timing won him legions of fans. He made $5-a-night and packed them in until "The Gaslight" in New York's Greenwich Village hired him away at $60-a-week. From there, he hit all the top clubs in the country, where America first fell in love with him. They came to know the comedian with the flexible, expressive face, large, beautiful, dark twinkling eyes that twinkled and dazzling smile. When performing live, his great gift is rapport with the audience. He said, "I feel that in-person contact with people is the most important thing in comedy. While I'm up on stage, I can actually put myself into the audience and adjust my pace and timing to them. I can get into their heads through their ears and through their eyes. Only through this total communication can I really achieve what I'm trying to do." This comic genius ironically broke new ground when he was the first African-American male to have a regular starring role, as a professional, not a flunky, in a weekly dramatic television series. He starred in the adventure show, "I Spy" (1965-'68), as secret agent Alexander Scott, scoring a major breakthrough for all African-American actors. This multi-Emmy Award winning actor has had four "Cosby" incarnations. First he played coach Chet Kincaid on "The Bill Cosby Show" (1969-'71). Second, he had a variety program called "The New Bill Cosby Show" (1972-'73). Third, he portrayed nice guy and terrific, lovable, but no-nonsense dad, Dr. Heathcliff (Cliff) Huxtable, on "The Cosby Show" (1984-'92). "The Cosby Show" is one of television's all-time most successful and popular family sitcoms. At its peak, more than half of America tuned in to watch the show! It was a phenomenon that rescued the genre of situation-comedy from the intensive care unit, and single-handedly helped propel NBC network into first place during the 1980s (a position that NBC has been able to hold onto through the late 1990s). His fourth sitcom, "Cosby" (1996-) airs on CBS, as does his Friday prime time family show, "Kids Say the Darndest Things," where he interviews children with oftentimes side-splitting results. Cosby has also made numerous specials. Cosby made his motion picture debut in the post-Civil War family drama *Man and Boy* (1972). That same year he re-teamed with his "I Spy" co-star Robert Culp, in *Hickey and Boggs*. Other movies include *Mother, Jugs and Speed* (1976) with Raquel Welch, *California Suite* (1978) with Richard Pryor, *Bill Cosby—Himself* (1982—concert film), *Meteor Man* (1993) with Robert Townsend, and *Jack* (1996) opposite Robin Williams. He co-stars with Sidney Poitier in three films, *Uptown Saturday Night* (1974—also with Harry Belafonte), its sequel *Let's Do It Again* (1975), and *A Piece of the Action* (1977). **ACHIEVEMENTS** Cosby is the recipient of hundreds of awards and honors. In 1998 he received the prestigious Kennedy Center Honor. Emmy-nominated eight times (it would have been more but he took himself out of the running during his highly popular Cosby television series), he won four Emmy Awards. He has won more than two dozen People's Choice Awards. Nominated for 17 Grammys, he has taken nine home. He earned a Master of Education degree (M.Ed.) in 1972, and his Doctorate in Education (Ed.D.) in 1977 from the University of Massachusetts. He and his wife, the former Camille Hanks, generously support many institutions of high-er education with considerable endowments, as well as their involvement with many other charities for social services and civil rights. Cosby is the best-selling comedian of all time on records. During the mid-1960s, he had as many as six albums on the charts at one time. Ten of Cosby's albums went Gold and five have been certified Platinum. He has earned seven Grammy Awards for best comedy album (and two others for best recording for children). His first success began with "Bill Cosby Is A Very Funny Fellow, Right?" On Geffen Records, he released "Those Of You With or Without Children, You'll Understand," sold close to a million copies, an almost unheard of phenomenon for a comedy record. He has also released a number of jazz recordings, including "hello, friend; to ennis with love" (1997). In 1986, he broke New York's famed Radio City Music Hall's attendance record for his concert appearance. He is the author of numerous best-selling books including *Fatherhood* (the fastest selling hard-cover book of all time), *Time Flies* (the largest single first printing in publishing history at 1.75 million copies), *Little Bill* (a book series designed to encourage literacy for children ages six through ten), *Love and Marriage*, *Childhood*, and *Congratulations! Now What? A Book for Graduates* (1999, published by Hyperion). **QUOTE** He received his Walk of Fame star on Nov. 23, 1977. At the ceremony, Cosby flashed his trademark grin, then took a wad of chewing gum out of his mouth, dropped it on his star, stepped on it, and remarked, "I wanted to be the first one to do that."

Carole Lombard 🎥　6922 Hollywood

Carole Lombard

Actress

BORN Jane Peters; Oct. 6, 1908, in Fort Wayne, IN. **SPOTLIGHTS** One of the finest comediennes to ever grace the silver screen, Lombard achieved goddess status in the glorious screwball comedies of the 1930s. Motion pictures include *Now and Forever* (1934) with Shirley Temple and Gary Cooper, *Twentieth Century* (1934) co-starring John Barrymore (who said of her, "She is perhaps the greatest actress I ever worked with"), *Hands Across the Table* (1935) with Fred MacMurray, *My Man Godfrey* (1936), opposite her real-life ex-husband William Powell, *Nothing Sacred* (1937) opposite Fredric March, Hitchcock's *Mr. and Mrs. Smith* (1941) with Robert Montgomery, and *To Be or Not to Be* (1942) co-starring Jack Benny. **HIGHLIGHTS** Married to actor William Powell (1931-'33) and Clark Gable (1939 until her death)...Fox dropped her $75-a-week contract in 1926 after she was in an automobile accident. Her subsequent plastic surgery, however, worked, and she looked as lovely as ever. In 1930 Paramount signed her to a seven-year contract. Died:

1942 in a plane crash while returning from a U.S. War Bond-selling tour of the Midwest. Clark Gable was originally requested to sell the bonds, but since his wife was a better saleswoman—and they wanted to make as much money as possible for the war effort—Lombard went in his place. Clark Gable never truly recovered from this major loss and tragic irony. He wished over and over again that he would have gone in her place as originally planned.

Bette Midler 🎙   6930 Hollywood

Bette Midler

Singer, actress, writer
BORN Dec. 1, 1945, in Honolulu, HI. (Her mother named her after Bette Davis.) **SPOTLIGHTS** Star of stage and screen, Midler initially gained recognition as an outrageously wacky, campy, bawdy and spontaneous entertainer at Manhattan's Continental Baths (yes, a bathhouse). Overflowing with wit, humor and *talent*, she became a popular nightclub entertainer, accomplished stage actress, and a successful recording artist. This energetic performer has won admiration worldwide. She has made close to two dozen albums. Her debut album—*The Divine Miss M*—went gold, winning her the coveted Grammy for the Best New Artist in 1972. But the title of her comedy album, *Mud Will be Flung Tonight!*, reveals her joy in lampooning life. As an actress, though, Midler is gifted with drama, too. She gives a riveting performance in her debut film, *The Rose* (1979). The picture, loosely based on singer Janis Joplin's life, earned Midler an Oscar nomination, and the album of the same title went platinum. But Midler quickly learned how fickle Hollywood could be when her second film, *Jinxed!* (1982), was just that. The Divine Miss M took a break from the silver screen and journeyed on a very successful, re-energizing world tour to sold-out audiences. She surprised critics and delighted fans with subsequent movies. Adept in comedy and drama, films include *Down and Out in Beverly Hills* (1986), *Ruthless People* (1986), *Outrageous Fortune* (1987), *Beaches* (1988), *Big Business* (1988), *For the Boys* (1991), *Gypsy* (1993), *Hocus Pocus* (1993), *Get Shorty* (1995), *The First Wives Club* (1996), *Isn't She Great* (2000), and *Drowning Mona* (2000). Any TV special she puts her personal stamp on is guaranteed to be great. After years of releases, "Wind Beneath My Wings" became her very first #1 hit. Another ballad, "From a Distance" also topped the charts. **ACHIEVE-MENTS** Four Grammys, two Emmys, a recipient of a Tony, and two Golden Globes. The Divine Miss M broke the box-office record at Radio City Music Hall, exceeding $11 million dollars during a 30-show run. That was the highest-grossing continuous concert engagement by a single

touring artist in one venue...She penned two best-selling books...She received her Walk of Fame star on Feb. 6, 1986. **QUOTE** In 1980, before marriage and motherhood, she talked *about her fans* stating, "In some strange way, they give—to me—meaning. I always feel more solid, more real, when they're around. They make me think that maybe there is more to me than I know." After her marriage and birth of their daughter, family became her #1 priority, offering new levels of joy and fulfillment.

George E. Stone 🎥   6930 Hollywood

George E. Stone

Actor
BORN George Stein; May 23, 1903, in Lodz, Poland. **SPOTLIGHTS** A shrewd, tough-looking character, his nicknames were: Toothpick Charlie, Society Max, and Georgie-Boy. He made his screen debut as a sewer rat in *Seventh Heaven* (1927). This dark-haired, dark-eyed supporting actor often played big-time criminals, and made 200 films. Another nickname—the Runt—came from the *Boston Blackie* series. Movies include *Little Caesar* (1931), *Five Star Final* (1931), *Viva Villa!* (1934), *The Racket* (1951), *Scared Stiff* (1953), *Guys and Dolls* (1955), *Some Like it Hot* (1959), and *Pocketful of Miracles* (1961). Died: 1967.

Mickey Gilley 🎙   6930 Hollywood

Singer, songwriter, pianist
BORN March 9, 1937, in Natchez, LA. **SPOTLIGHTS** With his boogie woogie piano style and open-faced good looks, Gilley had his first country hit with "Now I Can Live Again" in 1968. He successfully rerecorded the old George Morgan song, "Roomful of Roses," then hit again with "I Overlooked an Orchid," "City Lights," "Window Up Above," and "Don't the Girls Get Prettier at Closing Time." He remade Sam Cooke's "Bring It on Home to Me," and had more winners with "She's Pulling Me Back Again," "Here Comes the Hurt Again," "True Love Ways," "Stand By Me," "That's All That Matters," "A Headache Tomorrow (Or a Heartache Tonight)," "You Don't Know Me," "Lonely Nights," "Put Your Dreams Away," and "Talk to Me." **SIDELIGHTS** First cousin of famous singer Jerry Lee Lewis, and cousin of TV evangelist Jimmy Swaggart. Owned the world's largest honky-tonk, Gilley's, in Texas. Not only did Mickey Gilley himself symbolize the "Urban Cowboy" era, but his honky-tonk provided the setting for the movie *Urban Cowboy* (1980), starring John Travolta and Debra Winger. Gilley's became a worldwide tourist attraction until the Urban Cowboy fad ended at the end of the 1980s. It closed

and eventually burned down. Mickey Gilley, however, moved on to Branson, Missouri, where he owns a club and restaurant.

Richard Denning   6932 Hollywood

Richard Denning

Actor

BORN Louis A. Denninger; March 27, 1914, in Poughkeepsie, NY. **SPOTLIGHTS** A handsome, open-faced actor of 200 motion pictures. Denny made a variety of films, both "A" and "B" flicks, including *Million Dollar Legs*, *Union Pacific* (both 1939), *Geronimo, Golden Gloves, North West Mounted Police* (all 1940), *Adam Had Four Sons* (1941), *Black Beauty* (1946), *Unknown Island* (1948), *The Glass Web* (1953), *The Creature from the Black Lagoon* (1954), *Creature with the Atom Brain* (1955), *The Day the World Ended* (1956), *An Affair to Remember* (1957), and *I Sailed to Tahiti with an All-Girl Crew* (1969). He turned to TV with great success, as the publisher-turned-detective in the popular comedy-mystery "Mr. and Mrs. North" (1952-'54), "The Flying Doctor," and "Michael Shayne." He played Governor Philip Grey in the long-running police drama, "Hawaii Five-O" (1968-'80).

Dennis Weaver   6930 Hollywood

Dennis Weaver

Actor, singer, songwriter

BORN June 4, 1924, in Joplin, MO. **SPOTLIGHTS** A former collegiate track and field star, Weaver placed sixth in the decathlon at the U.S. national try-outs for the Olympic Games. Next, he became a Navy pilot. After his honorable discharge, he was accepted at New York's famous Actors Studio. He concentrated his talents onstage for several years, enjoyed success on Broadway, but became best known in television. His role as Chester in TV's longest-running Western series "Gunsmoke," made him a household name. A tall, lanky actor with a trustworthy face and pleasant heartland twang, he won America's admiration. He has starred for more than a quarter of a century in a number of TV series, including "Kentucky Jones," "Stone," and "Emerald Point, NAS." Motion pictures include *Mississippi Gambler* (1953), *Seven Angry Men* (1955), *Duel at Diablo* (1966) with James Garner and Sidney Poitier, and *Gentle Giant* (1967—it inspired the

family drama television series, "Gentle Ben," which Weaver also starred in). He has starred in a number of noteworthy TV movies: "Cocaine: One Man's Seduction," "The Ordeal of Patty Hearst," "The Ordeal of Dr. Mudd," and "A Winner Never Quits." He has written more than 75 songs. **ACHIEVEMENTS** 1959 Emmy for his role on "Gunsmoke." He was nominated for three Emmys for his own series "McCloud." He has been inducted into the Cowboy Hall of Fame. Weaver has made a strong commitment to world peace, the ending of hunger and homelessness in America, drug abuse prevention, and is one of the founders of Life (Love Is Feeding Everyone).

Ethel Clayton   6930 Hollywood

Actress

BORN 1884, in Champaign, IL. **SPOTLIGHTS** This lovely lady stars in "women's" films: *A Woman's Way* (1916) and *Women and Money* (1919). Died: 1966.

Stan Chambers   6930 Hollywood

Newscaster, special events coverage

BORN Aug. 11, in Los Angeles, CA. **SPOTLIGHTS** He signed on with Los Angeles TV station KTLA two months after its inception (March, 1947). Working daily with fellow Walk of Famer Gene Autry (who owned the station)—and friends Johnny Grant and Hal Fishman (who also have stars on the celebrated Walk of Fame), Chambers covered the 1952 atom bomb blast in Nevada; the bloody Watts riots in 1965; and the big, destructive earthquake of 1994. He continuously tackles challenging stories. Highly acclaimed and respected. He advises aspiring broadcasters, "It's one of the most rewarding fields, but there are many hurdles to overcome; be persistent." **ACHIEVEMENTS** 1987, Los Angeles Press Club Award; numerous Emmys. 1994, wrote his interesting autobiography, *Fifty Years with Stan Chambers—News at Ten*. Here's a quote from his book about the big earthquake: "In the blinding blackness of 4:31 AM January 17, 1994, a terrifying rumble roared up from the ground. It was as if demonic hands grabbed the eaves of the house and tried to rip it apart and yank it from its concrete foundation. As if, in a fit of rage, the giant of the night shook it viciously. I knew it would be only a moment before the shuddering walls, shattering glass, and the creaking, moaning roof would crash down upon me. My wife did the only sensible thing, she pulled the covers up over her head."

Elton Britt   6930 Hollywood

Singer, guitarist

BORN James Britt Baker; July 7, 1917, in Marshall, AR. **SPOTLIGHTS** Talent scouts discovered the half-Cherokee, half-Irish 15-year-old plowing a field. A premier yodeler, he became a country superstar of the 1940s. Hits include: "Wave to Me, My Lady," "Chime Bells," "Candy Kisses," and "I Hung My

Head and Cried." Duets with Rosalie Allen are "Beyond the Sunset" and "Quicksilver." During WWII he recorded the patriotic tune, "There's a Star Spangled Banner Waving Somewhere," earning his first gold record. He recorded 56 albums. Died: 1972.

Chad Everett 📺   6930 Hollywood

Actor
BORN Raymond Cramton; June 11, 1936, in South Bend, IN.
SPOTLIGHTS Everett possesses bright, beautiful aquamarine eyes, and with his heady good looks easily leads in dreamy, romantic roles. But he is also good in light comedy, and has some outstanding dramatic performances under his belt. Like Cary Grant, Everett ages beautifully. He enjoys a high popularity standing in television; with millions of fans eager to see what he will do next. He starred in four TV series, including "The Dakotas" (1963) and "Medical Center" (1969-'76).

During the 1980s he worked on "Hagen," and "The Rousters" series. Motion pictures include *The Singing Nun* (1965), and *Made in Paris* (1966). He gives an impressive psychological performance in the war drama, *First to Fight* (1967), and is interesting to watch in the Western, *The Last Challenge* (1967). Other movies include *Airplane II: the Sequel* (1982), and *Heroes Stand Alone* (1989). Everett is an accomplished stage performer.

Chad Everett

Stan Chambers covering the annual Tournament of Roses Parade, in Pasadena, California.

*Real estate developer/club owner Daniel Fitzgerald
and the fabulous Dionne Warwick*

*Walk of Fame Honorees: Jack Haley (left),
Rochelle Hudson and Arthur Treacher*

The Dead End Kids

7000 HOLLYWOOD

The Mills Brothers 🎵 7000 Hollywood

Singers

BORN Harry, Aug. 19, 1913; Donald, April 29, 1915; Herbert, April 2, 1912; and John, Jr., date unknown; all in Piqua, OH. Their father, John, Sr., Feb. 11, 1882, in Bellafonte, PA. **SPOTLIGHTS** Mellow harmony was this family's vocal trademark. Their successful career spanned decades, transcending the big band era, early rock 'n' roll, and pop. The terrific guitarist Norman Brown joined the group in 1936, and stayed through '69. Hit songs include "Lazy River," "Paper Doll," and "Glow Worm." They made many film and television appearances. **ACHIEVEMENTS** They were the first African American group heard nationwide on network radio—hired by CBS—in 1929. **SIDELIGHTS** John, Sr. joined the group when Jr. died. Then Sr. retired in 1957 after a leg amputation. Died: John, Jr., 1935; John, Sr., 1967; Harry, 1982.

Guy Mitchell 🎵 7000 Hollywood

Singer, actor

BORN Al Cernik; Feb. 27, 1925, in Detroit, MI. **SPOTLIGHTS** A former child star with Warner Bros, his recording career went big during the 1950s. Hits include "Singing the Blues," "My Heart Cries for You," "The Roving Kind" and "My Truly Truly Fair" (the last two with Mitch Miller's orchestra). This handsome baritone had his own musical variety program, "The Guy Mitchell Show" on ABC-TV. In the early 1960s, he co-starred with Audie Murphy in the Western detective show "Whispering Smith." The hit series used actual crime cases from police files out of Denver, Colorado dating back to the 1870s. Mitchell broke his shoulder after only seven episodes and the show was postponed.

Arthur Cohn 🎥 7000 Hollywood

Producer

BORN Feb. 4, 1941, in Basel, Switzerland. **SPOTLIGHTS** This elegant, but dynamic Swiss gentleman is one of the most successful independent producers of all time. He is the only producer in Hollywood history to be honored with five Academy Awards. In Europe, he has made memorable films with Vittorio de Sica, but has also discovered new talents such as French director Jean-Jacques Annaud. Cohn makes most of his films outside the U.S., but his sensitive pictures have gotten their big boost, both critically and at the box office, in America. Due to their popularity in the States, Cohn has been able to find distributors throughout the world. His motion pictures are unusual by Hollywood standards. They are intimate and personal and brave. Great care is taken in character development. He is a storyteller extraordinaire, no matter the genre, language or country. They are meaningful pictures that illuminate our times. For this reason, Cohn's exquisite productions have earned generous welcome and high praise at major international film festivals. But, they are more than cinema art pictures. They are major motion pictures that have found appreciative audiences around the globe. **ACHIEVEMENTS** Academy Awards include *Sky Above, Mud Below* (1963); *The Garden of the Finzi-Continis* (1973); *Black and White in Colour* (1978); *Foolish Immortals/La Diagonale du Fou* (1986); and *American Dream* (1991). His Brazilian motion picture, *Central Station* (1998), was Oscar-nominated as the "Best Foreign-Language Film." His

Arthur Cohn (right) and Al Pacino

production of *One Day in September* (2000), narrated by Michael Douglas, received high praise from critics and the public alike. Cohn was honored by the French Government with the Cultural Order *Commandant des Arts et des Lettres*—the highest title bestowed on non-French citizens. The prestigious Boston University honored Cohn with the *Doctor Honoris Causa*, the only film producer in its entire history to receive this title. His Hollywood Walk of Fame star, sponsored by Tichi and Arthur M. Kassel, was dedicated on Nov. 17, 1992. Hundreds showed up to celebrate Cohn's landmark tribute. By reputation, he is one of the most respected and widely admired producers in the international film community. **QUOTE** Cohn continually makes courageous decisions by choosing an actor based on talent, instead of fame. He allows relatively unknown talents to take on great movie roles. He declared, "I cast a film to be believable, not for the box office." His judgment and knowledge are impeccable, as evidenced by the number of Academy Awards and honors he has received.

Pauline Frederick 🎥 7000 Hollywood

Actress

BORN Beatrice Libbey; Aug. 12, 1883, in Boston, MA. **SPOTLIGHTS** A silent movie actress, she appears in *Slave Island* (1917), *A Slave of Vanity* (1920), and *Devil's Island* (1926). Died: 1938.

Jack Valenti 🎥 7000 Hollywood

Executive, author,

BORN Sept. 5, 1921, in Houston, TX. **SPOTLIGHTS** Elected as president of the Motion Picture Association of America in 1966, he has been the esteemed leader and spokesman for the organized American film production and distribution industry for more than three decades. His territories include the U.S. and more than 100 countries where American films are distributed. A true diplomat, he has negotiated film treaties and

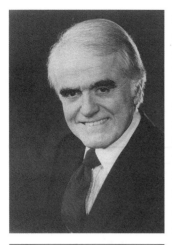

Jack Valenti

settled film issues with presidents, prime ministers and cabinet ministers of governments worldwide. To help audiences understand a movie's content, he created and implemented the movie rating system in use today. One of the busiest showmen in the world, he is much sought after for his extensive knowledge and valuable insight of the movie business. **ACHIEVEMENTS** A Harvard University graduate (M.B.A.), he became special assistant to the President of the United States during the Johnson administration. His intimate account of LBJ's White House is entitled *A Very Human President*. He is also the author of *Speak Up with Confidence: How to Prepare, Learn and Deliver an Effective* Speech, and *The Bitter Taste of Glory*. In 1988, he was honored as the Motion Picture Pioneer of the Year. **HIGHLIGHTS** His Hollywood Walk of Fame star was unveiled on Nov. 1, 1988. On hand for his dedication ceremony were Gregory Peck, Kirk Douglas, Arnold Schwarzenegger, Robert Wagner, Charlton Heston, Angie Dickinson and many of the industry's top executives such as Lew Wasserman, Robert Daly, Terry Semel and David Matalon. The significant date marked the 20th anniversary of the Valenti ratings for movies—G, PG, R and X.

Julie London ● 7000 Hollywood

Singer, actress

BORN Julie Peck; Sept. 26, 1926, in Santa Rosa, CA. **SPOTLIGHTS** A sensuous blues singer, her rendition of "Cry Me a River" turned audiences' eyes into the Blue Danube. She ventured into films in *The Great Man* (1956) with Jose Ferrer, *Drango* (1957) with Jeff Chandler, *Man of the West* (1958) opposite Gary Cooper, and *Voice in the Mirror* (1959) with Richard Egan. She also wrote the title song for the latter picture, but remarked, "Nobody believes I did it. They think composer Bobby Troup wrote it." She appeared as a guest in TV with Perry Como, and Steve Allen, among others. Her biggest album *Julie is Her Name* sold like hotcakes, especially to teenagers, who liked her offbeat, hip personality. **QUOTE** "I'm usually cast as a girl with a problem. So with all my films I'm trying to do all the social problems."

Stephen J. Cannell 📺 7000 Hollywood

Writer, producer, novelist

BORN Feb. 5, 1942, in Pasadena, CA. **SPOTLIGHTS** "I was told from first grade on that I was the stupidest kid in the class. I was trying to do well, but the teachers thought I wasn't," Cannell painfully recalled. He repeated second grade, and was flunked by an English teacher because he could not spell. School was a constant battle for him, but he excelled in athletics and won a football scholarship to the University of Oregon,

Stephen J. Cannell receives the America Star Award.

in Eugene. While taking a creative writing class he discovered his gift in crafting stories. Persistent enough to get what he wanted out of life, he began writing. In 1968 he got his breakthrough selling a script for a police show called "Adam-12." He became a television story editor, then skyrocketed as a creator. He created 30 prime time TV series during the 1970s, '80s and '90s including "The Rockford Files," "Baretta," "Baa Baa Black Sheep," "Hunter," and "Wiseguy," "The Greatest American Hero," "The A-Team," "Hardcastle and McCormick," "Renegade" and "Silk Stalkings." He is also an accomplished novelist. **SIDELIGHTS** It was not until 1981 when his daughter exhibited academic difficulties, that the disorder called dyslexia was mentioned. The doctors tested Cannell for the learning disability, too. The results revealed—for the first time—that he suffered from the disorder. It finally put a name on the problem. This Emmy Award-winning writer has set an extraordinary example in overcoming its difficulties.

Berry Gordy ● 7000 Hollywood

Songwriter, producer, executive

Berry Gordy

BORN Nov. 28, 1929, in Detroit, MI. **SPOTLIGHTS** Hitsville, U.S.A. A giant of the recording industry. An American success story. A genius. Born the seventh out of eight children he was raised by a loving mother, Bertha, and father, Berry Gordy, Sr. Sr. instilled a tough work ethic and shared the importance of family solidarity. While Jr. did not want to follow in his father's footsteps of grocery store ownership, plastering or printing, he did place high goals and standards for himself. Berry Gordy, Jr. set out to become a featherweight boxer. He won seven of his 14 pro fights by knockouts. In 1951 the U.S. Army called upon his services. Drafted into the military, his tour included Korea. Gordy served his country and was honorably discharged in 1953. His first foray into the music business was in the form of his 3-D Record Mart, a jazz-oriented store. Like other entrepreneurs, such as Walt Disney, his first business expedition went bust and he was forced to declare bankruptcy. In 1955 he became gainfully employed at the Ford Motor Company. There, he learned crucial business principles while working on the Lincoln-Mercury assembly line. At night he studied the Detroit's music scene, visiting both rhythm & blues, and jazz clubs. He began writing, and his song "Rite Petite" (performed by fellow former boxer, soul singer Jackie Wilson) became the first Gordy hit. At age 29, with an $800 loan from his family, Gordy founded Hitsville USA and the Motown Record Corporation. It was the first African American owned and operated record company in the country. They struck gold with Smokey Robinson's "Shop Around" in 1961. Gordy had a keen eye for selecting, shaping, developing, grooming and training unknown talent into polished stars. The visionary ordered remix after remix to get just the right sound. He could not afford to have any losers, money was too tight. He signed many greats, including The Temptations, Four Tops, Marvin Gaye, Diana Ross and the Supremes, Stevie Wonder, Jackson Five (and Michael Jackson), and Lionel Ritchie. Motown became a hit factory. Gordy had expanded the American entertainment industry with crossover; he integrated African Americans into the mainstream. It was a phenomenal accomplishment and long overdue. By 1977 he had the largest African American owned company in the United States. Gordy expanded into motion pictures, directing and/or producing: *The Wiz* (1978), *Mahogany* (1975), and *Lady Sings the Blues* (1972). **ACHIEVEMENTS** The recipient of hundreds of awards, Gordy was inducted into the Rock and Roll Hall of Fame in 1988, and bestowed the prestigious Gordon Grand Fellow in 1985 by Yale University. In addition he was honored with an ASCAP Lifetime Achievement Award. *To Be Loved: The Music, The Magic, The Memories of Motown: An Autobiography* (1994) by Berry Gordy, Jr., published by Warner Books. **QUOTE** About receiving his Hollywood Walk of Fame star on Oct. 24, 1996, Gordy said, "Music is the life blood of the soul. Music has been my life, my work and my luck. A star on the Hollywood Walk of Fame is especially rewarding. It just goes to show that the streets of Detroit and those of Hollywood, London, Paris and Peking are not as far apart as they seem to be on maps."

Maureen O'Hara 7000 Hollywood
Actress

Maureen O'Hara

BORN Maureen Fitzsimmons; Aug. 17, 1920, in Millwall, Ireland. **SPOTLIGHTS** Called "The Queen of Technicolor" for her extremely photogenic qualities, this oval faced, redheaded, green-eyed beauty started in show business in her hometown of Dublin. On radio at age 12, and onstage with the Abbey Players by 14, she was signed to a seven-year contract by actor Charles Laughton and his business partner when she 18. The next year, the high-spirited actress stars opposite Laughton in *The Hunchback of Notre Dame* (1939). This was the first sound version made of Victor Hugo's novel, and remains the finest. Her portrayal of the gypsy Esmeralda established her as one of Hollywood's most prominent leading ladies. She stars in the remake of *A Bill of Divorcement* (1940), opposite Adolph Menjou. O'Hara worked with writer-director Dorothy Arzner in *Dance, Girl Dance* (1940), then followed up with director John Ford in the tearjerker *How Green Was My Valley*. She and Ford established a lifelong, platonic friendship. Other Ford pictures include *Rio Grande* (1950), co-starring best friend John Wayne, *The Quiet Man* (1952) also with Wayne, and *The Long Gray Line* (1955), opposite Tyrone Power. She affectionately called director John Ford, "Pappy." In *Big Jake* (1971) she co-stars again with John Wayne. New generations of fans enjoy her in the Christmas classic *Miracle on 34th Street* (1947), which airs faithfully each Yuletide. O'Hara has continued to act into the 1990s, appearing both in top-rated Christmas specials and television movies, and films, including *Only the Lonely* (1991), opposite John Candy. **HIGHLIGHTS** Fred Cavens, a graduate of the Belgian Military Academy taught O'Hara how to fence for swashbuckling movies. He called her technique: "stupendous." **SIDELIGHTS** For reasons only her family could explain, her parents nicknamed her "Baby Elephant" as a child.

Andy Garcia 🎥 7000 Hollywood
Actor

Andy Garcia

BORN April 12, 1956, in Havana, Cuba. **SPOTLIGHTS** The son of a successful attorney, his family was forced to flee Castro's regime when Garcia was five years old. In the United States, his father established a lucrative cosmetics business. Beauty was not far from the teen himself; Garcia grew into a Latin Adonis. While attending the University in Miami, Florida, the handsome, dark-haired youth began performing. Garcia spent numerous years training in regional theater before moving to Los Angeles in the late 1970s. He brought fresh blood to gangster roles, but has been adept in playing a nice guy, too. He has created memorable characterizations in such notable films as *The Untouchables* (1987), *Stand and Deliver* (1988), *Clinton and Nadine* (1988), *Black Rain* (1989), *Internal Affairs* (1990), *The Disappearance of Garcia Lorca* (1997), *Hoodlum* (as Lucky Luciano—1997), *Night Falls on Manhattan* (1997), and *A Ticket to Ride* (1999). Garcia was nominated for both an Oscar and Golden Globe for his performancee in *The Godfather, Part III* (1990). He earned critical acclaim for his work opposite Meg Ryan in *When a Man Loves a Woman* (1994).

Ed McMahon
Actor, host, spokesman

7000 Hollywood

Ed McMahon

BORN March 6, 1923, in Detroit, MI. **SPOTLIGHTS** The tall, robust, affable McMahon appeared as a clown on TV's circus show "Big Top," which first aired in 1950. He hooked up with pal Johnny Carson on a daytime show called "Who Do You Trust?" (1957-'62) as the on-screen announcer. It was a version of the evening quiz show, "Do You Trust Your Wife?" The easy-going second banana enjoyed a 30-year run on "The Tonight Show Starring Johnny Carson" (starting in 1962). Other programs include the talent contest show, "Star Search," which launched the careers of Rosie O'Donnell, Dennis Miller, LeAnn Rimes, Sinbad and Drew Carey; "TV's Bloopers and Practical Jokes"; and "The Tom Show." **ACHIEVEMENTS** His career in TV has spanned more than five decades...He was a Marine fighter pilot of both WWII and the Korean War. He served bravely before his honorable discharge. Still disciplined, he works out every morning. His cardiovascular exercise is the treadmill, and McMahon builds muscular strength with weights...His 1998 autobiography, *For Laughing Out Loud: My Life and Good Times*, published by Warner Books. His website is www.edmcmahon.com **QUOTE** "Many people have told me that the thing I do best is make it look like I'm not doing anything...but believe me, that's not an easy thing to do. It took me years to convince an audience that I wasn't working."

Kirstie Alley
Actress

7000 Hollywood

Kirstie Alley

BORN January 12, 1955, in Wichita, KS. **SPOTLIGHTS** Alley soared to fame as Rebecca Howe on "Cheers." This hit television series was one of the most popular shows of all time. Playing the feisty, sometimes desperate, jinxed bar manager she earned the Emmy, Golden Globe, and People's Choice Awards for "Best Actress in a Comedy Series." Audiences loved her unique voice she used in the show. In a blink of an eye, she switched it from a graceful rhythm to one that was frantic and jocular. It gave her an added advantage in handling comedy. In 1997 this glamorous, high-strung female clown hit big again in the hugely successful sitcom "Veronica's Closet." On a dramatic note, she played a family member tied up with the mob in Mario Puzo's mini-series "The Last Don" (1998). Other TV performances include her portrayal of feminist Gloria Steinem in "A Bunny's Tale," her wonderful performance in the role of Virgilia Hazard in John Jakes' epic mini-series "North and South," and her Emmy Award-winning portrayal in "David's Mother." This versatile talent made her silver screen debut in *Star Trek II: The Wrath of Khan* (1982). Other motion pictures include *Blind Date* (1984), *Runaway* (1984), *Summer School* (1987) *Shoot to Kill* (1988), *Look Who's Talking* (1989) with John Travolta--and the sequels *Look Who's Talking Too* (1991) and *Look Who's Talking Now* (1993); children and teens absolute connect with her--*Sibling Rivalry* (1990), *It Takes Two* (1995), *Village of the Damned* (1995), *Sticks and Stones* (1996) and *Nevada* (1997). Her Walk of Fame star dedication ceremony took place on Nov. 9, 1995.

TIP If you're on a walking tour, cross the street to the *Hollywood Entertainment Museum*. Inside you'll find the original set of "Cheers," and you can sit on Norm's stool. Bring your camera—after all, this *is* Hollywood, so it's practically a law that you take pictures. Also available is the Eastman Kodak Spotlight Theatre. Guests can have their photographs taken in a variety of settings, including being "beamed up" the Starship Enterprise on the original "Star Trek" Children of all ages are welcome. Telephone: 323.465.7900; 7021 Hollywood (one block west of Grauman's Chinese Theatre).

Eddie Murphy
Actor, comedian, writer, producer

7000 Hollywood

BORN Apr. 3, 1961, in Brooklyn, NY. **SPOTLIGHTS** An accomplished stand-up comedian with a million-watt smile, Murphy first came to America's attention with several hilarious characters in TV's *Saturday Night Live*. Joining NBC's "not ready for prime time players" at age 19, Murphy spoofed the claymation figure "Gumby," created "Velvet Jones—the pimp," "Tyrone Green" the illiterate convict-poet, featured

From left: Brian Grazer, Johnny Grant, Eddie Murphy and wife Nicole.

"Buckwheat" (of *Our Gang/Little Rascals* Depression-era fame) in today's modern world, and did a hysterical parody of the revered children's show, "Mr. Roger's Neighborhood," with an imaginative ghetto character called "Mr. Robinson." It was during this time that the country fell in love with the fast thinking talent, whose broad, dazzling smile resembled Lewis Carroll's *Alice in Wonderland* Cheshire cat. His charisma translated to the silver screen. Murphy became an international movie star in his movie debut, *48 Hrs.* (1982), a comedy/action adventure that had its share of violence. This box office hit inspired the sequel *Another 48 Hrs.* (1990). In 1983, he gives a brilliant performance in the very funny and clever comedy, *Trading Places* (1983), co-starring Dan Aykroyd. In *Beverly Hills Cop* (1984), he plays a gutsy, streetwise, middle-class Detroit cop who finds himself in the lap of luxury, richness and snobbery in Southern California. It minted pure box office gold. Two sequels followed: *Beverly Hills Cop II* (1987) and *Beverly Hills Cop III* (1994). In 1988, he stars in the engaging comedy *Coming to America* (1988), with supporting talent by the talented actor Arsenio Hall. Other movies include *Distinguished Gentleman* (1992), *Vampire in Brooklyn* (1995—also co-produced), *The Nutty Professor* (1996—where Murphy plays seven roles), and *Dr. Dolittle* (1998). In 1999, Murphy stars in two smash hit comedies: *Life* and *Bowfinger*. Murphy is also a successful recording artist and stand-up comic.

W. C. Fields   7000 Hollywood
Actor, comedian, screenwriter

W. C. Fields

BORN William Claude Dukinfield; April 9, 1879, in Philadelphia, PA. **SPOTLIGHTS** Physically, verbally and mentally abused by his tyrannical father, Fields was fortunate to have been born with both an inner and outer strength. As early as age three, he apprenticed to his father selling fruits and vegetables. The muscular youngster was forced to work everyday as he was growing up, missing school. There were no toys, no amusement, except his father's singing—which Fields grew to detest. At age nine, he snuck into a vaudeville show where he saw jugglers perform. It was the first time something had excited him. When he returned to the cart, he slid some fruit into his pocket. After work, he hid in the stable juggling oranges and lemons (when his father wasn't looking). He later stated, "By the time I could keep two objects going, I'd ruined forty dollars worth of fruit." On Field's 11th birthday, his sadistic father picked up a shovel and slammed it on his son's head. That was it. Fields had had enough. For three days he planned his revenge, hiding in the stable's loft. When his father walked in looking for him, he dropped a heavy wooden box on his head knocking him out cold. Fields left home and never looked back. After considerable hardship, the street urchin rose from the ashes to become an international juggling celebrity, then a Ziegfeld Follies/Broadway star. When the 1929 financial crash dimmed Broadway's lights, he made his movie debut at 50 years old. With his own ingeniously, self-created verbose screen personas, he become the *first* talkies comedy hero and king of American comedy. A raspy-voiced, bulbous, cauliflower red-nosed anarchist, he was tough, bitter and cynical—*but* he pulled it off in an appealing, humorous, tongue-in-cheek way. He found absurdities in the small details of everyday work life. He used a clever turn of a phrase, such as: "If there's a will, prosperity can't be far behind." "You can fool half the people all of the time...and that's enough to make a good living." "I never worry about being driven to drink. I just worry about being driven home." "You can't cheat an honest man. He has to have larceny in his heart in the first place." "If at first you don't succeed, try, try again..then give up! No sense in making a fool of yourself!" "I wasn't being fresh, dear, I was just trying to guess your weight." And, "A rich man is nothing but a poor man with money." Before going to the studio in the morning (he detested mornings)—and *before* breakfast—he started with two martinis. And, as he put it, "Start every day with a smile and get it over with!" This comic genius stars in and/or wrote a number of zany, madcap films, including *Million Dollar Legs* (1932), *Six of a Kind*, *It's a Gift*, and *You're Telling Me* (all 1934), *The Man on the Flying Trapeze* (1935), *You Can't Cheat an Honest Man* (1939), *My Little Chickadee*, and *The Bank Dick* (both 1940 and both which he wrote on the back of envelopes), and *Never Give a Sucker an Even Break* (1941). He took his one dramatic role seriously; he portrayed Micawber in *David Copperfield* (1935). Completely self-taught, he always carried a dictionary. He wrote many scripts under the pen name of Mahatma Kane Jeeves (and others just as offbeat). His popular catchphrases include "Even a worm will turn!" and "Poppycock!" *Never Give a Sucker an Even Break* written by Ronald Fields (grandson of W.C. Fields), with Shaun O' L. Higgins, was published in 2000 by Prentice Hall Press. **QUOTE** "On or off the record, there may be some things better than sex, and there may be some things worse. But there's nothing exactly like it."...A lifelong agnostic, Fields was caught reading a Bible on his deathbed. He explained to those at his side, "I'm looking for a loophole." He passed away in 1946 on Christmas Day—a day he said he detested. He left part of his fortune for the establishment of an orphanage: "Where No Religion of Any Sort Is to Be Preached."

Hugh M. Hefner   7000 Hollywood
Publisher, Editor-in-Chief, Producer
BORN April 9, 1926, in Chicago, IL. **SPOTLIGHTS** Born the elder son of conservative Protestant parents, and a direct descendent of the distinguished Massachusetts puritanical colonists—Pilgrim Fathers William Bradford and John Winthrop—it would seem that Hugh M. Hefner's genetic des-

Hugh M. Hefner

tiny would have irrevocably appointed him to a life far different than the one he obtained. Although gifted with a genius IQ of 152, he was an average student at Steinmetz High School who distinguished himself by founding a school paper. Following graduation he enlisted in the Army, then studied art at the prestigious Chicago Art Institute. He earned his bachelor's degree at the University of Illinois in a speedy two and one-half years. It was during his college journalism days that Hef (his preferred nickname) introduced a new feature called "Coed of the Month." His first professional break was being hired as a promotion copywriter at *Esquire* magazine at $60 a week in 1951. When *Esquire* moved its offices to New York, his request for a five-dollar raise was denied. Hef decided to stay behind and start a magazine of his own. It took several years to raise the capital of $8,000 (including $600 of his own money borrowed from a bank using his apartment furniture as collateral). The first issue of *Playboy* magazine, featuring the now-famous calendar photo of Marilyn Monroe, was produced on a kitchen table in his South Side apartment by the 27-year-old dreamer. In creating the controversial *Playboy* publication—with its series of editorials entitled, "The Playboy Philosophy," proclaiming individual rights and personal freedom—Hef led the charge of America's sexual revolution. Early black-and-white TV sported a crewcut Hef hosting "Playboy's Penthouse" (syndicated 1960). Later, he lounged around on "Playboy After Dark" (syndicated 1969) entertaining a room full of celebrities and beauties while millions of American men watched with envy. He also produced a number of popular TV movies, and sponsored the restoration of vintage and silent films (shown on PBS TV). Meanwhile, *Playboy* became the largest-selling, most influential men's magazine in the world. Ultimately, Hugh M. Hefner is a man who profoundly influenced society in the second half of the 20th Century. **ACHIEVEMENTS** Contributed significantly to protecting the Constitutional Right of Freedom of Speech. He is a staunch supporter of women's rights; backs important jazz festivals; and came to the community's aid in 1980 by leading the restoration of the historic, world-famous Hollywood sign. He refers to the landmark as "Hollywood's Eiffel Tower." **HIGHLIGHTS** In the mid-1980s, daughter Christie Hefner (from his first marriage) took over as Chairman and Chief Executive Officer of Playboy Enterprises. His second marriage to Kimberley Conrad in 1990 produced two sons. To learn more about his life, see the 1996 A&E documentary "Hugh Hefner: American Playboy."

Brian Grazer 🎥   7000 Hollywood

Producer **BORN** July 12, 1951, in Los Angeles, CA. **SPOTLIGHTS** Many people do not recognize his name off the bat, but the entire world enjoys his work. This creative and prolific talent—with a special flair for comedy—has produced and/or executive produced more than 50 big motion pictures, including *Ed TV* (1999) with Matthew McConaughey, Woody Harrelson, Elizabeth Hurley and Jenna Elfman,

Brian Grazer (center), Mel Gibson (left), and Ron Howard (right)

Liar, Liar (1997) starring Jim Carrey, *Ransom* (1996) starring Mel Gibson, *The Nutty Professor* with Eddie Murphy (1996), *Apollo 13* (1995) starring Tom Hanks and Kevin Bacon, *Housesitter* (1992) with Goldie Hawn and Steve Martin, *Kindergarten Cop* (1990) starring Arnold Schwarzenegger, and *My Girl* (1991) starring Jamie Lee Curtis, Dan Aykroyd, and Anna Chlumsky—in her screen debut. In addition to his producer's credits, Grazer garnered an Oscar nomination for Best Screenplay for *Splash* (1984—along with co-writers Lowell Ganz and Babaloo Mandel). *Splash* was directed by his longtime pal Ron Howard (see Howard's bio in this book), and was the second film they worked on together. The two had met when Howard was just completing his seven-year run on the hit sitcom series "Happy Days." The relationship instantly clicked. Grazer first hired Howard to direct *Night Shift* (1982) starring Henry Winkler and Michael Keaton. Two years later, the mermaid story appeared. Two more years passed before Grazer and Howard inked a major industry production deal. They became co-chairmen and founders of Imagine Films Entertainment. In 1989 *Parenthood* became their first #1 box-office hit and was nominated for two Academy Awards. Throughout the next decade, Grazer delivered dozens of great motion pictures, including *Bowfinger* (1999), starring Steve Martin and Eddie Murphy. In 1999, he produced the highly acclaimed, entertaining wrestling documentary, *Beyond the Mat*. His films have won numerous Academy Awards and People's Choice Awards. He also executive produces and produces television shows and mini-series, including HBO's Emmy-winning "From the Earth to the Moon."

ACHIEVEMENTS Among his many honors, he is the recipient of the 1998 Cubby R. Broccoli Award of Excellence (see Broccoli's bio in this book); and the 1995 Darryl F. Zanuck Motion Picture Producer of the Year Award from the Producers Guild of America (see Zanuck's bio in this book). In terms of generating revenue—the grease that spins Hollywood's wheels—Grazer's films have grossed more than $4 billion to date. His Walk of Fame dedication ceremony on March 20, 1997 attracted celebrity friends, global media, and a large crowd of Hollywood enthusiasts.

John Drew Barrymore 📺 7000 Hollywood

Actor

BORN John Blythe Barrymore, Jr.; June 4, 1932, in Beverly Hills, CA. **SPOTLIGHTS** Descended from the important theatrical family, "the fabulous Barrymores," he made his screen debut at age 18 in *The Sundowners* (1950). After appearing in *High Lonesome* (1950), *The Big Night* (1951), and *While the City Sleeps* (1956), personal problems threw him off track time and again. **TV** He appeared in the game show "Pantomime Quiz" (1953-'54). Later work included guest spots on "Kung Fu" (with pal David Carradine in 1974). His greatest accomplishment was fathering actress-producer Drew Barrymore (child star of *E.T.*), who has successfully moved into major adult roles and has become a movie star/producer in her own right.

Julio Iglesias 🔘 7000 Hollywood

Singer, composer

Julio Iglesias (left) and Johnny Grant

BORN Julio Jose Iglesias de La Cueva; Sept. 23, 1943, in Madrid, Spain. Son of eminent physician Julio Iglesias Puga and Maria Del Rosario de La Cueva y Perignat. **SPOTLIGHTS** Iglesias studied law with the hopes of becoming a career diplomat, even though his first true love and ambition lied on the soccer field. As aspiring athlete, he signed with the world-famous professional soccer team, Real Madrid, as a goalkeeper. His budding sports career came to a crashing halt when an horrendous automobile accident left him near death and paralyzed at age 19. During his three-year long painful recuperation in a hospital, a physi-

cian's assistant provided Iglesias with a guitar to boost his spirits. There, he learned how to play the instrument, and started to write songs. He reflected, "Having that experience changed the direction and philosophy of my life. Going through all that made me who I am today. I was a sporting, flirty young guy before that. All that pain gave me sensitivity to everything around me. I became a poet without writing, a singer without singing." The gigantic artist within him had been roused. Since sports were no longer in his future, he dreamed of a life in music. After he took top prize at the acclaimed Benidorn Spanish Song Festival, singing his own "La Vida Sigue Igual," he was signed by Discos Columbia. The year was 1968, and by the 1970s, this dark, handsome crooner had become a superstar in Europe, Latin America, Russia, Australia and Asia. He became a star in America in 1984 with his multi-platinum album *1100 Bel Air Place*. Universally referred to as "the Latin Lover," he possesses an ultra-smooth, romantic singing style, yet radiates highly charged and deeply felt emotions. Iglesias, a legend in international entertainment, is sophisticated, suave and utterly charming on stage. Among his albums are *Julio Iglesias, Libra, Non-Stop, Raices, Romances, Starry Night, Crazy*, and *La Carretera. My Life: The Greatest Hits* marks his first "greatest hits" collection. Released on Sony in 1998, this double CD is a comprehensive package of "Iglesias' well-known hit recordings, including collaborations with other legendary artists such as Frank Sinatra, Dolly Parton, Willie Nelson and Diana Ross. Iglesias said, "This collection really is for all those fans who have made the whole story come true for me. They are the ones who made these songs the greatest hits. Without their support, there are no hits, no concerts, no career, and just a skinny guy with a little voice. All the awards and acclaim are very nice, but the ultimate award for me is to have the sort of fans who stay with you and your music year after year and allow you to keep growing as an artist and performer." His 1996 album, *Tango*, showcases his steamy interpretation of a dozen hot tangos, including the world's best known, "La Cumparsita." The tango is considered the most passionate, powerful dance music the world has ever known. For *Tango*, the artist received an award for "Favorite Latin Artist" at the 25th American Music Awards in 1998. The music "bible," *Billboard*, recognized Iglesias' astounding career sales as 120 million copies at the time, more than any other artist ever. His fans have come not only to expect, but respect his versatility. His music and charisma have touched every point of the globe, his following is unsurpassed and his career has more than once made the history books for his remarkable achievements. The artist believes "the *emotions* of the listeners are the same in every part of the world; only the *languages* are different." **ACHIEVEMENTS** Every minute of every day an Iglesias record is played on a radio station somewhere on the globe. Iglesias' more than 1,500 gold and platinum records and albums have made him the recipient of *The Guinness Book of World Records'* "Diamond Disc" award. They cited him for selling more albums in more languages than any other artist in history. He continues to record in Spanish, Portuguese, French, German,

Italian, Japanese, and English, in wildly varying styles with different musical approaches. Iglesias received a rare compliment from the Chinese government in Beijing, in January 1996, when he was awarded the prestigious "Golden Record Prize" for selling more albums than any other foreign artist in the history of China. In September 1997, the American Society of Composers, Authors and Publishers (ASCAP) honored him with "The Pied Piper Award," reserved solely for music legends. In all, he has released 76 LPs and sold more than 200 million records worldwide. In 1988, he received the Grammy Award for Best Latin Singer of the Year for his album *Un Hombre Solo*. Since 1988, he has given of himself as a Cultural Ambassador of the World for UNICEF. Iglesias is both passionate and humble of his efforts to help children in need. About recording the song "Can't Help Falling In Love," Iglesias commented, "You can't steal a song from the King. Elvis means to me what he means to anyone else. Like Frank Sinatra or Nat 'King' Cole, they mean the same thing universally. I recorded a song from each of them because I love them so. 'Can't Help Falling in Love' is just a timeless classic love song."...For the Official Julio Iglesias International Fan Club: Tel. 305.864.5749, Fax 305.861.0104. E-mail: Julio.fanclub@worldnet.att.com or www.julioiglesiasfanclub.com. The official U.S.A. contact is: The American Friends of Julio Iglesias Fan Club, P.O. Box 1425, La Mirada, CA 90637-1425. In addition to other activities, Southern Californian members meet the first Saturday of each month to keep his star shining bright when they polish the treasured landmark. **HIGHLIGHTS** His sons—Julio Iglesias, Jr. and Enrique—have followed in his footsteps, and have started what are expected to be major singing careers. About heading up this musical dynasty, papa Julio Iglesias proudly stated, "It is normal to follow a father's career. If a father is an attorney, then sometimes the kids are going to be attorneys. But it's a wonderful surprise to any father to have two champions." **QUOTE** His Hollywood Walk of Fame star was unveiled on Nov. 17, 1985. Family, friends, fans and the worldwide media attended the exciting dedication ceremony. Iglesias commented, "It would be great to see the surprised faces of my great grandchildren when they see I am part of this amazing constellation of talents."

Irving Thalberg 🎥 7000 Hollywood
Producer
BORN May 30, 1899, in Brooklyn, NY. **HIGHLIGHTS** The "Boy Wonder of Hollywood" became the head of production at Universal in 1919—at the tender age of 20. His record for spotting and developing stars and talent, and cleverly repairing scripts quickly led him into partnership with Louis B. Mayer. He was known for his enormous work loads and his fastidious attention to detail. Thalberg implemented the sneak preview (showing a movie to regular folks in a small community before its general release date). He personally attended--on average--five sneak previews of each of his films. Like a stealth bomber, he visited movie theatres incognito of an average Joe. He qui-

etly moved from seat to seat to gauge audience reaction. Associates knew that if he stuck around the lobby chatting nonchalantly with the folks--asking their opinions on different aspects of the movie they just viewed--he liked it. If he silently slipped out into the night, there was trouble. Thalberg had a string of hits at MGM, including *Ben Hur* (1925), *Anna Christie* (1930), *Mutiny on the Bounty* (1935), and *Romeo and Juliet* (1936). The Marx Brothers star in Thalberg's production, *A*

Irving Thalberg

Night at the Opera (1935). Offscreen, they learned the busy executive was not easy to see. Thalberg was so preoccupied with work that it was not uncommon to have people sitting in his outer office waiting to meet with him for several days. (Still, most people were affectionate toward him.) The Marx Brothers got tired of waiting, and literally lit a small fire in Thalberg's outer office to distract him long enough to talk to him. With Thalberg and Mayer, the glamorous studio was billed as having "more stars than there are in the heavens." His annual salary in 1935 was $151,762; Mayer's was a few dollars lower at $151,500. Another Thalberg picture, *The Good Earth* (1937), was released posthumously. During Thalberg's reign, his name did not appear on-screen, as Thalberg once stated, "Credit you give yourself isn't worth having." *Fortune* magazine described his MGM office in 1932: "Thalberg seats himself, in his moderne beavorboard office, at a massive shiny desk, in front of a dictograph which looks like a small pipe organ and partially hides a row of medicine bottles. Before him are huge boxes of cigarettes, which he never opens, and plates of apples and dates into which he sometimes dips a transparent hand."...He wed screen darling Norma Shearer in 1927. **ACHIEVEMENTS** In 1937 the Academy of Motion Picture Arts and Sciences instituted the Irving G. Thalberg Memorial Award "for the most consistent high level of production achievement by an individual producer." It is presented annually to one deserving individual at the annual Academy Awards. **QUOTE** About acquiring literary properties for the screen, Thalberg lamented, "No story ever looks as bad as the story you've just bought; no story ever looks as good as the story the other fellow just bought!" Died: 1936.

John Chambers 🎥 7000 Hollywood
Makeup artist
BORN Sept. 12, 1922, in Chicago, IL. **SPOTLIGHTS** Master of makeup artistry, his hands were busy ever since winning a national competition with his impressive sculpture, "Spirit of '76," an ambitious work depicting the three marching soldiers of the Revolutionary War. Unfortunately, it is no longer available for viewing. "You may say it went down the drain," said

John Chambers

Chambers. It was sculpted in Ivory Soap when he was nine years old. He won $20, plus a summer art course which introduced him to the wonders of human anatomy and taught him basic sculpture forms. After high school graduation, Chambers joined the military and was trained as a dental technician at the Army's Fitzsimmons General Hospital in Denver. Later assigned to a P-38 training group, he spent three years creating dental plates and prosthetic devices like artificial noses, jawbones, cheeks and ears for wounded soldiers. This gave the sculpture structured work with various forms of plastics, adhesives and rubber compounds. After WWII, he spent seven years at Hines Veterans Hospital in Chicago, developing new techniques for the painting of artificial eyes. He painted in such a manner to duplicate the coloring and texture of the patient's existing eye. He also designed and fabricated artificial limbs. Chambers' "body parts" replaced shoulders which had been blasted away in battle. He created individualized palates for use in reconstructive surgery of the mouth, allowing patients who had been unable to form words to speak again. A tender-hearted soul, he became too deeply involved with his patients, so that when anyone died, he took it as a personal loss. He decided to apply his skills elsewhere. "I'd been watching TV and noticed how poorly much of the makeup was done," he recalled. "I figured I could do as well or better. So I wrote NBC offering my services." For nine months he heard nothing, then in 1953 a job offer arrived in the mail. He disguised Charlton Heston as the beast in a Shirley Temple Storybook production of "Beauty and the Beast." For Paul Newman, who was playing a boxer in Hemingway's "The Battler" on live TV, Chambers had just seconds to make the actor appear sweaty and unscarred in one scene, then terribly beat up in the next. By 1959 he joined film crews. Movies include *True Grit* (1969) and *Patton* (1970). **ACHIEVEMENTS** 1969 Special Oscar for *Planet of the Apes* (presented by Walter Matthau and a chimpanzee in a tuxedo). 1974 Emmy for the "Struggle for Survival," a segment of David Wolper's "Primal Man" series. Winner of the world's most prestigious makeup awards, he donated much time/skill to making prosthetics for cancer victims. **SIDELIGHTS** Trekkies will appreciate this: Chambers fitted Leonard Nimoy, Mr. Spock, with his famous ears. The makeup man had several dozen ears left over because the series was cancelled. **BIG FOOT SIGHTING** Chambers created the hoax of Big Foot, by making a foot impression bigger and bigger.

Lily Pons   7000 Hollywood

Opera singer

BORN Alice Josephine Pons; April 12, 1904, in Draguignan, near Cannes, France. **SPOTLIGHTS** Soprano; Metropolitan Opera debut in 1931. She became incredibly popular on radio, widening her concert appeal to Americans. Studio producers lured her west to make musicals, much to the consternation of the Met! (The motion picture business was draining the great opera divas—such as Gladys Swarthout and Marta Eggerth—in droves.) The youthful looking Pons played romantic leading ladies. She was very good in RKO's *I Dream Too Much* (1935), co-starring Henry Fonda with supporting talent supplied by Lucille Ball. Look for an appearance of her husband, Andre Kostelanetz, who plays orchestra conductor. Highlights arias from *Rigoletto, Lakme*. Next, she made *That Girl from Paris* (1936)—a wonderful picture, and her best. She worked with Lucille Ball again in the musical comedy *Hitting a New High* (1937). Miss *Carnegie Hall* (1947); it has an all-star cast in a terrible picture! She became one of the Met's most popular performers—memorable for her exquisite trills—appearing in 280 performances. A town in Maryland was named in her honor, Lilypons. She was married to conductor Andre Kostelanetz (1938-'58). Died: 1976.

Walter Lantz   7000 Hollywood

Walter Lantz

Cartoon producer

BORN April 27, 1900, in New Rochelle, NY. **SPOTLIGHTS** He was the creator of the irresistible Woody Woodpecker. A gifted newspaper cartoonist, he started his career drawing the Katzenjammer Kids and Krazy Kat cartoons in 1916. Emerging from the comic ranks to a pioneer animator, he took over the job a young cartoonist named Walt Disney had vacated at the studio. Seems Mr. Disney had created a mouse that Universal rejected! (And I think we all know the ending to that story.) Lantz redesigned (and re-copyrighted) a loose-limbed character named Oswald Rabbit, which the young Walt Disney had originally worked on. Starting in 1928 he began the 300-cartoon short series of the rabbit. In 1930 he did the first Technicolor cartoon. He produced Andy Panda cartoons before a real-life noisy woodpecker started pounding on his roof. Well, if angels have wings, this might have been one. For his wife suggested he do a cartoon based on the pesky bird; he resisted at first, but the obnoxious bird kept coming back knocking at their roof. He relented and created a cartoon character based on this real-life nuisance; it turned out to be Lantz's most successful creation! Wife Gracie provided the voice for Woody. **ACHIEVEMENTS** 1979 Honorary Oscar for "bringing joy and laughter to every part of the world."**HIGHLIGHTS** Each cartoon took about four months to complete with about 5,000 drawings. Lantz produced 400 six-minute Woody shorts. **QUOTE** In 1993, he established the annual $10,000 animation prize/scholarship at California Institute of the Arts, in Valencia, California. He generously said, "I've been in this since I was 16 and I have done very well. I'd like to do something for somebody else." Died: 1994.

Errol Flynn   7000 Hollywood
See page 432.

Natalie Wood   7000 Hollywood
Actress

BORN Natasha Gurdin; July 20, 1938, in San Francisco, CA. **SPOTLIGHTS** When a Hollywood film crew went on location near her childhood home, her mother took her out for a walk to watch them at work. She was four years old at the time. Somehow she got separated from her mother. Mrs. Gurdin eventually found her sitting on director Irving Pichel's lap. He was so captivated by the little girl that he put her in his movie *Happy Land* (1943). Although she was in a crowd scene, the camera focuses on her as she cries over a dropped ice cream cone. She was so photogenic and performed her task with such ease, that Pichel remembered her and later called her to Hollywood. He changed her name to Natalie Wood with a $150-a-week Universal contract. It quickly climbed to $1,000-a-week 20th Century-Fox contract as a child star. Pichel cast her in a supporting role in *Tomorrow Is Forever* (1946), starring Orson Welles and Claudette Colbert. She was nine years old when she made her first classic, *Miracle on 34th Street* (1947). That same year, she appears with *The Ghost and Mrs. Muir*, co-starring Gene Tierney, Rex Harrison and George Sanders. She won the title of "Most Talented Juvenile Star of 1947." She made a number of other movies, including *The Green Promise* (1949), *The Jackpot* (1950), *The Blue Veil* (1951), and *The Star* (1952), before coming into her own as a young adult. She received an Oscar nomination for her role as a confused, angst-ridden teen in *Rebel Without a Cause* (1955). Co-star James

Natalie Wood

Dean gives a powerful performance as an anguished, tortured youth, and Sal Mineo lends terrific support. All were immortalized in this ultimate "alienated teen" classic. It is a movie of mythic stature. She made several other films before arriving as an adult. *Splendor in the Grass* (1961—in an Oscar-nominated performance) is a coming-of-age story about repressed sexuality and romance. She plays opposite Warren Beatty, in his screen debut. It was another hit. Wood delivers a dynamic performance in *West Side Story* (1961), establishing herself as the most popular actress of the decade. Other movies include her portrayal of Gypsy Rose Lee in *Gypsy* (1962), *Love with the Proper Stranger* (1963—in an Oscar-nominated performance; many critics cite this as her best performance), *The Great Race* (1965), *Inside Daisy Clover* (1966—another favorite of reviewers), and *Bob & Carol & Ted & Alice* (1969). **ACHIEVEMENTS** Her Walk of Fame star was dedicated posthumously on Hollywood's 100th birthday, February 1, 1987. She was married to Robert Wagner twice, 1957-'63 and 1972 until her untimely death in 1981, from drowning. Wagner attended the ceremony in her honor.

James Dunn   7000 Hollywood
Actor, singer, dancer

BORN Nov. 2, 1901, in New York, NY. **SPOTLIGHTS** A cheerful actor of Irish extraction, Dunn possessed a tenor voice and an open, smooth face. He toiled through his twenties to make it to Broadway musicals. He hit big onstage in 1930, then made the leap to movies in *Bad Girl*, and *Over the Hill* (both 1931). He appears in 35 films, including several Shirley Temple vehicles. When he first learned he had been cast opposite a child, he moaned, "All actors dislike working with children." The genial talent worked with Temple in *Stand Up and Cheer* (1934) doing a classic song-and-dance duet, *Baby Take a Bow* (1934—in a co-starring role), and *Bright Eyes* (1934—also in a co-starring role). After seeing how Temple sparkled onscreen and stole every scene, Dunn confirmed his earlier suspicions, "My worst fears were justified the minute I set foot in front of the camera with her." Offscreen, Dunn remained puzzled by the child's extraordinary acting abilities and intuitiveness. Other features include *The Living Ghost* (1942), *Leave It to the Irish* (1944), *Killer McCoy* (1947), *The Golden Gloves Story* (1950), and *The Oscar* (1966). He performed in live playhouses during TV's early days, and played Uncle Earl on the sitcom "It's a Great Life" (1954-'56). **ACHIEVEMENTS** 1945 Best Supporting Actor Oscar for *A Tree Grows in Brooklyn*. Died: 1967.

The Everly Brothers ● 7000 Hollywood

Singers, songwriters

BORN Don, Feb. 1, 1937; Phil, Jan. 19, 1939; both in Brownie, TX. **SPOTLIGHTS** The Everly Brothers are considered the most influential vocal duo in rock 'n' roll history. With their rich voices that intertwine in close harmony, they created a fresh, unique and famous sound by blending rock 'n' roll, rockabilly, country, blues, gospel and bluegrass. They are the sons of Midwestern country stars, Ike and Margaret Everly. Ike's roots were steeped in old Kentucky tradition. After teaching his sons to pick a guitar, the two toured with their parents. They performed on small radio shows as the Everly family act. During the hot, humid summer of 1955 the two brothers headed to Nashville. Initially they won jobs as songwriters. After they recorded the much-rejected "Bye Bye Love," it proved to be their breakthrough. The year was 1957 and the

The Everly Brothers (l and r) with Brian Beirne

song became an international smash hit. Over the next five years, Phil and Don produced a hit record every three months, often topping the pop, country and R&B charts simultaneously. Among their hits are "Wake Up Little Susie," "All I Have to Do Is Dream," "Cathy's Clown," "Bird Dog," "(Till) I Kissed You," "Claudette," and "When Will I Be Loved." The Everlys are known as important pioneers in the history of popular music. Through the years the brothers have influenced everyone from the Beatles, Simon and Garfunkle, the Beach Boys and a whole new generation of musicians, including Tom Petty. They split in 1973, but reunited on stage at the London's spectacular, and intimate, Royal Albert Hall in 1983. The reunion concert set the stage for their comeback album *EB '84*, which spun off the hit single "On the Wings of a Nightingale." They followed up with an album for the Mercury/Polygram label, *Born Yesterday*. **ACHIEVEMENTS** Among their numerous honors, the legendary Everly Brothers are among the first ten inductees into the Rock and Roll Hall of Fame in 1986. The brothers, through the years, have also donated generously of their talents to many children's charities, including the St. Vincent Orphanage here in Los Angeles. During the Vietnam War, they performed at a benefit concert in the war torn country with the proceeds benefitting a children's orphanage there. In 1962 the brothers served in the U.S. Marine Corps. While doing their military stint, their moving song, "Crying in the Rain" made it into the Top Ten.

Jo Van Fleet 🎥 7000 Hollywood

Actress

BORN Dec. 30, 1919, in Oakland, CA. **SPOTLIGHTS** A powerful character actress, she often portrayed women much older than herself. Films include *Gunfight at the O.K. Corral* (1957), *Wild River* (1960), *Cool Hand Luke* (1967—she played Paul Newman's mother) and *The Gang That Couldn't Shoot Straight* (1971). TV: She portrayed the wicked stepmother in the 1965 revival of Rodgers and Hammerstein's "Cinderella." **ACHIEVEMENTS** 1955 Oscar Best Supporting Actress in *East of Eden*, her very first movie role! In it she portrayed James Dean's madam mother, although in real life she was only 12 years older than him. In 1957 she won a Tony Award. Died: 1996.

Gene Autry 🐎 7000 Hollywood
See page 428

William Haines 🎥 7000 Hollywood
Actor

BORN Federico Nobile; Jan. 1, 1900, in Staunton, VA. **SPOTLIGHTS** He was a foppish silent screen actor seen in vain, showy roles. Pictures include *A Fool and His Money* (1925), and *Spring Fever* (1927). The talkies KO'd him, by 1931 he had been kicked out of movies. He became a successful interior decorator of stars' homes. Died: 1973.

Cybill Shepherd 📺 7000 Hollywood

Cybill Shepherd and Johnny Grant

Actress, singer, club entertainer **BORN** Feb. 18, 1950, in Memphis, TN. **SPOTLIGHTS** A dramatic actress. A hip comedienne. A cabaret singer. A tall, blonde, blue-eyed Southerner, she won her first beauty contest when she was a teenager. With thoughts of the bright lights of Broadway, this "Model of the Year" left her hometown of Memphis. She took her sweet, little ol' accent straight to New York. Before reaching age 20, the photogenic, fresh faced belle had graced countless magazine covers. Discovered by director Peter Bogdanovich, she made her critically acclaimed film debut in *The Last Picture Show* (1971). Other films followed: *The Heartbreak Kid* (1972), *Taxi Driver* (1976), *Special Delivery* (1977) and *The Long, Hot Summer* (1985). In 1985 television audiences discovered her anew on ABC's "Moonlighting," opposite Bruce Willis. The series lasted four seasons. Her second hit series "Cybill" (1995-'98) was a cleverly written show based on

Cybill Shepherd and club impresario Mark Fleischman

her own life. Adored by millions of women, it was a very honest, funny and wacky comedy. This four-time Golden Globe winner is also an accomplished singer, and swing dancer. The chanteuse performs live at intimate, sold-out venues across the country, providing first-rate entertainment.

Fred Niblo 🎥   7000 Hollywood

Director

BORN Jan. 6, 1874, in York, NE. **SPOTLIGHTS** A former legitimate actor, he earned the phenomenal sum of $500-a-week in the early 1900s. He toured with his pal, the multi-talented playwright George M. Cohan's troupe, where he met his future wife—George's sister—Josephine. In 1917 he switched to directing silent films. Movies include *The Three Musketeers* (1921), starring that swashbuckling heartthrob Douglas Fairbanks; *Blood and Sand* (1922), starring the divine Italian lover Rudolph Valentino; and *The Mysterious Lady* (1928), starring the beautiful Swede who graced the American screen, Greta Garbo. **QUOTE** A man of technical progress, he pioneered the use of film as an educational tool. He encouraged medical schools to shoot then view: "the operation again and again, until the student surgeons became letter perfect in their special line of surgical work. The surety of that camera picture would mean more to them than all the lectures they might listen to during a lifetime." He also lectured to elementary schools to "teach with motion pictures. Getting the child interested and then by repetition he could acquire that which might be difficult for him to learn otherwise." Died: 1948.

Angie Dickinson 📺   7000 Hollywood

Actress

BORN Angeline Brown; Sept. 30, 1931, in Kulm, ND. **SPOTLIGHTS** As a child, her parents owned and operated a weekly newspaper in North Dakota. They migrated to Burbank, California when she was age 10. An intelligent student, Dickinson attended parochial school, and later was educated at the Immaculate Heart High and Glendale College. She worked in an aircraft parts plant to finance acting lessons. On a lark, Dickinson entered a television beauty contest, "hoping just to win the prizes." A casting director spotted her. He was not the only one to notice her beauty. The long-legged, elegant blonde with her characteristic soft, well-modulated voice won the contest, and was given her first TV appearance on "The Jimmy Durante Show." Frank Sinatra was the special guest star; the show launched her career. Soon after, she made her screen debut in the Doris Day musical, *Lucky Me* (1954), then appeared opposite Robert Mitchum in the suspenseful Western, *The Man with the Gun* (1955). That same year, she worked with John Payne, Rhonda Fleming and Ronald Reagan in *Tennessee's Partner*. The Western about gambling and double cross had been adapted from a Bret Harte story. Several other good movies followed, including *China Gate* (1957) where she plays an Eurasian girl in the slick, fast-moving action picture opposite Gene Barry, with support from Nat King Cole and

Angie Dickinson and Johnny Grant

Lee Van Cleef. The suspense thriller, *Cry Terror* (1958), with James Mason and Rod Steiger was important as well, as a fine stepping stone to starring roles. Dickinson possesses both serenity and strength. These two fine qualities translate to screen, and without a doubt, make her one of America's most popular actresses. Following these early films, her breakthrough came in *Rio Bravo* (1959), opposite John Wayne. This is one of the best Westerns ever made. Director Howard Hawks called it "an exact inversion of Fred Zinnemann's *High Noon*." There's action, humor, a terrific Dickinson playing an extremely sultry, dance-hall girl named Feathers, who is also quite capable as a woman. The young Dickinson is absolutely compelling to watch. Other cast members—Dean Martin, Rick Nelson, and Walter Brennan—performed equally well under Hawks' direction and with the great script, making it a must-see movie. Next, she appeared with Richard Burton in *The Bramble Bush* (1960), a somewhat trashy melodrama. She joins the notorious "Rat Pack"—Frank Sinatra, Dean Martin, Sammy Davis, Jr., and Peter Lawford—in their first picture together, the crime caper *Ocean's Eleven* (1960). In the offbeat military comedy-drama, *Captain Newman, M.D.* (1963), she co-stars with Gregory Peck. Dickinson appears opposite Lee Marvin and John Cassavetes in the remake of a Hemingway story—*The Killers* (1964)—which did not strike a chord like the original of 1946. The 1964 version is notable for Ronald Reagan's unusual characterization of a gangster, as well as being his last film. A much better crime picture for this fine actress was the violent thriller *Point Blank* (1967) with Lee Marvin. With Marlon Brando, she co-stars in *The Chase* (1966). Director Roger Vadim made her super sexy in the black comedy *Pretty Maids All in a Row* (1971), opposite Rock Hudson. Other motion pictures include Roger Corman's *Big Bad Mama* (1974) with Tom Skerritt and William Shatner—it is a favorite video rental worldwide, *Jack London's Klondike Fever* (1979) with Rod Steiger, *Dressed to Kill* (1980) opposite Michael Caine, *Even Cowgirls Get the Blues* (1984), and *Sabrina* (1995) with Harrison Ford. **TV** She captured both the hearts and the imaginations of millions of viewers on her hit television series

Angie Dickinson quipped, "Now people can walk all over me."

"Police Woman" (1974-'78). Dickinson played the compassionate, sometimes tough, sometimes brassy Sgt. "Pepper" Anderson in this police drama. It is generally recognized that in this role she portrayed the first true feminist on the small screen, and inspired countless women to enter the police force. The significance of that for all future real-life police women cannot be underestimated in historic terms. Earl Holliman played Lt. Bill Crowley, who headed up her criminal conspiracy investigation team. "Police Woman" catapulted her to superstardom. Other television credits include "A Sensitive, Passionate Man" with David Janssen, "Overboard" with Cliff Robertson, the highly rated mini-series "Pearl," the Grace Kelly part in "Dial M for Murder," "A Touch of Scandal," the smash mini-series "Wild Palms," and the very popular mini-series "Hollywood Wives." **ACHIEVEMENTS** Among her awards are the Golden Globe Award presented by the Hollywood Foreign Press Association "for Best Dramatic Actress on Television," and two Emmy nominations as "Outstanding Lead actress in a Drama Series." She is active in several charities, particularly those involved with Alzheimer's, the Retinitis Pigmentosa Foundation, Sprint for Children and Toys For Tots. **QUOTE** At her Walk of Fame ceremony on Sept. 10, 1987, she commented, "I did absolutely nothing to deserve this great honor except to work hard, be kind to others, and love and enjoy my choice of work."

Sid Caesar 📺   7000 Hollywood
Actor, comedian, musician
BORN Sidney Caesar; Sept. 8, 1922, in Yonkers, NY. (The family's last name was given to his immigrant father by U.S. officials when he arrived at Ellis Island.) **SPOTLIGHTS** A saxophone player since his childhood days, as a teen he earned money playing at local gigs like weddings, and "gave to the house." In other words, his $6-a-week was used to help support his poor family who were suffering, like so many others, through the Great Depression. When he was older, he snuck into classes at the Juilliard School of Music. At the same time, he was always developing comic routines in his mind. His goal was to create a style of humor that did not require the degradation of another human being (for example, throwing a tomato in someone's face for a cheap laugh). During WWII, he served as seaman first class in the U.S. Coast Guard. Caesar found himself in the military revue "Tars and Spars." His star began rising during the show's tour, and he would also appear in the movie version. By the time Caesar performed on Broadway in hits like "Make Mine Manhattan" (1948), he was a full-fledged star. **TV** This master of comedy was matched

Sid Caesar

with Imogene Coca on the truly funny "Your Show of Shows" (1950-'54), where both enchanted audiences with their original comic brilliance, hilarious routines and movie spoofs. Along with "Caesar's Hour" (1954-'58), "Sid Caesar Invites You" (1958), "The Sid Caesar Show" (1963-'64), and his many inventive characters such as the eccentric psychiatrist, Caesar earned immortality in TV comedy. Another humorous character, the nutty professor, is once asked if the man who invented the first wheel was a genius. He answers, "the guy who invented the first wheel was an idiot. The guy who invented the other three wheels, *he* was a genius!" Caesar's cleverness, range of facial expressions and hilarious mugging have become legendary. The actor made his very funny motion picture debut reprising his Coast Guard role in the musical *Tars and Spars* (1946), then followed with the war drama, *The Guilt of Janet Ames* (1947), opposite Rosalind Russell, Melvyn Douglas and Nina Foch. Movies include *It's a Mad Mad Mad Mad World* (1963), *A Guide for the Married Man* (1967), *The Busy Body* (1967), *Ten from Your Show of Shows* (1973—an entertaining compilation of the favorite TV classic sketches with Imogene Coco, Carl Reiner, Howard Morris, and Louis Nye), *Airport '75* (1974), *Silent Movie* (1976), *The Cheap Detective* (1978), *Grease* (1978), *The Fiendish Plot of Dr. Fu Manchu* (1980), *The History of the World Part One* (1981), *Grease 2* (1982), *Cannonball Run II* (1984), *Stoogemania* (1985), and *The Emperor's New Clothes* (1987). **ACHIEVEMENTS** 1951 Best Actor Emmy. 1951 Emmy for "Your Show of Shows." 1956 Emmy, Best Continuing Performance by a comedian in a series, "Caesar's Hour." He penned his autobiography *Where Have I Been?* with Bill Davidson (published in 1982 by Crown Books).

Lionel Hampton 🎹   7018 Hollywood
Musician, band leader
BORN April 12, 1909, in Louisville, Kentucky. **SPOTLIGHTS** A vibraphone virtuoso, his musical talents extend to the piano, drums and singing. It all started with a drum he learned to play under the guidance of Catholic nuns. He fondly recalled, "Those wonderful women took a lamb into their fold and sent forth a cat." He played piano and drums in Les Hite's orchestra when Louis Armstrong took it over in 1930. Later, he formed his own band, landing gigs in such hip locales as Sebastian's Cotton Club and the Paradise Cafe in Los Angeles, where he originated the vibes. Jazz experts credit Hampton as

"one of the all time greats, and the only musician who has extracted genuine marvels from this unrewarding instrument (the vibraphone)." He has played every important venue in the U.S. ("Samsville"), along with Europe, the Middle East and the Far East. In addition to Armstrong, he's played with many great bands, including Benny Goodman. His own band performed in the Columbia's *Depths Below*. In *Pennies from Heaven* (1936), he is the masked drummer in Armstrong's band, and later appears in *The Benny Goodman Story* (1955). He was featured at President Jimmy Carter's White House Jazz Party (June 1978). **RECOMMENDED** *Hot Mallets Vol. 1* on Bluebird ND 86458 CD; *Tempo and Swing Vol. 3* on Bluebird 74321101612; *Midnight Sun* MCA GRP 16252 CD; *Chicago Jazz Concert* Columbia 21107 CD.

Louis Armstrong

Louis Armstrong ● 7018 Hollywood

Trumpeter, composer, singer

BORN Louis Daniel Armstrong; July 4, 1901, in New Orleans, LA. **SPOTLIGHTS** A genius. The most influential figure in jazz history grew up dirt poor with no adult supervision, in the red light district of New Orleans. Sent to the Home for Colored Waifs for juvenile delinquency at age 12, Armstrong was given his first musical instrument and reason for living. His sentence was the birth of his complex musical personality and devotion to the instrument. He said, "I just want to keep the horn in my chops 24 hours a day." Strongly influenced by the music of the streets and local honky-tonks, he became the father of jazz improvisation and one of jazz's greatest creators. He took the trumpet where no one thought it could go above High C. Then in the late 1920s, he recorded *Hot Fives and Sevens*, bringing new heights to jazz, overflowing with beauty and thrilling intensity: "Potato Head Blues," "Hotter Than That," "West End Blues," "Weather Bird," "Mahogany Hall Stomp," and "Cornet Chop Suey." (Available on CDs: JSP 312 *Hot Fives and Seven*, Volumes 1, 2 and 3.) His instinctive musical nature introduced a new school of thought. It focused on the virtuoso-soloist with sound created around him, with all music designed to move that sound into purposeful expression. He played an heroic and optimistic form of jazz, radiating warmth and good cheer. His virtuoso jazz trumpet playing, big smile and raspy voice were his trademarks. Some of his best-known recordings are: "Shine," "Ain't Misbehavin'," "Stardust," "I Can't Give You Anything But Love," "Tiger Rag," "Chinatown," "C'est Si Bon," "Jubilee," "Hello, Dolly!" "Got a Lot of Livin' to Do," "A Kiss to Build a Dream On," "When the Saints Come Marching In," and "Between the Devil and the Deep Blue Sea," to list a few. In 1949 he landed on the cover of *Time* magazine. Musician Jack Teagarden observed, "(He) wasn't much to look at...just a little guy with a big mouth. But, how he could blow that horn!" Armstrong, though, excelled in all arenas of entertaining. This incomparable artist made 23 films: *Pennies from Heaven* (1936), *Cabin in the Sky* (1943), *New Orleans* (1947—with a forgettable plot, but great music, including an performance by Billie Holiday in her only film appearance), *Here Comes the Groom* (1951), *The*

Glenn Miller Story (1953), *Jazz on a Summer's Day* (1959, a must-see documentary for jazz aficionados), and *Hello, Dolly!* (1969—his last film). **ACHIEVEMENTS** Sponsored by the U.S. Dept. of State on numerous international tours, he earned the title of "America's Ambassador of Goodwill" or, for those in the know, "Ambassador Satch." (Other affectionate nicknames to describe his large mouth were Satchelmouth, Satchmo, and Dippermouth. Musicians, though, referred to him as "Pops.") His enormous worldwide popularity required him to wear a catcher's mask anytime he disembarked from a plane in South America to keep the ardent and passionate fans from kissing him on his million-dollar lips...In America, he quietly helped break color barriers by being the first African-American to perform in dozens of previously segregated "whites only" venues. While he may have been invited everywhere—and he stated, "the horn don't know nothin' about these race troubles"—he made his personal indignation clear when he took a stand on public school desegregation. Regarding the problems in Little Rock, Arkansas, in 1957, he stated that President Eisenhower had "no guts" and declared Arkansas Gov. Orville Faubus an "uneducated plowboy." These words vibrated around the world, and helped shake off some prejudice. **QUOTE** When questioned if he thought that listeners in the former Soviet Union could grasp jazz, Armstrong stated, "I sometimes don't understand it myself." In a famous interview with newsman Ed Murrow—who was searching for a precise contrast between definite music like boogie-woogie and other forms of music—Armstrong observed, "There's two things in music: good and bad. If it's good, you don't have to worry what it is." When the great Armstrong died in 1971, Duke Ellington warmly remembered him, "He was born poor, died rich and never hurt anyone on the way."

David Hasselhoff ⌨ 7018 Hollywood

Actor, singer, executive producer

BORN July 17, 1952, in Baltimore, Maryland. **SPOTLIGHTS** He is the world's most popular television actor with the most watched series of all time, but the networks didn't see it com-

David Hasselhoff

ing. "Baywatch," the hour-long, soft drama series which made its television on NBC in 1989, was quickly cancelled by out-of-touch executives after only one season. Hasselhoff, having been in the business since 1975, knew he had a hit on his hands. Refusing to be discouraged by short-sighted corporate heads, Hasselhoff and his partners acquired the rights to the show, secured financing and gave mouth-to-mouth resuscitation to "Baywatch." With its hot California beach look, a cast of fit, slick and buff bodies, and its premise that revolves around the exciting adventures of Los Angeles County Lifeguards, "Baywatch" won viewers loyalties. With the force of a tsunami, their brawn and babes became part of American pop culture as well as an international phenomenon. *The Guinness Book of World Records* estimated the show is seen in 140 countries and is watched by more than one billion viewers each week. Hasselhoff had risen to global fame on an earlier hit series, "Knight Rider" (1982-'86), which still airs in 83 countries. Soap opera devotees remember him from "The Young and the Restless" (1975-'82), before he made his successful move to prime time. At 6'4", 185 pounds, with stunning blue/green eyes, the incredibly attractive star has flexed his acting muscles in a dozen made-for-television movies and three features. Lesser known to Americans are his numerous gold and triple platinum albums. Hasselhoff grew up dreaming about becoming a pop singing star, and has triumphed in the European market with hits such as *Looking for Freedom* and *You Are Everything.* **ACHIEVEMENTS** Recipient of the "People's Choice Award." Recognized by *TV Guide* as one of "TV's Ten Most Powerful Stars." His love for children is where his heart lies. Charitable contributions include Hasselhoff personally spending countless hours visiting children's hospitals throughout the world. He founded "Race for Life" which helps terminally ill and handicapped children in Indianapolis. A key participant in "Camp Baywatch" serving disadvantaged youths in Los Angeles., he is also active with the "Starlight" and "Make-A-Wish" foundations. He received his Hollywood Walk of Fame star on Jan. 12, 1996...He is married to the beautiful actress Pamela Bach Hasselhoff; they have two daughters.

Dudley Moore 🎥 7018 Hollywood
Actor, pianist, composer
BORN April 19, 1935, in London, England. **SPOTLIGHTS** The son of a railroad electrician, Moore was a child prodigy. He was educated at Guildhall School of Music, and later attended Oxford University on a full scholarship. While at school, he became interested in dramatics and formed a group with some Cambridge undergraduates. They became known for their

satirical revue called "Beyond The Fringe." By now he had also grown into an accomplished composer and jazz pianist. With his jazz trio, Moore was in constant demand. In addition to serious pieces, the charmer was known for having fun with his audience with ribald tunes. This led to his own popular television show in England. He made his screen debut in the hilarious British comedy, *The Wrong Box* (1966). This movie was adapted from a Robert Louis Stevenson story, and had an extremely capable cast, including John Mills, Michael Caine, Peter Cook, and Peter Sellers, as well as a delightful script. Moore appeared in/or composed songs or movie scores for

Dudley Moore

nine more British pictures, before making his American movie debut in *Foul Play* (1978), with Goldie Hawn, Chevy Chase and Burgess Meredith. On screen, he plays an eccentric character. Behind the scenes, he did the music. He stars as the romantic lead in the frothy sex comedy *10* (1980), opposite Julie Andrews, and Bo Derek in her breakthrough role. The lovable Moore triumphed in the role of *Arthur* (1981), showcasing his talent for wit and humor, and made the sequel

Arthur 2: On the Rocks (1988—also exec. producer). Both *Arthur* movies had these talented actors: Liza Minnelli, John Gielgud and Geraldine Fitzgerald. He appeared in the remake of *Unfaithfully Yours*, then made *Best Defense*, and *Micki and Maude* (all 1984). Other films include *Santa Claus: The Movie* (1985), *Koneko Monogatari* (1986—in Japan), and the engaging family comedy *Like Father, Like Son* (1987). Moore did a clever job performing the narrative voice-over for the children's dog-and-cat road story, *The Adventures of Milo and Otis* (1989). On location in scenic Venice, Italy, for *Blame It on the Bellboy* (1992), he appears as a desperate businessman on the verge of getting fired in a comedy of errors. The next year, he made *The Pickle*, with Danny Aiello, Dyan Cannon, Shelley Winters and Little Richard.

Patrick Swayze 🎥 7018 Hollywood
Actor, dancer
BORN Aug. 18, 1954, in Houston, TX. **SPOTLIGHTS** The son of choreographer Patsy Swayze, he grew up in a household where graceful body movements, physical strength, and excellent posture were the norm. He was schooled at the Joffrey Ballet (the dance requires more muscle power and endurance than football). The training paid off for the handsome, affable talent. He started in show business as a dancer in Disney on Parade. Then, the bright lights of Broadway beckoned. He appeared in the wildly successful play "Grease" to rave reviews. Swayze made his motion picture debut in *Skatetown, U.S.A.* (1979). His next film was Francis Ford Coppola's *The*

Outsiders (1983). The 1960s drama, adapted from S. E. Hinton's novel, showcases a young, up and coming cast, including Matt Dillon, Ralph Macchio, Rob Lowe, Diane Lane, Emilio Estevez and Tom Cruise. He landed a good supporting role in the Vietnam action story, *Uncommon Valor* (1983), starring Gene Hackman and Robert Stack. He would

Patrick Swayze

have to wait a number of years before his breakthrough role. *Dirty Dancing* (1987) launched the career of America's newest dancing heartthrob. With his extremely fit, professionally trained body, and his strapping good looks, Swayze leads as the romantic hunk at a resort set in the nostalgic 1960s. This movie made him an international star. He sparkled on-screen and his charisma was undeniable. *Dirty Dancing's* popular soundtrack helps sell copies of the movie on video/DVD at the rate of 40,000

units per month every year since its release. He was outstanding in the smash box office hit *Ghost* (1990), opposite Demi Moore. Whoopi Goldberg came along for the thrill and won a Best Supporting Actress Oscar. Other motion pictures include *Red Dawn* (1984), *Youngblood* (1986), *Point Blank* (1991), *City of Joy* (1992), *Father Hood* (1993), *To Wong Foo, Thanks for Everything Julie Newmar* (1995—a long title for a delightful movie about fairy godbrothers), and *Three Wishes* (1995). His Walk of Fame star dedication ceremony occurred on Aug. 18, 1997, with hundreds of screaming fans, cheering friends, family and the worldwide media.

Mary Margaret McBride 🎙 7018 Hollywood

Broadcaster, author

BORN Nov. 16, 1899, in Paris, MO. **SPOTLIGHTS** This small town gal achieved the greatest recognition and the largest audience of any female "conversation" radio personality. With Mary Margaret's homey presentation and burbling voice, she interviewed Presidents as well as the famous and celebrated. Millions of devoted fans listened to her daily at 1:00 PM on her own radio show (1935 to 1954), where she became an American institution. Playful ad-libs and homespun chitchat were her trademarks, and her catchphrase was: "Is everybody comfy?" Both on and off the air she was the same person: warm-hearted, unpretentious, with a straightforward, simple Missouri approach. But don't confuse simple with simpleminded; Mary Margaret was sharp as a tack. Her live performances could pack 75,000 people in venues like Yankee Stadium. She was so popular that roses were named after her, and she was called the "Female Arthur Godfrey." She did not, however, make the cut to the new medium of TV. Died: 1976.

Sonny & Cher 📺 7018 Hollywood

Singers, actors, producers, director

BORN Salvatore Bono on Feb. 16, 1935, in Detroit, MI. Cher: Cherilyn LaPiere Sarkisian on May 20, 1946, in El Centro, CA. **SPOTLIGHTS** The pair met at a coffee shop on Hollywood Boulevard when Cher was age 16, and Sonny was 28 years old. Sonny, a singer, already had recorded the pop hit "Needles and Pins." One afternoon, Cher accompanied Sonny to Phil Spector's Gold Star Studios. As luck would have it, a female singer failed to show up for a recording, allowing Cher to substitute. Thus, she began her professional career as a back-up singer for Spector, including performing on "Be My Baby," to "You've Lost That Loving Feeling." She also recorded duets with Sonny; "Baby Don't Go" rocketed to the top ten on the charts. In the 1960s, the two put together a nightclub act with jokes and songs. Their routine portrayed Sonny as the dumb,

Sonny & Cher

sweet, lovable guy, and Cher as the sarcastic, snooty, skinny femme fatale. Sonny was an ideal straight man to Cher's barbs. The couple married in 1964. The following year, Sonny and Cher turned out the first of several hit pop-rock 'n' roll songs, including their first chart topping, million seller, "I Got You Babe." They had five songs in the top 20 at one time, a feat accomplished only by them, Elvis Presley and the Beatles. Next, they co-star in the movie *Good Times* (1967). Cher's first solo effort was in *Chastity* (1969), with Sonny working behind the scenes. When their daughter was born that same year, she was christened with the film title. Their own variety show, "The Sonny and Cher Comedy Hour" premiered in 1971 on CBS and was an immediate smash hit. They became the hottest young couple in America. The highly popular, top-rated show ended in 1974, when the couple divorced. Cher had already started her solo recording career with the million sellers, "Gypsies Tramps and Thieves," "Half-Breed." "Dark Lady," all went gold. Cher did a number of opulent TV specials, while Sonny went on to become a restaurateur first in

Award. She won the Best Actress prize at the Cannes Film Festival for her portrayal of a troubled mother in Peter Bogdanovich's *Mask* (1985), and made the crime film, *Suspect* (1987), opposite Dennis Quaid. The dark-haired, exotic looking beauty co-stars with Jack Nicholson, Susan Sarandon and Michelle Pfeiffer in George Miller's *The Witches of Eastwick* (1987); this adult comedy was based on John Updike's novel. Other movies include *Mermaids* (1990), *The Player* (1992—cameo role), *Ready to Wear* (1994), *Faithful* (1996), and *Tea With Mussolini* (1999). In 1996, she made her directorial debut in "If These Walls Could Talk." She also released a number of albums, and enjoyed many hit songs, including "I Found Someone," "If I Could Turn Back Time," "Heart of Stone," and "Love Hurts." In 1999, Cher topped the charts again with her #1 hit dance song "Believe." Sonny, meanwhile went on to become Mayor of Palm Springs, then won a seat in Congress. He married again to the former Mary Whitaker of South Pasadena, and had two children, Chesare Elan and Chianna Maria. **ACHIEVEMENTS** Cher: Best Actress Oscar and Golden Globe Award for *Moonstruck* (1987). Her acceptance came with this comment, "I don't think this means I am somebody, but I guess I'm on my way." She also became known for her sensational and outrageous outfits worn to the annual Academy Awards ceremony. The "Sonny & Cher" Hollywood Walk of Fame star was dedicated on May 15, 1998. Cher was in attendance for the unveiling ceremony; it was a posthumous honor to Sonny. Died: Congressman Sonny Bono in Jan. 1998. Then, his politically minded Republican wife, Mary Bono, won his Congressional seat. Cher hosted an intimate and personal look back at their lives together on the highly rated CBS television special "Sonny & Me: Cher Remembers."

Mariette Hartley 📺 7000 Hollywood

Mariette Hartley

Actress, host, author, speaker **BORN** June 21, 1940, in Weston, Connecticut. **SPOTLIGHTS** A natural born talent, Hartley began studying theater at age 10, and had received a full drama scholarship five years later. A tour with the American Stratford Shakespeare Festival brought her to Los Angeles for a run at the Biltmore Theater. After excelling in stage work, she was chosen as one of the last young performers by MGM Studios to be groomed for motion picture stardom. This statuesque, warm, open faced talent conquered Hollywood in Sam Peckinpah's classic Western *Ride The High Country* (1962), opposite Randolph Scott. Other films include Alfred Hitchcock's *Marnie* (1964) with Sean Connery and Tippi Hedren, *Skyjacked* (1972) with Charlton Heston, *The*

West Hollywood, then Houston, Texas, and finally in Palm Springs, California. Cher was married briefly to rock star Gregg Allman, which produced her second child, a son, Elijah Blue. Next, Cher headed to Broadway, where director-producer Robert Altman cast her in the play, "Come Back to the Five and Dime, Jimmy Dean, Jimmy Dean." She delivered a brilliant performance and reprised her role on film in 1982; it was her first major movie. She earned an Academy Award nomination as Best Supporting Actress in Mike Nichols' *Silkwood* (1983) opposite Meryl Streep, and won a Golden Globe

Magnificent Seven Ride! (1972) opposite Lee Van Cleef, *O'Hara's Wife* (1983), and *Encino Man* (1992) with Brendan Fraser. Her first television exposure came with the incredibly popular, prime time melodramatic serial, "Peyton Place." She has appeared in numerous movies-of-the-week and guest-starred on many hit series. Hartley is consistently nominated for Emmy Awards for her outstanding performances. She won an Emmy for Best Actress for her guest starring role in "The Incredible Hulk." This warm, affable personality spent one year hosting "The CBS Morning Program," then continued to guest star in such series as "Caroline in the City." Hartley has also returned to her first love, the stage. Her performances are always sold out. **HIGHLIGHTS** She is granddaughter of the renowned psychologist, John B. Watson, founder of the psychological school of behaviorism. Active in M.A.D.D. (Mothers Against Drunk Driving) and a dedicated supporter of many causes to aid abused children. She has been instrumental in bringing mental illness out of the closet; she actively strives to raise public awareness and understanding about it. **QUOTE** "I've been so blessed—I have a star in the heavens that says, 'Keep working kid, you're doing fine! And keep working in all aspects of this business—see where it's going to take you!' Everything has taken me into another place."

Meryl Streep 🎥   7018 Hollywood

Meryl Streep

Actress, singer
BORN Mary Louise Streep, June 22, 1949, in Basking Ridge, NJ. **SPOTLIGHTS** A legendary award-winning actress of the American cinema, Streep is one of the finest artists of the 20th and 21th centuries. Before reaching her teens, she took singing lessons with dreams of becoming a professional vocalist. After repeatedly hearing the grand sweeping differences between her and another student, opera diva Beverly Sills, and feeling she was not making the necessary progress to make the grade, Streep opted for acting. She immediately became a leading lady in high school productions, then majored in drama at Vassar College, where she won the title role in the first production for which she auditioned. After graduation, the intelligent, determined, soft-spoken actress attended the Yale School of Drama for three years, earning a Master of Fine Arts degree in 1975. With her pale, fair-haired good looks, this gifted talent made the leap to the Broadway stage, immediately proving herself a thoroughly professional actress. She won the outer Critics' Circle Award and a Tony nomination for portraying two unique characters on the same night in the Phoenix Theater's productions of "A Memory of Two Mondays," and Tennessee Williams' "27 Wagons Full of Cotton." Next, she joined Joseph Papp's New York Shakespeare Festival. She performed in seven plays during her first season, including "Henry V" and "Measure for Measure." With self-assuredness and flawless delivery, Streep brought luminous beauty to the Bard's work *sans* theatrics. During this time, the busy, energetic actress also appeared in the Broadway musical "Happy End," and had the stamina to do the off-Broadway production of "Alice at the Place," for which she won an Obie. Turning to television, Streep won an Emmy Award for her portrayal of a devastated German wife, in the mini-series "Holocaust," opposite James Woods. She made her silver screen debut with a small part as a society lady in *Julia* (1977), opposite Jane Fonda, Vanessa Redgrave, and Jason Robards. Based on a compelling true story about fighting the Nazis from playwright Lillian Hellman, and directed by Fred Zinnemann, this film was nominated for nine Academy Awards and won three; two for cast members Robards and Redgrave, and one for screenplay (Alvin Sargent). It set the tone for Streep's career. She earned an Academy Award nomination as best supporting actress for her performance of a working-class Pennsylvania girl in *The Deer Hunter* (1978)—her second motion picture. The acclaimed, but controversial Vietnam War drama, starring Robert De Niro, earned five Oscars, including best picture, and best supporting actor for Christopher Walken. Streep did not take home the Oscar, but she did win the National Society of Film Critics Award. In 1979, she appears in *Manhattan*, and *The Seduction of Joe Tynan*—in which she won the David di Danatello Award (the Italian equivalent of the Oscar) for her portrayal of a mistress-lawyer, then won an Oscar in another role (see below). She is called the "mistress of accents" for her keen ear. With her composure in any milieu, Streep continually receives high praise and recognition for her diverse body of work. Her many Oscar nominations include *The French Lieutenant's Woman* (1981) in which she plays the dual roles of a sophisticated modern actress and a tragic 19th century heroine in this lush period piece; and *Silkwood* (1983) as a lower-class nuclear power plant worker who—to her own detriment—finds the courage to expose radiation leaks. While Streep wanted to do *Out of Africa* (1985), director Sydney Pollack did not think she was sexy enough. To prove she could make a man's heart race, her alluring and seductive feminine mystique to rose to the challenge. She donned a push up bra, a provocative low cut top and paid Pollack a visit. She landed the role of Dane Karen Blixen, and garnered another Oscar nomination. Other Academy Award winning roles include *Ironweed* (1987), *A Cry in the Dark* (1988—in which she won the Best Actress Award at the Cannes Film Festival and the New York Film Critics Circle Award), *Postcards from the Edge* (1990), co-starring Shirley MacLaine, and *The Bridges of Madison County* (1995), playing an Italian-born Iowa farm wife opposite Clint Eastwood. She scored another triumph in *One True Thing* (1998), in another Oscar-nominated performance. The radiant newcomer Renee Zellweger plays opposite Streep in the sophisticated tearjerker.

Enjoying the challenge of constantly reinventing herself, other movies include the comedies *She-Devil* (1989—in which she garnered a Golden Globe nomination) co-starring Roseanne, Ed Begley, Jr. and Linda Hunt, *Defending Your Life* (1991) with Albert Brooks and Rip Torn, and *Death Becomes Her* (1992—in which she garnered a Golden Globe nomination), co-starring Goldie Hawn, Bruce Willis, Isabella Rossellini and Sydney Pollack. She found the physical strength to do the all-action thriller, *The River Wild* (1994), with Kevin Bacon. Streep plays a white-water rafting heroine who encounters a batch of bank robbing villains. Behind-the-scenes, she got pulled beneath the treacherous rushing waters on the Rogue River in Oregon. She almost drowned in a watery grave as the panicked crew tried in vain to locate her. Fortunately, one of the safety kayakers (lifeguards) rescued her. Then, taking an entirely new direction, Streep joins an ensemble group of players in *Dancing at Lughnasa* (1998). An Irish stage play by acclaimed dramatist Brian Friel, it was adapted to the screen by the Irish writer Frank McGuinness, and directed by the Irish-born Pat O' Connor. It is a small movie, but meaningful with an interesting character study. She earned an Oscar nomination in *Music of the Heart* (1999). **HIGHLIGHTS** Married to artist-sculptor Donald Gummer since 1978, Streep is a devoted mother to their four children: Henry, Mamie, Grace and Louisa. **ACHIEVEMENTS** Streep plays the unsympathetic, ambitious wife and mother in the divorce drama *Kramer vs. Kramer* (1979) opposite Dustin Hoffman, winning the best supporting actress Oscar. Behind-the-scenes, Streep successfully argued to change crucial dialogue in the courtroom scene, when she found the screenplay lacking in emotional depth. She ended up improvising much of her courtroom plea. Streep also won the New York Film Critics award for the role. Her second Oscar was for her role as a Polish Catholic concentration camp survivor with horrific memories that haunt her postwar life in *Sophie's Choice* (1982--it was in the best actress category). One of the most respected and venerated actresses in the industry, she won the distinguished Women in Film Crystal Award in 1998, presented by her longtime friend, actress-writer Carrie Fisher. Called Magnificent Meryl, she has also been honored with the Bette Davis Lifetime Achievement Award given by Boston University. In terms of Academy Award nominations, the ranking is as follows: Katherine Hepburn was Oscar-nominated 12 times, and won four; Meryl Streep has received 12 Oscar nominations, and won two Academy Awards (to date, as of May 2000); and in third place, Bette Davis garnered 10 Oscar nominations, and took home two.

Anne Shirley 🎬   7018 Hollywood

Actress

BORN Dawn Evelyeen Paris; April 17, 1918, in New York, NY. **SPOTLIGHTS** A sweet and pretty five-year-old child star, she was originally billed as Dawn O'Day. By age 14, she was winning plum roles such as Anastasia in *Rasputin and the Empress* (1932). This is the only film ever to feature all three Barrymores (Ethel, John and Lionel). By age 16, this very per-

Anne Shirley

sonable talent felt she had outgrown her childhood stage name, so she borrowed the name Anne Shirley from her lead character in *Anne of Green Gables* (1934). The following year Shirley co-stars with Will Rogers in *Steamboat 'Round the Bend*. She earned a Best Supporting Actress Academy Award nomination for her role in *Stella Dallas* (1937) in the dramatic saga of mother love, opposite Barbara Stanwyck. Shirley was extremely well-liked by everyone in the industry and with her talent could have easily sustained a lifelong career. She retired after the classic film noir *Murder, My Sweet* (1945) to focus on marriage and family. In all, she made nearly 50 movies.

Reba McEntire 🔊   7018 Hollywood

Singer, actress

Reba McEntire

BORN March 28, 1955, Chockie, Oklahoma. **SPOTLIGHTS** One of America's favorite country singers, she began performing in her youth. Teamed with her sister Susie and brother Pake in a group called The Singing McEntires, the trio entertained with deeply rooted country tunes, straight along the rodeo circuit—a family tradition. When she was not singing, she followed in her daddy's footsteps, who possesses the world champion steer roper title. In her teens, this energetic, athletic and very pretty tomboy competed as a barrel rider. When she was age 20, her stirring rendition of the National Anthem at the 1974 National Finals Rodeo led to a recording contract with the Mercury/Polygram label. Two years later she hit the charts with the song "I Don't Want to Be a One Night Stand." Still her rise to the top was not overnight. She worked to define and perfect her style, and find the right kind of songs for her; a journey that took six years. After signing with MCA Records, she released three albums—*My Kind of Country, Have I Got a Deal For You*, and *Whoever's in New England*—back to back (1984, 1985 and 1986). Audiences fell in love with her big, emotional voice and lyric-driven songs. It has been said she befriends a song, then makes it her own. Hits include "Can't Even Get the Blues," "Whoever's in New England," "What Am I Gonna Do About You," "Little Rock," "One Promise Too Late, " The Last One to Know," "Fancy," "You Lie," "For My Broken Heart, " Is There Life Out There," "The Heart Won't Lie" (a duet with

Vince Gill), and "Does He Love You" (a duet with Linda Davis). She also went to the top of the charts with a remake of the 1960 Everly Brothers hit "Cathy's Clown." Recalling the beginnings of her career, she stated, "I think you spend a lot of your youth just trying to prove yourself. When I first started in this business 20 years ago, it definitely was a man's world. I had some great teachers, and I learned a lot from them. And I'll always be grateful for that education. But I always felt there needed to be a different way of doing things in my career. That sort of thinking takes a lot of energy. But through it all, my saving grace was music. I love looking for songs. Months before it's time to record an album, I listen to a ton of songs that writers from all over the country have sent to me. And when I find the song that just clicks, there are no words to describe how that makes me feel." Apparently fans feel that same thrill—during her career McEntire has sold 45 million records and has been honored with more than 60 major music awards. Her triple-platinum albums include *Greatest Hits Volume I* (1987), *For My Broken Heart* (1991), *It's Your Call* (1992), *Greatest Hits Volume* II (1993—quadruple -platinum), and *Read My Mine* (1994). Her release, *If You See Him* (1998), has joined her long list of successes. McEntire's artistry is apparent in front of the camera, too. The incredibly youthful-looking lady has starred in the highly rated 1998 CBS movie "Forever Love," opposite Tim Matheson. Two of her albums' songs—"All This Time" and "Forever Love"—were also featured. Previously she appeared opposite Kenny Rogers in the popular television movie series, "The Gambler IV," and co-starred with Anjelica Huston and Melanie Griffith in "Buffalo Girls." In addition she has starred in two network specials, "Reba Live" and "Celebrating 20 years." The red-headed beauty has also appeared as a movie actress, including the cult classic, *Tremors* (1989) starring Kevin Bacon, and in the family comedies *The Little Rascals* (1994—a special guest appearance), and *North* (1994) opposite Dan Aykroyd. In concert, her music runs the gamut from romantic ballads to high energy honky tonk, attracting audiences ranging from country to pop. With her vivacious and fun personality, McEntire enjoys the distinction of having the highest grossing tour in the history of country music in the late 1990s. **ACHIEVEMENTS** In 1985 she became a member of the Grand Ole Opry. She has won two Grammy Awards (1987 and 1994), eight People's Choice Awards for Favorite Female Musical Performer, among dozens of Country Music Association, American Music and Billboard awards. **QUOTE** Her Hollywood Walk of Fame dedication ceremony took place on Sept. 18, 1998. About the unveiling of her Walk of Fame star, she said, "Never has a kid from Oklahoma felt so proud."

Norman Jewison 🎥 7018 Hollywood

Director, producer, actor, writer

BORN July 21, 1926, in Toronto, Ontario, Canada.
SPOTLIGHTS Jewison studied piano and music theory at the Royal Conservatory, where he developed an ear and appreciation for sound and rhythm. He draws upon that training for

not only the music, but the dialogue in his films. For example, the Brooklyn-Italian dialect in *Moonstruck* (1987) is every bit as much music to Jewison as are the arias in "La Boheme." Previously, he made his professional debut in a college variety show, which he directed and co-wrote. Then Jewison put aside his career goals to enlist in the Royal Canadian Navy. He served bravely during WWII. Returning from his stint in the Navy, he attended University and worked at various odd jobs. He was a bartender, waiter, dishwasher, and taxi cab driver. It was a two-year work/study program at the BBC that opened doors for him. He landed a plum position in Canadian television, directing and producing some of their most popular musicals, dramas, and comedy-variety specials. America called in 1958: he directed "The Andy Williams Show," two Harry Belafonte specials, and Danny Kaye's television debut. His last TV special was the celebrated "Judy Garland Show" starring Frank Sinatra and Dean Martin. Collected three Emmys along the way. Stylish, diverse, intelligent, he turned motion picture director with *Forty Pounds of Trouble* (1963), starring Tony Curtis. His suspenseful, high-stakes poker film, *The Cincinnati Kid* (1965), stars Steve McQueen as a New Orleans cardsharper. This insightful director distilled sharp political satire on the Cold War in *The Russians Are Coming! The Russians Are Coming!* (1966) starring the dark-haired, handsome hunk, John Phillip Law, and introduced the talented Alan Arkin to the big screen. With his keen eye and sublime skills, Jewison offered the detective story, *In the Heat of the Night* (1967). This outstanding motion picture explores small town racial tensions. With its excellent cast and perfect timing, it became a favorite at the Oscars, as well as a classic, winning Best Picture and five other Academy Awards. Other directorial triumphs: *Send Me No Flowers* (1964), *The Thomas Crown Affair* (1968), *Fiddler on the Roof* (1971), *Jesus Christ Superstar* (1973), *Rollerball* (1975), *A Soldier's Story* (1984), *Agnes of God* (1985), *Moonstruck* (1987), *In Country* (1989), *Only You* (1994), *Bogus* (1996), and *The Hurricane* (1999--also prod.). His works are as varied as his own life experience. Jewison once commented, "I derive inspiration from the nature of the material I'm working on, and it's for this reason that I prefer a new subject matter on every film. As a director, I've got to know who and what I'm making a film about, so I have to spend a good deal of time researching the material." **ACHIEVEMENTS** Presented with the prestigious Irving G. Thalberg Memorial Award in 1999 "for the most consistent high level of production achievement by an individual producer." He is also a three-time Oscar-nominee for Best Director. His films have won 12 out of 45 nominations. He received his star on the Walk of Fame Nov. 14, 1988…When he's not working, he is a gentleman farmer on his 450-acre farm in Ontario, Canada. **QUOTE** "The film you present should preserve your intentions for all time. Film is forever."

Ivan Reitman 🎥 7018 Hollywood

Director, producer

BORN Oct. 27, 1946, in Komarmo, Czechoslovakia. **SPOT-**

Ivan Reitman (holding plaque) with friends: actress Natassja Kinski, and actors Billy Crystal (left) and Robin Williams.

LIGHTS After studying music at McMaster University in Ontario, a summer course in filmmaking captured his imagination. While a student, he directed three shorts. One — *Orientation*—was so well received that it was distributed to theatres across Canada. His breakthrough film was as co-producer of Universal's *Animal House* (1978—aka *National Lampoon's Animal House*), which introduced John Belushi to American filmgoers. Shot at the University of Oregon, in Eugene, and directed by John Landis, this hilarious college comedy was a gigantic box office triumph. With this hit under his belt, Reitman directed *Meatballs* (1979), a summer camp comedy starring Bill Murray. Next, he directed and co-produced *Stripes* (1981), starring Bill Murray and Harold Ramis. A stupendously successful military comedy, it showed that army life was nothing like the TV ads. In 1984 he directed/produced the immensely popular *Ghostbusters*. This big budget comedy was a spectacular triumph. The all-star cast was hip and fun: Bill Murray, Dan Aykroyd, Harold Ramis, Sigourney Weaver, Rick Moranis and Annie Potts. In 1997 he produced *Private Parts*, based on radio shock-jock Howard Stern's autobiographical book, and starring Stern as himself. The resulting film, cleverly directed by Betty Thomas, surprised critics and the public at large who had assumed it would be vulgar with low-brow comedy. *Private Parts* managed to be touching, entertaining, and revealing. A really good movie, it was overlooked by Academy voters. Reitman has directed and/or produced many hits, including *Twins* (1988), *Ghostbusters II* (1989), *Kindergarten Cop* (1990), *Beethoven* (1992), *Dave* (1993), *Junior* (1994), and *Space Jam* (1996). **ACHIEVEMENTS** The recipient of many honors and awards, including the 1984 Director of the Year Award given by the National Association of Theater Owners. In 1994, he was featured in *Variety* magazine, *in the special Billion Dollar Director issue*. His exciting Hollywood Walk of Fame ceremony took place on May 5, 1997.

Joyce Compton 🎥 7018 Hollywood
Actress

BORN Eleanor Hunt; Jan. 27, 1907, in Lexington, KY. **SPOTLIGHTS** Her speciality was playing dim-witted blondes in silent movies, but Compton proved to be a versatile talent during the Golden Era. She worked with screen giants Cary Grant and Irene Dunne in the box office smash, *The Awful Truth* (1937). Of her 200 movies, she made *Imitation of Life* (1934), *Trade Winds* (1938), *Mildred Pierce* (1945), *Sorry, Wrong Number* (1948), and *Mighty Joe Young* (1949). Died: 1999.

Lalo Schifrin 🔴 7018 Hollywood
Pianist, composer, conductor, arranger

Lalo Schifrin

BORN June 21, 1932, in Buenos Aires, Argentina. **SPOTLIGHTS** Think for a moment about pulsating theme to "Mission: Impossible." That's Schifrin's work. Not only did the tune define the urgent nature of the TV show (which first aired in Sept. 1966), but when the tune was released in 1968 as a single, it quickly climbed Billboard's "Hot 100" chart and stayed there for 14 weeks. Two "Mission: Impossible" albums also created a pop/jazz sensation in the 1960s. Schifrin is a true Renaissance man. Always in top form, whether conducting a symphony orchestra, playing piano in a jazz combo, scoring a film or television show, or composing works for a string quartet. Received early classical training from his father, Luis Schifrin, a pioneer of the Philharmonic Orchestra of Buenos Aires and for 35 years its formidable concertmaster at the famed Teatro Colon. Other illustrious artists who guided him are Juan Carlos Paz, Enrique Barenboim, and Mariano Drago. As a child he was exposed to such great talents as Toscannini, Callas, Heifetz, Ormandy, and Rubenstein. His desire for creative expression led him to search for new musical horizons, and typical of Schifrin's overwhelming desire to learn about all forms of music he embraced the advanced vortex of American jazz; the music of Miles Davis, Thelonious Monk, Charlie Parker, and Dizzy Gillespie (who later asked Schifrin to become the pianist for the Gillespie Band). He moved to America in 1958. He has since conducted more than 100 scores, including *Cool Hand Luke* (1967), *The Fox* (1968), *Dirty Harry* (1971), *Enter the Dragon* (1973), *Voyage of the Damned* (1976), *The Amityville Horror* (1979), *The Competition* (1980), *Mission: Impossible* (1996), and *Money Talks* (1997). TV credits include "Mannix," "Dr. Kildare," "Medical Center," "The Rise and Fall of the Third Reich," and "Hollywood Wives." His songs have been performed by such superior talents as Carmen McRae, Tony Bennett, Peggy Lee and Barbra Streisand. Traveled the world as conductor for national orchestras. Creator of classical works, he is also president/musical director of the Young Musicians Foundation.

Douglas Fairbanks 🎥 7018 Hollywood
Actor

Douglas Fairbanks

BORN Douglas Ulman; May 23, 1883, in Denver, CO. **SPOTLIGHTS** A former Broadway sensation, his charm, vitality, and athletic prowess made him one of the most famous silent screen stars. He was easily worth the $2,000-a-week salary back in 1914, appearing in social comedies and adventure stories. With his devil-may-care attitude, he became the silent movie's greatest swashbuckler. Motion pictures include *The Mark of Zorro* (1920), *The Three Musketeers* (1921), *Robin Hood* (1922), *The Thief of Bagdad* (1924), *Don Q Son of Zorro* (1925), *The Black Pirate* (1926), *The Gaucho* (1927), and *The Iron Mask* (1928). By 1931 he was making more than $5,000 a day. **ACHIEVEMENTS** In 1919, he co-founded United Artists with Mary Pickford, Charlie Chaplin, and D.W. Griffith. **HIGHLIGHTS** His marriage to Beth Sully (1907-'18) produced son Douglas Fairbanks, Jr. Then, he married the "Queen of Hollywood" Mary Pickford (1920-'35)—he was the "King." **QUOTE** "One of the best things in this little old world is enthusiasm. All children have it, but when they grow up they often lose it, and that's one of the world's tragedies. To be successful you have to be happy; to be happy you must be enthusiastic; to be enthusiastic you must be healthy; and to be healthy you must keep mind and body active. Whatever you undertake—whether it be grinding knives or building railroads—there will be plenty of competition. Learn the value of competition by competing with yourself. Make today's work be better than yesterday's." Died: 1939.

Four Step Brothers 7018 Hollywood
Dance team

The Four Step Brothers

BORN Stan Getz (Saxophonist), Feb. 2, 1927, in Philadelphia, PA; Bill Harris, (Trombonist); Ralph Burns (Arranger), June 29, 1922, in Newton, MA; Jimmy Guiffre (Arranger). **SPOTLIGHTS** There are many "firsts" in the careers of Rufus "Flash" McDonald, Maceo Anderson, Prince Spencer, and the late Al Williams. "America's greatest dance team" broke the "color barrier" in many venues. They were the first black attraction to play New York City's Radio Music Hall, and the Copa City in Miami Beach. They opened the doors for such performers as Lena Horne and Sammy Davis, Jr. Their fast rhythms, acrobatic leaps and boogie woogie jitterbug tap dancing excited audiences around the world. Died: Getz, 1991.

Ann Sheridan 7018 Hollywood
Actress

Ann Sheridan

BORN Clara Lou Sheridan; Feb. 21, 1915, in Denton, TX. **SPOTLIGHTS** Her prize for winning a beauty contest was a bit part in a Paramount's *Search for Beauty* (1934). Immediately signed, she worked in dozens of films, then switched to Warner Bros. Known as the redheaded "oomph girl," this sweet-natured, energetic beauty became one of Hollywood's love goddesses. Films include *Mrs. Wiggs of the Cabbage Patch* (1934), *Little Miss Thoroughbred* (1938), *Angels with Dirty Faces* (1938), *The Man Who Came to Dinner* (1942), *King's Row* (1942--her breakthrough dramatic role), *Shine on Harvest Moon* (1944), *The Unfaithful* (1947), *I Was a Male War Bride* (1949), and *Stella* (1950). She made 80 movies...Her hobby was dressing up as a clown in full makeup and curly wig. She performed for children at the circus, in hospitals, and at orphanages. No one knew it was her in a funny disguise. Died: 1967.

Tony Danza 7018 Hollywood
Actor, singer, dancer, producer

Tony Danza

BORN April 21, 1950, in Brooklyn, NY. **SPOTLIGHTS** Danza attended the University of Dubuque, in Iowa, on a wrestling scholarship. He graduated with a degree in History Education, but pursued his interest in boxing. It was at a gymnasium in New York that the agile, strong youth was discovered by a producer. This led to a part in James Brooks's critically acclaimed TV series, "Taxi." Danza was cast as an Italian middleweight who worked as a cabdriver. He has been a knockout ever since. The popular situation comedy "Who's The Boss" followed. He delivered a fine dramatic performance in the Showtime's "North Shore Fish" (1997). Academy Award-winning director William Friedkin pushed him harder in the tense remake of "12 Angry Men" (1997), where Danza turns in his best work ever. He appears in Disney's remake of *Angels in the Outfield*

(1994). An energetic song-and-dance man, this personable and charming talent has staged sold-out shows in Las Vegas and Atlantic City to enthusiastic crowds and rave reviews.

Wesley Snipes 🎥 7018 Hollywood

Actor, producer

Wesley Snipes

BORN July 31, 1963, in Orlando, FL. **SPOTLIGHTS** At age 11, his mother signed him up for a martial arts course at the Harlem YMCA, where he also became interested in dancing. A natural born talent, both athletic and graceful, Snipes attended Manhattan's High School for the Performing Arts to study acting. But, much to his dismay, his mother moved the family back to Orlando. During high school, he teamed up with friends to form Struttin' Street Stuff, a traveling puppet troupe. In the summer, they were paid by the city to perform in public parks, community centers and schools. A fun, creative outlet for entertaining, it allowed him to gauge audience reaction, and learn comic timing and delivery firsthand. In 1980, Snipes attended State University of New York, at Purchase. He commented, "I prepared to be a well-trained actor for the classical American stage." He subsequently landed roles on broadway in such productions as "Boys of Winter," "Execution of Justice," and Nobel laureate Wole Soyinka's "Death and the King's Horsemen." In 1985, he auditioned for a film role in Warner Bros.' *Wildcats*, starring Goldie Hawn, Swoosie Kurtz and James Keach. Snipes' charisma was apparent from the get-go, and his fresh appealing nature added humor to the comedy. He followed up his screen debut with a large supporting role in Joe Roth's boxing drama, *Streets of Gold* (1986), opposite Klaus Maria Brandauer and Adrian Pasdar. In 1987, the tall, very handsome actor was cast as the rival gang leader against Michael Jackson in the music video "Bad," directed by Martin Scorscsc. Snipes made several feature films, in both good supporting and starring roles, including playing the baseball player Willie Mays Hays in *Major League* (1989), and as the skilled jazz saxophonist, Shadow Henderson, in Spike Lee's *Mo' Better Blues* (1990). His breakthrough role was as the garish gangland drug lord, Nino Brown, in *New Jack City* (1991). The gangster persona had specifically been written with him in mind by screenwriter Barry Michael Cooper. Next, the versatile talent stars in Spike Lee's interracial romance drama, *Jungle Fever* (1991), opposite Annabella Sciorra. Snipes received both critical and public acclaim for his role, where the camera clearly picked up on his integrity. He possesses both serenity and intrigue, and when he flashes his smile, it is a dazzling one--ideal leading man material. Other motion pictures include the highly rated drama *The Waterdance* (1992), the excellent com-

edy *White Men Can't Jump* (1992), and the action picture *Passenger 57* (1992), which features his martial arts expertise and physical prowess. He portrays an LAPD special detective working to solve a murder in *Rising Sun* (1993) opposite Sean Connery, then is the diabolical Simon Phoenix who battles Sylvester Stallone in *Demolition Man* (1993). He stars in the fast-paced aerial action film *Drop Zone* (1994) as a U.S. marshal. In 1995 he appears in *Money Train* with Woody Harrelson, portrays one of a trio of drag queens stranded in a small Midwestern town in Universal's *To Wong Foo, Thanks for Everything, Julie Newmar*, and appears in the drama, *Waiting to Exhale*, based on the best-selling novel by Terry McMillan. He co-stars with Robert De Niro in *The Fan* (1996). His work with director Mike Figgis in *One Night Stand* (1997) won him the Best Actor Volpi Cup at the Venice Film Festival. Snipes stars in the title lead of *Blade* (1998), a vampire slayer based on the Marvel Comic book character. The dark action picture, which Snipes also produced, knocked the World War II movie, *Saving Private Ryan*, off its longstanding #1 position at the box office. *Blade* went on to become one of the top-selling DVDs of all time. He also produced the critically acclaimed Miramax feature film, *Down in the Delta*, which premiered Christmas 1998. It was Pulitzer Prize-winning poet Dr. Maya Angelou's directorial debut. This unforgettable story of discovery stars multi award-winning actress Alfre Woodard and has garnered several prestigious awards, including a Christopher, Prism, and a NAACP Image Award for Best Motion Picture. Snipes has also produced the highest rated cable special of all time, TNT's "The First Tribute to the Martial Arts Masters of the 20th Century," which showcased some of the greatest innovators of the martial arts. His Hollywood Walk of Fame star was unveiled on August 21, 1998. **QUOTE** "Not very many brothas from the boogie-down Bronx end up with a Star on the Walk of Fame. So, if they decide that they want to pull it up, let me know so I can take it back to the Bronx with me--see if I can trade it for a pair of Pumas!"

George Schlatter 📺 7030 Hollywood

Producer, director, writer

BORN in Birmingham, AL. **SPOTLIGHTS** One of Hollywood's most prolific producer-director-writers, his tremendous talent has given the gift of laughter to millions of fans. Schlatter has

George Schlatter

left an indelible mark on comedy/variety television programming. He is responsible for more than 1,000 hours of TV series and specials, Schlatter created such breakthrough series as "Rowan & Martin's Laugh-In." A main force in the discovery and development of many comedy stars, he began as a general manager and show producer for a Los Angeles nightclub. In Las Vegas he hired the stars as well.

Schlatter moved to television, where he produced shows for Dinah Shore, Andy Williams, Judy Garland, Frank Sinatra, Liza Minnelli, Bill Cosby, and others. Established the American Comedy Awards. **ACHIEVEMENTS** Among his countless honors are four Emmys, Golden Globe Awards, Image Awards, Directors Guild Award, and Producers Guild "Man of the Year" Award. **QUOTE** "Of all the work I've done, I am perhaps most proud of my involvement in the early careers of performers like Goldie Hawn, Lily Tomlin, Roseanne, Robin Williams and others who have gone on to greater heights. Working with stars is rewarding, but helping to create stars is the most fulfilling of all accomplishments."

James Brolin 7030 Hollywood
Actor, director

BORN July 18, 1940, in Los Angeles, CA. **SPOTLIGHTS** Raised in Los Angeles, and educated at UCLA, this tall, ruggedly handsome talent found acting work almost immediately upon graduation. He made his television debut in the controversial "Bus Stop" dramatic series, based on the play of the same name by playwright William Inge. The program revolved around the people (travelers, drifters, etc.) who stopped at the bus stop diner in the small town of Sunrise, Colorado. One episode, which featured a psychopath, was cited in Congressional hearings on violence in television. The president of ABC promptly cancelled the series. Due to his versatility, Brolin had little trouble finding work. He landed roles in TV Westerns, romance, comedy, drama and adventure shows. Brolin made his motion picture debut in the sweet, light family comedy, *Take Her, She's Mine* (1963), starring James Stewart, Sandra Dee and Audrey Meadows. Next, he lends terrific support in the gritty, nerve-racking action picture directed by Mark Robson, *Von Ryan's Express* (1965), starring Frank Sinatra. He appears in the sci-fi picture, *Fantastic Voyage* (1966), with Raquel Welch, then works with Tony Curtis, Henry Fonda and George Kennedy in the crime film, *The Boston Strangler* (1968). Brolin fluctuated between both the small and big screens. He became best known to television viewers on two long-running series. First, he played Dr. Stephen Kiley, the young assistant to Robert Young in the popular and highly successful medical series, "Marcus Welby, M.D." (1969-'76). Nominated four times for an Emmy Award, he won in 1970. Brolin also won two Golden Globes for Best Supporting Actor in 1971 and 1973. Brolin is also closely identified with his role as Peter McDermott, manager of the elegant, upscale "Hotel." This dramatic show, which he occasionally directed, ran from 1983-'88, and won Brolin millions of female fans attracted to his quiet and diffident charm. He possesses a soothing speaking voice and very masculine manner. Women find his sex appeal irresistible. One of TV's most popular stars, Brolin returned to series work in 1997 in "Pensacola: Wings of Gold." He portrays a tough, fearless Lieutenant Colonel and war hero whose new mission is to find and train the next generation of heroes. He has starred in some of the highest-rated television movies, including "Extreme," "Angel Falls," and the outstand-

James Brolin (left), Johnny Grant and Barbra Streisand

ing mini-series "And The Sea Will Tell." He has also directed numerous episodes of the ensemble Western series "The Young Riders." Other motion pictures include *Skyjacked* (1972) with Charlton Heston, *Westworld* (1973) co-starring Richard Benjamin and Yul Brynner, *Gable and Lombard* (1976—as Clark Gable), *Capricorn One* (1978) opposite Elliott Gould and Hal Holbrook, *The Amityville Horror* (1978) opposite Margot Kidder, *Gas, Food Lodging* (1991) with Brooke Adams, Ione Skye and Fairuza Balk, and *Cheatin' Hearts* (1993) co-starring Sally Kirkland and Kris Kristofferson. He made his directorial feature film debut with *Brothers in Arms* (1999). He married actress-singer-director Barbra Streisand in 1998. It proved to be a banner year for him, he received his star on the Hollywood Walk of Fame on Aug. 27, 1998...His hobby is NASCAR and stock car racing. More than enthusiast, he is a driver. He has raced stock cars throughout America.

Mary Hart 7030 Hollywood
Broadcaster, singer, dancer, producer

BORN Nov. 8, 1956, in Sioux Falls, SD. **SPOTLIGHTS** She is one of the most visible, respected, and articulate broadcast journalists in entertainment news. Although born in South Dakota, Hart moved with her family to Europe when she was eight years old. Thus, began an incredible life experience for Hart, who spent four years each in Denmark and Sweden

Mary Hart

before returning to the United States. In America, Hart attended a boarding school, then enrolled in Augusta College where she majored in English. Following her graduation she became a high school English teacher. Almost simultaneously Hart began her television career by hosting a local cable show. She moved into broadcasting full time when she relocated to Iowa, where she developed a public service radio and TV program. Invited to Oklahoma City, Hart produced and hosted the successful morning interview show, "Dannysday," as well as a variety of specials. She moved to Los Angeles and in 1981 became the co-host for NBC-TV's "Regis Philbin Show." Ingeniously, she produced her *own* customized video resume which won her the much coveted co-hosting position on "Entertainment Tonight" in 1982. Her work on "Entertainment Tonight" reflects both integrity and sensitivity; two traits which have gained Hart a huge, loyal following across North America. On May 12, 1989 this beautiful Emmy-nominated anchor led "ET" to its staggering 2,000th episode, a landmark in syndicated TV. (This is also the same day she received her star on the Walk of Fame.) She has interviewed the "Who's Who" of show business for nearly two decades. About this she stated, "People have always been fascinated with the stars we interview. What they're like, if they're real. Over the years, we've had the chance to interview so many Hollywood personalities and chronicle the ups and downs of so many careers, that now we have a truly unique, long-term perspective that can't be duplicated by any other show." Hart's trademark is her upbeat, zesty style, which inspired late-night TV host David Letterman to quip to her, "This perkiness must be stopped." Hart has also hosted Pasadena's annual Tournament of Roses Parade, the Macy's Thanksgiving Day Parade, and the Children's Miracle Network Telethon. She is in demand for speaking engagements throughout the United States. Audiences find her as eloquent as she is knowledgeable on such diversified subjects as women's issues, personal achievement and positive thinking. **HIGHLIGHTS** An accomplished entertainer, Hart has performed at major sold-out venues in Las Vegas and Atlantic City. Her live shows have won several awards for their outstanding stage qualities. She has starred in musical revues, sung the National Anthem at Dodger Stadium (and other sport events), has hosted and sung in the Presidential Inaugural Anniversary Gala at the Kennedy Center for a distinguished audience that included President and Mrs. Bush, and created platinum selling physical fitness videos: "Shape Up With Mary Hart," and "Mary Hart - Fit and Firm." This extremely fit, serious athlete is competitive in snow skiing, ice skating, jet skiing and hiking. **HIGHLIGHTS** In 1987 her stunning legs

were insured by Lloyd's of London for $1 million each. **QUOTE** When she received her star on May 12, 1989, Hart said, "I cannot believe in one month I got married *and* I'm getting my star on the Walk of Fame. I'm so happy. This is such an honor."

Engelbert Humperdinck
7030 Hollywood

Singer, musician

Engelbert Humperdinck and Johnny Grant

BORN Arnold George Dorsey; May 2, 1936, in Madras, India, while his father served as an officer in the British Army. **SPOTLIGHTS** Internationally known as "The King of Romance," he was born the ninth out of ten children. As a teen, he dreamed of fronting a big swing band. By age 17, Humperdinck was a professional saxophone player. When he entered a singing contest and won, his career focus shifted. Humperdinck never looked back, although he thought he might have to give up singing when he contracted tuberculosis. As if it were straight out of a Hollywood movie script, he fought his way back to health, then ironically got his big break when he substituted for a scheduled performer who fell ill. The year was 1967 and the appearance took British television by storm. This new sex symbol sang "Release Me" right up the Hit Parade pop charts to a platinum record, preventing "Penny Lane" from reaching the #1 spot. His "After The Lovin'" (1976) received two Grammy nominations, became a double platinum album and a #1 gold single. Other popular favorites include "There Goes My Everything," "The Last Waltz," "Am I That Easy to Forget," "(Lonely Is) A Man Without Love," "This Moment in Time," "Spanish Eyes," "Les Bicyclettes de Belsize," and "Winter World of Love." The 1998 release of *The Dance Album* has catapulted him onto the dance charts in the United States and Great Britain. *Billboard* magazine described it as "brilliantly cool." *The Dance Album* contains dance remixes of his classic hits, along with five new cuts. The music videos generated from this have received rave reviews. Humperdinck is tall, dark and handsome. His intimate styles and romantic ballads personify his elegance. Around the globe, this charming, charismatic entertainer has one of the largest, most devoted following with 250 fan clubs. Millions have been with him for more than 30 years, and now their children are his fans, too. About his enthusiastic reception, he commented, "Applause is the food of an artist." In all he has released more than 52 albums, and his annual world tour sells out. "Show business is a life of dedication. You have to dedicate yourself not only to your music and your work, but also to your audience," he declared. **ACHIEVEMENTS** One of the top-selling recording artists with more than 120 million records sold, 27 platinum albums, and

68 golds to his credit. Well-educated and highly intelligent, he records in English, German, Spanish and Italian. He devotes many resources to various charitable causes worldwide...And, besides Elvis, he was the only one to fill the showroom at the Las Vegas Hilton. **SIDELIGHTS** Known for his wit and sense of humor, with tongue-in-cheek he sang "Fly High Lesbian Sea Gull" on the movie soundtrack of *Beavis and Butt-head Do America*. **HIGHLIGHTS** He changed his name to that of the composer of "Hansel and Gretel," as "it was unique." His daughter, Louise Dorsey, is known professionally as Blu (her stage name). Blu has followed in her father's footsteps and has become a singer/songwriter, performing her original material regularly in Engelbert's shows. This talented prodigy has penned several songs for her father's albums. His son, Scott Dorsey, keeps a close eye on his dad's career as personal manager. Engelbert's youngest boy, Bradley, is responsible for road management, while eldest son, Jason, is raising a family of his own and looking into the show business bug himself. Engelbert maintains a home in Leicester, England (the family's hometown), with his wife of 35 years, Patricia. His Hollywood Boulevard Walk of Fame dedication ceremony was celebrated on Oct. 21, 1989. **QUOTE** "Pounding the pavement was an essential process for my growth as a human being and an entertainer. If life had been handed to me without the struggle, I probably would not have walked that extra mile that got me to where I am today...I am flattered and honored to be a part of this pavement of accomplishments. To those of you who ever feel that you just can't take another step, or knock on one more door to find your destiny, come stride the Walk of Fame. We'll give you the extra push and the pat on the back that you may need."

Tichi Wilkerson Kassel 🎥 7030 Hollywood
Publisher

Tichi Wilkerson Kassel and President George Bush

BORN In Los Angeles, CA. **SPOTLIGHTS** A daughter of the Verdugo family, her ancestors came to the continent around 1522 with the Spanish explorer and conqueror of Mexico, Hernan Cortes. Born of an American father and a Mexican mother, she was raised in Mexico City and returned to her native Los Angeles as a teenager. She grew into a raven-haired beauty. Her mentor, studio chief Joseph Schenck introduced her to William R. "Billy" Wilkerson, publisher and editor-in-chief of *The Hollywood Reporter*, a highly regarded entertainment news daily and Hollywood's first daily trade paper. After initially rejecting his advances, within a few months the two lovebirds were married, and had two children (see below). When the children began attending school, Tichi joined her husband in the office to learn how to run the paper. After her

husband passed away more than a decade later, she became the publisher and Editor-in-Chief. She continued in the tradition of excellence, as well as becoming a pioneer. This intelligent, savvy woman formulated new policies that dramatically increased its international circulation and the paper's impact on the entertainment industry. Among the programs she introduced was the Key Art Awards, which each year recognize outstanding artists in motion picture and television advertising and promotion. She also inaugurated *The Hollywood Reporter* Marketing Concepts Awards, which recognizes motion picture exhibitors who have originated the most imaginative and effective movie marketing campaigns. While continuing to run the paper, she married the world renowned security expert, businessman, and producer, Arthur M. Kassel. Proud of her heritage, *The Hollywood Reporter* was among the 100 most successful Hispanic companies in America. She is also the co-author of *The Hollywood Reporter—The Golden Years*, and *Hollywood Legends—The Golden Years of the Hollywood Reporter*. **ACHIEVEMENTS** In 1973, this energetic publisher called a small group of women together and founded the important organization, Women in Film. Her intent was to aid women in the entertainment business by increasing their visibility, helping them network with their peers, and unifying professional women in the industry. Throughout Women in Film's history, Wilkerson Kassel has been an emotional and inspirational guide. She is also a tremendous source of financial support, often giving her own money to keep the organization going and fund scholarship programs. The benefits of her original vision are now being enjoyed by thousands of creative women nationally and in 20 countries around the world. She also holds the title of Founder and President Emerita of Women in Film and its global branch, Women in Film International. "The Tichi Wilkerson Kassel, Women in Film Cottage and Garden" that she sponsored for the The Motion Picture & Television Fund (formerly known as the Motion Pictures Country Home and Hospital) is a special millennium site and serves as a retirement home and hospital for entertainment industry personnel who have fallen on hard times.

From left to right: Michael Jackson, Sophia Loren, Tichi Wilkerson Kassel and Sylvester Stallone

Among her many philanthropic gifts, Wilkerson-Kassel endowed the scholarship fund at the Hollywood Women's Press Club. As a major force behind the preservation of historic Olvera Street, as well as the Adobe House (the oldest house in Los Angeles), she was named "La Madrina de Los Angeles" by Los Amigos del Pueblo. (La Madrina translates to "godmother," and is the most respected woman. The title is reserved for someone very special who has helped the community the most.) In 1996, she was awarded the Hero of Los Angeles Award by the Hispanic Women's Council for her humanitarian efforts. She has received local, national and international recognition for her good Samaritan endeavors, but her humble nature has often kept her quiet about her contributions and honors. She received the Order of Arts and Letters from French President Mitterand, and later, the National Order of Merit, France's highest service award, from French President Jacques Chirac and the French Government. A patron of the arts and a civic leader, she founded and chairs the Beverly Hills-Cannes sister city committee, which linked the two largest film festivals in the world (the American Film Market and the Cannes Film Festival). **HIGHLIGHTS** Their son, William R. Wilkerson, Jr., became a composer of both classical and contemporary music, and their daughter, Cynthia Diane Wilkerson, became a theatrical agent and personal manager. Tichi's Walk of Fame star was dedicated on July 13, 1989. A fabulous post-party hosted by Arthur M. Kassel and Johnny Grant was held at the spectacular Hollywood Roosevelt Hotel—the original site of the Academy Awards ceremony. 1500 entertainment industry people attended Hollywood's social event of the year, the grandest ever for a Walk of Fame ceremony. **QUOTE** "All of our stars will be a reminder to future generations that we were here, were respected by our peers, and how important history and tradition are to the entertainment industry. I am honored to be a part of that history and tradition."

Joan Rivers   7030 Hollywood
Comedienne, author, actress

Joan Rivers

BORN Joan Molinsky, in Brooklyn, New York City, N.Y. **SPOTLIGHTS** Known as the "queen of the barbed one-liners," she is a witty, energetic, fast-talking comic. The throaty-voiced joker went from Greenwich Village coffee houses and cabarets—where a hat would be passed around after her performance to collect coins—to sold-out, prestigious concert venues across the country. Along the way, Rivers honed her comedic skills at Chicago's renowned "Second City." As an aspiring comic, she aimed for the biggest break in the business—landing an coveted spot on "The Tonight Show." Rivers

auditioned seven times unsuccessfully for the program. Even suffering repeated rejections, she refused to give up. Finally, she hit pay dirt in 1965 winning rave reviews from Johnny Carson himself. She appeared as a guest for 18 years before being named its sole permanent guest hostess in 1983, a position she held for the next three years. In 1986 she helped launch the fourth network (Fox) with her own "The Late Show Starring Joan Rivers" (1986), but it was short-lived. Next, she took her combination of humor and gossip to daytime with "The Joan Rivers Show" winning an Emmy. During her years doing stand-up comedy in the 1960s and early '70s she also wrote for Allen Funt's "Candid Camera" and the highly rated television movie "The Girl Most Likely To." As an actress, she made her screen debut in *The Swimmer* (1969) with Burt Lancaster. Reviewer Vincent Canby of *The New York Times* wrote she was "especially interesting." Later, she directed *Rabbit Test* (1978). She is an accomplished screenwriter, and has penned several best-selling books, including *Having a Baby Can Be a Scream, Enter Talking* (her autobiography), and *Bouncing Back: I've Survived Everything...and I mean Everything...and You Can Too!*, published by Harper-Collins. Radio: Host of "The Joan Rivers Show," two hours of talk radio airing nightly on WOR New York and syndicated nationally. She was granted a federal trademark on her popular catchphrase "Can we talk?" **ACHIEVEMENTS** First, her daughter Melissa. Second, Joan Rivers is the only performer ever to have been honored twice by the dramatic society at Harvard. She is a Grammy-nominated comedy recording artist. **QUOTE** Her Walk of Fame star was unveiled on a sweltering hot day on July 26, 1989. Johnny Grant mistakenly called her "Joan Collins." Rivers quipped, "I've been called a bitch before, so it's okay."

Jaclyn Smith   7030 Hollywood
Actress

Jaclyn Smith

BORN Oct, 26, 1947, in Houston, TX. **SPOTLIGHTS** An ultra-feminine, soft-spoken brunette, her classic beauty has been likened to that of the exquisite Gene Tierney (See Tierney's bio in this book.) Smith, like Tierney before her, is adored by women, even with her tremendous good looks. Men, of course, would like to marry her. This highly likable actress became a household name while starring in the smash television hit "Charlie's Angels" (1976-'81) with Farrah Fawcett and Kate Jackson. As a child, Smith studied ballet. Later she studied drama at Trinity University. She joined regional theatre in Boston, then moved to New York where she was signed as the "Breck Girl" and seen in magazine print ads and TV commercials. After she moved to Hollywood, she landed TV roles in

"The Rookies," "McCloud" and "Switch." In 1980 she starred as "Jacqueline Bouvier Kennedy" in one of the most successful TV movies of all time. A dear friend of author Sidney Sheldon, Smith has starred in numerous mini-series adapted from his novels, including "Rage of Angels." With her heavenly looks she became the key cosmetic spokeswoman for Max Factor makeup. Offscreen, she is a kind, gracious lady, and devoted mother. **ACHIEVEMENTS** Honored Chair of the Crippled Children's Society. She was honored with her Hollywood Walk of Fame star on Nov. 6, 1989.

Chuck Norris 🎥   7030 Hollywood

Chuck Norris

Actor, martial arts expert
BORN Carlos Ray Norris; March 10, 1940, in Ryan, OK. **SPOTLIGHTS** Born of an English-Irish mother and a Cherokee Indian father, Norris fought out his childhood on the mean streets in Los Angeles before suiting up with the United States Air Force. In the U.S.A.F. Norris began his martial arts training while serving in South Korea, where he earned a black belt in karate and a brown belt in judo. After his discharge he devoted his life to martial arts, opening his own studio in 1963, then competing in tournaments. In 1968 he became professional middleweight champion of the world, a title he held until retiring undefeated in 1974. One of his karate students, star Steve McQueen, suggested he take up acting, and in 1973 Norris made his screen debut eyeball to eyeball against kung fu hero Bruce Lee in the classic *Return Of The Dragon*. He starred in these action pics: *A Force of One* (1978), and the fearsome hit *Lone Wolf McQuade* (1983). With a flurry of fists and feet in awesome range, he got bigger and better in *Missing in Action* (1984), *Code of Silence* (1985) and *Delta Force II* (1990). TV: Stars in "Walker, Texas Ranger." He received his Walk of Fame star on Dec. 15, 1989. (See Gene Autry's bio in this book.) **RECIPE** His own special drink is called the "Chuck Norris Kicker." It's hot tea with Grand Marnier during the winter, and iced tea with Grand Marnier during the summer. (Don't drink and drive; or you know who will kick your...)

Lou Gossett, Jr. 🎥   7030 Hollywood

Actor, producer
BORN Louis Gossett, Jr.; May 21, 1936, in Brooklyn, NY. **SPOTLIGHTS** Born in the Coney Island section of Brooklyn, Gossett attended Abraham Lincoln High School where he grew into a tall (6'4"), strong, top athlete who won letters in

Lou Gossett, Jr.

three sports, including basketball, where he won all-city honors. When he suffered an injury, a drama teacher suggested he try his talents in a school production. He proved so riveting in the play that the same acting instructor urged him to try out for an open casting call on Broadway. At age 16 Gossett won the role, winning a Donaldson Award for "Best Newcomer in the Theater" (1953). He could not decide which he liked best—athletics or the stage—so he went to New York University on a double basketball and acting scholarship where he was an active star in both fields. The New York Knicks offered him a try out, but simultaneously he won a coveted Broadway role opposite Sidney Poitier in *A Raisin in the Sun*. He later reprised his role in the 1961 film—also his screen debut. Following his acclaimed theatrical performance, he has fluctuated between film, TV and stage. This well-respected, admired actor has been in more than 60 theatrical productions, and has been Emmy-nominated in "Sadat," "A Gathering of Old Men," "Palmer's Town," "The Century Collection Presents Ben Vereen—His Roots," "Backstage at the White House," and "Touched by an Angel." He has starred in numerous TV movies. Motion pictures include *Inside* (1997), *A Good Man in Africa* (1994), *Diggstown* (1992), *Keeper of the City* (1992), *Toy Soldiers* (1991), *Cover-Up* (1991), *The Punisher* (1990), *The Principal* (1987), *Firewalker* (1986), *Iron Eagle* (1996 + two sequels), *Enemy Mine* (1985), *Finders Keepers* (1984), *The River Niger* (1978), *The Deep* (1977), *The Laughing Policeman* (1974), *Travels With My Aunt* (1972), and *The Skin Game* (1971). **ACHIEVEMENTS** 1982 Oscar for his electrifying role as Sergeant Foley in the hit *An Officer and A Gentleman*. 1977 Emmy Award for playing Fiddler in the historic mini-series "Roots." His Walk of Fame star was dedicated on May 20, 1992. Among his many charitable works is the community project "The Family Tree" to help children without a solid family foundation...His great grandmother, a strong willed former slave who lived to be 117, inspired him for his role in *Roots*.

Woody Woodpecker 🎥 7030 Hollywood

Cartoon character
CREATED 1940. **SPOTLIGHTS** With the most famous laugh the world over, this irrepressible, nutty bird continues to bring joy and laughter to kids of all ages. Woody made his debut with Andy Panda in the cartoon "Knock Knock," which catapulted him to fame in "Woody Woodpecker (a.k.a. 'The Cracked Nut')" in 1941. Woody starred in 197 flicks. "The Woody Woodpecker Song" (1948) by Kay Kyser was on the Hit Parade for nine weeks and nominated for an Academy

Woody Woodpecker and Walter Lantz

Award. His creator, Walter Lantz, hosted "The Woody Woodpecker Show" on Saturday mornings for a two-year hit TV series. The gregarious redheaded bird is the official mascot of amusement parks in Japan and Sweden, and serves communities nationwide on behalf of environmental issues. (See the bio of Walter Lantz in this book.)

Keye Luke ▼   7030 Hollywood

Actor

Keye Luke

BORN June 1905, in Guangdong Province, China. **SPOTLIGHTS** He was one of the first male Asian actors to make a name for himself in motion pictures. Raised in Seattle, Luke studied architecture and design at the University of Washington. He moved to Los Angeles in 1928, and became an RKO advertising artist in the publicity department. The studio also utilized his expertise as a technical advisor in Chinese-themed movies. When a director requested a Chinese actor who spoke flawless English for a short film, Luke was cast in the part. With his ultra-photogenic, square-jawed, handsome, dignified face, he was cast as the Chinese doctor with Greta Garbo in *The Painted Veil* (1934). Then, Luke gained worldwide fame as Charlie Chan's "Number One Son" for thirteen movies in the long-running, popular series. His first one was *Charlie Chan in Paris* (1935). Luke also enjoyed a good stretch in his role as a rival doctor's assistant in MGM's *Dr. Gillespie* series—starting in 1942. He also played the fighting sidekick, Kato, in a couple of *The Green Hornet* film series, starting in 1940. Other movies include *The Good Earth* (1937—a must-see pic), *Mr. Moto's Gamble* (1938—in the same detective vein as Charlie Chan, but starring Peter Lorre for a twist), the thrilling drama *Across the Pacific* (1942—it reunited the cast from *The Maltese Falcon*,

starring Humphrey Bogart), *Love is a Many Splendored Thing* (1955), *Around the World in 80 Days* (1956), *The Hawaiians* (1970), and *Gremlins* (1984, and 1990 sequel). **TV** Already into his 80s, Luke portrayed the wise Master Po on TV's "Kung Fu" series; a new generation of fans came to admire him. **ACHIEVEMENTS** Honored with the first Lifetime Achievement Award by the Association of

Keye Luke (seated) & George Takei

Asian/Pacific Artists (1986). One of the founders of the Screen Actors Guild, he donated massive funds to many charities. He received his Hollywood Walk of Fame star on Died: 1991.

LeVar Burton ▼   7030 Hollywood

Actor, director, producer

LeVar Burton

BORN Feb 16, 1957, in Landsthul, West Germany. **SPOTLIGHTS** Burton's first career choice was the priesthood, and at age 13 he entered a Catholic seminary to fulfill his need to express himself spiritually and to be of service to others. After four years he decided an acting career would better fill those needs. He left the seminary and accepted a full academic scholarship at the University of Southern California to pursue a Bachelor of Fine Arts Degree. Burton, active in the USC drama department, saw an audition notice pinned up on a bulletin board. It was announcing a search for the role of Kunta Kinte in the planned mini-series "Roots." He signed up. His audition performance was riveting, and won Burton the role of a lifetime—and one that would launch his career. "Roots" (1977) was the most important and widely watched dramatic show in television history. Based on Alex Haley's research novel of his own roots, the mini-series was of significant historical value to our country. For the first time a face was affixed to the institution of slavery, the face of Kunta Kinte. Half of the entire population of America tuned in to watch Kunta (Burton) deal with life's horrendous blows amid fleeting moments of happiness. Following "Roots," Burton starred in a string of TV movies, but became best known to viewers in his role as Lieutenant Commander Geordi LaForge on the series "Star Trek: The Next Generation." Children know and love him, too, as the host of PBS' acclaimed children's series "Reading Rainbow" since its debut in 1983. He takes pride in the program's ability to encourage reading. He is delighted to help create "human beings who are passionate about literature." In addition to his acting credits, Burton's career as a director/producer keeps him very busy. He has directed several episodes of "Star Trek: The Next Generation," "Star Trek: Deep Space Nine," and "Star Trek: Voyager." In 1998 he received critical acclaim for directing his first dramatic television movie, "The Tiger Woods Story," for Showtime. Through his company—Eagle Nation Films—Burton is developing motion pictures and television projects to direct and produce. 1997 marked his debut as an author with his sci-fi novel, *Aftermath*; published by Warner Books.

Vivian Vance   7030 Hollywood

Actress

Vivian Vance

BORN Vivian Roberta Jones; July 26, 1907, in Cherryvale, KS. **SPOTLIGHTS** The world's most famous female second banana was immortalized as Ethel Mertz on "I Love Lucy." If Lucy was television's Queen of Comedy, Vivian was its Royal Princess. Playing best friend to Lucy was easy. In real life she adored Lucy (as did everyone else), and Lucy felt the same towards her. As the days, weeks, months then years passed, Ethel and Lucy were like two cozy and comfy slippers—they just felt better the more we had them on. "Ethel" emulated what a best friend is all about: support, love, humor, devotion, forgiveness and loyalty. The zany pair set about to fulfill Lucy's crazy schemes, which never worked out. Yet the two were duly ready to try the next new, odd idea that popped into Lucy's mind. You could almost see the gears working in both Lucy's and Ethel's brains. In the fantasy world of make-believe, there's not a gal around who wouldn't kill to have a die-hard pal like Ethel as best friend. In real life Vance was a self-taught actress born with an innate sense of timing and delivery. She appeared in numerous stage plays during the 1930s and '40s. Desi Arnaz caught her performance in "The Voice of the Turtle," at the La Jolla Playhouse, in Southern California, and decided that she would be perfect as Lucy's best friend and neighbor on the show. He was right and the rest is history. She also followed real life pal Lucy into other "Lucy" shows. Entertained millions for nearly 40 years. (Also see the bio of Lucille Ball in this book.) **HIGHLIGHTS** Devoted tireless efforts to the Prevention of Cruelty to Animals, and The National Mental Health Association. **NOTE** Her star was dedicated posthumously on St. Valentine's Day, Feb. 14, 1991. In attendance to honor her were Lucille Ball's daughter, Lucie Arnaz, and the original writers of the series, Bob Carroll and Madeline Pugh. Died: 1979.

The Original 5th Dimension

Vocal group

7030 Hollywood

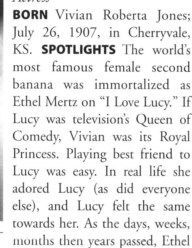
The Original 5th Dimension

BORN Marilyn McCoo, Sept. 30, 1943; LaMonte McLemore, Sept. 17, 1940; Florence LaRue Gordon, Feb. 4, 1944; Ron Townson, Jan. 20, 1941, and Billy Davis, Jr., June 26, 1940. **SPOTLIGHTS** One of the most popular singing groups in the world, the Original 5th Dimension has released more than a dozen top albums and received 14 Gold records. Their classy style and perfect harmonies created a string of pop-soul hits: "Go Where You Want To Go," "Aquarius/Let The Sunshine In," "One Less Bell To Answer," "The Worst That Could Happen," "This Is Your Life," "Wedding Bell Blues," "Stoned Soul Picnic," and "Sweet Blindness." Their special blend of "Champagne Soul" placed a staggering 30 songs on the pop charts in an eight-year period. **ACHIEVEMENTS** In 1967 their single "Up, Up, And Away" became one of the biggest smash hits in music history, leading to an unprecedented five Grammy Awards. The group catapulted to stardom, and their story has been one of success ever since. Billy Davis, Jr. and Marilyn McCoo, became the first African-American husband-and-wife couple to star in their own national television series, "The Marilyn McCoo and Billy Davis, Jr. Show" for CBS. The first single this husband and wife team recorded, "You Don't Have To Be A Star" became a #1 hit, a certified Gold seller, and earned them their first Grammy Award for best R&B Vocal Performance by a Duo. The group donates their time to Easter Seals, The Arthritis Telethon, and The United Negro College Fund. **HIGHLIGHTS** They were the first African American vocal group to break new ground by starring in a Broadway musical, "Ain't Misbehavin'." In the 1990s the group reunited for a concert, and the response was so overwhelming that they had to extend a number of dates with additional cities. Their Hollywood Walk of Fame star was dedicated on Aug. 9, 1991.

Liza Minnelli  7030 Hollywood

Actress, singer, entertainer
BORN March 12, 1946, in Los Angeles, CA. **SPOTLIGHTS**

Liza Minnelli

Born with talent to spare, she is the daughter of award-winning director Vincente Minnelli and the supremely gifted singer-actress, Judy Garland—both Walk of Fame honorees. Liza is a consummate performer in her own right, on stage, in film, television, and in concert. She is a vivacious, high-strung, multi-talented dynamo who can do it all. In 1988 she toured the world, performing with Frank Sinatra and Sammy Davis, Jr. She first appeared in motion pictures when she was only two years old, *In the Good Old Summertime* (1949), in one of her mother's star vehicles. Others include *The Sterile Cuckoo* (1969—in an Oscar-nominated performance), *Lucky Lady* (1975), *New York, New York* (1977), *Arthur* (1981), *The King of Comedy* (1983—cameo), and *Stepping Out* (1991). **ACHIEVEMENTS** In 1965, she became the youngest actress ever to win a Tony in her Broadway debut of "Flora, the Red Menace." Best Actress Oscar for *Cabaret* (1972). Awarded an Emmy for her own television special, "Liza with a Z" (1972). A sparkling entertainer, in 1987 she became the first to sell out

Liza Minnelli and Mark Fleischman

a three-week concert engagement at Carnegie Hall. She received her Walk of Fame star on Sept. 30, 1991. Her 1999 nostalgic Broadway show "Minnelli on Minnelli" (a tribute to her famous father) won the heart of the public. She performed with great spirit. Songs included "I Got Rhythm," "Love," "Shine on Your Shoes," "The Boy Next Door," "Limehouse Blues," "Happiness Is Just a Thing Called Joe," "If I Had You," and "Baubles Bangles and Beads."

Dean Stockwell 🎥 7030 Hollywood

Actor

BORN March 5, 1936, in North Hollywood, CA. **SPOTLIGHTS** A professional child actor, at nine years old he made his auspicious film debut in MGM's musical *Anchors Aweigh* (1945), starring Frank Sinatra and Gene Kelly. With a thick head of curly brown hair, sparkling brown eyes and a fetching charm, American audiences fell head over heels for him. That same year, he made four motion pictures including *Abbott and Costello in Hollywood*. Critics hailed his superb, intuitive talents. His shooting schedule remained hectic throughout his teenage years, including *Song of the Thin Man*

(1947), *Gentleman's Agreement* (1947), *The Boy with Green Hair* (1948), *Down to the Sea in Ships* (1949), the magical and best version of *The Secret Garden* (1949), the Post-Civil War drama *Stars in My Crown* (1950), and the dramatic *The Happy Years* (1950). He became the recipient of numerous acting honors before taking a breather from the business. Upon his return he won the Golden Globe Award for his remarkable performance in *Compulsion* (1959). He was equally brilliant in *Sons*

Dean Stockwell

and Lovers (1960) and *Long Day's Journey into Night* (1962). Other movie credits include *Paris, Texas* (1984), *Dune* (1984), *To Live and Die in L.A.* (1985), *Blue Velvet* (1986), *Beverly Hills Cop II* (1987), and a supporting actor Oscar nomination for his role in *Married To The Mob* (1988), *Tucker* (1988), *The Player* (1992), *Smokescreen* (1990), *Back Track* (1991), *Chasers* (1994), *Mr. Wrong* (1996), and *McHale's Navy* (1997). **TV** He played the quirky, sexy, wisecracking scientist, Albert, on NBC-TV's sci-fi series "Quantum Leap." He has also made numerous movies-of-the-week, and appeared in the Western mini-series "Son of the Morning Star." His Walk of Fame star was dedicated on Feb. 29, 1992, in a *leap* year.

Donna Summer 💿 7030 Hollywood

Singer, songwriter

BORN Donna Adrian Gaines; December 31, 1952, in Boston, MA. **SPOTLIGHTS** Born on New Year's Eve, the youngster grew up listening to the legendary singer Mahalia Jackson. She first tested her own voice at age 10 performing with church choirs. "It was then that I knew I had been given a very special gift from God," she recalled. "It was just a matter of how to best use it." At 18, she won a prime spot in the staged musical production of "Hair" which took her on a journey to Germany. She joined the Vienna Folk Opera, appeared in productions of American classics like "Show Boat" and "Porgy & Bess" eventually moving on to a recording career. Summer was christened the "Queen of Disco" for defining the 1970s musical generation with her well crafted dance minded records. Her hit songs of the era— "Love To Love You Baby," "I Feel Love," "Last

Donna Summer

Dance," and "Hot Stuff"—blended the primal groove urgency of disco and funk with symphonic strings. Summer's world-class vocals, richly enhanced by her dramatic talents, won her numerous Grammys. "Last Dance" won an Oscar for theme song to *Thank God It's Friday*. The pop superstar followed up the next decade with songs like "On the Radio," "She Works Hard For The Money," and "This Time I Know It's for Real." She has recorded children's tunes for Disney, and continues to tour to sold out audiences. **ACHIEVEMENTS** Summer is the first female vocalist to have a #1 single and #1 album on the Billboard Charts simultaneously. Her star was dedicated on March 18, 1992. It is a shining symbol of both her public and peer appreciation and remains a permanent tribute to the past, as well as to the future. **QUOTE** "Of all the songs from those days, I feel most connected to 'Last Dance.' Sing it and it brings tears to my eyes. For me it's a poignant song. There were a lot of people in my life who are not with us anymore. It's like I'm singing to the memory of people who are special to me."

Tom Hanks 🎥   7030 Hollywood

Actor, writer, director, producer

BORN July 9, 1956, in Oakland, CA. **SPOTLIGHTS** One of the world's most beloved and most respected actors, Hanks became interested in acting when he was a student at Skyline High School, in Oakland. Although he had tried soccer and the track team, he found the drama department to be more fun. The kids there appreciated the teen's goofy sense of humor. By the time he had arrived at California State University, in Sacramento, Hanks was beginning to take drama seriously. He appeared in a production of "The Cherry Orchard" and met director Vincent Dowling, who was also the resident director of the Great Lakes Shakespeare Festival in Cleveland, Ohio. Dowling invited Hanks to intern during the summer with the company, and he made his professional stage debut as Grumio in "The Taming of the Shrew." He appeared in the touring production of "The Two Gentlemen of Verona," for which he garnered the Cleveland Critics Award for Best Actor and about $50-a-week in salary. By 1978, he felt ready to head to the Great White Way. He sold his VW Beetle and took the $850. to New York City. He did not land a job on the Broadway stage, but answered a casting call for television's sitcom, "Bosom Buddies" (1980-'82). He was so poor at the time, that after completing the pilot, he asked to borrow $5,000 from the producers. They gave him twice that amount. When the network picked up the show, and he got his first paycheck, Hanks immediately started paying back the borrowed money. It was on this show—where the six-foot-tall actor donned a woman's wig and clothes—that critics first took notice of his comic timing and delivery. Hanks made his movie debut in a low budget, poorly written and executed horror flick, *He Knows You're Alone* (1980). Four years later, he inked a $100,000 deal to return to the silver screen in Ron Howard's romantic comedy hit, *Splash* (1984), opposite Daryl Hannah as a mermaid. This is when moviegoers first fell in love with Hanks' all-American good looks, appealing voice, and natural manner. He appeared in a number of movies, including working with the Great One, Jackie Gleason, in Garry Marshall's

Tom Hanks and wife Rita

Nothing in Common (1986). Playing the character David Basner, Hanks explores father-son psychological issues, which he does so honestly. It is a moving tribute to what would be Gleason's last film. This solid actor hit *Big* (1988) for his first Oscar nomination. Hanks was enchanting in this charming fantasy comedy about a child trapped in a businessman's body. Capturing the innocence, joy and confusion of childhood, his endearing portrayal of "Josh Baskin" won him his first Golden Globe Award. He was named Best Actor by the Los Angeles Film Critics Best Actor Award for his work in both *Big* and *Punchline* (both 1988). The following year, he appears in *Turner and Hooch* (1989), with a slobbering and gigantic drooling dog—ignoring W.C. Fields' advice about never appearing with small children or animals. The comedy fared well. He then made a couple of flops. Hanks came back stronger than before, establishing himself once and for all, both at the box office and with superior motion picture acting, in Penny Marshall's all-star baseball hit, *A League Of Their Own* (1992). He won a second Golden Globe Award for his work as the discouraged romantic lead in *Sleepless in Seattle* (1993), opposite Meg Ryan. (This was his second time Hanks worked with the actress; they were co-stars in *Joe Versus the Volcano* in 1990.) After winning two Oscars (see below), and making $20-million-a-picture, fans wondered if his career could soar any higher? The answer was yes. He was lauded for his portrayal of astronaut Jim Lovell in Ron Howard's Oscar-nominated space exploration epic, *Apollo 13* (1995). That same year, he originated the character of Cowboy Woody in Disney's animated classic, *Toy Story*. He made his writing and directorial debut in the delightful rock 'n' roll nostalgia feature *That Thing You Do!* (1996). Reminiscent of the 1960s Beatlemania that swept the country, Hanks set the story in 1964—a time prior to Vietnam, when America enjoyed an innocence and a sense of hopefulness. (During Vietnam, Hanks stated, "Everything went to hell in a handbag." This is a sentiment shared by former First Lady Jacqueline Kennedy Onassis right down through the baby boom generation.) In 1998, he delivered the breathtaking Emmy-winning 12-episode HBO mini-series "From Earth to the Moon." Not only did he executive produce, but he directed one episode and co-wrote half of the stories exploring the Apollo space program. Hanks stars in Steven Spielberg's bloody WWII remembrance, *Saving Private Ryan* (1998). It is the most realistic and gritty movie portrayal of the horrors of combat to date, and sheds a new moral light on the war. Hanks was Oscar-nominated for his role as Captain John Miller. There was the third felicitous pairing of Hanks and Meg Ryan in the romantic comedy, *You've Got Mail* (1998). He stars in a Stephen King drama (*not* horror), in *The Green Mile* (1999), playing prison guard Paul Edgecombe who builds a unique relationship with an inmate who possesses a miraculous gift. He also reprised his role as Cowboy Woody in Disney's animated sequel, *Toy Story 2* (1999). **ACHIEVEMENTS** 1994 Best Actor Academy Award for *Philadelphia*. He plays the AIDS-stricken lawyer Andrew Beckett. His performance in the title role of *Forrest Gump*, is perfection itself. He won the 1995 Academy Award for Best Actor. He is the first actor in nearly 60 years to win back-to-back Oscars. (The other was Spencer Tracy in *Captains Courageous* in 1937, and *Boys Town* in 1938.) Hanks was also honored with a Golden Globe for *Forrest Gump*, and a Screen Actors Guild Award. In 1994, Hanks was the apple of the Hollywood Women's Press Club's eye. He won two Golden Apple Awards; the Louella O. Parsons Award for the person "who best represents Hollywood and the entertainment industry to the world," and "the most newsworthy male star of the year" award. In 1999, Hanks was accorded the Box Office Star of the Decade, at Showest. His films since 1990 have earned a staggering 2.75 billion dollars. **HIGHLIGHTS** While filming *Volunteers* (1985), Hanks met the beautiful actress, Rita Wilson. Although the motion picture might have been a box office miss, it was a hit for love. The two are happily married and have two sons. Hanks is a devoted family man. **WALK OF FAME** Honorary Mayor of Hollywood, Johnny Grant, unveiled Hanks' Walk of Fame star on June 30, 1992. Hanks' lovely wife, Rita, was at his side rejoicing in the glorious moment. Both were blissfully unaware of a local controversy brewing over the dedication ceremony. There were a couple of unhappy shopkeepers who voiced their disapproval of the latest recipient. They thought the performer was too new and unworthy to receive such an honor, and that his name on a star reflected poorly on the Walk of Fame as a whole. Johnny Grant knew this was nonsense (there are always those who find something to criticize); he knew *Tom Hanks was a star*. Still, the cranky few complained vocally and managed to get a television news crew to come and interview them right at the very spot. They were moaning and groaning about what a huge scandal it was to have Tom Hanks on the Hollywood Walk of Fame. I personally remember having to rush to the boulevard to go on record *on the evening news* defending Tom Hanks. Of course, since 1992 Hanks has proven to be an outstanding actor of the highest caliber and quality. (I bet that those few skeptics are embarrassed now and would deny ever criticizing him. But the evidence exists on tape! That's Hollywood.)

Tom Hanks

Brock Peters   7030 Hollywood

Actor, producer, singer
BORN July 2, 1927, in Harlem, NY. **SPOTLIGHTS** He made his brilliant silver screen debut with *Carmen Jones* (1954), and followed up in *Porgy and Bess* (1959). He won a Golden Globe Award for *To Kill A Mockingbird* (1962), with Gregory Peck. In 1965, he appears in the exciting Peckinpah Western, *Major Dundee* with Charlton Heston, and in the important film *The Pawnbroker* opposite Rod Steiger. He lends support in *The Incident* (1967), in which

Brock Peters

Martin Sheen makes his film debut. He is the lead in *Lost in the Stars* (1974), opposite Melba Moore. (He earned a Tony nomination for the stage version of "Lost in the Stars.") Other movies include *Soylent Green* (1973), *Two-Minute Warning* (1976), *Star Trek IV: The Voyage Home* (1986), *Framed* (1990), *Star Trek VI: The Undiscovered Country* (1991), and *The Importance of Being Earnest* (1992). Known for his intense, well-crafted performances, he has also appeared regularly on stage to rave reviews in such plays as "The Great White Hope," "Othello," and "Showboat." He is a frequent guest star in major dramatic TV movies and mini-series including "Roots II--Second Generation," TV series, and with his beautiful voice is often asked to do narrations for documentaries, and he performs in radio dramas. **ACHIEVEMENTS** 1982 Emmy Award for "Voices of Our People." Like Paul Robeson (see his bio in this book), Peters' community involvement is legendary. A co-founder of the Dance Theatre of Harlem, he has also devoted himself to the free Southern Theatre, which brought free theater to rural areas, and the prestigious Media Forum, which presents distinguished public speakers and prominent media personalities at seminars. He co-founded the Communications Bridge Institute, which provides scholarships and training in media careers for troubled youth. He received his Hollywood Walk of Fame star on April 23, 1992.

Friz Freleng 7030 Hollywood
Cartoon animator, director, producer
BORN Isadore "Friz" Freleng; August 21, 1906, in Kansas City, MO. **SPOTLIGHTS** An animation pioneer, he was a major developer of Warner Bros.' characters. He produced and directed more than 300 beloved cartoons featuring Bugs Bunny, Daffy Duck, Porky Pig, Elmer Fudd, Speedy Gonzales, and other classic Looney Tunes characters. Born to immigrant parents, Freleng discovered at an early age his love of comic strips. As he grew up, he focused on drawing and illustration. The intelligent and funny Freleng became a superb draftsman and started his career in the early 1920s at Kansas City Film Ad. He relocated to Hollywood in 1927 to try to find work as a graphic artist in the motion picture industry. Three years later he struck gold when he landed a position at Warner Bros. He animated that studio's first cartoon ever released, "Sinkin' In The Bathtub" in 1930. By 1933 he had made his directorial debut with "Bosko in Dutch." Freleng quickly became known for his masterful handling of comic timing and musical synchronized animation. Working in Technicolor, he concentrated on "Merrie Melodies." He created and directed Porky Pig in Porky's debut short, "I Haven't Got a Hat" (1935). Still in the mid-1930s, Freleng created the rustic, raucous, hot-headed Yosemite Sam and sneaky Sylvester the Cat. His creation of sweet, innocent Tweety would follow. His other WB associates were animators/directors Chuck Jones, Bob Clampett and Tex Avery for more than a quarter of a century. Theirs was an outstanding teaming of sly wit, technical skills and artistic gifts, and was the driving force of Warner Bros.' legendary animation group, a department affectionately called Termite Terrace. In 1940, he ingeniously delivered his electrifying combination of live-action and animation in "You Ought To Be in Pictures," starring Porky Pig. This technical advancement was a true milestone. It inspired director George Sidney and actor Gene Kelly to make the famous dance scene in *Anchors Aweigh* (1945), where Kelly dances magically with the animated mouse Jerry (from the cartoon "Tom and Jerry").

And close to 50 years after Freleng's innovation, Steven Spielberg and Robert Zemeckis brought his concept to high art with help from computers in the technically brilliant, *Who Framed Roger Rabbit?* (1988). **HIGHLIGHTS** Using beautiful, clean penmanship, Freleng timed his musical pictures on musical bar sheets using extremely tiny lettering. **ACHIEVEMENTS** Winner of five Academy Awards: 1947 for *Tweetie Pie*. 1949 for *So Much For So Little*. 1955 for *Speedy Gonzales*. 1957 for *Birds Anonymous*. 1958 for *Knighty Knight Bugs*. 1981 Hugo Award for lifelong contribution to the animation/film industry. American Film Institute honoree. His career spanned 65 years. "That's All Folks!" Died: 1995, at age 89.

Patti La Belle 7030 Hollywood
Singer, actress

Patti La Belle

BORN Patricia Louise Holt; May 24, 1948, in Philadelphia, PA. **SPOTLIGHTS** The Queen of Rock 'n' Soul. Her shimmering voice brought joyful tears to the eyes of the Beulah Baptist Church congregation when first heard there. Remarkably this soul diva remained a gospel soloist even after embarking on a professional career. In the '60s she led the "girl group" the Bluebells—replete with sequin gowns, bouffant hair styles, and well-rehearsed choreography—to a multi-million seller, "I Sold My Heart to the Junkman." The '70s brought a stylistic change—rock's first all-female band, "LaBelle." It also brought the glitter costumes of the era with its now-famous lame space cadet suits. In 1974 Labelle appeared at the New York Metropolitan Opera House, the first black act to perform there. "Lady Marmalade" (*"Voulez-vous couchez avec moi, ce soir?"*), became the disco anthem of the '70s. In the late '70s she described herself as "Rock and rolled out" and turned to her husband, Armstead Edwards, to manage her solo career. In 1982 she took on Broadway with co-star Al Green in the revival of *Your Arm's Too Short to Box with God* receiving critical acclaim. Her 1985 album *Winner in You* went platinum with "On My Own," "Kiss Away the Pain," and "Oh, People." She had two major hits from the movie *Beverly Hills Cop* with "New Attitude" (it became the theme song for nationally syndicated radio psychologist Dr. Laura Schlessinger), and "Stir It Up." She recorded *Patti LaBelle, Live!* at the famed Apollo Theatre. **ACHIEVEMENTS** Three Emmy nominations for TV work, seven Grammy nominations and one Grammy Award—1991—for Best Rhythm-and-Blues

Female Vocal Performance for *Burnin'*. At Coretta King's request, she musically commemorated the inaugural celebration of the Martin Luther King, Jr. Federal holiday. Serves as spokeswoman for the National Cancer Institute to alert women to the importance of early breast cancer detection. A crusader to encourage adoptions and foster care for children (she's Mom to one son, two adopted sons, and the son and daughter of her sister—who she lost to breast cancer). This warm, loving lady is also humble, she means it when she tells fans, "I'm just like you, only I make records." Small surprise then, that growing up, she was the all-American wholesome teen; she ran track, sang in the glee club, and acted in plays at John Bartam High School. **READING** Her autobiography *Don't Block the Blessings,* published by Putnam Publishers.

Placido Domingo 🎭 7030 Hollywood
Opera singer, conductor

Placido Domingo

BORN January 21, 1941, in Madrid, Spain. **SPOTLIGHTS** The King of Opera descended from parents who were Zarzuela (traditional operettas) performers. When he was eight years old, the family moved to Mexico. There, he studied voice, piano and conducting at the Mexico City Conservatory. Ironically, his first professional singing role in Mexico in 1961 was as a *baritone!* (That was short-lived, although he occasionally sings baritone parts, like the prologue to *Pagliacci*.) Domingo, one of the best *tenors* of the twentieth century, arrived professionally in America in 1966 when he created the title role of Ginastera's *Don Rodrigo* at the New York City Opera. His Metropolitan Opera debut came in 1968, as Maurizio in *Adriana Lecouvreur*, and he has continued to appear there in 400 performances of 38 different roles spanning 30 consecutive seasons. This smooth, rich lyrical tenor plays all the world's grand opera houses: Milan's La Scala, Vienna State Opera, London's Covent Garden, Paris' Bastille Opera, San Francisco Opera, Chicago's Lyric Opera, Los Angeles Music Center Opera, and at the Bayreuth and the Salzburg Festivals. He is a prolific artist, with a tremendous range, who has made a staggering 93 complete recordings of 62 different operas. His breathtakingly beautiful voice—both sweet and powerful—is heard throughout the world on these best-selling gold records as well as in concert. His repertoire—110 different roles—extends from Mozart to Verdi, from Berlioz to Puccini, from Wagner to Ginastera, in Italian, French, and German. He is also well-known for both his love of and skill in conducting. **ACHIEVEMENTS** One member of the Three Tenors, the trio's performance entitled *In Concert with Carreras, Domingo, Pavarotti and Mehta* has become the highest selling classical video and CD of all time. He is the recipient of six Grammys; two Emmys Awards, among countless other honors and tributes. Domingo was seen by more people in one performance than any tenor in history. An estimated one and one-half billion people throughout the world watched the "Tosca" telecast from authentic Roman settings in 1993. He is also the first classical artist to hold a solo concert in Central Park, which attracted 400,000 people despite bad weather. Seven of his albums appeared simultaneously on Billboard's top-selling charts of classical and cross-over recordings. In 1998, Domingo surpassed Enrico Caruso's 1920 record for the most Metropolitan Opera opening night performances; he opened 18 times. **HIGHLIGHTS** *Newsweek* magazine proclaimed Placido Domingo "is the world's most important opera figure." On August 30, 1993, Domingo's star Hollywood Walk of Fame star was unveiled in a momentous dedication ceremony. He joined an elite group of opera stars on the landmark boulevard, including Enrico Caruso. Domingo became artistic director of the L.A. Opera in June 2000. **QUOTE** "I want to make the Hollywood community more enthusiastic about opera...I know how busy these producers, actors, designers, directors are. But, they have children, and it is very important that their children have a well-balanced background."

Charles Butterworth 🎥 7030 Hollywood
Actor

BORN July 25, 1895, in South Bend, IN. **SPOTLIGHTS** A solid graduate of Notre Dame University, and an accomplished stage actor, he played the indecisive sort like no other. This actor based his successful career on characterizing "the man who couldn't make up his mind." Loved for his vacillating and for being a follower-of-the-crowd, he enhanced *The Cat and the Fiddle* (1934), *Bulldog Drummond Strikes Back* (1934), *Thanks for the Memory* (1938), *Road Show* (1941), *This is the Army* (1943), and *Follow the Boys* (1944). Died: 1946.

James Gleason 🎥 7038 Hollywood
Actor, screenwriter

BORN May 23, 1886, in New York, NY. **SPOTLIGHTS** He made history when he co-wrote *Broadway Melody* (1929)—the *first* screen musical. This specialty character actor who thrived in identifiable wisecracking roles, like an army sergeant, a policeman, or an editor. His wiry body and thin-faced mug suited him well in films: *Arsenic and Old Lace* (1944), *The Clock* (1945), *A Tree Grows in Brooklyn* (1945), *The Bishop's Wife* (1947), *The Life of Riley* (1948), and *Joe Palooka in the Squared Circle* (1950). He continued to turn in superb performances right to the end. See the scary thriller *The Night of the*

Hunter (1955). Died: 1959.

Kathlyn Williams 🎥 7038 Hollywood

Actress

BORN 1888, in Butte, MT. **SPOTLIGHTS** A fine talent of the silent screen, she appears in dozens of pictures. Movies include *Lost in the Jungle* (1911), *The Adventures of Kathleen* (1913, a serial), and *The Spanish Dancer* (1923). She remained busy until 1947. Died: 1960.

Jack Webb 📺 7040 Hollywood

See page 258

Dick Jones 📺 7040 Hollywood

Actor

BORN Feb. 25, 1927, in Snyder, TX. **SPOTLIGHTS** A professional child actor since age five, Dickie was as comfortable sitting in front of the microphone as he was listening to radio. At age six, he performed in circus and rodeo stunts. At age eight, he made his screen debut in *Little Men*, then followed up that same year in *Westward Ho!* (both 1935), and *Daniel Boone* (1936). At age 13, his offscreen voice was immortalized in Disney's animated motion picture, *Pinocchio* (1940). Jones played the title character in that classic film. He returned to radio in "The Aldrich Family," but his service in the U.S. Army during WWII interrupted his career. Postwar, he played the buckskin-attired Western hero in TV's "The Range Rider," a series popular with children. Also in the 1950s, he starred in "Buffalo Bill, Jr." A star of TV and radio, he made 50 films, specializing in oaters. He retired to a California ranch.

Ernst Lubitsch 🎥 7040 Hollywood

Director, producer, screenwriter

BORN Jan. 28, 1892, in Germany. **SPOTLIGHTS** Master of romantic comedy, his motion pictures include *One Hour with You* (1932), starring Maurice Chevalier and Jeanette MacDonald; *Trouble in Paradise* (1932), with Herbert Marshall and Miriam Hopkins; *Ninotchka* (1939), with Greta Garbo; *Shop Around the Corner* (1940) starring James Stewart and Margaret Sullavan; *To Be or Not to Be* (1942) starring Jack Benny and Carole Lombard; and *Heaven Can Wait* (1943), with Don Ameche. **ACHIEVEMENTS** 1937 Special Academy Award for his "25-year contribution to motion pictures." **QUOTE** "When one considers that the motion picture art is the youngest of all the muses, so young, in fact, that the few decades of its existence appear almost negligible when compared to the age-old tradition of its sister art, the spoken drama, it is easy to realize that the screen, this latest medium of artistic creation, has not altogether found its proper mode of expression and is still borrowing many elements from outside sources which are alien to its very nature. To produce a perfect photoplay one must first of all realize that the art of the screen is wholly visual, that its only effect is upon the eye of the spectator. But the motion picture art, conscious that its technique lacks perfection and feeling that it cannot obtain all desired results by applying its own means, goes to the printed page and borrows from an art distinctly alien to the nature of motion pictures, interspersing the movement of pictures on the screen with words that either explain the action or tell a part of the story that is not shown on the screen. One of the results is that a photoplay today often is nothing else but the narration of a story told in subtitles and interrupted by a series of moving pictures. In some cases this goes so far that not only the telling of the plot but also the characterization, labeling 'The Hero,' 'The Villain,' 'The Neglected Wife,' etc. depriving the audience of the chance to use their own judgment and forcing them to accept the opinion of the man who wrote the title. The first step is to do away with the explanatory title. The screen should realize that it deals with a kinetic, dynamic, visual art and that it is more closely related to pantomime than to any other form of art." Died: 1947.

Elmo Lincoln 🎥 7044 Hollywood

Actor

BORN Otto Linkenhelter; June 14, 1899, in Rochester, NY. **SPOTLIGHTS** His first two dramatic appearances were in two of the most significant historical movies, D.W. Griffith's *The Birth of a Nation* (1915) and *Intolerance* (1916). He thrilled audiences with his greatest role, that of the lead in *Tarzan of the Apes* (1918). This was the screen's first adaptation of Edgar Rice Burroughs classic novel. He later made *The Return of Tarzan*. Died: 1952.

Ethel Merman 🎥 7044 Hollywood

See page 153

Lon Chaney 🎥 7046 Hollywood

Actor

BORN Alonso Chaney; April 1, 1883, in Colorado Springs, CO. **SPOTLIGHTS** "The man of a thousand faces" was the silent era's most versatile dramatic star. Creating menacing yet expressive characters such as Fagin in Charles Dickens' *Oliver Twist* (1922), Quasimodo in Victor Hugo's *The Hunchback of Notre Dame* (1923), and the disfigured musician in *The Phantom of the Opera* (1925), he set the industry standard. Only a handful of actors since have been able to hold a candle to the terror or empathy he evoked in audiences worldwide. His popularity extended beyond one-legged, one-armed, or one-eyed costumed-creatures. Underneath the masks—which were often painful to wear—Chaney proved himself a true acting talent. He was also one of the few star talents who fully understood the art of applying motion picture makeup, according to the

Lon Chaney

king of cosmetics, Max Factor. **HIGHLIGHTS** Skills to communicate ideas non-verbally (through facial expressions and body movements) were learned when he was a boy; both parents were deaf. James Cagney stars in the movie about Chaney's life, *Man of a Thousand Faces* (1957). Died: 1930.

Adele Jergens 7046 Hollywood
Actress

BORN Nov. 28, 1922, in Brooklyn, NY. **SPOTLIGHTS** Of model height with platinum blonde hair, this buxom beauty won the crown of "Miss World's Fairest" in 1939. She made her successful screen debut in the *Black Arrow* serial (1944), followed by dozens of flicks at Columbia Pictures. She was often cast as the wisecracking tootsie. TV: A regular on TV's "Pantomime Quiz" (1950-'52).

Samuel Z. Arkoff 7046 Hollywood
Producer

BORN June 12, 1918, in Fort Dodge, IA. **SPOTLIGHTS** Educated at the University of Colorado and the University of Iowa, Arkoff attended Loyola University School of Law and graduated with his Juris Doctor in 1948. This cigar-wielding executive became a stronghold of Hollywood's independent producers as co-founder of American International Pictures in 1954. Arkoff's companies have produced or released more than 500 movies, including the cult classic, *I Was A Teenage Werewolf* (1956) starring Michael Landon, the fun *Beach Party* (1963) starring Frankie Avalon and Annette Funicello, *Wild in the Streets* (1968), *Love at First Bite* (1979) starring George

Samuel Z. Arkoff

Hamilton, Susan St. James and Richard Benjamin, *Amityville Horror* (1979) starring James Brolin, and *Dressed to Kill* (1980) starring Michael Caine and Angie Dickinson. Retrospectives of his work have appeared throughout the country, including at the Museum of Modern Art, in New York, and the Bergamo Film Festival, in Italy. **ACHIEVEMENTS** Named: Producer of

the Year several times, Master Showman of the Decade Award given by the Theatre Owners of America, and has been honored by the Foundation of the Motion Picture Pioneers. During WWII, he served in the U.S. Army Air Corps as a cryptographer...His autobiography, *Flying Through Hollywood By The Seat Of My Pants*, reveals all about his motorcycle films, bikini pix, Edgar Allan Poe/Vincent Price pictures, other drive-in theater favorites, and his work with Roger Corman. His Hollywood Walk of Fame star was dedicated on Jan. 14, 1993.

George Marshall 7046 Hollywood
Director

BORN Dec. 29, 1891, in Chicago, IL. **SPOTLIGHTS** He co-directed the Laurel and Hardy feature *Pack Up Your Troubles* (1932), then directed *Their First Mistake* that same year. He helped Will Rogers make his best vehicle in *Life Begins at Forty* (1935). In 1938 he made the breakthrough Technicolor picture, *The Goldwyn Follies* (1938), which introduced the first flawless film makeup by Max Factor. He directed *You Can't Cheat an Honest Man* (1939), starring W.C. Fields—only he did not direct Fields, veteran Eddie Cline did. He directed the rest of the cast, Edgar Bergen (with dummies), Constance Moore and Eddie Anderson. In 1939 he hit his stride with the fabulous Western, *Destry Rides Again*, starring James Stewart as the sheriff who never raises his voice and Marlene Dietrich as the sultry dance hall singer, "Frenchy." Bob Hope was hilarious in *The Ghost Breakers* (1940) with Paulette Goddard. He broke out with the exciting action picture, *When the Daltons Rode* (1940), about the legendary outlaw brothers. *Texas* (1941), starring William Holden, Glenn Ford and Claire Trevor, is a terrific action picture about two Confederate veterans. Fred MacMurray showed his flair for slapstick in the hillbilly comedy *Murder, He Says* (1945), where he's up against a clan of demented killers, with Marjorie Main. (The film's secret coded message became a popular song in schoolyards across America: "Honors flyers, in cone beezers...") He directed Bob Hope and Joan Caulfield in *Monsieur Beaucaire* (1946). Died: 1975.

Dennis Day 7046 Hollywood
See page 428

Ann B. Davis 7046 Hollywood
Actress

BORN May 5, 1926, in Schenectady, NY. **SPOTLIGHTS** This likable comedienne worked in a number of family TV shows. She played Shultzy on "The Bob Cummings Show" (1955-'59), then was the beloved cook, housekeeper, and stable nurturer of common sense as Alice on "The Brady Bunch" (1969-'74). Millions of children grew up watching her and wishing "Alice" lived at their house. The show airs daily in syndication, attracting new generations of admirers of Davis. She was also a character actress in films. **ACHIEVEMENTS** 1958-'59 Emmy Best Supporting Actress.

Xavier Cugat (left) leading his dancers.

7050 HOLLYWOOD

Paul Newman 🎥

7050 Hollywood

Actor, director

Paul Newman and Tichi Wilkerson Kassel

BORN Jan. 26, 1925, in Cleveland, Ohio. **SPOTLIGHTS** An alumnus of Yale's Drama School and New York's Actor's Studio, he hit big with his first Broadway appearance in "Picnic" (1953). Newman made his screen debut in the ruinous religious movie, *The Silver Chalice* (1955), in the title role. A lesser actor might have put his tail between his legs and skipped town, but Newman managed to show his face again. Years later, when the picture was shown on television, Newman took out a newspaper ad to apologize for it. By the time he made *Somebody Up There Likes Me* (1956), he knew what he was doing. He gives a gritty portrayal of middleweight boxing champion, Rocky Graziano, in a role originally intended for James Dean. After this outstanding performance, Newman had set his course. Next, he appeared in the compelling courtroom drama, *The Rack* (1956), about war prisoners, brainwashing and treason. Based on Rod Serling's excellent TV play, Wendell Corey and Walter Pidgeon are also featured. Highly appealing, with his bedroom blue eyes and dreamboat good looks, he was widely recognized as Hollywood's leading male star of the 1960s and '70s. He received Oscar nominations in *Cat On A Hot Tin Roof* (1958), *The Hustler* (1961), *Hud* (1963), *Cool Hand Luke* (1967), *Absence of Malice* (1981), and *The Verdict* (1982). Other films include *The Rack* (1956), *The Long Hot Summer* (1958), *The Young Philadelphians* (1959), *Exodus* (1960), *Sweet Bird Of Youth* (1962), *Hombre* (1967), *Butch Cassidy And The Sundance Kid* (1969), *The Sting* (1973), and *Message in a Bottle* (1999). He stars with his wife Joanne Woodward in the quiet drama *Mr. and Mrs. Bridge* (1990), and pays homage to the 1950s with his wonderful performance in *The Hudsucker Proxy* (1994). He stars in the fun movie, *Where the Money Is* (2000). He directed the Oscar-nominated *Rachel, Rachel* (1968) starring his wife. Newman enjoys a reputation of remaining true to himself—a tremendous accomplishment for those who work in Hollywood. While talking to newsman Edward R. Murrow, Newman said, "I can't stand rebels. They're just as mediocre as the people they describe as conformists. They have to say 'no' just as the conformists have to say 'yes.' We live in what I call an age of conformity where you have to travel with the herd or be branded a rebel. *I* am trying desperately to be an *individual*...It seems as though in our society we try to go through life making as few enemies as possible, which makes Jack a pretty dull boy." **ACHIEVEMENTS** 1986 Best Actor Oscar, *The Color of Money*...A tremendous, humble and dedicated humanitarian. Newman has quietly donated 100 million dollars to worthwhile charities through his "all profits to charities" line of food products. **SIDELIGHTS** His hobby? Anything having to do with Formula One and NASCAR racing. **QUOTE** "Acting is like letting your pants down, you're exposed."

Sophia Loren 🎥

7050 Hollywood

Actress

BORN Sofia Scicolone, Sept. 20, 1934, in Rome, Italy. **SPOTLIGHTS** An international silver screen goddess, Loren grew up in the slums of Naples during WWII. She stood in breadlines, and was so skinny she was nicknamed *Stechetto*— "the stick." She described herself as a "scarecrow of a girl buried in poverty." As if out of a movie script, a notice went up announcing prize money for a local beauty contest. The 14-year-old and her mother made a dress from faded pink window curtains, while her grandmother painted a pair of black shoes white. Wearing this raiment, Loren entered and won the title "Princess of the Sea." Her prize was the equivalent of about $15, some beautiful wallpaper which her family put up in their bombed out rooms, and a trip to Capri. With no other means to earn money, her mother took her to Rome. Too poor to buy outfits, she wore dresses that were given to her by others. The family survived on Loren's small cash prizes from beauty contests, and modeling fees that she made doing

Sophia Loren

covers for pulp fiction novels. In 1949 she and her mother worked together as film extras in *Quo Vadis*. At 15 years old, she suddenly blossomed into a breathtaking stunner. Loren stated her growth spurt had come: "from eating spaghetti." She added, "It became a pleasure to stroll down the street." Along the way she won the "Miss Elegance" title among others. This led to her meeting and sustaining a relationship with film producer Carlo Ponti (they married in 1957, again in 1966, and later had two sons). Ponti helped her get her first starring role in the semi-documentary *Africa Under the Sea* (1953). The beauty followed with the lead role in *Aida* that same year, then took the world by storm. She is a striking, dark-haired, magnificent Italian creature. Unlike many movie queens, Loren possesses a sense of humor and a natural earthiness. She once stated, "Sex appeal is fifty percent what you've got and fifty percent what people think you've got." This statuesque goddess performed in European cinema before coming to Hollywood, where American men admired her ample bosom and ravishing beauty, and women her sympathetic temperament. She has starred in both comedies and dramas with equal skill. Motion pictures include *Boy on a Dolphin* (1957—a film she now detests, but both she and the Greek scenery are gorgeous), *The Key* (1958), *Houseboat* (1958—with Cary Grant), *The Black Orchid* (1959), *That Kind of Woman* (1959), *Heller in Pink Tights* (1960), *The Millionairess* (1960), *Madame* (1961), *El Cid* (1961), *Fall of the Roman Empire* (1964), *Operation Crossbow* (1965), *Man of La Mancha* (1972), *Ready to Wear* (1994), *Grumpier Old Men* (1996) and *Sun* (1997). She was superb in the social comedies *Yesterday, Today, and Tomorrow* (1963) and *Marriage Italian Style* (1964), both co-starring Marcello Mastroianni. She remains a veritable *grande dame* on the world stage...Superstitious by nature, ever since she was a little girl, she admits to always having something the color of witch's red on her. Even though it may be out of sight, never a day goes by without something red on her body. She believes, "that red brings me good luck and wards off negative, evil forces." She has also penned several cookbooks. **ACHIEVEMENTS** Loren garnered international acclaim along with a Best Actress Oscar for her role in *Two Women* (1961). This made motion picture history as she was the first actress to win the Academy Award for a foreign-language film. She mischievously declared, "You see, I am not just a sexy pot." Her second Oscar (1993) was for Lifetime Achievement. She received her Walk of Fame star on Feb. 1 (Hollywood's official birthday), in 1994. **QUOTE** When asked how she sustained her charms, the timeless beauty observed, "Beauty is love of all things: children, family, what you do, what you achieve. Be serene and look forward to the future."

The Supremes 🎵   7050 Hollywood

Singing group
BORN Diana Ross, Mar. 26, 1944; Mary Wilson, Mar. 4, 1944; and Florence Ballard, June 30, 1943. All three born in Detroit, MI. **SPOTLIGHTS** They are the girl singing group that

The Supremes

defined the great sound of Motown. With the leadership of Berry Gordy Jr., the Supremes burst onto the music scene in 1964 with "Where Did Our Love Go?" True trend setters, they became the first crossover group. With their special blend of style, elegance, and smooth sophistication, they appealed to people of all colors and classes. The Supremes rose to become the top-selling U.S. group. Their classics include "Baby Love," "Come See About Me," "Stop! In the Name of Love," "Back in My Arms Again," "I Hear a Symphony," "Love Child," "You Can't Hurry Love," "You Keep Me Hangin' On," among many others. The trio appeared on the highest rated television shows of the '60s and to sold-out concerts. Their fame and talent opened doors and inspired others to follow their lyrical dreams. **ACHIEVEMENTS** The only group to chart five consecutive #1 records in less than one year. In all, they had 12 #1 pop singles and numerous gold records. Died: Florence Ballard in 1976.

The Temptations 🎵   7050 Hollywood

Singing group
BORN Otis Williams (born Otis Miles), Oct. 30, 1949, in Texarkana, TX; Eddie Kendricks (a.k.a. Kendrick), Dec. 17, 1939, Union Springs, AL; Paul Williams, July 2, 1939, Birmingham, AL; Melvin Franklin (born David English), Oct. 12, 1942, in Montgomery, AL; Elbridge Bryant; David Ruffin, Jan. 18, 1941, MS; Richard Street, in Detroit, MI; Ron Tyson, in North Carolina; Ali-Ollie Woodson, in Detroit, MI. **SPOTLIGHTS** One of the all time, most successful, all male vocal groups, they started in the 1960s. Working with songwriter/producer Smokey Robinson, the Temptations rocked the music world. They caught the public's imagination with "The Way You Do the Things You Do," becoming another powerhouse in the Motown music machine. They enjoyed 14 classic Number One pop and rhythm-and-blues smashes including "My Girl," "The Way You Do The Things You Do," "Papa Was A Rollin' Stone," "I Can't Get Next to You," and "Just My Imagination (Running Away With Me)," among others. They also had a multitude of top 10 singles. Their exquisite vocals, incredible harmonies and choreography became the hallmark for others to emulate. Originals Otis Williams (group founder), Melvin Franklin, Elbridge Bryant, Eddie Kendricks and Paul Williams formed the group in the late '50s, which has served as a spawning unit for some of the world's greatest soul singers. (When Bryant left the group around 1963, David Ruffin joined. It was then that the group worked magic and became an "overnight" sensation.) The

1998 highly rated television mini-series based on Otis Williams' 1988 autobiography, *Temptations*, showcased the fascinating rise of the group. Died: Paul Williams, 1973; David Ruffin, 1991; Eddie Kendricks, 1992; Melvin Franklin, 1995.

Della Reese   7060 Hollywood

Actress, singer, ordained minister

Della Reese

BORN Deloreese Patricia Early; July 6, 1931, in Detroit, MI. **SPOTLIGHTS** At age six, the youngster was singing as a soloist with her Baptist choir on radio. She earned a few dollars a week, but it was a help to her family. As a teenager she toured with the great singer, Mahalia Jackson, in the segregated South. At 18, she was the first performer to take gospel music to Las Vegas. Her unique blend of jazz, blues and gospel led to "Don't You Know" and "And That Reminds Me," her biggest hits in the '50s. She had her first gold record in 1957. Reese appeared on many TV classics, including "The Perry Como Show," "The Jackie Gleason Show," and "The Ed Sullivan Show." She was the first African American female to host "The Tonight Show." This lively, warm, clever woman had her own talk show in 1969. Although she's had occasional lulls in her career, Reese made a powerful comeback in 1994 in television's popular, long-running show, "Touched by an Angel." She plays the feisty lead angel, Tess, who awakens people with the message that "God loves you," and helps steer them on the proper pathway for life. "Touched by an Angel" is an hour-long, feel good drama. An inspirational tonic for turbulent times, it is one of CBS's top-rated shows. **HIGHLIGHTS** She practices what she preaches. Offscreen, parishers call her the Rev. Della Reese-Lett, minister of Understanding Principles for Better Living. She holds services on Sunday morning at a nondenominational Christian church, in Los Angeles. Her divine Walk of Fame star was unveiled on July 12, 1994. **RECOMMENDED** *Angels Along the Way: My Life with Help from Above,* published by Putnam in 1997.

Luis Miguel ●   7060 Hollywood

Singer

BORN Luis Miguel Gallego; April 19, 1970, in San Juan, Puerto Rico. **SPOTLIGHTS** Raised in Mexico, he was given the gift of artistic drive from his father, singer Luisito Rey—who also managed his son's career. The young Miguel hit superstardom recording status in Latin America before his teen years. When he made his theatrical debut in the Spanish-language motion picture, *Ya Nunca Mas (Never Again)*—and won a gold

Luis Miguel

record for his interpretation of songs in it—he appealed to audiences as an actor, too. Miguel toured internationally, picking up prestigious accolades from Chile to Italy before hitting age 16 when he decided he needed more challenge musically, and took over the managerial reins of his career. To say he did a brilliant job of guiding himself artistically would be an understatement. His incredible discipline and unrivaled work ethic have made Luis Miguel one of the most respected artists in the world of Spanish music. He is considered the best singer in Latin pop who complements his mid-tempo, jazzy, brassy numbers with romantic love ballads. His blend of Latin music tradition is more than contemporary sensibilities though; it can include boleros and mariachi. Miguel is handsome enough to be a movie star in any country, dresses to the nines, and exudes just the right amount of machismo to attract millions of ladies admirers. But women aren't alone in their admiration of his talents. A stylish performer with plenty of snap, Miguel counted Frank Sinatra among his fans. In fact, the charismatic vocalist stole the show from Bob Dylan, Tony Bennett and Bruce Springsteen, when he sang "Come Fly with Me" in English at Sinatra's 80th-birthday salute televised from the Shrine auditorium in Los Angeles. (He recorded a duet with the legendary blue eyes Sinatra of that classic American standard for the album *Duet II*.) **ACHIEVEMENTS** Winner of four Grammy Awards: *Me Gustas Tal Como Eres (I Just Like You the Way You Are)*, a duet with Sheena Easton; *Segundo Romance*; *Nada es Igual*; and *Romances*. Dozens of gold and platinum records internationally (and the first Latin artist to be certified gold in the U.S. for a Spanish-language album). You don't have to speak Spanish to enjoy his recordings. **QUOTE** "The main thing for me has always been the music, not just the fame. I wanted to do it well. My father taught me that if you are going to do something, you do it well. He was very, very strict and it made an impression on me when I was young and getting started. It became important to me...to do things right and not embarrass yourself."

Stevie Wonder ●   7060 Hollywood

Musician, singer, songwriter

BORN Steveland Judkins Morris; May 13, 1950, in Saginaw, MI. **SPOTLIGHTS** A major force of creative energy and talent, he was signed by Motown Records at age 10. Called "Little Stevie Wonder," he earned his first Gold album at 12 with his career launching recording, "Fingertips I & II Live." He toured with the Supremes and Temptations in 1964. Mega-hits followed, including "Uptight (Everything's Alright)," "I Was Made To Love Her," "For Once In My Life," "Superstition,"

Stevie Wonder (left)

"You Are The Sunshine Of My Life," "My Cherie Amour," "Blowin' in the Wind," "We Can Work It Out," "Signed, Sealed, Delivered I'm Yours," "For Your Love," "That Girl," and "I Just Called to Say I Love You." His string of gold and platinum albums include *Talking Book, Journey Through the Secret Life of Plants, Innervisions, Songs In the Key of Life*, and *Hotter Than July*. This superb entertainer is universally recognized as one of America's greatest artists. His politically aware lyrics often carry a message of peace and hope. In 2000, Motown released an outstanding CD box set that covers many of his classic tracks from R&B to pop, *"Stevie Wonder: At the Close of a Century."* **ACHIEVEMENTS** Winner of more than 20 Grammys. He won an Oscar for best original song "I Just Called To Say I Love You," in *The Woman in Red* (1984). He received an Honorary Doctorate of Music from Howard University. His Walk of Fame star dedication ceremony took place on Feb. 1, 1994. **HIGHLIGHTS** Although blind since birth, on January 15, 1981 and 1982, he personally led a march and rally of hundreds of thousands in the nation's capital to demand that Congress declare Dr. Martin Luther King's birthday a national holiday.

Cristina Saralegui 📺 7070 Hollywood

Talk show host, writer, producer, editor-in-chief, publisher

Cristina Saralegui

BORN Jan. 29, 1948, in Havana, Cuba. **SPOTLIGHTS** The undisputed queen of Latin media, she is a one-woman empire with her own television and radio shows, magazine, and her own studio. A beloved Latina figure, she is affectionately known to her fans simply as Cristina. Brought up in the strict image of her grandfather, magazine publisher Don Francisco Saralegui, "The Paper Czar" of Latin America, he introduced her to journalism. In 1960, at age 12, Cristina emigrated to start anew in Miami, Florida's Cuban exile community. She attended the University of Miami, majoring in mass communications and creative writing, while beginning an internship with *Vanidades*, Latin America's #1 women's magazine. Since Cristina had received all of her formal training in

English, she then had to teach herself how to write in Spanish, which according to her, "proved to be a great challenge." In 1979, while still working for three successful magazines, Cristina was named Editor-in-Chief of the internationally distributed Cosmopolitan en Español. She held that position for ten years before resigning to become Executive Producer and host of "The Cristina Show." In 1989, "The Cristina Show" premiered on the Univision Network, the nation's leading Spanish-language television network and the fifth largest network in the United States. By 1991, "The Cristina Show" had received its first Emmy. Within ten years, a dozen more Emmys crowned this #1 rated talk show on Spanish-language TV with an audience of more than 100 million viewers worldwide. Highly articulate, dedicated, and well-respected, her show continuously reigns supreme in the United States and 30 other countries worldwide, as does her Monday night prime time version called "Cristina: Edición Especial" and her anniversary two-hour prime time specials. Cristina's website (http://www.cristinaonline.com) is also a popular forum. Her syndicated radio show, "Cristina Opina" ("Cristina's Opinion") airs daily throughout the United States and Latin America. Her company also develops radio programs, and produced the award-winning "Somos Hispanos" ("We're Hispanics"), hosted by Ricardo Montalban, "Auto World," "Desde Hollywood" ("From Hollywood") an entertainment show, and a program with Maria Elena Salinas, the national anchor for Univision News. Her magazine, Cristina La Revista, is distributed in the U.S. and Latin America. In 1996, in TV's prime time soap opera Te Sigo Amando, she made several guest appearances playing herself, opposite the Academy Award-winning actress Katy Jurado. **HIGHLIGHTS** Cristina is managed by her husband, Marcos Avila, a former musician and one of the founding members of the highly successful musical group "Miami Sound Machine." The couple resides in Miami Beach with their three children. **ACHIEVEMENTS** In Dec. 1995, on the Fiftieth Anniversary of the founding of the United Nations, Cristina was honored with the Award of Distinction for Leadership in Communications and Broadcasting. She is the recipient of countless honors, including awards from AmFAR, the National Association of Hispanic Journalists, the National Organization of Women in Communications--with its prestigious Outstanding Communicator of the Year Award, the GLAAD Media Awards, and The Council on Women's issues, among others. Cristina was featured on the cover of Time magazine's premiere issue of People en Español, as one of the "Ten Hottest Latin Stars." In 1998, she wrote her autobiography entitled *My Life as a Blonde*. Released simultaneously in both English and Spanish, it received critical acclaim and hit many bestseller lists. It has already had its third printing...She enjoyed being honored by New York's legendary Sardi's restaurant when they presented her with a caricature that now hangs in that famous show business landmark...Thousands cheered upon seeing her beautiful and happy face when her well-deserved star was unveiled on that momentous Nov. 4, 1999. **QUOTE** "It was a very incredible moment for Spanish-speaking people, Spanish TV, and Spanish media to be recognized with a star on the Hollywood Walk of Fame. I'm honored to join these legends as a neighbor. Johnny Grant and the Chamber were lovely, and my parents, who are very old, were thrilled to attend the dedication ceremony. Un besito."

Haskell Wexler 🎥   7070 Hollywood

Cinematographer, director, producer
BORN 1926, in Chicago, Il. **SPOTLIGHTS** As a child, Wexler was fascinated by the camera work in early talkies. By the time he had grown into his teens, Hollywood's Golden Era was producing one exciting motion picture after another. Technically inclined, with a good artistic eye for shooting a scene, he became an amateur filmmaker before reaching adulthood. He attended a California university, then earned a living making industrial films. He got his show business break on the well-received, semi-documentary film *The Savage Eye* (1959). He was director of photography on *The Hoodlum Priest* (1961), starring Don Murray, *Angel Baby* (1961), starring George Hamilton--a story about faith healing with gothic overtones, and the Oscar-winning *America, America* (1964). In 1965 he photographed/co-produced *The Loved One*--a caustic comedy about life and death in Southern California. Classic Wexler includes *In the Heat of the Night* (1967), *The Thomas Crown Affair* (1968), *Gimme Shelter* (1970), and *One Flew Over the Cuckoo's Nest* (1975, co-phot.). Important documentaries that he wrote, directed, edited, produced and photographed include *The Bus* (1965), and *Medium Cool* (1969), about the insanity of the riotous 1968 Democratic Convention. In 1996 he revisited the Democratic Convention in Chicago to explore the differences between then and now; this time his footage aired on ABC's "Nightline." Wexler's work remains detached, allowing viewers an opportunity to examine the citizens he has photographed. **ACHIEVEMENTS** 1966 Oscar for *Who's Afraid of Virginia Woolf?* 1976 Oscar for *Bound for Glory*. His Hollywood Walk of Fame star was dedicated on Feb. 28, 1996. Among the celebrities who attended were actress Daryl Hannah (his niece), and Oscar-winning producer, Arthur Cohn. **QUOTE** "People in 1968 were alive and interested and ready to fight and argue for the democratic process. There's nothing worse for democracy than when there is withdrawal."

Florence Henderson 📺 7070 Hollywood

Actress, singer, host
BORN Feb. 14, in Dale, IN. **SPOTLIGHTS** Here's the story of a lovely lady...The youngest of 10 children in a close-knit Midwestern family, Henderson learned her trade at the prestigious American Academy of Dramatic Arts. She first gained prominence as the lead in Rodgers & Hammerstein's national musical tour of *Oklahoma!*, but is best known as America's favorite baby boomer "Mom," Carol Brady, on "The Brady Bunch." Henderson has also appeared in films. The legendary Edward G. Robinson appears with her in the musical biopic,

Florence Henderson

Song of Norway (1970). He offered this advice on being an *actor*: "My dear, stars are in heaven. Just do you job and be professional. That's what it's all about." Her three decades plus entertainment career includes being the first woman ever to guest host "The Tonight Show." She hosted the Academy of Television Arts & Sciences second annual live "Prime Time Emmy Cast on the World Wide Web" with interactive internet audiences. She produced "Country Kitchen," on the Nashville Network Cooking, and has made countless guest appearances in variety shows and sit-coms. Then, she sidelined into hypnotherapy. (A proponent of the benefits of hypnotherapy, it freed her from stage fright, and her fear of flying that was so severe it almost ended her career). Much to America's delight, she returned to TV, and is seen daily weekdays on NBC's network morning show "Later Today." Intelligent and humorous, she is one of the country's most popular women. **HIGHLIGHTS** In 1996, she celebrated Valentine's Day (and her birthday) by unveiling her Hollywood Walk of Fame star.

Ray Walston 🎭   7070 Hollywood

Ray Walston

Actor
BORN Nov. 2, 1918, in New Orleans, LA. **SPOTLIGHTS** This extremely versatile and gifted actor began working with the notable Margo Jones Community Players, in Houston, Texas, in 1939. In 1949, Walston began an important 20-year association with George Abbott, the legendary director of the Great White Way. Walston performed in five of Abbott's productions, including the Broadway hit "Mrs. Gibbon's Boys." He appeared in many memorable Broadway productions, including "South Pacific," "Romeo and Juliet," "House of Flowers," and "Those Were the Good Old Days." This veteran Broadway actor received acclaimed critical reviews for his work. He was exuberant, superb, and absolutely terrific in the musical "Damn Yankees." Walston played the devilish Mr. Applegate, who traded souls for earthly delights. In this story, a man sells his soul for a chance for the baseball team, the Washington Senators, to beat a New York team. He won the Antoinette Perry (Tony) Award, before reprising the

character for screen in 1958. Make sure to watch for Gwen Verdon's sizzling song-and-dance "Whatever Lola Wants" (Lola gets!) in the movie. Feature films include *South Pacific* (1958), *The Apartment* (1960), *Kiss Me, Stupid* (1964), *Paint Your Wagon* (1970)—with a *singing* Clint Eastwood, *The Sting* (1973), *Silver Streak* (1976), and *Fast Times at Ridgemont High* (1982). His TV credits include the campy sci-fi comedy series classic, "My Favorite Martian." He plays the lovable, telepathic, sometimes invisible alien from Mars. His character, who looks human, pretends he is Bill Bixby's "Uncle Martin." Later, he received rave reviews for his portrayal of the cantankerous Judge Henry Bone on the popular Emmy Award-winning series "Picket Fences." His dream came true when he received his Walk of Fame star on December 8, 1995.

Dan Haggerty ▼■   7070 Hollywood

Dan Haggerty

Actor, animal trainer, stunt man
BORN Nov. 19, 1946, in Hollywood, CA. **SPOTLIGHTS** An animal trainer extraordinaire and stunt expert, he is best known for his movie portrayal of John Grizzly Adams in *The Life and Times of Grizzly Adams* (1975) and in the TV series of the same name. Millions of animal and nature lovers became his devoted fans. Describing the program's success Haggerty observed, "America is noted for its family relations. Everything is family-oriented: family restaurants, family carnivals, family television. But somewhere along the line family entertainment television got tainted with a lot of violence. People accepted this show because it basically went back to squirrels, bears and mountains. It was a good, hour-long entertainment show that anybody could watch: grandma or kids or teenage boys...On our show our message was to give people a chance, and it showed you didn't have to blow up animals. And also lessons in how to learn to live off the land, like the Native American Indians did." Haggerty played a similar role as Jacob Fremont in *The Adventures of Frontier Fremont* (1976). His innate skill in handling tigers, wolves, eagles and bears allows him to do scenes that other actors would find impossible. This brawny, rugged character—and former champion bodybuilder—made a number of motion pictures, including *Muscle Beach Party* (1964) with Frankie Avalon and Annette Funicello (he played Biff), *Girl Happy* (1965) with Elvis Presley, and *Born Champion* (1999)...His hobby is restoring and painting Harley Davidson motorcycles. Haggerty did the special red, white and blue paint job on the Peter Fonda's Harley in *Easy Rider*. (He also appears as a Hippie in that film.) **ACHIEVEMENTS** Devotes time to the Special Olympics, the annual Love Ride (in Glendale, CA) and various causes to aid battered and abused children. **HIGHLIGHTS** Declared clinically dead on May 24, 1994, after a motorcycle wreck and subsequent surgery caused a tear in his artery in his back. The tough

Haggerty astounded doctors by coming back to life. When asked if he saw "the Light," or "the Tunnel," he recalled, "I saw what appeared like a pathway of fireflies going through a revolving door and bright carnival lights. Somehow I sensed they weren't going to keep me." **QUOTE** "I don't believe in hitting animals—wild or domesticated. Anyone who would strike a bear or a lion is a fool. Just like people training, animal training is done on reward system with food, kindness and love. And just like humans, each animal is unique and has its own personality. You have to use common sense. For example, if you have a puppy, sit on the ground to be closer to the puppy's height. The puppy will relate to you a lot better than if you're a big, scary towering figure. If you're working with an 800-pound bear, it's like being married—you got to watch your step. Working with animals is working with your hands, and that's working with love."

Don Cornelius ▼■   7080 Hollywood

Don Cornelius

Producer
SPOTLIGHTS Cornelius is the legendary creator and executive producer of TV's popular dance program "Soul Train." Previously, he had dreamed of becoming a radio announcer. Attending broadcasting school in Chicago, Cornelius was advised that he and the majority of those enrolled in the course might never get jobs in broadcasting. Despite the odds against success, in 1967 he was offered a part-time position as news announcer on Chicago's WVON Radio, one of the nation's first African-American-oriented stations. During this time he became interested in TV production, and came up with the concept of an African-American-oriented dance show. After the completing the pilot, he could find no interested sponsors. In the summer of 1971, with support from The Johnson Products Company, he began commuting to Hollywood in hopes of making his artistic vision a reality. The syndicated version went on the air Oct. 2, 1971, and was an immediate success in the markets that carried the show. Unfortunately, the well-produced "Soul Train," was only shown in seven of the key 25 target cities. There remained resistance to it, but Cornelius persevered, and gradually picked up more stations. Staying at the cutting edge of soul and R&B music, Cornelius has made his show one of the most popular and longest-running programs. "Soul Train" celebrated its 25th season in 1995 with an all-star CBS TV special. In addition, Cornelius produces two major annual music awards events—"The Soul Train Music Awards," and "The Soul Train Lady of Soul Awards." Both awards shows are among the most revered and well-attended in the music/television industry and attract top

superstar talent. He received his Hollywood Walk of Fame star on Feb. 27, 1997, surrounded by a crowd of celebrities and fans who obviously loved the man.

Ernani Bernardi 💿   7072 Hollywood

Musician, arranger
BORN Oct. 29, 1911, in Standard, IL. **SPOTLIGHTS** He enjoyed a swingtime career as a professional musician and arranger for several famous big bands, including the Dorseys, Benny Goodman, Bob Crosby, and Kay Kyser. After retiring from show business, he was elected to the Los Angeles City Council. As a longtime council member, he has overseen and contributed to legislation benefitting Hollywood and the greater Los Angeles community.

George Fisher 🎤   7072 Hollywood

News broadcaster
SPOTLIGHTS A pioneer newsman, he began his career in the mid-1930s during Hollywood's Golden Era. The first time the Academy Awards were broadcast live on radio, his was the voice heard. When broadcast television first came to Los Angeles, the hazy image on the screen was his. He began "Hollywood Whispers," one of the earliest radio shows on show biz gossip. He appears in 40 motion pictures, mostly portraying himself—"an entertainment reporter of the highest credentials."

Terry Moore 🎥   7072 Hollywood

Actress
BORN Helen Koford, Jan. 1, 1932, in Los Angeles, CA. **SPOTLIGHTS** Her stage mother encouraged her darling baby to become a movie star. Little Terry began as a child model, attended Pasadena Playhouse in her teens, then made her screen debut in *Maryland* (1940). Movies include *My Gal Sal* (1942), *Since You Went Away, Gaslight* (both 1944), and *Son of Lassie* (1945). As the abducted heroine in *Mighty Joe Young* (1949), her magnetism was phenomenal. For years she appeared on the cover of every Hollywood film star publication. Her performance in *Come Back Little Sheba* (1952) earned her an Oscar nomination and world acclaim. Other films include *The Barefoot Mailman* (1951), *Man on a Tightrope* (1953), *Daddy Long Legs* (1955), *Bernadine, Peyton Place* (both 1957), *A Private's Affair* (1959), *Waco* (1966), *The Daredevil* (1972), and *Beverly Hills Brats* (1989--also co-story, and co-producer). **HIGHLIGHTS** While entertaining American troops in Korea, she made headlines by appearing in "almost enough fur to cover one tiny rabbit." The big brass asked her for more costume, so she added sequins to some flesh-colored cloth. They weren't too happy about it, but the soldiers sure were. **SIDELIGHTS** She is the best-selling author of *The Beauty and the Billionaire*, about her life and marriage to film mogul Howard Hughes.

Cleavon Little 🎥   7072 Hollywood

Actor
BORN June 1, 1939, in Chickasha, OK. **SPOTLIGHTS** He began his career on the New York stage, winning a Tony Award and The Drama Desk Award in 1970 for "Purlie." Perhaps best known for his portrayal of the sheriff in Mel Brook's Western spoof, *Blazing Saddles* (1974). Other major film roles: *Cotton Comes To Harlem* (1970), *Vanishing Point* (1971), *Arthur 2* (1988). Regular appearances in television scrics "Temperatures Rising," "Bagdad Cafe," and "True Colors." Co-starred in the Broadway hit, "I'm Not Rappaport," with Judd Hirsch. Emmy Award for his guest role in TV's "Dear John." Died: 1992.

Chuck Niles 🎤   7080 Hollywood

Chuck Niles

Jazz Disc Jockey
BORN June 24, 1927, in Springfield, Mass. **SPOTLIGHTS** Niles began playing the "licorice stick" (clarinet) at age seven. He added tenor saxophone to his bag by age 14, then began playing professional gigs. But it was in pursuit of a higher education that Niles found his niche. He commented, "During college I started announcing sports on the college station. Following graduation I went immediately into broadcasting professionally and that's what I've been doing for 50 years." Known as an ultra cool cat with a real affinity for swing, for bebop, he's the voice of jazz radio. In his basso profundo voice he hosts KLON-FM/88.1, America's Jazz Station—one of the premier jazz stations in the country. As the barometer of what's hip, he's meant the survival of many musicians. When the highly tuned one declares, "These cats can swing, man," he's shaping lives—one play at a time. **QUOTE** At his exciting Hollywood Walk of Fame dedication ceremony on March 5, 1998, some of jazz's top performers were there, as were family, friends and fans. He remarked, "I can satisfy my love for music—not necessarily as a musician playing it—but promoting and being around it as a 'talker.' That way I can still eat and pay the bills. I've done other things such as film, stage plays, voiceovers, produced concerts, hosted jazz cruises, emceed festivals, etc., but radio has always been my bread and butter and I hope to continue as long as the old pipes hold up."

John Lee Hooker 💿   7080 Hollywood

Singer, musician

BORN Aug. 22, 1917, near Clarksdale, Mississippi. **SPOTLIGHTS** A legendary and beloved blues originator, he is known

John Lee Hooker

as the "King of the Boogie." The son of a sharecropper, and one of 11 children, as a child Hooker sang in the local church. He wanted to play a musical instrument, and improvised by "playing" an inner tube that he had stretched across the barn door. His earliest musical influence on guitar came from his stepfather, William Moore, who entertained at community socials like fish fries and other regional events. By the late 1930s, Hooker had made his way through Memphis, Tennessee and Cincinnati, and finally settled in Detroit. In 1948 he made his first solo recording "Boogie Chillen." The song instantly became a #1 jukebox hit and his first million seller. He followed with "I'm In The Mood," an even bigger hit. Other classic tunes include "Crawling Kingsnake" and "Hobo Blues." He released more than 100 songs on Vee-Jay Records during the 1950s and '60s. When the young Bohemian generation "discovered" him, he found a new audience eager to hear him, and one who widely admired and respected his musical talents. He reached superstar status in mid-1960s England. By 1970 Hooker had moved to California and began working with rock musicians, notably Van Morrison and Canned Heat. For the next two decades he toured the world, and appeared in movies like *The Blues Brothers* (1980). Hooker's influence has contributed to a booming interest in the blues in the 1990s, and notably, its acceptance by the music industry as a commercially viable entity. Among his many splendid albums are *Mr. Lucky*, *Boom Boom*, *Chill Out*, and his release *The Best of Friends*, featuring the 50th anniversary version of his first hit "Boogie Chillen." For his album, *The Healer*, he was joined by guest appearances of Carlos Santana, Robert Cray, Los Lobos, George Thorogood, and others. With *Don't Look Back* for Pointblank (Virgin Records), Hooker forged forward in an already prolific career. The recording feature new and old original songs, as well as one new Van Morrison song destined to become a classic. This marked the 25th anniversary reunion of the two giants. Morrison and he had their first recorded collaboration on Hooker's *Never Get Out Of These Blues Alive*. **SIDELIGHTS** For product information, visit Virgin's website at www.virginrecords.com. **ACHIEVEMENTS** Winner of four Grammy Awards, he earned his first Grammy Award with Bonnie Raitt (a duet) for "I'm In The Mood." He later earned two from "Don't Look Back," including Best Traditional Blues Album and Best Pop Collaboration with Vocals on the title track duet with Van Morrison. In 1991 he was inducted into the Rock and Roll Hall of Fame. Lifetime Achievement awards were bestowed on him by The Blues Foundation in 1997, and The Rhythm and Blues Foundation in 1999. He received his star on the Hollywood Walk of Fame on August 29, 1997 in a tribute to his career that has spanned half a century. This Hollywood landmark is recognition of his lifelong contribution to the arts. It is a permanent monument of the past, as well as the present, and will be admired by countless generations of music lovers to come.

Jon Provost   7080 Hollywood

Actor

BORN March 12, 1950, in Los Angeles, CA. **SPOTLIGHTS** Possessing a gentle face, this blond lad warmed the hearts of all America in his role as Timmy, the young master of "Lassie" in

Jon Provost (then)

the classic TV series (1957-'64). Although he was just seven years old when he first appeared on "Lassie," he had, in fact, landed his first part in a major motion picture five years earlier. At the age of two and a few months, he appeared with Jane Wyman and Sterling Hayden in Robert Wise's *So Big* (1953). Other movies include *The Country Girl* (1954) with Grace Kelly and Bing Crosby, and Sydney Pollack's *This Property Is Condemned* (1966) with Natalie Wood, Robert Redford and Charles Bronson. He piled on an extensive list of TV credits, before leaving the entertainment industry to attend college. After graduation, he worked in special education, then switched to real estate. Investing his earnings wisely, he never had to work again, yet returned in the fall of 1989 for a role in

Jon Provost (now)

the new syndicated "Lassie" series, which allowed for a sweet and sentimental touchstone to the past. His talent had not diminished with age, and Provost found himself again inspired by the art, and resumed his acting career. **HIGHLIGHTS** He is a member of the board of governors of the N.W. Region of Canine Companions for Independence, which "supplies dogs to people with every kind of handicap other than blindness." He also works on behalf of Humane Societies and Easter Seals. Provost was named the recipient of the 1986 "Award for Outstanding Contribution as a Humanitarian" presented by the Motion Picture Council. **HIGHLIGHTS** His dedication ceremony took place on February 1, 1994, *Hollywood's* 107th birthday.

Don Johnson    7080 Hollywood

Actor, singer, director, executive producer
Born: Dec. 15, 1952, in Flat Creek, MO. **SPOTLIGHTS** This fair haired Midwesterner with striking good looks became a household name in the TV series "Miami Vice." The hip, glamorous, highly stylized show used rock music backgrounds and vivid colors. It virtually changed cultural tastes in America. Johnson played the rough edged Detective James "Sonny" Crockett, who lived on his sailboat called "St. Vitus' Dance." Instead of a guard dog, "Sonny" had a pet alligator with an attitude. He drove a slick, black, early 1970s Ferrari Daytona against the backdrop of the flashy Gold Coast. He got his feet wet behind-the-camera directing a handful of "Miami Vice" episodes, and was hooked. His second hit police drama series, "Nash Bridges," takes place an ocean away in a cosmopolitan area born of the Gold Rush. Both San Francisco and Johnson grace the screen with charm—the latter with roguish masculinity. The layout is *retro-moderne* and like the city itself, is enhanced by its multi-cultural diversity. Johnson plays "Captain Nash Bridges" who drives a 1981 Barracuda muscle car with a 426-Hemi engine. Johnson came upon acting as fast as the cars he drives, and quite by chance. Needing one more class to graduate from high school in Witchita, Kansas, he chose drama, a class he guessed would be easy. As it turned out he was very good at acting, and could sing, too. He won the lead role in the musical "West Side Story" on his first audition. A natural born talent with plenty of charisma, Johnson was awarded a full scholarship to the University of Kansas where he studied for a couple of years before joining The American Conservatory Theatre. He made an easy leap to motion pictures, appearing in the rock musical-cult classic *Zachariah* (1971), *The Harrad Experiment* (1973)—a drama which examines sexual mores of the day, and *A Boy and His Dog*—a black comedy classic sci-fi based on Harlan Ellison's novel (1974). Later films include *Goodbye, Lover* (1998), *Tin Cup* (1996), *Guilty as Sin* (1993), *Born Yesterday* (1993), *Paradise* (1991), *Harley Davidson & the Marlboro Man* (1991), *The Hot Spot* (1990) and *Sweet Hearts Dance* (1988). He's appeared in a number of television mini-series and television films: "From Here to Eternity," "First You Cry," "Elvis and the Beauty Queen," "Centerfold," "The Rebels," and "Beulah Land" to name a few. **HIGHLIGHTS** Although Johnson possesses "pretty boy" looks, his acting range is substantial. He has the emotional depth to mine any number of interesting characters, and devours meaningful dramatic roles with insight and clarity. His star was dedicated on July 26, 1996.

Don Johnson

Syd Cassyd    7080 Hollywood

Producer, writer
BORN Dec. 28, 1908; in Teaneck, NJ. **SPOTLIGHTS** Called television's renaissance man, Cassyd is founder of the Academy of Television Arts and Sciences (ATAS) with its world-famous Emmy Awards. Previously, during WWII he worked in the Signal Corps as a film editor under director Col. Frank Capra. After his honorable discharge, he worked as a reporter for a trade magazine, and moonlighted as a grip on Paramount's back lot. He teamed with TV pioneer Klaus Landberg, on an experimental station W6XYZ. At the time, there were only 5,000 television sets in the country. (Today's count is in excess of 500 million worldwide.) Watching the new medium grow, Cassyd felt the need to belong to a television organization where people of all levels could come share their ideas and thoughts, and engage in important and democratic discussions about the future of the business. Cassyd founded the Academy in 1946. Only seven people showed up for the first meeting. He reflected, "but by the fifth meeting, there were 250 members. That's how rapidly we grew...People could make connections, come up with ideas, and try to solve problems. For example, was something going to be filmed, or live? Which union was going to do what?" Cassyd stated, "our objective is to use television for enlightenment and education, as well as entertainment. Television is the greatest instrument that has ever been invented." He recruited popular radio and movie ventriloquist Edgar Bergen to be its first president on Jan. 7, 1947. One year later it was formally incorporated as a non-profit organization with its chief aim being "to promote the cultural, educational and research aims of television." He served as Academy president in 1950 and held various other positions over the years. A producer with a number of early television credits, he produced 105 episodes of the children's program "Candy's Playhouse" which won a Peabody Award. **ACHIEVEMENTS** In 1991 the board of governors instituted the Syd Cassyd Founders Award and named Cassyd as its first recipient, in recognition of his long and distinguished service to the Academy. He is also the recipient of three of its Governors Awards. Cassyd estimated that "20 billion people have seen the Emmy Awards all over the world, which has helped Hollywood immensely. The Emmy is a powerful symbol that means something today. You're proud of it. You love it." When Cassyd received his star on the Walk of Fame on Aug. 15, 1996, it was as part of the Academy's 50th anniversary celebration. He chose the placement of his star, stating, "At the very location where I am standing is the site of the former Hollywood playhouse. It is gone now, but in its time, it was glorious. I once produced a one-man show which starred the great actor John Carradine in "A Carousel of Famous Shakespearean Roles." **QUOTE** "Now that the Oscar Academy (the Academy of Motion Picture Arts and Sciences) resumes its rightful niche on Hollywood Boulevard, theaters, and other cultural events are coming back to life on the street. It's time that we old-timers return to our home in Hollywood. And

now at age 90, with my star on Hollywood boulevard, I am home."

Rod Steiger 🎥   7080 Hollywood

Actor

Rod Steiger

BORN Rodney Stephen Steiger; April 14, 1925, in West Hampton, NY. **SPOTLIGHTS** Nicknamed "Rodney the Rock" as a child because of his iron strength, Steiger has proven to be equally forceful on-screen. Wanderlust set in when he turned 16, and the teen dropped out of high school and ran away from home. Putting his acting talents to their first test, he invented a new birthday and enlisted in U.S. Navy. Steiger saw plenty of action and he withstood it with grit and might. He spent four years in the service and engaged in the major operations of the Third and Fifth fleets, including Iwo Jima and Okinawa campaigns during World War II. After his honorable discharge, he took advantage of the G.I. bill to study acting. He attended the New School for Social Research, The American Theatre Wing, the Dramatic Workshop and the Actors Studio in New York—where he immersed himself in Stanislavski's "Method" acting. He snared roles in 250 live television production of plays, including as the original lovesick, Bronx butcher in Paddy Chayefsky's "Marty." His portrayal of historic characters—Rudolph Hess, Andrei Vishinsky, Rasputin, and Romeo—in the Walter Cronkite series "You Are There" garnered him praise. Among his peers in the business, he received the greatest compliment when they recognized him as "an Actor's Actor." He made his motion picture debut in an interesting cultural study entitled *Teresa* (1951). In his second film, Steiger earned an Academy Award nomination for his compelling performance in the must-see *On the Waterfront* (1954). Next, he riveted audiences with his characterization of "Jud" in *Oklahoma!* (1955). Steiger sang for the first time and is the only actor known to have performed in the ballet. Among his legendary works run the gold thread of his uncommonly powerful screen presence. He is thrilling, captivating, and completely absorbing to watch. Motion pictures include *The Big Knife* (1955), *The Harder They Fall* (1956—he co-stars with Humphrey Bogart in Bogie's last film), *Cry Terror* (1958), *Seven Thieves* (1960), *The Pawnbroker* (1965), *Doctor Zhivago* (1965), *The Court-Martial of Billy Mitchell (1955), Al Capone* (1959), *No Way to Treat a Lady* (1968), *The Illustrated Man* (1969), *Waterloo* (1970), *Lucky Luciano* (1973), *The Naked Face* (1984), *Mars Attacks* (1996), *Shiloh* (1996), *Crazy in Alabama* (1999), and *End of Days* (1999). He appears in more than 85 films. And unlike many movie stars, he's not afraid to return to television—as he was a product of it. Back in the 1950s he commented, "television is an excellent training ground for new talent." This Emmy-winning actor has made numerous TV movies and mini-series including "Jesus of Nazareth." Steiger also returns to the stage as often as possible. **ACHIEVEMENTS** 1967 Best Actor Academy Award for *In the Heat of the Night*. At the podium accepting his Oscar, he exuberantly said, "I find it unbelievable. I find it overwhelming. I thank Mr. Sidney Poitier for the pleasure of his friendship, which gave me the knowledge and understanding of prejudice to enhance my performance." Then with a reference to Dr. Martin Luther King, Jr. he raised the statuette and declared, "We shall overcome!" When questioned later about the film which explored racial tensions, Steiger tried to put it in perspective. He said, "A very nice film and a very good film and, yes, I think it's good to see a black man and a white man working together, but it's not going to take the tension out of New York City; it's not going to stop the riots in Chicago." Maybe not, but the film made a big impact on him. Four days before the annual Oscar celebration Dr. Martin Luther King, Jr. was assassinated. Steiger voiced concerns about attending the ceremony if the show was to be scheduled before the historic funeral. He stated he would be a no-show; he was the only Caucasian star to openly do so. Alongside him stood Louis Armstrong, Sammy Davis, Jr., Sidney Poitier, and Diahann Carroll...He has received dozens of other accolades and awards, including the Lifetime Achievement Award by the Chicago International Film Festival. His Hollywood Walk of Fame dedication ceremony took place on April 10, 1997. A throng of movieland's top celebrities were in attendance to rejoice as his long overdue Walk of Fame star was unveiled. Also on hand were family, friends, fans and the international media. **SIDELIGHTS** Steiger was the original choice to play General Patton in the movie, but he turned it down. George C. Scott took the role.

Cicely Tyson 🎥   7080 Hollywood

Actress

BORN Dec. 19, 1933, in New York City. **SPOTLIGHTS** Raised in poverty in Harlem, the youngster helped supplement the family's income by peddling shopping bags on street corners. As she grew, she blossomed into a beauty. After high school graduation, Tyson became a model and participated in the local YMCA productions. She made her acting debut in "Dark of the Moon" with that organization, then quickly advanced to off-Broadway plays. In 1961 she was brilliant as Virtue (her character's full name was Stephanie Virtue Secretrose Drop), in Jean Genet's volatile, controversial, and timely drama, "The Blacks." Other talented members of this all African-American cast included James Earl Jones, Louis Gossett, Jr., Maya Angelou, Abbey Lincoln and Godfrey Cambridge. In 1962 she followed up with her performance in the wonderful play, "Moon on a Rainbow Shawl," for which she received rave reviews. In 1963 television discovered her. Tyson became the

Cicely Tyson (center), Angela Bassett, and Laurence Fishburne

first African American to win a leading role in George C. Scott's dramatic television series, "East Side, West Side" (CBS). That same year, she appeared in a then-unprecedented television program, "Who Do You Kill?" It explored the life crisis that can (and does) occur because of horrible housing conditions in the Harlem slums (or any ghetto). CBS received kudos for its bravery in airing the program; the racial issues it touched upon were shocking at the time. Motion pictures include *A Man Called Adam* (1966), *The Comedians* (1966), and *The Heart Is a Lonely Hunter* (1968). She earned an Academy Award nomination for *Sounder* (1972). Other films include *The River Niger* (1976), *The Blue Bird* (1976—notable chiefly for it being the first U.S.-Soviet co-production), *Fried Green Tomatoes* (1991), and *Hoodlum* (1997). Tyson has also established herself as a superior actress in television mini-series and movies. She has won several Emmys in this medium. **HIGHLIGHTS** Tyson's acting style dictates she stays in character whenever she's on the set—even when the cameras are turned off. And she insists others call her by her character name. About her acting rule she said, "That is the only way. They tease me all the time. But that's the only way I can function." A partial listing of her TV credits are: "Roots" (the most-watched mini-series of all time), "The Autobiography of Jane Pittman," "A Woman Called Moses," "The Oldest Living Confederate Widow Tells All," and "Heat Wave." In November of 1998 she starred in "Mama Flora's Family" and beat out the tough competition for the highest ratings. **QUOTE** "I am so blessed."

Earth Wind & Fire 🎵 7080 Hollywood

Singers, musicians, songwriters
BORN Maurice White (founder of group), Dec. 19, 1941, in Memphis, TN. **SPOTLIGHTS** A power group, they are an unparalleled force in music. White originated the troupe, naming it after the components of his astrological chart, and brazenly created music that defied categorization. The ingredients include soul, jazz, funk, rhythm & blues, pop, gospel and ethnic rhythms. EWF is a crossover band that appeals to every ethnic group in the world. White started the group in the early 1970s, and they're still going strong today. Though he no longer tours with the band, he still writes and produces for them in the studio. Currently lead singer Philip Bailey and bassist Verdine White (Maurice's brother) lead the 11-piece band, which features principals Ralph Johnson (percussion/vocals), Sheldon Reynolds (guitar/vocals), and

Earth, Wind & Fire

Sonny Emory (drums). These superb entertainers are famous for blending African and Latino rhythms, Southern gospel spirit, and intricate jazz arrangements with a rhythm-and-blues base. Great showmanship, harmonies, and horn section. Hits include "Shining Star," "After The Love Is Gone," "Let's Groove"; more. Their 1997 album, *In the Name of Love*, is available on Pyramid Records (website: www.rhino. com). **ACHIEVEMENTS** Six Grammy Awards, four American Music Awards, more than 50 Gold and Platinum albums.

Rita Moreno 🎥 7080 Hollywood

Actress, dancer, singer
BORN Rosita Delores Alveria; Dec. 11, 1931, in Humacao, Puerto Rico. **SPOTLIGHTS** She is a multi-talented actress, singer, dancer, and comedienne. Already performing on

Rita Moreno

Broadway at age 13, this versatile youth made her silver screen debut in *A Medal for Benny* (1945), at age 14. Signed by MGM when she was 17, she made *So Young So Bad*, *The Toast of New Orleans*, and *Pagan Love Song* (all 1950). Next, she co-stars in one of the best musicals ever made, *Singin' in the Rain* (1952), opposite Gene Kelly, Debbie Reynolds and Donald O' Connor. This gifted artist appears in a number of motion pictures, including *The Ring* (1952), *Latin Lovers*, *Fort Vengeance* (both 1953), *The Yellow Tomahawk*, *Garden of Evil* (both 1954), *Untamed* (1955), *The Lieutenant Wore Skirts* (1956), *The King and I*, *The Vagabond King* (both 1956), The *Deerslayer* (1957), *The Rebel Breed* (1960), *Popi*, and *Marlowe* (1969). As a member of a minority in Hollywood, Moreno has had to fight ethnic typecasting. After winning her Academy Award (see below) she said, "I was convinced producers would come pounding on my door with all sorts of exciting parts. But instead I was offered gypsy fortune tellers, Mexican spitfires, Spanish spitfires, Puerto Ricans—all those 'Yankee peeg, you steel me people's money' parts.'" Fortunately, she focused her artistic energy on Broadway and in Las Vegas until good roles, like *The Night of the Following Day* (1969) co-starring her former love of nine years—Marlon Brando—came her way. Among her other motion picture credits are *Carnal Knowledge* (1971), *The Boss's Son* (1978), *Evita Peron* (1981), *The Four Seasons* (1981), *Life in the Food Chain* (1991), *I Like It Like That* (1994), *Bogus* (1996), and *Slums of Beverly Hills* (1998). **ACHIEVEMENTS** Moreno became the first female performer (before Barbra Streisand) to win all four of the most prestigious show business awards: Oscar (1961) for her best supporting performance as Anita in *Westside Story*; Tony (1975) for her role as Googie Gomez in the Broadway play "The Ritz"; Grammy (1972) for her "Electric Company Album"; and two Emmys (1977, '78) for her appearance on "The Muppets" and her regular dramatic role in "The Rockford Files." Cheering fans, friends, family and media were there for her on July 20, 1995, at her thrilling Walk of Fame dedication ceremony.

Benny Carter 🎵　　　7080 Hollywood

Musician, composer, arranger
BORN Bennett Lester Carter, Aug. 7, 1907, in New York City. **SPOTLIGHTS** Best known as an alto saxophonist, Carter began performing at age 15. He worked with such bands as Horace Henderson, Chick Webb, and Cab Calloway, and wrote for Benny Goodman, Count Basie, Duke Ellington, Glenn Miller, Gene Krupa and Tommy Dorsey. Carter recorded with Billie Holliday, Ella Fitzgerald, Sarah Vaughn, Pearl Bailey and more. He was one of the first African American instrumentalists to score films, which include *Stormy Weather* (1943), *An American in Paris* (1951), and *The Guns of Navarone* (1961). TV credits include "Ironsides," "M Squad," and "Name of the Game." **ACHIEVEMENTS** Grammy, Lifetime Achievement (1987). Honorary Doctorates from Princeton (1974), Rutgers (1991), and Harvard (1994).

Signe Hasso 🎥　　　7080 Hollywood

Actress, songwriter
BORN Aug. 15, 1915, in Stockholm, Sweden. **SPOTLIGHTS** This beautiful international film star began her career on the Swedish stage at age 13. After starring in some wonderful films in her native country, and winning her country's equivalent of the Oscar for *Karrar* (1938), this cool sophisticate came to Hollywood. Hasso gained fame as a fine leading lady. Her strong, but low-key personality is highlighted is such movies as *Assignment in Brittany* (1943), *Heaven Can Wait* (1943), *The Seventh Cross* (1944), *House on 92nd Street* (1945), *Johnny Angel* (1945), *Where There's Life* (1947), *A Double Life* (1948), *The Black Bird* (1975), *I Never Promised You A Rose Garden* (1977), and *Evita Peron* (1981). **HIGHLIGHTS** An American citizen since 1948, Hasso has received numerous awards from around the world. She has been honored by the King of Sweden. Also a lyricist for number of popular Swedish songs. She received her star on the Walk of Fame on Feb. 1, 1994, in celebration of Hollywood's 107th Birthday.

Clint Black 🎵　　　7080 Hollywood

Singer, songwriter, director, producer, musician
BORN Feb. 4, 1962, in Long Branch, New Jersey.

Clint Black

SPOTLIGHTS One of the top contemporary country artists, he was raised in Houston, Texas. Black grew up in a family whose lives were filled with music. The first instrument he learned to play was the harmonica. At age 15, he wrote songs, played the guitar (self-taught), and got plenty of attention with that terrific voice of his. While in his teens he played both country, and rock 'n' roll, performing in the Full House Band with one of his brothers.

Before working in the country and western swing clubs full-time as a solo performer with just a guitar and harmonica, Black worked in construction to make ends meet. After almost ten years performing in night clubs around Houston, Texas, he found his way into the office of RCA Records. There he landed a recording contract in the big time. Black's debut album, *Killin' Time* (1989), exploded on the scene with a record-breaking five #1 hit songs: "A Better Man," "Killin' Time," "Nobody's Home," "Nothing's News," and "Walkin' Away." The album went platinum. A country music traditionalist with a gift for innovation, Black's album attracted new audiences who came over from pop, rock 'n' roll, and other forms of music. For millions, it was the first time they heard, bought, or even thought they could enjoy listening to country music, let alone go to a C&W concert. He helped blaze the C&W trail worldwide. In 1990 the supple, expressive tenor followed up with more #1 hit songs. He repeated his magic in 1992, 1993, 1994, 1996 and 1997, adding a string of platinum albums, including *Put Yourself in My Shoes*, *The Hard Way*, *No Time to Kill*, and *One Emotion*, to name a few. His 1997 CD surprised the music world. Collaborating with a wildly diverse group of artists, the results were nothing less than amazing. About the RCA album *Nothin' But the Taillights*, Black commented, "Every now and then I like to throw myself a curve-ball, just to see which way I'll move. You won't naturally move in any direction unless you make yourself. I thought it was time to confront myself with another challenge." *Nothin' But the Taillights* is a versatile collection of songs ranging from romantic "Something That We Do," to bluesy "Bitter Side of Sweet," and orchestral "Loosen Up My Strings," to bluegrass "Ode to Chet." He has done duets with Roy Rogers, Wynonna Judd, and the Pointer Sisters. He became an Opry member in 1991. **HIGHLIGHTS** Married to the beautiful actress Lisa Hartman since October 1991, Black occasionally acts in TV shows, and movies. He directs his own music videos. **ACHIEVEMENTS** He has won three awards from the Country Music Association, four from the Academy of Country Music, and was honored as the "Favorite New Country Male Artist," by the American Music Awards. *Billboard* magazine recognized him as the "Most Played Country Artist," and he is a nine-time Grammy nominee...Black arrived on Hollywood Boulevard on top a horse-drawn stagecoach (the same rig that was used in the 1994 movie *Maverick*, in which the handsome artist had a supporting role, as well as participating in the soundtrack with "A Good Run of Bad Luck." **QUOTE** His dedication ceremony took place on Dec. 12, 1996—a Christmas present from the community to him. Black commented, "I don't know if there is anyone in America who hasn't been affected by Hollywood. Many times we hear about how affected Hollywood is, and in our culture it seems to be more popular to accentuate the negative. I, without trying hard, have found many good people walking the streets of this town and would be proud to have them walk all over me."

Carlos Santana   7080 Hollywood

Musician, vocalist
BORN July 20, 1947, in the village of Autlan de Navarro, Mexico. **SPOTLIGHTS** A legendary pioneer of "World Music," Santana has thrilled and inspired millions of fans for more than three decades. Blending elements of 12-bar blues, fiery rock riffs, sensuous Afro-Cuban rhythms, and a multi-piece percussion session, and featuring his passionate guitar style, Santana created a unique, magical sound. His band, Santana, made its 1968 professional debut at San Francisco's Fillmore West. The audience's electric response won the group a coveted invitation to perform at the original 1969 Woodstock Festival in Bethel, New York. With their show-stopping performance, Santana's powerful, new Latin-flavored, salsa-rock sound swept the spirited crowd off their feet. The band's debut album,

Carlos Santana (holding star plaque) and Edward James Olmos.

Santana went double-platinum, and with hits like "Evil Ways," "Soul Sacrifice," and "Jingo" stayed on the charts for more than two years. His follow-up album, *Abraxas*, soared to #1 and went quadruple-platinum with hits "Black Magic Woman," "Oye Como Va," and "Gypsy Queen." *Santana III* included songs "Everybody's Everything," and "No One to Depend On." After winning a 1987 Grammy for Best Rock Instrumental Performance for his moving and highly personal *Blues for Salvador* (his eighth solo recording), he scored the feature film *La Bamba* (1987), based on the 1950s Chicano rocker Ritchie Valens. A whole new generation of appreciative listeners heard him for the first time at the 1985 Live Aid concert. In 1994, Santana returned to Woodstock for the 25th anniversary concert; they were one of three groups invited to attend that had performed at the original counterculture rock festival. Santana's legion of worldwide fans expanded with releases of his: comprehensive boxed-set retrospective *Dance of the Rainbow Serpent* (release in 1995), successful jazz-influenced solo projects, collaborations with other top artists such as John Lee Hooker and Lauryn Hill, and his riveting 1999 #1 release called *Supernatural* on Arista Records. Santana's creative strength, beauty and diversity is apparent on dozens of albums/CDs. **ACHIEVEMENTS** In 2000, Carlos Santana received 10 Grammy nominations, and won a record-tying eight Grammys. He was inducted into the Rock and Roll Hall of Fame, along with the Santana band in 1998. He won a Grammy in 1987 (see above). 1997 Latino Music Legend of the Year, Latin Rock Band of the Year by the Latin New York Music Awards, numerous Bammy Awards, voted the best pop-rock guitarist several times in the *Playboy* magazine's annual readers' poll, recipient of the *Billboard* Century Award, among countless other honors for excellence in music, and public service. He is a charitable individual without borders, giving and helping many worthy causes, including Earthquake Relief, orphans in Tijuana, Mexico, championing the rights of Indigenous Peoples, and education for Latin youth in association with the Hispanic Media & Education Group (HEMG). **HIGHLIGHTS** At age five, the young Carlos was introduced to traditional music by his father, Jose, an accomplished mariachi violinist and experienced musician. He taught his son the basics of music theory and an understanding of the value of a note. From this, the excitement of music was sparked. It ignited into Santana's lifelong passion.

Pearl Bailey   7080 Hollywood

Singer, actress, night club entertainer
BORN Mar. 29, 1918, in Newport News, VA. **SPOTLIGHTS** One of the greatest and most exciting jazz singers of all time, she started singing in the church where her father was a preacher. At age 13, she joined her famous tap dancing brother, Bill Bailey, touring in show business. Still in her teens she sang with Count Basie, Cootie Williams, and Cab Calloway, igniting the fire to her illustrious recording career. Bailey acted in nine films including *Carmen Jones* (1955) and *Porgy and Bess*

Pearl Bailey

(1959). She proudly stated, "Acting is living. It's being natural. The (African-American) is the greatest natural actor in the world. We're all great heart people." An accomplished Broadway performer, this dynamo garnered a Tony Award for the title role in the all-black Broadway musical production of "Hello Dolly." Her autobiography, *The Raw Pearl*, was published in 1962. **ACHIEVEMENTS** Active entertainer in U.S.O. tours for American troops since 1942. Hosted her own television show in 1971. Retired in 1975 and was named to the U.S. Delegation to the United Nations. **QUOTE** "It isn't the singing, it's the relaxing that does it." Died: 1990.

Frances Dee 🎥   7080 Hollywood

Actress
BORN Jean F. Dee, Nov. 26, 1907, in Los Angeles, CA. **SPOT-LIGHTS** A blue-eyed, brunette beauty, she co-stars with Maurice Chevalier in *Playboy of Paris* (1930). Then, she appears as leading ladies in numerous film productions: *If I Were King* (1938), with Ronald Coleman and Basil Rathbone; and *Wells Fargo* (1937), with Joel McCrea. She appears in the classic *Little Women* (1933), with Katherine Hepburn. In 1933 she married one of her leading men, Joel McCrea.

The Real Don Steele 🎙   7080 Hollywood

Radio personality, DJ
BORN April Fool's Day (April 1), 1936, in Hollywood, CA. **SPOTLIGHTS** Called the "Boss Jock," Steele "*introduced* rock 'n' roll to Southern California," becoming part of its culture. His light-speed patter and glib tongue captured the grooviest, hippest rockers from the late 1960s for two decades. He earned the highest ratings in KHJ station's history. *Billboard* magazine named Steele the #1 personality of 1967 and '68. **QUOTE** "We were standing literally at ground zero; then it became a huge giant. It was like a mushroom cloud that went up—heavy on the mushroom." Died: 1997.

The Dead End Kids 🎥   7080 Hollywood

Child actors
BORN Billy Halop on May 11, 1920, in Brooklyn, NY; Leo Gorcey on June 3, 1917, in New York, NY; Bernard Punsly on July 11 ("lucky 7-11"), 1923, in the Bronx, NY; Huntz Hall on Aug. 15, 1919 in New York, NY; Gabriel Dell on Oct. 7, 1919, in Brooklyn, NY; and Bobby Jordan on April 1, 1923, in New York, NY. **SPOTLIGHTS** The Dead End Kids snatched their name from their acclaimed roles as a gang of young hooligans in the 1935 hit Broadway production "Dead End." Two years later, movie mogul Samuel Goldwyn brought them to Hollywood for the highly theatrical movie version. The script, about New York's Lower East Side slum kids and gangsters, was toned down from Sidney Kingsley's dramatic play by Lillian Hellman. This meticulously stylized, socially conscious movie offers a graphic depiction of the powerful differences between Hell's Kitchen and the luxurious Sutton Place, between corruption and noble character. Directed by one of Hollywood's most honored, William Wyler, the film featured Joel McCrea, Sylvia Sidney, Humphrey Bogart, Wendy Barrie, Claire Trevor, and introduced The Dead End Kids to a delighted world. It received a 1937 Oscar nomination for Best Picture, and the Kids never left town. A film-making industry in themselves, they went from being known as the Dead End Kids to the Little Tough Guys, then to the East Side Kids. They finally became the Bowery Boys, where they worked in comedies with Laurel and Hardy, the Three Stooges and Abbott and Costello. They made a total of 88 feature-length films, an all-time motion picture record for an ensemble group—although not every Kid appeared in each film throughout the 21 years. The Kids did what came naturally. Basically, they were not acting, they were playing "pretend" with their friends and enjoying all the crazy things they got to do. However, about working with the legendary James Cagney, Punsly stated, "He wouldn't take any fooling around on the set." Movies include *Crime School, Angels with Dirty Faces* (both 1938), *They Made Me a Criminal, Hell's Kitchen* (both 1939), *The Dead End Kids on Dress Parade* (1940). **SIDELIGHTS** The Kids averaged from $350 to $650-a-week, with an occasional $900-a-week studio paycheck. As Punsly put it, "That was a lot of money back then." That was also before the passage of the Coogan Act, which protects child actors from financial abuses by their parents and/or managers. Several found themselves without a trust fund, or savings account, at the end of their show business career. One Kid grew up to discover his nest egg blown by his gambling addicted father at the four major Southern California Thoroughbred horse race tracks. **HIGHLIGHTS** When he retired from acting, Punsly joined the Army during World War II. After his honorable discharge, he attended the Univ. of Georgia School of Medicine on the G.I. bill. During the Korean War, he joined the Air Force, where the Captain served as a doctor. Since then, he has enjoyed a thriving practice specializing in internal medicine. **QUOTE** Their star was unveiled on Feb. 1, 1994 (Hollywood's 107th Birthday). Two surviving members—Hall and Punsly—attended. At the ceremony Punsly quipped, "My father told me I'd end up on the street, but I didn't think it would take 50 years." Died: Jordan in the late 1940s, Garcey a few years later, Halop in the 1950s, Dell in the late 1980s. Huntz Hall in 1999.

LA BREA GATEWAY

INAUGURATED Feb. 1, 1993, in Hollywood, CA. **SPOTLIGHTS** Created by studio production designer Catherine Hardwicke, this beautiful, stylized sculpture was unveiled as part of Hollywood's 105th Birthday Celebration. The 30-foot-high, stainless steel gazebo is supported by the likenesses of five actresses (all Walk of Fame honorees), whose careers were instrumental in the movie industry: Dolores Del Rio, Anna May Wong, Mae West, Dorothy Dandridge, and topped with a likeness of Marilyn Monroe. It is situated on a traffic island paved in terrazzo. There are also paved "film strip" crosswalks, rows of palm trees, accent lighting and landscaped medians.

The Beatles (left to right): Ringo, George, John and Paul
Ed Sullivan (center)

7095 HOLLYWOOD

Spanky McFarland 🎥 7095 Hollywood
Actor

Spanky McFarland

BORN George Emmett McFarland, Oct. 2, 1928, in Ft. Worth, TX. **SPOTLIGHTS** A darling baby boy, he came to the world's attention as "Spanky." This young fellow was already working by the age of two—modeling for the print ads of a Dallas bakery. He was kind of an early Pillsbury dough boy. At age three, he became the chubby little character in the endearing *Our Gang* comedy shorts; these evergreen skits were later released in television as "The Little Rascals." He appears in a number of features including *Honkey Donkey, The Trail Of The Lonesome Pine, General Spanky* (all 1936), *Peck's Bad Boy with the Circus* (1939), *Johnny Doughboy* (1943), and *The Woman In The Window* (1944). He remains one of cinema's early and most beloved child stars. McFarland occasionally returns to entertaining, and has penned an autobiography.

Eric Linden 🎥 7095 Hollywood
Actor

BORN Sept. 15, 1909, in New York, NY. **SPOTLIGHTS** He was a supporting talent in the action picture, *Robin Hood of El Dorado* (1936), starring Warner Baxter and Bruce Cabot. He appears in an American classic, *A Family Affair* (1937), with Lionel Barrymore and Mickey Rooney in the Hardy Family series. One of his last films was a small role in *Gone With the Wind* (1939).

Mako 🎥 7095 Hollywood
Actor, director

BORN Makoto Iwamatsu; Dec. 10, 1933, in Los Angeles, CA. **SPOTLIGHTS** An accomplished actor of stage, screen and television, Mako has earned numerous honors for his craftsmanship. His artistic successes include his Oscar nomination for Best Supporting Actor, in *The Sand Pebbles* (1966), starring Steve McQueen. Although the Oscar eluded him, he won a Golden Globe Award. Features include *Tora! Tora! Tora!* (1970), *The Hawaiians* (1970), *The Killer Elite* (1975), *The Big Brawl* (1980), *Conan the Barbarian* (1982), *Conan the Destroyer* (1984), *Pacific Heights* (1990), and *Seven Years in Tibet* (1997) with Brad Pitt, among many others in his long list of credits. He co-produced Japanese films *Chin Moku-Silence* (1979), and *Strawberry Road* (1990). In all, he has appeared in 300 television shows and movies. He performs—as well as directs—stage plays. In 1975 he received a Tony

nomination for Best Actor in "Pacific Overtures," a Broadway hit musical. He is the recipient of two Best Director Awards from the Los Angeles Drama Critics Circle. **ACHIEVEMENTS** Founder of East West Players, the first Asian-American theater company in the country. It is located in Little Tokyo, in Los Angeles, California. This company delivers outstanding work with four plays a season (from Jan. to June), and various command performances from conservatory during the summertime. Other activities include a writers institute. For ticket sales, or more information, please contact either by telephone (213) 625-7000; or e-mail: info@eastwestplayers.com; or their website: www.eastwestplayers.com.

Jerry Herman 🐺 7095 Hollywood
Composer, lyricist

Jerry Herman

BORN July 10, 1933, in New York, NY. **SPOTLIGHTS** A Broadway legend, this tremendous talent is known for his big, sweeping, emotionally moving scores. As a child growing up in New York, his mother took him to his first Broadway play, Irving Berlin's "Annie Get Your Gun." About that overwhelming excitement and experience, Herman reflected, "I came home starry-eyed. And I knew then that I had to have something to do with writing for the musical theater." Amazingly, he learned to play the piano by ear. After graduating from the University of Miami with a Bachelor of Fine Arts in drama, it was only a brief span of time before he wrote the score for "Milk and Honey." He said, "I found myself at a very tender age with a Broadway show. Not only a Broadway show, but a successful Broadway show." For more than four decades this brilliant, award-winning toast of Broadway has written the lyrics and music for hit extravaganzas. Classic Herman works include "Milk and Honey," "Hello, Dolly!" "Mame," "La Cage Aux Folles," "Jerry's Girls" (a revue of his life's work), and "Mack and Mabel." In the latter he created an instant classic with the song "Time Heals Everything." Many consider "Mack and Mabel," his finest score. Other favorite songs from a variety of the plays are "If He Walked Into My Life," "Hello, Dolly!" "I Am What I Am," "Mame," and "Kiss Her Now." In addition to musicals, Herman has created a wide spectrum of work, from ballads to waltzes. **ACHIEVEMENTS** Received numerous Grammy Awards, Tony Awards, and Gold records. He became the only composer/lyricist in history to have three shows running simultaneously for more than 1,500 performances each on Broadway: "Hello, Dolly!," "Mame," and "Dear World." He is also the recipient of the Songwriter's Hall of Fame and The Theater Hall of Fame. Herman received his star on the Walk of Fame on Feb. 1, 1994 (Hollywood's 107th Birthday). In 1987 he was presented with the Johnny Mercer Award. **RECOMMENDED READING** His autobiography *Showtune*, published by Donald I. Fine Books. **QUOTE** His positive, uplifting songs enjoy universal appeal. "I write songs about happy times. I want people to be able to hum my songs in the shower or dance to them at a wedding. And they do."

Irving Berlin 🎵   7095 Hollywood

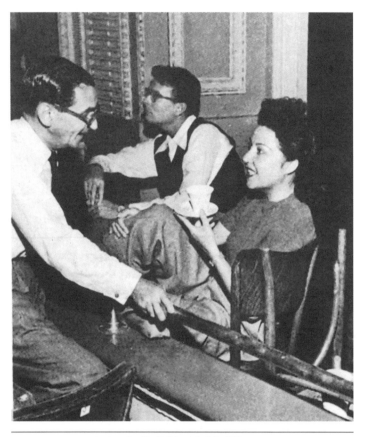

Irving Berlin (left) with Ethel Merman

Songwriter, composer

BORN Israel Beilin; May 11, 1888, in Mohilev, Russia. **SPOT-LIGHTS** Berlin *is* American music. Known as "the Prince of Melody," this musical genius produced more than 1500 ballads, dance numbers, novelty tunes and love songs that defined American popular music for much of the 20th century. One of the greatest in his field, he came to America from Russia at age five, and grew up in a ghetto, in New York's lower East Side. "Izzy" as he was called, sang on street corners and sold newspapers for pennies. At the end of the day he would return home to deposit the coins on his mother's apron. The streets are where he received much of his education. After his father's death, the family's financial situation worsened still. Berlin could not pull his own weight, and not wanting to burden his

family, he left home at age 14. The slim, reticent, private fellow got a job singing in cafes and in lodging houses. In 1902 he got his first theater job in the chorus of a musical called "The Show Girl." He published his first song in 1907 ("Marie from Sunny Italy"), and by 1911 had his first major international hit, "Alexander's Ragtime Band." This popular song heralded the advance of the Jazz Age. In 1914 he wrote the smash Broadway hit "Watch Your Step." During the course of his lifetime he had many hit shows including "As Thousands Cheer," filled with plenty of hit songs, such as "Easter Parade," that Berlin called, "singable." One of the most representative songwriters and composers, hits include "God Bless America," "Let's Face the Music and Dance," "Puttin' on the Ritz," "Anything You Can Do," and "Cheek to Cheek," among many others in his long list. "Oh, How I Hate To Get Up In The Morning" was written when he was an infantry sergeant at Camp Upton during WWI. After the war he formed his own publishing house. Many of his song titles became the basis for movies. erlin also wrote the scores for several cinema classics, including *Top Hat* (1935), with Fred Astaire and Ginger Rogers. In 1935, as composer, his Hollywood studio salary was $150,000, separate from royalties and recordings. He rewrote and published his original 1918 "God Bless America" in 1938. Kate Smith introduced it to the country on the radio. Megahits include "White Christmas" (1942--the best-selling single of all time), "Easter Parade" (1948), and "There's No Business Like Show Business" (1954). He also wrote the musical score for "Annie Get Your Gun" (1946). **ACHIEVEMENTS** Oscar (1942) Best Song, "White Christmas." U.S. Army's Medal of Merit from President Truman (1945); Congressional Gold Medal from President Eisenhower (1955); and the Freedom Medal from President Ford (1977). Through his various foundations, he donated millions of dollars that he earned in royalties to a number of charities. His centennial in 1988 was celebrated worldwide, culminating in an all-star tribute at Carnegie Hall. **HIGHLIGHTS** Calling himself a songwriter, not a composer, Berlin could neither read nor write music. He could only play the piano in the key of F sharp major in a "hunt and peck manner; ta-ta-ta-ta. **QUOTE** "All I can say is I'm a man with two interests—my family and my work." Died: 1989, at age 101.

Johnny Carson (left), producer Fred de Cordova (center), and Arthur M. Kasssel

7083 HOLLYWOOD

Frankie Lymon   7083 Hollywood

Singer

BORN Sept. 30, 1942, New York, NY. **SPOTLIGHTS** "Why Do Fools Fall in Love?" lifted the 13-year-old out of obscurity and into the limelight. It shot to #1 on the Rhythm & Blues charts and #6 on the pop charts. He became *the* first African-American teen idol, who, with his boyish soprano, paved the way for the likes of other singers, such as Michael Jackson. His life story reads like a movie. He sang in his father's gospel group, then along with four talented school chums they sang on the street corners of New York City. There, they were discovered and signed to a label. Frankie Lymon and the Teenagers were 1950s clean-cut with their letter sweaters and creased trousers. They were the personification of innocence, embraced by the American public, enjoying a string of hits: "I Promise to Remember," "I Want You to Be My Girl," and "The ABC's of Love." He appears in two Alan Freed films, *Rock, Rock, Rock* (1956) and *Mr. Rock and Roll* (1957). **ACHIEVEMENTS** Inducted into the Doo-Wop Hall Of Fame in 1991. Inducted into the Rock and Roll Hall Of Fame in 1993. **SIDELIGHTS** Ironically, Teenager first tenor vocalist Herman Santiago was slated to sing "Why Do Fools Fall in Love?" but could not record due to a cold. Frankie Lymon stepped in his place. In 1992 a Federal Court ruled regarding the copyright issue of the song writers. They ruling was in Santiago's favor, along with co-writer Jimmy Merchant who was the Teenagers second tenor vocalist. The judge awarded back royalties—estimated to be worth millions—for the evergreen song. Died in 1968.

Robert Urich   7083 Hollywood

Actor

Robert Urich with his wife

BORN Dec. 19, 1940, in Toronto, Ohio. **SPOTLIGHTS** Television's big, lovable, tough guy is one of the most prolific, popular and busy actors in the medium. He has starred in 11 series, including "Spenser: for Hire," "Vega$," "S.W.A.T.," "The Lazarus Man" and "Boatworks." His performances have kept TV audiences worldwide captivated by his charisma, intelligence and action sequences. **ACHIEVEMENTS** He has starred in more prime time television series than anyone else. **QUOTE** He bravely went public with his painful bout of a rare form of synovial cancer. He stated, "I wasn't sure I'd have a career anymore." He also commented, "I know I can beat this with your prayers." He visualized "the Golden Light of God comes through the top of my head, swirling through every fiber of my body and kills the poisonous cells." Urich continued some of his charity duties in between his chemotherapy sessions, remaining compassionate toward others even while he faced his own death. He affirmed, "Treatment works and people with cancer are cured everyday." He, too, was cured and inspired thousands of people.

Ben Johnson   7083 Hollywood

Actor

Ben Johnson

BORN June 13,1918, in Foreacre, OK. **SPOTLIGHTS** He worked as a cowboy and performed on the rodeo circuit until 1940. After he delivered a herd of horses to Howard Hughes, he decided to stay in Hollywood. He worked as a stuntman and riding double for both James Stewart and Joel McCrae. Johnson made his acting debut in John Ford's *3 Godfathers* (1948), starring John Wayne. He stars in the cult feature *Mighty Joe Young* (1949), before the 1950 Western *Wagon Master*. He worked with John Wayne again in the classics *She Wore a Yellow Ribbon* (1949) and *Rio Grande* (1950). In all, he appears in 300 films, including *Shane* (1953), *One-Eyed Jacks* (1961), *Will Penny* (1968), and *The Wild Bunch* (1969). **ACHIEVEMENTS** A Best Supporting Actor Oscar for *The Last Picture Show* (1971)...His "Cowboys for Kids" charity fund put on rodeos to help underprivileged children. Died: 1996.

Pedro Infante   7083 Hollywood

Singer, actor

BORN 1918. **SPOTLIGHTS** Crowned "the most popular singer-actor in Latin America," his devoted Spanish-speaking fans covered the globe. He made many personal, concert and hall appearances. Infante sparkled with charisma, and almost 40 years after his death, he is still one of the best-selling Latino recording stars of all time. He was honored universally as a world-class performer, and was the recipient of countless honors and awards. He has a street named after him in East Los Angeles. Died: 1957, in a plane crash, at age 39.

Gladys Knight   7083 Hollywood

Singer

Gladys Knight

BORN May 28, 1944, in Atlanta, GA. **SPOTLIGHTS** A natural born talent with an ease for performing, young Gladys began singing at Mount Mariah Baptist Church when she was four. As a first-grader she had already made it to the championship round of a talent competition held at Madison Square Gardens sponsored by the "Ted Mack Amateur Hour." On this nationally televised show— and only second in ratings to "Bonanza," the eight-year-old sang Nat "King" Cole's "Too Young" while "standing on a box because the microphone was too tall for me to reach." She won the National Grand Prize with a four-foot gold trophy that was taller than her. Later she formed a little family group, The Pips, and recorded their first hit record, "With Every Beat of My Heart" (1961). With her soulful voice, that "little group" lasted 39 years, with gigantic hits, "I Heard It Through The Grapevine," "Midnight Train To Georgia," "If I Were Your Woman," "The Best Thing That Ever Happened To Me," and "Love Overboard." She appeared in guest spots on popular TV sitcoms, landing her first co-starring role with Flip Wilson in the comedy series "Charlie And Company." She recorded the title theme for the James Bond movie, *License To Kill* (1990), and has led a successful solo career. Knight is also an accomplished Broadway performer. **ACHIEVEMENTS** The winner of numerous Grammy awards, Gladys Knight and The Pips were inducted into the Rock and Roll Hall of Fame. **RECOMMENDED READING** *Between Each Line of Pain and Glory—My Life Story* by Gladys Knight (published by Hyperion in 1997). **HIGHLIGHTS** Her paternal grandfather was a full-blooded Native American Cherokee Indian.

Vera-Ellen 🎥   7083 Hollywood

Actress, dancer

BORN Vera-Ellen Westmeyr Rohe; Feb. 16, 1926, in Cincinnati, OH. **SPOTLIGHTS** A natural born artist, when she began dance lessons at age 10 her obvious gift for the art was immediately recognized. After winning a Major Bowes talent contest, she became a regular dancer with his show, then segued into Ted Lewis' band, and later Billy Rose's Casa Manana night club. She also was a Rockette at the famed Radio City Music Hall. Energetic and petite, she appeared in a number of Broadway musicals, and was told by drama critic George Jean Nathan "you can dance on my desktop anytime." The beauty was signed by mogul Samuel Goldwyn for two Danny Kaye movies: *Wonder Man* (1945) and *Kid from Brooklyn* (1946).

Extremely accomplished, she starred opposite some of the world's greatest actor/dancers, including Gene Kelly and Fred Astaire. Movies include *Three Little Girls in Blue* (1946), *Carnival in Costa Rica* (1947), *On the Town* (1949), *Three Little Words* (1950), *Call Me Madam* (1953), and *White Christmas* (1954). Died: 1981.

Leiber & Stoller 🔘   7083 Hollywood

Song writing team

Leiber & Stoller with a "Hound Dog."

BORN Jerry Leiber, April 25, 1933, in Baltimore, MD.; Mike Stoller, May 13, 1933, in Belle Harbor, NY. **SPOTLIGHTS** The two met in Los Angeles in 1950, both families having moved there after WWII. Both were age 17, and they discovered a similar interest in the lyrics and musical progressions of African American music. Together they defined rock 'n' roll. By 20, their earliest songs were being recorded by such artists as Jimmy Witherspoon, Little Esther, Amos Milburn, Charles Brown, Little Willie Littlefield, Bull Moose Jackson, Linda Hopkins, Ray Charles and Willie Mae "Big Mama" Thornton. Then, they wrote the song "Hound Dog," which Elvis Presley performed. The combined energy of Presley and the genius of Leiber and Stoller was the realization of the creation of rock 'n' roll. After "Hound Dog," rock 'n' roll was here to stay. The two friends composed "Jailhouse Rock," "Treat Me Nice," "(You're So Square) Baby I Don't Care," and "I Want to Be Free," in one afternoon writing session of only four hours! Elvis recorded those, and more of their songs, including "Love Me," "Don't," and "Fools In Love." Hundreds of talented artists have recorded their songs, from

The Beatles and The Beach Boys, to Barbra Streisand and Aretha Franklin, as well as B.B. King and Muddy Waters. Considered the industry's first "independent producers" because of the strong demand for their product. They brought rhythm-and-blues into the national scene. **ACHIEVEMENTS** Inducted into the Songwriters Hall of Fame (1985), the Record Producers Hall of Fame (1986), and the Rock and Roll Hall of Fame (1987). **QUOTE** "We don't write songs, we write records."

Livingston & Evans 🎵 7083 Hollywood

Song writing team
BORN Jay Livingston, Mar. 28, 1915, in McDonald, PA; Ray Evans, Feb. 2, 1915, in Salamanca, NY. **SPOTLIGHTS** A power duo, their songs have sold 400 million copies. Among their more popular efforts: "Mona Lisa," "Golden Earrings," "Buttons and Bows," "Tammy," "Que Sera Sera," and "Silver Bells." **ACHIEVEMENTS** Three Oscars (seven Academy Award nominations). Inducted into the Songwriters Hall of Fame.

Nicholas Brothers 🎥 7083 Hollywood

Dance team
BORN Fayard Antonio Nicholas, Oct. 20, 1914, in Mobile, AL; brother: Harold. **SPOTLIGHTS** For 60 years this classic, superb tap dancing duo made entertainment history. Masters of style and flair, the "Nicholas Kids" began performing in vaudeville. In 1932 they opened at the Cotton Club, headlining with great orchestras like Duke Ellington and Cab Calloway. These great artists were invited to Hollywood to appear in *Kid Millions* (1934), with Eddie Cantor. They stayed to make 55 American films, including *Down Argentina Way* (1940), and *Tin Pan Alley* (1940). They also worked in

Nicholas Brothers

European cinema. They were pioneers in establishing tap as America's original dance art form. They enjoyed huge successes on the Broadway stage. The Nicholas Brothers worked in every medium of show business, even tap dancing *on radio*, and performed for British royalty and U.S. Presidents. **ACHIEVEMENTS** Emmy 1965-'66; Tony 1989. They were honored at the Academy Awards with a special tribute to their lifelong work in 1981. Their tireless efforts aid disadvantaged children and the homeless.

John Garfield 🎥 7065 Hollywood

John Garfield

Actor
BORN Julius Garfinkle; March 4, 1913, in New York, NY. **SPOTLIGHTS** Though raised on the tough lower East Side of the city, he managed to overcome a life of odd jobs and street gangs to win a state debating contest sponsored by the "New York Times." The resulting scholarship led him to the Broadway stage. Hollywood called. He stars in *Four Daughters* (1938), playing a cynical, defiant young man who charms and muscles his way to success (much like his own life). Other notable films include *Juarez* (1939), *The Sea Wolf* (1941), *Tortilla Flat* (1942), *Hollywood Canteen* (1944), *The Postman Always Rings Twice* (1946), and *Gentleman's Agreement* (1947). Died: 1952.

Katy Jurado 🎥 7065 Hollywood

Actress
BORN Maria Christina Jurado Garcia, Jan. 16, 1924, in Guadalajara, Mexico. **SPOTLIGHTS** With her heart-shaped face, large eyes, full pouty lips and a voluptuous figure, she was a true beauty. Jurado, one of Mexico's most exciting leading ladies during the 1940s, came to Hollywood in the 1950s. She arrived here as a columnist to cover tinsel town for several Mexican publications. With her fiery, dark-haired exotic looks and interesting personality, she was quickly signed by the studios. Jurado made her American silver screen debut in the compelling drama, *The Bullfighter and the Lady* (1950), co-starring Robert Stack and Gilbert Roland. This sensuous actress would be immortalized in her next film, *High Noon* (1952). She co-stars with Gary Cooper, Grace Kelly, and Lloyd Bridges in this classic Western masterpiece about "the story of a man who was too proud to run!" She made another Western, *Arrowhead* (1953), opposite Charlton Heston, Jack Palance, and Milburn Stone. In *Broken Lance* (1954), she was Oscar-nominated. It co-stars Spencer Tracy and Robert Wagner. Movies include *Trial* (1955), *Trapeze* (1956), *The Man from Del Rio* (1956), *The Badlanders* (1958), *One Eyed Jacks* (1961),

Pat Garrett and Billy The Kid (1973), *The Children of Sanchez* (1978), *Evita Peron* (1981), and *Under the Volcano* (1984). She has made 50 movies worldwide. TV movies and mini-series include "Four Women in Black," "A Little Game, " "Evita Peron" and "Lady Blue."

Sidney Poitier 🎥   7065 Hollywood

Sidney Poitier

Actor, director
BORN Feb. 20, 1924, in Miami, FL. **SPOTLIGHTS** A handsome, intelligent, charismatic talent with an elegant presence, he made his debut with the American Negro Theater on Broadway in "Lysistrata" (1946). He was the first African American actor to move into stardom by breaking away from "Negro" stereotypes. Careful about choosing roles, he once said, "I try to do and say nothing that might be a step backward."
He became one of Hollywood's most popular screen stars. Films include *No Way Out* (1950), *Cry the Beloved Country* (1951—his breakthrough film), *The Blackboard Jungle* (1955), *Something of Value* (1957), *A Raisin in the Sun* (1961), *A Patch of Blue* (1965), *The Bedford Incident* (1965), *Duel at Diablo* (1966), *In the Heat of the Night* (1967), *Guess Who's Coming to Dinner* (1967), *To Sir, With Love* (1967), and *They Call Me MISTER Tibbs!* (1970). He made his directorial debut with the Western *Buck and the Preacher* (1972). He also directed *Uptown Saturday Night* (1974), *A Piece of the Action* (1977), and *Stir Crazy* (1981). Poitier has also appeared in a number of television mini-series and special TV movie presentations. **HIGHLIGHTS** About Poitier's work in *The Defiant Ones* (1958), director Stanley Kramer stated: "He's the only actor I've ever worked with who has the range of Marlon Brando, from pathos to great power." Poitier earned a Best Actor Oscar nomination for this performance. **ACHIEVEMENTS** Best Actor Oscar for *Lilies of the Field* (1963). He portrays a construction worker persuaded into building a chapel for a group of German refugee nuns. It's an inspirational comedy/drama, which not only won Mr. Poitier an Oscar (the first time ever for an African-American male, and as 1999, the only African-American to win in the "best actor" category), but broke the 24-year-old dry spell since the last African-American, Miss Hattie McDaniel, won the prestigious award for *Gone With the Wind*. (McDaniel's had been in the "supporting" category, not lead. In between McDaniel and Poitier, James Baskett won an Honorary Award in 1947.) 1992 Lifetime Achievement Award given by the American Film Institute.

Lloyd Bridges 📽   7065 Hollywood

Actor
BORN Jan. 15, 1913, in San Leandro, CA. **SPOTLIGHTS** After studying drama at UCLA, this tall, blond, ruggedly handsome actor worked onstage with the acting group, The Playroom Club. In the late 1930s, he made his Broadway debut in a modernized "Othello," with Walter Huston and Brian Aherne. In 1940 he performed in the New York production of "Susanna and the Elders," then was signed by Columbia Pictures. Bridges' screen debut was in a "B" movie

Lloyd Bridges and Sandra Church

series, *The Lone Wolf Takes a Chance* (1941), a mystery. Next, he landed in the fantasy classic *Here Comes Mr. Jordan* (1941), starring Robert Montgomery, Evelyn Keyes and Claude Rains. Bridges made nearly 70 motion pictures, but no one can forget him as the athletic, swashbuckling ex-Navy frogman, Mike Nelson, in the TV adventure-swim series "Sea Hunt" (1957-'61). Yet his movie performances should not be missed. In Westerns and dramas he was often cast as a villain or a character significantly flawed. He delivered a gritty, compelling performance in the WWII drama *A Walk in the Sun* (1945). He played an all-too-human GI in the groundbreaking war drama that explored racism among fighting men in *Home of the Brave* (1949). Bridges is must-see as the gutless deputy in the Western masterpiece *High Noon* (1952). Directed by Fred Zinnemann, the movie employs the technique of "real time." The 85 minutes that retiring marshall Will Kane (Gary Cooper) sweats it out while waiting to confront an outlaw gang bent on killing him is the actual running time of the film. He appears with his son Jeff, in *Tucker—The Man and His Dream* (1988); it is an amazing real-life tale of an automotive genius going for the American dream. A capable talent in lighter works, he gave a riotous performance in the spoof *Airplane* (1980), and *Airplane II, The Sequel* (1982). Motion pictures include *The Talk of the Town* (1942), *Canyon Passage* (1946), *Colt .45* (1950), *The Whistle at Eton Falls* (1951—semi-documentary), *Plymouth Adventure* (1952), *The Kid from Left Field* (1953), *The Rainmaker* (1956), and opposite Kim Stanley in the Paddy Chayefsky written-and-produced tawdry Hollywood drama, *The Goddess* (1957). He appeared in a number of TV series, movies and mini-series, including "Roots," "How the West Was Won," "East of Eden," and "North and South, Book II." **ACHIEVEMENTS** Recipient of many honors, including the 1994 Ralph Bunche Peace Award commemorating the United Nations Year of the Family...The patriarch of one of the top contemporary Hollywood dynasties, two of his three sons, Beau and Jeff are successful actors. He was known as one of Hollywood's most-loving family men and a great father. **QUOTE** One of his last wishes was to attend one *particular* Hollywood ceremony. He told me, "My son,

Beau, deserves a star on the Walk of Fame, and it should be placed next to mine and Jeff's. I won't be happy until he has a star, too." Died: 1998.

Jeff Bridges   7065 Hollywood

Actor

Jeff Bridges

BORN Dec. 4, 1949, in Los Angeles, California. **SPOTLIGHTS** The son of actor Lloyd Bridges, he grew up on Hollywood soundstages. He made his silver screen debut around age one in *The Company She Keeps* (1950), a melodrama starring Lisabeth Scott, Jane Greer and Dennis O'Keefe. By age eight, he was professionally acting in his father's smash television show "Sea Hunt." As an adult, Bridges returned to the screen in *The Last Picture Show* (1971), earning a well-deserved best supporting actor Oscar nomination. It is a must-see movie. Well-built, with a charming grin and thick hair, he is easy on the eyes. Yet more than a ruggedly handsome talent, he is one of the most *natural* actors on-screen. This versatile leading man seemingly can play anything, excelling in both comedy and drama. Motion pictures include John Huston's *Fat City* (1972), opposite Stacy Keach and Susan Tyrell in a solid boxing drama, *Bad Company* (1972), with Barry Brown and Jim Davis in a thrilling, offbeat and action-packed Civil War era piece, *The Last American Hero* (1973), based on the true life story of stock car racer Junior Johnson, *The Iceman Cometh* (1973), adapted from Eugene O'Neill's masterpiece, and *Thunderbolt and Lightfoot* (1974—in an Oscar-nominated performance for best supporting actor), opposite Clint Eastwood. In 1976 he stars in the remake of *King Kong*, opposite Jessica Lange and Charles Grodin. He received his first Academy Award nomination—in the best actor category—for his role as the extraterrestrial in the sci-fi picture *Starman* (1984). Viewed as a romantic hero who is both out-of-this world "manly" and wistful, *Starman* remains a favorite film among his devoted base of female fans. He is outstanding in *Tucker—The Man and His Dream* (1988—based on a true story), co-starring Martin Landau and his father Lloyd Bridges. He works with his older brother, Beau, in *The Fabulous Baker Boys* (1989), while Michelle Pfeiffer sizzles as the love interest. He gives a stunning, utterly moving performance in the comedy-drama *The Fisher King* (1991). Other motion pictures include *Against All Odds* (1984), *Texasville* (1990—the sequel to The *Last Picture Show*), *Fearless* (1993), *Blown Away* (1994), with his father Lloyd Bridges and Tommy Lee Jones, *Wild Bill* (1995), *The Mirror Has Two Faces* (1996), opposite Barbra Streisand, *The Muse* (1999), co-starring Sharon Stone and Albert Brooks,

Arlington Road (1999), a suspense thriller with Tim Robbins, Joan Cusack and Hope Davis, and *Simpatico* (1999), a story of love, betrayal and money co-starring Nick Nolte and Sharon Stone, based on Sam Shepard's original play. **HIGHLIGHTS** Part of a well-known family dynasty, his star lies next to that of his famous father, Lloyd Bridges.

Richard Webb    7065 Hollywood

Actor

BORN Sept. 9, 1916, in Bloomington, IL. **SPOTLIGHTS** A Saturday morning hero, who, like his alter ego, "Captain Midnight," believed in the greatness of America and the goodness of mankind. Webb was immortalized as television's superhero "Captain Midnight" (1954-'58). His live-action TV show was frequently the nation's top-rated children's series. His character taught the principles of truth, fairness and honor, wrapped in an action-packed story. Each show would end

"Captain Midnight" Richard Webb

with: "This is Captain Midnight signing off with the code of the Secret Squadron. Justice through strength and courage. Out!" In a career spanning four decades, Webb appeared in more than 60 films and 260 television programs. Motion pictures include *Hold Back the Dawn* (1941), *O.S.S.* (1946), *The Big Clock* (1948), and *Sands of Iwo Jima* (1949). **ACHIEVEMENTS** In 1986 "Captain Midnight" was inducted in the Smithsonian Institution's National Air & Space Museum. It was one of Webb's most prestigious honors...He had a rewarding stint in the military. A graduate of Officer Candidate School, Webb was an explosives expert and extremely skilled in hand-to-hand combat and judo. He served with distinction as Captain in the Army Air Corps during World War II, ultimately achieving the rank of Lieutenant Colonel through the Army Reserves. He quipped, "I had to go into the military to prepare for 'Captain Midnight.'" **HIGHLIGHTS** A 1954 poll showed Captain Midnight the #1 hero of America's youth. In second place was President Eisenhower, in fourth place was "a new young man just breaking in named Elvis Presley." Four years later, Captain Midnight was in second place following "the King." Webb said, "Presley was really hot then." **QUOTE** "I feel very sorry for the current crop of actors. The junk they put them in. There really aren't any heroes anymore. They've gotten away from the actors and gone to special effects." Died: 1993.

Gil Cates   7065 Hollywood

Producer, director

Gil Cates

BORN June, 6, 1934, in New York, NY. **SPOTLIGHTS** The intelligent, artistically inclined Cates earned both his Bachelor of Science and Master of Arts degrees at Syracuse University, before embarking on his career in the entertainment business. Out of college, he started as director and producer of television games shows, including "Camouflage," "Haggis Baggis," "Picture This," and "Across the Board." From there he moved into variety shows, creating the landmark "Hootenanny" series. The first of the youth-oriented musical shows, it was taped before a live audience of college students at a different campus each Saturday. Aired in the early 1960s, "Hootenanny" specialized in the popular folk music of the day, with guests such as the Chad Mitchell Trio and the Smothers Brothers. When Cates headed to the Great White Way, he became associated with the noted American playwright Robert Anderson. On Broadway he produced several of Anderson's works: "I Never Sang For My Father," "Solitaire/Double Solitaire," and the comedy hit "You Know I Can't Hear You When the Water's Running." He also produced Murray Schisgals' "The Chinese and Dr. Fish," and directed an acclaimed production of Richard Lortz's "Voices," starring Julie Harris and Richard Kiley. In 1980 he directed George C. Scott and Trish Van Devere in "Tricks of the Trade." Cates achieved celebrity as film director for the movie version of Robert Anderson's *I Never Sang For My Father* (1970—which he had originally produced on Broadway). The movie, starring Melvyn Douglas, Gene Hackman and Estelle Parsons earned three Academy Award nominations. Cates also directed *Summer Wishes, Winter Dreams* (1973), starring Joanne Woodward and Sylvia Sidney which earned two more Oscar nominations. He has also distinguished himself as a director and/or producer in a number of superior, award-winning television dramatic specials, including "After The Fall," "Johnny, We Hardly Knew Ye," "Child's Cry," "Fatal Judgment," "Consenting Adults," "Do You Know the Muffin Man?" "Call Me Anna," "The Kid From Nowhere" and "Absolute Strangers." The Emmy Award-winning Gil Cates also took on the immense challenge of producing the Annual Academy Awards telecast from 1990-'95 and 1997, 1998 and 1999. He won widespread praise from film and television critics for restoring the luster surrounding the Oscar telecast, and bringing back its global audience. It is estimated more than one billion people watch the annual Oscar ceremony. **ACHIEVEMENTS** Served two terms as President of the Directors Guild of America (1983-'87). In 1989 he received the Robert B. Aldrich Award, the Guild's highest honor for extraordinary service to the membership. In 1991 he became a member of an elite group when the DGA

bestowed upon him Honorary Life Membership. He is the recipient of numerous other awards. In 1990 he was appointed Dean of the UCLA School of Theater, Film and Television, where he steadily reinvigorated one of the world's foremost academic programs in theater and film arts. He retired from the position in August of 1998 to pursue other projects. **QUOTE** Cates' dedication ceremony occurred on March 9, 1995. He commented, "I find it hard to believe that there is a star on the Walk of Fame with my name on it. What a thrill. Also, my family is very impressed."

Tyne Daly 📺   7065 Hollywood

Actress, singer

Tyne Daly

BORN Feb. 21, 1947, in Madison, WI. **SPOTLIGHTS** This incredibly talented actress is best known for her role as Detective Mary Beth Lacey, of the award-winning series "Cagney & Lacey" (1982-'88), which paired two working women in a rough New York police precinct. Daly's partner and best buddy was Sharon Gless, and the two shared a powerful screen chemistry that made the show really work. "Cagney & Lacey" amassed 14 Emmy Awards, and made a big impression on female viewers. The show was liberating and original. Daly has appeared in more than 200 television shows, not counting the 127 hours of "Cagney & Lacey" during its six-season run. Shows garnering her the greatest acclaim were roles in "The Entertainer' with Jack Lemmon, "The Women's Room," "The Man Who Talked to Kids," "Larry," and "Intimate Strangers." Daly is also an accomplished stage actress with an impressive list of theater credits: "Ashes," "Three Sisters," "Old Times," "Vanities," and "Come Back, Little Sheba." for which she won *Drama-Logue's* prestigious award for "Outstanding Performance by an Actress." She was the toast on Broadway during the 1989-'90 season in its 30th anniversary musical production of "Gypsy," receiving numerous awards for her brilliant work. Movie roles include *The Enforcer* (1976) with Clint Eastwood, *Zoot Suit* (1981) with Daniel Valdez and Edward James Olmos, and *Movers and Shakers* (1985) with Charles Grodin. By popular demand, she was brought back for a series of two-hour TV movies, "Cagney & Lacey: The Return" and "Cagney & Lacey: Together Again." **ACHIEVEMENTS** Unprecedented four Best Actress Emmys for "Cagney & Lacey." 1990 Tony Award for Best Actress in "Gypsy." Daly's Walk of Fame star was unveiled on March 29, 1995 in a dual ceremony with former TV partner Sharon Gless. **HIGHLIGHTS** Greasepaint runs in her veins. Her late father, James Daly, is best remembered for his seven years as star of TV's "Medical Center." Her mother, Hope Newell, and brother Timothy, are both involved in show business.

Sharon Gless 📺   7065 Hollywood

Actress

Sharon Gless

BORN May 31,1943, in CA. **SPOTLIGHTS** This charming, bright and dramatically powerful actress made television history as New York police detective Christine Cagney, opposite her Walk of Fame partner Tyne Daly, in "Cagney & Lacey" (1982-'88). Gless and Daly are also generally acknowledged to be the most successful dramatic acting duo in the history of television. This television series is well known for its pioneering spirit and controversial themes. Gless enjoyed another huge success with "The Trials of Rosie O'Neill," playing a recently divorced and well-to-do public defender, and winning her second Golden Globe. Many starring dramatic performances in TV movies such as "Honor Thy Mother" and "Separated By Murder" followed. Earlier TV series work includes "Marcus Welby, M.D." Lesser known to television audiences is her terrific sense of humor, her wit, and comic delivery. Gless performs in light comedy, and is an accomplished stage actress in America and England. **ACHIEVEMENTS** Two Emmys for "Cagney & Lacey." Two Golden Globe Awards. Gless' Walk of Fame star was unveiled in a rare double ceremony with her former TV partner, Tyne Daly, on March 29, 1995. Family and friends were present, and thousands of fans cheered them on as the worldwide media captured the thrilling event...Gless also plays an active role in several charities, including such worthy causes as Juvenile Diabetes, the Pediatric AIDS Foundation, and she is a great supporter of the Downtown Women's Center. She is married to producer Barney Rosenzweig. **HIGHLIGHTS** Gless is fifth generation native Californian; as anyone who lives in Los Angeles can tell you, this is a rarity. While performing in an actor's workshop, a publicist at Universal Studios saw her and was impressed with her performance. He set up an appointment for her with the West Coast head of the New Talent Program at Universal Studios, who promptly offered Gless a seven-year contract.

Doug McClure 📺   7065 Hollywood

Actor

Doug McClure

BORN May 11, 1935, in Glendale, CA. **SPOTLIGHTS** The muscular, fair-haired, blue-eyed versatile talent made his movie debut in *The Enemy Below* (1957), a suspenseful WWII sea drama, starring Robert Mitchum. A natural on a horse, McClure's career took off running when he appeared in the Western, *The Unforgiven* (1960), directed by John Huston. This four-star film about Native Americans and the settlers taking Texas stars Burt Lancaster, Audrey Hepburn and Audie Murphy. Other films include *Gidget* (1959), *Shenandoah* (1965), *Beau Geste* (1966) and *The Land That Time Forgot* (1975). TV: Played the cowhand Trampas in "The Virginian." He gave great performances in the TV mini-series "Roots" and "The Rebels." **SIDELIGHTS** His heavy drinking habits earned him the label: "the Dean Martin on horseback." Died: 1995.

Dizzy Gillespie 🔵   7065 Hollywood

Jazz trumpeter, band leader, composer, arranager

BORN John Birks Gillespie; Oct. 21, 1917, in Cheraw, SC. **SPOTLIGHTS** A jazz genius. A trumpet virtuoso. One of the founding fathers of bebop. Gillespie was known for his ballooning bullfrog cheeks and trademark trumpet's bell upturned at a 45-degree angle. (The story goes that a dancing partygoer slammed into his King Silver Flair trumpet while it was on a stand, and the Diz liked the sound of the damaged trumpet better. His trumpets were specially designed and built ever since that discovery.) He played the complete range of the horn, with clarity and command, and he played with all the greats: Ella Fitzgerald, Duke Ellington, Lionel Hampton, Earl Hines, Billy Eckstine, and Billie Holiday. The Diz revolutionized jazz music in the 1940s by being one of the acknowledged inventors of that progressive music, "Bebop." His complex harmonic alterations and dynamic ornamentation amazed the world. He introduced the rich rhythms of Afro-Cuban, Caribbean, and Brazilian music to an eager public. Classic songs include "Groovin' High," "Blue 'N Boogie," "Con Alma," and "Tin Tin Deo." **ACHIEVEMENTS** An American treasure, he was the first jazz artist to be sent abroad under the auspices of the U.S. government to spread goodwill throughout the world...In 1986 he donated his trademark trumpet to the Smithsonian Institution after blowing a few last bursts. **SIDELIGHTS**

During the 1950s, this chess-playing musician's trademark goatee, beret and horn-rimmed glasses marked him a cool cat. **QUOTES** "The instrument is always the boss." And, "If it doesn't hurt your ears, it isn't dissonance. But then, I'm a little deaf myself." Died: 1993.

Thelonious Monk ● 7059 Hollywood

Musician, pianist, composer
BORN Thelonious Sphere Monk; Oct. 10, 1917, in Rocky Mount, NC. **SPOTLIGHTS** A legendary force in the creative development of jazz. By age 13, he had won many amateur music contests. He pursued his studies of theory, harmony, and arranging at the prestigious Juilliard School of Music. At age 19 he collaborated with Charlie Parker, Dizzy Gillespie, Kenny Clarke, and Charlie Christian on a new musical sound, called "Bebop," becoming one of its founders. Although Monk is sometimes described as the "High Priest of Bebop," he went way beyond that to become one of the architects of the second-half century of jazz through composition and one of the giants of modern American music. With his distinctive playing style he toured internationally to great acclaim. His best known compositions are virtual classics, along with these recordings: "Round Midnight," "Straight, No Chaser," "Hackensack," "Ruby, My Dear," "Criss Cross," "Evidence," "Misterioso," and "Blue Monk." Recipient of numerous awards, his son T.S. carries on his father's musical legacy. Outstanding pieces include *Genius of Modern Music: Volume 1* on Blue Note 781510 CD. Died: 1982.

Herbie Hancock ● 7059 Hollywood

Herbie Hancock

Musician
BORN April 12, 1940, in Chicago, IL. **SPOTLIGHTS** A wizard on the keyboards, he was studying the piano by age seven; by 11 he was performing Mozart with the Chicago Symphony. Hancock became interested in jazz in high school along with his fascination of electronic musical instruments. Worked with many jazz artists along the way; wrote a Top Ten hit, "Watermelon Man." Got the call from Miles Davis to join his new group in 1968 and has been on the cutting edge of new technologies ever since. Always exploring new sounds, he released *Headhunters*, which became the largest-selling jazz album in history. Scored a number of films: *Action Jackson*, *Colors*; more. **ACHIEVEMENTS** 1987 Oscar for his soundtrack to *Round Midnight*. Numerous Grammys.

Mamie Van Doren 🎥 7057 Hollywood

Actress

Mamie Van Doren

BORN Joan Olander; Feb. 6, 1933, in Rowena, SD. **SPOTLIGHTS** This alluring siren was discovered by Howard Hughes while appearing in a Hollywood stage production of Clifford Odets' "The Big Knife." Van Doren became a 1950s blonde bombshell—with her platinum hair and famous bullet bra. This glamour puss made *Running Wild* (1956), the first film dealing with juvenile delinquency and rock 'n' roll. In *Teacher's Pet* (1958), she sang "The Girl Who Invented Rock and Roll" to Clark Gable. Cult classics include *Untamed Youth* (1957), *Born Reckless* (1959), *High School Confidential* (1958), *Sex Kittens Go To College*, *The Private Lives of Adam and Eve* (both 1960), and *Las Vegas Hillbillies* (1966). She penned *Playing the Field* (1987).

Farrah Fawcett 📺 7057 Hollywood

Actress

Farrah Fawcett on Feb. 23, '95

BORN Feb. 2, 1946, in Corpus Christi, TX. **SPOTLIGHTS** A blonde beauty with dazzling smile, her all-American cover-girl good looks captured the heart of our country. When the TV movie pilot for "Charlie's Angels" became a series, she became an overnight sensation. At first, idolized as a pinup girl with the most fabulous hair of all and a toothpaste smile, she went on to prove herself an accomplished actress. Taking a dramatic turn, she appeared onstage in "Extremities," then reprised her role on film in 1983. She won national acclaim and a Golden Globe and Emmy nomination for her portrayal of a battered wife in the TV movie "The Burning Bed." She starred as Barbara Hutton in the mini-series "Poor Little Rich Girl" and Diane Downs in "Small Sacrifices" (1989), again winning Emmy and Golden Globe nominations. Fawcett received critical acclaim for her dramatic work in the Hallmark Hall of Fame special, "The Substitute Wife." She co-stars opposite Robert Duvall in *The Apostle* (1997). Other movies include *Logan's Run* (1976), *Saturn 3* (1980), *The Cannonball Run* (1981), *See You In the Morning* (1989), and *Man of the House* (1995).

James Coburn 🎥 7055 Hollywood

James Coburn

Actor

BORN Aug. 31, 1928, in Laurel, NE. **SPOTLIGHTS** Whether sinister gangster, hard-nosed soldier, cowboy hero, comic spy, or romantic interest, this lean, personable performer with thick lips and a crooked smile has done them all. Coburn is a versatile talent who began his acting career at Los Angeles City College. It was there that he won his first award as supporting actor and was able to share the stage with such acting legends as Vincent Price. Moving to New York, he worked in various dramatic television series as "Studio One" and "General Electric Theatre." His motion picture debut was in *Ride Lonesome* (1959) starring Randolph Scott. His reputation soared with *The Magnificent Seven* (1960), *Hell is for Heroes* (1962), *The Great Escape* (1963), *Charade* (1963), *The Americanization of Emily* (1964), *Major Dundee*, and *A High Wind in Jamaica* (both 1965). The handsome wonder charmed fans with his cheetah-like agility and sex appeal in the *Our Man Flint* (1965) and *In Like Flint* (1967) spy spoofs. He followed up playing a secret psychiatrist in the satirical comedy *The President's Analyst* (1967). Other motion pictures include *Pat Garrett and Billy the Kid* (1973), *Harry in Your Pocket* (1973), *Midway* (1976), *Cross of Iron* (1977), *Young Guns II* (1990), *Sister Act 2: Back in the Habit* (1993), *Maverick* (1994), *Eraser* (1996), *The Nutty Professor* (1996), and *Payback* (1999). Upon learning that he had been Oscar-nominated for his performance in *Affliction* (1998), Coburn told actor Nick Nolte, "After 85 films, I guess I finally got it right." **ACHIEVEMENTS** 1999 Best Supporting Actor Academy Award for *Affliction*. Upon receiving the Oscar, Coburn stated, "Some you do for money, some you do for love. This is a love child." His star dedication ceremony occurred on April Fools Day, in 1994. A close friend of Bruce Lee (see his bio in this book), Coburn is an avid student of Eastern martial arts, exercise and philosophy.

Sam Cooke ●
7055 Hollywood

Singer, songwriter

Sam Cooke

BORN January 11, 1930, in Clarksdale, MS. **SPOTLIGHTS** A bright child with a precious voice, he sang with his family under the supervision of his father, the Reverend Charles Cook. At age 16, he was the lead singer for the world-renowned gospel group The Soul Stirrers. Cooke was exiled from the group when they discovered that he had cut a "worldly" song, "You Send Me" (1957). It became a #1 smash hit. Huge hits followed with "Only Sixteen," "Everybody Loves to Cha Cha Cha" and "Wonderful World" (1959), "Chain Gang" (1960), "Cupid" (1961), "Bring It on Home to Me" (1962). His silky voice and honeyed arrangements set the tone for the "sweet soul" sound, paving the way for singers Smokey Robinson, Marvin Gaye and Otis Redding. Died: 1964.

George Benson ●   7055 Hollywood

Singer, musician

George Benson

BORN March 22, 1943, in Pittsburgh, PA. **SPOTLIGHTS** A light soul vocalist and technically perfect jazz guitarist, this artist was never at a loss as to what to do for his career. At age four , "Little Georgie Benson" won a singing contest; soon thereafter he was performing on radio. This natural born talent began studying guitar at age eight, and sang with local rhythm & blues bands. By the time he got his driver's learner permit, he was performing as a musician. He moved to New York in the mid-1960s and was greatly influenced by Wes Montgomery. There he concentrated on the guitar, not vocals. In 1975 the gifted artist signed with Warner Bros. Persuaded to sing as well as play, Benson had his first hit album *Breezin'*— winner of three Grammy Awards. The hit song "This Masquerade" was the first in history to go all the way to #1 on the jazz, R&B, and pop charts. He is a handsome and all-around superb entertainer. Benson's successful career has spanned more than two decades with a number of gigantic hits: "On Broadway," "Give me the Night," and "Turn Your Love Around." His gold and platinum albums include *Tenderly*, *Love Remembers*, and *That's Right*, among many others. He received his star on the Hollywood Walk of Fame on Sept. 19, 1996. Many celebrities, friends and family attended, as well as fans and the worldwide media.

Efrem Zimbalist Jr.   7051 Hollywood

Actor

BORN Nov. 30, 1923, in New York, NY. **SPOTLIGHTS** His father was a world renowned violinist, his mother a leading figure in opera. This debonair, Yale-educated actor has played the handsome, dependable leading man right from the start. During the 1950s he was seen in TV's weekly show "Maverick." He also starred on the popular TV series "77 Sunset Strip." Zimbalist, though, was immortalized in the role of the stalwart Inspector Erskin in "The FBI." His character was so entrenched in the minds of viewers, that a large per-

*Efrem Zimbalist Jr.
and Lana Turner*

John Carradine (right) and Wallace Beery

centage of people actually thought he headed the real FBI agency, and told pollsters that! This fine actor has made numerous TV movies, including "The Black Dahlia," "The Gathering," "Harlow," "Scruples," "Charley's Aunt," and "Beyond Witch Mountain." Movie credits include *The House of Strangers* (1949), *Band of Angels* (1957), *Too Much, Too Soon* (1958), *The Deep Six* (1958), *Home Before Dark* (1958), *A Fever in the Blood* (1961), *By Love Possessed* (1961), *Wait Until Dark* (1967), *Airport 1975* (1974), and *Hot Shots!* (1991). With his distinctive, well-modulated voice, he provided talent in *Batman: Mask of the Phantom* (1994), an animated thriller that's suited for adults—*not* the kids. **ACHIEVEMENTS** His beautiful daughter is the clever film and television actress Stephanie Zimbalist (of TV's "Remington Steele" series fame). Zimbalist received his much-deserved Hollywood Walk of Fame star on Feb. 1, 1994, in celebration of Hollywood's 106th Birthday.

From left to right: Maurice Chevalier, George Burns, Dean Martin, Parkyakarkus (far right), and Jack Benny (standing)

7021 HOLLYWOOD

Jimmie Dodd  7021 Hollywood

Actor, songwriter

Jimmie Dodd

BORN March 29, 1910, in Cincinnati, OH. **SPOTLIGHTS** Walt Disney's children show, "The Mickey Mouse Club," was televised each weekday afternoon from 1955-'59. "Jimmie" (as he was known to oodles of kids) was the adult host of the young group of "Mouseketeers." He composed the "Mickey Mouse March": "Who's the leader of the club that's made for you and me? M-i-c, k-e-y, M-o-u-s-e." Wrote more than 50 songs for the show. He proudly wore his Disney Mouseketeer ears in his salute to youthfulness...His composition "Washington" became the official song of Washington, DC., in 1951. Died: 1964.

John Tesh 7021 Hollywood

Anchor, musician, composer

John Tesh

BORN July 7, 1952, in Long Island, NY. **SPOTLIGHTS** He came to the country's attention as the former host of "Entertainment Tonight" (1986-'96); a program featuring show business news. With his strapping, all-American good looks, affable personality and deep baritone voice, NBC selected him as commentator for the 1996 Olympic Games' gymnastics and water polo events. In addition to his broadcasting accomplishments, Tesh is a successful new age recording artist. With an emphasis on instrumental content, he performs with a 21-piece orchestra. His original themes have garnered four Emmys and an equal amount of derogatory remarks made by critics. His international following does not seem to mind those judgments placed on his music. Nor does Tesh himself. He commented, "I saw Billy Joel tear up a review onstage one time. You can't give critics that kind of power over you." Hit recordings include *The Games* (featuring music used by NBC in its 1992 Summer Olympics telecasts), *John Tesh Live at Red Rocks with the Colorado Symphony Orchestra*, *Grand Passion*, *Tour de France*, *Garden City*, *A Romantic Christmas*, *Monterey Nights*, and *Winter Song*. His video selection is entitled *The Avalon Concert*. He also creates music for TV series and various sports programs..A devoted family man, he is married to the beautiful actress Connie Sellecca...His Walk of Fame star was dedicated on Sept. 11, 1993.

Richard Boleslawski 7021 Hollywood

Director, actor

BORN Ryszard Boleslawsky; Feb. 4, 1889, in Poland. **SPOTLIGHTS** Taught method acting by Stanislavsky himself at the Moscow Arts Theater in 1905, he directed MGM's *Rasputin and the Empress* (1932), *Les Miserables* (1935), and *Theodora Goes Wild* (1936--a madcap comedy). Died: 1937.

Walt Disney 7021 Hollywood

Animator, writer, producer, executive

BORN Walter Elias Disney, Dec. 5, 1901, in Chicago, IL. **SPOTLIGHTS** A genius. A world-class dreamer. A creator whose ideas flowed like Niagara Falls. It all started when an elderly gentleman gave the six-year-old Walt one dollar to draw a picture. From that day forward he knew he wanted to be an artist. And although school teachers were not too happy about it, Disney was a non-stop doodler in the margins of textbooks and his homework. At age 16, he served as an ambulance driver in France during World War I. Two years later, he started his career in a Kansas City commercial art studio. There he met Ub Iwerks, who would become a longtime friend and associate. After the two successfully created and

Walt Disney (left) and Johnny Grant

sold animated cartoons locally, Disney's initial company, Laugh-O-Gram Films, went bankrupt. Disappointed, but willing to take more risks, he forged ahead to Hollywood. At age 22, Disney enlisted his responsible, older brother, Roy O. Disney, to become a new partner. The two Disneys and Iwerks teamed up to produce a live-action series, *Alice in Cartoonland* (1923). They made dozens of *Alice* comedies, but still struggled to make ends meet. In 1928, Mickey Mouse was "born." The Mouse was not an initial success. But by the third cartoon—entitled *Steamboat Willie*—he had caught on. Mickey Mouse became one of the most beloved animated figures worldwide. When Disney decided to make their first full-length animated motion picture, *Snow White and The Seven Dwarfs* (1938), it was a huge gamble. The brothers obtained loans to produce it. It went over budget and took longer than they had planned. The buzz in Hollywood was that the Disneys had a gigantic flop on their hands. Not one other studio executive had ever imagined audiences would want to—or pay to—watch a "cartoon feature film." It took Hollywood by storm with its box office receipts, winning Walt Disney honorary degrees from Harvard, Yale and USC. By now, the visionary had become an American institution. Other motion pictures followed and quickly became classics, including *Pinocchio* (1940), *Fantasia* (1940), *Cinderella* (1950), and *Peter Pan* (1953). The magical *Mary Poppins* (1964) is one of the finest films ever made, and is generally considered Disney's masterpiece. Nominated for 13 Academy Awards, the picture won five, and was embraced by the entire world. These outstanding productions made Disney the king of family fare. TV: "Walt Disney" (since 1954) garnered the largest family viewing audience in the history of television. "Walt Disney" became the longest-running prime-time TV series in network history. It also marked the first time a movie studio tapped into television production. About this time Disneyland theme park—his world of make-believe land—opened "as the happiest place on earth."...In 1954 *Time* magazine reported, "A friend explains that Disney is really 'a sort of visionary handyman, who has built a whole industry out of daydreams. He has the rarest of qualities, the courage of his doodles.'" **ACHIEVEMENTS** The all-time Oscar champion, he collected a total of 32 Academy Awards. He conceived and created Disneyland in Anaheim, CA in 1955; and conceptualized Disney World/EPCOT Center, in Florida...Even after having seen his dreams come true, with an empire at his feet, Disney rarely took time off from his labors. He said, "I get enough vacation from having a change of troubles." **SPECIAL NOTE** For theme park information, visit Disney's website: disneyland.com (and disney.com), or telephone 714.781.4000. See the bios in this book of: Roy O. Disney, Mickey Mouse, Snow White, Robert and Richard Sherman, Annette Funicello, and Jimmie Dodd. **QUOTE** Asked how he liked being a celebrity, Disney answered, "It feels fine when it helps to get a good seat at a football game. But it never helped me make a good film or a good shot in a polo game, or command obedience of my daughter. It doesn't even keep the fleas off our dogs—and if being a celebrity won't give

one an advantage over a couple of fleas, then I guess there can't be much in being a celebrity after all." Died: 1966. Millions worldwide mourned his death.

Charles M. Schulz 📺   7021 Hollywood

Cartoonist

Johnny Grant (left), Leron Gubler (right) and The Peanuts Gang prepare to unveil Charles M. Schulz's star on June 28, 1996.

BORN Charles Monroe Schulz; Nov. 26, 1922, in Minneapolis, Minn. **SPOTLIGHTS** The world's most popular cartoonist remembers his "first and only encouragement" came during kindergarten. The youngster's teacher watched him sketching a picture of a man shoveling snow. She remarked, "Someday, Charles, you're going to be an artist." That was music to his ears since all he really wanted to do was draw. In high school he was lured by a "Do You Like to Draw?" advertisement which he quickly responded to. He observed, "The truth is, I wasn't a very good student." The 14-year-old enjoyed a bit of beginner's good luck when his illustration of a black-and-white Pointer named Spike (the inspiration for Snoopy) was published in *Ripley's Believe It or Not*. Then during his senior year in high school an instructor requested Schulz sketch cartoons for the yearbook. When the yearbook came out, he eagerly flipped through its pages only to painfully discover his work had been edited out. "I never did find out why," he commented. His comic strip appeared on Oct. 2, 1950 in seven papers when Schulz was 27 years old. He was unhappy when his original title for his cartoon feature, "Li'l Folks," was changed to "Peanuts," a title he did not initially like. Young and old fans alike of "Peanuts" relate to the simple daily life issues of pain, angst, rejection, unrequited love, and desiring something that is perpetually elusive. There's the lonely, melancholy, moon-faced Charlie Brown who, at times, resembles a sincere welcome mat. Other characters include the crabby, inconsiderate, fussbudget Lucy who dotes on Schroeder—whose devotion is strictly Beethoven. There's Linus, the pee-wee-sized philosopher who clings to his security blanket. And, of course, there's the beagle Snoopy, who lives in a fantasy world and is now earth's most familiar dog. 200 million people read the strip daily. **TV** There have been dozens of "Peanuts" Specials, starting with the original Emmy Award-winning "A Charlie Brown Christmas." It has aired every Yuletide since 1965. Also in 1965 Snoopy and the Gang appeared on the cover of *Time* magazine. It coincided with Schulz's 25th Central High School reunion, in St. Paul, Minn. And although as a student he went unnoticed, one would think the low-keyed creator had gained his peers respect and admiration as an adult. Ironically his life mirrored that of good ol' Charlie Brown when his graduating class listed him as "whereabouts unknown" in their updated newsletter! **ACHIEVEMENTS** "Peanuts" animated specials have won five Emmys. *The Guinness Book of World Records* reports "Peanuts is the most widely syndicated comic strip in history appearing in 2,620 newspapers in 75 countries and 26 languages." Schulz has built a worldwide empire from his creations. Although it has brought him wealth beyond imagination, he lives a simple life and stated, "Who cares about being rich? The idea is to do something decent." **RECOMMENDED** Check this out of your local library—*Good Grief: The Story of Charles M. Schulz* (1989) by Rheta Grimsley Johnson, published by Pharos Books. **SIDELIGHTS** Nicknamed "Sparky" by an uncle from a character in the classic "Barney Google" comic strip, the name has stuck and he continues to be called "Sparky" by friends and colleagues...Camp Snoopy, the official home of the Peanuts Gang, is located at Knott's Berry Farm, in Buena Park, CA. Lushly themed to California's Yosemite, the six-acre kids' paradise features 30 hands-on attractions, rides, shows and adventures for the young. Telephone 714.220.5200 (website: www.knotts.com). **QUOTE** "We do nothing that even comes close to vulgar. I don't like ugly words. I've never sworn in my life. There's really nothing in life that can't be covered by 'rats' or 'good grief.'" Died: 2000.

Vilma Banky 🎥 7021 Hollywood

Vilma Banky

Actress
BORN Vilma Lonchit; Jan. 9, 1898, in Hungary. **SPOTLIGHTS** It was every actor's dream to be in a movie where the credits rolled: "Samuel Goldwyn Presents." Banky was even luckier; she was discovered by Goldwyn himself in Budapest. This fine actress—graceful, beautiful, aristocratic—fared brilliantly in romance pictures. The very ladylike Banky stars in *The Dark Angel*, with Ronald

Colman and *The Eagle*, with Rudolph Valentino (both 1925). Banky stole the breath of audiences in *The Son of the Sheik* (1926), again opposite Valentino. **ACHIEVEMENTS** Married to actor Rod La Roque in 1927, they were one of Hollywood's happiest couples. They had also invested wisely in California real estate with their early and large paychecks, providing them with a regal retirement. Died: 1991.

Gloria Estefan 🎵 7021 Hollywood

Gloria Estefan

Singer, songwriter
BORN Sept. 1, 1957, in Havana, Cuba. **SPOTLIGHTS** She was an infant when her refugee family moved from Cuba to the United States. As an adult, singer Gloria Estefan transcends both Spanish and English with her music, and is both widely admired and respected. Adored by her audiences, loud cheers are heard around the world for her songs, among them: "Anything for You," "Cuts Both Ways," "I See Your Smile," "Can't Stay Away From You," "Conga," "Bad Boy," "Words Get In the Way," "Rhythm Is Going to Get You," Here We Are," "Abriendo Puertas," and "Mi Tierra." Her description of her shows, sums up a fine description of the lady herself, "A high-energy show, but loose and relaxed. Laid-back, but fast-paced!" she laughed. Her balance of intimate ballads with sizzling salsa-spiced, up-tempo numbers, and seven to eight percussionists supplying the rhythm section, creates irresistible music in any language. Albums include: *Primitive Love, Greatest Hits, mi tierra, Hold Me, Thrill Me, Kiss Me, Abriendo Puertas, Into the Light, Christmas Through Your Eyes,* and *Destiny.* Estefan has garnered gold, platinum, double platinum and triple platinum for her outstanding recordings. **HIGHLIGHTS** Emilio Estefan (her future husband) persuaded her to sing with his band, the Miami Latin Boys. When she became their vocalist, the Miami Sound Machine was born. After she graduated summa cum laude from the University of Miami, they married and continue to blend business and love with phenomenal prosperity and success. They both share strong family values and have two beautiful children, a son and daughter. Her father, Jose Manuel Fajardo, was a superb athlete who was a member of the Cuban volleyball team. He won a bronze medal at the Pan American Games in the 1950s. **ACHIEVEMENTS** She was the first female Latin artist to successfully crossover to English. Among the many honors she has received: Named BMI's Songwriter of the Year; an American Music Award; Grammy Awards; and President Bush named her a "public delegate" to the United Nations in 1992. Her Hollywood Walk of Fame star dedication ceremony took place on Feb. 3, 1993. Estefan is one of the most successful enter-

tainers on the globe. She raised millions for victim relief after Hurricane Andrew devastated South Florida. **QUOTE** "Real success is having love in your life."

Noah Beery, Jr.   7021 Hollywood

Actor
BORN Aug. 10, 1915, in New York City, NY. **SPOTLIGHTS**

Noah Beery

Greasepaint ran in his veins, his father was actor Noah Beery, his uncle actor Wallace Beery. He literally grew up at the studios— emerged in the fantasy life of action heroes and cowboys—and later reflected how it was a life he loved. Beery made his motion picture debut at age five in *The Mark of Zorro* (1920), starring Douglas Fairbanks and his father, Noah. At age seven, he appeared in *Penrod*, then made its sequel *Penrod and Sam* (1923). He made an easy transition to talkies. In all, he made

more than 125 movies. Among his pictures are *The Champ* (1931) with his uncle Wallace Beery, *Of Mice and Men* (1940), *Sergeant York* (1941), and *Inherit the Wind* (1960). **TV** He played James Garner's genial father, Joseph (Rocky) Rockford, on the private eye detective series "The Rockford Files" (1974-'80). Beery performed his paternal role as a retired trucker with folksy charm, winning him two nominations for Emmy Awards. In television and films, Beery was a character actor best known for playing the sidekick. Other TV series include "Riverboat" and "Circus Boy" (as Joey the Clown). Died: 1994.

Anita Baker   7021 Hollywood

Singer, songwriter

Anita Baker

BORN Dec. 20, 1958, in Detroit, MI. **SPOTLIGHTS** Baker is an internationally renowned rhythm-and-blues, pop and jazz singer. Her magnificent voice is elegant and smoldering. Her music is a fusion of the jazz, gospel and blues influences of her early youth in Detroit. Singing in school and church choirs gave her an opportunity to explore a variety of musical styles. At age 16, she made her musical debut and performed with a succession of local bands. When an offer came to

join the area's hottest group, Chapter 8, she took advantage of the opportunity. The band was signed to a recording contract with Ariola Records in 1980, and riding the wave of radio's air play, toured the country. When Ariola merged with Arista, the group was caught in the transition and eventually disbanded. Baker became disenchanted with the business of music, and took a day gig as a receptionist. Eventually she signed with Elektra records label, recording her album, *Rapture*, in 1986. Baker wrote many of the top tunes. This beauty gained unanimous kudos from the music community, and traveled on a two-year road tour with sold-out performances throughout Europe and America. From Wembly Stadium to Radio City Music Hall, Baker had found her audience. Other albums, *Giving You the Best That I Got*, went double platinum in less than two weeks of its release, and *Compositions*, went platinum two months after its release. Her *Rhythm of Love*, debuted at #3 on the Billboard Charts and went platinum within a week. Hit songs include "Quiet Storm," "Angel," "Watch Your Step," "Sweet Love," "Caught Up in the Rapture," "Just Because," "Talk to Me," and "Giving You the Best That I Got." **ACHIEVEMENTS** NAACP Image Award for Best Female Vocalist and Best Album of the Year. Recipient of numerous awards and honors. Musical celebrities, family, friends and hundreds of cheering fans shared in her joy when her Hollywood Walk of Fame star was unveiled on Oct. 13, 1994. She is involved in many child-related causes, dedicated to improving the health and lives of children.

Jimmy Boyd ●   7021 Hollywood

Singer, actor
BORN Jan. 9, 1940; McComb, MS. **SPOTLIGHTS** This singing talent recorded the gigantic hit Christmas song, "I Saw Mommy Kissin' Santa Claus." After 2,200,000 copies of it had sold in less than three months, the press labeled him "The Early Boyd." At age 12, he earned $100,000 in royalties on that one song. The freckled face, redheaded kid always wore denims, a plaid shirt and cowboy hat. TV: Played Howard Meechim on "Bachelor Father" (1958-'61).

Kenny G ●   7021 Hollywood

Musician
BORN Kenneth Gorelick; June 5, 1956, Seattle, WA. **SPOTLIGHTS** Master of the saxophone and one of music history's all-time highest selling instrumentalists, G took piano lessons as a youngster growing up in Seattle, Washington. At age 10, he was mesmerized by a saxophone player performing on TV's "The Ed Sullivan Show," and immediately took up alto sax. Fascinated with the instrument, he also played tenor sax, and finally settled on soprano sax as his very own. G played sax in his school band, and landed his first professional gig as a sax *soloist* while still in his teens, backing up rhythm & blues/soul singer Barry White. He continued performing with R&B, pop, and jazz groups while attending college, where he

Kenny G

studied accounting (!). In the evenings G added to his musical resume, playing for such well-known entertainers as Johnny Mathis, the Spinners, Liberace and others who passed through his home state. He graduated *Phi Beta Kappa* and *magna cum laude* from the University of Washington, then immediately went to work as a musician. Initially remaining in the Pacific North, he worked in Jeff Lorber's popular Fusion Band, then gained his first experience of touring the country. G had a natural ability to communicate and relate with the audience—a trait of superb entertainers share. It was during this time that Arista Records president Clive Davis heard and saw G play, and offered him a solo recording contract, which led to the release of *Kenny G* in 1982. Two more albums, *G-Force* and *Gravity* followed, as G honed his writing and production skills and developed his signature heartfelt and emotional musical style. His breakthrough album, *Duotones* (1986), reached #6 on the pop charts and his single "Songbird" (inspired by beautiful model/actress, Lyndie Benson, who became his wife) went higher to #4 on the charts. G felt challenged, stating, "The history of the instrumentalist in pop is that you get a big hit and that's the end of it." *Duotones* tapped a new audience for instrumental music that crossed all genres, and his follow up album *Silhouette*, with the single "We've Saved the Best for Last," reached the Top Ten on the charts. He became one of the most sought after special guest performers in the recording industry, contributing his brilliant virtuosity with the queen of soul, Aretha Franklin, the dynamic Whitney Houston, among many others. The multi-platinum selling G has numerous other top albums including *Kenny G Live, Breathless, Miracles: The Holiday Album* (the best selling Christmas album of all time), *The Moment* (debuted at #1, with a number of hits including "Every time I Close My Eyes," "Havana," and "Innocence"), and his tenth album, *Kenny G Greatest Hits*. He has also composed and performed for movie soundtracks. **HIGHLIGHTS** G was honored when Frank Sinatra personally selected him to be the only non-singing star to be featured on Sinatra's *Duets* album. His Hollywood Walk of Fame star dedication ceremony took place on Nov. 25, 1997. The police shut down several streets so that a huge throng of music fans could share in his celebration. Typically a ceremony starts at 11:30 AM, and lasts about 30 minutes. That half hour is packed with guest celebrities and friends with brief speeches and tributes. G had planned to hold *one note for 45 minutes* (!)—it would have been a new *Guinness* world record—but the Hollywood Chamber of Commerce could not get a permit that would allow the police the extra time controlling the crowd. **QUOTE** "My first visit to Hollywood came after a 20-hour drive in a broken-down car using an already maxed-out credit card to pay for gas. My first stop was the Hollywood Walk of Fame to look at the stars. I can't begin to tell you the pride I have now, being amongst the names that I saw on my first day in Hollywood. I'll be forever grateful to Johnny Grant for allowing me into this very exclusive club."

Alan Curtis 🎥　　　　7021 Hollywood

Actor

BORN Harold Neberroth; July 24, 1909, in Chicago, IL. **SPOTLIGHTS** A tall, dark and handsome former model, he gave a strong supporting performance in the gangster picture, *High Sierra* (1941), starring Humphrey Bogart. He stars in *Phantom Lady, The Invisible Man's Revenge*, and *Destiny* (all 1944). His career spanned 13 years and 30 films. Died in 1953, at age 43, following kidney surgery.

Mary Tyler Moore 　　7021 Hollywood

Mary Tyler Moore

Actress, dancer, singer
BORN December 29, 1937, in Brooklyn, NY. **SPOTLIGHTS** America's first television sweetheart. This lovely, graceful, svelte brunette with a perfect heart-shaped face and flashing smile grew up in Southern California and received extensive training in ballet. Early on Moore set her sights on performing. By the time she graduated from high school, she had already danced professionally in television commercials and variety shows. Soon enough she had her big breakthrough as everyone's favorite perky suburban housewife. Moore made television history in her co-starring role as Laura Petrie on "The Dick Van Dyke Show" (1961-1966). She won two Emmy Awards (1964 and 1966) in the classic sitcom, which is still seen daily in worldwide syndication. In 1967 she appeared in the movie musical, *Thoroughly Modern Millie*, with Julie Andrews, Carol Channing and Beatrice Lillie. *Don't Just Stand There* (1968), *What's So Bad About Feeling Good* (1968) and *Change of Habit* (1969) followed. In 1970 she was immortalized in yet *another* TV series as the star of "The Mary Tyler Moore Show." She was endearing in this realistic, funny situation comedy about an ambitious single woman named Mary Richards, who makes it on her own. She earned three more Emmy Awards (1973, 1974 and 1976), plus a Special Award for "Series Actress of the Year"

(1974). "The Mary Tyler Moore Show" is one of television's most acclaimed series. Like her first series, this one went out on top in 1977, with its ratings high and quality undiminished. During its run of seven seasons and 168 episodes, "The Mary Tyler Moore Show" won a total of 29 Emmys. The following year she stunned audiences with her dramatic portrayal of TV news correspondent Betty Rollins and her real-life struggle with breast cancer, in "First You Cry." Moore garnered a Best Actress Emmy nomination. In 1979 she made her Broadway debut in "Whose Life Is It Anyway?" playing a hospitalized quadriplegic fighting to control her own destiny in this multi-award winning play. Moore earned a Special Tony Award. She plays a cold, complex wife and mother torn by family tragedy in *Ordinary People* (1980). Moore received a Golden Globe Award, and an Academy Award nomination for her powerful performance. She returned to TV portraying Mary Todd Lincoln in the NBC mini-series, "Gore Vidal's Lincoln." She won the highest praise from critics and garnered another Emmy nomination. She has appeared in numerous films and TV movies. **ACHIEVEMENTS** She has dedicated herself to numerous charities. As international Chairman of the Juvenile Diabetes Foundation, Moore was honored as their "Woman of the Decade." She serves on the Board of Juilliard School of Drama and the NYC Opera Company. She is a founding member of the Off-Center Ballet Company. Her Walk of Fame dedication ceremony occurred on Sept. 8, 1992.

Kitty Kallen 🎵   7021 Hollywood

Singer, actress

BORN May 25, 1926, in Philadelphia, PA. **SPOTLIGHTS** An ultra-feminine, exceptional singer from the 1940s and '50s, she was known as "Pretty Kitty." This swing era beauty sang for Jimmy Dorsey's incredibly popular big band around 1943. She became the vocalist for the great Harry James, a regular vocalist on radio's "Harry James and His Orchestra" in 1945, and the radio hostess for "Holiday for Music" in 1946. A terrific performer, she appears in a number of motion picture musicals as herself. For Artie Shaw, she recorded the gigantic hit, "My Heart Belongs to Daddy." Her biggest selling song was "Little Things Mean a Lot." While performing in Jack Teagarden's band as the female vocalist, she fell in love with and married clarinetist Clint Garvin. She retired after a later marriage to Hollywood press agent Buddy Granoff.

Chevy Chase 🎥   7021 Hollywood

Actor, comedian, writer, musician

BORN Cornelius Crane Chase, October 8, 1943, in New York City, NY. **SPOTLIGHTS** A native New Yorker, and grandson of plumbing tycoon Cornelius Crane (whom he was named after), he grew up in a privileged household. Chase was educated at Bard College where he took his B.A. degree. With writing skills inherited from his father, who was an esteemed book editor, he began his career in publishing. Instead of work-

ing for one of the prestigious literary houses, Chase went to work for a different institution. He started writing for the insane little world of the red-haired, freckle-nosed, impertinent grinner—with the missing front tooth—cover boy of *Mad Magazine*. Then, on the opposite end of the educational spectrum, he wrote and starred in the PBS series, "The Great American Dream Machine," and co-wrote and performed in "Lemmings," the National Lampoon off-Broadway musical spoof of Woodstock. Chase wrote and performed in the underground television revue "Channel One." It was a springboard for the audacious low-budget, underground parody film, *The Groove Tube* (1974), where he made his screen debut. He followed with Neal Israel/Brad Swirnoff's *Tunnelvision* (1976). Around this time, he met TV producer Lorne Michaels, who initially hired him as a writer for "Saturday Night Live." Chase's great gift was his irreverence. He later joined the fresh, cheeky and original "SNL" cast, winning two Emmy Awards. The handsome, cleft-chinned talent was featured doing broad physical comedy, and playing important political figures, like accident-prone President Gerald Ford. Chase, like the other cast members, did his own stunts. The wacky comedian took a number of hard falls making people laugh, although the public never knew what he sacrificed physically for humor's sake. His popular, cocky catchphrase was: "I'm Chevy Chase and you're not!" His first starring role in a motion picture was in the comedy-thriller *Foul Play* (1978), opposite Goldie Hawn. In 1980 he stars in the clever family picture *Oh Heavenly Dog!*, with Jane Seymour, Omar Sharif and Benji. He teams with "SNL" alumni, Bill Murray in the outrageous golf picture, *Caddyshack* (1980). Directed by Harold Ramis, it also stars Rodney Dangerfield, Ted Knight, and Michael O'Keefe. He became the bumbling, beloved head of the Griswold family in *National Lampoon's Vacation* (1983), and its sequels *National Lampoon's European Vacation* (1985), *National Lampoon's Christmas Vacation* (1989), and *Vegas Vacation* (1997). Other movies include *Fletch* (1985), *Three Amigos!* (1986), *L.A. Story* (1991), *Memoirs of an Invisible Man* (1991), and *Man of the House* (1995). **HIGHLIGHTS** His star dedication ceremony took place on Sept. 23, 1993. Hollywood Walk of Fame chairman Johnny Grant quipped to the cheering crowd of fans, "Chevy Chase is getting a star and you're not!" **QUOTE** "The very fact that my star is an inch and a half larger than any of the other stars makes me most proud. I would also like to thank my friends Martin Short and Tom Hanks for making sure it is polished weekly."

Chevy Chase

Charles Farrell 🎥   7021 Hollywood

Charles Farrell

Actor

BORN Aug. 9, 1901, in Onset Bay, MA. **SPOTLIGHTS** A very attractive, wavy-haired, romantic leading man of the 1920s and '30s, he co-stars opposite Janet Gaynor (see her bio in this book), in Frank Borzage's classic movie, *Seventh Heaven* (1927). Even though it is a silent film, this touching drama is well worth watching and stands the test of time. Farrell and Gaynor were coupled in a seven-year series of successful films. He appears in a number of important works, including *The Hunchback of Notre Dame* and *The Ten Commandments* (both 1923). In all, this incredibly popular star made more than 70 movies. TV: Played Vernon Albright on "My Little Margie" (1952-'55). **SIDELIGHTS** Founded The Palm Springs Racquet Club; later became the mayor of that desert city. Died: 1962.

DeForest Kelley 🎥   7021 Hollywood

DeForest Kelley

Actor, singer

BORN January 20, 1920, in Atlanta, GA. **SPOTLIGHTS** Kelley was immortalized in the phenomenally successful "Star Trek" sci-fi TV and motion picture series. Millions of fans worldwide worship his role as Dr. Leonard "Bones" McCoy, the acerbic chief medical officer of the U.S.S. Enterprise. His character is particularly fun to watch as he plays the genuinely human foil to the super-logical half-Vulcan, half-human Mr. Spock (Leonard Nimoy). Born and raised in Atlanta, Georgia, Kelley was a singer in his church choir. A radio performance on station WSB earned him a singing engagement with Lew Forbes and his Orchestra at the Atlantic Paramount Theater. After moving to Southern California, he joined the Long Beach Theater Group. During World War II, a Paramount Pictures talent scout noticed him in a U.S. Navy training film. He landed a studio contract, and made his motion picture debut in *Fear in the Night* (1947). Curiously, while he scored his biggest hit as the outspoken, somewhat cynical and eccentric, but thoroughly likeable McCoy, Kelley's earlier roles in motion pictures (several classics), TV and on the stage were mostly as sinister villains. His films include *The Man in the Gray Flannel Suit* (1956), *Gunfight at the O.K. Corral* (1957), *Raintree Country* (1957), *The Law and Jake Wade* (1959), *Warlock* (1959), and *Where*

Love Has Gone (1964). Thirteen years after originating the role of "Bones" for television, he reprised that role in *Star Trek: The Motion Picture* (1979). He appeared in five more motion picture sequels. **HIGHLIGHTS** A devout humanitarian, he makes innumerable goodwill hospital visits to children and veterans. His Hollywood Walk of Fame star was unveiled on Dec. 18, 1991. Died: 1999.

Mae Busch 🎥   7021 Hollywood

Mae Busch

Actress

BORN Jan. 20, 1897, in Australia. **SPOTLIGHTS** She rose to stardom in an extravagant million-dollar production, Erich Von Stroheim's *Foolish Wives* (1922). Comedy buffs recognize her in Laurel and Hardy films. **QUOTE** "I know that it is exceedingly difficult for the beginner in pictures. It is much more difficult for a girl. She must have a large wardrobe, and a goodly supply of money to keep her for at least a year. I started my career in comedies. I learned that they did not make the demands on my wardrobe that the other companies did. I believe it is more difficult to break into pictures now than it was a few years ago. The screen has an inexhaustible supply of good actors and actresses. A few years ago this talent had not been developed, and there was more of a demand for players. The person who starts work in pictures today must be satisfied with a small job every few days." Died: 1946.

Kim Basinger 🎥   7021 Hollywood

Kim Basinger, Johnny Grant and Brandon Tartikoff (far left)

Actress

BORN Dec. 8, 1953, in Athens, GA. **SPOTLIGHTS** Descended from a stunning combination of Swedish, German, and Native American Cherokee Indian blood, Basinger began studying dancing at age two, and later took up singing. While in high school, this hometown beauty queen won the national

Breck shampoo modeling title. (Amazingly her mother had also won the same title in her youth.) At age 17 she moved to New York, studied drama, and, at age 18 posed for *Playboy* magazine. With her breathtaking features, she signed with the highly reputable Eileen Ford Agency, where she established a lucrative career as a top fashion model during the next five years. The world became familiar with her face in a variety of cosmetic advertising campaigns for Revlon, Maybelline, and Clairol. She decided to try her luck in Hollywood. In 1977 she began performing in television, including "Charlie's Angels," and the TV movie "Katie: Portrait of a Centerfold." Then, she landed an important role in the mini-series "From Here to Eternity," from which she was able to leap to the silver screen. The sensitive actress made her film debut in *Hard Country* (1981) with Jan-Michael Vincent, playing a woman determined to escape from her small-town existence. In *Mother Lode* (1982), she co-stars opposite Charlton Heston, in a film directed by Heston, and written and produced by his son, Fraser Heston. Nick Mancuso also appears in the adventure picture. Rated on a scale of one to ten for sex appeal, this sensuous, voluptuous blonde gets a 20. She sizzles in a classic James Bond thriller, *Never Say Never Again* (1983), opposite Sean Connery—it was her third picture. Basinger co-stars with Burt Reynolds and Julie Andrews in the re-make of *The Man Who Loved Women* that same year. Barry Levinson's *The Natural* (1984), a baseball drama with Robert Redford, and the controversial *9 1/2 weeks* (1986) with Mickey Rourke, followed. Other films include *Fool for Love* (1985—adapted from Sam Shepard's play), *No Mercy* (1986), *Blind Date* (1987), *Nadine* (1987), *My Stepmother Is an Alien* (1988), and *Final Analysis* (1992). She portrays the character Vicki Vale in Tim Burton's darkly entertaining action picture, *Batman* (1989). She met her future husband, actor Alec Baldwin, on the set of *The Marrying Man* (1991). Their mutual attraction is apparent on screen in this gangster comedy. They later star in the re-make of the crime picture, *The Getaway* (1994). In 1992 she stars in a totally different kind of project; as an adult animated character who wants desperately to be human. *Cool World*, directed by Ralph Bakshi, is a mixture of cartoon and live action. Next, Basinger leads an all-star cast, including Sophia Loren, Marcello Mastroianni, Tim Robbins, and Julia Roberts in Robert Altman's glamorous comedy, *Ready to Wear* (1994). **HIGHLIGHTS** A vegetarian, she is actively involved in animal right issues. **ACHIEVEMENTS** 1998 Academy Award for best supporting actress in *L.A. Confidential*. Basinger joined the elite group of artists who won an Academy Award on their first nomination. She received her momentous Walk of Fame star on July 8, 1992. **QUOTE** After winning her Oscar, she enthusiastically and breathlessly stated, "Wait a minute. We only get 30 seconds. I just want to thank everybody I've ever met in my entire life...If anyone has a dream out there, please know I'm living proof that they do come true."

Pierce Brosnan 🎥   7021 Hollywood

Actor, producer
BORN May 16, 1953, in County Meath, Ireland. **SPOTLIGHTS** In a word—*elegance*. It is the long absent quality that Brosnan has brought back to the silver screen. This much yearned for trait, abundant during Hollywood's Golden Era with movie stars such as Cary Grant, flew off the story boards with the radical 1960s, then became missing-in-action with the stream of violent macho movies. It's been gone so long from cinema one wonders if today's producers are too

Pierce Brosnan (right) and Frank Mancuso

absorbed in repetitive sequels to know it ever existed. The team of Frank Mancuso and John Calley, (then) heads of MGM/UA, ushered in its welcomed return. When the tall, dark and handsome Brosnan made his much-anticipated bow in the role of the legendary James Bond in *GoldenEye* (1995), the picture became *the most successful Bond film in history*. It's no real surprise, though, as it was the elegant Cary Grant who was the original producer's choice to play the dashing 007. (Grant later expressed his deep regrets in turning down the role.) Brosnan fits the bill: he is man enough to play Bond. He is the confidant master of his own destiny, not with sweat, brawn and vulgarity, but with intelligence, humor and tremendous sex appeal. (Plus a lot of really hot high-tech weapons.) Men like his darker side, while women find him to be consummately romantic, their ideal lover. The camera picks up Brosnan's charisma with shining clarity, and viewers relish his sophisticated style. In this regard, Brosnan has renewed Hollywood and opened up a world of possible new stories in a genre we thought long lost. We are now hopeful. Other motion pictures include *The Thomas Crown Affair* (1999), *The World Is Not Enough* (1999—as James Bond; this is the 19th entry in the film series), *Tomorrow Never Dies* (1997—as James Bond), *The Mirror Has Two Faces* (1996) with Barbra Streisand and Jeff Bridges, *Mars Attacks!* (1996) with Jack Nicholson, *Mrs. Doubtfire* (1993) with Robin Williams and Sally Fields, and *The Fourth Protocol* (1987) with Michael Caine. Brosnan's background is all about acting. Trained as a youth at the Drama Centre in London, he participated in experimental theatre, then landed a job as an assistant stage manager at the prestigious York Theatre Royal. As luck would have it, after only six months there, the eminent playwright Tennessee Williams personally selected Brosnan to create the role of McCabe in the British premiere of "Red Devil Battery Sign." Other London stage productions include Franco Zeffirelli's "Filumena," and "Wait Until Dark." But it was the television detective series, "Remington Steele" (Oct. 1, 1982 - March 9, 1987), that brought the actor to America's attention. Amazingly he was offered the role of James Bond during this period, but could not get released from his television contract. (Timothy Dalton stepped into the role.) About the studio's second offer to him to play James Bond, after many years and another actor doing 007, Brosnan remarked, "It blows me away that it came around again." Some things are just meant to be. **ACHIEVEMENTS** In addition to the many critical accolades he's received for his work, and Golden Globe nominations, Brosnan serves as Ambassador for Women's Health Issues for The Entertainment Industry Foundation Permanent Charities. He has addressed key members of the U.S. Congress on ovarian cancer (he lost his beloved wife to the horrible disease in 1991), and has headed the annual Revlon Run/Walk for Women and other events which have raised milllions of dollars to combat ovarian and breast cancer. He has also assumed a passionate leadership role in environmental issues, on behalf of dolphin protection, ECO, Greenpeace and Sea Shepherd to keep our oceans clean. **HIGHLIGHTS** Brosnan received his Hollywood Walk of Fame star on Dec. 3, 1997. Among his guests were several celebrities, one mogul, family and dozens of friends. Fans were there, too, in such large numbers that the police had to shut down the streets. The cheering crowd delighted in seeing Brosnan's dedication ceremony. **QUOTE** "This is truly an honor. I am very happy to be associated with the great stars on the Hollywood Walk of Fame. Thank you for this fantastic tribute."

Fred Allen   7021 Hollywood

See page 53

David Bowie   7021 Hollywood

Superstar David Bowie and Johnny Grant, Honorary Mayor of Hollywood

Singer, songwriter, musician, actor
BORN David Robert Jones; Jan. 8, 1947, in London, England. **SPOTLIGHTS** Strange. Wonderful. Disturbing. This rare talent of pop music has managed to stay creative, experimental and cerebral through more than three decades of chameleon-like work. Considered cutting-edge and techno-stretching, Bowie always manages to captivate us with his artistry. Perhaps because of this he draws controversy with each new release. He has appeared as both an androgyne and an alien, a folk singer and a glam-rock star, into decadence on one cover and soulful on the next. Hits include: "Young Americans," "Fame," "Golden Years," "Space Oddity," "Scary Monsters," "Let's Dance,""China Girl," "Modern Love," and "Blue Jean." He has released more than 35 albums, and has recorded several movie soundtracks. He is also an actor of stage and film. Motion pictures include *The Man Who Fell to Earth* (1976) with Bowie in the title role, with support from Rip Torn, Candy Clark and Buck Henry, and *Basquiat* (1996) co-starring Gary Oldman, Christopher Walken and Dennis Hopper. His narration works include *Peter and the Wolf.* Worth about $900 million, Bowie is keeping up with the times, releasing some current work through the Internet only. Bowie made cyber-history by being the first to record a song "What's Really Happening," live on the Web on May 24, 1999. The song was co-written by Alex Grant. Grant beat out 80,000 other hopefuls who submitted their lyrics in an online contest. **QUOTE** Upon turning 50 years old, Bowie made this observation about aging in the youth-oriented rock business, "I think 40 was a much worse period. It was a struggle to let go of what I thought was imperative about being youthful. And it's not a coincidence that it came at the same time as my great depression...I've relaxed into this new plateau of age. In fact, I'm a lot happier now than I was then (in my young 20s)." He received his landmark Walk of Fame star on February 12, 1997.

NOTE TO MY READERS *WALKING* **THE WALK** Take time to visit the *Hollywood Entertainment Museum* (you are in front of it now). For less than the cost of a movie ticket, you can beam yourself aboard the Starship Enterprise from the original "Star Trek" set, sit on Norm's stool on the "Cheers" set, see props and costumes from the top movies, or have fun with the hands-on sound effects exhibit. Phyllis Caskey, HEM's president/CEO strives to bring the most interesting, entertaining, educational, historical and cultural facets of show business together in this superb museum. Bring your camera, after all this *is* Hollywood, it's almost a law that you take pictures.

Paula Abdul   7021 Hollywood

Singer, choreographer, dancer, actress
BORN June 19, 1962, in Los Angeles, CA. **SPOTLIGHTS** The bouncy, athletic former member of the L.A. Laker Girls cheer leading squad broke away from the ranks to rise to stardom. The charming talent became one of the most sought-after choreographers in the music and motion picture industries. This multi-media star propelled a generation of visually oriented artists, including ZZ Top, Duran Duran, and the Pointer Sisters, into the high-tech '90s. Adbul was behind Janet Jackson's highly energized choreography for her *Control* videos. Her own landmark *Forever Your Girl* album achieved world-

Paula Abdul

wide sales of more than 10 million copies. Hit songs include "Straight Up," "Forever Your Girl," "Cold-Hearted, "Opposites Attract," and "(It's Just) The Way That You Love Me." Her stylish music videos, some that have cleverly incorporated animation a la Gene Kelly in *Anchors Aweigh*, have received worldwide acclaim. Later albums have produced her first ballad hit, "Rush, Rush," and "The Promise of a New Day," "Blowing Kisses in the Wind," "Vibeology," and "Will You Marry Me." In 1999 this all-American beauty discussed making her stage debut as the lead in the touring production of "Sweet Charity." The revival show was given a contemporary edge, with her fantasy costuming and choreography. She said, "I could not have been selected or been chosen for a better role than Charity, the lovelorn dance hall hostess." She has appeared on talk shows, guest-starred and acted in a number of network and cable programs such as "The Tracy Ullman Show." **ACHIEVEMENTS** One Grammy, two American Music Awards, two People's Choice Awards, two Emmy Awards, four MTV Awards. Her Walk of Fame star was unveiled on Dec. 4, 1991. **QUOTE** "When I was growing up, I idolized the stars who could do it all: artist/entertainers like Gene Kelly, Judy Garland, and Fred Astaire."

Faye Dunaway 🎥　　7021 Hollywood

Faye Dunaway and James Coburn

Actress
BORN Jan. 14, 1946, in Bascom, FL. **SPOTLIGHTS** As the daughter of a career Army officer, the youngster was well-traveled and educated in both Europe and America. While attending the University of Florida, Dunaway blossomed into a stunning, blonde beauty with large, doe eyes, alabaster-smooth ivory skin, packaged in a perfect heart-shaped face. She transferred to Boston University before heading to New York. There, she joined the Lincoln Center Repertory Company appearing in plays for three years. Her screen debut in the comedy, *The Happening* (1967), led immediately to bigger and better things. She was not Warren

Beatty's first, second, or even tenth choice to play the bank-robbing Bonnie in his upcoming true crime film *Bonnie and Clyde* (1967). Beatty originally wanted Tuesday Weld, Natalie Wood, Jane Fonda, Sharon Tate or Ann-Margret, among others; all who turned him down. Dunaway, though, "knew it was a great role." She commented, "I really identified with Bonnie...a Southern girl who was dying to get out of the South. She wanted to take risks, she wanted to live." Nor was the actress frightened of the unusual character, a ruthless woman whom the audience is simultaneously fascinated and repelled by. Dunaway's delectable portrayal of the dangerous, charming female lead of the Barrows Gang won her an Academy Award nomination for Best Actress, and made her a superstar. It also started a new braless fashion craze where secondhand dresses (of the depression-era), and berets became the rage. This superb talent made a number of films, including *Hurry Sundown* (1966) with John Phillip Law, *The Thomas Crown Affair* (1968) with Steve McQueen, *Little Big Man* (1970) opposite Dustin Hoffman, *The Three Musketeers* (1973) with Michael York, and *The Towering Inferno* (1974) co-starring Steve McQueen, Paul Newman and William Holden. Then Dunaway's outstanding performance in *Chinatown* (1974) moved the earth. As the complex, elegant female lead in this *film noir*, she won her second Academy Award nomination. In *Network* (1976) she played the sophisticated, gutsy, career driven woman. Dunaway was brilliant and took home the Oscar statuette. Other motion pictures include *Don Juan DeMarco* (1995—co-starring Marlon Brando and Johnny Depp), *The Handmaid's Tale* (1990), *Wait Until Spring Bandini* (1990), and *Barfly* (1987). When she takes on a TV, it is always interesting. She starred in the title role in *Evita Peron*. She won the Golden Globe Award for her supporting role in HBO's original "Gia" (1998). Onstage, she was riveting as Maria Callas in "Master Class" (1997).

Fay Bainter 🎥　　7021 Hollywood

Actress
BORN Dec. 7, 1892, in Los Angeles, CA. **SPOTLIGHTS** After starring on the Broadway stage for more than two decades, she made her film debut in *This Side of Heaven* (1934). Movies: *The Shining Hour* (1938), *A Bill of Divorcement, Our Town* (both 1940), *Woman of the Year* (1942), *The Human Comedy* (1943), *The Virginian* (1946), *The Secret Life of Walter Mitty* (1947), *June Bride* (1948), and *The Children's Hour* (1962--in an Oscar-nominated performance). **ACHIEVEMENTS** 1938 Best Supporting Actress Academy Award for *Jezebel*. She was also Oscar-nominated in the Best Actress category that same year for *White Banners*. This combination forced the Academy to change their rules. Died: 1968.

Richard Dreyfuss 🎥　　7021 Hollywood

Actor, director
BORN Oct. 29, 1949, in Brooklyn, NY. **SPOTLIGHTS** His fam-

Richard Dreyfuss

ily moved from New York to Los Angeles when he was eight years old. Like any impressionable kid who gets a glimpse of the glamorous motion picture studios, he decided to become an actor. At age nine, the focused youth began acting at the local Westside Jewish Community Center. By the late 1960s and early 1970s he was commuting between both coasts doing Broadway, off-Broadway, repertory and improvisational comedy, features and television guest appearances. Along the way he was earning a reputation for his energy, speed, precision and intelligence. You can still see his early television work, which is really good, on "Bewitched" reruns. He has the fun distinction of making his big screen debut in *Valley of the Dolls* (1967)—one of the biggest dogs ever made; it's so bad it's laughable. (This is no fault of Dreyfuss, who had a bit part.) The actor fared better in his next work, the five-star production of *The Graduate* (1967). He had only one line, but things were looking up. He made several more films before his breakthrough year. 1973 brought his sensitive portrayal of an ambivalent, college-bound, cruising teen in the cult classic, *American Graffiti*, and the berserk bank robber, George "Baby Face" Nelson, in *Dillinger*. Dreyfuss had everyone's attention and the films got bigger. He played a caring scientist in the ocean thriller, *Jaws* (1975), where the terrifying action scenes have kept many swimmers out of the sea *permanently*. Dreyfuss slyly remarked, "In Jaws, the shark was the star of the film." Maybe so, but he came out of it a hero. He gave a stunning performance in the sci-fi blockbuster *Close Encounters of the Third Kind* (1977). That same year, he portrayed a failing actor in *The Goodbye Girl* and became the youngest actor to win an Academy Award. It was his first nomination—in a comedy, no less! (Only two other actors have won the Best Actor Oscar in comedic roles: Jimmy Stewart and Lee Marvin.) Other films include *Whose Life Is It Anyway?* (1981), *Down and Out in Beverly Hills* (1986), *Tin Men* (1987), *Stakeout* (1987), *Moon Over Parador* (1988), *Postcards From the Edge* (1990), *What About Bob?* (1991), *Prisoner of Honor* (1991), *James and the Giant Peach* (1996—voice only), and *Mr. Holland's Opus* (1995)—in an Oscar and Golden Globe Award-nominated performance. **ACHIEVEMENTS** This Oscar winner is extremely proud that three of the motion pictures he appears in were included in the American Film Institute's list of the 100 greatest films: *American Graffiti*, *Jaws*, and *Close Encounters of the Third Kind*...One of the many dimensions Dreyfuss has displayed throughout the years of success is his political and social activism. He has campaigned for candidates and causes, given testimony before Congressional and other governmental committees, worked with groups promoting solutions to the Arab/Israeli conflict, and encouraged community service and civic literacy. He has made his involvement a priority.

Edward James Olmos 🎥 7021 Hollywood

Actor, producer, director

BORN Feb. 24, 1947, in East Los Angeles, CA. **SPOTLIGHTS** With due respect and admiration among his peers, he is known as the "Olivier of the Latino world." His immense acting talents flow between deep, raging waters and a calm, bubbling brook. Born and raised in an East Los Angeles barrio, Olmos chose baseball over gang life, and became a Golden State Batting Champ. He recalled, "In the streets, to be a man was to be strong. You had to prove your machismo, prove your strength, by being able to walk the streets. There was a lot of role-playing and still is. They're all just trying to find out who they are..." At age 13, he decided to become an actor and singer. He graduated from Montebello High School and attended East Los Angeles City College and Cal State L.A. Beginning his entertainment career in the 1960s as a singer with various groups, Olmos was introduced to acting while helping a friend rehearse his part in a play. He then began to pursue parts in Equity-waiver productions, supporting himself by delivering furniture. His first professional acting jobs were bit parts in episodic television shows like the police dramas "Kojak" and "Hawaii Five-O." Still delivering furniture at the age of 31, Olmos attended an open cattle call audition for an Equity-waiver workshop about Latinos. Four callbacks and three months later, he won the part of El Pachuco in the musical "Zoot Suit." Pouring his entire life into the part, his Mexican heritage, his street savvy, his anger, as well as his ability to do perfect splits and "turning the brim of my hat as I came up," he gave a mesmerizing performance. He would stay with the show for its year-and-a-half run in Los Angeles—winning the Los Angeles Drama Critics Circle Award and a Theater World Award—and

Edward James Olmos

earning a Tony Award nomination on Broadway. He would later reprise his role for the 1981 film version. Olmos appears with Albert Finney and Diane Venora in the horror picture *Wolfen* (1981). He stars in the splendid Western, *The Ballad of Gregorio Cortez* (1982—also assoc. prod.). Directed by Robert M. Young, the story is based on true facts from 1901, about a Mexican cowboy being pursued by Texas rangers. This insightful, sometimes painful and beautifully told story explores the problems of language barriers and bigotry, and is interesting to watch both from an acting viewpoint and for the cinematography. That same year he appears in Ridley Scott's classic sci-fi motion picture, *Blade Runner*, with Harrison Ford, Rutger Hauer, Sean Young, and Daryl Hannah. If you rent this film, make sure to ask for the director's cut, as it features additional footage. Olmos is wonderful in *Saving Grace* (1986), a light comedy about the Pope trying to keep in touch with real people. Directed by Robert M. Young, it also stars Tom Conti, Fernando Rey, Giancarlo Giannini. He earned an Oscar nomination for his tour-de-force performance in *Stand and Deliver* (1988) as the hard-driving math teacher Jaime Escalante. Olmos made his directorial debut in *American Me* (1992). He received rave reviews for *My Family/Mi Familia* (1995), and stars in the Warner Bros. hit *Selena* (1997), in one of his most challenging roles to date. He portrays Abraham Quintanilla, the singer Selena's strong, supportive father, who plays the role of a dreamer and nurtures his family's ambitions against enormous odds. Olmos believes the film is "a celebration of life in the highest form. It's about the love of a family and how that helped them to reach success." Olmos transformed himself physically for the role, by gaining 60 pounds. Producer Robert Katz attested to the startling resemblance that Olmos was able to achieve. "Eddie and Abraham were together one day when the lights were down a little. At one point, someone asked me, 'Which one's Eddie?' One can imagine how well he approximated Abraham's appearance." Also in 1997 he appeared in *The Disappearance of Garcia Lorca*, opposite Andy Garcia. **TV** He garnered both a 1984 Emmy Award and Golden Globe Award for his role as Lt. Martin Castillo on the hit police series "Miami Vice" (1984-'89). Still seen in worldwide syndication, the show helped make Olmos an international star. Other work includes his co-starring role in William Freidkin's 1997 remake of "12 Angry Men" for Showtime cable, opposite Jack Lemmon, George C. Scott, and Tony Danza, to name just a few. In 1996 Olmos was honored with a Golden Globe Award and Emmy nomination for his work in the HBO production "The Burning Season," the story of the Brazilian political activist, Chico Mendes. **ACHIEVEMENTS** Olmos is a community activist and true humanitarian, speaking—on average—at 150 schools, charities and juvenile institutions a year across the country to help youth, and working in a national gang prevention program. He is also a Goodwill Ambassador for UNICEF, programs for the advancement for the arts, and many important organizations. He is on the board of Miami Children's Hospital and Los Angeles Children's Hospital, as well as the National Council on Adoption. Olmos is also the Executive Director of *It Ain't Love*, a program and documentary whose goal is to fight the growing problem of domestic abuse. His devotion to helping others has touched thousands of lives...Olmos has spearheaded several important Hispanic-related enterprises, including Latino Public Broadcasting, the annual Latino Book & Family Festival, and the Latino International Film Festival...His star was unveiled on his birthday, in 1992. Family, celebrity friends, a multitude of fans and the worldwide press were there to share in the joy.

Patrick Stewart 🎥   7021 Hollywood

Actor

BORN July 13, 1940; in Mirfield, England.

SPOTLIGHTS "There is a tide in the affairs of men
which taken at the flood, leads on to fortune;
omitted, all the voyage of their life
is bound in shallows and in miseries.
On such a full sea are we now afloat,
and we must take the current when it serves
or lose our ventures."
    —Shakespeare, *Julius Caesar,* Act IV, Scene III

Stewart came to America's attention as the evil Sir Janus in "I, Claudius," but it was as Captain Jean-Luc Picard in the hit sci-fi television series "Star Trek: The Next Generation" (1988-'94) that Americans took him to their hearts. His intelligence, Victorian posture, and deep, rich baritone voice perfectly suited the military character he conceived. That alone would have been enough to create a memorable figure. Stewart's composed, yet commanding presence made him a superstar in the role. This tremendous popularity helped him gain control behind-the-camera as well. Stewart directed several episodes, one of which ("A Fistful of Dates") won an Emmy. Devoted fans celebrate him in Paramount's futuristic, blockbuster movies, *Star Trek: Insurrection* (1998), *Star Trek: First Contact* (1996), and *Star Trek: Generations* (1994). He stars in dozens of features, including *Prince of Egypt* (1998—voiceover),

Patrick Stewart

Conspiracy Theory (1998), *Dad Savage* (1998), *Safe House* (1998), *Masterminds* (1997), *Jeffrey* (1995), *The Pagemaker* (1994), *Robin Hood: Men in Tights* (1993), *L.A. Story* (1991), *Lady Jane* (1985), *Excalibur* (1981), and *Hedda* (1975). But above all, this thespian is a great Shakespearean talent playing such roles as King John, Shylock, Henry IV, Cassius, and Titus Andronicus among others. Stewart projects the beauty and significance of the Bard's text without falling into theatrics interpretation. His performance as "Othello" was praised in *The New York Times* as "never anything less than uncanny in his psychological portrait: it's like watching an autopsy on human feeling." Diversified television roles—in the United States and United Kingdom—in TV movies, mini-series, and documentaries include his Emmy-nominated portrayal of Captain Ahab in "Moby Dick," "The Canterville Ghost," "In Search of Dr. Seuss," "The Shape of the World," "Tinker, Tailor, Soldier, Spy," "The Mozart Inquest," and "A Christmas Carol," as Scrooge. **ACHIEVEMENTS** Honorary Associate Artist of the Royal Shakespeare Company. 1996 "Will Award" (given annually to an individual who makes "a significant contribution to classical theatre in America"). 1996 Grammy for the "Best Spoken Word Album for Children"— *Prokofiev: Peter and the Wolf.* The recipient of countless stage awards, he is greatly admired for his one-man show, in which he plays 40 characters, in Charles Dickens "A Christmas Carol." **QUOTE** At his star dedication ceremony on Dec. 16, 1996, he commented, "The first time I visited the Hollywood Walk of Fame was as a tourist in 1968...what happened?!"

Bill Thompson   7021 Hollywood

Actor
BORN July 8, 1913, in Terre Haute, IN. **SPOTLIGHTS** A rascal of a child actor in vaudeville, he became a voice specialist/actor as an adult. Thompson could do a wide range of hilarious dialects, speech patterns, and tongue-twisters. At age 20, he went into radio, becoming a regular on NBC's variety show "The Breakfast Club." He used a very funny character he had created: Wallace Wimple—the hen-pecked husband who had "a big old wife." The terrified Wimple called her "Sweetie Face." A few years later he would bring wimpy Wally to "Fibber McGee and Molly" where he would play a host of other characters, too. Thompson signed on"Fibber McGee and Molly" in 1936, one year after the show had started, but it was still building. He played Greek restaurateur Nick Depopoulous, the film-flam man Widdicomb Blotto, the W.C. Fields' sounding con man Horatio K. Boomer, and the Old Timer. As the Old Timer, he'd respond to jokes with: "That's pree-tty good, Johnny, but that ain't the way I heerd it!" It was his amusing popular catchphrase. In 1941, after the bombing of Pearl Harbor, Thompson enlisted in the Navy. The voice of his four characters fell silent while he was gone. He served his country bravely during World War II. After his honorable discharge, he returned to the "Fibber" cast, and audiences were thrilled to have him back. This incredibly popular

radio show ended its long run in 1959. Thompson did not go on to the TV version. Instead he did voice-overs for several splendid animated classics produced by the Walt Disney Studios: *Alice in Wonderland, Peter Pan, Sleeping Beauty,* and *Lady and the Tramp.* Died: 1971.

Debbie Reynolds   7021 Hollywood

See page 433

Big Bird   7021 Hollywood

Giant puppet, educator
HATCHED 1969, in the Jim Henson Studios. **SPOTLIGHTS** The dazzling eight-foot-tall, yellow-feathered star of TV's "Sesame Street" is adored by more than a hundred million fans worldwide. Sweet Big Bird is the show's most popular character. Always portrayed as a six-year-old (no matter how many years the program has been on), Big Bird teaches kids that it is okay to "mess up" and make mistakes, they just have to keep trying. He's lumbering, naive, silly, but beloved in more than 130 countries and seven languages. Preschoolers and their parents alike recognize Big Bird's hearty laugh and pleasing manner. The difference is: children think Big Bird is a real person on the outside, while parents know there's a person inside. Carol Spinney, the award-winning puppeteer, has brought him to life for more than 30 years. Technically—once inside the costume—Spinney's right hand must stay over his head to operate Big Bird's beak. Ouch! His left arm moves the left wing, while an "invisible" string moves the right wing coordinated with the body movement. It can get pretty hot inside the feathered body under the studio lamps, or while making public appearances during the summer. No matter, Spinney is Big Bird once inside the costume, and Big Bird is a cheerful, flighty thing. Appeared in prime time television specials "Big Bird in China," "Big Bird in Japan," and the feature film *Follow that Bird* (1985), as well as cameo appearances in a variety of

Big Bird

movies. **ACHIEVEMENTS** 51 Emmys. Made the cover of "Time" and "Newsweek." Has visited four sitting U.S. Presidents at the White House. Big Bird is the most popular star in China. More than 100 million Asian viewers tune in to "Zhima Jie" every weeknight...Big Bird is of the globe's most recognizable children's characters...On April 21, 1994, he arrived on the street of dreams for his dedication ceremony wearing movie star sunglasses. That leaves us with one question. *Can you tell me how to get, how to get to Big Bird's star?*

Christopher Reeve 🎥   7021 Hollywood

Christopher Reeve celebrates with family, and friends Jane Seymour (left) and Glenn Close (behind him).

Actor, director
BORN Sept. 25, 1952, NYC, NY. **SPOTLIGHTS** Plucked from obscurity, Reeve won the highest flying part of his life—beating out 200 other candidates—to play the world's favorite comic book hero. The handsome, dark-haired actor was immortalized in the title role in *Superman— The Movie* (1978). His character subtleties clearly defined the meek, mild-mannered Clark Kent, and his alter ego, the strapping

Man of Steel. Reeve became an international superstar and followed up with three sequels *Superman 2* (1980), *Superman 3* (1983), and *Superman 4: The Quest for Peace* (1987). After the original action picture, he played an extremely romantic role in the drama *Somewhere in Time* (1979). He portrayed a playwright who falls in love with an antique portrait of an actress (played by Jane Seymour). It's a visually beautiful and tender film that appeals to women. (It's an entrancing video to rent on Valentine's Day.) Reeve was superb in the comic mystery, *Deathtrap* (1981), co-starring Michael Caine and Dyan Cannon. Again he is cast as a playwright, although this time it's *a la* Agatha Christie. The plot employs a number of fun twists. Other movies are *Anna Karenina* (1985), *Remains of the Day* (1993), *Speechless* (1994) and *Village of the Damned* (1995) to name a few. In 1997 he directed the television movie, "In the Gloaming." In his first acting job since the accident (see below), he starred in the television remake of "Rear Window" (1998). **ACHIEVEMENTS** 1999 Grammy for Best Spoken Word Album, "Still Me." His Walk of Fame ceremony took place on Apr. 15, 1997. **RECOMMENDED** His inspirational autobiography entitled *Still Me* published in 1998 by Random House. Reeve, educated at Cornel University and Juilliard, writes an uplifting, poignant story. He dedicated the book as

follows: "For Everyone Whose Life Has Been Touched by a Disability." **SIDELIGHTS** His life was drastically altered during a jumping competition in May of 1995. Reeve was thrown from his horse, and sustained a life-threatening injury. He has since been confined to a wheelchair. **QUOTE** When *Superman* became a worldwide hit, reporters frequently asked Reeve "what is a hero?" He said, "A hero is someone who commits a courageous action without considering the consequences." He would then give an example, like a brave soldier who returns to the battlefield to help another soldier get out alive. After his accident, he expanded his concept of "a hero." He observed, "I think a hero is an ordinary individual who finds the strength to persevere and endure in spite of overwhelming obstacles." Then he would give examples of average men, women and children who have overcome the odds and survived. Reeve, one of our heroes, is slowly, steadfastly making progress toward his goal of walking again. He has become a champion crusader for the rehabilitation of victims suffering spinal cord injury.

Nancy Kelly 🎥   7021 Hollywood

Actress
BORN March 25, 1921, in Lowell, MA. **SPOTLIGHTS** The brunette talent of *Stanley and Livingston* (1939), co-stars opposite Spencer Tracy and Cedric Hardwicke. She stars in the melodrama *Scotland Yard* (1941). By 1956 she was playing the sorrowful, worried mother of a manipulative eight-year-old in *The Bad Seed* (1956). Died: 1995.

Raquel Welch 🎥   7021 Hollywood

Actress, singer, dancer
BORN Raquel Tejada; Sept. 5, 1944, in Chicago, IL. **SPOTLIGHTS** As a child she was a ballerina, in her teens a beauty contest winner, and as a young woman she dreamed of becoming a movie star. She studied drama at San Diego State College performing in local repertory theater. With her voluptuous figure and sensuous face she landed a 20th Century-Fox contract. Welch generated a publicity blitz of the likes not seen

Raquel Welch and Bob Hope

since Jayne Mansfield. The campaign was wildly successful. The leggy, sultry stunner became a huge international celebrity *before* appearing in a single important film. This ultra-feminine bombshell defined the 1960s as *the* love goddess. She starred in a number of films in Italy, France, the United Kingdom, Germany and the United States. Movies include *Fantastic Voyage* (1966), *One Million Years B.C.* (1966), *The Magic Christian* (1969), *The Three Musketeers* (1974), *The Wild Party* (1975), and *Mother, Jugs & Speed* (1976), and *Naked Gun 33 1/3: The Final Insult* (1994). She has been a good sport guest starring in TV sitcoms like "Seinfeld" (1998) spoofing herself. She has made interesting TV movies: "Trouble in Paradise" (1988). Breaking away from her goddess role, she surprised critics and fans alike with her dramatic performance in "Right to Die." Welch is also an accomplished Broadway performer. Shows include "Woman of the Year," and "Victor/Victoria." Her Walk of Fame star was unveiled on June 8, 1996. Her daughter is actress Tahnee Welch.

Bob Hope ⚇   7021 Hollywood

See page 87

Dolores Hope ⚇   7021 Hollywood

Dolores Hope

Singer, entertainer
BORN Dolores DeFina; May 27, 1909, Bronx, New York. **SPOTLIGHTS** Descended from strong Italian-Irish stock, Hope was raised with the straightforward Italian philosophy that was a favorite of the late champion boxer, Rocky Marciano—"*Fa I fate, no parole.*" (Do it, don't talk about it.) In the 1930s, this auburn-haired beauty with a heart-shaped face, flawless porcelain skin, sparkling eyes, dazzling smile and comely figure was advised by her agent to change her name to Dolores Reade (after Broadway actress Florence Reed). Billed with her new stage name, she began her professional singing career on the New York nightclub circuit. While working at the Vogue Club on 57th Street she met a young actor/comedian, who was performing in the Broadway production of "Roberta." He had come with his friend/co-star George Murphy to "hear a pretty girl sing." That young man was Bob Hope. The year was 1933. As Bob Hope tells it, "she had a low, husky voice—soft and sweet. She sang 'It's Only a Paper Moon,' and 'Did You Ever See a Dream Walking?' That did it! It was love at first song: the look, the woman and the voice. From then on I was at the Vogue Club every night, waiting to take Dolores home. A few months later we tied the knot." Dolores changed her name again and joined her new husband in his vaudeville act. She exchanged her professional singing career for a role as a mother, singing lullabies to their four children—Linda, Tony, Kelly and Nora. She also kept in good voice entertaining friends—such as Rosemary Clooney (Clooney later became a singing partner) and Tony Bennett—at parties. In the late 1940s she returned to the stage where she entertained U.S. troops with her husband. Dolores became one of the most beloved performers in the U.S.O. show. In 1948 the Hopes did a special show overseas for the men and women involved in the Berlin Airlift. She bravely continued to tour with her husband during wartime. In Vietnam, Christmas 1966, there wasn't a dry eye in the house when Dolores sang "Silent Night." The hushed audience of soldiers treated her to a thunderous applause and a standing ovation after the song. When the Hopes traveled to Saudi Arabia to entertain the troops of "Operation Desert Storm" at Christmastime 1990, she was the only *female* entertainer allowed to perform there! In 1993, after waiting nearly 70 years, Dolores realized her musical dream with the release of her debut album, *Now and Then.* One reviewer was inspired to write that "she combines a 1930s style with today's technology to produce a pop sound that is truly timeless." Others include *Somewhere in Time: The Songs and Spirit of WWII, Hopes for the Holidays* (Christmas collection), *That's Love,* and in 1999 at age 90, she released her fifth album, *Young at Heart.* (For information, call 1-800-Bob-Hope.) **ACHIEVEMENTS** Dolores Hope has been honored, feted and esteemed—she has seven Honorary Doctorates. She is known as one of the most devoted, tireless and generous charity workers, who has literally helped thousands improve the quality of their lives. In 1998 both she and her husband shared honors as Cardinal Roger Michael Mahony of the Archdiocese of Los Angeles presented them with papal honors from Pope John Paul II—Knight and Dame of St. Gregory the Great with Star. Dolores is one of four women in the world to be presented the Dame of St. Gregory with Star...She received her Hollywood Walk of Fame star on May 1, 1997.

Ricardo Montalban ⚇   7021 Hollywood

Actor, singer, dancer
BORN Nov. 25, 1920, in Mexico City, Mexico. **SPOTLIGHTS** This suave, handsome, and gifted gentleman signed with MGM in 1947. Previously, he had made a handful of films in his native country. His flashing smile, rich, mellifluous voice enhanced by his romantic Latin accent helped make Montalban an international star. He made his American screen debut in the colorful musical, *Fiesta* (1947), opposite Esther Williams. Possessing an elegant presence, he plays a debonair bullfighter who wants to be a composer. He co-stars with Esther Williams in several other films; *Neptune's Daughter* (1949) is one of the best. At the beginning of his career, due to his striking good looks and popularity with female fans, he was most often cast as the Latin Lover. Montalban broke away from studio typecasting, proving a versatile talent in dozens of films. Motion pictures include *Across the Wide Missouri* (1949),

Ricardo Montalban (left) and Robert Stack

Battleground (1949), *Mark of the Renegade* (1951), *Sayonara* (1957), *Cheyenne Autumn* (1964), *The Singing Nun* (1966), *Sweet Charity* (1968), *Escape from the Planet of the Apes* (1971), *Conquest of the Planet of the Apes* (1972), *Star Trek: The Wrath of Khan* (1982), *Cannonball Run* (1984), and *The Naked Gun: From the Files of Police Squad.* In all, he made 40 films. **TV** He starred as the magical Mr. Roarke on the hit series, "Fantasy Island" (1978-'84). Other shows include "The Loretta Young Show," and "Dynasty II: The Colbys." He is an accomplished Broadway performer, and toured America with Agnes Moorehead and Paul Henreid playing the title role in George Bernard Shaw's "Don Juan in Hell." **ACHIEVEMENTS** 1977-'78 Emmy, "How The West Was Won, Part II." 1998 Recipient of the Easter Seals Lifetime Achievement Award. He is actively involved with many charities, especially those helping the world's children, and the Catholic Church.

Charlie Sheen 7021 Hollywood

Actor

BORN Carlos Estevez, Sept. 3, 1965, in New York City.

Charlie Sheen

SPOTLIGHTS He is a handsome, dark-haired young star of more than 25 motion pictures, including two Academy Award winners—*Platoon* (1986), as a young recruit, and *Wall Street* (1987), as a young stockbroker seduced by greed (and co-starring with his real-life father, actor Martin Sheen). Other movie credits are *Young Guns* (1988), *Major League* (1989, and the 1994 sequel), *The Rookie* (1990), *Navy Seals* (1990), *Hot Shots* (1991), *The Three Musketeers* (1993), *Terminal Velocity* (1994) and *Money Talks* (1997). **SIDELIGHTS** Sheen's brother Emilio Estevez is an actor of note. Also see the bio in this book of Martin Sheen. **QUOTE** He received his Walk of Fame star on Sept. 23, 1994. Sheen commented, "I grew up in Hollywood and there was nothing else I ever thought of doing."

Donald O'Connor 7021 Hollywood

See page 265

David Copperfield 7021 Hollywood

Magician, illusionist

David Copperfield (right, in black) and supermodel Claudia Schiffer celebrate the appearance of his own star one magical evening.

BORN David Seth Kotkin; Sept. 16, 1956, in Metuchen, N J . **SPOTLIGHTS** He is the dazzling maestro of the magic arts. The world's most popular illusionist. Copperfield is tall, dark and handsome with an angular face that could easily be translated to movie stardom from his spectacular wizardry. With no permanent residence of his own, the charmer travels the globe with his amazing bag of tricks. Known to dress in tight black jeans, black cowboy boots, black leather jacket, with his perfectly coiffed thick, black mane and dramatic eyebrows he wows audiences as he appears on stage striking a pose in a puff of smoke. He is not satisfied with a performance unless there is a lump in every throat at the end of the show. From Mexico City to Hong Kong, the dazzling entertainer performs in 500 sold-out shows a year personally making sure every aspect of his slick production is perfect. He is a showman *extraordinaire* creating the right mood with music, choreography and visuals. But that isn't enough. Copperfield works extremely hard creating new illusions for his shows whether it's with pyrotechnics or the latest high tech instruments. He observed, "Being cut in half with a laser doesn't exist in magic books. My death saw is also new technology. I take big risks and sometimes I fail. Every day is a battle for me." He does seem to be winning the war. He has been seen by more people worldwide than any other magician in history. His show, "The Magic of David Copperfield," has been an annual smash television special for 16 years. On television he has made a 747 airplane and the Statue of Liberty disappear, levitated himself across the Grand Canyon, walked through the Great Wall of China, and became the first person to successfully escape from Alcatraz. **ACHIEVEMENTS** The youngest person ever to be admitted to the Society of American Magicians; by age 16 he was teaching magic at New York University. Winner of dozens of Emmys for his series of specials: "The Magic of David Copperfield." The performer holds the all-time record for the highest weekly gross in box office receipts in Broadway history. (*The New York Times* wrote: "The Hottest Show on Broadway, Utterly Mesmerizing…Copperfield is our Era's Giant of Magic!") He has performed for seven U.S. Presidents. He was knighted by the French government, receiving *Le Chevalier des Arts et des Lettres*—the first ever for a magician. He received his Walk of Fame star on April 25, 1995. He developed Project Magic, a rehabilitative program to help strengthen dexterity and motor use in disabled patients by using simple sleight-of-hand magic. "It motivates a patient's therapy and helps to build self-esteem. There is nothing I do that is more important," Copperfield declared. Project Magic is implemented in 1,000 hospitals and 30 countries around the world. **QUOTE** His International Museum and Library of the Conjuring Arts is the world's foremost repository of historical documentation, artifacts and props on magic and illusion. It includes 80,000 supernatural pieces with a phenomenal 15,000 rare book library. "Every contemporary magician stands on the shoulders of giants," says Copperfield, "and this museum is eloquent proof of the rich mosaic of contributions by men and women throughout the ages to this most compelling of all art forms." Where exactly in Nevada is it located? That's a secret. It's not open to the public, but Copperfield stated, "If a scholar or journalist needs a piece of magic history, it's there."

Claire Windsor ♯   7021 Hollywood

Actress

Claire Windsor

BORN Clara Cronk; April 14, 1897, in Cawker City, KS. **SPOTLIGHTS** With her backlit pale blonde hair, and large, green eyes, this gifted enchantress was favored by the studios during the 1920s glamour period. At 5' 6 1/2" and 131 pounds, Windsor was considered svelte in silent movies, even with the camera adding 10 pounds. Her characters paraded around in a dizzying array of fashion. In those days, by and large, the actors had to provide their own wardrobe, so this expense came directly out of Windsor's own bank account. Off screen, she was romanced by moviedom's leading men, including Charlie Chaplin, and married the handsome actor Bert Lytell. Windsor specialized in dramatic, melodramatic and love roles. Films include *To Please One Woman* (1920), *Two Wise Wives* and *What Do Men Want?* (both 1921), *Rich Men's Wives* (1922), *Strangers Banquet Little, Church Around the Corner, The Acquittal* and *The Eternal Flame* (all 1923), *Nellie, The Beautiful Cloak Model* and *Born*

Rich (both 1924), *The White Desert* and *Souls for Sables* (both 1925), *Dance Madness* and *Money Talks* (both 1926), and *Blondes by Choice* (1927). In all, she made more than 60 pictures, including a handful of talkies. **QUOTE** "I know a great many people say that beauty is not the greatest asset to a girl who would climb the ladder to stardom. But beauty, if not vitally essential, is a big asset." Died: 1972.

James Woods ♯   7021 Hollywood

Actor, producer

James Woods

BORN April 18, 1947, in Vernal, Utah. **SPOTLIGHTS** Educated at MIT, where he majored in political science on a full scholarship, Woods is one of Hollywood's most intense actors. He is a multiple Golden Globe winner, a multiple Emmy winner, a Peabody Award winner, and a multiple Oscar nominee among his wide array of film, stage and television honors. Raised in Warwick, Rhode Island, his father was in the military, his mother a preschool (nursery) teacher and a nationally recognized expert in early education. Woods himself was an altar boy, who began his lifelong devotion to attending Catholic Church. When he was age 12, his father died, but not before leaving him with a legacy of values, like responsibility, decency and honor, and a strict code of ethics. Woods took his father's lessons to heart, and would adhere to them as he matured until they were fully integrated into his own character. As he grew up, a kindly immigrant neighbor—who had survived the horrors of WWII in Europe—became his father figure, taking him fishing, and helping to reinforce the values of hard work. Smart as a whip, Woods excelled in academics. During his college years, he joined the drama workshop, taking to the arts like a duck to water. Woods appeared on stage in the Boston area at Harvard's Loeb Theater. With one semester of school left to go before graduation, he headed to the Great White Way with a part on Broadway in "Borstal Boy." His MIT days were now behind him. He won his first major theatrical honor, the Obie Award, for his performance in "Conduct Unbecoming." Then, the artist made his silver screen debut in Elia Kazan's Vietnam vet comedy, *The Visitors* (1972). Woods appeared that same year in TV's "The Streets of San Francisco" with Karl Malden and Michael Douglas. Unlike many motion picture actors who shun television, Woods has never been afraid to work in the medium. This has availed him to several worthwhile projects on important subjects and/or real-life figures such as "And Your Name Is Jonah," the Hallmark Hall of Fame special "All the Way Home" opposite Joanne Woodward, the mini-series "Holocaust" with Meryl Streep, "Promise" for which he won his first Emmy Award and Golden Globe as the schizophrenic brother opposite James Garner, "My Name is Bill W..." a movie about the founder of Alcoholics Anonymous for which he won his second Emmy, "Citizen Cohn" for cable for which he won the first American Television Critics Best Actor Award—voted by the nation's critics, as well as the prestigious Peabody Award, and the highly rated "Jane's House" where he played a vulnerable and endearing leading man. He has distinguished himself in many superb television productions. In motion pictures, Woods initially became known as a villain. In his breakthrough role, he plays the despicable, sociopathic cop killer in *The Onion Field* (1979). Woods' passion comes through the camera lens, and viewers find him a compelling and riveting individual. He has an exciting personality. His powerful performance in *The Onion Field* led to more "bad guy" roles. None were boiler plate, they were each as unique as a soiled snowflake. He co-stars with Robert De Niro in Sergio Leone's last work, the sprawling gangster crime epic, *Once Upon a Time in America* (1984). This picture was voted one of the top ten films of the decade. After "the first lady of the screen," Bette Davis, viewed his impressive body of work to date, she steely declared, "Woods is the best young actor in America." This extremely gifted talent received two Academy Award nominations; one in the Best Actor category as the sleazy journalist who finally discovers his own well-hidden principles in Oliver Stone's *Salvador* (1986), and the Best Supporting Actor Oscar nomination portraying racist, white supremacist murderer, Byron De La Beckwith, in Rob Reiner's *Ghosts of Mississippi* (1996). His performance in Stone's *Killer: A Journal of Murder* (1995) earned him the first Golden Satellite Best Actor Award, in a tie with Geoffrey Rush's performance in *Shine*. Other films include Oliver Stone's *Any Given Sunday* (2000), *True Crime* (1999), *The General's Daughter* (1999), *The League* (1999), John Carpenter's *Vampires* (1998—in his first adventure hero role), *Another Day in Paradise* (1998—which he also produced), *Contact* (1997), *Casino*, *Nixon* (both 1995), *Diggstown* (1992), *Chaplin* (1992), *The Boost* (1988), *Best Seller* (1987), *Cop* (1987—also producer), *Against All Odds* (1984), and *Hickey and Boggs* (1972). When Woods did voiceover work for Disney's *Hercules* (1997), the studio suggested that he give the pitiless Greek god of the underworld, Hades, a booming voice. Woods thought otherwise about the mythological creature. He decided to give Hades a "slick, aggressively charming persona, as unctuous people can be the most dangerous." His instincts proved correct, and he won critical raves. He is a powerful and versatile motion picture actor, capable in both drama and comedy, of playing the villain or the hero. On Oct. 15, 1998 family and celebrity friends (who call him Jimmy—his preferred name), the worldwide media, and a legion of devoted fans watched the unveiling of his Walk of Fame motion picture star at the dedi-

cation ceremony. **QUOTE** "I don't care how big the role is, I don't care how big the check is, I don't care if I'm playing a spear-carrier if the script is good, and the director is good...For a great filmmaker, any role, anytime, any place."

David Brian   7021 Hollywood

Actor

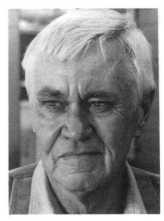

David Brian

BORN Aug. 5, 1914, in New York, NY. **SPOTLIGHTS** A tall, light-haired actor with pale, penetrating eyes, he made his screen debut in the melodramatic tale of a manipulative dancer (Joan Crawford) in *Flamingo Road* (1949). It co-stars Zachary Scott and Sydney Greenstreet, and Brian lends good support. He stars in *Intruder in the Dust* (1949), a compelling adaptation of William Faulkner's novel. Other movies include *The High and the Mighty* (1954) starring John Wayne, *The Rabbit Trap* (1959) co-starring Ernest Borgnine, *A Pocketful of Miracles* (1961) with Bette Davis, and *How the West Was Won* (1962). He starred in TV drama-adventures, as he liked the steady work and regular paychecks. In 1954, he became "Mr. District Attorney." In the 1970s, he starred in "The Immortal" as the rich, callous Arthur Maitland. Died: 1993.

Nicolas Cage   7021 Hollywood

Actor

BORN Nicolas Coppola, Jan 7, 1964, in Long Beach, CA. **SPOTLIGHTS** There is no one else similar to Nicolas Cage onscreen. Like a stealth fighter pilot he continually surprises us with where he ends up. The journey could be a fascinating study of quirkiness—like in the comedy *Raising Arizona* (1987)—or take us to the nethermost regions of the mind—like in the drama *Leaving Las Vegas* (1995). By fearlessly maneuvering his career, by being courageous, open and honest in his roles, Cage has left audiences curious, impressed, and fiercely loyal to him. And unlike other actors who bring a cartoonish quality to their work, Cage remains all human—without sparing humankind's weaknesses. It is his rare ability to give himself fully to his craft—instead of trying to be a movie star—that makes Cage unique. He is truly an original. His distinctive rugged looks showcase Italian eyes that reincarnationists believe have viewed many millenniums. Through these expressive orbs he convinces us to come along for a time to meet some *new* characters. In 1984 his portrayal of a tormented Vietnam vet in *Birdy* established him as a serious actor. The film won the jury prize at Cannes. In 1987 he appeared as an opera-loving, lovesick, one-armed baker in the romantic comedy *Moonstruck*, starring Cher. His performance was sublime,

Nicolas Cage

and he earned a well-deserved Golden Globe nomination. In *Honeymoon in Vegas* (1992), he plays a very funny character fearful of commitment, who gambles his fiance Sarah Jessica Parker away to James Caan. Other motion pictures include *Racing with the Moon* (1984), *Cotton Club* (1984 — directed by his uncle Francis Ford Coppola of *The Godfather* fame), *Peggy Sue Got Married* (1986), *Guarding Tess* (1994), *It Could Happen to You* (1994), *The Rock, Con Air, Face/Off, City of Angels* (all 1997), *Snake Eyes* (1998), and Martin Scorsese's *Bringing Out the Dead* (1999). **ACHIEVEMENTS** 1995 Best Actor Academy Award for *Leaving Las Vegas*. He was also named Best Actor by the Los Angeles and New York Film Critics Associations, and the Golden Globes. About the film's grim ending he stated, "Tragedy is rarely seen anymore, but it's a necessary part of the preparation for tragedy in one's own life. Shakespeare wrote tragedies, and they had a medicinal purpose, along with an artistic purpose." Offscreen he is one of the nicest, kindest people you would ever hope to meet—and staying that way is an accomplishment in this town. He received his Walk of Fame star on July 31, 1998. **QUOTE** "Oh, wow, what an amazing day. I want to thank all of you people who came out here on this very hot day to share this most amazing day in my life. You stuck by me for a long time and I know that I wouldn't be here if it weren't for you. (A fan shouts out "I love you, Nicholas!") He responds with 'I love you, too.' And I want you to know that I'm an L.A. boy. This is my city. This is where I'm from. I was born here, I was raised here. I used to live a block away from here in this old apartment building and I can remember over 20 years ago as a young kid, with my, you know, science fiction mind walking up and down this street and thinking, 'Man, if I could just get my name on one of these. And God forbid, if a meteor hit, or the world blew up,

at least I'd have my name floating around in outer space on a star.' I love you. Thank you."

Lewis Milestone 🎥   7021 Hollywood

Director

BORN Sept. 30, 1895, in Russia. **SPOTLIGHTS** He spent 40 years in Hollywood; his work went from excellent to good. He directed and produced *Of Mice and Men* (1940). He also did a remake of *Les Miserables* (1952); it was good, but not outstanding like the 1935 original. He then did the 1962 remake of *Mutiny on the Bounty*. In 1950 he directed the World War II action picture, *The Halls of Montezuma*. **ACHIEVEMENTS** 1927-'28, Best Director for *The Arabian Nights*, at the first-ever Academy Awards presentation. 1929-'30, Best Director, *All Quiet on the Western Front*. Died: 1980.

Leeza Gibbons 📺   7021 Hollywood

TV and Radio Producer/Personality

BORN March 26, 1961, in Hartsville, South Carolina. **SPOTLIGHTS** Blonde, beautiful and smart, Gibbons graduated *magna cum laude* from the University of South Carolina's School of Journalism. In her home state she became news anchor for WSPA-TV in Spartanburg, and for National Public Radio in Columbia. She moved to Texas to co-host "PM Magazine," then tested herself in New York on WCBS-TV's "Two on the Town." In 1984 Gibbons hit the big time by signing a prestigious contract as an anchor/reporter of "Entertainment Tonight"—a television program that revolutionized entertainment news. She spent more than a decade on the hugely successful show, becoming a familiar and friendly face to millions. When Paramount offered her the opportunity of hosting and producing her own show, "LEEZA," she not only took the chance, but earned 21 Daytime Emmy nominations in the process. She wisely steered her show away from the current tide of exploitation and sensationalism, instead offering viewers an examination of a subject's universal underpinnings. Gibbons also produces and hosts prime time network

Leeza Gibbons

specials. Her voice has become well-known on radio with her two programs syndicated throughout the United States and Canada: the daily "Entertainment Tonight on the Radio with Leeza Gibbons" and the weekly "Top 25 Countdown with Leeza Gibbons." Gibbons co-hosted the annual Hollywood Christmas Parade broadcast for many years. **ACHIEVEMENTS** LEEZA has won two Emmys. She is devoted to several charities which help children, is the March of Dimes' National Ambassador Program celebrity spokesperson, the recipient of Childhelp USA's 1997 Woman of the Year Award, and the national spokesperson for KidsPeace. **QUOTE** "I wanted to take in every detail of the day (May 7, 1998) I got my star. The sounds coming from the crowd, the flashes from the photographers, right down to the color of the sky. It was like an out-of-body experience...I dedicated the star to my children who are the brightest stars in any galaxy, and my husband who lets me be the star in his life everyday, as he certainly is in mine...My six year old had zero interest in going to the ceremony so I had to negotiate with him. I bribed him with a 'Happy Meal.'...Since I grew up professionally in the entertainment business, my first thought upon arriving at the ceremony on Hollywood Boulevard was that I was there to cover the ceremony as a reporter. I feel I have a pretty well-rounded, fully dimensional view on show business and knowing what's behind the veneer makes me love it even more."

Regis Toomey 🎥   7021 Hollywood

Regis Toomey

Actor
BORN Aug. 13, 1902, in Pittsburgh, PA. **SPOTLIGHTS** He was a gentle faced, fair haired, popular character actor in 200 films from 1925-'77. He studied drama at the University of Pittsburgh. After he graduated in 1921, Toomey became a song-and-dance man with George M. Cohan. While touring England in the stage production of "Little Nelly Kelly" he lost his singing voice due to illness. Toomey switched to films. An enthusiastic type, he played good guys—the average American Joe—to perfection, but he was good in a variety of roles. He plays opposite Chester Morris in *Alibi* (1928), the first all-talkie gangster flick. He appears in the early talkie *Rich People* (1929), co-starring Constance Bennett, then works with the "It" girl, Clara Bow, in her first talkie, *Kick In* (1931). Movies include *Union Pacific* (1939), *His Girl Friday* (1940), *Meet John Doe* (1941), *The Big Sleep* (1947), *The Bishop's Wife* (1947), *The Boy With the Green Hair* (1948), *Show Boat* (1951), *The High and the Mighty* (1954), *Guys and Dolls* (1955), *Dakota Incident* (1956), *Warlock* (1959), and *Voyage to the Bottom of the Sea* (1961). Died: 1991.

Nina Foch 📺   7021 Hollywood

See page 370

David Carradine 📺   7021 Hollywood

David Carradine

Actor, singer, songwriter
BORN Dec. 8, 1936, in Hollywood, CA. **SPOTLIGHTS** Carradine is the son of the highly respected actor, John Carradine (see his bio in this book). Like his dad, he is eccentric, tall and lanky. Yet he did not immediately follow in his famous father's footsteps. Carradine did a variety of manual jobs before settling on acting. He had a bit part in *Taggart* (1964) before heading to Broadway for a production of "The Royal Hunt of The Sun." Next, he experimented with TV in a quick-lived series based on the Western classic "Shane." His following attempt at a series worked magic around the globe. "Kung Fu" (1972 - '75) was a gigantic hit. Everyone watched it. "Kung Fu" was a philosophical Western that blended Eastern spiritualism and martial arts (karate and judo) action. Carradine started a national martial arts trend. Carradine returned to motion picture work. He delivered a poignant performance of Depression-era folk singer/activist Woody Guthrie in *Bound for Glory* (1976). Other movies include *The Serpent's Egg* (1977), *Lone Wolf McQuade* (1983), *Double Trouble* (1992) and *Bird of Prey* (1996). His Walk of Fame star dedication ceremony took place on April Fool's Day, 1, 1997; his actor-brother Keith Carradine (see his bio in this book), and actor John Phillip Law joined in the excitement.

Stan Laurel 🎥   7021 Hollywood

Actor, comedian
BORN Arthur Stanley Jefferson; June 16, 1890, in Ulverston, England. **SPOTLIGHTS** Bewildered. Sweet. Innocent. A comic genius. Laurel, along with partner Oliver (Ollie) Hardy, were *the most successful comedy team in motion picture history.* Laurel was the creative force of the team. When asked what made Laurel and Hardy so funny, Jack Benny stated, "Their humor will always be great because they do not rely on jokes. Instead, by placing themselves into basic situations and then having something go wrong, they are understood by people of all ages and all walks of life. Jokes may become outdated, but the type of comedy Laurel and Hardy did will always live with us." The two performed their original, delightful routines in all seriousness and played farce comedy to the optimum. They were visual comedians who employed character identifications: a befud-

Stan Laurel (far left) and Oliver Hardy (center)

Dick Van Dyke

dled Laurel scratching his head, or a flustered Hardy fumbling with his necktie. When they filmed movies during the Great Depression, vast numbers of their audience could relate to the two screen characters who were always trying to improve their lot in life. For status, they politely referred to each other as "Mr. Laurel" and "Mr. Hardy." But when things unraveled—which they always did—Hardy would confront baby-faced Laurel. The thin, dim-wit removed his derby hat and, with a dazed stare scratch his head. When all hope was lost, Laurel got teary-eyed, choked up, then began whimpering. Ollie's standard comment to the simpleton was: "Here's another fine mess you've gotten me into." Laurel made audiences laugh in 200 silent and talkie films—76 were made before the famous teaming. Movies include *Leave 'Em Laughing* (1928), *From Soup to Nuts* (1928), and *Angora Love* (1929). Other classics (talkies): *The Music Box* (1932), *Helpmates* (1932), *Towed in a Hole* (1932), *The Devil's Brother* (1933), *Wild Poses* (1933), *Babes in Toyland* (1934), *Them Thar Hills* (1934), *Way Out West* (1937), and *Blockheads* (1938). **SPECIAL NOTE** Their wonderful film, *Sons of the Desert* (1933), inspired a legion of Laurel and Hardy devotees. This fraternal order of fans assembles annually around the globe...For an excellent overview of their finest silent work, check out *Laurel and Hardy's Laughing 20s* (1965). **ACHIEVEMENTS** 1960 Special Oscar. **SIDELIGHTS** When Oliver Hardy died in 1957, Laurel was so heartbroken he pledged never to perform again. (See Oliver Hardy's bio in this book.) **QUOTE** "What is comedy? I don't know. Does anybody? All I know is that I learned how to get laughs and that's all I know about it. *You have to learn what people will laugh at, then proceed accordingly.*" This divine comedian died in 1965.

Dick Van Dyke   7021 Hollywood

Actor, dancer, singer **BORN** Dec. 13, 1925, in West Plains, M O . **SPOTLIGHTS** A legendary talent. The personification of great American entertainment. He grew up in Danville, Illinois, in a town that could easily define Middle America. Even his father depicted the American way of life as a traveling salesman for the Sunshine Biscuit Company. In his youth he practiced magic, and had a captive audience with his younger brother, Jerry. At age 18, he enlisted in the Army Air Corps to serve in World War II. After auditioning for the local military radio station, he was assigned the show "Flight Time." The program gave Van Dyke the opportunity to develop his voice and personality. After his honorable discharge, he teamed with Phil Erickson and hit the nightclub circuit. Their record-pantomime act was known as "The Merry Mutes" and lasted six years. In 1955 he entered television with his own variety show in New Orleans. Meanwhile, Bryon Paul, an old buddy from his Army Air Corps days, had become a TV director. He invited Van Dyke to New York to host "The CBS Morning Show." It proved to be his breakthrough. Guest appearances quickly followed on all the top TV shows of the day: Ed Sullivan, Perry Como, and Dinah Shore. Off to the Great White Way, this bundle of talent made his 1958 Broadway debut in "The Boys Against the Girls." He then won the lead in the hit musical production, "Bye, Bye, Birdie," which made him a major star. Hollywood called. Creator-producer Carl Reiner starred him in his own series, "The Dick Van Dyke Show." He was immortalized as Rob Petrie in this classic hit comedy series that initially ran from 1961-'66, but is still seen in worldwide syndication. In 1963 he repeated his award-winning performance for the exuberant film version of *Bye, Bye, Birdie*, co-starring Janet Leigh and Ann-Margret. It was a fantastic screen debut for him. During that same span of time he would be immortalized in yet another role, in Disney's masterpiece motion picture, *Mary Poppins* (1965). Van Dyke gave a flawless performance. He was utterly magical as Bert, the gentle, wise, but fun chimney sweep, who also doubled as a one-man-band, and kite seller. Playing opposite Julie Andrews, he attained the highest level of perfection. Van Dyke's endearing Bert will charm children for centuries to come. This classic musical also featured a fine cast of veteran talents—David Tomlinson, Glynis Johns, Ed Wynn, and Arthur Treacher—with a superb score by Robert B. Sherman and Richard M. Sherman. Van Dyke appeared in a handful of films, including *Divorce American Style* (1967) and *Chitty Chitty Bang Bang* (1968). This Emmy-winning talent starred in a number of his own "Dick Van Dyke Variety Specials" for CBS television. In 1991 he developed the character of the crime-solving M.D. Mark Sloan in the made-for-television movie "Diagnosis of Murder." The weekly series, "Diagnosis Murder" soon followed (fall of 1993). Van Dyke's son, Barry, plays police Lt. Steve Sloan in this popular long-running series. **ACHIEVEMENTS** Five Emmys. **QUOTE** Van Dyke's star was placed next to the star of his idol and friend, Stan Laurel. About the dedication ceremony, Van Dyke commented, "I was just so impressed that Johnny Grant and the Hollywood Chamber of Commerce had placed my star next to Stan Laurel's. I was wearing the bow tie he gave me that day. When my star was uncovered and my name was misspelled, I laughed. It was a perfect Stanley situation...*another fine mess*. They corrected it later." **AUTHOR'S NOTE** When his star was unveiled on February 25, 1993, there, etched in terrazzo and bronze, was his *misspelled* name: "Vandyke." He politely requested a black felt marker, drew a line separating Van and Dyke, and gave fans a big, beautiful smile.

Ella Raines 🎥   7021 Hollywood

Actress

BORN Ella Raubes; Aug. 6, 1921, in Snoqualmie Falls, WA. **SPOTLIGHTS** A beautiful brunette, she enjoyed a 10-year run in pictures starting with *Corvette K-225* (1943)—the only woman in the movie. This extremely talented actress made only 22 pictures, but appeared in such five-star classics as the psychological thriller, *Phantom Lady* (1944—a must-see movie), the satirical comedy, *Hail the Conquering Hero* (1944—another must-see film), and the psychological suspense piece, *Uncle Harry* (1945—aka *The Strange Affair of Uncle Harry*). She was known for her wide range of roles, and her ability to delve deeply into each character. **HIGHLIGHTS** Wed Brigadier General Robin Olds in 1947. Died: 1988.

Mitch Miller 💿   7013 Hollywood

Musician, conductor, producer

BORN Mitchell William Miller; on the Fourth of July, 1911, in Rochester, NY. **SPOTLIGHTS** Regarded as one of the best classical oboists during the 1930s—and known for his trademark long hair—Miller changed his Tin Pan Alley appearance and emerged an authority in the pop record world. His updated image was his mustache and uniquely shaved beard which landed him the title "the Beard." But it was his finely tuned ear for new talent that made stars out of so many singers. He pro-

Mitch Miller

duced many hits by covering tunes no one else really knew what to do with. Never one to shy from a marketing angle or gimmick, Miller saw gold when 12-year-old Jimmy Boyd gave his spirited rendition of "I Saw Mommy Kissing Santa Claus." Johnnie Ray wailed with "Cry" and Frankie Laine pounded with "Mule Train." Rosemary Clooney's thrilling rendition of "Come On-a My House," with lyrics by William Saroyan remains a classic. Miller's musical background made these and hundreds of other greats possible as Director of Popular Artists and Repertoire at Columbia Records. Baby boomers recall his "Sing Along with Mitch" albums and 1960s TV show of the same name. These "Sing Alongs" introduced the joy of singing—with a bouncing ball keeping beat with the lyrics—to many Americans. (Miller's concept was the forerunner to karaoke.) In 1993 he was appointed principal pops conductor of the New Jersey Symphony Orchestra. (Also see bios of Hank Williams and Johnny Mathis in this book.). **QUOTE** Because he never liked rock 'n' roll, as a producer he passed on signing Buddy Holly. He bid for Elvis Presley, but not thinking much of Elvis, refused to meet Col. Parker's price of $18,000. Miller stated, "Oh, forget it, nobody's worth that much."

Oliver Stone 🎥   7013 Hollywood

Director, screenwriter, producer

BORN William Oliver Stone; Sept. 15, 1946, New York, NY. **SPOTLIGHTS** Brilliant. Controversial. A modern-day pioneer. The young writer first penetrated the world's consciousness as the creator of the dark screenplay, *Midnight Express* (1978). This grim, harrowing and graphic drama was based on the true story of Billy Hayes, an American jailed in Turkey for drug smuggling. It set a new standard for prison stories, and scared the hell out of anyone who fantasized about running drugs for a profit, or a thrill. In 1982 he co-wrote *Conan the Barbarian,* a violent action pic starring Arnold Schwarzenegger in his breakthrough role. The next year Stone wrote *Scarface,* a remake of the classic gangster motion picture with an added Cuban-cocaine twist. By now the screenwriter had a reputation for the volume of violence seen in his work. The question became:

Oliver Stone

Was it gratuitous, or honestly reflective of the plot and its characters? This was not a difficult one for Stone. The Yale University dropout had enlisted in the Army and served in the U.S. Infantry. On the eve of his 21st birthday, Stone and the rest of the 25th Infantry Division were heading to War Zone C in the Hobo Woods, right next to Vietnam's Cambodian border. These fresh-faced American kid soldiers were attacked in a night ambush. Stone sustained injuries while many of his buddies were brutally killed. This twice-wounded, twice decorated—Purple Heart and Oak Leaf cluster—Vietnam veteran had seen the unholiest of unholy human practices. Deep inside of him a slumbering creative giant had been disturbed. It was now awakening. After his honorable discharge, he found an artistic outlet at New York University's film studies. It was the birth of another life for him. Before a decade had passed he would be holding his first Academy Award for *Midnight Express*. Stone became a world-class director with *Platoon* (1986), which he also wrote based on his own war experiences. The film took these honors from the Academy: Best Picture, Best Director, Best Sound and Best Editing. *Platoon* was the first in the series of his Vietnam trilogy. In 1987 he co-wrote and directed *Wall Street* starring Michael Douglas. Douglas won an Oscar for Best Actor in his role as Gordon Gekko, the villain (or is he?). The character's evergreen slogan—"Greed is Good"—lives on around the globe with an unrelenting stream of nefarious workers in pursuit of the Almighty Dollar. In 1989 Tom Cruise stars in Stone's *Born on the 4th of July*. The director also co-wrote the second in his war trilogy, based on the true story of Ron Kovic. Stone took home the Academy statuette for Best Director; another was awarded for Best Editing. He directed and co-wrote the screenplay (with J. Randal Johnson) for *The Doors* (1991), and the highly rated *JFK* that same year. His final entry to his Vietnam trilogy *Heaven and Earth* (1993), was based on the memoirs of a Vietnamese woman named Le Ly Hayslip. In *Natural Born Killers* (1994), he created a horrifying pair of psychotic sociopaths who are glorified by media frenzy. *Nixon* (1995) which he also co-wrote earned an Academy nomination. As a producer, his films include *Assassinated* (1998), *The People vs. Larry Flynt* (1996), *The Joy Luck Club* (1993), *South Central* (1992), and *Reversal of Fortune* (1990), among others. **QUOTE** On March 15, 1996, the director's Walk of Fame star was dedicated. Stone stated, "I love this town! Hollywood has been very generous to me and when all is said and done, it is still one of the last bastions of true democracy. No matter who you are or where you come from, here you are measured by the size of your talent, character, and dreams. I shall always be proud of my cubic centimeter on Hollywood Boulevard."

Alfred Hitchcock 📽   7013 Hollywood

Director
BORN Aug. 13, 1899, in London, England. **SPOTLIGHTS** The Master of Suspense once said, "Movies are delightfully simple. What you do is take a piece of time, add color and pattern, and

Alfred Hitchcock

you have a movie. Quite." One of the greatest directors of all time, his films explored human emotions: terror, bloodcurdling chill, and painful exploration of identity. Hitchcock blended in mordant humor, dark guilt, and romance. Here is a treasure trove of his British and American thrillers: *The Man Who Knew Too Much* (1934), *The Thirty-Nine Steps* (1935), *The Lady Vanishes* (1938), *Rebecca* (1940), *Foreign Correspondent* (1940), *Shadow of a Doubt* (1943—Hitchcock's favorite), *Lifeboat* (1944—a drama based on a John Steinbeck story), *Notorious* (1946), *Strangers on a Train* (1951), *Dial M for Murder* (1954), *Rear Window* (1954), *The Man Who Knew Too Much* (1956—a remake of his earlier work), *Vertigo* (1958—many consider this work his masterpiece), *North by Northwest* (1959), *Psycho* (1960), and *The Birds* (1963—inspired by a true story of crazed birds in Monterey Bay, California). Yet throughout his career, Hitchcock never saw any of his films in movie theaters with audiences. Someone asked him, "Don't you miss hearing them scream?" Hitchcock replied, "No. I hear them when I'm making the picture." **HIGHLIGHTS** In 1944 he directed actress Ingrid Bergman in the psychological drama, *Spellbound*. Bergman was having considerable trouble in one scene opposite Gregory Peck. The actress told the director: "I don't think I can do that naturally." Then she started explaining alternatives. Hitchcock appeared to listen to her, nodding his head occasionally in understanding. The actress thought she had made her point and won Hitchcock over to her way of thinking. After Bergman had finished, Hitchcock looked at her and stated, "All right, if you can't do it naturally, then *fake* it." (Years later the three-time Academy Award winner recalled that was the single, most important piece of acting advice she had *ever* received.) **TV** "Alfred Hitchcock Presents" (1955-'65), and "The Alfred Hitchcock Hour" (1962-'65)...He has two stars on the Walk of Fame; the other is in motion pictures. **QUOTE** He summed up a typical Hitchcock situation as "murder in sunlight, beside the babbling brook. In real life, most horrible things happen in very commonplace surroundings—living rooms, poppy fields—rather than in dark alleys and haunted houses." Died: 1980.

Roger Corman 📽   7013 Hollywood

Director, producer, distributor
BORN April 5, 1926, in Detroit, MI. **SPOTLIGHTS** A maverick. An outlaw filmmaker. The saga of this great independent—who has produced more than 550 films and directed 50 others—ranks as one of the most amazing motion picture success stories. Corman, following in his father's engineering foot-

Roger Corman (left), Bridget Fonda and William Hurt

steps, studied engineering at Stanford University. In 1947, with his bachelor's degree in hand, he decided not to use it. After a brief stint in the Navy, he took a job at 20th Century-Fox, and by 1949 was a story analyst. Disenchanted with studio protocol, he left for England, where he did post-graduate work in modern English literature at Oxford's Balliol College. Upon his return to Hollywood, Corman worked briefly as a literary agent. In 1953 he sold his first screenplay, *Highway Dragnet*, and served as associate producer on the film. With the proceeds of the sale he made *The Monster from the Ocean Floor* (1954)—his first film as an independent producer, on the remarkable budget of $18,000. The triumph of his initial endeavor proved that a quality film could be made inexpensively. He began producing a wide array of low-budget features for American International Pictures; all were extremely successful. The movies ranged from Westerns to gangster, from science fiction to teen hot rod to rock 'n' roll. Riding the wave of financial success, he made eight Vincent Price-Edgar Allen Poe films, for which he won international acclaim. When the French Film Institute honored him with a retrospective in 1964, Corman became the youngest producer-director ever to receive such an accolade. Always a trend setter, Corman originated the first "biker" movie with *Wild Angels*, starring Peter Fonda and Nancy Sinatra. *The Trip*, written by and starring Jack Nicholson, began the "psychedelic" film craze of the late 1960s. He launched careers of actors such as Robert DeNiro and Bruce Dern in films like *Bloody Mama* (1969), with Shelley Winters. He enjoys legendary acumen for discovering talented writers, directors, producers and actors, such as Jack Nicholson, Ellen Burstyn, Francis Ford Coppola, Martin Scorcese, and Dennis Hopper..."Roger Corman—Hollywood's Wildest Angel" is both his nickname and the title of a documentary by Christian Blackwood...*How I Made a Hundred Movies in Hollywood and Never Lost a Dime*, written by Roger Corman (with Jim Jerome), was published by Da Capo Press (800.321.0050). Also available is *Roger Corman: An Unauthorized Biography of the Godfather of Indie Filmmaking* by Beverly Gray (beverly@beverlygray.com), published by Renaissance in 2000.

Lilli Palmer ☖   7011 Hollywood

Actress

BORN Lilli Peiser; May 24, 1914, in Posen, Germany. **SPOTLIGHTS** She worked on London stage and in European films before fleeing war-torn Europe. Arriving in Hollywood in 1945, she made several films. Movies include *Cloak and Dagger* (1946) opposite Gary Cooper, *Body and Soul* (1947—a must-see, five-star movie co-starring John Garfield), the fascinating study of the history of one marriage in *The Four-Poster* (1953) with her real-life husband Rex Harrison, and *Operation Crossbow* (1965) with George Peppard and Sophia Loren. Palmer observed the universal truth about Hollywood: "There is no film capital as you have here." She also worked in dramatic plays made for television. **HIGHLIGHTS** Appeared with her husband, Rex Harrison (married 1943-'57) in "The Man in Possession" and "The U. S. Steel Hour." Responding to a reporter's questions after their divorce Palmer stated, "Of course we're friends—why not? No reason to be enemies just because we're no longer married. I don't think you can hate each other after being married fifteen years. One year, perhaps, but not fifteen." **QUOTE** "My first part was in a film called *First Offense*—which is exactly what it was!" Died: 1986.

David Janssen 📺   7011 Hollywood

David Janssen

Actor

BORN David Meyer; March 27, 1931, in Naponee, NE. **SPOTLIGHTS** His stage mother, a former beauty queen who enjoyed minor success in films, guided her son into show business. After working in theater, he made his screen debut at age 16 in *Swamp Fire* (1946). Several movies followed: *Yankee Buccaneer* (1952), *Chief Crazy Horse* (1955) and *To Hell and Back* (1955). Thereafter, he interspersed movie roles between his starring roles in television. Actor/director Dick Powell chose Janssen to star in the title role of "Richard Diamond, Private Detective" (1956-'60), a character Powell had created on radio. But Janssen was immortalized as "The Fugitive" (1963-'67). Each week, as Dr. Richard Kimball, he portrayed a man on the run who had been falsely accused of murdering his wife. He searched for the one-armed man who did kill her. He received three Emmy Award nominations for outstanding actor in a TV series. In 1968, he co-stars with John Wayne in *The Green Berets*. He made 28 movies. Died: 1980, at age 49, of a massive heart attack.

Lloyd Bacon 🎥   7011 Hollywood

Director, actor

BORN Dec. 4, 1887, in San Jose, CA. **SPOTLIGHTS** One of his many significant contributions to motion pictures was direct-

Lloyd Bacon (left), Frances Marion, Carole Lombard, William Randolph Hearst (as a Mississippi riverboat gambler), Bacon's wife Nadine, Clark Gable and Marion Davies at Hearst's 70th birthday "pioneer days" costume party.

ing the first all-talkie, *The Singing Fool* (1928), starring Al Jolson. (This immediately followed the historic and immensely successful 1927 picture, Alan Crosland's *The Jazz Singer*. That movie also stars Jolson and introduced *sound* with several songs and a few spontaneous lines of dialogue.) *The Singing Fool* is a full-talkie melodrama with a script that showcases Jolson's singing, dancing, and chatting up a storm. Audiences poured into the theater seats over and over again, and the movie held one of the highest box office records for 11 straight years! Many credit Bacon's exquisite timing in directing the classics *42nd Street* (1933) starring Ruby Keeler, Dick Powell, Ginger Rogers, and Warner Baxter with Busby Berkeley supervising choreography, and *Footlight Parade* (1933) starring James Cagney, Joan Blondell, Ruby Keeler, and Dick Powell, as setting the pace for all future musicals. As true as these gifts were, Bacon abilities extended far beyond that genre. He directed gangster, dramas, comedy, and sports movies, too. On Bacon's film, *Marked Woman* (1937), producer Hal Wallis came to the set and threw a fit. He strongly disapproved of one actor who had been cast as the gangster's hit man. He tried to insult Bacon's casting choice in front of stars Bette Davis, Humphrey Bogart, and supporting talent Lola Lane, Isabell Jewell, and Eduardo Ciannelli, as well as the crew. Wallis demanded defiantly, "Who is that monkey? Why the hell didn't you get a menacing looking character? He looks like some five-dollar extra. Couldn't you see he wasn't right for the part of a gangster?" Davis and Bogart busted up when Bacon replied, "I'm sorry to tell you that he's one of Lucky Luciano's favorite gang members. We put him in the picture for realism." A real mobster. That's a classic Lloyd Bacon touch. Other motion pictures include *Son of a Sailor* (1933) with Joe E. Brown and Thelma Todd, *Gold Diggers of 1937*, *A Slight Case of Murder* (1938) with Edward G. Robinson, *Brother Orchid*

(1940) starring Edward G. Robinson, Ann Sothern and Humphrey Bogart, the landmark football movie which set the tone for all future sports picture, *Knute Rockne, All American* (1940) with Pat O'Brien and (future U.S. President) Ronald Reagan with his famous scene as "The Gipper," *Larceny, Inc.* (1942) with Edward G. Robinson and Jane Wyman, *The Sullivans* (1944) starring Anne Baxter, and *It Happens Every Spring* (1949) with Ray Milland and Jean Peters. Earlier, he was an actor in silent movies, often playing the villain opposite Charlie Chaplin in several time-honored comedics, including *The Champion*, *The Tramp* (both 1915), *The Fireman* and *Vagabond* (both 1916). **SIDELIGHTS** Born into a show business family, his father Frank Bacon was a famous star of the Broadway stage. His talents included acting, writing (one of his popular works is the play "Lightnin'" which was later made into a film starring Will Rogers), and producing. The New York celebrity also founded Actors Equity Association in 1913. The union continues to protect artists to this day. **HIGHLIGHTS** Lloyd Bacon was married four times. The first was to Floy Brightwell, which produced a daughter, Frances Bacon, who followed with a granddaughter, Jennifer (Guiol). His third marriage in 1935 was to Nadine Coughlin (see photo) who, coincidentally, was a Busby Berkeley dancer and appears in *42nd Street* and *Footlight Parade*. That marriage produced one son, Frank Bacon (whom Papa Bacon urged to become an attorney—and, he did), and seven grandchildren— Lloyd Bacon, Eve Marie Bacon, Jennifer Bacon-Blaine, John Bacon, Jacqueline Quinn (Gelber), Maureen Bacon, and William Bacon. **QUOTE** Since Bacon was renowned for turning out quality work really fast, in his words, making "accessible movies, not art house work," he felt neglected by the Academy. But he refused to sacrifice his realism and common touch that audiences loved. After several years of being ignored, he finally declared, "I wouldn't accept a damn Oscar even if they dropped it on my house!" Died: 1955.

Chuck Jones 🎥   7011 Hollywood

Animation creator, director, producer

BORN Charles Martin Jones; Sept. 21, 1912, in Spokane, WA. **SPOTLIGHTS** America's master of animation, his motto is: "Animation isn't the illusion of life; it *is* life." Jones' work is often compared with that of classic screen comedians. Growing up in Hollywood, Jones observed firsthand the talents of comic geniuses Charlie Chaplin and Buster Keaton while working as a child extra in the wacky, slapstick Mack Sennett comedy shorts. After graduating from Chouinard Art Institute in Los Angeles (now

Chuck Jones

California Institute of the Arts), he drew pencil portraits for a dollar-a-piece on Olvera Street, a popular and charming turn-of-the-century Mexican shopping and dining tourist area located in downtown L.A. Jones began his professional career in 1932 in the fledgling animation industry when former Disney animator Ub Iwerks (of Mickey Mouse fame *et al*) hired him as a cel washer. Jones' rare artistic gift was apparent early on, he advanced quickly, and in 1936 he landed a position as an animator for the Leon Schlesinger Studio. Later he became an integral part of the world-famous Warner Bros. team that created "Looney Tunes" and "Merrie Melodies." Working in the unit headed by Fred "Tex" Avery, Jones and other Warner Bros. animators, the team affectionately nick-named their back-lot building "Termite Terrace." It was here, during Hollywood's Golden Era, that the clever personalities, unique characteristics, and personality animation of Porky Pig, Bugs Bunny, Elmer Fudd, Yosemite Sam, and Daffy Duck, among others, were developed. At the young age of 25, Jones directed his first animated film, *The Night Watchman*, utilizing approximately 5,000 animation drawings for a six-minute cartoon. As a director, he timed the picture, finalized all of the writing, drew more than 300 layouts for the key scenes, directed the art design, music, sound effects and animation. Released in 1938, it was to be the first in more than 300 timeless films that Jones would direct and/or produce. 1938 also marked the beginning of his legendary career that would span more than six and a half decades, delight several generations of children, and bring him international acclaim. From his original ideas, and proving he never suffered from lack of wit, he created Road Runner, Wile E. Coyote, Marvin Martian, Pepe Le Pew, Michigan J. Frog, Gossamer, and many other favorites. He explained, "'Full' or character animation is the art of breathing heart, soul and life into design, producing characters who are both understood and understandable. Films must be made for ourselves. By making each other laugh, the audience will follow. We must maintain, nurture, and ensure the ability to recognize and communicate the characteristics we, ruefully, recognize in ourselves. We must never write down to children. We should take our work, but not ourselves, seriously." Pictures include *Elmer's Candid Camera* (1940), *Little Orphan Airedale* (1947), *Haredevil Hare* (1948), *Fast and Furry-ous* (1949), *For Scent-imental Reasons* (1949—Academy Award Winner), and *So Much for So Little* (1949—Academy Award Winner), and *Operation: Rabbit* (1952). Jones has become a true icon of creativity by directing such mini-epics as *What's Opera, Doc?* (1957), which was inducted into the National Film Registry for being "among the most culturally, historically or aesthetically significant films of our time." Jones turned his classic cast of animated characters into some of the world's most enduring film stars. His later work at MGM included 34 *Tom & Jerry* theatrical short films. **HIGHLIGHTS** Jones recalled, "A small child once said to me: 'You don't draw Bugs Bunny, you draw pictures *of* Bugs Bunny.' That's a very profound observation because it means that he thinks the characters are alive, which as far as I am concerned is true." **ACHIEVEMENTS** A three-

time Academy Award winner, and nominated two other times. 1996 Honorary Oscar. 1972 Oscar as producer for *A Christmas Carol*. 1965 Oscar as director for *The Dot And The Line*. Jones received the highest civilian honor awarded by the Minister of Culture in France, the *Chevalier des Arts et Lettres* (12/98). He was inducted into the Director's Hall of Fame (11/98). 1966 Recipient of the prestigious Peabody Award for the utterly spectacular *Dr. Seuss' How the Grinch Stole Christmas* as well as in 1971 for *Dr. Seuss' Horton Hears a Who*. Jones is the recipient of countless awards and honors, too numerous to list here. **SIDELIGHTS** Extremely fit, active, and still working, on his 85th birthday he wryly remarked, "I don't feel like an old man, I feel like a young man with problems." **RECOMMENDED** If you're a fan of animation and comedy, check out these excellent books: *Chuck Amuck: The Life and Times of an Animated Cartoonist*, by Chuck Jones, with a foreword by Steven Spielberg, published by Avon Books. A second outstanding book is: *Chuck Jones—Chuck Reducks: Drawing from the Fun Side of Life*, by Chuck Jones, with a foreword by Robin Williams, published by Warner Books. He received his Walk of Fame star on Feb. 13, 1995. **QUOTE** "It takes a peculiar and rather acrobatic technique to walk down Hollywood Boulevard without stepping on one of my heroes or heroines. At last I have a perch where I am safe from *lese majeste* by perching on my own square and wondering 'how the hell do I rate to be in such august company.' I've found that you don't have to deserve something in order to enjoy it."

Lurene Tuttle   7007 Hollywood

Actress

BORN Aug. 20, 1906, near Phoenix, AZ. **SPOTLIGHTS** A phenomenal character actress, she was respectfully called the "First Lady of Radio." (The category on the Walk of Fame is incorrect. It should be a "radio" star.) Tuttle grew up on an Arizona ranch, but was driven into Phoenix every week by her father for acting lessons. Her professional career began in Burbank,

Lurene Tuttle

California where she won a regular role with Murphy's Comedians. In theater, she graduated into ingenue roles, then traveled across America doing summer stock. After the 1929 stock market crash, Tuttle wisely moved to Hollywood, where, it was joked, "There's nothing depressing about the Depression." Tuttle, a Hollywood regular on radio, became steadily employed. Her vast radio experience is encyclopedic in scope. Take radio's notorious crime drama "The Whistler": "I am the Whistler, and I know many things, for I walk by night. I know many strange tales, many secrets hidden in the hearts of men and women who have stepped into the shadows. Yes, I know the nameless terrors of which they dare not speak..." Producer-director George Allen offered her the highest praise. He stated, "Lurene can be anything. She may change her performance on the air as she finds another facet of the character. She picks out the parts of her character-ization that didn't ring right in rehearsal and corrects them." Other shows include "Blondie," "The Adventures of Ozzie and Harriet" (as Harriet's Mother, a frequent telephone caller), "The Red Skelton Show" (as the Mother of Junior, "the mean widdle kid"), "The Great Gildersleeve," "Dr. Christian," "Yours Truly, Johnny Dollar," and "Suspense (radio's outstand-ing theater of thrills)." In the latter, rotating guest stars depended on her strength and guidance. Her films include *The Ghost and Mr. Chicken* (1966)...Many of her radio shows are still available in full fidelity. A wonderful organization, the Pacific Pioneer Broadcasters, preserves and honors radio's past. Write to: Pacific Pioneer Broadcasters, P.O. Box 4866, North Hollywood, CA 91617. Miss Tuttle died in 1986.

Bugs Bunny 🎥   7007 Hollywood

Cartoon character

CREATED On the Warner Bros. lot, in Burbank, CA.
SPOTLIGHTS A comic hero. The world's most famous rabbit. Like many stars, Bugs had to pay his dues. He first appeared as an unbilled extra, receiving little screen time as a hyperactive bit player in *Porky's Hare Hunt* (1938). The following year, he played screwball in *Hare-Um Scare-Um*, where a connection is made between the rabbit and his name. Then, he made his breakthrough in the Technicolor film short, *A Wild Hare* (1940). Fans loved his mischievous, intelligent personality and Brooklyn-Bronx accent. When Bugs stood upright, munched a carrot, and, while staring down Elmer Fudd's shotgun barrels, casually asked, "Eh, what's up, Doc?", a star was born.

Bugs Bunny & friends at Mel Blanc's star dedication ceremony

Depression-era audiences identified with the character. They viewed themselves as the underdog, just like Bugs. In each car-toon, Bugs survives an aggressor by his wits and confidence. He never runs from conflict, but merrily outsmarts the fools who dare to go after him. This "wascawwy wabbit" has been featured in more than 175 cartoons including such classics as "What's Opera, Doc?" and "Carrotblanca." In addition he has made numerous cameos and special appearances, as well as appearing in feature films including *Space Jam* (1996).
ACHIEVEMENTS Nominated several times for an Oscar, Bugs' cartoon, *Knighty Knight Bugs*, won an 1958 Academy Award. This beloved "pesky wabbit" has delighted children and adults alike for six decades. In 1997 Bugs Bunny became the first animated character to appear on a United States postage stamp. The Bugs Bunny stamp, costing 32 cents, became one of the most popular and collectible stamps of all time, even outselling stamps featuring Elvis Presley and Marilyn Monroe! Bugs Bunny's Walk of Fame star was dedicated on Dec. 21, 1985. **HIGHLIGHTS** With monumental help from Warner Bros., Bugs Bunny earned a service record with the U.S. Marine Corps during WWII, he also popped-up wearing the uniform of other military branches. His impertinent likeness became the mascot insignia for the U.S.S. Comfort hospital ship, and was painted on the nose of more than one Liberator bomber. Bugs Bunny also sponsored a War Bond selling cam-paign. Thereafter, he was an American institution. **QUOTE** Bugs describes himself—with carrot in cheek—as "a stinker."

Rory Calhoun 🎥   7007 Hollywood

Actor, writer, director, producer

Rory Calhoun

BORN Francis Timothy McCown Durgin; Aug. 8, 1922, in Los Angeles, CA.
SPOTLIGHTS Born into an impover-ished, troubled household, his father—a gambling addict—frequently beat him throughout his childhood. Calhoun became a runaway juvenile delinquent, adept at hot-wiring cars. He served time for his crimes—"three years, three months and four days"—in a federal reformatory in Oklahoma. Inspired to seek the path of righteousness by a Catholic priest, Calhoun promised himself "never to do anything that would get me locked up again." He did reform himself. As a young adult, he tried his hand as a cowpuncher, lumberjack, forest firefighter and miner before finding his pot of gold at Hollywood's end.

While horseback riding in Griffith Park, the outdoorsman met movie star Alan Ladd. Ladd brought him home to meet his wife, agent Sue Carol. She took one look at the tall (6'3"), black-haired Calhoun and immediately got on the phone to get him a studio contract. The half Spanish and half Irish Calhoun had devastating good looks, and was nicknamed "Smoky" for his gorgeous, gray bedroom eyes. Gossip columnist Hedda Hopper described him as "one of the handsomest men in the industry, all male." After bit parts and small roles, his breakthrough came in the 1945 boxing film, *The Great John L.* After that his career took off galloping. He landed important supporting roles and eventually the lead in 50 motion pictures, including *Nob Hill* (1945) starring George Raft and Joan Bennett, *The Red Horse* (1947), starring Edward G. Robinson, *I'd Climb the Highest Mountain* (1951) with Susan Hayward, *With a Song in My Heart* (1952) opposite Hayward again, *How to Marry a Millionaire* (1953) with Marilyn Monroe, Betty Grable and Lauren Bacall, *River of No Return* (1954) with Robert Mitchum and Marilyn Monroe, *The Treasure of Pancho Villa* (1955), *The Hired Gun* (1957—a Western which he also produced and directed), and *Requiem for a Heavyweight* (1961). Calhoun made nearly 30 Westerns, although many were minor oaters, including *Way of a Gaucho* (1952—filmed in Argentina), *The Silver Whip* (1953) with Dale Robertson, Robert Wagner and Kathleen Crowley, *Powder River* (1953), and *Black Spurs* (1965) co-starring Terry Moore. **TV** Played Bill Longley in 79 episodes of the post-Civil War Western, "The Texan" (1958-'60). He also hosted "Western Star Theater." **HIGHLIGHTS** To help troubled youths avoid prison, Calhoun dedicated himself and serious funds to help combat juvenile delinquency. Died: 1999.

George Sanders 📺   7005 Hollywood

See page 275

Diahann Carroll 🎤   7005 Hollywood

Diahann Carroll

Singer, actress
BORN Carol Diahann Johnson, July 17, 1935, in Bronx, NY. **SPOTLIGHTS** The gifted child began singing at age six in the church choir. By age 10, she had won a Metropolitan Opera House scholarship to attend New York High School of Music and Art. After graduation, she enrolled in New York University to study sociology. A ravishing young woman, she earned extra money by modeling, and performing in nightclubs. In 1952 she made her brilliant Broadway debut in Truman Capote's "House of Flowers." Subsequently,

Richard Rodgers created the Broadway production "No Strings" as a starring vehicle for Carroll, for which she won her 1962 Tony Award. In Hollywood, she made her film debut in *Carmen Jones* (1954) with Dorothy Dandridge, Harry Belafonte and Pearl Bailey. Other motion pictures include *Porgy and Bess* (1959) opposite Sidney Poitier, Dorothy Dandridge, Pearl Bailey, and Sammy Davis, Jr., *Paris Blues* (1961) co-starring Paul Newman and Sidney Poitier, *Hurry Sundown* (1967) with Michael Caine, Jane Fonda and John Phillip Law, *Claudine* (1974—in an Oscar-nominated performance for Best Actress) with James Earl Jones, *The Five Heartbeats* (1991) with Robert Townsend, and the critically acclaimed *Eve's Bayou* (1997) co-starring Samuel L. Jackson. **TV** She was Emmy-nominated for outstanding single performance by an actress in a leading role for her work in the police drama series "Naked City." Next, she made television history. Carroll was the first black actress to star in her own series, "Julia" (1968-'71). Her character, Julia Baker, played a nurse—a *professional* woman, not a servant. Her inspiration for other black women cannot be underestimated in historic terms. She was articulate and dignified. The ground breaking sitcom was Emmy-nominated. During the excessive 1980s, this remarkable beauty starred as Dominique Deveraux in TV's wildly popular primetime soap opera "Dynasty." Still seen in worldwide syndication, she has millions of devoted fans. She was also Emmy-nominated as outstanding actress in the acclaimed NBC-TV series, "A Different World." For Showtime, she delivered another Emmy-nominated portrayal in "The Sweetest Gift" (1998). In 1999, she portrayed one of the celebrated Delany sisters in CBS-TV's "Having Our Say," which was based on the hit Broadway play and best-selling book. It swept the ratings. In 1995, the artist returned to the stage to star as Norma Desmond in the Toronto premiere of Andrew Lloyd Webber's international hit spectacle "Sunset Boulevard." She "gave a bold and exciting performance," the producer said. Critics hailed her as "the ultimate Norma Desmond." This talented actress also appears in television movies, and is a Las Vegas headliner. In 1999, she completed a cross country sell out concert tour starring in "Almost Like Being in Love—The Lerner & Loewe Songbook," underlying this legendary performer's top box office draw. Her album, *The Time of My Life*, includes many Broadway show stoppers and has received rave reviews. She is the consummate entertainer, who astounds fans and critics alike with her versatility and magnetism. Her autobiography is entitled *Diahann* (1986). **ACHIEVEMENTS** Throughout her lifetime she has given generously in support of civic and humanitarian concerns. Carroll received the Women in Film Crystal Award for her excellence in work and for the accomplishment and contributions she has made to the advancement of women in the entertainment industry in 1992. That same year, she was awarded the Black Women of Achievement Award for her work and charitable activities given by the NAACP Defense and Education Fund. She was awarded her second Women in Film Crystal Award in 1998, and is the only person so honored.

Robert Stack 🎥
Actor

7005 Hollywood

Robert Stack

BORN Robert Modini; Jan. 13, 1919, in Los Angeles, CA. **SPOTLIGHTS** A tall, ruggedly handsome, leading man with a crooked smile and pale blue eyes, he made headlines in his screen debut as the first boy to kiss the sweet-as-pie singing sensation, Deanna Durbin, in *First Love* (1939). He followed up with *The Mortal Storm* (1940), *A Little Bit of Heaven* (1940), and *Badlands of Dakota* (1941), without reaching the fame he seemed destined for. Stack was very good in Ernst Lubitsch's wonderful classic *To Be or Not to Be* (1942), then made the *Eagle Squadron* (1942), before enlisting in the U.S. Navy and serving during WWII. After his honorable discharge, he returned to movies with *A Date With Judy*, *Fighter Squadron*, and *Miss Tatlock's Millions* (all 1948). He stars in the compelling drama *The Bullfighter and the Lady* (1950) opposite Gilbert Roland, and Katy Jurado—in her American film debut. Stack finally became a superstar in *The High and the Mighty* (1954), opposite John Wayne. He felt it was his first challenging role and commented, "If I had *The High and the Mighty* as my first picture, I would have been a star sooner." He earned an Academy Award nomination for his brilliant performance as the alcoholic playboy in *Written on the Wind* (1956). Decades later, his zany characterization in *Airplane!* (1980) proved he was still flying high with a new generation of fans. He co-stars opposite Gene Hackman in the Vietnam action story, *Uncommon Valor* (1983). A versatile actor, he is gifted in both comedy and drama. Other movies include *The Bullfighter and the Lady* (1951), *House of Bamboo* (1955), *The Tarnished Angel* (1957), *The Scarface Mob* (1959—as Elliot Ness, the famed treasury department gangbuster vs. Al Capone; this also served as the pilot for the television series), *The Caretakers* (1963), *Is Paris Burning?* (1966), *Plain Clothes* (1988), *Caddyshack II* (1988), and *Joe Versus the Volcano* (1990). **TV** He starred as Elliot Ness, fighting a variety of crime lords, in the popular, long-running police drama, "The Untouchables" (1959-'63). Due to the loud, rapid machine-gun fire, the sound of speeding, screeching tires, and a new level of mindless violence, the show almost begged for controversy. And it got it, along with high ratings. One defense "The Untouchables" had was that it was historically accurate. Sort of. On one occasion, the FBI got involved when the writers used creative license to show Ness capturing Ma Barker, when in reality, it had been their agency. On another, the producers were hit with a lawsuit by the heirs and descendants of mobster Al Capone, who had died in 1947. They sued not for inaccuracy, but rather that Capone's name and likeness were being used for profit. In other words, it was a licensing issue to the tune of one million dollars. And Italian-Americans, one of the largest populations in the country, were not pleased that so many of the criminals portrayed in "The Untouchables" were called by Italian names. Finally the producers closed each show with a disclaimer that the show had been fictionalized. Other series include "The Name of the Game" (1968-'71), and "Strike Force" (1981-'82). He has hosted the ongoing series, "Unsolved Mysteries" since 1991. **ACHIEVEMENTS** 1960 Emmy for "The Untouchables." **QUOTE** "When things have been going rotten, my career has gone well. When things have gone well with the industry, I couldn't walk in the back door."

Gene Nelson 🎥

7005 Hollywood

Gene Nelson -- Sept. 24, 1990

Dancer, actor, singer, director
BORN Eugene Berg; March 24, 1920, in Seattle, WA. **SPOTLIGHTS** One Saturday afternoon changed his life. He went to see the matinee *Flying Down to Rio* (1933) starring Fred Astaire in his film debut. So inspired by the dancing-singing-acting talent, that he decided "most definitely" on a career in the entertainment field. The blond-haired, boyish looking, athletic Nelson started in 1937 with cold feet—skating in Olympic medalist/actress Sonja Henie's Hollywood Ice Revue. Credits include big movie musicals, Broadway stage, directing and choreography. Best remembered as the definitive cowboy Will Parker in *Oklahoma!* (1955). He played his character with a nice, easy drawl, and was immortalized with a high-steppin' lasso dance. With a charm that won audiences hearts and his loose-limbed, physical agility he tap-danced his way through many movies: *I Wonder Who's Kissing Her Now* (1947), *Tea For Two* (1950), *The West Point Story* (1950), *Lullaby of Broadway* (1951). He put his best foot forward with James Cagney in *Three Sailors and a Girl* (1953). He directed two Elvis Presley movies, *Kissin' Cousins* (1964) and *Harum Scarum* (1965). He also directed TV. **HIGHLIGHTS** During WWII, he entertained troops by touring with Irving Berlin's "This Is the Army." He was active in the Professional Dancers Society. Died: 1996.

Gene Raymond 🎥

7003 Hollywood

Actor, composer
BORN Raymond Guion; April 13, 1908, in New York, NY. **SPOTLIGHTS** He studied at the Professional Children's School, then landed a part on Broadway as Bill Potter in J.P. McEvoy's "The Potters." Next, he won the role as the Big Swede in the

"Cradle Snatchers," opposite Humphrey Bogart. The play ran for two years. He spent his childhood on stage and loved it. As an adult, the fair-haired, strapping gent made his debut in *Personal Maid* (1931), then appeared in a number of comedies. Kept busy throughout the 1930s: *Red Dust* (1932), *Flying Down to Rio* (1933), and *The Woman in Red* (1935), to name just a few. Sporadic film appearances throughout 1940s, '50s, and '60s. TV: Host of "Fireside Theater" (1953-'55), and feature film revivals. Also star of the weekly series, "The Amazing Mr. Malone." **HIGHLIGHTS** Married to soprano Jeanette MacDonald (from 1937 until her death in 1965). Raymond wrote several tunes for her— among them: "Let Me Always Sing," and "Release." He co-starred with her in the film *Smilin' Through* (1941). After the bombing of Pearl Harbor, he enlisted in the Army Air Corps (Air Force) and was dispatched as an Intelligence Officer. He served bravely and was honorably discharged in the rank of Major in 1945. Died: 1998.

Phyllis Diller 📺   7003 Hollywood

Comedienne, actress, wit, pianist

Phyllis Diller

BORN Phyllis Driver; July 17, 1917, in Lima, OH. **SPOTLIGHTS** One of America's greatest comediennes, she is queen of the one-liners. Diller, a former stand-up comic, possesses a stinging sharp wit. She first became world famous for her self-deprecating humor. She once quipped, "You know what keeps me humble—mirrors! I considered changing my name when I entered show business, but with a face like this, who cares!" Her hearty laugh— enhanced by her wide, open mouth and thrown back head—produced her trademark deep, throaty guffaw: "aah ha ha haaa!" At the beginning of her career, Diller wore outlandish costumes and outrageous hair styles. Dressed like a drag queen for a Mardi Gras parade, she brought fans along for the hilarious ride, winning over club audiences across the country. At one vacation resort she wisecracked, "I wore one of those topless swimsuits to the beach the other day. It took me twenty minutes to get arrested—and then it was because I was parked by a fire hydrant. That night I had a phone call from a Peeping Tom. He asked me to pull my window shades down!" She has enjoyed a long-running, successful series of zany comedy albums starting in 1959 with *Wet Toe in a Hot Socket*. In the 1960s, she played the wacky, scheming Mrs. Poindexter Pruitt on TV's "The Pruitts of Southhampton." She also had her own comedy-variety run with "The Beautiful Phyllis Diller Show," and countless TV guest spots through several decades. Motion pictures include *Splendor in the Grass* (1961), *Boy, Did I Get a Wrong Number!*

(1966), and *Antz* (1998—voice-over). Offscreen, she is as funny as they come, an accomplished pianist, and gourmet chef! Diller is a true delight and a madcap American treasure. A candid individual, she was the first actress to bring plastic surgery out of the closet. When asked what her first procedure was, she responded, "I paid the doctor before having anything done." **HIGHLIGHTS** On her 80th birthday, she declared, "I go back so far, I know everybody in show business. I mean everybody. I knew Moses, he had a water act." **QUOTE** "I don't have hecklers. My timing is so precise, a heckler would have to make an appointment to get a word in."

Roger Wagner ⬤   7003 Hollywood

Musician

BORN 1914, in LePuy, France. **SPOTLIGHTS** A pioneering chorale director, Wagner's remarkable ability to interpret music written for chorus brought him a prominent identity in choral ensembles. He organized his Roger Wagner Chorale in 1949, then this widely popular director founded the Los Angeles Master Chorale in 1964. His breathtakingly beautiful concerts offered music from Palestrina and Gregorian chants, secular Renaissance works, right through to 20th-century songs. One of Wagner's signature pieces was "Ave Maria" of Tomas Luis de Vittoria. Among his many recordings: *Bach's Cantata No. 65 and Cantata No.106; Roger Wagner Chorale in Lyrichord; Monteverdi's Madrigals; Lyrichord.* **HIGHLIGHTS** The Los Angeles Master Chorale continues Wagner's musical legacy. For concert information, call 213.626.0624, or 800.787.5262. Website: lamc.org This master died in 1992.

Barbara Eden 📺   7003 Hollywood

Actress, singer

Barbara Eden

BORN August 23, 1940, Tucson, AZ. **SPOTLIGHTS** Blonde, pretty and perky, she is the female counterpart to Dick Clark with her perpetually youthful appearance. Eden set her sights on a career in show business while in high school. Her family, who recognized her talent, encouraged her. As a teenager she studied drama, then graduated to studying music at the San Francisco Conservatory. On weekends, she earned extra money by singing with bands in the Bay area. At age 19, she won a scholarship to a theater group. One year later, the poised talent headed to Hollywood with confidence and high hopes. She landed an interview with a producer at Warner Bros. who took one look at her fresh face and advised her, "You're a nice kid from a nice family. Go home!" Instead she settled in Studio

City, took a bank job to make ends meet, and roomed with other aspiring actresses. Eden soon found stage work. When a director from 20th Century-Fox discovered her in "The Voice of the Turtle" at the Laguna Playhouse, he instantly signed her to Fox's new television series, "How To Marry A Millionaire." This led to starring roles in feature films *Voyage to the Bottom of the Sea* (1961) with Walter Pidgeon, *The Wonderful World of the Brothers Grimm* (1962) with an all-star cast, and *7 Faces of Dr. Lao* (1963) opposite Tony Randall. She has also starred in several well-received and sold out tours of such staged musicals as "Woman of the Year," "South Pacific," and "The Best Little Whorehouse in Texas." **TV** Eden was immortalized in the hit television series "I Dream of Jeannie." She enchanted audiences with her magical and mischievous role as a contemporary 2015-year-old genie in-a-bottle. The "I Dream of Jeannie" series continues to air daily worldwide making Eden one of the most popular actress/comedians in TV history. When she starred in the smash hit comedy film *Harper Valley PTA* (1978), it was the only program to out-rate the Olympics in its time slot. A capable craftsman in dramas, an accomplished singer and all-around entertainer, this delightful personality also headlines at Las Vegas and Atlantic City hotel casinos. **ACHIEVEMENTS** A recipient of dozens of awards and honors, Eden generously helps charities that improve the lives of children: The March of Dimes, Save the Children and Childhelp. **SIDELIGHTS** Contact Barbara Eden's Official Fan Club, P.O. Box 5556, Sherman Oaks, CA 91403. Or, visit the website: www.fansource.com...Her Hollywood Walk of Fame star dedication ceremony took place on Nov. 17, 1988. **QUOTE** "When I was a young, aspiring actress in Hollywood, just down from San Francisco, I remember thinking that if I could ever really be a part of the entertainment industry it would be like having the impossible dream come true. But, somehow, I did get there—and having my own star placed on the Walk of Fame, with Johnny Grant and Bob Hope there presiding over the ceremony, was one of the true highlights of my life."

Barry Fitzgerald ⊠   7001 Hollywood

See page 249

Mike Douglas ⊠   7001 Hollywood

Talk show host, singer, author
BORN Michael Delaney Dowd, Jr.; Aug. 11, 1925, in Chicago, IL. **SPOTLIGHTS** The son of a poor Irish railroad worker, Mike began singing for nickels in a local pub when he was five years old. He grew up during the Great Depression and worked after school to help support the family. With no formal musical education, Douglas picked up his singing style and love of show business from listening to the top radio singers of the era. After serving on active duty with the Navy in World War II, Douglas signed on as a singer with America's #1 big band, Kay Kyser and his Kollege of Musical Knowledge—which showcased on both radio and television. He moved onto an experi-

Mike Douglas (center) and Sammy Davis, Jr. (left) are preparing to duke it out with the great heavyweight prizefighter, Muhammad Ali (right).

mental daytime entertainment show in 1961. Two years later it launched nationally, and two years after that "The Mike Douglas Show" was a smash hit coast-to-coast making Mike the king of daytime talk. His innovations are legendary. He was the first to: feature co-hosts, invite major stars to join him for a full-week, emerge from behind-the-desk to sing, dance, joke and participate in stunts. He broke ground by being the first to: take his show on the road from Honolulu to Las Vegas, Miami to Monaco. In his 23-year run he featured both established personalities and those he thought would become future stars. His guest list includes Bill Cosby, Billy Crystal and 30,000 more. His favorite guest was a 20-year-old Barbra Streisand playing a skit with Nelson Eddy and Jeanette MacDonald. He fondly remembers "John Lennon and Yoko Ono talking about love, peace and women's lib. Lennon sang *Imagine*." **HIGHLIGHTS** The Emmy-award winning host's friendly style and interesting show format greatly influenced and inspired future TV talk show host Rosie O'Donnell. **ACHIEVEMENTS** Douglas received the TV Academy's first Emmy Award for "Individual Achievement in Daytime Television." He is the recipient of hundreds of honors, including a gold record. His Hollywood Walk of Fame star was unveiled on Feb. 4, 1976.

Wallace Beery 🎥   7001 Hollywood

Actor
BORN April 1, 1885, in Kansas City, MO. **SPOTLIGHTS** He first became known for his comic impersonation of *Sweedie*, a

Wallace Beery

witless, clumsy Swedish maid (the proverbial bull in a china shop), in a universally popular film series at Essanay starting in 1914. Beery made dozens of the *Sweedie* silent shorts during a four-year period. Then, for more than a decade, the tall, six-foot, 200-pound, dark-haired, dark-eyed Beery played tough, sometimes brutish guys. He enjoyed a smooth transition to talkies, fluctuating between leading and supporting roles, in both comedy and drama. Movies include *Grand Hotel* (1932), *Flesh* (1932), *Tugboat Annie* (1933), *Dinner at Eight* (1933), *The Bowery* (1933), *Viva Villa!* (1934), *Treasure Island* (1934), *The Mighty Barnum* (1934), *China Seas* (1935), and *Barnacle Bill* (1941). **SIDELIGHTS** He dropped out of school *after third grade—at age 14*, to become an elephant pooper scooper with the Ringling Bros. Circus. **ACHIEVEMENTS** 1931 Best Actor Oscar for *The Champ*, as the washed-up boxer. **QUOTE** "A heavy man need not, necessarily, be a villain in real life. He earns a living by being villainous in pictures and, therefore, he gets very weary of carrying it forward into his domestic relationships. There is a certain pleasure in displaying to the world—for a moral lesson—those forces which actuate us, at times, to evil. We, who portray these parts, are an essential and integral part of drama because we shed light upon the virtue of the hero and teach a moral lesson." Died: 1949.

Houdini 🎥   7001 Hollywood

Magician, escape artist, actor, writer, director, producer
BORN Ehrich Weiss; March 24, 1874, in Budapest, Hungary. **SPOTLIGHTS** This master illusionist baffled the world with his mystifying magic, and death-defying escape acts. Known the world over as Harry Houdini, he first captured the imagination of the public when he offered rewards to anyone who could successfully restrain him. He escaped from handcuffs, leg irons, a mail pouch, packing crates, milk cans, coffins and the famous "water torture cell." Upon close examination there were no clues as to how Houdini accomplished the release. He also escaped from locked jail and prison cells—located in the various towns or cities he played—with newspaper reporters present to record the feat and to ensure a headline story. Other great escapes, such as the straight jacket, or being tied with a hundred feet of rope, he accomplished in full view of an astounded audience. Houdini's breathtaking acts were amazingly scary to watch. Yet, few could resist the lure of watching him struggle to survive. He went to Europe in 1900 and stayed five years as a headliner. Hollywood called. Houdini co-wrote and stars in five feature-length silent films, and numerous shorts, including *Deep Sea Loot*, *The Master Mystery* (serial),

Harry Houdini

The Grim Game (all 1919), and *Terror Island* (1920). He also stars in and produced: *The Soul of Bronze* (1921), *The Man from Beyond* (1922), and *Haldane of the Secret Service* (1923). The movie *Houdini* (1953), stars Tony Curtis as the legendary artist. (Contrary to Hollywood film scripts, Houdini did not die in an escape.) A superior cable movie was made in 1998, with an outstanding cast. **ACHIEVEMENTS** Houdini's name is still invoked as the "King of all magicians." Houdini has become internationally synonymous for daring and ingenious feats of escapology...He was the first magician to be honored with a star on the Hollywood Walk of Fame...The word "Houdini" entered the Funk & Wagnall's 1920 dictionary as a noun and a new verb; "*hou'di-nize*: to release or extricate oneself from (confinement, bonds, or the like), as by wriggling out." **NOTE** The Houdini museum is located at 1433 No. Main Street, in Scranton, PA. Co-directors of this fun and mysterious institution are world-class magicians Dorothy

Dietrich and John Bravo. (Dietrich is considered one of the world's leading female magicians. She has duplicated many of Houdini's original escapes, and has gone one step further by including "The Jinxed Bullet Catch Stunt"—the one Houdini himself backed away from.) It is the authorized site to purchase movie posters, sweatshirts, and a magical array of related gift items. Call 717.342.5555. Website: www.houdini.org (e-mail magicusa@microserve.net)...An avowed occultist, he pledged to communicate a message from the "Other Side," just before his death on October 31, 1926. His devoted wife, Bess, attended a seance for 10 consecutive Halloween nights in an attempt to reach him, but Houdini remained silent. **QUOTE** "My brain is the key that sets me free."

Ethel Barrymore 🎥   7001 Hollywood

Ethel Barrymore

Actress

BORN Ethel Mae Blythe; Aug. 15, 1878, in Philadelphia, PA. **SPOTLIGHTS** Called "The First Lady of the American theater," Barrymore was a shy, reserved, supremely talented actress. She became known for her appealing manner, deep voice, and wit, first on stage, then in motion pictures. She possessed a dignified beauty, but had a tendency to appear older than her age. Ethel is one of the remarkable descendants of the noted Barrymore theatrical family— her father was Maurice Barrymore, a famous actor of the '90s, and her uncle was the celebrated John Drew, her mother having been Georgiana Drew. Ethel Barrymore dominated the American stage for decades, and when she appeared onscreen, her dramatic craftsmanship had not diminished one iota. She made her first appearance at the Empire Theatre in New York City in 1895 in "That Independent Young Person." Also in the cast were Maude Adams and John Drew. She distinguished herself as a member of the Empire Theatre Stock Company in "Secret Service" both in the States and in London. While in England, producer Henry Irving engaged her to play three important roles in "Peter the Great," where she received widespread acclaim by the English critics and press. Barrymore's first starring role on Broadway was in "Captain Jinks of the Horse Machine" in 1900. A number of other critical successes followed, including "A Doll's House," "Alice Sit-by-the-Fire,""The Silver Box," and "The Corn is Green." She made her silver screen debut in *The Nightingale* (1914). She made a dozen other silents, then returned to her first love, the stage. After sound had arrived, Barrymore graced the screen in the cinematic event of the year, MGM's *Rasputin and the Empress* (1933). This classic movie is historic for another reason, it is the only film that all three Barrymore siblings appeared in together. Along with her two actor brothers, Lionel and John, the family was known as the "Fabulous Barrymores." She plays the Czarina in this extravagant film. MGM considered the project so important that they brought and introduced a new "sound-camera" to the set. The crew nicknamed the mechanical contraption "Grandma." When Ethel crossed the set to meet her brothers for a scene, an assistant director, who wanted to find out if the film was in place, called out: "Is Grandma ready?" Of course she believed the comment was intended for her. She stiffened, then whirled around. It was said she glared sharply enough that apples could have fallen from trees. Her brother John became so convulsed with laughter that he was unable to complete the scene. Other motion pictures include *The Spiral Staircase* (1946—in an Oscar-nominated performance), *The Farmer's Daughter* (1947), *The Paradine Case* (1948—in an Oscar-nominated performance), *Portrait of Jennie* (1949) *Pinky* (1949—in an Oscar-nominated performance), *Deadline U.S.A.* (1952), and *The Story of Three Loves* (1953). She also appeared in television and radio. **ACHIEVEMENTS** 1944 Best Supporting Actress Oscar for *None but the Lonely Heart*...An avid reader, she collected an impressive library during her lifetime. Her other hobby had to do with anything associated with baseball—a sport she adored. **HIGHLIGHTS** Movie fans recognize another Barrymore, the vivacious Drew, who started out as the cute youngster in Spielberg's *E.T.* Miss Ethel died: 1959.

Laurel and Hardy

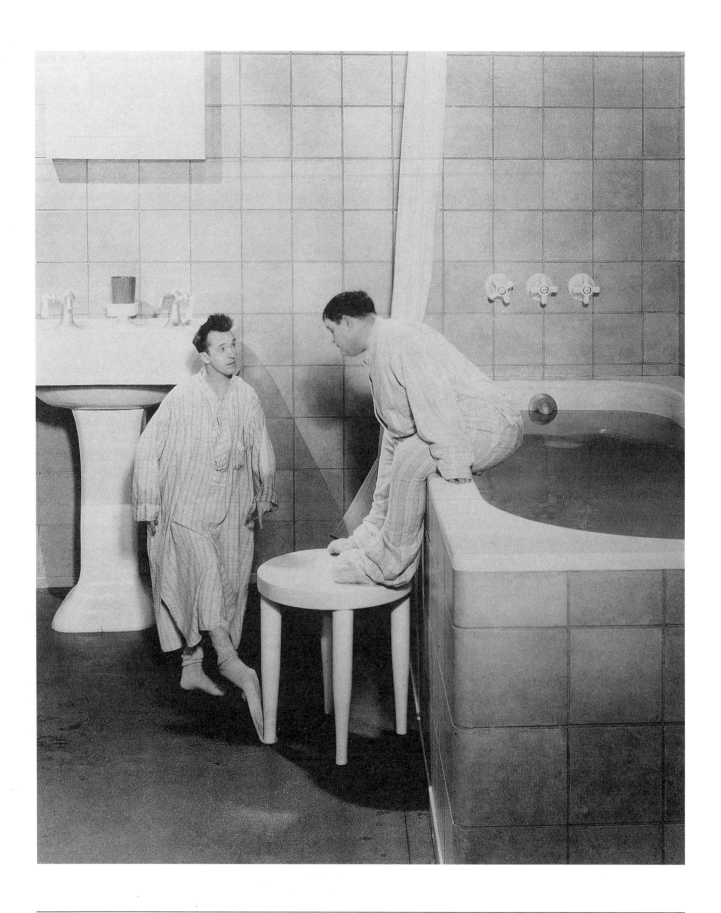

Laurel and Hardy

6935 HOLLYWOOD

Pola Negri 🎥

Pola Negri

6935 Hollywood

Actress

BORN Appolonia Chalupec; Dec. 31, 1894, in Poland. **SPOTLIGHTS** She arrived in Hollywood during the Roaring Twenties, when the champagne poured freely and the stars lived out their wildest dreams. This black-haired beauty with fair skin and dark red lips strolled with her tiger (on a leash) down Sunset Boulevard! Her romance with Rudolph Valentino was front-page news and the envy of millions of women worldwide. And her dalliance with Charlie Chaplin was not chopped liver either. She was dubbed "The Dark Pole" for her sultry, exotic looks. Films include *The Cheat* (1923), *Forbidden Paradise* (1924), *Good and Naughty* (1926), *Hotel Imperial* and *Barbed Wire* (both 1927). **SIDELIGHTS** She bought hundreds of bottles of imported perfume each year. **QUOTE** A reporter asked her: "At what time in your life did you do the hardest work?" "Now," she answered promptly. "Because when I was young and unknown, I had very few people to criticize the way I did things. Today there are millions of people who have that right. If I am to please all those who see my pictures, I must work harder than ever before in my life." Died: 1987.

Lee Majors 📺

Lee Majors

6935 Hollywood

Actor

BORN April 23, 1942, in Wyandotte, MI. **SPOTLIGHTS** Orphaned when he was an infant, Majors was later adopted. Then, in his early 20s, and at a million-to-one odds, he landed the plum role of Heath Barkley in "The Big Valley" (1965-'69). He made television history of sorts, as it was his *first* audition, and he had only taken acting lessons for six months. Majors also had the extremely good fortune of working with the show's star, Barbara Stanwyck. Stanwyck, one of motion picture's all-time finest actresses, was a generous, kind and thoughtful talent. She offered him expert acting advice, dramatic tips and support. He came out of the action-filled Western adventure series a pro. Next, he went high-tech as super hero Colonel Steve Austin, in "The Six Million Dollar Man" (1974-'78). His character, an astronaut, had been critically injured when testing a moon-landing craft in the desert. Doctors implanted atomic-powered devices into him in an effort to save his life. In doing so, they made him a bionic man, with machine-like strength and rocket speed to catch international villains and mad scientists. Majors won international fame in the role. In the 1980s he played Hollywood stuntman Colt Seavers in "The Fall Guy." Films include *Will Penny* (1968), and *High Noon, Part II: The Return of Will Kane* (1980). His former wife is actress Farrah Fawcett. Majors received his Walk of Fame star on Sept. 5, 1984.

Robert Young 🎥

Robert Young

6935 Hollywood

Actor

BORN Feb. 22, 1907, in Chicago, IL. **SPOTLIGHTS** Six feet tall with brown eyes and a wholesome demeanor, Young was both a supporting and leading man in films. He played every woman's dream of a decent, dependable husband, and every boy's ideal father. Motion pictures include *Strange Interlude* (1932), starring Norma Shearer and Clark Gable; *The Bride Comes Home* (1935), with Fred MacMurray; and *Florian* (1940), with Helen Gilbert. He was wonderful in *The Enchanted Cottage* (1945). He co-stars opposite Dorothy McGuire and Herbert Marshall in this love story about inner beauty when a man returns horribly disfigured from the war. Young, though, became immortalized in a role he originated on radio in "Father Knows Best." He starred as Jim Anderson, a loving father and warm family man. The program moved successfully to TV (1954-'63). Later, he starred as the caring physician "Marcus Welby, M.D." (1969-'76). In real life, he had been a medical student. **ACHIEVEMENTS** 1956 and 1957 Emmys for "Father Knows Best." 1970 Emmy for "Marcus Welby, M.D." Happily married since 1932: "We're still in love." **QUOTE** "Sooner or later everything I've ever wanted has come to me...I've been so lucky." Died: 1998.

Lou Rawls 🎵

6935 Hollywood

Singer

BORN Dec. 1, 1935, in Chicago, IL. **SPOTLIGHTS** Raised in the South Side of Chicago where he sang in church, he joined the gospel group The Pilgrim Travelers in the 1950s. Then, he enlisted in the Army and served in the U.S. Army 82nd Airborne Division (1956-58). Upon his honorable discharge, he toured with singer Sam Cooke. While traveling to a concert the two were in a horrible auto accident. Cooke was fine, but Rawls was pronounced dead at the scene! He lay in a coma for five days clutching life, before regaining consciousness. Once out of bed, he sang the blues for a few years. Singing R&B/Pop hit big for Rawls in the 1960s: "Love Is a Hurtin' Thing," and "Dead End Street." 1970s: "You'll Never Find Another Love Like Mine," "See You When I Git There," "Lady Love," "Let Me Be Good to You." TV: Acting ("77 Sunset Strip"), variety shows, and voiceovers for "Garfield the Cat" Specials. Films: *Believe in Me* (1971). **ACHIEVEMENTS** 1961, 1971, and 1977 Grammys. He has several gold and platinum albums, including *Lou Rawls Live;* and *All Things in Time.* A tremendous humanitarian, he has raised more than $110 million for African-American colleges.

Larry Semon 🎥   6935 Hollywood

Actor, producer, director, screenwriter
BORN July 16, 1889, in West Point, MI. **SPOTLIGHTS** A casualty of fame, his meteoric rise to stardom included a brief worldwide popularity that rivaled top silent screen comedians, more money than he ever dreamed existed, and marriage to two beautiful actresses—not simultaneously. Pictures include *Spooks and Spasms* (1917) and *Babes and Boobs* (1918). Died: 1928.

Paul Williams ⏺   6933 Hollywood

Singer, songwriter, actor
BORN Sept. 19, 1940, in Omaha, NE. **SPOTLIGHTS** After working as a motion picture set painter and stuntman, he was cast as a 10-year-old genius in the movie *The Loved One* (1964). He was 24 years old at the time. In *The Chase* (1966) starring Marlon Brando, he plays a hooligan in the drama. While not busying shooting—and there's ample down time during a film—Willliams picked up a pen and began writing songs. He quickly discovered he had a natural talent for it. The following year the gifted writer teamed up with lyricist Roger Nichols to write songs for The Carpenters ("We've Only Just Begun" and "Rainy Days and Mondays"), Helen Reddy ("You and Me Against the World"), and Three Dog Night ("An Old Fashioned Love Song"). He has also scored numerous films: Title song, *Grease* (1978); *The Muppet Movie* (1979); *Rocky IV* (1984). He continued to act, in *Smokey and the Bandit* (1977-'83 series), and *The Doors* (1991). **ACHIEVEMENTS** 1976 Oscar for the song "Evergreen" (*A Star is Born*). 1976 Grammy.

Jon Hall 📷   6933 Hollywood

See page 178

The Carpenters ⏺   6933 Hollywood

Singers, musicians
BORN Richard, Oct.15,1945; Karen, March 2,1950; both in New Haven, CT. **SPOTLIGHTS** This sister and brother singing team were discovered by Herb Alpert, who signed them to his A&M label in 1969. Karen's unique, throaty delivery complemented Richard's style with vocal harmony. Their densely-layered, pop-oriented tunes propelled them to stardom. Million-sellers: "Close to You," "We've Only Just Begun," "Rainy Days and Mondays," "Superstar," "It's Going to Take Some Time," "Hurting Each Other," "Goodbye to Love," "Sing," "Yesterday Once More," "Top of the World," "I Won't Last a Day Without You," "Please Mr. Postman," and "Only Yesterday." Although the duo had a sweet image, Karen is acknowledged by female rock musicians such as Chrissie Hynde, Madonna, and Sheryl Crow as a "pioneer." **ACHIEVEMENTS** 1970 Academy Award, Best Song, "For All We Know." **SIDELIGHTS** Richard studied classical piano at Yale, while Karen played the drums. Died: Karen, in 1982, of cardiac arrest caused by anorexia nervosa. In 1988, a sensitive, made-for-TV movie "The Karen Carpenter Story" told her life story.

Glenn Ford 🎥   6933 Hollywood

Glenn Ford

Actor
BORN Gwyllyn Newton; May 1, 1916, in Quebec, Canada. **SPOTLIGHTS** His breakthrough role, as a nasty and twisted hero, came opposite the gorgeous Rita Hayworth in *Gilda* (1946). Ford, though, is best known for his relaxed sincerity, likable screen presence and meticulous care he brings to each role. He's incredibly versatile and very good in dramas, comedies, westerns, action-adventure and romance films. He is a superb craftsman. After making 60 films he quipped, "Heck, I'm no actor. I just act as a hobby. My real business is stamp collecting." A selection of his 90 motion pictures include *Texas* (1941), *The Big Heat* (1953), *Human Desire* (1954), *The Blackboard Jungle* (1955), *Teahouse of the August Moon* (1956), *The Fastest Gun Alive* (1956), *Don't Go Near the Water* (1957), *Pocketful of Miracles* (1961), *Experiment in Terror* (1962), *The Courtship of Eddie's Father* (1963), *Midway* (1976), and *Superman* (1978). **ACHIEVEMENTS** He served as a sergeant in the U.S. Marine Corps in WWII, then after the war received his commission in the Naval Reserve achieving the rank of Captain, before his military retirement. **QUOTE** "Nobody survived more bad pictures than I have. I've done some of the worst dogs ever released."

Jerry Weintraub 🎥   6933 Hollywood

Jerry Weintraub (right) and Johnny Grant

Producer, manager, promoter

BORN Jerome Weintraub; Sept. 26, 1937, in New York, NY. **SPOTLIGHTS** As a producer he made *Oh God!* (1977), starring George Burns playing the Almighty One, and John Denver—in his screen debut—as the one chosen to spread the Good Word. His motion picture *Diner* (1982) proved to be an excellent vehicle for a group of at-the-time unknown talents, such as Steve Guttenberg, Daniel Stern, Mickey Rourke, Kevin Bacon, and Ellen Barkin. His *Karate Kid* (1984) knocked blocks off the competition and spawned a number of sequels. Other films include *Vegas Vacation* (1997), and *The Avengers* (1998). He has been involved with the production of more than 100 television specials. Earlier in his career he managed top talents: the Beach Boys, Neil Diamond, Bob Dylan, and Waylon Jennings. **ACHIEVEMENTS** 1974 Emmy for "John Denver's Rocky Mountain Christmas."

Gloria De Haven 🎞   6933 Hollywood

Actress, vocalist

BORN July 23, 1926, in Los Angeles, CA. **SPOTLIGHTS** She got her break at age nine, while visiting her father, an assistant director, on the set of Charlie Chaplin's *Modern Times* (1936). The great director himself selected her to be in his film. Cast as one of Paulette Goddard's sisters, Chaplin said she was "perfect" for the role of a tattered kid running away from a truant officer. From this role as an extra, she enjoyed a bit role in Chaplin's important political satire film, *The Great Dictator* (1940). This pretty young lady with photogenic high cheekbones became a popular starlet. MGM utilized her wonderful singing voice in their musical revues including *Thousands Cheer* (1943). Delightful in *The Thin Man Goes Home* (1944), she was charming and funny in *Summer Holiday* (1948) starring Mickey Rooney. She also sang during the Big Band era in Bob Crosby's band. In 1997 she appears in *Out to Sea* with

Walter Matthau and Jack Lemmon. In 2000, she starred in a celebration of the "Classic Hollywood Musicals" at the Pasadena Civic.

Gail Russell 🎥   6933 Hollywood

Actress

BORN Sept. 21, 1924, in Chicago, IL. **SPOTLIGHTS** Russell had it all. A beautiful oval face. Large eyes. Full lips. Dark, thick curly hair. A Paramount contract. At age 19 she made *Henry Aldrich Gets Glamor* (1943), but is best remembered for her roles as the helpless heroine. In *The Uninvited* (1944), she plays a woman haunted by the ghost of her dead mother; and in the supernatural melodrama, *Night Has a Thousand Eyes* (1948), a former vaudeville clairvoyant (Edward G. Robinson) predicts tragedy for her. Died: 1961.

Guy Madison 🎙   6933 Hollywood

See page 123

Ward Bond 📺   6933 Hollywood

Ward Bond

Actor

BORN April 9, 1903, in Denver, CO. **SPOTLIGHTS** While playing on the USC Trojan football field, director John Ford spotted him. Ford told his assistant, "Get me that one with the ugly face." Ford also recruited Bond's teammate and roommate, John Wayne. Both of these large, strapping men made good in Hollywood. Bond, like the Duke, became one of Ford's favorite actors, and the three men often worked together. Bond appeared in a number of John Ford films, including his screen debut in *Salute* (1929), *The Long Voyage Home* (1940), *The Grapes of Wrath* (1940), *Tobacco Road* (1941), *They Were Expendable* (1945), *Wagon Master* (1950), *The Quiet Man* (1952), *The Long Gray Line* (1955), and *Mister Roberts* (1955—which Ford co-directed). Born with an aggressive nature and jutting lip, he relished playing a rowdy heavy in countless Westerns and war pictures. Occasionally, he was cast as a good guy. Bond was an important and reliable supporting actor in some 150 films, and made, on average, $250,000-a-film. He stated, "I preferred not to be the star. When a director wanted Ward Bond, no other actor would do. Who else has a face like mine?" **TV** He was the California-bound wagon master Major Seth Adams (1957-'60) on "Wagon Train." This was one of television's biggest and most popular Westerns, set in the post-Civil War days. After working in Hollywood for four decades, Bond was enjoying his greatest fame on the

"Wagon Train" series. It was during this happy period of his life when he suffered a massive heart attack while taking a shower and died in 1960.

Herb Alpert 🎵   6933 Hollywood

Musician, songwriter, executive
BORN March 31, 1936, in Los Angeles, CA. **SPOTLIGHTS** Affectionately known as "the King of South of the Border." This trumpet virtuoso began taking lessons at age eight. He played while serving in the U.S. Army. Busy days required he perform taps for up to 20 military funerals a day. After his honorable discharge, he attended USC for a brief time, then in 1962 became co-founder of A&M Records with Jerry Moss. Each man had to scrape together $100 to form the company. They worked out of Alpert's garage. He was also band leader of the instrumental group, Tijuana Brass. Their distinct "Ameriachi" style music (Americanization of the mariachi) and first hit "The Lonely Bull" made enormous sound waves around the world that same year. Of the stylized group, he once said, "The seven who made up the TJB sound were not of Spanish-American descent. We were four salamis, two bagels and an American cheese." Alpert built A&M Records on hits like "The Lonely Bull" (1962), "A Taste of Honey" (1965), "This Guy's in Love with You" (1968), "Diamonds" (1969)— featuring Janet Jackson, "Rise" (1979) and signing such groups as The Carpenters and recording artists as Carole King, Cat Stevens, and later rock 'n' roll artists Styx, Peter Frampton, Sting, and the versatile Janet Jackson. Alpert's albums include *Under a Spanish Moon* (1988), *North on South Street* (1991) and *Midnight Sun* (1992). **ACHIEVEMENTS** Three Grammy Awards for "A Taste of Honey" in 1965; 1966, Two Grammy Awards for "My Love" in 1966; 1979 Grammy for "Rise." In 1990 Alpert and Moss sold their record company for more than $500 million.

Claire Trevor 🎥   6933 Hollywood

Claire Trevor

Actress
BORN Claire Wemlinger; March 8, 1909, in New York, NY. **SPOTLIGHTS** Trevor attended the American Academy of Dramatic Arts, worked onstage, then made her screen debut in the Western *Life in the Raw* (1933). A man's star, she played the hard-drinking broad, saucy show girl, wisecracking newsgal, or gangster sidepiece. Somehow Trevor managed to breathe new life into these cynical, tough and warm-hearted characters and remained steadily employed for decades, as well as being adored by the public. Motion pictures include *Dante's Inferno* (1935), opposite Spencer Tracy, John Ford's landmark Western *Stagecoach* (1939), as a prostitute named Dallas opposite John Wayne in his breakthrough role as Ringo Kid, *I Stole a Million* (1939), with George Raft, *Dark Command* (1940), opposite John Wayne again, *Texas* (1941), with William Holden and Glenn Ford, *Murder My Sweet* (1945), co-starring Dick Powell, Robert Wise's *Born to Kill* (1947), *Man Without a Star* (1955) opposite Kirk Douglas, *The Stripper* (1963), opposite Joanne Woodward, and *How to Murder Your Wife* (1965), with Jack Lemmon. **ACHIEVEMENTS** 1948 Best Supporting Actress Oscar for *Key Largo* (1948), playing gangster Edward G. Robinson's boozy moll. She was Academy Award-nominated two other times for: William Wyler's *Dead End* (1937), as Humphrey Bogart's streetwalking ex-girlfriend, and *The High and the Mighty* (1954), as a loose lady opposite John Wayne. **QUOTE** "I never liked to see myself in any of my pictures. I didn't like myself in any movie I did." Died: 2000.

Tito Puente 🎵   6933 Hollywood

Tito Puente

Musician, composer, conductor
BORN Ernesto Anthony Puente, Jr., April 20, 1923, in New York, NY. **SPOTLIGHTS** A legendary Latin jazz master, he brought his music into the American mainstream. The percussionist-arranger's rhythmic history covers 50 years beginning with his days as a teenager. At age 15, his paying gigs included drumming for a society band in Miami Beach. Admiring the big bands of Benny Goodman and Duke Ellington, yet greatly influenced by Cuban music, he became an expert on many instruments and styles. After serving three years in the Navy, he completed his formal education using the G.I. bill at the Juilliard School of Music. He studied conducting, orchestration and theory. Puente's signature sound became popular as a mix of spicy dance beats and red-hot jam sessions, incorporating jazz harmonies and extended improvisation into his music. He is a master drummer, pianist, saxophonist, percussionist, and vocalist. His other musical gifts have earned him the titles of composer, conductor, arranger and orchestrator. As a band leader with his Latin Jazz Ensemble, he has won international critical acclaim, performing on stage, in TV, and in film, including *The Mambo Kings* (1992). This beloved musical giant is affectionately adored by millions of fans. **ACHIEVEMENTS** Four Grammy Awards. Puente has recorded more than 100 albums. His Hollywood Walk of Fame star was dedicated on August 14, 1990. It is a permanent tribute to this great artist. His wonderful recordings on the Concord Records label: *On Broadway*; *Mambo Diablo*; and *Goza Mi Timbal.*

Lois Wilson 🎥   6933 Hollywood

Actress

BORN June 28, 1896, in Pittsburgh, PA. **SPOTLIGHTS** A youthful schoolteacher, she broke into show business as an extra. Her career spanned six decades—starting during the silent era. Among her 100 credits are James Cruze's classic Western *The Covered Wagon* (1923), *Ruggles of Red Gap* (1923), *The Great Gatsby* (1926), *Bright Eyes* (1934—with Shirley Temple singing "On the Good Ship Lollipop"), and *Wedding Present* (1936). **QUOTE** "What Chance Has the Extra Girl in Pictures? This is a more difficult question to answer than it really appears to be. I was once an extra girl myself and I'm not ever going to forget it when another girl comes to me for advice. I would answer the question this way: If you have that 'something'—call it personality—which lifts you above the common run of humanity, if you have special talents—riding, dancing, swimming, etc.—if you have the instinct for pantomime and are intelligent, and if you photograph well, why— then I should say you have a pretty good chance. But it is well to remember that less than one in 500 of the girls who play as extras ever reach stardom. Possession of merely a pretty face will not get you by in competition for screen work today. Just one more thing: I would urge you not to come to Hollywood with the sole idea of working in the 'movies.' It is unfortunately true that there has been such an influx of talented boys and girls that there are literally a hundred applicants for every bit to be played." Died: 1983.

Casey Kasem 🎙   6933 Hollywood

Casey and Jean Kasem

Disc jockey, TV host, actor
BORN Kemal Amen Kasem, April 27, 1932, in Detroit, MI. **SPOTLIGHTS** He is the smooth-voiced, easy-going, articulate creator and host (1970-'88) of the popular radio program "American Top 40," a music countdown heard around the world. Since 1989, he has hosted "Casey's Top 40," "Casey's Hot 20" and other shows on Westwood One Entertainment. His countless voiceover jobs include Shaggy on the animated "Scooby Doo," and Robin on "Batman and Robin," among 2000 other cartoons. He first acted on professional radio at age 18 in "The Lone Ranger" in Detroit, Michigan. During military service he performed in radio drama on the Armed Forces Network in Korea. Later, a full-time disc jockey in Detroit, Cleveland, Buffalo, then in Oakland, where he developed the now widely used "teaser/bio" format. His station manager there told him to change his format and quit doing wild comedy characters; instead, describe the artists and their music. Just minutes before his next show—still stuck for ideas—Casey found a discarded copy of *Who's Who in Pop Music*, 1962, atop a trash barrel wedged in the studio's doorway. The magazine was full of short biographies of recording artists, just what he needed! "I pulled my career out of a trash barrel," Casey quipped. And he's talked about the artists ever since. Relocating to Los Angeles in 1963, he continued broadcasting, then branched into acting in commercials, TV, and motion pictures. One of the highlights from the "American Top 40" radio show is the legendary long-distance dedication segment dealing with requests and dedications from listeners. His famous upbeat sign-off: "Keep your feet on the ground and keep reaching for the stars!" **ACHIEVEMENTS** He was the youngest inducted member into the National Association of Broadcasters' Radio Hall of Fame. Recipient of numerous honors for activist work in social and humanitarian causes. **HIGHLIGHTS** Married to Jean Kasem, a statuesque blonde actress lauded by *People* magazine as "the dumbest blonde in the history of television" for her comedic presence. This talent has proven adept in dramatic roles, too. She is also CEO of the *Little Miss Liberty Round Crib Company* and *Little Miss Liberty of Beverly Hills* that manufactures round cribs and a full service nursery line of products that are safer by design. For information, contact (800) RND-CRIB (E-mail: liberty@crib.com. Website: www.crib.com). The company's name was inspired by their daughter, Liberty. Casey's three adult children from a prior marriage are Kerri, Michael and Julie.

John Charles Thomas 🎵   6933 Hollywood

Opera singer

BORN Sept. 6, 1891, in Meyersdale, PA. **SPOTLIGHTS** Known as "America's beloved baritone," Thomas was as American as apple pie, but openly admired Italy's superior musical culture. He stated, "The adult Italian was singing arias when he was a child; Americans were singing 'Yes, We Have No Bananas.'" This lusty, charming baritone—with a warm, rich, powerful voice—started by performing in music halls, then singing light opera. He made his grand opera debut in *Pagliacci* as Tonio at the Theatre de la Monnaie, in Brussels. A huge bear of a man, he made his American operatic debut in Verdi's *Aida* (his favorite opera) at President Coolidge's inauguration, in Washington, DC. He triumphed with every opera company he worked with across the United States. Thomas sang with the Los Angeles Civic Light Opera House (1930-'34), then made his spectacular Metropolitan Opera debut in 1934 in *Traviata*. He stayed with the Met for a decade. He was a celebrated vocalist on radio's "Bell Telephone Hour" (1942-'47), and his own NBC show (1943-'46) where the theme song was "Home on the Range" (sung hardily). Thomas was also a popular screen, and TV personality...Known for his sense of humor and preference for comfort over style, he often showed up barefooted for rehearsals. Died: 1960.

Bruce Lee 🎥   6933 Hollywood

Bruce Lee

Actor, author

BORN Lee Yuen Kam; Nov. 27, 1940, in the Hour of the Dragon, in the Year of the Dragon, in San Francisco, CA. He was later known by the name Lee Siu Yoong (it means "Little Dragon"). **SPOTLIGHTS** The son of a Chinese opera star—Lee Hoi-chuen—the child's theatrical ambitions and talents appeared almost immediately. When his family returned to live in Hong Kong, Lee made his motion picture debut at age six. Even then his charisma was evident; he immediately became a child star in dozens of Chinese films. At 18 he returned to the U.S. intent on becoming a movie star. He also set out to simplify, harmonize and modernize the art of Kung Fu. A true Zen philosopher, Lee created the method of Jeet Kune Do, more a spiritual discipline than a fighting system. Passionate, focused, intense, he was a master of martial arts with a style of fighting uniquely his own. He hand picked the best moves from every other type of martial art, assembling them into an unbeatable force. Using his athletic talents and his magnetic personality he won his breakthrough role in America. He first displayed his unique talents in the television series "The Green Hornet" (1966-'67). He played the supporting role of Kato. Lee was so fast that the director had him slow down his rapid-fire kicking and punching so that the camera could catch it. Although it lasted only one season, when he returned to Hong Kong he was surprised to find out he had risen to legendary status. The show in Asia was a huge hit known as "The Kato Show." He was mobbed by fans everywhere. In 1971 he made his first martial arts film, *The Big Boss* (known in America as *Fists of Fury*), on a modest budget. It broke all previous box office records in Asia. By showcasing his electrifying presence Lee instantly achieved movie superstar status in Asia and attracted a cult-like following in America. Fans—such as Sugar Ray Leonard— began to follow his straight and narrow path of discipline and clean living. His other motion pictures overseas surpassed all box office expectations. Still Hollywood showed prejudice in hiring Asians. In the early 1970s Lee co-created and co-developed the television series "Kung Fu" as a star vehicle for himself. Narrow-minded network executives declared he looked "too Chinese" and gave the role to David Carradine, a Caucasian. Carradine was good in it, but the series would have been spectacular if Lee had

been allowed to do his part. Finally, the dynamic actor got a starring role in an American-made film, *Enter the Dragon* (1973). A phenomenal success, it shot him into the stratosphere as a global superstar, and especially important to him, in America, his main objective. Now a classic, it was unfortunately to be his only American-made picture. **ACHIEVEMENTS** Revered for breaking Hollywood's color barrier against Asian actors, as a Eurasian youth growing up in Hong Kong, he was subject to much prejudice, as he was in the United States later. He popularized martial arts around the world and paved the way for motion picture and television *action heroes*. He became an inspiration—*and remains an inspiration*—to millions of fans by personally overcoming the many obstacles life dealt him. His nearsightedness was so severe he was almost legally blind. He suffered from a speech impediment, had one leg shorter than the other and was epileptic. He overcame all these problems by creating his own self-help philosophy. **HIGHLIGHTS** He married a blonde American beauty, Linda Emery, who proved to be a key guiding force in his life's work. The devoted husband became the devoted father of a daughter, and a son, Brandon, who followed in his footsteps. Bruce Lee died in 1972, at age 32, from a stroke brought on by taking the wrong medicine. More than 25,000 people attended his funeral in Hong Kong. Laid to rest in Seattle, his cemetery plot has become a pilgrimage for devotees. In 1993 *Dragon— The Bruce Lee Story* hit big as a feature film. Loosely based on his wife's book, *Bruce Lee: The Man Only I Knew*, it is an exciting biography of the martial arts hero. He was honored posthumously with a Hollywood Walk of Fame star on April 28, 1993, directly in front of the west corner of the world-famous Chinese Theatre. **RECOMMENDED** Learn more about Bruce Lee from the legend's own words. *The Bruce Lee Library* by Bruce Lee and edited by John Little, published by Tuttle Publishing, is a twelve-volume series of books. Available at bookstores, or by calling 800.526.2778.

Dorothy McGuire 🎥   6933 Hollywood

Actress, singer

BORN June 14, 1918, in Omaha, NE. **SPOTLIGHTS** Under David O. Selznick's wing, and encouraged by producer John Golden, McGuire stars in her first film, *Claudia* (1943). This very pretty, light-haired leading lady with an open face and kind eyes was wonderful in *The Enchanted Cottage* (1945), a love story. She co-stars opposite Robert Young and Herbert Marshall. It is about discovering inner beauty when a man returns horribly disfigured from the war. She was outstanding as the deaf-mute servant in the spooky suspense thriller *The Spiral Staircase* (1946). Her Oscar-nominated performance in *Gentleman's Agreement* (1947) opposite Gregory Peck was flawless. She co-stars opposite Burt Lancaster and Edmund Gwenn in the comedy, *Mister 880* (1950). *Three Coins in the Fountain* (1954) remains a classic 1950s romance-fantasy picture. She stars opposite Glenn Ford in *Trial* (1955), about a witch hunt. McGuire moved into wholesome character roles for Walt

Disney in *Old Yeller* (1957) and *The Swiss Family Robinson* (1960). TV includes *Rich Man, Poor Man* (1976), among others. **SIDELIGHTS** Educated in a convent in Indianapolis, Indiana. **ACHIEVEMENTS** Co-Founded the famed La Jolla Playhouse in Southern California with Gregory Peck, Jennifer Jones, Joseph Cotten and Mel Ferrer in 1946.

Glen Campbell ●   6927 Hollywood

Glen Campbell

Singer, guitarist, host
BORN April 22, 1936, in Delight, AR. **SPOTLIGHTS** If you believe in lucky numbers, Campbell is the seventh son of a seventh son. Although born to a poor sharecropper, his voice and music earned him fame and fortune. This country-pop star had two hits in 1967—"Gentle on My Mind" and "By the Time I Get to Phoenix"—which shot him to stardom. Other hits include "Wichita Lineman," "Rhinestone Cowboy," "Gentle on My Mind," "Southern Nights," and "Country Boy (You Got Your Feet in L.A.)." TV: "The Glen Campbell Goodtime Hour" (1969-'72) was a variety program that showcased country singers and comedy sketches. Films include *True Grit* (1969) starring John Wayne. He performs live at his Goodtime Theatre, in Branson, Missouri. **ACHIEVEMENTS** Grammys: 1967 (four); 1968 Album of the Year. Wrote *Rhinestone Cowboy: An Autobiography* in 1994. **QUOTE** He finally found inner peace saying, "I have a ministry in my music, much of which is focused on God and all of which is performed for God."

Hattie McDaniel ▯   6927 Hollywood

See page 144

Army Archerd ■   6927 Hollywood

Journalist, host
BORN Armand Archerd; Jan. 13, 1923, in New York, NY. **SPOTLIGHTS** Archerd is "Hollywood's Must-Read." He initially trained as a reporter for the Associated Press and a local Los Angeles newspaper. He joined Associated Press Hollywood Bureau in 1945 and became an immediate success in making friends throughout the entertainment industry. Gifted at cultivating great sources, always remaining tactful and diplomatic, and maintaining friends decades after decade, Archerd's files contain the world's most sought after personal telephone numbers—which speaks volumes for the man himself. This well-respected and admired newsman is also the town's hardest

Army Archerd (center), his wife Selma, Johnny Grant (left, kneeling), Bill Welsh (right, kneeling), family, and celebrity friends: Marty Allen (left), James Stewart, and Carol Burnett.

working columnist. Under pressure to report the inside scoop—the *exclusive* news—on a *daily* basis, Archerd has utilized a system to stay competitive. He takes calls himself, without a secretary running interference. He remains sincerely excited over the genius and creativity of show business—the art of the business, as well as the deal. He takes time to meet each newcomer on a one-to-one basis. In doing so, he has survived and thrived with four different generations of stars. His column, entitled "Just for Variety," has appeared in the *Daily Variety* show business trade paper since 1953. Although his name may not be widely recognized outside the industry, everyone who's anyone, or hopes to be, reads "The Column." If you're Somebody in Hollywood, you're in Army. **HIGHLIGHTS** It is estimated that he has broken more news stories than any other Hollywood entertainment writer. He has also broken key stories (that ultimately affect the global population). He revealed that Rock Hudson had died from AIDS. Archerd said, "It turned out to be the most important Hollywood story of all time, really, because it created a sensitivity about the most horrible plague that has ever hit the world. And everyone, including journalists at the *L.A. Times* and *New York Times* agreed that had I not printed the story, Rock Hudson might have died of liver cancer, and AIDS would never have been the subject." His disclosure had the whole world talking about the disease. **TV** Fans have seen Archerd interviewing and welcoming the glamorous parade of stars on the red carpet leading into the annual Academy Awards ceremonies. A frequent guest star on various other shows, he appears regularly on E! cable television's the "Gossip Show." **ACHIEVEMENTS** Among his many honors, he is the founder/president of the Hollywood Press Club, and recipient of numerous "Newsman" awards. His momentous Walk of Fame dedication ceremony occurred on June 27, 1984.

Lefty Frizzel ●   6927 Hollywood

Country-and-western performer
BORN William Orville Frizzel; March 31, 1928, in Corsicana, TX. **SPOTLIGHTS** The Honky-Tonk Man, his first job was his own radio show (KELD in El Dorado, Arkansas) when he was 12 years old. He became one of the greatest male country singers post-WWII, and one of the most influential country vocalists of all time. He sang with an open, warm tonal quality and soulful resonance. He wrote many of his own songs, the first ("I Love You a Thousand Ways") while in jail. His original record, "If You've Got the Money (Honey), I've Got the Time," and "I Love You a Thousand Ways," sold at the incredible rate of 42,000 copies daily. Top ten hits: "Always Late," "Mom & Dad's Waltz," "Don't Stay Away," and "Forever." He did the folk-flavored ballad, "The Long Black Veil," then did the story-song, "Saginaw, Michigan." In the 1960s, Lefty recorded the masterpiece "Honky Tonk Stardust Cowboy." In 1982, he was inducted into the Country Music Hall of Fame. Lefty's "It Hurts to Face Reality" became the theme song for the Academy Award- winning movie *Tender Mercies* (1983), starring Robert Duvall. **SIDELIGHTS** When he was a teenager, he earned his nickname "Lefty" after punching an eye of a schoolyard bully. The name stuck as he grew into a feisty, rambunctious, hard-drinking adult. Died: 1975; he stubbornly refused to take his high-blood pressure medicine because he'd have to give up booze.

Michael Jackson ●   6927 Hollywood

Michael Jackson

Singer, actor
BORN Aug. 29, 1958, in Gary, IN. **SPOTLIGHTS** He enjoyed one of the most successful careers of any contemporary performer. Formerly teamed with family members, he became even more famous on his own. His *Off the Wall* and *Thriller* solo albums crossed pop, rhythm and blues, jazz, and rock 'n' roll. *Thriller* was the highest selling album, until 1997 when the rock group the Eagles tied with Jackson matching record sales. He has enjoyed an unprecedented number of singles on the chart, including "Don't Stop 'Til You Get Enough," "Billie Jean," and "Beat It." Recipient of numerous Grammys, and countless music awards, his Nov. 10, 1984 Walk of Fame star dedication ceremony was witnessed by thousands of screaming fans.

Lupe Velez 🎥   6927 Hollywood

Actress, dancer
BORN Maria Velez de Vallalobos; July 18, 1908, in Mexico City, Mexico. **SPOTLIGHTS** She was a gorgeous, dark eyed, dark haired, temper-tantrum-throwing artist. In the 1920s she appeared opposite a slew of handsome hunks including Douglas Fairbanks in *The Gaucho* (1927), and Gary Cooper in *Wolf Song* (1929). Velez stars with Warner Baxter in the important remake of the classic *Squaw Man* (1931). Other films are *Hot Pepper* (1933), *Palooka* (1934), and *The Girl From Mexico* (1939). RKO fashioned the *Mexican Spitfire* (1940) comedy series around her. "Tarzan" Johnny Weissmuller and she endured a tempestuous marriage (1933-'38)...The spirited Velez was a die-hard boxing fan, who joined other celebrities at the Hollywood Post of the American Legion each Friday night. Hers was not a quiet crowd. Along with the zany Marx Brothers, and other A-list types, they shouted and cheered for the fighters. until the wee hours of the morning. Died: 1944.

Tommy Lee Jones 🎥   6925 Hollywood

Actor

Tommy Lee Jones

BORN Sept. 15, 1946, in San Saba, TX. **SPOTLIGHTS** He is a macho, intense, brooding artist who exudes confidence. A man's man, he typically plays figures of authority, but is convincing as a villain. In 1969 Jones made his Broadway debut in John Osborne's "A Patriot For Me." His first film role was in Arthur Hiller's *Love Story* (1970). He made a number of films and TV movies, giving a solid performance as Loretta Lynn's husband in *Coal Miner's Daughter* (1980), and becoming an Emmy nominee for his exceptional performance in the Western mini-series "Lonesome Dove." Motion pictures include *Rolling Thunder* (1977), *The River Rat* (1984), *Black Moon Rising* (1986), *The Big Town* (1987), *JFK* (1991), *Under Siege* (1992), *The Client* (1994), *Blown Away* (1994), *Blue Sky* (1994), *Cobb* (1994), *Natural Born Killers* (1994), *Batman Forever* (1995), the cartoon-like, sci-fi blast *Men in Black* (1997), *Small Soldiers* (1998—voiceover), and *Double Jeopardy* (1999). Jones' ruggedness is uniquely complemented by his intelligence, creating a potent aphrodisiac; a combination far more devastating than mere looks alone. Jones' talents can honestly be compared to Hollywood's best Golden Era artists, such as Spencer Tracy. Both audiences and critics like him. **ACHIEVEMENTS** 1993 Academy Award for Best Supporting Actor in *The Fugitive*. 1992 Best Actor Emmy Award for his portrayal of convicted killer, Gary Gilmore, in "The Executioner's Song." He received his Walk of Fame star on Nov. 30, 1994. **SIDELIGHTS** In his youth, he worked in the local oil fields with his father...He graduated *cum laude* from Harvard University with a degree in English literature; his roommate was future Vice President of the United States, Al Gore.

Mickey Mouse 🎥   6925 Hollywood

Cartoon character

CREATED Nov. 18, 1928, in Hollywood, CA. **SPOTLIGHTS** According to legend, Walt Disney created Mickey Mouse on a train to Hollywood. He originally named him "Mortimer," but Mrs. Disney thought it sounded too haughty and suggested Mickey. In 1928 the animated creature, which seemed to think for itself, made his film debut *in sound* in *Steamboat Willie*. Disney used his own voice for Mickey's squeaky falsetto. At first Disney had a tough time persuading distributors to handle this unique new personality. Studio executives and theatre owners alike thought the mouse would scare ladies from their seats. Refusing to be discouraged, the 26-year-old persevered, and in time was able to get Manhattan's Colony Theater to screen it. The rest is history. Mickey Mouse has starred in many pictures, among them, *Fantasia* (1940). Mickey is well-loved by children and adults alike. **HISTORIC MILITARY NOTE** On D-Day, June 6, 1944, the Allied Forces used "Mickey Mouse" as a code word. **ACHIEVEMENTS** 1931-'32 Special Oscar to Disney "for the creation of Mickey Mouse." Mickey Mouse is one of the most recognizable characters on earth. **QUOTE** Once while television cameras were scanning Disneyland, Walt Disney commented: "I hope we never lose sight of one fact...that this was all started by a Mouse."

Sharon Stone 🎥   6925 Hollywood

Actress

BORN March 10, 1958, in Meadville, PA. **SPOTLIGHTS** As hard as it is to believe, Stone considered herself an ugly duck-

Sharon Stone (holding star plaque), Faye Dunaway, and Johnny Grant share a laugh.

ling while growing up. Her younger sister Kelly got all the dates while the self-proclaimed bookworm stayed home. The tall, skinny teenager with thick glasses could not even get a date to her senior prom. Her destiny changed when she was discovered by Manhattan model agent Eileen Ford during a Christmas school break. The brainy Stone blossomed into an elegant high fashion model on the runways of Paris and Milan, studying acting along the way. Seemingly, she was on the fast track to fame and fortune. But it was not to be. (Stone later reflected, "If I'd gotten really famous really fast back then, I'd be dead now.") Her silver screen debut in Woody Allen's *Stardust Memories* (1980)—as a fleeting vision of a blonde goddess—foreshadowed legendary silver screen status. If she had been born during Hollywood's Golden Era, studio moguls would have rushed to have scripts written for her. Instead she had to singlehandedly fight the actor's movie game where there are neither rules nor fair play. She struggled for four years until she landed the role of the sexy, funny, conniving mistress to Ryan O'Neal's duplicitous character in *Irreconcilable Differences* (1984). It co-stars a young Drew Barrymore dealing with the tough issue of divorcing her immature parents. Although Stone was very, very good in the role, the celluloid gods were intent on making her pay more dues. Her next pictures—*King Solomon's Mines* (1985) and *Police Academy 4* (1987)—would detract rather than enhance her career, although many fans like the support she gave in the action film, *Above the Law* (1988). She exposed herself in *Playboy* magazine, estimating Hollywood executives would take notice of her again (they did). And Stone plays dangerous in the futuristic sci-fi thriller *Total Recall* (1990), opposite Arnold Schwarzenegger. Her breakthrough film was all the more surprising since the piercing beauty was not the first, second, third, or even fourth choice for the role. Nor did Michael Douglas even want her as his co-star. The blonde husky-voiced, determined talent did, of course, eventually win the part that would catapult her to superstardom. She plays the ice-pick murderess in *Basic Instinct* (1992), causing more than a stir in the now-classic police interrogation scene. There was no gambling with her career in *Casino* (1996), starring opposite Robert De Niro and Joe Pesci. She delivers a brilliant and gutsy performance and was Oscar-nominated. Bold and beautiful, this intelligent broad sizzles onscreen. Other films include the animated feature *Antz* (1998--voiceover), and the remake of *Gloria* (1999). Stone also plays the title character in *The Muse* (1999), with Albert Brooks and Jeff Bridges. Both critics and audiences loved her in the comedy, and she garnered a Golden Globe nomination. That same year, she co-stars with Nick Nolte and Jeff Bridges in *Simpatico*, a story of love, betrayal and money, based on Sam Shepard's original play. **WALK OF FAME** What made Stone and her gal pal Faye Dunaway laugh at her Walk of Fame dedication ceremony on Nov. 16, 1995? Johnny Grant whispered into her ear, "I heard that when you were at the U.S. Embassy in France you got the Marines so excited their dog tags were panting." **QUOTE** Her Walk of Fame star was unveiled on Nov. 16, 1995. She graciously commented, "When I a kid in Pennsylvania, I dreamed of coming to Hollywood and becoming a movie star. I'm enchanted. You've made my dreams come true. And I thank you for that."

Sherry Lansing 🎥   6925 Hollywood

Executive

BORN July 31, in Chicago, Illinois. **SPOTLIGHTS** Articulate. Beautiful. Talented. This incredible woman has worked on many of Hollywood's biggest blockbusters, including *The China Syndrome* (1979), *Kramer vs. Kramer* (1979), *9 to 5* (1980), *Chariots of Fire* (1981), *The Verdict* (1982), *Fatal Attraction* (1987), *The Accused* (1988), and *Indecent Proposal* (1993). So who is she? Sherry Lansing is the savvy Chairman of Paramount Pictures Motion Picture Group. Since her 1992 promotion to that position, three of the studio's feature films

Sherry Lansing (center) receives a great birthday present from Hollywood, her own Walk of Fame star (July 31, 1996). Officiating are: Johnny Grant (left) and Leron Gubler (right). Sharing in her joy (in the second row) are: Sharon Stone (wearing white hat), L.A. Mayor Richard Riordan, Michael Douglas, Jackie Goldberg and Lansing's son (partially hidden).

have won the Academy Award for Best Picture: *Forrest Gump* (1994), *Braveheart* (1995), and *Titanic* (1997)—the highest grossing film of all time. Critically acclaimed motion pictures include *Face/Off* (1997), *The Truman Show* and *Saving Private Ryan* (both 1998). But nobody, including Lansing herself, could have predicted her meteoric rise through the studio system. She graduated *cum laude* from Northwestern University with a degree in Speech Communications, then headed to Southern California. Teachers were desperately needed in L.A.'s inner city. Most had been scared off by the violent and bloody Watts Riot. There, in a tough area of Los Angeles that could make strong men faint, she taught high school math, English and drama. After three years, she began pursuing a modeling and acting career. She had a couple of movie roles, then realized acting was not for her. (She later admitted, "I was a *terrible* actress!") She took a $5-an-hour job as a script reader, and driven by ambition rose to executive story editor at MGM. After a stopover at Columbia, Lansing was appointed President of 20th Century-Fox in 1980, the first woman *ever* to head production at a major motion picture studio. About one year earlier, she was questioned about the invisible glass ceiling professional women encountered. She stated, "I doubt that I will see a woman as the president of a movie company in my working lifetime." After her promotion, she remarked, "I'm very happy to have to eat my words. I hope this is the last time a woman holding a position like this will be newsworthy. It should be natural." **QUOTE** "When I was growing up, I loved *Gentleman's Agreement*, *To Kill a Mockingbird*, and *The Pawnbroker*—all movies that came out of somebody's passion. I want to make movies that stir up your emotions, movies where you really root for the people."

Paramount Pictures moguls Sherry Lansing (right) and Jonathan Dolgen, with wife Susan

bling country home to get away from the hustle and bustle of the big city. It was his dream home come true...with one exception. The deal came with a gravelly voiced talking horse named Mr. Ed. (The horse's voice was provided by Allan "Rocky" Lane.) Mr. Ed, a beautiful palomino, would only talk to Wilbur, because Wilbur was the first human being worth talking to. Picked up in syndication, this beloved nonsensical series in still seen worldwide. And that's straight from the horse's mouth.

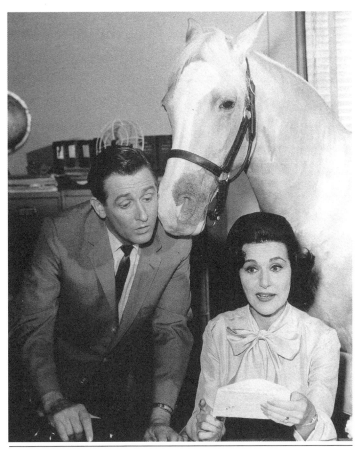

Alan Young receives some good advice from Mr. Ed and Dear Abby.

Alan Young ●   6925 Hollywood

Actor, comic, cartoonist

BORN Angus Young; Nov. 19, 1919, in North Shields, England. **SPOTLIGHTS** Raised and educated in Canada, one of his first acting jobs was in "Stag Party," where he was basically the whole party. When the overworked comic asked radio station CJOR for a raise from his $15-a-week paycheck, they promptly axed him. In search of work, he headed to the States. In America, this delightfully funny, but truly bashful 25-year-old landed his own radio series. "The Alan Young Show" (1944-'49) was a popular 30-minute sitcom. *Newsweek* magazine wrote he was a "meek, washed-down blond with saucer eyes and a perpetual woebegone manner...(with) flashes of Harold Lloyd and Charlie Chaplin." Being compared to legendary silent screen comedy giants did not hurt his career. During this same time, he also worked on the air in "The Jimmy Durante Show," then Young made his silver screen debut in the 1920s musical *Margie* (1946), starring Jeanne Crain. Next, he appears in *Chicken Every Sunday*, and *Mr. Belvedere Goes to College* (both 1949). Other movies include the fairy tale *Tom Thumb* (1958), *The Time Machine* (1960), *The Cat from Outer Space* (1978), *The Great Mouse Detective* (1986—voice-over), *Duck Tales: The Movie* (1990—voice-over), and *Beverly Hills Cop III* (1994). Young, though, gained national fame and became a household name as the fumbling architect, Wilbur Post, on TV's *Mr. Ed* (1961-'65). His character had purchased a ram-

James Garner 📺   6925 Hollywood

James Garner

Actor, producer

BORN James Scott Baumgarner; April 7, 1928, in Norman, OK. **SPOTLIGHTS** Lacking inspiration in high school, Garner dropped out to seek adventure. In 1944, at age 16, he joined the Merchant Marine. After his honorable discharge he met up with his father in Southern California and returned to school to get his degree. He attended Hollywood High, and did some part-time modeling, getting his first taste of show business. Drafted into the Army in 1950, Garner saw combat in Korea (see below). After his honorable discharge in 1952, he enrolled at the University of Oklahoma on the GI bill. He was a gas pump jockey, a traveling salesman, and a carpet installer. With his tall, dark, rugged good looks, he modeled swim trunks. Then an old buddy, Paul Gregory, whom Garner had known when Gregory was a soda jerk, called. Gregory, now a Broadway producer, offered Garner theatrical work in "The Caine Mutiny Court-Martial." Garner became an understudy, cued the principles, and handled costumes. He got his chance to be on stage in the last months of the show, replacing John Hodiak. Although Garner recalled, "I didn't even register beyond the sixth row," he was able to parlay his strapping good looks and his stage credit to land a small part in the new medium of television. It was in the Western "Cheyenne," and Warner Bros. signed him to a contract. Garner quickly acquired the acting skills necessary to make his silver screen debut in *Toward the Unknown* (1956) starring William Holden. He was a natural born talent. Other early motion pictures include the exquisite drama *Sayonara* (1957), the fun comedy *Boys' Night Out* (1962), and the excellent WWII action film *The Great Escape* (1963). He handled each genre with equal aplomb. Returning to the small screen to work for the Warner Bros. television arm, this incredibly videogenic actor won the lead as Bret Maverick on the hit "Maverick" (1957-'60). The series was unique for a Western, as it employed humor and satire without straying too far from the cowboy's beaten path. By now Garner was a huge star, and his horse opera even attracted large numbers of women viewers. Female fans were especially attracted to the divinely handsome hunk who had a twinkle in his eyes. The appealing Garner had conquered both TV and films. Motion pictures include *Move Over, Darling* (1963), *The Americanization of Emily* (1964), *Duel at Diablo* (1966), *Grand Prix* (1966), *Marlowe* (1969), *Support Your Local Sheriff* (1969), *Skin Game* (1971), *Victor/Victoria* (1982), *Murphy's Romance* (1985—in an Academy Award-nominated performance), and *My Fellow Americans* (1996). When his old television series *Maverick* was made into a film in 1994, Mel Gibson played the role Garner originated. Garner appears in a supporting role as a gambler. In between movies, this affable, well-liked actor returned to television as private eye, ex-con Jim Rockford in "The Rockford Files" (1974-'80), where he confronted danger from modern thugs. **ACHIEVEMENTS** 1976-'77 Emmy, Outstanding Lead Actor in a drama series for "The Rockford Files." Wounded in action during the Korean War, Garner was awarded two Purple Heart medals for wounds suffered. **QUOTE** After achieving weekly success on "Maverick," Garner said, "If we fall apart now, we've had our day. I'm eatin' good, and if I want a new suit of clothes I can buy it. I don't have to save up for it which I did a few years back."

Charles McGraw 6925 Hollywood

Actor
BORN May 10, 1914, in New York. **SPOTLIGHTS** A veteran tough guy with steely blue eyes, he came to Hollywood via an extensive stage and radio career. In the latter he specialized in police dramas and adventure serials. McGraw made his screen debut in the archetypal gangster drama, *Angels with Dirty Faces* (1938). The film is one of the best in the crime genre. It set the tone for McGraw's career, where he was usually cast as the heavy. He is a throat-grabbing, vindictive killer in *The Threat* (1949). The husky, light-haired character actor stars in the classic B-movie thriller, *The Narrow Margin* (1952), opposite Marie Windsor. Don't let the part about it being a "B" picture fool you, it's wonderfully suspenseful. It is a thriller-on-a-train classic. In all, he appeared in more than 60 movies, including Westerns, war, action and thrillers. Motion pictures include *Blood on the Moon* (1948), *Armored Car Robbery* (1950), *The Defiant Ones* (1958), *Spartacus* and *Cimarron* (both 1960), *The Birds* (1963), *In Cold Blood* (1967), *Hang 'Em High* (1968), *Johnny Got His Gun* (1971), and *A Boy and His Dog* (1975). **TV** He intermittently appeared on the small screen. McGraw starred in dozen of live playhouse dramas, as well as in series. He portrayed Rick in "Casablanca" (1955), and Captain Hughes in "The Smith Family" (1971-'72) co-starring Henry Fonda. Died: 1980.

Barbra Streisand 6925 Hollywood

Singer, actress, director, producer
BORN Barbara Joan Streisand; April 24, 1942, in Brooklyn,

Barbra Streisand and Johnny Grant

NY. **SPOTLIGHTS** One of the greatest female vocalists of the 20th and 21st centuries, she is also a distinguished, multi-faceted artist, with the gift of genius. This phenomenal entertainer made her Broadway debut in the musical, "I Can Get It For You Wholesale," winning the New York Critics Award, and becoming an overnight sensation. Celebrated on Broadway, she was a full-fledged star by age 21. She made her film debut as Fanny Brice in *Funny Girl* (1968), a role which she had played for twenty months on stage. America fell in love with her, her spectacular recordings with her big, emotional voice, and her television specials. She gave an effervescent performance in *Hello Dolly* (1969); co-stars with Robert Redford in the romantic picture, *The Way We Were* (1973); and stars in, sang, co-wrote, directed and produced *Yentl* (1983). She would wait a number of years before directing again. This time it was the compelling psychological drama, *The Prince of Tides* (1991). She co-stars opposite Nick Nolte, and also produced this highly acclaimed piece. There was much controversy when the Academy honored the picture with many nominations, including Best Picture, but overlooked her for the Best Director category even though she had been nominated for The Directors Guild of America award. At the Academy Awards presentation, master of ceremonies Billy Crystal referred to *The Prince of Tides* as: "the film that apparently directed itself." Streisand's third directorial effort, *The Mirror Has Two Faces* (1996), challenged traditional notions of romantic love and beauty. About this picture, she said, "I wanted to make an uplifting, life-affirming, hopeful picture about love. And that people do find each other at later ages, that everything's possible." She co-stars with Jeff Bridges, and also produced, wrote the love theme and was nominated for Best Song Oscar for the second time for "I Finally Found Someone." She is one of the highest paid actresses, and has helped pave the way toward more equality with women's pay in Hollywood—although there is still some distance to be traversed. Other motion pictures include *On a Clear Day You Can See Forever*, and *The Owl and the Pussycat* (both 1970), *What's Up, Doc?* and *Up the Sandbox* (both 1972), *For Pete's Sake* (1974), *Funny Lady* (1975—reprising her role as Fanny Brice), *A Star Is Born* (1976; plus song composer), *The Main Event* (1979—also co-produced), and *Nuts* (1987). After a 27-year absence from paid concert performances, she returned to the concert stage on New Year's Eve 1993, at the MGM Grand Hotel and Casino, in Las Vegas. The record-breaking, two performance engagement sold out in 20 minutes. When her 1994 tour of an additional six cities was announced, more than a million ticket requests were received in the first hour, and the tour broke virtually all existing records. Barbra Streisand is the top-selling female recording artist of all time, with 12 multi-platinum albums and 24 platinum, the most ever for a female in each case. Her total of 39 gold albums is exceeded only by Elvis Presley and The Beatles. Ms Streisand has had #1 albums in each of the last four decades. Her #1 albums span a period of more than 40 years, the greatest longevity in that statistic for any recording artist or group. **ACHIEVEMENTS** Her 1968 Best Actress Academy Award for *Funny Girl* was one of the rare instances of an actor winning for her *first* film. She won another Oscar in 1977 for composing the song "Evergreen," from her film *A Star Is Born*—making her the first female to achieve that honor for composing music. She has also won eight Grammy Awards, numerous Emmys and Golden Globes, and is the recipient of countless honors for her art, charity and political and social activism, including an Honorary Doctorate of Arts and Humanities from Brandeis University. She is the only artist of either gender to be accorded the Oscar, Tony, Emmy, Peabody, Golden Globe, Cable ACE and Grammy Awards. Through her Barwood films, she recently has produced and continues to make series of award-winning, issue related motion pictures for television. The first of these, "Serving in Silence: The Margarethe Cammermeyer Story" earned the Peabody Award and several Emmys, while others, such as "The Rescuers" were also honored. **HIGHLIGHTS** She is a lifelong student of many subjects and an influential political activist and defender of civil liberties. Her first marriage was to actor Elliott Gould, father of her son, Jason Gould. Her second marriage is to Emmy-winning actor/director James Brolin. (Also see James Brolin's bio in this book.)

Donald O' Connor

Nazimova

Plain page numbers denote pages where a star for that individual appears without a biography.
Page numbers in **bold** denote pages where a photograph of that star appears.

INTERNATIONAL LUMINARIES

Jackie Chan (right), and Deputy Sheriff Sam Storm

Actor, director, screenwriter, producer, stuntman, comedian and martial arts expert Jackie Chan is one of the world's most popular and talented movie stars.

Cari Valero

Born in Switzerland, of Spanish heritage, actress Cari Valero speaks several languages. She appears in Hollywood and European movies, and hosts a TV show in Paris.

John Phillip Law

The versatile and charismatic stage, motion picture and television actor, John Phillip Law, receives worldwide praise for his tremendous, ongoing global body of work.

Cylk Cozart

Part Native American Indian and African American, he combines the athletic grace of an action-hero with the romantic charm of a leading man. Actor Cylk Cozart is blazing his trail to stardom. His talent is marked by intelligence and emotional depth.

Dr. Ava Cadell

Dr. Ava Cadell is frequently called the "new Dr. Ruth." She combines intelligence, beauty and humor in her advice to radio listeners, television viewers and to audiences who hear her live on her global speaker circuit (E-mail: acadell@earthlink.net).

Hollywood Walk of Fame honoree, Jack Nicholson (wearing sunglasses), proudly receives the California Star Award. The Los Angeles and the Orange County Sheriff's Departments organize the annual benefit for the Rescue Our Children program.
Offering their support (from left) are Los Angeles County Sheriff Leroy Baca, California Governor Gray Davis, motion picture producer-director and Star Award's co-producer Rudy Durand, Star Award's Founder and event co-producer Arthur M. Kassel, producer Daphna Ziman, and Orange County Sheriff Mike Carona.

(Photo credits continued on next page)

Mary Hart

Stefanie Powers

Photo credits:

Anita Baker, by Harry Langdon, courtesy of Elektra Entertainment

Bob Barker, by Monty Brinton, courtesy of CBS

Astronauts Collins, Armstrong and Aldrin, courtesy of NASA

Tony Bennett, by Nigel Parry, courtesy of Columbia

George Benson, by Debbie Leavitt

James Brolin and Barbra Streisand, by Lisa O'Connor (E-mail: lisaocon@earthlink.net)

Rosemary Clooney, by Fergus Greer

Arthur Cohn (with Al Pacino), by Peter C. Borsari, collection of Arthur Cohn

David Copperfield, by Roger Karnbad/Michelson, courtesy of Johnny Grant

Gloria Estefan, by Alberto Tolot, collection of Gloria Estefan

Charles Fries (with Peter Chernin and Aaron Spelling), by Lee Salem Photography (copyright 1999)

La Brea Gateway by Carlos Figueroa, courtesy of the Community Redevelopment Agency

Leeza Gibbons, courtesy of Berliner Studio/BEI.

Leonard and Wendy Goldberg, by Alan Berliner, and courtesy of Berliner Studio/BEI.

Brian Grazer by Berliner Studios, courtesy of the Hollywood Chamber of Commerce and courtesy of Berliner Studio/BEI.

Chick Hearn by Andrew D. Bernstein, courtesy of the NBA

Florence Henderson, by Jonathan Exley

Chuck Jones by Dean Diaz, courtesy of Warner Bros.

Gladys Knight by Randee St. Nicholas, courtesy of MCA

Sherry Lansing by Berliner Studios, courtesy of Paramount Pictures

Carl Laemmle, coutesy of Universal Studios (copyright 1982)

Lassie by Delmar Watson

John Lennon by Bob Gruen, courtesy of Capitol Records

The Lennon Sisters by Harry Langdon, collection of The Lennon Sisters

Reba McEntire by Dana Fineman, courtesy of MCA Nashville

Luis Miguel by Daniela Federici, courtesy of Wea Latina, Inc.

Steve Miller by David Stahl, courtesy of Capitol Records

Jack Nicholson (squating),and courtesy of Berliner Studio/BEI.

Chuck Niles by Bill Jackson

Donald O'Connor (and Samantha Hart), by Roger Karnbad

The Pointer Sisters by Norman Seeff

Stefanie Powers, by Elise Lockwood

Pat Sajak, courtesy of "Wheel of Fortune" and King World

Vin Scully, courtesy of the Dodgers

Alex Trebek, by Steve Crise, courtesy of "Jeopardy!"

Tommy Tune, by Carmine Schiavone, collection of Tommy Tune

Paul Winchell (and Samantha Hart), by John Mejia

Joanne Woodward, courtesy Bruce Torrence Historical Collection

Various Hollywood Walk of Fame star photographs by the Chamber's past photographer Buzz Lawrence, and current photographer Bob Freeman, courtesy of the Hollywood Chamber of Commerce, and/or Johnny Grant.

Group shot on page 316 of Frank Sinatra, Carol Burnette, Florece Henderson, et al, by Alan Berliner, and courtesy of Berliner Studio/BEI.

Also see the "Acknowledgment" page in this book. Thank you.

Placido Domingo at Walk of Fame star ceremony

Tom Cruise at Walk of Fame star ceremony

Tommy Lee Jones at Walk of Fame star ceremony

Arnold Schwarzenegger and Johnny Grant at star ceremony

Alistair Cooke visits America's beloved treasure, the Statue of Liberty

Key to the United States

AL - Alabama	**IN** - Indiana	**NE** - Nebraska	**SC** - South Carolina
AK - Alaska	**IA** - Iowa	**NV** - Nevada	**SD** - South Dakota
AZ - Arizona	**KS** - Kansas	**NH** - New Hampshire	**TN** - Tennessee
AR - Arkansas	**KY** - Kentucky	**NJ** - New Jersey	**TX** - Texas
CA - California	**LA** - Louisiana	**NM** - New Mexico	**UT** - Utah
CO - Colorado	**ME** - Maine	**NY** - New York	**VT** - Vermont
CT - Connecticut	**MD** - Maryland	**NC** - North Carolina	**VA** - Virginia
DE - Delaware	**MA** - Massachusetts	**ND** - North Dakota	**WA** - Washington
FL - Florida	**MI** - Michigan	**OH** - Ohio	**WV** - West Virginia
GA - Georgia	**MN** - Minnesota	**OK** - Oklahoma	**WI** - Wisconsin
HA - Hawaii	**MS** - Mississippi	**OR** - Oregon	**WY** - Wyoming
ID - Idaho	**MO** - Missouri	**PA** - Pennsylvania	**DC**- Washington, D.C.
IL - Illinois	**MT** - Montana	**RI** - Rhode Island	(not a state)

FINIS